# Dedication

**Marriage of**
**Peter Shier & Anna Burbage**
**September 24, 1883**
**Bismarck, Dakota Territory**

To my first North Dakota ancestors, representing the hearty pioneers whose efforts against all odds formed the foundation of our heritage.

Peter Shier (1856-1925) was born to German-immigrant parents in Minnesota Territory, and came to Bismarck in the late 1870's. He homesteaded in northern Emmons County in the early 1880's where his Dinner Ranch became one of that area's most successful ventures. A salty frontiersman who was able to outdrink and outcuss most of his contemporaries, he nevertheless was widely admired for his honesty, loyalty, and generosity. He was a popular five-term sheriff of Emmons County, and later operated a small restaurant in Linton and served as the town constable.

Anna Burbage Shier (1860-1937) was born in Ireland and came to North Dakota about 1879. A prim and proper Victorian lady who is remembered for hosting annual Saint Patrick's Day parties, she raised five children while more than holding her own with work on the ranch.

# NORTH DAKOTA PLACE NAMES

by
Douglas A. Wick

PEMBINA
FEB
12
MIN.

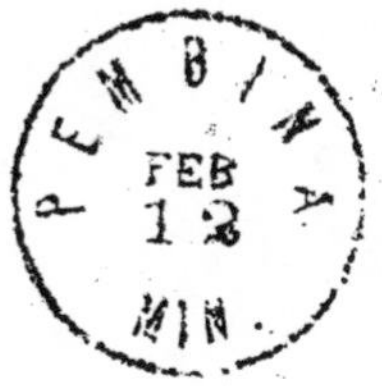

*Rare postmark from Pembina
prior to the creation of
Dakota Territory in 1861.*

## HEDEMARKEN COLLECTIBLES

P.O. Box 7399 — Northbrook Station
Bismarck, ND 58502

First Printing 1988

ISBN: 0-9620968-0-6

Published and distributed by:

**HEDEMARKEN COLLECTIBLES**
P.O. Box 7399 — Northbrook Station
Bismarck, ND 58502

# Acknowledgements

In 1978 I began to compile a listing of North Dakota place names, and while the effort was at first quite casual, it soon grew into a monster. Thirteen large three-ring binders held the basic source information, and an almost endless collection of loose notes could be found here and there throughout my home. The decision to publish was made in 1987, which initiated a year-long editing process to reduce this mass of trivia into a manageable finished product.

North Dakota stands out among the fifty states in having one of the best selections of local "jubilee" books, and many of these were published during the period of this research. I attempted to review each and every one of these references, and supplemented this effort as much as possible with on-site visitations. Countless local residents graciously shared their first-hand expertise, and it was a continually humbling experience to discover the vast amount of knowledge literally walking the streets.

To name all of these people would be utterly impossible. Beginning in 1985, I contacted many local officials, and found their supportive efforts to be invaluable. Among these public servants were Helen Christenson of Bottineau, Ramona Hoffman of Ashley, Susan Froemke of Lisbon, Brenda Arnold of Bowbells, Joyce Delebo of Langdon, Dr. George M. Christensen of Minot, Reuben Brownlee of Wahpeton, Jane Dunham of New Rockford, Dwayne Oster of Washburn, and Corabelle Brown of Towner. Private citizens who offered their assistance included Sandy Cole of Watford City, Vida Gunderson of Bathgate, Olive Benson of Bottineau, Harry Middaugh of Lansford, and Thomas Elliott of Valley City.

The resources and staff of the North Dakota State Historical Society deserve a special recognition, for without this valuable resource, any book of this type would be virtually impossible. Of particular assistance was Forrest Daniel, a veritable walking encyclopedia of North Dakota history, who recently retired from his post at the Heritage Center in Bismarck.

The illustrations included in this book are from the personal collections of Gordon Twedt of Maddock, Murray Pearce of Bismarck, and the author. Mr. Pearce provided special assistance with North Dakota's postal history at a time when this information was essentially unpublished, and frequently served as a consultant when attempting to sort out seemingly contradictory findings.

Finally, recognition must be given to the members of my immediate family who volunteered many hours of proofreading, consultation, support, and general perseverence. Our amateur efforts have produced what we hope will be a worthwhile addition to the preservation of North Dakota history.

# Introduction

Since the beginning of recorded history, we have given names to the places that are a part of our very existance. Although there is evidence that our distant ancestors were intrigued with the origins of place names, the systematic accumulation of such data is primarily a twentieth-century phenomenon. This pursuit is now considered to be a "science" with its own name—onomastics.

Warren Upham's *Minnesota Geographic Names* of 1920 is generally considered to be the standard of this field by which all other works are judged. While some features of his book are dated, its thoroughness and general accuracy were at levels which were previously unknown. It is a fitting and probably unique fact that a city in North Dakota was named in Mr. Upham's honor.

Books on place names are never complete, nor are they ever completely accurate. The establishment and naming of a new settlement is rarely documented, and the passage of time coupled with the emergence of local folklore complicates any research project. The relative newness of North Dakota would seem to make this effort relatively easy, yet this same newness makes the elusiveness of such name origins as Zap that much more frustrating.

Place names are usually divided into two categories, natural and artificial, and it is the intended scope of this work to concentrate on the latter, which I prefer to call man-made. The scope is further restricted to places which were at some point intended to represent a place of habitation. The existing fifty-three counties of North Dakota are covered by capsule histories in the county-by-county index following the main body of this book. Townships, those political subdivisions that generally are six-by-six mile squares, are not included within the scope of this work, but represent a major area for future study.

Chronologically, the first names in this book were the direct result of the fur trade, beginning with the Chaboillez Post of 1797. The later enterprises called Fort Union, Fort Berthold, Fort Clark, etc., have acquired an almost legendary status when discussing the pre-territorial history of North Dakota.

Formal military presence in the state began in the 1850's with the establishment of Fort Abercrombie, and similar installations have taken their rightful place in history along with the various camps, posts, cantonments, etc., that preceded or supported the forts. In a special category are the named campsites of the 1863 Sibley Expedition, which were in most cases literally one-night stands, but still seem worthy of inclusion within the scope of this book.

Permanent settlement by white people in what is now North Dakota began in the Pembina area in the 1840's, and by the time of the Civil War this region had begun to take on an air of civilization. River traffic was beginning to open other areas to settlement, but without doubt the single greatest catalyst to development occurred in 1871, when the Northern Pacific Railway crossed the Red River at what would become Fargo. Within two years the railroad had reached the Missouri River, and new townsites began every few miles along its route. The next few years saw a period of unparalleled growth as railroad branch lines were built in all directions, and when statehood was achieved on November 2, 1889, maps of eastern North Dakota closely resembled those of today.

Many different railroads operated in North Dakota during territorial days, but by the turn of the century, mergers and reorganizations had greatly reduced that number. For this book I have not used the names of these short-lived pioneer lines, instead using the following generic names and abbreviations for what would become the five major lines in the state: NPRR (Northern Pacific), GNRR (Great Northern), Soo Line RR (Minneapolis, St. Paul, & Sault Ste. Marie), Milwaukee Road RR (Chicago, Milwaukee, St. Paul & Pacific), and C&NW RR (Chicago & Northwestern). Because the merger of the NPRR and GNRR as part of the Burlington Northern system occurred long after the state's initial development, I have used the appropriate original railroad's name. Small independent railroads that thrived during the boom period of North Dakota development, most notably the Midland Continental, are identified by their proper names.

Although agriculture continues to dominate North Dakota's economy, its settlements have provided an identification for all residents of the state. While most cities owe their existence to the railroad, their survival is now influenced by the automobile. This form of personal transportation has caused many smaller villages to become ghost towns. A review of population figures will show that most smaller cities in the state have steadily declined during the last half century, while the major cities have continued to grow. This trend is found nationwide.

A large percentage of the place names in this book are rural post offices. A few of these facilities had their own buildings, and many were housed in country stores, but most were located in the homes of the postmasters and moved about as different people assumed the duties of the position. The period from about 1890 until 1910 saw thousands of these post offices established nationwide, some serving only a handful of patrons. While they were not settlements in the literal sense, they did fill a void in an era when rapid communications was becoming a necessity.

The post office, of course, has always provided a sense of community identification. In 1982 co-authors Alan H. Patera and John S. Gallagher published their excellent *North Dakota Post Offices 1850-1982*, which is strongly recommended for any readers interested in this aspect of North Dakota history. A considerable amount of postal history will be found in this book, including a thorough review of post offices which received government approval, but never went into operation. The abbreviation "pm" is used throughout the book, and should be read postmaster or postmistress, whichever is applicable.

In a special category are the so-called "copyright" towns. Cartographers for many years have engaged in the practice of placing fictitious towns on their maps as a means of detecting unauthorized copying of their products. Attempts at contacting officials of the major map publishers to discuss this practice were consistently met with evasive hedging, yet such places continue to appear on many state maps. It is amusing that several rural Interstate exits were "unnamed" in the mid-1980's because of confusion for tourists, yet the practice of using copyright towns continues to flourish. If some travelers searched in vain for Geck, Lippert, Dengate, etc., I wonder how many have searched with equal futility for Yandell, Coryell, Dixboro, etc?

The main body of this book is alphabetical in format, with each place name having its own entry. All entries are placed in their appropriate present-day counties, although it should be remembered that today's county boundaries date only from 1916. Most of the places in this book have locations per the Rectangular System for land surveys adopted in 1785, which remains in the opinion of many the best such system ever devised. In addition, most places that are now either very small or nonexistant are reported in miles and direction from an existing place.

Many places have had more than one name, with each name receiving separate treatment. During the 1890's the federal government attempted to standardize place names, eliminating such things as two-word names, romantic spellings, possessive spellings, etc. Examples of this effort can be found throughout this book, but public sentiment caused many original spellings to be restored after about ten years. To facilitate cross-referencing, subject and alternate names are completely capitalized when appearing within an entry.

This book is by no means the first study of North Dakota place names, nor will it likely be the last. The collecting of such information is an endless pursuit. As early as 1929 a cursory listing of North Dakota place names was included in Walter E. Spokesfield's *The History of Wells County, North Dakota and its Pioneers.* Mary Ann Barnes Williams of Washburn published *Origins of North Dakota Place Names* in 1966. This often criticized book in truth was a great advance over what existed at the time, and undoubtedly would have been more error-free had Mrs. Williams lived long enough to complete her research.

My contribution to this ongoing effort contains well over three thousand entries, with major emphasis on the small, and virtually forgotten places of our not so distant past. While each individual entry is a collection of trivia, the entire book hopefully provides a history of the state with a somewhat offbeat twist. Fargo, Bismarck, Grand Forks, Minot, etc., take their rightful places in the book, but such places as Mondak, Krem, Mardell, Wamduska, and Whynot are included as equals. Likewise, the giant figures of North Dakota's history, from Lewis and Clark to Lawrence Welk, receive mention, but stand together with Joseph Colton, Emery Mapes, Ernest Jacobi, Elling Ulness, Linda Warfel Slaughter, and thousands of other North Dakotans who contributed to our heritage.

Ten years passed from the start of this project, and while it rarely took top priority, nevertheless countless hours were spent compiling the information. It quickly became apparent that the book could never be complete, or error free, but every effort was made to approach that goal. The subject of the book is ever changing. Indeed, during the period of research, many settlements virtually disappeared and dozens of post offices closed their doors, yet during that same time new cities were born. My only hopes are that readers will consider my efforts worthwhile, and that it might someday inspire another writer to continue the pursuit.

*Douglas A Wick*

Bismarck, ND August 1988

# A

**AAE** (Grand Forks). Kittle Olson Aae settled in SW¼ Sec. 33-150-53, Pleasant View Twp., about six miles ENE of Northwood, in 1881. About 1886 he began operating a mail distribution service for his neighbors, who were not on the mail route out of Northwood, and also ran a private community library service from his home. (3, 69)

**ABBOTTS** (Barnes). This was a farm post office established June 7, 1880 in Sec. 34-143-58, Sibley Trail Twp., on the west bank of the Sheyenne River fifteen miles north of Valley City, with Frank H. Abbott pm. Abbott is a Hebrew word meaning father. It was discontinued October 31, 1882 with mail to Valley City. Abbot's is an erroneous spelling. (2, 3, 19, 40, 76)

**ABBOTTSFORD** (Benson). This rural post office was established April 16, 1884 with James C. Gibson pm. It was located in NW¼ Sec. 21-154-67, Riggin Twp., about two miles north of Minnewaukan. In 1887 it was moved two miles NE to the home of James Egbert in NW¼ Sec. 14-154-67. The post office closed February 26, 1894 with mail to Jackson. Some say the name honored W. L. Abbott, a famous naturalist who visited here in 1879, and some say it was named for Gerard Alan Abbott, an authority on waterfowl. The "ford" noted its location at a crossing point of Big Coulee. Abbotsford is an erroneous spelling. (2, 3, 34, 40, 110, 240)

**ABERCROMBIE** (Richland). This townsite was founded in 1884 at the site of Fort Abercrombie in Sec. 4-134-48, Abercrombie Twp., which had been named for the fort's builder, Lt. Col. John Joseph Abercrombie (1802-1877). The post office retained the name FORT ABERCROMBIE until longtime pm Nellie Hutchison shortened the name to simply ABERCROMBIE on May 21, 1892. The village, elevation 935, incorporated in 1904, and reached a peak population of 299 in 1910. Its Zip Code, 58001, is the lowest in the state. (1, 2, 13, 33, 40, 147)

**ABSARAKA** (Cass). This GNRR station was founded in 1882 in S½ Sec. 33-141-55, Empire Twp., and NE¼ Sec. 5-140-53, Wheatland Twp. It was just NW of Ripon, and was begun by settlers who felt this site offered better chances for development than its nearby rival. Mrs. John Hay, nee Jane Boyd, is credited with selecting the name, and Indian word meaning home of the crows. The name is often applied to the earliest known Indian tribe of the area, the Absaroke, or sparrow-hawk people, who later became the Hidatsa, Gros Ventres, and Minitari. Col. Chester G. Thompson platted the townsite on his land in 1885, and offered free lots to settlers. Among the takers were William Staples, a merchant, and Thomas Monilaws (1849-1933), a blacksmith. On February 25, 1890 the Ripon post office relocated here with John B. Meacham pm. The Zip Code is 58002, and while this town

did in fact prove to be better than Ripon, it never counted more than 50 residents. (2, 18, 34, 40, 77, 79, 296)

**ACKLIN** (Hettinger). This was a rural post office established November 15, 1907 in the country store of pm Willaim A. Acklin, who came here in 1906 from IL, and claimed to be the only Democrat in the county. It was located in SW 1/4 Sec. 8-132-93, Kern Twp., eight miles south of Mott. The post office closed June 30, 1909 with mail to Mott. Mr. Acklin then sold the store and his farm, moved into Mott, and died in 1938. (2, 3, 40, 178, 179, 180, 414)

**ACKWORTH** (Rolette). This was a rural post office established February 27, 1905 with Albert Hiatt pm in his country store. It was located in SE¼ Sec. 6-163-73, Willow Lake Twp., in the extreme NW corner of the county. Norwegian settlers in the area are credited with the name, but its meaning is unknown. The post office and store were later operated by William Stokes and William McDonald, but the post office was discontinued August 31, 1926 with mail to Kelvin. It remained on most maps into the 1930's. (1, 2, 3, 18, 40, 123)

**ACORN** (Dunn). This was a rural post office established November 4, 1914 with Ramona Bailey pm. It was located in NE¼ Sec. 20-148-97, on the west bank of the Little Missouri River in the extreme NW corner of the county. The nut of the native oak trees in the area provided the name, derived from the Middle English *akern*, a corruption of a Russian word meaning berry. The post office was discontinued May 31, 1918 with mail to Schafer. (1, 2, 3, 4, 40, 53, 79)

**ACTON** (Walsh). This Red River townsite was founded in 1871 in NW¼ Sec. 25-157-51, Acton Twp., and called KELLY'S POINT. Pm Antoine Girard changed the name to ACTON on May 27, 1879, commemorating his hometown of Acton, Ontario, Canada, which was named for Acton, Middlesex, England, a suburb of London that had its greatest fame during the Oliver Cromwell regime in the 1600's. It is said that the town had a population of over 400 in 1881, but when it was bypassed by the railroad, it decline rapidly, with a 1890 population of just 25. In 1913 the post office moved across the section line to NE¼ Sec. 26-157-51, the home of new pm Emil Hoenke, but operated here only until September 30, 1913, when mail went to Fork, MN. (1, 2, 3, 10, 18, 40, 75, 79, 414)

**ADAMS** (Adams). This is thought to be a copyright town that appears on a 1930 roadmap published by the General Drafting Co. It is one of several such places on this map that duplicates the name of its county, which was named for Milwaukee Road RR official John Quincy Adams, a distant relative of the President of the same name. It is shown approximately midway between Mott and Lemmon, SD. (3)

**ADAMS** (Richland). This was a rural community founded in 1881 in SE¼ Sec. 22-132-49, Mooreton Twp., consisting mainly of laborers at the Fairview bonanza farm run by John Quincy Adams of Wheaton, IL, who was a benefactor of the state science school in Wahpeton. Adams is a contraction of Adam's son, Adam being a Hebrew name meaning man of the red earth, noting the Palestinian soil. William P. Adams, the son of J. Q. Adams, was the site manager until 1927. A NPRR siding was built here in 1885, but little development occurred. (1, 2, 19, 242)

**ADAMS** (Walsh). This was a farm post office established June 23, 1890 with Erick T. Grove pm. It was located in NE¼ Sec. 27-157-58, Adams Twp., which was named by settlers from Adams County, WI, which was named for John Quincy Adams (1767-1848), 6th President of the United States. The pm's wife, Christina, suggested the name. In 1905 the Soo Line RR founded a townsite in Secs. 13 & 14-157-58, three miles to the SE, naming it SARLES, but because of duplication the ADAMS name was transferred to the new location. The village incorporated in 1905, the Zip Code is 58210, and a peak population of 411 was reached in 1950. Neil Levang, longtime guitarist with the Lawrence Welk band, was born here. (1, 2, 3, 18, 33, 40, 70, 75, 79)

**ADDISON** (Cass). This GNRR station was established in 1880 as WILLIAMS, and a short-lived post office was here 1881-1882. That year the new townsite of Davenport became dominant in the area and this site, Secs. 15 & 22-138-51, Addison Twp., was renamed ADDISON for Addison Leach, who had purchased the interests of Mr. Williams. Leech owned at one time 47,000 acres, and served at the Constitutional Convention in 1889. Addison is an Old English name meaning son of Adam. The post office was established March 30, 1888 with Douglas E. Austin pm, and was discontinued November 30, 1920 with mail to Davenport. The station, at the junction of a branch line to Chaffee, survived as a small village for many years. Louie Gillan, living here in 1957, was its last resident. (1, 2, 3, 18, 19, 34, 40, 77, 79, 303)

**ADELAIDE** (Bowman). This was a rural community founded in 1908 when several families, mostly from Valley City, homesteaded a few miles south of Rhame. The center of the community was the rural school in NE¼ Sec. 33-131-104, Adelaide Twp. The origin of the name is unknown. (3)

**ADIE** (Stark). This was a proposed townsite on the Dickinson, Lefor, & New Leipzig RR effort of 1917, which failed to be built. It would have been located in SW¼ Sec. 3-137-96, twelve miles south of Dickinson, and was to be a junction point, one line going north to Dickinson, and another west to the terminus of Wylie. Joseph Dukart owned the townsite. The origin of the name is unknown. (3, 18, 74)

1

**ADLER** (Nelson). This was a rural post office established May 29, 1882 with Charles Adler pm. It was located in Mr. Adler's store in SW¼ Sec. 3-151-57, Adler Twp., midway between McVille and Petersburg. Adler is German for eagle. A village of 30 people was reported here in 1890. Paul Severson took over the post office duties and moved it into his rural hotel in Sec. 5-151-57, but the post office closed October 31, 1902 with mail to Petersburg. (2, 3, 18, 25, 34, 40, 53, 124, 128, 130)

**ADRIAN** (LaMoure). This settlement in NW¼ Sec. 13-136-63, Adrian Twp., was first settled in 1885 and called PORTERVILLE. The NPRR arrived in June 1886, and superintendent J. N. Graham renamed it for his hometown of Adrian, MI, which had been named for Adrian, or Hadrian (76-138 A.D.), the scholar, militarist, and Emporer of Rome. His name came from the Italian city of Adria, and has been borne by six popes. The post office was established January 15, 1887 with James D. Bradway pm. Development was slow with the population never exceeding 150. It was platted by John A. Whipple in 1933, but the village never incorporated. It claims to have the largest elm tree in the state. The elevation is 1379. The post office, Zip Code 58410, closed April 22, 1977 with the retirement of Mrs. Edna S. Miller, who had been pm since 1942, mail service now coming from Montpelier. (1, 2, 3, 10, 18, 19, 33, 40, 138, 151)

**AETNA** (Burleigh). This was a farm post office established July 20, 1907 with Mrs. Charles W. (Louella) Lyman pm. It was located in NW¼ Sec. 8-141-76, Lyman Twp., seven miles SSW of Wing. The name is said to have been transferred from Aetna Twp., Pipestone County, MN, which was named for Aetna Johnson, step-daughter of Christ Gilbertson who came there in 1878 from Norway. The post office was moved to the home of Gilbert Cotes in Sec. 6-141-76 in 1909 when the Lyman family moved to St. Hilaire, MN, and it closed May 31, 1914 with mail to Wing. (2, 3, 8, 13, 14, 40, 63)

**AGATE** (Rolette). This was a Soo Line RR station in Sec. 1-159-69, Pleasant Valley Twp., between Mylo and Bisbee. The railroad workmen selected the name to note the many moss agates found in this region. The post office was established March 29, 1907 with Noah O. Narveson pm. Anton Landmark ran a general store here, but little development occurred beyond that. A population of 25 was reported in 1920. The post office, Zip Code 58310, became a rural branch of Bisbee on July 3, 1964. (2, 18, 33, 40, 79, 123)

**AGRICULTURAL COLLEGE** (Cass). This post office was established September 14, 1897 with Louise B. Evans pm on the campus of North Dakota Agricultural College in SW¼ Sec. 36-140-49, Reed Twp., in NW Fargo. The college had been founded in 1890. On November 30, 1925, it was made a branch of the Fargo post office, with a name change to AGRICULTURAL COLLEGE STATION, and in 1961 the name was again changed to STATE UNIVERSITY STATION, noting the new name of the institution. (2, 3, 18, 40, 77)

**AGRICULTURAL COLLEGE SPUR** (Cass). This was a GNRR spur built in 1914 to the power house on the campus of North Dakota Agricultural College in NW Fargo, SW¼ Sec. 36-140-49, Reed Twp. (2, 3, 18, 34, 77)

**AGRICULTURAL COLLEGE STATION** (Cass). The independent post office at North Dakota Agricultural College became a branch of the Fargo post office on December 30, 1925, officially under this name. When the institution became a university, the name was changed to STATE UNIVERSITY STATION on December 8, 1960. (2, 3, 34, 40, 77)

**AKRA** (Pembina). This rural community was founded in 1882 in NW¼ Sec. 14-161-55, Akra Twp., by settlers from Iceland. The post office was established January 2, 1890 with Sigur Thorwaldson pm. The name, meaning cultivated fields, comes from Akranes, Iceland, just north of the capital city of Reykjavik. The post office, Zip Code 58211, closed November 1, 1973 with mail to Cavalier. It was located in the same country store throughout its history, and the store is still in operation. (2, 3, 18, 33, 40, 79, 108)

**ALAMO** (Williams). This GNRR station was founded in 1916 in Sec. 22-159-99, Rock Island Twp., and absorbed the old village of COTTONWOOD LAKE one mile to the east. *Alamo* is Spanish for cottonwood, and was suggested by a Texan who lived here, both to maintain a continuity with the old settlement, and to note the restoration being done at the time at the famous TX shrine in San Antonio. The post office moved from COTTONWOOD LAKE on April 16, 1917 with Roy Whitaker pm. Andrew Smith was the GNRR agent from its establishment in 1916 until 1952. The Zip Code is 58830, and a peak population of 214 was reported in 1940. In 1973 the old depot was moved to the Frontier Museum in Williston. (2, 10, 33, 40, 50, 79)

**ALBERT** (Benson). A rural community existed here as early as 1882, and was called ALBERT for pioneer settler O. A. Albertson. A post office was established July 2, 1891 with Anne T. Jacobson pm, and was located in NW¼ Sec. 27-153-69, Albert Twp., about six miles north of Maddock. Mrs. Jacobson retained the name in part to note her former home of Albert Lea, MN, which was named for Albert Miller Lea (1808-1891), a pioneer surveyor in the upper Mississippi and Missouri River valleys. The post office closed December 14, 1895 with mail to Minnewaukan. It was reestablished May 5, 1898 about two miles SE of the original site, but closed for good on October 31, 1906 with mail to Maddock. (2, 10, 11, 33, 34, 40)

**ALBERTHA** (Dickey). This was a farm post office established August 5, 1896 with Mark Hambrook pm. It was located in NE¼ Sec. 5-129-66, Albertha Twp., in the extreme western side of the county, eleven miles NW of Forbes. The name was coined from ALlen Dodge Town, an early resident of the area, and his fiancee, BERTHA Dickie, a teacher in the local school. The post office was discontinued September 14, 1905 with mail to Wirch. (2, 40, 154, 264)

**ALBION** (Stutsman). This was a farm post office established February 13, 1885 with Frederick B. Fancher pm. Mr. Fancher was the Governor of North Dakota 1899-1901. It was located in NW¼ Sec. 34-141-63, Fried Twp., four miles NE of Jamestown, and was named for the hometown of J. J. Eddy, Albion, MI, which was named for Albion, ME. The name is derived from *albus*, the Latin word for white, and was the Roman name for England, probably influenced by the White Cliffs of Dover. Sir Francis Drake in 1579 named what is now CA as New Albion, the first of many instances that this name was used in North America. The post office closed December 16, 1896 with mail to Fried. (2, 3, 10, 18, 25, 35, 50, 158, 240, 415)

**ALCIDE** (Rolette). This was a rural post office established December 11, 1900 with Arias M. Riendeau, later a merchant at Thorne, as pm. It was located in NW¼ Sec. 6-161-71, Shell Valley Twp., seven miles east of Dunseith, and the site once contained a general store, blacksmith shop, and a cheese factory. The post office closed September 30, 1909 with mail to Laureat. The origin of the name is unknown, although it is a common masculine given name among people of French ancestry. (1, 2, 3, 18, 40, 123)

**ALDEN** (Hettinger). This was a rural post office established November 5, 1906 with John A. Lein pm. It was located in NE¼ Sec. 14-133-95, Alden Twp., six miles south of Regent. Mr. Lein was the township clerk from 1908 until his death in 1937. The name was selected by settlers from Alden, Polk County, WI, and is an Anglo-Saxon name meaning old friend. The post office closed July 31, 1917 with mail to Regent, although its only reported population of 30 was reported in 1920. (1, 2, 3, 18, 19, 40, 178, 179, 181)

**ALDEN** (Sargent). This was a farm post office established July 2, 1901 with Lars M. Hansen pm. It was located in NW¼ Sec. 27-129-53, Marboe Twp., in the extreme SE corner of the county. After the names Larson, Lanitan, and Maxwell had been rejected, the post office was named ALDEN, for Alden, MN, which had been named in 1858 for unknown reasons. The name is generally traced to John Alden of the *Mayflower*. The post office closed January 14, 1904 with mail to Marlow, SD. (2, 3, 13, 40, 414)

**ALDERIN** (Mercer). This was a rural community in SW¼ Sec. 26-144-84, one mile NW of old Fort Clark. It was named for Goran Alderin (1831-1896), a native of Sweden who came here from McKeesport, PA, and was the first white settler in the area. Some say that Mr. Alderin started a post office here in 1881, but government records do not support this claim. The name is perpetuated by a creek, and a cemetery in NW¼ Sec. 26-144-84. (2, 3, 18, 40, 64, 232)

**ALDERMAN** (Barnes). This was a rural post office established January 16, 1885 with John Alderman (1851-1937) as pm. A population of 20 was reported in 1890. It was located in SW¼ Sec. 26-142-58, Ashtabula Twp., twelve miles north of Valley City, until 1901, when it moved three miles NW to the home of new pm Francis Logan in NE¼ Sec. 20-142-58. The post office closed June 30, 1902 with mail to Valley City. (2, 3, 25, 34, 40, 76, 414)

**ALDRIDGE** (McLean). This was a rural store located in NW¼ Sec. 3-150-86, Blue Hill Twp., seven miles SSE of Ryder. It was operated by Abe Aldridge, who is said to have also run a post office, although this claim is unsupported by government records. It is found only in a 1914 county atlas. (3, 18, 28)

**ALEXANDER** (McKenzie). This GNRR townsite was founded in 1905 in Sec. 5-150-101, Alex Twp., and was at first called RAGGED BUTTES, but within a short time it was renamed for Alexander McKenzie (1856-1922), the political boss from Bismarck, who is also the namesake of the county. Some say it was named for Alexander F. Bell, the town's first barber, for whom nearby Bell's Butte is named. The post office was established August 14, 1905 with Herbert W. Moore pm. It was made county seat when the county organized in 1905, but lost the honor to Schafer in 1909. The elevation is 2154, the Zip Code is 58831, and a peak population of 415 was reached in 1940. Arthur A. Link, Governor of ND 1973-1981, was born here in 1914. (1, 2, 3, 18, 33, 40, 77, 226, 227, 230)

**ALFRED** (LaMoure). This NPRR townsite was founded about 1903 in SE¼ Sec. 8-136-66, Glen Twp., and named by promoter Richard Sykes for Alfred the Great (c.848-899), King of England. Alfred is a Teutonic name meaning supernaturally wise. The streets of this town carry classic English names such as Avon, Warwick, Winchester, etc. The post office was established September 8, 1904 with David W. Barr pm. The elevation is 1902, the Zip Code is 58411, and the population peaked at about 150 in 1930. (1, 2, 3, 10, 18, 19, 33, 40)

**ALGEO** (Barnes). This was a farm post office established December 19, 1890 with Alex K. Algeo pm. It was located in NE¼ Sec. 12-143-57, Baldwin Twp., two miles NW of Pillsbury, and closed May 15, 1909 with mail to Hope. (2, 3, 18, 34, 40, 79, 414)

**ALHALSTEAD** (Traill). This rural post office established February 3, 1892 with James H. McVeety pm. It was located in SW¼ Sec. 27-146-52, Mayville Twp., five miles SE of Mayville on the GNRR branch line. The name is credited to site owner Andreas C. Ulland (1849-1907), a Norwegian who came here in 1873, although its meaning is unknown. Frank A. West became pm December 7, 1892, and on December 23, 1897 received the authorization to change the name to MURRAY. Mr. Ulland became pm on February 16, 1898, but the facility closed April 14, 1898 with mail to Blanchard. The name change to MURRAY was rescinded for official purposes on April 25, 1898, and it believed that that name was never acutally used by the post office, although the station adopted this name and used is until abandonment about 1940. (2, 3, 29, 40, 187, 414)

**ALICE** (Cass). This NPRR townsite was founded in 1900 in SW¼ Sec. 18-138-54, Eldred Twp., and SE¼ Sec. 13-138-55, Clifton Twp., and named by R. S. Lewis of Fargo for his wife and daughter, both of whom were named Alice. Mr. Lewis was a banker and onetime Lt. Governor of North Dakota. Alice

*Alexander, circa 1906.*

is a Teutonic name meaning noble and of good cheer. The post office was moved from Petersen, two miles ESE of here, on June 15, 1901 with Joseph F. Wellentin pm. Frank Blasl (1866-1942), owner of the townsite, platted it in 1900, and it incorporated as a village in 1925. The elevation is 1149, the Zip Code is 58003, and a peak population of 181 was reached in 1940, with a steady decline to just 66 in 1980. (1, 2, 3, 18, 19, 34, 40, 77, 79, 310)

**ALICETON** (Ransom). This was a pioneer settlement in NW¼ Sec. 20-133-55, Aliceton Twp., nine miles SSE of Lisbon on the east bank of Dead Colt Creek. It was named for Alice Ringdahl Melby (1873-1948), oldest daughter of pioneer settler Lars Ringdahl. Some sources say it was named for Alice Bemis, daughter of another pioneer settler. The post office was established February 12, 1884 with James W. Barry pm, and it closed July 9, 1886 with mail to Lisbon. A population of 18 was reported in 1890, but the site soon became a ghost town. (2, 40, 77, 201, 203)

**ALICIA** (Sargent). This was a Soo Line RR station in NE¼ Sec. 14-13053, Kingston Twp., just NW of the GNRR townsite of Geneseo. The name is said to have been suggested by a Soo Line RR employee for his girl friend. The post office was established February 1, 1898 with James H. FitzGerald pm, but it closed May 24, 1899 with mail to Geneseo, which was becoming the dominant townsite in the area. In 1904 a compromise townsite called Veda was promoted between the two communities, but little came of this venture. ALICIA reported a population of 40 as late as 1920, but the Geneseo name is now used by the entire settlement. (1, 2, 3, 18, 19, 40, 414)

**ALKABO** (Divide). This Soo Line RR townsite was founded in 1913 in NE¼ Sec. 14-162-103, Westby Twp., and given a name coined from two types of soil in the area, ALKAli and gumBO. The post office was established December 19, 1913 with Nels H. Nelson pm. The Zip Code is 58832, and after

reporting a population of 100 in 1920, the village has declined to just 19 residents in 1976. (2, 18, 34, 38, 40, 79)

**ALMA** (Cavalier). This was a farm post office established December 24, 1882 with John McBride, later a delegate to the Constitutional Convention and a state senator, as pm. It was located in NE¼ Sec. 16-160-57, East Alma Twp., seven miles ENE of Osnabrock. Settlers from Alma, Ontario, Canada gave it its name, which in 1885 was also given to the township. Alma is a name derived from the Latin word meaning nourishing, and an Arabic word meaning learned. The post office closed February 7, 1896 with mail to Osnabrock. (2, 3, 18, 19, 40, 117)

**ALMA** (Pembina). This was a farm post office established February 9, 1880 with William Hogg pm. It was named by settlers from Alma, Ontario, Canada, and located on the west bank of the Red River in Sec. 5-161-50, Lincoln Twp., eight miles north of Drayton. The post office moved one mile north to the new townsite of Bowesmount on August 2, 1880. (2, 3, 40, 108, 366)

**ALMIRA** (McKenzie). This rural post office, approximately twenty-two miles SSE of Alexander on the north bank of the Little Missouri River, was authorized June 11, 1904 with Almira Sandercock pm. Her name is Arabic for princess. That order was rescinded December 6, 1904, but the office was reestablished January 4, 1905 with Percy S. Sanford pm at his home in SW¼ Sec. 9-147-101, on the SW bank of Redwing Creek. It closed September 30, 1907 with mail to Alexander. Alnura is an erroneous spelling. (2, 3, 19, 40, 53, 414)

**ALMONT** (Morton). This NPRR townsite was founded in 1883 in Sec. 35-138-86, Sims Twp., and owed its existance to the escalating property values in Sims. Real settlement began about 1906, promoted by Eber W. Hyde, a native of Rauville, SD. The name is derived from the nearby landmark, ALtaMONT Moraine, French for moraine high hill. The post office was established October 15, 1906 with Egbert E. Templeton (1881-1966) pm. The elevation is 1935, the Zip Code is 58520, and the village, which incorporated in 1936, reached a peak population of 232 in 1940. The NPRR tracks were removed in 1947 when the mainline was rerouted, but the little city has continued to thrive. (1, 2, 3, 17, 25, 33, 40, 52, 79, 107, 109)

**ALPHA** (Golden Valley). This was a rural community founded in 1906 in NE 1/4 Sec. 32-137-104, Bullion Twp., twenty miles south of Sentinel Butte. The post office was established May 3, 1907 with Benjamin George Odiorne, a druggist from Minneapolis, MN, as pm. Mrs. Catherine Ferney Odiorne, who actually performed the postal duties, suggested the name of the first letter of the Greek alphabet, both to note a new beginning for the settlers, and to express their hopes that it would become the premier settlement in the area. In 1917 it was moved one-half mile south to NE¼ Sec. 2-136-105, Bull Run Twp., where Enoch Johnson became the pm. A population of 10 was listed in 1920, and the site boasted of a general store, town hall, school, and two churches. Robert L. Johnson and Mrs. Helen Sonnek ran the post office until it closed September 9, 1947 with mail to Sentinel Butte. (1, 2, 3, 18, 40, 53, 79, 80, 82)

**ALSEN** (Cavalier). This Soo Line RR townsite was founded in August 1905 in Sec. 6-159-62, Storlie Twp., and Sec. 31-160-62, Gordon Twp., and named by the Tri-State Land Co. for local settlers who had come here from Alsen Island off the coast of Denmark. On August 31, 1905 the Storlie post office was moved here, with Martin Martinson continuing as pm. The Zip Code is 58311, and the village, which incorporated in 1920, reached a peak population of 358 in 1930. Mike Wipf (1887-1929), longtime pm, is remembered as the founder of the Mirolene Co., local manufacturers of patent medicines. (1, 2, 3, 18, 23, 33, 40, 79, 212)

**ALSOP** (Stutsman). This was a NPRR station built in 1875 in Sec. 3-139-67, Stirton Twp., now the south part of Cleveland. Later maps show ALSOP about two miles east of Cleveland in Sec. 36-140-67, Wold Twp. The station was named for H. W. Alsop and his brother, C. R. Alsop, engineers on the NPRR during its early years, who later operated steam boats on the Red River. Used for supplying water to locomotives, ALSOP was dismantled in 1882. (2, 3, 156, 414)

**ALTA** (Barnes). This NPRR station was built in 1884 in Sec. 20-140-57, Alta Twp., between Valley City and Oriska, and named PEAK. On July 29, 1923 it was renamed ALTA for its township, which is named for Alta Ridge, a high point on the moraine belt east of the Sheyenne River valley. A population of 20 was reported in 1920, but the site never experienced any real development, and the station was removed in 1960. (1, 2, 3, 18, 25, 34, 281)

**ALTA** (Burleigh). John Anderson (1875-1963) settled in SE¼ Sec. 4-144-78, Steiber Twp., in 1901 and about 1906 opened a country store on his land. On May 23, 1906 he was appointed pm of a post office he named ALTA, the abbreviation for the Canadian province of Alberta, which he had noticed on a recently received letter from a friend living near Calgary. Ole Anderson, father of the pm, was the mail carrier. In 1919 the business was sold to James R. Jones, who moved it one mile SSW to NW¼ Sec. 8-144-78. The post office was discontinued June 30, 1930 with mail to Regan. (1, 2, 3, 8, 12, 18, 40)

**ALTA** (McHenry). This place appears on a 1978 roadmap published by the H. M. Gousha Company, apparently in SW¼ Sec. 9-156-77, Denbigh Twp., about two miles north of Denbigh. It is a copyright town, inserted to protect against unauthorized copying by competitors. (3, 34)

**ALTON** (Hettinger). This NPRR station was founded in 1910 in NE¼ Sec. 6-133-91, Cannon Ball Twp., and named for Alton M. Burt, Superintendent of the Dakota Division of the NPRR. Alton is an Old English name meaning from the old manor. The townsite was platted in 1910, and the post office was established April 27, 1910 with George W. Bysom pm. There was confusion with Alton Junction in Traill County, so on September 17, 1910 the name was changed to BURT. (2, 3, 18, 19, 40, 181)

**ALTON** (Traill). This was a GNRR spur and loading station built in SW¼ Sec. 21-145-50, Hillsboro Twp., three miles SSE of Hillsboro, and one-half mile north of Alton Junction. It was founded in the 1890's to serve the Alton Farm, a 2,000 acre operation named for Alton R. Dalrymple, the only son of legendary bonanza farmer Clark C. Dalrymple. Sometimes shown on maps as Alton Siding, it was served by the Kelso post office. About 1905-1915, it was shown on maps as DALRY, or Dalry Siding, quite obviously coined from the Dalrymple family name. ALTON is still shown on some detailed county maps. (1, 2, 3, 18, 29, 187)

**ALTON JUNCTION** (Traill). This is a point in NW¼ Sec. 28-145-50, Hillsboro Twp., about one-half mile south of Alton, and two miles north of Kelso, where the GNRR branches off to Halstad, MN. Today it is approximately the intersection of US Highway 81 and ND Highway 200. (3)

**AMANDA** (Mountrail). This was a rural post office established March 23, 1906 with Henry H. Rustad pm. It was located in SW¼ Sec. 25-153-91, Crane Creek Twp., eight miles NE of New Town. Sadie Pettingill became pm in 1907 in Sec. 36-153-91. She married John W. McNamara in 1908, and was the area's first school teacher. Gus Sather (1881-1962) became pm in 1911, moving it to his country store in NW¼ Sec. 32-153-91. He moved to Van Hook in 1914, and the post office closed September 7, 1915 with mail to Van Hook. The name is said to honor Amanda Fulton Chaffee, wife of Eben Chaffee, President of the Amenia and Sharon Land Co., a holding company doing most of its business in Cass County. Others say it was named for Amanda Pettingal, an early settler. The name is derived from the Latin word meaning love. (2, 18, 19, 40, 53, 72)

**AMBRO** (Cavalier). This was a Bohemian settlement founded about 1891 in SE 1/4 Sec. 18-163-60, Mount Carmel Twp., about thirteen miles NNW of Langdon. The origin of the name is unknown. The post office was established November 27, 1893 with George Reidhammer pm, and closed August 15, 1901 with mail to Mount Carmel. (2, 3, 40, 249, 414)

**AMBROSE** (Divide). This city was platted in 1905 by the Tri-State Land Co. in SW¼ Sec. 12-163-99, Ambrose Twp., at the terminus of the Soo Line RR branch line from Flaxton. It was named for Ambrose Olson, right-of-way agent for the Soo Line RR. Ambrose is a Greek name meaning immortal. The post office was established August 18, 1906 with Elstone McKoane pm. It became a Canadian port-of-entry in 1907, the same year it became the first settlement in Divide County to incorporate as a village. It became a city in 1910, and was the first county seat, losing that honor to Crosby in 1912 by just three votes. The Zip Code is 58833. Called "The Queen City of Divide County", it reached a peak population of 389 in 1920, but reported just 58 residents in 1980. (2, 18, 19, 33, 40, 52, 73, 79)

**AMENIA** (Cass). This NPRR station was founded in 1880 in NE¼ Sec. 26-141-52, Amenia Twp., and named by Eben Chaffee of the Amenia-Sharon Land Co., formed in 1875 in Amenia, NY and Sharon, CT. Amenia, NY was named by Dr. Thomas Young, who chose a name of unclear Latin origin. The company acquired thousands of acres of NPRR land, and this was essentially a company town until the firm was disbanded in 1920. The GNRR had acquired the railroad in 1882. The post office was established January 20, 1880 with Edwin McNeil pm. The village incorporated in 1927, becoming a city in 1967. The elevation is 952, the Zip Code is 58004, and a peak population of 127 was reached in 1950. Armenia is an erroneous spelling. (2, 10, 33, 40, 45, 77)

**AMERICAN CITY** (McLean). This was a Garrison Dam boom town, founded in 1947 in NE¼ Sec. 5-146-83, Longfellow Twp., just east of Sitka. Its name was promotional in nature, said to demonstrate the post-WWII patriotism of the residents. The Ranger Bar was the sole business venture in AMERICAN CITY. (3, 28)

**AMERICAN SETTLEMENT** (Cass). This was a rural community founded about 1871 in W½ Sec. 33-141-49, Harwood Twp., just west of present-day Harwood, and straddling the Sheyenne River. Simon V. Hoag and John M. Bender were the first settlers. The name noted the nationality of the settlers, as opposed to the Norwegian community six miles to the NE called Osterdahl Settlement. (3, 77)

**AMES** (Traill). This was a GNRR loading station in SE¼ Sec. 13-147-53, Viking Twp., three miles NNW of Mayville, and one mile SSE of Portland Junction. It appears on maps circa 1915-1920, and was named for Francis Wilbur Ames (1851-1926), a native of CT who was one of the county's first lawyers. He came to Caledonia in 1881, moved to Mayville in 1886, and was involved in banking and politics. (1, 2, 29, 187)

**AMIDON** (Slope). This townsite was founded in 1910 in NW¼ Sec. 25-135-101, East Sand Creek Twp., as the anticipated terminus of the Milwaukee Road RR branch line from McLaughlin, SD. It was named for Judge Charles F. Amidon of Fargo. The post office was established May 13, 1911 with James E. Dinsmore pm. The railroad never did build beyond New England, but AMIDON beat Marmarth, Bessie, and Slope Center for county seat honors in 1915, and its survival was thus virtually assured. It incorporated as a village in 1915, and became a city in 1918. The peak population was 162, reached in 1930, but the 1980 count was just 41, making it one of the smallest county seats in the nation, challenged only by Manning in Dunn County. The elevation is 2800, and the Zip Code is 58620. (1, 2, 40, 79, 82)

**AMOR** (Bowman). This was a farm post office established July 31, 1908 with Martin C. Nelson pm. It was located in NE¼ Sec. 29-130-103, Amor Twp., fourteen miles south of Rhame, and named for its township, which was named for Amor, MN by settlers from that village, which had been named in 1879 by Norwegian settlers for the Latin word meaning love, only after their first choice of Cupid had been rejected. The post office closed July 31, 1920 with mail to Bowman. (1, 2, 3, 13, 18, 34, 40, 120)

**AMOR** (Walsh). This was a farm post office established October 24, 1881 with Almon Wamben pm. It was located in SE¼ Sec. 16-156-56, Vernon Twp., midway between Park River and Lankin. The name is Latin for love. Ed Wamben (1853-1954) was a state legislator. The post office closed May 31, 1882 with mail to Kensington. (3, 25, 40, 75)

**AMOR** (Ward). This was a rural post office established July 26, 1904 with Albert Larsen pm. The order was rescinded January 24, 1905. The location of this proposed post office is unknown. (3, 40)

**AMUNDSVILLE** (McLean). This was a farm post office established December 1, 1913 with Joseph O. Amundson pm in his country store. It was located in SE¼ Sec. 27-150-88, Amundsville Twp., five miles NW of Roseglen. The name honored both the pm and his brother, Henry, who came here in 1912 from Glencoe, MN. It closed May 31, 1916 with mail to Ryder. (2, 3, 28, 40, 278)

**AMY** (McHenry). This was a farm post office established April 21, 1904 with Tabitha B. Collins pm. It was located in NW¼ Sec. 26-158-79, Little Deep Twp., midway between Bantry and Deering, on the farm of her husband, James E. Collins. Her father, Eli Harmon, lived just to the NW in SE¼ Sec. 22-158-79, and served as the mail carrier. The post office closed October 31, 1907 with mail to Saline. The name, of Latin origin meaning beloved, was chosen to honor the daughter of Rev. C. M. Rees, the local Methodist minister. (2, 3, 18, 19, 40, 412)

**ANAMOOSE** (McHenry). This settlement was founded about 1893 by Romanians who came here from Saskatchewan, Canada. The Soo Line RR arrived and a townsite was established in Secs. 22 & 23-151-75, Anamoose Twp. The post office was established September 7, 1898 with Albert

Albrecht pm, and the village incorporated in 1922. The name is credited to the daughter of a Soo Line RR official, and is a corruption of the Chippewa word *uhnemoosh*, meaning female dog. It is a favorite of collectors of unusual place names. The elevation is 1620, the Zip Code is 58710, and a peak population of 669 was reached in 1910. (1, 2, 3, 18, 33, 40, 79)

**ANDERSEN** (Grant). Jeppe G. Andersen became pm of the SANDERS post office on September 9, 1908, moving the facility to his home in NW¼ Sec. 24-133-88, Rock Twp., two miles south of the original location. During his tenure as pm, local residents usually referred to the post office as ANDERSEN, but no official name change was ever made. The SANDERS post office closed February 28, 1911 with mail to Elm. (3, 40, 177, 414)

**ANDREWS** (Burleigh). This was a rural community founded in 1891 about five miles NE of Regan, and named for William E. Andrews, one of the first settlers. The post office was established April 15, 1898 with David Z. Keeler pm, with the facility being in his home in NE¼ Sec. 20-143-77, Canfield Twp. In 1905 it moved one mile SW to the home of new pm John W. Olson in SW 1/4 Sec. 30-143-77. About this time a small settlement called Canfield started at the original location, and the ANDREWS post office closed January 31, 1906 with mail to Canfield. (2, 3, 8, 12, 40, 414)

**ANDREWS** (Golden Valley). This was an original NPRR siding built on the mainline in SE¼ Sec. 28-140-103, Sentinel Butte Twp., seven miles east of Sentinel Butte. It was named for nearby Andrews Creek, which had been named for a member of the construction crew. No development occurred at the site, and it disappeared from most maps before 1900. (3, 18, 25, 79, 179, 414)

**ANETA** (Nelson). A rural community named HOILAND began about 1881 in NE 1/4 Sec. 32-149-57, Ora Twp., but when a post office was established September 3, 1883 with

LeRoy W. Mitchell pm, the name was changed to ANETA, coined from the name of the pm's wife, ANna RosETA Mitchell. In 1896 the GNRR built into this area, and the post office was moved one-half mile SW to W½ Sec. 32 & E 1/2 Sec. 31-149-57, with a continuation of the name. The town incorporated as a city in 1903 with George F. Thayer, known as the "Father of Aneta", as first mayor. The elevation is 1491, the Zip Code is 58212, and a peak population of 662 was reached in 1920. ANETA is known as the "Queen City of the Upper Sheyenne." (1, 2, 3, 18, 33, 40, 52, 79, 124, 130, 131)

**ANGIE** (Williams). This was a rural post office in SW¼ Sec. 28-158-98, Rainbow Twp., about thirteen miles NW of Ray. It was established June 25, 1904 with Joseph M. Wiltse pm, and closed May 15, 1914 with mail to Ray. The name was suggested by area resident John Ryan using the nickname of the pm's wife, Angelica. A store operated here until 1917. (2, 18, 40, 50, 53)

**ANGORA** (Burleigh). This NPRR siding was built in 1906 in Sec. 27-139-76, Sterling Twp., two miles NE of Sterling, and named for Angora, MN, which was named for the ancient city in Galatia, Turkey, famed for its goats wool. Little development occurred here, and the siding was dismantled in 1941. (2, 12, 13, 18, 34, 35)

**ANNIE** (Foster). This was apparently a proposed name change for the HAVEN post office when Mrs. Annie Wentworth Parker became pm on April 11, 1905. The facility was then located in the home of her husband, Clarence Parker (1862‑1947), in SE¼ Sec. 12-146-64, Haven Twp. The proposed name change, noting the given names of both the pm and her daughter, is mentioned in many local histories, but is not reflected in government records, which state that the post office operated as HAVEN until closing April 15, 1909 with mail to Kensal. (3, 40, 97, 414)

**ANNIS** (Pierce). This was a rural post office in NW¼ Sec. 3-152-72, Alexanter Twp., ten miles north of Selz. It was established September 12, 1900 with Walter McPeek

*Main Street, Aneta, circa 1910.*

pm, who suggested the name Buffalo Lake. Postal officials did not allow two-word place names at that time, and since there was an existing Buffalo post office in Cass County, they selected the name ANNIS, of unknown origin and no local significance. The post office closed January 15, 1905 with mail to Selz. (2, 40, 113, 114, 414)

**ANSELM** (Ransom). This Soo Line RR station was built in 1891 in SE¼ Sec. 5-135-54, Shenford Twp., and by the next year had absorbed much of the pioneer settlement of Shenford, four miles to the south. The post office was transferred here January 21, 1892 from Shenford, with railroad agent Denis C. Cullen becoming the pm. A Soo Line RR official's wife selected the name from the famous medieval Archbishop of Canterbury, St. Anselm. Anselm is a Teutonic name meaning divine protector. The elevation is 1085, and the peak population of 50 was reached in 1921. The post office closed June 30, 1942 with mail to Sheldon. (1, 2, 3, 18, 19, 40, 79, 85, 201, 206)

**ANTELOPE** (Benson). This was a NPRR siding built in June 1885 in SW¼ Sec. 2-151-67, Oberon Twp., and named to note its location in the extreme NW end of Antelope Valley, named in 1883 by the area's first settler, Henry U. Thomas, to note the many antelope that roamed the prairie here. When the post office was established January 25, 1886, the name was changed to OBERON. (2, 18, 79)

**ANTELOPE** (Richland). This place appears sporadically on maps as late as the 1950's in SE¼ Sec. 16-133-50, Antelope Twp., and was named for the common range animal. It consists of a rural school and church. (3)

**ANTELOPE** (Stark). This NPRR station was founded in 1881 in N½ Sec. 33-140-93, Taylor Twp., and named for the prong-horned antelope that grazed in the area. The post office was established July 21, 1882 with John M. Tracey pm. On September 4, 1882 the name was changed to TAYLOR. (2, 18, 40, 74, 407)

**ANTELOPE** (Stark). This NPRR siding was built in 1881 in Sec. 18-139-91, twelve miles SW of Hebron. It was at first called FIFTH SIDING, and then for a few months called YOUNG MAN'S BUTTE SIDING, but in 1882 it was renamed ANTELOPE by NPRR official H. V. Thomas to note the nearby creek and valley that were named to note the large population of prong-horned antelope in the area. The post office was established January 11, 1886 with Jacob Heidhardt pm. ANTELOPE at one time had a store and a grain elevator, and reported a population of 35 in 1920. The post office closed June 30, 1954 with mail to Richardton. The site is marked today as Exit –18 on Interstate 94. (1, 2, 3, 18, 25, 40, 74, 79)

**ANTELOPE STATION** (Stark). This was the seventh station on the Bismarck-Fort Keogh mail route, established in 1878 in Sec. 18-138-95, eight miles SSE of Dickinson, and named for nearby Antelope Creek. The exact site is subject to debate, as no positive remains can be identified today. The station was abandoned in 1882 after completion of the NPRR mainline. (2, 3, 417)

**ANTLER** (Bottineau). This rural post office was established June 21, 1898 with Duncan McLean pm. In 1902 it moved two miles SW

to the GNRR terminus in SE¼ Sec. 3-163-82, Antler Twp. The townsite was platted in 1905. The elevation is 1542, the Zip Code is 58711, and a peak population of 342 was reached in 1910, although just 101 residents lived here in 1980. Harley "Bud" Kissner brought national attention to ANTLER in 1981 when he offered free land to families with children who would move here. The intent was to keep the school open, and the plan worked for a few years. The name was chosen because of its location near Antler Creek, named because its north and south branches resemble the antlers of a deer when drawn on a map. (1, 2, 18, 33, 34, 40, 52, 79, 101, 153)

**ANTWERP** (Towner). This was a rural post office in SW¼ Sec. 22-163-66, Bryan Twp., about nine miles north of Rocklake. It was established May 8, 1901 with Peter Geyer, who came here in 1897, as pm. After postal officials rejected the name Dover, it was named for ANTWERP, Belgium at the suggestion of a local resident who had come from there. The Belgian city dates from before the eighth century, when the Ganerbians, or Antwerpians, were converted to Christianity. The name was never very popular with local residents, but a name change to Midway was rejected by postal officials in 1902, and the post office operated as ANTWERP until it closed July 31, 1907 with mail to Saginaw. (2, 3, 5, 18, 40, 196, 414)

**APLIN** (Oliver). This was a rural post office in Sec. 20-143-87, Springvale Twp., about five miles SE of Beulah. It was established October 5, 1906 with Harry C. Aplin pm, and closed August 31, 1916 with mail to Evans. The name officially honored Henry Clay Aplin and Lillian Kraus Aplin, who came here in March 1906 from Knob Noster, MO. (1, 2, 3, 7, 40, 121)

**APPAM** (Williams). This was a GNRR station founded in 1916 on the Stanley-Grenora line. It is located in NE¼ Sec. 27-159-100, Blue Ridge Twp. The post office was established August 17, 1917 with Mrs. Frances E. Pilgrim pm, who held the post until 1954. Her husband was a pioneer merchant in the community. The population never was much more than 100. The post office, Zip Code 58834, closed November 30, 1972 with mail to Alamo. GNRR officials coined the name, which has no known local significance. (2, 33, 40, 41, 50, 79)

**APPLE CREEK** (Burleigh). This was a NPRR loading station built before 1890 in NE¼ Sec. 10-138-79, Apple Creek Twp., seven miles east of Bismarck. It was named for nearby Apple Creek, which was called Qui Apelle by the early French explorers to note the thorn apple thickets along its banks. Local Indians called it *Taspan Wakpala*, meaning thorn apple creek. It appeared on maps into the 1930's. (1, 2, 8, 18, 25, 79)

**APPLETON** (Burleigh). This was a rural post office established June 9, 1880 with Monroe D. Dawes pm, who named it for Mary E. Appleton, a pioneer homesteader. On September 29, 1880 the name was changed to MAINE. It was located in E½ Sec. 23-138-77, Logan Twp., five miles SSE of McKenzie. (2, 8, 18, 40)

**APPLE VALLEY** (Burleigh). This is a rural subdivision founded in the early 1970's in NW¼ Sec. 36-139-79, Gibbs Twp., three miles west of Menoken, and just south of US Highway 10. The owners of the site were

Ralph E. and Roberta Small. The name notes its location near Apple Creek, and although it remains an unincorporated settlement, it is the largest population center between Bismarck and Steele. (3, 18, 34)

**ARCIS** (Mercer). This was a farm post office established May 24, 1894 with George Kuch Jr. pm. It was located in NW¼ Sec. 24-145-86, six miles NE of Hazen, and named for Arcis, South Russia, hometown of many local settlers. In 1899 it moved eight miles NW to SW¼ Sec. 10-146-87, the home of new pm William Fischer. The post office closed July 15, 1901 with mail to Expansion. (2, 3, 40, 64, 414)

**ARCTIC** (Stutsman). This NPRR station was founded in 1882 in NW¼ Sec. 3-140-64, Midway Twp., five miles NNW of Jamestown. The post office was established September 22, 1882 with Henry Griffin pm, who suggested the name Forrest. This was rejected by postal officials who felt there would be confusion with Forest River, and Forestburg, which is now in South Dakota. Instead, it was given a name which certainly did not serve to attract settlers. Little development occurred, and the post office closed October 2, 1885 with mail to Jamestown. (2, 3, 40, 414)

**ARDOCH** (Walsh). This GNRR station was founded in 1881 in NW¼ Sec. 33-155-52, Ardoch Twp., and platted that year as CLARE. The first settlers called the place KIMBALL, which was found to be duplicated in what is now South Dakota. The post office was established February 27, 1882 with John Stevenson pm, who named it for his hometown of Ardoch, Ontario, Canada. For some years the GNRR station was spelled ARDOCK, creating a bit of confusion. The townsite had an early boom period, claiming a population of 300 in 1890. High hopes continued in 1905, when the Soo Line RR came, making ARDOCH a two-railroad town. Since that time, however, the village, which incorporated in 1886, has been in a decline, reporting a population of just 79 in 1980. The elevation is 821, and the Zip Code is 58213. On August 31, 1975 the post office became a CPO of Grand Forks. (1, 2, 3, 25, 33, 40, 52, 75, 79)

**ARDOCK** (Walsh). This GNRR station was founded in 1881 in NW¼ Sec. 33-155-52, Ardoch Twp., and was called CLARE and KIMBALL before being named ARDOCH on February 27, 1882. The depot itself was acutally across the section line in NE¼ Sec. 32-155-52, and for some time its name was spelled ARDOCK. It is claimed without support that the post office used this spelling for a time as well. (2, 3, 18, 75)

**ARENA** (Burleigh). A rural post office was established January 23, 1906 with Harry A. Mutchler (1874-1956) pm, located in S½

Sec. 10-142-75, Harriett Twp., between Wing and Tuttle. Mr. Mutchler named it to note its location in a shallow valley surrounded by hills, a natural arena, which curiously is the Latin word meaning sand. When the NPRR built the Pingree-Wilton line in 1910, they angled the line a bit to the south and entered what was becoming a thriving little inland townsite. A population of 150 was claimed in 1920, but just 35 residents were counted here in 1930. The elevation is 1903, and the Zip Code is 58412. Bernice Wenaas Asbridge, State Treasurer in the 1960's, was born here. (1, 2, 3, 8, 12, 13, 18, 33, 40, 41, 63, 200, 263)

**ARGUSVILLE** (Cass). This settlement was founded in 1880 in SW¼ Sec. 6-141-49, Harwood Twp. The GNRR arrived in 1881, and the post office was established April 12, 1881 with John M. Olds pm. It was platted in August 1881 by Frank W. Aldrich and incorporated as a village on May 31, 1921. The elevation is 884, the Zip Code is 58005, and a peak population of 147 was reached in 1980. The name was coined from *The Fargo Argus*, a daily newspaper founded in 1879 by A. W. Edwards. Argus was the Greek mythological watchman with a hundred eyes. (1, 2, 18, 19, 25, 33, 40, 77, 79)

**ARICKAREE** (McLean). This was a farm post office established March 17, 1898 with Annie Minehan pm. It was located on the farm owned by her husband, Patrick J. Minehan, in NW¼ Sec. 6-148-87, Blackwater Twp., seven miles SE of Roseglen, and named for the Arikara Indians, a local tribe, whose name means horns of the elk, referring to their hair styles. The spelling of the post office name was an alternate form in vogue at the time. The post office was discontinued April 20, 1899 with mail to Fort Berthold. (2, 3, 10, 28, 40, 415)

**ARMOURDALE** (Towner). This was a farm post office established April 24, 1900 with Daniel M. Armour pm, who named it for his brother, Angus Armour. It was located in SE¼ Sec. 6-162-67, Armourdale Twp., four miles south of Hansboro. In 1904 this name was adopted by the new Soo Line RR terminus townsite in Sec. 7-162-67, although the post office was later moved two miles SE to the home of Angus Armour in NW¼ Sec. 21-162-67. The post office closed December 15, 1912 with mail to Elsberry, but the townsite reported a population of 25 as late as 1930, and remained on most maps into the 1960's. (1, 2, 3, 18, 40, 79, 414)

**ARMSTRONG** (Emmons). This was a rural post office established February 13, 1886 with Cymontho J. Walker pm. After postal officials rejected the name Walker, it was named for Moses K. Armstrong, who came to Dakota in 1859 and was influential in securing its territorial status in 1861. He was active in politics for twenty years, and served as the Congressional delegate 1871-1875. Armstrong is an Old English name meaning as it implies, strong of arm. The post office was located in NE¼ Sec. 22-136-74, Campbell Twp., two miles NW of Kintrye, and a population of 24 was reported in 1890. In 1898 it moved four miles WSW to the home of new pm John Anderson in NE¼ Sec. 30-136-74, and closed May 15, 1909 with mail to Braddock. (2, 3, 18, 19, 36, 40, 66, 113, 414)

**ARMSTRONG** (McLean). This was a community center of the Arikara tribe founded about 1894 in NE¼ Sec. 29-147-88, Nishu Twp., on the Fort Berthold Indian Reservation. It was named for Charles Armstrong, a well known scout, guide, and Indian interpreter at the Standing Rock Indian Reservation, and was located across the Missouri River from Ree, Mercer County. The principal structure here was the Armstrong School. Wilbur Wilde Howard (1905-1971), a famous concert violinist, was born here. The site was renamed NISHU in the early 1920's, and is now inundated by Lake Sakakawea. (1, 2, 3, 18, 28)

**ARNDT** (Towner). This was a farm post office established October 1, 1896 with Richard Euler pm, who named it for local pioneer Wilhelm Arndt. It was located in SE¼ Sec. 31-160-66, Crocus Twp., five miles west of Egeland. A few years later the name was adopted by the Soo Line RR townsite in NE¼ Sec. 1-159-67, Ideal Twp., about one mile to the SW. In 1903 the post office moved one mile NE to the home of new pm Henry L. Kahl in NW¼ Sec. 28-160-66, and closed February 28, 1906 with mail to Crocus. The post office was authorized to reopen at the townsite on July 20, 1907 with H. F. Goode pm, but that order was rescinded December 27, 1907. Little development occurred at the townsite, and after reporting a population of 5 in 1940, it disappeared from most maps. (1, 2, 3, 18, 40, 195, 197, 414)

**ARNEDO** (Bottineau). This was a GNRR siding established in 1888 in NE¼ Sec. 28-161-75, Amity Twp., about six miles SE of Bottineau. E. J. Hurt owned the site, and Lillburn Stair (1872-1927), a state legislator and penitentiary warden, operated a brick factory here about 1900. The factory was abandoned in 1909, the elevator was destroyed by fire in 1937, and the siding was abandoned in 1939. The origin of the name is unknown. Arneido and Arneida are erroneous spellings. (2, 3, 34, 101, 153)

**ARNEGARD** (McKenzie). This was a rural post office established July 14, 1906 with Gerhard A. Stenehjem pm. The name honors pioneer settler Oscar Arnegard, and was perpetuated by the GNRR when it platted a townsite in SE¼ Sec. 14-150-100, Arnegard Twp., on June 14, 1913. The elevation is 2245, the Zip Code is 58835, and the village, which incorporated in 1920, reached a peak population of 254 in 1930. (1, 2, 3, 33, 40, 52, 79, 434)

**ARNOLD** (Burleigh). This Soo Line RR station was founded in 1900 in NE¼ Sec. 27-140-80, Burnt Creek Twp., eight miles north of Bismarck, and named by townsite owner

Gen. William D. Washburn for G. T. Arnold, original owner of the site. Arnold is a Teutonic name meaning mighty as the temple. The post office was established October 31, 1901 with Robert A. Yeater pm, and it closed April 30, 1909 with mail to Grove. People continued to live here for many years, and recently the area has begun to grow with the out growths of Bismarck. (1, 2, 3, 18, 19, 40)

**ARNOLD'S POST** (Traill). This was a Hudson's Bay Compnay trading post established in 1871 in Sec. 31-147-52, Lindaas Twp., by Alvin Lewis Arnold (1833-1891). The site is just west of Mayville, and is considered to be the beginning of settlement in the Mayville-Portland area. The Arnold family played a major role in the founding of both cities. This site was later known as MAY, for Mr. Arnold's daughter. (2, 3, 187, 359, 395)

**ARRETON** (Bottineau). This rural post office was established August 14, 1901 with Pleasant O. Heald pm. Mr. Heald lived in SW¼ Sec. 10-161-82, Renville Twp., seven miles west of Maxbass, and was an organizer of the township and its first Justice of the Peace. The post office order was rescinded October 18, 1901 with the entry "no papers" in government records. On January 6, 1902 another post office, called RENVILLE, was established here, operating until 1906. The origin of the name ARRETON is unknown. (2, 3, 18, 40, 153)

**ARROWWOOD** (Stutsman). This was a farm post office established August 23, 1887 with George F. Armstrong pm. It was located in SE¼ Sec. 6-144-64, Kensal Twp., five miles west of Kensal, and named for a natural widening of the James River, Arrowwood Lake, so named because the Indians used the juneberry shoots growing on its shore for making arrows. The post office moved two miles east to SW¼ Sec. 4-144-64, the home of new pm Henry Tufford, and closed August 16, 1893 with mail going to the new Soo Line RR townsite of Kensal. Arrow Wood, Arrowood, and Arrowhead Park are erroneous spellings. (2, 3, 40, 79, 158, 161, 415)

**ARTHUR** (Cass). This NPRR townsite was founded in 1881 as ROSEDALE in NW 1/4 Sec. 24-142-52, Arthur Twp., but was quickly renamed for President Chester Alan Arthur (1830-1886), who had just succeeded the assassinated James A. Garfield. Arthur is both a Welsh name meaning bear-man, and a Celtic name meaning rock. The post office was established October 31, 1881 with John Brandenberg pm, and the townsite was platted in 1882 by Samuel B. Johnson. The elevation is 979, the Zip Code is 58006, and the city, which incorporated as a village in 1921, has shown a steady growth to a peak population of 448 in 1980. (1, 2, 10, 19, 25, 33, 34, 40, 77, 265)

**ARVID** (Golden Valley). This was a farm post office established July 18, 1916 with Kate Shucha pm. It was located in NE¼ Sec. 8-143-105, Henry Twp., twenty-four miles north of Beach, and named for H. J. Arvid, an area settler. The site also had a rural school, and listed a population of 10 in 1920. The post office closed October 31, 1919 with mail to Wibaux, MT. (2, 18, 40)

ARVIDSON (McLean). This proposed townsite was platted about 1905 by J. W. Arvidson in SW¼ Sec. 28-147-80, Lake Williams Twp. Promotional efforts failed, and it is today the eastern section of Turtle Lake. (2, 28, 271)

ARVILLA (Grand Forks). Settlement began here in 1878, and the following year the ORANGE post office was established. In May 1882 a GNRR townsite was platted in SE¼ Sec. 1-151-54, Arvilla Twp., about two miles east of ORANGE on land owned by Dudley H. Hersey. On June 28, 1882, pm Frank B. Merriman moved the ORANGE post office to the new townsite, changing the name to honor the owner's wife, Arvilla Estella Wardwell Hersey. The elevation is 1021, the Zip Code is 58214, and the population has been approximately 100 for many years. (1, 2, 3, 25, 31, 40, 69, 79, 414)

ASH (Bowman). This was a farm post office established June 8, 1909 with Bridget Agatha Phalen pm, at her home in SE¼ Sec. 17-129-102, Ladd Twp., fourteen miles south of Bowman. She married August A. Halm, her neighbor, who had come here in 1907 from Minneapolis, MN. The name honored Frank C. Ash, pm at the old Beaver post office which operated 1903-1908. ASH post office closed October 15, 1913 with mail to Swartwood. (1, 2, 3, 18, 40, 53, 120)

ASHEM (Nelson). This was a farm post office established June 30, 1884 with Louis N. Ashem pm. It was located in NE¼ Sec. 11-154-58, Sarnia Twp., three miles NE of Whitman, and closed October 20, 1885 with mail to Michigan. (2, 3, 25, 34, 40, 415)

ASHGROVE (Emmons). This was a farm post office established April 6, 1899 with Patrick Kinsella pm. It was located in NW¼ Sec. 24-129-79, two miles north of the SD border on the east bank of the Missouri River. The name is said to have been descriptive of the locale. It closed February 14, 1903 with mail to Pollock, SD. (2, 3, 40, 66, 414)

ASHLEY (McIntosh). The Soo Line RR established this townsite in 1887 in Sec. 30-130-69, Kisslingberry Twp., and named it for Ashley E. Morrow of the Northwestern Construction Co., builders of the railroad grade here. Some state that it was named for Ashley Morrell, who was related to the owners of the townsite. Ashley is an Old English name meaning dweller in the ash-tree meadow. The post office was established May 4, 1888 with Thomas J. Lamunyon pm. That year it was made McIntosh county seat, replacing Hoskins. The elevation is 2001, the Zip Code is 58413, and the peak population of 1,423 was reached in 1950. (1, 2, 3, 19, 33, 40, 79, 134, 211)

ASHTABULA (Barnes). This farm post office was established October 23, 1882 with John B. Rich pm. It was located in SE¼ Sec. 4-142-58, Ashtabula Twp., fifteen miles NNW of Valley City, and named for the nearby lake, which was named for Ashtabula County, OH. John Hubbard selected the name, which is an Algonquin Indian word meaning there are always enough fish moving in the river. In 1883 it moved one mile NE to the home of new pm Andrew T. Anderson in Sec. 34-143-58, Sibley Twp., and in 1893 it moved one mile SE to Sec. 2-142-58, where a townsite was

platted in anticipation of a railroad. The railroad did not get built, but the post office survived until May 13, 1913 when mail went to Luverne. James Scott was the first pm at the "townsite", and many early accounts refer to the site as SCOTT'S. (2, 10, 18, 40, 76)

ASTER (Oliver). This was a farm post office established May 18, 1904 about three miles SE of Sanger with Peter Mortensen pm. On March 16, 1906 it was moved one mile west to the home of Sherman Hickle in NE¼ Sec. 8-142-82, Manley Twp. It closed March 15, 1911 with mail to Yucca. The name, Greek for star, notes the many asters, a wild flower, found in the area. (2, 3, 4, 18, 40, 121)

ATCOAL (Burke). This was a Soo Line RR loading station in NW¼ Sec. 32-163-94, Forthun Twp., that was promoted as a rival townsite to the GNRR station at Larson. No real settlement ever occurred in ATCOAL. The name is thought to note the station's use as a loading site for the lignite mined just south of the site. (1, 2, 3, 18, 67)

ATKINSON (Bowman). This was a station on the Milwaukee Road RR in NE¼ Sec. 34-132-103, Marion Twp., between Rhame and Bowman, and named for William Atkinson, a local Justice of the Peace. The post office was established May 22, 1907 with James H. Kratzer pm, and on February 9, 1908 the name was changed to GRIFFIN. (2, 3, 18, 34, 40)

ATWILL (Stutsman). This was a rural post office established September 28, 1883 in the home of pm Clarence F. Atwill in NW¼ Sec. 12-137-64, Severn Twp., five miles west of Montpelier. Postal officials suggested using the pm's name after rejecting his suggested name of Allen. Mr. Atwill and his friend, E. A. Webb, came here in 1882 from Baltimore, MD. A small settlement began, with a population of 25 being reported in 1890, but the lack of a railroad resulted in a quick decline. The post office closed March 2, 1895 with mail to Montpelier. (2, 18, 25, 40, 158, 414)

AUBURN (Walsh). This was a farm post office established March 26, 1883 with Donald McKenzie pm. It was located in S½ Sec. 25-158-54, Glenwood Twp., five miles NW of Grafton, and named for Auburn, Ontario, Canada, which was named for Auburn, Yorkshire, England, a city featured in Oliver Goldsmith's poem *The Deserted Village*. In 1884 the post office moved four miles NE to the new GNRR townsite known as AUBURN STATION in NW¼ Sec. 14-158-53, Farmington Twp. This place became generally known as AUBURN. An initial boom resulted in a population of 240 in 1890, but all census reports since 1920 have been under 100. The post office closed March 31, 1943 with mail to Grafton. Harley Ralph Kingsbury, a longtime state legislator, was born here in 1913. (1, 2, 3, 10, 18, 25, 38, 40, 75)

AUBURN STATION (Walsh). This GNRR station was built in 1884 in NW¼ Sec. 14-158-53, Farmington Twp., six miles north of Grafton, and named for the nearby farm post office. That facility moved here later in the year, and the site soon became known simply as AUBURN. (3, 18)

AURELIA (Ward). This settlement was founded in 1900 by Moravians from Hector, MN along the GNRR tracks in Sec. 34-158-87, Carbondale Twp., three miles south of Donnybrook. Railroad officials named it using the Latin word for golden, signifying the opportunites in the area. Others say it noted the golden color of the butterflies at the site. A station was built in 1904 with two elevators, and a post office was established March 29, 1907 with William D. Cooper pm. A population of 125 was reported in 1920, but by 1960 the count was just 25. The post office was discontinued May 31, 1954 with mail to Donnybrook, and the Aurelia Moravian Church conducted its last service in 1970. (1, 2, 18, 19, 40, 41, 79, 100, 375)

AUSTIN (Bowman). This was a rural post office established May 13, 1908 with Walter W. "Bill" Austin pm. It was located in SW¼ Sec. 12-130-106, sixteen miles SW of Rhame. Austin is derived from the Latin name Augustus, meaning exalted. The post office closed September 15, 1919 with mail to Rhame. (1, 2, 3, 19, 40, 120)

AUSTIN (Cavalier). This was a rural community of Scotch-Irish settlers from Canada about two miles south of Sarles. The post office was established September 19, 1895 with William Hay pm. It was named for the local Presbyterian minister, Rev. James Austin. In 1902 it was moved a few miles east to NE¼ Sec. 29-163-63, Byron Twp., and closed May 15, 1903 with mail to Hannah. (2, 3, 40)

AUSTIN (Slope). This name was once applied to a rural community centered along the Little Missouri River in East Yule Twp. (135-105), about twenty-five miles west of Amidon. The name honored William Leslie Austin (1860-1941), a local rancher. (2, 18, 34, 82, 415)

AVOCA (Williams). This was a GNRR loading station in SE¼ Sec. 3-154-100, Stony Creek Twp., about five miles NE of Williston. During the 1890's large stockyards operated at the station. A post office was established October 4, 1904 with Arthur L. Cosmer pm, and closed May 31, 1910 with mail to Williston. The name is Latin for called away, or withdrawn. It is said that GNRR officials named it for Avoca, MN, which had been named in 1879 by Archbishop Ireland for the river and valley in Ireland about forty miles south of Dublin, made famous in the poetry of Thomas Moore. Avoka is an erroneous spelling. (2, 3, 13, 18, 40, 50, 79)

AYE (Cass). A post office called DUNLOP was established in SW¼ Sec. 11-141-54, Ayr Twp., on October 17, 1883 with Frank Howard Dickinson pm. On December 4, 1883 he changed the name to AYR, but postal officials erroneously approved the name change as AYE. While filing the paperwork necessary to correct the mistake, efforts were made to change the name to

ELGIN, but on January 7, 1884 the name AYR was officially put into use. It is assumed that the AYE spelling was never actually put into use. (3, 40, 297)

**AYLMER** (Pierce). This was a GNRR station established in the early 1900's straddling Sec. 6-151-74, White Twp., and Sec. 31-152-74, Antelope Lake Twp. A rural school was located here in 1916 and there have always been a few residents, but it never did have a post office. A population of 45 was reported in 1910, and 11 residents were here as late as 1981. It was named for Aylmer, Ontario, Canada, which was named for Lord Aylmer, Governor-in-Chief of Canada 1831-1835. Aylmer is a Teutonic name meaning of awe-inspiring fame. (2, 3, 10, 19, 53, 68, 79, 114)

**AYR** (Cass). This post office was established October 17, 1883 as DUNLOP, but pm Frank H. Dickinson changed the name to AYR on December 4, 1883. Postal officials erroneously entered the change as AYE, and this mistake was corrected January 7, 1884. Meanwhile some people tried to change the name to ELGIN, and it took action by the territorial legislature in 1885 to kill this effort. Mr. Dickinson named the post office for Ayrshire, Scotland, home of many area settlers. Ayr, Scotland dates from 1197, when King William the Lion built a castle at the site. The village incorporated in 1925, and reached a peak population of 107 in 1940, with a decline to just 32 in 1983. The elevation is 1203, and the Zip Code is 58007. Mayor Keith Johnson's efforts in 1983 allowed local residents to secure vehicle license plates with the prefix "AYR". (1, 2, 3, 18, 25, 33, 34, 40, 52, 77, 79, 297)

# B

**BABCOCK** (Sargent). This was a rural community in NE¼ Sec. 5-130-58, Jackson Twp., named for Luther Verner Babcock, a pioneer settler who was the county judge 1884-1886. Some sources report that a post office was here in 1883, but government records do not confirm this. A Soo Line RR townsite was founded later in 1883 two miles to the north named Verner, also for Mr. Babcock. (2, 3, 25, 165, 167)

**BABY MINE** (Morton). This was a rural post office established June 21, 1880 with Robert McKee pm. It was located in SW¼ Sec. 22-138-86, Sims Twp., two miles SW of Sims, and named to note that it served a small coal mine. The post office closed May 24, 1881 with mail to Bismarck. It reopened June 15, 1881, but closed for good August 3, 1881 with mail again to Bismarck. (2, 3, 40, 107, 415)

**BAC** (Cavalier). This was a farm post office established August 24, 1891 with Wilson McCann pm, and was located in NW¼ Sec. 4-163-64, Mount Carmel Twp., four miles west of Maida near the Canadian border. The origin of the name is unknown. The post office closed February 14, 1903 with mail to Maida. Bae is an erroneous spelling. (2, 3, 40)

**BACHELOR** (Rolette). This was a rural post office established January 23, 1901 with Newton J. Morris pm. It was at first located in Hutchinson Twp. (163-71), but was later moved to NE¼ Sec. 24-163-72, Holmes Twp., about three miles SW of the original site. The name noted the fact that many of the patrons were bachelors. The post office closed April 30, 1918 with mail to Jarves. The Helium post office operated at this site 1922-1923. (1, 2, 3, 18, 40, 123)

**BACHELOR'S GROVE** (Grand Forks). This was a stage stop on the Grand Forks-Fort Totten trail, sometimes called THOMSON'S GROVE, in Sec. 30-153-55, Agnes Twp., about two miles NW of McCanna. The name was coined by James H. Mathews and W. N. Roach while establishing the mail route, noting that most settlers in the area were Norweigians, and only one had a family. He was Hans Hanson, and the township was named for his daughter, the first white baby born here. The later part of the name noted the many trees along the nearby Turtle River. The site was abandoned after the building of the GNRR in the late 1880's. (2, 31, 69, 79)

**BACKOO** (Pembina). This is a GNRR townsite in Secs. 23 & 24-162-55, Advance Twp. A post office was established September 26, 1887 with William L. Weeks pm. The population never exceeded 50, and the post office, Zip Code 58215, closed July 1, 1985. Some sources say the name was coined from the Barcoo River in Australia by pioneer settler John Mountain, who wanted to pick a name that was unique to this country.

Others say it is derived from Baku, the Russian port on the Caspian Sea. (2, 3, 18, 25, 33, 40, 79, 108)

**BACONVILLE** (Nelson). This was a farm post office established November 21, 1883 with James Cromar pm, and located in Sec. 35-154-57, Dahlen Twp., three miles south of Dahlen. The name honored J. D. Bacon, the owner of the Dacotah Hotel in Grand Forks, who had interests in this area. In 1904 the post office was moved to SE¼ Sec. 17-154-57, three miles west of Dahlen with Martha Helland pm, but it closed October 31, 1905 with mail to Petersburg. (2, 3, 18, 25, 40, 124, 125, 126, 128, 130)

**BADEN** (Ward). This Soo Line RR loading station in S½ Sec. 14-159-88, Baden Twp., replaced the Galva station just to the east in 1904. The Galva post office moved here January 15, 1904, taking the name BADE? to honor settlirs from that province of Germany. Olof Rudolph was the pm and the township clerk. A population of 25 was reported in 1920, but the post office closed November 15, 1920 with mail to Kenmare, and BADEN disappeared from maps in the late 1930's. (1, 2, 18, 40, 79, 100, 375)

**BADLAND** (Bowman). This place appears on maps circa 1910-1915 in Langberg Twp. (129-104), near the source of the North Fork of the Grand River, about twenty miles south of Rhame. No significant development occurred here, and it is thought that it was a rural community named for the Badlands, a range of highly-eroded territory extending throughout the western portions of both Dakotas. Early French explorers called the area Mauvaises Terres, meaning bad-for-traveling lands. The township at this time was served by the Langberg post office. (2, 3, 18, 36, 79)

**BADLAND** (Slope). This was a rural post office established September 10, 1908 with Frethjob A. "Fred" Halbakken, a Norwegian who had come here in March 1908 from Fergus Falls, MN, as pm. It was located in Sec. 18-135-103, Richland Center Twp., twelve miles west of Amidon, and named to note its location in the Badlands. The French called this area Mauvaises Terres, meaning bad-for-traveling lands, the Sioux called the area *Maka Seeche*, or bad earth, and the Mandan called the area *Wahs Chon Choka*, meaning where the hills look at each other. Forest Lambert was the mail carrier. The post office closed July 6, 1916 and was replaced the following day by the Bierman post office, but BADLAND continued to appear on maps into the 1940's. (2, 3, 10, 40, 53, 79, 82)

**BAHM** (Morton). This was a rural post office established March 7, 1912 with John Bahm Sr. (1874-1941) pm. He was born in MN and came here in 1877 with his parents, William and Mary (Kasper) Bahm, natives of Bohemia and Germany respectively. The

post office was located in S½ Sec. 32-137-84, sixteen miles south of New Salem, from which it received mail twice weekly. It was discontinued September 30, 1916 with mail to New Salem. (1, 2, 3, 17, 40, 107)

**BAILEY** (Dunn). This was a rural post office established September 8, 1905 with Jedekiah B. Smith pm. It was located in the sod house of rancher J. W. Bailey in SW¼ Sec. 32-146-93, about six miles NE of Dunn Center, although some insist that it was named for Dr. S. W. Bailey. It closed March 31, 1916 with mail to Dunn Center. (1, 2, 3, 18, 40)

**BAIRD** (Barnes). This NPRR loading station was built in 1897 in SW¼ Sec. 19-140-57, Alta Twp., just west of the Alta, or Peak, station. About 1905 the name was changed to GORMAN, and it was removed in 1924. The origin of the name is unknown. (2, 34)

**BAKER** (Benson). This Soo Line RR townsite was founded in early 1911 in NW 1/4 Sec. 15-154-70, Broe Twp. Because three prominent citizens were named William, the name Williamsburg was submitted to postal officials, but it was rejected. The name BAKER, for C. E. Baker, an early area settler and former Register of Deeds, was accepted, and the post office opened September 23, 1912 with George Olson pm. Lots were sold July 11, 1912, and this day has since been celebrated as Baker Day. The first rural electric cooperative in ND was founded here in 1937, but it moved to Cando in 1942. A population of 150 was claimed in 1920, but a steady decline has reduced that county to just 20 in 1976. The post office, Zip Code 58312, closed March 12, 1976 with mail to York. (2, 33, 34, 40, 41, 149)

**BALDT** (Dunn). This was a farm post office established October 2, 1911 with Olive Baldt pm, and named for her husband, John P. Baldt. It was located in NW¼ Sec. 22-146-94, seven miles NNW of Dunn Center, and closed March 31, 1913 with mail to Bailey. (3, 34, 40, 53, 415)

**BALDWIN** (Burleigh). This Soo Line RR townsite was founded in 1900 in Sec. 13 & 24-141-80, Glenview Twp., and Secs. 18 & 19-141-79, Crofte Twp., and named for Frank Baldwin, the son-in-law of Soo Line RR founder Gen. William Drew Washburn. Mr. Baldwin was a correspondent for *Outlook* magazine. The post office was established November 16, 1901 with Charles A. Johnson, the railroad agent, as pm. A boom occurred, and by 1920 the city boasted of 200 residents, a bank, car dealerships, etc., but a steady decline reduced the population to just 49 in 1940, and it has remained about that size to this day. The Zip Code is 58521. (2, 12, 14, 18, 33, 40, 79)

**BALDWIN** (Dickey). This was a Soo Line RR siding built in 1917 in NW¼ Sec. 22-131-61, Yorktown Twp., six miles east of Fullerton.

It was named for George Baldwin, a native of Appleton, WI, who purchased many sections of land in the area. After his death his son, George B. Baldwin, in partnership with C. S. Dickinson and W. J. Fitzmaurice, continued the farming operation, and were responsible for building this facility. Because of confusion with Baldwin in Burleigh County, also on the Soo Line RR, timetables listed the site as KEYES SPUR. The elevator was moved to Westport, SD in 1953. (2, 3, 154)

**BALFOUR** (McHenry). This Soo Line RR station was founded in 1898 in Sec. 28-152-77, Balfour Twp., and named by railroad officials for Arthur, Lord Balfour, a British statesman and essayist. The post office was established February 9, 1899 with Ador Jevnager pm. The elevation is 1613, the Zip Code is 58712, and the village, which incorporated in 1921, reported a peak population of 399 in 1910, but has declined steadily to just 51 in 1980. (1, 2, 3, 18, 33, 40, 52, 79, 184)

**BALLVILLE** (Burleigh). This was an early name for the community in Secs. 32 & 33-139-76, Sterling Twp. It had been built by the NPRR as SIXTEENTH SIDING, and since 1882 has been known as STERLING. This name, which never had any official status, honored Oscar Ball, a pioneer settler who became the first pm of STERLING. The local school district is currently named BALLVILLE. (2, 3, 8)

**BALTA** (Pierce). This Soo Line RR station was founded in 1911 in SW¼ Sec. 10 & NW¼ Sec. 15-154-73, Balta Twp., and named EGAN. Because of duplication in SD, the name was changed to BALTA when the post office opened February 6, 1913 with William H. Ortwein pm. Most area settlers were Germans from Russia, and the name is taken from a town in South Russia. The village incorporated in 1930, the Zip Code is 58313, and a peak population of 263 was reached in 1940. (2, 33, 40, 79, 114, 149)

**BALTIMORE** (Pembina). This rural post office was established August 24, 1882 with Edward Sing pm. It was located in Sec. 35-161-53, Hamilton Twp., and named for George Calvert, Lord Baltimore (1580-1632), the founder of MD. His hereditary title was seated in the barony of Baltimore in Ireland, with Baltimore being a Celtic word meaning large town. When the GNRR established the townsite of Glasston just across the section line to the south, the post office was transferred to that townsite on September 20, 1886. (2, 3, 10, 40, 45, 108, 146)

**BALTON** (Towner). This was a farm post office established May 8, 1901 with Moses S. Peters pm. It was located in SE¼ Sec. 13-161-67, Howell Twp., three miles SW of Rocklake, and said to have been named by Mrs. Peters for a hotel in her home state of OH. The post office closed April 2, 1906 with mail to Rocklake. (2, 3, 40, 415)

**BANKS** (McKenzie). This was a ranch post office established December 7, 1900 with Frank Banks pm. It was located in NW¼ Sec. 33-154-96, about twenty-six miles NE of Watford City near the south bank of the Missouri River. In 1904 the post office moved ten miles SW to SW¼ Sec. 30-153-97, Twin Valley Twp., nineteen miles NNE of Watford City where a rural settlement developed. A peak population of 25 was reported in 1920. The post office, which had been run for many years by members of the Sax family, closed September 15, 1955 with mail to Watford City. Mr. Banks, one of the county's first pioneers, came here in 1884 with W. L. Richards, forming the Birdhead Cattle Ranch. BANKS reported a population of 10 in 1960, but disappeared from maps a few years later. (1, 2, 3, 34, 40, 79, 228)

**BANKS** (McKenzie). This name was first applied to the GNRR townsite in SW 1/4 Sec. 19-150-98, Schafer Twp., when it was founded in 1913. The name noted the coal banks in the area, but had to be changed because the name was already used by a rural post office in the county established in 1900. In 1914 Dr. Vaughan C. Morris, the town's first physician, suggested naming it for his hometown of Watford, Ontario, Canada. This was done, but because of confusion with Wolford, Pierce County, the name was changed to WATFORD CITY in 1916. (2, 3, 18)

**BANNER** (Cavalier). This was a farm post office established October 26, 1899 with Elias W. Scott pm in the country store of E. I. Birch located in Sec. 33-159-63, Banner Twp., six miles SW of Alsen. It was named for its township, which was named by settlers who felt it would be the "banner" township of the county. Banner County, NE was named for similar reasons in 1888. The post office closed May 30, 1903 with mail to Starkweather. (2, 3, 18, 35, 40)

**BANTRY** (McHenry). This GNRR station was founded in 1905 in NE¼ Sec. 21-158-77, Bantry Twp., and named for Bantry, county Cork, Ireland, a city of about 3,000 at that time. The Milroy post office moved here July 10, 1905 with John F. Shafer continuing as pm. The elevation is 1466, the Zip Code is 58713, and a peak population of 315 was reported in 1920, with a decline to just 28 in 1980. (1, 2, 3, 18, 40, 52, 79, 412)

**BAQUAL** (Williams). This post office was established September 14, 1903 with Richard Calvin Ike (1880-1945) pm. It was located in his log cabin in NW 1/4 Sec. 34-154-99, Twelve Mile Twp., about ten miles east of Williston, and said to have been named for a local rancher. The post office closed February 15, 1909 with mail to Williston. Bagnal and Baquol are erroneous spellings. (2, 3, 40, 50)

**BARBER** (Renville). From 1896 until 1904 this was a mail drop for local residents who were served by the somewhat distant post offices of McKinney and Pleasant. On March 4, 1904 it became an official post office with Anthony Berg pm. It was located in Sec. 6-162-86, Grover Twp., on the west bank of the Souris River about ten miles south of the Canadian border. William Mattern opened a grocery store here in 1904. The name came from nearby Barber Bridge, said to have been named for a pioneer rancher. It closed July 31, 1909 with mail to Tolley. (2, 40, 69, 71)

**BARBY** (Rolette). This was a GNRR station built about 1905 in NW¼ Sec. 3-159-71, Rice Twp., between Rolette and Nanson. The origin of the name is unknown. Very little development occurred here, and the site disappeared from maps during the 1920's. (1, 2, 18, 123)

**BARKER** (Benson). This name is associated with OBERON in some sources, complete with a post office and a NPRR station. No confirmation that the BARKER name was used here has been found. (2, 3, 18, 40, 321)

**BARKER** (Benson). This post office was established June 11, 1886 with Jacob Fultz pm, who named it for John Ryan Barker, a local settler. It was located in Secs. 31 & 32-156-68, Leeds Twp., which is the present site of LEEDS. It closed November 11, 1886 without having been in operation. Mail service was provided by the New Rockford post office until the Leeds post office was established in 1887. (2, 3, 18, 25, 34, 40)

**BARKER** (Eddy). An 1893 map shows a place called BARKER in Bush Twp. (150-65), about one mile west of the Sheyenne River near Goose Lake. Nothing has been discovered about this place, but it is thought that this might be the BARKER associated in some sources with Oberon, about twelve miles to the NW in Benson County. (3, 18, 240, 321)

**BARKER** (Emmons). This was a farm post office established June 21, 1890 with Mary Johnson pm. It was located in NW¼ Sec. 26-129-76, eleven miles south of Strasburg, and closed June 23, 1892 with mail to Westfield. It was supposedly named for Barker, TX. (2, 3, 34, 40, 66, 415)

**BARKER'S STATION** (Grand Forks). This was a stop on the Grand Forks-Fort Totten trail in Sec. 6-152-56, founded in 1879 on the land of George D. Barker. Settlers here were mostly from Niagara County, NY, and they called the site the NEW YORK SETTLEMENT. In 1882 the site was relocated one mile south to the new GNRR townsite of Niagara. (2, 3, 31, 69)

**BARLOW** (Foster). This NPRR townsite was founded in 1883 in Sec. 7-147-66, Estabrook Twp., and Sec. 12-147-67, Birtsell Twp., and named for Frederick George Barlow (1839-1901), the town's founder and first merchant. He was a charter county commissioner and served in the first state legislature. The post office was established June 3, 1884 with Mr. Barlow as pm, and the NPRR arrived here in 1885. A population of 600 was claimed in 1909, but for most of its life BARLOW has had fewer than 100 residents. Bayard Amundson became pm in 1934, and the post office closed when he retired on November 19, 1965, with mail going to Carrington, ten miles to the south. (1, 2, 18, 40, 79, 97, 324)

**BARNES** (Barnes). This rural settlement began in the early 1880's as BURBANK, but because of duplication the name was changed to BARNES for its county, which was named for Alanson H. Barnes, an Associate Justice of the Dakota Territory Supreme Court 1872-1881. The post office

was established September 29, 1884 with Edward R. Byhre pm, and was located in Sec. 24-137-60, Rosebud Twp., just north of Litchville. A population of 27 was reported in 1890, but the post office closed January 31, 1901 with mail to Griswold. Later that year the new townsite of Litchville began to develop. (2, 18, 25, 34, 36, 40, 76)

**BARNES** (Morton). This was a rural post office established August 5, 1908 with Franklin Moreland pm, who is said to have never actually served in that capacity, turning the duties over to Walter Hone. It was named for Henry Barnes (1830-1918), who had come here in 1878 from Saginaw, MI. The post office was located in NE¼ Sec. 8-136-83, ten miles west of Saint Anthony, until 1912 when it moved two miles west to NW¼ Sec. 12-136-84, DeVaul Twp., the home of new pm William Woll, who was replaced in 1917 by Francis X. Roedl. In 1919 the post office moved four miles ESE to SW¼ Sec. 10-136-83, the home of pm Mrs. Ida Corey Dawson, who closed the facility October 31, 1929 with mail to Mandan. (1, 2, 3, 17, 34, 40, 107)

**BARNETT** (Stutsman). This was a farm post office established February 16, 1903 with Martin Albrecht pm. It was located in SE¼ Sec. 24-142-63, Ashland Twp., thirteen miles north of Jamestown, and named for Fremont Barnett, who settled two miles to the west in Sec. 22-142-63 in 1895. Barnett is an English name meaning a place cleared by burning. The post office was discontinued August 31, 1907 with mail to Gray. Barnet is an erroneous spelling. (2, 3, 40, 45, 415)

**BARNEY** (Richland). A post office named OBERWEIS operated here 1882-1884. This post office was established October 26, 1899 with Frederick Henkel pm. It was located in Sec. 7-132-50, Barney Twp., between Mooreton and Wyndmere, and opened in anticipation of the NPRR loading station that was built here in 1900. It was named for A. H. Barney, a former NPRR President, although some say that the name came from the nearby St. Barnard's Catholic Church. A population of 225 was reached in 1940, but a sharp decline since then has reduced the count to just 70 in 1980. The post office, Zip Code 58008, became a CPO of Wyndmere on July 31, 1973. Hans N. Langseth (1846-1927), a local farmer, attained national fame with his beard, the world's longest at 17'4", and it is now on display at the Smithsonian Institution in Washington, DC. Ray Thompson, ND Treasurer in the 1950's, was born here in 1911. (1, 2, 18, 33, 40, 79, 242, 248, 348)

**BARNEY STATION** (Richland). This was a NPRR loading station in Sec. 7-132-50, Barney Twp., built about 1882, and named for NPRR President A. H. Barney. A post

office called OBERWEIS operated here 1882-1884, and in 1899 a village called simply BARNEY was founded at this site. (2, 77)

**BARRETT** (Richland). This was a GNRR station in Sec. 15 & 22-134-49, Abercrombie Twp., two miles NW of Galchutt. It appears only on territorial maps, and was served by the Kongsberg post office. The origin of the name is unknown. (3, 25, 77)

**BARRIE** (Richland). This was a rural settlement begun in the 1870's on the Fort Abercrombie-Fort Ransom trail. A post office was established September 20, 1878 with Joseph T. Larkin pm in his log cabin in SE¼ Sec. 20-136-51, Barrie Twp., ten miles west of Walcott. Mr. Larkin named it for his former home of Barrie, Ontario, Canada, which was named for an early military hero of that region. The post office was later moved to the home of Charles H. Morgan in SW¼ Sec. 20-136-51, where it was sometimes called MORGAN, although the name officially remained BARRIE. A population of 25 was reported in 1890, and 10 people were still here in 1920, although the post office had closed November 30, 1907 with mail to Walcott. (1, 2, 3, 10, 25, 40, 147)

**BARRIE CROSSING** (Richland). This was the site of an early crossing of the Sheyenne River in NW¼ Sec. 32-136-51, Barrie Twp., which had earlier been known as NOLAN CROSSING. Peter Vang was the first operator of the ferry, and he was succeeded by Anthony Nolan in 1869. A government bridge was later built here to help the settlers reach homestead lands to the west. Some of the log buildings still exist. (2, 3, 147)

**BARRON** (Burleigh). This rural post office was established July 22, 1911 in the home of pm Henry Espeseth (1888-1957) in NE¼ Sec. 25-140-75, Clear Lake Twp. The Espeseth family came here in 1910 from Barron County, WI, which was named for Henry D. Barron, a state legislator and judge. Some claim it was named for George E. Barron. The post office, located about five miles NE of Driscoll, closed August 14, 1915 with mail to Driscoll. Barren is an erroneous spelling. (2, 3, 8, 14, 18, 40, 70, 200)

**BARTLETT** (Ramsey). This settlement began in the fall of 1882 as the famous END OF THE TRACK boomtown on the GNRR mainline, just inside the Ramsey County line in SE¼ Sec. 25-153-61, Bartlett Twp. The post office was established January 4, 1883 with Thomas Thorson pm, who used the name of the township, which had been named for Frank B. Bartlett, part owner of the townsite. Population estimates ran as high as 2,000 in late 1882, but the GNRR resumed construction in the spring of 1883, and Lakota, four miles to the east, became the Nelson County seat in June 1883 as BARTLETT quickly declined to a population of just 75 in 1890. The elevation is 1535, and the village, which incorporated in 1904, reached an official peak population of just 120 in 1910, declining to just 19 in 1970. The post office, Zip Code 58314, closed January 24, 1975 with mail to Lakota. (1, 2, 3, 18, 25, 33, 40, 41, 79, 103)

**BARTON** (Pierce). This GNRR townsite had been founded in 1887 as DENNEY in SE¼ Sec. 14-158-74, Barton Twp. The name was changed to BARTON on June 13, 1893 by pm James A. Tyvand. Many GNRR townsites had English names, and this name is said to have been chosen for one of twenty-six places of this name in England. Some say it was named for a GNRR official. The village incorporated in 1906, and a peak population of 202 was reached in 1910, with a decline to just 38 in 1980. The elevation is 1511, the post office, Zip Code 58315, became a rural branch of Rugby on May 31, 1964, and the school closed in 1965. (1, 2, 3, 18, 25, 33, 40, 52, 79, 114)

**BASKIN** (Mountrail). This was a GNRR loading station in Ross Twp. (156-92), between Stanley and Ross. The origin of the name is unknown, and no development took place at this site. (2, 3, 72, 377)

**BASS STATION** (Sheridan). This was the halfway station on the Fort Totten-Fort Stevenson trail, established in SW¼ Sec. 13-150-76, Rosenfield Twp., about seven miles SW of Anamoose in 1867. More commonly called MIDDLE STATION, this name noted the linden, or basswood, trees along nearby lake shores. The trail fell into disuse after completion of the NPRR mainline in 1872. (3, 60, 417)

**BASTO** (McLean). This rural post office was established June 18, 1901 with John A. Lundquist pm in his home in NW¼ Sec. 30-145-83, Basto Twp. His daughter, Esther (1885-1965), acutally performed most of the duties of the office. Located about twelve miles SSE of Riverdale, the post office closed December 31, 1912 with mail to Wahsburn. The origin of the name is unknown. (2, 18, 28, 40, 53)

**BATESVILLE** (McLean). F. N. Bates platted a townsite in Sec. 5-149-87, Roseglen Twp., in anticipation of a railroad which never materialized. When the area was opened for settlement by whites in 1916, however, a small village did develop, but the post office at nearby ROSEGLEN was moved here, and the BATESVILLE name became just a memory. (2, 277, 278)

**BATHGATE** (Pembina). This settlement in SE¼ Sec. 3-162-53, Bathgate Twp., was founded in 1879 as BAYVIEW, but was renamed when the post office was established November 2, 1881 with William Foster pm. It was platted that year by the Comstock and White Co, and Mr. Comstock named it for Bathgate, West Lothian, Scotland, the hometown of his wife. Its elevation is 828, the Zip Code is 58216, and the city, which incorporated in 1907, reached a peak population of 825 in 1890, with a decline to just 68 in 1980. The ND School for the Blind was founded here in 1908 with B. P. Chapple as Superintendent, but it was relocated to Grand Forks in 1960. Norval Baptie (1879-1966), the world ice skating champion in 1905, moved here from his native Canada in 1880. (1, 2, 3, 18, 25, 33, 40, 79, 108, 235)

**BATTLEVIEW** (Burke). This was a farm post office established September 10, 1908 with David Davidson pm. Mr. Davidson was a native of Evansville, MN, coming here in 1906, and he named the post office to note his view of an Indian battle field several miles to the south. Later research at the site turned up many Indian relics, but the site proved to be an abandoned Hidatsa village with no concrete evidence of any battle being fought here. In 1911 the post office was moved three miles SSW to Sw¼ Sec. 23-159-94, the site of a new GNRR townsite, which adopted this name. The elevation is 2197, the Zip Code is 58714, and a peak population of 100 was reported in 1920, with a decline to 52 in 1930, at which level it has remained for many years. (1, 2, 3, 18, 34, 40, 67)

**BAY CENTER** (Pembina). This was a farm post office established December 20, 1882 with Wentworth J. Dumble pm. The origin of the name is unknown, and seems to have no descriptive significance. It was first located in NE¼ Sec. 5-163-55, Saint Joseph Twp., seven miles NE of Walhalla. In 1885 it moved across the section line to NW¼ Sec. 4-163-55, the home of new pm Andrew J. Lindsay. In 1888 it moved two miles WNW to the home of pm William H. Best in SW¼ Sec. 31-164-55, Saint Joseph Twp., who spelled the name as BAY CENTRE. In 1894 it again moved, this time a bit to the east in SE¼ Sec. 31-164-55, the home of Albert Noice, who restored the BAY CENTER spelling to comply with new government regulations for place names. The post office closed January 15, 1906 with mail to Walhalla. (2, 3, 18, 25, 40, 45, 235, 414)

**BAY CENTRE** (Pembina). William H. Best was appointed as the pm of what was officially known as the BAY CENTER post office in 1888 at his home in SW¼ Sec. 31-164-55, Saint Joseph Twp., six miles NE of Walhalla. His Site Report filed July 30, 1888 shows the "romantic" spelling, BAY CENTRE, which apparently went unnoticed by postal officials. When Albert Noice became pm in 1894, the original, and official, spelling was restored in part, no doubt, due to newly enacted government regulations for place names. Several postmarks are known from the Best tenure, all showing BAY CENTRE, indicating that he had clearly intended to alter the spelling, and had carried out his plans. (3, 40, 414)

**BAYFIELD** (McLean). This was a farm post office established November 17, 1905 with James Fielding pm. It was located in SE¼ Sec. 20-146-80, five miles south of Turtle Lake and named for Bayfield County, WI, which also has a county seat named Washburn, named for the same C. C. Washburn that the McLean County city is named for. The WI county was named for Henry W. Bayfield, a British naval officer. The post office closed March 15, 1907 with

mail to Turtle Lake. (2, 3, 5, 10, 28, 40, 70, 414)

**BAYNE** (Richland). This was a NPRR loading station in Sec. 11-131-50, Belford Twp., that was the terminus of a thirteen-mile spur into the 7,000 acre Keystone Farm on the Wild Rice River. It operated during the 1890's, then was dismantled. The origin of the name is unknown. (2, 18)

**BAYVIEW** (Pembina). This was a pioneer settlement founded in 1879 by Isaac Foster in Sec. 3-162-53, Bathgate Twp., and named to note the view of a bay, actually a bend in the Tongue River. When the post office was established November 2, 1881, it was renamed BATHGATE. (2, 18, 108)

**BEACH** (Golden Valley). The NPRR built a section house here in 1881 and named it for Capt. Warren C. Beach of the 11th Infantry, U. S. Army, who had escorted the first railroad surveyors through this area in 1880. Settlement began in 1900, and by 1910 a city of 1,003 people spread across Secs. 23, 24, 25 & 26-140-106, Beach Twp. The post office was established October 27, 1902 with Frank E. Heath pm. The village incorporated in 1908, it became a city in 1909, and when Golden Valley County organized in 1912, BEACH was named as the county seat. The elevation is 2779, the Zip Code is 58621, and a peak population of 1,460 was reached in 1960. (1, 2, 3, 18, 33, 40, 80, 369, 370)

**BEAN** (Grand Forks). This was a NPRR station founded in 1887 in NE¼ Sec. 32-153-53, Gilby Twp., three miles south of Gilby, and named for S. S. Bean, who came here in 1886 and built an elevator at the site. A post office was established March 29, 1888 with Samuel White pm, and it was discontinued April 27, 1891 with mail to Gilby. In 1882 the post office was reestablished, but it was named HONEYFORD for new pm William J. "Bob" Honeyford. The station continued using the BEAN name until 1906, when it changed to the more frequently used HONEYFORD. (2, 25, 31, 40, 69, 240, 338)

*Beach about 1925*

**BEAR CREEK** (Dickey). This was a relay stage station on the line from Jamestown to Columbia, SD built in 1880. It was located at the corner of Secs. 4, 5, 8 & 9-131-59, Bear Creek Twp., just north of Oakes. The township and this station were named for Bear Creek, which had been named in 1839 by the explorers Nicollet and Fremont. The Indian name for this creek translated as the place where the grizzly bear has his den. (2, 3, 18, 154)

**BEAULIEU** (Cavalier). This historic settlement was founded about 1880 in NW¼ Sec. 26-162-57, North Olga Twp., and named for Paul H. Beaulieu, a descendant of the famous fur trader Joseph Beaulieu, who had come here in the 1830's from WI. The name is French, and can be translated as beautiful place. The post office was established July 11, 1882 with James R. Copeland pm. A thriving little village developed, and the general stores of Alex Montpetit and the Xerxa brothers are remembered by many. A population of 39 was reported as late as 1930, but the post office closed July 31, 1935 with mail to Walhalla, six miles to the NE, and the site is now largely abandoned. Bealieu is an erroneous spelling. (2, 3, 18, 40, 79, 115, 292)

**BEAULIEU** (Pembina). The 1884 Andreas Historical Atlas of Dakota Territory shows this place in NW¼ Sec. 18-162-56, LaMoure Twp., two miles NE of the pioneer settlement of this name in Cavalier County. A 1890 map published by Rand-McNally also shows it in Pembina County. It is assumed that these two locations were one and the same, but no explanation has been found for the dual locations. (3, 18, 25)

**BEAUMONT** (Mercer). This was a rural post office established August 6, 1906 with Sarah Jane Brown pm. It was located in NE¼ Sec. 28-144-85, six miles SW of Stanton, and named for L. S. Beaumont, the operator of a saw mill in Stanton and an owner of the nearby Maichel Ranch, who was instrumental in securing this post office. His name is French for beautiful mountain. On April 11, 1907 the name was changed to HUB. (2, 3, 10, 18, 40, 64, 232)

**BEAVER** (Bowman). This was a farm post office established April 10, 1903 with Mae E. Ash as pm, but she declined the appointment. Her husband, Frank L. Ash, received the appointment on April 17, 1903. The post office was located in the Ash home in SE¼ Sec. 23-132-107 on the banks of Beaver Creek in the extreme NW corner of the county. It closed December 31, 1908 with mail to Marmarth. (2, 3, 40, 53, 120, 415)

**BEAVER** (Stutsman). This place is listed in a 1890 guide to ND as being in Stutsman County, and served by the Jamestown post office. The name honors Adolph Beaver, a pioneer of Plainview Twp. (142-65), between Pingree and Buchanan, although the exact location of BEAVER is unknown. (3, 25, 158, 415)

**BEAVER CREEK** (Logan). This Soo Line RR station appears on a 1890 map of ND in the center of Johannesdale Twp. (133-71), between Burnstad and Wishek, with a notation in the index that it was served by the Youngstown post office, a predecessor of Wishek. Several lifetime residents of the township were asked about this place, and the general conclusion is that it was a planned townsite that never developed. The name came from the creek which flows through the township. (2, 3, 25, 116)

**BEAVER CREEK** (Stutsman). An 1882 map shows this place in Sec. 12-137-63, Montpelier Twp., six miles south of Ypsilanti on the Chicago, Milwaukee, & St. Paul RR, later part of the NPRR. The name apparently comes from Beaver Creek which empties into the James River just south of this site. Nothing came of this townsite, but in 1885 development began here under the name Montpelier. The area had been served by the Tarbell post office. (3, 40, 414, 415)

**BEAVER LAKE** (Logan). This was a Soo Line RR loading station SW of Beaver Lake in SW¼ Sec. 32-134-71, Red Lake Twp., just south of Burnstad. The lake had been named to note the large population of beavers living there. This station was replaced by the village of Burnstad in 1906. (2, 3, 116)

**BECHYNE** (Walsh). This is a rural community centered around Sts. Peter and Paul Catholic Church in Secs. 12 & 13-155-58, Perth Twp. A townsite was developed by the brothers Frank and John Hodny, and Msgr. Vaclav F. Mikolasek (1878-1950) was the longtime priest at the church. The name is taken from Bechyne, Bohemia, a holy place in Czechoslovakia. Pioneer settler Joseph Bosh was born there in 1858, and is thought to have suggested the name. (3, 49, 75)

**BEDFORD** (Cass). This was a GNRR station built in 1911 in SE¼ Sec. 6-142-54, Rich Twp., two miles SE of Page on the Surrey cutoff line. George S. Barnes, founder of the Northern Pacific Elevator Co., named it for his hometown of Bedford, OH, which was named for the city and county in England. A population of 10 was reported in 1920, but the site never developed beyond that. The name was changed to NOLAN on August 15, 1944, but the original name is perpetuated by a nearby picnic grounds. (2, 10, 34, 77)

**BEICEGEL** (McKenzie). This was a ranch post office established June 2, 1902 with Fred Hoerauf pm. It was located in NW¼ Sec. 33-145-99, Rhoades Twp., five miles SW of Grassy Butte, and closed September 15, 1906 with mail to Fayette. It was named for nearby Beicegel Creek, which was named for George and August Beisigl, area pioneers who came here in 1884, with an Anglicization of the spelling. Another post office operated here 1916-1935, and was likewise named for the Beisigl brothers, but this time the name was wildly corrupted into Bicycle. (2, 3, 18, 34, 40, 414)

**BELAIR** (Mountrail). This was a GNRR loading station a few miles north of Stanley on the Grenora branch line. The name is French for good air. It is thought that was an alternate name for WASSAIC, the GNRR station in NE¼ Sec. 25-157-91, James Hill Twp. (2, 3, 10, 72)

**BELCOURT** (Rolette). This settlement dates from 1883, when it was called TURTLE MOUNTAIN. It was renamed in 1888 for Father George Antoine Belcourt (1803-1870), a Roman Catholic priest who was doing missionary work in the area as early as 1845. Father Belcourt was a man of many interests and talents, and is considered to be the first Canadian to own an automobile, importing a crude steam machine from America in 1866. The post office was established February 11, 1888 with Adolph LeBurn (1854-1922) pm. It was located in SE¼ Sec. 20-162-70, Couture Twp., but the town now sprawls over Secs. 20, 21, 28 & 29-162-70. BELCOURT, which has never incorporated, is the agency headquarters for the Turtle Mountain Indian Reservation. The Zip Code is 58316, and its 1980 population was about 1,900. Longtime state senator Phillip Berube was born here in 1905. (1, 2, 3, 18, 33, 40, 79, 123, 253)

**BELDEN** (Logan). A post office named BELDEN was authorized June 28, 1890 with Morris M. Crepps pm, but on March 15, 1892 the entry "no papers" was made in government records. The location is unknown. Some say it was named for W. L. Belden, U. S. Indian Agent for ND, who was Logan County Auditor 1893-1894, while others say it was named for Belden, NE, which was named for Scott Belden, an official of the Burlington RR in Sioux City, IA. (1, 2, 35, 40, 116)

**BELDEN** (Logan). On April 18, 1892 postal officials authorized the RICHVILLE post office to change its name to BELDEN, for W. L. Belden, U. S. Indian Agent for ND. It is believed that the name change was never enacted, and nearly three years later, on January 28, 1895, the order was rescinded. An earlier Belden post office in Logan Coun-

ty existed 1890-1892, but likewise did not operate, was related only by coincidence of name. (2, 3, 40)

**BELDEN** (Mountrail). This was a settlement founded in 1904 in Secs. 14, 15, 22 & 23-154-91, Sikes Twp., primarily by settlers from Finland. A post office was established July 25, 1904 with Garrett F. Jarrell pm. Most sources credit the name to W. L. Belden, U. S. Indian Agent-at-Large at Fort Berthold, although some local sources say that the pm named it for his hometown in IN, or Stanley attorney Ray Miller named it for one of his nephews. The village has maintained a population of about 25 for decades, and has never allowed a saloon in town. The Belden Store, owned for years by Marvin Husa, is a well known landmark. During the 1930's BELDEN was the center of a Communist movement, but most local residents strongly deny this today. The post office, Zip Code 58715, closed August 28, 1986. (2, 18, 33, 40, 72, 79)

**BELDEN** (Sioux). This was the junction of NPRR branch lines in NW Sec. 23-134-79, just north of present-day Cannon Ball, built in 1910 and named for William L. Belden, U. S. Indian Agent-at-Large at Fort Berthold, and Superintendent of the Standing Rock Indian Agency 1906-1911. It was later renamed CANNON BALL JUNCTION. (2, 3, 18, 127)

**BELFIELD** (Stark). This NPRR townsite was founded in 1883 in Sec. 5-139-99, just NW of the old military post known as Camp Houstin, and named for Belle Field, daughter of a NPRR official. Others say it was coined from BELle, French for beautiful, and FIELD, noting the agricultural economy of the area, while still others claim it was named to note bluebells growing in the surrounding fields. The post office was established September 16, 1883 with Hugh I. McBirney pm. The city had a population of just 50 in 1890, but grew rapidly after Ukrainian settlement began in 1897, reaching a count of 1,268 in 1980. The elevation is 2603, and the Zip Code is 58622. Herbert L. Meschke, a ND Supreme Court Associate Justice, was born here in 1928. (1, 2, 3, 18, 33, 40, 74, 79, 253, 414)

**BELLE PLAINE** (Sargent). This was a GNRR loading station in SE¼ Sec. 25-130-56, Forman Twp., four miles south of Forman. The site was served by the Rutland post office, and named by settlers from Belle Plaine, MN, which was named by Andrew G. Chatfield, an Associate Justice of the Minnesota Territory Supreme Court, for the French words meaning beautiful plain, descriptive of both sites. Little development occurred at the site, but it appeared on maps into the 1950's. Belleplaine and Belle Plain are erroneous spellings. (2, 3, 13, 18, 25, 165, 167)

**BELLEVILLE** (Grand Forks). This was a farm post office established June 19, 1882 with Neil Bell pm. The name came from Belleville, Ontario, Canada, home of many area settlers, and is French for beautiful city. The name is also said to honor the pm. A townsite was platted in SE¼ Sec. 6-154-56, Elkmount Twp., in anticipation of a railroad, but this hope was not realized. On April 15, 1907 the post office was discontinued with mail to Medford. In 1910 the Medford site was renamed Fordville, coined from the last syllables of MedFORD and BelleVILLE. Bellville is an erroneous spelling. (2, 10, 31, 40, 69, 293)

**BELLEVUE** (Grand Forks). This townsite was platted in July 1879 adjacent to the townsite of CHRISTIANI in SE¼ Sec. 35-154-51, Turtle River Twp., three miles NNE of Manvel. The name is French for beautiful view. Development here was limited to a couple mills. At various times 1877-1902 a post office operated here using the name TURTLE RIVER. The site was bypassed by the GNRR, and fire destroyed the mills, leaving only the old Evans Hotel at BELLEVUE. (2, 3, 10, 31, 40, 238)

**BELLEVYRIA** (Steele). This was a rural post office established June 6, 1882 with Watson E. Boise pm in his home in SW¼ Sec. 26-144-56, Carpenter Twp., about four miles south of Hope on the east bank of the Maple River. A route from Oriska to Hope brought mail here three times weekly. The unusual name was coined by Mr. Boise using his birthplace, Bellevue, OH, named for pioneer settler James Bell, and his wife's birthplace, Elyria, OH, named for the town's founder, Herman Ely (1775-1852). The post office was discontinued August 24, 1898 with mail to Hope. (2, 10, 25, 40, 99, 240)

**BELLMONT** (Traill). This historic place was founded in 1871 as FROG POINT in NE¼ Sec. 22-148-49, Belmont Twp. On August 20, 1879 pm Robert Ray, brother of the previous pm, David Ray, changed the name to BELLMONT, said to be for Belle Mont, the daughter of the local bartender, although descendants of the Ray family deny this story. A townsite was platted in 1880, and a population of 75 was reported in 1890. Without a railroad the town declined, and the post office closed April 30, 1909 with mail to Buxton, ten miles to the west. Most of the town was destroyed by fire in 1912, and it was never rebuilt. The site today is marked by a plaque, and is now an old settlers' park. Although BELLMONT was the official name, nearly all references spell the name as BELMONT. (1, 2, 3, 25, 29, 40, 187)

**BELMAR** (Bottineau). Founded as a GNRR grain loading station in NE¼ Sec. 27-160-75, Willow Vale Twp., about four miles NW of Willow City, the name was coined from the French words meaning beautiful sea. A post office was established December 28, 1906 with Walter J. McDougall pm, but it closed May 31, 1909 with mail to Omemee. (2, 3, 10, 18, 40, 101, 153)

**BELMONT** (Richland). This place is shown in a 1890 guide to ND as being in Richland County, and served by the Fairmount post office. No other information is available. (3, 25)

**BELMONT** (Traill). This settlement was founded in 1871 as FROG POINT, and from 1879 to 1909 a post office called BELLMONT operated here as a small village developed. During its existance and afterwards, the name has usually been spelled as BELMONT, said to have been the intended spelling suggested by the Ray family, and taken from Belmont, Ontario, Canada. The name is French for beautiful mountain, certainly not descriptive of its location in the Red River valley. (2, 3, 10, 29, 77, 187)

**BEMENT** (Towner). This was a GNRR station in SE¼ Sec. 22-160-68, Grainfield Twp., two miles NW of Bisbee. The origin of the name is unknown, although it is thought to be the name of a local resident or a GNRR official. It appeared on maps circa 1910-1920. (1, 2, 3, 18)

**BENEDICT** (McLean). This townsite was founded in 1906 one-half mile NW of the townsite platted by the Soo Line RR in June 1908 in NE¼ Sec. 7-150-81, Andrews Twp. The post office was established October 8, 1906 with Alexander Munns pm. Some sources say the name is based on the term benedict, meaning a longtime bachelor who has recently married, and applicable to many local pioneers. Others say it was named for the Order of St. Benedict to which most Roman Catholic priests in the area belonged. The Zip Code is 58716, and the village, which incorporated in 1916, reached a peak population of 195 in 1920, but has declined to just 68 in 1980. (1, 2, 3, 4, 18, 28, 33, 40, 79)

**BENNETT** (Bottineau). The Comstock & White Land Co. of Fargo founded this townsite in 1884 in Secs. 12 & 13-159-75, Ostby Twp., and named it for one of their officials. Local residents disliked the name, and less than one month later managed to get it changed to McRAE. The post office opened in 1886 using this name, but changed it to WILLOW CITY on November 9, 1889. (2, 40, 153)

**BENNIEPIER** (McKenzie). This was a ranch post office just inside the MT border about 34 miles WSW of Watford City in SE¼ Sec. 10-148-105. It had been established about three miles NE in 1910 as RUBY, but when it moved to the home of new pm Silas R. Bryant on February 17, 1912 the name was changed to note nearby Bennie Peer Creek, which had been named for a Fort Buford soldier who had settled in the area. The one-word corrupted spelling was apparently done to satisfy postal officials. The community served by this post office was sometimes called Bryant's Farm. It closed October 15, 1919 with mail to Earl. Bennie Pierre is an erroneous spelling. (1, 2, 3, 18, 40)

**BENOIT** (Rolette). This was a farm post office established December 2, 1886 with John A. Benoit pm. It was located in SW¼ Sec. 9-161-70, Maryville Twp., five miles south of Belcourt, and closed January 17, 1889 with mail to Island Lake. Mr. Benoit was a pioneer settler in the Turtle Mountains who later ran a store in Rolla and was a great promoter of that city as a new county seat. (2, 25, 40, 123, 414)

**BENSON** (LaMoure). A post office was established October 2, 1905 with Carl E. Dunham pm in his country store in Sec. 18-135-60, Greenville Twp., about nine miles NE of LaMoure. The name honored Peter E. Benson, who homesteaded on this site in 1882. The post office closed November 15, 1909 with mail to Litchville, although the store operated until 1957. The site was locally known as BENSON CORNERS. (2, 40, 53)

**BENSON CORNERS** (LaMoure). This was the local name for the country store in Sec. 18-135-60, Greenville Twp., nine miles NE of LaMoure. It was named for the BENSON post office of 1905-1909, and noted the location at a rural crossroads. (2, 3)

**BENSVILLE** (McIntosh). This was a rural post office established August 26, 1909 with the Rev. Henry G. Bens pm. Rev. Bens was the pastor at a country church located in SW¼ Sec. 7-131-68, Rosenthal Twp., nine miles SE of Lehr, and also operated a quarter-section homestead just north of the church. The post office closed April 30, 1910 with mail to Lehr. (2, 3, 18, 40, 211)

**BENTLEY** (Adams). This was a rural post office established December 18, 1906 with Homer O. Bentley pm. It was located in Mr. Bentley's sod house in Sec. 4-131-92, Cedar Butte Twp., about twenty miles NNW of Lemmon, SD. In 1907 he built a country store at this site, which he ran in conjunction with the post office until about 1910 when he sold the entire operation to his brother, Arthur A. Bentley, who had just moved here from LaCrosse, WI. About 1915 Arthur A. Bentley moved the building fifteen miles north to a new townsite in Hettinger County, which was named BENTLEY in his honor. (2, 3, 18, 34, 40, 189)

**BENTLEY** (Hettinger). This rural post office was founded in 1906 in Adams County by Homer O. Bentley. Later housed in a country store, it moved about 1915 to the new NPRR townsite in SW¼ Sec. 13-133-91, Cannon Ball Twp., which was named for his brother, Arthur A. Bentley, who now owned the operation. The village experienced an initial boom, reporting an unofficial population of 200 in 1920, but the count had declined to just 51 in 1960. The elevation is 2447, and the post office, Zip Code 58522, closed April 15, 1985. (1, 2, 3, 33, 38, 40, 79, 179, 181)

**BENTLEY** (Oliver). This post office was established in 1881 as SANGER with George Sanger pm. On May 17, 1890 Charles P. Thurston became pm at his home in SE¼ Sec. 31-143-81, Sanger Twp., just west of the SANGER townsite, and changed the name to honor Dr. W. A. Bentley, a local physician. George Sanger regained the pm position on September 23, 1891, and promptly changed the name back to SANGER. (2, 3, 18, 40, 121)

**BENTON** (Mercer). This was an 1870's Missouri River boat landing in Sec. 14-147-85, opposite Fort Stevenson. It was named for the steamboat *Benton*, which plied the river between Saint Louis, MO and Fort Benton, MT. Both the boat and the MT fort were named for Sen. Thomas Hart Benton (1782-1858), the MO politician who was also a noted historian. (2, 3, 13, 18, 64)

**BENTRU** (Grand Forks). This was a rural settlement on the Red River in Sec. 4-149-49, Bentru Twp., eight miles east of Thompson, and named for its township which was named for Halvor Hanson Bentru, who came here from IA with his family in June 1871. The post office was established June 23, 1900 with Torkel A. Torkelson pm, and it closed August 14, 1906 with mail to Thompson. A population of 10 was listed in 1920. (1, 2, 18, 31, 40, 69)

**BENZION** (Ramsey). This was a rural post office established January 30, 1891 with Benie Greenbergh, later known as Ben Greenberg, as pm. It was located in SW¼ Sec. 33-157-63, Sullivan Twp., seven miles SE of Starkweather. Mr. Greenberg suggested the name Zion, which was rejected due to duplication in Cass County, but postal officials added the pm's given name as a prefix to coin this unique place name. In 1898 the post office was moved one mile NE to NE¼ Sec. 33-157-63, the home of new pm Phillip Greenberg. It closed August 15, 1903 with mail to Iola. Benzoin is an erroneous spelling. (3, 4, 40, 103, 414)

**BERDELLA** (Rolette). This was a rural post office established June 2, 1909 with Theodore M. Brekke pm at his home in Sec. 28-163-72, Holmes Twp., eight miles NE of Dunseith. Mr. Brekke is said to have selected the name from a list of young girls in the area. Anton Julseth became the pm in 1910, and is best remembered as the county Register of Deeds 1922-1953. The post office closed December 15, 1916 with mail to Bachelor. (2, 40, 53, 123)

**BEREA** (Barnes). This was a NPRR loading station founded in 1884 in NW¼ Sec. 23-140-59, Hobart Twp., four miles west of Valley City. It was named for Berea, KY, which was named for the Biblical city in Macedonia by Sen. Cassius M. Clay, who envisioned the KY city as a refuge for freed slaves. The post office was established January 4, 1896 with Ellsworth J. Holliday pm, but it closed October 24, 1896 with mail to Valley City. (2, 3, 10, 18, 25, 34, 35, 40, 76, 87)

**BERG** (McKenzie). This was a rural post office established June 23, 1905 with Julius I. Berg (1863-1945) pm, who came here in 1904 from Solor, Hedmark, Norway. Others say it was named for local pioneer Hans Berg. It was located in a large sod building in SW¼ Sec. 13-151-96, Blue Butte Twp., eighteen miles ENE of Watford City. A population of 10 was reported in 1920. It moved two miles SW in 1936 to NW¼ Sec. 26-151-96, the home of pm Florence Ellen Rice, and closed October 31, 1944 with mail to Keene. (1, 2, 18, 40, 79, 229, 434)

**BERGEN** (McHenry). A post office was established November 7, 1905 with Oscar Sawby pm, and named for Bergen, Norway,

homeland of many area settlers. The Soo Line RR reached here in 1907, and the village located in Sec. 12-152-79, Voltaire Twp., incorporated in 1929. A population of 98 was reported in 1930, but that figure declined to just 24 in 1980. The post office, Zip Code 58717, closed January 9, 1979. (2, 3, 18, 33, 40, 41, 52, 79)

**BERGER** (Slope). This was a Milwaukee Road RR station in NE¼ Sec. 36-133-105, Hughes Twp., six miles east of Marmarth. The origin of the name is unknown. It appeared on maps circa 1907-1918, when it was replaced by the Mazda station about two miles to the west. Neither site experienced any real development. (3, 53, 82, 414)

**BERLIN** (Grant). This was a farm post office established October 17, 1896 with August Beck pm. It was located in Sec. 20-135-90, nine miles NNE of New Leipzig, and named by local German settlers for the capital of their homeland, which was founded about 1230. Most believe that the name is of Slavic origin, although others feel it is derived from *barlein*, noting the fact that the city's coat of arms features a bear. The post office closed September 20, 1898 with mail to Leipzig. (2, 5, 34, 40, 177)

**BERLIN** (LaMoure). This NPRR station was founded by John Young in the 1890's and named for the capital of Germany to honor the many German settlers in the area. It is located in Sec. 33-134-62, Henrietta Twp. The post office was established October 18, 1892 with Mr. Young as pm, and closed October 31, 1895 with mail to LaMoure. It reopened May 19, 1902 as significant settlement began, reaching a peak population of 137 in 1910. The elevation is 1491, and the Zip Code is 58415. Milton R. Young (1897-1983), a U. S. Senator 1945-1980, was a lifelong resident of BERLIN. (1, 2, 3, 18, 33, 40, 52, 79, 143, 144, 262)

**BERLIN** (Richland). This was a rural post office established July 8, 1875 with George Worner pm. Mr. Worner, who came here in 1874, named it for the capital of Germany to note his own ancestry as well as that of many of his neighbors. It was located in SE¼ Sec. 29-131-49, Brandenburg Twp., three

miles SW of Great Bend. In 1882 the post office moved to the home of new pm Franklin S. Dwyer in NE¼ Sec. 9-131-49, a site just NW of present-day Great Bend. It closed July 13, 1883 with mail to Wahpeton. (2, 3, 18, 40, 77, 147, 347, 414)

**BERLIN** (Sheridan). This was a farm post office established June 20, 1899 with Jacob Weisser, who came here in 1897, as pm. It was located in SE¼ Sec. 18-149-74, Berlin Twp., eight miles south of Martin, and named for the capital of Germany. The post office closed December 20, 1899 with mail to Casselman. (2, 3, 18, 21, 40)

**BERNDT** (Richland). This was a NPRR siding built in 1899 in Sec. 7-132-51, Danton Twp., and named WARNER. The name was changed to BERNDT in October 1915 to honor Albert and Christian F. J. Berndt, who had come here in 1886 and owned the right-of-way used for the siding, which was dismantled in 1943. (2, 3, 18, 147)

**BERNER** (Stutsman). This was a NPRR loading station in SE¼ Sec. 30-140-64, Midway Twp., about four miles west of Jamestown. The origin of the name is unknown, and it disappeared from maps about 1920. (2, 18, 158)

**BERRIER** (Morton). This townsite was founded in 1902 in NW¼ Sec. 3-134-84, Flasher Twp., and named IOWA CITY by founder William H. Brown. This name was rejected by postal officials, and it was renamed BERRIER for storekeeper and pm-to-be William Frank Berrier (1866-1915). This name was also rejected by postal officials who felt it was too similar to others names in ND. A third name was submitted, FLASHER, and this was accepted. (3, 40, 106)

**BERRY** (Hettinger). This was a rural post office established April 2, 1907 with William G. Berry pm in his home in NE¼ Sec. 8-134-91, Solon Twp., about ten miles NE of Mott. It closed April 30, 1911 with mail to Hoosier. (3, 18, 40, 180, 181)

*Berg post office about 1920*

**BERTHA** (Rolette). This was a farm post office established June 6, 1903 with Bertha Rigstad as the first and only pm. Bertha is the female form of Albert, a Teutonic name meaning bright or glorious. The post office was located in NE¼ Sec. 5-162-72, Hillside Twp., seven miles NE of Dunseith, and closed March 15, 1914 with mail to Dunseith. (1, 2, 18, 19, 40, 123)

**BERTHOLD** (Ward). This GNRR mainline station was founded in April 1900 in SE¼ Sec. 21-156-86, Berthold Twp., about 25 miles west of Minot. The name came from Fort Berthold, which was named for Bartholomew Berthold, who ran the trading post there in 1845. The post office was established October 1, 1900 with Frederick C. Walther pm. The elevation is 2087, the Zip Code is 58718, and the village, which incorporated in 1902, reached a peak population of 523 in 1920. (1, 2, 18, 25, 33, 40, 100)

**BERWICK** (McHenry). This was a farm post office established October 22, 1890 in the sod house of James Cocks, with his wife Mary as pm. It was named by GNRR officials for Berwick, Dorsetshire, England. The site in Sec. 1-156-75, Berwick Twp., had been designated as a railroad townsite, but no development began. The post office closed August 18, 1893 with mail to Towner. A section house was built in 1897, and Elmer Greene purchased the townsite in 1899 just as settlers began to arrive. The post office reopened November 17, 1899 with Mr. Greene as pm. A boom followed, and the unofficial population was 300 in 1920. The village incorporated in 1929, but a steady decline has reduced the population to just 24 in 1980. The post office, Zip Code 58719, closed April 4, 1969 with mail to Towner. (1, 2, 10, 18, 25, 40, 41, 79, 288)

**BESSIE** (Slope). This was a rural post office established August 4, 1908 as DEMORES, with Caroline C. Desforges pm. It was located in S½ Sec. 11-133-102, Cash Twp., twelve miles SW of Amidon. Miss Desforges declined the appointment, and the position was given to Theodore Gilbertson on January 20, 1909, who renamed it BESSIE for attorney A. J. Bessie. The site developed into a rural community, challenging for the county seat in 1915 and reporting a population of 30 in 1920. Henry J. Burke ran a country store at this site, and his wife was the last pm, closing the post office October 30, 1926 with mail to Rhame. The Burke family owned this site into the 1970's. (1,2, 18, 40, 82, 400)

**BESSOBA** (Burleigh). For approximately half a century, beginning about 1895, this place has appeared on various maps in Sec. 22-137-76, Long Lake Twp., at or near what is now the crossing of the NPRR and the Soo Line RR. The origin of the name is unknown, and nothing ever developed at this townsite. The settlement of Moffit is adjacent to BESSOBA. (2, 3, 8, 18)

**BESTON** (Towner). This was a farm post office established May 5, 1898 with Charles P. Beston pm. It was located in SW¼ Sec. 3-158-65, Bethel Twp., nine miles NE of Cando, and closed July 31, 1902 with mail to Cando. (2, 3, 40, 414)

**BETHEL** (Morton). This was a rural post office established May 11, 1909 with Rev. Gustav Sturm pm. The name is a Hebrew word meaning the house of God, and was chosen by Mrs. Sophia Albrecht who arrived here from Germany on May 20, 1889, and was married that very day. It was located in SE¼ Sec. 24-138-85, eight miles ENE of Almont, and closed April 30, 1913 with mail to Judson. (2, 3, 13, 17, 18, 40, 107)

**BEULAH** (Mercer). This NPRR townsite was founded in 1914 in Sec. 25-144-88, replacing the settlement called TROY, and absorbing the post offices of Bowdish and Farrington, just to the east and west respectively. Lee Pettibone, agent for the Tuttle Land Co., named it for his niece, Beulah Stinchcombe Bishop of Calgary, Alberta, Canada. Mr. Bishop visited here in 1917, 1928, and 1964, the latter occasion noting the city's 50th anniversary jubilee. The name is of Biblical origins meaning land flowing with milk and honey. The post office was established April 29, 1914 with Joseph C. Evans pm. The elevation is 1797, the Zip Code is 58523, and the village, which incorporated in 1916, has become a center of the energy industry, reaching a population of 2,878 in 1980, more than double its 1970 count. Realtor Louis F. Temme, druggist Theo P. Herman, and grocer Fred Galloway were prominent among local businessmen. (1, 2, 7, 19, 34, 40, 79)

**BEYROUT** (Pierce). This rural post office was established March 5, 1901 with Atlas David pm, who suggested the name David. This name was rejected in favor of BEYROUT for the capital of Lebanon, now usually spelled Beirut. Many Assyrian people settled in this area in the 1890's, but most have long since departed. The post office was located in SW¼ Sec. 2-154-72, Elverum Twp., three miles NE of Silva. In 1904 it moved to the home of pm Martin Timboe in SE¼ Sec. 17-154-72, one mile SW of Silva. Mr. Timboe (1879-1924) ran a grocery store in conjunction with the post office, which closed August 15, 1906 with mail to Fillmore. (2, 40, 114, 149, 414)

**BICYCLE** (McKenzie). This was a rural post office established November 22, 1916 with Mrs. William (Anna) Fane as pm. It was located in NW¼ Sec. 2-145-100, Rhoades Twp., six miles WNW of Grassy Butte until 1920, when it was moved six miles west to the home of new pm Reuben A. Lyon in NE¼ Sec. 2-145-101, Rhoades Twp. Louis K. Elstrand and Mrs. Frances Cook then held this position at their homes just to the north in Township 146-101, with the post office closing October 31, 1935 with mail to Grassy Butte. The name was a heavily-Anglicized corruption of nearby Beicegel Creek resulting in a recognition, of sorts, of the popular two-wheeled vehicles. (1, 2, 3, 40, 79, 415)

**BIERMAN** (Slope). This was a rural post office established August 20, 1916 with Elizabeth Beirman pm. It was located in E½ Sec. 20-135-103, Richland Center Twp., sixteen miles west of Amidon, and one mile SE of the old BADLAND post office which it replaced. It was named for the pm and her brother, Frank, who ranched at this site. The post office closed August 5, 1927 with mail

to Rhame. A population of 10 was reported in 1920, and a count of 13 was made in 1930. (1, 2, 3, 40, 82)

**BIG BEND** (McLean). This was by many standards the most successful of the Garrison Dam boom towns that developed before the creation of the government-sponsored town of Riverdale. BIG BEND was favored locally as the name of Riverdale, and was adopted here only after the government town's name had been chosen. The name noted the major change in direction from east to south made by the Missouri River in central ND. The post office was established October 1, 1946 with Agnes Butts pm, and the site boasted among its businesses a grocery store, hardware store, cafe, and a bowling alley. After an initial boom, the first census in 1950 showed just 207 people living here, and the site declined rapidly when construction ended a few years later. The post office closed August 31, 1957 with mail to Coleharbor, and the last census in 1960 showed a count of just 39. BIG BEND was located in Sec. 6-146-83, Longfellow Twp., just SE of Riverdale. (2, 3, 28, 40)

**BIG BEND** (Mercer). This was a speculative townsite in SE¼ Sec. 18-147-84, two miles NNE of Pick City. Dr. Alexander Shutt of Milwaukee, WI promoted the site on land owned by J. E. Hedeen, but it is said that only one person ever lived here, even though several hundred lots were reported sold, mostly to people in WI. A post office was established June 27, 1905 with Paul H. Spangenberg pm, who must have been that one person, and it closed July 14, 1906 with mail to Mannhaven. The name noted the big bend of the Missouri River in the area, where it begins its more southerly course. This site is now inundated by Lake Sakakawea. (2, 3, 18, 34, 40, 64, 232, 414)

**BIG COULEE** (Towner). This was an alternate name for LaCROSSE, the first settlement in southern Towner County. It was located in NW¼ Sec. 6-157-65, Coolin Twp., five miles SE of Cando, and named to note its location on the east bank of the Mauvais Coulee. (3, 18, 103)

**BILLINGS** (Slope). This was a ranch post office established March 7, 1910 with Bert E. Sanford pm in his country store located in SW¼ Sec. 4-133-103, Deep Creek Twp., seventeen miles SW of Amidon. It was named for Frederick K. Billings (1823-1890), a native of VT who served as President of the NPRR 1879-1881, and is also the namesake of both Billings County and Billings, MT. Mr. Sanford closed the post office May 31, 1914 with mail to Rhame, and moved back to his hometown of LaCrosse, WI. (1, 2, 3, 10, 40, 82, 416)

**BINFORD** (Griggs). Settlers were here as early as 1877, and when Gabriel Gilbertson homesteaded in Sec. 8-147-60, Addie Twp., a rural community called BLOOMING PRAIRIE began. In 1899 the NPRR built a station on this site and named it for Ray Binford, an attorney from Charles City, IA with interests in this area. Some say it was named for J. R. Binford, who is likely the same man as above. The post office was established November 17, 1899 with Oscar A. Greenbaum pm. The village incorporated

*Birchwood Store about 1911*

April 2, 1906 and reached a peak population of 393 in 1920. The elevation is 1543, and the Zip Code is 58416. Dr. J. R. Truscott has been the town's only physician, but he practiced here for fifty years beginning in 1902. (1, 2, 18, 40, 65, 285)

**BINGHAMTON** (Barnes). This townsite was platted in 1884 by Mortimer Webster, a Soo Line RR official, at the north edge of KIBBY in NE¼ Sec. 25-138-56, Binghampton Twp. He named it for his hometown of Binghamton, NY, which was named for William Bingham (1752-1804), a Philadelphia merchant who founded the NY city. The KIBBY post office moved here on August 29, 1884 with Reuben P. Jennings pm. In 1887 it was moved four miles SW to the new Soo Line RR townsite in Sec. 11-137-56, Raritan Twp. The 1890 population was listed as 38. In 1891 the townsite was moved one-half mile north to NE¼ Sec. 11-137-56 and renamed LUCCA. The BINGHAMTON post office changed its name to LUCCA on October 19, 1891, and the old BINGHAMTON plat was abandoned in 1909. No explanation is given for the variation in the spelling of Binghampton township. (2, 3, 10, 18, 25, 40, 76, 118)

**BIRCH** (Barnes). This was a rural post office established May 1, 1894 with James Burchill pm. The order was rescinded May 20, 1896 before it had gone into operation. Its location is something of a mystery. Mr. Burchill was a member of a prominent family with vast land holdings north of Valley City, and his own home was in SW¼ Sec. 8-142-57, Grand Prairie Twp., fifteen miles NNE of Valley City, but some historians believe that the post office was intended to be located just NW of Kathryn on Birch Creek, about fifteen miles south of Valley City. (2, 3, 18, 34, 40, 76)

**BIRCHWOOD** (Rolette). This was a rural post office established September 7, 1910 with John Jay pm. It was located in E½ Sec. 10-163-71, Hutchinson Twp., on the west shore of Lake Upsilon about five miles west

of Saint John. It closed March 31, 1914 with mail to Saint John. It was reestablished November 29, 1915, closing for good November 30, 1920 with mail again to Saint John. A population of 25 was reported in 1920. A resort called Birchwood Park was platted on the opposite shore of this irregular shaped lake, and this post office no doubt served that venture, as well as the neighboring resorts of Wye, Eagles Nest, and Oak Springs. (1, 2, 3, 18, 40, 123)

**BIRCHWOOD PARK** (Rolette). This was a resort platted on the east shore of Lake Upsilon in E½ Sec. 10-163-71, Hutchinson Twp., five miles west of Saint John. The name notes the birch trees surrounding the lake. A post office called Birchwood operated on the west shore of the lake 1910-1914 and 1915-1920, just opposite this resort, which appears only in county atlases published in 1910 and 1928. (2, 3, 18, 40, 123)

**BIRDSALL** (Grant). This was a NPRR station founded in 1910 in W½ Sec. 5-133-90, five miles west of New Leipzig and named for

John Summerfield Birdsall, a prominent grain dealer and rancher who came here from Gladstone. He later was a bank president in New Leipzig. The post office was established October 22, 1910 with Emanuel Arhom pm, and on July 19, 1911 the name was changed to ODESSA. (2, 3, 17, 18, 40, 177)

**BISBEE** (Towner). This townsite was founded in 1888 in W½ Sec. 1-159-68, New City Twp., and is now at the junction of the GNRR and Soo Line RR. It was named by a vote of the people for Col. A. Bisbee, a Civil War veteran who lived two miles south of town. On March 29, 1890 pm John K. Aanes of Hanson moved that post office to BISBEE, assuming the name of the townsite. The elevation is 1605, the Zip Code is 58317, and a peak population of 531 was reached in 1930. (1, 2, 3, 18, 25, 33, 40, 79)

**BISCHOF** (McIntosh). This was a farm post office established September 5, 1919 with Thomas G. McClelland pm. It was located in NW¼ Sec. 32-132-73, Friedensthal Twp., fourteen miles WSW of Wishek, and sixteen miles north of Zeeland. It was named for John Bischof, a Zeeland banker and businessman who came here in 1905 from South Russia, and closed March 31, 1922 with mail to Zeeland. Bischoff is an erroneous spelling. (1, 2, 3, 18, 34, 40, 79, 211)

**BISMARCK** (Burleigh). Founded as the NPRR's Missouri River terminus, this townsite had many unofficial names before it became EDWINTON in May 1872. On July 17, 1873 it was renamed BISMARCK for the Chancellor of Germany, Prince Otto Eduard Leopold von Bismarck-Schonhausen (1815-1898), to please German investors in the railroad. It became the county seat in 1873, and became the capital of Dakota Territory in 1883, assuming that role for ND in 1889. The Soo Line RR reached BISMARCK in 1902. The elevation is 1674, and the base Zip Code is 58501. It incorporated as a city in 1875 with Edmund Hackett mayor, and has grown to a peak population of 44,502 in 1980, second only to Fargo. It sprawls over much of Lincoln Twp. (138-80) and Hay Creek Twp. (139-80),

*Bismarck about 1925*

and is the site of the state penitentiary, Bismarck State College, and the University of Mary. As the capital, nearly every politician of note in the state's history has a connection to BISMARCK. Notable pioneers included journalists Col. Clement A. Lounsberry and Marshall H. Jewell, riverboat captain Grant Marsh, and the colorful Dennis Hannifin. (2, 3, 9, 14, 33, 40, 79)

**BISMARK** (Burleigh). This erroneous spelling of BISMARCK has undoubtedly occurred thousands of times over the years, and its own post office has been one of the offenders. (3)

**BISON SPUR** (Ward). Commercial atlases of the 1970's list this place as being in Ward County. No other information is available. (3)

**BITUMIA** (McLean). This was a Soo Line RR siding built in 1908 in SE¼ Sec. 4-144-82, Washburn Twp., between Washburn and Falkirk. It served the Black Diamond Coal Company's mine at this site which was owned by Washburn pioneer "King" John Satterlund, and was given a name derived from bituminous coal. The siding was removed in 1939. (2, 3, 18, 28)

**BJELLAND** (Bottineau). This was a farm post office established October 31, 1901 with Chris H. Knudson pm who named it for his father, Knud Bjelland. It was located in NE¼ Sec. 12-159-83, Lansford Twp., two miles SE of Lansford, and closed December 14, 1903 with mail to Lansford. (2, 3, 34, 40, 101, 153)

**BJORN** (Grand Forks). This was a farm post office established July 19, 1880 with Andrew Hallockson pm. It was located in Sec. 20-152-51, Rye Twp., three miles south of Manvel, and closed November 29, 1881 with mail to Grand Forks. *Bjorn* is Norwegian for bear, and one of these animals had been seen in the area, resulting in the name. Bijorn is an erroneous spelling. (2, 31, 40, 69)

**BLABON** (Steele). This was a GNRR townsite was founded in 1896 in SW¼ Sec. 3-145-56, Melrose Twp., and named for Joseph Ward Blabon (1858-1933), a GNRR official who visited the new townsite in 1897. The post office was established March 3, 1900 with

Edward J. Baldner pm in his general store. The townsite was platted in 1903, but never incorporated, reaching an unofficial peak population of 150 in 1914, with a decline to just 17 in 1983. The elevation is 1337. The post office closed July 31, 1957 with mail to Hope. Gilbert Johnson (1887-1975) was the GNRR agent here 1910-1960. (1, 2, 18, 33, 40, 79, 99, 325)

**BLACK** (Ward). This was a rural post office established July 14, 1886 in the country store of pm Nathan D. Terrell, who named it for the Black brothers, local ranchers. It was located in NE¼ Sec. 11-153-81, Sawyer Twp., just east of present-day Sawyer. Mr. Terrell's daughter, Amy, became pm August 6, 1886, and following her marriage to William H. Wilson, moved the facility one mile SE to the Wilson home in SW¼ Sec. 12-153-81 on August 18, 1887 with a name change to ECHO. (2, 3, 40, 373, 414, 415)

**BLACKMER** (Richland). This was a Milwaukee Road RR station in Sec. 21-129-47, Fairmount Twp., five miles south of Fairmount, and named for John Blackmer who came here about 1885 from MI to manage an 800 acre farm. A post office was established December 29, 1897 with Otis D. Forte pm, and it closed May 15, 1905 with mail to Fairmount. The elevator was razed in 1974 leaving the site vacant. Blackmere is an erroneous spelling. (1, 2, 18, 40, 53, 79, 147)

**BLACKSTONE** (Sargent). This townsite was platted in early 1883 in Secs. 13 & 14-130-57, Sargent Twp., two miles south of Cogswell. Promoters George S. Montgomery and Pat H. Rourke named it for Mr. Rourke's hometown of Blackstone, IL. The post office was established June 25, 1883 with Ford D. Benton pm. On December 31, 1883 the name was changed to SARGENT. (2, 40, 165, 167)

**BLACKWATER** (McLean). This post office opened December 22, 1906 with Ira Matheny (1873-1945) pm. Mr. Matheny came to Fort Berthold in 1902 as a teacher at the mission school, and in 1906 built a country store in SW¼ Sec. 17-148-87, Blackwater Twp., nine miles north of the fort, whose post office was replaced by the BLACKWATER facility. It was named for nearby Blackwater Lake, named by the Indians to note the murkiness of its water, thought to be caused by the coal deposits in the area. Mr. Matheny operated the facility until 1923. A population of 10 was reported in 1930, and a count of 6 was made in 1940, but the post office closed May 31, 1941 with mail to Emmet. (1, 2, 3, 18, 28, 40, 79, 278)

**BLAINE** (Burleigh). The NPRR built SEVENTEENTH SIDING in 1873 in Sec. 33-139-78, Menoken Twp. Pioneer settlers in the area were mostly from the state of ME, and they named the community for that state's U. S. Senator, James Gillespie Blaine (1830-1893), who was the Republican candidate for President in 1884, losing to Grover Cleveland. A post office was established here in 1880 with the official name CLARKE'S FARM, with a name change to MENOKEN in 1883. The NPRR was not happy with this name, and called its station BURLEIGH from 1891 un-

til it closed in 1957. (2, 3, 8, 10, 13, 40)

**BLAINE** (Sheridan). Joseph T. Wyard was appointed pm of BLAINE on August 21, 1902. He was a merchant in the new town of GOODRICH, just recently formed by a merger of the rival townsites of CLARK and DUDLEY, and in a rare example of quick government action, the BLAINE order was rescinded and replaced with paperwork appointing Mr. Wyard as pm of GOODRICH in just nine days. The first name is thought to honor James Gillespie Blaine (1830-1893), the well known politician from the state of ME. (2, 3, 5, 18, 40)

**BLAISDELL** (Mountrail). This GNRR station was founded in the late 1880's as DELTA, and in 1904-1905 was known as RONESS, BLENHEIM, GRENADA, and HANLEY. It is located in NE¼ Sec. 14-156-89, McGahan Twp., between Palermo and Tagus. The post office was established as GRENADA on February 28, 1905, but was changed to BLAISDELL on October 21, 1905 by pm Christian S. Vie, honoring Alfred Blaisdell, a young Minot attorney and partner in the Blaisdell-Bird Land Co. that platted the townsite. Mr. Blaisdell was ND Secretary of State in 1907-1910. The elevation is 2263, the Zip Code is 58720, and a peak population of 175 was reported in 1920, with a decline to just 30 in 1979. (1, 2, 3, 18, 33, 40, 52, 72, 79)

**BLAKELY'S CROSSING** (Grand Forks). Robert Blakely came here in 1877, settling at the site of a pioneer crossing of the Turtle River on the Grand Forks-Fort Totten mail route. It was located in SE¼ Sec. 20-152-53, Mekinock Twp., four miles SW of present-day Mekinock. Mr. Blakely established a post office here in 1879 which he named MECKINOCK. (2, 3, 31, 40, 69)

**BLANCHARD** (Traill). This GNRR townsite was founded in 1880 in E½ Sec. 25-145-52, Blanchard Twp., and named for S. S. Blanchard, an area bonanza farmer originally from Boston, MA, and a brother-in-law of J. L. Grandin, the king of the bonanza farmers. The post office was established November 29, 1880 with Douglas Robertson pm. The elevation is 932, the Zip Code is 58009, and a population of 100 has been reported at various times since 1890, although the current population is under 50. Since January 2, 1976 the post office has been operated as a Community Post Office affiliated with Hillsboro. In the 1960's BLANCHARD billed itself as the city with the world's tallest manmade structure, the 2063 foot KTHI-TV tower just SW of town. (1, 2, 3, 25, 29, 33, 40, 79, 187)

**BLENHEIM** (Mountrail). This GNRR siding was founded in the late 1880's in NE¼ Sec. 14-156-89, McGahan Twp., as DELTA. When settlement began in 1904 it was at first called RONESS, but soon the name was changed to BLENHEIM for unknown reasons. In 1905 the post office was established as GRENADA, a name unpopular with local residents who began calling the town HANLEY. This name was rejected by postal officials, citing possible confusion with nearby Stanley, and on October 21, 1905 the name was changed to BLAISDELL. (2, 40, 72)

**BLOOM** (Stutsman). This is a NPRR loading station built before 1890 in Sec. 27-140-63, Bloom Twp., and named by construction crews for the many flowers in bloom at the time this railroad was built. The township name was changed from Harmony to Bloom in 1905. Anton Klaus had a brickyard here, and in 1913 Pierce Blewett and Jacob Yeager built an elevator at the site. A village of about 10 people has existed here for years, but the site has always been served by the Jamestown post office. In recent years BLOOM has been most familiar to motorists as Exit –61 on Interstate 94, four miles east of Jamestown. (1, 2, 3, 18, 25, 38, 79, 158)

**BLOOMENFIELD** (Stutsman). This was a farm post office established February 28, 1898 with Heinrich Odenbach pm. It was located in SE¼ Sec. 14-137-68, Germania Twp., seven miles ENE of Streeter, and named for Blumenfeld, South Russia, the home of many area settlers. The adjoining township to the north was also named Bloomenfield, but in this case the name is said to note the wild flowers blooming on the prairie. In 1905 the post office moved to the Alix Anderson home in NW¼ Sec. 26-137-69, Streeter Twp., which later that year became the new NPRR terminus townsite of STREETER. The BLOOMEN-FIELD post office adopted the new name on March 2, 1906. (2, 3, 23, 40, 158, 162, 414, 415)

**BLOOMFIELD** (Traill). This was a rural post office in NE¼ Sec. 33-146-51, Norway Twp., five miles WNW of Hillsboro. It was established in 1877 as STONY POINT, but on March 24, 1879 pm Rev. Jonas Ostlund changed the name to BLOOMFIELD to note the wild flowers that bloomed here each summer. The post office closed July 10, 1882 with mail to Hillsboro. (2, 3, 18, 25, 40)

**BLOOMING** (Grand Forks). This NPRR townsite was founded in 1887 in Sec. 1-152-53, Mekinock Twp., and named for the adjacent township, Blooming (152-52), which was named by settlers from Blooming Prairie, MN. It was just west of Mekinock, which soon became the site of development in the area. (2, 31, 69, 338)

**BLOOMING PRAIRIE** (Griggs). The first settlers were here about 1877 and named this rural community for Blooming Prairie, MN, which had been founded in 1868 and named to note the many wild flowers blooming in the area. Some say this name noted the wild flax that grew here prior to settlement. Included in the community was the home of Gabriel Gilbertson in Sec. 8-147-60, Addie Twp., which in 1899 became the NPRR townsite of BINFORD. (2, 13, 18, 65, 285)

**BLUEBELL** (McKenzie). This was a farm post office established February 8, 1911 with Helen G. Raze pm, who named it to note the many blue flowers native to the area. It was located in NE¼ Sec. 4-151-97, twelve miles NE of Watford City, and closed December 15, 1912 with mail to Tobacco Garden. (2, 18, 40, 53)

**BLUE GRASS** (Morton). This NPRR siding in SW¼ Sec. 25-139-86, Caribou Twp., three miles SW of New Salem, was built in 1880 and temporarily named SECOND SIDING. Sometime before 1884 it was named BLUE GRASS by NPRR officials to note the wide-bladed, blue-colored bunch grass common to the area. Local legend says that the grass had been brought here from KY by soldiers serving under Gen. Custer. Little development occurred here, and the station disappeared from maps during the 1920's. The site was served by the Sims post office, and was abandoned in 1946 when the NPRR rerouted its mainline. (1, 2, 3, 18, 18, 25)

**BLUEGRASS** (Morton). This was a rural community founded in 1890 in NE¼ Sec. 18-140-86, Bluegrass Twp., twelve miles NW of New Salem, and named for the NPRR siding just SW of New Salem. The post office was established July 2, 1902 with buttermaker Wilhelm C. Michaels as pm. To comply with government spelling regulations the post office name was spelled as one word. John Moos ran the Blue Grass Cooperative Creamery Association for many years. George Conitz became the pm in 1923, and the post office operated until August 31, 1955 when mail went to New Salem. A peak population of 20 was reported in 1920, and the 1960 count of just 7 was the last report from BLUEGRASS. (1, 2, 3, 17, 18, 40, 107, 109)

**BLUESHALE** (McKenzie). This was a rural post office established August 4, 1916 with Mrs. John (Mary R.) Barnett pm. It was located in SE¼ Sec. 22-146-103, twenty-six miles WSW of Grassy Butte, until October 29, 1918 when it moved three miles SW to the home of new pm Emma May Scott in NE¼ Sec. 30-146-103. The post office closed August 30, 1919 with mail to Trotters. The post office application was submitted with the name Poker Jim, which was rejected in favor of BLUESHALE, the origin of which is unknown, although it would seem to be descriptive. (3, 40, 415)

**BLY'S MINE** (Morton). This was a pioneer coal mining settlement in Sec. 14-138-86, Sims Twp., just SW of Sims, and about three miles north of Almont. It was named for owner Eber H. Bly, who came to Dakota Territory from NY in 1872 and worked with the NPRR locating townsites along the mainline. He was later involved in various business ventures from Bismarck to Medora. BLY'S MINE was absorbed by the Sims townsite in the early 1880's. (2, 3, 25, 72, 79, 416)

**BOBTOWN** (Emmons). This was a rural post office established August 18, 1894 with Robert Buchanan (1850-1930) pm. It was located in NW¼ Sec. 30-136-77, seven miles SE of Glencoe, and one mile NW of the old Buchanan post office which had closed May 23, 1894. Upon hearing of the closing of the Buchanan post office, officials of the Rio post office in Stutsman County had initiated the paperwork required to change their name to Buchanan. When the Emmons County facility decided to reopen, it was discovered that the rights to the Buchanan name had been lost, so this new name was coined from the pm's nickname. The BOBTOWN post office closed September 28, 1896 with mail to Livona. (2, 3, 40, 66, 415)

**BOGUSVILLE** (Cass). As the NPRR approached Dakota Territory in 1870, great efforts were made to disguise the planned crossing point of the Red River at what would become Fargo-Moorhead. This squatters' town, which bears a name that obviously dates from after its heyday, is generally believed to have been about seven miles north of the actual crossing point, but on the MN side of the river. Some insist that it was on the Dakota side in Cass County. (3, 199, 307, 420)

**BOHAN** (Burleigh). This was a farm post office established May 27, 1903 with John P. Bohan pm. It was located in S½ Sec. 8-141-77, Trygg Twp., thirteen miles east of Baldwin, and closed March 31, 1909 with mail to Baldwin. (2, 3, 8, 18, 40, 63)

**BOLACK** (Grand Forks). This was a NPRR siding built in SE¼ Sec. 21-152-51, Rye Twp., four miles NW of Grand Forks, and named for pioneer settler Joseph Napoleon Bolack, the owner of the land at this site. Little development took place, and the site is now the Grand Forks International Airport. (1, 2, 31, 69)

**BOLAKER** (Renville). L. L. Goheen had established a mail drop for settlers at his home in NW¼ Sec. 10-163-84, Eden Valley Twp., four miles east of Sherwood. On November 8, 1902 the BOLAKER post office was established one-half mile SW in SE¼ Sec. 9-163-84 with Stener V. Svennungsen pm, who named it for his hometown in Norway. The post office was relocated to the new GNRR townsite of Sherwood on January 24, 1905. (2, 3, 40, 71)

**BOLKEN** (Nelson). This was a farm post office established November 7, 1905 with Peder L. Bolken pm. Mr. Bolken came here in 1887 from Norway and founded the Plainview Farm in NE¼ Sec. 27-149-61, Forde Twp., eight miles SW of Pekin. The post office closed October 31, 1907 with mail to Pekin. (2, 3, 18, 40, 53, 124, 132)

**BOLLINGER** (Rolette). This was a farm post office established February 14, 1888 with Charles A. Bollinger pm. It was located in NE¼ Sec. 27-159-69, Pleasant Valley Twp., in the extreme SE corner of the county. Mr. Bollinger ran a store and blacksmith shop in conjunction with the post office, which closed January 17, 1891 with mail to Island Lake. (2, 3, 18, 25, 40, 123, 415)

**BONETRAILL** (Williams). This was a rural settlement founded in 1903 in NW 1/4 Sec. 23-157-102, Bonetraill Twp., about twenty miles NNW of Williston, and named for its location on an old trail used by pioneers when hauling buffalo bones to Williston. The post office was established June 19, 1905 with Charles O. Borstad pm. Oscar I. Wilson was a merchant and the pm here 1915-1938. A peak population of 100 was

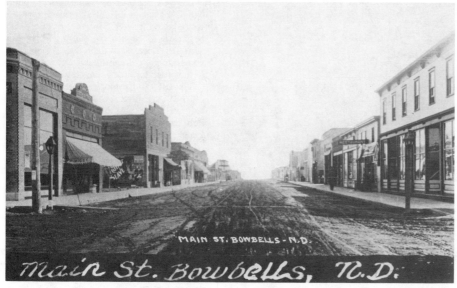

*Bowbells about 1915*

reported in 1920, with a decline to just 14 in 1960. The post office, Zip Code 58836, closed September 8, 1978 with mail to Williston, although the official date of closing was March 16, 1979. (1, 2, 3, 18, 33, 40, 41, 50, 79)

**BONNERSVILLE** (Ransom). Peter Bonner settled here in 1870 and is considered to be the first homesteader in the county. About 1873 a settlement started on his land in SW¼ Sec. 11-135-54, Shenford Twp., seven miles south of Sheldon, and a post office was established April 8, 1878 with Mr. Bonner as pm. A population of 12 was reported in 1884, and a count of 15 was made in 1890, but without a railroad the townsite could not compete with neighboring towns, and the post office closed April 21, 1890 with mail to Shenford. (2, 3, 40, 77, 85, 201)

**BONNIE VIEW** (Golden Valley). This was a farm post office established April 23, 1915 with Renovia B. Hubbard as pm in the home of O. R. Krull in SE 1/4 Sec. 20-142-105, Elmwood Twp., thirteen miles north of Beach. The name was coined by Alexander McCaskey (1834-1911), who came here in 1906 at the age of 72 to try his luck ranching in the west. He thought of the name while looking at the countryside from a nearby butte. A population of 10 was reported in 1920, and the site included the Bonnieview School one-half mile to the south. The name is often spelled as one word. The post office closed August 31, 1920 with mail to Beach. (1, 2, 3, 18, 40, 80)

**BOOTH** (Barnes). This was a rural community founded in 1881 as EDNA. The post office was established as BOOTH on July 25, 1882 with Albert Anson Booth (1850-1914) as pm. He was the father of Edna Booth, and is credited with suggesting both names. It was located in NE¼ Sec. 24-142-60, Edna Twp., three miles NW of Rogers, and closed November 18, 1884 with mail to Odell. (2, 3, 18, 25, 40, 76, 328)

**BORDULAC** (Foster). This Soo Line RR station was founded in 1892 as CHIHAUN, but adopted the name BORDULAC in 1895. The

new name was coined from the French words meaning border of the lake, noting its location on the west shore of Lake George. The lake was named for George M. Palmer of the Carrington-Casey Land Co., and the new name for the townsite was suggested by Mrs. Palmer. Lake George has receded since BORDULAC was founded, and is now several miles from the edge of town. The post office was established June 3, 1895 with Charles M. Porter pm. The elevation is 1530, the Zip Code is 58417, and a peak population of 200 was claimed for many years, although an official count in 1960 showed just 85 people living here. James Morris, an Associate Justice of the ND Supreme Court, was born here in 1893. (1, 2, 3, 18, 33, 38, 40, 52, 79, 97)

**BOSTONIA** (Kidder). This was a farm post office established February 8, 1908 with Theodore A. Stramblad pm at his home in SE¼ Sec. 30-144-73, Stewart Twp., eight miles north of Tuttle. Mr. Stramblad had attended a few college courses in Boston, MA as a young man, and suggested this Latinized version of the name along with others to postal officials. Boston, MA was named for Boston, Lincolnshire, England, which had been a hotbed of Puritan activity in the 1600's. The post office was discontinued August 31, 1913 with mail to Tuttle. (2, 3, 4, 10, 18, 40, 53, 122)

**BOTTINEAU** (Bottineau). This GNRR townsite was founded in 1884 in Secs. 30 & 31-162-75, Whitteron Twp., and Secs. 25 & 36-162-76, Pickering Twp., and absorbed most of the pioneer settlement of Oak Creek one mile to the NE. The post office was established March 3, 1884 with Augustine Thompson pm. Ten days later Bottineau County was organized, and BOTTINEAU was named the county seat. Both are named for Pierre Bottineau (1812-1895), a voyageur, guide, interpreter, and frontiersman who is often considered to be the first white baby born in ND, although he was part Chippewa Indian. The elevation is 1638, the Zip Code is 58318, and a peak population of 2,828 was reached in 1980. It incorporated as a village in 1888 and

became a city in 1904. It is the site of the State School of Forestry, now affiliated with NDSU in Fargo. (1, 2, 3, 18, 25, 33, 34, 40, 52, 79, 97, 101, 153)

**BOUNDARY** (Rolette). This was a farm post office established March 9, 1903 with Frank Laberge pm. It was located in S½ Sec. 28-164-69, Fairview Twp., in the extreme NE corner of the county and just south of the international boundary with Canada. The post office closed December 31, 1909 with mail to Saint John. (2, 18, 40)

**BOUNDARY LINE** (Pembina). This place appears on postmarks used by the railroad mail service, and notes the point at which the NPRR reaches Canada just north of Pembina in Sec. 28-164-51, Pembina Twp. Commercial guides refer to the place as INTERNATIONAL BOUNDARY. (3)

**BOUNTY** (Divide). This was a Soo Line RR siding in E½ Sec. 30-163-96, Long Creek Twp., six miles east of Crosby on land owned by Charles Atherton. The origin of the name is unknown. The site consisted of a grain elevator which operated into the 1920's, although the site was shown on maps into the 1940's. (2, 3, 18, 73)

**BOWBELLS** (Burke). This Soo Line RR townsite was founded in 1896 in Sec. 5-161-89, Bowbells Twp., and SE¼ Sec. 32-162-89, Minnesota Twp. Railroad officials named it for the bow bells at the Church of St. Mary-le-Bow in London, England. The post office was established January 29, 1898 with John Lesh pm. BOWBELLS was named the county seat when Burke County organized in 1910, and it became a two-railroad town in 1913 with the arrival of the GNRR. The elevation is 1961, the Zip Code is 58721, and a peak population of 806 was recorded in 1950. (1, 2, 4, 18, 34, 40, 67, 79, 375)

**BOWDISH** (Mercer). This was a rural post office established June 3, 1908 with James A. Bowdish pm. This order was rescinded, but a second application was approved October 30, 1908 and the office went into operation. It was located in NW¼ Sec. 27-144-88, two miles west of Beulah, and closed February 15, 1915 with mail to Beulah. (1, 2, 3, 18, 40)

**BOWDON** (Wells). This NPRR townsite was founded in 1899 in NW¼ Sec. 15-146-71, Haaland Twp., and was for several years the terminus of a branch line from Carrington. It was named, with local consent, for Bowdon, Cheshire, England, the birthplace of townsite owner Richard Sykes. The post office was established August 26, 1899 with Frank Lathrop pm, who also built the town's first business, a drugstore, and served as the mayor when the village incorporated in 1905. It became a city in 1952 with Lloyd Jones as mayor, and reached a peak population of 348 in both 1940 and 1950. The elevation is 1832, and the Zip Code is 58418. (1, 2, 3, 18, 38, 40, 79, 267, 364)

**BOWESMONT** (Pembina). This townsite was founded as PETTIT in 1888 in SE 1/4 Sec. 11-160-51, Lincoln Twp., but when the post office was established May 7, 1888 with Volney S. Waldo pm, it adopted the name of the recently closed rural post office of

*Braddock about 1915*

BOWESMOUNT, about three miles to the north, with a slight change in the spelling. That office had been named for William Bowes, although some sources say the railroad townsite was named for another pioneer, George Bowes. A population of just 18 was reported in 1890, but the city has had a population of about 150 for much of the twentieth century. The elevation is 819, and the post office, Zip Code 58217, closed January 8, 1983 with mail to Drayton. Gen. Harold K. Johnson, former Army Chief of Staff, was born here. (1, 2, 3, 18, 33, 38, 40, 79, 108, 366, 414, 415)

BOWESMOUNT (Pembina). This was a rural post office established August 2, 1880 with Edward L. Brooks pm, who named it for William Bowes, a local storekeeper, and "mount" to note its location on some high ground just west of the Red River. It was located in NW¼ Sec. 8-160-50, Lincoln Twp., just south of Alma which it replaced. On December 16, 1886 it was moved three miles NW to SE¼ Sec. 25-161-51, Joliette Twp. The post office closed April 20, 1888 with mail to Drayton, but reopened seventeen days later at the new NPRR townsite of PETTIT. The post office and townsite adopted the name BOWESMONT, the erroneous spelling which had been commonly used by local residents. (2, 3, 40, 108, 414, 415)

BOWMAN (Bowman). This city was founded in 1907 in Sec. 11-131-102, Bowman Twp., and named TWIN BUTTES. It was apparently also called EDEN for a time until July 26, 1907, when the post office was established as LOWDEN. On October 19, 1907 pm Arthur L. Lowden changed the name to BOWMAN for its county and township, both of which were named for territorial legislator William Bowman. Others say it was named for E. M. Bowman, an official of the Milwaukee Road RR which runs through this site. The city was named county seat when Bowman County organized July 5, 1907. The elevation is 2954, the Zip Code is 58623, and a peak population of 2,070 was reached in 1980. (1, 2, 3, 18, 33, 34, 40, 57, 79, 120, 383)

BOYDTON (Rolette). This was a pioneer townsite in NW¼ Sec. 8-162-69, Mount Pleasant Twp., named for the brothers Samuel and David C. Boyd who came here in 1882 from Utica, NY. The post office was established January 25, 1886 with David C. Boyd pm. The site was crossed by the GNRR in 1888, but railroad officials felt it was too close to Saint John and established the new townsite of ROLLA one mile to the SE. Mr. Boyd adopted the ROLLA name for the post office on November 9, 1888, but it remained at the old location until he left the pm position in 1893. (2, 3, 34, 40, 123, 415)

BOYLE (Stark). This NPRR siding in NW¼ Sec. 9-139-94, Heart River Twp., three miles NE of Gladstone, was built in 1890 and named KNOWLTON. In 1907 it was renamed BOYLE to honor Daniel Boyle who had been promoted to Assistant General Superintendent of the NPRR in 1906. Little development occurred here, and the site disappeared from most maps during the 1920's. (1, 2, 18, 74)

BOYNTON (Dickey). This Soo Line RR station was built in 1887 as the terminus of its Oakes Branch in NE¼ Sec. 21-131-63, Keystone Twp., two miles SE of Monango. The line was extended in 1888, ending BOYNTON's brief period of importance. The name honored C. A. Boynton of Saint Paul, MN, who was involved in railroad land management throughout central ND. The post office was established December 15, 1888 with W. C. Church pm, and closed March 21, 1892 with mail to Monango. The site is now vacant. (2, 3, 18, 25, 40, 154)

BRACKETT (Barnes). This was a NPRR station built in 1907 in N½ Sec. 22-140-56, Oriska Twp., three miles east of Oriska on Lake Howard, actually a wide spot of a stream. It was named for either a local settler, or for George Brackett, a member of the Sibley Expedition of 1863. Because of confusion with Brocket in Ramsey County, the name was changed to KOLDOK on December 10, 1915. (2, 3, 18, 34, 281)

BRADDOCK (Emmons). The first settlers came to this area in 1883, and a townsite was platted in 1888, but real development began in 1898 with the coming of the Soo Line RR. Located in SE¼ Sec. 27-136-75, it was named by Soo Line RR official Fred D. Underwood for his friend Edward Braddock (1856-1920), Emmons County Auditor 1897-1900 and a former employee of the railroad. The post office was established February 24, 1899 with John C. Brown pm. Isaac Elba Sheppard was the longtime mail carrier, and established the first Rural Free Delivery service in the county in 1908. The village incorporated in 1916 with J. D. McCusker as mayor. The Zip Code is 58524, and a peak population of 216 was reported in 1920, with a decline to just 86 in 1980. BRADDOCK is considered to be the oldest town in Emmons County. (1, 2, 3, 18, 33, 34, 40, 66, 79, 113, 234, 402)

BRAMPTON (Sargent). This was a farm post office established February 7, 1884 with Charles A. Finch pm, who named it for his hometown of Brampton, Ontario, Canada. It was located in SE¼ Sec. 12-129-57, Brampton Twp., and closed August 31, 1897 with mail to Newark, SD. A Milwaukee Road RR townsite had been platted in 1882 by Charles H. Cooper just to the west in SW¼ Sec. 12-129-57, but development had not occurred. About 1900 settlement began at the townsite, and the post office was reestablished there on September 1, 1904 with Giles Sink pm. A village of about 75 people existed here for many years, but recent decline has greatly reduced the importance of the town. The school closed in 1955, the depot was removed in 1958, and the post office, Zip Code 58010, closed December 15, 1984. (2, 18, 25, 33, 40, 79, 167).

BRAND'S SUBDIVISION (Bottineau). This platted area is shown in a 1910 county atlas in N½ Sec. 8-160-75, Willow Vale Twp., one mile west of Omemee on the south side of the Soo Line RR tracks. The land just to the south of the platted area was owned by W. D. Nicholson. The origin of the name is unknown, and the site did not develop. (3, 18)

BRANTFORD (Eddy). Settlement began about 1910 in anticipation of the GNRR which reached here in 1912. Located in NW¼ Sec. 35-148-65, Pleasant Prairie Twp., the post office was established July 26, 1910 with Oliver Z. Row pm. It was named for Brantford, Ontario, Canada by either GNRR officials or pioneer settler Thomas Adam. The elevation is 1526, and a peak population of 200 was claimed in 1920. The town has declined in recent years, and pm S. R. "Tim" Ludwig closed the post office, Zip Code 58419, on March 31, 1973 with mail to New Rockford. (2, 18, 33, 40, 119, 272)

BRAZIL (Pierce). This was the lifetime passion of Albert B. Fox (1861-1947), who founded the townsite in 1899, platted it, and was appointed pm when the post office was established April 27, 1900. It was located in SE¼ Sec. 20-155-73, Tuscarora Twp., eight miles SSW of Rugby. He began the Brazil Grain & Shipping Co. to market the farmers' crops, and labored long and hard to entice the GNRR to build a branchline into his little city. The railroad never came,

and his dream town died. The origin of the name is unknown, although some say it was named for Brazil, IN, which was named for the country in South America. The post office closed October 31, 1914 with mail to Rugby. It reopened February 15, 1918 with Hazel A. Fox pm, but was closed for good by pm Hilma Dahl on December 31, 1930 with mail to Orrin. A peak population of 40 was reported in 1920. (2, 3, 18, 23, 40, 114, 149, 287)

**BREIEN** (Morton). This NPRR station was founded as PARKIN in 1915 in NW 1/4 Sec. 36-134-82, New Hope Twp., six miles west of Solen. The post office was established May 6, 1916 with Ellen J. Ring pm, but it was renamed BREIEN by town founder Edward Jacobson, the local elevator manager, for one of his Norwegian relatives. It was chosen from a list of twelve names submitted to postal officials after PARKIN had been rejected due to assumed confusion with the recently discontinued rural post office of that name sixteen miles NNE of this site. Breien is a Norwegian word meaning to spread or broaden. The population never exceeded 40, and the post office, Zip Code 58525, closed June 21, 1985. (2, 3, 17, 34, 40, 106, 107)

**BREMEN** (Wells). This GNRR townsite was founded in 1910 on the Surrey cutoff line in SE¼ Sec. 5-149-68, Bremen Twp., just west of the old Twist post office which had closed the previous year. It was named for Bremen, Germany, the point of departure for many immigrants in this area. The German city reached a level of importance in 787 A.D. during the reign of Charlemagne, and derives its name from the original *Bremun*, meaning on the boundaries, describing its location 75 miles from the mouth of the Weser River. In 1827 it was the first German city-state to sign a treaty of friendship with the United States. The BREMEN post office was established May 12, 1910 with William F. Johnson pm. The elevation is 1548, the Zip Code is 58319, and a population of 200 was claimed in 1920, although the count has been under 100 since 1950. (1, 2, 3, 26, 33, 40, 53, 79, 364)

**BREMER'S RANCH** (Stutsman). An 1890 guide to ND lists this place as being in Stutsman County, and served by the Jamestown post office. No other information is available. (25)

**BRENIZER** (Golden Valley). This was a farm post office established June 1, 1908 with Hugh H. Brenizer pm at his farm in SW¼ Sec. 32-142-105, Elmwood Twp., nine miles north of Beach. Raleigh Brenizer, Hugh's brother, farmed one mile to the NW. On April 9, 1909 the post office was moved two miles west to the home of new pm Herman Gregory, which was in the state of MT. Postmarks exist with the ND identification as late as June 1909, thought to indicate that a new device had not been received by the MT facility, which closed September 30, 1919 with mail to Beach. (3, 40, 88, 415)

**BRENNAN'S LANDING** (Emmons). This was an early 20th-century Missouri River boat landing on the east bank of the Missouri River opposite Cannon Ball, and very near

the old ferry service at Gayton's Landing. No other information is available. (3)

**BRENNER** (Eddy). This was a rural post office established October 4, 1880 with Ernest William Brenner pm. It was located in Sec. 35-150-64, Hillsdale Twp., about seventeen miles NE of New Rockford, and closed April 23, 1887 with mail to New Rockford. The site was also known as Brenner's Crossing to note the location at a crossing point of the Sheyenne River. Mr. Brenner was a charter county commissioner of Foster County before Eddy County was created from it in 1885. (2, 40, 112, 119)

**BREWERS CORNERS** (Burleigh). This place appears on some maps circa 1915-1920 in Grass Lake Twp. (143-79), about six miles NE of Wilton. Although it was thought to be a copyright town, it was very close to the medical treatment center operated by Dr. John Sandelin 1914-1924. (3, 12, 18)

**BRIARWOOD** (Cass). This is one of the new cities of the 1970's, created primarily to avoid high city taxes and annexation by larger cities. BRIARWOOD, a euphonic name, is located in NW¼ Sec. 7-158-48, Stanley Twp., just north of Fargo, and incorporated as a city August 8, 1978 by a vote of 27-0. The population at the time was 57, just above the legal minimum of 50, with a drop to 47 in 1980. (3, 34)

**BRICKMINE** (Cavalier). Charles Major operated a brick manufacturing plant in NW¼ Sec. 34-161-57, South Olga Twp., four miles SW of Concrete, from 1905-1912. A settlement of about 80 people was here in 1910, but the operation failed due to its remote location, poor quality of clay at the site, and the lack of funds. (2, 3, 18)

**BRIGHTWOOD** (Richland). Herman Mittag began a townsite in Sec. 13-130-50, Brightwood Twp., in 1886 which he named for the township. He sold his interests September 17, 1886, and the site was absorbed by the new townsite of HANKINSON. (3, 147)

**BRINSMADE** (Benson). This NPRR station was built in 1889 in SW¼ Sec. 6-154-67, Riggin Twp., and named by E. S. Rolfe, a Minnewaukan attorney and owner of this townsite, for his friend Rev. S. Brinsmade of Beloit, WI. Some claim the name honors the first railroad engineer in the area. The post office was established June 6, 1892 with William Evans pm. The village incorporated in 1904 with Goodard Hofstrand as first board president, and reached a peak population of 206 in 1940, with a rapid decline to just 36 in 1970. The post office, Zip Code 58320, became a rural branch of Leeds on April 29, 1972. The well known Brinsmade Gopher Days celebration began here in 1902. Longtime Bismarck music instructor Belle Mehus was born in BRINSMADE. (2, 18, 33, 40, 79, 110, 236, 257, 259)

**BRISBANE** (Grant). This Milwaukee Road RR station was founded in 1910 in SE¼ Sec. 9-133-86, Brisbane Twp., and named for Arthur Brisbane (1864-1936), a famous nationally syndicated newspaper columnist. Others say it was named for a railroad official. The post office was established October 1, 1910 with Edward H. Robinson pm in his general store. The town attracted several German-Russian families from Emmons County and reported a population of 100 in 1920, but the count had declined to just 6 in 1960. Brisbane High School operated 1927-1936, graduating just 32 students. The post office closed March 31, 1956 with mail to Carson. (1, 2, 3, 10, 17, 38, 40, 79, 174, 176, 177)

**BRITTIN** (Burleigh). This was a Soo Line RR station built in 1902 in N½ Sec. 4-137-77, Morton Twp., six miles NW of Moffit, and named for pioneer homesteaders George and William Brittin. The post office was established February 25, 1903 with Edward F. Mutchler pm. Ellison M. Whiteaker and F. E. Galloway opened stores here as a small village began to develop. A population of 30 was reported in 1920, and the 1930 count was 23, but most residents left during the Great Depression and the post office closed January 31, 1933 with mail to Moffit. (1, 2, 8, 12, 14, 18, 40, 79)

**BROCKET** (Ramsey). F. H. Stoltze purchased 80 acres in SW¼ Sec. 27-155-60, Lillehoff Twp. on June 25, 1900, opened a lumber and hardware store at the site and announced the new townsite of BROCKET, named for John Brocket, a pioneer in the area, although others say the name is a corruption of Henry Raketti, another local pioneer. The post office was established August 21, 1901 with Daniel F. Humphreys as the pm and manager of the Stoltze businesses. The GNRR reached the site in May 1902, and the village incorporated in 1907, reaching a peak population of 291 in 1940, with a decline to just 74 in 1980. The elevation is 1519, and the Zip Code is 58321. Dr. John A. D. Engesather (1886-1968) was the town's physician 1919-1950. (1, 2, 18, 33, 40, 58, 103)

**BROCKWAY** (Ransom). This townsite was promoted in Sec. 35-133-57, Alleghany Twp., eight miles south of Elliott, which served this area's postal needs. It was to be a station on the Great Southern Railway, but that venture failed to materialize. The name was chosen by settlers from Brockwayville, PA, which was founded in 1839 by Alonzo Brockway, and changed its name to Brockway in 1925. (2, 3, 25, 251)

**BROFY** (Emmons). This post office was established January 3, 1906 with Alice L. Brophy pm. It was located in NE¼ Sec. 5-133-76, McCulley Twp., in the store run by her husband, L. W. Brophy. Mr. Brophy had applied for the post office as Brophyston, but the authorization for this office was approved October 21, 1905 as BROFY. Mr. Brophy declined this appointment, and his wife assumed the position the following January. The Brophys moved away, and new pm William A. Foell changed the name to LARVIK on January 28, 1908. Meanwhile a rival townsite called TEMPELTON began on the opposite side of the NPRR tracks, and the two merged in 1911 as TEMVIK. (2, 3, 18, 40, 66)

**BRONCHO** (Mercer). This was a ranch post office a few miles NW of Goldenvalley, closely associated with the Haven family during most of its existance. It was established

April 11, 1890 with Fannie K. Haven pm, who had come here in 1884 from Detroit Lakes, MN with her husband Harvey. It was first located in SE¼ Sec. 26-143-90, moving four miles SW in 1897 to SE¼ Sec. 4-142-90. In 1907 it was moved six miles north to NE¼ Sec. 5-143-90, and two years later moved to NW¼ Sec. 10-143-90. In 1912 it moved two miles north to SE¼ Sec. 32-144-90, operating here until it closed May 15, 1916 with mail to Goldenvalley. The name honors the native Mexican horse, named by the Spanish to mean rough and wild. This name became a cowboy colloquilism for any untamed horse. Mail carrier Lee E. Haven, a nephew, is credited with the selection of this name, and he operated the Broncho Stock Farm here for many years following the closing of the post office. (1, 2, 3, 4, 18, 40, 79, 232, 414, 415)

**BROOKBANK** (Mountrail). This was a ranch post office established March 14, 1907 with William Gibbs pm. It was located in SE¼ Sec. 31-154-92, Brookbank Twp., ten miles NNW of New Town, and received mail three times each week from Ross. Mr. Gibbs submitted Brookbank, Brookside, Brumbrae, and Ashcroft to postla officials. The latter two noted his Scottish ancestry, while the first two noted the location of this post office on the bank of a small brook. The post office closed October 14, 1916 with mail to Sanish. (2, 18, 40, 72)

**BROOKFIELD** (Burleigh). This was a rural post office established October 22, 1906 with Arnold P. Nelson pm. The order was rescinded January 17, 1907 before the post office had gone into operation. It bears a common descriptive name, and is thought to have been located about seven miles NW of Regan. (2, 3, 8, 13, 18, 40)

**BROOKLAND** (Sargent). This GNRR townsite was founded in 1890 in SW¼ Sec. 30-130-56, Forman Twp., four miles north of Brampton. On February 15, 1890 pm Jacob C. Noteman changed the name of the existing post office from MOHLER to BROOKBANK to honor local pioneers Gilbert Brooks and his son Andrew, who came here in 1888. Little development occurred, and the post office closed February 28, 1901 with mail to Cogswell, although the site had a depot, elevator, store, and lumber yard as late as 1918. (2, 3, 18, 25, 40, 165, 167)

**BROOKS** (Dunn). This was a farm post office established March 31, 1908 with Emma M. Brooks pm. It was located in W½ Sec. 14-145-95, just north of present-day Killdeer, and officially named for the pm's husband, Walter P. Brooks. The post office was replaced by the facility at the new NPRR townsite of Killdeer on April 30, 1915. (2, 3, 18, 34, 40, 223, 415)

**BROWN'S LANDING** (Traill). An 1890 guide to ND lists this place as being in Traill County, and served by the Fargo post office. No other information is available, although it is thought that it was an early Red River boat landing. (3, 25)

**BRUCE** (Pembina). This post office was established April 27, 1882 with Robert McConnell, who came here in 1878 from Ontario, Canada, as pm. It was located in his home in NW¼ Sec. 34-163-54, Felson Twp., five miles SW of Neche, and named for Bruce County, Ontario, the home of many area settlers. On October 31, 1883 the name was changed to McCONNELL, only to be changed back to BRUCE on December 23, 1889, but now located two miles north at the home of new pm David McFadden in SW¼ Sec. 22-163-54. The post office closed November 15, 1906 with mail to Neche. Midway between the two post office locations in SE¼ Sec. 28-163-54 was the Bruce Methodist Church, built in 1887 and holding services until 1939. (2, 3, 40, 235)

**BRUMBAUGH** (Towner). This was a Soo Line RR townsite in SW¼ Sec. 20-161-66, Virginia Twp., three miles south of Rocklake. It was named for J. A. Brumbaugh, a pioneer settler in the Egeland area, although some sources say it was named for N. G. Brumbaugh, President of Juniata College in Huntington, PA. The post office was established November 29, 1905 with John Deal pm, and closed December 31, 1910 with mail to Rocklake. The station was abandoned about 1930. (1, 2, 3, 18, 40)

**BRUSHLAKE** (McHenry). This rural post office was established April 24, 1900 with Henry R. W. Bentley (1854-1942) pm, and named for nearby Brush Lake, so called because the shore was lined with brush. The one-word spelling was necessary to comply with government spelling regulations. It was located in SE 1/4 Sec. 7-151-76, Spring Grove Twp., four miles west of Drake, and closed September 15, 1902 when the Drake post office was established. The lake itself was later renamed for Mr. Bentley, a native of MI who came here in 1885. (2, 18, 40, 183)

**BUCHANAN** (Emmons). This was a stopping point on the Bismarck-Williamsport stage route located at the home of Willis W. Goodwin in SW¼ Sec. 29-136-77, eight miles NW of Hazelton. A post office was established November 17, 1884 with Isena A. Goodwin pm, and it closed May 23, 1894 with mail to Williamsport. A population of 50 was reported in 1890. It was named for the Buchanan Valley in which it was located, which was named for Robert Buchanan (1850-1930), a native of Ireland who came here in 1872. The post office reopened August 18, 1894 with Mr. Buchanan as pm, but was renamed BOBTOWN because the Buchanan name had been claimed by the Rio post office in Stutsman County. (2, 3, 25, 40, 66, 240, 401)

**BUCHANAN** (Stutsman). This NPRR station was built in 1881 in NE¼ Sec. 6-141-64, Buchanan Twp., and was first called RIO due to the existance of a Buchanan post office in Emmons County. The name BUCHANAN was officially adopted September 6, 1894 during the term of pm Amanda Farnsworth, who claimed the new name when the Emmons County facility closed. The name honored pioneer settlers John and James A. Buchanan who came here from Rio, WI. James A. Buchanan (1859-1937) was the unsuccessful candidate for Governor of ND in 1912. The elevation is 1571, the Zip Code is 58420, and a population of 200 was claimed in 1920, with a decline to just 76 in 1960. (1, 2, 3, 18, 33, 38, 40, 79, 158)

**BUCYRUS** (Adams). This Milwaukee Road RR townsite was founded in Secs. 22 & 23-130-97, Bucyrus Twp., in 1907 as WOLF BUTTE, and later that year changed its name to DOLAN. Because of confusion with Doland, SD, the name was changed to BUCYRUS on February 11, 1908. Pm William N. Worra wanted to name it May for his daughter, but instead chose a compromise name that was taken from one of the steam shovels used to build the railroad grade at this site. The name originates in Bucyrus, OH, named by a surveyor named Kilbourne who coined the name by adding "bu", for beautiful, to Cyrus, a Persian general. Some sources say the name is derived from Busirus, an ancient city of Egypt. The elevation is 2775, and a peak population of 124 was reached in 1930, with a decline to just 32 in 1980. The post office, Zip Code 58624, closed April 19, 1984. (1, 2, 3, 10, 18, 33, 34, 40, 52, 79, 189)

**BUDAPEST** (Hettinger). This was a proposed townsite on the Dickinson, Lefor, and New Leipzig RR of 1917. It was to be located in Secs. 26 & 35-136-92, Highland Twp., near the Willa post office, or about thirteen miles NNE of Mott, but the town was doomed when the railroad project was abandoned. John J. Schmidt, Frank Barth, and Andrew Dietz were landowners at the site, which was named for the capital of Hungary to honor local settlers from that country. (3, 18, 74)

**BUE** (Nelson). This was a rural post office established February 27, 1882 with Lars O. Bue pm. Mr. Bue (1860-1902) came to this location, NW¼ Sec. 1-149-60, Bergen Twp., three miles SE of Pekin, in 1880. Tobias Holm operated a blacksmith shop here for a time. The post office closed January 31, 1907 with mail to Pekin. (2, 3, 25, 40, 124, 128)

**BUELL** (Eddy). In 1884 three Minneapolis, MN men, O. S. Buell, A. P. W. Skinner, and William R. Guile attempted to established a town in NE¼ Sec. 29-149-66, New Rockford Twp., just north of the NPRR townsite of New Rockford. The town was platted with much pageantry and was billed as "the future county seat of Foster County," but scathing reports in the *Jamestown Weekly Alert* ended whatever legitimacy may have existed. The site is now a cemetery. (2, 3, 119)

**BUELSDALE** (Golden Valley). This was a rural post office established August 2, 1912 with Buel W. Richards pm. Its name was coined from the pm's given name, plus "dale" to note its location in the valley of Beaver Creek in SW¼ Sec. 27-143-104, Pearl Twp., seventeen miles north of Sentinel Butte. The post office closed June 30, 1914 with mail to Beach. (2, 3, 18, 40, 53, 414)

**BUFF** (Cass). This name is shown on a NPRR map of the 1870's in SW¼ Sec. 19-140-54, Buffalo Twp. This site was established as THIRD SIDING, and became NEW BUFFALO about 1875, with a final name change to BUFFALO in 1883. It is likely that BUFF was a cartographer's error. (2, 3, 266)

**BUFFALO** (Cass). This NPRR station was founded in 1872 as THIRD SIDING and became NEW BUFFALO about 1875. Pm Charles A. Wilder shortened the name to BUFFALO on June 5, 1883. The village, located in Secs. 19 & 30-140-54, Buffalo Twp., incorporated April 8, 1883 with A. H. Lowry mayor. The elevation is 1211, the Zip Code is 58011, and a peak population of 410 was reported in 1890, with the recent population averaging about 250. (2, 3, 25, 33, 40, 52, 77, 266)

**BUFFALO LODGE PARK** (McHenry). This townsite was platted in Sec. 24-156-79, Egg Creek Twp., five miles NE of Granville. It was located just south of Buffalo Lodge Butte on the SW shore of Buffalo Lodge Lake, but failed to develop, appearing only in a 1910 county atlas published by the George A. Ogle Co. (3, 18, 34)

**BUFFALO SPRINGS** (Bowman). This Milwaukee Road RR townsite was founded in 1907 as INGOMAR, but when the post office was established July 18, 1907 with Gilbert Gilbertson pm, the name was changed to BUFFALO SPRINGS to note its location near Buffalo Creek and the natural springs in the area. It is located in N½ Sec. 18-131-100, Scranton Twp., between Bowman and Scranton. The elevation is 2850, and it reached a peak population of 100 in 1920, with a decline to just 23 residents in 1960. The post office closed June 30, 1955 with mail to Bowman, but the community has recently shown some growth with the construction of some new houses and buildings. (1, 2, 3, 18, 34, 40, 79, 120, 381)

**BUFORD** (Williams). This GNRR station was built in SW¼ Sec. 10-152-104, Buford Twp., and named for the old military post of Fort Buford one mile to the SW which it replaced. The post office was established February 5, 1897 with Thomas R. Forbes, the former post trader at Fort Buford, as the pm. Many buildings from the fort were moved to the new townsite. A population of 240 was reported in 1910, but a steady decline reduced the count to just 23 in 1960. The post office, Zip Code 58837, closed December 6, 1975 with mail to Trenton. (1, 2, 33, 38, 40, 41, 50, 79)

**BUNKER** (Kidder). This was an alternate name used for the mail distribution service provided by Mr. and Mrs. Byron Dexter at their home in Sec. 4-137-72, Bunker Twp. in the early 1900's. The name came from the township, which originally was called Belden, but had been renamed to honor pioneer settler Robert Bunker (1848-1915). (1, 2, 3, 18, 61)

**BURBANK** (Barnes). This rural settlement began in Sec. 11-137-60, Rosebud Twp., three miles NNW of Litchville, and was named for John A. Burbank, Governor of Dakota Territory 1869-1874. A town in Clay County, SD had been named for him in 1873, so when the post office was established on September 29, 1884 two miles to the south, it was named BARNES for its county. (2, 34, 36)

**BURDETTE** (Slope). This was a rural community dating from about 1900, centered in Sec. 8-134-101, Chalky Butte Twp., five miles SW of Amidon. The name came from Charles Burdette Williams (1861-1917), the son of Frood B. Williams, who along with Thomas Frank Roberts (1859-1954), were pioneer ranchers in this area. Reports of a post office here are not confirmed by government records. (2, 3, 74, 82, 415)

**BURDICK** (Burleigh). This was a NPRR siding and loading station built in NW¼ Sec. 36-138-77, Logan Twp., midway between McKenzie and Moffit. It was named for C. C. Burdick, Traffic Manager of the Twin City Rapid Transit Co. and a NPRR official, although local legend says that it was named for Usher L. Burdick, the politician who was not yet well known. It appeared on maps circa 1910-1940. (1, 2, 8, 18, 79)

**BURGESS** (Morton). This NPRR station was built in 1966 in Sec. 29-135-82, eleven miles ENE of Flasher on the newly-built shortcut line from Mandan to Flasher. No development occurred at the site. The origin of the name is unknown. (3, 34)

**BURKEY** (Golden Valley). This was a rural settlement in SW¼ Sec. 4-137-105, Lone Tree Twp., three miles SE of Golva. The post office was established September 9, 1905 with John Burkey pm, and the site included a Roman Catholic church, school, bank, general store, dance hall, cheese factory, blacksmith shop, and several houses. The NPRR bypassed the site in 1914, and most of BURKEY soon moved to the new townsite of Golva. The post office closed December 30, 1916 with mail to Golva. (2, 3, 18, 34, 40, 80)

**BURLEIGH** (Burleigh). The NPRR built SEVENTEENTH SIDING in 1873 in Sec. 33-139-78, Menoken Twp. The first settlers called it BLAINE, and the post office opened in 1880 with the official name CLARKE'S FARM, with a name change to MENOKEN in 1883. The NPRR did not like this name, and claimed that too many stations on its lines began with the letter "M". On September 23, 1891 the railroad renamed its station BURLEIGH for the county, which was named for Dr. Walter Atwood Burleigh (1820-1896), a physician, attorney, territorial legislator, Indian agent, and territorial delegate to Congress. The post office persisted with the name MENOKEN which was also favored by the local residents, but the depot continued to show the BURLEIGH name until it closed in 1957. (1, 2, 3, 10, 12, 14, 18)

**BURLEIGH** (Burleigh). This is another place that appears only on a 1930 roadmap published by the General Drafting Co. It is shown about seven miles south of Regan, uses the name of its county, and is a copyright town. (3)

**BURLEIGH CITY** (Burleigh). This settlement, often claimed to be the first in Burleigh County, was founded in 1872 in SE¼ Sec. 15-138-80, Lincoln Twp., and named for its county, which was named for Dr. Walter Atwood Burleigh, the prominent politician who also was a physician and attorney. It was located on a NPRR grade, but this route was abandoned after railroad of-ficials witnessed spring floods and replaced by another grade two miles to the north. The latter site became Bismarck, and many have speculated that BURLEIGH CITY was an attempt to confuse squatters. Several modern sources show this place as Burleigh Town or Burleightown, but all original maps of the period show this place as BURLEIGH CITY. The site was soon abandoned, but later became Fort Lincoln. (2, 3, 9, 15, 414)

**BURLINGTON** (Ward). First known as COLTON, the first post office in Ward County was established here February 26, 1884 as BURLINGTON with James Johnson (1850-1932), the son-in-law of townsite founder Joseph L. Colton, as pm. It is located in E½ Sec. 2-155-84, Burlington Twp., and was named for Burlington, IA, hometown of Frank Hatton, the Assistant Postmaster General at the time. The IA city was named for Burlington, VT, which was named for either Richard Boyle (1695-1753), or John Boyle (1707-1763), the 3rd and 4th Earls of Burlington, by their relative, Gov. Benning Wentworth of NH. As the only town in Ward County, BURLINGTON was named county seat in 1885, but lost that honor to Minot in 1888. The elevation is 1590, the Zip Code is 58722, and the village, which did not incorporate until 1957, maintained a population of about 200 for decades, but recent outgrowth from Minot has swelled the count to a peak of 761 in 1980. (1, 2, 3, 10, 33, 40, 79, 95, 100, 371)

**BURNSTAD** (Logan). This was a Soo Line RR townsite founded in 1906 in Sec. 29-134-71, Red Lake Twp., and named for Christ P. Burnstad who donated the land for the townsite. He was known as the "Logan County Cattle Baron of North Dakota," and owned 54 sections of land in the region. The post office was established March 16, 1907 with Nellie Smith pm. A population of 200 was claimed in 1930, but the count has been under 100 since the 1940's. The post office, Zip Code 58526, closed in 1979 although government records did not record this fact until May 8, 1984. (1, 2, 3, 18, 40, 79, 116)

**BURNT CREEK** (Burleigh). This was a farm post office established October 24, 1924 with Annie Kocher pm. It was located in NE 1/4 Sec. 6-140-80, Burnt Creek Twp., four miles SW of Baldwin, and named for its township which was named to note an early incident where Indians ambushed and massacred some returning miners at the mouth of what was first called Burnt Boat Creek, named after searchers found the charred ruins of the miners' boat. Mrs. Linda Warfel Slaughter, the famous Bismarck pioneer, wrote that the name actually noted charred tree stumps along the creek's banks following a prairie fire. The post office closed November 19, 1929 with mail to Bismarck. (2, 3, 8, 9, 18, 40)

**BURT** (Hettinger). This NPRR townsite was founded in NE¼ Sec. 6-133-91, Cannon Ball Twp., and named ALTON, but after some confusion with Alton Junction in Traill County, the name was changed to BURT on September 17, 1910. Both names honored Alton M. Burt, Superintendent of the Dakota Division of the NPRR. George W. Bysom was pm before and after the name change. The elevation is 2383, the Zip Code is 58527, and a peak population of 200 was reported in 1920, with a decline to just 70 in 1960. (1, 2, 3, 18, 33, 40, 79, 179, 181)

**BURTON** (Stutsman). The NPRR built a siding in Sec. 35-140-65, Eldridge Twp., in 1872 and called it TENTH SIDING. Settlement began about 1879, and the townsite was platted May 3, 1880 and named for Burton Towne, son of Charles Towne, a NPRR official and part owner of this site. The post office was established July 21, 1880 with Jerry Collins pm, who changed the name to ELDRIDGE on September 20, 1880. (2, 40, 158)

**BUSHNELL PARK** (Grand Forks). This was a rural post office established November 17, 1881 with Omar Bushnell, a native of Saint Paul, MN, as pm. It was located in W½ Sec. 29-152-56, Niagara Twp., three miles SE of Niagara, and closed June 5, 1882 with mail to Orange. (3, 25, 40)

**BUSHTOWN** (Dickey). This pioneer settlement was founded in 1883 in Sec. 2-129-60, Port Emma Twp., two miles WNW of Ludden, and named for its founder, Thomas W. Bush (1836-1898), who came here from Ontario, Canada in 1882. Located on the west bank of the James River, it quickly attained considerable importance in the area, but the railroad was built on the east side of the river, and BUSHTOWN declined. It was also known as OTTAWA, but the most common name for this place was PORT EMMA. The post office operated here 1883-1887 as EMMA. (2, 3, 154,164)

**BUTLER** (Walsh). This was a farm post office established July 13, 1883 with Thomas Hare pm. It was located in NE¼ Sec. 11-158-52, Martin Twp., three miles north of Cashel and nine miles NE of Grafton. The origin of the name is unknown. The post office closed February 18, 1884 with mail to Grafton. Butter is an erroneous spelling. (2, 3, 34, 40, 415)

**BUTTE** (McLean). This Soo Line RR townsite in SW¼ Sec. 4-150-78, Dogden Twp., was founded in 1906 as DOGDEN, but on January 2, 1927 the name was changed to BUTTE, both names noting the nearby landmark, Dodgen Butte, a 2291-foot sentinel of the prairie first reported by the explorer David Thompson in 1797. The pm at the time was Mrs. Cassie Stewart, whose husband William had earlier held the position. The Zip Code is 58723, and since the name change the peak population has been 272 reported in 1950. (2, 3, 28, 33, 40, 79, 357)

**BUTTE** (Oliver). This was a ranch post office established April 27, 1898 with John Day pm. It was located in Sec. 6-141-81, Butte Twp., two miles SW of Price, and named for Square Butte, a landmark in Sec. 10-141-81,

three miles to the SE. Charles V. Day became pm in 1899, serving in that capacity until the post office closed August 15, 1913 with mail to Harmon. (2, 3, 18, 40, 53, 121)

**BUTTERCUP** (Divide). This place appears on current maps published by Hearne Brothers, approximately in Sec. 31-161-96, Upland Twp., eight miles north of Wildrose. An official of the map company hedges that it is a copyright town. (3)

**BUTTZVILLE** (Ransom). This NPRR station was founded in 1881 in Sec. 17-135-55, Casey Twp., five miles NE of Lisbon, and platted in 1882 by the townsite owners, the Carrington-Casey Land Co. It was named for Maj. Charles Wilson Buttz, a Civil War veteran from PA, who with his brothers David H. and John R. came here in 1880 and were involved in farming and various business ventures. The post office was established January 25, 1883 with David H. Buttz pm. The elevation is 1194, and a peak population of 100 was claimed in 1920, with a decline to just 15 in 1960. The post office closed April 30, 1955 with mail to Lisbon. Butzville and Buttsville are erroneous spellings. (1, 2, 3, 18, 25, 38, 40, 77, 79, 94, 201, 206)

**BUXTON** (Traill). This GNRR townsite was founded in 1880 in SE¼ Sec. 25-148-51, Buxton Twp. Budd Reeve (1842-1933) obtained the townsite from the railroad in exchange for the land used for the old Union Depot in Minneapolis, MN. He was a prolific writer known as "The Sage of Buxton," and named the town for his friend, Minneapolis Treasurer Thomas J. Buxton. The post office was established November 8, 1880 with Arne A. Moen pm. The elevation is 930, the Zip Code is 58218, and a peak population of 410 was reached in 1930. Dr. James Grassick, namesake of the childrens' camp near Dawson, practiced medicine here 1885-1905. Chester Fritz (1892-1983), the famous businessman, financier, and UND benefactor, was born here. (1, 2, 3, 29, 33, 40, 52, 77, 187)

**BYE** (Ward). A country store was opened in SE¼ Sec. 31-152-86, Anna Twp., by Ole J. Bye, who then established a post office August 12, 1903 which served only seven people with mail brought twice weekly from Minot. The post office closed October 15, 1906 when Mr. Bye became the new pm at Ryder, recently relocated to the new Soo Line RR townsite two miles to the SE. (2, 18,40, 100, 277, 373)

**BYERS** (McLean). This was a farm post office established April 21, 1904 with Henry A. Kenny pm in SW¼ Sec. 4-149-78, Byersville Twp., five miles south of Butte. It was named for its township, which was named for Jacob Byers, a pioneer settler in the area whose home had been used as a mail distribution point. The post office later moved to the home of new pm Peter Preisinger in NE¼ Sec. 1-149-78, and moved again to SW¼ Sec. 12-149-78, the home of pm Walter Bjorhus. It closed December 15, 1913 with mail to Dogden. (2, 28, 40, 357)

**BYRON** (Cavalier). This was a rural post office established June 15, 1888 with Donald

Shaw pm. It was located in NW¼ Sec. 5-163-63, Byron Twp., seven miles west of Hannah, and named for Byron St. Clair Kelly, a pioneer stage operator here in the 1870's whose name was the basis of several places throughout the region. Byron is a Teutonic name meaning from the cottage. The post office closed August 31, 1904 with mail to Woodbridge. (2, 3, 18, 19, 25, 40, 240)

# C

**CABLE** (Grand Forks). This was a farm post office established July 20, 1888 with Jesse H. Cable pm. It was located in Sec. 14-149-56, Loretta Twp., which was named for Mrs. George Hart, the township's first white woman. The post office was discontinued July 7, 1893 with mail to Northwood. On June 23, 1900 it was reestablished two miles NW in SW¼ Sec. 3-149-56, changing its name to LAKEWOOD on October 17, 1903. (2, 3, 25, 31, 40, 240, 241)

**CAITHNESS** (Ward). This was a farm post office established September 16, 1902 with Henry P. Rygmyr pm. It was located in NE¼ Sec. 26-154-84, Burt Twp., twelve miles SW of Minot. Caithness is a northern county in Scotland, but the name of the post office is said to honor Beth Caithness Stephenson, a stenographer in Minot. The post office closed June 15, 1903 with mail to Minot. (2, 3, 40, 100, 414)

**CALCITE** (Slope). This was apparently a rival townsite of Chenoweth, as it was located in NE¼ Sec. 10-133-101, Sheets, Twp., just one mile north of the more established townsite, and fourteen miles SW of Amidon. Chenoweth itself did not develop anywhere near original expectations, and the only venture to locate in CALCITE was the general store of Ben Etzwiler. The name noted the mineral content of the nearby Chalky Buttes. (2, 3, 82, 400)

**CALEDONIA** (Traill). This settlement was founded in 1875 in SE¼ Sec. 15-146-49, Caledonia Twp., absorbing the adjacent pioneer community of GOOSE RIVER. The post office opened as CALEDONIA on August 19, 1875 with Asa Sargeant (1844-1935) pm. He came here in 1870 from Vermont, and was a county official and state legislator. Caledonia is the ancient name for Scotland, and was Mr. Sargeant's home county in Vermont. Joseph P., Chester M., and Oliver P. Clark, cousins of Mr. Sargeant, were pioneer merchants here. CALEDONIA became the county seat by default in 1875 when it absorbed GOOSE RIVER, but lost that honor to Hillsboro in 1890, having survived several previous challenges. The population had been as high as 1,000 in 1890, but has been in the 150 range for most of this century. The Zip Code is 58219. (1, 2, 3, 10, 13, 18, 29, 33, 40, 45, 79, 187, 393)

**CALIO** (Cavalier). This Soo Line RR townsite was founded in 1905, replacing the old rural post office of Etna. It was located in NE¼ Sec. 5-159-64, Seivert Twp., and SE¼ Sec. 32-160-64, Trier Twp., and given a name said to be used on Soo Line RR sleeping cars, meaning repeated calls. The Etna post office moved here September 8, 1905 with William T. Townsend assuming the pm duties. The Zip Code is 58322, and a peak population of 152 was reached in 1930. (1, 2, 3, 18, 33, 40, 79)

**CALMAR** (Rolette). This was a rural post office established July 22, 1902 with Aaron

*Calvin about 1920*

G. Falardeau pm. It was located in N½ Sec. 22-159-72, Finnegan Twp., seven miles SW of Rolette, and was also the site of a country store. The name was drawn from several suggestions by local residents, with the winning name being the entry of Mrs. A. W. "Tony" Huber, who lived two miles south of the post office, and chose the name of her hometown, Calmar, IA. The post office closed April 15, 1907 with mail to Rolette. Calmer is an erroneous spelling. (2, 3, 18, 40, 123)

**CALVIN** (Cavalier). This GNRR townsite was founded in 1902 in SE¼ Sec. 16-162-64, Glenila Twp., between Sarles and Clyde. The name honors Presbyterian Church founder John Calvin (1509-1564), born Jean Chauvin, and was selected by Rev. David J. Sykes, who became the pm when the post office opened May 23, 1902. Calvin is Latin for bald. The elevation is 1623, the Zip Code is 58323, and a peak population of 350 was reported in 1920, although a steady decline has reduced the count to just 61 in 1980. (1, 2, 3, 4, 18, 19, 33, 40, 79)

**CALVIN** (Rolette). This was a rural post office established October 23, 1899 with Ira. C. Eisenhour pm. The order was rescinded October 5, 1900. It would have been located in NW¼ Sec. 22-160-69, Ellsworth Twp., four miles NE of Mylo. The origin of the name is unknown, although it probably honored the religious leader John Calvin. (3, 40)

**CAMBRIDGE** (Mercer). This was a farm post office established December 18, 1906 with Hans J. Johnson pm. It was located in SE¼ Sec. 10-144-86, four miles east of Hazen. This was the headquarters of the Cambridge Farm, operated by Mr. Johnson, who had come from Cambridge, MN, which was named for Cambridge, ME, which was named for Cambridge, England, so named because it

lies on both sides of the River Cam. The post office was discontinued October 14, 1916 with mail to Hazen. (1, 2, 3, 10, 13, 18, 40, 53, 64, 386)

**CAMPAGNA** (Burleigh). This was a rural post office established May 17, 1905 with Frank Campagna pm. It was located in NW¼ Sec. 7-137-79, Missouri Twp., seven miles SE of Bismarck, and closed September 15, 1906 with mail to Bismarck. Campagne is an erroneous spelling. (2, 3, 8, 11, 12, 40)

**CAMP AMBLER** (Cass). This was a Sibley Expedition camp used August 17-19, 1863 on the return to Fort Abercrombie. It was located in NW¼ Sec. 36-138-53, Walburg Twp., six miles NW of Leonard, and named for Capt. Rufus C. Ambler of the expedition. This site was near the crossing of the Maple River that had been used by gold seekers, fur traders, soldiers, and settlers since the 1820's. A plot of land for a historic site was donated by owner Alvin Zaeske. (3, 411, 417)

**CAMP ARNOLD** (Barnes). This was a stopping point of the Sibley Expedition, used August 15, 1863. It was located in Sec. 34-141-56, Weimer Twp., four miles north of Oriska, and named for Capt. John K. Arnold of the expedition. On June 25, 1933 a historical site was dedicated, although it was in NE¼ Sec. 32-141-56, two miles west of the actual campsite. (2, 34, 281, 411)

**CAMP ATCHISON** (Griggs). This was the campsite used July 18, 1863 by the Sibley Expedition. It was located on the NE shore of Lake Sibley in Sec. 29-147-60, Addie Twp., four miles south of Binford, and traces remain today. It was named for Capt. Charles B. Atchison, an aide of Maj. Gen. John Pope, who was on temporary assignment to Gen. Sibley. Atchison joined the army in 1861 in his native IL, and served until his death on

May 10, 1876. Camp Atcheson is an erroneous spelling. (1, 2, 65, 79)

**CAMP BANKS** (Burleigh). This was a Sibley Expedition campsite used August 2, 1863, and named for Capt. Rolla Banks. The return journey continued to follow the original route, and this campsite was just beyond the earlier Camp Schoenemann, probably about three miles north of Driscoll in Driscoll Twp. (139-75). The trusted Indian scout, Chaska, died suddenly and unexpectedly during the night, and was buried near the camp. He is memorialized by the so-called Camp Chaska Historical Site in SW¼ Sec. 34-140-75, Clear Lake Twp., just to the north of the probable site of CAMP BANKS. (3, 411)

**CAMP BARBOUR** (McKenzie). This was a military camp of the Second Yellowstone Expedition, established August 17, 1825 using the abandoned remains of Fort Henry in Sec. 27-152-104, Yellowstone Twp., on the Yellowstone River just above its confluence with the Missouri. Gen. Henry Atkinson and Major Benjamin O'Fallon, an Indian agent, named it for their Secretary of War, James Barbour (1775-1842), who earlier had served as Governor of VA and as a U. S. Senator. After a few days, the expedition continued up the Yellowstone, but met with little, if any, success in locating renegade Indians. (3, 5, 15, 438)

**CAMPBELL** (Emmons). This name was used for a planned settlement east of Braddock as early as 1898. Dugald Campbell (1855-1937) and his brother, Hugh Campbell (1850-1928) had come here in 1882 from Campbelltown, Scotland, and operated the 6,000 acre Northwestern Livestock Co. Ranch, with headquarters in SW¼ Sec. 28-136-74, Campbell Twp. When a townsite was begun two miles ESE of here in 1905, this name and Campbelltown were apparently rejected by postal officials, and the new town became Kintyre. (2, 3, 18, 66, 113)

**CAMP BRADEN** (Burleigh). This was the first campsite of the Sibley Expedition's return march, used August 1, 1863 and named for Capt. William W. Braden. It was probably just NE of present-day Menoken in Menoken Twp. (139-78), as soldiers' logs note it was just beyond Camp Stees, used three days earlier. (3, 411)

**CAMP BUELL** (Sargent). This was a campsite of the Sibley Expedition used July 3, 1863, and located on the south shore of Stump Lake in Sec. 9-132-54, Milnor Twp., at the present site of Milnor. It was named for Major Salmon E. Buell of the First Regiment Minnesota Mounted Rangers, who would be a hero at the Battle of Big Mound on July 24, 1863. Camp Buel is an erroneous spelling. (2, 3, 165, 171, 411)

**CAMP BURKE** (Ramsey). This name was applied to the newly-acquired National Guard training center south of Devils Lake in 1891 to honor Andrew H. Burke, the second Governor of ND. The name was used until 1902, when it was renamed CAMP LAWTON. When John Burke became Governor in 1907, the camp again was named CAMP BURKE, using the name until

1913, when Louis B. Hanna became Governor. In 1924 the name was changed to CAMP GRAFTON, by which name it is known today. (2, 3)

**CAMP BURT** (Griggs). This was a Sibley Expedition campsite used August 12-13, 1863 during the return to Fort Abercrombie. It was located in NE¼ Sec. 35-145-59, Ball Hill Twp., two miles NE of Hannaford, and named for Capt. William H. Burt of the expedition. (3, 411, 417)

**CAMP CARTER** (Foster). This was a campsite used by the Sibley Expedition on August 8, 1863, and named for Capt. Theo. G. Carter. It was located in Sec. 2-145-64, Bucephalia Twp., eleven miles south of Grace City. (3, 97)

**CAMP CHASE** (Richland). This was a campsite used August 19, 1863 by the Sibley Expedition on the return from the Missouri River, with the name honoring Capt. Jonah Chase of the expedition. Pioneer homesteaders erased all traces of the site and trail at this point in the journey, but soldiers' journals indicate that it must have been in the NE part of Barrie Twp. (136-51), just SW of Kindred on the banks of the Sheyenne River. (3, 411, 417)

**CAMP CHASKA** (Burleigh). Chaska was the Indian scout for the Sibley Expedition who died August 3, 1863 at Camp Banks, probably just north of Driscoll. Chaska is the Sioux word meaning first-born son, as opposed to Winona, which is Sioux for first-born daughter. The Sioux pronounced the word "Chas-kay", although this form is rarely heard today. Louis A. Slaatenhus (1854-1945) donated a parcel of land in SW¼ Sec. 34-140-75, Clear Lake Twp., three miles north of Driscoll, and on July 25, 1937 a bronze and granite monument was dedicated to the honor of Chaska. The site is usually referred to as CAMP CHASKA, although this name was not used by the Sibley Expedition itself. (2, 3, 10, 12, 13, 200, 411)

**CAMP COMFORT** (Pembina). This was an early stopping point at a crossing of the Tongue River on the Old Hunters Trail in Sec. 9-161-55, Akra Twp., two miles west of Akra. The name, which honored pioneer settlers Nicklaus and Patrick Comfort, had a double meaning for travelers, most of whom were fur traders. The site is now Icelandic State Park, a popular wooded picnic grounds. (2, 3, 34)

**CAMP CORNING** (Barnes). This was the camp used July 16-17, 1863 by the Sibley Expedition. It was located in SE¼ Sec. 7-143-58, Sibley Twp., about seven miles NE of Dazey. A granite monument marks the site, which was named for Capt. Edward Corning, Quartermaster to Sibley's staff. (2, 34)

**CAMP EDGERTON** (Richland). This was the August 20, 1863 campsite of the Sibley Expedition, named for Capt. Alonzo J. Edgerton. It was one day's march from Fort Abercrombie, probably in Walcott Twp. (136-50) just NW of present-day Walcott, but physical evidence of the site was destroyed by pioneer homesteaders long before historians could trace this portion of the journey. (3, 411, 417)

**CAMP FORBES** (Foster). This was the camp used July 20, 1863 by the Sibley Expedition, and named for Capt. William H. H. Forbes. The site, SW¼ Sec. 33-146-63, Rolling Prairie Twp., is about six miles south of Juanita. (1, 97)

**CAMP GILBERT C. GRAFTON** (Ramsey). Although the National Guard training center south of Devils Lake had been unofficially known as CAMP GRAFTON since 1924, it was not until May 16, 1952 that Governor C. Norman Brunsdale issued a proclamation naming it CAMP GILBERT C. GRAFTON, honoring the guard's Lt. Colonel, who was a veteran of the Spanish-American War and World War I. Col. Grafton died in France February 5, 1919. Four days after Gov. Brunsdale's proclamation, Adjutant General Heber L. Edwards ruled that for the sake of brevity, all official correspondence should use the name CAMP GRAFTON, the name generally used today. (2, 3, 34, 103)

**CAMP GILFILLAN** (Stutsman). This was a campsite used by the Sibley Expedition on August 5, 1863. It was located in SW¼ Sec. 13-143-68, Wadsworth Twp., six miles NE of Woodworth, and named for Capt. James Gilfillan of the expedition. (3, 411, 417)

**CAMP GRAFTON** (Ramsey). This is the National Guard training center in Secs. 19, 20, 21, 28, 29 & 33-153-64, Creel Twp., five miles SW of Devils Lake. After coming into the guard's hands in 1891, it went through a number of names until CAMP GRAFTON came into general, although unofficial, usage in 1924. On May 16, 1952, Governor C. Norman Brunsdale issued an Executive Order naming the facility CAMP GILBERT C. GRAFTON. Four days later, Adjutant General Heber L. Edwards ruled that for brevity all official business would use the name CAMP GRAFTON. Modern detailed county maps show the facility as Gilbert C. Grafton State Military Reservation. (2, 3, 34)

**CAMP GRANT** (Stutsman). This was a campsite of the Sibley Expedition used July 23, 1863. It was located in SW¼ Sec. 24-143-69, Gerber Twp., five miles NW of Woodworth, and named for Capt. Hiram P. Grant of the expedition. It is now marked as a historic site. (3, 34, 158, 411)

**CAMP GRASSICK** (Kidder). A group of Dawson men first platted this site on the south shore of Lake Isabel, SW¼ Sec. 34-139-72, Sibley Twp., two miles south of Dawson, in 1921. The ND Tuberculosis Association acquired the site in 1928 for a sanitarium, and named it for Dr. James Grassick (1850-1944), a pioneer physician in Buxton and Grand Forks, who had come to this country from Scotland as a young man. In 1947 it was purchased by the State Elks Association, and since that date has been used as a camp for handicapped and underprivileged children. (2, 3, 18, 28, 61, 79, 122, 187)

**CAMP GREELEY** (Burleigh). On August 8, 1872 Company D, 17th Infantry, came here on the Missouri River steamboat *Ida Stockdale*, and established a camp in Sec. 4-138-80, Lincoln Twp., which today is on

West Main Street in Bismarck. The name undoubtedly honored Horace Greeley (1811-1872), at the time the Democratic and Liberal Republican candidate for President, who lost in November to Ulysses S. Grant. In 1873 the name was changed to CAMP HANCOCK. (2, 3, 5, 9, 11, 343)

**CAMP GREENE** (Morton). This was a military supply camp established in April 1872 in anticipation of approaching NPRR construction crews. It was located at the mouth of the Little Heart River, which would put it in Sec. 14-137-80, about midway between Fort Rice and present-day Mandan. Garrisoned by soldiers from Fort Rice under the command of Lt. O. D. Greene, it was at first thought that this would become a permanent post, but within a few months Fort McKeen was established to the north, and CAMP GREENE was abandoned. (2, 3, 107, 343, 420)

**CAMP HACKETT** (Richland). This was the August 21, 1863 campsite of the Sibley Expedition, and was located in or adjacent to Fort Abercrombie in Sec. 4-134-38, Abercrombie Twp. It was named in honor of Capt. Charles W. Hackett, and marked the last campsite in what is now ND. The expedition left here two days later and arrived at Fort Snelling, MN on September 12, 1863, marking the end of the expedition. (3, 411, 417)

**CAMP HALL** (Foster). This was the campsite used August 7, 1863 during the return of the Sibley Expedition. It was named for Capt. Thomas G. Hall, and located in Sec. 24-145-66, Melville Twp., about midway between Melville and Bordulac. (1, 3, 97)

**CAMP HANCOCK** (Burleigh). This military post in Sec. 4-138-80, Lincoln Twp., on what is today West Main Street in Bismarck, was founded in 1872 as CAMP GREELEY, and was the supply depot for Fort Abraham Lincoln across the Missouri River. In 1873 the name was changed to honor Gen. Winfield Scott Hancock (1824-1886), a Civil War veteran who led the first extensive exploration of Yellowstone National Park. Mr. Greeley had lost the race for President the previous year, and Gen. Hancock would lose the same race in 1880, both running as Democrats. A MN township, a St. Paul, MN street, and a McLean County pioneer settlement were also named for the General. CAMP HANCOCK today is a well-preserved historical site in downtown Bismarck. (2, 3, 9, 11, 13, 343)

**CAMP HANNA** (Ramsey). This name was used by the National Guard training center south of Devils Lake during the 1913-1916 administration of Governor Louis B. Hanna. The camp then was nameless for six years while members of the guard were on active duty. In 1922 it assumed the name ROCK ISLAND MILITARY RESERVATION, becoming CAMP GRAFTON in 1924, its current name. (2, 3)

**CAMP HAYES** (Ransom). This was the campsite used July 3-5, 1863 by the Sibley Expedition, and named for Major Oren T. Hayes of the First Regiment Minnesota Mounted Rangers. The troops remained at this site for three days while waiting for supplies to arrive from Fort Abercrombie. It was

located in S½ Sec. 36-134-55, Big Bend Twp., eight miles SE of Lisbon. (2, 201, 204, 411)

**CAMP HOUSTIN** (Stark). This was a military camp founded in 1876 to protect NPRR work crews. It was located in SE¼ Sec. 5-139-99, just SE of present-day Belfield, and named by Col. Merrill, the commander of the camp, for his son. The site was intended to be a station on the 1878 Bismarck-Fort Keogh mail route, but operators of the route felt that the continuation through the Badlands was too rugged, and the route angled to the south of this site. NPRR officials proceeded with the more northern route, however, and Belfield was founded here in 1883. (2, 3, 74, 417)

**CAMP JOHNSON** (Barnes). The explorers, Jean Nicollet and John C. Fremont, camped here in 1839, and it was the site of a major Sioux council in 1853, but the name dates from August 11, 1863, when the place was used as a campsite by the Sibley Expedition. It was located in Sec. 18-137-58, Oakhill Twp., two miles east of Hastings, and was named for Lt. Daniel B. Johnson of the expedition at the suggestion of Col. Samuel McPhail. The site was later a stopping place on the Fort Totten-Fort Ransom trail, and today is the Clausen Springs State Game Management Area, named for the pioneer family that came here from Norway. This much-used site is officially marked as the Birch Creek Historic Site. (2, 3, 34, 76, 411)

**CAMP KENNEDY** (Kidder). This was a campsite of the Sibley Expedition used August 3-4, 1863, and named for Capt. John Kennedy. Although no physical traces of the camp survived the efforts of the pioneer homesteaders, it can be guessed with some accuracy that the site was in Vernon Twp. (140-72), about ten miles NE of Steele. (3, 411)

**CAMP KIMBALL** (Foster). This was the camp used July 22, 1863 by the Sibley Expedition. Some say it was named for Surgeon General James P. Kimball of Fort Buford, while others say it was named for Capt. William H. Kimball, Asst. Quartermaster for Gen. Sibley. The site, NE¼ Sec. 16-145-67, Longview Twp., is about five miles SW of Carrington, and is today a state historic site. (1, 2, 97)

**CAMP LAWTON** (Ramsey). This name was used by the National Guard training center south of Devils Lake 1902-1905, honoring Gen. Henry W. Lawton (1843-1899), a hero of the Spanish-American War in the Philippines, under whom many ND guardsmen served. (2, 3, 5)

**CAMP LIBBY** (Barnes). This was a Sibley Expedition campsite used August 13-14, 1863 during the return to Fort Abercrombie. It was located in SW¼ Sec. 13-142-58, Ashtabula Twp., fourteen miles NNE of Valley City, and named for Capt. Asa Libby Jr. of the expedition. (3, 411, 417)

**CAMP LIBBY** (Richland). This was the first campsite used by the detachment of soldiers that left Fort Abercrombie on July 6, 1863 to join the main column of the Sibley Expedition at Camp Hayes, about fifty-six miles to the west. This campsite, named for

Capt. Asa Libby Jr., was about five miles west of the fort, just across the Wild Rice River, probably in Abercrombie Twp. (134-49), although all traces of the trail have disappeared under the homesteaders' plows. Capt. Libby was also honored at the August 13-14, 1863 campsite in Barnes County. (3, 411, 417)

**CAMP MILLER** (Ramsey). This name was used by the National Guard training center south of Devils Lake 1905-1907 honoring Adjutant General Elliott S. Miller. After frequent name changes, the present name of CAMP GRAFTON came into use in 1924. (2, 3)

**CAMP OLIN** (Foster). This was the campsite used July 21, 1863 by the Sibley Expedition, and named for Capt. Rolin C. Olin, who had been a 2nd Lt. in the 3rd Minnesota Infantry. He was captured by the Confederates on July 19, 1862, and formally exchanged and released. He was promoted to Captain May 11, 1863 and assigned to Gen. Sibley's staff. The site, in Sec. 33-145-64, Buchephalia Twp., is about midway between Kensal and Bordulac. (1, 97)

**CAMP PARKER** (Sargent). This was a campsite of the Sibley Expedition used July 2-3, 1863. It was located at the east end of Lake Tewaukon in SW¼ Sec. 32-129-53, Marboe Twp., and named for Major John H. Parker of the First Minnesota Mounted Rangers. (2, 3, 165, 171)

**CAMP PFAENDER** (Kidder). This was a campsite of the Sibley Expedition used July 26-27, 1863, and it became the site of one of the few actual battles during the entire operation. The remains of the trail in this area were plowed under by pioneer settlers, leading to considerable confusion as to its location. A map of the battle, done shortly after it had occurred, shows CAMP PFAENDER on the shore, apparently the south, of Dead Buffalo Lake, thought to be the lake of that name in Sec. 33-140-72, Vernon Twp., two miles NW of Dawson. The origin of the name Pfaender is unknown. All other Sibley campsites bear names of various senior officers taking part in the expedition, but no one named Pfaender appears on the roster of men. (3, 61, 62)

**CAMP POPE** (Griggs). This was a campsite used July 17, 1863 by the Sibley Expedition. It was located in NW¼ Sec. 4-145-59, Ball Hill Twp., five miles east of Sutton, and named for Capt. Douglas Pope of Gen. Sibley's staff. 676 men were encamped here. Capt. Pope later married Augusta Sibley, the General's eldest daughter. (1, 2, 13, 65, 411)

**CAMP RUSTEN** (Griggs). This was a campsite used in 1863 by Col McPhail, who led a party of soldiers who were flanking Gen. Sibley's column on the way to Bear Den Hill. It was located in Sec. 23-145-60, Helena Twp., three miles SE of Sutton. The origin of the name is unknown. (1, 65)

**CAMP SCHOENEMANN** (Burleigh). This was the Sibley Expedition campsite used July 27, 1863. Remains of the trail were plowed under by pioneer settlers, making a positive siting impossible, but it was probably located near SE¼ Sec. 18-139-75, Driscoll Twp., two miles west of Driscoll, the site of Driscoll Sibley Park. The Battle of Stony Lake was fought the following day about one mile NE of the campsite, which was named for Capt. Rudolph Schoenemann. (3, 411)

**CAMP SHEARDOWN** (Barnes). This was the campsite used July 14, 1863 by the Sibley Expedition, and named for Dr. Samuel B. Sheardown of the Tenth Minnesota Infantry. Located in NW¼ Sec. 2-139-58, Marsh Twp., about three miles south of Valley City, the site is today marked by a bronze tablet. (1, 2, 34)

**CAMP SHIELDS** (Emmons). This was a wintering camp on the east bank of the Missouri River, used by pioneers as a refuge before homesteading in the spring. It was about eighteen miles west of Williamsport, the county seat, and was named for N. Shields, thought by some to be the same man that became associated with the community of that name in Grant County. (3, 66)

**CAMP SIBLEY** (Kidder). This was a Sibley Expedition campsite, used July 24-25, 1863, and named apparently for General Henry Hastings Sibley himself. The trail from Camp Grant to the site did not survive the farming efforts of the first homesteaders, and the exact site is therefore subject to debate. It was on the bank of a large lake, possibly Kunkel Lake in Buckeye Twp. (141-71), and the site became the scene of the Battle of Big Mound. Dr. Weiser, for whom the adjacent township is named, was killed here. These events are commemorated at the Burman Historic Site in NW¼ Sec. 24-141-71, on a parcel of land donated by John Burman, who homesteaded here in 1906. (3, 62, 411).

**CAMP SILL** (Grand Forks). An 1890 guide to ND lists this place as being located in Grand Forks County, and served by the Walshville post office. No other information is available. (3, 25)

**CAMP SLAUGHTER** (Burleigh). This campsite marked the end of the Sibley Expedition's march to the Missouri River before returning to Fort Snelling, MN. Named for Capt. Thomas I. Slaughter, the camp was just above the mouth of Apple Creek, in Sec. 28-138-80, Lincoln Twp., four miles south of Bismarck, at what was then called Burned Boat Island from an incident during the 1834 visit of Prince Maximilian of Wied. It is now renamed Sibley Island, and is a popular picnic grounds. Sibley's troops, numbering 3,674, arrived here July 29, 1863, and spent the next three days driving the Indians, with considerable brutality, to the west side of the Missouri River. The return march began August 1, 1863. (3, 34, 411, 420)

**CAMP SMITH** (Barnes). This was the campsite used July 15, 1863 by the Sibley Expedition, named for Dr. Lucius B. Smith, Surgeon of the 7th Regiment. It was located in W½ Sec. 30-141-57, Noltimier Twp., six miles NE of Valley City. (1, 2, 34, 411)

**CAMP STEES** (Burleigh). This was a Sibley Expedition campsite used July 28-29, 1863, and named for Capt. Charles J. Stees. Although the site can no longer be positively identified, it was about eighteen miles from Camp Schoenemann on the banks of Apple Creek, most likely about two miles NW of Menoken in Menoken Twp. (139-78). (3, 411)

**CAMP STEVENS** (Cass). This was a Sibley Expedition campsite used August 15-17, 1863 on the return to Fort Abercrombie. It was located in SE¼ Sec. 2-139-55, Hill Twp., six miles SE of Tower City on the east bank of the Maple River, and named for Capt. Albert H. Stevens of the expedition. (3, 411, 417)

**CAMP SYKES** (Stutsman). On November 26, 1871 sixteen soldiers under the command of Lt. Joseph S. Stafford arrived at the projected NPRR crossing of the James River, and established CAMP SYKES in SE¼ Sec. 26-140-64, Midway Twp., naming it for Col. George Sykes of the 20th Infantry. On June 3, 1872 the name was changed to CAMP THOMAS. In September of that year the post was upgraded to a fort, taking the name FORT CROSS. It was renamed FORT SEWARD in November 1872 and remained active until 1877. (2, 34, 158)

**CAMP TATTERSALL** (Richland). This was the second campsite used by the detachment of soldiers that left Fort Abercrombie to join the main column of the Sibley Expedition at Camp Hayes. Used the evening of July 7, 1863, it was named in honor of Capt. William K. Tattersall. Remains of the campsite and trail have vanished, but it was probably located in Freeman Twp. (134-52), about ten miles NW of Wyndmere. (3, 411, 417)

**CAMP THOMAS** (Stutsman). Founded in 1871 as CAMP SYKES, this military post in SE¼ Sec. 26-140-64, Midway Twp., was renamed CAMP THOMAS on June 3, 1872 to honor its commanding officer, Capt. Henry Goddard Thomas, a descendant of Isaiah Thomas, publisher of the first Bible in New England. The post, established to protect NPRR construction crews, became an official military post on September 7, 1872, taking the name FORT CROSS. Two months later, it was renamed FORT SEWARD. (2, 158)

**CAMP WEISER** (Barnes). This was the campsite used July 13-14, 1863 by the Sibley Expedition, named for Dr. Joseph H. Weiser, Surgeon with the First Minnesota Mounted Rangers. He was later killed at the Battle of Big Mound north of Tappen. The site, N½ Sec. 33-137-57, Thordenskjold Twp., is about four miles SW of Nome, and is today part of the Gernard Storhoff farm. (2, 34, 61, 79, 118)

**CAMP WHARTON** (Ransom). This was the campsite used July 11-12, 1863 by the Sibley Expedition, and named for Dr. Alfred Wharton of the Sixth Minnesota Volunteer Infantry. The site, Sec. 19-135-56, Tuller Twp., is about five miles NW of Lisbon. (1, 2, 204)

**CAMP WHITNEY** (Kidder). This was a campsite used July 25-26, 1863 by the Sibley Expedition following the Battle of Big Mound, and named for Capt. Joseph C. Whitney.

Destruction of the trail by homesteaders makes positive siting impossible, but it was thought to be about eight miles north of Tappen in Westford Twp. (140-71). In 1951 John DeKrey Jr. donated a three acre plot in NW¼ Sec. 5-140-71, known today as the McPhail Butte Historic Site. (3, 62, 411)

**CAMP WILLISTON** (Kidder). This was a campsite used August 4-5, 1863 during the return of the Sibley Expedition. It was named for Capt. William C. Williston, and was on the same lake, but not the same site, as Camp Sibley, used eleven days earlier. Obliteration of the trail has made positive siting impossible, but it probably was on Kunkel Lake in Buckeye Twp. (141-71). Soldiers' logs note the fine fresh water springs here, and state that it was "the nicest camp we have had." (3, 411)

**CAMP WILSON** (Ransom). This was the third and last campsite used by the detachment of soldiers that left Fort Abercrombie to join the main column of the Sibley Expedition at Camp Hayes. Used July 8, 1863, the campsite was named in honor of Capt. Eugene M. Wilson, and was only a few miles east of Camp Hayes, probably in Scoville Twp. (134-54), on the west bank of the Sheyenne River about ten miles ESE of Lisbon. The following day the detachment reached Camp Hayes, and the combined forces resumed their march to the Missouri River. (3, 411, 417)

**CANAAN** (Cass). This was a rural community founded in 1881 in NE¼ Sec. 18-138-51, Addison Twp., ten miles SSE of Casselton, and was the site of a Moravian church. Karl A. Piper (1842-1899) donated the land for the church, with the present brick building dating from 1914. The name is of Biblical origin, meaning land of promise in Greek, and lowland in Hebrew. (3, 4, 10, 77)

**CANDO** (Towner). The site was selected February 14, 1884 to be the county seat. J. W. Connelly objected to this action, but was told by Commissioner Prosper T. Parker that they did, in fact, have the power to do this, and proposed the name CANDO to prove it. Located in SW¼ Sec. 20-158-66, Cando Twp., the post office was established March 31, 1884 with Guy W. Germond pm. The town was platted in 1886, and it became a city in 1901 with C. J. Lord as mayor. The elevation is 1490, the Zip Code is 58324, and the population has leveled off at about 1,500. People from here founded a town in Saskatchewan, Canada in 1907 and used this name for their new home. Two famous sons of CANDO are William F. Lemke, U. S. Representative 1933-1950, and professional football player Dave Osborn. (1, 2, 18, 33, 40, 52, 79, 83, 102)

**CANFIELD** (Burleigh). This small settlement began in 1905 in NE¼ Sec. 20-143-77, Canfield Twp., on the north shore of Canfield Lake. This was the original site of the ANDREWS post office, just recently moved one mile to the SW. The township, settlement, and lake were all named for Charles E. Canfield, a pioneer rancher who sold his interests to Louis D. McMunn in 1896, who in turn sold the ranch to Lewis H. Ong in 1902. The township name was changed from Andrews to Canfield in 1912 at the suggestion of C. F. Lindsey and S. L. Jordahl. The CANFIELD post office was established July 6, 1905 with Arthur H. Knowlton pm. Axel H. Lundberg (1880-1948) operated a grocery store here, and his son, Bismarck attorney Robert Lundberg, currently owns the old townsite. In 1912 the post office moved one mile SW to SE¼ Sec. 30-143-77, the home of new pm Martha E. Ong, but it closed August 31, 1912 with mail to Regan. (1, 2, 3, 8, 12, 18, 34, 40, 63, 414)

CANFIELD (Cass). This NPRR station was built in 1882 in NW¼ Sec. 2-139-50, Mapleton Twp., three miles east of Mapleton, and named for Thomas H. Canfield, President of the Lake Superior & Puget Sound Land Co., a subsidiary of the NPRR. He is sometimes called the father of Fargo. On June 2, 1907 the name was changed to FIFE. (2, 3, 34, 77, 79, 301)

CANNON (Adams). This was a rural community shown on some maps of the 1920's, centered in Sec. 28-130-91, South Fork Twp., about three miles from the eastern border of Adams County. It is on the north bank of Cedar Creek, which flows into the Cannon Ball River. (3)

CANNON (Morton). The CANNON BALL post office in NW¼ Sec. 16-134-79 was reestablished October 12, 1889 with Robert Goudreau pm, but postal officials crossed out the "Ball" part of the name, resulting in the locally unpopular name CANNON. Protests that CANNON BALL was an established name with historical importance were filed, and the full name was restored November 19, 1889. It is interesting to note that the CANNON name was used for just five weeks, yet exists during both statehood and territorial times. (2, 3, 40, 414)

CANNON BALL (Grant). This was the fourth stage station out of Bismarck on the Bismarck to Deadwood trail established in 1876. It was located in SW¼ Sec. 29-132-86, Two Mile Twp., twelve miles SW of Raleigh at a crossing of the Cannonball River still used today. (3, 34, 418)

CANNON BALL (Morton). This was a pioneer settlement in NW¼ Sec. 16-134-79, on the north bank of the Cannonball River at its confluence with the Missouri River. The smaller river's name noted the many limestone boulders found in its bed and banks, which were said to resemble cannon balls. The Sioux called the river *Inyan Wakagapi*, meaning Stone Idol River. The post office was established June 21, 1880 with Richard M. Johnston pm, and it closed August 1, 1881, being replaced on that date by the Gayton post office on the opposite side of the Missouri River in Emmons County. It reopened October 12, 1889 as CANNON with Robert Goudreau pm. Following protests from local settlers, the full CANNON BALL name was restored November 19, 1889. The post office closed again on March 31, 1915 with mail to Fort Rice. On December 3, 1915 the name was transferred to the Hekton post office on the south bank of the Cannonball in Sioux County. (2, 3, 40, 79, 240, 414)

CANNON BALL (Sioux). This village in Secs.

22 & 23-134-79, on the south bank of the Cannonball River at its confluence with the Missouri River, dates from the 1870's, and was at first called HEKTON. On December 3, 1915 the name was changed to CANNON BALL by pm Chester R. Wilcox, taking the name of the adjacent Morton County post office which had closed March 31, 1915. The city was served by the NPRR branch line for many years, and has generally had a population of about 200. The post office, Zip Code 58528, became a rural branch of Fort Yates on November 17, 1966, effective December 2, 1966. (1, 2, 3, 18, 33, 40, 127, 414)

CANNON BALL JUNCTION (Sioux). This was the junction of NPRR lines in NW 1/4 Sec. 23-134-79, just north of present-day Cannon Ball. It was built in 1910 as BELDEN, and assumed this name when the townsite on the south bank of the Cannonball River began to develop about 1915. (2, 3, 127)

CANTON (Pembina). This was a pioneer Icelandic settlement founded in 1879 in SE¼ Sec. 12 & NE¼ Sec. 13-160-55, Park Twp., and named by townsite officials to note that it was a "canton" for several rural communities at the headwaters of the Tongue River. Canton is French for small territorial division, and is the term used for the political division, or states, of Switzerland. The HENSEL post office, founded in 1887 three miles NW of here, moved to the townsite in 1889, retaining its name, and since that date the town has usually been called HENSEL, although CANTON remains its legal name, and as late as 1940 has been used on maps. (2, 3, 4, 10, 40, 108, 366)

CARBON (Morton). This NPRR station was founded in 1878 in Sec. 11-138-86, Sims Twp., in anticipation of the railroad. Charles W. Thompson started the Carbon Pressed Brick and Lime Co. here, supplying most of the brick for the buildings at SIMS, a boom town started on this site in 1883, as well as for the new territorial Capitol in Bismarck and the Morton County court house in Mandan. (2, 3, 107)

CARBURY (Bottineau). This GNRR station was founded in 1901 in N½ Sec. 5-162-76, Pickering Twp., and SW¼ Sec. 32-163-76, Dalen Twp. Folklore tells of a mixup, either by GNRR officials or by the Secretary of State, which resulted in the names of this site and Roth, formerly Faldet, being reversed. There does appear to be some truth to the story, but this site has always been called CARBURY, for a city in county Kildare, Ireland. The post office was established April 16, 1906 with George O. Aal pm. CARBURY never experienced a boom period, reaching a peak population of 50 in 1920, with a count of just 5 in 1980. The post office, Zip Code 58724, closed February 13, 1984. (1, 2, 3, 18, 33, 34, 40, 101, 153, 380)

CARDER (McHenry). This was a farm post office established May 19, 1891 with Alfred Booker House pm. It was located in SE¼ Sec. 23-158-76, Poplar Grove Twp., eight miles east of Bantry, and just west of the LANE post office, which it replaced. The origin of the name is unknown. It closed

June 30, 1903 with mail to Towner. (2, 40, 412, 415)

CARIGNAN (Sioux). This was a NPRR station seven miles north of Fort Yates, just north of Battle Creek, straddling Sec. 1 & 2-131-80. The name honored John W. Carignan, who came to Fort Yates from Quebec, Canada in 1883 as a teenager, and was a merchant, legislator, and pm. He was beloved by the Indians, who called him Mata Kokipapi, meaning afraid of bear. Carrignan and Carrigan are erroneous spellings. (2, 3, 18, 52, 127)

CARL (Grant). This was a farm post office established May 13, 1907 with Carl Thompson pm. It was located in NW¼ Sec. 14-135-86, eight miles NE of Carson. Carl is a variant of Charles, which means man. Mail service was provided three times each week from Almont. The post office closed June 30, 1922 with mail to Almont. (1, 2, 17, 18, 19, 40, 174, 177)

CARLETON CITY (Burleigh). This was one of the pre-1872 settlements at what would become BISMARCK, and is said to have been named for Carlton, MN, near the NPRR railhead at Duluth. The MN city was named for Reuben B. Carlton (1812-1863), a pioneer settler, but no explanation is found for the variation in the spelling. CARLETON CITY, essentially a collection of saloons, was opposite Camp Greene, the predecessor of Forts McKeen and Abraham Lincoln, probably in Fort Rice Twp. (137-80), about six miles south of present-day BISMARCK, and the actual site is said to have been washed out by the shifting channel of the Missouri River in 1874. (2, 3, 10, 15, 420)

CARLISLE (Pembina). This was an early rural community in SW¼ Sec. 10-162-52, Carlisle Twp., about four miles SE of Bathgate. Settlers arrived here about 1876, and the post office was established August 21, 1878 with Adolph Carl, a former soldier at Fort Pembina, as pm. Charles Wesley Argue (1871-1942) ran a country store here for many years. Some say the name honors Mr. Carl, and others say the name came from Carlisle, Ontario, Canada. Carlisle is an Old English residence name meaning from the walled city. The post office was discontinued March 31, 1912 with mail to Hamilton. (2, 3, 18, 19, 25, 40, 108, 146)

CARLSON (Kidder). This was a rural post office established February 5, 1910 with Alarik W. Carlson pm, located in NE¼ Sec. 34-144-73, Stewart Twp., about eight miles NNE of Tuttle. Mr. Carlson had settled here in 1904. On October 27, 1910 the name of the post office was changed to CARLSONDALE. (2, 3, 18, 40, 122)

CARLSONDALE (Kidder). On October 27, 1910 the name of the CARLSON post office was changed to CARLSONDALE, the "dale" apparently added to note its location in a valley. It closed December 31, 1912 with mail to Moyersville. (2, 3, 4, 18, 40, 53, 122)

CARL'S POINT (Pembina). This was a stopping point on the old Pembina to Cavalier trail in Sec. 10-162-52, Carlisle Twp., twelve miles west of Pembina. It was named for

Adolph Carl, pm of the CARLISLE post office at this site beginning in 1878. All traces of the settlement and the trail have vanished. (3, 25, 40, 440)

**CARLTON** (Barnes). Soon after settlement began on the NPRR mainline site of FOURTH SIDING, a post office became necessary. It was established September 12, 1879 with John M. Dennett pm, who named it for his wife, Mary Carlton Dennett, a native of Maine and the daughter of a Congregationalist minister. She is remembered as the first organist of the local Congregational church. The original site, NW¼ Sec. 21-140-56, was replaced by a new townsite in Sec. 20 in 1880, and the following year it was again moved west, this time to Sec. 19. Due to confusion with the neighboring town of Casselton, the name was changed to ORISKA on September 18, 1881. (2, 34, 40, 76, 279, 281)

**CARLTON** (Traill). This was a pioneer post office established January 9, 1871 with Jacob Lowell pm. It was located in NW¼ Sec. 26-144-49, Elm River Twp., in the extreme SE corner of the county, and is said to be named for Carleton County, Ontario, Canada, which was named for Sir Guy Carleton (1724-1808), a British statesman active in early Canadian affairs. The change in the spelling is not explained. The post office, which may never have actually operated, closed February 9, 1872 with mail to Georgetown, MN, thirteen miles south on the east side of the Red River. Mr. Lowell is shown on an 1884 map in Sec. 13-154-58, Sarnia Twp., Nelson County, three miles east of present-day Whitman. He was active in the founding of Lakota, the Nelson County seat. (2, 3, 10, 34, 40, 130, 414)

**CARPENTER** (Rolette). This was a rural community founded in 1901 in Sec. 24-164-72, Holmes Twp., about eleven miles WNW of Saint John. The name came from nearby Carpenter Lake, which had been named for Henri Scharpenter, a Frenchman who had settled here in 1878, and drowned in the lake in 1888. The post office was established March 9, 1903 with Anton T. Julseth pm, and closed August 15, 1938 with mail to Saint John. A population of 25 was listed in 1960, and the place appeared on some maps into the 1970's. (2, 18, 38, 40, 123)

**CARPIO** (Ward). This Soo Line RR station was founded in 1896 in NE¼ Sec. 12-157-86, Carpio Twp., and has grown into parts of three adjacent sections. The post office was established July 7, 1898 with Austen E. Kjontvedt pm. The elevation is 1696, the Zip Code is 58725, and the village, which incorporated in 1906, reached a peak population of 344 in 1930. Many theories exist concerning the origin of the name, the most well known being the folklore version about the first post office being housed in a box car, quite literally a "Car P. O." Some say Mrs. Pennington, the wife of a Soo Line official, named it for a Spanish novel of this name, which means tents. Others say it was named for Carpio de Vega, a Spanish poet, while still others say it was named for Bernardo del Carpio, a Spanish explorer. (1, 2, 3, 18, 33, 40, 79, 100)

**CARRINGTON** (Foster). Henry A. Soliday

*Carrington*

(1836-1923), a respected judge and businessman, is credited with being the first settler here in 1882. A post office was established February 15, 1883 with Arthur C. Halsey pm, and the town was chosen as the county seat of Foster County. It was named for Miles D. Carrington (1823-1887) by his partner, Lyman R. Casey, the two men being influential in townsite development throughout central North Dakota. The city, which incorporated in 1900, is located mostly in Sec. 19-146-66, Carrington Twp., has an elevation of 1605, and the Zip Code is 58421. The population has increased steadily, reaching 2,636 in 1980. (1, 2, 3, 40, 97)

**CARSON** (Grant). This rural post office opened August 11, 1902 with David Pederson pm. John Erickson suggested the name Zelma, for the daughter of a local rancher, but the selected name was coined from the names of local settler Frank CARter, and Simon and David PederSON. In 1906 it moved one mile east to Sec. 24-134-87, Carson Twp., and a small settlement began to develop. The following year a rival townsite, NORTH CARSON, started two miles to the north. When the NPRR built between the two, they merged as CARSON in Sec. 13-134-87. CARSON became the county seat when Grant County organized in 1916. The court house burned in 1978, and was replaced in 1980. The elevation is 2341, the Zip Code is 58529, and a peak population of 501 was reached in 1960. (1, 2, 3, 17, 18, 33, 40, 52, 79, 171, 173, 174, 175)

**CARTWRIGHT** (McKenzie). This was a farm post office established June 28, 1901 with Samuel George Cartwright pm. Mr. Cartwright came to Dakota Territory in 1882, and with his sons became well known as a rancher and trail blazer in the Souris River valley. He came here in 1900, settling in NW¼ Sec. 31-151-103, Sioux Twp. In 1913 the post office moved to the new GNRR townsite in Sec. 31-151-103 and Sec. 36-151-104, Sioux Twp. The elevation is 1904, the Zip Code is 58838, and a peak population of 200 was claimed in 1920, but the 1930 count of 50 is probably more realistic. Grace Johnson, later the wife of Governor Arthur A. Link, was born here. (1, 2, 3, 18, 33, 40, 79, 227)

**CASEY** (McLean). This was a rural post office established September 3, 1902 with Mary B. Casey pm. Casey is a Celtic name meaning valorous. It was located in SW¼ Sec. 17-148-80, Wiprud Twp., eight miles north of Turtle Lake. On July 25, 1904 Stener T. Wiprud became pm, changing the name to WIPRUD, and he operated the facility along with a country store until 1914. (2, 3, 18, 19, 28, 40)

**CASHEL** (Walsh). This is the first NPRR station NE of Grafton, located in NE¼ Sec. 26-158-52, Martin Twp. The name honors John Lyons Cashel Sr. (1848-1926), a Grafton banker, realtor and politician who owned the townsite. The family name comes from the ancient city of Cashel, county Tipperary, in southern Ireland. The post office was established December 17, 1887 with Charles Moore pm, and closed March 15, 1943 with mail to Drayton. A population of 80 was listed in 1920. (1, 2, 13, 18, 25, 40, 75, 79)

**CASSELMAN** (Emmons). This was a rural post office established February 23, 1886 with William S. Casselman pm. He came here from Ontario, Canada in 1883 with his wife, Ella Hough Casselman, a pioneer school teacher. It was located in SE¼ Sec. 8-136-75, four miles NW of Braddock, and closed April 2, 1887 with mail to Steele. The Casselman family moved to Bismarck in 1892. (2, 18, 25, 40, 66)

**CASSELMAN** (Sheridan). This area was first settled by Romanians in 1893, and the Soo Line RR made plans to build through here as early as 1896. The post office was established January 15, 1898 with Patrick Walsh pm. The settlement was located in Sec. 10-150-74, Martin Twp., and named for the townsite agent. On November 6, 1902 the name was changed to MARTIN. (2, 3, 21, 30, 40)

**CASSELTON** (Cass). This site, Sec. 35-140-52, Casselton Twp., was first settled in 1870, and known as GOOSE CREEK, SWAN CREEK, and CASSTOWN. When the post office was established August 8, 1876 with William Craswell pm, the name was stylized as CASSELTON, for George Cass, namesake of the county. It became an incorporated village in 1880, and a city in 1883. The elevation is 928, the Zip Code is 58012, and it has grown steadily, reaching a population of 1,658 in 1980. William Langer, the state's most famous politician, was born near here in 1886. George A. Sinner, Governor of ND since 1985, is a resident, and M. G. Strauss, the clothing store founder, began his business here in 1897. Max G. Taubert is remembered for his service station, which featured a towering conical formation of empty oil cans, said to be the world's largest such structure. (1, 2, 3, 13, 25, 33, 34, 40, 77, 79, 299, 300)

**CASSTOWN** (Cass). This settlement in Sec. 35-140-52, Casselton Twp., began in 1870 and was known as both GOOSE CREEK and SWAN CREEK. The NPRR built a station here in 1876, and local citizens Mike Smith and Emil Priewe suggested renaming it to honor George Cass, namesake of the county and NPRR President 1872-1875. Some sources spell the name as two words. When the post office was established August 8, 1876, the name was stylized as CASSELTON. (2, 18, 19, 77)

**CATHAY** (Wells). This Soo Line RR townsite was founded in 1892 in NW¼ Sec. 13-147-69, Cathay Twp., and platted that year by the Minnesota Loan & Trust Co. The name was suggested by Soo Line official Fred D. Underwood and a Chinese cook working with the construction crew to recognize China, using the ancient Tartar name for that country. CATHAY is a corruption of the original *Khitai*. The post office was established June 17, 1893 with Marcus L. Peck pm. The elevation is 1578, the Zip Code is 58422, and the village, which incorporated in 1907, reached a peak population of 255 in the 1925 special census. Dr. John G. Johns was a well known pioneer physician and druggist in the area. (2, 18, 23, 33, 40, 52, 79)

**CATHMERE** (McKenzie). This was a rural post office established May 12, 1914 with William Grant Heisler pm. He coined the name by using part of his wife's given name, CATHerine, and "MERE", meaning meadow, after postal officials had rejected Catherine. Others claim the name was chosen by Mrs. Charlotte Winter Walton, the area's first school teacher, without explaining its origin. It was located in NE¼ Sec. 19-149-103, thirteen miles south of Cartwright, and moved two miles south in 1917 to SE¼ Sec. 32-149-103. Mr. Heisler moved to CA in 1920, and Henry Derudder, a Belgian immigrant, became pm. The post office closed October 31, 1930 with mail to Cartwright. (2, 3, 40, 227)

**CATLIN** (McKenzie). This was a ranch post office established November 25, 1908 with Sarah J. Catlin pm. The Catlin Ranch was established in 1906 in SW 1/4 Sec. 26-150-96, Pershing Twp., seventeen miles east of Watford City. Some claim it was named for the noted western artist George Catlin. On March 23, 1915 William B. Croff became pm, moving the post office two miles south to his home in SW¼ Sec. 2-149-96, Bear Den Twp., where he also ran a small store. Mr. Croff, and many local residents, thought that the store and post office should have the same name, so on October 29, 1915

the name of the post office was changed to CROFF. (2, 3, 18, 40, 79, 229)

**CATO** (Ramsey). This was a farm post office established September 7, 1898 with Erik Kalhagen pm. With his brother, Einar, and two sisters, they had been the first settlers in the area, coming here from Norway in 1882. The post office closed December 28, 1899 without ever being in operation. It was located in SW¼ Sec. 26-156-62, Cato Twp., about ten miles west of Lawton. No one knows where the name came from, although some suggest that it was named for Marcus Porcius Cato (95-46 B.C.), an ancient Roman official. Cato is Latin for sagacious. (1, 2, 3, 10, 19, 40, 103)

**CAUGHEY** (McHenry). This was a farm post office established February 15, 1901 with Andrew Caughey pm. It was located in SW¼ Sec. 23-153-78, Lake Hester Twp., four miles SW of Karlsruhe. Emil Bredeson, who lived one mile SW of the post office in SW¼ Sec. 27-153-78, was the mail carrier. The post office was discontinued June 15, 1906 with mail to Bergen. (2, 3, 34, 40, 412, 415)

**CAUSEY** (Mercer). This was a rural community founded in 1882 about three miles north of present-day Stanton. The post office was established October 10, 1882 with Peter C. Causey pm, running the facility at his home in SE¼ Sec. 16-145-84. He was a Civil War veteran who had come here in the 1870's, and his name was chosen by townsite promoters August and Edward Heinemeyer, who had just come here from Germany. Mr. Causey died in 1883, and the post office was moved to the home of Edward Heinemeyer in NE¼ Sec. 30-145-84. The post office closed June 29, 1894 with mail to Stanton. (2, 18, 25, 40, 64, 121, 232, 414)

**CAVALIER** (Cavalier). This place is shown on a 1930 roadmap published by the General Drafting Co., one of several such places on this map that utilize their county names. It is shown about eight miles NNW of Langdon, and is believed to be a copyright town. (3)

**CAVALIER** (Pembina). This settlement was founded in 1875 in Sec. 4-161-54, Cavalier Twp., and received this name in 1877 after being known as DOUGLAS POINT, DEWEY, PENNINGTON, and several unofficial names. Although it is generally assumed to have been named for Charles Turner Cavileer (1818-1902), the county's famous pioneer, an 1879 inquiry by postal officials as to the correct spelling resulted in the response that it was named for Rene Robert Cavalier, Sieur de la Salle (1643-1687), the explorer. The CAVALIER post office was established June 20, 1877 with John Bechtel (1828-1898) pm, who wanted to name it for Gen. George A. Custer, but that name had already been awarded to a town in what is now SD. It incorporated as a village in 1892, and became a city in 1903. Because of its central location, it replaced Pembina as county seat in 1911. The elevation is 896, the Zip Code is 58220, and a peak population of 1,496 was reached in 1980. In 1902 settlers from here founded Cavalier, Saskatchewan, Canada. (1, 2, 3, 18, 25, 33, 40, 79, 83, 108, 199, 366, 414, 440)

**CAVILEER** (Cavalier). Official records indicate that the name of this city has always been CAVALIER, but a postmark exists from 1881, nearly four years after the establishment of the post office, with the spelling as CAVILEER, the proper version of the family name of the prominent pioneer Charles Turner Cavileer, generally believed to be the city's namesake. (3)

**CAYUGA** (Sargent). This GNRR station was founded in 1886 and named SENECA. Because of the existance of a town of that name in what is now SD, the name was changed to CAYUGA in 1887, both names being tribes of the Iroquois nation. The post office was established October 13, 1887 with Albert K. Maloy pm. The village, located in Sec. 18-130-53, Kingston Twp., and Sec. 13-130-54, Ransom Twp., incorporated in 1909, and reached a peak population of 219 in 1930, although a steady decline has reduced that count to just 75 in 1980. The elevation is 1131, and the Zip Code is 58013. (1, 2, 3, 10, 18, 25, 33, 40, 52, 79)

**CECIL** (Pierce). This farm post office was established in Towner County in 1887, and named for pm Uriah Cecil Miller. On July 8, 1902 it was moved to the farm home of Rhoe C. Hatch in NE¼ Sec. 3-158-69, Union Twp., in Pierce County, about eight miles NE of Wolford. It closed August 31, 1911 with mail to Wolford. (1, 2, 3, 18, 40, 53, 414)

**CECIL** (Towner). This was a farm post office established February 25, 1887 with Uriah Cecil Miller pm. Cecil is a Latin word meaning blind. Jacob C. Siple, who came here in 1883, was appointed pm March 17, 1890, and the post office was moved about four miles SW to his home in the center of Sec. 31-159-68, New City Twp., eight miles SW of Bisbee. On July 8, 1902 Rhoe C. Hatch was appointed pm, and the post office moved to his home about three miles WSW of the Siple home, a move which resulted in CECIL now being in Pierce County. (2, 3, 18, 19, 25, 40)

**CEDAR** (Adams). This was a rural post office established March 4, 1908 with Anton J. Serbus pm. It was located in NW¼ Sec. 14-132-95, Maine Twp., sixteen miles SW of Mott, and named for the red cedars that grow in abundance on the NW sides of the buttes in the area. On May 29, 1912 the post office was moved about four miles NE into Hettinger County, closing in 1918. (2, 3, 40, 79, 415)

**CEDAR** (Hettinger). This rural post office was established March 4, 1908 in Adams County. On May 29, 1912 it moved four miles NE to the home of new pm Herman F. Schneider in Sec. 30-132-94, Ashby Twp., thirteen miles SW of Mott, a move which put CEDAR into Hettinger County. It was discontinued June 31, 1918 with mail to Mott according to postal records. There is, of course, no such date, and with June 30, 1918 being a Sunday, it is assumed that the correct date of closing was July 1, 1918. (1, 2, 3, 40, 179)

**CEDAR CANYON** (Billings). This name has primarily been used for a rest stop and scenic overlook on US Highway 10, and now Interstate 94, eight miles east of Medora, in Sec. 36-140-101, West Fryburg Twp. For motorists driving west, it offers the first good look at the North Dakota Badlands. The first development of the site occurred in the 1930's. (3, 34)

**CEDAR RIVER** (Sioux). This was the fifth and last stage station, in what is now North Dakota, on the Bismarck to Deadwood trail established in 1876. It was located on the south bank of the Cedar River in Sec. 6-129-87, nine miles NE of Morristown, SD. Traces of the stables and living quarters were still visible in recent years. (3, 127, 418)

**CENTER** (Dickey). This was one of several names used by townsite promoter Myron Henry Puffer, along with CENTRALIA, CENTROPOLIS, COLDWATER, and MENASHA CENTER, in SW¼ Sec. 32-130-60, Hudson Twp., now the NE section of GUELPH. The name reflects Mr. Puffer's desire for this town to become the center of activity in the area. (2, 3, 18, 154)

**CENTER** (Oliver). Settlement occurred here as early as 1900, but the townsite was officially founded in 1902 as a new, centralized county seat for Oliver County, hence the name. The site was platted in 1903 by H. H. Harmon, and the post office was established February 9, 1903 with Frank J. V. Kiebert pm. It is located in Secs. 14 & 15-142-84, Lincoln Twp., incorporated as a village in 1928, and became a city in 1967. The Zip Code is 58530, and the city has shown a steady growth, reaching a population of 878 in the 1983 special census. (2, 3, 23, 33, 40, 79, 121)

**CENTERVILLE** (Ward). This was an inland town in SE¼ Sec. 24-151-86, Ryder Twp., founded in 1902. It had a bank, general store, hotel, and a newspaper, *The Centerville News*, edited by Guy F. Humphries. The name is thought to be indicative of the settlers' hopes for the importance of their community. This name was rejected by postal authorities because of duplication in SD, and the name was changed to DeKALB, which likewise was rejected. Finally the name RYDER was accepted, and it became a thriving city on the newly-built Soo Line RR. (2, 3, 28, 100, 277)

**CENTRALIA** (Cass). This was the site of the NPRR entrance into Dakota Territory, Sec. 7-139-48, Barnes Twp. It was first called THE CROSSING, and unofficially TENT CITY, but when a post office was established October 6, 1871 with Gordon J. Keeney pm, it was named CENTRALIA to note its place as a central point of development in the territory. On February 12, 1872 the name was changed to FARGO, and this wretched little town grew into the metropolis of ND. (2, 3, 10, 40, 77, 79, 199)

**CENTRALIA** (Dickey). This was one of several names used by townsite promoter Myron Henry Puffer (1842-1921), along with CENTER, CENTROPOLIS, COLDWATER, and MENASHA CENTER, in SW¼ Sec. 32-130-60, Hudson Twp., now the NE section of GUELPH. Forty acres were platted with the CENTRALIA name by W. P. Butler of Aberdeen, SD, and application was made for a post office, but officials rejected this name, with GUELPH being adopted in 1887. (2, 3, 154, 264)

**CENTROPOLIS** (Dickey). This was one of several names used by townsite promoter M. H. Puffer in SW¼ Sec. 32-130-60, Hudson Twp., now the NE section of GUELPH. The name was promotional for the site, which was hoped to be a center of activity in the area. *Polis* is Greek for city. (2, 3, 10, 154)

**CHABOILLEZ POST** (Pembina). This fur trading post was built in 1797 in SW 1/4 Sec. 4-163-51, Pembina Twp., at the confluence of the Red and Pembina Rivers, by Charles Baptiste Chaboillez, and can claim to be the first white settlement in ND. Five buildings were erected, staffed by 15 men, but the site abandoned in April 1798 when the Pembina River flooded the area. The site was also called RIVIERE PEMBINATI, and in 1801 another attempt was begun to establish a settlement at the site, now part of the city of Pembina. (2, 3, 18, 79, 108, 365, 366)

**CHADWICK** (Sioux). This was a Milwaukee Road RR loading spur in Sec. 23-131-83, between Shields and Selfridge. The name honored Earl Chadwick Sr., who operated a stockyard at the site. Chadwick is a Celtic name meaning from the warrior's town. CHADWICK consisted of an old railroad car used as a bunkhouse, and a corral. (1, 2, 19, 53,, 127)

**CHAFFEE** (Cass). This GNRR station was founded in 1893 as RITA, and was the terminus of a twelve mile branch line built westward from Addison. It is located in Sec. 10-138-53, Walburg Twp., and was renamed CHAFFEE in 1894 to honor Eben W. Chaffee, President of the Amenia-Sharon Land Co., promoters of this site. The post office was established April 21, 1894 with Herman Frederick pm. A village was platted in 1898, and a peak population of 126 was recorded in 1920. The elevation is 960, and the post office, Zip Code 58014, became a rural branch of Wheatland on December 2, 1966. Chester Fritz, the engineer, international financier, and benefactor of the University of North Dakota, was born here in 1892. (1, 2, 3, 18, 33, 34, 38, 40, 77, 79)

**CHAFFEES** (Foster). This was a Soo Line RR siding and loading station in NE¼ Sec. 10-146-67, Wyard Twp., four miles NW of Carrington. It was originally known as CHAFFEE SPUR, but during the 1930's it began to be called simply CHAFFEES. (2, 18, 77, 97)

**CHAFFEE SPUR** (Foster). This was a Soo Line RR siding and loading station in NE¼ Sec. 10-146-67, Wyard Twp., four miles NW of Carrington. It was named for Frank Newton Chaffee (1861-1914), who came here in 1883 and ran the 2,400 acre Vermont Farm. He later moved to Carrington where he engaged in banking and ran a general store. He served two terms in the state legislature, and was mayor of Carrington 1911-1913. In the 1930's the site became known as CHAFFEES. (2, 18, 97)

**CHAHINKAPA** (Richland). This settlement was founded in 1869 as RICHVILLE, and on October 13, 1873 pm D. Wilmot Smith changed the name to CHAHINKAPA, a word of the Sisseton and Wahpeton tribes meaning end of the woods. The townsite was platted by founder Morgan T. Rich, a New

Yorker, in 1874, and the name proved to be difficult for many officials. On July 24, 1874 the name was changed to WAHPETON. The CHAHINKAPA name survives as the name of a park. (1, 2, 3, 40, 242)

**CHAMA** (Golden Valley). This was a NPRR station and spur located in Sec. 34-140-105, Beach Twp., between Beach and Sentinel Butte. Its elevation is 2804, making it the highest NPRR station in the state. It was built in 1888, but development was very slow. A post office was established June 7, 1913 with Minnie B. Whipple pm, but it was discontinued July 15, 1914 with mail to Sentinel Butte. A population of 15 was listed in 1920. The name is said to have come from the Chama River in TX. It is a common place name in the SW United States, and is derived from the Tewa Indian word *tzama*. J. P. Harrington says it means here they have wrestled, while Edgar L. Hewett says it means red, describing the color of the water in the river. (1, 2, 25, 34, 40, 79)

**CHANDLER** (Adams). This was a rural post office established March 18, 1907 in NE¼ Sec. 24-131-94, Chandler Twp., fifteen miles NE of Hettinger, with David E. Elliott pm. He came here in 1906 from Indiana, and named it for his wife, the former Hulda J. Chandler. Others say it was named for local rancher Shad Chandler. Chandler is a French name meaning candle maker. The post office moved two miles SSE in 1910 to NW¼ Sec. 31-131-93, Jordan Twp., the home of new pm John W. Clark. In 1916 it moved three miles NNW to the home of pm Edna E. McNeely in NW¼ Sec. 13-131-94, and in 1928 it moved one mile south to SW¼ Sec. 13-131-94, the home of Tabitha Kymm, before closing April 30, 1929 with mail to Haynes. (1, 2, 3, 18, 19, 40, 189, 414)

**CHANTAPETA** (Adams). This was a rural post office located in NE¼ Sec. 13-132-96, Cedar Twp., just north of Chata Peta Creek, and about twenty miles north of Hettinger. Chanta Peta is a Teton Sioux word meaning fire-heart. The post office was established April 10, 1919 with Mrs. Arntina Olstad pm, who came here in 1906 from Minneapolis, MN with her husband, Ole. It closed August 15, 1929 with mail to Hettinger. (3, 18, 25, 40, 79, 188, 189, 414)

**CHAPIN** (Burleigh). This was a coal miners' settlement one mile east of Wilton in NW¼ Sec. 1 & NE¼ Sec. 2-142-80, Ecklund Twp. Gen. William D. Washburn named the settlement for his son Edward Chapin Washburn. Chapin is a French name meaning chaplain or clergyman. Twelve blocks were platted here to serve the Washburn Lignite Coal Mine No. 1, and development featured an 80-room hotel and a Soo Line RR siding. The site dates from 1902, but as the mines became less feasible from an economic standpoint, it was eventually abandoned, and the principal remains of the site are the spoil banks left at the mines. (2, 3, 18, 19)

**CHARBONNEAU** (McKenzie). This was a GNRR station founded in 1913 in SE¼ Sec. 32-151-102, Charbon Twp., seven miles west of Alexander, and named for nearby Charbonneau Creek, which was named for Touissant Charbonneau, the interpreter for the

Lewis & Clark Expedition, and the husband of Sakakawea. The post office was established March 21, 1914 with Ira E. Wolcott pm, and a village of 125 was reported here in 1920. A decline began shortly after that, and by 1960 the population was down to just 15. The post office closed September 22, 1967 with mail to Alexander. (1, 2, 3, 40, 79, 226)

**CHARLESTON** (Barnes). This was a farm post office established March 17, 1881 with Francis E. Sherman pm. It was located in Sec. 5-141-57, Noltimier Twp., ten miles north of Oriska. The origin of the name is unknown, although it was likely named after one of several Charlestons in the United States, all of which ultimately are traced to Charles II (1630-1685), King of England. This short-lived post office closed December 21, 1881 with mail to Tower City. Charlestown is an erroneous spelling. (2, 3, 10, 40, 76)

**CHARLSON** (McKenzie). This rural post office was established December 23, 1904 with Thorsten E. Charlson pm at his home in NE¼ Sec. 22-153-95, Elm Tree Twp. In 1907 he lad out a townsite in SW¼ Sec. 23-153-95, and a population of 125 was reported in 1920, although the village never incorporated. The almost inevitable decline began in later years, and the 1960 population was just 20. Rose C. Boots retired as pm November 14, 1980 after more than thirty years on the job, and the post office closed with mail to New Town, although government records did not record this fact until Mary 19, 1982. (1, 2, 3, 20, 40, 79, 228, 253)

**CHASE** (Burleigh). This was a short-lived Soo Line RR siding between Stewartsdale and Brittin, thirteen miles SE of Bismarck, probably located in Sec. 4-137-78, Telfer Twp. It appeared on maps circa 1890, and was named for Elmer C. Chase, a pioneer homesteader in N½ Sec. 11-137-78. Mail service came from Glasscock. (3, 12, 25)

**CHASE** (Cass). This was a GNRR loading station built in 1899 in SW¼ Sec. 23-140-49, Reed Twp., three miles NW of Fargo. The origin of the name is unknown. It was removed in June 1936. (1, 2, 34)

**CHASE** (Hettinger). This was a farm post office established January 19, 1901 with Charles Mutschelknaus pm. According to local accounts, Mrs. Mutschelknaus actually performed the duties at the post office. It was located in NW¼ Sec. 31-134-93, Mott Twp., five miles west of Mott, and was named for Osborn S. Chase, who had begun a ranch here in 1890. On September 17, 1904 the post office was replaced by the facility in the new townsite of Mott. (2, 3, 18, 40, 53, 181)

**CHASELEY** (Wells). This NPRR townsite was founded in 1902 in NW¼ Sec. 23-146-72, Chaseley Twp., and named by the ever-present Richard Sykes for the estate of a friend in England. The post office was established July 27, 1905 with George Brower pm. The elevation is 1880, the Zip Code is 58423, and a population of 125 was claimed in 1920, with a decline to just 76 in 1960. Chasely is an erroneous spelling. (1, 2, 3, 18, 33, 38, 40, 79, 267, 363, 364)

**CHAUTAUQUA** (Ramsey). In June 1892 a group of Devils Lake citizens conceived the idea of organizing a Chautauqua Assembly at the nearby namesake lake. A site was acquired, and the first assembly began June 28, 1893. These religious and educational meetings had begun at Chautauqua Lake, NY in 1874. That lake has an Indian name of uncertain origin, some of the suggested meanings being where the fish was taken out, foggy place, bag tied in the middle, place of easy death, and place where a child was washed away. A railroad line was built from Devils Lake to the site, W½ Sec. 18-153-64, Lake Twp., in 1899, and a post office called NORTH CHAUTAUQUA was opened here in 1902. The last assembly was held in 1929, and the site gradually became a residential area known as LAKEWOOD PARK, with three additions at first called GREENWOOD. The area became part of the city of Devils Lake in 1949. (2, 3, 10, 18, 103)

**CHENOWETH** (Slope). This was the dream town of Mrs. Chester Chenoweth, a wealthy widow from Chicago, IL, who came to Slope County in 1910 with farm machinery unlike anything ever seen in these parts, and began both a large-scale farming operation and a townsite in NE¼ Sec. 15-133-101, Sheets Twp. No less than eighty blocks were platted, and at first a few settlers were attracted to the development, but after failing to obtain either a railroad or the county seat, the site began to decline. The post office was established September 16, 1910 with Lloyd Wetzel pm, and closed October 31, 1918 with mail to Bowman. Chenowith is an erroneous spelling. (1, 2, 3, 40, 82, 400)

**CHERRY** (McKenzie). This was a rural post office established October 26, 1908 with Olof P. Transtrom pm, who named it for nearby Cherry Creek, which was named for his daughter, Cherry, although others say the creek was named to note the many chokecherry trees along its banks. It was first located in SE¼ Sec. 17-149-99, Ellsworth Twp., seven miles SW of Watford City, and made several moves, ending up in NW¼ Sec. 29-148-98, thirteen miles SSE of Watford City when it closed May 31, 1929 with mail to Watford City. A population of 4 was reported in 1930. (1, 2, 3, 18, 40, 79, 434)

**CHESS CROSSING** (Wells). This was a crossing point of Pipestem Creek used circa 1884, and built by Henry B. Chess, a bricklayer, plasterer, livery operator, contractor, lawyer, and county official from nearby Sykeston. The actual site is probably in NE¼ Sec. 13-146-69, Sykeston Twp., just east of a present-day bridge over the creek at the west edge of Sykeston. (2, 3, 18, 79, 268, 364)

**CHESTER** (Grand Forks). This place appears on an 1882 map of North Dakota in SW¼ Sec. 2-151-51, Brenna Twp., six miles east of Ojata on the GNRR. The planned townsite did not develop, although a quarter-century later the Powell elevator was built just to the west. It was named for Chester Alan Arthur (1830-1886), who had just become President of the United States following the assassination of James A. Garfield. The name is traced to the ancient city of Chester, England. (3, 4, 5, 69, 414)

**CHESTER** (Mountrail). This was a farm post office established November 26, 1908 with Charles L. Ellis pm. It was located in SE¼ Sec. 14-153-92, Knife River Twp., about seven miles north of New Town. The origin of the name is unknown, although it is an Old English name meaning dweller in a fortified town. Mail was carried here three times weekly on the route from Stanley through Belden to this place. The post office closed May 14, 1910 with mail to Belden. (2, 18, 19, 40, 72)

**CHICOTA** (McHenry). This was a rural post office established July 31, 1902 with Arthur C. Kampson pm. It was located in SW¼ Sec. 9-157-80, Deering Twp., two miles NE of Deering. The name came from Chicota, TX, which was first called Center Springs. It was renamed Chicota when the post office was established in 1880. Col. W. E. Wilkins submitted three names to postal officials, one of which was Checotah, the name of an Indian who had served with the Colonel in the Confederate Army. The name was accepted with a change in the spelling. The post office at CHICOTA, ND closed May 15, 1903 with mail to Granville. (2, 3, 18, 40, 98)

**CHIDA** (Mountrail). This was apparently a mail drop for local residents on the Samuel Steele farm in SE¼ Sec. 18-158-91, Lostwood Twp., four miles NNW of what would become the town of Lostwood. Several sources indicate that a post office existed here, but government records do not support that claim. The origin of the name is unknown. An alternate name was STEELE, which undoubtedly proved confusing with the county seat of Kidder County. CHIDA disappeared after the establishment of the Lostwood post office in 1907. (2, 3, 40, 72)

**CHIHAUN** (Foster). This Soo Line RR station was founded in 1892 in SW¼ Sec. 9-145-65, Bordulac Twp., and given an Indian name of uncertain meaning. In 1895 the name was changed to BORDULAC. Chilhaun and Chemaun are erroneous spellings. (2, 3, 97)

**CHILCOT** (Mountrail). This was a rural post office established November 24, 1896 with Frederick W. Hannah pm. It was located in SE¼ Sec. 8-153-93, twelve miles NW of New Town, and named for an early settler who operated a saw mill in the area. Most believe this man would have been James E. Chilcote, who homesteaded in Sec. 18-153-88, Spring Coulee Twp. Mail was carried here by horseback from Nesson, 26 miles away. The post office closed February 15, 1909 with mail to White Earth. (2, 3, 40, 72)

**CHITUTAH** (McLean). This was a rural post office established January 25, 1886 with Ollie M. Hudson pm. It was located in Sec. 23-146-82, Underwood Twp., two miles east of Underwood, and named for nearby Coal Lake, which the Indians called CHITUTAH, meaning coal. The post office closed June 1, 1887 with the entry "no papers" in the records. It is said to have never sent or received a single piece of mail. (2, 28, 40)

**CHOLA** (Renville). This was a Soo Line RR station in SW¼ Sec. 2-159-84, Lockwood Twp., between Grano and Lansford. The origin of the name is unknown. It appears on several maps circa 1910-1925. (1, 2, 3, 18, 71)

**CHRISTIANI** (Grand Forks). This townsite was platted in April 1978 in SE 1/4 Sec. 35-154-51, Turtle River Twp., and named for the owners of the site, August and Margaret Christiani. Mr. Christiani had come here in the 1870's, operating a grist mill and a saw mill at the site. In July 1879 a new site was platted adjacent to this site, and it was called BELLEVUE. A post office existed just west of here 1877-1902 called TURTLE RIVER. (2, 69, 238)

**CHRISTINE** (Richland). This Milwaukee Road RR townsite was founded in 1883 in SE¼ Sec. 23-136-49, Eagle Twp., at a site midway between the Red and Wild Rice Rivers. The post office was established November 17, 1884 with Johannes O. Manger pm in his general store. There are several stories as to its name, the most likely being that it was named for Christine Nilsson, a Swedish opera singer of that era who was much admired by local settlers. Another theory is that it was named for Kristine Lien Norby, wife of pioneer settler Knute Norby, who wanted to have it named for himself, but townsite officials are said to have disliked both of his names. The village has never incorporated, and generally has had a population of about 150. The elevation is 926, and the Zip Code is 58015. (1, 2, 18, 25, 33, 40, 79, 147, 345)

**CHURCH** (Hettinger). This was a rural post office established July 27, 1912 with Forest Church pm in his country store in NW¼ Sec. 25-135-93, Acme Twp., eight miles north of Mott. It replaced the HOOSIER post office of 1906-1911, which had been located in this store the last two years of its existance. The CHURCH post office was officially named for all seven Church brothers, Forest, James, George, William H., Charles E., Oliver L, and Lester, all of whom came here in 1905. It closed September 15, 1917 with mail to Mott. (1, 2, 3, 18, 40, 53, 178)

**CHURCH** (Ramsey). This was a rural post office established December 12, 1883 with Irvine Church pm. Mr. Church came here in 1882 from Northfield, MN, and operated a ferry service across the Mauvaise Coulee. It was located in SW 1/4 Sec. 7-155-66, Coulee Twp. On November 13, 1886 it was moved one mile north to the GNRR townsite in SW¼ Sec. 6-155-66, and the name was changed to CHURCH'S FERRY. Irvine Twp. (156-67), in Benson County, just west of the new townsite, and Lake Irvine, just NE of the townsite, were also named for Mr. Church. (2, 3, 18, 40, 79, 103)

**CHURCH'S FERRY** (Ramsey). This GNRR townsite was founded in the summer of 1886 in SW¼ Sec. 6-155-66, Coulee Twp., and named for the ferry service operated by Irvine A. Church one mile to the south. Mr. Church moved his CHURCH post office here on November 13, 1886, adopting the new name. The ferry service ended when the coulee dried up, and Mr. Church moved to Alhambra, CA, where he died in 1925. To conform to new government spelling regulations, the name was changed to CHURCHS FERRY on November 30, 1894. (2, 3, 18, 25, 40, 79, 103)

**CHURCHS FERRY** (Ramsey). The GNRR townsite in SW¼ Sec. 6-155-66, Coulee Twp., adopted this spelling on December 1, 1894, dropping the apostrophe from the original CHURCH'S FERRY to conform to new government spelling regulations. The elevation is 1458, the Zip Code is 58325, and the village, which incorporated in 1897, reached a peak population of 457 in 1910. Churches Ferry is a frequently encountered spelling, which may look more correct, but it is an erroneous spelling. (1, 2, 3, 18, 25, 33, 40, 52, 79, 103)

**CHURCHTOWN** (Oliver). This was a community center founded March 12, 1888 in NW¼ Sec. 32-141-84, Church Twp., ten miles SSW of Center. The site included Christs Lutheran Church, a school, and several houses, but no store or post office. For many years a rock and flower garden was maintained at the site, spelling "Churchtown". (3, 121)

**CITY OF DEVILS LAKE** (Ramsey). When DEVILS LAKE incorporated as a village in February 1884, one month after the post office adopted this name, the papers and the plat were filed as CITY OF DEVILS LAKE, no doubt to differentiate the settlement from the inland sea for which it was named. This official name was never in vogue, and in 1887 was changed to DEVILS LAKE, although several detailed county atlases continued to show the longer name for many years. (2, 3, 18, 103)

**CLARE** (Stutsman). This was a farm post office established April 14, 1904 with Martin B. Olson pm at his home in SW¼ Sec. 17-142-66, Round Top Twp., eight miles SW of Pingree. On January 3, 1905 it was relocated two miles SW to the home of new pm Michael Kinnane in NW¼ Sec. 24-142-67, Paris Twp. The name came from the homeland of Mr. Kinnane, county Clare, Ireland. It closed August 31, 1911 with mail to Pingree. (1, 2, 18, 40, 53, 158, 160, 414)

**CLARE** (Walsh). The first plat of the townsite in NW¼ Sec. 33-155-52, Ardock Twp., in 1881 was titled CLARE, probably for county Clare, Ireland. Later plats continued to show this section of town as the "Original Town Site of Clare," but the name never appears to have been actually used by local residents. When settlement began, the site was called KIMBALL, and when that name was found to be duplicated in what is now SD, the name was changed to ARDOCH. Clair and Claire are erroneous spellings. (2, 3, 75)

**CLARENA** (Towner). This was a farm post office established June 25, 1890 with George F. Elsberry pm. It was located in Sec. 6-161-66, Virginia Twp., the site of present-day Rocklake. The origin of the name is unknown, and the post office closed October 18, 1892 with mail to Rolla. (2, 3, 40, 240)

**CLARK** (Sheridan). This town was founded in 1901, and platted in 1902 in SE¼ Sec. 8-146-74, Goodrich Twp., with its name honoring promoter James Clark of Hurdsfield. Five blocks were platted as the "Town of Clark," with main street being called Clark Avenue. A rival townsite, DUDLEY, was platted both east and west of CLARK, and after a few good rounds of country politics, the two merged in 1902 as GOODRICH. (2, 3, 18, 21, 30)

**CLARK CITY** (Barnes). David W. Clark, a printer in Valley City, platted this townsite in 1882 in SE¼ Sec. 11-138-61, Meadow Lake Twp., ten miles SSW of Eckelson, but no development took place. (2, 3, 34, 76)

**CLARKE** (Traill). This was a GNRR station in SE¼ Sec. 18-146-50, Eldorado Twp., between Hillsboro and Cummings. It is mentioned in a state guide of 1890 as GUNDIN FARM, and appears as CLARKE on a 1904 map. It has been suggested that the name honors Hopewell Clarke of Minneapolis, MN, who led an expedition in October 1886 to confirm that Lake Itasca was the true source of the Mississippi River. Starting about 1910 the site is shown on maps as TAFT. (3, 13, 18, 25)

**CLARKE FARM** (Burleigh). The CLARKE'S FARM post office opened August 2, 1880, changing its name to MENOKEN on March 6, 1883. All known postmarks from this office read CLARKE FARM, which is the name used on the post office siting report. (3, 414)

**CLARKE'S FARM** (Burleigh). The NPRR built SEVENTEENTH SIDING in 1873 in Sec. 33-139-78, Menoken Twp., and the first settlers called it BLAINE. A post office called CLARKE'S FARM was established August 2, 1880 with John I. Steen pm, although all known postmarks read CLARKE FARM. It was named for C. J. Clarke of Pittsburgh, PA, the owner of the townsite, who sold it to Col. S. G. Magill of Fargo in 1882. The name of the post office was changed to MENOKEN on March 6, 1883. The NPRR was not happy with this name, and called its station BURLEIGH from 1891 until it closed in 1957. (2, 3, 14, 18, 40)

**CLAYTON RANCH** (Stutsman). This was a ranch, saloon, and stage station on the Fort Totten-Fort Seward trail, founded in the 1870's by "Limpy" Jack Clayton, a colorful and somewhat uncouth character who came here from New York shortly after the founding of Jamestown. It was located in Sec. 22-144-64, Kensal Twp., three miles SW of Kensal, near the banks of Stoney Creek in the Grasshopper Hills. For several years the site, which consisted of little more than several dugout caves, was an important stop on this much-traveled route, but after the railroads were built, it declined, and "Limpy" Jack Clayton moved on in 1883. (3, 25, 158)

CLEMENT (Dickey). This Soo Line RR station was founded in the 1880's in Sec. 18-131-60, Clement Twp., between Fullerton and Oakes. It was named for J. C. Clement, foreman of the construction crew building the grade at the site. Clement is a Latin name meaning merciful. The post office was established June 7, 1888 with Gustavus H. Goecke pm, and closed June 30, 1944 with mail to Oakes. A small village existed here for some time, with a population of 25 reported in 1920, and a count of 10 made as late as 1960. (2, 18, 19, 25, 38, 40, 154, 264)

CLEMENTSVILLE (Stutsman). This was a Midland Continental RR station built in SE¼ Sec. 11-141-62, Rose Twp., seven miles north of Spiritwood, and named for an English stockholder in the railroad. The post office was established March 12, 1914 with pioneer merchant Frank L. Papstein pm. Barney Sorem was the original owner of the townsite, which had grown to 57 residents in 1917, and claimed 125 in 1920. A decline reduced the population to just 16 in 1940, and pm William Rick closed the post office December 31, 1941 with mail to Wimbledon. (2, 33, 38, 40, 79, 158)

CLEVELAND (Stutsman). This NPRR townsite was founded in June 1882 by settlers from Cleveland, OH, which was founded in 1796 by Moses Cleaveland (1754-1806), an associate of George Washington. Like its Ohio namesake, the main street in this town is called Euclid Avenue. It is located in Sec. 3-139-67, Stirton Twp., and Sec. 34-140-67, Weld Twp., and was platted in 1882 by Samuel Reynolds. The post office was established September 21, 1882 with Rev. David Wirt pm, and closed October 2, 1884 with mail to Windsor. After years of stagnation, a second boom began, and the post office reopened October 1, 1900. The elevation is 1874, the Zip Code is 58424, and a peak population of 341 was recorded in 1920, with a decline to just 129 in 1980. It became a city in 1968 with Earl Smith as first mayor. Lenus Carlson, a baritone with the Metropolitan Opera in New York City, was born here in 1945. (1, 2, 10, 11, 13, 33, 40, 52, 154, 156, 158)

CLIFFDALE (McHenry). This was a farm post office established July 11, 1901 with Adam A. Black, a native of OH who came here in 1900, as pm. It was located in SW¼ Sec. 32-158-77, Bantry Twp., three miles SW of Bantry. The name is descriptive, although seemingly not for this location. The post office authorization was rescinded August 10, 1901. (2, 3, 18, 40)

CLIFFORD (Traill). This GNRR townsite was founded in 1881 in NW¼ Sec. 27 & NE¼ Sec. 28-145-53, Norman Twp., and named for Clifford F. Jacobs of Hillsboro, a promoter of the townsite. Others say it was named for a pioneer settler in the area. Clifford is an Old English name meaning dweller at the ford near the cliff. The post office was established February 15, 1883 with George A. Swaren pm, and he was replaced the following year by his brother, Andrew A.

Swaren (1856-1937). The elevation is 1061, the Zip Code is 58016, and a peak population of 175 was reached in 1940. Anton T. Kraabel (1862-1934), a prominent businessman, was Lt. Governor of ND 1917-1918. (1, 2, 3, 18, 19, 25, 29, 33, 40, 79, 187, 394)

CLIFTON (Pierce). This was a GNRR station on the Surrey cutoff line built in 1912 in NE¼ Sec. 20-151-73, Truman Twp., eight miles NW of Selz. It was named by GNRR officials for the Clifton District of Bristol, England, although local folklore says that the name notes its location in Antelope Valley surrounded by high, rocky, cliff-like hills. Clifton is an Old English name meaning from the farm at the cliff. Development was very slow, the post office not being established until October 17, 1938 with Alice H. Lockrem pm. It closed March 31, 1954 with mail to Martin. A population of 7 was listed in 1960, but CLIFTON is a ghost town today. (1, 2, 3, 38, 40, 68, 114)

CLINE (Foster). This was a farm post office established November 22, 1899 with David L. Andes pm. It was located in Sec. 32-147-65, Nordmore Twp., about eight miles NE of Carrington, and named for A. Cline, a bachelor who had come here in 1882 from Carroll County, IL, who would bring the mail to this post office from Carrington on his bicycle. In 1900 the post office moved across the road to the Henry Miller home in Sec. 29-147-65, and closed July 30, 1904 with mail to Carrington. (2, 18, 40, 97)

CLINTON (Divide). This was a farm post office established August 7, 1908 with George Clinton E. Goetze pm. It was located in SW¼ Sec. 17-162-101, Clinton Twp., two miles ESE of Alkabo, and named for the pm and his oldest son. Mr. Goetze had applied for the post office with the name Hillside, but postal officials substituted CLINTON, which is a Teutonic name meaning from the headland farm. The post office closed October 31, 1911 with mail to Norge. (2, 3, 18, 19, 40, 414)

CLINTON (Grand Forks). This was a farm post office established May 24, 1880 with Hezekiah Willett pm. It was located in Sec. 23-149-50, Americus Twp., about five miles NE of Reynolds, and named by settlers from Clinton, IA, which was named by settlers from NY for DeWitt Clinton (1769-1828), a famous politician of that state and unsuccessful candidate for President in 1812. The post office was discontinued March 27, 1882 with mail to Walle. (2, 10, 31, 40)

CLIVE (Barnes). This was a Soo Line RR townsite founded in 1892 in NW¼ Sec. 31-142-59, Rogers Twp., adjacent to the NPRR townsite of Odell, which it later absorbed. The post office at Odell relocated here on July 11, 1893 with Galencia J. Parker pm in her husband's store. The name was intended to be Olive, but an error by a telegrapher resulted in CLIVE, which was accepted by the townspeople. Some say it was named for Clive, England, which is an Old English name meaning cliff dweller. In October 1897 the railroad station was moved to the new townsite of Rogers, and the CLIVE post office followed on April 25, 1898, although yet another error was made,

resulting in the name Roger, which was used until 1917. By the spring of 1899, the CLIVE townsite had been vacated. (2, 19, 34, 40, 76)

CLYDE (Cavalier). This GNRR townsite was founded in 1905 in NE¼ Sec. 14-161-64, Bruce Twp., between Calvin and Munich. The post office was established November 20, 1905 with J. Peter Larsen pm, who named it for the River Clyde in Scotland to please the many Scottish settlers in the area. Clyde is a Welsh name meaning heard from afar, and the river was given this name to note the roar of its waterfalls. The elevation is 1621, and a peak population of 275 was claimed in 1920, but by 1940 the count had declined to just 80. The post office closed August 27, 1965 with mail to Munich. (1, 2,3, 18, 19, 40, 79)

COALBANK (Hettinger). This was a rural post office established July 24, 1917 with William I. Sadler (1891-1963) pm. Mr. Sadler requested his own family name for the post office, but postal officials substituted the name COALBANK, apparently to note the banks of lignite coal in the area. It was located in SW¼ Sec. 5-134-95, Indian Creek Twp., five miles WNW of Regent, and closed December 31, 1927 with mail to Regent when Mr. Sadler moved to Seattle, WA. A population of 10 was reported in 1920. (2, 3, 18, 40, 79, 414)

COAL CITY (Hettinger). This Milwaukee Road RR station was built in 1909 in SE¼ Sec. 28-135-96, Havelock Twp., ten miles SE of New England, and named to note the site's chief economic activity. Local accounts tell of a post office here in August 1909 with E. W. Adams pm, but government records do not confirm this. When efforts were begun to secure a post office, the name Adams was rejected due to duplication in Walsh County, then Adamsville was rejected due to possible confusion with the same. Adrian, for the first baby born here, was rejected because of duplication in LaMoure County. Finally, on June 24, 1910 the post office opened as HAVELOCK. (2, 3, 18, 40, 181, 385)

COAL HARBOR (McLean). This Missouri River port was founded in the spring of 1882 in Sec. 34-147-84, Coal Harbor Twp., and named by site owner George S. Gilbert to note the exposed coal veins at this natural boat landing. The post office was established June 6, 1883 with Mr. Gilbert as pm. Later that year George Laidman Robinson (1842-1923), a longtime storekeeper here, became pm. In 1885 it moved one mile east to the center quarter of Sec. 35-147-84, the site of the town of VICTORIA. This name fell into disuse when the post office retained the COAL HARBOR name. On October 1, 1905 the post office moved seven miles ENE to the new Soo Line RR townsite of COLEHARBOR in NW¼ Sec. 23-147-83, Victoria Twp., continuing to use the old two-word name until January 1, 1923. The old site existed for a number of years, generally known as OLD COAL HARBOR. (1, 2, 3, 18, 28, 40, 79, 387)

COAL LAKE (McLean). This was the terminus townsite on a proposed Soo Line RR spur that would serve a coal mine in SE¼ Sec.

23-146-82, Underwood Twp., three miles ESE of Underwood, and just NW of a small lake called Coal Lake. The mine was operated by Washburn interests around 1920, but closed before the railroad spur or townsite became a reality. (3, 34, 414)

**COBURN** (Ransom). This was a NPRR station in S½ Sec. 5-136-53, Coburn Twp., six miles NE of Sheldon. A post office was established May 9, 1883 with Alonzo B. Rudd pm, but it closed October 4, 1883 with mail to Sheldon. It reopened December 28, 1889 with Robert Kreeger pm, and closed June 15, 1895 with mail again to Sheldon. It opened for the third time on February 14, 1896 with Magnus Johnson pm, and closed for good February 27, 1897 with mail to Sheldon. It was named, along with its township, for Abner Coburn, a former Governor of ME, who bought thousands of acres of land for the NPRR in this area. (2, 10, 25, 40, 77, 201)

**COGSWELL** (Sargent). This townsite was founded in 1889 in NE¼ Sec. 2-130-57, Sargent Twp., and SE¼ Sec. 35-131-57, Harlem Twp., at the junction of the Soo Line RR and Milwaukee Road RR. Some say it was named for a Soo Line RR official, while others say it was named for Maj. Thomas Cogswell, a Revolutionary War hero. The post office was established August 27, 1890 with William L. Straub pm. Most of the settlers in the bypassed towns of Harlem and Sargent moved here. The elevation is 1294, the Zip Code is 58017, and a peak population of 445 was reported in 1920. (1, 2, 3, 33, 40, 45, 52, 166, 167)

**COLBEN** (LaMoure). This was a rural post office established Feburary 6, 1902 with Irene Croswell McLeod (1864-1910) pm. She was born in WI, came to LaMoure County in 1886, and married David McLeod in 1887 in the first wedding performed in Dean Twp. (133-61). The post office was located in NE¼ Sec. 8-135-63, Russell Twp., eight miles west of Dickey on the south bank of Bone Hill Creek, and it was discontinued November 15, 1902 with mail to Dickey. The origin of the name is unknown, although it has been suggested that it was coined from the COLd Spring Co., with interests in the area, and H. GarBEN, a neighbor of the McLeods. Calben is an erroneous spelling. (2, 3, 40, 410)

**COLD SPRING** (Morton). This was a water supply facility on the NPRR mainline between Sims and Almont, probably in NW¼ Sec. 25-138-86, Sims Twp., and named to note its location near Hailstone Creek. Its existance covered no more than two years, as it was soon replaced by facilities built at Bly's Mine. (3)

**COLDWATER** (Dickey). This was one of several names used by townsite promoter M. H. Puffer in SW¼ Sec. 32-130-60, Hudson Twp., now the NE section of GUELPH. The significance of this name is unknown. The others, CENTER, CENTRALIA, CENTROPOLIS, and MENASHA CENTER, all promoted Mr. Puffer's idea of this place becoming the center of area activities. (2, 3)

*Cogswell business district about 1910.*

**COLDWATER** (McIntosh). This was a longtime stopping point in rural eastern McIntosh County, named for nearby Coldwater Lake, which was named for Coldwater, MI, which had been named for the Coldwater River which runs through it. The post office was established August 21, 1884 with Charles Valentine Bayse (1854-1909) pm. It was located on the Bayse ranch, a stopping place on the Bismarck-Ellendale trail, in NW¼ Sec. 3-129-67, Coldwater Twp., fifteen miles east of Ashley. In 1912 it moved to the Selmer J. Kubrud farm in SW¼ Sec. 34-130-67, Beresina Twp., just across the section line from the Bayse ranch. Christopher R. Weisz and Jacob Kosel followed as pms before the office closed May 15, 1918 with mail to Ashley. It was then reestablished April 19, 1923 with Jacob R. Ley pm, at his home in NE¼ Sec. 19-130-67, three miles NW of the original site, and closed for good December 31, 1924 with mail again to Ashley. A general store and gas station were at this site for many years after the post office had closed. (1, 2, 3, 18, 25, 40, 46, 53, 79, 134, 211, 414)

**COLEHARBOR** (McLean). This Soo Line RR townsite was founded in 1904 in NW 1/4 Sec. 23-147-83, Victoria Twp., and named for Soo Line RR official W. A. Cole, with a reference to the historic Missouri River port of COAL HARBOR, seven miles WSW of here. The COAL HARBOR post office, in fact, moved here on October 1, 1905, keeping the old name which was the source of much confusion. Finally, pm John W. Vogel adopted the station name of COLEHARBOR on January 1, 1923. The Zip Code is 58531, and the peak population of 315 was reported in 1950 at the height of construction activity on the nearby Garrison Dam. In recent years the little village has again enjoyed some economic growth as Lake Sakakawea increases as a recreational area. (1, 2, 3, 28, 33, 40, 387)

**COLFAX** (Richland). This GNRR station was founded in 1881 and named for Schuyler Colfax (1823-1885), a former Vice President of the United States who owned land in the area. The post office was established February 10, 1881 with Horace B. Crandall pm, who wrote a history of Richland County in 1886. Because of the many artesian wells in the area, COLFAX is known as "The Fountain City." The elevation is 951, the Zip Code is 58018, and it has maintained a population of about 100 for many years, reporting a population of 105 in 1980. It incorporated as a village in 1954, and became a city in 1968, claiming to be the smallest city in the state with a public swimming pool. (1, 2, 3, 10, 18, 25, 33, 40, 79, 147, 243, 344, 349)

**COLGAN** (Divide). A rural post office was established November 9, 1905 with Mae Colgan pm. Edward L. Colgan, a county commissioner, had established a country store, the first in the area, at this site, NE¼ Sec. 14-163-100, Gooseneck Twp. In 1913 the Soo Line RR built through the area, and a small village began, reaching a peak population of 125 in 1920. The population declined to just 20 in 1960, the school closed in 1963, and the post office closed December 6, 1974 with mail to Fortuna. (2, 18, 31, 40, 73)

**COLGATE** (Steele). This GNRR townsite was founded in 1882 in SE¼ Sec. 33-144-55, Colgate Twp., and named for James B. Colgate, who had purchased 5,000 acres in Steele County from the NPRR in 1880 and was the county's largest landowner. He was the son of William Colgate, founder of what became the Colgate-Palmolive Co. The village never incorporated, but it had grown to nearly 200 people when the Surrey cutoff line was built in 1912, reducing this town's market significance. The elevation is 1167, and the town was platted in May 1898. The post office, Zip Code 58019, opened June 20, 1883 with William Orser (1840-1912) pm, and closed September 30, 1972 with mail to Hope. (1, 2, 3, 18, 40, 41, 99)

**COLLINS** (Dunn). This was a rural post office established July 6, 1905 in Sec. 32-144-92, about eight miles SSW of Halliday. It was named for Ben Collins, who came here in 1904 from WI. His wife, Jane, was the pm. After Ben Collins' death in 1920, she moved to OR, where she died in 1942. The post office closed January 15, 1914 with mail to Marshall. (1, 2, 3, 18, 40, 221, 223)

COLTON (Ward). After the initial settlement at THE FORKS, the party of settlers led by Joseph Lynn Colton (1840-1896) moved one-half mile NW to the higher ground in E½ Sec. 2-155-84, Burlington Twp., and founded the first village in Ward County. Mr. Colton, the founder of Lisbon, left that settlement in 1883 after losing the mayoral election, and operated a general store, hotel, and coal mine at his new home. A post office application was submitted in August 1883 as COLTON, but the name was rejected, supposedly due to duplication in Dakota Territory, although Colton, SD was not established until 1898. On February 26, 1884, the post office was established as BURLINGTON, the first in the county. Coltan is an erroneous spelling. (2, 3, 36, 100, 201, 371)

COLUMBUS (Burke). This post office was established January 10, 1903 with Gustaf Bjorkman pm in SE¼ Sec. 16-163-94, Forthun Twp., but the order was rescinded February 3, 1903. On that date, however, a new order was approved, but with Columbus Larson as pm, for whom the facility had been named. It is thought that this is the only place of this name in the United States not named for Christopher Columbus. An inland town began to form, but in 1906 it moved six miles SE to NW¼ Sec. 32-163-93, Short Creek Twp., the site of a new Soo Line RR townsite. There was an attempt to name the new townsite NEW COLUMBUS, but instead the remains of the old site lingered on as OLD COLUMBUS. The Zip Code is 58727, and a peak population of 672 was reported in 1960. (1, 2, 3, 18, 33, 40, 52, 67, 79)

COLVILLE (Emmons). This was a rural community in Twp. 130-79 in SW Emmons County, south of Winona, which was opposite Fort Yates. It flourished about 1900, and was named for local landowner William Colville, a native of Scotland. Some accounts refer to it as NORTH GLANAVON, years before the Glanavon post office was established. (3, 18)

COMBA (Billings). This post office was established December 13, 1880 with Frank S. Moore pm, located in Sec. 22-140-102, Medora Twp., and serving the frontier settlement of LITTLE MISSOURI and the military post called LITTLE MISSOURI CANTONMENT. This site was just across the Little Missouri River to the west of present-day Medora. The name honored Capt. Comba, the commanding officer of the Seventh Infantry at the cantonment. On November 13, 1883, the post office was replaced by the facility at the new townsite of Medora. (2, 40)

COMMUNITY (Stutsman). This post office was established July 6, 1918 with Mary G. Karr pm in her home in SE¼ Sec. 31-142-62, Gray Twp., on the south shore of Spiritwood Lake. The application was made out with "not yet established" for the name, and after much heated discussion the generic name of COMMUNITY was chosen as a compromise. In 1921 it moved one mile SW to the home of pm Alice G. Wojcik in NE¼ Sec. 1-141-63, Fried Twp. In 1925 it moved one mile east to NW¼ Sec. 6-141-62, Rose Twp., the home of new pm Charles Gospodar, and

finally, in 1937 it moved one mile NE to the home of pm Veronica G. Reck in NW¼ Sec. 32-142-62, once again on the south shore of Spiritwood Lake. The only population figure reported was 10 in 1930, and the post office closed September 14, 1940 with mail to Jamestown. (2, 3, 40, 414)

COMSTOCK (Benson). Settlement began here in 1883, and a Soo Line RR siding was built in the early 1900's. The site, NE¼ Sec. 21-154-68, McClellan Twp., just SW of Brinsmade, also featured a stockyards and an elevator, but no lasting settlement occurred. It was named for Oliver D. Comstock (1864-1945), the site's owner and ND Attorney General 1901-1903. (2, 18, 34, 110)

COMSTOCK (Traill). Settlers first came into this area in the late 1870's, and in 1880 a small settlement began in NE¼ Sec. 5-145-50, Hillsboro Twp. Asa W. Morgan, a native of ME and a resident of Caledonia, established the post office here September 14, 1880, which he named for Solomon Gilman Comstock, also a native of ME, who was a lawyer and politician from Moorhead, MN. The site was platted in September 1880 as HILL CITY, but it was discovered that a place of that name already existed in the Black Hills, so the post office and the town were renamed HILLSBORO on August 12, 1881. (2, 13, 40, 187, 393, 396)

CONCORD (Bowman). This was a rural post office established February 15, 1909 with George W. Lampson pm. It was first located in Sec. 33-129-106, in the extreme SW corner of the county, and moved to NE¼ Sec. 35-129-106 in 1916 with the appointment of Mrs. Lloyd Jones as pm, moving again in 1919 to Sec. 29-129-106 with the appointment of Mrs. Frank Stevens, nee Cora E. Pierce, as pm. It closed August 31, 1925 with mail to Rhame. The name commemoratates the Concord style stagecoaches that ran through this area in the 1870's. The name, popular in colonial times, is said to have been coined in MA as a hope for peace between the Indians and the white man. (1, 2, 3, 18, 40, 45, 120)

CONCRETE (Pembina). Prof. Earle Babcock of UND discovered cement-making clay here in 1891, and a settlement called McLean began in 1892 just across the line in Cavalier County. On August 27, 1908 the McLean post office moved to SW 1/4 Sec. 32-161-56, Beaulieu Twp., with Walter P. Strong pm, and was renamed CONCRETE by Mrs. Webster Merrifield, wife of the UND President, who had an interest in the mine. In 1915 the settlement was moved one mile NW to the site of the new Soo Line RR terminus in NE¼ Sec. 30-161-56. A population of 200 was here in 1920 as the mine prospered, but the cost of transportation soon made the venture impractical, and by 1960 the population had declined to just 10. The elevation is 1214, and the post office, Zip Code 58221, closed December 15, 1984. (1, 2, 3, 18, 33, 38, 40, 79, 108)

CONGER (Burleigh). This was a pioneer settlement in W½ Sec. 22-141-80, Glenview Twp., two miles south of Wilton. Some say it was named for Conger, NY, which was named for Abraham B. Conger, a local politi-

cian, while others say it was named for Conger, MN, which was named by railroad officials for reasons unknown. The post office was established January 11, 1886 with Myron B. Hatch pm, and it closed June 30, 1905 with mail to Baldwin. A population of 12 was reported in 1890. (2, 3, 10, 13, 40)

CONKLING (McLean). This was a pioneer settlement in SE¼ Sec. 15-144-83, Conkling Twp., eight miles west of Washburn, named for Roscoe Conkling (1829-1888), a Congressman and U. S. Senator from NY, who was very prominent at the time. The post office was established April 12, 1883 with James L. Crosley pm, and it was discontinued August 15, 1913 with mail to Washburn. A population of 25 was reported in 1890. Leslie R. Burgum, ND Attorney General 1961-1969, was born here in 1890. (2, 3, 18, 25, 28, 40, 121)

CONNOLLY (Dunn). This was an inland townsite founded in 1908 in Sec. 19-143-94, twelve miles south of Dunn Center, and named for William Connolly, a pioneer area rancher and county commissioner, who along with C. L. Melby and J. W. Bailey, had donated the land for the townsite. A post office was established August 27, 1908 with Erasmus O. Baker pm, and on March 30, 1909 the name was changed to EMERSON. (2, 3, 40, 223)

CONSIDINE (Towner). This was a GNRR station in SE¼ Sec. 27-159-67, Ideal Twp., between Cando and Bisbee, named for Martin Considine, a local pioneer who lived in Sec. 15-159-67, two miles to the north. The post office was established July 5, 1902 with George D. Levitte pm, and it closed July 15, 1911 with mail to Cando. The only population figure reported was a count of just 2 in 1930. (1, 2, 3, 18, 40, 75, 79)

CONWAY (Walsh). This was a farm post office established November 26, 1884 with James Francis pm, who named it for Conway, Ontario, Canada. Conway is a Celtic name meaning hound of the plain. It was located in SW¼ Sec. 11-155-55, Eden Twp., two miles north of the GNRR station called Kelner, which was renamed Conway in 1885. This first CONWAY post office operated only until December 23, 1884, when mail was sent to Kelner. (2, 3, 19, 34, 40, 75, 79, 415)

CONWAY (Walsh). This GNRR station was founded in 1884 in NE¼ Sec. 23-155-55, Eden Twp., and named by GNRR officials for Conway, Wales to please British stockholders. The KELNER post office was at this site, and on January 12, 1885 pm Norman Kelner adopted the new name. A farm post office named Conway, about two miles to the north, had operated for twenty-seven days in late 1884, and may have had some influence in the naming of the station. The village incorporated in 1895, and reached a peak population of 228 in 1890, with a decline to just 33 in 1980. The elevation is 993, and the Zip Code is 58232. Since October 27, 1961 the post office has been a rural branch of Fordville. Lloyd Bennett Omdahl, a former Tax Commissioner and ND Lt. Governor 1987- , was born here in 1931. (1, 2, 3, 18, 25, 33, 40, 75, 79, 253, 293)

**COOK** (Adams). This was a ranch post office established April 22, 1908 with Ella Cook pm. It was located in NE¼ Sec. 15-130-93, Dakota Twp., ten miles NE of Haynes on the south fork of the Cannonball River. The Cook Ranch was run by the pm's husband, Walter Cook, and his brother, Jay D. Cook, who had homesteaded in SW¼ Sec. 15-130-93. The post office closed September 16, 1911 with mail to Lemmon, SD. (2, 3, 18, 34, 40, 414, 415)

**COOKRANCH** (Slope). This was a ranch post office, as the name clearly states, established April 10, 1915 with Charles T. Bock (1881-1959) pm. It was located in N½ Sec. 2-135-99, Moord Twp., thirteen miles ENE of Amidon, and named for Elmer E. Cook, a native of VT who came to Hettinger County in 1888 with the New England colony, and moved to Slope County in 1895, starting a large cattle and sheep ranch. The site was a popular stopping place for travelers, and included a general store for their convenience. W. C. McKenzie purchased the ranch and Mr. Bock purchased the store when Mr. Cook decided to retire in 1910. The post office closed December 7, 1917 with mail to New England. (1, 2, 3, 33, 40, 53, 82)

**COOLEY** (Pembina). This was a pioneer Icelandic settlement in Sec. 24-161-56, Beaulieu Twp. The post office was established March 29, 1881 with Sigurdur J. Bjornsson pm. The origin of the name is unknown. On September 18, 1882 the name was changed to HALLSON. (3, 25, 40, 108)

**COOLIN** (Towner). This was a farm post office established April 17, 1884 with Albert S. Gibbens pm. It was located in Sec. 6-157-65, Coolin Twp., in the extreme SE corner of the county, and named for its township. Several theories exist for the origin of the name. Most sources say that it honors Jacob Coolin, a pioneer saloon operator in the area, or his sons, John and David, who with their widowed mother, operated a store in the area. Others say it was named for Coolin LaCrosse, a pioneer innkeeper in the area, which was sometimes called the Coolin Inn. The post office closed November 15, 1894 with mail to Cando. It reopened March 22, 1898 and closed for good July 15, 1910 with mail to Garske. The last two years of its existance were in the home of pm R. J. Armstrong in NE¼ Sec. 27-157-65, five miles SE of the original site. (1, 2, 3, 18, 25, 40, 53, 102)

**COOPERSTOWN** (Griggs). The townsite was founded in 1882 in Sec. 24-146-59, Cooperstown Twp., and named for bonanza farmer Rollin C. Cooper (1845-1938) and his brother Thomas, who had come here in 1880 after some successful mining ventures in CO. The site was platted in October 1882, and the post office was established December 28, 1882 with George W. Barnard pm. It incorporated as a village in 1892, and became a city in 1906 with John Syverson as first mayor. It became the county seat November 7, 1882 after a bitter fight with Hope. The NPRR reached here in 1883. The elevation is 1430, the Zip Code is 58425, and the population has held at just over one thousand for decades, with a peak of 1,485 in 1970. Edwin Reiten founded the well known plow manufacturing firm here in 1937. (1, 2, 18, 40, 65, 79, 283, 284)

**CORATON** (Dickey). This was an early day settlement in Sec. 20-130-59, Riverdale Twp., six miles south of Oakes, named for Cora Devendorf, a young lady of the community. Cora is a variant of Corinna, a Greek name meaning maiden. An application for a post office about 1882 was rejected, and the townsite failed to develop. This place was sometimes called DeCORA. (2, 3, 19, 40, 154)

**CORBINSVILLE** (Emmons). Benjamin Corbin Sr. (1829-1912), a beloved pioneer of northern Emmons County known as "Uncle Ben," purchased the so-called Wilson place in September 1893. This building, which he converted into a store and hotel, was located in Sec. 31-135-78, about thirteen miles west of Hazelton, or about midway between the old post offices of Livona and Gayton. In 1901 he promoted his business as CORBINSVILLE. The site remained a local landmark until it was torn down in 1966. Corbin is a Latin name meaning raven. (2, 3, 4, 19, 66, 96, 415)

**CORDELIA** (Bottineau). This was a farm post office established March 3, 1893 with Laurits Larson (1855-1911) pm in his country store. It was located in NE¼ Sec. 7-162-74, Cordelia Twp., and named for the township, which was named for a young girl living in the area. The site was about seven miles NE of Bottineau. The post office closed March 31, 1910 when Mr. Larson became ill, with mail going to Bottineau. (1, 2, 34, 40, 101, 153)

**CORDES** (Oliver). This was a rural post office established June 6, 1903 with Christoph Friedrich Skubinna (1862-1936) pm. It was located in NE¼ Sec. 6-141-83, Bremer Twp., five miles SE of Center, and named for Henry Cordes (1851-1947), in whose home the post office was first located. Mr. Cordes came to America in 1868 from Germany, and settled here in 1885. For several years a cheese factory was also located at this site. John M. Walkup and Oswald K. Wildgrube later served as pms before the post office closed August 14, 1909 with mail to Center. (2, 33, 40, 121)

**CORINNE** (Stutsman). This was a rural settlement in NE¼ Sec. 22-144-62, Corinne Twp., five miles NE of Courtenay in the ex-

treme NE corner of the county. The post office was established February 26, 1884 with Dr. Daniel A. Langworthy pm. He was a country physician from Bay City, MI, who came to Jamestown in 1882, and homesteaded here in 1884. It was named for his wife, and for his daughter, Belle Corinne Langworthy, who filed on NW¼ Sec. 22-144-62, just west of her father's place. Corinne is derived from the Greek name Corinna, meaning maiden. The population was 82 in 1890, but after being bypassed by the Soo Line RR, the site declined. The post office closed June 14, 1906 with mail to Courtenay. (2, 18, 19, 25, 40, 79, 158, 415)

**CORINTH** (Williams). This GNRR townsite was founded in 1916 in Sec. 10-159-98, Big Stone Twp., and named for Corinth, NY, which was named for the great city of ancient Greece in the Peloponnesus district frequently mentioned in the Bible. The post office was established January 29, 1917 with Laur S. Evenson pm. The site was at first a thriving village, recording a population of 108 in 1920, but it declined steadily after that date. The post office became a rural branch of Wildrose on May 24, 1963 with the retirement of pm Olaf Haugen, and it became a rural branch of Alamo December 31, 1965, finally closing May 2, 1969 with mail to Alamo. The elevator burned in 1966, and the Lutheran church closed in 1970, leaving CORINTH virtually deserted. (1, 2, 3, 10, 38, 40, 41, 50, 79)

**CORYELL** (Nelson). This place appears on road maps of the late 1930's and early 1940's published by the H. M. Gousha Co., approximately eight miles south of Tolna in Forde Twp. (149-61). It was a copyright town, purely ficticious and inserted to detect unauthorized copying by competitors. (3)

**CORYELL** (Sargent). This place appears on

*Cooperstown about 1905*

road maps of the early 1970's published by the H. M. Gousha Co., approximately in SW¼ Sec. 12-131-57, Harlem Twp., between Stirum and Cogswell. This site happens to be a rural cemetery. CORYELL is a copyright town, and the Gousha people had previously used this same name for similar purposes just before World War II, placing it in Nelson County. (3, 34)

COTEAU (Burke). This GNRR townsite was founded in 1906 in NW¼ Sec. 23-161-90, Ward Twp., and named for the Coteau du Missouri, a range of hills in the area that separates the Missouri and Souris River basins, in effect being part of the north-south continental divide. Coteau is French for hillock. The post office was established February 12, 1907 with F. J. Glenn pm, and on June 30, 1973 it became a rural branch of Bowbells. The elevation is 1994, the Zip Code is 58728, and a population of 150 was claimed in 1920, with a count of just 82 being recorded in 1960. Albert Jacobson coined the nickname "The Biggest Little Town in North Dakota" for COTEAU. (1, 2, 10, 18, 34, 40, 67, 79, 375)

COTTER (Cass). This NPRR station was built in May 1881 at the corner of Secs. 15, 16, 21 & 22-139-49, Barnes Twp., four miles SW of Fargo, and named COTTERS. On July 25, 1915 the name was shortened to simply COTTER. Charles Cotter was an early fireman on the NPRR locomotives of the area. The station was removed in the fall of 1949. (1, 2, 3, 77)

COTTERS (Cass). This NPRR station was built in May 1881 at the corner of Secs. 15, 16, 21 & 22-139-49, Barnes Twp., four miles SW of Fargo. It was served by the Fargo post office, and named for Charles Cotter, an employee of the NPRR since 1870, and the original owner of this site. On July 25, 1915 the antiquated possessive form of the name was changed to simply COTTER. (1, 2, 3, 18, 25, 77)

COTTONWOOD (Griggs). This was a rural post office established July 7, 1892 in Sec. 25-148-60, Willow Twp., about seven miles north of Jessie, with Torger O. Torgerson pm. It replaced the nearby rural post office of WILLOWS, with a name change, so it is said, because this area had more cotton-woods than willows. The post office moved two miles SSE in 1896, and closed January 15, 1900 with mail to Jessie. (2, 40, 65)

COTTONWOOD (Williams). This rural community began about 1904 in Sec. 24-159-99, Rock Island Twp., and was named by Lem Heen, who came here in 1899, to note the large stand of cottonwood trees in the area. When the post office was established in 1907 the name was changed to COTTONWOOD LAKE, and in 1917 it was relocated two miles west to the new GNRR townsite of ALAMO. (2, 3, 33, 40, 50)

COTTONWOOD LAKE (Williams). This rural community was begun about 1904 in Sec. 24-159-99, Rock Island Twp., as COTTON-WOOD, but when the post office was established July 26, 1907 with Nellie E. Mellor Heen (1864-1951) pm, it was moved one mile west to Sec. 23-159-99 and renam-ed COTTONWOOD LAKE, on whose east

end it was now located. A small village began to develop, but a fire in 1911 destroyed most of the buildings. In 1917 it was moved one mile west to the new GNRR townsite of ALAMO, which is Spanish for cottonwood. The post office moved to ALAMO, taking that name, on April 16, 1917. (2, 3, 18, 40, 50, 53)

COULEE (Mountrail & Ward). This is a GNRR townsite founded in 1906 in NW 1/4 Sec. 2-158-88, Lowland Twp., Mountrail County. A tiny portion of the town extends into SW¼ Sec. 35-159-88, Baden Twp., Ward County. It was named to note the deep coulee NE of the townsite. The land for the townsite was donated by William Atkins. The post office was established April 18, 1907 with Marius N. Peterson pm in his hardware store. The elevation is 2058, and a peak population of 125 was recorded in 1920, with a steep decline in later years. Lillian Jacobsen became pm in 1943, and when she retired October 1, 1975, the post office, Zip Code 58729, closed with mail to Don-nybrook. (1, 2, 18, 20, 33, 40, 72)

COUNTY LINE (Morton & Oliver). This was the first stop to the north on the Glen Ullin Northern Stage Line operated 1910-1915 by Gust A. Falk. Its exact location is unknown, although it is said to have been on the coun-ty line NE of Glen Ullin. (3, 105)

COURTENAY (Stutsman). This Soo Line RR townsite was founded in 1892 in Secs. 5 & 8-143-62, Courtenay Twp., and named for a place in England. The post office used an erroneous spelling, COURTNEY, from its establishment in 1893 until June 17, 1905, when pm Henry Theodore Nelson corrected the spelling. The elevation is 1523, the Zip Code is 58426, and a peak population of 539 was reached in 1910. The village, incor-porated in 1902, has declined steadily to just 110 residents in 1980. (1, 2, 3, 18, 33, 40, 52, 79, 158)

COURTNEY (Stutsman). This Soo Line RR townsite was founded in 1892 in Secs. 5 & 8-143-62, Courtenay Twp., and named for a place in England. John H. Reid was the original owner of the townsite, which was platted in 1892. When the post office was established August 9, 1893 with Elbridge F. Horn pm, the name was erroneously spell-ed COURTNEY, and this name was used by the post office until the corrected spelling was adopted June 17, 1905. (3, 40, 158)

COWAN (Cass). This was a farm post office established April 8, 1884 with William Cowan pm. It was located in NE¼ Sec. 22-137-54, Highland Twp., ten miles west of Leonard, and closed October 18, 1888 with mail to Sheldon. (2, 3, 25, 34, 40)

CRARY (Ramsey). This GNRR station was founded in 1883 as MIDWAY, but when the post office was established January 14, 1884 with Alfred Slighter pm, the name was changed to CRARY to honor William A. Crary, the owner of the townsite, and his brother John Hopkins Crary, a local hotel operator. The name was suggested by pioneer settler James Whelan, the elevator agent, and a native of Massena, NY. It is located in Secs. 16 & 17-153-62, Stevens Twp., ten miles east of Devils Lake. The

elevation is 1491, the Zip Code is 58327, and a peak population of 307 was reported in 1920. (1, 2, 3, 18, 25, 33, 40, 52, 79, 103)

CREAMERY (Morton). This was a rural post office established June 12, 1900 with Ed-ward F. Letterly, a native of OH, as pm. It was located in NW¼ Sec. 22-137-81, four miles NNE of Saint Anthony, and named to note a nearby rural creamery. The order establishing the post office was rescinded August 14, 1900. (2, 3, 18, 40)

CREEL CITY (Ramsey). This townsite was founded in 1882 by Heber M. Creel and named CREELSBURGH. On February 28, 1883 Mr. Creel, who was the pm, changed the name to CREEL CITY. The name change is said to have coincided with a slight relocation within SE¼ Sec. 28-154-64, Lake Twp., in anticipation of the GNRR, which arrived here in May 1883. At that time CREEL CITY moved one mile SE to Secs. 33 & 34-154-64, where the new town began to grow at a rapid pace as the site became a center of both railroad traffic, and boat traffic on nearby Devils Lake. On January 10, 1884 the name was changed to DEVILS LAKE. The 1883 population was 521. (2, 3, 25, 40, 79, 103)

CREELSBURGH (Ramsey). Lt. Heber Mansfield Creel (1855-1932) was a topographical engineering graduate of West Point stationed at Fort Totten. The MO native resigned from the military in the spring of 1882 and founded a townsite in SE¼ Sec. 28-154-64, Lake Twp., which he named for himself. The post office was established November 15, 1882 with Mr. Creel as pm. At this time the fledgling town had a population of about 50. On February 28, 1883 the name was changed to CREEL CITY. (2, 18, 40, 103)

CREMERVILLE (McLean). This was a rural post office established June 12, 1913 in the country store of pm Andrew J. Cremer. It was located in SE¼ Sec. 22-150-89, Cremer-ville Twp., about three miles north of Raub, and closed August 14, 1915 with mail to Raub. (2, 3, 28, 40, 289)

CRESCENT HILL (Dickey). This was a Soo Line RR siding in Sec. 26-130-59, Riverdale Twp., about six miles ENE of Ludden. The name seems to have been transferred from somewhere else, as there are no hills in the area. It was served by the Ludden post of-fice. (1, 2, 18, 25, 264)

CRETE (Sargent). This NPRR station was founded in 1900 as ELIZABETH, but when the post office was established February 20, 1901 with Charles Gray pm, the name was changed to CRETE. This was the nickname of Lucretia Steele, daughter of John M. Steele, who sold the right of way here to the

NPRR in return for this favor. Some claim it was named for the island off the coast of Greece. The elevation is 1339, the Zip Code is 58020, and a population of 200 was claimed at various times, although the 1960 count was just 33. (1, 2, 3, 18, 33, 38, 40, 79, 165)

**CROCUS** (Towner). This was a farm post office established June 21, 1898 with Solomon Henricks pm. It was located in NW¼ Sec. 11-160-66, Crocus Twp., four miles north of Egeland, and named for the pasque flower, incorrectly called the crocus, that grows profusely in the area. It is the state flower of SD. In 1906 the post office moved one mile NW to the new Farmers Grain & Shipping Co. RR (later the GNRR) townsite in SW¼ Sec. 3-160-66. A population of 37 was reported in 1920, and a count of 20 was made as late as 1960, but the post office closed January 31, 1955 with mail to Rocklake. (1, 2, 3, 18, 38, 40, 52, 79)

**CROFF** (McKenzie). William B. "Bert" Croff (1869-1954) became pm of CATLIN on March 23, 1915, moving it to his country store in SW¼ Sec. 2-149-96, Bear Den Twp., sixteen miles east of Watford City. On October 29, 1915 he changed the name to CROFF. Mr. Croff, who came here from Alexandria, MN in 1907, ranched about 8,000 acres, and held the pm position until retiring in 1940. Although CROFF was never really a settlement, a population of 10 was reported in 1920, and a count of 9 was made in 1930. Paul L. Gruetzner and Ole Mathistad served as pms before the post office closed July 31, 1945 with mail to Watford City. (1, 2, 3, 34, 40, 229, 253)

**CROFTE** (Burleigh). This farm post office was established January 12, 1885 as CUMBERLAND, and on June 19, 1886 it moved slightly SW, but still in Sec. 4-141-79, Crofte Twp., the home of new pm George C. Wainwright, who changed the name to CROFTE, matching the name of the township which was named for an early settler. A population of 20 was reported in 1890. The post office closed December 31, 1900 with mail to Conger. (2, 9, 12, 25, 40)

**CROMWELL** (Burleigh). This was a rural community in S½ Sec. 22-141-78, Cromwell Twp., nine miles east of Baldwin. The post office was established August 21, 1884 with Catherine Hubbard pm, who named it for Edward Cromwell, a pioneer settler in the area. Cromwell is an Old English name meaning dweller by the winding brook. A population of 25 was reported in 1890. The post office closed May 15, 1909 with mail to Baldwin. (1, 2, 9, 12, 19, 25, 40)

**CROSBY** (Divide). This GNRR terminus station was platted in 1903 in SE¼ Sec. 30-163-97, Fillmore Twp., and named for S. A. Crosby, a Portal businessman involved in the founding of this townsite. The post office was established June 25, 1904 with Samuel S. Nelson pm. In 1908 it was relocated one mile east to SE¼ Sec. 29-163-97, a site crossed by the GNRR and the Soo Line RR, and by this action, in effect absorbing the old townsite of Imperial. When Divide County was organized in 1910, CROSBY was named the county seat, and won that honor officially in the 1912 election. It incorporated as a city in 1911 with

J. C. Rousseau as mayor. The elevation is 1959, the Zip Code is 58730, and a peak population of 1,759 was reached in 1960. The original site became known as OLD CROSBY. (1, 2, 3, 18, 33, 40, 73, 79)

**CROSIER** (Nelson). This was a farm post office established June 27, 1882 with Leonard H. Higgins pm. It was located in NW¼ Sec. 12-150-61, Dayton Twp., two miles east of Tolna. The origin of the name is unknown. In 1901 it was moved two miles south to NW¼ Sec. 24-150-61, the home of new pm Edward Hollander, and had several other locations within this general area before closing August 11, 1906 with mail to Tolna. A population of 15 was reported in 1890. (2, 18, 25, 40, 124, 128, 132)

**CROSSING** (Ransom). This junction of the NPRR and Soo Line RR in Sec. 24-136-55, Liberty Twp., two miles SW of Sheldon, was at first called SHELDON JUNCTION. About 1910 the generic name CROSSING was used for the site, and since 1915 the name has generally been WILLARD. No development occurred here. (2, 3, 18)

**CROSSING** (Richland). This name appears on a 1912 map in SW¼ Sec. 20-133-47, Dwight Twp., three miles north of Wahpeton, and is the site of the junction of the GNRR and Milwaukee Road RR. (3, 18)

**CROSSING** (Sargent). This was a generic name appearing on a 1912 map to identify the junction of GNRR and Milwaukee Road RR lines in E½ Sec. 26-130-57, Sargent Twp., four miles north of Brampton. No development occurred at the site, and it became just an unnamed crossing. (3, 18, 414)

**CROWN BUTTE** (Morton). This is an alternate name for the SAINT VINCENT rural community in NW¼ Sec. 2-139-83, Sweet Briar Twp., twelve miles WNW of Mandan. It takes this name from the nearby butte, and is also the name of a manmade lake just south of the site, near Interstate 94. (2, 3, 107)

**CRYSTAL** (Pembina). This village was founded in 1879 in Sec. 13-159-55, Crystal Twp., and named for the crystal clear water found in nearby Cart Creek. Crystal is derived from the Greek word meaning frost. The post office was established May 26, 1880 with Albert F. Appleton pm. The GNRR reached the site in 1890, when the population was just 78. The village incorporated in 1891, and it became a city in 1893. The elevation is 917, the Zip Code is 58222, and a peak population of 429 was reached in 1950. (1, 2, 18, 19, 25, 33, 40, 79, 108, 366)

**CRYSTAL SPRINGS** (Kidder). This NPRR siding was built in 1873, and named for the numerous springs in the area. The springs had been named by Gen. H. H. Sibley during his Indian campaign of 1863. A townsite was platted in 1882, and the post office opened May 28, 1884 with Augustus C. Sheldon pm, but it closed November 15, 1889 with mail to Tappen. It reopened February 11, 1890, and from December 1, 1895 until May 31, 1910 it was called CRYSTALSPRINGS to comply with new government regulations for spelling geographic names. The elevation

is 1802, the Zip Code is 58427, and the population has never exceeded 100, with just 20 residents counted here in 1960. The famous fountain on US Highway 10 was a popular stopping point for many years until being bypassed by Interstate 94 in 1960. (1, 2, 3, 18, 25, 33, 40, 62, 79, 122, 148)

**CRYSTALSPRINGS** (Kidder). To comply with new government standards for the spelling of geographic names, the post office at CRYSTAL SPRINGS used a one-word spelling of its name from December 1, 1895 until May 31, 1910 when the old two-word spelling was restored. The one-word rule was virtually ignored by larger, established places such as New York, San Francisco, etc., and the sometimes ridiculous results of this regulation are quite obvious here. (3, 40)

**CUBA** (Barnes). Settlers first came here in 1892, and on December 15, 1900 a post office was established with Lewis O. Lund pm. It was located in SW¼ Sec. 27-139-57, Cuba Twp., nine miles SE of Valley City. The township had been renamed in 1895 for Cuba, NY, hometown of area land owner J. E. Weiser, who came here in 1880. Some say it was named by Soo Line RR officials for the large island south of Florida, at that time a colony of Spain. The post office closed January 14, 1905 with mail to Fingal. In 1907 the Soo Line RR came through, and a townsite was platted by John Anderson. The post office reopened July 1, 1907 with Thomas C. Lillethun pm. Development was very slow, with a 1920 population of 50 being the town's high point. The post office closed October 31, 1959 with mail to Valley City. (1, 2, 18, 34, 40, 79, 118)

**CUMBERLAND** (Burleigh). This was a farm post office established January 12, 1885 with Ada Cumberland pm, who submitted CUMBERLAND, Wilmington, Corwin, and Elliott as suggested names to postal officials. It was located in Sec. 4-141-79, Crofte Twp., three miles NE of Baldwin. On June 19, 1886 it moved about one mile to the SW and was renamed CROFTE. (2, 3, 8, 25, 40)

**CUMINGS** (Traill). The GNRR founded this townsite in SE¼ Sec. 30-147-50, Ervin Twp., and named it for Henry Cumings, a GNRR employee in the area. The post office was established January 26, 1881 with William Comfort pm. No real boom occurred, and the population stabilized at about 100. Because the name was often misspelled, the name was changed to CUMMINGS on March 15, 1922. (2, 3, 18, 25, 29, 40, 77, 187)

**CUMMINGS** (Traill). Founded in 1880 as CUMINGS, and named for GNRR employee Henry Cumings, the name of this village was so frequently misspelled that on March 15, 1922 the spelling was officially changed to CUMMINGS. Burnett L. Myers pm at that time. The elevation is 936, the Zip Code is 58223, and the population has remained between 50 and 100 during the entire life of the town. (1, 2, 18, 29, 33, 40, 187)

**CURLEW** (Morton). This was a NPRR loading station built in 1879 in Sec. 27-138-86, six miles NW of Almont. The section house and depot were used until 1917, but little development took place here. It was named by NPRR officials for nearby Curlew Creek, now called Big Muddy Creek, which was named for the long-billed curlew, a large shore bird common to the area during the summer months. The name is derived from the French *curlieu*, meaning messenger. Some sources say it was named for a Capt. Curlew, killed by Indians in the area. It disappeared from maps about 1940. (1, 2, 3, 18, 25, 79, 105)

**CURTIS** (Sheridan). This was a farm post office established December 11, 1908 with Elizabeth C. Curtis pm, who came here in 1903 from IA with her husband, Ben. Curtis is a French name meaning courteous. It was located in NW 1/4 Sec. 32-145-75, Sperry Twp., ten miles south of Denhoff, and closed November 30, 1912 with mail to Denhoff. Cuptis is an erroneous spelling. (2, 3, 18, 19, 21, 40)

**CUSHMAN** (Morton). Although the official name was MANDAN, pm Andre Thompson changed the name of the post office to CUSHMAN on March 11, 1879 to honor local settler Charles Cushman. The name MANDAN was restored September 26, 1879. (2, 40, 107, 343)

**CUSTER** (McLean). This was a Soo Line RR siding in NE¼ Sec. 25-148-84, Garrison Twp., six miles SE of Garrison, serving the Custer Mine, which was established by the Truax-Traer Coal Co. about 1945. It is quite safe to assume that it was named for Gen. George Armstrong Custer (1839-1876), the controversial commander of Fort Abraham Lincoln who died at the Battle of the Little Big Horn. The mine flourished for about twenty years, and a small community developed at the site, reporting a population of 20 in 1970. The siding and the mine are now abandoned. (3, 34)

**CYNCH** (Morton). This was a farm post office established January 28, 1895 with Conrad Hoeffler pm. It was located in NE¼ Sec. 2-136-82, about two miles NW of Saint Anthony, and closed April 8, 1897 with mail to Mandan. The origin of the name is unknown. (2, 40, 107)

**CYNTHIA** (Bowman). This was a rural post office authorized June 21, 1898 with Cynthia A. Stark pm. Cynthia is a Greek name associated with lunar mythology. The Stark home was at the confluence of Spring Creek and the Little Missouri River, about twenty-four miles west of Bowman in what was then uncharted territory. Today the site would be in SE¼ Sec. 13-131-105. The order for this post office was rescinded April 21, 1899. Mrs. Stark served as pm of the Paoli post office at this site 1902-1904. (2, 3, 19, 40, 414)

**CYPRESS** (Cavalier). This was a rural post office established November 20, 1896 with James Kyle pm. It was located about three miles west of Hannah, and named for its township, Cypress (163-64), which was named for Cypress Creek flowing through it, so named to note the evergreen trees along its banks. The post office was discontinued September 9, 1897 with mail to Hannah. (2, 3, 40, 249, 265)

# D

**DAGLUM** (Stark). This was a rural community founded in 1900 about ten miles south of South Heart. The post office was established November 12, 1906 with John O. Daglum pm in his country store located in W½ Sec. 2-137-98, Simpson Twp. Most early settlers were Norwegians coming here from Beresford, SD. The post office closed March 31, 1920 with mail to South Heart. A population of 10 was reported in 1920. A school operated here 1907-1961, when it merged with the New England school district. (1, 2, 3, 18, 40, 74, 385)

**DAHL** (Grand Forks). This was a farm post office established March 13, 1879 with Lewis Knudson pm. It was located in Sec. 6-152-52, Blooming Twp., just SE of present-day Mekinock in the Turtle River valley. The name is an Anglicized version of *dal*, meaning valley in all Scandinavian languages. The post office closed August 12, 1881 with mail to Stickney. (2, 3, 40)

**DAHLEN** (Nelson). This Soo Line RR townsite was built in SE¼ Sec. 14-154-57, Dahlen Twp., in the extreme NE corner of the county. The post office was established August 20, 1913 with George B. "Byron" Frost pm. The township and this community were named for Elling N. Dahlen, who had settled here with his eight sons in 1881. Family members were involved in the area's business affairs for many years. A population of 200 was reported in 1920, but a more realistic count of 75 was made in 1960. The post office, Zip Code 58224, closed June 30, 1983 with mail service now being handled by several rural mail routes, although government records did not record this fact until May 1, 1985. (2, 40, 69, 79, 124)

**DAILY** (Barnes). This post office replaced the SHEYENNE post office just to the north on March 28, 1882 when it moved to the country store of Ole P. Hjelde (1844-1930) in NW¼ Sec. 2-137-58, Oakhill Twp., two miles north of Kathryn. Mr. Hjelde was the first and only pm, and he named the post office for James Daily, who had established the SHEYENNE post office in his home in 1881. Mr. Daily came here in 1879, and was known as an expert builder of wooden bridges. The post office closed November 15, 1908 with mail to Fingal. Dailey and Baily are erroneous spellings. (1, 2, 3, 18, 25, 34, 40, 76, 118, 331)

**DAISY** (Oliver). A post office was authorized February 2, 1907 in the farm home of George Maxwell in SW¼ Sec. 28-143-82, Marysville Twp., about five miles west of Sanger. It was named for the flower common to the area, which derives its name from the Middle English *dayeseye*, or day eye. Postal officials rescinded this order February 27, 1907 before the office had begun operations, apparently deciding that the name would prove to be confusing with Dazey in Barnes County. On March 9, 1907, the post office opened as SILO. (1, 3, 4, 40, 121)

**DAKEM** (Emmons). This was a rural post office established April 21, 1890 with Sarah V. Braddock pm. She was the wife of Edward Braddock, for whom that Soo Line RR townsite was named. The name was coined by combining the state, North DAKota, with the county, EMmons. DAKEM was first located in SE¼ Sec. 20-132-74, fourteen miles ESE of Linton. In 1903 it moved three miles NE to the home of new pm Thomas E. Thorn in NE¼ Sec. 10-132-74. It later moved back to a site near the original location, and closed November 15, 1909 with mail to Linton. (2, 3, 18, 40, 66, 415)

**DAKOTA CITY** (Cass). This was an effort by Frank Durand and David Auge to begin a frontier settlement in 1859. It was located at the mouth of the Sheyenne River in SW¼ Sec. 13-141-49, Harwood Twp., about nine miles north of Fargo. *Dakota* is a Sioux word meaning friend or ally, and its selection as a name for this venture is interesting in that it occurred two years before the establishment of Dakota Territory. DAKOTA CITY was abandoned during the 1862 Indian wars. (1, 2, 3, 77, 199)

**DAKOTA CITY** (McLean). This was a Garrison Dam boom town located in SW¼ Sec. 32-147-83, Coleharbor Twp., across ND Highway 7 (now 200) from Sitka. It was named in 1947 by resident construction workers to note its location in ND. Businesses in the town were a service station and a night club. (2, 3, 28, 387)

**DALE** (Emmons). This was a rural community in NW¼ Sec. 7-129-77, eight miles west of Westfield, and five miles north of the SD border. The post office was established June 13, 1891 with Joseph Clark (1851-1930), a native of England, as pm, and named to note its location in a valley. The post office moved several times within this township, closing November 30, 1923 with mail to Pollock, SD. Over the years, DALE included a church, store, school, Grange Hall, and a stage depot. The original post office building was a log house with a dirt roof. (1, 2, 3, 4, 18, 40, 66)

**DALLAS** (Eddy). This unsuccessful townsite venture was located in NE¼ Sec. 25-148-65, Pleasant Prairie Twp., about three miles NE of Brantford. A perfectly square nine-block site was platted, and the post office was established July 17, 1906 with William A. Coleman pm. It was named for Dallas L. Draper, who came here from IA in 1902. Dallas is a Celtic name meaning dweller by the waterfall. The post office closed October 15, 1907 with mail to Morris, as DALLAS failed to develop. (2, 18, 19, 40, 119)

**DALLAS** (Pierce). This townsite was established in 1910 by the Northern Town & Land Co. in anticipation of the GNRR. It was located in NW¼ Sec. 33-151-72, Hagel Twp., six miles NE of Harvey, and named for Dallas, TX, which was named for George

Mifflin Dallas (1792-1864), a U. S. Senator from PA, Minister to Russia and Great Britain, and Vice President under President James K. Polk. Postal officials rejected the name, however, and the townsite was renamed SELZ. (1, 2, 3, 10, 40, 68, 114)

**DALRY** (Traill). This name appears on several maps circa 1905-1915 at the exact site of ALTON, a GNRR spur and loading station in SW¼ Sec. 21-145-50, Hillsboro Twp., three miles SSW of Hillsboro. The more commonly used name, ALTON, honored Alton R. Dalrymple, and it is assumed that DALRY was simply a shortened version of his family name. One map shows the site as Dalry Siding. (3, 18, 187)

**DALRYMPLE** (Cass). This is a NPRR station built in 1875 in S½ Sec. 31-140-51, Harmony Twp., two miles east of Casselton, and named for Oliver P. Dalrymple, owner of the 75,000 acre Dalrymple Farm, the first bonanza farm in Dakota Territory. The station is still in use, and descendants of Oliver Dalrymple still farm nearby. Shown on some maps as Dalrymple Station, it has always been served by the Casselton post office. (2, 25, 77, 79, 300)

**DANA** (Emmons). This was a NPRR siding built about 1910 in E½ Sec. 16-136-76 at the intersection of the road from US Highway 83 to Braddock, about eight miles to the east. NPRR official E. C. Blanchard named it for Charles A. Dana (1819-1897), a famous journalist. Dana is a Scandinavian name meaning one who comes from Denmark. Little development occurred here, with a population of 10 in 1920 being its only census report, and it disappeared from most maps in the 1960's. The Kertzman post office operated 1919-1922 in NE¼ Sec. 18-136-76, two miles south of DANA. (2, 3, 19, 66)

**DANA'S GROVE** (Bottineau). This was a rural community in Sec. 19-162-75, Whitteron Twp., one mile north of Bottineau. It was located on the site of the first settlement in the county, Oak Creek, and named for Lorenzo Dow Dana, a native of NY who came here in 1893, and was a county commissioner, probate judge, and political activist. "Grove" noted the large stand of trees nearby. Little development took place at the site, which is now a popular picnic spot. (2, 3, 101, 153)

**DANA'S GROVE** (Ramsey). This was a rural settlement on the north shore of Devils Lake in Sec. 12-153-64, Lake Twp., three miles SE of the city of Devils Lake. It flourished for a time in the early 1880's, but disappeared shortly after the name was rejected by postal officials. The origin of the name is unknown. (2, 3, 18, 103)

**DANBURY** (Emmons). This was a farm post office established April 25, 1887 with Mrs. Rachel A. Procunier pm. It was located in

Sec. 12-134-77, four miles SW of Hazelton, and named for the pm's husband, Dan Procunier. Some sources say it was named for Danbury, IA, which was named for Danbury, Essex, England. A population of 25 was reported in 1890. Abraham Lincoln Geil (1865-1940), his father John F. Geil (1831-1904), and Lot S. Koker served as pms at various sites in Sec. 12-134-77 before the post office closed July 5, 1894 with mail to Williamsport. (2, 25, 40, 66, 113, 415)

**DANEVILLE** (Divide). This was a rural post office established May 23, 1906 with Theodore Nelson Fischer pm, and was located in NE¼ Sec. 24-161-103, Daneville Twp., seven miles south of Alkabo. It was named for its township, named to note that many of its pioneers were natives of Denmark, and closed January 31, 1913 with mail to Westby, MT. (2, 3, 18, 34, 40, 415)

**DANIELS** (Cavalier). This was a rural post office established July 28, 1890 with Orville R. Daniels pm. It was located for a time in SW¼ Sec. 3-162-62, Minto Twp., and later moved to NW¼ Sec. 4-162-62. It moved about frequently, for a time being in Grey Twp. (162-63), and closed August 15, 1910 with mail to Calvin. (2, 3, 18, 40)

**DANISH SETTLEMENT** (Grand Forks). This was the name used to identify a tract of land in the vicinity of Larimore, set aside in 1904 by the Elk Valley Land Colonization Company for settlement by Danish immigrants. (2)

**DANTON** (Richland). This was a rural community centered in NW¼ Sec. 34-132-51, Danton Twp., just NE of Wyndmere. The name honored Daniel Nulph (1823-1910), who came here from IA in 1879 with his family as the first settler in the township. (2, 3, 147, 350)

**DANZIG** (McIntosh). Germans from Russia arrived here in the 1890's and named this settlement for the free city of Danzig, or Gdansk, in Poland. The post office was established June 21, 1898 with William J. P. Giedt at his home about eight miles north of Venturia. In 1900 it was relocated to the Soo Line RR townsite in Secs. 20 & 29-131-70, Danzig Twp., retaining the name. This site was midway between Ashley and Wishek, but little development occurred, and the post office closed August 15, 1903 with mail to Ashley. A spurt of activity began in 1911, the townsite was platted, and the post office reopened May 13, 1911, but the population never exceeded 100 as development again slowed. The post office closed for good June 30, 1955 with mail again to Ashley. (2, 3, 23, 40, 134)

**DARBY** (Ramsey). This GNRR townsite was platted in 1912 on the farm of Pat G. Crilly in Sec. 13-154-65, Grand Harbor Twp., just SE of Grand Harbor. The origin of the name is unknown, no settlement ever occurred here, and the site was abandoned in the 1950's. (2, 53, 103)

**DARLING** (McLean). This rural post office was established June 28, 1902 with Arthur Logan Maxwell (1869-1943) pm. He was well known in the area as a politician and businessman. It was named for D. M. Darl-ing, a local homesteader, and was located in SE¼ Sec. 33-148-81, Lake Nettie Twp., about seven miles NW of Turtle Lake. It closed November 15, 1907 with mail to Coal Harbor. (2, 28, 40, 79)

**DARMSTADT** (Oliver). This was a farm post office established September 18, 1916 with Adam A. Buman, or Bumann, as pm. The name was transferred from the city in Germany, and can be translated as sausage-skin city. The order was rescinded July 31, 1917. The 1915 census shows Adam Bumann, his wife Riska, and a young daughter Iola, living in Township 141-87, in the SW corner of the county, and a 1938 county atlas shows H.E. Buman living in S½ Sec. 12-141-87. County records indicate that Adam Buman, or Bumann, never owned land in the county, so the exact location of the post office-to-be is unknown. (3, 40, 121)

**DARTMOOR** (Cass). This GNRR station was built in 1907 in N½ Sec. 28-142-54, Rich Twp., between Ayr and Page. No development ever took place. Some claim it was named for a Mr. Dartmoor, said to be an early landowner in the area, but it seems more likely that the name came from the Dartmoor Forest in Devonshire, England. A high mound in Rich Twp. was known as Dartmoor Hill prior to the founding of the railroad station, which was removed in August 1926. (1, 2, 3, 34, 38, 77)

**DASH** (Towner). This was a rural community originally in SE¼ Sec. 32-164-65, Dash Twp., four miles west of Sarles. It was named for its township, which as a compromise was named for a famous rabbit-chasing dog owned by a pioneer settler. The post office was established June 21, 1890 with William E. Williams pm. In 1900 it moved one mile SE to SE¼ Sec. 4-163-65, Dash Twp., the site of a country store operated by new pm H. P. Poe. The post office closed January 15, 1906 with mail to Sarles, and Mr. Poe moved his store to that new townsite at that time. (2, 3, 18, 40, 208, 240)

**DAVENPORT** (Cass). This townsite was founded in 1882 at the junction of NPRR and GNRR lines in NW¼ Sec. 1-137-51, Daven-port Twp. It was platted by G. E. Channing and Henry D. Cooke Jr. in March 1882, and the post office was established April 6, 1882 with Elmer E. Smith pm. Mr. Channing named the town for Mary Buckland Davenport, a friend in MA who in 1845 became the second wife of William Claflin (1818-1905), the Governor of MA 1869-1872, and later a Congressman from that eastern state. The main street in DAVENPORT is named for Gov. Claflin. The village incorporated in 1895, and reached a peak population of 226 in 1910. The elevation is 912, and the Zip Code is 58021. (1, 2, 3, 18, 33, 34, 40, 52, 77, 79, 303)

**DAVIDSON** (Pierce). This was a pioneer community in Wolford Twp. (157-70), founded in 1883 and named for William S. Davidson, a Williston banker who had once homesteaded in Bottineau County. (2, 3)

**DAVIS** (Ward). This was a Soo Line RR loading station in SW¼ Sec. 12-155-84, Burlington Twp., one mile south of Burlington, serving the Davis Coal Co., which later became the Northern Briquetting Co. L. M. Davis established the first coal mine in the area in 1893. The station appeared on maps circa 1910-1920. (2, 3, 18, 100, 371)

**DAVISVILLE** (Ramsey). This place appears on a 1903 map of ND in Hammer Twp. (157-64), at what was then the temporary terminus of the Farmers Grain & Shipping Co. RR. The name apparently honored William M. K. Davis, a prominent area promoter of the railroad. A townsite did develop in this township, but it was named STARK-WEATHER. (3, 103)

**DAWSON** (Kidder). The NPRR founded this place in 1872 in Sec. 10-139-72, Sibley Twp., and called it THIRTEENTH SIDING. Settlement began in 1880, and the name was changed to DAWSON to honor pioneer settler Joshua Dawson Thompson, or Thomson, who had come here from PA. The post office was established October 14, 1881 with Irving E. Philleo pm. Two of the county's most influential men, William P. Tuttle and Lee C. Pettibone, lived here in the early years,

*Dawson about 1911*

and DAWSON reported a population of 300 in 1890, but it lost the county seat battle to Steele in 1882. The village incorporated in 1917, and reached a peak population of 306 in 1930. The elevation is 1771, and the Zip Code is 58428. Lake Street was paved in 1935, funded in part by Mr. Pettibone, and for a time DAWSON was able to boast of the only paved street in Kidder County. (1, 2, 18, 25, 33, 40, 52, 61, 79, 122)

**DAYOU** (Nelson). A 1902 article by prominent historian Col. Clement A. Lounsberry mentions a DAYOU post office in Nelson County with Charles Dayou pm. Postal and census records yield no confirmation of the existence of either the post office or the man. (2, 3, 40, 423)

**DAYTON** (Morton). This place is listed in an 1890 guide of ND as being in Morton County, but served by the Williamsport post office in Emmons County. This would seem to indicate that its was located in the vicinity of Fort Rice. The Dayton-Clark Land Co. once had extensive holdings in Morton County, but no connection between this place and that firm has been established. (3, 17, 25)

**DAZEY** (Barnes). This NPRR station was founded in 1883 in Sec. 19-143-59, Dazey Twp., and named for Charles Turner Dazey (1855-1938), who came here in 1882 to start a bonanza farm, and donated the land for the townsite. He later returned to his native IL, and achieved considerable success as a playwright. The post office was established January 7, 1884 with John H. Little pm. The elevation is 1453, the Zip Code is 58429, and the village, which incorporated in 1904, reached a peak population of 293 in 1920. (1, 2, 18, 25, 34, 40, 76, 79, 328)

**DEAPOLIS** (Mercer). This pioneer settlement was founded in the late 1880's in NE¼ Sec. 28-144-84, four miles SE of Stanton. The post office was established April 28, 1888 with Herman Danielson pm, who coined the name with the initial of his last name replacing the first letter of Neapolis, a city mentioned in the Bible. The result was a name which could be loosely translated as the goddess city. O. R. Thue later was the pm in his general store, but the post office closed January 31, 1916 with mail to Stanton. Populations of 15 were reported in 1890 and 1910. A cemetery near the site perpetuates the name. Diapolis and Dapolis are erroneous spellings. (1, 2, 3, 18, 25, 40, 64, 79, 232)

**DEASAM** (LaMoure). This NPRR station had been built in 1880 in SW¼ Sec. 6-134-64, Nora Twp., but development did not begin until after 1900. The site, named for pioneer settler Christian S. Deisem, was erroneously spelled DEASAM when the plat was made in May 1905, but the cartographer's error never came into actual usage. (3, 18, 143)

**DeCORA** (Dickey). This was an alternative name for CORATON, a pioneer settlement of about 1882 in Sec. 20-130-59, Riverdale Twp., six miles south of Oakes. Both names were coined to honor Cora Devendorf, a young lady of the community. (2, 154)

**DEEHR** (Nelson). This was a farm post office established June 17, 1891 with Oscar Deehr pm in Sec. 8-149-61, Forde Twp., nine miles SW of Pekin. Mr. Deehr, a native of Germany, came here in 1886 with his parents from Sheboygan, WI, and lived in the area until his death in 1937. The post office closed October 31, 1907 with mail to Pekin. Dehr is an erroneous spelling. (2, 3, 18, 40, 124, 128, 132)

**DEEP** (Bottineau). This townsite was founded in 1905 in SE¼ Sec. 23-160-79, Tacoma Twp., at the junction of the GNRR's Towner-Maxbass line, and the Soo Line RR. It was named for nearby Deep Creek, a tributary of the Souris River. The post office was established November 29, 1905 with William H. Bennett pm. The only population figure reported was 50 in 1920, and the post office closed June 30, 1936 with mail to Upham. DEEP was shown on some maps as late as the 1960's. (1, 2, 3, 18, 34, 40, 79, 101)

**DEEPRIVER** (McHenry). This was a rural post office established March 23, 1901 with August J. Buchholz pm. It was located in SW¼ Sec. 20-159-79, Deep River Twp., eight miles west of Upham, and named for nearby Deep Creek. The post office, which used the then mandatory one-word spelling, closed September 15, 1909 with mail to Upham. (1, 2, 3, 18, 40, 53, 75)

**DEERING** (McHenry). This GNRR townsite was founded in 1903 in NW¼ Sec. 30-157-80, Deering Twp., and named for William Deering of the Deering Harvester Co. of Minneapolis, MN, although some say it was named for a GNRR official. The Peebler post office, run by William H. Allen, moved to this site on November 9, 1903 from its original location one mile to the west in Ward County. The elevation is 1547, the Zip Code is 58731, and the village, which incorporated in 1909, reached a peak population of 194 in 1930. (1, 2, 3, 18, 33, 40, 79, 100, 412, 414)

**DEER LAKE** (Stutsman). This was a rural post office established March 13, 1905 with Elwin L. Pendergast pm, and named for the small lake nearby which had been named to note the large numbers of deer that watered there. The post office was located in Sec. 6-141-66, Deer Lake Twp., twelve miles west of Buchanan, and was closed by pm Lee Wright on May 31, 1913 with mail to Buchanan. (1, 2, 18, 40, 53, 79, 158)

**DEFIANCE** (Mercer). This was a farm post office established December 23, 1908 with Mark P. Malcom pm. It was located in NW¼ Sec. 2-146-90, thirteen miles NNW of Goldenvalley, and named for the old fur trading post of Fort Defiance, which some sources say was is in Mercer County. In 1916 the post office moved one mile south to the home of new pm Emma Kettner in SW¼ Sec. 20-146-90, and closed December 14, 1918 with mail to Dodge. (1, 2, 3, 18, 40, 64)

**DeGROAT** (Ramsey). This was a farm post office established June 10, 1884 with George B. DeGroat pm. It was located in Sec. 24-156-65, DeGroat Twp., five miles NW of Webster. A population of 35 was reported in 1890 as the site developed into a rural community. On July 29, 1895 the spelling was changed to DEGROAT to comply with new government spelling regulations. (2, 25, 40, 79, 103)

**DEGROAT** (Ramsey). This was a farm post office in Sec. 24-156-65, five miles NW of Webster, which had been established in 1884 as DeGROAT. On July 29, 1895 the spelling was changed to DEGROAT to comply with new government spelling regulations. It was discontinued July 14, 1906 with mail to Evanston. (2, 25, 40)

**DEISEM** (LaMoure). This NPRR station was founded in 1880 in SW¼ Sec. 6-134-64, Nora Twp., between Jud and Edgeley, and named for Christian S. Deisem (1848-1919), one of the first settlers in the county and a longtime politician in local affairs.. Mr. Deisem opened a store here in 1880, but development did not begin until the early 1900's. The site was platted in May 1905 as DEASAM, a cartographer's error that never saw actual usage. The post office was established May 22, 1907 with Arthur A. Bunker pm. A population of 50 was reported in 1920, but when the town's general store burned to the ground on January 30, 1943, the post office housed in it closed with mail to Edgeley. The town continued to decline, and the railroad abandonment in 1984 literally closed the book on DEISEM. (2, 3, 18, 40, 79, 143, 144, 152)

**DeKALB** (Ward). This inland town was founded in 1902 in SE¼ Sec. 24-151-86, Ryder Twp., as CENTERVILLE, but that name was rejected by postal officials because of duplication in SD. The name DeKALB was selected, but was similarly rejected. The origin of this name is unknown, but traces to Johann, Baron de Kalb (1721-1780), a German-born French soldier who fought with the Americans in the Revolutionary War. This townsite next chose the name RYDER, which was accepted, and after being relocated in 1906 to the nearby Soo Line RR branchline, it became a thriving village. (2, 3, 10, 100, 277)

**DELAHUNT** (Bowman). This was a farm post office established August 27, 1915 with Inez Fulks pm at the farm of her husband, John W. Fulks, in SW¼ Sec. 15-131-106, Sunny Slope Twp., sixteen miles WSW of Rhame. It was named for their neighbor, Charles Delahunt, who lived two miles to the SW in SE¼ Sec. 29-131-106, and closed April 30, 1918 with mail to Marmarth. (1, 2, 3, 18, 34, 40, 415)

**DeLAMERE** (Sargent). This NPRR station was founded in 1885 in Sec. 9-132-53, Hall Twp., and named for Thomas DeLamere of Brainerd, MN, a dispatcher for the NPRR in its early years. The post office was established May 28, 1886 with John Rustad, the town's founder, as pm. From December 1, 1895 to November 30, 1905 the post office name was spelled DELAMERE to comply with government regulations. The elevation is 1086, and the village reached a peak population of 220 in 1930, declining to just 103 in 1960. The post office, Zip Code 58022, became a rural branch of Milnor March 12, 1965, and closed March 6, 1982. (1, 2, 3, 18, 33, 38, 40, 79, 171)

**DELAMERE** (Sargent). The post office at the village of DeLAMERE changed its spelling to DELAMERE on December 1, 1895 to conform to new government specifications for geographic names. It reverted to the original spelling on November 30, 1905. (3, 40)

**DELGER** (Wells). This was a farm post office established March 20, 1900 with Caleb, or Conrad, A. B. Delger (1838-1920) as the first and only pm. It was located in NW¼ Sec. 4-147-72, Delger Twp., nine miles north of Chaseley, and mail was supplied from Bowdon. The first settlers in the area were Mennonites from Freeman, SD. The post office was discontinued February 15, 1903 with mail to Manfred. (2, 18, 40, 79, 267, 364)

**DELL** (Kidder). This was a farm post office established May 27, 1907 with Martha Dell pm. It was located in Sec. 20-144-70, Rexin Twp., twelve miles NNW of Pettibone, but the order was rescinded November 7, 1907 before the office had gone into operation. (2, 3, 18, 40)

**DELNO** (Cass). This was a rural post office established June 28, 1880 with Joseph Sayer pm. It was located in NW¼ Sec. 12-143-52, Hunter Twp., and is said to have been named for Francis Roach Delano (1823-1887), who came to MN in 1853 from his native MA, and had a long career in railroads and politics. No explanation is given for the change in spelling. On June 15, 1881 the post office was replaced by the facility at the new NPRR, later GNRR, townsite of Hunter. (2, 3, 13, 40, 77, 298, 415)

**DELTA** (Mountrail). This GNRR siding was built in the late 1880's in NE 1/4 Sec. 14-156-89, McGahan Twp., and called DELTA for unknown reasons. H. O. Phelps was the first section foreman, and the site was served by the Des Lacs post office. When settlement began in 1904, the settlers began using the name RONESS, and later BLENHEIM. A post office was established in 1905, and it was named GRENADA, but this name was unpopular with many local residents, who began calling the town HANLEY. This name was rejected by postal officials because of possible confusion with Stanley. Finally, on October 21, 1905, the name was changed to BLAISDELL. (2, 25, 40, 72)

**DeMORES** (Golden Valley). This was a NPRR siding in Sec. 24-140-104, Sentinel Twp., five miles east of Sentinel Butte. It was named for Antoine Amedee Marie Vincent Manca de Vallombrosa, the Marquis de Mores (1858-1896), the flamboyant French nobleman who played a major role in the early history of nearby Medora. A population of 4 was reported here in 1930. (1, 2, 3, 18, 34, 79)

**DEMORES** (Slope). This was a rural post office established August 4, 1908 with Caroline C. Desforges pm. It was located in S½ Sec. 11-133-102, Cash Twp., twelve miles SW of Amidon, and named for the Marquis de Mores, the legendary pioneer of Medora, with the spelling modified to comply with current government spelling regulations. The pm, however, declined her appointment. On January 20, 1909 Theodore Gilbertson

was appointed as pm, but he renamed the post office BESSIE. (2, 3, 40, 82)

**DeMORRIS** (Kidder). This was a farm post office established August 6, 1884 with Robert B. Burslem pm. It was located in SE¼ Sec. 18-141-73, Haynes Twp., eight miles SSE of Tuttle, and closed November 15, 1887 with mail to Steele. The name is thought to be a misspelling of DeMores, intentional or otherwise. The Marquis de Mores, the famous pioneer of Medora, and his brother-in-law, Nicholas von Hoffman, owned thousands of acres of Kidder County farmland at this time as part of their planned beef packing empire. (2, 3, 18, 25, 40, 122)

**DENBIGH** (McHenry). This GNRR station was founded in the 1890's in SE¼ Sec. 20-156-77, Denbigh Twp., and named for Denbigh, Wales, the birthplace of the explorer Henry M. Stanley. Others say it was named for Basil Fielding, the Earl of Denbigh (1719-1799), an aide to Kings George II and George III. The post office was established May 12, 1900 with James A. Pendroy pm. The elevation is 1523, and a population of 250 was reported in 1920, with a decline to just 37 in 1960. The post office, Zip Code 58732, closed April 29, 1988. (1, 2, 3, 18, 40, 45, 79, 240)

**DENEVITZ** (Logan). When this community was founded in 1904 in Sec. 15-133-67, Haag Twp., settlers from Dennewitz, Bessarabia gave it an Anglicized version of the name of their hometown, which had been settled in 1834 by German Evangelicals. A store and elevator were built, but when the post office was established February 1, 1905, the name was changed to FREDONIA. (2, 23, 40, 79, 116, 334)

**DENGATE** (Morton). This was a NPRR siding built in June 1946 in Secs. 22 & 23-139-87, midway between New Salem and Glen Ullin on the newly rerouted mainline. It was named in honor of Pvt. Roy William Dengate (1915-1943), a Jamestown employee of the NPRR who was killed in World War II, and is buried in the famous Punchbowl cemetery in Honolulu, HI. His father, William J. Dengate, came to Jamestown in 1917 from Albert Lea, MN, and was a longtime NPRR employee. The siding never experienced any development, but the name became familiar to motorists as Exit #24 on Interstate 94, just north of the siding at the junction of Secs. 10, 11, 14, & 15-139-87. (2, 3, 34, 107)

**DENHOFF** (Sheridan). This NPRR station was founded in 1901 in SW¼ Sec. 8-146-75, Denhoff Twp. The post office was established December 21, 1901 with John Steinbrecker pm, who named it for his former hometown of Alt-Donhoff, South Russia, which had been settled in 1766 by Germans, who named it for Count Donhoff of Berlin. The Russian name for the village was Cololobowka. The elevation is 2042, the Zip Code is 58430, and a peak population of 323 was recorded in 1920. (1, 2, 3, 21, 23, 30, 33, 40, 79, 93)

**DENNEY** (Pierce). This GNRR townsite was platted by Comstock & White of Moorhead, MN in SE¼ Sec. 14-158-74, Barton Twp., and named for a popular conductor on this branch line. The post office was establish-

ed July 7, 1887 with Christian Evanson pm. A small village began which tried unsuccessfully to capture the county seat in 1889. The 1890 population was listed as 40. On June 13, 1893 the name was changed to BARTON. Denny is an erroneous spelling. (2, 3, 25, 40, 114, 414)

**DENVER** (Rolette). This was a rural post office established January 13, 1901 with William C. Tabor pm. It was located in Sec. 25-159-73, South Valley Twp., eleven miles SW of Rolette. The origin of the name is unknown. The post office closed June 30, 1908 with mail to Barton. (2, 3, 40, 53, 123)

**DERRICK** (Ramsey). This GNRR station was founded in 1891 in SE¼ Sec. 29-158-61, Prospect Twp., between Edmore and Hampden. The name notes a high derrick used to support a lantern to guide nighttime travelers. Some sources say it was named for P. O. Derrick, a pioneer settler in the area, although a search of original records did not locate such a person. Derrick is a Teutonic name meaning ruler of the people. The post office was established May 14, 1900 with Joseph E. Moscrip pm. His brother, John T. Moscrip, moved to Saskatchewan, Canada in 1911 and founded a town called Derrick. A population of 100 was claimed in 1920, but a rapid decline reduced the count to just 12 in 1960. The general store was razed in 1955, the post office closed April 30, 1957 with mail to Edmore, and the last church services were held in 1979. The site is now vacant. (1, 2, 3, 18, 19, 40, 79, 103)

**DESART** (Slope). This was a farm post office established October 25, 1906 with Ora R. DeSart (1850-1916) pm. Mr. DeSart and his wife, nee Anna Hill, came here in 1905 from IA, although they were both natives of WI. The post office was located in SE¼ Sec. 18-134-98, Carroll Twp., fourteen miles ESE of Amidon. In 1911 it moved four miles SE to NW¼ Sec. 35-134-98, where a small settlement began to develop. On June 19, 1912 the name was changed to DeSart, the correct spelling of the first pm's name. The original spelling had been required, even though erroneous, to comply with government spelling regulations. (2, 3, 40, 53)

**DeSART** (Slope). This was a rural settlement in NW¼ Sec. 35-134-98, Carroll Twp., about seventeen miles SE of Amidon. It had been founded about 1911, and took its name from the nearby farm post office, which moved here that year as DESART. On June 19, 1912 pm Ora R. DeSart officially changed the name to DeSART following the lifting of unpopular government regulations on the spelling of place names. A population of 75 was reported in 1920, but by 1960 the count had declined to just 6. The post office was closed by pm Robert Krenz on August 31,

1955 with mail to Reeder. (1, 2, 3, 18, 38, 40, 82)

**DES LACS** (Ward). This was a rural community along the GNRR tracks in SE 1/4 Sec. 11-155-85, Des Lacs Twp. A post office was established March 15, 1888 with Tobias Welo pm, who named it for the nearby lakes and river. The name is literally translated from the French as the lakes. The post office closed July 6, 1898 with mail to Minot. A townsite was platted in 1900, and the post office reopened July 27, 1900 as DESLACS to comply with government spelling regulations, changing back to the two-word spelling on February 15, 1948. Fred B. Becker (1865-1934) is considered to be the first resident of the new townsite, which incorporated as a village in 1911, and reached a peak population of 211 in 1980. The elevation is 1931, and the Zip Code is 58733. (1, 2, 3, 18, 33, 40, 79, 100, 373)

**DESLACS** (Ward). This post office in SE¼ Sec. 11-155-85, Des Lacs Twp., operated 1888-1898 as DES LACS, but when it was reestablished July 27, 1900 the name was spelled as one word to comply with government regulations for the spelling of geographic names. The village received national attention in 1922 when all eight elective positions were captured by women. On February 15, 1948 the original two-word spelling was restored by popular demand. (2, 3, 40, 100)

**DeVAUL** (Morton). This was a farm post office established September 9, 1905 with Elmer H. DeVaul pm. It was located in NE¼ Sec. 30-136-84, DeVaul Twp., nine miles NNE of Flasher. Mr. DeVaul ran a general store at this site, and was a promoter of the nearby Heart River bridge which was built in 1908. Otis Malone (1875-1945) took over the operation in 1909, and closed the post office April 30, 1914 with mail to Heart. He later moved to Almont, where he served as pm of that city 1934-1945. (1, 2, 17, 18, 40, 107)

**DeVILLO** (Richland). This was a Soo Line RR station built in 1880 in Sec. 20-130-47, Fairmount Twp. The post office was established July 12, 1880 with Warren Spaulding pm. Noah Davis chose the name, honoring DeVillo Crafts, a relative of the pm. On June 5, 1884 the name was changed to FAIRMOUNT. (2, 3, 18, 40, 355)

**DeVILLO** (Richland). This was a rural post office established September 3, 1888 with Jacob Keller pm. It was located in SE¼ Sec. 24-130-48, DeVillo Twp., two miles west of Fairmount, which had originally been named DeVillo in 1880. The name honored DeVillo Crafts, a relative of Fairmount's first pm, Warren Spaulding. On July 29, 1895 the spelling was changed to DEVILLO to comply with new government regulations, and on October 21, 1895 the post office closed with mail to Fairmount. The site had developed into a thriving little village at a new Soo Line RR station, and reported a population of 22 in 1890. Charles Whitehead (1873-1959) managed the local elevator 1907-1959, but after his death, use of the station declined, and DeVILLO is now virtually abandoned. (1, 2, 3, 25, 40, 147, 355)

*Devils Lake about 1908*

**DEVILLO** (Richland). This spelling was adopted July 29, 1895 by the DeVILLO post office to comply with government spelling regulations for geographic names. The DEVILLO post office closed October 21, 1895 with mail to Fairmount, although the site remained an active Soo Line RR shipping point until 1959. (3, 40, 355)

**DEVILS LAKE** (Ramsey). This city was founded in 1882 as CREELSBURGH, and was also known as CREEL CITY before the post office adopted the name DEVILS LAKE on January 10, 1884 with Henry C. Hansbrough pm. It incorporated as a village the following month, officially taking the name CITY OF DEVILS LAKE, and it became a city in 1887 with Mr. Hansbrough as the first mayor. It has been from its beginning the major city between Grand Forks and Minot, reaching a peak population of 7,441 in 1980. The elevation is 1469, the Zip Code is 58301, and it is the county seat of Ramsey County. It sprawls over five sections of Lake Twp. (153 & 154-64), just north of the large lake of this name, which owes its name to a misunderstanding by French explorers of the Indian name for the lake, *Mini-waukan*. Among the native sons of DEVILS LAKE are William Lewis Guy, Governor of ND 1961-1973, and John T. "Jack" Traynor, a lawyer and Past Grand Exalted Ruler of the Benevolent and Protective Order of Elks, a national service club. (1, 2, 3, 18, 25, 33, 40, 52, 79, 103)

**DEVIL'S LAKE AGENCY** (Benson). This was the headquarters of the Devils Lake Indian Reservation, the predecessor of the Fort Totten Indian Reservation. It was located near Fort Totten in Totten Twp. (152-65), and was served by the new NPRR branch line from Jamestown, and the Jamestown post office during the 1880's. (3, 25, 423)

**DEWAR** (Walsh). This was a Soo Line RR loading station built in 1911 in NE 1/4 Sec. 17-155-56, Medford Twp., five miles NW of Fordville. It is said to have been named for an uncle of Mrs. Victor Potulny of Fordville. Albert Harazim was the elevator manager here 1916-1935, but no major development

ever occurred. DeWar is an erroneous spelling. (1, 2, 3, 75, 254, 293)

**DEWEY** (Pembina). This was a townsite in SW¼ Sec. 4-161-54, Cavalier Twp., promoted by George Adam Douglas, who named it for Admiral George Dewey (1837-1917). Postal officials rejected this name, and the post office was established June 20, 1877 as DOUGLAS POINT. On that same date the Cavalier post office was established just to the west, and a few weeks later the DOUGLAS POINT post office was discontinued. The city of Cavalier now covers both sites. (3, 25, 40, 414, 415, 440)

**DEXTER** (Kidder). This was a mail distribution service run by Byron William Dexter (1850-1919), and his wife, the former Isabella McCoy (1859-1950), at their home in NE¼ Sec. 4-137-72, Bunker Twp., ten miles south of Dawson. Some sources refer to the place as BUNKER. The Dexters came here in 1907, and were highly respected pioneers in the area. Dexter is Latin for right-handed. Mrs. Dexter operated a post office at this site in 1916-1919, but postal officials rejected the name DEXTER, and named it PORTNER. (1, 2, 3, 18, 19, 122, 414)

**DEXTER** (Richland). This was a pioneer townsite platted in March 1880 in SE¼ Sec. 24-132-52, Dexter Twp., three miles south of Wyndmere. It was named for Dexter Carlton, who with his sons Lowell and George, were the first settlers in the area. No development occurred at the site. (2, 3, 243)

**DIAMOND** (Morton). This was a rural post office established July 6, 1905 with Harry W. Potter (1856-1909) pm, and located on the Diamond C Ranch in SE 1/4 Sec. 1-134-82, New Hope Twp., six miles north of Breien. Mr. Potter, who came here in 1903 from IA, was killed in a train wreck, and the post office moved two miles SW to SE¼ Sec. 14-134-82, closing June 15, 1911 with mail to Timmer. (2, 3, 17, 18, 40, 107, 414)

**DICKEY** (LaMoure). This NPRR townsite was founded in 1884 in Sec. 3-135-62, Roscoe

Twp., just south of the pioneer settlement of SARATOGA. It was named for Alfred M. Dickey (1846-1901), the original homesteader of this site, who came here in 1880 from IN, was a partner in the Wells-Dickey Land Company, and served as Lt. Governor of ND. Dickey County is also named for him. The post office was established October 28, 1884 with John C. Courtney pm. It incorporated as a village in 1907, reached a peak population of 203 in 1940, and became a city in 1968. The elevation is 1384, and the Zip Code is 58431. John Arthur Youngman (1886-1961) was the NPRR depot agent here from 1907 until his death, and holds the national record for tenure in such a position. (1, 2, 3, 19, 18, 25, 33, 40, 52, 79, 139)

**DICKEY'S LANDING** (LaMoure). This was a pioneer boat landing on the James River in Sec. 3-135-62, Roscoe Twp., located on the Alfred M. Dickey homestead. This section also contained the pioneer settlement of SARATOGA, and in 1884 became the site of the NPRR townsite of DICKEY. DICKEY'S LANDING was still shown as a separate place into the 1890's. (2, 25, 139)

**DICKINSON** (Stark). This site was named PLEASANT VALLEY SIDING in 1880, but was renamed in 1881 for Wells Stoughton Dickinson (1828-1892), a land agent and politician from Malone, NY, who had visited here in 1880. His brother, Horace L. Dickinson, lived here to oversee its development. The post office was established October 6, 1881 with F. H. Longley pm. It became the county seat in 1883, incorporated as a village in 1899, and became a city in 1900 with Daniel Manning mayor. The elevation is 2430, the Zip Code is 58601, and the city has shown a steady growth, reaching a population of 15,893 in 1980. Dickinson State University opened here in 1921. DICKINSON is a NPRR division point, has played a leading role in the energy boom, and is the major city of SW ND. (1, 2, 3, 18, 25, 33, 34, 40, 52, 74, 79, 406)

**DILLINGHAM** (McLean). This was a farm post office established April 18, 1891 with James Dillingham pm. It was located in SE¼ Sec. 2-149-80, Horseshoe Valley Twp., sixteen miles north of Turtle Lake, and closed August 18, 1893 with mail to Turtle Lake, then a rural post office itself. (2, 3, 28, 40)

**DIMOCK** (Pembina). This was a GNRR station established in Sec. 26-160-53, Saint Thomas Twp., two miles north of Saint Thomas. Promoters predicted that it would become the county seat, but this hope was never realized as development failed to occur. The post office was established August 3, 1882 with John McIntyre pm, who named it for his hometown of Dimock, PA, which was named in 1832 for Dr. Davis Dimock, a pioneer physician and county judge. The PA city is near McIntyre Hill, likely named for a relative of the pm. The post office closed October 10, 1882 with mail to Saint Thomas. Dirnock is an erroneous spelling. (2, 40, 251, 252)

**DION LAKE** (Rolette). This was a farm post office established October 23, 1906 with John C. Hathaway pm. It was first located in NE¼ Sec. 6-163-71, Hutchinson Twp., nine miles WNW of Saint John, but was later relocated across the section line to SE¼ Sec. 31-164-71, Hutchinson Twp. It closed August 15, 1910 with mail to Carpenter. The name noted nearby Dion Lake, named for Pascal and Joseph Dion who settled here in 1885. Dion is derived from Dionysos, the Greek god of wine. (2, 18, 19, 40, 123)

**DISSMORE** (Nelson). This was a farm post office established January 23, 1901 with William A. Dissmore pm. It was located in SW¼ Sec. 21-151-61, Leval Twp., five miles NW of Tolna, and closed October 31, 1908 with mail to Lakota. Dinsmore and Dismore are erroneous spellings. (2, 3, 40, 124)

**DIVIDE** (Divide). This place appears on a 1930 roadmap published by the General Drafting Co., and like several others on this map, is believed to be a copyright town using its county name. It is shown about seven miles SSE of Alkabo, probably in Writing Rock Twp. (161-101). (3, 50, 73)

**DIVIDE** (Eddy). This was a NPRR station between New Rockford and Sheyenne in NW¼ Sec. 33-150-66, Gates Twp. A post office was established September 27, 1907 with John Moe, who also ran a general store, as pm. The elevation is 1632, and it was named to note its location on the north-south continental divide. Settlement never materialized, and the post office closed March 15, 1910 with mail to Sheyenne. (1, 2, 40, 112)

**DIXBORO** (Mercer). This place appears on a 1936 roadmap published by the H. M. Gousha Company, located just across the Morton County line about midway between Glen Ullin and Zap. It is a copyright town, purely ficticious and put on the map to detect unauthorized copying by competitors. (3)

**DODGE** (Dunn). This NPRR station was founded in 1914 in Sec. 10-144-91, Loring Twp. Railroad official Lee C. Pettibone named it for George W. Dodge, a banker from Anoka, MN who owned the townsite, although local residents had suggested Loring or Mittelstedt as the name of the town. The post office was established December 21, 1915 with Hans A. Burgess pm. The elevation is 2004, the Zip Code is 58625, and the village, which incorporated in 1917, reached a peak population of 251 in 1950. (1, 2, 3, 18, 33, 40, 52, 79, 222)

**DOGDEN** (McHenry). This rural post office operated June 30, 1890 to November 13, 1897 in McLean County. It was reestablished March 4, 1898 with Matilda J. Jones pm in SW¼ Sec. 32-151-79, Olivia Twp., in McHenry County, about seven miles NNW of the original location. On February 12, 1900 it moved one mile SE to the home of new pm Frank B. Park in NW¼ Sec. 4-150-79, Butte Twp., once again in McLean County. (2, 3, 28, 40, 414)

**DOGDEN** (McLean). This was a rural post office established June 30, 1890 with John E. Park pm, and named for the nearby landmark, Dogden Butte. It was located in NW¼ Sec. 34-150-79, Butte Twp., eight miles SW of Butte, and closed November 13, 1897 with mail to Velva. It was reestablished March 4, 1898 in McHenry County, about seven miles NNW of the original location. On February 12, 1900 it moved one mile SE to the home of new pm Frank B. Park in NW¼ Sec. 4-150-79, and was once again in McLean County. In 1902 it moved one mile SW to the home of pm Emma Perley in SW¼ Sec. 5-150-79, and changed its name to PERLEY on September 6, 1904. A new townsite was founded in 1906, taking the name Dogden, and the PERLEY post office closed in 1907. (2, 3, 28, 40, 414, 415)

**DOGDEN** (McLean). This Soo Line RR townsite was founded in 1906 in SW¼ Sec. 4-150-78, and named for the nearby landmark, Dogden Butte, which was the site of many wolf dens. Verendrye had called it *Maison de Chien*, or Prairie Dog's Home. The post office was established August 27, 1906 with John Schroth pm. DODGEN grew quickly, reaching a peak population of 320 in 1910. On January 2, 1927 the name was changed to BUTTE, also in recognition of the nearby landmark. This change was

*Dickinson about 1920*

generally opposed by local citizens, who liked their unusual name, but it is said that the change was mandated by postal and railroad officials who found the name to be frequently confused with Doyon. (1, 2, 3, 18, 28, 40, 79, 357)

**DOGTOOTH** (Grant). This place began as the third stage station on the 1876 Bismarck-Deadwood trail, located in NW¼ Sec. 11-133-85, Raleigh Twp., and named for the nearby range of sandstone buttes, said to resemble the molars of a dog's lower jaw when viewed from the east. The stage station closed in the 1880's after completion of the NPRR, but settlers began coming into the area, and a post office was established at this site on March 20, 1900 with Robert Pearce pm. Charles C. Leonard operated a store at the site, and became the first pm at Raleigh, the new Milwaukee Road RR townsite one mile to the ENE, when the DOGTOOTH post office moved there October 1, 1910. (2, 3, 17, 40, 79, 174, 177, 414, 418)

**DOKKEN** (Bottineau). This farm post office was established October 14, 1901 with Ole N. Dokken pm in his country store in SE¼ Sec. 3-162-82, Sherman Twp., seven miles south of Antler. The post office was later located in Sec. 10-162-82, the home of pm Sherman Hatton, and closed August 31, 1909 with mail to Antler. Dakken and Bokken are erroneous spellings. (1, 2, 3, 34, 40, 101, 153)

**DOLAN** (Adams). This post office in Secs. 22 & 23-130-97, Bucyrus Twp., was established as WOLF BUTTE. On September 14, 1907 pm William N. Worra changed the name to DOLAN, honoring C. R. Dolan, a Milwaukee Road RR employee who had built the grade through this site, then decided to stay and build a general store. The new name was found to be confusing with Doland, SD, and on February 11, 1908 the name was changed to BUCYRUS. (2, 3, 40, 189)

**DOLAND** (Wells). This was a Soo Line RR station built in 1893 in SW¼ Sec. 31-148-69, Germantown Twp. The origin of the name is unknown, and almost immediately it proved to be confusing with Doland, SD, so before the year was over this site was renamed EMRICK. (2, 18, 79)

**DON** (Stutsman). This was a NPRR siding built in 1905 in SE¼ Sec. 35-140-68, Flint Twp., three miles east of Medina. Some sources credit the name to Mrs. Alton M. Burt, wife of the Superintendent of the NPRR's Dakota Division, who cited the Don River of Russia, while others say it was named for Don S. Colb, a NPRR work train conductor for the crew that built this siding. Don is a diminutive of Donald, a Celtic name meaning brown-haired stranger. Little development took place here, but the site was shown on maps until the 1950's. (1, 2, 3, 18, 19, 158)

**DONE WORKIN BEACH** (Rolette). This was a platted resort on the east shore of Fish Lake in SE¼ Sec. 5-162-70, Couture Twp., two miles north of Belcourt. It appears only in a 1928 county atlas published by Brock & Co. The intent, and humor, of the name is obvious. (18, 123)

**DONNYBROOK** (Ward). This post office was established March 20, 1895 with Martha J. Power pm. It was located in Sec. 14-158-87, Carbondale Twp., and named for the famous Donnybrook Fair in Ireland. On December 29, 1897 new pm Edward C. Henry changed the name to GOETZ. Meanwhile a townsite was forming just to the west at the Soo Line RR tracks in Sec. 15-158-87, and on March 9, 1898 a new Donnybrook post office was established with Delos R. Hunnewell pm. The population was just 30 in 1898, but when the village incorporated in 1904, it reported a population of 504. The elevation is 1760, the Zip Code is 58734, and the population has declined to just 139 in 1980. (1, 2, 3, 18, 33, 40, 52, 79, 100, 375)

**DONOVAN** (Stutsman). This was a NPRR station founded in 1882 in NE¼ Sec. 3-142-65, Plainview Twp., two miles SE of Pingree. The post office was established July 21, 1882 with George W. Vennum pm, and closed January 4, 1883 with mail to Pingree. The origin of the name is unknown. (2, 3, 25, 40, 414)

**DORE** (McKenzie). This GNRR townsite was founded in NE¼ Sec. 7-151-104, Yellowstone Twp., five miles north of East Fairview. The post office was established April 18, 1901 with George Dore, one of the area's first settlers, as pm. The town never experienced any major development, and population figures of 50 reported in both 1920 and 1960 were probably somewhat exaggerated. The post office closed December 27, 1968 with mail to Fairview, MT. (1, 2, 3, 18, 33, 40, 79)

**DOUBLE WALL STATION** (Stark). This was the eighth relay station on the Bismarck-Fort Keogh overland mail route established in 1878, and closing in 1882 after the completion of the NPRR. It was located eighteen miles south of Belfield in Sec. 31-137-99, Grand Meadow Twp., in the extreme SW corner of the county, and named for Double Wall Creek on whose banks it was located. Adobe Walls Station, Dooby Walls Station, and Doby Walls Station are found in some accounts of this place, and are thought to be erroneous, or slang, interpretations of the correct name. (2, 3, 18, 74, 82)

**DOUGLAS** (McLean). This was a country store operated by Otis J. Marks in SE¼ Sec. 1-150-85, Douglas Twp. A post office was established in the store July 25, 1903 with Mr. Marks as pm. He named it for nearby Douglas Creek, which had been named earlier to honor a Major Douglas who was stationed at Fort Stevenson in the 1870's. The creek is now called Garrison Creek. Douglas is a Celtic name meaning dweller by the dark stream. The Soo Line RR built into this area in 1906, and on November 2, 1906 the post office relocated to the new townsite one mile to the north, which put it into Ward County. (2, 3, 19, 28, 40, 79, 100, 295)

**DOUGLAS** (Ward). This townsite was founded along the newly-built Soo Line RR branch line from Max to Plaza in Sec. 36-151-85, Cameron Twp. On November 2, 1906 the post office in Otis J. Marks' country store known as DOUGLAS moved to the townsite from its original location one mile to the

south in McLean County, although Arthur C. Bates assumed the duties of pm at this time. The site was platted in December 1906, and incorporated as a village in 1908 with A. G. Burgeson mayor. The Zip Code is 58735, and it reached a peak population of 313 in 1940, declining to just 112 in 1980. (2, 18, 33, 40, 52, 100, 295)

**DOUGLAS POINT** (Pembina). This townsite in SW¼ Sec. 3-161-54, Cavalier Twp., was promoted by George Adam Douglas as DEWEY, but this name was rejected by postal officials. The post office was established June 20, 1877 as DOUGLAS POINT with Mr. Douglas as pm. This site was adjacent to Cavalier, whose post office was established on the same date, and two post offices were, of course, unnecessary. Through the influence of Charles T. Cavileer, the DOUGLAS POINT post office closed July 30, 1877, and the site is now part of the city of Cavalier. (2, 3, 40, 108, 414, 415, 440)

**DOVER** (Wells). This NPRR station was founded as ROSS, but on August 27, 1903 the name was changed to DOVER, a name favored by local dispatcher W. E. Berner because it was easy to telegraph. The name is ultimately traced to Dover, Kent, England. The post office was established June 22, 1907 with Elmer E. Evans pm. Development at this station in SE¼ Sec. 13-146-68, Bilodeau Twp., five miles east of Sykeston, was very slow, with a peak population of 10 being reported in 1920. The post office closed April 30, 1924 with mail to Sykeston. Frank Augustus Wenstrom, a Lt. Governor and longtime state legislator, was born here in 1903. (1, 2, 3, 18, 40, 45, 79, 363)

**DOW** (Williams). This rural post office was established July 9, 1914 with Fred Dow Larkin pm. Some say it was named for Wilmont Dow, a native of ME who was associated with Theodore Roosevelt in the Badlands during the 1880's. It was first located in NE¼ Sec. 10-153-98, Truax Twp., fourteen miles south of Wheelock. It moved about within Truax Twp. as new pms were appointed, and closed January 31, 1938 with mail to Wheelock. (2, 3, 40, 50, 53)

**DOWNING** (Richland). This NPRR loading station was built before 1890 in Sec. 5-132-49, Mooreton Twp., one mile east of Mooreton, and named for J. F. Downing of Erie, PA, the owner of the site. Mr. Downing's nephew, Frederich Austin Bagg (1858-1950), managed the Downing Farm at this site 1889-1914, which was served by the Mooreton post office. (2, 3, 18, 25, 242)

**DOWNTOWN** (Ward). This was a classified station of the Minot post office, sharing Zip Code 58701 with the parent office. It opened July 1, 1964, and closed August 15, 1977. (33, 40)

**DOYON** (Ramsey). This GNRR station was founded in 1883 in SE¼ Sec. 19-153-61, Bartlett Twp., and named for Charles Herrick Doyon (1871-1937), a local bonanza farmer from VT who sold the right-of-way to the railroad. The post office was established June 19, 1900 with Frank Wilson pm. The elevation is 1518, the Zip Code is 58328, and a peak population of 222 was reached in 1930, although DOYON has had a population of under 100 since 1950. (1, 2, 18, 40, 103)

**DRADY** (Ward). This was a rural post office established January 16, 1906 with John Drady (1852-1932) pm. He came here in 1901 from Moorhead, MN to open a general store in Sec. 13-154-84, Burt Twp., twelve miles SW of Minot, and ran the business until retiring in 1929. Iver Monshaugen then operated the post office in NE¼ Sec. 23-154-83, Afton Twp., until it closed May 31, 1934 with mail to Minot. Brady is an erroneous spelling. (1, 2, 3, 18, 40, 100)

**DRAKE** (McHenry). This village was founded in 1899 in Secs. 2, 3, 10 & 11-151-76, Spring Grove Twp., at the junction of the Devils Lake-Max and Valley City-Minot lines of the Soo Line RR. The post office was established September 15, 1902 with Henry R. W. Bentley (1854-1942) pm. The village incorporated in 1906, and became a city in 1916. The Zip Code is 58736, and it reached a peak population of 831 in 1950. It was named for Herman Drake (1860-1947), the original homesteader of the townsite who was active in village and school affairs. (2, 3, 18, 33, 40, 52, 79, 183)

**DRAYTON** (Pembina). First known as HASTINGS LANDING, the first settlers in April 1878 renamed it for their hometown of Drayton, Ontario, Canada, which was named for Drayton, England. The post office was established July 1, 1878 with Ezra A. Healy pm. Located on the Red River in Sec. 26-159-51, Drayton Twp., the village incorporated in 1888, and became a city in 1896. The elevation is 825, the Zip Code is 58225, and a peak population of 1,095 was reported in 1970. The city has a reputation as a sports center, having ND's first curling club in 1904, and twice (1958, 1962) being the state Junior Legion baseball champions, the first time also winning the regional competition against much larger cities from other states. (1, 2, 3, 10, 18, 25, 33, 40, 79, 108, 366)

**DRESDEN** (Cavalier). This GNRR townsite was founded in June 1897 in Sec. 25-162-61, South Dresden Twp., and named for Dresden, Ontario, Canada, which was named for Dresden, Germany. The German city was founded about 922 A.D., became the capital of Saxony in 1485, and has become famous for its artistic heritage. The post office was established October 21, 1897 with Harvey J. Mathisen pm. The elevation is 1587, and a peak population of 250 was claimed in 1920, with a count of just 26 made in 1960. The post office, Zip Code 58226, closed June 30, 1975 with mail to Langdon. (1, 2, 3, 5, 18, 33, 40, 79, 214)

**DRISCOLL** (Burleigh). This NPRR station was founded in 1883 in Secs. 21 & 22-139-75, Driscoll Twp., and named for Frederick Driscoll (1834-1907), Manager of *The St. Paul Pioneer Press*, the official organ of the NPRR. Driscoll is a Celtic name meaning interpreter. The post office was established June 5, 1884 with William W. Wilcox pm, and closed January 20, 1888 with mail to Sterling. It reopened January 29, 1890, and closed April 15, 1891 with mail again to Sterling. It again reopened December 15,

1900 with H. E. Johns pm, with the post office located in the NPRR depot. The elevation is 1895, the Zip Code is 58532, and a population of about 200 has been claimed for many years. Era Bell Thompson, a member of one of ND's few pioneer black families, and once the editor of *Ebony* magazine, lived here as a child. Driscoll, Saskatchewan, Canada was named for DRISCOLL, ND by its first pm, Engebret Olsen, who had come from here. (1, 2, 14, 18, 25, 33, 40, 79, 83, 200)

**DRY FORKS** (Burleigh). This place is listed in an 1890 Rand-McNally & Co. guide to ND as being in Burleigh County, and served by the Bismarck post office. It is thought to refer to a rural area several miles north of Bismarck along the eastern bank of the Missouri River. (3, 25)

**DUANE** (Dickey). This was a Milwaukee Road RR station built in 1897 in SE 1/4 Sec. 15-130-63, Elden Twp., midway between Ellendale and Monango. A store and elevator were built here, but the site was always served by the Ellendale post office. Frank Letson, Ed Byers, and George Rose, a state legislator, were the organizers of the elevator, which was considered to be one of the best equipped in ND. The name came from Duane, NY, which was named for Robert L. Duane, a prominent local citizen. A peak population of 19 was reported in 1920. The elevator was destroyed by fire in 1970. (1, 2, 3, 18, 25, 154, 316)

**DUANE** (Traill). This was a farm post office established September 10, 1894 with Theodora Miller Hurley pm, who had married Harry Duane Hurley (1853-1942) in 1893. It was located in NE¼ Sec. 19-145-49, Caledonia Twp., seven miles east of Hillsboro on the 2,200 acre farm run by Mr. Hurley, who later served two terms as a state legislator. The post office closed January 30, 1904 with mail to Hillsboro. (2, 3, 18, 40, 187)

**DUBAY** (Pierce). This was the dream town of John and Minnie Dubay of Willow City, who purchased four acres in Sec. 27-153-73, Girard Twp., midway between Rugby and Harvey. A townsite was platted August 28, 1937 and divided into lots, but few people seemed interested. The Dubays established a country store with a bar and a gas pump, and for a few years did a good business. ND Highway 3 was rerouted four miles to the east after World War II, isolating the store from traffic. The Dubays closed the store and their dreams in 1949. (3, 114)

**DUDLEY** (Ramsey). This was a farm post office established December 28, 1900 with Mary E. Grimes pm. The name, of no local significance, was chosen by postal officials after rejecting Grimes and Highland. It was located in NE¼ Sec. 19-158-63, Royal Twp., five miles NE of Starkweather until March 6, 1903, when it moved three miles ESE to SE¼ Sec. 27-158-63, the home of new pm John R. Foster. It closed August 31, 1903 with mail to Starkweather. (2, 3, 40, 414)

**DUDLEY** (Sheridan). This town was founded in 1900, platted in 1902 in SE 1/4 Sec. 8-146-74 as the "Town of Dudley", and named for a partner of James Clark, for whom

an adjacent rival townsite was named. DUDLEY consisted of seven blocks to the west of CLARK, and two blocks to the east of CLARK. Later in 1902 the two merged as GOODRICH. (2, 3, 18, 21, 30, 40)

**DUKE SPUR** (Morton). This was a little used NPRR loading station about midway between Mandan and Harmon, named for G. M. "Duke" deLambert, a NPRR official at Mandan. (2, 3, 107, 431)

**DUNBAR** (Sargent). This settlement was founded by Neil Laughlin in 1883 in NW¼ Sec. 18-131-55, Dunbar Twp., four miles north of Forman. The Sargeant post office, located two miles to the NE, moved here August 20, 1883 with Willis W. Bradley continuing as pm. It was named for its township, which some say was named for Clarence S. Dunbar, who settled south of Lisbon in 1882 and moved here in 1887. Others say it was named by local pioneer C. P. Chesney for his aunt, while yet another theory says that it was named by pioneer Philander N. Brown for one of his wife's relatives. The town was on an expected railroad line from Valley City to Watertown, SD, but the line failed to materialize, and DUNBAR was doomed. The post office closed December 8, 1887 with mail to Forman. (2, 3, 25, 34, 40, 165, 166, 171, 414, 415)

**DUNDAS** (Dickey). This was a settlement promoted by the township's first settler, Abram L. Beggs, on his land in SW¼ Sec. 2-129-60, Port Emma Twp., one-half mile SW of Port Emma, the historic James River townsite. Mr. Beggs came here in 1880 from Dundas, Ontario, Canada, which was named for Henry Dundas, Lord Melville (1742-1811), a Scottish statesman and Secretary of War 1794-1804 under Prime Minister William Pitt. DUNDAS was overshadowed by Port Emma in the 1880's and abandoned. Mr. Beggs moved to Ellendale where he was elected Dickey County Register of Deeds in 1896. (2, 3, 5, 10)

**DUNDAS** (Eddy). This was a GNRR station established in 1912 on the Surrey cutoff line. Its location, NW¼ Sec. 13-148-66, Superior Twp., placed it between New Rockford and Brantford. John Dodds, who lived just north of the station, named it for Dundas, Ontario, Canada, which was near his hometown of Seaforth, Ontario. A population of 25 was claimed in 1960. Dandus is an erroneous spelling. (2, 3, 10, 18, 38, 119)

**DUNDEE** (Walsh). This was a rural community located in Sec. 17-158-55, Dundee Twp., six miles ENE of Edinburg. Some say it was named for Dundee Twp., Fond du Lac County, WI, while others say it was named for Dundee, Ontario, Canada, both of which were named for Dundee, Scotland. The post office was established April 12, 1881 with Ole Oveson pm, and closed December 31, 1887 with mail to Lampton. It reopened March 22, 1888, and closed for good October 31, 1902 with mail to Edinburg. A population of 25 was reported in 1890, but the lack of a railroad led to its demise. (2, 25, 40, 75)

**DUNKER COLONY** (Towner). This was the original name used to describe the colony of Dunkards that came from IN in 1894 to the area west of Cando. This group, members of the Church of the Brethren, were descended from German Baptists, practiced trine immersion, and refused to take oaths or perform military service. The religion originated in Germany in 1708. The colony developed into a small village, which was named ZION for its township. (2, 3, 4, 18, 102)

**DUNLOP** (Cass). This townsite in Sec. 11-141-54, Ayr Twp., was founded in 1883 and named for James Dunlop, manager of the Park Bonanza Farm which donated land for this townsite. The post office was established October 17, 1883 with Frank H. Dickinson pm. On December 4, 1883 the name was changed to AYR, but an error by postal officials resulted in the name being approved as AYE. During the period necessary to correct this error, efforts were made to change the name to ELGIN, but on January 7, 1884 the name AYR was approved, and the ELGIN name was declared invalid in 1885. Dunlap is an erroneous spelling. (3, 25, 40, 77, 297)

**DUNN** (Dunn). This was a rural post office established June 2, 1909 with John Johnson pm. It was located in N½ Sec. 12-144-92, four miles west of Dodge, and named for its county, which was named by Erastus A. Williams, a state legislator, for his friend, John P. Dunn, a former mayor of Bismarck. Mr. Johnson, a native of Sweden, came to America in 1887. The post office closed January 15, 1914 with mail to Loring. (2, 3, 10, 18, 40, 415)

**DUNN** (Eddy). This was an early settlement in Sec. 32-149-66, New Rockford Twp., which today is the south part of the city of New Rockford. The post office was established July 2, 1883 with Capt. Walter G. Dunn pm. He had arrived here in 1882 from Meadville, PA, along with Hugh Peoples of Boston, MA. The post office merged with the newly formed New Rockford office on December 18, 1883. (2, 25, 40, 41)

**DUNN CENTER** (Dunn). This NPRR townsite was founded in 1913 in N½ Sec. 26-145-94, Decorah Twp., and named to note its location in the center of Dunn County, which was named for John P. Dunn of Bismarck. The Melby post office was relocated here on May 7, 1914 with Gustave B. "Bert" Nyhagen as pm. The elevation is 2191, the Zip Code is 58626, and the village, which incorporated in 1916, reached a peak population of 276 in 1930. (1, 2, 3, 10, 18, 33, 40, 52, 79, 223)

**DUNNING** (Bottineau). This was a GNRR grain loading station established in 1905 in SE¼ Sec. 33-161-80, Brander Twp., three miles east of Maxbass. A townsite was platted in 1905, but little development occurred. Populations of 15 in 1920, and just 4 in 1960 were the only reports from the site. Three elevators were built, two of which still exist, but the site never had a post office. It was named for Dunning, NE, which was named for the brothers R. A. and Samuel Dunning. A 1912 county atlas shows this townsite owned by S. O. Birk, with "Chas. W. Dunning" in parenthesis, indicating that the name may have had more local significance that the NE version of its origin would imply. (1, 2, 3, 18, 34, 35, 89, 101, 153)

**DUNN'S CREEK** (Eddy). This was a locally used name for the pioneer post office of DUNN, now part of the city of New Rockford. (2, 119)

**DUNSEITH** (Rolette). This townsite was founded in 1881 in Sec. 36-162-73, Gilbert Twp., and named by founder William Eaton for his mother, Jeannette Dunseith Eaton. Some say it was named for Dunseith, Scotland, a city whose name means City of Peace in Gaelic. The post office was established March 31, 1884 with Giles M. Gilbert pm. DUNSEITH was named county seat when Rolette County organized in 1884, but it lost the honor to Saint John in 1886. The GNRR finally arrived here in 1905, making the town the terminus of its line from York. The elevation is 1713, the Zip Code is 58329, and a peak population of 1,017 was reached in 1960. The International Peace Garden, a few miles north of town at the Canadian Border, was dedicated July 14, 1932. (1, 2, 3, 18, 33, 40, 79, 123, 396, 398)

**DURBIN** (Cass). This townsite was settled in the late 1870's, and platted by C. W. Redmore in SW¼ Sec. 32-139-51, Durbin Twp., on the new GNRR line from Wahpeton to Casselton. The post office was established May 19, 1881 with Albert Bazemiel pm, and closed April 30, 1906 with mail to Addison, but reopened June 19, 1906. The village was named for a GNRR employee who worked on locomotives at the local roundhouse. A population of 100 was claimed in 1890, although the count has been less than 30 for most of the twentieth century. The post office, Zip Code 58023, closed July 12, 1985. (1, 2, 3, 18, 25, 33, 34, 40, 77, 300, 303)

**DURHAM** (Griggs). This was a rural post office established January 26, 1880 with Frank H. Tappen pm. It was located in Sec. 8-147-58, Romness Twp., seven miles ENE of Jessie, and named by Mr. Tappen for his sister, Mrs. Durham, who was his assistant. The post office closed March 10, 1881 with mail to Newburgh, with the area later being served by the Lee post office in Nelson County. (1, 2, 3, 25, 40, 65)

**DURHAM** (Stutsman). This was a farm post office established May 5, 1884 with Elbridge F. Horn pm. It was located in SW¼ Sec. 20-143-62, Courtenay Twp., three miles south of Courtenay, and named for the township just to the west, which was at first named Spinarski. The name DURHAM is said to come from the city and county of that name in England. On January 20, 1887 the post office was renamed HORN. (2, 25, 40, 158, 415)

**DURKEE** (Stutsman). This was a Midland Continental RR station in Sec. 31-140-62, Spiritwood Twp., eight miles ESE of Jamestown, named for J. B. Durkee, a merchant at Courtenay. Little development occurred at the site. One map shows it as Dyrkee, and a MCRR publication shows it as Dyrkes, both of which are thought to be erroneous spellings. (3, 34, 158)

**DURUM** (Stutsman). This was a NPRR station in Sec. 32-140-63, Bloom Twp., three miles east of Jamestown, and named for durum wheat, first grown in ND about the time this station was established. The name is deriv-

ed from the Latin word meaning hard. Little development occurred at the site. (2, 3, 18, 79, 432)

**DURUPT** (Stutsman). This was a Midland Continental RR station in Sec. 25-142-62, Gray Twp., six miles SSW of Wimbledon, and named for Wimbledon businessman and farmer Paul Durupt (1851-1921). It appears on maps circa 1915-1925. (1, 3)

**DUVAL** (Bowman). This was a rural post office established February 17, 1911 with C. E. Berquist pm. It was located in SE¼ Sec. 33-130-104, Nebo Twp., thirteen miles SSW of Rhame. Mr. Berquist applied for the post office as Berg Valley, but postal officials renamed it DUVAL, which has no local significance. The post office closed December 15, 1911 with mail to Amor. (2, 3, 18, 40, 414)

**DWIGHT** (Richland). This GNRR townsite was founded in 1880 in SE¼ Sec. 29-133-48, Dwight Twp., principally to serve the New York Farm, owned by Jeremiah Wilber Dwight (1819-1885), a Congressman from Dryden, NY who owned 27,000 acres in Richland County. Dwight is a Teutonic name meaning white or fair. The post office was established February 2, 1881 with John Miller (1843-1908) as pm. Mr. Miller, also from Dryden, NY, was elected in 1889 as the first Governor of ND. The village incorporated in 1914, and became a city in 1968, reaching a peak population of 168 in 1940. The elevation is 944, and the post office, Zip Code 58024, became a rural branch of Wahpeton on December 31, 1975. (1, 2, 3, 18, 19, 33, 40, 77, 79, 243, 351, 352)

**DYMOND** (Mountrail). This was a farm post office established September 8, 1902 with Per A. Anderson pm in NW¼ Sec. 26-154-90, Austin Twp., fifteen miles SE of Stanley. Mr. Anderson, who was the first chairman of the Austin Township Board, carried the mail twice weekly from Palermo by horseback. It was named for Chester S. Dymond, a Civil War veteran who was the first settler in the area. On March 13, 1906 the post office was relocated one mile south to the new inland town of Epworth, which was first called Indiana. (2, 18, 40, 72, 289)

# E

**EAGLE'S NEST** (Morton). This was a NPRR loading station in SW¼ Sec. 16-139-89, Classen Twp., five miles NW of Glen Ullin, whose post office served the site. It was named for nearby Eagle's Nest Butte in Sec. 10-139-89. Little development occurred at the site, although the name was familiar to travelers on Interstate 94 as Exit #20. The site was the scene of a marooned NPRR passenger train during the great blizzard of March 1966. Because the virtual non-existance of this site caused confusion for motorists, the name was removed from highway signs in 1987. (1, 2, 3, 17, 18, 25, 34, 79)

**EAGLES NEST** (Rolette). This was a platted resort on the SW shore of Lake Upsilon in SW¼ Sec. 10-163-71, Hutchinson Twp., five miles west of Saint John. The name is euphonic and appropriate for a resort community. It was shown on maps circa 1910-1930. (3, 18)

**EARL** (McKenzie). This was a farm post office established August 13, 1910 with Ida Empie pm, who named it for her son, Earl Empie. Earl is an Anglo-Saxon name meaning nobleman or chief. It was located in SE¼ Sec. 26-147-104, twenty-four miles south of Cartwright, and moved four times within this general area before closing August 15, 1925 with mail to Cartwright. (1, 2, 3, 18, 19, 40)

**EASBY** (Cavalier). This GNRR townsite dates from 1881, and is located in NE¼ Sec. 4-160-59, Easby Twp., and named by settlers from Easby, Ontario, Canada. The post office was established June 17, 1884 with Charles Wrightson pm. The elevation is 1656, and a peak population of 125 was listed in 1920, which was surely an exaggeration, with the count of 18 in 1890, and 15 in 1960 representing more realistic figures. No real boom ever occurred at EASBY, and the post office closed July 31, 1957 with mail to Langdon. Eastby is a frequently encountered erroneous spelling. (1, 2, 3, 18, 25, 38, 40, 79)

**EAST CARLYLE** (Golden Valley). This name applies to eight families, as of 1985, that have telephone prefix 688 under the exchange in Carlyle, MT, which was named in 1907 by pm Arthur C. Knutson for his son. (3, 55, 88)

**EASTEDGE** (Barnes). This NPRR station was built in 1900 in NE¼ Sec. 29-137-57, Thordenskjold Twp., and named for the old railroad construction camp here, which had been named to note its location at the east edge of the Sheyenne River valley, between Kathryn and Nome. The post office was established June 27, 1902 with Bernt A. Brorby pm. A population of 80 was reported in 1920, but this had declined to just 14 in 1960. The post office closed July 15, 1954 with mail to Kathryn, and only a few foundations mark the site today. (1, 2, 3, 18, 34, 40, 76, 79, 118)

**EAST FAIRVIEW** (McKenzie). This is a GNRR station in E½ Sec. 31-151-104, and is the portion of Fairview, MT that lies on the ND side of the border. Fairview was named in 1904 by pm L. E. Newton to note the beautiful view of the Yellowstone River valley from his home. About 175 people live in EAST FAIRVIEW, which is almost universally considered to be a part of the MT city. (1, 2, 3, 52, 88)

**EAST LINTON** (Emmons). Newspapers carried a story in August 1902 about a new rival townsite of Linton, the new county seat of Emmons County. It was located in Sec. 8-132-76, just east of Linton, more or less representing that part of the town that is today east of US Highway 83. Despite negative publicity by the *Emmons County Record*, much of Linton moved to this new site, which offered better flood protection during the spring thaws of Beaver Creek, and EAST LINTON soon assumed the original townsite's name, which today is locally called Old Town. (2, 3, 66)

**EASTMAN** (McLean). This was a rural post office established April 23, 1903 with Ida O. Pace pm, located in the home of her husband, Frank Pace, in NW¼ Sec. 24-145-79, Park Twp., eight miles south of Mercer. This order was rescinded, but Mrs. Pace was again appointed as pm on October 8, 1903, and the facility became a reality. Carl Goessele, who lived just to the west in NE¼ Sec. 23-145-79, was appointed pm October 13, 1904, but this appointment was rescinded. The post office continued to be at the Pace home until it closed May 31, 1905 with mail to McClusky. It was named for Philip Kimball Eastman (1867-1949), a prominent area pioneer who was the first pm at Wilton. (2, 3, 18, 28, 40, 379, 415)

**EAST MICHIGAN CITY** (Nelson). A townsite just east of Michigan City, or Michigan, was platted August 8, 1883 in SW¼ Sec. 33-153-58, Michigan City Twp., by W. G. Marshall, but it failed to develop. (3, 124)

**EAST MONDAK** (Williams). A plat was filed August 14, 1908 for a townsite in NE¼ Sec. 7-152-104, Buford Twp., and named EAST MONDAK. It was, as the name indicated, the eastern portion of the notorious town of MONDAK that straddled the ND-MT border, although the shorter name was generally used for the entire community. Charles V. Dietes and Wilfred Lemeiux were the town's founders. (3, 50)

**EASTON** (Steele). This rural post office was established in 1882 as GRAIN, and in 1883 became PICKERT. It was located in Sec. 7-146-56, Easton Twp., two miles south of Finley. Elsie J. Pease, the new pm, changed the name to EASTON on March 18, 1896 to match the name of the township, which had changed its name from Pickert in 1895. The new name was suggested by settlers from Easton, MN, which was named in 1873 for Jason Clark Easton (1823-1901), the

original townsite owner who later was prominent in banking at LaCrosse, WI. On January 29, 1897 the post office closed, being replaced on that date by the facility at the new GNRR townsite of Finley. (2, 13, 40, 99, 326)

**EAST OSNABROCK** (Cavalier). This was an early platted townsite in NW¼ Sec. 21-160-58, Alma Twp., just east of Osnabrock, that failed to develop. (3, 18)

**EAST SIDNEY** (McKenzie). This name is used for residents of western McKenzie County with telephone prefix 481, affiliated with the exchange in Sidney, MT, which was named for Sidney Walters, the son of a prominent pioneer. (3, 55, 88)

**EAST SOURIS** (Bottineau). This was a platted townsite in NW¼ Sec. 32-163-77, Haram Twp., just SE of Souris. It appears only in a 1910 county atlas, apparently as a rival site of the GNRR's station, but little development occurred at the site. (3, 18)

**EAST SPRINGBROOK** (Williams). This was a rival townsite of SPRINGBROOK begun in 1903 in Sec. 10-155-99, Springbrook Twp., three miles ENE of the pioneer settlement in Sec. 18-155-99. When the GNRR decided to locate their station at the newer site, most of the original site and its name were transferred here. (2, 3, 50)

**EAST WESTBY** (Divide). This name is used for residents of western Divide County with telephone prefix 985, part of the exchange in Westby, MT, which had been founded in ND. (3, 55, 88)

**EAST WYNDMERE** (Richland). This site, Secs. 6 & 7-132-52, Danton Twp., just east of WYNDMERE, began to develop shortly after the Soo Line RR crossed the NPRR tracks here in 1888. A townsite was platted in 1899, and the next year most of WYNDMERE moved to the new site, which adopted the old name. (2, 3, 147)

**EATON** (Dickey). This was a pioneer settlement founded in 1883 in SE¼ Sec. 27-129-60, Port Emma Twp., five miles SW of Ludden on the west bank of the James River. The post office was established June 11, 1883 with Hamlin F. Eaton (1838-1928) pm. He had come to Dakota Territory in 1882 after running a boarding school in his native ME for twenty-two years. Eaton is an Old English name meaning from the riverside village, which was a most appropriate name for this site. A ferry service was about the only development here that met with success, and the post office closed May 26, 1887 with mail to Ludden. (2, 3, 19, 25, 40, 154, 264)

**ECHO** (Ward). Miss Amy Terrell had succeeded her father as pm of the BLACK post office on August 6, 1886, shortly before she married William H. Wilson, the son of their neighbor, James Wilson, a pioneer from Sioux Falls, now in SD. The post office was then moved to the Wilson home in SW¼ Sec. 12-153-81, Sawyer Twp., just south of present-day Sawyer. It was decided that a name change was appropriate for the post office, and Lyman, Seymour, Stella, Echo, and Edna were submitted as choices. Postal officials selected ECHO, which had been submitted by the pm's husband to note the echo he heard in the woods after shooting a deer. Alois Hartl became pm in 1895, and Fred L. Hartleip took over the position in 1897. On April 26, 1898 the post office was replaced by the facility in the new Soo Line RR townsite of Sawyer, with Mr. Hartleip continuing as the pm. (2, 3, 25, 40, 100, 240, 414)

**ECKELSON** (Barnes). This NPRR station was built in 1872 in S½ Sec. 18-140-60, Potter Twp., and named SEVENTH SIDING. About 1879 it was renamed ECKELSON for A. O. Eckelson, a NPRR civil engineer, with the name also being given to a nearby lake. The post office was established July 21, 1882 with Ephraim S. Lawrence pm. A major effort was made that year to secure the territorial capital, which was awarded to Bismarck in 1883. A population of 65 was reported in 1890, but the townsite began to decline until it was moved two miles to SE¼ Sec. 14-140-61, Eckelson Twp., in 1897. The original site was located on a slope, and the NPRR locomotives often had trouble restarting on the steep grade. The new townsite has an elevation of 1497, the Zip Code is 58432, and a peak population of 130 was reported in 1920. The post office became a rural branch of Jamestown on December 2, 1966. (1, 2, 3, 25, 34, 40, 76, 79)

**ECKMAN** (Bottineau). This was a Soo Line RR townsite founded in 1906 in Sec. 30-160-80, Newborg Twp., and Sec. 25-160-81, Lewis Twp. The post office was established April 16, 1906 with Anton A. Bakke pm. The townsite was platted about 1908 during its brief boom period, but after reaching a population of 84 in 1910, it declined rapidly, and is now a virtual ghost town. The post office closed July 31, 1956 with mail to Maxbass. The town was named for A. Eckman, an agent for the Tri-State Land Co., owners of the site. (1, 2, 18, 34, 40, 101, 153)

**EDBERG** (Burleigh). This was a farm post office established February 13, 1886 with Marcus A. Edberg pm. It was located in

NW¼ Sec. 28-140-78, Frances Twp., seven miles north of Menoken. A rural community began to develop, and a population of 42 was reported in 1890. The post office moved one mile SE on March 26,1894, changing its name to FRANCES. (2, 3, 8, 14, 18, 25, 40, 414)

**EDDVILLE** (Dickey). This was a GNRR siding and loading station built in 1905 in SE¼ Sec. 18-129-63, Ellendale Twp., between Ellendale and Forbes. It was named for Edward Pehl, a prominent land owner in the area, and was soon renamed PEHL SPUR. (2, 154)

**EDDY** (Eddy). This was a post office authorized July 21, 1887 with John J. Anderson, who came here in 1882 and was a county commissioner, as pm. He named it for its county, which was named for E. B. Eddy, founder of the First National Bank of Fargo. Government records show "no papers" entered for the EDDY post office on October 7, 1887. In 1890 a post office called FREEBORN was established on this same site, SE¼ Sec. 33-150-62, Freeborn Twp., and Mr. Anderson became its pm in 1893. (2, 3, 18, 40, 119, 321)

**EDEN** (Bowman). This settlement was founded in 1907 in Sec. 11-131-102, Bowman Twp., and called TWIN BUTTES. The post office was established July 26, 1907 as LOWDEN, changing its name to BOWMAN on October 19, 1907. Government records indicate it was also called EDEN for a time in 1907, but no local residents know when or why, indicating that the official records might be in error on this matter. (2, 3, 34)

**EDEN** (Walsh). This was a pioneer settlement founded in 1882 in Sec. 23-155-55, Eden Twp. It failed to develop, but in 1884 a farm post office called KELNER was established at this site, and the following year it became the new townsite of CONWAY. The first settlers had chosen to name their community for the Biblical Garden of Eden to note the area's fertile soil and general attractiveness. (2, 75, 293)

**EDEN** (Wells). This was a rural post office established December 24, 1896 with Julius J. Bondelie pm. It was named by an early settler from Eden, LaMoille County, VT, which was named for the Biblical Garden of Eden to note the fertile soil in the area. EDEN, ND was first located in NE¼ Sec. 9-150-68, Valhalla Twp., nine miles NE of Hamberg, and in 1900 it moved to Sec. 10-150-68, the home of new pm Halford Erickson. Later it was located in a country store in Sec. 4-150-68, and in 1905 it moved about five miles SW into Norway Lake Twp. (150-69), where Nels Presetter Hanson was the pm. It closed February 28, 1907 with mail to Twist. (2, 3, 40, 53, 79, 112, 364)

**EDGAR** (Dunn). This was a ranch post office established December 23, 1908 with Edgar E. Palmer pm. It was located in SW¼ Sec. 28-143-96, near Crooked Creek five miles SW of Manning. The site was used as a place for changing horses on the daily mail stage to area post offices. EDGAR closed July 15, 1913 with mail to Fayette. Edgar is an Anglo-Saxon name meaning fortunate

spear, and is often loosely translated as the happy warrior. (1, 2, 3, 18, 19, 40)

**EDGELEY** (LaMoure). This NPRR townsite was founded in 1886 in Sec. 3-133-64, Golden Glen Twp., replacing the pioneer settlement of Saint George. The new townsite was platted by the everpresent developer, Richard Sykes, who named it for his birthplace, Edgeley Park, Stockport, Cheshire, England. He later founded Edgeley, Saskatchewan, Canada, reusing this name. EDGELEY, ND became the terminus of the Milwaukee Road RR and the Midland Continental RR. The post office was established November 16, 1886 with John B. Kesler pm. The elevation is 1568, the Zip Code is 58433, and the village, which incorporated in 1911, reached a peak population of 1,040 in the 1964 special census. (1, 2, 3, 18, 25, 40, 52, 79, 83, 140)

**EDGELEY JUNCTION** (LaMoure). This was the junction of the NPRR, Midland Continental RR, and Milwaukee Road RR one mile NE of Edgeley in Sec. 35-134-64, Nora Twp. The NPRR listed it as a station for many years. (1, 3)

**EDINBURG** (Walsh). On November 17, 1892 EDINBURGH pm John E. White changed the spelling to EDINBURG to comply with new government spelling regulations. When these rules were relaxed a few years later, many affected names were restored to their previous spellings, but EDINBURG has continued with its new name. The elevation is 1194, the Zip Code is 58227, and a peak population of 378 was reached in 1940. (1, 2, 3, 18, 25, 33, 40, 75, 392)

**EDINBURGH** (Walsh). This settlement was founded in 1882 in NW¼ Sec. 5-158-56, Lampton Twp. The post office was established November 1, 1882 with Christian Buck (1849-1912) pm. Mr. Buck, a native of Tromso, Norway, named it for Edinburgh, the capital of Scotland. He had attended Edinburgh University before coming to America, and was a much revered citizen of this community until he was murdered by a transient in 1912. The village incorporated in 1886, and the following year moved about three miles SE to the new GNRR townsite in E½ Sec. 21-158-56. On November 17, 1892 pm John E. White changed the name to EDINBURG to comply with new government spelling regulations. (2, 3, 40, 75, 392)

**EDISONS** (Grand Forks). This was a GNRR loading station built in 1895 in Sec. 28-152-55, Elm Grove Twp., three miles south of McCanna. It was named for Thomas S. Edison, owner of a 3,100 acre farm at this site, and the owner of the privately held loading facilities. He came here in 1882 from Canada to manage the bonanza farm owned by Jameson Larimore, and was a first cousin of the famous inventor, Thomas Alva Edison. (2, 3, 18, 69, 342)

**EDMORE** (Ramsey). This GNRR townsite was founded in July 1901 as STOLTZVILLE, and some consideration was given to adopting the name of Lunde, a nearby farm post office, but when the new post office was established July 19, 1901 with Henry Richard Aslakson (1857-1945) pm, it was named EDMORE. Some say the name was coined from the name of local settler Edward E. Moore, while others say it was similarly coined from the name of E. J. Moore, of Fargo, an official of the Ancient Order of United Woodmen, a masonic order. The village incorporated in 1902, and it became the second city in Ramsey County in 1920, the year it reached its peak population of 501. The elevation is 1524, and the Zip Code is 58330. Edmore, Saskatchewan, Canada was named by Canadian Pacific RR officials for this city. (1, 2, 18, 33, 40, 52, 79, 83, 103)

**EDMUNDS** (Stutsman). This NPRR station was founded in the summer of 1885 in Sec. 31-144-65, Edmunds Twp., and named by the local twin brother physicians, Drs. Albert and Alfred Richmond, for their friend, U. S. Senator George Franklin Edmunds (1828-1919) of VT, a famous Constitutional lawyer. The post office was established November 23, 1885 with Caleb C. Cochrane, a pioneer merchant, as pm. The elevation is 1619, and a peak population of 125 was reported in 1920, with a decline to just 34 in 1960. The post office, Zip Code 58434, closed March 1, 1975 with mail to Pingree. (1, 2, 5, 18, 33, 40, 41, 79, 158)

**EDNA** (Barnes). This was a rural community in NE¼ Sec. 24-142-60, Edna Twp., three miles NW of Rogers. It was named for Edna Booth, who on July 7, 1881 was the first white child born in the township. Edna is a Hebrew name meaning pleasure. In 1882 her father established a post office, but decided to name it BOOTH. (2, 3, 19, 40, 76, 328)

**EDSON** (Renville). This was an early settlement in SW¼ Sec. 29-163-87, Stafford Twp., about twelve miles north of Norma. At one time it included a store, a meeting hall, a church, and a blacksmith shop. Some sources state that it had a post office, but government records do not confirm this claim. The site was named for George Edson, whose family name literally means the son of Ed, which is an Anglo-Saxon name meaning prosperous. (2, 3, 19, 40, 71)

**EDTON** (Hettinger). This was a NPRR townsite in NW¼ Sec. 26-134-95, Indian Creek Twp., about three miles SW of Regent. A post office was established November 15, 1907 with Mons J. Nelson (1857-1941), a native of WI, as pm. He coined the name using his son's name, Ed, plus a contraction of "town". Ed Nelson later lived at Sarles. The founding of Regent in 1910 doomed this townsite, and the post office closed December 31, 1911 with mail to Regent. (2, 3, 18, 40, 179, 181)

**EDWINTON** (Burleigh). This was the first official name for what is now BISMARCK, then the western terminus of the NPRR, and honored that railroad's late Chief Engineer, Edwin F. Johnson (1803-1872), who had routed the entire NPRR mainline to this point. The name was suggested by Thomas P. Canfield, the NPRR townsite agent, who like Mr. Johnson, was a native of VT. Edwin is an Anglo-Saxon name meaning valuable friend. *The Bismarck Capital* of June 17, 1947 stated that the name honored Edwin McMasters Stanton (1814-1869), the Secretary of War during the Civil War, but many contemporary sources confirm that the name was indeed chosen to honor Mr. Johnson. The post office was established February 7, 1873 with Major Samuel A. Dickey pm, but on July 17, 1873 the name was changed to BISMARCK by the NPRR Board of Directors, who felt it was important to compliment German investors in the firm. Ewinton is an erroneous spelling. (2, 3, 9, 14, 18, 19, 40, 79, 416)

**EGAN** (Pierce). This Soo Line RR station was founded in 1911 in SW¼ Sec. 10 & NW¼ Sec. 15-154-73, Balta Twp., and named for Egan Pierce, an official of the railroad. It is unknown if he was any relation to Gilbert A. Pierce, namesake of the county. Egan is a Celtic name meaning ardent, and a Teutonic name meaning formidable. When application for a post office was made, postal officials cited potential confusion with Egan, SD, named for a Milwaukee Road RR official, and the name was changed to BALTA. (2, 19, 33, 40, 114, 149)

**EGELAND** (Towner). This Soo Line RR townsite was founded in 1905 in NW¼ Sec. 6-159-65, Victor Twp., and NE¼ Sec. 1-159-66, Lewis Twp., a site originally homesteaded by Rasmus Rasmussen in 1894. It was named for Axel Egeland, a banker in Bisbee and an official of the Soo Line RR. Lots were sold August 9, 1905, and on August 23, 1905 the country store and post office called Lakeview relocated here, John M. Borgerson continuing as pm and storekeeper. The village incorporated October 18, 1905, and reached a peak population of 333 in 1930. The Zip Code is 58331. (1, 2, 18, 33, 40, 79, 197)

**EIGHTH SIDING** (Stutsman). The NPRR built this siding in 1873 in Secs. 15 & 22-140-62, Spiritwood Twp., and named it to note the chronological numbering of sidings as they were built westward from Fargo. Settlement began in 1879, and the site was renamed SPIRITWOOD. (2, 3, 158)

**ELAND** (Stark). This was a NPRR loading station in SE¼ Sec. 11-139-97, Ash Coulee Twp., five miles west of Dickinson. It was built in the 1880's, and starting about 1890 was considered to be the largest stockyards in the world, loading about 10,000 horses in one day in 1907. The elevation is 2453, and it was served by the Dickinson post office. The name is thought to have come from the large antelope found in South Africa, although why it was chosen for this site is unknown. The station was dismantled about 1920. (1, 2, 3, 5, 13, 18, 25, 34, 74, 81, 240)

**ELBOWOODS** (McLean). Father DeSmet, the Roman Catholic missionary, conceived this place in the 1860's, but development did not begin until about 1889 in Sec. 4-147-90, Elbowoods Twp. The name noted a peculiar bend in the Missouri River and the heavy wooded river bottoms at this site. Both the Mandan and Arikara tribes called this place Elbow Woods in their native languages. A post office was established July 31, 1893 with Mary Farrell pm, and it was the agency headquarters for the Fort Berthold Indian Reservation 1893-1953. After many years of effort, the Catholic mission school was founded in 1910, and it was the center of activity in the community until it burned in 1939. A population of 175 was reported in 1930, and a famous bridge across the Missouri River was completed here in 1934. The post office closed April 15, 1954 with mail to Emmet, and the site is now inundated by Lake Sakakawea. (2, 28, 40, 79, 189)

**ELDRED** (Cass). This was a rural post office established April 5, 1882 with James M. Watson pm. It was located in NE¼ Sec. 18-138-53, Walburg Twp., three miles west of Chaffee, and named for L. F. Eldred, and early settler in the area, and an uncle of the pm's wife, Caroline Eldred Watson. Eldred is an Anglo-Saxon name meaning sage counselor. The post office closed September 11, 1895 with mail to Watson. (2, 19, 25, 34, 40, 77)

**ELDRIDGE** (Stutsman). The NPRR built a siding in Sec. 35-140-65, Eldridge Twp., in 1872 and called it TENTH SIDING. A settlement called BURTON began here about 1879, but on September 20, 1880 the post office was established and named for J. H. Eldridge of Davenport, IA, who owned a bonanza farm in the area. He was the father-in-law of Judge S. L. Glaspell of Jamestown. The pm was Henry Vessey, who built a Victorian-styled store in 1881 that was pictured in many national publications. The elevation is 1563, and a peak population of about 100 was reported in the early years, with a count of just 63 in 1960. The post office, Zip Code 58435, closed in 1982. (1, 2, 33, 38, 40, 79, 158)

**ELDRIGE** (Stutsman). This is an erroneous spelling of ELDRIDGE that was used for a time during 1909 by the post office. (3)

**ELEVENTH SIDING** (Stutsman). This NPRR siding was built in 1873 in Secs. 31 & 32-140-68, Flint Twp., and named to note the chronological order of the sidings as they were built westward from Fargo. In 1880 the site was called MIDWAY, and later that year came to be known as MEDINA. In 1888 an effort was made to adopt the name MEADOW, but the MEDINA name was retained. (2, 3, 158)

**ELGIN** (Cass). A post office called DUNLOP was established in SW¼ Sec. 11-141-54, Ayr Twp., on October 17, 1883 with Frank H. Dickinson pm. He changed the name to AYR on December 4, 1883, but the change was erroneously recorded on government records as AYE. While correcting the mistake, there was an effort made to change the name to ELGIN, to honor bonanza farmer Thomas Park, a native of Harrington, Elginshire, Scotland, who had donated land for the townsite. The name officially became AYR on January 7, 1884, although some local citizens persisted with the name ELGIN for over a year. In March 1885 the territorial legislature ordered the discontinuance of the name ELGIN for any purpose, citing the existance of a post office of this name in Cavalier County. (2, 3, 25, 40, 77, 297)

**ELGIN** (Cavalier). This was a rural post office established April 2, 1883 with Josiah Ritchey pm. It was located in SW¼ Sec. 14-159-58, Osford Twp., four miles SW of Milton, and named for Elgin, MN, which was named for the city and county in Scotland. The post office closed May 18, 1888 with mail to Milton. (2, 13, 25, 40, 117, 249)

**ELGIN** (Grant). This NPRR townsite was first named SHANLEY, but became ELGIN in 1910. The residents were having difficulty agreeing on a new name, and Isadore Gintzler is said to have looked at his pocket watch to check the time at a very late hour, and suggested its brand name, Elgin, as a compromise name for the townsite. Elgin watches are made in Elgin, IL, which was named by founder James T. Gifford for Elgin, Scotland. ELGIN, ND is located in S½ Sec. 22 & N½ Sec. 27-134-89, Minnie Twp. The post office was established August 11, 1910 with Julius Heil pm in his general store. It incorporated as a village in 1911, and reached a peak population of 944 in 1960. The elevation is 2355, the Zip Code is 58533, and for many years its was a station on both the NPRR and Milwaukee Road RR. Frederick Charles Lorenzen (1881-1969) was a longtime physician in the city, and is the namesake of the local hospital. (1, 2, 3, 10, 17, 33, 40, 52, 79, 111)

**ELIDAH** (McKenzie). This was a rural post office established January 20, 1908 with Roland T. Muzzy pm, who named it for his wife. Both Roland and Elidah Muzzy were natives of ME, and Mrs. Muzzy carried the mail by horseback from Charlson to their home in NE¼ Sec. 12-152-97, eighteen miles NE of Watford City, until Maxwell Ove, a neighbor, was hired as the mail carrier. The post office closed December 15, 1919 with mail to Keene. (1, 2, 3, 18, 40, 53, 228, 415)

**ELISA** (Rolette). This was a rural post office established May 6, 1898 with John Thorson pm, who named it for his wife. The name is of Hebrew origin, meaning consecrated to God. It was located in SW¼ Sec. 9-159-71, Rice Twp., five miles south of Rolette. For a short time in 1901 it was located in NE¼ Sec. 20-159-71, the home of new pm John K. Ness, then later that year moved five miles north to the home of pm Andrew R. Thompson in NE¼ Sec. 33-160-71, Leonard Twp., which was just two miles south of Rolette. The post office closed November 30, 1905 with mail to Rolette. Eliza is an erroneous spelling. (2, 3, 19, 40, 123, 414, 415)

**ELIZABETH** (Cass). This NPRR station was established in 1900 in E½ Sec. 31-138-55, Clifton Twp., seven miles SW of Alice. Elizabeth is a Hebrew name meaning God of the oath, and several versions of its local origin exist. Some say it was named for Elizabeth Miller, daughter of Joseph Miller, the town's founder. Others say it was named for Elizabeth Fee, daughter of C. S. Fee, a NPRR official. Still others say it was

chosen by E. H. McHenry, Chief Engineer of the NPRR, for an unknown person. The post office was established March 5, 1904 with Emma Miller pm, and closed November 30, 1905 with mail to Alice. The elevator was destroyed by fire in 1922, leaving the site vacant. (1, 2, 18, 19, 34, 40, 77, 79, 118)

**ELIZABETH** (Sargent). This NPRR station was founded in 1900 in Sec. 33-132-58, Denver Twp. The origin of the name is unknown, and in early 1901 the name was changed to CRETE. (2, 3, 18)

**ELK LANDING** (McKenzie). This was a rural post office established September 14, 1915 with Raymond Robinson pm, who also had a store and lumberyard at this site in NW¼ Sec. 31-154-94, River View Twp., on the south bank of the Missouri River, opposite the Williams-Mountrail County border. The name noted that the site was a place where herds of elk forded a creek. The post office closed September 15, 1917 with mail to Charlson. Elk's Landing is an erroneous spelling. (1, 2, 3, 18, 40, 53, 79)

**ELKWOOD** (Cavalier). This was an early Canadian port-of-entry in NE¼ Sec. 3-163-59, West Hope Twp., five miles ESE of Maida. The name was coined from the fact that early pioneers had shot seven ELK near here in the heavy WOODs along the Pembina River. The post office was established January 2, 1883 with Ole M. Lillsater pm. Little development occurred, and the site was replaced first by Mowbray, then later by Maida. The post office closed August 30, 1930 with mail to Homen. Elkton is an erroneous name for this place. (1, 2, 3, 18, 25, 40, 79, 240, 292)

**ELLA** (Divide). This was a ranch post office established November 2, 1907 with Syver Peterson pm, who named it for his wife. Ella is an Anglo-Saxon name meaning elfin. It was located in NE¼ Sec. 35-161-99, Burg Twp., sixteen miles SW of Crosby. The site was part of the Ella Farm, owned by John August and Nels Z. Anderson. A rural school and cemetery completed this rural community. The post office closed March 31, 1914 with mail to Plumer. (2, 3, 19, 34, 40, 415)

**ELLEFSON** (Mountrail). This was a farm post office established March 28, 1904 with Edward Ellefson pm in his home in NE¼ Sec. 1-157-92, Cottonwood Twp., about twelve miles NW of Stanley. R. A. Hovey became pm in 1906 in his home in Sec. 2-157-92, just west of the original site. Mail was supplied on a Star Route from Ross. The post office closed April 30, 1909 with mail to Lostwood. (2, 3, 40, 53, 72)

**ELLENDALE** (Dickey). This townsite was founded in 1881 in Secs. 11 & 12-129-63, Ellendale Twp., in anticipation of the Milwaukee Road RR that arrived in 1882. The GNRR established a terminus here in 1887 before building on to Forbes in 1905. This was the first permanent white settlement in the county, and it became the county seat in 1882. The post office was established May 22, 1882 with William E. Finch pm. It incorporated as a village in 1883, and became a city in 1889 with Thomas Sefton as mayor. A state teachers college was located here 1899-1970. The elevation is 1499, the Zip Code is 58436, and a peak population of 1,967 was reported in 1980. The name honored the wife of Milwaukee Road RR official S. S. Merrill, who was born Mary Ellen Dale. By coincidence, Ellendale, MN was named for another railroad official's wife, whose maiden name was Ellen Dale. (1, 2, 3, 13, 18, 33, 40, 79, 154, 264, 316)

**ELLERTON** (Cavalier). This was a rural post office established June 27, 1888 with William H. Conn pm. It was located in NW¼ Sec. 31-164-61, Dresden Twp., six miles north of Wales, and closed August 6, 1894 with mail to Hannah. Mr. Conn had suggested the name Linden, but this was rejected by postal officials who wrote in ELLERTON, which has no known local significance. (2, 3, 25, 40, 240, 249, 414)

**ELLING** (Pierce). This was a rural post office established July 8, 1902 with Charles

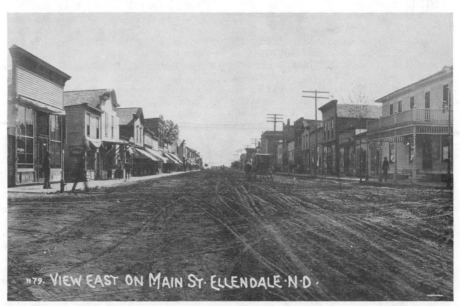

*Ellendale about 1910*

Stackhouse pm. It was located in SE¼ Sec. 12-153-74, Elling Twp., about three miles ESE of Orrin. The post office is said to have been named for Elling N. Enger (1864-1928), who had settled in 1885 on the land that would become the townsite of Barton. The township was named for Elling Jensen, who owned the country store in which this post office was located. George Youmans became pm on September 12, 1905, but the post office closed May 14, 1906 with mail to Brazil. (2, 18, 40, 114, 149)

**ELLIOTT** (Ransom). This NPRR station was platted by townsite owner Thomas M. Elliott, who came here in 1879 from Canada, in the shape of a wheel, with a park at the hub, streets forming the spokes, and a race track around the rim, but the town was built along conventional lines. The post office was established April 17, 1884 with Mr. Elliott as pm, and closed December 6, 1886 with mail to Lisbon. It reopened December 27, 1886, and closed September 15, 1904 with mail again to Lisbon. It reopened December 13, 1906, closing for good January 31, 1972 with mail to Englevale. The village, located in Sec. 23-134-57, Elliott Twp., has an elevation of 1352, the Zip Code was 58025, and a peak population of 118 was reached in 1940. 1, 2, 18, 33, 40, 77, 79)

**ELLIS** (Oliver). This was a farm post office established August 10, 1903 with Alfred B. Marshall pm. It was located in the home of Byron Ellis in Sec. 8-143-82, Marysville Twp., about four miles SW of Hensler. Ellis is a variant of the Hebrew name Elias, meaning Jehovah is God. E. G. Merriam operated one of several country stores in the area. Eliza Brown became pm in 1904, and James Thompson Jr. took over the duties in 1905, moving the post office to his farm in Sec. 18-143-82, one mile to the SW. It was closed June 26, 1908, being replaced on that date by the Seroco post office in Sec. 24-143-83, another mile to the SW (2, 19, 40, 53, 121)

**ELLISON** (Towner). This was a rural post office established October 23, 1899 with Harry H. Horner pm. It was located in SE¼ Sec. 6-161-65, Teddy Twp., six miles east of Rocklake, and was named for Thomas H. Ellison, a pioneer settler in the area. Ellison literally means son of Ellis, which is a derivatve of the Hebrew name Elias, meaning Jehovah is God. The post office closed August 31, 1912 with mail to Rocklake. (1, 2, 18, 19, 40, 53, 197)

**ELLSBURY** (Barnes). This was a farm post office established December 20, 1880 with Wallace L. Humphrey pm. It was located in NE¼ Sec. 20-143-56, Ellsbury Twp., two miles SE of Pillsbury, and named for its township which was named for George H. Ellsbury, manager of the Charlemagne Tower properties in the area. A small village began, with a population of 25 reported in 1890. The post office was discontinued December 15, 1900 with mail to Algeo. (2, 25, 34, 40, 76, 79)

**ELLSWORTH STATION** (Richland). This was a NPRR loading station in Secs. 6 & 7-132-48, Center Twp., just outside Farmington, and named for local land owner A. D. Ellsworth. It appeared on maps circa 1884-1900, sometimes simply as Ellsworth. (2, 3, 25, 77)

**ELLWOOD** (Benson). Ellwood Jenson was the son of a rural storekeeper in Sec. 29-152-69, North Viking Twp., just SW of Maddock. Plans were being made to establish a post office here, but the railroad townsite of Maddock was founded before the papers were filed, and the plans were dropped. (2, 18, 33, 34)

**ELM** (Grant). This was a farm post office established February 10, 1904 with Henry Heil Sr. pm. It was located in NW¼ Sec. 10-134-88, Elm Twp., seven miles NE of Elgin, and named for nearby Elm Butte, which was named to note a lone elm tree in the area. Heil had been rejected as its name by postal officials. In 1907 it was moved one mile SE to the home of new pm Charles H. Davison in SW¼ Sec. 14-134-88. *The Carson Press* of December 8, 1910 reported that the Elm post office had moved to the townsite of KAISER in NE¼ Sec. 31-134-88, with Mr. Davidson (sic) continuing as pm. The post office adopted the townsite's name officially on February 20, 1911. (1, 2, 3, 17, 18, 40, 111, 177, 414)

**ELMGROVE** (Dunn). This was a rural post office established February 10, 1908 with Mrs. Howard H. Fleek, nee Una Case, as pm. It was given a name descriptive of its location in SE¼ Sec. 32-148-97, in the extreme NW corner of the county on the banks of the Little Missouri River. The Fleeks moved to CA in 1913, and for a short while the post office was located in SE¼ Sec. 28-147-96, the home of acting pm Charles L. Butler, eight miles to the SE. Later that year it moved six miles NW to SW¼ Sec. 2-147-97, the home of new pm Mae E. Thorp. The post office closed March 31, 1915 with mail to Oakdale. (1, 2, 3, 40, 53, 223, 414, 415)

**ELMO** (LaMoure). This townsite was founded by the NPRR in 1900 and named ELMO for unknown reasons. It was the terminus of the Casselton-Alice branch line, famous for having several stations with female names. When the post office was established January 19, 1901 with Otto Dersch pm, there was some local talk about changing the name, and on November 26, 1902 the name was changed to MARION. (2, 3, 18, 40, 145)

**ELMO** (Ramsey). This was a Soo Line RR station built in 1900 in Sec. 13-154-61, Nixon Twp., eight miles NW of Lakota. No real development ever occurred here, with a 1930 population of 5 being the only such report. The origin of the name is unknown, although it is traced to Saint Elmo, a martyr killed at Formiae, Italy in 303 A.D., who is now the patron saint of sailors in Italy, with his feast kept on June 3 of each year. The station disappeared from maps about 1940. (1, 2, 5, 103)

**ELMPOINT** (Cavalier). This was a rural post office established May 5, 1899 with Henry Porter pm. It was located in NE¼ Sec. 8-163-57, Fremont Twp., in the extreme NE corner of the county, and given a name descriptive of the location. It closed June 8, 1900 with mail to Walhalla. (2, 3, 18, 40)

**ELM POINT** (McLean). The Lewis & Clark Expedition had camped here during the winter of 1804, the actual site being Sec. 5-144-84, Lewis and Clark Twp., across the Missouri River from Stanton. In later years the site was used as a steamboat landing, and for a time a mail drop for local settlers was maintained, but no actual post office was ever established. The name is descriptive of the locale. (25, 28)

**ELM RIVER** (Traill). This was the post office established March 18, 1874 to serve the stage station in NE¼ Sec. 26-144-49, Elm River Twp., known as ELM RIVER STATION. Fred Freebel was the first pm, and he chose to drop the "Station" from the post office's name, and simply note its location on the Elm River at its confluence with the Red River in the extreme SE corner of the county. A settlement began to develop, and on February 16, 1880 the name was changed to QUINCY. (2, 3, 18, 29, 40, 187)

**ELM RIVER STATION** (Traill). This was a stage station at the confluence of the Elm and Red Rivers in NE¼ Sec. 26-144-49, Elm River Twp., in the extreme SE corner of the county. It was run by George H. F. "Dutch Ferdinand" Johnson (1843-1912), who settled here in 1874. "H. F." stood for Henry Ford, although Mr. Johnson was born twenty years before the famous automobile manufacturer. This site was once thought to have been the NPRR crossing point into Dakota Territory, but it actually happened several miles to the south at Fargo. A post office called ELM POINT operated here 1874-1880, taking the name QUINCY in that year. (2, 3, 18, 29, 187)

**ELORA** (Walsh). This post office was established October 24, 1895 with William Sell pm. It was located in NW¼ Sec. 16-158-51, Saint Andrew Twp., serving the NPRR station called SAINT ANDREWS STATION, which had been built in 1887 and at first called NEW SAINT ANDREWS. The post office was named for Elora Jennings, the daughter of James Jennings. She later married George Welch and lived NW of Langdon in Cavalier County. Elora is a Greek name meaning light. The post office closed January 15, 1903 with mail to Cashel. At this time the NPRR renamed the station HERRICK. (2, 3, 19, 40, 75)

**ELSBERRY** (Towner). This was a station on the Farmers Grain & Shipping Co. RR (later the GNRR) founded in 1906 in SW¼ Sec. 11-162-67, Armourdale Twp., six miles NW of Rocklake. It was named for pioneer settler George F. Elsberry, formerly the pm at Clarena, and at this time the Justice of the Peace in Egeland. The post office was established January 10, 1906 with Albert L. Tennis pm, and it closed May 31, 1918 with mail to Rocklake. A peak population of 15 was reported in 1930, but the site is now a ghost town. Ellsberry is an erroneous spelling. (1, 2, 3, 18, 40, 197)

**ELSWORTH** (McKenzie). This was a rural post office established May 22, 1907 with John Gerard pm at his home in Sec. 33-149-100, Ellsworth Twp., near the source of Cherry Creek. After the name Gerard had been rejected by postal officials, it was named for its township, which was named for pioneer settler Elsworth E. Earley who served as the mail carrier, bringing it here from Schafer. The township's name is now spelled Ellsworth. The post office closed June 15, 1915 with mail to Arnegard. (1, 2, 18, 40, 53)

**ELTON** (Mountrail). This was a GNRR station two miles west of Palermo in NW¼ Sec. 16-156-90, Palermo Twp., and was the site of a water tank for servicing the steam locomotives of the era. It was served by the White Earth post office, and appears on maps only during the 1890's. Many GNRR stations were given English names, and it is likely that this place was named for one of six towns of that name in England, or possibly for Charles Isaac Elton (1839-1900), a famous jurist and archaeologist of the time. (1, 3, 5, 18, 25, 72, 240)

**ELY** (Bottineau). This was a pioneer settlement founded in 1892 in SW¼ Sec. 35-160-78, Stone Creek Twp., and named for John A. Ely, U.S. Land Commissioner in Minot. Ely is a variant of Elias, a Hebrew name meaning Jehovah is God. The post office was established June 29, 1892 with William Schroeder pm. On August 15, 1905 the post office closed, being replaced on that date by the Kramer post office at the new Soo Line RR townsite four miles to the north. (2, 19, 40, 101, 153)

**ELY** (McHenry). This was a rural post office established March 9, 1888 with Frederick W. Schroeder pm. It was located in NW¼ Sec. 1-159-78, Meadow Twp., four miles NE of Upham on the NE bank of the Souris River, and named for Col. John A. Ely, who came here in 1885, served in the territorial legislature in 1887, and was influential in getting the three northern tiers of townships (157, 158, and 159) added to McHenry County. The post office closed December 15, 1891 with mail to Wines. (3, 18, 25, 40, 412)

**ELZAS** (Emmons). This name refers to the rural community in Elzas Twp. (129-75), SE of Strasburg, west of Zeeland, and just north of the SD border. The majority of settlers, who first came here in 1886, were from Elsas, South Russia, which was named for the Alsace reion of Germany (now France), to which the ancestry of many of the residents could be traced. The variation in the spelling is not explained. Descendants of these pioneers now make up much of the population of Hague. (3, 18, 23, 66)

**EMBDEN** (Cass). This was a rural post office established February 26, 1883 with Enos Gray pm. It was located in NW¼ Sec. 32-139-53, Gill Twp., and named by Mr. Gray for his hometown of Embden, ME, which was named for Emden, Germany, which was named to note its location on the Ems River. The "b" was added to clarify the pronunciation. On May 6, 1886 the post office was moved to NW¼ Sec. 35-139-53, the home of new pm William M. Smylie, who renamed it GILL. (1, 2, 3, 10, 40, 77, 78, 79)

**EMBDEN** (Cass). A farm post office of this name operated 1883-1886 with Enos Gray pm, after which it became known as Gill. On February 8, 1888 a new EMBDEN post office was established in NE¼ Sec. 1-138-54, Eldred Twp., with Mr. Gray again serving as pm, closing July 31, 1891 with mail to Gill. It reopened October 24, 1891, and closed September 30, 1895 with mail to Petersen. It reopened February 18, 1896, and in 1900 the NPRR built a new branch line through the site, which was at first called KRUEGERSVILLE. Its namesake, local landowner William F. Krueger, declined the honor and it was agreed that the name EMBDEN should continue as the name of the new townsite. A small village of less than 100 people existed here for many years, but in recent years has declined. The post office closed May 31, 1969 with mail to Wheatland. (2, 3, 18, 25, 34, 40, 77)

**EMERADO** (Grand Forks). Henry Hancock sold the GNRR 40 acres for a townsite in 1882 in SE¼ Sec. 1 & NE¼ Sec. 12-151-53, Chester Twp. The townsite was platted in 1885 and named in a stylized fashion for the nearby Emery Farm, owned by Lewis Emery Jr., an oilman from Bradford, PA. The post office was established November 25, 1885 with Edmund Gale Jr. as pm. The little town experienced a belated boom period when the Grand Forks Air Force Base was founded in the 1950's just north of town. EMERADO incorporated as a city in 1955, and reached a peak population of 596 in 1980, although higher figures were claimed during the major construction phases at the air base. The elevation is 910, and the Zip Code is 58228. (1, 2, 25, 31, 33, 40, 69, 79, 336)

**EMERSON** (Dunn). This was an inland townsite founded in 1908 as CONNOLLY. It was located in SE¼ Sec. 19-143-94, twelve miles south of Dunn Center, and renamed EMERSON on March 30, 1909 to honor Ed Emerson, who ran a roadside inn here. Emerson means literally son of Emery, which is a Teutonic name meaning industrious. Erasmus O. Baker continued as pm after the name change. A peak population of 90 was reported in 1920, but without a railroad it began to decline. The 1930 population was just 15, and the post office closed November 15, 1933 with mail to Gladstone. It became a ghost town in the 1940's. (1, 2, 3, 18, 19, 40, 223)

**EMMA** (Dickey). This historic townsite was founded in 1883 in Sec. 2-129-60, Port Emma Twp., on the west bank of the James River two miles WNW of Ludden. It was known as BUSHTOWN and OTTAWA until 1884, when the more familiar name of PORT EMMA was coined. The post office was established February 8, 1883 with town founder Thomas W. Bush as pm, but was called simply EMMA, for Emma Williams, the first woman homesteader in the area, who on March 4, 1884 would marry Mr. Bush in the first wedding performed in the area. Emma is a Teutonic name meaning ancestress or grandmother. The post office closed March 8, 1887 with mail to Ludden. (2, 19, 25, 40, 154, 264)

**EMMET** (McLean). This farm post office was established in 1903 in NW¼ Sec. 28-148-86, Emmet Twp., twelve miles WSW of Garrison, and named ROBINSON. On September 2, 1905 the name was changed to EMMET for the infant son of new pm Charles Laudenbeck, who came here in 1904. Emmet is an Anglo-Saxon name meaning ant, with the implication of diligence. In 1910 it moved one mile NW to NE¼ Sec. 20-148-86, and in 1938 it moved two miles north to SE¼ Sec. 8-148-86. A population of 3 was reported in 1930, and in the next three federal censuses the count was 100, which surely included a wide rural area around the site. The post office, Zip Code 58534, considered by many to be the last rural post office in ND, closed February 17, 1984, although government records did not record this fact until November 25, 1985. (2, 3, 18, 19, 28, 34, 40, 278, 387)

**EMMONSBURG** (Emmons). This was a pioneer settlement in SW¼ Sec. 14-132-79, at the mouth of Big Beaver Creek on the east bank of the Missouri River. It was named for its county, which was named for James A. Emmons, a native of VA who came to Dakota in 1872 as the post trader at Camp Hancock. The post office was established October 17, 1883 with Harmidas Archambault pm, and closed November 30, 1912 with mail to Hartford. It reopened September 3, 1924 with Mrs. Sophie Ketchum pm, and closed for good November 30, 1934 with mail to Livona. A population of 28 was reported in 1890, a count of 40 was made in 1930, and the last report was a count of 25 in 1940. (1, 2, 3, 18, 25, 40, 66, 415)

**EMPIRE** (Cavalier). This was a pioneer village in Sec. 8-160-63, Henderson Twp., two miles NE of Munich. It once had a general store, blacksmith shop, and a printing office. The post office was established March 13, 1903 with William Ellenbaum pm, and given a name with no local significance. It closed March 31, 1905 with mail going to the new GNRR townsite of Munich. (2, 3, 40)

**EMPIRE CITY** (Dickey). This was a pioneer settlement in SW¼ Sec. 17-131-61, Yorktown Twp., founded in April 1883 by settlers from central New York state. The name noted their old home state's nickname, but was rejected by postal official and changed to YORKTOWN in June 1883. (2, 3, 154)

**EMRICK** (Wells). This is a Soo Line RR station in SW¼ Sec. 31-148-69, Germantown Twp., between Fessenden and Cathay. It was first called DOLAND, but because of confusion with Doland, SD, the name was changed to EMRICK, derived from Emmerich, Germany. The post office was established December 20, 1895 with Ophelia Kellner pm, and it closed January 31, 1903 with mail to Fessenden. It reopened December 12, 1903 with Gustav E. Ellingson pm, and closed November 18, 1905 with mail to Cathay. It opened for the third time August 1, 1906 with Fred C. Clough pm, and closed for good March 31, 1973 with mail again to Cathay. Development was very slow, with a peak population of just 25 being reported in 1920. Emrich is an erroneous spelling. (1, 2, 3, 18, 33, 40, 41, 54, 79, 364)

*Enderlin about 1929*

**ENDERLIN** (Ransom). This Soo Line RR townsite was founded in 1892 in Secs. 3 & 4-136-55, Liberty Twp., at the southernmost bend of the Maple River. The name is said to be a fictional character in a book, suggested by either Mrs. A. L. Allen or Mrs. Fred D. Underwood, both wives of Soo Line RR officials, but folklore insists that the name is coined from German workers in the region when the site was the terminus of the branch line, or the "end der line." The post office was established October 10, 1891 with Nels O. Akre pm. It became a city in 1897 with Dr. Olaf Sherping mayor. The elevation is 1082, the Zip Code is 58027, and a peak population of 1,919 was recorded in 1920. Hjalmer Nygaard, a Congressman from ND 1961-1963, was born here. (1, 2, 3, 18, 25, 33, 40, 52, 79)

**END OF THE TRACK** (Sargent). The NPRR reached this point, SW¼ Sec. 1-132-54, Milnor Twp., in April 1883 and the construction of its Fergus Falls-Black Hills branch line was temporarily halted. Severt A. Olson, owner of the site, started a town, and gave it this generic name. Later that year it was named GRABALL, and still in 1883 it was renamed LINTON. A boom town was just beginning when the NPRR built another three miles westward, and everything in LINTON was moved to the new terminus of Milnor. (2, 3, 171)

**ENDRES** (McLean). This was a rural post office established July 25, 1904 with Nick C. "Con" Ulrich pm. It was located in NE¼ Sec. 26-149-83, Endres Twp., eight miles south of Max, and named for Elizabeth Endres, who had become his wife in 1901. His brother, John Ulrich, married Johanna Endres in 1905. St. Adolph's Catholic Church in SW¼ Sec. 24-149-83 was the center of this community 1907-1956. The post office closed August 14, 1909 with mail to Max. (2, 3, 18, 28, 30, 389)

**ENERGY** (McLean). This blueprint townsite was platted in 1885 by T. L. Stanley of Fargo in Sec. 29-146-84, North Hancock Twp., on the Missouri River about five miles SSW of Riverdale. He gave it a name in hopes that it would lead to development at the site. The

plat showed stores, churches, a college, factories, and steamboat landings, all of which were imaginary. A post office was established August 8, 1910 with Richard C. Olson pm, and although a quarter-century had passed, he knew of this pioneer effort and revived the ENERGY name. The post office didn't last much longer than the townsite, closing May 31, 1911 with mail to Underwood. (2, 28, 40, 79)

**ENERSON** (Grand Forks). This was a rural post office established May 17, 1905 with Edward Enerson pm, but the order was rescinded November 1, 1905. Mr. Enerson, a native of Sweden, came to Dakota in 1883 from Michigan with his parents, and starting in 1899 operated one of the largest farms in the region. The post office would probably have been located at his home in SE¼ Sec. 32-154-56, Elkmount Twp., about eight miles north of Niagara. Emerson and Everson are erroneous spellings. (2, 3, 31, 40, 69)

**ENGER** (Traill). This was a post office established July 15, 1910 with Mrs. Bella Halland pm. It was located at the GNRR station known as PORTLAND JUNCTION in SE¼ Sec. 11-147-53, Viking Twp., five miles NW of Mayville, and was named for Fingal G. Enger (1846-1913), who came here in 1872 and ran a 20,000 acre bonanza farm, later serving four terms in the state senate. Others say it was named for Carl F. Enger, a local farmer. The post office closed December 15, 1912 with mail to Mayville. (2, 40, 79, 187, 240)

**ENGLEVALE** (Ransom). This NPRR townsite was originally named MARSHALL, but due to duplication in what is now SD, the post office was established November 5, 1883 as ENGLEVALE with Austin F. Taylor pm in his hotel. The townsite was in Sec. 30-134-57, Elliott Twp., and Sec. 25-134-58, Hanson Twp., and was named for Mathias L. Engle, who came here in 1881 from NY and was an avid promoter of the new townsite. The elevation is 1364, and a peak population of about 200 was maintained between the two World Wars, although the population is now less than 100. The post

office, Zip Code 58028, closed March 26, 1985. (1, 2, 3, 18, 25, 33, 40, 77, 79, 201)

**ENLOE** (Richland). This was a Milwaukee Road RR station built in the 1890's as SPERRY, named for elevator manager William Enloe Sperry, who started a post office in 1892. It was located in SW¼ Sec. 17-135-48, Eagle Twp., four miles NW of Abercrombie. About 1910 the station began to be listed as ENLOE, and on March 12, 1913 pm Peter Bolme renamed the post office to match. The post office closed May 31, 1923 with mail to Abercrombie, and the elevator was moved into Christine in 1967. Enlo is an erroneous spelling. (1, 2, 3, 18, 40, 147, 345)

**ENTERPRISE** (Ward). This was a rural post office established May 3, 1904 with William H. Von Ehr pm. It was located in SE¼ Sec. 15-159-88, Baden Twp., eight miles NW of Donnybrook. The order was rescinded on November 23, 1904 before the post office had gone into operation. The name is thought to have been promotional. (3, 40, 415)

**EPPING** (Williams). This GNRR station in Sec. 1-155-99, Springbrook Twp., was named by railroad officials for the city of Epping, Essexshire, England, and the forest in this region. Queen Victoria made the area a public recreation park in 1882. Postal officials selected this name from six that were submitted, probably because the only other Epping in the country is in New Hampshire, resulting in little chance for confusion with other sites. The post office was established March 10, 1906 with Asa D. Lawrence pm, and the village incorporated in 1913. The elevation is 2221, the Zip Code is 58843, and the peak population of 183 was reached in 1930. In the early days, EPPING billed itself as "The Biggest Little Town on the Great Northern." (1, 2, 5, 18, 33, 40, 50, 79)

**EPWORTH** (Mountrail). This inland town was first called INDIANA, but the name was rejected by postal officials. The post office was established March 13, 1906 with Francis A. Newnam (1839-1923) pm, replacing the rural post office of Dymond one mile to the north. EPWORTH was located in NW¼ Sec. 35-154-90, Austin Twp., and because of its central location in newly formed Mountrail County, it had high hopes of securing the county seat. Cora Newnam, a daughter of the pm, chose the name to remember their former home of Epworth, MO, which was named for Epworth, England, the birthplace of religious leader John Wesley. The Epworth League is a society of Methodist young people and had two million members worldwide at this time. A small village began, with a store, printing office, bank, and post office, but the lack of a railroad eventually ended the town's hopes. The post office closed December 31, 1942 with mail to Palermo. (2, 3, 5, 40, 72, 289)

**ERICKSON** (McLean). This was a rural post office established February 13, 1886 with Par "Preacher" Erickson pm, who suggested the name Paradise. Postal officials rejected this name, substituting the name of the pm. It was located in his country store in SE¼ Sec. 10-144-84, twelve miles WNW of Washburn, and just north of what is now believed to be the true site of Fort Mandan, the 1804-1805 winter headquarters of the Lewis & Clark Expedition. A population of 25 was reported in 1890, but the post office closed January 7, 1890 with mail to Conkling. (2, 3, 25, 28, 40, 414)

**ERIE** (Cass). This GNRR station was built in the spring of 1881 in NE¼ Sec. 16-142-53, Erie Twp. The post office was established October 30, 1882 with John McKee, a pioneer merchant, as pm. The owner of the townsite, H. W. Noble, had come here from Erie, PA. Others say it was named by settlers from Erie County, NY. Both of these places, and the Great Lake, are named for the Iroquois Indian word meaning long tail, referring to the tribe's nickname of "Cat Nation." The townsite was platted in 1904, and a small village of about 150 people has existed here for many years. The elevation is 1115, and the Zip Code is 58029. (1, 2, 10, 11, 33, 34, 40, 77, 79)

**ERIE JUNCTION** (Cass). This name is shown on a state map published about 1940 at the junction of GNRR lines in SW¼ Sec. 22-142-53, Erie Twp., just south of Erie. Earlier maps show this place as MASON JUNCTION. (1, 3, 34)

**ERNEST** (Pembina). This was a farm post office established February 25, 1880 with Henry McGuire pm. The origin of the name is unknown, although it is a Teutonic name meaning intent in purpose. It was located in Sec. 13-163-56, Walhalla Twp., four miles NE of Walhalla. A small village began to develop, and a population of 47 was reported in 1890, but when the site failed to attract a railroad, it declined, and the post office closed June 30, 1904 with mail to Walhalla. (2, 19, 25, 33, 40, 53, 108, 240)

**ERROR** (Renville). This place name appears on a state map included in a 1922 atlas published by the John Thomas Co. It is on the east bank of Cut Bank Creek, a few miles SSE of Sherwood. Nothing else has been found concerning ERROR, ND, and perhaps it is what the name implies. (3)

**ESLER** (Stutsman). This was a station on the Fort Totten-Fort Seward trail in NE¼ Sec. 16-143-64, Lyon Twp., seven miles SW of Kensal, named for pioneer settlers Alexander and William Esler. The post office was established June 7, 1882 with Alexander Esler pm, and it was discontinued September 29, 1906 with mail to Kensal. (2, 3, 18, 25, 40, 158, 415)

**ESMOND** (Benson). This NPRR townsite was founded in 1901 as RHODES, but the post office was established August 5, 1901 as ESMOND, with Jens A. Lyngved pm, and named for Henry Esmond, the fictional hero of a novel by British author William Makepeace Thackeray. Esmond is an Anglo-Saxon name meaning gracious protector. A village in SD was founded in 1883 and named for the same reason. The site, NE¼ Sec. 34-153-71, Esmond Twp., was platted in 1901, and is called "The Terminal City" because it is the terminus of the NPRR's Oberon branch line. The elevation is 1646, the Zip Code is 58332, and a peak population of 535 was reached in 1910. The village incorporated in 1906, and it became a city in 1952 with Albert Horner as mayor. The

well known politician, Sebastian Fabian "Buckshot" Hoffner, is a native of ESMOND. (1, 2, 3, 18, 33, 36, 40, 79, 110, 149)

**ESSEX** (Ramsey). This was a Soo Line RR station built in 1913 in Sec. 33-154-63, Minnewaukan Twp., five miles east of Devils Lake. Some sources say it was named for Essex County, NY, while others say it was named for the Earl of Essex. Both trace their origin to Essex County, England, just east of London. A population of 3 was reported in 1930 and 1940, but the site was abandoned shortly after the latter date. (1, 2, 10, 45, 103)

**ESTES** (McKenzie). This was a rural post office established May 2, 1908 with Fred Roche Estes (1869-1949) pm. It was located in NE¼ Sec. 6-149-104, eight miles SW of Cartwright near the east bank of the Yellowstone River, and closed September 15, 1916 with mail to Cartwright. (1, 2, 3, 18, 40, 227)

**ESTHER** (Grant). This was a rural post office established June 3, 1907 with George E. Miles pm. It was located in Secs. 20 & 21-133-84, Brisbane Twp., and closed August 15, 1911 with mail to Brisbane, two miles to the north. The origin of the name is unknown, although it is traced to Hebrew, Latin, and Greek roots, and in ancient Persia signified the planet Venus. (2, 17, 18, 19, 40, 177)

**ETHEL** (Emmons). This was a pioneer post office established February 13, 1886 with George A. Peters pm. It never went into operation, and no other entries are found in government records. The location and origin of the name are unknown. (3, 40)

**ETHEL** (McLean). This was a farm post office established January 15, 1898 with Dan Williams pm. It was located in NW¼ Sec. 27-147-79, Wise Twp., twelve miles NE of Turtle Lake on the shore of Brush Lake. It was named for nearby Ethel Lake, named for the daughter of John Merry, a local rancher. Ethel is a Teutonic name meaning noble. The post office closed October 15, 1900 with mail to Turtle Lake. (2, 19, 28, 40)

**ETNA** (Cavalier). This was a farm post office established September 13, 1902 with Mark J. O'Brien pm. It was located in SW¼ Sec. 6-159-63, Banner Twp., and on September 8, 1905 moved five miles west to the new Soo Line RR townsite of Calio, assuming that name. The origin of the name ETNA is unknown. (2, 3, 18, 40, 249)

**EVANS** (Oliver). This was a rural post office established June 1, 1908 with Bernard E. Evans as the first and only pm. It was located in Sec. 7-142-87, Bert Twp., about ten miles south of Beulah just inside the county line, and closed March 15, 1917 with mail to Beulah. (2, 7, 18, 33, 40, 121)

**EVANSTON** (Ramsey). This farm post office was established April 14, 1898 with George W. H. Davis pm. It was located in SE¼ Sec. 18-157-64, Hammer Twp., four miles SW of Starkweather, and one mile NE of the original Evanston post office established in 1895 in Towner County. Will Davis succeeded his father as pm in 1907, and the post

office closed July 15, 1910 with mail to Starkweather. (2, 3, 18, 40, 103, 415)

**EVANSTON** (Towner). This was a farm post office established November 4, 1895 with William J. Evans pm. It was located in NE¼ Sec. 24-157-65, Coolin Twp., five miles SW of Starkweather, just inside the Towner County line. It closed March 15, 1898 with mail to Starkweather. It reopened April 14, 1898 at a new site one mile to the NE, which was in Ramsey County. (2, 3, 18, 40, 103, 415)

**EVEREST** (Cass). This was a GNRR station built in 1881 in NE¼ Sec. 15-139-52, Everest Twp., two miles south of Casselton. A village was platted in 1881 and the post office was established May 24, 1882 with Carl Knuppel pm. A population of 175 was reported in 1890, but the GNRR revised their long-range plans, removed this station in 1895, and took up the tracks in 1896. The post office closed August 13, 1904, reopened September 17, 1904, and closed for good November 30, 1908 with mail in both closings going to Casselton. The village existed for many years, reporting a population of 10 as late as 1960. All sources say the town was named for the editor of *The Lisbon Star*, but his name was actually Charles A. Everitt, not Everest. (2, 3, 18, 25, 34, 40, 77, 202, 300)

**EWEN** (Foster). This was a farm post office established June 6, 1890 with Henry S. Ewen pm. He settled in Sec. 14-146-65, Rosehill Twp., sixteen miles east of Carrington, in 1885. On October 3, 1895 the post office was moved four miles west to the home of new pm Joseph Haven in Sec. 18-146-64, Haven Twp. On June 19, 1896 the name was changed to HAVEN. A name change to MARIA in 1902 was at first approved, but was later rescinded, and it operated as HAVEN until closing in 1909. (2, 3, 40, 97)

**EXETER** (Emmons). This was a rural post office established March 2, 1887 with Florentine J. Brown pm, who named it for Exeter, Ontario, Canada, which was named for Exeter, Devonshire, England, which was named to note its location on the left bank of the River Exe. It was located in Sec. 30-132-74, twelve miles ESE of Linton, and closed October 30, 1897 with mail to Dakem. It reopened January 8, 1898 with Hiram Scott pm at his home in N½ Sec. 26-131-74, eight miles SE of the original site, and closed for good March 30, 1907 with mail to Dakem when pm-to-be Joseph Schmaltz declined his appointment. (2, 3, 5, 10, 25, 34, 40, 66, 415)

**EXPANSION** (Mercer). This was a pioneer Missouri River port established in 1899 in NE¼ Sec. 27-147-86, about fifteen miles north of Hazen. Town founders John Bloodgood and Jacob Kruckenberg named it to announce their confidence in its growth. The post office was established April 18, 1901 with Mr. Kruckenberg as pm. A population of 75 was reported in 1920, but the post office closed December 15, 1922 with mail to Krem. The town continued to appear on many maps until it was inundated by Lake Sakakawea in the 1950's. (2, 3, 18, 40, 64)

**EYFORD** (Pembina). This was a farm post office established January 11, 1887 with

Jacob Eyford pm. It was located in NE¼ Sec. 33-160-56, Thingvalla Twp., midway between Mountain and Gardar. A small Icelandic settlement began here, with a population of 10 being reported in 1890, but the post office closed September 5, 1895 with mail to Mountain. (2, 3, 25, 40, 108, 414)

**EYRESVILLE** (Traill). This was a rural post office established November 8, 1880 with Joseph G. Eyres pm. It was located in Sec. 24-144-52, Greenfield Twp., five miles south of Blanchard, and closed March 2, 1881 with mail to Casselton. It reopened April 11, 1881 with Mr. Eyres again serving as pm, but closed for good February 7, 1882 with mail again to Casselton. The EYRESVILLE community survived into the 1890's, and was served by the Kelso post office. Eyersville is an erroneous spelling. (2, 3, 40, 415)

**FABIAN** (Cass). This NPRR station was built in October 1901 in SW¼ Sec. 9-138-54, Eldred Twp., just NE of Alice, serving as a grain loading facility. The name honored Harry A. Fabian, Chief Clerk to the President of the railroad. Fabian is a Latin name meaning bean farmer. The facilities were removed in April 1940. (1, 2, 18, 19, 34)

**FAIRCHILD** (Walsh). This was a rural post office established May 5, 1884 with George O. Sevinson pm. It was located in NW¼ Sec. 4-157-54, Fertile Twp., seven miles NE of Park River, and closed February 19, 1885 with mail to Perry. The origin of the name is unknown. (25, 40, 414)

**FAIRDALE** (Walsh). This Soo Line RR station was founded in 1905 in SE¼ Sec. 22 & SW¼ Sec. 23-158-59, Kinloss Twp., and given a descriptive name noting its pleasant location in the Park River valley. The post office was established September 27, 1905 with Ole J. Nordlie pm. The Zip Code is 58229, and the village, which incorporated in 1907, reached a peak population of 192 in 1920. Al Van Dahl, the pioneer editor of *The Fairdale Times*, later achieved success in Mill City, OR as the publisher of *The Western Stamp Collector*, a national periodical serving that popular hobby. (1, 2, 3, 18, 33, 40, 75) •

**FAIRFIELD** (Billings). A post office was established August 10, 1911 with John Tester pm in his home in SE¼ Sec. 18-143-98, twenty miles NNE of Belfield. Mr. Tester declined suggestions to name it for himself, instead choosing a name to note the area's fair fields of grain. In 1922 the post office moved to a new townsite in Sec. 22-143-99, about four miles WSW of the original site, with Mark Brandt as pm. John Petryzak ran a store and the post office 1945-1972, when the townsite was relocated to Sec. 10-142-99, about four miles south, absorbing the Gorham post office. This last move was related to the booming oil industry development in the region. The Zip Code is 58627. (2, 3, 40, 81)

**FAIRGROUND** (Cass). This was a contract station of the Fargo post office that operated July 17, 1922 until July 22, 1922, the dates of the 1922 State Fair, which was held in Fargo for many years. The site was in NW¼ Sec. 31-140-48, Reed Twp., at the time the extreme north end of Fargo. (3, 40, 414)

**FAIRLAWN** (Grand Forks). This was a platted subdivision in SW¼ Sec. 5-151-50, Grand Forks Twp., at a junction of GNRR lines just west of the city of Grand Forks. It appeared on maps during the 1920's, and is now a part of Grand Forks. The name is descriptive. (3, 18)

**FAIRMOUNT** (Richland). This village began as the DeVILLO post office in 1880, and officially was founded in 1883 in Sec. 20-130-47, Fairmount Twp. The post office adopted this name June 5, 1884 with War-

*Fairdale    about 1910*

ren Spaulding continuing as pm. The new name was suggested by Joseph C. Henvis for Fairmount Park in his native Philadelphia, PA, which was the site of the original Quaker settlement in that city. The elevation is 983, the Zip Code is 58030, and the village, which incorporated in 1887, reached a peak population of 706 in 1920. Before the locally-formed Fairmount & Veblen RR merged with the Soo Line RR in 1915, this town claimed to be the only place in the state with four different railroads, having been previously reached by the Milwaukee Road RR in 1884, and the GNRR and Soo Line RR in 1886. (1, 2, 3, 10, 18, 25, 33, 40, 52, 79, 147, 354)

**FAIRVIEW** (Cavalier). This was an early platted townsite in SE¼ Sec. 23-161-60, Elgin Twp., just south of Langdon near the present Langdon Reservoir. The name is descriptive, and it has long since become part of the city of Langdon. (3, 18, 34)

**FAIRVIEW** (Griggs). This was a GNRR station built in 1910 in NW¼ Sec. 20-144-58, Broadview Twp., between Hannaford and Luverne. It was named by the Luverne Land Co. to note the fair view of the Sheyenne River from this site on the bluffs west of the river. Henry Curtis, original townsite owner, sold the site to the GNRR, but no settlement occurred. In 1912 it was renamed KARNAK. (1, 2, 3, 65)

**FAIRVIEW GARDENS** (Ward). This was a platted townsite in NE¼ Sec. 21-155-83, Harrison Twp., two miles west of Minot, on land originally owned by F.L. Metcalf. The name was descriptive of its location in the Souris River valley, and it appeared only in a 1915 county atlas. (3, 18)

**FAIRVIEW JUNCTION** (Richland). This was a NPRR loading station built in 1913 in Sec. 9-132-49, Mooreton Twp., two miles east of

Mooreton. The owner of the land at this short spur was originally from Fairview, PA. The site was served by the Wahpeton post office. (2, 3, 18, 25)

**FALCONER** (McLean). This was a rural community founded in the 1880's, and named for Samuel Falconer, a native of Lancaster, Ontario, Canada, who had been a United States Receiver of the Ports in Stika, AK before homesteading in this area. He originally spelled his family name as Faulkner. Others say it was named for Angus Falconer, another local pioneer. The post office was established April 14, 1884 with Samuel Falconer pm. It was located in NE¼ Sec. 33-143-81, Nettle Creek Twp., one mile SE of the Reed post office which it replaced. J. C. Every operated a hotel on Painted Woods Lake two miles to the north, and the community also had a school. The post office closed October 31, 1905 with mail to Washburn. It reopened September 14, 1910, closing for good July 15, 1913 with mail again to Washburn. The school was the first in McLean County, and the hotel was for many years a popular stopping point on the trail between Fort Stevenson and Bismarck. (2, 3, 12, 25, 28, 40, 79)

**FALDET** (Bottineau). This GNRR station was built in 1904 in Secs. 29 & 32-163-78, Scandia Twp., and named for Faldet, Norway, the hometown of a local pioneer named Christofferson. English-speaking residents had trouble pronouncing and spelling the name, and the Norwegians were fearful that the name might get corrupted into "Foldet", as in *syndefoldet*, meaning falling into sin. In 1905 the station was renamed ROTH, although the post office was first established in 1907 as HEWITT. Some sources say this site was named Faldot, for a city in Canada, which appears to be an erroneous statement of fact. (2, 3, 34, 101, 153, 380)

**FALKIRK** (McLean). This Soo Line station was founded in 1913 in W½ Sec. 23-145-82, Buffalo Lake Twp., between Washburn and Underwood, and named MINDEN. When the post office was established December 16, 1916 with Walter C. Jertson pm, the name was changed to FALKIRK to avoid confusion with Mandan. The new name was chosen by postal officials because it was the only place with this name in the entire country, and traces to Falkirk, Stirlingshire, Scotland, the site of a famous battle on July 22, 1298. The new townsite had grown to a population of 50 in 1920, but it has declined to less than half that figure today. The post office closed April 30, 1955 with mail to Washburn. (2, 5, 28, 40, 79)

**FALLON** (Morton). This rural settlement dates to the late 1890's in NW¼ Sec. 4-135-83, eight miles NE of Flasher. The post office was established April 2, 1900 with James A. Fallon, a native of Ireland, as pm. In 1909 it was relocated to NE¼ Sec. 15-135-83 with H. S. Freiz pm. This site was on the old Mandan-Black Hills stage trail. About 10 people have lived here since its founding, as the inland village never attracted any real development. The post office closed November 15, 1914 with mail to Flasher. (2, 17, 40, 107)

**FALSEN** (McHenry). This GNRR station was founded in 1912 in Sec. 31-154-78, Falsen Twp., between Simcoe and Karlsruhe. The post office was established March 10, 1913 with Oliver H. Wolhowe pm. The area was largely settled by Germans from Kandel and Selz, South Russia. The origin of FALSEN is unknown, and on March 1, 1925 it was changed to VERENDRYE. (1, 2, 18, 23, 33, 40)

**FANCHER** (Stutsman). This rural post office was established September 19, 1900 with Martha Arms pm. It was located in Sec. 34-142-62, Gray Twp., ten miles north of Spiritwood, and two miles north of Spiritwood Lake. It was named for Frederick Bartlett Fancher (1852-1944), the first pm at nearby Albion, who was the President of the ND Constitutional Convention in 1889, ND Insurance Commissioner in 1894, and Governor of ND 1899-1901. The post office closed May 15, 1909 with mail to Wimbledon. Francher is an erroneous spelling. (2, 3, 18, 40, 53, 158)

**FARGO** (Cass). This city began in 1871 as THE CROSSING, was unofficially called TENT CITY, and was known as CENTRALIA until becoming FARGO on February 12, 1872, honoring William George Fargo (1818-1881), President of the Wells-Fargo Express Co., and a director of the NPRR. Known as "The Biggest Little City in the World," it has become the metropolis of ND, reaching a population of 61,281 in 1980, and a metropolitan area population of well over 100,000. Gordon J. Keeney, an attorney, continued as pm after the name change in 1872. It became a city in 1875 with George Egbert as mayor. The elevation is 903, the base Zip Code is 58102, and the city sprawls over parts of four townships. Many famous people have called FARGO home, including Roger Maris (1934-1985), the man who broke Babe Ruth's single season homerun record in 1961. It is the county seat of Cass

*Fargo business district 1909*

County, and in many ways the dominant city of ND. (1, 2, 3, 5, 10, 13, 33, 40, 44, 77, 79, 199, 307)

**FARIBAULT** (Ransom). This was an alternate name for the early stage station called PIGEON POINT that operated 1867-1872 under the management of David Faribault. (3, 153, 201, 206)

**FARLAND** (McKenzie). This was a rural post office established November 2, 1907 with Jens G. Walla (1871-1925) pm. Peter Vidmo opened a store here that same year, and in 1909 the Farland Lutheran Church was built. The location was NW¼ Sec. 29-151-99, Farland Twp., six miles NNE of Arnegard. The name was coined to note that this place was very far from everywhere else. The post office moved one mile NE to SE¼ Sec. 20-151-99 just before it closed November 30, 1916 with mail to Arnegard. (1, 2, 40, 53, 79, 229)

**FARMINGTON** (Richland). This was a NPRR station built in the 1880's to serve a bonanza farm colony in Sec. 7-132-48, Center Twp., six miles WSW of Wahpeton. The name noted the occupation of the people in this area. A post office was established May 6, 1886 with William O. Rogers pm, and a population of 75 was reported in 1890. The post office closed September 30, 1909 with mail to Wahpeton. (2, 3, 18, 25, 40, 79)

**FARQUER** (Foster). This was a NPRR station built in the 1880's in Secs. 4 & 9-145-66, Melville Twp., about four miles NW of Melville, and six miles SE of Carrington. It was named for William Farquer (1835-1912), a Civil War veteran who settled in Sec. 2-145-66 in 1883, moving into Carrington in 1889. He was a justice of the peace, and a county Superintendent of Schools. Although little development ever occurred at this site, it appeared on maps into the 1940's. Farquar is an erroneous spelling. (2, 3, 34, 79, 97)

**FARRINGTON** (Mercer). This was a rural post office established July 15, 1909 as THOMAS in SW¼ Sec. 30-144-87, one mile east of Beulah. On February 21, 1910 the

name was changed to FARRINGTON, both names honoring pm Thomas P. Farrington. It was discontinued April 29, 1914 when it was transferred to Beulah, taking the name of the new NPRR townsite. (2, 3, 40)

**FAUST** (Barnes). This was a Soo Line RR station built in 1892 and named IVAN. It was located in SW¼ Sec. 31-141-58, Getchell Twp., six miles NW of Valley City. In 1898 it was renamed for Aaron, Jacob, Charles, Otto and Peter Faust, five brothers who came here in 1882. The station was removed in 1939. (2, 18, 34, 76)

**FAYETTE** (Dunn). This was a much remembered farm post office established May 5, 1898 in the sod house of pm Elizabeth French Little (1858-1946), who served in that capacity until retiring in 1940. Her husband, Frank A. Little, named the post office for his business partner, Dr. Fayette D. Kendrick of Saint Paul, MN. Fayette is an Old French name meaning little fairy. It was located in SE¼ Sec. 26-144-97, eight miles WNW of Manning. Anna Fisher became pm in 1940 and served until the post office closed July 31, 1956 with mail to Manning. The original sod house was used for the post office during the entire life of the facility. (1, 2, 3, 18, 19, 40, 79)

**FERDINAND** (Eddy). This was a farm post office established June 27, 1906 with Pasquale DeFiore pm. It was located in E½ Sec. 18-150-63, Eddy Twp., about twenty miles NE of New Rockford, and about six miles SW of Warwick. The origin of the name, which is Teutonic and means adventurous in life, is unknown. The post office was discontinued May 31, 1907 with mail to Morris. (2, 3, 40, 321)

**FERGUS** (Grand Forks). This was a rural post office established July 11, 1893 with Michael Kent pm. It was located in NW¼ Sec. 22-150-56, Logan Center Twp., just across the road from the community known for years as Logan Center. Most sources state that the name honored pioneer settler Peter Ferguson, although some say a mail carrier named McEvins named it for his hometown in Ontario, Canada. Fergus is a Celtic name meaning of manly strength. The country store containing the post office burned in 1918, and the post office closed September 30, 1919 with mail to Kempton. (1, 2, 3, 18, 19, 31, 40, 69, 241)

**FERN** (Burke). This was a farm post office established January 4, 1904 with Ole Haugen pm. It was located in NW¼ Sec. 22-162-93, Fay Twp., five miles SSE of Columbus. The origin of the name, Greek for feather, is unknown. The post office closed November 15, 1907 with mail to Macroom. (2, 19, 40, 53, 67)

**FERNWOOD** (Towner). This was a rural post office established February 9, 1905 with William B. Underwood pm, and located in SW¼ Sec. 12-163-68, Picton Twp., one-half mile NW of Hansboro. The name was coined from the names of F. H. FERNyhough and the pm, W. B. UnderWOOD, who homesteaded adjoining quarter sections. The post office closed April 2, 1906 with mail to Hansboro. (2, 3, 18, 40)

**FERO** (Pierce). This was a GNRR station on the mainline five miles east of Rugby in Sec. 3-156-72, Meyer Twp., named for Charles W. Fero, a GNRR engineer. The post office was established August 4, 1905 with Michael Savage pm, and closed February 15, 1911 with mail to Rugby. It reopened January 24, 1917, closing February 14, 1920 with mail again to Rugby. It again went into operation June 9, 1922, closing for good April 30, 1942 with mail to Pleasant Lake. FERO was a long-lived small village, recording a population of 15 in 1920, and showing 4 residents as late as 1960. (2, 3, 18, 40, 114)

**FERTILE** (Divide). This was a rural post office established September 20, 1907 with Jens Sorenson pm in Sec. 5-160-102, Fertile Valley Twp., ten miles south of Alkabo. The name came from the township, which was named by settlers from Fertile, MN, which was named by settlers from Fertile, IA. All of these places can claim that the name is descriptive of the soil in the area. The post office was discontinued March 31, 1924 with mail to Grenora. (2, 13, 18, 34, 40)

**FERTILE** (Walsh). This was a farm post office established March 22, 1881 with Osmund T. Hjemdal pm, and named by settlers from Iowa to note the fertile soil at their new home. The township adopted the name in 1882. It was located in SW¼ Sec. 26-157-54, Fertile Twp., nine miles WSW of Grafton, and closed June 7, 1883 with mail to Grafton. Roger Allin came here in 1880 from Ontario, Canada, and lived in SE¼ Sec. 22-157-54, one mile NW of the post office. Mr. Allin was the first township clerk, and was Governor of ND 1895-1896. (2, 3, 25, 40, 75, 415)

**FESSENDEN** (Wells). This Soo Line RR townsite was founded in 1893 in Secs. 7 & 8-148-70, Oshkosh Twp., at the site of the rural post office called WELLS. On November 23, 1893 the old post office was replaced by the FESSENDEN post office, with John Austin Regan pm. It was named for Cortez Fessenden (1825-1910), Surveyor-General for Dakota Territory 1861-1885,

*Fessenden about 1960*

and because of its central location, became the county seat in 1894, taking that honor away from the pioneer settlement of Sykeston. The elevation is 1605, the Zip Code is 58438, and the village incorporated in 1904, becoming a city in 1905 with E. F. Volkman mayor. The peak population of 920 was recorded in 1960. (1, 2, 3, 18, 33, 40, 54, 79, 363)

**FIFE** (Cass). This NPRR station in NW¼ Sec. 2-139-50, Mapleton Twp., three miles east of Mapleton, was built in 1882 and called CANFIELD. The name was changed on June 2, 1907 to honor Joe Fife of Ontario, Canada, who developed Scotch Fife wheat in 1872, which was the leading hard spring wheat grown in the Red River valley. The elevator at this site closed during the 1920's, and the site is currently used to store railroad cars for use at the stockyards in West Fargo. (1, 2, 18, 77)

**FIFTEENTH SIDING** (Kidder). This NPRR siding was built in 1873 in SW¼ Sec. 19-139-74, Pleasant Hill Twp., right on the Burleigh County line eight miles west of Steele. It was named for its chronological order as sidings were built westward from Fargo. About 1882 the name was changed to GENEVA, and about 1915 it was moved a mile west into Burleigh County. No development took place at either site. (2, 18, 25, 122)

**FIFTH SIDING** (Barnes). The NPRR changed the name of SECOND CROSSING OF THE SHEYENNE when the siding was completed in October 1872. The new name noted the chronological order of sidings as they were built westward from Fargo. Later that year settlers began to call the place WAHPETON, a name never recognized by the NPRR. The name WORTHINGTON was adopted in 1874, and in 1878 it became VALLEY CITY. It was located in SE¼ Sec. 21-140-58, just west of the actual crossing of the Sheyenne River. (2, 3, 76, 275)

**FIFTH SIDING** (Stark). This NPRR siding

was built in 1881 in Sec. 18-139-91, twelve miles SW of Hebron. The name noted the chronological order of sidings as they were built westward from Mandan. Later that year it was named YOUNG MAN'S BUTTE SIDING, and in 1882 it was named ANTELOPE. (2, 3, 74)

**FILLMORE** (Benson). This was a farm post office established September 27, 1901 with Erick E. Arness pm. It was located in SE¼ Sec. 8-154-71, Impark Twp., and named by settlers from Fillmore County, MN, which was named for Millard Fillmore (1800-1874), thirteenth President of the United States. In 1912 the post office was moved to the new Soo Line RR townsite in SW¼ Sec. 4-154-71, one mile NNE of the original site, with Ole Vold pm. The Zip Code is 58333, and a peak population of 150 was reported in 1920, with a decline to just 74 in 1960. (2, 3, 10, 18, 33, 34, 40, 79, 149)

**FINCH** (Morton). This was a farm post office established March 30, 1909 with Bert H. Finch pm, located in SE¼ Sec. 32-134-82, New Hope Twp. On July 21, 1910 it was replaced by the post office at Timmer, a new NPRR townsite just SE across the section line, with Mr. Finch continuing as pm. (2, 3, 18, 40, 107)

**FINGAL** (Barnes). This Soo Line RR townsite was founded in 1891 in SE¼ Sec. 18-138-56, Binghampton Twp., between Lucca and Cuba, and named by settlers from Fingal, Ontario, Canada, which was named for Fingal's Cave, Scotland. Fingal was the King of Morven on the NW coast of ancient Scotland who invaded and defeated Ireland, these events being the subject of the 1762 epic poem by James MacPherson. The post office was established December 11, 1891 with Thorkel A. Thorkelson (1860-1912) pm. The village, which incorporated in 1920, reached a peak population of 324 in 1930, but has declined to just 153 in 1980. The elevation is 1277, and the Zip Code is 58031. (1, 2, 5, 18, 33, 34, 40, 52, 76, 79, 118)

FINLAND (Nelson). This was a Finnish community that developed in the 1890's about two miles NW of Pelto. A school and town hall were built in Sec. 8-154-59, Enterprise Twp., the cemetery was just east in Sec. 9-154-59, and a church was built just to the north in SE¼ Sec. 5-154-59, on land homesteaded by John and Erick Kyllonen. Some sources say a post office operated here 1899-1903, but government records do not confirm this. (2, 3, 18, 124)

FINLAND (Ramsey). This was a farm post office established October 29, 1898 with Charles Hango pm, who suggested the name of Great Finland, which was shortened by postal officials to simply FINLAND. Mr. Hango was one of a large colony of Finnish settlers in this area. The post office was located in NE¼ Sec. 22-155-60, Lillehoff Twp., two miles north of Brocket, and closed December 31, 1901 with mail to Brocket. (2, 40, 58, 103, 414)

FINLEY (Steele). This GNRR townsite was founded in 1896 as WALKER, changed its name to FINLEY, and absorbed its rival adjoining townsite of GILBERT in January 1897. It was named for W. W. Finley, a GNRR official. The post office was established January 29, 1897 with Alfred Kenning Cochrane (1855-1949) pm. The village incorporated in 1903, and it became a city in 1926 with Benton J. Long as first mayor. In 1918 it succeeded the inland town of Sherbrooke as county seat. The elevation is 1448, the Zip Code is 58230, and a peak population of 809 was reached in 1970. Peter O. Sathre (1876-1978), a Justice of the ND Supreme Court and ND Attorney General began his law career here, and Harvey B. Knudson (1903-1979), also a Justice of the ND Supreme Court, was born here. Finlay is an erroneous spelling. (1, 2, 18, 33, 40, 52, 79, 99, 326)

FISCHBEIN (Bowman). This settlement began in 1907 in Sec. 32-131-99, Fischbein Twp., just NW of present-day GASCOYNE. The post office was established November 8, 1907 with Max F. Fischbein, who had just come here from Saint Paul, MN, as pm. As this townsite began to grow along the new Milwaukee Road RR tracks, it was said that the railroad telegraphers were having difficulty with the name, resulting in a change to GASCOYNE, which doesn't seem to be very easy either. The change officially took place on March 25, 1908, but postmarks of FISCHBEIN are known dated much later in that year. The son of Max Fischbein related in later years that his father retained the old name for the post office until January 1, 1909, explaining this discrepancy. (2, 3, 18, 34, 40, 120, 381)

FISHER (Barnes). This was a farm post office established August 20, 1883 with Edwin Fisher pm. It was located in Sec. 12-140-60, Potter Twp., nine miles NW of Sanborn, and closed September 25, 1885 with mail to Sanborn. (2, 3, 25, 40, 76)

FISHER (Rolette). This was a rural post office established September 7, 1898 with John Fisher pm, located in NW¼ Sec. 26-160-72, Wolf Creek Twp., four miles west of Rolette, serving the rural community known as WOLF CREEK. The post office was discontinued June 29, 1907 with mail to Rolette. Peter Henkes operated a blacksmith shop here for many years. (2, 3, 40, 75, 123)

FISHLAKE (Benson). This was a farm post office established February 23, 1899 with Daniel Olson pm. It was located in NE¼ Sec. 6-153-69, Albert Twp., five miles SW of Harlow, and named for Fish Lake just to the east. The lake was noted for its abundance of fish, but one year it froze completely, killing all the fish. Later it dried up, and today no longer exists. The one-word spelling was intentional, conforming with recently enacted government rules for geographic names. The post office was discontinued October 31, 1906 with mail to Maddock. (2, 18, 34, 40)

FLASHER (Morton). This NPRR townsite was founded in 1902 in NW¼ Sec. 3-134-84, Flasher Twp., by William H. Brown (1860-1943), who named it IOWA CITY, and then BERRIER. Both names were rejected by postal officials. Mr. Brown then named it FLASHER, for his secretary and niece, Mabel Flasher (1880-1934), later Mrs. Owen Vrooman of Saint Paul, MN, and this name was accepted. The post office was established January 3, 1903 with William F. Berrier pm. The elevation is 1929, the Zip Code is 58535, and the village, which incorporated in 1914, reached a peak population of 515 in 1960. (1, 2, 3, 17, 18, 33, 40, 79, 106)

FLAXTON (Burke). This Soo Line RR townsite was founded in 1900 in Secs. 31 & 32-163-90, Richland Twp., and named to note the dominant crop of the area, flax. Pm William Henry Post (1847-1934) moved his farm post office of Postville here on May 31, 1901. The village incorporated in 1904, and it became a city in 1920. The Zip Code is 58737, and a peak population of 436 was reached in 1950. (1, 2, 3, 18, 34, 40, 52, 67, 79)

FLEAK (Grant). This was a rural community about eight miles south of New Leipzig. The post office, located in NE¼ Sec. 14-132-90, just north of Coffin Butte, was established March 30, 1904 with Jennie Fleak pm. St. Paul Lutheran Church was built in 1909, serving the area until 1946 when the building was moved into New Leipzig. Henry B. Johnson operated a store here for some years, and a rural school existed here 1917-1960. The various facilities were scattered over a three-township area, with a population of 10 being reported in 1920. The post office closed November 30, 1921 with mail to Pretty Rock. (1, 2, 3, 17, 18, 40, 176, 177, 358)

FLEECE (Pembina). This was a NPRR station in NW¼ Sec. 23-161-51, Joliette Twp., four miles SSW of Joliette. The post office was established October 15, 1912 with Walker F. Moody pm, and the name is said to be a family name of the pm's. It closed September 30, 1913 with mail to Joliette, after which the site was often shown on maps as Fleece Station. The only population figure reported for FLEECE was a count of 10 in 1930. (1, 2, 3, 18, 40, 108)

FLEMING (Cass). This was a GNRR loading station built in the fall of 1881 in NW¼ Sec. 25-140-53, Wheatland Twp., four miles WNW of Casselton, whose post office served this station. It was named for Rufus E. Fleming, owner of the farm served by this station. Former President Ulysses S. Grant visited here in 1883 to view farming operations. The station was removed in 1943. (1, 2, 3, 18, 25, 34, 77)

FLETCHER (Richland). For one month in 1883 a post office called JASPER existed here, Sec. 21-132-51, Danton Twp., three miles SE of Wyndmere. On February 19, 1891 a new post office was established with Milton L. Hilliard pm, who named it for Fletcher, OH. Fletcher is a Teutonic name meaning featherer of arrows. This was a Soo Line RR station, and Mr. Hilliard also managed the local elevator and the Cleveland Farm Store. On January 26, 1892 the name was changed to MOSELLE. (2, 3, 18, 19, 40, 147)

FLORA (Benson). This NPRR townsite was founded in June 1901 in SW¼ Sec. 30-152-68, Aurora Twp., four miles ESE of Maddock, and named SCHUYLER, but within a few months was renamed FLORA by George F. Leslie, NPRR material clerk, for the sister of townsite owner William H. S. Schuyler. Others say it was named for the sister of Dr. Frank Wheelon, and still others say it was named for Flora Bjerken, sister of Mrs. Herman Rice, and a popular young lady of the area. Flora is a Latin name meaning flower. The post office was established December 11, 1901 with William T. Kennedy pm, and it closed August 31, 1971 with mail to Maddock. The elevation is 1596, the Zip Code was 58334, and a peak population of 100 was claimed in 1920, but by 1982 the count had declined to just 8. (1, 2, 18, 19, 34, 40, 79, 110, 239)

FLORADALE (Ward). This was a platted townsite in SW¼ Sec. 19-155-82, Nedrose Twp., just east of Minot. It appears only in a 1915 county atlas, and the origin of the name, descriptive in nature, is unknown. (3, 18)

FLORENCE (Griggs). This was a NPRR station built in 1899 in Sec. 4-147-61, Bryan Twp., between Binford and McHenry. It was named for Florence Phipps, the first baby born here, but the name was never officially used. The railroad named the station LEWIS, and in 1904 renamed it MOSE. (1, 2, 3, 65)

FLORINE (Richland). This was a rural post office established April 19, 1901 in the country store of pm David C. Geary. It was located in NE¼ Sec. 23-129-51, Duerr Twp., eight miles south of Lidgerwood. The origin of the name is unknown. The post office closed May 14, 1904 with mail to Lidgerwood. (2, 18, 40, 53)

FLOYD (LaMoure). This was a farm post office established October 26, 1899 with James Withnell pm. It was located in Sec. 25-136-65, Mikkelson Twp., two miles WNW of Nortonville on the south bank of Bone Hill Creek. There is a theory that it was named for Charles Floyd, a member of the Lewis & Clark Expedition, but it seems more likely that it was named for some local resident. Floyd is a Celtic name meaning gray. The post office was discontinued

August 31, 1911 with mail to Jud. (1, 2, 3, 10, 18, 19, 40, 53)

**FLUSHING** (Grand Forks). This was a GNRR loading station in NW¼ Sec. 6-154-54, Strabane Twp., and NE¼ Sec. 1-154-55, Inkster Twp., three miles north of Inkster at the Walsh County line. It appears on maps circa 1915-1925, and reported a population of 5 in 1920. The name probably traces to Flushing, NY, which is a part of Queens Borough of New York City, whose name is an Anglicized version of Vlissingen, the name given it by Dutch settlers in 1645. (1, 2, 3, 5, 31, 53)

**FOGARTY** (Billings). This was a settlement of railroad construction workers that developed in 1879 in NE¼ Sec. 9-139-100, East Fryburg Twp., and was named for a contractor working on the project. In 1883 the name was changed to SUMMIT, and in 1911 it was renamed FRYBURG. (1, 2, 18, 34, 81)

**FONDA** (Rolette). This was a Soo Line RR station built in 1905 in Sec. 24-160-73, Kohlmeier Twp., eight miles west of Rolette. The townsite was platted in 1905, and the post office opened June 7, 1907 with Edmond Florentine pm in his general store. Jay Edwards, a local resident, named it for his hometown of Fonda, IA, the name being Spanish for hotel. A small village began to develop, but the population never exceeded 25, and the post office closed March 31, 1944 with mail to Rolette. (1, 2, 18, 38, 40, 79, 123)

**FORBES** (Dickey). This GNRR terminus was founded in 1905 in SE¼ Sec. 35-129-65, Lorraine Twp., fourteen miles SW of Ellendale just above the SD border. It came into existance after the GNRR extended its line beyond Ellendale following the expiration of a twenty-year agreement with the Milwaukee Road RR not to build west of their tracks in this area. It is the youngest town in Dickey County. The post office was established December 11, 1905 with George H. Ladd pm. The village incorporated in 1911, and reached a peak population of 293 in 1920, with a decline to just 84 in 1980. The elevation is 1554, and the Zip Code is 58439. The name honors S. F. Forbes, a pioneer storekeeper here, and later an official of the GNRR. (1, 2, 3, 18, 40, 52, 79, 154, 316, 317)

**FORDVILLE** (Walsh). The Soo Line RR townsite of MEDFORD was founded in 1905 in Sec. 26-155-56, Perth Twp., and changed its name to FORDVILLE officially on July 1, 1910 to end confusion with similarly named stations. The new name was coined from MedFORD and BelleVILLE, a rural post office that had merged with MEDFORD in 1907. The FORDVILLE post office adopted the new name on May 21, 1910 during the term of pm William J. Henry. The village incorporated in 1911 with Karl Isackson as mayor. It is the eastern terminus of the Drake-Fordville line. The Zip Code is 58231, and a peak population of 442 was reported in 1930. (1, 2, 3, 40, 52, 70, 75, 79, 293)

**FOREST CITY** (Ransom). This townsite was founded in Sec. 11-135-57, Springer Twp., eight miles NW of Lisbon, as a station on the Dakota Great Southern RR. A grade was constructed through the site which is still visible today, but the project did not develop beyond that point. The name apparently notes the heavily wooded Sheyenne River valley at the site. A short while later the townsite of WISNER, and a post office called PLYMOUTH, were located at this site. (2, 18, 201)

**FOREST RIVER** (Walsh). This was a rural settlement in Sec. 28-155-53, Forest River Twp., named for the Forest River which flows through the area. The river was originally called the Big Salt River until 1878 when the name was changed to note the heavy growth of trees along its banks. The post office was established September 20, 1878 with Jesse B. Warren pm. This site was crossed by both the NPRR and the Soo Line RR, and in 1893 incorporated as a village, reaching a peak population of 236 in 1950. The elevation is 868, and the Zip Code is 58233. Dr. Alexander B. Field (1863-1949) was the town doctor from his arrival in 1892 until his death fifty-seven years later. (1, 2, 18, 25, 33, 40, 52, 75, 79)

**FORFAR** (Bottineau). This GNRR station was founded in 1903 as JEFFERSON in Secs. 20 & 29-159-82, Elms Twp., six miles SE of Lansford. On September 27, 1905 the name was changed to FORFAR, for either Forfar, Ontario, Canada, of Forfar, Angushire, Scotland. Development here was virtually nonexistant, and the post office closed March 30, 1907 with mail to Lansford. The site was shown on maps into the 1960's as elevator facilities were maintained here for the use of local farmers. (2, 3, 5, 18, 34, 38, 40, 101, 153)

**FORK** (Traill). This was a farm post office established December 2, 1879 with Even Larson pm at his home in Sec. 12-146-52, Mayville Twp., seventeen miles ENE of Finley. It was located at the fork of the Goose River and its north branch, hence the name, and closed March 16, 1881 with mail to Mayville. (2, 3, 40, 77)

**FORMAN** (Sargent). This townsite was founded in 1882 at the exact center of the county, touching Sec. 1-130-56, Sec. 6-130-55, Sec. 31-131-55, and Sec. 36-131-56. It replaced Milnor as county seat in 1886, and is called "The Hub City." The post office was established October 18, 1883 with William H. Groff pm, and named for Col. Cornelius Hageman Forman (1833-1923), who came here from MI in 1883 and donated land for the townsite. It incorporated as a village in 1889, and became a city in 1954. The elevation is 1250, the Zip Code is 58032, and it is a station on the Soo Line RR. The population has grown continuously since its beginning, reaching a peak of 629 in 1980. (1, 2, 10, 18, 25, 33, 40, 52, 79, 168)

**FORSBY** (Sargent). This post office was established June 21, 1890 with John Ek pm, and was located in his country store in Sec. 13-132-56, Whitestone Hill Twp. Mr. Ek named it for his hometown of Forsby, Sweden, the name meaning village by the waterfall or stream. It closed September 30, 1901 with mail to the new townsite of Gwinner, one mile SW of here. Forsburg is an erroneous spelling. (2, 3, 40, 165, 169, 240)

**FORT ABERCROMBIE** (Richland). The first military post in what is now ND, this fort in Sec. 4-134-48, Abercrombie Twp., just east of the present-day city of Abercrombie, was built by the authority of an Act of Congress passed March 3, 1857. Lt. Col. John Joseph Abercrombie (1802-1877) arrived here August 28, 1857, and the fort was named in his honor. The fort was dismantled in 1858, but was rebuilt in 1860, serving many years as a gateway into Dakota Territory. It was the major origination point for many early Indian campaigns. The post office was established December 13, 1858 with Ferdinand DeCoursey pm, and closed November 25, 1859. It reopened August 29, 1860 with Jesse M. Stone pm, and about 1884 moved to the new townsite of Abercrombie, dropping the "Fort" from its name on May 21, 1892. Much of the fort still stands, or has been rebuilt, and it is one of ND's most historic places. (2, 3, 13, 18, 40, 79, 147, 243)

**FORT ABRAHAM LINCOLN** (Morton). This military post was established June 14, 1872 as FORT McKEEN in Sec. 13-138-81, just south of Mandan. On November 19, 1872 it was renamed FORT ABRAHAM LINCLON to honor the martyred sixteenth President of the United States. The infantry post, consisting of three block houses and supporting structures, was built on a high bluff, and the cavalry post was built just to the east at the bottom of the bluff. The post office was established February 7, 1873 with Col. Robert Wilson, the post trader, as pm. Gen. George Armstrong Custer was the post commander, and it was from here that he began his expedition to the Little Big Horn in 1876. During most of its existence as an active military post, it had a population of between 500 and 700, and can be considered as the first white settlement in Morton County. The fort was abandoned July 22, 1891, and the post office closed March 9, 1894 with mail to Mandan. (2, 3, 9, 18, 25, 40, 79, 107, 127, 343)

**FORT ATKINSON** (McLean). This fur trading post was built in 1858 or 1859 in Secs. 30 & 31-147-87, Like-a-Fishhook Twp., and Secs. 25 & 36-147-88, adjacent to its rival post of Fort Berthold. Henry Boller was the manager of the post, which was named for Gen. Henry Atkinson, the negotiator of an 1825 treaty between the Teton and Yanktonai tribes. The post was never much of a threat to Fort Berthold, and when the latter post was burned by the Sioux on December 24, 1862, its owners acquired FORT ATKINSON, renaming it FORT BERTHOLD, often referred to as Fort Berthold II to differentiate it from the original facility. (2, 3, 28, 387, 417)

**FORT BERTHOLD** (McLean). This was a fur trading post built in 1844 by the Chouteau

Company of Saint Louis, MO, and located in Sec. 31-147-87, Like-a-Fishhook Twp., on the north bank of the Missouri River. It was first managed by James Kipp, who had previously run a small post upriver near the mouth of the White Earth River. The post was named for Bartholomew Berthold, a prominent fur trader in Saint Louis. The famous Mandan-Hidatsa settlement, Like-a-Fishhook village, was built adjacent to this post. It enjoyed a near monopoly in the area until Fort Atkinson was built nearby in 1859. FORT BERTHOLD was destroyed by the Sioux on December 24, 1862, after which Fort Atkinson was acquired and occupied as a new Fort Berthold, sometimes called Fort Berthold II by historians. The destruction of the original post called for an increased military presence, leading to the building of Fort Stevenson in 1867. (2, 3, 28, 127, 387)

**FORT BERTHOLD** (McLean). This fur trading post resulted from the destruction of the original post of this name in 1862 by Sioux Indians. The defunct post of FORT ATKINSON, also in Sec. 31-147-87, Like-a-Fishhook Twp., was acquired and renamed FORT BERTHOLD, often referred to by historians as Fort Berthold II. Fort Berthold Indian Reservation was created April 12, 1870, and this post became the agency headquarters. The post office was established September 1, 1874 with William Courtenay pm. The site developed into a thriving village, with several stores, a doctor, and a school. The 1890 population was reported to be 125. Among its residents was Mattie Grinnell (1866-1974), credited with being the last full-blooded Mandan Indian. On December 22, 1906 the post office was moved nine miles north to SE¼ Sec. 17-148-87, Blackwater Twp., and renamed BLACKWATER. (2, 3, 28, 40, 389)

**FORT BUFORD** (Williams). This military post in Sec. 16-152-104, Buford Twp., was established June 15, 1866 by Gen. Alfred Sully to protect overland and water routes in the area. It was named for Maj. Gen. John Buford (1825-1863), a hero of the Battle of Gettysburg, by the detahcment commander, Capt. William G. Rankin. The post office was established September 11, 1867 with Charles W. Hoffman pm, and it closed June 20, 1870 with mail to Fort Abercrombie at the opposite corner of ND. The post office reopened December 6, 1871 and closed November 14, 1895 with mail to Williston. The fort had been disbanded that year, and many of its buildings were moved to Buford, a new townsite founded one mile to the north in 1897. A state park was dedicated at the old site on July 31, 1929. (2, 3, 5, 18, 40, 50, 79)

**FORT CLARK** (Mercer). This trading post was established in 1829 in SE¼ Sec. 36-144-84, in the extreme SE corner of Mercer County, by the American Fur Co. They built a building 197' x 132', and named it for William Clark (1770-1838) of the Lewis & Clark Expedition, who camped across the Missouri River from here in 1804. James Kipp was the first manager of the fort, which was the center of the terrible smallpox epidemic of 1837 that killed most of the Mandan Indian tribe. It was abandoned in the 1860's. Later maps continued to

show the fort as OLD FORT CLARK. Fort Clarke is an erroneous spelling. (2, 3, 5, 64, 121, 127)

**FORT CLARK** (Oliver). This townsite was platted in 1909 by Robert W. Livingston in SW¼ Sec. 31-144-83 and NW¼ Sec. 6-143-83, Fort Clark Twp., immediately ESE of the abandoned ruins of the old fur trading post of this name. The post office was established May 28, 1910 with Edgar W. Chamberlain pm, and the NPRR arrived in 1911. A population of 86 was reported in 1920, but this had declined to just 13 in 1960. The post office became a rural branch of Stanton on July 31, 1967, and it closed November 30, 1969 with mail to Stanton. (1, 2, 3, 33, 40, 41, 121)

**FORT CROSS** (Stutsman). Founded in 1871 as CAMP SYKES in SE¼ Sec. 26-140-64, Midway Twp., and later known as CAMP THOMAS, this site became an official military post on September 7, 1872, taking the name FORT CROSS at the suggestion of Maj. A. W. Edwards, a Fargo newspaperman, who wanted to honor his Civil War commander, Col. Edward S. Cross, who had been killed at Gettysburg on July 2, 1863. On November 9, 1872 the name was changed to FORT SEWARD. (2, 18, 79, 158, 420)

**FORT DAER** (Pembina). This fur trading post was built by Lord Selkirk in 1812 in Sec. 4-163-51, Pembina Twp., on the exact site of Chaboillez Post, the pioneering post of 1797-1798. It was on the south bank of the Pembina River, opposite Fort Paubian, with which it was in direct competition. The name is said to honor a patron of this effort. The site was sometimes called FORT GIBRALTAR, and the whole affair ended in July 1823 when Maj. Stephan H. Long ousted the British tenants, driving them into Canada. (2, 3, 108, 365)

**FORT DEFIANCE** (Mercer). This was a short-lived fur trading post founded in 1845 by Alexander Harvey and Francois A. Chardon, supposedly to show their defiance toward their former employers at Fort McKenzie. Its connection to Mercer County is strong enough to have resulted in a rural post office being named for this fort, however it is the opinion of several historians that FORT DEFIANCE was actually in what is now SD, near Pierre. (2, 3, 64, 420)

**FORT DILTS** (Bowman). In September 1864 a large party of men were proceeding from Fort Ripley, MN to the gold fields of Montana under the military escort of Capt. James L. Fisk. After thirteen of his men were ambushed and killed by Hunkpapa Sioux, Capt. Fisk had a circular enclosure constructed from six-foot thick sections of native sod to protect the men from further attack. Troops from Fort Rice arrived after sixteen days, and the party proceeded on their journey. This site became known as FORT DILTS, for Jefferson Dilts, a scout for the group. It is located in Sec. 11-132-105, midway between Marmarth and Rhame. L.G. Dawes donated the site to the State Historical Society, and it was dedicated as a State Park on September 4, 1932. (2, 3, 34, 120, 383, 384)

**FORT FLOYD** (Williams). This fort was built in 1828 in SE¼ Sec. 7-152-104, Buford Twp., by the American Fur Company, owned by John Jacob Astor (1763-1848), to compete with the Hudson's Bay Company for business in the area. The origin of the name is unknown, and it was renamed FORT UNION in 1830. Fort Lloyd is an erroneous spelling. (2, 5, 50, 88)

**FORT GEORGE H. THOMAS** (Pembina). This military post was established July 9, 1870 in Sec. 16-163-51, Pembina Twp., just south of the village of Pembina, and named for Gen. George Henry Thomas (1816-1870), a Civil War hero. On September 6, 1870 the name was changed to FORT PEMBINA by Gen. William T. Sherman, a West Point classmate of Gen. Thomas, to establish a precedent that forts should not be named after living persons, although Gen. Thomas had died four months before the fort had been named for him. (2, 3, 5, 18, 79, 108)

**FORT GIBRALTAR** (Pembina). This was a seldom-used alternate name for FORT DAER, the fur trading post operated by Lord Selkirk 1812-1823. It was likely named for the famous British colony on the southern coast of Spain, noted for its prominent rock. The name is a corruption of the Arabic *gebel al tarik*, meaning the rock of Tarik. Tarik ibn Zeaid was a general from Valid who led a Moorish invasion of Spain in 711 A.D. After Selkirk's party was driven into Canada, this name was used for a fort at the mouth of the Assiniboine River in Manitoba, Canada. (2, 3, 5, 10)

**FORT GILBERT** (McKenzie). This was a little known fur trading post established in 1871 at or near the site of the long-abandoned Fort Henry of 1822-1823 just above the mouth of the Yellowstone River. To avoid military control, founders Alvin and James Leighton, and Walter B. Jordan, purposely built it just outside the military reach of Fort Buford, although they named it for Col. Charles C. Gilbert of that post. It proved to be of little merit, and no mention of the fort is found after September 1874. (3, 438)

**FORT HANKINSON** (Richland). This was not a military post, but a sardonic attempt at humor by Col. R. H. Hankinson, who platted the original portion of his namesake townsite in Sec. 13-130-50, Brightwood Twp., using this name in 1886. The site was reached by the GNRR and Soo Line RR in that year, with the two rival railroads building virtually parallel lines. The GNRR wanted to angle south at this point into SD, but was north of the Soo Line RR, which wanted to continue straight west. Tempers flared concerning a GNRR crossover, and a one-shot "war" was staged, but order was restored, and a crossover was built in Sec. 16-130-50, three miles west of HANKINSON. (25, 147, 360)

**FORT HANNIFIN** (Stark). Dennis Hannifin (1835-1917) came to America from his native Ireland at the age of ten, and moved to Bismarck in 1872, becoming one of its more colorful pioneers. In September 1873, he joined three other men in battling Sioux Indians near a coal seam west of Mandan.

The men pursued the Indians to a point on the Green River, near Dickinson, where they built FORT HANNIFIN, which was occupied for about two weeks. The exact location is unknown, and the whole affair is little more than an anecdote of history. A street in Bismarck is named in Mr. Hannifin's honor. (3, 9, 52)

**FORT HENRY** (McKenzie). This was an early trading post established by the Rocky Mountain Fur Company of Saint Louis, MO in 1822. It was located in Sec. 27-152-104, Yellowstone Twp., on the south bank of the Yellowstone River, just above its confluence with the Missouri River. William H. Ashley (1778-1838), later a Congressman from MO, was the money behind this venture, but active management was the responsibility of its namesake, Andrew Henry (1775-1833), a native of PA. The venture was unsuccessful, and it was abandoned in 1823. (3, 438)

**FORTIER** (Divide). This was a rural post office established May 19, 1905 with Fred G. Fortier pm. Mr. Fortier, a native of IL, was later a hardware dealer in Wildrose and Grenora. It was located in Sec. 17-160-96, Hayland Twp., eighteen miles SE of Crosby. The post office closed September 30, 1908, and the following day reopened one mile to the north as PADDINGTON. (2, 3, 33, 40, 50)

**FORT KIPP** (Mountrail). This fur trading post was built in 1825 near the mouth of the White Earth River. It was named for James Kipp, the well known trader, scout, and interpreter, who built this fort but actually spent very little time at the post. He was born in Canada in 1788 of German ancestry, and is known to have been in the Red River valley as early as 1808. He married twice, both to daughters of Mandan chiefs, and was a great friend of the Indian people. He retired in 1865, and had an emotional reunion with the Mandan people in 1876 shortly before his death. Racing against the rising waters of Lake Sakakawea, historians positively identified the site of this historic post, probably abandoned between 1827 and 1830, as being in Sec. 1-153-94, about ten miles NW of New Town. (2, 3, 64)

**FORT LEWIS** (Mercer). This was an alternate name for FORT LISA, the pioneer fur trading post probably located in Sec. 13-146-85, ten miles NNW of Stanton. It was built by Manuel Lisa in 1809, and run by Reuben Lewis, brother of Meriwether Lewis of the Lewis & Clark Expedition, until it was abandoned in 1812. the post was occupied in 1822-1823 as FORT VANDERBURGH. (2, 3, 417)

**FORT LINCOLN** (Burleigh). This military post was authorized by Congress in 1896, and built in 1902 in SE¼ Sec. 15-138-80, Lincoln Twp., just SE of Bismarck. In many ways it replaced the abandoned post of Fort Abraham Lincoln across the Missouri River, just south of Mandan. It served various functions throughout its active period, including use as an internment camp for German, Italian, and Japanese nationals during World War II. After the war the military population was generally about 150, and the fort was gradually phased out of military

plans. It was converted into a Job Corps center in 1966, and became the United Tribes Educational Training Center in 1969. (2, 3, 8, 14, 18, 34)

**FORT LISA** (Mercer). This early fur trading post was built in 1809 under the direction of Manuel Lisa, a Spaniard from New Orleans, LA, who came into the Missouri Basin in 1807 and established many posts along the upper portion of the river. The exact site is subject to debate, although it can safely be placed in Secs. 13 & 24-146-85, and Secs. 12 & 19-146-84, just south of Mannhaven, and about ten miles NNW of Stanton, with scanty evidence seemingly pointing to Sec. 13-146-85 as the actual site. The post was sometimes called FORT LEWIS for its operator, Reuben Lewis. It was abandoned in 1812, only to be reopened for a brief time circa 1822-1823 as FORT VANDERBURGH. (2, 3, 417)

**FORT MANDAN** (McLean). The Lewis & Clark Expedition reached this site on November 20, 1804, and built an enclosed compound for their winter headquarters, naming it for the Mandan Indians, whose villages were nearby. The exact location is subject to debate. Early county maps place the "probable site" in SW¼ Sec. 14-144-82, Washburn Twp., just west of present-day Washburn, although later research puts the probable location about ten miles upriver, almost opposite Stanton. The fort was abandoned April 7, 1805 when the expedition resumed their journey. A site was donated to the State Historical Society in 1926 in NW¼ Sec. 16-144-82, two miles west of Washburn, and a replica was built in 1969-1972, with the site dedicated as a State Park on July 23, 1972. (2, 3, 28, 34, 127)

**FORT MANEURY** (Mountrail). This was an obscure, short-lived fur trading post of the middle 1800's, said to be named for Charles Malnouri, a trader at Fort Berthold, with a rather severe corruption of the spelling. The site was about eighteen miles SSE of New Town, in SE¼ Sec. 34 and/or SW¼ Sec. 35-150-92, opposite the mouth of Skunk Creek. The site is now inundated by Lake Sakakawea, and unless contemporary accounts are discovered, its history will remain unknown. (2, 3, 417)

**FORT McKEEN** (Morton). This military post replaced Camp Greene, and had a primary purpose of protecting NPRR construction crews from hostile Indians. It was established June 14, 1872 in Sec. 13-138-81, just south of present-day Mandan, and named for Col. H. Boyd McKeen, Commander of the PA Volunteers, who was killed at the Battle of Cold Harbor on June 3, 1864. On November 19, 1872 the fort was renamed FORT ABRAHAM LINCOLN. (2, 3, 18, 79, 127, 343, 409)

**FORT MORTIMER** (Williams). This outpost was built in 1842 in SE¼ Sec. 16-152-104, Buford Twp., the approximate site of the earlier Fort William, and the later Fort Buford. Fox, Livingston & Co. built the fort for the Union Fur Co. to compete with the American Fur Co., but the venture failed and was absorbed by the latter firm in 1846. It was abandoned in 1858, with the material used to construct Fort Buford in 1866. The origin of the name is unknown. (2, 50)

**FORT PAUBIAN** (Pembina). This fur trading post was built in 1801 by Alexander Henry of the Northwest Fur Co., after he had abandoned his Park River Post to the south on May 4, 1801. Construction of this post was begun September 8, 1801, with completion on October 1, 1801. Mr. Henry named his post for the Pembina River, which he called Paubian, meaning entrenchment. It was one hundred yards north of the confluence of the Pembina and Red Rivers, just north of the old CHABOILLEZ POST of 1797-1798, and closed in 1823. Some accounts give the name of this place as Fort Panbian or Fort Paubna. (2, 3, 79, 108, 127, 365, 366)

**FORT PEMBINA** (Pembina). This military post was established July 9, 1870 as FORT GEORGE H. THOMAS, but the name was changed to FORT PEMBINA on September 6, 1870 by order of Gen. William T. Sherman. It was located just south of the village of Pembina in Sec. 16-163-51, Pembina Twp., and was staffed by a force of 200 men. It was one of a series of forts designed to protect settlers from hostile Indians. The 1,920 acre reservation was abandoned in 1878, and the facilities were auctioned to the public in 1895. (2, 3, 18, 25, 79, 108)

**FORT PRIMEAU** (Mercer). This was an obscure, short-lived fur trading post, said to have been located a few miles north of Fort Clark. It was named for founder Charles Primeau, who had come to Fort Union in 1831, and later lived at Fort Yates until his death in 1897. (2, 3, 64, 420)

**FORT RANSOM** (Ransom). This historic military reservation in Sec. 12-135-58, Fort Ransom Twp., was founded June 17, 1867 by Gen. Alfred Terry, and named for Gen. Thomas Edward Greenfield Ransom (1834-1864) of the 11th IL Volunteers, who was killed in battle during the Civil War. The fort, built to accomodate 200 men, was part of a network of forts extending from Fort Abercrombie to protect settlers from hostile Indians. The fort was abandoned July 31, 1872 after the arrival of the NPRR at Jamestown. The ruins are now part of Fort Ransom State Park. (2, 5, 18, 77, 79, 206)

**FORT RANSOM** (Ransom). This village was founded in 1880 in Sec. 12-135-58, Fort Ransom Twp., adjacent to historic Fort Ransom, the military post of 1867-1872. The post office was established June 23, 1880 with Isaac J. Oliver pm. The elevation is 1180, the Zip Code is 58033, and the peak population of 225 was reported in 1930, with a decline to just 99 in 1980. It became a city in 1977, and is considered by many to be one of the most picturesque settlements in the state. (1, 2, 3, 18, 33, 40, 77, 201, 207)

**FORT RICE** (Morton). This military post was established in July 1864 in Secs. 13 & 14-135-79, on the west bank of the Missouri River a few miles above the mouth of the Cannonball River, and named for Gen. James Clay Rice, who was killed in May 1864 at the Battle of the Wilderness. It was the second fort built by Gen. Alfred Sully in what is now ND, and it played major roles in Indian campaigns and railroad construction until it was replaced in 1878 by Fort Yates. The average

population was 235. A post office was established January 8, 1866 with J. Shaw Gregory pm, and it closed June 6, 1870 with mail to Fort Sully. It reopened September 2, 1873, closing January 15, 1879 with mail to Bismarck. The site was donated to the State Historical Society in 1911 by owner Robert Gwyther, although all original buildings had long been dismantled. It was made into a State Park, and a replica fort was built by the WPA in the 1930's. (2, 3, 9, 25, 34, 40, 79, 107, 127, 343, 409)

**FORT RICE** (Morton). This settlement was founded in 1891 in W½ Sec. 11-135-79, one mile north of the abandoned military post from which it took its name. The post office opened September 2, 1891, changing its name to GWYTHER on May 6, 1909 to honor pioneer settler Robert Gwyther, whose wife was the pm. The name FORT RICE was restored August 3, 1910 when the NPRR built a line through the site. The elevation is 1654, the Zip Code is 58537, and a peak population of 215 was reached in 1930. Pius Uselmann purchased the general store in 1917, and operated it for over fifty years. A tornado destroyed most of the town on May 29, 1953, and the 1960 population was just 25. (1, 2, 3, 33, 34, 40, 107, 409)

**FORT RICE LANDING** (Morton). This was a Missouri River boat landing used for several years before 1900. It was located in NW¼ Sec. 23-135-79, on the west bank of the river, just south of the old abandoned military post from which it derived its name. (3, 429)

**FORT SAUERKRAUT** (Morton). An Indian scare alarmed the residents of Morton County in 1890. At Hebron the women and children were evacuated to Bismarck, and the men constructed a stockade in NE¼ Sec. 32-140-90, Custer Twp., just NW of the city, which was named for the German ethnic food which had been stockpiled here due to its unlikelihood of spoiling. The scare proved to be false, and after a few days things had returned to normal. Its walls survived for many years, but the farming efforts of subsequent landowners eventually destroyed most physical evidence of the fort. (1, 2, 3, 34, 107, 419)

**FORT SEWARD** (Stutsman). This military post was founded in 1871 in SE¼ Sec. 26-140-64, Midway Twp., to protect NPRR construction crews. It was known as CAMP SYKES, CAMP THOMAS, and FORT CROSS before assuming the name FORT SEWARD on November 9, 1872. This last name change was made by commanding officer Capt. John Colter Bates, the son of Edward Bates, President Lincoln's Attorney General, to honor William Henry Seward (1801-1872), the late Secretary of State noted for his purchase of Alaska. The fort was adjacent to Jamestown, and the rapid

growth of that city reduced the importance of the military post. Nathan Myrick was the post trader until it was abandoned September 30, 1877. (2, 5, 25, 34, 79, 153, 155, 158, 420)

**FORT STEVENSON** (McLean). This military post was established June 12, 1867 in NE¼ Sec. 10-147-85, Stevenson Twp., as NEW FORT BERTHOLD, but on July 9, 1867 the name was changed by the War Department to FORT STEVENSON, honoring Brig. Gen. Thomas Greely Stevenson, who was killed May 12, 1864 at the Battle of Spottsylvania in VA. Philippe Regis Denis de Kerendon de Trobriand (1816-1897), a native of France, was made the post commander, with Lt. Col. A. M. Powell and Capt. John Platt as his assistants. The post office was established April 30, 1873 with Julius Schmidt pm. The military abandoned this post August 7, 1883, turning it over to the Fort Berthold Indian Agency August 31, 1883. The post office closed October 26, 1883 with mail to Bismarck. It operated 1885-1894 under civilian control. Fort Stephenson is an erroneous spelling. (2, 3, 18, 28, 40, 79, 387)

**FORT STEVENSON** (McLean). This military post was abandoned on August 7, 1883, and on August 31, 1883 turned over to the Fort Berthold Indian Agency, after which it was an important community center on the reservation for a number of years. The post office was established February 10, 1885 with Frank B. Wells pm. The 1890 census reported 125 residents, but a decline began shortly afterwards. The post office closed December 18, 1894 with mail to Coal Harbor. The site remained on maps as OLD FORT STEVENSON into the 1920's. It was inundated by Lake Sakakawea in the 1950's, but the name is remembered as a state park south of Garrison. (2, 3, 28, 40)

**FORT TILTON** (Mercer). This post was built in 1822 by the American Fur Co., under the direction of James Kipp, about three miles upriver from Fort Clark, probably in Sec. 16-144-84, near the present-day power plants SE of Stanton. It was named for J. P. Tilton, who led a six-man garrison at the post, and whose American citizenship provided legal status for the operation. Actual construction occurred May-November 1823, in response to an Arikara uprising, but the venture proved to be uneconomical, and the site was abandoned in 1824. It was sometimes called Tilton's Post, or Tilton's Fort. Reports that it was relocated across the Missouri River in 1823 are subject to debate, as is its location in Mercer County. (2, 3, 417)

**FORT TOTTEN** (Benson). This military post was established July 17, 1867 in NW¼ Sec. 21-152-65, Third Commissioner District, with Capt. S. A. Wainwright as commanding officer. It was named for Gen. Joseph Gilbert Totten (1788-1864), chief of the U. S. Army Engineers. A post office was established February 5, 1868 with Thomas P. Fuller pm, but it closed October 17, 1868 with mail to Fort Abercrombie. It reopened January 27, 1869, operating until July 31, 1895 when mail went to Devils Lake. The military post was closed December 31, 1890, and transferred to the U. S. Department of the Interior for use as an Indian School in concert with the Indian mission that had been establish-

ed here in 1874. The buildings of FORT TOTTEN are considered to be among the best preserved of their type in the nation, and the whole complex was put under the jurisdiction of the State Historical Society in 1960. (2, 5, 18, 25, 40, 79, 260, 261)

**FORT TOTTEN** (Benson). This civilian community began in 1885 in SE¼ Sec. 17-152-65, just NW of the military post for which it was named. A population of 50 was reported in 1890, and the post office, Zip Code 58335, opened August 3, 1895. It is the administrative center of the Fort Totten Indian Reservation, and reached a peak population of 215 in 1960. (2, 3, 18, 33, 34, 40)

**FORT TOTTEN STATION** (Benson). This NPRR station was built in 1885 in SE 1/4 Sec. 15-152-67, Lallie Twp., about nine miles west of the military post for which it was named. After 1886 mail service was provided from Oberon. In July 1887 the name was shortened to simply TOTTEN, and in 1889 it was renamed LALLIE. (2, 3, 18, 79, 110)

**FORT TOTTEN STATION** (Ramsey). This was a GNRR station in SE¼ Sec. 29-153-64, Lake Twp., six miles south of the city of Devils Lake at the crossing point of Devils Lake called the narrows. The site served military facilities on both sides of the lake, and appears on maps of the 1920's using this name, while earlier maps called it simply MILITARY SPUR. (3, 18)

**FORTUNA** (Divide). This Soo Line RR townsite was founded in 1913 in SE¼ Sec. 27-163-101, DeWitt Twp., and named by railroad officials at the suggestion of Rosie Jeglum to note the settlers expectations of prosperity with the coming of the railroad. Fortuna was the Roman god of good luck. The new townsite absorbed the nearby community of Norge, with pm Clarence C. Gilday moving that post office here October 11, 1913. The Zip Code is 58844, and a peak population of 214 was reached in 1940, which remained fairly constant until a general decline in the 1970's, resulting in a 1980 count of just 97. (2, 3, 18, 19, 34, 40, 73, 79)

**FORT UNION** (Williams). This historic fur trading post was built in 1828 as FORT FLOYD, and renamed FORT UNION in 1830 to note the merger of the American Fur Company and the Columbia Fur Company, and because this site was regarded as a point where all trade routes could be united. Kenneth McKenzie (1797-1861) was the builder of the outpost, which was visited by the famous naturalist John James Audubon in 1843. Corruption by officials of the site led to its termination in 1865, and much of the material was salvaged to build the military post of Fort Buford three miles downstream in June 1866. Reconstruction of FORT UNION began in 1986, and the replica of the majestic bourgeois house, circa 1851, was opened to the public in 1987. (2, 3, 9, 50, 79, 127)

**FORT VANDERBURGH** (Mercer). In 1822 a group of men led by Maj. Joshua Pilcher of the Missouri Fur Co. occupied the ruins of old FORT LISA, probably located in Sec. 13-146-85, ten miles NNW of Stanton. It was renamed for Capt. William Henry Vanderburgh, a member of Gen. Leavenworth's company which had subdued an Arikara uprising in 1822, in part resulting in this venture. It proved to be economically impractical, and the post was soon abandoned. Scavenging and the environment virtually destroyed all evidence of the site, and its exact location is subject to debate. (2, 3, 64, 79, 232, 417)

**FORT WILLIAM** (Williams). This outpost in Sec. 16-152-104, Buford Twp., was built in 1833 by William Lewis Sublette (1799-1845) and Robert Campbell of Saint Louis, MO, who hoped to capture a share of the fur trading market in the area. Their venture, named for Mr. Sublette, was short-lived as the monopolistic tactics of the nearby American Fur Co. at Fort Union forced this effort out of business in 1834. It is thought that it was on the same site later occupied by Fort Mortimer, and still later by Fort Buford. (2, 10, 50)

**FORT YATES** (Sioux). The Standing Rock Indian Agency was established here January 11, 1875. On June 6, 1875 a small military garrison arrived to replace Fort Rice. The fort received official recognition by Congress on March 2, 1889 when it replaced Fort Abraham Lincoln. Because of the lack of railroad connections, FORT YATES was abandoned July 25, 1903 with their responsibilities moved to Fort Lincoln, just SE of Bismarck. FORT YATES was named for Capt. George W. Yates, who was killed June 25, 1876 at the Battle of the Little Big Horn. The post office was established May 7, 1879 with Henry Sidney Parkin, a native of Pittsburgh, PA who came here in 1872, as pm, replacing the old STANDING ROCK post office. With the end of the military presence here, the site became a civilian settlement. (2, 3, 18, 34, 40, 79, 127)

**FORT YATES** (Sioux). This settlement evolved from the old military post founded in 1875 in Secs. 12 & 13-130-80. The fort was officially abandoned July 25, 1903, although by this time the site was a thriving civilian settlement, officially declared as such in 1909. The post office, established in 1879 under military control, continued without interruption. The elevation is 1670, the Zip Code is 58538, and the city, which incorporated in 1964, reached a peak population of 1,153 in 1970. It is the county seat of Sioux County, and the headquarters of the Standing Rock Indian Reservation, which was opened for general settlement February 14, 1913. Jean Mason, later the wife of ND Governor William L. Guy, was born here in 1922. Father Bernard Strassmeier (1861-1940) was a Roman Catholic missionary here for fifty-four years. (1, 2, 3, 18, 33, 34, 40, 44, 127, 253)

**FOURTEENTH SIDING** (Kidder). This NPRR siding was built in 1872 in SE¼ Sec. 17-139-73, Woodlawn Twp., and given a name using the simple chronological order of the sidings as they were built westward from Fargo. This site was the terminus of railroad construction during the winter of 1872-1873, as the project was halted by an October snow storm. Settlement began in 1881, and the name was changed to STEELE. (2, 9, 18, 25, 122)

**FOURTH SIDING** (Barnes). The NPRR built this siding in 1872 in NW¼ Sec. 21-140-56, Oriska Twp., and named it to note the chronological order of the sidings as they built westward from Fargo. A post office opened here in 1879 with the name CARLTON. It moved one mile west in 1880, and the following year was renamed ORISKA. (2, 25, 76, 281)

**FOURTH STATION** (Morton). This was, as the name implies, the fourth station out of Bismarck on the Bismarck-Fort Keogh mail route established in 1878 in NE¼ Sec. 21-140-89, eight miles NE of Hebron, and just west of the rural community of Haymarsh. Unlike the other stations, it does not appear to have had a formal name. The entire route was abandoned in 1882 following completion of the NPRR mainline. (3, 417)

**FOX** (LaMoure). The Smith Land Co. platted this townsite in 1904 in NE¼ Sec. 7-135-65, Bluebird Twp., and named it for an official of that firm, even though a post office had been established here on July 16, 1904 with the name GUNTHORP. The site was on an expected NPRR branch line, and when it was built in 1905, plans were begun to end the confusion. On October 6, 1906 the names of both the town and the post office were changed to JUD, honoring the politician Judson LaMoure, namesake of the county. (2, 3, 18)

**FOXHOLM** (Ward). This was a Soo Line RR station built in 1886 in NW¼ Sec. 2-156-85, Foxholm Twp., between Burlington and Donnybrook. The post office was established May 7, 1894 with Jens Glein pm. Peter Fugelso, later pm at Minot, owned the townsite, which was named by railroad officials for Foxholm, England. The elevation is 1657, the Zip Code is 58738, and a population of about 200 was maintained for many years, although there has been a sharp decline since 1960. On April 21, 1967 the post office became a rural branch of Burlington. (1, 2, 18, 38, 40, 79, 100)

**FOX LAKE** (Ramsey). This was a rural post office established May 31, 1888 with James R. Henley pm. It was located in SW¼ Sec. 24-155-62, Noonan Twp., ten miles west of Brocket, and initially served a large rural area. It was named for Fox Lake, WI, which was named in 1838 by Jacob Brower after he was told that the Indian name for the place was hos-a-rac-ah-tah, meaning fox. On March 6, 1896 the name was altered to the one-word FOXLAKE to comply with new government regulations for geographic names. (2, 18, 25, 40, 70, 103, 282)

**FOXLAKE** (Ramsey). The 1888 rural post office of FOX LAKE changed its name to a one-word spelling on March 6, 1896 to comply with new government regulations for geographic names. James R. Henley continued to serve as pm. The post office closed August 31, 1910 with mail to Crary. The place was still shown on some maps into the 1920's, but always as FOX LAKE. (2, 18, 40, 53, 103)

**FRANCE** (Bottineau). This was a GNRR servicing station in Sec. 5-162-79, Eidsvold Twp., between Westhope and Landa. The

origin of the name is unknown. There were large colonies of French-Canadians in Bottineau County, but this area was settled primarily by Norwegian immigrants. It is shown on maps circa 1905-1920, usually as WATER TANK to note its principal function of replenishing water supplies on the steam locomotives of the GNRR. (2, 3, 18)

**FRANCES** (Burleigh). This was a farm post office established March 26, 1894 with Frank Durette pm. It was located in NW¼ Sec. 34-140-78, Frances Twp., seven miles NNE of Menoken and named for its township, which was named for Frances Hood, a pioneer settler. Frances is the feminine form of Francis, a Teutonic name meaning free. The post office, which replaced the old EDBERG facility, closed December 15, 1921 with mail to Menoken. (1, 2, 8, 12, 14, 18, 19, 34, 40)

**FRANKLIN** (LaMoure). This was a station on the Midland Continental RR founded in 1912 in Sec. 28-135-64, Glenmore Twp., eight miles north of Edgeley. It was named for Franklin Bull, President of the J. I. Case Threshing Machine Co., and a major stockholder in the new railroad. Others say it was named by settlers from Franklin County, MI, which was, like most places of this name, named for Benjamin Franklin (1706-1790), the great statesman. Franklin is a Teutonic name meaning a freeman. The only development here was an elevator built in 1915. It closed in 1948 and was moved into Edgeley on March 29, 1952, leaving the site vacant. (1, 2, 3, 19, 46, 143)

**FRAZIER** (Barnes). This was the northern terminus of the Midland Continental RR, built in 1913 in SE¼ Sec. 30-143-61, Pierce Twp., at the north edge of Wimbledon. The origin of the name is unknown, although some have speculated that it was named for Lynn J. Frazier of Hoople, who shortly afterwards would be a U. S. Senator and Governor of ND. (2, 3, 34)

**FREDA** (Grant). This Milwaukee Road RR station was founded in 1910 in SE 1/4 Sec. 7-133-83, Freda Twp., between Shields and Raleigh. The post office opened November 11, 1910 with Charles Alphonso Thompson pm, replacing the nearby rural post office of Pearce on that date. It was named for Freda Van Sickle, the daughter of the railroad construction foreman. The name is the feminine variant of Frederick, a Teutonic name meaning peaceful. Although the town once had a thriving business section, including a bank, the peak population was only 50, reached in 1920. The last pm, Mrs. Elizabeth M. Fraase, closed the post office, Zip Code 58539, on April 12, 1975 with mail to Shields, which itself was a rural branch of Flasher. The 1976 population was just 2. A meteorite fell here in 1919 and is now on display at the Smithsonian Institution in Washington, DC. (1, 2, 3, 17, 18, 19, 33, 40, 176, 177)

**FREDERICKSON** (Williams). This was a farm post office established March 19, 1907 with Frederick R. Frederickson pm. It was located in NW¼ Sec. 26-155-102, Mont Twp., eight miles NW of Williston, and closed November 15, 1909 with mail to Williston. (2, 3, 40, 50, 53)

**FREDONIA** (Logan). This village in Sec. 15-133-67, Haag Twp., was founded along the Soo Line RR in 1904 and named DENEVITZ. When the post office was established February 1, 1905 with storekeeper Daniel Flaig pm, the name was changed to FREDONIA. Some say the name was suggested by Mr. Derrick of the Soo Line RR, while others say French laborers in the area came up with the name. The origin of the word, coined from the Latin for place of freedom, is traced to Samuel Latham Mitchell, and was once seriously considered as the name for the United States of America. The village incorporated in 1914, and reached a peak population of 394 in 1930, although a steady decline has reduced that figure to just 83 in 1980. The Zip Code is 58440. (1, 2, 10, 18, 23, 33, 40, 79, 116, 334)

**FREEBORN** (Eddy). This was a rural post office established October 6, 1890 with Simon Anderson pm. It was located in SE¼ Sec. 33-150-62, Freeborn Twp., about six miles SSW of Hamar. In 1887 an attempt to establish a post office named EDDY had failed at this site. The name was chosen by settlers from Freeborn County, MN, which had been named for William Freeborn (1816-1900), a prominent businessman and state legislator from Saint Paul. Some claim the name came from nearby Free People's Lake, noting the residents lack of affiliation with Fort Totten. The post office closed June 30, 1908 with mail to Hamar. (2, 10, 13, 40, 79, 119)

**FREMONT** (Emmons). This was a farm post office established February 3, 1906 with Willie C. Noble pm. It was located in Sec. 2-133-74, fourteen miles east of Temvik. The origin of the name is unknown, although it probably traces to John Charles Fremont (1813-1890), the famous soldier, explorer, and politician who was the first Republican candidate for President in 1856. The order for the FREMONT post office was rescinded September 6, 1906. (3, 10, 34, 40, 415)

**FRETTIM** (Kidder). This was a rural community in SW¼ Sec. 20-143-71, Frettim Twp., five miles NE of Robinson. A lake at the site also bears the name of Hans Frettim (1865-1921), who came to America from Norway in 1866, and homesteaded in Kidder County in 1899. When the post office was established October 24, 1904, Mr. Frettim was appointed as pm. The site also had a creamery, store, and several houses, but the NPRR bypassed the site in 1911 and most of the town moved to the new townsite of Robinson. The post office closed April 30, 1913 with mail to Robinson. Frettin and Frettum are erroneous spellings. (2, 3, 18, 40, 61, 93, 122)

**FRIED** (Stutsman). This small village was founded in the late 1800's by Roman Catholics of German/Austrian/Polish ancestry who had previously lived in Wisconsin. The post office was established April 30, 1896 with Ida A. Fried pm. She was the wife of John B. Fried, who was the son of townsite owner Peter U. Fried. It was located in Sec. 10-141-63, Fried Twp., about ten miles NE of Jamestown. The population never exceeded 100, and a 1983 count showed just 16 people living here. The post office was discontinued July 31, 1957 with mail to Jamestown. (2, 18, 38, 40, 79, 158)

**FRIEDENTHAL** (Mercer). This was a rural post office established February 24, 1908 with Peter Boeckel pm. It was located in NE¼ Sec. 26-145-88, about six miles north of Beulah, and named by settlers from Friedental, Crimea, South Russia, which had been settled by Germans in 1804 in the Suja District. The post office closed June 15, 1909 with mail to Krem. Fredenthal and Friedental are erroneous spellings. (2, 3, 18, 23, 40, 64)

**FROG POINT** (Traill). This settlement was founded in 1871 in NE¼ Sec. 22-148-49, Belmont Twp., as a Red River port and the site of a Hudson's Bay Company trading post. The county's namesake, Walter J. S. Traill, was in charge of the trading post, and when a post office was established March 6, 1872, Mr. Traill was appointed pm. Folklore says the name can be traced to 1860, when Samuel Painter was leading a group of 300 soldiers through the area. The party encountered frogs so thick at this point that they could not steppping on them as they watered their horses. Mr. Painter erected a wooden sign with "Frog Point" painted on it, and this sign was found by the first settlers in 1871. The town declined in 1875 when it lost the county seat battle to Caledonia, and the post office closed June 21, 1875. It reopened June 4, 1877 with David Ray pm, and on August 20, 1879 changed its name to BELLMONT. (2, 3, 25, 29, 40, 79, 187, 393, 395)

**FRONTIER** (Cass). This is a rural subdivision in NW¼ Sec. 2-138-49, Stanley Twp., five miles south of Fargo. The name apparently recalls the area's past. It incorporated as a city in the late 1970's with a population of 119, and in 1980 had grown to 152 residents. (3, 34)

**FRYAR** (Logan). This was a rural post office established March 26, 1896 with Orson T. Fryar pm. It was located in Sec. 36-133-68, Lautt Twp., about twelve miles SSW of Gackle, and closed April 25, 1899 with mail to Kulm. (2, 3, 40, 116)

**FRYBURG** (Billings). This NPRR station began in 1879 as a settlement of railroad construction workers, and was named FOGARTY. In 1883 the name was changed to SUMMIT, and when a post office was established May 13, 1911 the name was again changed, this time to FRYBURG honoring James Barnet Fry (1827-1894), a Civil War general. The first pm was Myra Fitzsimmons. This is the first NPRR station west of Belfield, in NE¼ Sec. 9-139-100, East Fryburg Twp. The elevation is 2790, and the village, platted in 1909, reached a peak population of 140 in 1920. The post office, Zip Code 58628, closed October 29, 1971 with mail to Belfield. U. S. Senator Gerald P. Nye, a newspaperman, published *The Fryburg Pioneer* here for a number of years. (1, 2, 3, 4, 5, 18, 34, 40 81)

**FULDA** (Pierce). Paul Goldade was appointed pm of this rural post office November 18, 1903, but the appointment was rescinded May 5, 1904. The post office took its name from the Roman Catholic community centered around St. Anselm's Church which had been built in 1899 in Sec. 7-155-74, Jefferson Twp., eight miles SE of Towner. The church still exists, although the original building was destroyed by fire on March 6, 1946. The name was chosen by German-Russian settlers for the 90-mile long Fulda River in Germany, and the city of the same name that dates from 744 A.D. (1, 2, 3, 13, 40, 114)

**FULLERTON** (Dickey). This Soo Line RR townsite was founded in 1887 in Sec. 15-131-62, Maple Twp., on land donated by Edwin F. Sweet, who named it for the family of his wife, the former Sophia F. Fuller, in particular Philo Case Fuller (1787-1855), Mrs. Sweet's grandfather, who was a former Congressman. Mr. Sweet was later mayor of Grand Rapids, MI and a Congressman himself. The post office was established August 8, 1888 with George F. Bartlett pm. Benjamin C. Porter had received the appointment, but did not qualify for the post. The elevation is 1439, and the Zip Code is 58441. The village incorporated in 1908, and reached a peak population of 206, a count reported in 1910, 1930, and 1950. (1, 2, 3, 18, 25, 33, 40, 52, 79, 154, 316)

**FUNSTON** (McHenry). This was a Soo Line RR station in Sec. 3-152-75, Schiller Twp., between Drake and Orrin about nine miles north of Anamoose. A population of 18 was reported as late as 1940, but little development ever took place here. It was named for H. S. Funston, Soo Line RR Land Commissioner at the time, although some believe it was named by a Mr. Ruehl for Gen. Frederick Funston, a Spanish-American War hero. (1, 2, 3, 5, 18, 79, 183)

# G

**GACKLE** (Logan). Sec. 8-135-67, Gutschmidt Twp., was the site of an early settlement called HACKNEY, which on June 3, 1903 was renamed GACKLE for George Gackle, a prominent farmer and businessman in the area. The post office was established July 22, 1903 with George Elhard pm. In the fall of 1904 it was moved six miles north to the NPRR townsite in NE¼ Sec. 6-136-67, Finn Twp., with a continuation of the GACKLE name. The old site was renamed MINISTER, but it soon became a ghost town. The new site incorporated as a village in 1914, and reached a peak population of 604 in 1950. The elevation is 1951, and the Zip Code is 58442. (1, 2, 3, 18, 23, 40, 79, 116)

**GADSDEN** (Adams). This was a Milwaukee Road RR station built in 1906 in NW 1/4 Sec. 29-129-94, Clermont Twp., and named for an official of the railroad. In 1907 the name was changed to HAYNES. Gadsen is an erroneous spelling. (2, 3, 18, 34, 188)

**GADY** (McLean). This was a farm post office established April 23, 1898 with Paul Gady pm. It was located in NW¼ Sec. 30-143-80, four miles WNW of Wilton, and closed September 15, 1899 with mail to Falconer. (2, 3, 34, 40, 415)

**GAGE CITY** (Logan). This was a pioneer settlement founded in 1883 in Sec. 15-135-72, Kroeber Twp., on the west bank of the lake to the west of present-day Napoleon. Nine men from Steele, one of whom was J. R. Gage, a surveyor, came here June 16, 1883 and built a shack using the first lumber hauled into Logan County. GAGE CITY anticipated a proposed NPRR branch line, but it never materialized. A population of 1 was reported in 1884 as a new townsite, Napoleon, began to develop at a nearby Soo Line RR townsite. (2, 3, 116)

**GAINES** (Oliver). This was a rural post office established October 21, 1901 with Alfred B. Peterson pm. It was located in Sec. 26-143-83, Nebo Twp., about seven miles NE of Center, and named for A. D. Gaines who owned the ranch on which it was located. Mr. Gaines, who came here in the 1880's and was a former professor of classical languages at the University of Minnesota, was a major promoter of Oliver County. He was the local agent for the NPRR, and kept his records in classical Greek. The post office closed September 30, 1910 with mail to Seroco. The ranch was purchased from the Gaines family in 1956 by Robert Levis II of Alton, IL, who changed the name to the Cross Ranch, parts of which are now being developed as a recreational area. (2, 3, 18, 40, 48, 121)

**GAINESVILLE** (Oliver). A. D. Gaines, an energetic promoter of the area, founded this townsite about 1902 in Sec. 15-142-83, Center Twp., six miles west of Center. A blacksmith shop and a store were built, and

Mr. Gaines hoped that this would become the new county seat. Support from the residents of Yucca did not materialize as had been hoped. In late 1902 Center was established by county officials, and GAINESVILLE became a ghost town. (1, 121)

**GALCHUTT** (Richland). This GNRR station was founded in SE¼ Sec. 26-134-49, Abercrombie Twp., and named for Hans Galchutt, a Norwegian who came here in 1882 and built a store, warehouse, and an elevator. The post office was established January 30, 1891 with Mr. Galchutt as pm. The elevation is 940, and a population of about 100 has been recorded here for most of the twentieth century. Mrs. Marvin Johnson retired as pm in 1978 after more than thirty years service, and the post office, Zip Code 58034, closed although government records do not note this fact. (1, 2, 18, 40, 41, 147)

**GALESBURG** (Traill). This GNRR station was founded in 1881 in SW¼ Sec. 21 and SE¼ Sec. 20-144-53, Norman Twp. The town was platted in 1882 by Isaac Wood, who named it for Josiah Hallis Gale, an early homesteader just south of the site, and it incorporated as a village in 1885. The post office was established August 3, 1882 in the store of pm Joseph S. Kemp. The elevation is 1066, the Zip Code is 58035, and a peak population of 328 was reached in 1930. Ole Soholt was Mayor of GALESBURG 1947-1968. (1, 2, 25, 33, 40, 79, 187, 246)

**GALEY** (Bowman). This was the name of the early settlement in Secs. 25 & 36-129-100, Goldfield Twp., and Secs. 30 & 31-129-99, Haley Twp., honoring William Galey, or Gay, who discovered gold near here in 1887. Postal officials erroneously entered the name of the post office as HALEY, and it retains that name to this day. (1, 2, 3, 18, 34, 120)

**GALL** (Morton). This was a NPRR loading station built in 1910 in W½ Sec. 17-134-83, Harmon Twp., four miles east of Flasher. The post office was established April 12, 1910 with Simon G. Russell pm, who named it for Chief John Gall of the Teton Sioux. Mr. Russell, who came here from MO in 1902, also operated a store at the site. Little development occurred, and the post office closed November 30, 1913 with mail to Flasher. (1, 2, 3, 17, 18, 40, 79, 107)

**GALLATIN** (Griggs). This was a rural settlement founded in 1881 in NW¼ Sec. 24-145-58, Sverdrup Twp., about seven miles SE of Cooperstown, and named for Gallatin County, IL, which was named for Albert Gallatin (1761-1849), the Swiss-born statesman and diplomat who came to America in 1780 and was Secretary of the Treasury 1801-1814, and later Minister to France and Great Britain. The post office was established October 24, 1881 with John H. Atchison pm, and closed July 14, 1905

with mail to Cooperstown. A population of 25 was reported in 1890. (2, 10, 25, 40, 65, 99, 284)

**GALLOWAY** (Rolette). This pioneer settlement was started in 1888 in Sec. 12-161-69, Oxford Twp., about seven miles SE of Rolla. The post office was established September 11, 1902 with George F. Galloway pm. The GNRR built through this area in 1905, and established a townsite called Gronna just south of GALLOWAY. The post office transferred to Gronna December 1, 1905. Mr. Galloway later lived in Rolla, where he was a successful cheese manufacturer. (2, 40, 123)

**GALT** (Walsh). This was a country store established in 1882 in NE¼ Sec. 22-156-57, Norton Twp., two miles west of Lankin. The post office was established February 5, 1883 with Thomas H. Woods pm, who named it for his hometown of Galt, Ontario, Canada, which was named for John Galt, a politician and friend of town founder William Dickson. The post office moved twice within this general area before closing May 21, 1892, the date a new post office called Norton began operations. (2, 3, 10, 18, 40, 75, 356)

**GALVA** (Ward). This was a Soo Line RR loading station in SW¼ Sec. 13-159-88, Baden Twp., three miles north of Coulee, between Kenmare and Donnybrook. It was named for Galva, IL, which was named for Gelfe, Switzerland with an Anglicized spelling. The post office was established July 13, 1899 with Josie Clipper pm. She was succeeded by Minnie Price in 1901. The post office closed January 15, 1904 when it was relocated one-half mile west to the new townsite of Baden in S½ Sec. 14-159-88. (2, 3, 10, 40, 100, 375)

**GAMBETTA** (Williams). This was a rural post office established January 13, 1909 with Isaac Decker pm. It was located in SW¼ Sec. 9-156-101, Tyrone Twp., about fifteen miles NNW of Williston, and closed September 30, 1912 with mail to Bonetraill. The origin of the name is unknown, although it seems likely that it may have been named for Leon Michel Gambetta (1838-1882), a French statesman. (2, 3, 5, 18, 40, 50, 53)

**GARDAR** (Pembina). This is an Icelandic settlement founded in 1879 in SW 1/4 Sec. 16-159-56, Gardar Twp., and named by Stephen G. Stephenson for the Swedish Viking who discovered Iceland, which was once known as Gardars Holmi, or the Islet of Gardar. The name was also given to a town in Greenland founded by Eric the Red in 985 A.D., which flourished for four centuries, then vanished. The post office was established March 15, 1881 with Eirikur Bergman pm, but through an error by postal officials, the name was GARDER until August 23, 1883, when the error was corrected. The elevation is 1172, and a peak population of 100 was reached in 1920. The post office, Zip

Code 58234, closed August 15, 1984 with government records noting this fact on September 27, 1984. Helgi Johannesson, ND Attorney General 1963-1973, was born here in 1906. (1, 2, 3, 18, 33, 40, 79, 108, 366)

**GARDENA** (Bottineau). This Soo Line RR station was founded in 1905 in Secs. 8 & 9-160-76, Oak Creek Twp., and named to note that it was a garden spot in the Souris River valley. Others say it was named for the daughter of a local settler, or for a Soo Line RR official. The post office was established October 18, 1905 with Carl Hahn (1862-1946), a native of Germany who settled here in 1899, as pm. Five elevators were built during the initial boom, and the village incorporated in 1908, reporting a peak population of 134 in 1970. The post office, Zip Code 58739, became a rural branch of Kramer on April 23, 1965. (1, 2, 18, 33, 34, 40, 79, 101, 153)

**GARDER** (Pembina). This was an Icelandic settlement founded in 1879 in Sec. 16-159-56 as GARDAR. When the post office was established March 15, 1881 with Eirikur Bergman pm, postal officials erroneously entered the name as GARDER. The error was officially corrected on August 23, 1883. (2, 18, 40, 108)

*A so-called "complete" postmark, with both the county and the pm's name*

**GARDNER** (Cass). This townsite on the GNRR was founded in 1881 after efforts to develop Larson just to the south had failed. The name honored Stephen Gardner, an extensive land owner in the area. The post office was established December 8, 1881 with Cornelius Byerly pm. The village incorporated in 1929, and reached a peak population of 136 in 1950. The elevation is 886, and the Zip Code is 58036. Dr. Charlotte Campbell Pratt, a pioneer female physician, practiced here for many years. (1, 2, 33, 40, 52, 77, 79, 305)

**GARFIELD** (Cass). This was a farm post office established May 25, 1895 with C. C. Furnberg pm. It is likely that the name memorialized James Abram Garfield (1831-1881), twentieth President of the United States. It was located in NW¼ Sec. 33-139-49, Barnes Twp., between Fargo and Horace, and on April 29, 1899 changed its name to OSGOOD. (2, 40, 77)

**GARFIELD** (Divide). This was a farm post office established August 29, 1905 with Hattie Zimmerman pm. It was located in SW¼ Sec. 9-161-95, Border Twp., six miles south of Noonan, and closed August 31, 1908 with mail to Kermit. It was likely named for President James A. Garfield. (2, 3, 18, 40)

**GARFIELD** (Walsh). This pioneer settlement was founded in 1880 in Sec. 21-157-56, Golden Twp., seven miles west of Park River, and named for James Abram Garfield, the 1880 Republican candidate for President, who won the election, but was assassinated within a few months after his inauguration. The post office was established October 18, 1880 with Knute P. Levang (1851-1919) as pm, at first in his home one mile north of the townsite. The little village thrived, at one time having a newspaper, three general stores, a drugstore, two doctors, two hotels, two blacksmiths, two saloons, three land offices, etc., but when the GNRR bypassed the site in 1884, an exodus began to the new townsite of Park River on the railroad. The post office closed May 21, 1886 with mail to Vesta, and GARFIELD was soon a ghost town. (2, 3, 25, 40, 75, 356)

**GARLAND** (Foster). This was a NPRR station in SE¼ Sec. 16-146-67, Wyard Twp., four miles west of Carrington. It was named for the Garland family in the township. Christian Garland came here in 1883, and Claude, Preston, and Frank V. Garland arrived in 1890. Garland is an Old French name meaning crowned for victory. It appeared on maps circa 1900-1965, but little development ever occurred at the site. A population of 200 was reported on one 1940 map, surely a cartographer's error. (3, 19, 97)

**GARNES** (Burke). This was a farm post office established December 29, 1904 with Ole H. Garnes (1859-1960) pm., and was located in SW¼ Sec. 31-159-92, Garness Twp. On April 2, 1906 Mr. Garnes moved the facility one mile NE to SW 1/4 Sec. 29-159-92, the site of the new GNRR station called Powers Lake. The post office name was spelled GARNES, but the namesake and pm, who was the patriarch of Powers Lake and lived to celebrate a jubilant 100th birthday, later spelled his name as Garness, leading to some confusion. (2, 3, 34, 40, 67, 376)

**GARRISON** (Eddy). This was an early name for NEW ROCKFORD, which was used for a time in 1883, but was rejected by postal officials. It is said to honor either Lloyd Garrison, a stockholder of the NPRR, or William Lloyd Garrison (1805-1879), the famous abolitionist. (2, 3, 5, 119)

**GARRISON** (McLean). Theodore and Cecil H. Taylor founded this townsite in 1903 in NW¼ Sec. 6-147-84, Coal Harbor Twp., and named it for nearby Garrison Creek, which had been named in 1864 to note the troops of Fort Berthold garrisoned on its banks. The post office was established January 17, 1903 with Cecil H. Taylor pm. In 1905 it was moved five miles NNE to the new Soo Line RR townsite in SW¼ Sec. 8-148-84, Garrison Twp., on land originally owned by Andreas Pankratz (1848-1917). It incorporated as a village in 1907, and became a city in 1916 with Otis F. McGray as mayor. The Zip Code is 58540, and the peak population of 1,890 was reached in 1950. It is about twelve miles north of the giant Missouri River dam that uses this name. The original site, called OLD GARRISON after 1905, is now inundated by Lake Sakakawea. (1, 2, 3, 18, 28, 33, 40, 52, 79, 387)

**GARSKE** (Ramsey). This was a rural settlement founded in 1882 in NW¼ Sec. 10-156-64, Webster Twp., and named for William Garske (1845-1919), Gust Garske (1859-1924), and their cousins Charles, Herman Julius, and Louis Garske. In 1900 it moved one mile NE to the new GNRR townsite in SE¼ Sec. 3-156-64, between Webster and Starkweather. The post office was established December 28, 1900 with Charles Garske pm, and closed September 30, 1960 with mail to Webster. The elevation is 1480, and a peak population of 75 was reported in 1920. (1, 2, 3, 18, 40, 79, 103)

**GASCOYNE** (Bowman). This Milwaukee Road RR townsite was founded in 1907 as FISCHBEIN, and on March 25, 1908 the name was officially changed to GASCOYNE to honor a construction foreman of the railroad. Others say it is a coined name to note the large natural gas deposits in the area. The townsite is in Sec. 4 & 5-130-99, Gascoyne Twp., and Secs. 32 & 33-131-99, Fischbein Twp. The elevation is 2754, and the village, which incorporated in 1911, reached a peak population of 97 in 1930, with a decline to just 23 in 1980. The post office, Zip Code 58629, closed March 19, 1982. (1, 2, 3, 18, 34, 40, 79, 120, 381)

**GASSMAN** (Ward). This was a GNRR station built in 1883 in Sec. 19-155-83, Harrison Twp., five miles west of Minot, and named for Henry C. Gassman (1856-1938), a native of WI who was the first settler in Gassman Coulee. A small coal mine settlement developed here about 1915, but it disappeared by 1940. (1, 2, 3, 18, 100, 371)

**GATES** (Eddy). This was a pioneer settlement in SW¼ Sec. 16-150-66, Gates Twp., about one mile SSW of Sheyenne. A post office was established July 20, 1883 with Frank M. Gates, who was an early settler in the area who practiced law, as pm. The township adopted this name in 1906. Philip Brandt became the pm a short time later, but the office closed March 8, 1886 with mail to New Rockford. (2, 18, 40, 112)

**GATEWAY** (McLean). This was one of many boom towns that sprang up with the construction of Garrison Dam. It was founded in 1946 in Sec. 31-147-82, Linder Twp., just east of the junction of US Highway 83 and ND Highway 200A. The Soo Line RR station of RIVERDALE JUNCTION was also at this site. William Shillingstad, the owner of the townsite, named it to note its location at the point where people left the main highway to approach the construction site. (2, 28)

**GAYLORD** (Stark). This was a rural community located in SE¼ Sec. 32-138-99, Gaylord Twp., eleven miles south of Belfield. The name is said to have been selected by postal officials with no known local significance when the post office was established December 9, 1907 with Howard Molm (1874-1940) pm. The town consisted of the post office, a store, and a blacksmith shop, and claimed a population of 50 in 1930. The post office closed December 15, 1917 with mail to Belfield. (1, 2, 18, 40, 44, 53, 74)

**GAYTON** (Emmons). This was a rural community in SW¼ Sec. 11-134-79, about twenty miles NW of Linton, and just east of the Missouri River port of Gayton Landing.

Both were named for James Bennett Gayton (1833-1909), who came here as early as 1868 from Ohio, and was the first white settler in the county. He was a county commissioner and delegate to the ND Constitutional Convention in 1889. The post office was established August 2, 1881 with John L. Kennedy pm. Daily mail service began in 1886 when a stage line from Bismarck to Winona was begun by GAYTON rancher Peter Shier (1856-1925), who later served as the pm and was a five-term sheriff of the county. His Dinner Ranch was the midway stopping point on this stage line. A population of 15 was reported in 1890, and the site included a school, post office, stage station, and ferry service to Cannon Ball. Longtime pm Dennis W. Casey closed the post office November 15, 1915 with mail to Livona, and the site is now inundated by Lake Oahe. (1, 2, 3, 18, 25, 40, 66, 127, 368, 401, 414)

**GAYTON LANDING** (Emmons). This was an early Missouri River crossing located on the homestead of James B. Gayton in E½ Sec. 36-134-79, opposite Cannon Ball, and just west of the rural community of Gayton. A ferry service operated here for many years, but the site is now inundated by Lake Oahe. (3, 66, 96)

**GECK** (Morton). GECK appeared in the 1960's as the name of Exit #23 on Interstate 94, six miles east of Glen Ullin at the corner of Secs. 7 & 8-139-87, and Secs. 12 & 13-139-88, Curlew Twp. The name honored the Geck family, whose patriarch Philip G. Geck (1860-1950), came here in 1883 from Hessen, Germany, and with his brother, Peter, farmed over 5,000 acres. There never was a settlement at the site, and because this caused confusion for travelers, the name was dropped in 1987. (3, 17, 34, 107)

**GEM** (Stutsman). This was a rural post office established November 7, 1905 with Dallas L. Draper pm. It was located in Sec. 4-142-68, Strong Twp. until August 4, 1911, when it was replaced by the post office in the new NPRR townsite of Woodworth, one mile to the south. The name was chosen by postal officials from three—Gem, Hawkeye, and Dallas—that had been submitted by Mr. Draper, and is thought to be for Gem, Clayton County, Iowa. (2, 3, 18, 40, 158, 414)

**GENESEO** (Sargent). This GNRR townsite was founded in 1886 in Sec. 13-130-53, Kingston Twp., and called GOLTZ. When the post office was established October 13, 1887 with John Fink pm, the name was changed to GENESEO, for Geneseo, NY, the home of many local settlers. It is a name of Iroquois Indian origins, meaning beautiful valley. The town was rivaled by the adjacent Soo Line RR townsite of Alicia, and Veda, a compromise town between the two. Both were eventually absorbed by GENESEO. The elevation is 1155, and a peak population of 220 was recorded in 1930. The post office, Zip Code 58037, closed August 30, 1985. (1, 2, 3, 10, 18, 25 33, 40, 79, 434)

**GENEVA** (Burleigh). This NPRR siding was built in 1873 in SW¼ Sec. 19-139-74, Pleasant Hill Twp., just across the line in Kidder County, and called FIFTEENTH SIDING. In 1882 the name was changed to GENEVA, and about 1915 was moved one mile west to Sec. 24-139-75, Driscoll Twp., which is in Burleigh County. No development occurred at the site. (1, 2, 3, 14, 18)

**GENEVA** (Kidder). This NPRR siding was built in 1873 in SW¼ Sec. 19-139-74, Pleasant Hill Twp., eight miles west of Steele, and called FIFTEENTH SIDING. About 1882 it was renamed GENEVA, but no development occurred at the site. Some say it was named for Geneva, MN, which was named in 1855 by pm Edwin C. Stacy for Geneva, NY. Others say it was named directly for the NY city. Both American cities would ultimately trace their name to Geneva, Switzerland, which was given a name derived from the French word meaning juniper tree, a common site in that area. About 1915 GENEVA was moved one mile to the west, putting it into Burleigh County. (2, 3, 13, 14, 18, 19)

**GENIN** (Benson). An early rural settlement existed in SW¼ Sec. 36-152-68, Aurora Twp., before 1900, and was named for Father Jean Baptiste Marie Genin, a Canadian Roman Catholic missionary in Dakota Territory, and later the Bishop of Duluth, MN. When a NPRR townsite was founded here in 1901, it was renamed JOSEPHINE. (2, 18, 34, 44)

**GENOA** (McHenry). This was a GNRR station built in Sec. 5-154-80, North Prairie Twp., four miles south of Norwich, and probably named for Genoa, Italy, the birthplace of Christopher Columbus. A population of 10 was reported in 1920, but it became a ghost town shortly after that. (1, 2, 3, 13, 18)

**GEOFF** (Walsh). This was a rural post office established September 22, 1899 with Geoffrey R. B. Green pm. It was located in Sec. 14-157-59, Dewey Twp., nine miles west of Adams, and was moved two miles east in 1900 to the home of new pm Lars Dahlgren. It was given Mr. Green's nickname. Geoffrey is a Teutonic variant of Godfrey, meaning God's peace. The post office closed June 30, 1908 with mail to Adams. Goeff is an erroneous spelling. (2, 19, 40, 75)

**GERBER** (Stutsman). This was a rural post office established April 24, 1900 with George W. Gerber pm in his home about five miles NW of Woodworth. In 1909 it moved about five miles WSW to Sec. 30-143-69, Gerber

Twp., near the Kidder County line. On September 1, 1910 it was replaced by the post office at the new NPRR townsite of Pettibone. (2, 18, 40, 158)

**GERMANTOWN** (Oliver). A rural post office was established July 23, 1903 with L. W. Kadus pm, but the order was rescinded March 10, 1904. It was located in Mr. Kadus' country store in Sec. 11-142-87, Bert Twp., two miles west of Hannover. The area was settled primarily by people of German ancestry. The first German settlement in the United States, now a part of Philadelphia, PA, was given this name in 1683. (1, 3, 40, 121)

**GERTRUDE** (Cavalier). This was a rural post office established April 24, 1883 with John J. Strate pm, and closed August 20, 1883 with mail to Elgin. It was reestablished August 25, 1884 with Henry Hanson pm, and closed for good April 27, 1895 with mail to Milton. It was located in Sec. 25-159-58, Osford Twp., five miles SW of Milton, later moving to Sec. 27-159-58, two miles to the west. The post office was in a sod house with the door propped open by a pole, and was often called the STRATE post office in early accounts. The origin of the unofficial name is obvious, but the origin of GERTRUDE is unknown. It is a Teutonic name meaning spear maiden, and in Norse mythology Gertrude was a maiden who bore the souls of slain warriors to Valhalla. (2, 3, 19, 25, 40, 117, 247)

**GETH** (Renville). This was a rural settlement in Secs. 28 & 29-158-86, Whiteash Twp., between Carpio and Donnybrook. A store, blacksmith shop, and a mail drop were established here to serve the employees of the Mandt Mine, owned by the White Ash Coal Co., but when a Soo Line RR spur was not built to the site, it became a ghost town. Reports of an official post office in GETH are not confirmed by government records. The origin of the name is unknown, although some say it was the name of a local resident. (3, 71)

**GIBSON** (Barnes). John Henry Gibson (1844-1921) came to MN from his native VT in 1866 and settled here in 1882. His home in SW¼ Sec. 30-143-61, Pierce Twp., served as a mail drop, although it was never an official post office. When the Soo Line RR arrived in 1893, he sold land that became the new townsite of WIMBLEDON. (2, 3, 18, 34, 76, 269)

**GIEDT** (McIntosh). This was a farm post office established July 22, 1891 with Johann P. Giedt, who came here in 1886, as pm. It was located in SE¼ Sec. 3-130-71, Albright's Valley Twp., seven miles north of Venturia. In 1895 it was moved eleven miles WNW to the home of new pm Jacob Gaub in NE¼ Sec. 35-131-73, Frieda Twp., eleven miles NNE of Zeeland. The post office closed January 31, 1902 with mail to Danzig. Geidt is an erroneous spelling. (2, 3, 18, 40, 211, 240)

**GIESE** (Slope). This farm post office was established in 1908 as HOLTON. On April 30, 1910 pm George F. Giese moved it four miles SSW to the country store run by Ed Hess in NW¼ Sec. 2-134-102, Slope Center

Twp. William F. Hess became pm in 1913, and the facility closed March 31, 1914 with mail to Bessie. The community now became known as HESS, but when Mr. Giese reestablished the post office in 1917, he called it SLOPE CENTER. (2, 3, 40, 82, 414)

GILBERT (Steele). This townsite was platted by Mary E. Patterson in September 1896 in NW¼ Sec. 32-147-56, Finley Twp. Considerable development took place, with several lots sold for business and residential purposes. C. K. Norcott opened a general store, and his wife was preparing to establish a post office when the sales of lots were found to be invalid, and all property was returned to the original site owner, W. H. M. Phillip. In January 1897 the townsite was purchased by the GNRR, which annexed it to their adjacent townsite of FINLEY. The origin of GILBERT, a Teutonic name meaning illustrious pledge, is unknown. (2, 19, 99, 326)

GILBY (Grand Forks). This was a farm office established May 2, 1881 with John Braithwait pm. It was located in SW¼ Sec. 22-153-53, Gilby Twp., and named for John Gilby Jr., one of the brothers who came to this area in 1878. In 1887 it was moved to the new NPRR townsite in SE¼ Sec. 8 & SW¼ Sec. 9-153-53, two miles NW of the original site. The townsite was platted in August 1887, and reached a peak population of 544 in 1930. The elevation is 906, and the Zip Code is 58235. Notable among its pioneers were physician Robert Machray McLean (1867-1930), and merchant Lars P. Bjerklie. (1, 2, 25, 31, 33, 40, 69, 79, 240, 338)

GILL (Cass). This post office was established May 6, 1886 in the home of pm William M. Smylie in NW¼ Sec. 35-139-53, Gill Twp., replacing the EMBDEN post office about three miles to the west. It was named for its township, which was named for James C. Gill, owner of a 4,000 acre farm in the area, and later a state legislator. It closed September 30, 1895 with mail to Chaffee. (2, 40, 77, 240)

GILMA (Mercer). This was a farm post office established February 29, 1916 with Knute C. Stai pm. He came here in 1906 from Norway and operated the Triplet Spring Farm in NW¼ Sec. 2-142-90, nine miles south of Goldenvalley. He named the post office for his wife, the former Gilma Pederson. It closed October 15, 1917 with mail to Hebron. (2, 18, 40, 64)

GILSTRAP (Adams). This was a rural post office established February 2, 1907 with Thomas R. Sarver pm. It was located in SW¼ Sec. 33-129-93, Gilstrap Twp., seven miles ESE of Haynes, and just north of the SD border. It was named for Charles Gilstrap, the original settler at this site. It moved a couple times in the same general area, the last of which amounted to only about one-quarter mile, but this move put GILSTRAP into SD. On December 31, 1909 GILSTRAP, ND became White Butte, SD. (2, 3, 40, 189, 414)

GINGREY (Stutsman). An 1890 guide to ND lists this place as being in Stutsman County, and served by the Esler post office. The

name likely honors Frank Gingrey, a county pioneer who was active in establishing rural schools. No other information is available. (3, 25, 148, 415)

GIRARD (Pierce). This was a rural post office established April 18, 1901 with Carl E. Ellertson pm. It was located in Sec. 19-153-72, Rosedale Twp., at the NE end of Girard Lake about eight miles SE of Balta. On January 31, 1904 it was moved two miles ESE to the home of new pm Ole J. Olson in NW¼ Sec. 29-153-72, at the SE end of Girard Lake near the place where ND Highway 3 crosses Buffalo Lake. The post office was named for the lake, which was named for Antoine Girard, a famous pioneer of the Red River valley. It closed August 31, 1909 with mail to Fillmore. (2, 3, 40, 53, 79, 114, 149)

GLACIS (Cass). This NPRR station three miles west of Casselton had been founded in 1882 as SIDNEY, and at the time was promoted as a replacement for Casselton. None of this happened, and the station's development stagnated for many years. On November 19, 1905 it was renamed GLACIS, operating as a loading station until it was removed in 1940. A glacis is a gentle slope or incline, and is descriptive of the locale. (2, 3, 18, 34)

GLADSTONE (Stark). This city was founded in the spring of 1882, and platted in February 1883 in N½ Sec. 17-139-94, Heart River Twp., one mile SE of the Green River construction camp. It was named for William Ewart Gladstone (1809-1898), the British Prime Minister at the time. The post office was established June 7, 1882 with Oliver C. Bissell pm. It challenged for county seat honors in 1883, but lost to Dickinson. The elevation is 2348, the Zip Code is 58630, and the village, which incorporated in 1939, reached a peak population of 316 in 1980, although a population of 400 had been claimed in 1890. It became a city in 1965 with Anton Degel Sr. (1889-1974), who had been mayor since 1939, continuing in that position under the new form of municipal government. (1, 2, 3, 10, 13, 18, 25, 33, 40, 52, 74, 79, 244)

GLADYS (Williams). This was a rural community founded in 1905 in SE¼ Sec. 23-158-102, Good Luck Twp., ten miles SE of Grenora. At one time it had a general store, bank, printing office, blacksmith shop, and a post office which was established April 1, 1906 with William H. Rowe pm. The town was founded by Richard Evans, who name it for his wife, the former Gladys McCurdy. Gladys is a Welsh feminine form of the Latin name Claudius, and means lame. The town failed to attract a railroad and declined. The post office closed March 15, 1918 with mail to Grenora. (2, 18, 19, 40, 50, 53)

GLANAVON (Emmons). This was a rural post office established January 17, 1903 with Martha Whitney pm on the ranch owned by her husband, Ben W. Whitney. It was located in NW¼ Sec. 28-129-78, one mile north of the SD border on the east bank of the Missouri River. The name is of Scottish origin, but its meaning is unknown. The post office closed November 2, 1907 with mail to Winona. (2, 3, 18, 40, 66)

GLASCOCK (Burleigh). This was a farm post office establshed July 14, 1886 with James B. Glascock pm, whose suggested name of Logan was rejected because of duplication in Barnes County, although that office had closed a few months earlier. It was located in SW¼ Sec. 26-138-77, Logan Twp., eight miles SSE of McKenzie. In 1888 it moved three miles SW to NE¼ Sec. 4-137-77, Morton Twp., the home of new pm David W. Rittenhouse. A population of 30 was reported in 1890. The post office closed July 16, 1895 with mail to Sterling. Glasscock is an erroneous spelling. (2, 3, 25, 40, 414)

GLASSER (McKenzie). This was a rural post office that was authorized, and rescinded, on three occasions. It was first authorized July 14, 1906 with Lenora K. Glasser as pm, and rescinded November 6, 1906. She was reappointed pm January 4, 1907, and on February 6, 1907 a new order appeared, but listing John K. Glasser as pm. Both of these orders were rescinded May 24, 1907. The reasons for these actions and the location of the post office remain unknown. (2, 3, 40)

GLASSTON (Pembina). This GNRR station was founded in 1886 in Sec. 2-160-53, Saint Thomas Twp., just south of the Baltimore post office, which was transferred here on September 20, 1886 with Archibald Glass pm. The new townsite was named in honor of Mr. Glass. A small village has continued to exist at this site, with its population rarely exceeding 100. The elevation is 844, and the Zip Code is 58236. Conrad W. Leifur (1897-1982), a well known educator and author, was born here. (1, 2, 3, 18, 40, 108, 146)

GLEASON (Towner). This was a rural post office established November 3, 1888 with Charles W. Gleason pm. The order was rescinded November 25, 1893, over five years after its authorization, with the notation "no papers." The location of GLEASON is unknown. (2, 3, 40)

GLENBURN (Renville). This GNRR townsite was founded in 1903 in NE¼ Sec. 14-158-82, Ensign Twp., as LINCOLN. Because of duplication the name was changed to GLENBURN when the Walter post office moved here October 9, 1903 with Wilson Walter continuing as pm. Some say the name came from Glenburn, Ontario, Canada, while others say it was named for a GNRR official. Folklore tells of a young newspaper boy, Glenn D. Colcord, whose zeal for his job prompted the remark, "Look at Glenn burn up the road with his bicycle." Mr. Colcord, many years later, did not deny that GLENBURN's name was derived from this tale. The elevation is 1577, the Zip Code is 58740, and the village, which incorporated in 1903, reached a peak population of 454 in 1980. Among its notable citizens are Reinhart Gilbertsen, longtime pm and newspaper editor, and Richard John Backes, a prominent state legislator. (1, 2, 3, 18, 33, 40, 52, 71, 79, 253, 322, 323)

GLENCOE (Burleigh & Emmons). This was a rural community named by pioneer settlers for Glencoe, Argyllshire, Scotland. It was located primarily in Sec. 6-136-78 and Secs. 1 & 12-136-79 in Emmons County, although the well known and still existing

Glencoe Church is just north of the main settlement in SE¼ Sec. 32-137-78, Telfer Twp., in Burleigh County. The post office was established May 2, 1883 with Cyrus M. Robinson pm, and it moved several times within the community until closing November 29, 1930 with mail to Bismarck. A population of 18 was reported in 1890. The site once boasted of a store, dance hall, hotel, school, and church, but the settlement is now largely abandoned. (1, 2, 3, 13, 18, 25, 40, 66, 401)

**GLENFIELD** (Foster). This was a rural post office established December 15, 1886 with Robert Clendenning pm, and closed September 30, 1897 with mail to Corinne. It reopened February 11, 1898 and closed October 31, 1902 with mail to McHenry. Both of these post offices were located within three miles of a GNRR townsite founded in May 1912 in NE¼ Sec. 21-146-62, Glenfield Twp., on the newly-built Surrey cutoff line. A post office was established here September 12, 1912 with Lottie Posey pm, who revived the old name, which is descriptive of the locale. Mrs. Posey served as pm until 1958. The village incorporated in 1953, and reached a peak population of 164 in 1980. The elevation is 1500, and the Zip Code is 58443. (1, 2, 33, 40, 97)

**GLENILA** (Cavalier). This post office was established November 8, 1902 with Richard H. O'Neale pm. It was rescinded January 8, 1903 before it went into operation. GLENILA was to be located in Glenila Twp. (162-64), near Calvin. The origin of the township name is unknown. (2, 3, 40)

**GLEN LAUREL** (Dunn). This post office was established February 8, 1911 with Henry B. Schaffner pm, who gave it a descriptive name. Mr. Schaffner owned six full sections of land in the township, and it is thought that the post office was housed in a rural school in S½ Sec. 15-142-91, thirteen miles south of Dodge. The post office was discontinued December 31, 1912 with mail to Hebron. (2, 3, 40, 223)

**GLENN** (Renville). This was a rural post office established May 22, 1903 with Fred H. Giddings pm in SW¼ Sec. 21-160-85, Grassland Twp., ten miles SW of Mohall. It was named to note its location at the mouth of a large ravine, and to honor Mr. Giddings son, Glenn. The name is of Gaelic origin, and means valley. The post office closed July 14, 1906 with mail to Mohall. (2, 3, 18, 19, 40, 71)

**GLENORA** (Richland). This was a Milwaukee Road RR station in Sec. 5-131-47, Summit Twp., five miles south of Wahpeton. It was shown on many maps during the first twenty years of this century. The origin of the name is unknown. (1, 2, 3, 18)

**GLENULLEN** (Morton). This spelling was used on the NPRR station at GLEN ULLIN from the time it was built in 1883 until the depot was replaced by a new building in 1949. The difference in spelling was the source of much confusion, and it is a continuing topic of conversation as to why the sign on the depot was not changed. It is apparent that the spelling had some influence, with the Glen Ullen State Bank of

1905-1908 using a name containing elements of both the railroad and official names. (2, 3, 105)

**GLEN ULLIN** (Morton). This NPRR station was built in 1879 in Sec. 31-139-88, Curlew Twp., and settlement began in 1883. NPRR land agent Alvin E. Bovay, known as the father of the Republican Party, coined the name from "glen", Gaelic for valley, and "Ullin", taken from *Lord Ullin's Daughter*, a ballad by Thomas Campbell. The post office was established June 4, 1883 with Dr. Sid O. Morgan pm. From November 30, 1895 to December 1, 1905 the name was spelled as one word to conform to government spelling regulations. From 1883 until 1949 the NPRR depot displayed the town's name as GLENULLEN. The village incorporated in 1901, and it became a city in 1910 with Michael Tschida (1866-1956) as mayor. The reservoir at nearby Heart Butte Dam is named in his honor. The elevation is 2067, the Zip Code is 58631, and a peak population of 1,324 was reached in 1950. (1, 2, 3, 17, 25, 33, 40, 52, 79, 105)

**GLENULLIN** (Morton). This one-word spelling was officially used by the post office at GLEN ULLIN from November 30, 1895 to December 1, 1905 to conform with goverment regulations for place names. (40)

**GLOVER** (Dickey). This Chicago & NW RR station was founded in 1886 in Secs. 13 & 24-132-60, James River Valley Twp., eight miles NNW of Oakes, and named for Samuel Glover of Delaware, OH, who traded his NPRR stock for 30,000 acres of land in this area. He had originally settled in KS, but did not like that area of the country. The post office was established January 26, 1887 with Elling O. Ulness pm. He had been pm at the nearby Ulness post office, and later started another Ulness post office in Richland County. The elevation is 1396, and the population has been under 100 during its entire existance. The post office closed February 28, 1943 with mail to Oakes. (1, 2, 3, 18, 25, 38, 40, 154, 318)

**GOA** (Benson). This was a farm post office established January 8, 1900 with Elisabeth Hunter pm. It was located in SE¼ Sec. 22-152-71, Rich Valley Twp., seven miles SE of Esmond. Area residents wanted to name it Roberts for Robert Hunter, who had petitioned for the office, while Mr. Hunter wanted to name it for mail carrier William August Preuss (1868-1937). Some sources credit Mr. Preuss with suggesting the compromise name of Go, which evolved into GOA, although postal records show Roberts as the submitted name, with GOA apparently substituted by postal officials. The post office closed November 30, 1905 with mail to Esmond. (2, 18, 40, 53, 149, 414)

**GODKIN** (Emmons). What became TEMVIK was first called GODKIN, which according to folklore resulted from a 1904 conversation between either two local settlers, or two railroad crewmen. One is said to have asked, "Who could possibly see much of a future at this desolate location?", and the other answered in broken English, "God kin." When the post office was established the following year, it was called BROFY. The rival townsites of LARVIK and

TEMPELTON began here, with a merger in 1911 as TEMVIK. (2, 3, 66)

**GOETZ** (Ward). The first DONNYBROOK post office was established in 1895 in Sec. 14-158-87, Carbondale Twp., and on December 29, 1887 new pm Edward C. Henry changed the name to GOETZ, for unknown reasons. On March 9, 1898 a new Donnybrook post office was established one-half mile to the west at the new Soo Line RR townsite. Both post offices operated until GOETZ closed April 13, 1899 with mail to Donnybrook. (2, 40, 100)

**GOHRING** (McIntosh). This was a farm post office established October 5, 1896 with Jacob Gohring pm at his home in NE¼ Sec. 26-132-69, Lowenthal Twp., six miles SE of Lehr. It closed July 31, 1899 with mail to Kulm. (2, 3, 40, 133)

**GOLDEN LAKE** (Steele). This pioneer settlement was founded as INTERLAKEN, but when the post office was established February 26, 1885 with Isaac Golden pm, the name was changed to GOLDEN LAKE. The site, Sec. 2-147-55, Golden Lake Twp., nine miles NE of Finley, was between Golden Lake, named for Isaac and Fannie Golden, who came here in 1883, and Swan Lake. The post office closed June 14, 1902 with mail to Hatton, reopened January 27, 1903, and closed for good October 15, 1904 with mail again to Hatton. A population of about 15 was here for many years, centered around the Golden Lake Store, but this business closed in 1936 ending the history of GOLDEN LAKE as a rural community. John Arthur Engen (1897-1963), longtime ND Tax Commissioner, was born here. (1, 2, 3, 25, 40, 99, 240, 326)

**GOLDENVALLEY** (Mercer). This post office was established May 11, 1909 with George Bratzell pm, who chose a name descriptive of the location in the Knife River valley. In 1913 it moved one mile south to E½ Sec. 15-144-90, where the NPRR had established a townsite. The elevation is 1946, the Zip Code is 58541, and a peak population of 400 was reported in 1940. The post office name has always been officially spelled as one word, but the two word spelling is used so often that it is almost a *de facto* correct spelling. (1, 2, 3, 18, 33, 34, 40, 64)

**GOLDWIN** (Stutsman). This NPRR station was founded in 1914 in Sec. 5-142-67, Paris Twp., six miles east of Woodworth, and named RAMONA. The post office was established November 5, 1915 with Nels Handevidt pm, and the name was changed at this time to GOLDWIN at the suggestion of W. H. Stripp, a local pioneer, although there in no known significance to the name. The townsite never experienced a boom, reaching a peak population of just 45 in 1930. The post office closed December 31, 1943 with mail to Woodworth. (2, 3, 40, 158)

**GOLTZ** (Sargent). This GNRR townsite was founded in 1886 in Sec. 13-130-53, Kingston Twp., and named for one of its employees, said to be the construction foreman. The first settlers did not like the name, and changed it to GENESEO in 1887. (2, 18, 434)

GOLVA (Golden Valley). This is a NPRR station founded in 1914 in SW¼ Sec. 30-138-106, Lone Tree Twp. The name was coined by townsite owner A. L. Martin from the name of the county, GOLden VAlley. The post office was established February 15, 1916 with Johanna Christensen pm. Many buildings were moved here from the inland town of Burkey. The village incorporated in 1947, and it became a city in 1967. The Zip Code is 58632, and its 1980 population was 101. (2, 33, 40, 52, 79, 80)

GOODALL (McKenzie). This was a rural post office established October 6, 1902 with Carrie E. Goodall pm. It was located on the W. J. Goodall ranch in NW¼ Sec. 10-152-93, River View Twp., opposite Sanish, moved two miles west to NW¼ Sec. 8-152-93 in 1909, and closed September 15, 1916 with mail to Sanish. (1, 2, 18, 40, 79)

GOODRICH (Sheridan). This NPRR townsite was founded in 1902 as the result of the merger of the rival townsites of CLARK and DUDLEY. It is located in S 1/2 Sec. 8-146-74, Goodrich Twp., and named for F. H. Goodrich, the NPRR civil engineer in charge of construction in this area. The post office was established August 30, 1902 with Joseph T. Wyard pm. Mr. Wyard, a pioneer merchant, had established the post office August 21, 1902 as BLAINE, but in an example of swift government action, this order was rescinded and replaced with the GOODRICH paperwork in just nine days. The elevation is 1994, the Zip Code is 58444, and the village, which incorporated in 1909, reached a peak population of 476 in both 1920 and 1940. (1, 2, 3, 18, 21, 23, 30, 40, 52, 79)

GOOLER (Ward). This was a rural post office established April 12, 1902 with Rose Gooler pm. The order was rescinded October 17, 1902. The location of GOOLER is unknown. (3, 40)

GOOSE CAMP (Sioux). This was an Indian settlement of the late 1880's in Sec. 34-130-82, just SE of present-day Selfridge, and named for Chief Joe Goose. (127)

GOOSE CREEK (Cass). This was the popular name used for the settlement in Sec. 35-140-52, Casselton Twp., during the early 1870's. The NPRR preferred SWAN CREEK. In 1876 the name CASSTOWN was adopted, and when the post office opened August 8, 1876, the name was stylized as CASSELTON. (2, 3, 77, 300)

GOOSENLAND (Traill). This was a rural community founded in 1871 by a colony of mostly Norwegian settlers. Rev. Jonas Ostlund, a Swede, led the group and settled in NE¼ Sec. 33-146-51. Among the others were Olaf Varnson, who settled in SE¼ Sec. 34-146-51, Anders Johnson, who settled in SE¼ Sec. 36-146-51, Ole Hovde, and Lars Hovde. They named their new home with a coined word noting the nearby Goose River. It was later renamed NORWAY for its township, and when Rev. Ostlund started a post office in 1877, he called it STONY POINT, and later BLOOMFIELD. (3, 187)

GOOSE RAPIDS (Traill). Some accounts refer

Goodrich about 1908

to the pioneer settlement of GOOSE RIVER as GOOSE RAPIDS, said to note the rapids of the Goose River as it flows into the Red River. It appears that Asa Sargeant, who became pm in 1872, did in fact try to change the name, but government records indicate that the official name was always GOOSE RIVER. (2, 3, 29, 40, 414)

GOOSE RIVER (Traill). This was the first settlement in Traill County, founded in 1870 in NW¼ Sec. 14-146-49, Caledonia Twp., by Asa Sargeant and Chester M. Clark. George E. Weston (1832-1903) ran the Hudson's Bay Company post here, and became the pm when the post office was established November 2, 1871. The settlement's name noted its location near the mouth of the Goose River, named Aux Outardes by early French explorers to note the flocks of geese that fed and nested here. When Traill County organized February 23, 1875, GOOSE RIVER was chosen as the county seat, with Mr. Clark as Sheriff, and Mr. Weston as Register of Deeds, but on August 19, 1875 the court house and post office were relocated one mile SW to the new townsite of CALEDONIA, and GOOSE RIVER soon became a ghost town. (2, 3, 29, 40, 79, 187, 393, 414, 415)

GORDER (Dunn). A rural post office was established June 18, 1908 with Martin Gorder pm, who declined the appointment, and the order was rescinded October 3, 1908. It is thought that this was the same man as the Martin Goarder who settled in SW¼ Sec. 4-145-94, Decorah Twp., five miles NW of Dunn Center, in 1905. (2, 3, 18, 40, 415)

GORDON (Bottineau). This GNRR townsite was founded in 1902 in Sec. 3-159-83, Lansford Twp., and changed its name to LANSFORD the following year. The origin of GORDON, an Old English name meaning three-cornered hill, is unknown. (2, 18, 19, 34, 101)

GORHAM (Billings). This post office was established July 28, 1899 with Thomas J. McDonald pm in NW¼ Sec. 1-142-99, about sixteen miles north of Belfield. The name honored Frederick Eldridge Gorham, a pioneer rancher in the area who came here from MA. In 1907 it moved to Sec.

12-142-100, about six miles west, and moved one mile NW to Sec. 2-142-100 in 1914. In 1917 a small community began in Sec. 1-142-100, and the GORHAM post office moved there about 1920, when the population was reported to be 40. On June 30, 1973 the post office, Zip Code 58633, closed with mail to Fairfield, which had just relocated to Sec. 10-142-99. Mike Baranko, pm at GORHAM since 1948, became the new pm of Fairfield on that date. (2, 3, 18, 33, 34, 40, 41, 79, 81)

GORMAN (Barnes). This NPRR loading station was built in 1897 in SW¼ Sec. 19-140-57, Alta Twp., just west of the Alta, or Peak, station. At first it was called BAIRD, but about 1905 the name was changed to GORMAN for unknown reasons. The station was removed in 1924. (2, 34)

GOSHEN (Cass). This is a rural community founded in 1878, and centered around a Moravian church in NE¼ Sec. 5-138-52, Maple River Twp., nine miles SW of Casselton. The first pastor was Frank Wolff in 1880, and the present church building was built in 1884. The first settlers, most of whom came from Winona, MN, felt that the soil was as rich as that in the Biblical land of Goshen, the homeland of the Israelites prior to the Exodus. (3, 10, 77)

GOSS (Burke). This was a rural post office established March 21, 1906 with William G. Bennett pm in his country store in SE¼ Sec. 25-160-91, Dimond Twp., seven miles SSW of Coteau. It was named for Evan B. Goss, a District Judge from Minot who was an Associate Justice of the ND Supreme Court 1911-1916. For a time Peter Melquist operated a blacksmith shop here, but the site failed to develop beyond this, and the post office closed April 30, 1908 with mail to Kenmare. (2, 3, 40, 67, 100)

GRABALL (Sargent). This townsite was founded in April 1883 in SW¼ Sec. 1-132-54, Milnor Twp., and was called END OF THE TRACK until a permanent name, GRABALL, was chosen. The origin of the name is unknown. After a short time this name was changed to LINTON, which experienced a brief boom until August 1883 when the NPRR was extended three miles further, and a new terminus, Milnor, was founded. (2, 171)

**GRABER** (Hettinger). This was a rural post office established November 30, 1907 with Mary E. Gray, nee Rutherford, as pm. She came here with her husband, A. D. Gray, the township's Justice of the Peace and Road Overseer, from IA in 1906. The post office was located in NW¼ Sec. 20-136-94, Madison Twp., and named for the Graeber family, prominent local ranchers, with a change in the spelling. It closed January 15, 1914 with mail to Regent. (1, 2, 3, 18, 40, 53)

**GRACE** (Cavalier). This was a farm post office established June 19, 1902 with Mary M. Watson pm. The order was rescinded March 4, 1903. Records also show a GRACE post office authorized November 17, 1902 with Mary A. S. Hudson pm, and this also failed to go into operation. They are thought to be one and the same, located in SW¼ Sec. 8-161-64, Bruce Twp., three miles WNW of Clyde. The origin of the name is unknown, although some speculate that the name honored Thomas Langdon Grace (1814-1884), Roman Catholic Bishop of Saint Paul, MN 1859-1884. (2, 3, 13, 40, 249)

**GRACE CITY** (Foster). This GNRR townsite on the Surrey cutoff line was founded in 1910 in Sec. 15-147-64, Larrabee Twp., and named for Grace Enos Bradley, wife of townsite owner Edgar Ralph Bradley, who promised the surveyors a keg of beer if they would agree to name the town for his wife. Bradley, SD was named for Mr. Bradley for having broken up a fight between railroad construction supervisors and laborers. The post office was established January 1, 1911 with Ole Bonderud moving his operation into town from the old Larrabee post office four miles ESE of here. Mr. Bonderud's sister, Ida Louise (1893-1974), was pm here 1919-1959. The elevation is 1514, the Zip Code is 58445, and the population reached a peak of about 225 in 1920. (1, 2, 3, 33, 36, 40, 79, 97)

**GRACEVILLE** (Bowman). This was a farm post office established June 17, 1910 with Charles F. Malm pm. It was located in NE¼ Sec. 25-129-101, Minnehaha Twp., six miles west of Haley, and named by settlers from Graceville, MN, which was named for Thomas Langdon Grace (1814-1897), the Roman Catholic Bishop of Saint Paul, MN 1859-1884. The post office closed February 29, 1916 with mail to Swartwood. (1, 2, 3, 13, 18, 34, 40, 120, 414)

**GRAFTON** (Walsh). The post office was established May 20, 1879 with Thomas E. Cooper pm, and by 1883 the city claimed to have 2,000 residents. It is located in Secs. 13 & 24-157-53, Grafton Twp., and Secs. 18 & 19-157-52, Oakwood Twp., and was designated as county seat of Walsh County in 1881, the year it incorporated as a village and was reached by both the NPRR and GNRR. Mr. Cooper named it for his wife's home of Grafton County, NH, which was named for Augustus Henry FitzRoy, 3rd Duke of Grafton (1735-1811). Folklore says that Mr. Cooper planned to raise fruit in the area by grafting on branches, and coined the term "graft-on." The village became a city in 1883 with Stewart Cairncross as mayor, and the State Institute for the Feeblemind-ed was founded here in 1903 with Dr. L. B. Baldwin as Superintendent. The elevation is 827, the Zip Code is 58237, and a peak population of 5,946 was recorded in 1970. (1, 2, 10, 18, 25, 40, 45, 75, 79)

**GRAGREEN** (Barnes). This was a rural community eight miles SW of Valley City. The post office was established February 28, 1881 with Gilbert B. Green pm at his home in SW¼ Sec. 24-139-59, Green Twp., and closed December 20, 1882 with mail to Valley City. The name was coined from the names of the pm and A. H. Gray, both of whom had settled here in 1879. GRAGREEN was known as "The Colorful Community" due to the fact that its settlers were named Gray, Green, Brown, Black, and White. (2, 3, 25, 40, 76)

**GRAHAM** (Benson). On December 6, 1887, the LAROSE post office in Sec. 25-153-66, seven miles ESE of Minnewaukan, was renamed GRAHAM, honoring Duncan Graham, the first white settler on Graham's Island who came here about 1814 and ran a fur trading post. A native of Scotland, his wife was the daughter of the Sioux Chief Wayagoenagee, one of his daughters married Alexander Faribault, the namesake of Faribault, MN, and a granddaughter, Louise Buisson, married Major James McLaughlin, the namesake of McLaughlin, SD. The GRAHAM post office closed February 11, 1888 with mail to Grand Harbor. (2, 3, 18, 40, 79, 110)

**GRAHAM'S ISLAND** (Benson). This post office was established December 30, 1889 with Angeline Lindersmith Hoadley pm, who named it for its location in SE 1/4 Sec. 14-153-66, on Graham's Island, which had become a peninsula due to the receding waters of Devils Lake. It replaced the old Graham post office two miles to the SE which had closed in 1888. To comply with government spelling regulations the name was changed to GRAHAMS ISLAND on November 30, 1894, operating under this name until it closed in 1919. Usher Lloyd Burdick (1879-1960), a longtime Congressman from ND, lived here from about 1884 until 1900. (1, 2, 3, 18, 40, 110, 414)

**GRAHAMS ISLAND** (Benson). This spelling was adopted by the GRAHAM'S ISLAND post office on December 1, 1894 to comply with new government spelling regulations. Angeline Lindersmith Hoadley was pm at her home in SE¼ Sec. 14-153-66 until 1902, when she was succeeded by David Denoyer, who moved the facility one mile south to his home in SE¼ Sec. 23-153-66. Sophia Schultz assumed the position at the same location in 1919, but the post office closed May 31, 1919 with mail to Minnewaukan. (1, 2, 3, 18, 40, 110, 414)

**GRAIN** (Steele). This was a rural post office established August 18, 1882 with James H. McLean pm, who named it to note the large grain fields in the area. It was located in Sec. 7-146-56, Easton Twp., two miles south of Finley. On June 22, 1883 James A. Pickert became pm, and he changed the name to PICKERT. On March 18, 1896 new pm Elsie J. Pease changed the name to EASTON, and on January 29, 1897 it relocated to the new townsite of FINLEY. (2, 25, 40, 99, 326)

**GRAND FORKS** (Grand Forks). Settlers arrived here in 1868, making GRAND FORKS the oldest of ND's four major cities, and the second oldest permanent white settlement in the state. The post office was established June 15, 1870 with Sanford C. Cady pm, who named it using the English translation of *Les Grandes Fourches*, the name given this place by early French explorers to note the confluence of the Red and Red Lake Rivers. Capt. Alexander Griggs, owner of most of the original townsite, platted GRAND FORKS in 1875. It incorporated as a village in 1878, and became a city in 1881 with William H. Brown as mayor. It was named county seat when Grand Forks County organized in 1873, and sprawls over six sections of Grand Forks Twp. (151-50) and two sections of Falconer Twp. (152-50). It reported a population of 30 in 1870, but had grown to a city of over 7,000 residents when ND became a state in 1889. For most of this century it was the state's second largest city, but its 1980 population

*Grafton about 1940*

GRAND PRAIRIE ??

*Grand Forks December 24, 1907*

of 43,760 allowed Bismarck to move into second place. The University of North Dakota was founded in 1883, making GRAND FORKS the state's center for higher education. The State Mill and Elevator was built in 1922, and the ND School for the Blind moved here from Bathgate in 1961. The elevation is 836, and the Zip Code is 58201. Arthur G. Sorlie (1874-1928), governor of ND 1925-1928, was born here. (1, 2, 3, 31, 33, 40, 69, 79, 240, 341)

**GRAND FORKS AIR FORCE BASE** (Grand Forks). This military facility was authorized by Congress in 1954, and 5,400 acres in Meckinock Twp. (152-53) were purchased, partly with local contributions, with construction beginning in 1956. It is just NW of Emerado, and was named for the nearby city of Grand Forks. A classified branch of the Grand Forks post office operated here from June 22, 1959 until January 26, 1980. The population on base generally exceeds 16,000. (3, 69, 240)

**GRAND FORKS JUNCTION** (Grand Forks). This is the GNRR station at the junction of their main lines just west of Grand Forks in NW¼ Sec. 7-151-50, Grand Forks Twp. It was built in 1881, and appeared on maps until about 1915. (2, 31, 240)

**GRAND HARBOR** (Ramsey). This townsite was founded in 1882 in NE¼ Sec. 22 & SE¼ Sec. 15-154-65, Grand Harbor Twp., at the head of Teller's Bay, and named by local settlers who felt that this was the best harbor on Devils Lake. The post office opened December 20, 1882 when Michael Donohue relocated his Swan post office to this site. A population of 225 was reported in 1890, but later counts would never exceed 50. In 1897 it moved one mile north to the GNRR siding in SE¼ Sec. 10-154-65, with George McDevitt running the post office. Being only seven miles NW of the city of Devils Lake, the site failed to show any major development, and the post office closed March 31, 1914 with mail to Devils Lake. E. Bruce Hagen, a longtime ND Public Service Commissioner, was born here in 1930. (1, 2, 3, 18, 25, 40, 79, 103, 414, 415)

**GRANDIN** (Cass & Traill). This GNRR

townsite was founded in 1880 in NW¼ Sec. 3, 143,50, Kinyon Twp., Cass County, and was platted in November of that year by Comstock & White. The post office was established April 21, 1881 with John D. Taylor pm. Sometime before 1892 an addition was platted at the north edge of town called North Lindsey's Addition to Grandin, which was in SW¼ Sec. 34-144-50, Kelso Twp., Traill County. GRANDIN became an incorporated village in 1926, and reached a peak population of 211 in 1980, although it showed an unofficial population of 318 in 1890. The elevation is 891, and the Zip Code is 58038. It was named for John Livingston Grandin of Tidioute, PA, who was a pioneer in the oil industry in his home state, then acquired 72,000 acres of Red River valley farm land as a credit settlement with the NPRR and became a leading bonanza farmer in Dakota Territory. (1, 2, 18, 25, 33, 34, 40, 77, 79, 187)

**GRAND RAPIDS** (LaMoure). Founded in 1880 in Sec. 5-134-61, Grand Rapids Twp., this NPRR station was the first settlement in LaMoure County. It was platted in June of that year by Edward P. Wells and Homer T. Elliott, the latter of whom became pm when the post office was established June 17, 1880. It was named for the cataracts of the James River at this site, sometimes called the stepping stones, although some say it was named for Grand Rapids, MI, which was named to note the rapids on the Grand River at that site. It was the county seat 1881-1886, and reported a population of 300 in 1890, but years of decline resulted in a count of just 50 in 1960. The elevation is 1321, and the post office, Zip Code 58446, became a rural branch of LaMoure on December 31, 1966, and closed altogether on October 31, 1973. (1, 2, 10, 18, 25, 33, 40, 41, 79, 144)

**GRANO** (Renville). This Soo Line RR station was founded in 1905 in NE¼ Sec. 12-159-85, Callahan Twp., midway between Tolley and Lansford. A thriving little village was incorporated in 1911, reaching a population of 112 in 1920. The post office was established July 27, 1905 with John Cleven pm. The population declined drastically, and the post office closed January 31, 1956 with mail to

Lansford. Several versions exist to explain the name, several of which are interrelated. It was coined from the names of Charles GRAce and LaNO Robert Ortberg, newspapermen from Mohall, or it was coined from A. D. GReene and Charles LANO, Soo Line RR officials (Mr. Lano was the Mohall pm), or it was suggested by Mr. Lano from a tradename of a breakfast cereal, *Grain-0*, or some combination of the above. (2, 18, 38, 40, 52, 71, 75, 79)

**GRANT** (McKenzie). This was a rural post office established December 4, 1911 with Charles W. Dean pm. It was located in SE¼ Sec. 34-150-104, Yellowstone Twp., seven miles SSW of Cartwright, and closed November 30, 1912 with mail to Fairview, MT. After the name Horse Creek was rejected, it was named for D. W. Grant, a NPRR official involved with the construction of the mainline westward from Mandan in 1879. Grant is a Latin name meaning great. (2, 3, 19, 40, 53, 415)

**GRANT RIVER** (Traill). An 1890 guide to ND lists this place as being in Traill County, and served by the Caledonia post office. No other information is available. (25)

**GRANVILLE** (McHenry). This GNRR station was founded in 1886 in NE¼ Sec. 8-155-79, Granville Twp., and named for Granville M. Dodge, a civil engineer with the railroad who was later an executive with the Union Pacific RR. Granville is an Old French name meaning from the large town. The post office was established March 31, 1888 with Morley W. Ludlow pm. The elevation is 1521, the Zip Code is 58741, and the village, which incorporated in 1907, reached a peak population of 455 in 1910. (1, 2, 3, 18, 19, 25, 33, 40, 79)

**GRASS LAKE** (Burleigh). This was a farm post office established October 19, 1892 with John H. Noon (1835-1917) pm, but the entry in the postal records is then marked "no papers." On October 29, 1892 the problem apparently had been taken care of, and the post office became official. It was located in SE¼ Sec. 18-143-79, Grass Lake Twp., three miles NE of Wilton, and named for the nearby lake which was named to note the rank grass growing along its banks. The post office closed November 25, 1893 with mail to Wilton. Mr. Noon was in Ford's Theater in Washington, DC on the day Abraham Lincoln was assassinated, and was one of the group of men that chased John Wilkes Booth. (1, 2, 9, 12, 14, 18, 40)

**GRASSLAKE** (Pierce). This was a rural post office established September 17, 1896 with John Edes pm. It was located in NE¼ Sec. 1-158-70, Wolford Twp., three miles NE of Wolford, and named for the nearby lake. In 1903 it moved two miles south to the home of new pm James W. Farrier in SE¼ Sec. 12-158-70. Mr. Farrier moved it across the section line to NE¼ Sec. 13-158-70 later that year, and the following year it moved to NW¼ Sec. 18-158-69, Union Twp., the home of new pm Abraham R. Gingerich. The post office was discontinued June 15, 1909 with mail to Wolford. (2, 40, 114, 414)

**GRASSNA** (Emmons). This is a rural community centered at the junction of Secs. 10, 11, 14, & 15-130-77, eight miles SW of Strasburg. The first settlers came here in 1890 from Krassna, Bessarabia, and the change in spelling is thought to be intentional, noting the prairie grass growing at their new home while remembering their old home. The focal point of the community is the country church and cemetery dating from the early twentieth century. The community still appears on some maps. (3, 18, 23, 34)

**GRASSY BUTTE** (McKenzie). This rural community was founded about 1910 in NW¼ Sec. 12-145-99, Rhoades Twp., thirty-five miles south of Watford City, and named for the nearby butte which was named to note the fact that it was the only butte in the area that was not bare of vegetation. The post office was established in a sod house on September 10, 1913 with Donald McKenzie pm. He and James Warren operated it from this building until 1964. The Zip Code is 58634, and the population has been quoted at about 100 since its founding, although that figure includes some outlying areas. (1, 2, 3, 18, 33, 40, 79)

**GRAVEL PIT** (McHenry). This place appears on a circa-1905 ND map as a station on the Soo Line RR between Velva and Voltaire, approximately in NE¼ Sec. 36-153-80, Velva Twp. Its name would seem to be self-explanatory as to its purpose. (3, 18)

**GRAVLY** (Bottineau). This was a rural post office established March 30, 1904 with Lars John Gravly pm. It was located in his country store in SW¼ Sec. 27-161-80, Brander Twp., six miles ENE of Maxbass, and replaced the Sommers Store located two miles to the north. The post office closed November 15, 1905 with mail to Maxbass. (2, 3, 34, 40, 101, 153, 415)

**GRAY** (Stutsman). This was a pioneer settlement founded in 1879 in SW¼ Sec. 31-142-62, Gray Twp., on the south shore of Spiritwood Lake about ten miles south of Courtenay. It was named for the four Gray brothers, John T., Robert, Lewis, and George, who led a group of settlers here from Toledo, OH, and later operated a ranch near Velva. The post office was established February 26, 1884 with Robert Lewis pm. A population of 12 was reported in 1890. It moved about four miles east in 1900, and returned to the

original site in 1905, closing April 15, 1914 with mail to Long Pine according to postal records, although there has never been a post office of this name in ND. (2, 3, 18, 25, 40, 79, 158)

**GREAT BEND** (Richland). This NPRR townsite was founded in 1885 in Secs. 14, 15 & 23-131-49, Brandenburg Twp., and named for its location on a wide bend of the Wild Rice River. The post office was established May 31, 1888 with Malcolm Cornelius MacLeod pm. From November 30, 1895 until November 30, 1905 the official name was one-word, GREATBEND, to comply with government spelling regulations. The elevation is 998, and the village, which incorporated in 1908, reached a peak population of 198 in 1940. The post office, Zip Code 58039, has been a community post office affiliated with Wahpeton since October 1, 1975. (1, 2, 3, 18, 25, 33, 40, 52, 79, 147, 347, 414)

**GREATBEND** (Richland). To comply with government spelling regulations, the post office at GREAT BEND used a one-word name from November 30, 1895 until November 30, 1905, when the two-word spelling was restored. (40)

**GREATSTONE** (McLean). This was a rural post office established January 5, 1904 with Hareton Sabrovitch pm. It was located in E½ Sec. 7-149-81, Greatstone Twp., six miles south of Benedict, and named for its township, which was named by settlers to note the many large glacial stones that had to be moved from their fields. In 1907 it moved one mile east to SE¼ Sec. 8-149-81, the home of new pm Mabel E. Griffith, and closed September 30, 1912 with mail to Coal Harbor. (2, 3, 18, 28, 40, 389)

**GREEN** (McKenzie). This was a farm post office established March 26, 1907 with Charles Green pm. It was located in SE¼ Sec. 1-151-102, Charbon Twp., six miles NNW of Alexander on the bank of Timber Creek. The post office was discontinued November 15, 1907 with mail to Alexander. (2, 3, 40)

**GREENE** (Cass). This was a NPRR station built in 1882 in Sec. 34-140-51, Harmony Twp., between Casselton and Mapleton. The site was served by the Casselton post office, and named for Eli Greene who had just purchased the bonanza farm served by this station. On May 24, 1912 the name was changed to NORPAK. (2, 3, 18, 25, 34, 77)

**GREENE** (Renville). This Soo Line RR townsite was founded in 1909 in NE 1/4 Sec. 30-160-85, Grassland Twp., eight miles SE of Tolley, by Martin O. Hall, also the founder and namesake of Mohall. It was named for Thomas Greene, Chief Engineer of the Soo Line RR. The post office was established October 9, 1909 with Minnie Hall pm, but development was very slow, and the post office closed January 31, 1945 with mail to Tolley. The peak population was 75 in 1920, with a decline to just 16 in 1960. (2, 18, 40, 71, 79, 322)

**GREENFIELD** (Traill). This was a GNRR station built in 1881 in W½ Sec. 24 & E½ Sec. 23-144-52, Greenfield Twp., six miles south

of Blanchard. It was named for its township, which seems to have been given a name descriptive of the locale. A post office called WEIBLE operated at the site 1883-1909. A population of 10 was reported in 1930, and a count of 4 was made in 1940. The site is still shown on detailed county maps. (1, 2, 3, 18, 25, 29, 40, 77, 187)

**GREENMAN'S SPUR** (Richland). This was the first station SW of Fairmount on the Fairmount & Veblen RR. It was built about 1911 in Sec. 34-130-48, DeVillo Twp., six miles SW of Fairmount, and named for Dr. N. H. Greenman, owner of the site, who came here in 1899 from MI and was the surgeon for the Soo Line RR, practicing his profession in Fairmount. The station appears on maps only into the 1920's, and is sometimes shown as simply Greenmans. (1, 2, 3, 18, 147)

**GREENRIVER** (Ransom). This is a Hutterite settlement begun in 1977 in Sec. 21-133-54, Sydna Twp., twelve miles SE of Lisbon. The initial colony included 40 settlers, and they raise grain and turkeys. The group is called the Sundale Hutterian Association, and they are served by the Milnor post office. (3, 171)

**GREEN RIVER** (Stark). This NPRR siding was built in 1880 in SE¼ Sec. 7-139-94, Heart River Twp., and served as a railroad construction camp for the crossing of the Green River. In 1883 a townsite was platted in N½ Sec. 17-139-94, one mile to the SE, which was named Gladstone. (2, 3, 25, 74, 244)

**GREEN RIVER** (Traill). An 1890 guide to ND lists this place as being in Traill County, and served by the Caledonia post office. No other information is available. (25)

**GREEN RIVER STATION** (Stark). This was the sixth station on the Bismarck-Fort Keogh mail route established in 1878, and was located in NW¼ Sec. 7-139-94, Heart River Twp., one mile NW of Gladstone on the east bank of the Green River. It was discontinued in 1882 when the NPRR mainline was completed. (2, 3, 18)

**GREEN VALLEY** (Grant). This is a rural community centered around a rural school in Sec. 13-132-84, Shields Twp., two miles north of Shields. The name is descriptive, noting its location in a scenic valley of green shrubbery and tall trees, with a creek running through it. (3, 34, 177)

**GREENWOOD** (Ramsey). In the 1920's, before LAKEWOOD PARK became an official place, three platted additions were made in N½ Sec. 18-153-64, Lake Twp., at the north end of the old Chautauqua resort. They are named Stotlar's 1st, 2nd, and 3rd additions to GREENWOOD, and it is unclear as to whether they were intended to be a rival development, or simply expansions of the original site. The name is thought to be descriptive in origin. (2, 3, 18, 103)

**GRELLAND** (Ward). This was a farm post office established October 11, 1902 with Johann W. Rode pm. It was located in NE¼ Sec. 23-153-85, Vang Twp., sixteen miles SW of Minot, and made several moves within the immediate area before closing August 15, 1918 with mail to Drady. The origin of the name is unknown. (2, 3, 18, 40, 53, 100)

**GRENADA** (Mountrail). This GNRR siding was founded in the late 1880's as DELTA, and was located in NE¼ Sec. 14-156-89, McGahan Twp. When settlement began in 1904 it was renamed RONESS, then BLENHEIM, but when the post office was established February 28, 1905 with William F. Thompson pm, it was called GRENADA, probably for the British colony in the West Indies, but only after postal officials had rejected the suggested name of ROUEN, which nevertheless saw limited use. The name GRENADA was unpopular with local citizens, who began calling the town HANLEY. When this name was rejected by postal officials, citing possible confusion with nearby Stanley, the name was officially changed to BLAISDELL on October 21, 1905. (2, 18, 40, 72)

**GRENORA** (Williams). This GNRR station was built in 1916 in NE¼ Sec. 12-159-103, Grenora Twp., as the terminus of their branch line from Stanley. The name was coined from that of the railroad—GREat NOrthern RAilroad. The post office was established November 25, 1916 with Lydia E. Elstad pm, who moved the post office from Howard to this site. The village incorporated in 1917 with Rasmus A. Johnson (1865-1954) as mayor. The Zip Code is 58845, and a peak population of 525 was reached in 1950. (1, 2, 33, 40, 50, 52, 79)

**GRESHAM** (Cavalier). This was a rural post office established June 11, 1881 with George W. Colborn pm. It was located in Osford Twp. (159-58), about five miles south of Osnabrock, and was likely named for Walter Quinion Gresham, who held three different cabinet positions during his long political career, and was the United States Postmaster General at the time this post office was established. Gresham is an Old English name meaning from the grass land. The post office closed October 18, 1883 with mail to Grafton. (2, 3, 5, 19, 40, 117)

**GRIFFIN** (Bowman). This post office and Milwaukee Road RR station in NE 1/4 Sec. 34-132-103, Manley Twp., was named ATKINSON until February 10, 1908, when the name was changed to GRIFFIN to honor H. T. Griffin, the Assistant General Passenger Agent for the railroad. James H. Kratzer continued as pm. A population of 67 was listed in 1930, but the post office closed March 31, 1930 with mail to Rhame. (2, 3, 18, 34, 40, 79)

**GRIFFIN** (Richland). This was a name adopted by the NPRR for its station in Secs. 6 & 7-132-49, Mooreton Twp., in May 1883 at the site of the TRIEST post office, to honor F. T. Griffin, an official of the railroad. On April 21, 1884 both the station and the post office were renamed MOORETON. (2, 18, 25, 77, 147, 242)

**GRINNELL** (Morton). This was an alternate name for the NPRR townsite of the 1880's in SW¼ Sec. 6-138-82, four miles ESE of Sweetbriar. DeWitt C. Grinnell was the pm of the short-lived SYLVAN post office located here. The site was abandoned by 1890. (2, 3, 40, 107)

**GRINNELL** (Williams). This rural post office was established May 11, 1881 with George W. Grinnell (1840-1888), the first white settler in Williams County, circa 1862, as pm. It closed November 27, 1882 with mail to Fort Buford. It reopened November 3, 1884 with Amos H. Blood pm, and closed July 9, 1888 with mail again to Fort Buford. It opened once again November 4, 1895, and in 1910 moved from its original site, SE¼ Sec. 20-154-95, thirteen miles SSE of Tioga, to the farm of new pm Albert L. Eustis in SW¼ Sec. 35-155-95, Dry Fork Twp., five miles to the NE. The post office closed for good December 31, 1920 with mail to Hofflund. A settlement of about 15 people lived at the original site for many years, and it was shown on some maps as late as the 1940's. (1, 2, 18, 25, 40, 50, 79)

**GRINNELL'S LANDING** (Williams). This was an early river boat landing on the north bank of the Missouri River in S½ Sec. 29-154-95, named for the nearby post office and rural community. (3, 50, 429)

**GRISWOLD** (LaMoure). This was a pioneer settlement in Sec. 11-136-60, Prairie Twp., eight miles east of Marion, and named for the abandoned gold rush town in Ransom County. The post office was established May 24, 1886 with John M. Olson pm. A population of 25 was reported in 1890, but when the NPRR bypassed the site in 1900, most residents moved to the new townsites of Marion and Litchville. The post office closed October 15, 1909 with mail to Litchville, and only indentations and a cemetery remain to mark the site. (1, 2, 3, 18, 25, 40, 76, 201, 204, 240)

**GRISWOLD** (Ransom). This town resulted from the discovery of gold nearby by Henry W. Griswold, a surveyor for the Chicago & NW RR. With Frank E. Fry and Edward P. Barker, the three men bought up land in the area, but abandoned their dream of instant wealth after it was found that the ore was of such poor quality that it cost more to mine the gold that it was worth. A townsite was platted in SW¼ Sec. 10-135-57, Springer Twp., and the post office was established December 11, 1883 with Mr. Fry as pm, but the development slowed to virtually nothing, and the post office closed July 30, 1884 with mail to Fort Ransom, four miles to the west. (2, 3, 25, 40, 77, 201, 204)

**GROAT** (Adams). This was a very early regional post office established September 19, 1891 with Lillian E. Howe pm. It was named for P. B. Groat, General Immigration Agent for the NPRR. The post office closed November 4, 1892 with mail to New England City, twenty miles to the north. The post office siting report states that it was located in the unsurveyed area that later became Cedar Twp. (132-96), on the north fork of the Cannonball River, two miles south of Chanta Peta Creek. It would seem that the reference to the Cannonball River was actually intended to mean today's Cedar Creek, which if true would place GROAT in the area of Sec. 20-132-96. (2, 3, 40, 414)

**GRONNA** (Rolette). This was a GNRR station built in 1905 in Sec. 12-161-60, Oxford Twp., seven miles SE of Rolla and just south of the old village of Galloway which it replaced. The post office was relocated here from Galloway December 1, 1905 with John D. Crosby pm. The name honored Asle J. Gronna of Lakota, who was elected to the United States Senate in 1910. The site never experienced a boom period, and the post office closed July 31, 1913 with mail to Rolla. A population of 10 was reported in 1920. (1, 2, 3, 18, 40, 79, 123)

**GROUSE** (Kidder). This was a NPRR siding built in 1905 in S½ Sec. 7-139-72, Sibley Twp., five miles east of Steele, and named for the native game bird of the area. This name is now applied to several species that range across the whole of North America, but it was originally the name of the moorfowl, or red grouse, the only bird absolutely restricted to the British Isles. On January 1, 1909 the name was changed to SIFTON. (2, 5, 18, 122)

**GROVE** (Burleigh). This was a post office established May 7, 1908 at the ND Penitentiary, just SE of Bismarck in SW¼ Sec. 2-138-80, Lincoln Twp. Warden Frank Hellstrom was the pm, and its name noted the large grove of cottonwood trees growing at the entrance to the facility. Governor John Burke used his political influence to establish the post office, and Governor Louis B. Hanna used his political influence to have it closed on August 31, 1913 with mail to Bismarck. (1, 2, 3, 8, 18, 33, 40)

**GRUND** (Pembina). Postal records indicate that the GRUND post office was established July 9, 1894 with S. A. Anderson as pm, and closed June 17, 1895 without having gone into operation. The name is Icelandic for grassy field, and is said to have been named by pioneer settler Jonathan Arnason for his hometown in Iceland. It is believed to have been located in Sec. 36-161-56, Beaulieu Twp., about three miles south of Hallson, while others think it was about two miles SE of this site in NE¼ Sec. 8-160-55, Park Twp., the site of the Arnason homestead. Despite the notation in postal records, and the fact that no postmarks are known to exist from GRUND, several longtime residents of the area insist that the post office actually did operate for a time. (2, 3, 40, 436, 437)

**GUELPH** (Dickey). This GNRR station was founded in 1886 in Secs. 31 & 32-130-60, Hudson Twp., and Secs. 5 & 6-129-60, Port Emma Twp. This site was settled in 1883, and parts of it had borne the names CENTER, CENTRALIA, CENTROPOLIS, COLDWATER, MENASHA CENTER, THATCHER, and THATCHERVILLE. The post office was established March 8, 1887 with Silas R. Dales pm, and named for his hometown of Guelph, Ontario, Canada, which had been named for Manfred von Guelph, the son of Duke Karl Otto of Hanover, Germany. GNRR President James J. Hill was born near the Canadian city. The elevation is 1360, the Zip Code is 58447, and a peak population of 158 was reached in 1930. (1, 2, 3, 18, 25, 33, 40, 79, 154, 264)

**GUNDERSON** (Griggs). Aslak Gunderson settled here in 1880, and in 1899 the NPRR built a station on the land of his son, Peter, in Secs. 29 & 30-144-59, Greenfield Twp.

Local people referred to the new site as GUNDERSON, but the railroad named its station WALUM. (65)

**GUNDIN FARM** (Traill). This was a GNRR station in SE¼ Sec. 18-146-50, Eldorado Twp., between Hillsboro and Cummings. It appears in a state guide published by Rand, McNally & Co. in 1890, with the notation that it was served by the Fargo post office. An 1892 county atlas shows the siding, but it is unnamed. It is thought that the 1890 guide's name was in error, and was referring to the Grandin interests, which spread across Cass and Traill Counties at the time. A 1904 map shows the site as CLARKE, and beginning about 1910 the name is given as TAFT, which grew into a small settlement on US Highway 81. (3, 25, 77, 187)

**GUNTHORP** (LaMoure). This was a rural post office established July 16, 1904 with Julius Johnson pm, who also ran a general store housed in a tent. It was located in NE¼ Sec. 7-135-65, Bluebird Twp., the site of an expected NPRR branch line, and was named for Charles Gunthorp, the pm at Edgeley, who co-signed the petition for this post office. The Smith Land Co. platted a townsite here in late 1904, naming it FOX for an official of that firm, but the post office remained GUNTHORP. The NPRR did arrive in late 1905, and on October 4, 1906 the names of the town and post office were changed to JUD, honoring the famous politican Judson LaMoure. Gunthorpe and Gunthrop are erroneous spellings. (2, 3, 18, 40, 414)

**GUPTILL** (Foster). This was a NPRR station built in the early 1900's in SW 1/4 Sec. 30-147-66, Estabrook Twp., four miles north of Carrington, and named for Emery T. Guptill, a pioneer settler in the area who was the first clerk of Estabrook School District in 1884, and later was a prominent resident of Carrington. Others say it was named for A. B. Guptil, a Republican politician from Fargo at the turn of the century. A large grain elevator was at the site for many years, but GUPTILL disappeared from maps during the 1940's. Guptel and Guptil are erroneous spellings. (1, 2, 3, 18, 53, 79, 97)

**GUTHRIE** (McHenry). This was a GNRR station founded in 1910 on the Surrey cutoff line in NE¼ Sec. 10-152-76, Strege Twp., five miles north of Drake. It was named for Archibald Guthrie, head of the Saint Paul, MN firm doing the grade work during the construction of this line. Guthrie is a Celtic name meaning war serpent, and is derived from Guthrum, an early Danish king who invaded England. The post office was established January 18, 1911 with Robert H. Schatz pm. The elevation is 1588, and for a few years GUTHRIE became a thriving little settlement, claiming a population of 100 as late as 1930. The post office closed June 30, 1946 with mail to Drake, although a population of 24 was reported here in 1960, and it remained on most maps into the 1970's. (1, 2, 3, 18, 19, 40, 53, 79, 183)

**GUYSON** (Logan). This was a Soo Line RR townsite founded in 1922 in NW¼ Sec. 35-133-68, Lautt Twp., between Lehr and Fredonia. It was platted in 1926, and the post office was established April 21, 1926

with Lester L. Meads pm. The name was coined to honor Guy Welsh, the son of pioneer area homesteader Alonzo P. Welsh. Guy is a name found in four languages—Celtic, meaning sensible, Old French meaning guide, Teutonic meaning warrior, and Latin meaning life. A population of 14 was recorded in 1940, but the village could not compete with its older, more established neighbors, and the post office closed March 31, 1947 with mail to Lehr. (2, 19, 33, 40, 116)

**GWINNER** (Sargent). This NPRR station was founded in 1900 in Secs. 23 & 26-132-56, Whitestone Hill Twp., and named for Arthur von Gwinner (1856-1932), President of the Deutsche Bank in Berlin, Germany, and a large stockholder in the NPRR. The post office was established May 15, 1901 with Josephine A. Carlblom pm. Her husband, Albert, was a pioneer banker and merchant. The elevation is 1083, the Zip Code is 58040, and the peak population was 330 in 1930 until a boom started with the founding of the Melroe Manufacturing Co. in 1947 by E. G. Melroe. Now a division of the Clark Corp., this firm's hometown plant has swelled the population of GWINNER to 724 in 1980, and the Melroe name is known throughout the world. (2, 3, 18, 33, 40, 52, 79, 165, 169)

**GWYNNE** (Wells). John Gwynne Vaughan came here from England in 1881 and purchased 1,000 acres from the NPRR. He platted a townsite in Sec. 12-146-49, Sykeston Twp., one mile NW of Sykeston, and began a grand promotion of the place, complete with purely ficticious brochures showing a large city on a mighty river, actually Pipestem Creek. He duped many Eastern investors on the scheme. A post office was actually established on July 5, 1882 with Mr. Vaughan as pm, but the plan failed and the post office closed February 9, 1883 with mail to Jamestown. Mr. Vaughan later was extridited back to England to stand trial for previous crimes committed there. Some sources call this place GWYNNE CITY. (2, 40, 76, 79, 268)

**GWYNNE CITY** (Wells). This was an alternate name for GWYNNE, the paper townsite of promoter John Gwynne Vaughan that was platted in 1882 in Sec. 12-146-49, Sykeston Twp., one mile NW of Sykeston. (2, 79, 268)

**GWYTHER** (Morton). On May 6, 1909 pm Martha Gwyther renamed the FORT RICE post office for her husband, Robert, a native of Wales who came to America in 1882. It was located in W½ Sec. 11-135-79, and was renamed FORT RICE on August 3, 1910 when the NPRR reached the site, which then became a station on the Mandan-Mott branch line. Mr. Gwyther, who was involved in farming and banking, donated the site of the abandoned military post to the State Historical Society in 1911. (2, 3, 17, 18, 34, 40, 107, 343, 409)

# H

**HAARSTAD** (Williams). This was a GNRR station in SW¼ Sec. 26-157-96, Golden Valley Twp. The post office was established July 16, 1906 with Ole G. Haarstad (1838-1923), who came to Otter Tail County, MN from Norway in 1883, and came here in 1904, as pm. On March 12, 1908 the station and post office were moved one-half mile west to the new townsite of Temple, with Mr. Haarstad continuing as pm. (2, 18, 40, 50)

**HAASE** (Bottineau). This was a farm post office established July 1, 1902 with William F. Haase pm. It was located in Sec. 11-162-83, Hoffman Twp., eight miles SW of Antler, and closed March 31, 1908 with mail to Mohall. (2, 34, 40, 101)

**HACKETT** (Barnes). This was a farm post office established February 1, 1882 with Dan D. Hackett pm at his home in SE¼ Sec. 12-137-57, Thordenskjold Twp., one mile north of Nome. Marcus A. Smith became pm in 1887, and a rural community began to develop, reporting a population of 50 in 1890. The post office closed October 2, 1891 with mail to Binghamton. (2, 3, 40, 118)

**HACKETT FALLS** (McHenry). This was a pioneer settlement, usually called SOURIS CITY, that was promoted in 1882 by Edmund Hackett, the first mayor of Bismarck. It was located in Sec. 31-156-76, Newport Twp., six miles SW of Towner. Mr. Hackett was a professional carpenter, and built many of Bismarck's first buildings. Besides serving as mayor, he served in the territorial legislature, and after coming to McHenry County, served as a county commissioner. The "falls" part of the name noted the nature of the Souris River at this location. Remains of a saw mill are still recognizable here. (2, 3, 412)

**HACKNEY** (Logan). This was an early name for the pioneer settlement in Sec. 8-135-67, Gutschmidt Twp., which was officially named GACKLE in 1903. The origin of the name is unknown. GACKLE was relocated six miles north in 1904 to a new railroad townsite, and the old site became known as MINISTER. (2, 3, 116)

**HAGEN** (Ward). This was a farm post office established May 22, 1907 with Ole E. Hagen as the first and only pm. Mr. Hagen (1876-1957) came to Portland, ND in 1898 from Norway and settled in Ward County in 1904, first in the Carpio area, then in Sec. 31-154-87, Shealey Twp., thirteen miles SSW of Berthold and the site of this post office which closed May 31, 1909 with mail to Berthold. Mr. Hagen moved to Berthold in 1913, and was active in politics for many years. (2, 3, 18, 40, 100)

**HAGGART** (Cass). A post office called HAGGART'S was here 1874-1875, and it reopened as HAGGARTS on July 9, 1883. On August 13, 1883 pm Peter Miller shortened the name to HAGGART, all of these named honoring John E. Haggart (1846-1905), who came here in 1871 from St. Lawrence County, NY and was the first sheriff of Cass County, later serving as a U. S. Marshall in Fargo. This post office closed December 7, 1885 with mail to Fargo. About 1920 an industrial settlement began to develop, taking the name WEST FARGO, and is now known as RIVERSIDE. (2, 3, 18, 40, 77, 79, 199, 210)

**HAGGARTS** (Cass). A post office operated here 1874-1875 called HAGGART'S, serving the SHEYENNE STOCKYARDS. It reopened as HAGGARTS on July 9, 1883 with Peter Miller pm, who shortened the name to HAGGART on August 13, 1883. This site in Sec. 5-139-49, Barnes Twp., later developed into WEST FARGO, and since 1974 has been the city of RIVERSIDE. (2, 3, 40)

**HAGGART'S** (Cass). This post office was established June 18, 1874 with Arthur Deacon pm. It was located in Sec. 5-139-49, Barnes Twp., and served the SHEYENNE STOCKYARDS station. The post office closed May 14, 1875 with mail to Fargo. It reopened in 1883 as HAGGARTS, with the name changed to HAGGART after just one month, closing in 1885. About 1920 the site began to develop as WEST FARGO, and since 1974 has been the city of RIVERSIDE. Hoggart's is an erroneous spelling. (2, 3, 40)

**HAGUE** (Emmons). This Milwaukee Road RR station was founded in 1902 in SW 1/4 Sec. 31-130-74 and NW¼ Sec. 6-129-74, midway between Strasburg and Zeeland. It was named by railroad officials for the Hague, Netherlands to honor Dutch settlers in the area, although most of these people later moved farther west, with this community now being populated largely by Germans from Russia. The post office was established November 24, 1902 with Franz Wolf pm. The elevation is 1899, the Zip Code is 58542, and the village, which incorporated in 1908, reached a peak population of 442 in 1940. (1, 2, 18, 33, 40, 66, 79)

**HAGUE** (Traill). This was a rural post office established March 31, 1882 with John A. Hague pm. He was also the manager 1876-1883 of the Grandin Bros. Bonanza Farm, which at 40,000 acres was the largest wheat farm in the world. The post office existed primarily to serve this farming enterprise, and was located in NW¼ Sec. 25-145-49, Herberg Twp., seven miles south of Caledonia. It closed December 31, 1900 with mail to Halstad, MN. (2, 3, 25, 29, 40, 240, 396)

**HAGUE** (Traill). A map published approximately 1905 shows the Hague post office as well as this place, a station on a railroad spur east of Alton Junction. The site, NE¼ Sec. 17-144-49, Elm River Twp., near the confluence of the Elm River and its north branch, never saw any development, and this place must be considered either a car-

tographer's error, or an anticipated development that failed to materialize. (3, 18)

**HAILSTONE CREEK STATION** (Morton). This was the third relay station on the Bismarck-Fort Keogh mail route. It was established in 1878 in SE¼ Sec. 36-140-87, thirteen miles NE of Glen Ullin, and named for the creek on which it was located. Hailstone Butte is about three miles WNW of the site. It was closed in 1882 after completion of the NPRR mainline. (1, 2, 105)

**HAIR HILLS** (Pembina). This name is frequently found in early accounts of the fur trading days as the name of an outpost in Sec. 30-163-56, Walhalla Twp., the present site of the city of Walhalla. The name refers to the nearby Pembina Mountains, and is said to have been chosen by Scottish travelers to note the hairbell flowers in the area. Others claim that the name was chosen by either Charles Baptiste Chaboillez, the builder of the fur trading post near Pembina in 1797, or Alexander Henry, the builder of another post near this same site in 1801. (2, 3, 79, 108, 365, 366, 367)

**HALEY** (Bowman). This settlement in Secs. 25 & 26-129-100, Goldfield Twp., and Secs. 30 & 31-129-99, Haley Twp., began in 1898 as GALEY, named for William Galey, or Gay, who discovered gold near here in 1887. An error by postal officials resulted in the post office being established as HALEY on December 9, 1898 with Bertie W. Jackson pm. She was the daughter of Richard Ludlow Jackson (1842-1915), the first settler in the townsite. The post office was located in the Jacksons sod hotel until it was destroyed by fire in 1921. The village has never experienced a real boom, reporting a peak population of 112 in 1950, but now having a count of under 50 residents. (2, 3, 18, 34, 40, 79, 120)

**HALF WAY HOUSE** (Renville). This was a wayside inn for travelers built in Sec. 30-161-87, Fairbanks Twp., near present-day Norma. The name noted the fact that it was half way between Kenmare and some coal mines. (2, 71)

**HALL** (Grand Forks). This farm post office was established July 6, 1907 with Lewis A. Lorenson pm, but the order was rescinded before it went into operation. The name is Old English meaning from the hall or manor, but why it was used for this post office is unknown. Its location is also unknown. (2, 3, 19, 40)

**HALL** (Renville). This townsite was founded in 1901 in SW¼ Sec. 13-161-84, Brandon Twp., and named for founder Martin O. Hall (1853-1925). Because of an alleged duplication of the name, it was changed to MOHALL, coined from the founder's name, when the post office was established February 24, 1902. (3, 40, 71)

**HALLIDAY** (Dunn). This was a rural post office established March 19, 1900 with Nathan C. Halliday pm. It was located in a sod dugout on the ranch of his father, William Halliday, a native of Scotland, in SE¼ Sec. 12-145-92. The Hallidays moved to CA in 1903, and the post office moved east across the section line to a country store in SW¼ Sec. 7-145-91. In 1913 it moved three miles south to the new NPRR townsite in NE¼ Sec. 25-145-92 with H. N. Wimmer assuming the pm position. He was soon replaced by Jeremiah Palmer (1859-1945), who was Dunn County's first Register of Deeds. The elevation is 2073, the Zip Code is 58636, and a peak population of 509 was reported in 1960. (1, 2, 3, 18, 33, 40, 220, 221, 223, 414)

**HALLSON** (Pembina). This was a pioneer Icelandic settlement founded in Sec. 24-161-56, Beaulieu Twp., as COOLEY. On September 18, 1882 pm Gisli Egilsson changed the name to HALLSON for pioneer settler John S. Hallson, who came here in 1878. A population of 25 was reported in 1890, but the town failed to develop without a railroad. The 1960 population was just 3, and the post office closed May 31, 1960 with mail to Cavalier. (1, 2, 3, 18, 25, 40, 79, 108)

**HALL'S TRADING POST** (Mountrail). Edward S. Hall opened a wood business with Charley Baldwin at the mouth of Knife Creek in 1882. In 1883 he opened a trading post in NE¼ Sec. 35-154-94, ten miles NW of Sanish, and two miles above the mouth of White Earth Creek on its west bank. This was a landmark for early ranchers, hunters, trappers, and the Indians until it closed in 1893. A stone monument marks the site today. (2, 72)

**HAMAR** (Eddy). This settlement began in 1905 in advance of the GNRR which arrived in 1906. The post office was established August 18, 1906 with Erland Christofferson pm, who named it for Hamar, Norway, the county seat of his home county of Hedemarken, now simplified to Hedmark. The townsite was in NE¼ Sec. 3-150-62, Freeborn Twp., and was originally owned by Stena Peterson, known as "The Prairie Queen." The elevation is 1478, the Zip Code is 58336, and a peak population of 150 was claimed in 1920, although the population has been less than 100 since World War II. On January 31, 1974 the post office became a Community Post Office affiliated with Tolna. (1, 2, 33, 40, 119, 272)

**HAMBERG** (Wells). This GNRR townsite was founded in SE¼ Sec. 52-150-69, Norway Lake Twp., in 1910 and named VIKING, but local German residents soon began calling it HAMBURG, for the great German seaport on the Elbe River founded by Charlemagne about 808 A.D. As a compromise, the name HAMBERG was officially adopted May 29, 1913 by pm Amil F. Pforr. The elevation is 1548, the Zip Code is 58337, and the village, which incorporated in 1921, reached a peak population of 187 in 1930, but declined to a count of just 41 in 1980. (1, 2, 33, 40, 54, 79, 363, 364)

**HAMBURG** (Wells). This name was used unofficially during 1912-1913 by German residents of VIKING. On May 29, 1913 the town was officially renamed HAMBERG, a compromise name between the German and Scandinavian residents. (2, 3, 5, 13, 79, 363)

**HAMILTON** (Pembina). This was a farm post office established October 30, 1879 with Donald M. McIntosh pm, located in NW¼ Sec. 27-162-53, Hamilton Twp. Some say it was named for Sam Hamilton, an early settler in the area, while others say it was named for Hamilton, Ontario, Canada, which was named for George Hamilton (1787-1835), who founded the city in 1813. Hamilton is a Norman name meaning from the beautiful mountain. In 1882 it moved one mile SE to the new GNRR townsite in SE¼ Sec. 35-162-53. The elevation is 831, the Zip Code is 58238, and a peak population of 300 was claimed in 1890. After a period of decline, HAMILTON rebounded to an official population of 255 in 1940, but recent decline has reduced the count to just 109 in 1980. The Bank of Hamilton, chartered in 1886, is the oldest state bank still in operation. (1, 2, 3, 10, 18, 19, 33, 40, 52, 79, 108, 146)

**HAMLET** (LaMoure). This was a farm post office established March 2, 1911 with William Havens pm, who named it for Hamlet, NY, a small village in Chautauqua County that had a post office 1850-1954. HAMLET, ND was located in S½ Sec. 4-136-64, Kennison Twp., four miles north of Nortonville, and closed November 30, 1911 with mail to Adrian. (2, 3, 34, 40)

**HAMLET** (Williams). This GNRR townsite was founded in 1911 in Sec. 2-159-96, Big Meadow Twp., and named HANKEY, but when the nearby Harry post office relocated to this site on April 10, 1913, pm Edward W. Battleson changed the name to HAMLET, from the French *hamelet*, meaning a small village, and descriptive of this place. A boom occurred, with a peak population of 219 in 1930, but a steady decline after that date left just 25 residents here in 1960. The elevation is 2276, and the post office, Zip Code 58742, closed January 31, 1975 with mail to Wildrose. (1, 2, 3, 4, 33, 38, 40, 50, 79)

**HAMLIN** (Sargent). This was the first settlement in Sargent County, founded in SE¼ Sec. 11-131-53, Herman Twp., seven miles north of Geneseo. It was first called POSTVILLE, and then HERMAN, but when the post office was established April 18, 1881 with Ezra D. Post pm, it was renamed HAMLIN at the request of settlers from Hamlin Twp., Eaton County, MI, which was named in 1869 for Samuel Hamlin, a local road builder. It was bypassed by the Soo Line RR, and began to decline. The post office closed November 10, 1888 with mail to Milnor. It reopened February 4, 1889, but closed for good April 30, 1912 with mail to DeLamere. (2, 3, 18, 25, 33, 40, 46, 165, 171)

**HAMMERFEST** (Renville). This was a farm post office established February 9, 1905 with Simon Olson pm, located in SE¼ Sec. 33-162-85, Hamerly Twp., ten miles WNW of Mohall. The name was suggested by Mr. Olson's uncle, Rev. Jakob Mikaelson, for the city in extreme northern Norway. The post office closed January 15, 1907 with mail to Mohall. (2, 3, 18, 40, 71, 322)

**HAMPDEN** (Ramsey). This GNRR townsite was founded in 1903 in NE¼ Sec. 4-158-62, Northfield Twp., and soon absorbed most of the nearby townsite of NORTHFIELD, whose post office moved here on July 15, 1903 with Joseph A. Elliott pm. The NORTHFIELD name was disliked by GNRR officials because of confusion with Northfield, MN. Some say the name honors Frank Hampden, a pioneer settler in the area, while others say it was named for a John Hampden. The elevation is 1569, the Zip Code is 58338, and the village, which incorporated in 1917 and became a city in 1968, reached a peak population of 222 in 1930. (2, 18, 33, 40, 52, 75, 79, 103)

**HAMPLE** (Sargent). This farm post office was established February 9, 1897 with Hannah S. E. Hample pm, and was located in Sec. 30-131-58, Hample Twp., five miles south of Crete. Within a short time the Soo Line RR established a station here, and a village with three elevators, a lumberyard, grist mill, creamery, general store, blacksmith shop, church, and several homes developed. The boom was short-lived, and the post office closed July 14, 1905 with mail to Oakes. By the 1930's, only the siding was left at this site. (2, 3, 18, 40, 165)

**HAMPTON** (Emmons). This was a rural post office established October 4, 1888 with Mills Beach pm. It was located in NE¼ Sec. 6-133-78, thirteen miles west of Temvik on the east bank of the Missouri River, and named for Hampton, IA, which was named for Hampton Roads, VA, which was named for the Earl of Southampton. In 1893 the post office moved one mile NE to the home of new pm Hiram Fuller in SW¼ Sec. 32-134-78. It closed August 15, 1906, being replaced on that date by the Hartford post office. (2, 3, 10, 34, 40, 66, 415)

**HANCOCK** (McLean). This townsite was in NE¼ Sec. 32-146-84, North Hancock Twp., and was primarily an early ferry service across the Missouri River. The first settlers in the 1880's were mostly from VA, and they named it for Gen. Winfield Scott Hancock (1824-1886), a veteran of the Civil and Indian Wars, and the Democratic candidate for President in 1880. He led one of the first explorations of what would become Yellowstone National Park. On July 24, 1886 the post office at WALKERTOWN, one mile to the NE, moved here with pm James Mann continuing at that post. A population of 100 was reported in 1890, but as the railroad replaced the river as the principal method of transportation, the site declined, and the post office closed May 31, 1908 with mail to Underwood. The area today is known as Hancock Bottoms. (2, 13, 25, 28, 40, 79)

**HANKEY** (Williams). This GNRR townsite was founded in 1911 in Sec. 2-159-96, Big Meadow Twp., between Wildrose and McGregor, and named for Frank D. Hankey (1857-1929), the first settler in the township who had come here in 1901 from IA. The nearby rural post office of Harry moved here April 10, 1913, and pm Edward W. Battleson changed the name to HAMLET. (2, 3, 33, 40, 50)

**HANKINSON** (Richland). This townsite was

founded in 1886 in Secs. 13, 14 & 24-130-50, Brightwood Twp. Col. Richard Henry Hankinson (1841-1911) was at this time promoting a townsite called Kelly a few miles to the south, but development shifted to the new site, which had just been reached by both the GNRR and Soo Line RR, who were engaged in a vigorous rivalry to establish control in the area. The post office was established December 6, 1886 with Col. Hankinson as pm, and the new town was named in his honor. The elevation is 1068, the Zip Code is 58041, and a peak population of 1,503 was reached in 1910, two years before HANKINSON incorporated as a city. (1, 2, 3, 18, 25, 33, 40, 79, 147, 360)

**HANKS** (Dunn). This was a rural post office established August 2, 1909 with David Hanks pm. It was located in NW¼ Sec. 12-145-93, seven miles NW of Halliday, and closed October 15, 1912 with mail to Halliday. (1, 2, 3, 18, 40)

**HANKS** (Williams). This GNRR townsite in NE¼ Sec. 13-159-102, Barr Butte Twp., was founded in 1916 as MESA, but when the post office was established December 19, 1916 with Charles W. Johnson (1892-1949) as pm, the name was changed to HANKS for W. F. Hanks, a Powers Lake banker who was associated with the Northern Town and Land Co., developers of this townsite. Mr. Johnson served as the pm until his death. The town had an early boom, reaching a population of 223 in 1920, and unofficially claimed to have a population of 300 in 1926, but since that time HANKS has steadily declined, and the 1980 population was just 10. The post office closed June 30, 1964 with mail to Zahl. (2, 3, 38, 40, 50, 79)

**HANLEY** (Mountrail). This GNRR siding was founded in the late 1880's as DELTA in NE¼ Sec. 14-156-89, McGahan Twp. When settlement began in 1904 it was at first called RONESS, then BLENHEIM, and when the post office was established February 28, 1905, it was named GRENADA. This name was unpopular with local residents, who began calling the town HANLEY for area homesteader Michael Hanley, who had come here in 1901. Citing possible confusion with Stanley, postal officials rejected this name, and on October 21, 1905 the name was changed to BLAISDELL. (2, 3, 40, 72)

**HANLY** (Billings). This ranch post office was established November 19, 1908 with Luroff Holdren pm. It was located in Sec. 24-137-102, seventeen miles south of Medora, and was the only post office in Billings County to be located south of the NPRR tracks. The name honored the Hanly family of the area. Maggie was the wife of the pm, and her sister Edna was the wife of an area rancher named German. Their brother,

Jack, was a Confederate veteran of the Civil War, and had come here to start a new life. The post office closed November 30, 1920 with mail to Medora. Hanley is an erroneous spelling. (2, 3, 40, 53, 81)

**HANNA** (Cavalier). The new GNRR townsite in NW¼ Sec. 4-163-62, Linden Twp., was platted in 1896 as HANNA, probably for Marcus Alonzo Hanna (1837-1904), a powerful politician from OH. In 1897 the nearby HANNAH post office relocated here, and residents were divided over which name to use for their town. HANNAH was chosen, mostly because it was the name of the pm, who was a member of one of the area's most respected pioneer families. (3, 5, 18, 215)

**HANNAFORD** (Benson). This was one of several townsites competing for dominance at the west end of Devils Lake. It was founded in SE¼ Sec. 34-154-67, Riggin Twp., three miles NNE of Minnewaukan, and the post office was established June 25, 1883 with Milton B. Brown pm, also serving the rival townsites of New Chicago and West End. It was named for Jules M. Hannaford, a NPRR official, no doubt in hopes that this would entice the railroad to build through this site. Minnewaukan, however, got the railroad, and the post office closed March 12, 1884 with mail to Minnewaukan. (2, 40, 79, 110, 255)

**HANNAFORD** (Griggs). The NPRR founded this townsite in 1883 in Secs. 5 & 8-144-59, Greenfield Twp., and named it for Jules M. Hannaford, General Freight Agent and later the President of the railroad. Reuben C. Brophy platted the townsite and became the pm when the post office was established November 20, 1886. In 1912 the GNRR built its Surrey cutoff line through HANNAFORD, giving the village two-railroad status. The elevation is 1433, the Zip Code is 58448, and the village, which incorporated in 1906, reached a peak population of 431 in 1920. (1, 2, 18, 25, 40, 65, 79, 286)

**HANNAH** (Cavalier). This was a farm post office established November 24, 1884 with Alpheus Adams pm, who named it for his father-in-law, Frank Hannah, who had come here in the early 1880's from Ontario, Canada. In 1897 it moved one mile east to NW¼ Sec. 4-163-62, Linden Twp., the site of the new GNRR terminus which had been platted as HANNA. Frank Hannah's son, John, was at this time the pm, and largely through his efforts the GNRR agreed to rename the town HANNAH. The elevation is 1569, the Zip Code is 58239, and a peak population of 262 was recorded in 1930. Russell Reid, longtime head of the ND Historical Society was born here in 1900, and Ethel Catherwood, who won a gold medal at the 1928 Olympics representing her adoptive country of Canada, was born here in 1908. (1, 2, 3, 18, 33, 40, 52, 79, 83, 212, 215, 262)

**HANNAH JUNCTION** (Grand Forks). This site, NE¼ Sec. 3-151-55, Larimore Twp., two miles NW of Larimore, was the junction of the GNRR mainline and a branch line built in 1884 to Park River. It was at that time called PARK RIVER JUNCTION, and when this branch line was extended to Hannah in 1897, the name was changed according-

ly. (1, 2, 3, 18, 31)

**HANNONS** (Mountrail). This was a rural community in NW¼ Sec. 32-154-92, Brookbank Twp., fourteen miles south of Ross. It was named in possessive form for John Hannon, who is said to have established a post office here in 1908, a claim not supported by government records. (1, 2, 3, 18, 40, 53)

**HANNOVER** (Oliver). This was a rural settlement that began in 1884 in Sec. 23-142-85, Hannover Twp., six miles west of Center. Town founders August and Edward Hannemier named it for their hometown of Hanover, Germany, which is named for its location on a high bank of the Leine River. *Hoen overe* in the early Germanic tongue meant high bank. The variation in the spelling is said to have been influenced by the founders' name. The post office was established April 28, 1888 with Henry Albers (1844-1914) pm. In 1912 the townsite was moved one-quarter mile NE to a newly graded road. A population of 31 was reported in 1885, and a count of 28 was made in 1960, as the little town maintained a consistent, if tiny, existance. The post office, Zip Code 58543, closed December 14, 1978 with the death of pm Mrs. Harold Henke, although governments records did not record the closing until March 22, 1985. (2, 3, 18, 25, 26, 40, 109, 121)

**HANSBORO** (Towner). This townsite on the Farmers Grain & Shipping Company RR was founded in 1905 in SW¼ Sec. 7-163-67, Sidney Twp., as the northern terminus of the railroad, which later became part of the GNRR system. It was named for Henry Clay Hansbrough (1848-1933), a Devils Lake newspaperman and mayor who served as a Congressman 1889-1891, and as a U. S. Senator 1891-1909. The stylized spelling was intentional. The post office was established November 17, 1905 with Alexander Messer pm. The village incorporated in 1917 and reached a peak population of 218 in 1920, but a steady decline has reduced that count to just 43 in 1980. The elevation is 1597, and the Zip Code is 58339. On January 27, 1967 the post office became a rural branch of Rocklake. (1, 2, 18, 33, 40, 52, 79, 196)

**HANSON** (Grand Forks). This was a post office in Sec. 18-152-54, Hegton Twp., six miles north of Larimore on the old Grand Forks-Fort Totten mail route. Several contemporary accounts refer to this place as HANSON, for pm Hans E. Hanson, but the post office, which operated 1879-1882, was officially named HEGTON. (2, 3, 31, 40, 69)

**HANSON** (Rolette). Some circa-1900 accounts mention a HANSON post office in Rolette County, but government records do not confirm this. The pm was said to be Carl Hanson in Rice Twp. (159-71), just SW of Nanson, but the only "Carl Hanson" in the county at this time was a Carl F. Hanson who lived in NW¼ Sec. 4-163-71, Hutchinson Twp., eight miles WNW of Saint John. (2, 3, 40, 123, 415)

**HANSON** (Towner). This was a farm post office established November 6, 1888 with John K. Aanes pm. It was located in NE¼ Sec. 6-159-67, Gerrard Twp., one mile east of Bisbee, and named for pioneer settler Henry Hanson. The post office closed March 29, 1890 when it was replaced by the facility in the new GNRR townsite of Bisbee. (2, 3, 40, 415)

**HAPPY** (Divide). This was a rural post office authorized August 5, 1908 with Benjamin Happy pm at his home in SW¼ Sec. 18-161-96, Upland Twp., eleven miles SE of Crosby. Mr. Happy declined the appointment and the order was rescinded. (2, 3, 40, 415)

**HARDY BEET SIDING** (McKenzie). This is a GNRR siding serving the Hardy Feed Lot, Inc. in NW¼ Sec. 28-151-104, Yellowstone Twp., three miles NE of Fairview, MT. John W. Hardy and members of this family operate an extensive farming operation in the area. The siding appears is lists of commercial places beginning in the early 1970's. (3, 34)

**HARLEM** (Sargent). This townsite was founded in 1885 in Secs. 10 & 11-131-57, Harlem Twp., at the terminus of the Milwaukee Road RR branch line from Andover, SD. It was named for its township, which was named for Haarlem in the Netherlands. The post office was established March 8, 1887 with Frank E. Kendall pm. The village incorporated in 1888, and by 1890 the population was 225. The building of the NPRR line from Milnor to Oakes in 1900 resulted in many HARLEM residents moving to Cogswell, five miles to the south. The post office closed October 31, 1907 with mail to Cogswell. It reopened May 17, 1909 but closed for good April 30, 1912 with mail again to Cogswell. The railroad was taken up in 1923, completing the demise of HARLEM. (2, 3, 18, 25, 40, 79, 165, 167)

**HARLOW** (Benson). This Soo Line RR station was founded in 1912 in NW¼ Sec. 15-154-69, Butte Valley Twp. The site had been homesteaded by Louis Larsen Ulvestad in 1896, but was now owned by Olai O. Ronning. It was named for an official of the Soo Line RR, although some say it was named for the famous Harlow House in Plymouth, MA. The post office was established March 2, 1914 with August C. "Gust" Wicken pm. The village never incorporated, and had a population of about 100 at its peak of development. The post office, Zip Code 58340, closed February 28, 1978 with mail to Leeds when pm Ruth Knutson retired after holding that position since 1944. (1, 2, 34, 40, 79, 110, 236, 257, 258)

**HARMON** (Morton). This was a ranch post office established March 16, 1895 with C. F. Massingham pm, who revived the name of the Oliver County post office 1886-1893 just to the north. It was located in SE¼ Sec. 1-140-82, ten miles NNW of Mandan. In 1912 it moved one mile SE to SW¼ Sec. 7-140-81, the site of a new station on the NPRR branch line from Mandan to Killdeer. Frank A. Larson became the pm in 1917 and moved the post office to his property in SE 1/4 Sec. 7-140-81. A population of 50 was reported in 1917, and a count of 21 was made in 1928. The post office closed March 31, 1943 with mail to Mandan. (1, 2, 3, 17, 18, 40, 79, 107, 414)

**HARMON** (Oliver). This was a ranch post office established January 11, 1886 with Alonzo Gerrish pm. It was located on the Square Butte Ranch in W½ Sec. 30-141-81, Butte Twp., about fifteen miles NW of Mandan, and named for George W. Harmon, who came to this area in 1872 and was the first sheriff of Morton County. The post office closed November 30, 1893 with mail to Mandan. It reopened in 1895 in Morton County, operating until 1943. (2, 3, 18, 25, 40, 79, 107)

**HAROLD PETERSONS** (Williams). This place is shown on a 1917 state map in SW¼ Sec. 11-156-103, Bull Butte Twp., seven miles SSW of Bonetraill. The owner of the site at that time was Harald M. Pedersen, whose name was apparently Anglicized by the cartographer. It is thought that this place was a rural stopping point for travelers. (3, 53, 415)

**HARRIET** (Burleigh). This was a pioneer settlement in Sec. 10-142-75, Harriet Twp., about one mile west of Arena on the north shore of Harriet Lake, for which it was named. (3, 63, 200)

**HARRISBURG** (Nelson). Pm John O'Brien changed the name of HARRISBURGH to HARRISBURG on September 6, 1895 to comply with government spelling regulations. At the time it was located in his home in NE¼ Sec. 26-151-60, Wamduska Twp., just south of the old townsite which had been promoted with great fanfare in 1882, but was now virtually a ghost town. The plat was officially abandoned in 1902, and the post office closed July 31, 1909 with mail to Pekin. The site is now an old settlers' park. (1, 2, 3, 40, 124, 128)

**HARRISBURGH** (Nelson). This post office was established June 20, 1882, replacing the Parkhurst post office. It was at first located in the home of pm Cicero T. Harris, but it soon moved to SE¼ Sec. 23-151-60, Wamduska Twp., two miles to the SE, where a magnificent city of 54 blocks had been platted. Promoters of the site included Judson LaMoure, Alexander Griggs, and Col. Oscar M. Towner, all powerful figures in the territory. It was billed as the future county seat of Ramsey County (Nelson County was not yet in existance), and the new capital of Dakota Territory, but when it was bypassed by the GNRR, its short boom went bust. A population of just 30 was reported in 1890. On September 6, 1895 the name was changed to HARRISBURG, but the plat was abandoned in 1902, and the post office closed in 1909. (1, 2, 3, 18, 25, 40, 82, 124, 126, 128, 415)

**HARRISON** (Ward). This was a pioneer settlement which soon became an annexed part of the city of Minot. The name is credited to T. E. Olsgard, the Register of the U. S. Land Office, who chose to honor the then current President of the United States, Benjamin Harrison (1833-1901). The name is perpetuated by the township (155-83) in which most of Minot is located. (2, 3, 100)

**HARRY** (Williams). This was a rural post office established January 18, 1912 with Edward W. Battleson (1890-1945) pm. He came here and operated a hardware store with an agency for Dort automobiles, later moved to

OR, and drowned in the Pacific Ocean. He named it for a relative, Harry Battleson, although some say it was named for Harry V. Johnston, a pioneer rancher in the Badlands. Harry is a form of Harold, a Teutonic name meaning mighty in battle. It was located in SE¼ Sec. 9-159-96, Big Meadow Twp., and on April 10, 1913 it moved two miles NE to the GNRR townsite of HAMLET, originally called HANKEY. Hatry is an erroneous spelling. (2, 3, 19, 40, 50)

**HARTE** (Dunn). Paul Ziner (1866-1918) and his twin brother left their native Norway for America about 1889. Paul Ziner came to what is now Dunn County shortly after his arrival, settling in Sec. 5-142-93, Myron Twp., eighteen miles SW of Dodge. He was appointed pm of the HARTE post office, probably named for the author Francis Bret Harte (1839-1902), on June 30, 1892, six weeks after the establishment of the Rand post office, the first in the county. The authorization for HARTE was rescinded November 25, 1893 with the notation "no papers". The Ziner ranch was just west of the well known Paulson ranch. (2, 3, 5, 40, 223)

**HARTFORD** (Emmons). This was a rural post office established August 15, 1906 with Ellen Chamley pm. It was located in Sec. 32-134-78, twelve miles west of Temvik, and adjacent to the old Hampton post office which it replaced on this date. The new name was coined from J. H. Hart, who unsuccessfully tried to promote a townsite here, and "ford", apparently to note its location on the east bank of the Missouri River. The HARTFORD name was adopted because of confusion with Hampden in Ramsey County. The post office closed December 31, 1918 with mail to Livona. Daniel C. Monford was appointed pm on July 3, 1919 in an attempt to reestablish this office, but the order was quickly rescinded. (1, 2, 3, 18, 40, 66, 415)

**HARTINGER** (Dunn). This was a rural community in M. R. Township (142-95), named for William Hartinger, who lived in Sec. 28-142-95, nine miles SE of Manning. When the post office was established June 24, 1909, the name was changed to LIBBY BUTTE. (2, 3, 18, 40)

**HARTLAND** (Ward). This was a GNRR townsite in NE¼ Sec. 30-157-86, Carpio Twp., seven miles NW of Berthold. The post office was established March 23, 1908 with Mons J. Hoff pm. Local resident Martin D. Johnson chose the name for his birthplace, Hartland Twp., Worth County, IA, which was named for Hartland, VT, which was founded in 1761 as Hertford, but was changed to Hartland in 1782 to avoid confusion with nearby Hartford. The new name was suggested by settlers from Hartland, CT, which was in Hartford County. The CT town was named for Hartland, Devonshire, England, and the name means stag island town. Ward County folklore says that the name was meant to show the town as the heart of the area. The elevation is 2091, and a peak population of 150 was claimed in 1920, but by 1940 the population was less than 100. The post office closed May 6, 1966 with mail to Carpio. (1, 2, 3, 13, 18, 38, 40, 47, 100, 372)

**HARTLEY** (Cass). Guilford G. Hartley (1853-1922) left his native New Brunswick, Canada as a teenager for MN, and for several years divided his time between logging near Brainerd, and farming in the Red River valley. In 1883 he started the Hartley Stock Farm in the Page vicinity, and although he moved to Duluth, MN in 1885, he continued to be active in Page affairs. Prior to this time, he lived "somewhere north of Fargo", and while there became pm of the HARTLEY post office which was established May 12, 1881. Mrs. A. N. Gilman assumed that position February 23, 1882, but the post office closed April 24, 1882 with mail to Mapleton. HARTLEY continued to be listed in some guides into the 1890's, in later years being served by the Harwood post office. Hartley is an Old English name meaning from the stag's meadow. (2, 3, 19, 40, 308)

**HARTSLAND** (Traill). This was a farm post office established May 20, 1879 with Ole N. Sunby pm. It was located in SW¼ Sec. 14-146-52, Mayville Twp., four miles SE of Mayville, and closed April 5, 1880 with mail to Bloomfield. The origin of the name is unknown. (2, 3, 15, 34, 40, 415)

**HARVARD** (Barnes). This was a way station on the NPRR branch line to McHenry, replaced in 1883 by the townsite of DAZEY, near which it was probably located. The origin of the name is unknown, although it would seem probable that it had some connection to the famous university in MA. (3, 76)

**HARVARD** (Sargent). This was a planned townsite on the shore of Sprague Lake in Sec. 2-129-55, Weber Twp., said to have been named in honor of a young college student who visited the site. Nothing came of this venture, but in 1887 settlers founded RUTLAND three miles to the NE. (3, 434)

**HARVEY** (Wells). This Soo Line RR townsite was founded in 1892 in NW¼ Sec. 31-150-72, Wells Twp., and named for Col. James S. Harvey, a stockholder from Milwaukee, WI, although this explanation is not confirmed by the railroad. Some sources say it was named for Harvey, IL. Harvey is derived from Houery, an ancient bard of Brittany, and means bitter. A post office with Carl W. Brauer pm was authorized August 31, 1893, but the order was rescinded. On October 2, 1893 Miss Sara L. Beaubier was appointed pm, and HARVEY replaced the nearby rural post office of Whitby. The village incorporated in 1903, and became a city in 1906 with Aloys Wartner mayor. The elevation is 1599, the Zip Code is 58341, and a peak population of 2,529 was reached in 1980. (1, 2, 19, 40, 44, 68, 79)

**HARWOOD** (Cass). This GNRR townsite was founded in 1880 in SE¼ Sec. 33 and SW¼ Sec. 34-141-49, Harwood Twp., and named for A. J. Harwood, a Fargo realtor and part owner of the site. The post office was established October 3, 1881 with Cyrus G. Bradley pm. The elevation is 887, the Zip Code is 58042, and recent outmigration from nearby Fargo has increased the population to a peak of 326 in 1980. (1, 2, 18, 25, 38, 40, 77, 79)

**HASTINGS** (Barnes). This was a farm post office established May 13, 1890 with Carlton B. Cross pm. It was located in Sec. 20-138-59, Skandia Twp., and named for Hastings, MN, which was named for Gen. Henry Hastings Sibley (1811-1891), Governor of MN 1858-1860, and the leader of the 1863 expedition against the Sioux. In 1900 it moved eight miles south to the new NPRR station in NW 1/4 Sec. 14-137-59, Spring Creek Twp. The elevation is 1478, and a peak population of 199 was reported in 1930. Although the population was still 102 in 1960, the post office closed October 7, 1967 with mail to Kathryn. (1, 2, 3, 10, 18, 34, 38, 40, 76, 79)

**HASTINGS LANDING** (Pembina). This place in Sec. 26-159-51, Drayton Twp., was named for the captain of a Red River steamboat. When settlers began arriving in 1878, they renamed it DRAYTON. (2, 18, 108, 366)

**HATTON** (Traill). This GNRR townsite was established in 1881 in NE¼ Sec. 18-148-53, Garfield Twp., in anticipation of the coming of the railroad, which reached here in July 1884. The post office was established December 19, 1881 with Lawrence O. Fisk pm, who requested the name Garfield for the recently martyred President. This name was rejected due to duplication, and instead named for Frank Hatton (1846-1894), Assistant Postmaster General at the time and later the Editor of the *Washington Post*. Mr. Hatton named several post offices in the country for himself, this being one of five that still exist, and he is considered to be the inventor of special delivery service. The village incorporated in 1885, and it became a city in 1901. The elevation is 1068, the Zip Code is 58240, and a peak population of 991 was reached in 1950. HATTON calls itself "The City of Action." Carl Benjamin Eielson (1897-1929), the famous aviator, and author Agnes Kjorlie Geelan were born here. (1, 2, 3, 5, 18, 40, 52, 79, 187)

**HAVANA** (Sargent). This GNRR station was founded in 1883 as WEBER, but the name was changed to HAVANA in 1886. The new name was suggested by Lewis Jones, a local realtor, who came from Havana, IL, which was named for the capital city of Cuba. Havana is Spanish for haven or harbor. The post office was established August 23, 1887 with Lewis Johnson pm. The elevation is 1287, the Zip Code is 58043, and a peak population of 387 was reached in 1910, with a decline to just 144 in 1980. In 1987 the town received national attention when it kept its last cafe open by running it with volunteer labor from local residents. (1, 2, 3, 13, 18, 33, 40, 52, 79, 170)

**HAVELOCK** (Hettinger). This Milwaukee Road RR townsite in SE¼ Sec. 28-135-96, Havelock Twp., ten miles SE of New England, was founded in 1909 as COAL CITY, and such names as Adams, Adamsville, and Adrian were suggested before the post office was established June 24, 1910 with Fred R. Hunter pm. Some sources say it was named for an English stockholder of the railroad, while others say it was named for Havelock, NE, both of which would ultimately trace to Sir Henry Havelock (1795-1857), a British military hero. The elevation is 2566, and the village, which never incorporated, reported a population of 175 in 1920, but declined to just 15 residents in 1960. Charles L. Rafferty (1873-1962) ran a grocery store here for many years, and was the pm from 1934 until the post office closed January 31, 1948 with mail to New England. (1, 2, 3, 13, 18, 35, 40, 79, 89, 179, 181, 385)

**HAVEN** (Foster). This farm post office was established in 1890 as EWEN, but on June 19, 1896 pm Joseph P. Haven renamed it for himself. He was a Civil War veteran who had settled in Sec. 18-146-64, Haven Twp., in 1894 and became pm in 1895. New pm Frank Settle moved the post office to SW¼ Sec. 8-146-64 in 1901, and was authorized to change the name to MARIA on May 6, 1902, but that order was rescinded September 13, 1902 without the change having been made. The post office closed January 21, 1905, effective February 15, 1905 with mail to Carrington, but that order was rescinded. On April 11, 1905 Annie W. Parker became the new pm, and tried unsuccessfully to change the name to ANNIE. Now located in E½ Sec. 12-146-64, it

*Havana about 1940*

operated as HAVEN until closing April 15, 1909 with mail to Kensal. (2, 3, 18, 40, 53, 79, 97)

**HAY CREEK** (Burleigh). This was a pioneer rural community in Hay Creek Twp. (139-81), then just north of Bismarck, although the capital city's growth has now engulfed much of that township. It does not appear on maps, but guides to ND in the 1890's listed it with the notation that it was served by the Bismarck post office. (3, 25, 34)

**HAYES** (Ransom). This was a farm post office established May 1, 1894 with William A. Hayes pm. It was located in NW¼ Sec. 13-133-56, Bale Twp., twelve miles south of Lisbon, and closed April 12, 1899 with mail to Lisbon. Hayes is an Old English name meaning from the hedged place. (2, 3, 19, 40)

**HAYMARSH** (Morton). This was a rural community founded in 1891 around St. Clement's Catholic Church in NE¼ Sec. 15-140-89, eleven miles NNW of Glen Ullin. The area, a favorite of waterfowl, is named to note its boggy soil, and the fact that area farmers harvested the hay annually after the summer waters had receded. The post office was established July 22, 1911 with Simon J. Nagel, who came here in 1886 and served on the county commission, as pm. In 1920 a Roman Catholic school was built, operating into the 1960's. Minnie Nagel, daughter of Simon, became pm in 1917, but the post office closed October 15, 1920 with mail to Glen Ullin. (1, 2, 3, 17, 40, 44, 104, 105, 107

**HAYNES** (Adams). This Milwaukee Road RR station was founded in NW¼ Sec. 29-129-94, Clermont Twp., in 1906 as GADSDEN, but in 1907 the name was changed to HAYNES, for George B. Haynes, President of the railroad. The post office was established April 2, 1908 with Albert Guerkink pm. The elevation is 2540, the Zip Code is 58637, and the village, which incorporated in 1910, reached a peak population of 210 in 1940, but declined to a count of just 53 in 1970. (1, 2, 18, 34, 40, 52, 79, 189)

**HAZELTON** (Emmons). This NPRR townsite was founded in 1902 in NE¼ Sec. 30-135-76, Hazelton Twp., and named by John Ithamer Roop (1865-1958) for his daughter, Hazel. The post office was established July 6, 1903 with Mrs. Elise Longpre Perras (1854-1918) pm. The elevation is 2000, the Zip Code is 58544, and a peak population of 500 was reached in 1940. The village incorporated in 1916, and it became a city in 1950. Among its more prominent pioneers were William Lewis Yeater (1848-1952) and Abraham Lincoln Geil (1865-1940), both of whom were long active in county affairs. HAZELTON bills itself as "The Flax Capital of the Nation." (1, 2, 3, 18, 33, 34, 40, 66, 79, 401)

**HAZEN** (Emmons). This place is shown on a circa 1905 state map as a station on the Milwaukee Road RR, at or very near the site of Hague. There is nothing to indicate that this was a prior name for Hague, and HAZEN is probably a cartographer's error. (3)

**HAZEN** (Mercer). This rural community was founded in 1882 by Richard Farrington and Alexander F. "Sandy" Roberts, both of whom homesteaded in Sec. 18-144-86. The post office was established February 12, 1885 with Zacariah L. Jones pm, who named it for A. D. Hazen, Third Assistant Postmaster General. Others say it was named for Gen. William Babcock Hazen (1830-1897), a hero of the Dakota Indian campaigns, and a former post commander at Fort Buford. The 1890 population was 27. In 1912 it moved to the NPRR townsite in NE¼ Sec. 18-144-86, and incorporated as a village in 1914. The elevation is 1760, and the Zip Code is 58545. The energy boom of the 1970's nearly doubled the 1970 size of HAZEN, reaching a population of 2,376 in 1980. (1, 2, 3, 18, 25, 33, 34, 40, 64, 79, 231, 415)

**HAZLEBROCK** (Kidder). This was a farm post office established March 8, 1886 with George Hasselbrock pm, who named it for himself but changed the spelling to reflect the correct pronunciation. It was first located in SW¼ Sec. 34-142-71, Lake Williams Twp., seven miles SE of Robinson, and later moved one mile NW to SW¼ Sec. 28-142-71. The post office closed December 5, 1887 with mail to Steele. (2, 3, 18, 25, 40, 414)

**H. B. JUNCTION** (Ward). This is a GNRR junction in Sec. 21-156-86, Berthold Twp., just west of Berthold. It first appears on a 1912 state map, and its name is thought to note that it is between Hartland and Berthold. (3, 18, 100)

**HEART** (Grant). This was a rural post office established July 6, 1905 with Anton Johnson pm. It was located in NW¼ Sec. 17-136-85, about twelve miles NE of Carson in the extreme NE corner of the county, and named for the nearby Heart River. The post office was discontinued January 31, 1911 with mail to Carl. It reopened May 13, 1911 about four miles NNE of the original site, and closed for good August 31, 1916 with mail to Almont. (1, 2, 3, 17, 40, 53, 177)

**HEART RANCH** (Oliver). This was a trading post operated by C. M. Whitman on the Heart Ranch in Sec. 17-141-82, Butte Twp., beginning about 1882. In 1901 a post office was established here and named YUCCA. (2, 3, 33, 40, 121)

**HEART RIVER STATION** (Morton). This was the first relay station on the Bismarck-Fort Keogh mail route. It was established in 1878 in SE¼ Sec. 5-138-82, about eight miles WSW of Mandan, and closed in 1882 after completion of the NPRR mainline. It was named for the Heart River on whose banks it was located. The Mandan Indians called the river *Natka Passahe*, and the Sioux called it *Ta Chanta Wakpa*. Both names

translate as river of the heart, meaning that its headwaters were in the heart, or middle, of their territory. (2, 3, 25, 79)

**HEATON** (Wells). This NPRR townsite was founded in 1899 in SE¼ Sec. 11-146-70, Speedwell Twp., and named for George Heaton, Manager of Land Sales for the railroad. The post office was established July 27, 1903 with Augusta Faulk pm. The elevation is 1727, the Zip Code is 58450, and a population of 400 was claimed in 1930, but a decline had reduced the count to just 62 in 1960. Bishop A. A. Leiske (1901-1983), who founded the *Town Hall* religious broadcasts in 1953, was born here. (1, 2, 3, 18, 38, 40, 79, 267, 363)

**HEBBARD** (Emmons). This place appears on several pre-1900 maps in Sec. 14-136-76, about eight miles NE of Hazelton. It is thought to have been a planned townsite on either the NPRR or Soo Line RR, but the site was bypassed and failed to develop. No one of this name ever resided in the area, indicating that it was probably named for a railroad official. (2, 3, 415)

**HEBRON** (Morton). This NPRR townsite was founded in 1885 in Sec. 33-140-90, Custer Twp., and named by either Rev. J. G. Koch or Rev. John L. Kling for Hebron, Palestine, whose locale is said to be similar. Hebron means enclosure. The post office was established October 22, 1885 when pm Charles Krauth moved his KNIFE RIVER post office here from its original location one mile to the west. Ferdinand Leutz (1854-1934) is generally considered to be the town's founder, with the first influx of settlers coming here from Johannestal, Crimea, South Russia. The elevation is 2180, the Zip Code is 58638, and the city, which incorporated in 1916 with Peter S. Jungers mayor, reached a peak population of 1,412 in 1950. HEBRON is called "The Brick City," noting the famous Hebron Brick Company which was established here in 1904. (1, 2, 3, 10, 17, 18, 25, 33, 40, 52, 79, 104)

**HECKER** (Ward). A rural post office operated here 1887-1898 and 1903-1904 as LOGAN, and when a Soo Line RR townsite was founded, the LOGAN pm, Owen Hecker, moved his facility to the railroad site on March 30, 1905 and renamed it for himself.

When Anna A. Beebe became pm November 15, 1909, she changed the name back to LOGAN. (2, 3, 18, 40, 100)

**HEERMAN'S LANDING** (Ramsey). This was an early boat landing on Devils Lake in Sec. 18-153-64, Creel Twp., on the eastern shore of Creel's Bay, four miles SW of the city of Devils Lake. It was named for Capt. Edward Heerman (1834-1929), a native of VT who was in Dakota Territory as early 1858, and came to Ramsey County in 1882. He built and operated the *Minnie H*, named for his daughter Minnie Etta Heerman, which was the most famous of the steamers that operated on the lake during its heyday. The site became the location of the Chautauqua assembly. (3, 103)

**HEFFERNAN** (Kidder). This was a farm post office established April 10, 1909 with James E. Heffernan pm. Mr. Heffernan came in 1903 from Ardoch in Walsh County, where his family had located in 1882, coming there from Toledo, Ontario, Canada. It was located in E½ Sec. 8-142-73, Clear Lake Twp., eight miles north of Tuttle, and closed December 31, 1911 with mail to Tuttle. Most sources and historical accounts refer to this place as Hefferman, which is an erroneous spelling. Mr. Heffernan apparently had difficulty with his name as well, for in later years he shortened it to Heffern. (2, 3, 18, 40, 75, 122)

**HEGTON** (Grand Forks). This was a rural post office on the Grand Forks-Fort Totten mail route in Sec. 18-152-54, Hegton Twp., six miles north of Larimore. It was established February 6, 1879 with Hans E. Hanson pm, who coined the name from his hometown of Hegstad, Norway. The post office was unofficially known as HANSON, and closed February 14, 1882 with mail to Larimore. (2, 3, 31, 40, 69)

**HEIL** (Grant). This NPRR townsite was founded in 1910 in SE¼ Sec. 26-134-88, Elm Twp., and named for William Heil, owner of the townsite. He was the son of Elm pm Henry Heil, and operated a store here before moving to Lodi, CA. The HEIL post office was established May 12, 1911 with Joseph Schafer pm. The elevation is 2275, and a peak population of 100 has been reported several times, although a 1985 count showed just 22 residents. Mrs. Freda Ketterling, who was appointed pm in 1948, retired January 22, 1981, and the post office, Zip Code 58546, closed at that time, although it is still listed as operational by the U. S. Postal Service. (1, 2, 3, 17, 40, 79, 111, 176, 414)

**HEIMDAL** (Wells). This GNRR station was founded in 1912 in SE¼ Sec. 20-150-70, Heimdal Twp., on the newly-built Surrey cutoff line. It was named for its township and the large coulee within the township, which were named for Heimdall, the watchman for the gods and guardian of the gate Bifrost at the rainbow bridge in Norse mythology. The post office was established September 22, 1910 with Ole H. Backen pm. The elevation is 1556, the Zip Code is 58342, and a peak population of 148 was reached in 1960. (1, 2, 33, 40, 54, 79, 363)

**HEKTON** (Sioux). This village on the south bank of the Cannonball River at its confluence with the Missouri River dates from as early as 1877. The name is based on the Sioux word *hecta*, meaning set back, which describes its location near the two rivers. The site was served by the Gayton post office in Emmons County, and later by the Cannon Ball post office on the north bank of the Cannonball River. On June 27, 1913 the HEKTON post office was established with Chester R. Wilcox pm in SW¼ Sec. 23-134-79. On December 3, 1915 the name was changed to CANNON BALL, taking the name of the old Morton County facility which had closed March 31, 1915. (2, 3, 40, 53, 127, 414)

**HELENA** (Griggs). This was a rural post office established November 21, 1882 with Peter Fiero pm, who named it for his wife. Helena is a Latin form of the Greek name Helen, meaning light, and made famous by Helen of Troy, whose name is derived from Helios, the Greek sun god. It was located in NE¼ Sec. 29-145-60, Helena Twp., five miles SE of Sutton. It moved twice within the immediate area before closing December 15, 1912 with mail to Hannaford. (2, 19, 25, 40, 53, 65, 284)

**HELIUM** (Rolette). This was a rural post office established May 24, 1922 with Eugene A. Demers pm. It was located in NE¼ Sec. 24-163-72, Holmes Twp., ten miles west of Saint John, and closed November 30, 1923 with mail to Saint John. The origin of the name is unknown, although it has been suggested that it was named for the light, gaseous element. Hellium is an erroneous spelling. (2, 3, 40)

**HELLWIG** (McIntosh). This rural post office was established December 6, 1900 in the home of pm Ludwig Hellwig in SW¼ Sec. 19-131-67, Antelope Twp., about fourteen miles NE of Ashley. Bernard Hellwig ran a general store here, and when the store was destroyed by fire in 1917, the post office was moved a few miles east to the home of new pm P. C. Anderst. It closed October 15, 1920 with mail to Kulm. (2, 3, 18, 40, 53, 211)

**HENDLEY** (Adams). This was a rural post office established May 13, 1907 with Clara E. Hurd pm. It was located in SE¼ Sec. 4-129-94, Clermont Twp., five miles NNE of Haynes, and named for Hendley, NE, which was named for a pioneer settler. Later that year William Little became pm at the same location. In 1908 the post office moved two miles north to the home of new pm Albert Guerbink in NE¼ Sec. 33-130-94, Kansas City Twp., and it closed November 15, 1909 with mail to Haynes. (2, 3, 40, 89, 414)

**HENLEY** (Mountrail). This post office was established December 24, 1904 with William F. Thompson pm, but the order was rescinded October 2, 1905. It would have been located in E½ Sec. 31-157-90, Clear Water Twp., about four miles NNE of Stanley. The origin of the name is unknown. (3, 40, 442)

**HENRICO** (McHenry). This place appears on a state map included in an atlas published by John Thomas in 1922, although the map is probably about twenty years older. It is shown just SSW of Velva in Velva Twp. (153-80), and is thought by local residents to be a copyright town, although the name seems to be coined from the name of the county. (3)

**HENRY'S POST** (Walsh). This was an alternate name for PARK RIVER POST, a short-lived fur trading post built in 1800 by Alexander Henry (1739-1824) of the North West Fur Co. Mr. Henry was one of the major figures in the fur trading business from the Great Lakes to the Rocky Mountains. It was located in Sec. 36-158-51, Saint Andrew Twp., just above the mouth of the Park River. A replica of this post is on display at the Interstate 29 rest area just north of Grafton. (2, 3, 5, 75)

**HENSEL** (Pembina). This was a rural post office established November 1, 1887 with Joseph Erwin pm, who named it for his hometown of Hensel, Ontario, Canada. It was located three miles NW of CANTON until it moved to that townsite in 1889, retaining its name. The townsite is now generally called HENSEL, although its legal name remains CANTON. The elevation is 929, the Zip Code is 58241, and a peak population of 139 was reported in 1950. (1, 2, 3, 18, 33, 40, 79, 108, 366)

**HENSLER** (Oliver). This was a farm post office established January 4, 1882 on the Missouri River, virtually opposite Washburn. Louis Connolly (1846-1911) was the pm, and he named it for his wife, Mary, the daughter of P. Hensler. Mr. Connolly was later the mayor of Mandan. In 1886 an inland townsite was founded in SE¼ Sec. 24-144-83, three miles SW of the original site, where John C. Ellis and James O. Kyser served as pms. In 1909 it moved again, this time two miles west to SW¼ Sec. 28-144-82, where the NPRR arrived in 1911. A peak population of 65 was reported in 1960, and with the closing of the Hannover post office in 1978, HENSLER, Zip Code 58547, became the last Oliver County post office dating to territorial times. (1, 2, 3, 18, 25, 33, 38, 40, 79, 121)

**HERMAN** (Sargent). This was the first settlement in the county, founded in 1879 in SE¼ Sec. 11-131-53, Herman Twp., seven miles north of Geneseo, and named POSTVILLE. Ezra D. Post began an unofficial mail service in 1880, calling it HERMAN for John Herman, in whose store it was located. Mr. Herman, a Civil War veteran known locally as "Honest John," was one of the first county commissioners. Herman is a Teutonic name meaning warrior. When the post office officially opened April 18, 1881 with Mr. Post as pm, he renamed it HAMLIN. (2, 3, 19, 40, 171)

**HERR** (Sheridan). This was a farm post office established February 16, 1903 with Fred G. Herr pm. It was located in NW¼ Sec. 26-148-77, Harris Twp., nine miles north of McClusky, and closed June 30, 1909 with mail to McClusky. Mr. Herr also operated a country store at this site. (2, 3, 18, 21, 30, 40)

**HERRICK** (Walsh). This NPRR station was built in 1887 and called NEW SAINT ANDREWS. About 1893 it was renamed SAINT ANDREWS STATION. A post office operated here from 1895-1903 called ELORA. After it closed NPRR officials renamed the station HERRICK for Frank and Job Herrick, who had settled here in 1870. Two elevators were at this site for many years, one operated by John C. Stewart (1857-1948), who came here in 1900. (1, 2, 3, 18, 40, 75)

**HERRIOTT** (Walsh). This was a GNRR station built in 1886 in SE¼ Sec. 1-156-53, Walsh Centre Twp., five miles SE of Grafton. It was named for William Herriott, a grain buyer who moved to the site in 1896 after the original elevator was destroyed by fire. He built a new, smaller elevator here, operating it until 1915. It still exists, having been operated since 1923 by William H. Gorder and his descendants. (1, 2, 18, 75)

**HESNAULT** (Ward). This was a farm post office established June 30, 1903 with John A. Berg pm. It was located in Sec. 35-154-86, Tolgen Twp., fourteen miles SSE of Berthold, and named for the Hesnault family who were pioneer settlers in the area. Mildred Hesnault was the private secretary to Gen. Arthur MacArthur, father of Gen. Douglas MacArthur. Bernt E. Edwardson (1880-1939) became pm in 1916, moving the facility across the section line to his home in SE¼ Sec. 34-154-86. The post office closed September 29, 1917 with mail to Deslacs. (2, 18, 40, 100, 374)

**HESPER** (Benson). This was a farm post office established April 13, 1899 with Charlie Jacob Camp pm. It was located in NE¼ Sec. 8-152-70, Hesper Twp., and named by pioneer settler Perry Roth for his hometown of Hesper, IA. Mr. Camp (1862-1926) and many others in the area also came from that IA city. About 1905 the post office was relocated to the NPRR townsite in NE¼ Sec. 16-152-70, about one mile to the SE, with a continuation of the name. Leonard Nelson was the first pm at the townsite, which reached a peak population of about 50 in 1920, but declined to just 4 in 1974. The post office closed April 15, 1955 with mail to Maddock. (2, 18, 40, 79, 110, 149, 239)

**HESS** (Slope). Ed Hess ran a country store in NW¼ Sec. 2-134-102, Slope Center Twp., seven miles SW of Amidon. As this store became a community gathering place,

George F. Giese decided to move his HOLTON post office, established in 1908 four miles to the NNE, to the store. This move occurred April 30, 1910 with a name change to GIESE. William F. Hess became pm in 1913, but the post office closed March 31, 1914 with mail to Bessie. At this time the community became known as HESS, but when Mr. Giese reestablished the post office on January 10, 1917, he called it SLOPE CENTER. (3, 40, 82, 414)

**HETTINGER** (Adams). This Milwaukee Road RR townsite was founded in 1907 in Secs. 11, 12, 13 & 14-129-96, Hettinger Twp., and named by popular demand for the county from which this area was about to separate as a new county. The name is credited to Erastus A. Williams of Bismarck, who was the son-in-law of Mathias Hettinger of Freeport, IL. HETTINGER was named county seat in 1907, incorporated as a village in 1908, and became a city in 1916. The post office was established May 17, 1907 with Edward C. Barry pm. The elevation is 2668, the Zip Code is 58639, and a peak population of 1,769 was reached in 1960. Ole Abelseth (1886-1980), one of the last living survivors of the sinking of the *Titanic* in 1912, was a longtime resident of HETTINGER, and Joris O. "Bud" Wigen (1917-1987), a three-term ND Insurance Commissioner, was born here. (1, 2, 3, 18, 33, 40, 79, 188, 189)

**HETTINGER** (Hettinger). This place appears on a 1930 road map published by the General Drafting Company. It is shown on ND Highway 8 about six miles SSE of Regent, and is believed to be a copyright town. (3)

**HETTINGER** (LaMoure & Stutsman). This place appears on a 1930 road map published by the General Drafting Company on ND Highway 46 which was built along the county line at this point. It is about three miles east of the James River, and is believed to be a copyright town. (3)

**HEWITT** (Bottineau). This GNRR station in Secs. 29 & 32-163-78, Scandia Twp., was founded in 1904 as FALDET, but in 1905 the name was changed to ROTH. When the post office was established May 22, 1907 with Joseph H. Carl pm, it was named HEWITT for William Hewitt, a native of Ontario, Canada, who came here in 1899 from Hillsboro. The GNRR station retained the name ROTH, creating a confusing situation until May 14, 1908, when new pm John W. Reep changed the name of the post office to ROTH. (2, 34, 40, 101)

**HICKSON** (Cass). This Milwaukee Road RR townsite was founded in 1883 in N 1/2 Sec. 24-137-49, Pleasant Twp., by Richard S. Tyler, a Fargo realtor. The name notes the 1869 arrival in this area of Ole, Andrew, Lewis, Haakon, Martin, August and Carl, all sons of Haakon Hicks. The post office was established June 23, 1884 with Alfred M. Hovland pm. The elevation is 915, and the village, which never incorporated, reached a peak population of 125 in 1890, with a decline to just 47 in 1975. The post office, Zip Code 58044, closed December 31, 1975 with mail to Horace. (1, 2, 18, 25, 38, 40, 41, 77, 79, 304)

**HIDDENWOOD** (McLean). This was a pioneer rural settlement on the south shore of Hiddenwoods Lake, named by early settlers to describe a grove of native trees there. It was located primarily in NW¼ Sec. 3-150-87, Gate Twp., about seven miles NNE of Roseglen. The post office was established June 11, 1903 with William W. Wright pm, and closed August 14, 1909 with mail to Ryder. An annual picnic was first held in 1903, a tradition that far outlived the settlement. Old Settlers' Picnics are still held here, a replica sod house has been built, and the site is known as "The Whist Capital of North Dakota." 18, 25, 33, 40, 52, 79, 187, North Dakota." The name is perpetuated by the Hiddenwood National Wildlife Refuge nearby. Hiddenwoods is an erroneous but commonly found spelling. (2, 3, 28, 40, 277)

**HIGH BRIDGE** (Barnes). This was a short-lived NPRR station at the east end of the famous highline bridge in Secs. 15 & 16-140-58, at the north edge of Valley City. The bridge was built in 1906-1908, and is 3,860 feet in length. The NPRR operated a water pumping station here. Some sources spell the name as one word. (2, 3, 18, 34, 76, 77, 266)

**HIGLEY** (Williams). This was a farm post office established December 11, 1905 with Van DeVere Bernard pm, and was named for Lyman O. Higley, who came here in 1903 and was appointed as the pm, but it was found that his farm was just beyond the maximum distance allowed for a one-day round to Williston to pick up the mail. Mr. Higley served as Register of Deeds 1908-1918, and died in 1919. The post office was located in NE¼ Sec. 18-155-101, Missouri Ridge Twp., eight miles NW of Williston, or six miles closer than the Higley farm. It closed May 31, 1909 with mail to Williston. (2, 18, 40, 50)

**HILL** (Cass). HILL emerged as a place name in the 1960's when it was assigned as the name of Exit #75 on Interstate 94 between Tower City and Buffalo. It refers to Hill Twp. (139-55), which was named for Cullen William Hill (1846-1924), a native of VT who came here from MN, and is said to be the first person in ND to make and market cheese. (3, 34, 77, 266)

**HILL CITY** (Traill). This settlement in NW¼ Sec. 5-145-50, Hillsboro Twp., was founded as COMSTOCK, but when it was platted in September 1880, the same month that the GNRR arrived at the site, it was renamed HILL CITY to honor GNRR President James J. Hill, "The Empire Builder." Others insist that it was named to note its location on a hill. Because a Hill City already existed in the Black Hills, the name was changed to HILLSBORO on August 12, 1881. (2, 3, 29, 77, 393, 395)

**HILLS** (Mountrail). This was a rural post office established April 18, 1901 with August Peterson pm on his farm in SW¼ Sec. 11-157-89, Redmond Twp., eight miles NE of Palermo. William Delaney became pm in 1904 and moved it to his farm in NW¼ Sec. 31-158-88, Lowland Twp. Rozeneth E. Mayham became pm in 1905 and moved it to his farm in NW¼ Sec. 6-157-88, Stave

Twp. Named for Adrian B. Hills, a pioneer homesteader in the area west of Minot, the post office closed June 30, 1906 with mail to Donnybrook. (2, 40, 72)

**HILLSBORO** (Traill). This city was founded in 1880 as COMSTOCK in Sec. 5-145-50, Hillsboro Twp. When it was platted in September 1880, it was renamed HILL CITY to honor GNRR President James J. Hill. It was discovered that a Hill City already existed in the Black Hills, so when the post office was established August 12, 1881 with Asa W. Morgan pm, it was named HILLSBORO, again honoring the GNRR President. The elevation is 901, the Zip Code is 58045, and the city, which incorporated in 1882 with John DeGroat mayor, reached a peak population of 1,599 in 1980. In the election of 1890, HILLSBORO was awarded the county seat, but legal challenges prevented the removal of the court house from Caledonia until 1896. (1, 2, 3, 13,18, 25, 33, 40, 52, 79, 187, 393, 396)

**HILLSDALE** (Dickey). This was a rural post office established August 22, 1887 with Thomas W. Bush, formerly associated with the pioneer settlement of Port Emma, as pm. It was located in E½ Sec. 25-130-60, Riverdale Twp., about three miles NW of Ludden on the west bank of the James River. Early accounts mention local parties going to nearby sand hills for picnics and to pick strawberries, and the name is thought to have noted this fact. The post office closed February 15, 1890 with mail to Ludden. It reopened April 21, 1890, but closed for good July 15, 1893 with mail again going to Ludden. (2, 3, 25, 40, 154, 264)

**HILLSIDE** (Rolette). This was a country store located in SE¼ Sec. 25-162-72, Hillside Twp., which was named in 1893 to note its location on the edge of the Turtle Mountains. The store was run by S. C. Pigeon, who came here in 1901 and later served on the county commission. It opened about 1903, and operated into the 1930's at this site about six miles ENE of Dunseith. (2, 3, 18, 103, 123)

**HILLTOWN** (Barnes). This blueprint townsite was promoted in Sec. 4-142-61, Uxbridge Twp., about two miles SE of Wimbledon. The Soo Line RR had widened its right of way here, suggesting a future siding, but instead opted for the nearby community of Gibson, which was renamed Wimbledon in 1893. The name was descriptive of its locale, but the site failed to develop. (2, 3, 34, 269)

**HINGER** (Kidder). This was a farm post office established May 22, 1907 with William Hinger (1872-1961) pm. This order was rescinded, but on July 15, 1908 the post office was again authorized, and was located in Mr. Hinger's home in NW¼ Sec. 2-143-70, Petersville Twp., eight miles north of Pettibone. Mail was carried by wagon from Medina until the post office closed August 31, 1909 with mail to Heaton. (2, 3, 40, 314, 315, 414)

**HIRSCHVILLE** (Dunn). This was a rural post office established January 5, 1911 with Casper Hirsch pm. Hirsch is German for deer. It was located in NW 1/4 Sec. 2-141-94, Coon Twp., fifteen miles SE of Manning, and

closed September 15, 1920 with mail to Taylor. (1, 2, 3, 40)

**HOBART** (Barnes). This NPRR siding was built in 1872 and named SIXTH SIDING. It was located in SE¼ Sec. 17-140-59, Hobart Twp., three miles east of Sanborn, and in 1882 was renamed for its township, which was named for C. F. Hobart, a NPRR official, by Charles Hokenson of Valley City. Hobart is a Teutonic name meaning bright-minded. Mr. Hokenson and Charles A. Robert of Fargo platted the townsite in August 1882, but little development occurred, with most area settlers choosing to live in Sanborn. The site was served by the Valley City post office, and disappeared when the siding was removed in the spring of 1925. (1, 2, 18, 19, 25, 34, 76, 79)

**HOBO KINGDOM** (Burke). Robert Blomquist, Conrad Peterson, Walfred Forsgren, and Gust Edlund settled in Sec. 12-159-94, Battleview Twp., three miles NE of Battleview in 1905. All four men were bachelors, and local settlers bestowed this name on the community to humorously note the cooking habits of the four men. (18, 67)

**HOBSON** (Morton). This was a rural post office established October 29, 1898 with Laura Gipp pm. It was located in NW¼ Sec. 6-136-79, one mile NW of Huff, and named for Richmond P. Hobson, a U. S. Navy officer acquainted with the Gipp family. In 1903 it moved two miles NW to the home of new pm Johanna Melzner in SE¼ Sec. 31-137-79, and closed September 14, 1905 with mail to Fort Rice. It reopened March 12, 1908 with Mrs. Dorothy Wead pm at her home in SW¼ Sec. 28-136-79, four miles SE of Huff, and closed for good July 30, 1910 with mail again to Fort Rice. (2, 3, 17, 18, 40, 414, 415)

**HOE** (Emmons). This was a farm post office established April 30, 1907 with Orson Ott pm, although his wife Verna usually performed the duties. It was located in the Ott's sod house in SW¼ Sec. 18-134-77, eight miles SW of Hazelton, and Allie Linderman was the mail carrier. It was discontinued December 31, 1907 with mail to Hazelton. Some historians believe that it was never in operation, yet the *Emmons County Record* of January 9, 1908 mentions its discontinuance, which would seem to indicate that it had been in operation. Folklore says that the name was chosen after local settlers were unable to agree on a name, and agreed to name it for the common gardening tool as a compromise. (3, 18, 40, 66)

**HOFFLUND** (Williams). This rural settlement began about 1888 in Sec. 11-154-96, Hofflund Twp., fifteen miles SSW of Tioga, and was named for its township, which was named for John C. Hoff. The post office was established December 6, 1895 with Mr. Hoff as pm. He was succeeded in 1897 by Ole Danielson (1858-1946), who changed his name to Hoff when he became pm. The post office closed April 30, 1907, but reopened February 17, 1908 with August Mattson (1874-1959) pm. Mrs. Jennie Mattson (1879-1953), his wife, became pm in 1910, and served until the post office closed October 31, 1936 with mail to White Earth. A population of 12 was reported in 1900. (2, 3, 18, 40, 50, 53, 79)

**HOILAND** (Nelson). Peter L. Hoiland, his wife, and three children settled in NE¼ Sec. 32-149-57, Ora Twp., in 1881, and a small rural community named in his honor began to develop, but when a post office was established September 3, 1883, the name was changed to ANETA. (3, 40, 124)

**HOLMES** (Grand Forks). This was a country store in SW¼ Sec. 15-149-52, Union Twp., nine miles WNW of Reynolds. Some say it was named for David M. Holmes, who helped survey the township in 1872, while others say it was named for Holmes Wyman, the first clerk of the township. Holmes is a Teutonic name meaning son of Holman, which means from the river island. A post office was established Februry 13, 1886, a year after the store opened, with Lars P. Hjelmstad pm. Herman Frederick Schroeder (1874-1943) bought the store in 1902 and became pm, and his son Ralph took over the duties following the elder Mr. Schroeder's death. The post office closed January 31, 1954 with mail to Reynolds, and the store closed in 1962 marking the end of an era. A population of about 25 lived at the site for many years. (1, 2, 3, 18, 19, 25, 31, 40, 69, 79, 241, 276)

**HOLTON** (Slope). This was a farm post office established December 17, 1908 with George F. Giese pm. It was located in SW¼ Sec. 24-135-102, West Sand Creek Twp., five miles west of Amidon, and named for Charles Holton, who lived in SW¼ Sec. 14-135-102, one mile to the NW from 1892-1900, and was well known as a cowboy and bartender. On April 30, 1910 Mr. Giese moved the post office to NW¼ Sec. 2-134-102, Slope Center Twp., four miles to the SSW, and renamed it GIESE. (2, 3, 18, 40, 82, 414)

**HOLY CROSS** (Cass). This name referred to a very early Roman Catholic community that began on both sides of the Red River in 1868, promoted by Father J. B. Genin as a new home for French-Canadians from Quebec. A log church was built in SE¼ Sec. 13-138-49, Stanley Twp., one mile north of Wild Rice, but it was destroyed by fire in 1871. A post office of this name existed on the MN side of the river 1869-1889. The name noted a large wooden cross at the church site that was clearly visible on both sides of the river. (3, 13, 309, 312)

**HOMEN** (Cavalier). This was a rural post office established January 28, 1895 with Halvor Homen pm. He later changed his name to Halvor Torgerson. It was located in NE¼ Sec. 7-163-58, Hope Twp., sixteen miles NE of Langdon, and closed July 31, 1933 with mail to Langdon. (1, 2, 3, 18, 40, 79)

**HOMER** (Stutsman). This was a Midland Continental RR station in NE¼ Sec. 19-139-63, Homer Twp., one mile SE of Jamestown. An elevator was built to serve the Homer Stock Farm owned by Russell R. Wright. It is said that the name came from Homer, NY, which was named for the ancient poet. Homer is a Greek name meaning a pledge. The population was listed as 10 in 1920, but the site never developed beyond the elevator, which was destroyed by fire in 1981. (1, 2, 13, 19, 79, 158)

**HOMESTEAD** (Richland). This was a rural post office established May 7, 1894 with James Nelson, the township clerk and Justice of the Peace, as pm at his home in NW¼ Sec. 4-133-51, West End Twp., seven miles north of Wyndmere. He named it for the popular method of acquiring title to land, and the name was adopted by the township in May 1895. About 1907 the post office was moved three miles north to the farm of I. T. Braaten in Sec. 28-134-51, Garborg Twp., and it closed July 15, 1930 with mail to Wyndmere. (1, 2, 3, 18, 40, 79, 147, 361)

**HONEYFORD** (Grand Forks). A NPRR station named BEAN was founded in 1887 in NE¼ Sec. 32-153-53, Gilby Twp., three miles south of Gilby, and grew into the adjacent NW¼ Sec. 33-153-53. A post office operated here 1888-1891. When it was reestablished July 25, 1892 in the store of Andrew Redwing, new pm William J. "Bob" Honeyford named it for himself. The railroad station retained the name BEAN until the townsite was platted in 1906 as HONEYFORD. A peak population of 75 was reported in 1920, but a count of just 6 residents was made in 1981. The post office, Zip Code 58242, became a rural branch of Gilby on April 7, 1967, and closed July 31, 1973 with mail to Gilby. (1, 2, 3, 18, 31, 33, 40, 69, 79, 338)

**HONG** (Pierce). This GNRR station was founded in 1905 in SW¼ Sec. 24-157-70, Rush Lake Twp., six miles NE of Knox. It was named for P. B. Hong, a banker in nearby Wolford who later was a bank president in Willmar, MN. A small village existed here for years, but HONG never had a post office. Elevators were built in 1907 and 1909, but both were destroyed by fire in 1967. The 1920 population was reported to be 15. Jesse M. Palmer, the townsite owner, came here in 1897 and was known as the largest man in Pierce County, weighing over 450 pounds. Meat dealer Frank Fay was the honorary mayor of HONG until 1926, when he lost his land for non-payment of taxes. (1, 2, 18, 79, 114)

**HOOPLE** (Walsh). This GNRR townsite was founded in 1890 in SW¼ Sec. 5-158-54, Glenwood Twp., and named for Allan Hoople (1849-1923), who owned the townsite and operated a drug store. The post office was established January 7, 1890 with Merrit B. Bronson pm. The elevation is 903, the Zip Code is 58243, and the village, which incorporated in 1898, reached a peak population of 447 in 1950. Lynn J. Frazier, Governor of ND 1917-1921 and a U. S. Senator 1923-1940, was a native and longtime resident of HOOPLE, which is known as "The Potato Capital of North Dakota." (1, 2, 3, 18, 33, 40, 75, 391)

**HOOSIER** (Hettinger). This was a rural post office established August 16, 1906 with William H. Hendricks pm, who named it for the nickname of his home state of IN. The term is generally thought to be a corruption of husher, a slang term of the early 1800's meaning a bully. It was located in NW¼ Sec. 12-134-93, Mott Twp., four miles north of Mott, but the order was rescinded September 14, 1906 before it went into operation. It was again established December 18, 1906 with David S. Helms pm,

about a mile further north. In 1910 it was moved to NW¼ Sec. 25-135-93, Acme Twp., about eight miles north of Mott, where it was located in a country store operated by Forest Church. The post office closed May 31, 1911 with mail to Mott, and reopened July 27, 1912 with Mr. Church as pm, who then renamed it CHURCH. (1, 2, 3, 5, 18, 40, 53, 179, 181)

**HOOSIER** (McHenry). On August 8, 1902 postal officials authorized the SHIGLEY post office in SE¼ Sec. 18-158-77, Bantry Twp., two miles WNW of Bantry, to change its name to HOOSIER, the request having been made by local settlers who had come from IN, "The Hoosier State." The new name never saw actual usage, and on December 12, 1902 the name was changed to MILROY. (2, 3, 18, 40, 415)

**HOPE** (Steele). This GNRR station was founded in 1882 in Sec. 1-144-56, Carpenter Twp., and Sec. 31-145-56, Hugo Twp., and named for Hope A. Hubbard Steele, wife of E. H. Steele, the namesake of the county. The post office had been established March 29, 1881 with Herbert Smart pm, one mile NE of the townsite, to which it moved in 1882. It incorporated as a village in 1890, and became a city in 1904 with George A. Warner (1857-1948) as mayor. The elevation is 1231, the Zip Code is 58046, and a peak population of 909 was reported in 1910. It was the first county seat of Griggs County in 1882, and after some boundary changes it became the first county seat of Steele County in 1883. Because it was not centrally located, however, it lost the court house to Sherbrooke in 1885. Elmer D. Wallace, a ND Lt. Governor, and Charles Emerson Murry, a ND Adjutant General, were onetime residents of HOPE. (1, 2, 3, 18, 25, 33, 40, 52, 79, 99, 233, 320, 327)

**HORACE** (Cass). This place began as a rural post office established March 12, 1875 with Henrik Clemenson pm. In 1882 the NPRR built near the post office, and established a station called Horace Station. An unplatted village began in NE¼ Sec. 19-138-49, and adopted the name of the rural post office, which had been named for Horace Greeley (1811-1872), the losing Presidential candidate in 1872 who had been supported by most local residents. He is famous for his quote: "Go west young man, and grow up with the country." Horace is a Latin name meaning time keeper. The village incorporated in 1942, and as a result of outmigration from nearby Fargo, reached a peak population of 497 in 1980. The elevation is 940, and the Zip Code is 58047. The general store operated here by Henry Helge Thue and his son for 58 years is now at the Bonanzaville museum in West Fargo. (1, 2, 5, 18, 19, 40, 52, 77, 79, 309)

**HORACE STATION** (Cass). This was a NPRR station built in 1882 in NW¼ Sec. 20-138-49, Stanley Twp., just east of Horace, soon becoming a part of that settlement. (2, 77, 309)

**HORN** (Stutsman). This rural post office was established in 1884 as DURHAM in SW¼ Sec. 20-143-62, Courtenay Twp., three miles south of Courtenay. On January 20, 1887 pm Elbridge F. Horn renamed it for himself.

A small settlement began, reporting a population of 10 in 1890. On August 9, 1893 the post office moved to the new Soo Line RR townsite of Courtenay, assuming that name, although an error by postal officials resulted in the name being Courtney until 1905. (2, 3, 25, 40, 158, 415)

**HORSWILL** (Hettinger). This was a rural post office established September 9, 1905 with Nancy Horswill pm. It was located in the country store operated by James O. Horswill in NW¼ Sec. 30-135-94, St. Croix Twp., four miles NNE of Regent, and closed June 30, 1910. The following day Nancy Horswill became the first pm of Regent. (2, 3, 18, 40, 178, 179, 181)

**HOSKINS** (McIntosh). This was the first settlement in McIntosh County, founded in 1884 in Sec. 33-130-70, Hoskins Twp., on the shore of the lake which had been named by Col. Clement A. Lounsberry, founder of *The Bismarck Tribune*, for his wife's maiden name. The post office was established August 21, 1884 in the grocery store of pm George W. Abbott. It was the county seat of McIntosh County from 1884 until 1888, when everything in the town except the school moved three miles east to the new Soo Line RR townsite of Ashley. The post office closed May 4, 1888 when pm Thomas J. Lamunyon moved to Ashley. (2, 3, 40, 79, 134, 211)

**HOVE MOBILE PARK** (Cavalier). This is a rural subdivision begun in the 1960's by Howard J. Hove in NE¼ Sec. 22 & NW¼ Sec. 23-159-59, Osnabrock Twp., six miles east of Nekoma. The population is approximately 20. (3, 34)

**HOVING** (Sargent). This NPRR station in NW¼ Sec. 5-132-55, Willey Twp., was the first station west from Milnor after construction of the line resumed in 1900. For a time it was the new terminus, but dreams of a boom ended when construction continued westward. The town was named for John Hoving, NPRR roadmaster at the time. A population of 20 was reported in 1920, but the 1960 count was just 2. HOVING never had a post office, and the last business place closed in 1922, although some maps continued showing the place into the 1970's. (2, 3, 18, 40, 165, 171)

**HOWARD** (Williams). This was a rural post office established November 30, 1906 with Howard W. Nelson pm in his country store. Mr. Nelson came here in 1906 from Northwood, and returned to that Grand Forks County settlement in 1909 with James E. Haskett taking over this store and post office. Howard is a Teutonic name meaning chief warden. Some sources say it was named for William A. Howard, Governor of Dakota Territory 1878-1880. It was located in SW¼ Sec. 25-159-102, Barr Butte Twp., six miles SE of Grenora, and closed November 25, 1916 with mail to Grenora. On December 19, 1916 a post office opened at the new GNRR townsite of Hanks, two miles NE of the old HOWARD store. (2, 18, 19, 40, 50, 53, 79)

**HOWE** (Grant). This was a farm post office established June 16, 1900 with Alphonso Thompson pm. It was located in SW¼ Sec.

28-130-89, Howe Twp., twenty-five miles south of Elgin on the north bank of Cedar Creek. The origin of the name is unknown. The post office closed June 30, 1916 with mail to Morristown, SD. (1, 2, 3, 17, 18, 40, 53, 176, 177)

**HOWES** (Cass). This was a GNRR loading station built in 1885 in SW¼ Sec. 11-140-52, Casselton Twp., two miles north of Casselton, and named for the brothers William J. and Thomas W. Howe, owners of a bonanza farm in the area. It was served by the Casselton post office. A rural school, later called the Howes Siding School, had been built in 1879 in SE¼ Sec. 10-140-52, just across the tracks, and operated until 1947. The station was removed in April 1955. (2, 3, 18, 25, 34, 77, 266, 300)

**HOWSER** (Hettinger). This was a rural post office established October 3, 1906 with Orville Williams pm. It was located in NW¼ Sec. 2-134-93, Mott Twp., five miles north of Mott. In 1908 it moved nine miles north to SW¼ Sec. 24-136-93, Campbell Twp., the home of new pm Thomas R. Sarver, and closed November 15, 1909 with mail to Hoosier. The origin of the name is unknown. (2, 3, 40, 181, 414)

**HUB** (Mercer). This rural post office was established in 1906 as BEAUMONT in NE¼ Sec. 26-144-85, six miles SW of Stanton. On April 11, 1907 pm Sarah Jane Brown changed the name to HUB for her husband, Hub Brown. It closed November 30, 1912 with mail to Stanton. (1, 2, 3, 18, 40, 53)

**HUBBARD PIT** (Grand Forks). An 1890 guide to ND lists this place as being located in Grand Forks County, and served by the Reynolds post office. It is thought to have been a GNRR engine servicing facility just north of Reynolds, and was probably named for Newton K. Hubbard, a Fargo developer and partner of W. A. Kindred. (3, 25, 430)

**HUBERTON** (McLean). This townsite was platted about 1913 in NE¼ Sec. 9-149-89, Loquemont Twp., in anticipation of a railroad that never was built. It was named for P. H. Huber, a local landowner who was a promoter of the site. In 1915 a post office was established in Sec. 8-149-89, just to the west of this site, but it was named Raub. That name was retained when it moved two miles SW in 1916 to Sec. 19-149-89, the location of a new townsite. (2, 3, 28)

**HUDSON** (Dickey). This was a pioneer settlement founded in April 1883 in Secs. 1 & 2-130-60 and Secs. 6 & 7-130-59, all Hudson Twp., on the west bank of the James River about four miles SW of Oakes. Many of the first settlers had come from NY, and they named it for the Hudson River in their home state, which was named for Henrik Hudson ( ? -1611), the famous explorer. The post office was established June 11, 1883 with Thomas J. Millham pm, and the townsite was platted by the Dakota Midland Railway. A village began to develop, complete with a newspaper, a hotel, and other luxuries, but when the railroad failed to materialize, development shifted to the new NPRR townsite of Oakes in 1886. The post office closed December 6, 1886 with mail to Oakes. (2, 10, 40, 154, 264, 319)

**HUDSON COLONY** (McLean). This rural community was founded in 1882 by several Scandinavian families who had come from Hudson, WI, which was named in 1852 by Alfred Day, who thought that the St. Croix River here resembled the Hudson River in NY. It was located in Sec. 5-143-81, Nettle Creek Twp., on the east bank of the Missouri River four miles SE of Washburn. In 1883 it was renamed SVERDRUP. (3, 34, 70, 390)

**HUFF** (Morton). This NPRR station was built in 1910 in SE¼ Sec. 6-136-79, nineteen miles SE of Mandan, and called NINETEENTH SIDING. The post office was established May 12, 1911 with Emmett W. Dobson pm, who named it for John S. Huff, who had settled here in 1888. HUFF never had a population greater than 60. The post office, Zip Code 58555, became a rural branch of Mandan on April 30, 1960, and the last train passed through the town in October 1966. Local postal service ended December 28, 1985 when the rural branch closed with mail now coming directly from Mandan. (1, 2, 3, 17, 33, 40, 79, 107)

**HULL** (Emmons). This rural community was started about 1887 by Dutch settlers from Hull, IA. It is located in NW¼ Sec. 6-129-75, Elzas Twp. and SW¼ Sec. 31-130-75, about seven miles west of Hague. The post office, in Sec. 6-129-75, was established December 18, 1888 with George Pekelder pm, and it closed June 13, 1892 with mail to Westfield. It reopened July 12, 1892 with Peter G. Rooks pm, and closed June 30, 1954 with mail to Hague. Its population has generally been about 40 throughout its existance. (1, 2, 3, 18, 34, 40, 66)

**HULT** (Oliver). This was a farm post office established February 26, 1904 with John Anderson pm. Mr. Anderson, a native of Sweden, came to America in 1885 and settled here in 1895. The post office was located in SW¼ sEC. 18-143-83, Nebo Twp., three miles south of Fort Clark, and closed June 15, 1910 with mail to Center. Hult is a Swedish word meaning coppice, which is a thicket, or grove of small trees, and was probably chosen to describe the location. (3, 4, 18, 40, 121)

**HUME** (Slope). This was a rural post office established February 24, 1908 with James Samuel Hume pm. He came here in 1907 from WI, served as Auditor of Slope County, and operated a telephone exchange along with the post office, which closed January 31, 1917 with mail to Stillwater. HUME was located in SW 1/4 Sec. 18-134-99, Hume Twp., eight miles SE of Amidon. Home is an erroneous spelling. (1, 2, 3, 18, 40, 82)

**HUNGARY** (Stark). This was a rural post office established December 28, 1900 with Frank Lefor pm, who named it for his homeland. The order was rescinded February 27, 1901. It was reestablished February 23, 1906 with John Grundhauser (1860-1946) pm in his home in NW¼ Sec. 32-137-94, three miles south of Lefor, and closed November 30, 1906 with mail to Gladstone. (2, 40, 74)

**HUNSKOR** (Bottineau). This was a pioneer settlement in SE¼ Sec. 29-163-79, Scotia Twp., one mile NW of Landa. It was centered around the country store operated by Arne Hunskor beginning in 1902. HUNSKOR declined after the establishment of the GNRR townsite of Landa in 1904, and is now a ghost town. (18, 101, 153)

**HUNTER** (Cass). This NPRR (later GNRR) townsite was founded in 1880 in NE 1/4 Sec. 23 & NW¼ Sec. 24-143-52, Hunter Twp., and named for John C. Hunter, a major landowner in the area. The Delno post office, located two miles to the north, moved here June 15, 1881 with Josiah H. Gale pm, although postmarks with the HUNTER name are known as early as April 7, 1881. The elevation is 966, the Zip Code is 58048, and the village, which incorporated in 1885, reached a peak population of 446 in 1960. David H. Houston (1841-1906) was a local farmer who was a poet and inventor on the side. He invented the roll-type film process, named it *Kodak*, and sold the rights to George Eastman of Rochester, NY. (1, 2, 3, 18, 25, 33, 40, 77, 79, 297, 298)

**HURD** (Bottineau). This was a Soo Line RR station founded in 1905 in NE 1/4 Sec. 35 & SE¼ Sec. 26-160-82, Mount Rose Twp., seven miles east of Lansford. It was developed by the Tri-State Land Co., and named for T. E. Hurd of Minneapolis, MN, the townsite agent for the Soo Line RR. The post office was established June 2, 1906 with Andrew C. Scott pm. A population of 50 was claimed in 1920, but the 1940 count was just 14, and the post office closed September 30, 1942 with mail to Lansford. (1, 2, 18, 34, 40, 53, 79, 101, 153)

**HURDSFIELD** (Wells). This NPRR station was founded in 1902 in SE¼ Sec. 23-146-73, Bull Moose Twp., and named for Warren W. Hurd, a prominent area farmer and developer. Mr. Hurd built the famous Round House on his land in SE 1/4 Sec. 6-145-73, Lynn Twp., about nine miles SE of town. This historic home was restored in 1977. The post office was established April 13, 1903 with Howard F. Miller pm. The elevation is 1923, the Zip Code is 58451, and the village, which incorporated in 1926, reached a peak population of 258 in 1940. (1, 2, 3, 18, 33, 40, 79, 364)

**HURNING** (Stutsman). This was a Midland Continental RR station in SE¼ Sec. 19-140-62, Spiritwood Twp., six miles east of Jamestown at the junction with the NPRR. It was named for H. H. Hurning, the Jamestown City Engineer and an official of the MCRR who drew many of its early maps. Little development occurred, and HURNING disappeared from company literature about 1930, although the 21.78 acre site remained company property until the corporation was dissolved in 1970. (2, 3, 18, 79)

*Hurdsfield about 1910*

**HURON CITY** (Pembina). This was a platted townsite in Sec. 28-164-51, Pembina Twp., one mile north of Pembina in the absolute NE corner of ND, bounded on the north by Canada, and on the east by the Red River. It was one of four sites platted here in the 1880's at this intersection of ND, MN and Manitoba. Going clockwise from HURON CITY were West Emerson, Manitoba, Emerson, Manitoba, and Interapolis, MN. Only Emerson, Manitoba developed into a permanent settlement. The name honors the tribe of the Iroquois nation, whose name is of French derivation meaning ruffian or wild boar. (3, 10, 36)

**HURRICANE LAKE** (Pierce). This was an early stage station on the Devils Lake-Bottineau trail founded by Moses Levine in Sec. 2-157-69, Hurricane Lake Twp., six miles SE of Wolford. A post office was established November 26, 1886 with Fannie J. Halloway pm. She came here in 1885 and built a hotel at the north of Hurricane Lake, which was named to note the whirlwinds that frequently passed over its surface. William R. Runcorn (1861-1954) ran the post office for a few years, and later was succeeded by Otto Schultz, who moved the facility to Sec. 34-158-69, Union Twp. It closed August 31, 1905 with mail to Grasslake. (2, 25, 40, 79, 114, 236)

**HUTCHINSONVILLE** (Rolette). Alexander Hutchinson ran a saw mill in SW¼ Sec. 15-163-70, Baxter Twp., beginning in 1881, to which he later added a boarding house. After his death the mill was run by Barney Cain for a number of years. The site was at one time promoted as a rival townsite to Saint John, but it is now part of the Varty addition to Saint John. (2, 3, 18, 123)

**HYDE PARK** (Pembina). This was a farm post office established December 20, 1878 with James Hyde (1836-1914) pm. He came to this site, NE¼ Sec. 31-164-54, Felson Twp., in 1878 from Quebec, Canada. Some say it was named for John D. Hyde, another local settler, and others claim it was named for the famous park in London, England. The "park" probably notes the location in a wooded area along the Pembina River. In 1886 it moved to a rural community that was developing in NW¼ Sec. 1-163-55, Saint Joseph Twp., three miles SW of the original site. On July 20, 1895 the name was changed to HYDEPARK to conform to new government regulations for place names. (2, 3, 18, 25, 40, 79, 108, 235)

**HYDEPARK** (Pembina). On July 20, 1895 the HYDE PARK post office became HYDEPARK to conform to new government spelling regulations. The village had recorded a population of 28 in 1890, but it was now in decline. The post office closed December 31, 1902 with mail to Bay Center. It reopened February 16, 1903, but closed for good November 14, 1905 with mail to Neche. (2, 40, 108)

**HYLAND** (Towner). This was a country store in Sec. 8-160-65, Twin Hill Twp., operated by Julius C. Syfford, who established a post office January 10, 1903 in his store. The name is said to be coined from high land, descriptive of the locale. The post office closed November 30, 1905 with mail to Crocus, and Mr. Syfford moved his store six miles SSW to Egeland in 1906. (2, 3, 18, 40, 197)

**HYLAND PARK** (Cass). This place appears on some maps of the early 1880's in Sec. 13-141-53, Empire Twp., four miles NE of Absaraka. It was a proposed townsite on a proposed railroad, neither of which ever materialized. The origin of the name is unknown. (3, 414, 415)

**HYLAND PARK** (Stutsman). This was a resort platted by W. C. Hyland in 1925 in NW¼ Sec. 30-144-64, Kensal Twp., four miles SW of Kensal on the SE shore of Arrowwood Lake. A large pavilion was built for dances, but little other development took place. Today the site is a picnic grounds. (2, 3, 158)

# I

**IBSEN** (LaMoure). This was a rural post office established February 20, 1899 with Nicolai Nilson pm, located in NE¼ Sec. 8-135-59, Black Loam Twp., eleven miles NNW of Verona. It was named for the Norwegian poet and dramatist, Henrik Ibsen (1828-1906). It was adjacent to a country store run by Knute Saeter, and closed September 19, 1900 with mail to Verona. (2, 3, 4, 34, 40, 415)

**IMPERIAL** (Divide). This townsite was founded in 1906 in NW¼ Sec. 27-163-97, Fillmore Twp., three miles ENE of the original site of Crosby. It was a Soo Line RR station, apparently named to imply that it was the more important townsite in the area, its rival being the adjacent GNRR townsite of Crosby. The post office was established February 14, 1907 with Anna LaFlame pm. V. F. Snyder established a newspaper, *The Imperial News*, but beyond that it soon became apparent that Crosby would become the dominant townsite at this location. The post office closed November 15, 1907 with mail to Crosby, and in 1908 Crosby was replatted in SE¼ Sec. 29-163-97, about midway between the two original townsites. (1, 2, 3, 18, 34, 40, 73)

**INA** (Rolette). This was a Soo Line RR loading station built in 1905 in NW 1/4 Sec. 28-160-70, Union Twp., six miles east of Rolette. A post office was established December 31, 1909 with Jens A. Berg, and closed September 30, 1910 with mail to Rolette. It was named for a daughter of August Cooper, a local pioneer. Ina is a feminine suffix as used in names such as Paulina, Katherina, etc., that had a brief vogue as a name by itself. Two elevators and two houses were built, but one elevator burned down, and the other buildings were moved away. All that remained by 1953 was an abandoned pump. Sometime after 1910 the station was renamed UMBRIA. (2, 3, 18, 19, 40, 123)

**INDEPENDENCE** (Dunn). This was an early settlement founded in 1885 in Sec. 11-149-91 on the west bank of the Missouri River, opposite Lucky Mound in McLean County. The founder of the town, Wolf Chief of the Gros Ventres, named it to express his desire that his tribe be independent of other tribes at Fort Berthold. A Christian Day School was built here in 1894 by the Congregational Church, and St. Anthony's Catholic Church was built in 1912. John Stahl operated a ferry here 1927-1942. The site is now inundated by Lake Sakakawea. (1, 3, 18, 28)

**INDEPENDENCE** (LaMoure). This NPRR junction in Sec. 11-133-60, LaMoure Twp., five miles east of LaMoure was built in 1886 and called VALLEY JUNCTION. In 1897 the name was changed to OAKES JUNCTION, and on April 26, 1910 a post office was established here with David Sorenson pm. It was called INDEPENDENCE, a name chosen by local settlers who had come

here from Independence, WI, which was named by Giles Cripps in 1876 during the centennial celebration of American independence. A small village existed for a time, but the post office closed March 15, 1919 with mail to LaMoure. On November 20, 1919, eight months after the post office had closed, the NPRR officially changed the name of the junction from OAKES JUNCTION to INDEPENDENCE. (1, 2, 3, 18, 40, 70)

**INDIANA** (Mountrail). This was the first name of EPWORTH, but it was rejected by postal officials when papers were filed to replace the nearby rural post office of Dymond. The name apparently was the suggestion of a local resident with ties to the Hoosier State. (2, 3, 40, 72)

**INEZ** (Hettinger). This was a rural post office established August 26, 1912 with Wilburn Traylor pm. Mr. Traylor, a native of IN, came here in 1909 and was the local Justice of the Peace. It was located in SW¼ Sec. 14-136-93, Campbell Twp., fifteen miles north of Mott, and moved one mile SE to Sec. 24-136-93 in 1913. It closed May 15, 1916 with mail to Mott. The origin of the name, a female name of Greek-Spanish origin meaning pure, gentle, and meek, is unknown. (3, 18, 19, 40, 181)

**INGERSOLL** (McLean). This was a rural community in Sec. 20-146-81, Veeder Twp., seven miles ESE of Underwood, and named for Col. Robert Green Ingersoll (1833-1899), a Civil War veteran, lawyer, and agnostic lecturer. The name was chosen by John P. Lindeleaf, who came here in March 1883 from Rantoul, IL, and was an admirer of Col. Ingersoll. The post office was established December 4, 1883 with Mr. Lindeleaf pm, and a school was built in 1884. On October 27, 1887 the post office was moved one mile SE to the home of pm John O. Fjaerli in SE¼ Sec. 28-146-81. Col. Ingersoll died July 21, 1899, and on that date a tornado struck this site, turning the school on its foundation. The tale was later featured in a column of *Ripley's Believe It or Not*. The post office closed September 14, 1905 with mail to Underwood. (2, 3, 5, 18, 25, 28, 40, 390)

**INGOMAR** (Bowman). This Milwaukee Road RR townsite was founded in 1907 in N½ Sec. 18-131-100, Scranton Twp., between Bowman and Scranton. Some sources say it was named for Ingomar, TX, while others assume that it was named for a local Norwegian settler. When the post office was established July 18, 1907, the name was changed to BUFFALO SPRINGS. (2, 3, 34, 120, 381)

**INGRAM** (Richland). This was a Milwaukee Road RR station in Sec. 29-132-47, Dwight Twp., three miles north of Wahpeton. It was named for the Ingram brothers, gunsmiths at Wahpeton. The name is Teutonic for Ing's raven, Ing being a hero of Scandinavian

mythology. The site appears on maps circa 1910-1930. (1, 2, 3, 19, 147, 351)

**INKSTER** (Grand Forks). Founded as MATHIE in 1879, this rural settlement in Sec. 12-154-55, Inkster Twp., was renamed INKSTER when the post office was established August 9, 1880 with William Mathie pm. The name honored George T. Inkster, a local settler from a prominent family in Winnipeg, Manitoba, Canada, where a street is named for his uncle, John Inkster. George T. Inkster (1848-1901) later was a cattle rancher in the Souris River valley. In 1885 the post office moved to Secs. 13 & 24-154-55, the site of a new GNRR townsite, with a continuation of the old name. The elevation is 1040, the Zip Code is 58244, and a peak population of 368 was recorded in 1920, with a decline to 135 in 1980. (1, 2, 3, 18, 31, 33, 40, 69, 79, 293, 337)

**INTERLAKEN** (Steele). This was a rural settlement begun in the early 1880's in Sec. 2-147-55, Golden Lake Twp., nine miles NE of Finley. The name noted that it was located between Golden Lake and Swan Lake. When the post office was established February 26, 1885, it was named GOLDEN LAKE. (2, 3, 77, 99)

**INTERNATIONAL BOUNDARY** (Pembina). This place appears in commercial guides throughout the history of ND, and is the point at which the NPRR reaches the Canadian border just north of Pembina in Sec. 28-164-51, Pembina Twp. Railroad post office postmarks refer to this place as BOUNDARY LINE. (3)

**INVERLAC** (Morton). This was a NPRR siding built in 1966 in S½ Sec. 2-135-82, six miles SSW of Saint Anthony, on the newly-built shortcut line between Mandan and Flasher. No development occurred at the site, and the origin of the name is unknown. (3, 34)

**IOLA** (Ramsey). This was a farm post office established December 23, 1889, replacing the SCHAPERA post office located· four miles to the NW. IOLA was located in NW¼ Sec. 22-156-63, Harding Twp., seven miles NE of Webster, and was named by pm John A. G. Dahlen (1859-1954) for his hometown of Iola, WI, which was named for the daughter of Old Red Bird, a brother of Chief Waupaca of the Potawatomi tribe. She married a son of Chief Schenectady, and moved from WI to his home in NY. IOLA post office closed May 15, 1903 with mail to Benzion. Clyde Duffy (1890-1977), Lt. Governor of ND 1957-1959, was born here. (2, 3, 40, 70, 103, 414, 415)

**IONE** (LaMoure). This was a farm post office established March 3, 1903 with Fred T. Wood pm. It was located in Sec. 1-136-66, Glen Twp., seven miles north of Jud, and named for a local female settler. The post office was discontinued December 15, 1911 with mail to Alfred. (2, 3, 18, 40, 79)

**IOWA CITY** (Morton). This name was given to the new NPRR townsite in NW 1/4 Sec. 3-134-84, Flasher Twp., by founder William H. Brown to honor William F. Berrier, a native of IA who was to be its pm. The name was rejected by postal officials, who at the time were not allowing state names to be used for post offices. The name was changed to BERRIER, but this too was rejected. Finally, the townsite received an acceptable name, FLASHER. (3, 106)

**IRENE** (Cavalier). This post office was established September 15, 1905 with Henry F. Baker pm, replacing the Morton post office located five miles SSW of here. IRENE was located in Sec. 33-160-61, Loma Twp., six miles WNW of Nekoma, and was named for Irene Campbell, step-daughter of a storekeeper in the area. It is a Greek name meaning peace. On February 23, 1906 the name was changed to LOMA. (2, 3, 18, 19, 40)

**IRON HEART** (Benson). Iron Heart, a Sioux chief and veteran of the 1862 Minnesota uprising, later converted to Christianity, and sometime between 1867 and 1871 located in SW¼ Sec. 8-151-62, Minco Twp., at the extreme SE end of Devils Lake, about seven miles NE of Warwick. The site was the intersection of several early trails, including the much-used Grand Forks-Fort Totten trail. Chief Iron Heart built a mail station and hotel here, which operated into the 1890's. Ruins of the buildings still exist. (3, 417, 425)

**ISAAC** (Burleigh). This was a farm post office established November 21, 1902 with John Isaak pm. Postal authorities changed the spelling of his name, probably assuming that they were correcting an error, instead of making one. It was located in SW¼ Sec. 7-144-79, Wilson Twp., eleven miles NNE of Wilton in the extreme NW corner of Burleigh County. This township was named Hawkeye until 1914, when it was renamed for President Woodrow Wilson, even though few area residents were Democrats. The post office closed July 31, 1905 with mail to Wilton. Isaac is a Hebrew name meaning he who laughs. (2, 8, 12, 19, 40)

**ISLAND LAKE** (Rolette). This was a rural community in NE¼ Sec. 10-159-70, Island Lake Twp., named for the large lake near its center, which featured an island covered with trees. The lake has receded over the years, and the island is now a peninsula. The post office was established January 14, 1885 with Charles "Dugout" Beaver as pm, and in 1889 it was relocated to the Hanna Farm with James Hanna pm. A population of 20 was reported in 1890. The post office closed October 15, 1907 with mail to Mylo, four miles to the NE. (2, 3, 25, 40, 123, 257)

**IVAN** (Barnes). This was a Soo Line RR station built in 1892 in SW¼ Sec. 31-141-58, Getchell Twp., six miles NW of Valley City. The origin of the name, a Russian form of John, is unknown. In 1898 the station was renamed FAUST, and it was removed in 1939. (2, 19, 34)

**IVES** (Bowman). This Milwaukee Road RR station was built in 1907 in SW¼ Sec. 7-132-104, Rhame Twp., four miles NW of Rhame, and named for L. C. Ives of Co. G, 2nd MN Regiment, who fought in the Battle of the Killdeer Mountains on July 28, 1864, and on the fiftieth anniversary of this battle in 1914 he located the graves of its two casualities, George Northrup and Horatio Austin. A post office was established April 13, 1909 with Olof Iverson pm, but little development occurred at the site, and the post office closed March 15, 1916 with mail to Rhame. The only population figure reported was a surprisingly large count of 51 in 1930. (1, 2, 3, 18, 34, 40, 79, 120)

# J

*Jamestown about 1920*

**JACKSON** (Ramsey). This was a rural post office established March 11, 1884 with Jacob H. Fulkerson pm. It was located in NW¼ Sec. 9-154-66, Pelican Twp., four miles SW of Penn, and named for Abraham Jackson who led a group of homesteaders here in 1879 from Houston County, MN. A small settlement developed, reporting a population of 25 in 1890. Lars Ellingson was the last pm, closing the post office July 30, 1910 with mail to Churchs Ferry. (1, 2, 18, 40, 53, 103)

**JACOBSON** (Nelson). This was a rural post office established June 26, 1890 with Lars E. Jacobson, who came here about 1884 from Norway, as pm. It was located in SW¼ Sec. 4-150-59, Hamlin Twp., about five miles NE of Pekin. Jacob is a Hebrew name meaning the supplanter. Government records show the JACOBSON post office closing January 14, 1893 with the entry "no papers", and it is assumed that the facility never actually operated. (2, 3, 19, 40, 415)

**JAMESTOWN** (Stutsman). This NPRR townsite was founded in 1871 adjacent to Fort Seward and named by Gen. Thomas LaFayette Rosser for his hometown of Jamestown, VA, which also is on a James River. The names of all of these places ultimately trace to King James I of England (1566-1625). The post office was established December 23, 1872 with Arthur Wellesley Kelley (1832-1908) as pm. It incorporated as a village in 1881, and became a city in 1883 with J. J. Flint mayor. It is the county seat, and in 1883 and 1932 made unsuccessful attempts to become the capital city. The ND State Hospital was founded here in 1884, and the city is the home of Jamestown College. The elevation is 1497, the Zip Code is 58401, and the population has increased steadily to a high of 16,281 in 1980. Native sons include drugstore chain founder H. E. White and author Louis L'Amour (1908-1988). JAMESTOWN occupies much of Midway Twp. (140-64) and calls itself "The City Beautiful". (1, 2, 3, 13, 33, 40, 52, 79, 155, 157, 158)

**JAMESTOWN JUNCTION** (Stutsman). This was the junction of the Midland Continental RR and NPRR two miles SE of Jamestown in SW¼ Sec. 8-139-63, Homer Twp., just NE of Homer station. (2, 3, 158)

**JANESBURG** (Grant). This was a rural post office established December 13, 1894 with Henry E. Comfort pm. It was located in SW¼ Sec. 18-132-87, Janesburg Twp., eight miles south of Leith, from which it received mail three times each week. The origin of the name is unknown. The post office closed April 29, 1899 with mail to Wade, but reopened August 25, 1899. Mary L. Clark was the last pm, and she closed the facility for good on November 15, 1919 with mail to Leith. (1, 2, 3, 17, 18, 40, 53, 176, 177)

**JANET** (Dickey). This was a NPRR loading station built in 1901 in SE¼ Sec. 11-131-59, Bear Creek Twp., four miles NE of Oakes. The origin of the name is unknown. It is a variant of Jane, a Hebrew name used as a feminine form of John, meaning God's gracious gift. Jeanette is an erroneous spelling. (2, 3, 18, 19, 154)

**JARDINE** (Mountrail). This was an early GNRR station in Myrtle Twp. (156-94), between Manitou and White Earth. The origin of the name is unknown, and JARDINE has been found only on maps of the 1920's. (3, 377)

**JARVES** (Rolette). This was a rural post office established February 9, 1905 with Daniel Danielson pm. It was located in SW¼ Sec. 27-163-71, Hutchinson Twp., six miles SW of Saint John, and was named for nearby Jarves Lake, which was named for Fred Jarves who had surveyed this area in 1897. The post office closed November 30, 1921 with mail to Carpenter. Jarvis is an erroneous spelling. (2, 3, 18, 40, 123)

**JARVIS** (Towner). This was a GNRR loading station in NW¼ Sec. 17-159-67, Ideal Twp., three miles SE of Bisbee. F. E. Pew owned the site, which some say was named for Joseph Jarvis who settled here as early as 1872, while others say it was named for Jarvis, Ontario, Canada. The name is Teutonic and means keen as a spear. JARVIS appeared on maps circa 1905-1920. (1, 2, 18, 19, 79)

**JASPER** (Richland). This was a farm post office established October 18, 1883 with Joseph B. Wilcox pm, who named it for Joseph Jasper who settled in the Abercrombie area in 1873. Jasper is a name based on the precious stone worn by Hebrew high priests as a breastplate. It was located in Sec. 21-132-51, Danton Twp., three miles SE of Wyndmere, and closed November 19, 1883 with mail to Dwight. In 1891 the FLETCHER post office opened at this same site, changing its name to MOSELLE in 1892. It closed in 1900 but still appears on some maps. (2, 19, 40)

**J. D. SWITCH** (Ward). This GNRR station was the junction of the mainline and the temporary spur built to Tatman. It was located in Nedrose Twp. (155-82) between Minot and Surrey, and disappeared from maps in the 1970's. (3)

**JEANETTE** (McLean). This was a farm post office established June 23, 1905 with Peder Romsaas (1876-1939) pm. It was located in SE¼ Sec. 3-149-86, Romsaas Twp., eight miles east of Roseglen. The township was named Jeanette at this time, but the origin of the name is unknown. Located in a country store, the post office closed June 30, 1908 with mail to Oscar. All known postmarks from this post office are spelled JEANNETTE, and this spelling also is used on several maps, so it is debatable which spelling is correct. The site today is a military installation built in 1961 to control several underground missiles in the area. (2, 3, 28, 40, 277)

**JEANNETTE** (McLean). This is the spelling used on all known postmarks from the JEANETTE post office in SE¼ Sec. 3-149-86, Romsaas Twp., eight miles east of Roseglen which operated 1905-1908. (3, 40)

**JEFFERSON** (Bottineau). This GNRR station was founded in 1903 in Secs. 20 & 29-159-82, Elms Twp., six miles SE of Lansford, and named for Thomas Jefferson (1743-1826), 3rd President of the United States. The post office was established February 9, 1904 with Samuel J. Parker pm. On September 27, 1905 the name was changed to FORFAR. (2, 3, 18, 34, 40, 101, 153)

**JENKINS** (Stutsman). This was a rural post office established August 26, 1904 with William Jenkins pm, but the order was rescinded January 25, 1905. The exact location is unknown, although it is thought to have been in the Eldridge vicinity. (2, 3, 40)

**JENKSVILLE** (Cass). This was a farm post office established January 6, 1881 with Barnabus D. Wilcox pm. It was located in Sec. 22-137-54, Highland Twp., and named for his wife, whose maiden name was Jenks. It closed July 20, 1881 when it was relocated to the new NPRR townsite six miles to the south in Ransom County. Mr. Wilcox had purchased this townsite June 22, 1881, but sold it within a few days to E. E. Sheldon who took the liberty to see that it was renamed for himself. (2, 3, 40, 77, 85)

**JENKSVILLE** (Ransom). Barnabus D. Wilcox operated a rural post office named Jenksville about six miles north of here in Cass County. In anticipation of the NPRR he purchased the townsite in Secs. 17 & 20-136-54, Greene Twp., on June 22, 1881 for $3,200, and closed his post office July 20, 1881 with plans to reestablish it at the new location. It is quite certain that the site was known as JENKSVILLE for a short time, but within a few days Mr. Wilcox sold the townsite to E. E. Sheldon for $3,800, who renamed it for himself. (2, 3, 18, 280)

**JENNIE** (Morton). This was an NPRR siding on the branch line from Mandan to Mott, and was named for local resident Jennie Slayton. It was probably located in Sec. 31-138-80, seven miles SSE of Mandan, but little development occurred and it appeared only on a 1911 map published by the NPRR at the time of the line's construction. (2, 3, 432)

**JEROME** (Ward). This was a farm post office established May 19, 1906 with Herbert Jerome Young as the first and only pm. Jerome is a Greek name meaning of sacred name. It was located in NE¼ Sec. 13-152-85, Rice Lake Twp., ten miles north of Douglas, and closed January 31, 1914 with mail to Grelland. (2, 18, 19, 40, 100)

**JERUSALEM** (Ramsey). James G. Lamoreaux founded this town in 1881 in SE 1/4 Sec. 28-152-62, Odessa Twp., eight miles SSE of Crary at the east end of Devils Lake. He called the place LAKE CITY, but postal officials would not accept a two-word name, so Mr. Lamoreaux submitted JERUSALEM, not for religious reasons, but because he sought revenge and felt that it would be a difficult name to spell. One wonders why he didn't use his own name. The name of the holy city is derived from Greek, Hebrew, and Assyrian roots and is usually translated as the city of peace. The post office was established October 24, 1881 with Mr. Lamoreaux as pm. JERUSALEM included

a general store and a tavern, and reported a population of 35 in 1890. The post office closed March 31, 1914 with mail to Crary, and the building itself was demolished in 1940. (2, 10, 18, 40, 79, 103)

**JESSIE** (Griggs). This was a rural post office established October 14, 1884 with William Thomas McCulloch pm. It was located in SE¼ Sec. 14-147-60, Addie Twp., at the SE end of Jessie Lake. The lake was named in 1839 by Lt. John C. Fremont, the famous explorer, for his fiancee Jessie Benton, the daughter of Sen. John D. Benton of KY. Jessie is a form of Jessica, a Hebrew name meaning grace of god. In 1899 the NPRR built a townsite five miles WSW in NW¼ Sec. 19-147-59, Tyrol Twp., which was at first called MELLEMVILLE, but pm Wilson J. Humimer moved the JESSIE post office to the new townsite later that year and retained the old name. The elevation is 1487, the Zip Code is 58452, and the population has always been less than 100. (1, 2, 3, 10, 18, 19, 25, 33, 40, 65, 79, 284)

**JEWELL** (McIntosh). This was a farm post office established July 14, 1886 with Jacob Mayer pm, who named it for Marshall H. Jewell (1857-1911), the editor of *The Bismarck Tribune*, who made several trips to this area and was a leading promoter of settlement here. The post office was located in NW 1/4 Sec. 4-129-68, Jewell Twp., eight miles east of Ashley. In 1898 it moved three miles SSW to NE¼ Sec. 19-129-68, the home of new pm Andrew Linn (1822-1909). W. A. Linn was the last pm, closing the facility January 15, 1906 with mail to Ashley. (2, 3, 23, 25, 40, 211)

**JIM LAKE** (Stutsman). This place appears on some maps of the early 1880's in Sec. 33-143-64, Jim River Valley Twp., on the SW shore of what was then called Jim Lake, actually one of a series of natural widenings of the James River. The town never developed and the site is now inundated by the Jamestown Reservoir. (3, 414)

**JIM RIVER CROSSING** (Wells). This was the slang name used by pioneers for a much-used crossing of the James River in Sec. 19-149-71, Manfred Twp., just NW of present-day Manfred. (2, 3, 18)

**JOE** (McKenzie). This was a rural post office established August 15, 1913 with Fred Horstman pm at his home in NW¼ Sec. 17-148-103, sixteen miles SW of Alexander. Mr. Horstman had submitted the names Frederick, Ida, Joe, Gunder, Center, and Horse Creek, and postal officials chose JOE, which honored Joe Stroud who came here from TX in 1891 with his brother Robert. The post office closed June 30, 1916 with mail to Moline. (1, 2, 3, 40, 227, 414)

**JOHNSON** (McLean). This was a farm post office established June 13, 1906 with Mary A. Johnson pm at her home in Sec. 20-150-86, Blue Hill Twp., nine miles SSW of Ryder. The order was rescinded September 11, 1906 before operations could begin. (2, 28, 40, 277)

**JOHNSON** (Stutsman). This was a Midland Continental RR loading station built about 1920 in Sec. 4-140-62, Spiritwood Twp., four

miles NNW of Spiritwood. It was named for J. A. Johnson, an area farmer, and is sometimes shown as Johnson Spur and Johnson's. No development took place at the site, although a population of 15 was reported in 1960. (1, 3, 38, 158)

**JOHNSONS CORNERS** (McKenzie). This is the junction of ND Highways 23 and 73, sixteen miles east of Watford City. Since about 1930 the site has been at the corner of Secs. 14, 15, 22 & 23-150-96, with most development in NE¼ Sec. 22-150-96. There have been several Johnson families in this area over the years, but the name is thought to honor L. L. Johnson, who lived in NW¼ Sec. 14-150-96, just west of the rural school, as early as 1916. Johnson's Corner and Johnson Corners are alternate spellings of the name. (3, 18, 34, 229)

**JOHNSON'S SIDING** (Pembina). This was a way station on the short-lived Northern Dakota RR, built in 1909 in Sec. 27-161-56, Beaulieu Twp., three miles east of Concrete. Several Johnsons lived in this area, but it seems most likely that the station was named for Wilfred Johnson, who farmed in this section during the station's existence. It was removed in 1920. (1, 3, 108, 436)

**JOHNSTOWN** (Grand Forks). This rural settlement was called MILAN, but when the post office was established December 13, 1880 with John Ryan Barker pm, it was renamed JOHNSTOWN. Some say it was named for the pm, while others say it was named for townsite owner Isaac N. Johnson. Both men claimed the honor during their own lifetimes. A third theory exists stating that the name honors the three members of the first township board, the pm, John Gabb, and John Sparks. It was located in NE¼ Sec. 20-154-53, Johnstown Twp., until 1887 when it moved one-half mile east to the new NPRR townsite in NW¼ Sec. 21-154-53. The population has remained at about 50 since its founding. On January 3, 1964 the post office, Zip Code 58245, became a rural branch of Gilby. (1, 2, 18, 31, 38, 40, 69, 79, 338)

**JOLIETTE** (Pembina). This was a rural post office established August 7, 1879 with John R. Rivitt pm. It was located in Sec. 35-162-51, Joliette Twp., and moved one mile WNW to the new NPRR townsite in Secs. 27 & 34-162-51 in the 1880's. Frank LaRose, the first settler in the area, named it for his hometown of Joliette, Quebec, Canada, which was founded in 1823 by saw mill operator Barthelemy Joliette. The elevation is 821, the Zip Code is 58246, and a peak population of 319 was recorded in 1930, with a sharp decline to just 36 in 1960. (1, 2, 10, 18, 25, 38, 40, 79, 108)

**JORDAN** (Hettinger). This was a planned townsite on the Dickinson, Lefor, & New Leipzig RR proposed in 1917 but never built. The town was to have been in Sec. 19-136-93, Campbell Twp., about sixteen miles NNW of Mott, and named for pioneer settler Frank Jordan. Mr. Jordan was born Frank Jorda, and lived three miles to the north in SE¼ Sec. 6-136-93. (3, 18, 74)

**JOSEPHINE** (Benson). This NPRR townsite

was founded in 1901 in SW¼ Sec. 36-152-68, Aurora Twp., on the site of the pioneer settlement of GENIN. It was named by Dr. Frank Wheelon, a railroad official, for Dr. Josephine Lindstrom Stickelberger (1870-1962), a pioneer settler in the area and one of ND's first female physicians. Josephine is the feminine form of Joseph, a Hebrew name meaning he shall add. The post office was established May 3, 1902 with Frank D. Hoadley pm, and closed April 30, 1906 with mail to Oberon. It reopened June 13, 1906 and closed for good June 30, 1943 with mail again to Oberon. The townsite was platted in 1901 but never incorporated, and the only population report was a count of 30 in 1920. Two vacant elevators and the old railroad sign remained here in 1983 to mark the site. (2, 3, 18, 19, 34, 40, 79, 110, 239)

**JOSLYN** (Renville). This was a rural post office established January 12, 1888 with Frank P. Madison pm. It was located in NW¼ Sec. 1-160-86, Roosevelt Twp., four miles ESE of Tolley, and was the first post office in what is now Renville County. The name honored E. E. Joslyn and his cousin Clyde Joslyn, both of whom were pioneers in the area and cousins of Otis F. McKinney, the namesake of that pioneer village. On December 19, 1905 the post office was relocated to the new townsite of Tolley, assuming that name. (2, 3, 25, 40, 71, 75, 79, 240, 322)

**JUANITA** (Foster). This GNRR station was founded in 1911 in SW¼ Sec. 34-147-63, Florence Twp., on the Surrey cutoff line. The name came from the nearby lake which had been known as Townsend, Smith, and Belland before being named Wanitah by newspaperman A. L. Lowden in 1900. Wanitah is thought to be an Indian name, but for some reason the townsite planners changed the spelling into the Spanish form, which is the feminine version of Juan, or John, a Hebrew name meaning God's gracious gift. The post office was established October 26, 1911 with William Walter Hazlett, a native of PA, as pm. The elevation is 1508, and a peak population of 150 was claimed in 1920, although the count is less than 50 now. The post office, Zip Code 58453, closed May 7, 1985. (1, 2, 3, 19, 38, 40, 79, 97)

**JUD** (LaMoure). This townsite was founded in 1904 in NE¼ Sec. 7-135-65, Bluebird Twp., in anticipation of the NPRR which arrived in 1905. It was platted as FOX, but the post office was established as GUNTHORP. On October 4, 1906 the name was changed to JUD, honoring Judson LaMoure (1839-1918), the famous politician who was also the namesake of the county. Orcutt R. Bennett was the first pm. The elevation is 1745, the Zip Code is 58454, and the village, which incorporated in 1909, reached a peak population of 202 in 1940. (1, 2, 3, 18, 33, 40, 79, 94, 141)

**JUDSON** (Morton). This NPRR townsite was first settled in the 1890's. It was located in NW¼ Sec. 27-139-84, Dettman Twp., seven miles east of New Salem, and named for pioneer politician Judson LaMoure (1839-1918). The post office was established October 3, 1901 with Henry M. Seethoff

pm. The elevation is 1971, and a peak population of over 200 was reached between the two World Wars, although the town has experienced a sharp decline in recent years. The post office, Zip Code 58548, became a rural branch of New Salem on February 9, 1968, and closed August 10, 1979 with mail to New Salem. (1, 2, 3, 17, 18, 33, 38, 40, 107, 109, 144)

**JUNCTION** (Traill). This is the junction of the GNRR lines running through Mayville and Portland. Located in SE¼ Sec. 11-147-53, Viking Twp., four miles north of Portland, this name appears on maps of the 1890's, and was later renamed PORTLAND JUNCTION. (3, 25)

**JUNCTION SWITCH** (Burleigh). This is the crossing of the NPRR mainline and the Soo Line RR in Sec. 2-138-80, Lincoln Twp., in what is now the eastern part of Bismarck near the ND Penitentiary. The name appears on maps circa 1900-1920. (3, 14, 18)

**JUNE** (Dunn). This was a farm post office established June 17, 1907 with Lewis Y. June pm at his home in N½ Sec. 14-149-93, seven miles SW of Halliday. June is a Latin name meaning youthful. It closed February 29, 1908 with mail to Rockspring. (2, 3, 18, 19, 40)

**JUNIATA** (Pierce). This was a rural post office established August 21, 1901 with Charles M. Guss pm. It was located in SE¼ Sec. 23-158-71, Juniata Twp., four miles WSW of Wolford. Mr. Guss had led a group of settlers here from Juniata, PA, which has an Indian name meaning they stay long, or beyond the great bend. The post office closed April 30, 1906 with mail to Pleasant Lake. (2, 10, 18, 40, 53, 114)

**JUNIPER** (McKenzie). This townsite was founded about 1915 in SW¼ Sec. 25-149-97, thirteen miles SE of Watford City. It owed its existance to a planned extension of the GNRR from Watford City to New Rockford, but JUNIPER failed to develop when these plans were abandoned. The name notes the native evergreen trees in the area. (2, 3, 34, 53)

**JUNKERS** (Richland). This was a Soo Line RR station in Sec. 17-131-50, Belford Twp., just south of present-day Mantador. It was named for C. H. Junkers, an official of the Keystone Farm at this site, although some claim, tongue-in-cheek, that the name noted the fact that the railroad left worn out equipment at the site. It was built in 1886 and replaced the following year by the new townsite of Mantador. Junker is an erroneous spelling. (2, 3, 18, 147)

**JUNKET** (Williams). This was a GNRR loading station built about 1888 in NW 1/4 Sec. 32-154-101, Williston Twp., about three miles SW of Williston. The origin of the name is unknown, and the station was abandoned about 1930. (3, 50)

**JUNO** (Divide). This was a GNRR siding in Sec. 31-163-96, Long Creek Twp., one mile south of the Soo Line RR siding called Bounty. Both were located about six miles east of Crosby. The site was owned by Henry Jacob-

son, and named for the queen of heaven and wife of Jupiter in Roman mythology. JUNO was shown on maps until about 1950. (3, 18, 19, 34)

**JUNO** (Rolette). This was a farm post office established March 19, 1904 with John Halls pm at his farm in NW¼ Sec. 7-162-73, Gilbert Twp., seven miles NW of Dunseith. The name, in phonetic form, honored Francois Jeanotte (1806-1905), the son of French trapper Justras Jeanotte and Assiwenotok, a Turtle Mountain Indian, who spent most of his long life in this area. The order for the post office was rescinded, but shortly thereafter Simon Johnson applied for a post office to be called WILLOW LAKE at his home in SW¼ Sec. 6-162-73, just across the section line to the north. This name was rejected because of the ban on two-word place names, and on January 25, 1905 Mr. Johnson opened the facility with the original name of JUNO. The post office closed March 15, 1914 with mail to Dunseith. (1, 2, 3, 18, 40, 123)

# K

**KAHLER** (Benson). This was a farm post office authorized May 23, 1901 with Andrew J. Feiring pm, at his home in Sec. 14-154-71, Impark Twp., just east of the new townsite of Fillmore near Cranberry Lake. This order was rescinded on June 10, 1902. On July 28, 1903 it was again authorized with Gust Johnson pm, but on March 4, 1904 this order was rescinded. This post office-to-be was named for Mrs. Lloyd Harwood, nee Eva Kahler, who came here in 1898 with her husband from Cass County, MI. (2, 18, 34, 40)

**KAISER** (Grant). This Milwaukee Road RR townsite was founded in 1911 in NE 1/4 Sec. 31-134-88, Elm Twp., two miles SE of Elgin, and named for local farmer William Kaiser, known locally as "Kaiser Bill." *The Carson Press* noted on December 8, 1910 that pm Charles H. Davidson (sic) had moved the Elm post office to the new townsite, but government records give the official date for the establishment of the KAISER post office as February 20, 1911 with Charles H. Davison pm. There was some initial interest in the townsite, but its proximity to Elgin led to a quick decline. The depot was moved into Elgin in 1914, and the post office closed June 30 of that year with mail to Elgin. The settlement persisted for several years, changing its name to KARY during World War I due to anti-German sentiments. (1, 2, 3, 17, 23, 40, 176, 177, 414)

**KALUGA** (McHenry). This was a Soo Line RR station in Sec. 30-152-75, Schiller Twp., between Drake and Funston. It was named for the Russian city and district of Kaluga, just southwest of Moscow. No development occurred. Kuluga is an erroneous spelling. (2, 3, 18)

**KANDEL** (Pierce). Roman Catholic Germans from Russia came here in 1903 and started a rural community centered around St. Mathias Church in SW¼ Sec. 15-153-74, Elling Twp., just SW of Orrin to which the community had merged by 1917. The name came from the Kandel area of South Russia, which had been settled by ancestors of these pioneers in 1808. (3, 23, 114)

**KANDIOTTA** (Sargent). This rural post office was established July 2, 1883 in SW¼ Sec. 20-131-54, Shuman Twp., eight miles south of Milnor, with Anna L. Canfield pm. It was named for nearby Lake Kandiotta, which bears a Wahpeton Indian name meaning buffalo fish, which were plentiful here. Sibley's Expedition of 1863 called the lake Buffalo Lake. Mail service came from Hamlin. The post office was discontinued November 16, 1887 with mail to Milnor. (2, 25, 40, 79, 165, 171)

**KAPETO** (McLean). This was a farm post office established June 5, 1884 with Anton Peterson, a native of Denmark, as pm. It was located in NE¼ Sec. 2-145-82, Buffalo Lake Twp., four miles SE of Underwood, and clos-

ed October 20, 1885 with mail to Weller. The origin of the name is unknown. (3, 6, 25, 28, 40, 415)

**KARLOPOLIS** (Stutsman). This was a rural post office established September 12, 1889 with Thomas Jefferson Young pm. It was located in SW¼ Sec. 2-143-62, Courtenay Twp., three miles east of Courtenay, and closed February 28, 1894 with mail to Courtenay. The origin of the name is unknown. (2, 40, 415)

**KARLSRUHE** (McHenry). The first settlers arrived in this area about 1902, with many of them being German Catholics. A GNRR station was built here in 1912 in Sec. 7-153-77, Karlsruhe Twp., on the Surrey cutoff line. The post office was established May 15, 1912 with John E. Sauer pm. The village was named for Karlsruhe, Baden, Germany, and translates literally as Charles' rest. The elevation is 1546, the Zip Code is 58744, and the village, which incorporated in 1927, reached a peak population of 289 in 1940. (1, 2, 3, 18, 33, 40, 44, 52, 79)

**KARNAK** (Griggs). This GNRR station was built in 1910 in NW¼ Sec. 20-144-58, Broadview Twp., between Luverne and Hannaford. It was first called FAIRVIEW, but because of confusion it was renamed KARNAK on November 20, 1912. The new name was said to have been chosen at random by GNRR officials, taking the name from Karnak, IL, which was named for the ancient city of Egypt, also known as Thebes. The post office was established February 27, 1913 with John J. Hogness pm, and a small village began. The elevation is 1410, and a peak population of 90 was reported in 1920, with a decline to just 9 in 1960. The post office closed August 31, 1954 with mail to Hannaford. (1, 2, 38, 40, 65, 79)

**KARY** (Grant). This Milwaukee Road RR townsite was founded in 1911 in NE 1/4 Sec. 31-134-88, Elm Twp., two miles SE of Elgin, and named KAISER. The post office and depot closed in 1914, but the town lingered on, changing its name to KARY for local saloon owner Philip Kary in 1917 because of anti-German sentiments during World War I. Carl Schmidt ran the elevator, and Adolph Hartstein had a general store, but both eventually moved to Elgin, and the siding was removed in 1942. (2, 3, 17, 177)

**KASMER** (Mercer). This was a small community located in SE¼ Sec. 21-146-88, about eleven miles north of Zap. The post office was established March 12, 1908 with Kasmer Mastel pm. J. B. Field of MN opened a bank in 1911, Ole Viken started a creamery, and Eli Gunderson opened a general store, but when the NPRR passed far to the south the village was doomed. The post office closed January 31, 1915 with mail to Ree. (2, 3, 18, 40, 53, 64, 414)

**KASSEL** (McIntosh). This was a farm post of-

fice established October 18, 1893 with Jacob Breitling pm in his home in NW¼ Sec. 15-129-72, Berlin Twp., six miles west of Venturia. It was named for the district in South Russia that had been the homeland of many area settlers. Mr. Breitling (1862-1928) came here in 1884 from South Russia, and was later a county judge and treasurer. The post office was moved a few years later to the home of Friedrich Strobel in NE¼ Sec. 10-129-72. In 1904 it moved two miles WSW to NE¼ Sec. 17-129-72, the home of pm Christian Rempfer, who closed the facility May 13, 1905 with mail to Ashley. Kessel is an erroneous spelling. (2, 3, 18, 40, 134, 211)

**KATHRYN** (Barnes). This NPRR townsite was founded in 1900 in W½ Sec. 14-137-58, Oak Hill Twp., and named for Kathryn Mellon, the daughter of NPRR President Charles S. Mellon. It was platted in September 1900 by John Runck on land purchased from Frank Lynch of Casselton, and the post office was established February 6, 1901 with John K. Dye pm. The elevation is 1238, the Zip Code is 58049, and the village, which incorporated in 1917, reached a peak population of 289 in 1920, but has declined to just 95 in 1980. (1, 2, 3, 18, 19, 34, 40, 76, 79)

**KAYTOWN** (Dickey). This was a rural settlement founded in 1883 in Sec. 31-129-59, Lovell Twp., and named for Edward F. Kay, one of the original settlers. Later that year postal officials changed the name to TICEVILLE because of confusion with Keystone. (3, 264)

**KEENE** (McKenzie). Several families, mostly Scandinavians, came here in 1905 from Ulen, Keene Twp., Clay County, MN, which had been named for a Civil War veteran who homesteaded there. The post office was established May 13, 1911 with Swend A. Martinson pm at his home in SE¼ Sec. 11-152-96, Keene Twp. The name KEENE was adopted only after Mr. Martinson's suggested name of Pioneer had been rejected. By 1915 a small townsite had begun to develop, and the post office was moved to the drugstore run by new pm Olof T. Kjorlaug. A population of 26 was reported in 1920. In October 1934 pm Catherine Schuman moved the facility five miles SSW to NW¼ Sec. 2-151-96, Blue Butte Twp., which was the site of a new community called UNION CENTER. There is evidence that the actual move had taken place as early as October 15, 1932. Within a short time, KEENE was almost universally accepted as the name of the new location. This small settlement about twenty miles NE of Watford City still exists, although its population has never exceeded 50. The Zip Code is 58847. (1, 2, 3, 13, 18, 33, 40, 228, 253)

**KEGO** (Cass). This place appears on current maps published by Hearne Brothers, and is shown just south of Fargo in the area occupied by several of the incorporated rural subdivisions that were conceived in the 1970's. An official of the map company hedges that KEGO might be a copyright town. (3)

**KEITH** (Ramsey). This GNRR loading station was built in 1885 in NE¼ Sec. 9-153-63, South Minnewaukan Twp., between Devils Lake and Crary. Real development at the site never occurred. A post office was established Feburary 6, 1900 with Charles Anderson pm, but it closed June 15, 1905 with mail to Devils Lake. The origin of the name is unknown, although it is a Welsh name meaning wood-dweller. After the post office closed, the site was sometimes called Keith Station, but the station itself was removed about 1944. (2, 18, 19, 40, 103)

**KELLOGG** (Walsh). This was a NPRR station in NE¼ Sec. 3-156-53, Walsh Centre Twp., about four miles SSW of Grafton, named for H. C. Kellogg, a pioneer settler from Plainfield, WI. The post office was established January 15, 1898 with Frank J. Votava pm, and closed June 5, 1910 with mail to Grafton. (1, 2, 18, 40, 75, 79)

**KELLY** (Richland). This townsite was established, platted, and promoted by Col. Richard H. Hankinson in 1886 on the shore of Lake Elsie in SW¼ Sec. 26-130-50, Brightwood Twp. Col. Hankinson was appointed pm of the post office on November 13, 1886, with the facility to be located in his general store, but before it could become functional the order was rescinded by postal officials, and everything moved two miles NE to the new townsite of Hankinson on the GNRR and Soo Line RR. The origin of the name KELLY is unknown. (2, 3, 40, 360)

**KELLYS** (Grand Forks). This was the post office serving the adjacent NPRR station of KELLY'S STATION in SE¼ Sec. 13-152-52, Blooming Twp., ten miles WNW of Grand Forks. It was established February 14, 1889 with Daniel B. Thompson pm, and named for Henry and Mary Kelly, who operated an inn for travelers at the site, although others say it was named for Byron St. Clair Kelly, a pioneer mostly associated with Walsh County. E. H. A. Fischer ran a general store here for many years as a small village of about 10 people developed. The post office closed October 15, 1935 with mail to Grand Forks. Kelley's, Kelly's, and Kelly are erroneous spellings. (1, 2, 3, 25, 31, 38, 40, 69, 338)

**KELLY'S POINT** (Walsh). This Red River port dates from about 1871, when Byron St. Clair Kelly established a stage station in Sec. 25-157-51, Acton Twp., due east of Grafton on the river. The post office was established August 23, 1878 with Antoine Girard pm, and a townsite was platted in 1879. On May 27, 1879 the name was changed to ACTON. Kelley's Point is an erroneous spelling. (2, 3, 40, 75, 79)

**KELLY'S STATION** (Grand Forks). This NPRR station was built in 1881 in SE 1/4 Sec. 13-152-52, Blooming Twp., ten miles WNW of Grand Forks, and named for Henry and Mary Kelly, who operated an inn at the site. Others claim it was named for Walsh County pioneer Byron St. Clair Kelly. The station was removed in September 1957. A

post office called KELLYS operated here 1889-1935. (2, 3, 31, 33, 40, 69, 338)

**KELNER** (Walsh). This was a farm post office established June 2, 1884 with Norman Kelner pm. It was located in Sec. 23-155-55, Eden Twp., at approximately the same site as the earlier community called EDEN. Later in 1884 a GNRR townsite was founded in NE¼ Sec. 23-155-55, which adopted the name CONWAY from another nearby rural post office, although Mr. Kelner became its pm, changing KELNER on January 12, 1885. Kilner is an erroneous spelling. (2, 3, 18, 40, 75)

**KELSO** (Traill). This GNRR station was founded in 1880 in NE¼ Sec. 5-144-50, Kelso Twp., and named SAFFORD. On February 1, 1882 pm Augustus L. Wentworth, who came here from ME in 1879, changed the name to KELSO for its township, which was named for Kelso, MO, which was named for Kelso, Scotland, a city on the Tweed River. Some say it was named for a GNRR official. The site never experienced a boom, with a peak population of just 50 in 1890. The post office closed October 6, 1967 with mail to Hillsboro. (1, 2, 3, 13, 18, 25, 29, 40, 79, 187)

**KELVIN** (Pembina). This was a rural post office established February 13, 1886 with Reuben F. Kenney pm, but the order was rescinded August 27, 1887 with the entry "no papers" in government records. The location and name origin are unknown, although it has been suggested that it was named for William Thomson, Lord Kelvin (1824-1907), the British mathematician and physicist who made a much-publicized visit to the United States in 1884. (2, 3, 5, 40)

**KELVIN** (Rolette). This was a rural community founded in 1888 in Sec. 24-163-73, Willow Lake Twp., and named for the British physicist William Thomson, Lord Kelvin (1824-1907) by local storekeeper Albert Hurst. The post office was established January 7, 1901 with James S. Leyde pm. During the 1930's it moved a mile NNE to Secs. 13 & 24-163-73 to take advantage of traffic on the newly-built ND Highway 3. The post office closed December 21, 1953 with mail to Dunseith. The population had never been listed as higher than 10. (2, 5, 18, 38, 40, 123)

**KEMPTON** (Grand Forks). This GNRR station was founded in 1884 in E½ Sec. 7-150-54, Avon Twp., six miles south of Larimore, and named for W. S. Kemp, a GNRR roadmaster. The post office was established March 16, 1887 with Elmer A. Bickford pm, who came here in 1886 as the manager of the Cargill elevator. The elevation is 1110, and a thriving village existed here for a time with an exaggerated population of 216 being reported in 1930. The actual population has probably never exceeded 100. The post office, Zip Code 58247, became a rural branch of Northwood on August 2, 1963, and closed altogether October 31, 1970, with mail to Northwood. (1, 2, 3, 25, 33, 38, 40, 41, 69, 79, 241)

**KENASTON** (Ward). This GNRR station was founded in 1906 in NE¼ Sec. 12-159-89, Spencer Twp., four miles SSW of Kenmare, and named for F. E. Kenaston, President of

the Minneapolis Thresher Co. and a stockholder of the GNRR. The post office was established October 23, 1907 with Thomas Dodds pm. A village of about 50 people existed for many years, but a decline began after World War II and the post office closed July 2, 1965 with mail to Kenmare. (1, 2, 3, 18, 40, 100)

**KENMARE** (Ward). A settlement named LIGNITE existed here 1894-1896, mainly to support local lignite mines. In 1897 a new settlement was founded in Secs. 17, 18, 19 & 20-160-88, Kenmare Twp., and named KENMARE by the wife of a Soo Line RR official for Kenmare, Ireland. The post office was established April 30, 1897 with John H. Clapper pm. The village was platted in May 1899, and incorporated in December 1901. It has maintained a population of about 1,500 for many years, with a peak of 1,712 in 1950. Its elevation is 1799, the Zip Code is 58746, and it claims to be the only city in ND with its business district built around a central park. It is the principal city of Ward County's so-called "Gooseneck", which resulted when neighboring Burke and Renville Counties excluded the region to prevent KENMARE from becoming the county seat of either of the new counties. (1, 2, 3, 18, 33, 40, 52, 79, 100)

**KENNEDY** (Hettinger). This was a rural community founded in 1908 in NE¼ Sec. 34-133-97, Kennedy Twp., seventeen miles SW of Regent on the Star Mail Route from Reeder. The post office was established July 15, 1908 with William H. Kennedy pm, and closed November 30, 1915 with mail to Reeder. (2, 18, 40, 53, 179)

**KENSAL** (Stutsman). This Soo Line RR station was founded in 1892 in Sec. 12-144-64, Kensal Twp., and named by local settlers for their former home of Kensale, county Cork, Ireland, although some say it was named for an early surveyor in Stutsman County. The post office was established August 16, 1893 with George F. Armstrong of the nearby Arrowwood post office taking over the new facility. John Putnam and C. J. Croonquist opened the first stores, and the village incorporated in 1907. The elevation is 1541, the Zip Code is 58455, and a peak population of 456 was reached in 1910 with a decline to 210 in 1980. (1, 2, 3, 18, 33, 40, 52, 79, 158, 161)

**KENSINGTON** (Walsh). This was a rural community in the heart of a colony of Scandinavian immigrants. The post office was established September 23, 1879 with Edwin O. Faulkner pm. The name was suggested by a Canadian settler for Kensington, England, a borough of London. A village of this name in MN was founded in 1887 by Gen. William D. Washburn, later to have a major influence in central ND, and was the site of the discovery of the famous Viking runestone in 1898. The ND community was located in Sec. 11-158-55, Kensington Twp., about six miles north of Park River. The post office closed September 15, 1884 with mail to Park River. (2, 10, 13, 25, 40, 75)

**KENYON** (Grant). This was a farm post office established May 15, 1912 with John Kennedy pm. It was located in Sec. 18-136-86, midway between Almont and Carson, and named for Kenyon, MN, which was named in 1855 for a pioneer storekeeper, while others say its name was based on the pm's name, which was already being used by a post office in Hettinger County. The KENYON post office closed November 30, 1912 with mail to Almont. (2, 3, 13, 17, 40, 177)

**KEOGH** (Stark). This place honors Patrick Keogh, a native of Ireland, who came here in 1882 and was associated with NPRR interests until his death in 1909. He promoted, without success, a settlement at the Knife River siding west of Hebron, and NPRR officials erected a commemorative plaque in SE¼ Sec. 24-140-91, just NW of Hebron, which is shown on some maps although it is likely that the site was never intended to be developed as a townsite. (3, 18, 104)

**KERMIT** (Divide). This Soo Line RR townsite was founded in the summer of 1906 in Sec. 30-163-95, Mentor Twp., two miles NW of Noonan. The post office was established December 28, 1906 with Ole O. Christenson pm, and the village incorporated in 1907. The name is said to honor President Theodore Roosevelt's son, Kermit, who was killed in World War I, and was suggested by Ambrose Olson, a Soo Line RR official. Kermit is a Celtic name derived from Kermode, which in turn was a contraction of MacDermott, which means son of Diarmaid, the god of arms. A population of 108 was reported in 1910, but it declined sharply to just 23 in 1940, and the post office closed October 31, 1943 with mail to Noonan. (2, 3, 18, 19, 33, 40, 52, 79)

**KERRY** (Walsh). This was a GNRR station in Sec. 6-157-55, Kensington Twp., between Park River and Edinburg, but no settlement occurred at the site. The origin of the name is unknown, although it is a Celtic name meaning the dark, and is the name of a county in Ireland. (1, 2, 3, 18, 19, 75)

**KERTZMAN** (Emmons). This post office was first authorized as KURTZMAN on March 6, 1919 with Gail Wade pm, but she declined the appointment. John S. Schott was named pm on July 3, 1919, but the name was entered as KERTZMAN. It was located in NE¼ Sec. 28-136-76, two miles south of the Dana siding, and closed June 15, 1922 with mail to Hazelton. It is thought that the name was intended to honor the Kurtz family of this area, but the apparent error coincides with the family name of John C. Kertzman (1893-1967), who came here in 1911, served on the Dana school board, and in 1937 was named "ND Corn King." Many local sources insist that this post office was named for him, although when it was established Mr. Kertzman was a young, virtually unknown farmer in the area. (2, 3, 40, 66, 401, 414)

**KEYES SPUR** (Dickey). This was a Soo Line RR siding built in 1917 in NW 1/4 Sec. 22-131-61, Yorktown Twp., six miles east of Fullerton. The locally used name was BALDWIN, but because of confusion with Baldwin, Burleigh County, also on the Soo Line RR, timetables called the site KEYES SPUR, for George H. Keyes, an associate of George Baldwin. Both men were natives of WI, and Mr. Keyes was active in county

politics, serving as a county commissioner. The elevator was moved to Westport, SD in 1953. (2, 3, 154)

**KEYS COVE** (Williams). This is a resort community on the north shore of Lake Sakakawea in NW¼ Sec. 14-154-97, Nesson Valley Twp., twelve miles SSE of Ray. It first appeared on maps in the late 1960's, and was named for developer James G. Key. (3, 34, 50)

**KEYSTONE** (Dickey). This pioneer settlement was founded in 1882 by settlers from PA, "The Keystone State," so named because it was in the center, or keystone, position geographically among the original thirteen colonies. The community in Sec. 10-131-63, Keystone Twp., two miles east of Monango, was usually called KEYSTONE CITY, but the post office was established July 5, 1882 as KEYSTONE with William A. Caldwell pm. Bypassed by the Milwaukee Road RR in 1886, most residents moved to the new site of Monango. The post office closed September 17, 1886, being replaced by the Monango post office which was established the following day. (3, 40, 154, 264)

**KEYSTONE CITY** (Dickey). This pioneer settlement was founded in March 1882 in Sec. 10-131-63, Keystone Twp., two miles east of Monango, by settlers from PA, "The Keystone State." A population of 51 was reported during the first summer, and the new town seemed destined for success, but the Milwaukee Road RR bypassed the site in 1886, and most residents moved to Monango. The Soo Line RR was to have built through here in 1890, but they too bypassed the site, and KEYSTONE CITY became a ghost town. The KEYSTONE post office operated here 1882-1886. (2, 3, 25, 40)

**KEYSTONE JUNCTION** (Richland). This was a NPRR station built in the 1890's at the corner of Secs. 10, 11, 14 & 15-131-49, Brandenburg Twp., just north of Great Bend. It served a farm colony at a large bonanza farm, and was named by settlers from PA, "The Keystone State." (2, 3, 13, 18)

**KIBBY** (Barnes). This townsite was founded in Cass County in 1881 as KIBBYVILLE, and shortened its name when the post office was established. A new townsite was platted in 1882 just to the west in SE¼ Sec. 25-138-56, Binghampton Twp., Barnes County, and the post office moved there September 18, 1882 with Eli C. Northrup, the son-in-law of Dinah Kibby, as the new pm. Nearly all the settlers were from OH. In 1884 another townsite was platted just to the north called BINGHAMTON. The KIBBY post office moved there on August 29, 1884. (2, 3, 18, 22, 40, 76, 118, 280)

**KIBBY** (Cass). Founded in 1881 as KIBBYVILLE, the post office was established August 1, 1881 as KIBBY with Dinah Kibby pm. She built a hotel here, and was the mother-in-law of townsite promoter Eli C. Northrup and the sister of George Ellsbury, land dealer and agent for Charlemagne Tower. Mr. Northrup platted the townsite in Sec. 30-138-55, Clifton Twp., just inside the Cass County line, but the townsite was replatted just to the west in Barnes County in 1882. The post office moved to the

Barnes County site on September 18, 1882. (2, 3, 18, 22, 40, 76, 118, 280)

**KIBBYVILLE** (Cass). This was a pioneer settlement in Sec. 30-138-55, Clifton Twp., right on the border of Barnes County. The post office was established August 1, 1881 as KIBBY with Dinah Kibby pm. (3, 40, 281)

**KIDDER** (Kidder). This was one of several places that appear only on a 1930 roadmap published by the General Drafting Co., and apparently named for its county, which was named for Jefferson Parish Kidder (1815-1883), a judge who had successful political careers in his native VT, as well as in MN and Dakota Territory. KIDDER is shown about ten miles NE of Robinson, and it is a copyright town. (3, 57, 122)

**KIDVILLE** (Ransom). This townsite was founded in 1898 in Sec. 14-135-58, Fort Ransom Twp., one mile SW of Fort Ransom. Andrew J. Olson, a merchant, and Alfred Thompson, a blacksmith, led a group of young men in what was apparently a rival townsite to the established village of Fort Ransom. Merchants in the older town coined the name to note that most of the residents in the new town were teenagers or very young adults. The last business in KIDVILLE folded in 1919, and the site is now abandoned. (2, 18, 201, 207)

**KIEF** (McHenry). This Soo Line RR station was founded in 1906 in NW¼ Sec. 34-151-77, Land Twp., about eight miles SW of Drake. The post office was established March 13, 1909 with Herman H. Hohenstein pm. The Zip Code is 58747, and a peak population of 307 was reported in 1920, with a decline to just 36 in 1980. The name was suggested by settlers from South Russia to note the capital city of the Ukraine, Kiev, using the spelling that was in common usage at that time. (2, 3, 18, 33, 40, 52, 79)

**KILBERNIE** (Dickey). This place began about 1880 as a planned Milwaukee Road RR station about two miles south of Monango, at a time when the Soo Line RR terminus was at Boynton, just east of Monango. After construction had determined the site of Monango, the KILBERNIE name was transferred to a Soo Line RR station in NE¼ Sec. 13-131-64, Hamburg Twp., three miles west of Monango. The site had an elevator and a loading chute, but little development happened beyond that, and it disappeared from maps during the 1920's. The name was of Scottish origin, and was chosen by J. C. Hamilton, a native of Scotland who was the depot agent in Boynton. (1, 2, 3, 18, 79, 154)

**KILDAHL** (Ramsey). This rural post office was established February 16, 1885 with Andrew J. Kildahl pm, who later served as a county commissioner. It was located in NE¼ Sec.5-156-66, Chain Lakes Twp., seven miles north of Churchs Ferry. A population of 25 was reported in 1890, indicating that a community of sorts had begun to form. The post office closed January 16, 1893 with mail to the new GNRR townsite of Maza. (2, 18, 40, 103)

**KILDEER** (Dunn). This was a rural post office established February 8, 1911 with Ida Tift pm. It was located in SE¼ Sec. 24-147-96, eleven miles NW of Killdeer. Both names were for the nearby Killdeer Mountains, the scene of an Indian battle in 1864. The Sioux called the place *Tah-kah-o-kuty*, or place where they kill the deer. Others say the name came from the killdeer, a bird with a black breastband and a penetrating cry. The name of this post office was spelled with just one "L" for unknown reasons. It closed October 31, 1911 with mail to Oakdale. (2, 3, 18, 40, 79, 83, 223)

**KILLDEER** (Dunn). This city was founded in 1914 in NW¼ Sec. 23-145-95 as the terminus of the NPRR branch line built NW from Mandan, and named to note the nearby Killdeer Mountains. The post office was established May 1, 1915 with George Norred pm, although his wife acutally performed the duties of the office. It incorporated as a village in 1915 with J. F. "Jack" Whetstone as President of the Village Board. The elevation is 2258, the Zip Code is 58640, and a peak population of 791 was reported in 1980. The townsite attracted many settlers from nearby Manning and Oakdale, and is called "The Fawn City."

**KIMBALL** (Walsh). The GNRR station founded in 1881 in NW¼ Sec. 33-155-52, Ardoch Twp., was platted as CLARE, but generally called KIMBALL by the first settlers. The origin of the name is unknown, and when it was found to be duplicated by a town in what is now SD, the name was officially changed to ARDOCH on February 27, 1882. (2, 3, 75)

**KINCAID** (Burke). Some sources say this name was intended for the village of Lignite, but through error it was given to this GNRR spur in Sec. 5-162-93, Fay Twp., one mile south of Columbus. It was named for a GNRR official, and about the only development here was the Kincaid Power Plant operated by the Montana-Dakota Utilities Co. 1925-1966. It was shown on detailed county maps into the 1970's. (2, 18, 34, 67)

**KINCAID** (Rolette). This was a farm office established March 9, 1903 with James G. Rowley pm. Mr. Rowley submitted the names Anna, Maria, and Gideon on his application, but postal officials crossed out these names and wrote in KINCAID, which has no local significance. It was located in SE¼ Sec. 5-160-72, Wolf Creek Twp., eight miles WNW of Rolette, and closed September 30, 1903 with mail to Fisher. (3, 40, 414)

**KINDRED** (Cass). A post office called SIBLEY was established in Richland County in 1876, and moved two miles north to this site, SE¼ Sec. 29-137-50, Normanna Twp., in 1879. The GNRR founded this townsite in 1880 and named it for William S. Kindred, a pioneer Fargo realtor and that city's mayor 1882-1883. Pm Albert Vangsness adopted the new name on May 18, 1881. The village incorporated in 1920, and became a city in 1949. The elevation is 938, the Zip Code is 58051, and a peak population of 580 was reported in 1960. Sam T. Lykken, a local resident, developed the popular cash crop, Kindred Barley. (1, 2, 3, 18, 25, 33, 34, 40, 52, 77, 79, 302, 306)

**KINDRED MILL SPUR** (Richland). This was

a GNRR siding one mile SE of Kindred in Sec. 5-136-50, Walcott Twp. It was also known as MILL SIDING, and the post office that operated here 1898-1905 was called ULNESS. (3, 40)

**KINER** (Wells). This was a farm post office established March 17, 1890 with John F. Goss pm at his home in Sec. 26-149-69, Hamburg Twp., four miles SSW of Bremen. Mr. Goss named it for his wife who was born Vina M. Kiner. The Goss family moved to New Rockford in 1902, and on July 1, 1902 the post office was moved three miles ESE to SW¼ Sec. 29-149-68, Bremen Twp., the home of new pm Jacob Adams. It closed April 30, 1909 with mail to Cathay. Kinner is an erroneous spelling. (2, 3, 18, 40, 53, 79, 364)

**KING** (Logan). This was a rural post office established August 24, 1889 with Peter Koenig pm, who named it using the English translation of his own German surname. It was located in Sec. 19-134-69, Hillsburg Twp., near the center of the county, and because of this location it made a challenge for the county seat in the 1898 election, winning 105-50. The county seat moved to the new KING townsite in SW¼ Sec. 6-134-69 on January 17, 1899, but Judge Glaspell of Jamestown overturned the vote on a technicality, and the county seat was returned to Napoleon on September 30, 1899. The post office closed May 14, 1914 with mail to Lehr. Kuig is an erroneous spelling. (1, 2, 18, 40, 79, 116)

**KINLOSS** (Walsh). This was a rural post office established February 13, 1886 with John N. McDaniels pm. It was located in the country store operated by John Fauchner in Sec. 3-158-59, Kinloss Twp., four miles NE of Fairdale, and closed February 12, 1887 with mail to Gertrude. Mr. Fauchner named it for his birthplace of Kinloss, Ontario, Canada, which was named for Kinloss, Moray, Scotland. It reopened August 25, 1887 at a new site two miles to the west, and after a couple more moves in this general area, closed for good September 27, 1905 with mail to the new townsite of Fairdale. (2, 3, 25, 40)

**KINSLEY** (McKenzie). This was a rural post office established March 6, 1908 with Fred Kramer pm. It was located in NW¼ Sec. 8-152-95, Hawkeye Valley Twp., seven miles NE of Keene, and closed February 15, 1910 with mail to Charlson. The origin of the name is unknown. Kingsley is an erroneous spelling. (2, 18, 40)

**KINTYRE** (Emmons). This settlement was founded in 1905, replacing the rural community of Campbell. It is located in Sec. 35-136-74, Campbell Twp., on the Soo Line RR seven miles ESE of Braddock, and was

named for the Kintyre peninsula in Scotland. The name is derived from the clan name McIntyre, and means the head of land. The post office was established January 21, 1905 with Michael Farrell pm. He was succeeded by Myron B. Fallgatter who operated it in conjunction with a general store until 1934. The Zip Code is 58549, and a peak population of 300 was claimed in 1920, although the 1960 count was just 78. Thomas S. Kleppe, a U. S. Representative and Secretary of the Interior under President Gerald R. Ford, was born here. (1, 2, 3, 18, 33, 34, 40, 66, 79, 113, 262)

**KIPP'S POST** (Mountrail). This was an alternate name for FORT KIPP in Sec. 1-153-94, about ten miles NW of New Town. The fur trading post was built in 1825 by James Kipp, and the site is now inundated by Lake Sakakawea. (2, 3)

**KIRK** (Bottineau). This was a post office established May 13, 1891 at a Lake Metigoshe resort hotel owned by William H. Kirk. It was located in SE¼ Sec. 34-164-75, Roland Twp., eleven miles NNE of Bottineau, with Mr. Kirk as pm. Kirk is a Teutonic name meaning dweller by the church. The post office closed May 12, 1894 with mail to Bottineau. (2, 3, 19, 40, 101, 414, 415)

**KIRK** (Bowman). This was a farm post office established August 25, 1911 with Samuel Goldhirsch pm, who was a member of a Jewish colony that had come to Bowman County from Chicago, IL about 1910. It was located in Sec. 17-129-106, Mud Butte Twp., twenty-two miles SW of Rhame, in the extreme SW corner of the county, and named for Edwin Kirk, a local rancher. A grocery store was also built at the site. The post office closed February 15, 1914 with mail to Concord. (2, 3, 18, 40, 120)

**KIRKWOOD** (Burleigh). This is a postal station of the Bismarck post office located in the Kirkwood Plaza shopping center in SW¼ Sec. 4-138-80, Lincoln Twp., in the south part of the city of Bismarck. It opened August 2, 1982 with Paul C. Wachter as Officer-in-Charge. The shopping mall had its official grand opening on May 14, 1971, and was named for Robert C. Kirkwood, a native of UT who managed the Bismarck F. W. Woolworth Co. store 1935-1936 on his way to attaining the presidency of that large retail chain. Woolco, a division of F. W. Woolworth, was the first major tenant of the shopping mall. (3, 18, 34, 424)

**KLARA** (Benson). This was a rural post office established June 21, 1898 in Wells County with Carl G. Johnson pm. On April 6, 1901 it moved one-half mile NW to SW¼ Sec. 32-151-70, Arne Twp., Benson County, ten miles SW of Maddock, with Mr. Johnson continuing as pm. The post office closed February 15, 1909 with mail to Maddock. (1, 2, 3, 18, 34, 40, 239)

**KLARA** (Wells). This was a rural post office established June 21, 1898 with Carl G. Johnson pm. It was located in NE¼ Sec. 5-150-70, Heimdal Twp., four miles NE of Heimdal, and named for the Klaralven River in western Sweden, the homeland of many area settlers. Others say it was named by Nelson Olson for his mother. On April 6, 1901 Mr. Johnson moved the post office one-half mile NW, which put it into Benson County. (1, 2, 3, 18, 34, 40, 239, 414)

**KLEIN** (Cavalier). This rural post office was established July 26, 1898 with Cornelius Gresbrecht pm, who named it for pioneer settler Gottfreid Klein after his suggested name of Rosa was rejected. It was located in SW¼ Sec. 21-160-63, Henderson Twp., about two miles east of Munich. In 1901 it moved to NE¼ Sec. 31-160-63, about two miles south of Munich, where new pm Peter D. Walde tried unsuccessfully to change the name to Walde, and closed December 12, 1904 with mail to Munich. (2, 3, 40)

**KLEIN** (Oliver). This was a rural post office established May 27, 1887 with William Klein pm. It was located in Sec. 26-141-85, Fair View Twp., nine miles SW of Center, and closed April 21, 1890 with mail to Hannover. (3, 25, 40, 121)

**KLEPOL** (Sargent). This name was apparently used on an unofficial basis in the early 1880's as an alternate name for RANSOM, a rural community centered at the home of pm Randolph Holding in SE¼ Sec. 1-130-54, Ransom Twp. The origin of the name is unknown. (2, 3, 40, 165, 415)

**KLOEPPEL** (Richland). This was a farm post office established February 26, 1885 with Peter Kloeppel pm. It was located in SE¼ Sec. 8-129-51, Moran Twp., seven miles SE of Lidgerwood. On December 16, 1890 it moved one mile west to SW¼ Sec. 8-129-51, the home of new pm Lena Bremer, and it was discontinued July 20, 1892 with mail to Lidgerwood. Some sources state that it was at first located in what is now SD, but both post office sites were approximately four miles north of what became the border between ND and SD. (2, 3, 40, 147, 362, 414, 415)

**KLOSE** (Stutsman). This was a Midland Continental RR loading station built about 1912 in Sec. 3-138-64, Sydney Twp., three miles north of Sydney, and named for site owner August Klose. It was first known as KLOSE SIDING, and about 1920 was renamed KLOSES SPUR. The simplified name KLOSE was adopted during the 1930's, but the site disappeared from maps during the 1940's. Kloze is an erroneous spelling. (2, 3, 158)

**KLOSE SIDING** (Stutsman). This was a Midland Continental RR loading station built about 1912 in Sec. 3-138-64, Sydney Twp., three miles north of Sydney, and named for site owner August Klose, who settled here about 1894. About 1920 the site was renamed KLOSES SPUR, and in the 1930's it became simply KLOSE. (3, 158)

**KLOSES SPUR** (Stutsman). This was a Midland Continental RR loading station built about 1912 in Sec. 3-138-64, Sydney Twp., and originally called KLOSE SIDING. About 1920 it was renamed KLOSES SPUR, and during the 1930's the name was simplified to KLOSE, all names honoring site owner August Klose. (1, 3, 158)

**KLOTEN** (Nelson). This GNRR station was founded in 1906 in Secs. 15, 16, 21 & 22-149-58, Lee Twp., and named by Charles Colson (1860-1926) to honor local settlers from Kloten, Sweden. The post office was established March 2, 1907 with Sadie H. Severson pm. The elevation is 1520, and the population has remained at about 150 for many years. The post office, Zip Code 58248, closed August 30, 1985, although government records did not record this fact until April 11, 1987. (1, 2, 3, 18, 33, 38, 40, 79, 124, 128)

**KNIFERIVER** (Dunn). This was a rural post office established September 25, 1907 with Lewis L. Fixen (1855-1929) pm. It was located in S½ Sec. 32-143-93, fourteen miles south of Dunn Center on the north bank of the Knife River, so called because of its use as a source of flint for making arrowheads. Others say the name is a translation of the Indian name *Mina Wakpa*, noting that this was where the local tribes obtained their first metal knives, trading with wandering tribes from the southwestern United States who had gotten them from the early Spanish explorers. The one-word spelling was done to comply with government spelling regulations, with a change to the more popular two-word spelling on July 22, 1911. (3, 18, 40, 79, 223)

**KNIFE RIVER** (Dunn). The rural post office of KNIFERIVER had been established in 1907 in S½ Sec. 32-143-93, fourteen miles south of Dunn Center. On July 22, 1911 pm Robert Tesch changed the spelling to the more popular two-word form after government spelling regulations had been relaxed. The post office closed January 15, 1914 with mail to Emerson. (2, 3, 18, 40, 223)

**KNIFE RIVER** (Morton). This rural post office was established January 14, 1885 with Charles Krauth pm, who named it for the Knife River, which was nearly twenty miles to the north. It was located in Sec. 32-140-90, Custer Twp., and closed October 22, 1885 when it moved one mile east to the new NPRR townsite of HEBRON. (2, 3, 25, 40, 107)

**KNIFE RIVER** (Stark). This was a NPRR siding built in 1882 in SW¼ Sec. 35-140-91, three miles west of Hebron, and named for the nearby Knife River. It appeared on maps into the 1940's, although little development ever occurred at the site. (1, 2, 3, 18, 74, 104)

**KNOFF** (Divide). This was a farm post office established December 27, 1904 with Peter Christian Olson pm. It was located in SW¼ Sec. 31-163-95, Mentor Twp., three miles WNW of Noonan, and named for Ludwig Knoph, the owner of the store in which the post office was located, with an intentional Anglicization of the name. It closed January 2, 1907 with mail to Columbus. (2, 3, 40, 414)

**KNOWLTON** (Stark). This NPRR siding in NW¼ Sec. 9-139-94, Heart River Twp., was built in 1890 and named for G. A. Knowlton, a member of the railroad construction crew in the area. Located three miles NE of Gladstone, the name was changed to BOYLE in 1907. (2, 3, 18, 240)

**KNOX** (Benson). This GNRR station was founded in 1883 in Secs. 8 & 17-156-70, Knox Twp., and named for either Gen. Henry Knox (1750-1806) of Revolutionary War fame, or the Scottish religious reformer John Knox (1505-1572). The post office was established September 26, 1887 with Zada C. Crowell pm. It was platted in 1889, and incorporated as a village in 1906. The elevation is 1610, the Zip Code is 58343, and a peak population of 330 was reported in 1910, with a steady decline to just 69 in 1980. (1, 2, 5, 13, 18, 25, 34, 40, 52, 79, 236, 237)

**KNUDSON** (Bottineau). This was a country store started about 1890 by Chris H. Knudson in SW¼ Sec. 2-159-83, Lansford Twp., one mile SE of Lansford. Mr. Knudson

*Knox about 1909*

started a post office called Bjelland in 1901 one mile further SE, and in 1903 moved his entire operation to the new townsite of Lansford. Knutson is an erroneous spelling. (2, 3, 18, 153, 378)

**KOEPPEL** (McIntosh). This was a rural post office established November 17, 1896 with Jacob Koeppel pm, but the order was rescinded January 19, 1897 before it had gone into operation. The location is unknown. (2, 3, 40)

**KOLDOK** (Barnes). This was a NPRR station built in 1907 and named BRACKETT, but because of confusion with Brocket the name was changed to KOLDOK on December 10, 1915. The new name was coined from "coal dock", noting the main structure at this site in N½ Sec. 22-140-56, Oriska Twp., three miles east of Oriska. For many years it was an important service point for NPRR locomotives, but a fire in 1929 severely damaged the facilities. The dawn of the diesel era further reduced its importance, and in 1951 a huge derailment right at the site virtually destroyed the remaining buildings, and only the passing track could be salvaged. Joe Gray was foreman here 1926-1944. The name is perpetuated at a nearby State Game Management Area. Koldock and Kolkock are erroneous spellings. (2, 3, 18, 34, 281)

**KONGSBERG** (McHenry). This village was founded in 1900 as OLIVIA on the Soo Line RR in Secs. 32 & 33-151-79, Olivia Twp., midway between Ruso and Butte. When the post office was established January 15, 1916 with Rudolf Christiansen pm, the name was changed to KONGSBERG at the suggestion of local elevator manager I. L. Berg, taking the name from his hometown in Norway. Although the OLIVIA name saw occasional use into the 1970's, KONGSBERG became the official name. The population never exceeded 50, and the post office closed April 30, 1958 with mail to Voltaire. (2, 3, 40, 412)

**KONGSBERG** (Richland). This was a pioneer settlement in NW¼ Sec. 4-133-48, Dwight Twp., three miles SE of Galchutt. The post office was established September 19, 1879 with Hans C. N. Myhra pm, who named it for his hometown of Kongsberg, Buskerud, Norway. Mr. Myhra came here in 1871, and was the first assessor for the township. A population of 25 was reported in 1890, but the post office closed August 31, 1905 with mail to Abercrombie. Kongsburg and Keongsberg are erroneous spellings. (2, 3, 25, 40, 243, 351)

**KOVASH** (Morton). This is a rural subdivision founded in 1976 by Albert G. Kovash, who had founded West Acres subdivision, three miles to the west, in 1975. KOVASH is

located in SE¼ Sec. 14 & NE¼ Sec. 23-139-83, Sweet Briar Twp., twelve miles WNW of Mandan. (3)

**KRAMER** (Bottineau). This Soo Line RR townsite was founded in 1905 in Secs. 10, 11, 14 & 15-160-78, Stone Creek Twp., and named for a Soo Line RR surveyor. The post office was established August 15, 1905 with Alfred G. Chadbourn pm. Consideration was given to naming the site Crossroad City, but compound names were not allowed by government officials at the time. The village incorporated in 1908 and reached a peak population of 220 in 1940, but many years of decline have reduced that count to just 83 in 1980. The Zip Code is 58748. (1, 2, 18, 33, 34, 40, 79, 101, 153)

**KREM** (Mercer). This was a rural post office established September 17, 1888 with Samuel Sprecher pm at his home in NW¼ Sec. 1-146-86. Carl Semmler selected the name, a corruption of the Crimea in South Russia, which was the homeland of many area settlers, although some claim it was named for Krems, Austria. In 1894 it moved three miles SSE to SW¼ Sec. 18-146-85, and in 1898 it moved five miles SSW to Secs. 11 & 12-145-86, where a thriving townsite developed. The population is said to have reached about 300, but when the NPRR bypassed the site by several miles in 1914, most of the residents moved to Hazen. KREM lingered on, but by 1940 the population was just 5, and the post office closed November 14, 1942 with mail to Hazen. Two cemeteries and the ruins of several buildings mark the site today. (2, 3, 18, 23, 40, 64, 79, 232, 414)

**KRINGEN** (Rolette). This was a farm post office established July 29, 1899 with Marie Eikness pm. Her husband, Rev. C. D. Eikness, named it for Kringen, Oppland County, Norway. It was located in Sec. 19-160-73, Kohlmeier Twp., thirteen miles west of Rolette, and closed August 13, 1904 with mail to Twala. (2, 3, 40, 123)

**KRONTHAL** (Mercer). This was a rural community founded in June 1898 by settlers from Kronental, South Russia, who chose an Anglicized version of this name for their new home. The post office was established in NW¼ Sec. 14-146-87, thirteen miles NNE of Beulah, on September 13, 1902 with Robert Heiser pm, and closed October 31, 1905 with mail to Expansion. It reopened July 9, 1909 in SE¼ Sec. 20-146-87, just SW of the original site, but closed for good on May 15, 1911 with mail again to Expansion. The community consisted of Eli Gunderson's general store, Trinity Lutheran Church founded by Rev. P. L. Wohlfeil, and a few homes, and survived intact into the 1930's before starting to decline. The church was the last building, and that was moved to Stanton in 1963, leaving only a cemetery to mark the site. (2, 3, 7, 18, 23, 40, 64, 232, 414)

**KRUEGERSVILLE** (Cass). The NPRR established this townsite in NE¼ Sec. 1-138-54, Eldred Twp., in 1900 on its newly built Marion branch line, naming it for local land owner William F. Krueger. He declined this honor, and the name was changed to EMBDEN, the name of the rural post office

that had just moved to the townsite. (3, 40, 77)

**KUCK** (Grant). The Dickinson, Lefor, & New Leipzig RR was heavily promoted in 1917, and the first station north of New Leipzig was to be VIENNA in Secs. 9 & 16-135-90. The railroad plans were virtually dead in 1918 when New Leipzig challenged unsuccessfully for the county seat. Its newspaper, in promoting this effort, printed a rather crude map from April until June 1918, showing the D, L, & NL RR extending north from New Leipzig, but the first station was KUCK. It is thought that this name represented a name change for VIENNA, apparently to honor either Fred or John Kuck, both of whom were residents in Township 135-90. John Kuck was at that time a Deputy Sheriff of the county. (3, 17, 74, 358, 427)

**KULM** (LaMoure). This Soo Line RR townsite was founded in 1892 in NW¼ Sec. 26-133-66, Norden Twp., and named by Christian Flegel (1859-1937) for his hometown of Kulm, Bessarabia, which was settled by Germans in 1815. The first colony of settlers in ND had lived for a short time in Kulm Twp., Hutchinson County, SD before coming to this area. The post office was established January 9, 1893 with Friedrich Buechler (1869-1904) pm. KULM was the terminus of the branch line until 1898, when it was extended to Wishek. The elevation is 1966, the Zip Code is 58456, and the city, which incorporated in 1906, reached a peak population of 742 in 1930. Angie Dickinson, the actress, was born here in 1936. (1, 2, 3, 18, 23, 33, 40, 52, 142)

**KUNTZ** (Emmons). This is a rural community in S½ Sec. 22 & N½ Sec. 27-133-74, seventeen miles ENE of Linton. It was founded in 1914 when plans were made to erect a rural Roman Catholic church, and during the 1920's several country stores operated at this site. The church was named St. Michael's, and the community is often called by this name. The more commonly used name of KUNTZ honors pioneer merchants Leo and Christian Kuntz. (3, 18, 34)

**KUROKI** (Bottineau). This GNRR siding was founded in 1905 in Secs. 22 & 23-163-81, Wayne Twp., between Antler and Westhope, and named for General Itei Kuroki, a Japanese military leader who defeated the Russians at the Yalu River during the Russo-Japanese War of 1904-1905. He had recently visited North America to enlist financial support for his cause. A townsite was platted, and the post office opened September 3, 1909 with John H. Zeigler pm, but it closed October 15, 1920 with mail to Westhope. A population of 20 was reported in 1920, and a count of 10 was made as late as 1960, as KUROKI continues to appear on some maps. (1, 2, 3, 18, 34, 40, 79, 833, 101, 153, 379)

**KURTZ** (Morton). This was a NPRR station built in 1879 in Sec. 36-139-88, Curlew Twp., five miles east of Glen Ullin. It was named for Thomas C. Kurtz of the H. A. Bruns Co. of Moorhead, MN, supply agents for the NPRR construction crews, although others say it was named for George W. Kurtz, a Private at Fort Rice in 1864 who carved his name on a nearby butte. The post office was established May 31, 1888 with Joseph Beesinger pm, and it closed February 17, 1890 with mail to Glen Ullin. Little development occurred, and all buildings were sold and moved in 1929. The NPRR mainline was rerouted in 1946, and KURTZ was bypassed and forgotten. (1, 2, 3, 17, 18, 25, 40, 79, 105)

**KURTZMAN** (Emmons). The community just south of the Dana siding in Township 136-76 became known as KURTZMAN, and Gail Wade was named pm on March 6, 1919 when the post office was authorized, but she declined the appointment. John W. Schott was appointed pm July 3, 1919, but the name was changed to KERTZMAN by postal officials, apparently through an error. It operated under this name until it closed June 15, 1922. It is thought that the original name honored the Kurtz family of the area. (3, 40)

# L

**LaCROSSE** (Towner). This community began in 1883 in NW¼ Sec. 6-157-65, Coolin Twp., five miles SE of Cando, and was the first settlement in southern Towner County. The name is said to note its location at a crossing of the Mauvais Coulee, although some say it was named for a somewhat elusive pioneer named Coolin LaCrosse, a pioneer innkeeper in the Turtle Mountains. The site was sometimes called BIG COULEE, and while it appears on an 1884 map as "LaCrosse P. O.", the local post office was called COOLIN. By 1884 most of the settlers had moved to Cando. (2, 3, 34, 40, 102)

**LADD** (Bowman). This name is used to describe the residents of southern Bowman County who have telephone prefix 574, and are part of the exchange out of Ludlow, SD. The name is taken from Ladd Twp. (129-102), and the area receives its mail service from Bowman. (3, 34, 55)

**LADOGA** (Kidder). This was a NPRR station built in 1905 in NW¼ Sec. 7-139-70, Crystal Springs Twp., four miles west of Crystal Springs. The name was selected by Mrs. A. M. Burt, wife of a NPRR official, for Lake Ladoga on the Finnish-Russian border. That lake is the largest lake in Europe (7,156 square miles), and today is entirely within the Soviet Union. Little development occurred here, and LADOGA disappeared from maps during the 1940's. (1, 2, 3, 5, 18, 122)

**LaFOLLETTE** (Ward). This was a farm post office established July 18, 1904 with George W. Smith pm, who named it for Sen. Robert Marion LaFollette (1855-1925), the WI Governor and U. S. Senator who achieved a large national following as an Independent candidate for President. The post office was located in SW¼ Sec. 18-153-87, Lund Twp., nine miles NW of Makoti, and just inside the Ward County line, although virtually all of its patrons were in Mountrail County. It closed January 2, 1907 with mail to Plaza. LaFolette is an erroneous spelling. (2, 4, 5, 18, 40, 72, 100)

**LAKE** (Rolette). This was a farm post office established May 26, 1902 with Charles Paulson pm. It was located in N½ Sec. 30-163-73, Willow Lake Twp., on the west edge of Willow Lake about eight miles NW of Dunseith, and closed February 6, 1903 with mail to Kelvin. (2, 3, 18, 40, 123)

**LAKE CITY** (Ramsey). Former Indian trader James G. Lamoreaux promoted this townsite at the east end of Devils Lake on a bay he named for himself. When he applied for a post office in 1881, postal officials rejected LAKE CITY because they were not accepting two-word place names at the time. Mr. Lamoreaux then submitted the name JERUSALEM, which was accepted, and the post office was established October 24, 1881 in Sec. 28-152-62, Odessa Twp., eight miles SSE of Crary. (2, 3, 40, 103)

**LAKE ECKELSON** (Barnes). An 1890 guide to ND lists this place as being in Barnes County, and served by the Sanborn post office. The townsite of Eckelson was several years old in 1890, so perhaps this place name referred to settlers living east of Lake Eckelson in Potter Twp. (140-60), and west of Sanborn. (3, 25)

**LAKE IBSEN** (Benson). This was a rural post office established July 14, 1886 with Peter E. Morden pm. It was located in NE¼ Sec. 8-155-68, Lake Ibsen Twp., five miles SE of Leeds near Lake Ibsen, named by L. P. Havrevold, a local state legislator, for the Norwegian poet and dramatist Henrik Ibsen (1828-1906). Mr. Havrevold introduced legislation requiring the teaching of Scandinavian languages at the University of North Dakota. The post office closed July 7, 1887 with mail to Church's Ferry. Lake Ebsen is an erroneous spelling. (2, 3, 5, 18, 34, 40, 79, 236)

**LAKE METIGOSHE** (Bottineau). This is a post-World War II commercial development in Secs. 11 & 14-163-75, Roland Twp., at the junction of ND Highway 43 and a county road to the east shore of Lake Metigoshe. (3, 34)

**LAKE METIGOSHE PARK** (Bottineau). This was a platted resort community in NE¼ Sec. 2-163-75, Roland Twp., on the east shore of Lake Metigoshe, just west of the Metigoshe post office. It appeared as such only in a 1910 county atlas, although the lake area had been a popular resort for many years, and continues in that role. The Chippewa name for the lake is *Metigoshe Washegum*, meaning clear water lake surrounded by oaks. (3, 18)

**LAKE TOBIASON** (Steele). Tobias Johnson settled in NW¼ Sec. 15-148-55, Beaver Creek Twp., twelve miles NE of Finley, in 1881 near a natural slough on the Middle Fork of the Goose River, which came to be called Tobias Slough. In 1931 efforts began to build a small dam at the site, which resulted in an artificial lake called Lake Tobiason, derived either from the name of the old slough, or according to some, for Tollef Tobiason (1862-1947), who lived just SW of the new lake. A resort community called LAKE TOBIASON began to develop, featuring a popular lakeside store to serve area residents and tourists. In 1946 the ND Farmers Union built a camp and auditorium here, and this site has hosted numerous meetings, rallies, and conventions over the years. (3, 18, 34, 59)

**LAKE VIEW** (Adams). This was a platted site in SW¼ Sec. 13-129-96, Hettinger Twp., just south of HETTINGER. The name notes its location on the shore of Mirror, or Crystal, Lake. Little development occurred, and it is now a part of HETTINGER. (3, 18)

**LAKEVIEW** (Burleigh). This was a farm post office established May 17, 1907 with Paul C. Burhaus pm. It was located in NW¼ Sec. 3-143-76, Richmond Twp., seven miles NNW of Wing, and closed September 15, 1908 with mail to Ong. Postal officials rejected the name Highland, after which the name LAKEVIEW was chosen to note the ability to see two small lakes, Lone Tree Lake in Secs. 15 & 22, and Horseshoe Lake in Secs. 1 & 12, from the post office site. (2, 3, 8, 14, 18, 40, 414)

**LAKEVIEW** (LaMoure). This was a farm post office established June 25, 1884 with John A. Baughman pm. It was located in NE¼ Sec. 35-133-62, Badger Twp., eight miles SW of LaMoure, which supplied this office with its mail. The name noted the view of Cottonwood Lake about one-half mile to the east in Sec. 36. The post office closed November 18, 1887 with mail to LaMoure. (2, 3, 25, 40)

**LAKEVIEW** (Towner). This was a country store located in SW¼ Sec. 11-159-65, Victor Twp., where a post office was established June 26, 1903 with John M. Borgerson pm. The name notes the view from this store of two small unnamed lakes, one just to the north in Secs. 2 & 11, and the other just to the south in Sec. 14. The post office closed August 23, 1905, being replaced on that date by the facility at the new Soo Line RR townsite of Egeland, four miles WNW of here. Mr. Borgerson moved his store to Egeland and became the first pm in that community. (2, 18, 40, 197)

**LAKEVIEW PARK** (Stutsman). This was the descriptive name given to an area platted about 1910 by promoter and site owner A. B. Koltze on the SW shore of Jim Lake in SW¼ Sec. 19-143-64, Lyon Twp., five miles east of Pingree. Development was minimal, and the project was abandoned. (1, 2, 18, 158)

**LAKE WILLIAMS** (Kidder). This was a NPRR siding built in 1915 in Sec. 12-142-71, Lake Williams Twp., between Robinson and Pettibone. It was originally named WILLIAMS for the nearby lake, but when postal officials rejected this name, it was renamed LAKE WILLIAMS. The new name is said to note the nearby lake which was named for Jeremiah D. Williams, and also honors Joseph Molesworth Williams, a founder of the townsite which began to develop in 1916. The post office was established August 9, 1916 with Martha K. Cook pm. A peak population of 83 was reported in 1930. The post office, Zip Code 58457, closed September 17, 1971 with mail to Robinson. (1, 2, 18, 33, 38, 40, 79, 122)

**LAKEWOOD** (Grand Forks). The CABLE post office operated 1888-1893 in Sec. 14-149-56, Loretta Twp. In 1900 it was reestablished in SW¼ Sec. 3-149-56, ten miles west of Northwood. On October 17, 1903 pm George W. Hart changed the name to LAKEWOOD, coined to note the nearby wooded shore of Hart Lake, an artificial lake built by Mr. Hart on his tree claim. The post office closed August 31, 1906 with mail to Northwood. (2, 18, 40, 241)

**LAKEWOOD PARK** (Ramsey). As the Chautauqua Assembly in W½ Sec. 18-153-64, Lake Twp., four miles SW of the city of Devils Lake, began to decline in the early 1920's, the site began to develop into a residential area. It was felt that it should have a new name, and a contest was held in 1922, with Lakewood being the overwhelming choice of the people. Mrs. Mary E. Holmes had submitted the earliest entry with this name, so she won the $10 prize and the distinction of having named the settlement. The last Chautauqua was held in 1929, and the NORTH CHAUTAUQUA post office changed its name to LAKEWOOD PARK on April 1, 1931 with Mrs. Nellie A. Barr pm. It closed September 30, 1942 with mail to Devils Lake, and since 1949 the area has been a part of that city. (2, 3, 40, 103)

**LAKOTA** (Nelson). This GNRR townsite was founded in 1882 in Sec. 27-153-60, Lakota Twp., and named by Governor Nehemiah G. Ordway for the Teton Sioux word meaning allies. The Santee Sioux word for allies is *Dakotah*, with the suffix "otah" meaning many in both languages. Some say it means land of plenty, and the name is shared with a small community in northern IA and a lake in VT. The post office was established July 16, 1883 with Francis J. Kane pm. It was designated as the county seat in 1883, incorporated as a village in 1885, and became a city in 1889. The elevation is 1514, the Zip Code is 58344, and a peak population of 1,066 was reached in 1960. The famous Berriedale Farm operated by the eccentric British nobleman John Sutherland Sinclair, the Earl of Caithness, was located six miles NE of LAKOTA 1884-1905. Asle J. Gronna (1858-1922), a U. S. Representative and U. S. Senator 1904-1921, was a longtime resident here. (1, 2, 3, 10, 18, 19, 25, 33, 40, 45, 79, 124, 130)

**LALLIE** (Benson). This NPRR station was built in 1885 in SE¼ Sec. 15-152-67, Lallie Twp., and named FORT TOTTEN STATION for the military post nine miles to the east. In 1887 the name was shortened to TOTTEN, and on March 3, 1889 the name was changed to LALLIE. Some say it was named by NPRR official A. J. McCabe for his sister, while others say it was named for James Lallie, a NPRR engineer. This rather undeveloped site was served by the Oberon post office until June 21, 1916, when the LALLIE post office was established with Mary Fevog pm. She was succeeded by Fern Mullvain, who closed the facility January 15, 1936 with mail to Oberon. The highest population figure quoted was a count of 10 in both 1920 and 1930. (1, 2, 3, 18, 25, 34, 40, 79, 110)

**LaMARS** (Richland). This was a Soo Line RR station built in 1913 in NW¼ Sec. 27-129-48, LaMars Twp., eleven miles SW of Fairmount. It was named for its township, which was named by a Mr. Britton who came here from LeMars, IA, although no explanation is given for the change in the spelling. Levi Johnson operated a store here for several years, and a population of 10 was reported in 1920, but nothing developed beyond this modest beginning. The store closed in 1948 and was moved to Hankinson after township officials refused to let the owner add a beer parlor. (1, 3, 147)

**LAMBERT** (Walsh). This was a rural post office established February 13, 1886 with Robert Vernon pm. It was located in NW¼ Sec. 22-155-58, Perth Twp., eight miles SW of Lankin, and said to have been named for Louis A. Lambert, a famous Roman Catholic priest of the time who founded the *Catholic Times* magazine in 1874. Lambert is a Teutonic name meaning literally land bright, and interpreted as glory of his country. In 1895 it was moved four miles NNE to the home of new pm Joseph Bosh (1858-1930), who also ran a blacksmith shop at this site in SE¼ Sec. 2-155-58. The post office closed May 31, 1907 with mail to Lankin. (2, 3, 5, 19, 25, 40, 75)

**LAMOINE** (Kidder). This was a rural post office established June 3, 1907 with Emma V. Virgin pm, who came here in 1906 with her husband, Bruce. It was located in NE¼ Sec. 21-144-74, Northwest Twp., ten miles NNW of Tuttle. The origin of the name is unknown, although it is French for the monk. Postal officials had changed the spelling from LaMoine to LAMOINE. The post office closed August 31, 1916 with mail to Tuttle. (2, 10, 18, 40, 122, 313, 414)

**LAMONT** (Sheridan). This NPRR townsite was founded in 1902 in SE¼ Sec. 6-146-76, Lamont Twp., three miles east of McClusky, and became that town's rival in a losing battle for the county seat. The name honored Daniel Scott Lamont (1851-1905), Secretary of War under President Grover Cleveland 1894-1897, and Vice President of the NPRR 1897-1905. The post office was established November 1, 1904 with Arthur Steinbrecker pm, and closed November 30, 1905 with mail to McClusky. Lamont is a Scandinavian name meaning lawyer. (2, 3, 5, 19, 21, 30, 40)

**LaMOURE** (LaMoure). This townsite in Sec. 1-133-61, Bean Twp., was platted in October 1882 by the Wells-Dickey Land Co. as a station for the NPRR, which came in 1883. It was named for Judson LaMoure (1839-1918), who came to Dakota Territory from Quebec, Canada in 1860 before it was a territory, and served in the territorial and state legislatures until 1912. LaMoure County, and the villages of Jud and Judson are also named for Mr. LaMoure. The post office was established December 13, 1882 with Norris B. Wilkinson pm. It was designated as county seat in 1886, and incorporated as a city in 1905 with C. W. Davis mayor. The elevation is 1329, the Zip Code is 58458, and a peak population of 1,077 was reached in 1980 as the city has maintained a stability throughout the twentieth century. (1, 2, 3, 18, 25, 33, 40, 52, 79, 144, 152)

**LAMPTON** (Walsh). This was a pioneer settlement founded by George Michi in 1879 in Sec. 12-158-56, Lampton Twp., three miles NE of Edinburg. The post office was established January 9, 1882 with Mr. Michi as pm, and closed December 14, 1887 with mail to Edinburgh. It was named for its township, which is said to have been named for William James Lampton, a popular newspaper columnist of the time. (2, 3, 5, 25, 40, 75)

**LANDA** (Bottineau). This GNRR townsite was first planned in 1903 as STRABANE, but when settlement began in 1904, the Norwegian settlers changed the name to LANDA for Daniel D. Landa (1875-1953) and his cousin Theodore T. Landa (1859-1945), both of whom were natives of Norway who settled here in 1900. It was located in SE¼ Sec. 33-163-79, Scotia Twp. The post office was established as LAUDA on August 9, 1904 with Jonas J. Johnson, a pioneer merchant, as pm, but that order was soon rescinded. It was reestablished January 13, 1905 with Andrew Helgeson pm, with the spelling corrected. During its boom years it was said that the depot agent was the only person in LANDA who was not of Norwegian ancestry. The elevation is 1488, the Zip Code is 58749, and the village, which incorporated in 1922, reached a peak population of 154 in 1920. (1, 2, 3, 18, 33, 40, 79, 101, 153)

*Lakota 1951*

*LaMoure about 1915*

**LANDON** (Grant). This townsite was platted in 1913 in NE¼ Sec. 34-137-90, eighteen miles NNW of Elgin near the rural post office of Worms. No development occurred, and the origin of the name is unknown. (3, 40, 414)

**LANE** (McHenry). This was a farm post office established February 13, 1886 with Omar C. Lane, who came here in 1885, as pm. Lane is an Old English name meaning from the rural road. It was located in SW¼ Sec. 24-158-76, Poplar Grove Twp., nine miles east of Bantry. On May 19, 1891 it moved one mile west, changing its name to CARDER. (2, 3, 19, 25, 40, 412, 415)

**LANGBERG** (Bowman). This was a farm post office established February 5, 1910 with Suzie Cook Parks (1875-1961) as pm. She was a young widow homesteader who married Odin Angell Ostness in 1911. The post office was first located in SW¼ Sec. 26-129-104, Langberg Twp., eighteen miles south of Rhame, and named for its township, which was named for Trygve Langberg, a pioneer settler in SE¼ Sec. 27-129-104. Mr. Langberg left his Bowman County farm in 1913 for CA, where he became a Seventh Day Adventist minister. The post office was moved at times within the general area, winding up in SW¼ Sec. 24-129-104 in 1917, and closed June 30, 1919 with mail to Amor. (1, 2, 3, 18, 34, 40, 120)

**LANGDON** (Cavalier). This town was designated as the county seat almost before settlement began in 1884. The GNRR founded the town as a terminus station, and the nearby McHugh post office moved here June 25, 1886 with Charles Crawford pm. It is located in Secs. 14 & 23-161-60, Elgin Twp., and was named for Robert Bruce Langdon (1826-1895), a MN legislator and official of the GNRR, who donated a bell for the local school. The elevation is 1615, the Zip Code is 58249, and the village, which incorporated in 1888, has grown consistently to a peak population of 2,335 in 1980. It calls itself the "Durum Capital of the World." The father of LANGDON is often considered to be pioneer merchant Edward James Fox

(1857-1931). Thomas John Clifford, longtime President of the University of North Dakota, was born here in 1921. (1, 2, 3, 13, 18, 25, 33, 40, 52, 79, 209, 216, 253)

**LANGEDAHL** (Kidder). This was a pioneer rural community in SW¼ Sec. 12-141-74, Chestina Twp., seven miles south of Tuttle. The post office was established March 22, 1888 with Lars S. Langedahl (1861-1946) pm, who had come here in 1880 from Norway. His last name translates as long valley, probably a description of his home in the old country. A population of 18 was reported in 1890, but without a railroad any hope of developing a permanent townsite was dashed. The post office closed December 31, 1915 with mail to Tuttle. (2, 3, 18, 25, 40, 79, 122, 200, 240, 313)

**LANGERS** (Cass). This was a NPRR loading station built in 1900 in NE¼ Sec. 4-139-52, Everest Twp., two miles SW of Casselton, and named for the brothers Joseph and Frank J. Langer, area farmers who came here in 1877. Frank J. Langer was an official of a bank in Casselton, and the father of the famous politician William Langer. No development occurred here, and the station was removed in 1950. (1, 2, 3, 34, 77)

**LANGHORNE** (Burleigh). This was a coal miners' settlement in SE¼ Sec. 1-142-80, Ecklund Twp., two miles east of Wilton, at the Washburn Lignite Coal Co. Mine No. 2. It was founded about 1912 and named for the maiden name of one of Gen. W. D. Washburn's daughters-in-law. (2, 3, 18)

**LANGTON** (Pembina). This was a farm post office established April 7, 1884 with James Langton pm. It was located in E½ Sec. 32-164-52, Pembina Twp., six miles west of Pembina, and closed April 7, 1886 with mail to Pembina. In 1893 five different Langton families were living on farms within two miles of this site. (2, 3, 25, 40, 108)

**LANKIN** (Walsh). This Soo Line RR townsite was founded in 1904 in SW¼ Sec. 24-156-57, Norton Twp., and named for townsite owner James Lankin. The Young post office mov-

ed here on July 27, 1905 with John Matejcek continuing as pm. The Zip Code is 58250, and the village, which incorporated in 1908, reached a peak population of 341 in 1910. Among the town's residents were Jack McDonald, a trumpet player with John Philip Sousa's famous band, and Herman Witasek, a member of LANKIN's 1930 State Class C High School basketball champions, who is considered to be ND's first professional player of that sport. (1, 2, 3, 18, 33, 40, 52, 75, 79)

**LANONA** (Barnes). The first settlement occurred in this area about 1891, and on February 20, 1892 the post office was established with John H. Ehlers pm. Some believe the name came from a place in England, but it is much more likely that the name derives from the ancient lake of some 160 square miles that covered this area about 14,000 years ago. The Soo Line RR came through the site, NW¼ Sec. 31-140-57, Alta Twp., in 1896, and a townsite was platted in 1906. No boom ever occurred here, with a population of 40 being claimed at one time, and even that is believed to have been an exaggeration. The post office closed December 31, 1910 with mail to Valley City, its two elevators were destroyed by lightning in 1939, and the station was removed in July 1940. Two slabs of concrete remain to mark the site. (2, 40, 76, 79, 281)

**LANSFORD** (Bottineau). This GNRR townsite was founded in 1902 as GORDON, but the name was changed to LANSFORD in 1903 by townsite owner Martin Olson, who named it for his hometown of Lansfjord, Norway. Others say it was named for a GNRR construction foreman at the site. The post office was established July 25, 1903 with Clarence C. Banks pm. It incorporated as a village in 1904, and became a city in 1907 with J. G. Walstad mayor. In 1905 it became a two-railroad town with the arrival of the Soo Line RR. The elevation is 1633, the Zip Code is 58750, and a peak population of 456 was reached in 1910, with a decline to 294 in 1980. (1, 2, 18, 33, 40, 79, 101, 153, 378)

**LANSING** (Towner). This was a rural post office established May 27, 1903 with John D. McDonnell pm. It was located in NE¼ Sec. 17-162-65, Lansing Twp., nine miles NE of Rocklake, and named by settlers from Lansing, MI, which was named in 1837 for Lansing, NY, which was named for Revolutionary War hero John Lansing (1754-1837), who later served as Chief Justice of the NY Supreme Court. The post office closed March 15, 1907 with mail to Ellison. (3, 5, 10, 18, 40, 46)

**LARAMORE** (Grand Forks). This was an erroneous spelling of LARIMORE used as a postmark by the post office during 1882-1883. (3)

**LARIMORE** (Grand Forks). This GNRR townsite was founded in 1881 in Sec. 12-151-55, Larimore Twp., on land owned by Albert Clark. It was named for Newell Green Larimore, a native of KY who developed the 15,000-acre Elk Valley Bonanza Farm in this area. Many members of his family still live in LARIMORE. The post office was established October 31, 1881 with Lyman P. Goodhue pm. The elevation is 1134, the Zip Code is 58251, and a peak population of 1,714 was reached in 1960. (1, 2, 3, 18, 31, 33, 40, 52, 69, 79, 94, 342)

**LARK** (Grant). This was a rural post office established July 26, 1907 with Hiram D. Larkee pm, who used a shortened version of his family name as the name of the post office. It was located in SE¼ Sec. 6-134-85, Lark Twp. In 1910 a townsite was platted one mile to the NE in NW¼ Sec. 5-134-85 on the new NPRR branch line from Mandan to Mott, and the post office and its name were transferred to the new village. The elevation is 2092, and the village reached a peak population of 125 in 1930, with a decline to just 11 in 1960. Mrs. Don Whiteman became pm in 1951, and when she retired in 1980 the post office, Zip Code 58550, closed with mail to Flasher, although this fact was not entered in government records until July 28, 1985. (1, 2, 3, 17, 18, 33, 40, 41, 175, 177)

**LARKEE** (Grant). This was a rural community centered at the home of Hiram D. Larkee in SE¼ Sec. 6-134-85, Lark Twp. Mr. Larkee, a native of IA, was the first white settler in this area, coming here as a teenager in 1901. He was appointed pm of a post office here on July 26, 1907, and chose LARK, a shortened version of his own name, as the name of the facility. (2, 3, 17, 40, 176, 177, 415)

**LAROSE** (Benson). Octave LaRose, a native of Canada, came to the area called Graham's Island about 1880 and operated a ferry service across Devils Lake. On June 10, 1884 he became pm of a post office bearing his name, although postal officials changed the capital "R" in his name to lower case. It was located in Sec. 25-153-66, about seven miles ESE of Minnewaukan. On December 6, 1887 the name was changed to GRAHAM by pm Thomas Fitzgerald, who had assumed that position in 1886. (2, 3, 18, 34, 40, 110)

**LARRABEE** (Foster). Capt. William H. Larrabee was a Civil War P.O.W., a veteran of various Indian wars, and an officer at Fort Totten, but when he refused reassignment to Fort Abraham Lincoln in the early 1870's, he was sentenced to "ten years on the Dakota prairie" for his act of insurrection, an thus by fate did not wind up at the Little Big Horn with Gen. Custer. In 1876 he established a stage stop at his home in SE¼ Sec. 24-147-64, Larrabee Twp., two miles SE of Grace City, and opened a post office here on September 4, 1882. He was well past the completion of his "sentence" when his buildings were destroyed by fire in 1886, and a disgruntled Capt. Larrabee decided to return to his native New England. Five other pms continued the post office, first in Sec. 19-147-63, Florence Twp., then in Sec. 14-147-64 from 1887-1896. It moved to Sec. 10-147-64 in that year, where new pm

Jerome C. Warren's efforts to change the name to Warren were rejected by postal officials. In 1906 it moved to SW¼ Sec. 21-147-64, the home of new pm William Black, and in 1908 it moved to NE¼ Sec. 20-147-64, the home of pm Ole Bonderud, who closed the post office on December 31, 1910, becoming pm at the new GNRR townsite of Grace City, two miles to the east. Larrabees is an erroneous spelling. (2, 3, 18, 25, 40, 97, 414)

**LARSON** (Burke). This GNRR townsite was founded in 1907 in NE¼ Sec. 3-162-94, Keller Twp., about four miles SSE of the original inland townsite of Columbus, later known as Old Columbus, and about four miles WSW of the new Soo Line RR townsite of Columbus. At the suggestion of Gust Bjorkman and Ole Forthun, it was named for Columbus pm Columbus Larson, giving him the unusual distinction of having two adjacent townsites named for him. The LARSON post office was established September 23, 1907 with Herman E. deVilliers pm. The elevation is 1928, the Zip Code is 58751, and the village, which incorporated in 1911, reached a peak population of 114 in 1920, with a decline to just 21 in 1980. Local residents state that the post office closed in 1980, but government records do not confirm this statement. Larsons is an erroneous spelling. (1, 2, 3, 18, 34, 40, 52, 67, 79)

**LARSON** (Cass). In 1881 the GNRR planned to build a townsite in NW¼ Sec. 12-142-50, Gardner Twp., just south of Gardner on land owned by Henry Larson. Despite promises to name the town for him, Mr. Larson refused to sell his land, and the railroad relocated the town one mile north, naming it GARDNER. (77, 305)

**LARVIK** (Emmons). This was a farm post office established May 27, 1899 with Brynhjolf Stolee pm in NW¼ Sec. 35-129-76, twelve miles south of Strasburg. It was named for Larvik, Vestfold, Norway, and closed October 31, 1902 with mail to Westfield. (2, 3, 34, 40, 66, 415)

**LARVIK** (Emmons). This name was adopted by new pm William A. Foell on January 28, 1908 as a name change for the BROFY post office, which served the townsite founded in 1904 as GODKIN. The new name honored townsite owner Edward Larvick, with a slight change in the spelling, who platted six blocks in NE¼ Sec. 5-133-76, McCulley Twp., and three blocks in SE¼ Sec. 32-134-76, Danbury Twp., in February 1908 on the west side of the NPRR tracks. Some say the change in spelling was influenced by the Norwegian city of Larvik, which had been the namesake of an earlier Larvik post office in Emmons County. In May 1908 Franz and Balthazar Tempel platted TEMPELTON on the east side of the NPRR tracks, and the two adjoining townsites engaged in a lively rivalry until May 9, 1911, when they merged as TEMVIK. (2, 3, 18, 40, 66)

**LATONA** (Walsh). This was a farm post office established February 18, 1884 with John Lennon pm. It was located in SW¼ Sec. 9-156-58, Latona Twp., seven miles south of Adams, and named for its township, which

was named for Latona, Ontario, Canada. The name is derived from Leto, a Greek mythological goddess and the mother of the sun god, Apollo, and the moon goddess, Diana. In 1905 the post office moved one mile SSW to SE¼ Sec. 17-156-58, the home of new pm George McIntyre, and closed May 31, 1908 with mail to Adams. (2, 5, 18, 19, 40, 75)

**LAUDA** (Bottineau). A post office of this name was established August 9, 1904 with Jonas J. Johnson pm, but the order was rescinded November 3, 1904. Mr. Johnson was at the time a merchant in the new GNRR townsite of LANDA, and it is assumed that this was an erroneous spelling entered by postal officials. The post office of LANDA, with the corrected spelling, was established January 13, 1905 with Andrew Helgeson pm. (3, 40)

**LAUREAT** (Rolette). This was a rural post office established March 25, 1887 with Euclyde Lamoureaux pm. It was located in SW¼ Sec. 3-161-71, Shell Valley Twp., five miles SW of Belcourt, and named for Laureat Martineau, a son of a pioneer family from Quebec, Canada. Joseph Plante operated a store and blacksmith shop here for many years. The post office was discontinued August 31, 1913 with mail to Rolla, but the store was still operating in the mid-1960's. Laureate is an incorrect spelling. (1, 2, 3, 18, 40, 123, 240)

**LAURENS** (Ramsey). This townsite was platted in 1882 by townsite owner Fred Lau in anticipation of the coming of the GNRR. It was located in NW¼ Sec. 25-155-66, Coulee Twp., five miles SE of Churchs Ferry, and the name is generally believed to have been coined from the last name of Mr. Lau. When the GNRR arrived in 1883, officials of the railroad renamed it PENN. Lauren is an erroneous spelling. (2, 18, 25, 103)

**LAWTHER** (Grant). Several maps circa 1910-1911 show a NPRR station named LAWTHER in Sec. 26-134-88, Elm Twp., seven miles east of Elgin. This was apparently a proposed name for the townsite that officially became HEIL in 1911, with the name honoring townsite owner William Lawther of Dubuque, IA. (3, 18, 414)

**LAWTHER** (Grant). The city of NEW LEIPZIG was renamed LAWTHER on January 15, 1912, apparently due to confusion with the still thriving inland village of Leipzig. The new name honored original townsite owner William Lawther of Dubuque, IA, who had also been the original namesake of Heil, but this name proved to be confusing with Lawton, Ramsey County, and the name NEW LEIPZIG was restored on August 2, 1912. Mike C. Rausch was the pm during this era. (2, 3, 17, 18, 40, 111, 177)

**LAWTON** (Ramsey). This post office was established October 10, 1899 with Norman Anderson pm in E½ Sec. 28-156-60, Lawton Twp. The GNRR reached the site in 1902, and the townsite incorporated as a village in October 1911. It was named for Gen. George Lawton, a veteran of the Spanish-American War, who led a group of ND National Guard volunteer infantrymen in the Philippines. Lawton is an Old English name meaning from the hillside farm. The elevation is

1522, the Zip Code is 58345, and a peak population of 233 was recorded in 1930. (1, 2, 18, 19, 40, 52, 103, 282)

**LEAKEY** (McKenzie). This was a rural post office established April 5, 1930 with John Leakey pm at his home in NE¼ Sec. 2-145-102, eighteen miles west of Grassy Butte. It was discontinued September 15, 1931 with mail to Bicycle. Leskey is an erroneous spelling. (2, 3, 34, 40, 414, 415)

**LEAL** (Barnes). This Soo Line RR townsite was founded in 1892 in NW¼ Sec. 20-142-60, Edna Twp., and was named by railroad officials to honor the Scottish-English settlers who came here from Canada in 1883. Leal is Scottish for faithful and true, and is used to represent heaven, and is derived from Old French and Latin roots. Joseph J. Bascom (1840-1918) moved the Uxbridge post office here on December 28, 1892. The village incorporated in 1911, and became a city in 1968. The elevation is 1465, the Zip Code is 58459, and a peak population of 105 was reached in 1930. The post office became a rural branch of Jamestown on November 1, 1975. (1, 2, 18, 33, 34, 40, 52, 76, 79, 328, 332)

**LEE** (Divide). This was a farm post office established October 2, 1911 with Peter J. Hansen pm. It was located in SW¼ Sec. 5-162-99, Twin Butte Twp., six miles SW of Ambrose. Most sources say it was named for Iver E. Lee (1885-1972), who homesteaded three miles south of here, while some say it was named for either Clarence W. Lee or Hans C. Lee, both area pioneers. The post office closed March 31, 1914 with mail to Ambrose. (2, 18, 40, 73)

**LEE** (Nelson). This was a rural settlement in SE¼ Sec. 30-149-58, Lee Twp., three miles SW of Kloten, and named for its township, which was named for Samuel and John M. Lee, pioneer settlers in the area. The post office was established September 5, 1881 with Ole Knutson Kjorvestad (1856-1933) pm in his country store. A population of 20 was reported in 1890, but the lack of a railroad prevented further development, and the post office closed August 31, 1905 with mail to Aneta. (2, 18, 25, 40, 53, 124, 128, 240)

**LEECHES** (Cass). This was a NPRR siding built in 1881 in NW¼ Sec. 33-138-50, Warren Twp., three miles NE of Davenport, and named for Addison Leech, a bonanza farmer just north of this siding. It was served by the Davenport post office. On April 10, 1887 it was renamed WARREN, and from 1908-1915 it was known as SCHAIBLE, after which it was again called WARREN. (2, 25, 34, 303)

**LEEDS** (Benson). A settlement called BARKER was here in 1886, and in the spring of that year the GNRR founded the townsite of LEEDS in Secs. 31 & 32-156-68, Leeds Twp., at the junction of the GNRR and the NPRR. It was named for Leeds, Yorkshire, England, an important manufacturing center dating back to 616 A.D., when it was called Loidis. The post office was established August 31, 1887 with Thomas Howrey pm. It incorporated as a village in 1899, and became a city in 1903 with Elisha

Bartlett Page as mayor. The elevation is 1519, the Zip Code is 58346, and the peak population of 797 was reached in 1960. Dr. A. B. Lund (1880-1972) was the town doctor for sixty-five years beginning in 1907. (1, 2, 5, 10, 18, 25, 34, 40, 52, 79, 236, 257)

**LEES RANCH** (Stutsman). This was a stopping point on the Fort Totten-Fort Seward trail in Sec. 33-143-64, Lyon Twp., about six miles east of Pingree. James Lees (1849-1926) came here in 1872 from Scotland and established a ranch on the prairie just north of Jim Lake. He handled most of the freight work on this early stage line before settling in Homer Twp., just SE of Jamestown. The site is served by the Jamestown post office, and is now part of the DePuy farm. Lee's Ranch is an erroneous spelling. (3, 25, 158, 160)

*Leff, ND postmark of July 1, 1908, the day the new name of Reeder is said to have been put into use*

**LEFF** (Adams). This was a ranch post office established November 15, 1907 with Henry W. O'Dell pm. It was located in SE¼ Sec. 10-130-98, Reeder Twp., one mile east of present-day Reeder, and named for the Leff brothers, pioneer area ranchers and miners. Albert Leff (1872-1941) came here in 1904 from IL, and was later a county commissioner and a merchant in Reeder. Charles G. Leff (1881-1918) managed the family ranch in S½ Sec. 24-130-98, two miles to the SE. A townsite began to develop in anticipation of the Milwaukee Road RR, but the railroad built the siding one mile to the west, naming it Reeder. The LEFF post office moved to Reeder on March 16, 1908, and officially changed its name to REEDER on May 29, 1908, although the new name was said to have not been actually used until July 1, 1908. (2, 34, 40, 189, 414, 415)

**LEFOR** (Stark). This rural community was founded in the 1890's as the center of a large colony of German-Hungarians. The post office was established February 8, 1911 with Adam A. Lefor pm. He had come here with his parents, four brothers, and their families from Schwaben Banat, Hungary in 1893. In 1917 the post office moved across the section line to SW¼ Sec. 16-137-94, the home of new pm John Reiner Jr., returning to approximately the original site in 1942. The Zip Code is 58641, and a peak population of 224 was reached in 1930. Prior to the establishment of the post office, the community was sometimes called SCHNELLREICH or SAINT ELIZABETH. (1, 2, 3, 18, 33, 40, 44, 74, 414)

**LEHIGH** (Richland). This GNRR station was built before 1890 in Sec. 8-133-47, Dwight Twp., about six miles NNW of Wahpeton,

and named for Lehigh, PA. Some years later it was renamed LURGAN. No development occurred here. (1, 2, 18, 25)

**LEHIGH** (Stark). This NPRR station was built in 1883 in Sec. 8-139-95, four miles east of Dickinson, to serve the coal mines in the area. The name was chosen to note the area's similarity to Lehigh, PA, also a coal mining town. Lehigh is a corruption of the Algonquin word *lechauweking*, meaning where there are forks. The post office was established April 29, 1893 with mine operator Anthony F. Reilly pm, closing March 28, 1921 with mail to Dickinson. A small settlement of about 25 people has existed here for many decades. The elevation is 2372. (1, 2, 10, 18, 25, 40, 74, 79)

**LEHR** (Logan & McIntosh). This townsite was founded in 1898 and named for Andreas and Johann Lehr, who had come here in 1886 from SD. It is located in Sec. 5-132-69, Lowenthal Twp., McIntosh County, and Sec. 34-133-69, Koepplin Twp., Logan County. The post office was established in McIntosh County on April 6, 1899 with John F. George pm. After existing as an incorporated village for a few years, LEHR became a city in 1909 to end the problem of having to have separate village boards for the portion of the settlement in each county. It billed itself as "The Smallest Incorporated City in the U.S.A. Situated in Two Counties." The Soo Line RR arrived here in 1898, but rail service virtually disappeared after 1970. The elevation is 2017, the Zip Code is 58460, and a peak population of 536 was reached in 1940, with most of the residents living in McIntosh County. (1, 2, 3, 18, 33, 40, 79, 115, 133, 134)

**LEIGH** (Adams). This was a rural post office established May 17, 1907 with Wendell White pm. After the name White was rejected by postal officials, it was named for Leigh, NE, which was given the maiden name of the wife of townsite owner A. M. Walling. Leigh is an Old English name meaning dweller in the meadow. It was first located in SE¼ Sec. 31-132-95, Taylor Butte Twp., fifteen miles north of Hettinger, and in 1908 moved one mile NW to SW¼ Sec. 30-132-95. In 1910 it moved one mile SE to SW¼ Sec. 32-132-95, the home of new pm Belle White. In 1912 it moved one mile NE to SE¼ Sec. 28-132-95, the home of Emil S. Nelson, where his wife Mary was the new pm. The post office closed September 30, 1918 with mail to Hettinger. (2, 3, 18, 19, 35, 50, 189, 414)

**LEIGHTON** (Williams). This was an early post office in the upper Missouri River region of Dakota Territory, established March 12, 1883 with Alva D. Landrum pm, operating only until July 13, 1883 when mail went to Fort Buford. Its location is thought to have been in NE¼ Sec. 15-154-97, Nesson Valley Twp., about twenty miles east of Williston. The name honors either Alvin C. Leighton, who was appointed post trader at Fort Buford in 1871, or Joseph Leighton, who was appointed pm at Fort Buford in 1876. (3, 40, 50, 420, 421)

**LEIN** (Burleigh). This was a farm post office established August 29, 1905 with Bernt M. Lein pm, who named it for his brother John

Martin Lein (1859-1943), who came here in 1904. Bernt Lein died in 1908, and John took over the pm duties until the post office closed July 31, 1914 with mail to Driscoll. It was located in NW¼ Sec. 34-141-75, Lein Twp., eleven miles north of Driscoll until 1908, when it was relocated one mile ENE to SW¼ Sec. 26-141-75, these sites being the homesteads of the Lein brothers. (1, 2, 8, 12, 18, 40, 63, 200)

**LEIPZIG** (Grant). This rural post office was established September 19, 1896 with Michael Nuss pm, and named by Daniel Sprecher for Leipzig, Bessarabia, which in turn had been named in 1815 for Leipzig, Germany, a city founded about 1017 and named with a corruption of the Slavonic word *lipa*, meaning lime tree. It was located in Sec. 29-135-89, Leipzig Twp., eight miles north of Elgin, until about 1902 when a townsite began to develop in NW¼ Sec. 32-135-89. Mr. Sprecher became pm at the townsite, which reached a population of about 200 in 1909, but the following year both the NPRR and Milwaukee Road RR bypassed the site, and many residents moved to the new railroad townsite of New Leipzig. The post office was closed by pm Orthelo W. Shadduck (1855-1920) on July 31, 1915 with mail to Elgin, and the site became known as OLD LEIPZIG. (2, 3, 5, 17, 18, 23, 40, 176, 177, 358)

**LEITH** (Grant). This was a Milwaukee Road RR station founded in 1910 in SW 1/4 Sec. 5-133-87, Valley View Twp., six miles SW of Carson. It was named by railroad officials for Leith, Scotland, the seaport just north of Edinburgh, which dates from 1128, and bears a Celtic name meaning wide, in reference to the Firth of Forth at this site. The post office was established August 24, 1910 with Elmer E. Carter pm. The town had an initial boom, incorporating as a village in 1915 and reaching a peak population of 174 in 1930, but a sharp decline has reduced the count to just 40 in 1984. The elevation is 2353, and the Zip Code is 58551. The depot closed in 1964, the last train ran in 1982, and the track was taken up in 1983, as LEITH struggles to survive into the next century. (1, 2, 3, 5, 17, 19, 33, 40, 79, 175, 176, 177)

**LELAND** (Mountrail). This area was first called MANSFIELD, but postal officials rejected this name, and the post office was established March 30, 1904 as LELAND with Iver F. Nelson pm. It was located on his farm in NE¼ Sec. 24-153-89, Shell Twp., ten miles NW of Plaza, and named by settlers from Leland, IA. Leland is an Old English name meaning from the meadow land. In 1904 it moved to NE¼ Sec. 18-153-88, Spring Coulee Twp., and in May 1907 it moved to the country store of new pm George T. Erickson in NE¼ Sec. 24-154-89, Oakland Twp. The post office closed September 30, 1907 with mail to Shell, and the store was moved into the new townsite of Plaza. (2, 19, 40, 72)

**LEMERT** (Foster). This Soo Line RR station was built in NW¼ Sec. 31-147-67, Birtsell Twp., eight miles NW of Carrington. The post office was established April 29, 1893 with Judge Joshua Lemert (1829-1918) pm, who came here in 1883 from OH and was

a longtime county judge, commuting daily to Carrington to perform his duties. The post office closed April 30, 1904 with mail to Carrington. The tiny village reported a population of 20 in 1920, and appeared on maps until the 1960's. (1, 2, 18, 40, 79, 97)

**LEMON** (Cavalier). This was a rural post office established January 4, 1883 with Amelia Burnett pm. It was located in Sec. 3-162-59, Harvey Twp., ten miles NE of Langdon, and named for George W. Lemon, a pioneer settler in the area. Julia M. Lemon became the pm in 1887, but the post office closed July 18, 1888 with mail to Elkwood. In 1889 the Stilwell post office was established in this same section as a small settlement developed, and operated until 1920. (2, 18, 25, 40)

**LENDRUM** (Kidder). This post office was established February 7, 1883 with George W. Chase pm. It was located in NE¼ Sec. 10-139-72, Sibley Twp., which is Coulter's Addition, the north end of the village of Dawson. The post office closed May 25, 1883, presumably because postal officials discovered that there were two post offices in Dawson, although mail was curiously sent to Tappen, not Dawson. The origin of the name is unknown. Sendeum is an erroneous spelling. (2, 3, 40)

**LEONARD** (Cass). This NPRR townsite was founded in 1881 in E½ Sec. 28-137-52, Leonard Twp., and named for Leonard C. Stiles, who was named pm when the post office was established December 19, 1881. Others say it was named for pioneer settler Leonard Stroble, or the name was selected by Mary Hewitt Watts, the original townsite owner, for a friend. Her husband, Edgerton Watts, donated money for a free library in 1913 to be built in her memory. The elevation is 1075, and the Zip Code is 58052. The village became a city in 1951, and the peak population of 535 was reached in 1930. (1, 2, 19, 25, 33, 34, 40, 79, 250)

**LEROY** (Pembina). This inland townsite was founded in 1887 in SE¼ Sec. 21-163-55, Saint Joseph Twp., on the south bank of the Pembina River. It was named for the old trading post at the site, which had been named for Julien Leroy, a French horologist and author. Leroy is an Old French/Latin name meaning royal. The post office was established August 30, 1887 with Albert Noice pm. The 1890 federal census showed 34 residents in LEROY, with a peak population of 64 being reported in 1930. The post office, Zip Code 58252, closed February 13, 1984. (2, 18, 19, 25, 38, 40, 41, 79, 108, 235)

**LEROY'S TRADING POST** (Pembina). This was a fur trading post established and run by Metis, French-Canadian/Chippewa halfbreeds, in the 1850's. It was located in Sec. 21-163-55, approximately the site of present-day Leroy, and named for the French author Julien Leroy. The Saint Joseph mission was moved here in 1873 from Walhalla. (2, 3, 108)

**LEVANT** (Grand Forks). This was a GNRR siding built in 1881 in SE¼ Sec. 24-154-52, Levant Twp., six miles NW of Manvel, with a station added to the site in March 1882. The name was chosen by settlers from Le-

vant, Ontario, Canada, and is a name associated with the lands around the eastern Mediterranean Sea, centering on Syria. The name translates as sunrise, or orient. A post office was authorized January 8, 1900 with Isaiah Steen pm, but the order was rescinded October 5, 1900. A school house was here for many years, and a population of 10 was reported in 1920, but no real development ever took place, and the site is now generally considered to be a part of the Manvel community. (1, 2, 3, 18, 25, 31, 40, 59, 75, 238, 338)

**LEVERICH** (Pierce). This was a GNRR loading station in SE¼ Sec. 9-157-73, Walsh Twp., between Rugby and Barton, and said to be named for a GNRR official. Fire destroyed the elevator at the site in 1927, but it was rebuilt. Ernest Tuff was the elevator manager for many years. A population of 20 was reported in 1920, and 5 residents were counted as late as 1960, but LEVERICH never had a post office. Leverich and Liverich are erroneous spellings. (1, 2, 38, 79, 114)

**LEWIS** (Griggs). First known as FLORENCE, this NPRR station built in 1899 in Sec. 4-147-61, Bryan Twp., was renamed by railroad officials for E. W. Lewis, a NPRR employee. Lewis is a Teutonic name meaning famous in battle. A post office was discussed as early as 1903, but because of duplication the name was changed to MOSE in 1904. Some railroad maps of the period continued to show this place as Lewis Siding. (2, 3, 19, 40, 65)

**LEWIS** (Renville). This was a pioneer settlement in NE¼ Sec. 21-161-87, Fairbanks Twp., four miles NE of Tolley. The post office was established December 28, 1900 with John E. Lewis pm. The village had a hotel, several stores, a livery, blacksmith shop, land office, and at one time about 100 residents, but when it was bypassed by the Soo Line RR, most residents moved to the nearby townsites of Norma and Tolley. The post office closed November 3, 1907 with mail to Norma, whose post office opened the following day. (2, 3, 40, 71, 322)

**LEWIS** (Sargent). Some sources list a LEWIS post office in Sargent County, operated 1894-1900 by one T. S. Lewis, a charter county commissioner. Government postal records do not list such a post office, nor is T. S. Lewis shown to a resident of this county, much less one of its officials. (2, 3, 40, 165)

**LEWIS** (Towner). This was a rural post office established January 10, 1895 with Emily Vinter pm at the home of her husband, Frederick J. Vinter, in SW¼ Sec. 1-159-66, Paulson Twp., two miles SE of Egeland. Some sources say it was named for James Seneca Lewis (1868-1953), later a prominent resident of Rolla, although it seems more likely that it was named for Thomas D. Lewis, a neighbor of the Vinters, who came here in 1889 at the age of 69 with his large family, many of whom homesteaded in Paulson Twp. The post office closed May 26, 1899 with mail to Arndt. (2, 3, 18, 40, 415)

**LEYDEN** (Pembina). This was a GNRR station in NE¼ Sec. 7-162-55, Advance Twp., between Walhalla and Backoo. The post office was established February 16, 1898 with John P. Myhre pm, and closed November 15, 1913 with mail to Backoo. It reopened March 1, 1915, closing for good December 31, 1956 with mail again to Backoo. The station was named for Leyden in the Netherlands, where the Pilgrims lived for about twelve years before coming to America in 1620. LEYDEN reported a population of 20 in 1920, and once had a depot, general store, drug store, blacksmith shop, lumber yard, and two grain elevators, but it is now a ghost town. (2, 33, 40, 108, 292)

**LIBBY BUTTE** (Dunn). This rural community was first known as HARTINGER, but when the post office was established June 24, 1909 with Elizabeth Hewson pm, it was renamed LIBBY BUTTE, combining the pm's nickname and noting the many buttes in the area. It was located in SW¼ Sec. 22-142-95, M. R. Twp., nine miles SE of Manning, and moved two miles north in 1915 to SW¼ Sec. 10-142-95, the home of new pm Charles W. Jones. The post office closed March 15, 1917 with mail to Emerson, although LIBBY BUTTE reported a population of 10 in 1920. (1, 2, 3, 18, 40, 223)

**LIBERAL** (Nelson). This was a rural post office established March 9, 1887 with Erick Erickson pm. It was located in NE¼ Sec. 33-149-59, Nesheim Twp., six miles SSW of McVille, and closed June 23, 1887 with mail to Bue. The origin of the name is unknown. (2, 25, 40, 415)

**LIBERTY** (Hettinger). This was a rural post office established February 15, 1909 with Della Hopwood pm in the country store operated by her husband, James Hopwood, in NE¼ Sec. 28-133-91, Cannon Ball Twp., five miles SW of Bentley. The store burned to the ground in 1911, and the post office was moved to the home of new pm A. F. Beasley in Sec. 31-132-92, Merrill Twp., twelve miles SW of Bentley. Pm C. M. Twitchel closed the post office January 2, 1916 with mail to Watrous. No explanation is given for the choice of this patriotic name. (1, 3, 18, 40, 53, 178, 179, 181)

**LIBERTY** (Ward). This was a farm post office established August 12, 1905 with Martin O. Hulberg (1869-1945) as pm, who was born in Norway and came here in 1902 from MN. It was named for its township, which was given this patriotic name, chosen by the local residents over the other suggested name of Foster. Later it was discovered that the township name was duplicated, and to comply with a state law prohibiting such duplication, the name was changed to Freedom. The post office was located in SW¼ Sec. 2-153-83, Freedom Twp., nine miles south of Minot, and closed March 15, 1906 with mail to Minot. (2, 3, 40, 100)

**LIDGERWOOD** (Richland). This townsite was founded in 1886 as the GNRR and Soo Line RR built westward with nearly parallel lines. It is located in Secs. 13 & 14-130-52, Grant Twp., and named for George I. Lidgerwood, the right-of-way agent for the Soo Line RR who platted the site with his partners, Gen. William D. Washburn and R. N. Ink. The post office was established March 2, 1887 with Jacob A. Rickert pm. The village

incorporated in 1895, and became a city in 1900 with J. D. Mulloy mayor. The elevation is 1090, the Zip Code is 58053, and a peak population of 1,147 was reached in 1950. Historical author Z'Dena Trinka (1893-1967) was born near here, and sculptor Ida Bisek Prokop Lee began her career in this city. For many years the Movius family dominated local affairs, achieving success in many fields. (1, 2, 3, 18, 33, 40, 52, 79, 147, 362)

**LIDSTROM** (Morton). George Monson (1878-1939) is credited with discovering coal south of Glen Ullin in 1901, but real development did not begin until about 1920 when Andrew, Ernest, Hadley, and Leonard Lidstrom, all sons of pioneer Charles Lidstrom, developed an underground mining operation in Secs. 21, 22, 27 & 28-138-88, four miles SE of Glen Ullin. A two-story headquarters building, several houses, several temporary buildings, and a store operated by William Moskie were built here, but the mine closed in 1924 and LIDSTROM became a ghost town. (3, 17, 105)

**LIGNITE** (Burke). Some sources say this GNRR station was intended to be named KINCAID, but since its founding in April 1907 in NW¼ Sec. 12-162-92, Vale Twp., it has been called LIGNITE to note the coal veins located in the area. Lignite coal is partially carbonized fossil wood retaining its woody fiber. The post office was established April 22, 1907 with Thorvald Kopsland pm. LIGNITE was a principal contender for county seat honors when Burke County was organized in 1910, but it lost to Bowbells. The elevation is 1575, the Zip Code is 58752, and the village, which incorporated in 1915, reached a peak population of 355 in 1960. (1, 2, 3, 5, 18, 33, 34, 40, 52, 67, 79)

**LIGNITE** (Ward). A Soo Line RR station was built in 1894 in Sec. 20-160-88, Kenmare Twp., to serve the many lignite coal mines in the area. The post office was established December 27, 1894 with Augustine Rouse, one of the mine operators, as pm, but Mr. Rouse was killed in a quarrel in 1896, and the post office closed November 20, 1896 with mail to Donnybrook. A new townsite was founded the following spring, but the name was changed to KENMARE. (2, 3, 40, 100)

**LILAC** (Bottineau). This was a farm post office established March 17, 1900 with Emil Olson (1877-1928), a native of Sweden, as pm. It was located in NE 1/4 Sec. 1-163-78, Scandia Twp., five miles NW of Souris, and named for the purple-flowered shrub common to the area. The name is derived from *lilak*, Arabic for bluish. The post office closed January 31, 1902 with mail to Bottineau. (2, 3, 4, 34, 40, 101)

**LILLA** (McHenry). This was a farm post office established Janaury 25, 1901 with Jennie H. O'Brien as the first and only pm. It was located on the farm owned by her husband, Donophan O'Brien, in NE¼ Sec. 23-152-76, Strege Twp., four miles NNE of Drake. Mr. O'Brien was a native of Ireland, coming to America in 1885, while Mrs. O'Brien was born in MN of Welsh ancestry. The post office was discontinued June 30, 1904. The origin of the name is unknown. Several

sources and accounts refer to this post office as Lillian, but all post office records show the name as LILLA. (2, 3, 18, 40, 182, 412, 414, 415)

**LINCOLN** (Burleigh). This was a rural subdivision started in the early 1970's as Fort Lincoln Estates, named for the nearby military post which had recently been abandoned. It was located in N½ Sec. 19-138-79, Apple Creek Twp., about five miles SE of Bismarck. The residents chose to incorporate as a city in 1977, shortening the name to LINCOLN at that time. Warren Enyart was elected as the first mayor, and the city reported a population of 657 in 1980. (3, 34)

**LINCOLN** (Morton). A group calling itself the Lincoln Townsite Company approached the first Morton County commissioners on October 7, 1878 with a proposal to donate a site in Sec. 28-139-81 for a courthouse, with the "new" town to be named LINCOLN. The proposal was accepted, although the post office chose the name MORTON. On December 14, 1878 the same commissioners changed the name to MANDAN, and the post office followed suit on March 3, 1879. The name LINCOLN honored the martyred President, and was undoubtedly influenced by nearby Fort Abraham Lincoln. (2, 3, 343)

**LINCOLN** (Renville). When it was founded in 1903 in NE¼ Sec. 14-158-82, Ensign Twp., this GNRR townsite was named LINCOLN for the sixteenth President of the United States, but it was discovered that a village in Sheridan County already had this name, so the name was changed to GLENBURN. (2, 3, 19, 71, 322)

**LINCOLN** (Sheridan). George Reiswig sold this site, SW¼ Sec. 13-148-75, Lincoln Twp., to the GNRR in 1899, but the planned railroad never materialized, and Mr. Reiswig repurchased the land. In 1900 a townsite nevertheless was begun and named for its township, which was named for President Abraham Lincoln (1809-1865). Lincoln is a Celtic name meaning from the settlement by the pool. The post office was established February 14, 1904 with Conrad C. Reiswig, George's brother, as pm, with John Diede as the mail carrier. On October 18, 1912 the name was changed to LINCOLN VALLEY. (2, 3, 10, 21, 40)

**LINCOLN VALLEY** (Sheridan). This inland townsite was founded in 1900 by George and Conrad C. Reiswig as LINCOLN. On October 18, 1912 the name was changed to LINCOLN VALLEY at the suggestion of local banker Herman H. Hohenstein, who became the pm later that year. The "valley" part of the name described the location, and set this town apart from the many places in the country with this now common place name. It was located in SW¼ Sec. 13-148-75, Lincoln Twp., twelve miles north of Denhoff. The population never exceeded 100, and the post office closed July 7, 1961 with mail to Denhoff. Joe Leintz became the subject of national publicity in December 1972 as the last resident of this once bustling village, but shortly afterwards he moved to New Rockford, making LINCOLN VALLEY a ghost town. (2, 21, 30, 38, 40)

**LINDEN** (Burleigh). A map of ND circa 1901 shows the "Linden P. O." in NW 1/4 Sec. 8-142-76, Wing Twp., three miles west of present-day Wing. This site was at the time known as the Linden Ranch, said to be named for the native trees, and managed by Lewis Ong, a native of IA who later was associated with the post offices at Andrews, Canfield, and Ong. Postal records do not confirm the existence of the LINDEN post office. The ranch was later called the Boynton, Soder, or Dawson Ranch. (3, 12, 34, 40, 414)

**LINSTAD** (Walsh). This was a rural post office established November 16, 1896 with Louis Swenson pm. It was located in NW¼ Sec. 11-156-59, Shepherd Twp., eight miles SW of Adams on the west bank of the Forest River. It was named for Ole Linstad, a pioneer settler in the area, and closed January 31, 1914 with mail to Adams. (1, 2, 18, 40, 53, 75)

**LINTON** (Emmons). This city was founded in 1898 in SE¼ Sec. 7-132-76, and has grown north into Sec. 6 and east into Sec. 8, with the original section commonly called Old Town. It is a double railroad terminus, with the NPRR coming here from the north, and the Milwaukee Road RR coming here from the south. LINTON was named for attorney George W. Lynn, who rejected using Lynn as the name, and only accepted this name because it was sufficiently camouflaged to make his own name virtually unrecognizable. It was founded as a potential new county seat, and won that honor in the election of November 1898. The post office was established February 21, 1899 with Charles A. Patterson pm. It incorporated as a village in 1906, and became a city in 1914. The elevation is 1731, the Zip Code is 58552, and a peak population of 1,826 was reached in 1960. (1, 2, 3, 10, 18, 33, 34, 40, 66, 79)

**LINTON** (Sargent). This townsite was founded in April 1883 at the terminus of the NPRR's projected line from Fergus Falls, MN to the Black Hills. It was located in SW¼ Sec. 1-132-54, Milnor Twp., and was called END OF THE TRACK and GRABALL before being named LINTON for Nathan Linton, a pioneer merchant here. A boom town complete with a newspaper began to form, but the NPRR was unable to obtain additional right-of-way at their price, and another three miles of track were built westward in August 1883. Everything in LINTON was soon moved to the new terminus in Sec. 9-132-54, three miles to the west, which became Milnor. (2, 3, 165, 171)

**LINUSVILLE** (McHenry). This was a rural post office and country store in SE¼ Sec. 2-153-77, Karlsruhe Twp., eleven miles NNE of Balfour on the north shore of a small lake. The post office was established March 23, 1904 with Linus Peterson, originally spelled Pettersen, as pm. It closed March 31, 1909 with mail to Balfour. (2, 3, 18, 40, 53, 183, 412, 415)

**LIPPERT** (Stutsman). This place name appeared in the 1960's as Exit #55 on Interstate 94 west of Jamestown, and is the name of the township in which this exit is located. Lippert Twp. (139-65) was settled by Germans from Russia, and named for George Lippert, a prominent member of this group, who settled here in 1880. Because motorists expected to find a townsite at this exit, the name was removed from signs in 1987. (3, 23, 158)

**LISBON** (Ransom). This townsite was founded in 1880 by Joseph L. Colton (1840-1896). His wife, Diana Robinson, was from Lisbon Center, NY, which was named for Lisbon, Portugal, whose ancient name was Olisipo. The new townsite was platted on both sides of the Sheyenne River in Secs. 1, 2, 11 & 12-134-56, Island Park Twp. The post office was established January 23, 1880 with Mr. Colton as pm, and his brother-in-law, George Murray, as the first mail carrier. LISBON became the county seat in 1881, and the NPRR reached the site in 1882. It incorporated as a city in 1883 with G. B. Green mayor. Mr. Green defeated Mr. Colton for this honor, after which Mr. Colton moved to Ward County and founded the new townsite of Burlington. The elevation is 1112, the Zip Code is 58054, and the peak population of 2,286 was reached in 1980 as the city has maintained a steady growth since its founding. The ND Soldiers Home was built here in 1891. (1, 2, 3, 5, 18, 25, 33, 40, 52, 77, 79, 100, 201, 202)

**LITCHVILLE** (Barnes). The NPRR founded this townsite in 1900 in E½ Sec. 25-137-60, Rosebud Twp. Hans Jacob Hanson, pm at the rural post office of LITCHVILLE, six miles SSE in LaMoure County, moved his business to the new townsite in October 1900 and managed to persuade railroad officials to retain the old name. Because he did not notify postal officials of this move, government records do not show the move taking place until September 5, 1901. The village incorporated in 1903, and reached a peak population of 528 in 1920. The elevation is 1488, and the Zip Code is 58461. Fred George Aandahl, Governor of ND 1945-1950, was born here in 1897. (1, 2, 3, 18, 33, 34, 40, 52, 76, 262, 329, 333)

**LITCHVILLE** (LaMoure). This was a rural post office established February 13, 1886 with Hans Jacob Hanson as the first and only pm. It was located in his country store in Sec. 10-136-59, Litchville Twp., six miles SSE of the future NPRR townsite of LITCHVILLE in Barnes County. Mr. Hanson named it for his hometown of Litchfield, MN, which was named for the brothers Egbert S., Edwin C., and E. Darwin Litchfield of London, England, financiers of railroad activities in MN in the 1860's. The change from "field" to "ville" was apparently a matter of personal preference on the part of Mr. Hanson. In October 1900 he moved his business to the new NPRR townsite of LITCHVILLE, but did not notify postal officials, so government records show the transfer as occurring on September 5, 1901. Mr. Hanson served as pm at the new townsite until 1910. (2, 3, 10, 13, 25, 40, 76, 240, 333)

**LITHIA** (Richland). Accounts differ as to whether William T. Montgomery was a freed slave, or the son of a slave, but it is clear that this black man had had considerable formal education when he homesteaded in Sec. 11-136-49, Eagle Twp., in the 1880's. About 1888 he built an elevator where the Milwaukee Road RR crossed his land, and named it for his mother, although some sources say it was named for Lithia, MA. In the early 1900's a small village began, and a general store operated at the site 1909-1920. The elevator closed in 1963 and was moved into Walcott in the 1970's, leaving the site vacant. (1, 2, 3, 18, 147, 345)

**LITTLE CHICAGO** (Traill). This was a speculative pioneer settlement founded in 1879 just south of present-day Mayville in anticipation of the GNRR. Albert F. Anderson, who settled in SW¼ Sec. 18-146-52, Mayville Twp., in 1878, operated a business called The Chicago Store, and the town took its name from this venture. The exact location of LITTLE CHICAGO is the subject of debate, with some sources placing it in Sec. 8-146-52, one mile NE of the Anderson land. When Mayville was founded in 1881, LITTLE CHICAGO soon disappeared. (3, 34, 225, 359, 395, 415)

**LITTLE CHICAGO OF THE WEST** (Dunseith). This townsite was founded in 1882 by Giles W. Gilbert, Lemuel G. Welton, and Edward J. Oakes, all of whom filed in Sec. 36-162-73, Gilbert Twp. The site was platted by the Turtle Mountain Coal & Land Co., and named to note the promoters' hopes that it would soon rival the great city in IL, which bears an Algonquin name meaning garlic field. A settlement did in fact begin here, but it was soon given the more manageable name of DUNSEITH. (2, 3, 10, 123, 398, 415)

**LITTLE FARGO** (Bottineau). This was a rural community of French-Canadians founded about 1889, and centered around the Roman Catholic Mission of St. Genevieve in NW¼ Sec. 35-160-74, Cecil Twp., two miles SW of Overly. Hyacinth Richard (1866-1952), Edmond Fortin (1861-1943), Joseph Cyrille Marcotte (1842-1904), and Theophile Dostaler were the first settlers, coming here from Quebec. They passed through Fargo on their way to this site, and were sufficiently impressed by the Cass County city to transfer its name to their new home. Most of the community's residents had moved to Overly by 1921. (18, 101, 153)

**LITTLE FORK** (Steele). This was a farm post office established May 27, 1878 with Tosten Erickson pm. It was located in NW¼ Sec. 12-147-54, Enger Twp., nine miles NW of Portland, just inside the Steele County line, and named to note its location near the confluence of the Goose River and its north fork. The post office closed February 11, 1879 with mail to Newburgh. (2, 3, 25, 40, 414, 415)

**LITTLE HEART** (Morton). This was the first stage station out of Bismarck on the Bismarck-Deadwood trail laid out in 1876. The structures here were moved away or dismantled long ago, but recent historical exploration has found evidence that places the station in NE¼ Sec. 29-137-81, four miles NNW of Saint Anthony, at a crossing of the Little Heart River. (3, 418)

**LITTLE HEART** (Morton). This was a pioneer community of primarily Roman Catholic

Germans from Russia, founded about 1890 in Secs. 6 & 7-136-81, and named for Little Heart Butte which was just to the north. About 1896 it was renamed for the local church, SAINT ANTHONY. (2, 3)

**LITTLEHEART** (Morton). This was a rural post office established August 14, 1900 with Carl Hartwig pm. It was located in SW¼ Sec. 15-137-81, five miles north of Saint Anthony, and named by the pm for the nearby river. The one-word spelling was required to comply with government spelling regulations. The post office closed August 15, 1902 with mail to Saint Anthony. (2, 3, 40, 414)

**LITTLE HEART** (Morton). This was a farm post office established March 1, 1905 with Javan G. Nead pm. It was located in SW¼ Sec. 22-137-81, four miles north of Saint Anthony, and named for the nearby butte and river. The post office closed May 5, 1914 with mail to Mandan. (2, 3, 17, 18, 40, 107, 414)

**LITTLE LAKE** (Pembina). An 1890 guide to ND lists this place as being in Pembina County, and served by the Drayton post office. No other information is available. (25)

**LITTLE MISSOURI** (Billings). This frontier settlement began in 1879 in Sec. 22-140-102, Medora Twp., just west of present-day Medora on the west bank of the Little Missouri River. The civilian population lived adjacent to the new NPRR station and the military post called LITTLE MISSOURI CANTONMENT. A post office called COMBA served the area 1880-1883. This was the first settlement in Billings County, but it declined rapidly after the establishment of Medora across the river in 1883. The Indian name for the Little Missouri River was *Takchaokuti Wakpa*, meaning shooting deer river. Missouri was the name of an Indian tribe living near the Missouri River's mouth just north of Saint Louis, MO. They called the river *pekitanoul*, meaning muddy water. (2, 3, 10, 18, 25, 34, 36, 40, 79)

**LITTLE MISSOURI CANTONMENT** (Billings). This was the military post located in Sec. 22-140-102, Medora Twp., which was founded November 10, 1879 to protect railroad crews and settlers at the adjacent civilian townsite of LITTLE MISSOURI. The post office serving the site was named COMBA. Capt. Stephen Baker of the Sixth Infantry from Fort Abraham Lincoln was the first commanding officer here. The cantonment officially closed March 4, 1883 and the buildings were dismantled. An 1890 map still shows this place, but with the name Cantonment Bad Lands. (2, 3, 25, 81)

**LITTLE MISSOURI STATION** (Slope). This was the tenth station on the Bismarck-Fort Keogh mail route established in 1878 in NW¼ Sec. 16-136-104, Wilkens Twp., near the old Yule Ranch. It was first located on the east bank of the Little Missouri River, but was later moved to the west bank. It closed in 1882 when the route was replaced by the newly-built NPRR mainline. (3, 82)

**LITTLE MUDDY** (Williams). This pioneer settlement was begun about 1875 in Sec. 19-154-100, Stony Creek Twp., and named for the Little Muddy River which flows into the Missouri River at this site. The post

office was established September 30, 1878 with Robert C. Mathews (1848-1922) pm. Other pioneers here were merchant Gustave B. Metzger (1853-1932) and Luther S. "Yellowstone" Kelly (1849-1929), a scout and mail carrier. The post office closed November 29, 1882 with mail to Fort Berthold. It reopened January 15, 1884 with Philip J. Cates pm, closing July 12, 1887 when it was replaced by the post office at the new GNRR townsite of Williston on the west, or opposite, bank of the river. (2, 3, 25, 40, 50)

**LITTLE NORWAY** (Ransom). This was an unofficial name for the civilian townsite of FORT RANSOM in the early days, noting the fact that almost all of the residents were of Norwegian ancestry. (2, 3)

**LITTLE SALT** (Pembina). An 1890 guide to ND lists this place as being in Pembina County, and served by the Grafton post office. No other information is available. (25)

**LIVONA** (Burleigh). This was a rural post office 1885-1955, located in Emmons County on the east bank of the Missouri River, opposite Fort Rice. On June 30, 1955 it became a rural branch of the Bismarck post office, moving ten miles north to the farm home of Larry K. Schramm in SW¼ Sec. 33-137-78, Telfer Twp., Burleigh County. It shares Bismarck's Zip Code of 58501, but retains the old LIVONA name as a mailing address. (3, 33, 34, 40, 405)

**LIVONA** (Emmons). This was a rural post office established December 31, 1883 with Lavina Livingston pm. It was named for the pm, with an unexplained change in the spelling, although others say it was named for the Livonia District in Russia. It was located in Sec. 18-135-78, thirteen miles WNW of Hazelton. For over fifty years the post office was run by members of the Wesley Baker (1847-1929) family, either from a farm home in NE¼ Sec. 19-135-78, or from a country store in SE¼ Sec. 12-135-79. A population of 32 was reported in 1890. On June 30, 1955 pm John Henry Baker, a grandson of Wesley, closed the facility and it was relocated ten miles north into Burleigh County, where it became a rural branch of the Bismarck post office. (1, 2, 3, 18, 25, 33, 40, 66, 79, 113, 401, 405)

**LLOYD** (Adams). This was a rural post office established June 8, 1908 with William M. Vanderly pm. It was first located in NE¼ Sec. 31-130-92, Spring Butte Twp., twelve miles ENE of Haynes at the forks of the South Cannonball River. In 1911 it moved one-half mile SE to NW¼ Sec. 5-129-92, North Lemmon Twp., with Mr. Vanderly continuing as pm. The origin of the name is unknown, although it is a Celtic name meaning gray. The post office closed August 31, 1911 with mail to Petrel. (2, 18, 19, 34, 40, 414)

**LLOYD'S SPUR** (Ward). This was a Soo Line RR loading station in NE¼ Sec. 32-156-84, Kirkelie Twp., one mile SE of the Vanderwalker station. It served the Lloyd Coal Co. mine in Secs. 31 & 32-156-84, owned by Harold Lloyd, who shared his name with a famous actor of the era. The station was

built about 1900, and was removed in 1920. (1, 2, 18, 100)

**LOCKE** (Ramsey). This was a farm post office established September 4, 1882 with James A. Locke pm. It was located in NW¼ Sec. 28-155-63, Morris Twp., five miles ESE of Webster at the NE end of Sweetwater Lake, and closed September 30, 1892 with mail to Devils Lake. It was reestablished July 9, 1898, closing for good February 1, 1899 with mail again to Devils Lake. A townsite was planned for the site, and a population of 13 was reported in 1890, but not much happened beyond that small beginning. (2, 3, 18, 25, 40, 103)

**LOGAN** (Barnes). This was a farm post office established November 17, 1884 with Henry Barden pm, and named for John Logan who settled in this area in 1880 and was a state legislator in 1895. It was located in SW¼ Sec. 20-142-58, Ashtabula Twp., thirteen miles NNW of Valley City, and closed January 14, 1886 with mail to Sanborn. (2, 3, 18, 25, 40, 76)

**LOGAN** (Ward). This was a rural post office established April 13, 1887 with Robert A. Davidson pm, who named it for Gen. John Alexander Logan (1826-1886), a Civil War hero who later was a U. S. Senator from IL and was the Republican Vice Presidential candidate in 1884. It was located between Minot and Sawyer, and closed May 31, 1898 with mail to Sawyer. It reopened April 14, 1903 with Owen Hecker pm, closing April 20, 1904. Later that year a townsite was founded on the Soo Line RR in NE¼ Sec. 24-154-82, Sundre Twp., and Mr. Hecker reestablished the post office, naming it for himself. On November 15, 1909 new pm Anna A. Beebe restored the LOGAN name. The post office closed September 30, 1931 with mail to Minot, but the community still exists, reporting a population of 60 in 1960. (1, 2, 3, 10, 13, 18, 25, 40, 79, 100)

**LOGAN CENTER** (Grand Forks). This was a rural community founded in 1886 in SW¼ Sec. 15-150-56, Logan Center Twp., and named for Gen. John A. Logan, a Civil War hero and prominent politician who had recently died. The name was suggested by area resident W. P. Wilson, also a veteran of the Civil War. The "center" part of the name noted the fact that it was sixteen miles NW of Northwood, sixteen miles SW of Larimore, sixteen miles NE of Aneta, and sixteen miles SE of Niagara. The post office was located just across the road to the south from 1893-1919, but operated under the name Fergus. The Logan Center Consolidated School operated 1904-1960, and was the first of that type in ND. (2, 31, 40, 65, 241)

**LOMA** (Cavalier). This post office was established in 1905 in SW¼ Sec. 33-160-61, Loma Twp., as IRENE, and on February 23, 1906 pm Henry F. Baker changed the name to LOMA for its township, which bears a Spanish name meaning broad-topped hill. The site became a Soo Line RR station, and experienced a boom period that saw the population rise to 293 in 1930, but a steady decline has reduced the count to just 6 in 1970. The post office became a rural branch of Alsen on December 30, 1964, and closed

December 10, 1965 with mail to Alsen. (1, 2, 3, 12, 18, 40, 41, 52)

**LOMICE** (Walsh). This was a rural post office established June 12, 1900 with Frank Kvasnicka pm, and named for Lomnice, Bohemia, the hometown of many area settlers, with a slight change in the spelling. It was located in NE¼ Sec. 3-155-59, Sauter Twp., eleven miles SW of Adams. The post office closed October 4, 1905 with mail to Lawton. In 1937 St. Catherine's Catholic Church was built at this site. (2, 40, 75)

**LONE TREE** (Oliver). This was the second stop to the north on the Glen Ullin Northern Stage Line, operated 1910-1915 by Gust A. Falk. Its exact location is unknown, although logic would put it somewhere in the western half of Oliver County. (3, 105)

**LONE TREE** (Richland). This was a mail relay station on the Fort Abercrombie military trail during the 1870's. It was located in Eagle Twp. (135-49), about three miles NW of Fort Abercrombie, and named to note a single large cottonwood tree at the site that guided travelers across the open prairie. (2, 3, 147)

**LONE TREE** (Ward). This was a GNRR townsite in SW¼ Sec. 32-156-85, Foxholm Twp., four miles west of Des Lacs, and named by GNRR officials for the lone tree fifty rods west of town. The post office was established March 20, 1888 with Theodore Schufelt pm, but the order was rescinded. It was reestablished February 14, 1890 with Nicholaus Zirbes pm, but closed November 11, 1891 with mail to Minot. Later this area was served by the Des Lacs post office until the local post office reopened August 1, 1902 using the one-word spelling, LONETREE. (2, 3, 18, 25, 40, 79, 100, 372)

**LONETREE** (Ward). This was a GNRR townsite in SW¼ Sec. 32-156-85, Foxholm Twp., four miles west of Des Lacs, where a post office called LONE TREE operated 1890-1891. Development was very slow, but about 1900 a small townsite did begin to develop, and the post office reopened August 1, 1902 with Benjamin F. Stump pm, who used a one-word spelling of the old name to comply with current spelling regulations. The elevation is exactly 2000, and a peak population of 75 was reported in 1920, with a decline to just 37 in 1960. The post office closed December 31, 1957 with mail to Berthold. (3, 18, 40, 100)

**LONG LAKE** (Kidder). This is the name of Exit #42 on Interstate 94 at the corner of Secs. 8, 9, 16 & 17-139-74, Pleasant Hill Twp., six miles west of Steele. It is named for the large lake about six miles to the south, which was named for its shape. (3)

**LONG LAKE CITY** (Burleigh). This was a city founded about 1880 at the western end of Long Lake, which was named for its shape. Maps of the period show it in either SW¼ Sec. 22-137-76 or NW¼ Sec. 35-137-76, Long Lake Twp. This was the expected location of a number of proposed railroads, and great things were predicted for the site. The NPRR and Soo Line RR did eventually build through here, and their intersection is in this area, but nothing anywhere near the

hopes of the promoters ever developed. A permanent settlement, Moffit, did not develop until the early 1900's, and promoters again predicted great things, including an effort to create a new county, but LONG LAKE CITY is today a ghost town, and Moffit is, and always has been, a very small village. (2, 3, 8, 14, 79)

**LORAIN** (Renville). Although the post office of this tiny village operated as LORAINE from 1907-1976, the GNRR station used the name LORAIN. Both names were corruptions of Fort LaReine in Canada. (3, 40)

**LORAINE** (Renville). This GNRR townsite was founded in 1907 in SE¼ Sec. 9-162-84, Hurley Twp., between Sherwood and Mohall. The name is said to have been suggested by Mohall banker Sherwood H. Sleeper, the namesake of Sherwood, for Fort LaReine, Verendrye's fort on the Assiniboine River in Manitoba with a corruption of the spelling. The post office was established as LORAINE on December 13, 1907 with Pearl Robertson pm, although the GNRR station was called LORAIN. The village incorporated in 1913, but development was very slow, with a peak population of just 92 being reported in 1930. The post office, Zip Code 58753, closed July 1, 1976. (2, 3, 18, 33, 40, 41, 71, 79)

**LORDSBURG** (Bottineau). This was a rural community in SE¼ Sec. 14-161-74, Lordsburg Twp., twelve miles ESE of Bottineau. The majority of the first settlers were French-Canadian Roman Catholics. The name honored either Frank Lord, a pioneer merchant, or C. J. Lord, another pioneer settler in the area. The post office was established October 15, 1884 with David Miller pm. The village recorded a population of 42 in 1890, but a decline began about 1900, and the post office closed June 30, 1910 with mail to Omemee. The name is perpetuated by a National Wildlife Refuge at the site. (2, 18, 25, 40, 101, 153)

**LORING** (Dunn). This rural post office was established April 13, 1909 with Charles Jacobson pm. It was first located in NE¼ Sec. 6-143-91, but in 1910 it was moved three miles NE to SW¼ Sec. 20-144-91, Loring Twp., the home of new pm Clarence N. Lee (1881-1959), who came here from Norway in 1903, and was a state legislator 1927-1931. Loring is a High German name meaning famous in war, said to be derived from Lorraine. Some have speculated that it may have been named for Loring Park in Minneapolis, MN, which was named for Charles M. Loring, a pioneer promoter of parks in that city. The post office closed January 31, 1916 with mail to Dodge. (1, 2, 3, 10, 18, 19, 40, 222, 223)

**LORRAINE** (Dickey). This was a farm post office established April 9, 1884 with Alexander D. Walker pm. It was located in SW¼ Sec. 2-129-65, Lorraine Twp., twelve miles west of Ellendale. In 1897 it moved three miles west to the Theodore Graf farm in NW¼ Sec. 5-129-64, Elm Twp., which was on the stage route from Ellendale to Ashley. The post office closed March 31, 1904 with mail to Ellendale, and the following year the area began receiving mail service from Forbes. It is thought that the name came

from the province of Lorraine in France. Lorraine is a French word derived from the High German, and means famous in war. (1, 2, 3, 10, 19, 40, 154, 240, 264, 316)

**LOSTWOOD** (Mountrail). This was a rural post office established September 25, 1907 with Samuel Steele pm in SE¼ Sec. 18-158-91, Lostwood Twp., and named for its township, which owes its name to the story of a man who about 1900 cut some wood to be used for making slaked lime and left it here to dry. Others found it and used it as fuel to heat their homes that winter. The man returned the next spring, and the wood was "lost." Others say the name commemorates the legend of a load of wood that was lost in a blizzard. The post office moved to the new GNRR townsite in Sec. 23-158-91 in 1912, retaining its name. The elevation is 2343, and a population of 100 was reported in 1920, but the town has declined rapidly and is now nearly a ghost town. The post office, Zip Code 58754, closed April 1, 1974 with mail to Stanley. (1, 2, 33, 40, 72, 79)

**LOUREN** (Walsh). This was a farm post office established August 9, 1880 with Ole A. Moe pm. It was located in SW¼ Sec. 10-158-55, Dundee Twp., four miles WSW of Hoople, and closed December 20, 1880 with mail to Mount View. The origin of the name is unknown. Lowren is an erroneous spelling. (2, 3, 40, 415)

**LOVDOKKEN** (Richland). This was a farm post office established June 22, 1894 with Ole Lovdokken pm. Mr. Lovdokken (1863-1919) came here in 1890 from Norway, and was active in school, church, township, and county affairs. He visited Norway in 1914 during that nation's 100th Jubilee as the personal representative of Governor Hanna, and founded *Hallingen*, a Norwegian-language magazine. The post office was located in Sec. 4-134-51, Garborg Twp., eleven miles west of Colfax, but the order was rescinded October 13, 1894 before it had gone into operation. Loodokken is an erroneous spelling. (2, 3, 40, 147)

**LOVELL** (Griggs). This was a NPRR station founded in 1899 in Sec. 3-146-59, Cooperstown Twp., between Cooperstown and Jessie, and named for Alfred Lovell, Superintendent of Motive Power for the railroad. No development occurred at the site. (1, 2, 18, 79)

**LOWDEN** (Bowman). The settlement founded in 1907 in Sec. 11-131-102, Bowman Twp., was first called TWIN BUTTES, and apparently for a short time it was also known as EDEN, although this latter name was probably never used on a local basis. The LOWDEN post office was established July 26, 1907 with Arthur L. Lowden pm, who with his brother, W. O. Lowden, had erected the first building at the site. On October 19, 1907 the name of the post office was changed to BOWMAN. (2, 34, 40)

**LOWELL** (McIntosh). Settlement began here about 1890, and on June 30, 1890 the post office was established with James Beveridge, a native of Scotland, as pm. Located in Sec. 36-129-70, Lowell Twp., the name was chosen by settlers from Lowell,

MI, which was named for Lowell, MA, which was named for Francis Cabot Lowell (1775-1817), a pioneer processor of cotton in New England. Lowell is derived from the Old English lovell, which means beloved. Elvin Edison Amburn (1863-1920) became pm on September 17, 1902 and moved the post office to his home in NW¼ Sec. 31-129-70, eight miles SW of Ashley. His family continued to operate the post office after his death, but it closed April 30, 1926 with mail to Ashley. Local residents usually referred to this place as LOWELL VALLEY. (1, 2, 10, 18, 19, 40, 45, 53, 134, 211)

**LOWELL VALLEY** (McIntosh). This was the locally used name for the area around the rural post office named LOWELL, which operated 1890-1926. (2, 3, 10, 45, 134)

**LOWRY** (Barnes). This was a NPRR station built in 1893 in NW¼ Sec. 20-141-59, Stewart Twp., four miles south of Rogers. It was named for John Lowry, who settled here in 1879 and was a promoter of the station. In October 1897 it was relocated to the new townsite of Rogers. (2, 34)

**LOWRY** (Logan). In 1887 a Mr. Richards of the Soo Line RR chose a site in Sec. 11-134-72, Starkey Twp., six miles SE of Napoleon, for a new townsite which he named LOWRY for unknown reasons. Along with T. J. Butler, they predicted that it would become the most important city between Bismarck and Aberdeen, SD. It tried to get the county seat in a special election in 1887, but lost to Napoleon 24-21. The lone building was soon moved to Napoleon, and LOWRY was vacant until 1912, when the Soo Line RR built a loading station here called PETERS. (3, 25, 116)

**LOYAL** (McKenzie). This was a rural post office established May 22, 1914 with Claud M. Murray pm, who named it for his hometown of Loyal, WI, which was named during the Civil War when it was claimed that every eligible male in the town had enlisted in the military. It was located in SE¼ Sec. 18-146-104, Loyal Twp., about forty miles SW of Watford City, and closed April 15, 1916 with mail to Trotters. (1, 2, 3, 18, 40, 70, 414)

**LUCCA** (Barnes). This Soo Line RR townsite was founded in 1891 in NE¼ Sec. 11-137-56, Raritan Twp., just north of the townsite of BINGHAMTON, whose post office was moved here on October 19, 1891 with William Gruff pm. Mrs. Fred D. Underwood, wife of a Soo Line RR official, named the town for Pauline Lucca (nee Lucas), a popular opera singer of that era. Some say it was named for Lucca, Tuscany, Italy. In 1900 the NPRR crossed the Soo Line RR tracks one mile to the north in SW¼ Sec. 2-137-56, and the town moved there with Lottie Miller taking over the post office. A population of 150 was claimed in 1920, but by 1940 the count was just 37. The post office, Zip Code 58055, closed June 28, 1968 with mail to Enderlin. The 1891-1900 site survived for a number of years, generally being called OLD LUCCA. (1, 2, 3, 5, 18, 34, 40, 41, 76, 79, 118)

**LUCKY MOUND** (McLean). This was an Indian settlement in Sec. 9-149-90, Lucky Mound Twp., on the east bank of the Missouri River opposite Independence in Dunn County. The name is a corruption of the French name for the area, *l'eau qui monte*, meaning water that rises. Loquemont Twp. (149-89), just to the east, also derives its name from this French phrase. The village had a Roman Catholic church and a store, but no post office. The backwaters of the Garrison Dam inundated the site in the 1950's. (2, 3, 28, 40)

**LUDDEN** (Dickey). This pioneer settlement was founded in 1883 in Secs. 1 & 12-129-60, Lovell Twp., and named by townsite owner Frank E. Randall for Mr. and Mrs. John D. Ludden of Saint Paul, MN, with whom Mr. Randall had lived in 1875 while attending business college. Mr. Randall came here from Ortonville, MN, where he had operated a grocery store. The post office was established May 26, 1884 with Ogden Lovell pm. In 1886 the townsite was moved one mile to the east where the Chicago & NW RR had established a station in Secs. 6 & 7-129-59, Lovell Twp. This new site absorbed most of the pioneer settlements of Port Emma and Eaton, as well as the old townsite of Ludden, which became known as OLD LUDDEN. The elevation is 1303, and a peak population of 400 was claimed in 1890, but since the village incorporated in 1909, the peak population has been just 164 in 1930, with a steady decline to 47 in 1980. The post office, Zip Code 58462, closed April 26, 1986. (1, 2, 3, 18, 25, 33, 40, 41, 52, 79, 154, 264)

**LUDWIG HEINS CORNER** (McIntosh). Ludwig Hein came here in 1887 from South Russia, and was a longtime rural mail carrier. He also operated a stage line before the days of the railroad, and his home in Sec. 6-129-67, Coldwater Twp., became a popular stopping point, being midway between Ellendale and Ashley. Ludwig Hems Corner is an erroneous spelling. (3, 53, 134, 211)

**LUNDE** (Ramsey). This was a farm post office established August 12, 1898 with Nils Christopher Lunde (1864-1933) pm. Mr. Lunde came to America in 1888 from his native Norway, returned home in 1893, and came back to America in 1895, settling here in 1898. The post office was located in SW¼ Sec. 24-157-61, Fancher Twp., one mile SW of Edmore, and closed August 31, 1901 with mail to Edmore. Lund is an erroneous spelling. (2, 3, 40, 103)

**LUNDSVALLEY** (Mountrail). This was a rural post office established November 15, 1909 with Jens Madson Lund pm, who had been the first settler in this large valley. In 1911 a GNRR townsite was established just NW of the post office in Sec. 15-158-92, Powers Twp., and the post office relocated there with a retention of the name. The elevation is 2223, and the tiny village survives today, although its population has never exceeded 100. The post office closed May 31, 1957 with mail to Lostwood when pm Clemmen Christianson retired. Most maps show the village name as two words. (1, 2, 3, 40, 67, 72)

**LURGAN** (Richland). This GNRR station was built before 1890 in Sec. 8-133-47, Dwight Twp., about six miles NNW of Wahpeton, and called LEHIGH. Sometime before 1920 the name was changed to LURGAN for Lurgan, PA, which was named for Lurgan, Armaghshire, Northern Ireland. The station disappeared from maps during the 1930's. (1, 2, 3, 18, 83)

**LUVERNE** (Steele). This GNRR station was founded in 1910 in NW¼ Sec. 32-144-57, Willow Lake Twp., and platted by the Luverne Land Co. of Willmar, MN. The post office was established February 17, 1912 with Peter F. Orn pm. Many of the original settlers came here from Denmark, and the place is known in local slang as Little Denmark. The elevation is 1417, the Zip Code is 58056, and a peak population of 241 was reported in 1920, with a steady decline to just 65 in 1980. A prominent feature in the area is the GNRR high bridge nearby, very similar to the more familiar structure at Valley City. (1, 2, 3, 33, 40, 79, 99)

**LUZON** (Renville). This post office was established January 13, 1904 with Charles Edward Johnston pm, but the order was

*Luverne about 1912*

rescinded July 6, 1904. It would have been located in NE¼ Sec. 15-162-85, Hamerly Twp., five miles west of Loraine. It was named for the principal island in the Philippines, which was the first to come under American control in the Spanish-American War of 1898. (3, 5, 40, 442)

**LYBECK** (Griggs). This was a farm post office established February 17, 1881 in Sec. 25-147-58, Romness Twp., about eight miles NE of Cooperstown near the Steele County line. Andrew C. Knutson was the first pm, and he is said to have named it for a place of this name in MN. Lybeck is Norwegian for quiet stream, and the name may refer to the Sheyenne River at this point. Mail was brought here from Newburgh until the post office closed June 28, 1882 with mail to Mardell. Sybeek is an erroneous spelling. (2, 3, 13, 18, 25, 29, 40, 65)

**LYNCH** (Ward). This was a farm post office established March 1, 1902 with Robert Dumond pm, who named it for John Lynch, a pioneer area homesteader who came here in 1886 and was clerk of the District Court for many years. It was located in SW¼ Sec. 30-157-82, Tatman Twp., twelve miles north of Minot, and just east of the present-day Minot Air Force Base. Joshua H. Humphreys became the pm in 1903, and operated it in conjunction with a country store, insurance agency, and justice of the peace service. The post office closed October 15, 1909 with mail to Glenburn. (2, 3, 18, 40, 100)

**LYNCHBURG** (Cass). This GNRR station was founded in 1893 in S½ Sec. 9-138-52, Maple River Twp., five miles east of Chaffee. It was the middle station on the Addison-Chaffee branch line, and was named for Frank Lynch, the President of the Red River Valley & Western RR which built this short line, later selling it to the GNRR. The post office was established September 6, 1895 with Lillie B. Peart pm. A small village began, but the population never exceeded 30. The post office closed July 29, 1911 with mail to Durbin. Lynchberg is an erroneous spelling. (2, 18, 38, 40, 77)

**LYNDALE** (Williams). This was a farm post office established June 24, 1909 with Edward G. Sutton pm. It was located in SW¼ Sec. 14-156-103, Bull Butte Twp., eighteen miles NW of Williston near the source of Painted Woods Creek. The name is thought to have come from Lyndale Avenue, a major thoroughfare in Minneapolis, MN, that was named for the Lyndale Farm owned by William S. King, and located between Lakes Calhoun and Harriet within the city limits. The farm had been named for Mr. King's father, Rev. Lyndon King, who had been named for Josiah Lyndon, the Governor of RI 1768-1769. The post office closed August 31, 1910 with mail to Scott. (2, 3, 10, 18, 40, 50)

**LYNWOOD** (Morton). This NPRR station was built in 1966 in Twp. 137-81, just north of Saint Anthony on the newly-built Mandan-Flasher line. No development occurred at the site. The origin of the name is unknown. (3, 34)

**LYONS** (Morton). This was a NPRR loading station built about 1910 in NE 1/4 Sec. 32-139-82, seven miles west of Mandan at the same site as the old station of MARMOT. LYONS was platted with considerable enthusiam, and named for Hiram R. Lyons, a Mandan banker and Vice President of the Russell-Miller Milling Co., but little development occurred at the site, which disappeared from maps during the 1920's. (1, 2, 3, 18, 79, 107)

# M

**MACK** (Cavalier). This was a farm post office established May 24, 1899, and given the nickname of the pm, Austin E. McEwen. This surname prefix is common in Scotland, and is derived from the Celtic word meaning son of. It was located in NW¼ Sec. 10-162-64, Glenila Twp., two miles NNE of Calvin,, until 1902 when it moved one mile NW to SE¼ Sec. 5-162-64. In 1905 it moved another mile NW to NW¼ Sec. 5-162-64, and closed January 31, 1906 with mail to Calvin. (2, 19, 40, 414)

**MACKINOCK** (Grand Forks). This NPRR station was founded in 1887 as MEKINOCK in Sec. 1-152-53, Mekinock Twp., but when the post office was established January 30, 1888 with Mathew Ladwell pm, it was erroneously entered in government records as MACKINOCK. The error was corrected on February 14, 1888, and it is assumed that the erroneous spelling was never actually used by the post office. (2, 3, 40, 69)

**MACOMBER** (Burleigh). This was a Soo Line RR siding at the Washburn Lignite Coal Mining Co. in Sec. 1-142-80, Ecklund Twp., three miles east of Wilton. It was named for Walter P. Macomber, the mine superintendent, who was also a realtor in Wilton. (2, 3, 18)

**MACROOM** (Burke). This was a rural post office established May 9, 1903 with Peder E. Barmoen pm. It was located in NE¼ Sec. 8-161-92, Foothills Twp., eight miles SW of Lignite, and named for Macroom, county Cork, Ireland. The post office closed June 30, 1911 with mail to Lignite. Macroon is an erroneous spelling. (1, 2, 3, 34, 40, 67)

**MADDOCK** (Benson). This was a farm post office established February 4, 1898 with Ludwig Ellingson pm, in SW¼ Sec. 17-152-69, North Viking Twp. In 1901 it moved one mile south to the new NPRR townsite in Secs. 19, 20, 29 & 30-152-69. Some say it was named for pioneer settlers John R. and David E. Maddock, while others say it was named for Michael Maddock, another pioneer settler in the area. The village incorporated in 1908, and became a city in 1917 with E. C. Olson mayor. The elevation is 1604, the Zip Code is 58348, and a peak population of 740 was reached in 1950. Merton Blaine Utgaard, director of the music camp at the International Peace Garden 1956-1983, was born here in 1914. (1, 2, 3, 18, 33, 40, 52, 79, 239, 253, 414)

**MAGNOLIA** (Cass). This was a NPRR siding built before 1890 in NE¼ Sec. 25-140-54, Buffalo Twp., three miles west of Wheatland, with mail service being provided from that village. For many years MAGNOLIA was an important station for replenishing the water supply on the steam locomotives of the day. A population of 5 was reported here as late as 1940, but the switch to diesel power ended the site's reason for existance. It was named for the magnolia tree, which was named for the French

*Coal mines at Macomber about 1915*

botanist Dr. Pierre Magnol. The name was chosen for euphonic reasons rather than local significance, and is perpetuated by a nearby state game management area. (1, 2, 3, 18, 19, 34, 77, 266)

**MAGNUS** (Burleigh). This was a Soo Line RR townsite platted in SE¼ Sec. 30-138-79, Apple Creek Twp., five miles SE of Bismarck. A post office was authorized January 15, 1901 with Olof J. Magnuson pm, but the order was rescinded February 27, 1901. A second authorization was made on March 30, 1901 with Mr. Magnuson again as pm, but this too was rescinded. The name was derived from that of the pm, *magnus* being Latin for great. The original owner of the townsite was John Robidou (1809-1905), one of the first settlers in Burleigh County. (2, 12, 18, 19, 33, 40)

**MAHONEY SPUR** (Dickey). This was a Soo Line RR station in SW¼ Sec. 24-131-60, Clement Twp., three miles west of Oakes. It was also known as NORWAY and NICKOLS CROSSING. The origin of this name is unknown. (2, 3, 18)

**MAIDA** (Cavalier). This post office was established September 8, 1884 with Charles Howatt pm. It was located in NW¼ Sec. 2-163-60, Mount Carmel Twp., fifteen miles north of Langdon and just west of the pioneer settlement of Seven Lakes, and given an Anglo-Saxon name meaning maiden. Some say the pm chose the name from a dog in a book he had read, presumably a work by Sir Walter Scott, while others say it was named for a local female dog. MAIDA never experienced a boom, reporting a 1960 population of just 19, but in 1919 it moved two miles north to SW¼ Sec. 25-164-60, Mount Carmel Twp., right on the Canadian border, and survives as a port-of-entry. The post office, Zip Code 58255, became a rural branch of Langdon on April 21, 1967. (2, 3, 18, 19, 38, 40, 79)

**MAIL STATION** (Griggs). Between 1867 and 1872 a cave in Sec. 14-147-60, Addie Twp., on the east side of Lake Jessie, was used as a shelter for mail carriers on the Fort Abercrombie-Fort Totten trail. An 1875 map of what was then Foster County shows this place as MAIL STATION. The cave still exists near the site of the old Jessie rural post office. (3, 153, 284)

**MAINE** (Burleigh). This was a rural post office established as APPLETON on June 9, 1880 about six miles ESE of Bismarck. On September 29, 1880 it was moved one mile NE to the home of new pm Lamont O. Stevens in NW¼ Sec. 2-138-79, Apple Creek Twp., who renamed it MAINE. Some state that the new name honored Burleigh County pioneer L. M. Maine, although it is more likely that the name noted that many area residents were natives of the state of ME. The post office closed September 12, 1887 with mail to Bismarck. (2, 3, 8, 18, 40, 414)

**MAKOTI** (Ward). This Soo Line RR townsite was founded in 1911 in NW¼ Sec. 27-152-87, Orlein Twp. The name was coined by townsite promoter Edward Kamrud from *maakoti*, a Mandan Indian word meaning largest of the earthen lodges. He learned of this word from James Holding Eagle, an Indian who was building a replica Mandan-type earthen lodge on the Capitol grounds in Bismarck at the time. The post office was established December 18, 1911 with William J. Nutting pm, a position which was held by Erhart Petersen 1934-1970. The Zip Code is 58756, and the village incorporated in 1916, reaching a peak population of 276 in 1930. Clarence Schenfisch organized the first Makoti Threshing Show in 1961, and that event has become a popular annual attraction for people throughout ND. (2, 33, 40, 79, 100, 373)

**MALCOLM** (McLean). This was a farm post office established March 3, 1902 with Ole C. Peterson pm. It was located in Sec. 4-148-82, Malcolm Twp., ten miles NE of Coleharbor, and named for its township, which was named by Swedish settlers from Detroit Lakes, MN for unknown reasons. Malcolm is a Celtic name meaning servant of St. Columbia, the sixth-century Scottish missionary whose name means the dove in Latin. The post office closed March 31, 1912 with mail to Coal Harbor. Malcom is an erroneous spelling. (2, 18, 19, 28, 40)

**MALETTE** (Cass). This was a farm post office established June 23, 1880 with Charles A. Malette pm. It was located in NW¼ Sec. 12-142-52, Arthur Twp., two miles north of Arthur, with mail carried once each week from Casselton. Mr. Malette, who sometimes spelled his name Mallette, came here in 1879 and operated a 1,500 acre farm. On October 31, 1881 the post office was replaced by the facility at the new NPRR townsite of Arthur. (2, 40, 77, 265, 415)

**MALLOY** (Benson). This was a farm post office established September 7, 1906 with Nora Malloy pm. It was located in Sec. 8-151-65, Twin Tree Twp., nine miles east of Oberon, and closed August 31, 1907 with mail to Fort Totten. (2, 3, 18, 40, 112)

**MALTBY** (Bottineau). This place appears on maps circa 1935-1940 published by the H. M. Gousha Company, and is shown approximately in SW¼ Sec. 15-162-83, Hoffman Twp., seven miles NE of Mohall. A rural school is located at this site. Local residents have no knowledge of such a place, and MALTBY is assumed to be a copyright town. (3, 34, 101)

**MANDAN** (Morton). The first settlers were here in 1872, and it was known as MORTON and LINCOLN before officially becoming MANDAN, for the Indian tribe of that name, on December 14, 1878. MANDAN is derived from *Mantahni*, or people of the river bank. Pm Arthur Linn adopted the new name March 3, 1879, but on March 11, 1879 new pm Andre Thompson changed the name to

CUSHMAN. The MANDAN name was restored September 26, 1879 by popular demand. MANDAN occupies about half of Twp. 139-81, on the west bank of the Missouri River opposite Bismarck, and is the county seat of Morton County. It incorporated as a village in 1881, and has grown steadily to a city of 15,496 in 1980. The elevation is 1667, and the Zip Code is 58554. It is a major railroad center, and is the home of the State Industrial School. (1, 2, 3, 18, 33, 40, 44, 79, 107, 343)

**MANDAREE** (McKenzie). This is a community founded in 1954 in Sec. 14-149-94, thirty miles ESE of Watford City, as the Western Segment Sub-Agency for the Fort Berthold Indian Reservation, and was intended to be a home for those people displaced by the rising backwaters of the Garrison Dam. The name was suggested by Father Reinhard Kauffman, a longtime Roman Catholic missionary on the reservation, using parts of the names of the three affiliated tribes here— MANdan, HiDAtsa, and REE, or Arikara. The post office was established May 20, 1955 with Mrs. Beatrice E. Balliet as acting pm. Her appointment became official July 1, 1955. The Zip Code is 58757, and a population of 115 was reported in 1960. (2, 3, 28, 33, 40, 289)

**MANDT** (Walsh). This was a small inland settlement in Sec. 15-157-54, Fertile Twp., nine miles west of Grafton. The post office was established July 22, 1893 with Ole H. Wig pm, who named it for Peter Mandt, owner of the store in which the post office was located. Ed Herwick was a pioneer merchant at this site. The post office closed February 28, 1903 with mail to Grafton. It reopened May 21, 1903, but closed for good June 10, 1904 with mail to Park River. A population of 20 was reported in MANDT as late as 1920. Harvey Tallackson, a state senator and Grafton businessman, was born here. (1, 2, 3, 18, 40, 75)

**MANFRED** (Wells). This Soo Line RR townsite was founded in 1893 in NE¼ Sec. 28-149-71, Manfred Twp., between Harvey and Fessenden, and just SE of the Jim River

Crossing that had been used by pioneers on their way to the Souris River valley to the north. English settlers in the area chose the name for the fictional hero of a work by the famous author, Lord Byron. The post office was established May 3, 1894 with Thorstein K. Rogne pm. The elevation is 1605, the Zip Code is 58465, and the village, which has never incorporated, claimed a population of 439 in 1920, although by 1960 the count was just 70. (1, 2, 3, 13, 18, 33, 39, 40, 68, 79, 363)

**MANGER** (Williams). This was a farm post office established December 18, 1906 with Johannes O. Manger pm. Mr. Manger came here from McIntosh, MN in 1906, settling in NE¼ Sec. 12-158-100, Winner Twp., six miles SW of Alamo, and died in 1936. The post office closed September 30, 1913 with mail to Zahl. (2, 18, 40, 50, 53)

**MANITOU** (Mountrail). This was a GNRR station founded in 1887 in NE¼ Sec. 16-156-93, Manitou Twp., between Ross and White Earth. It was served by the White Earth post office until June 22, 1905, when a post office was established here with Ole P. Fladeland pm, closing December 15, 1917 with mail to Ross. It reopened July 29, 1920 as a small settlement began, reporting a peak population of 43 in 1930, but closed for good June 14, 1941 with mail again to Ross. It was named for its township, which bears a Chippewa Indian name meaning great spirit. The word was popular among Indians, and all tribes west of the Mississippi River used it to mean spirit. (2, 5, 10, 13, 25, 40, 72, 79)

**MANNHAVEN** (Mercer). This was a Missouri River townsite founded in 1896 in NW¼ Sec. 7-146-84, on the west bank of the river two miles south of the present-day Garrison Dam. It was named for William Henry Mann, a merchant and politician from New Salem, who was active in the townsite's development. He was an owner of the Mannhaven Mercantile & Transportation Co., operators of the steamboat *Bismarck*. The "haven" part of the name noted the natural boat landing at the townsite. The post office was established January 15, 1898 with Henry M. Pfenning pm. The site declined after 1914 when it was bypassed by the NPRR, reporting a population of 40 in 1920, and a last report of just 12 in 1930. The post office closed March 15, 1928 with mail to Krem. John Young, known as "The Laird of Mannhaven", was its last resident, living here until the 1960's. (1, 2, 3, 18, 40, 64, 79, 232)

**MANNING** (Dunn). This inland town in SW¼ Sec. 6-143-95, eleven miles south of Killdeer, was named for Daniel Manning, a pioneer rancher in the area, after county organizer W. P. Owens rejected the suggestion of naming it Owensville in his honor. It was designated as the county seat in 1910, and regularly competes with Amidon, in Slope County, for the honor of being the smallest county seat in the nation. MANNING claimed a population of 300 in 1920, but it has not reported a population greater than 100 since that time, with a 1980 count of just 42. The post office, Zip Code 58642, was established March 16, 1908 with Ethel V. Owens pm. (1, 2, 3, 18, 33, 40, 79)

*Mandan about 1925*

**MANNING** (Sargent). This was a farm post office established December 14, 1895 with Miss Therissa Manning pm. It was located in SE¼ Sec. 10-129-53, Marboe Twp., five miles south of Geneseo in the extreme SE corner of the county, and closed July 28, 1896 with mail to Geneseo. (2, 3, 40, 165, 415)

**MANSFIELD** (Mountrail). This was the name chosen by Iver F. Nelson when he applied for a farm post office, but it was rejected by postal officials. The origin of the name is unknown, although local residents continued to use this name even after the post office was established March 30, 1904 as LELAND. (3, 40, 72)

**MANTADOR** (Richland). This Soo Line RR townsite was founded in 1886 in NE 1/4 Sec. 8-131-50, Belford Twp., replacing the nearby station of Junkers. Folklore says that before settlement began a solitary home was here, and its owner would always appear at the door to watch passing trains, prompting the comment "There's the man at the door." No better explanation of the name has surfaced. The post office was established November 7, 1893 with Anton Kabella pm. The townsite was originally built north of the Soo Line RR tracks, but about 1914 development shifted to the south side, leaving the original townsite to decline as OLD MANTADOR. The elevation is 1027, the Zip Code is 58058, and the village, which incorporated in 1949, reported a population of 138 in 1950, with a decline to just 76 in 1980. (1, 2, 3, 18, 33, 40, 79, 147)

**MANTAHNI** (Morton). This is a rural subdivision founded in 1977 in NE¼ Sec. 9-139-81, three miles north of Mandan, and named for the Mandan, or Mantahni, Indians, whose tribal name means people of the river bank. (3, 79, 107)

**MANVEL** (Grand Forks). This place was founded in 1879 as a stage stop named TURTLE RIVER STATION in NE¼ Sec. 15-153-51, Ferry Twp. The GNRR arrived in 1881 and built a station which they named for Allen A. Manvel, General Passenger Agent for the GNRR. A street in Saint Paul, MN is also named for him. Manvel is a Latin name meaning from the great estate. The post office was established as MANVEL on January 16, 1882 with Ernest R. Jacobi, the great-grandfather of actress Jane Russell, as pm. The elevation is 827, the Zip Code is 58256, and the village, which incorporated in 1930, has grown in recent years to about 300 residents as some people who work in nearby Grand Forks have chosen to live here and commute. (1, 2, 3, 13, 18, 19, 25, 31, 40, 52, 69, 79, 238)

**MAPES** (Nelson). This GNRR station was built in 1883 in NW¼ Sec. 34-153-59, Rubin Twp., and named for Emery Mapes, the owner of the townsite. Mr. Mapes is famous as the inventor of Cream of Wheat, the breakfast cereal first produced in Grand Forks, who served as that firm's President after it relocated to Minneapolis, MN. A peak population of 100 was reported in 1890, with a decline to just 55 in 1960. The post office, Zip Code 58349, was established April 24, 1883 with Martin Thurin pm, and closed August 1, 1980. (2, 3, 18, 25, 34, 38, 40, 79, 124, 128)

**MAPLE** (Cass). This rural community began in 1895 in SE¼ Sec. 8-137-53, Watson Twp., six miles SSW of Chaffee, on the banks of the Maple River near the Ransom County line. The post office was established January 15, 1898 with Arnold Mostul pm in his general store, and closed November 15, 1904 with mail to Leonard. The store burned in 1906, Mr. Mostul moved to OR, and the townsite was abandoned. (2, 3, 10, 40, 77)

**MAPLE RIVER** (Cass). This settlement began about 1870 in NW¼ Sec. 6-139-50, Mapleton Twp., but when NPRR surveyors arrived in 1871 they found only the cabin of Mary Bishop. The NPRR station was built in 1872, and named for the nearby Maple River, so named because of the maple trees in the area. In 1875 the name was changed to MAPLETON. (2, 10, 34, 77, 304)

**MAPLE RIVER TANK** (Dickey). This was a Soo Line RR siding in Sec. 17-131-62, Maple Twp., two miles west of Fullerton. The site consisted of a water tank for replenishing the steam locomotives of the day, and took its name from its township, which was named for the Maple River, whose name noted the maple trees along its banks. Although the diesel locomotives have long since made this site obsolete, it appeared on some detailed maps into the 1970's. (3, 154)

**MAPLETON** (Cass). Settlement began here in 1870, and a place called MAPLE RIVER was christened by the NPRR in 1872 at their station in NW¼ Sec. 6-139-50, Mapleton Twp. The post office was established as MAPLETON, noting the nearby Maple River, on July 21, 1875 with Mary Bishop, the area's first settler, as pm. It was platted in 1876, and the village incorporated in 1884, reaching a peak population of 307 in 1980. The elevation is 929, and the Zip Code is 58059. The husband and wife physicians, Drs. Albion A. Andrews (1844-1904) and Ada Jane Healy Andrews, were prominent among the area's pioneers, and they are the grandparents of MAPLETON's most famous native son, Mark Andrews, a U. S. Representative 1963-1981 and a U. S. Senator 1981-1987. (1, 2, 3, 18, 25, 34, 40, 52, 77, 79, 304)

**MARDELL** (Griggs). This was a boom town promoted by Richard P. Sherman, George H. Ellsbury, and Samuel R. Reynolds in 1881 in W½ Sec. 13-146-58, Washburn Twp., about six miles SW of Finley. Mr. Sherman coined the name from MARvelous DELL, descriptive of the location. A surge of settlers and construction took place in 1882 in anticipation of the coming of the railroad. The post office was established April 3, 1882 with Dr. Theodore F. Kerr, a physician, as pm. When the railroad did not materialize, the settlers left as fast as they had come, and MARDELL was doomed. The post office was moved to a farm site in Steele County on April 15, 1885, although a population of 48 was reported in 1890. The site today is vacant, and is marked by a small sign. (2, 25, 40, 65, 79, 99, 284, 285)

**MARDELL** (Steele). After the Griggs County boom town of MARDELL went bust, the name was transferred to a rural post office in Sec. 20-146-57, Greenview Twp., five miles SW of Finley, on April 15, 1885 with Mrs.

Bertha Margarete Marum Nelson (1852-1896) pm. She was the wife of Steen H. Nelson (1854-1929), a delegate to the ND Constitutional Convention in 1889 and later a state legislator. In 1895 Carl G. Carlson became pm at his home in Sec. 22-146-57, two miles to the east, and the post office closed December 30, 1899 with mail to Finley. (1, 3, 40, 99)

**MARIA** (Foster). This was a name change of the HAVEN post office that was approved May 6, 1902 under pm Frank Settle, but the order was rescinded September 13, 1902, and is believed to have never been actually used at the facility. The origin of MARIA is unknown. The post office had been established in 1890 as EWEN, assuming the HAVEN name in 1896. In 1905 attempts were made to change the name to ANNIE, but nothing came of this effort either, and the post office closed as HAVEN in 1909. (2, 40, 97)

**MARIE** (Cavalier). Road maps of the 1970's published by the H. M. Gousha Company show this place just north of Osnabrock. It is believed to be a copyright town. (3)

**MARIE** (Emmons). This was a rural post office established April 28, 1905 with Katie B. McGuire pm. It was located in NW¼ Sec. 17-133-74, twelve miles ENE of Linton. The origin of the name is unknown. *The Emmons County Record* of July 12, 1910 carried the following report: "The Marie post office has been discontinued due to lack of interest in the large headaches and little margin for profit." This was not quite true, as James Green moved the facility to his home in NW¼ Sec. 10-133-74, two miles NE of the McGuire home, with his wife actually performing the duties. It closed May 15, 1914 with mail to Omio. *The Emmons County Record* of May 28, 1914 stated: "The Marie P. O. has closed. Mrs. Green quit, and no one wanted it." The building housing the MARIE post office was moved to the Wendelin Wangler farm in 1938, and attached to his house. (1, 2, 3, 18, 40, 66, 113, 415)

**MARION** (LaMoure). This NPRR townsite was founded in 1900 as ELMO as the terminus of its branch line from Casselton, famous for having several stations with female names. On November 26, 1902 the name was changed to MARION, honoring Marion Mellen, daughter of NPRR President Charles S. Mellen, at the suggestion of E. H. McHenry, NPRR Chief Engineer. Louis O. Berg was the pm at this time, and his daughter, the first baby born in town, was named Marion. The village incorporated in 1911 with Dr. L. W. Myers as mayor. The elevation is 1481, the Zip Code is 58466, and a peak population of 309 was reached in 1960. (1, 2, 3, 18, 33, 40, 52, 79, 145)

**MARKILLIE** (Bottineau). This was a farm post office established December 19, 1901 with William B. Markillie pm. It was located in SE¼ Sec. 25-159-83, Lansford Twp., just west of Forfar, and about four miles SSE of Lansford. On March 7, 1905 it moved about six miles south to the farm home of new pm Robert D. Clark, which was in Renville County. (2, 3, 40, 71, 101, 323)

**MARKILLIE** (Renville). This post office had been established by William B. Markillie in 1901 on his farm in Bottineau County. On March 7, 1905 it was moved about six miles south to the farm home of new pm Robert D. Clark in NE 1/4 Sec. 25-158-83, Van Buren Twp., six miles WSW of Glenburn. The Clarks had come here in 1901 from Van Buren County, MI, and ran the post office in their dining room until it closed June 30, 1906 with mail to Glenburn. Markville is an erroneous spelling. (2, 3, 18, 40, 71, 323)

**MARLEY** (Williams). This was a GNRR station in SW1/4 Sec. 35-153-103, Hardscrabble Twp., between Trenton and Buford. The origin of the name is unknown, and it disappeared from maps during the 1920's. (1, 2, 3, 50)

**MARMARTH** (Slope). This Milwaukee Road RR townsite was founded in the fall of 1907 in S1/2 Sec. 30-133-105, Hughes Twp., and named for MARgaret MARTHa Fitch, the granddaughter of the railroad's President, Albert J. Earling. Her father, Harry Fitch, was an official of the railroad as well, and was fond of naming new townsites for members of his family. The NEVA post office moved here on February 29, 1908, taking the name MARMARTH with Neva M. Woods continuing as pm. It incorporated as a village in 1909, and became a city in 1915, the same year it lost the county seat election to Amidon. It reached a peak population of 1,318 in 1920, but declined rapidly after 1922 when the railroad shop was closed following a bitter labor strike, reporting a population of just 190 in 1980. The elevation is 2707, and the Zip Code is 58643. Since July 31, 1974 the post office has been a community post office affiliated with Dickinson. Eugene "Bus" Leary, a Bismarck grocer and onetime mayor of the capital city, was born here in 1916. (1, 2, 3, 18, 33, 40, 52, 79, 82, 253)

**MARMON** (Williams). This was a long-lived rural post office established July 26, 1902 with Stephan Marmon (1862-1952) pm at his home in SW1/4 Sec. 29-157-100, Athens Twp., twenty miles north of Williston. Mr. Marmon, a onetime sheriff, was one of Williams County's more colorful pioneers. William Kelly became pm in 1903 in NE1/4 Sec. 8-157-100, followed by E. C. Smith in 1906 in SE1/4 Sec. 5-157-100. Thomas Wright assumed the duties in 1916, and he was replaced by Alvin Henry Brown in 1918. Ruth Koepke, a daughter of Stephan Marmon, became pm back at the original site in late 1918, serving until 1928 when the facility moved to the home of new pm Inger Skindrud Sylte in SW1/4 Sec. 30-157-100, which was the site of the crossing of the Little Muddy Creek by US Highway 85. She retired November 30, 1956, and the MARMON post office was discontinued with mail to Williston. (1, 2, 3, 18, 38, 40, 50, 79)

**MARMOT** (Morton). This was a NPRR station in NE1/4 Sec. 32-139-82, seven miles west of Mandan, and named for the large ground squirrel, although it is thought that the actual animal inspiring the name was the prairie dog. The site, at the confluence of the Heart and Sweet Briar Rivers, was selected by Major T. J. Mitchell of Mandan. The post

office was established June 1, 1883 with James Maxwell pm. Little development occurred here, and on June 3, 1886 the post office closed, being replaced on that date by the facility at the new townsite of Sweet Briar, five miles to the west. About 1910 a new townsite, LYONS, was platted at this site, but it did not develop beyond the construction of a loading station. (2, 3, 5, 25, 40, 107, 121)

**MARS** (Rolette). This was a country trading post in NW1/4 Sec. 6-160-70, Union Twp., six miles NE of Rolette, which was opened about 1889 by Auguste Demers, who came here in 1887 from Canada. The name is that of the Roman god of war, and the fourth planet of the Solar System, but it is said to have been coined from the last name of Mr. Demers. The post office was established June 21, 1898 with Mr. Demers pm, and it closed March 31, 1909 with mail to Rolette. The store building was still standing in the 1960's, and was being used as a granary. (2, 3, 18, 40, 123)

**MARSHALL** (Dunn). This is a rural community founded about 1900 in NW1/4 Sec. 12-142-92, on the Knife River about fifteen miles south of Halliday. The post office was established July 24, 1901 with John Kyseth pm, and it has been located at the above location, with periods in Secs. 10 & 14-142-92, ever since. It was named for Thomas Frank Marshall (1854-1921), U. S. Representative from ND 1901-1909 who was instrumental in securing this post office. Marshall is an Old French name meaning an officer in charge of horses. Appropriately, the community's most famous native son is Bradley Jay Gjermundson, several times a national saddle bronc rodeo champion, who was born in Richardton in 1959, but calls MARSHALL his home. The Zip Code is 58644, and the little community reported a population of 8 in 1980. (1, 2, 3, 18, 19, 33, 40, 223)

**MARSHALL** (Ransom). This NPRR townsite was founded in 1880 in Sec. 25-134-58, Hanson Twp., and Sec. 30-134-57, Elliott Twp., and named for Marshall T. Davis, the townsite owner, who came here in the late 1870's from Friendship, NY. When the post office was established November 5, 1883, the name was changed to ENGLEVALE due to the existance of a Marshall in Moody County, SD. (2, 18, 25, 201)

**MARS JUNCTION** (Emmons). This place appears on current maps published by Hearne Brothers at the junction of county roads in Secs. 1 & 2-129-76, and Secs. 35 & 36-130-76, three miles east of Westfield, one mile west of Hull, and eight miles south of Strasburg. An official of the map company hedges that the place is a copyright town. (3, 34)

**MARSTON** (Stutsman). This was a NPRR station built about 1912 in SE1/4 Sec. 9-142-69, Marstonmoor Twp., and named for the nearby post office and store called Marstonmoor. Hugh Marston and his father, James D. Marston, came here in 1893. Marston is an Old English name meaning from the farm by the pool. The station disappeared from maps shortly after 1920. (1, 2, 3, 19, 158)

**MARSTONMOOR** (Stutsman). This was a rural post office established April 2, 1904 with Alva C. Thomas pm. The name honored Hugh Marston and his father, James D. Marston, pioneer settlers in the area, with the "moor" noting the huge swampy area at nearby Chicago Lake. By coincidence, a Marston Moor in Yorkshire, England is a famous site where Oliver Cromwell defeated the royal army led by Prince Rupert in 1644. The post office was first located about eight miles SW of Woodworth, and moved several times within this general area until 1917, when it moved to the country store in Sec. 26-142-69, Marstonmoor Twp., six miles WSW of Woodworth, which was operated by new pm Ross Lowe. A population of 20 was reported in 1920, but the post office closed December 12, 1921 with mail to Woodworth. Marston Moor and Marstonmoore are erroneous spellings. (1, 2, 3, 5, 18, 40, 158)

**MARTELLS** (Ward). This Soo Line RR station appears on maps circa 1895-1905 in Kirkelie Twp. (156-84), a few miles NW of Burlington, and is believed to have served a small coal mine. The origin of the name is unknown. (3)

**MARTHA** (McHenry). This was a farm post office established April 7, 1903 with Robert H. Thom pm. His home in NE1/4 Sec. 24-153-76, Lake George Twp., nine miles north of Drake, had been used as a mail drop as early as 1900. The choice of the name is unexplained, but it is an Aramaean name meaning mistress. The post office closed October 14, 1905 with mail to Drake. (2, 3, 4, 19, 40, 412)

**MARTIN** (Sheridan). This Soo Line RR station was founded in 1896 as CASSELMAN, and is located in E1/2 Sec. 10-150-74, Martin Twp., in the extreme NE corner of the county. On November 6, 1902 pm Maggie Herr changed the name to MARTIN for William Leslie Martin, a Soo Line RR conductor. Martin is derived from Mars, the Roman god of war. The Zip Code is 58758, and the city, which incorporated in 1910, reached a peak population of 228 in 1940. It is the oldest settlement in Sheridan County, and because of its location it has been more closely affiliated with adjacent towns in Wells and McHenry Counties than with other places in its own county. (1, 2, 3, 18, 19, 21, 30, 33, 40, 52, 68, 79)

**MARY** (McKenzie). This was a farm post office established August 16, 1906 with William N. Crist pm, who named the post office for his wife. The name Mary commemorates the Virgin Mary, and during the Middle Ages it was translated as star of the sea, although it traces to the Hebrew name *Mara*, meaning bitter. It was located in SW1/4 Sec. 25-147-99, Rhoades Twp., nine miles north of Grassy Butte, moved to Sec. 34-147-99 in 1914, and SE1/4 Sec. 33-147-99 before closing January 26, 1932 with mail to Grassy Butte. (1, 3, 4, 18, 19, 40, 79, 414)

**MASON** (Cass). This GNRR station was built about 1888 in SW1/4 Sec. 10-141-53, Empire Twp., on the Ripon-Erie branch line about five miles south of Erie. It was named OATLAND, but when the post office was established June 24, 1895 with John M. Johnson pm, it was renamed MASON for

Mr. Johnson's young nephew, Mason G. Palmer (1892-1970). Mason is a French/Teutonic name meaning worker in stone. The station name was changed to match that of the post office, but development was slow, and the post office closed November 30, 1900 with mail to Erie. In 1913 the Ripon-Erie line was removed, and the MASON station was relocated three miles NE to NE¼ Sec. 36-142-53, Erie Twp., three miles SE of Erie on the newly-built Surrey cutoff line. (1, 2, 3, 18, 19, 34, 40, 77)

**MASON JUNCTION** (Cass). This was the GNRR station in SW¼ Sec. 22-142-53, Erie Twp., located just NW of Mason on the Surrey cutoff line, and just south of Erie on the Portland branch line. No development took place here, and the site remained simply a railroad junction on the prairie. After 1940 the site was generally called ERIE JUNCTION. (1, 3, 34)

**MASTEL** (Emmons). This was a farm post office established July 1, 1912 with Thomas H. Mastel pm. It was located in NE¼ Sec. 18-131-74, nine miles north of Hague, and for a time also served as an overland stage station. The post office closed October 15, 1913 with mail to Hague. (2, 3, 18, 40, 66)

**MATHEWS** (Richland). This NPRR farm loading station was built in W½ Sec. 15-132-49, Mooreton Twp., three miles SE of Mooreton, and named for James H. Mathews, founder of the New York Bonanza Farm, who came to Richland County from Orange County, NY in 1878. It appeared on maps from about 1915 until the 1970's. (2, 3)

**MATHIAS** (Oliver). This was a farm post office authorized July 6, 1908 with Mathias Miller pm. It was located in NW¼ Sec. 30-141-87, in the extreme SW corner of the county thirteen miles NNE of Glen Ullin. The order was rescinded January 13, 1909. (3, 40)

**MATHIE** (Grand Forks). This rural settlement began in 1879 when William Mathie and his brother, Neil, came here from Ontario, Canada. It was located in Sec. 12-154-55, Inkster Twp., but when the post office was established in 1880 with William Mathie pm, he renamed it INKSTER. Mr. Mathie was the first chairman of Inkster Twp. Matthie is an erroneous spelling. (2, 3, 40, 69, 337)

**MATSON** (LaMoure). This NPRR station was founded in 1883 in Sec. 2-133-59, Ovid Twp., and named for its township, which was originally named Matson for unknown reasons. Because of duplication, the township name was changed to Ovid, and when the post office was established at the townsite in 1886, the name was changed to VERONA. Before 1886, MATSON had been served by the LaMoure post office. (2, 3, 25, 40, 150)

**MATTESON** (Barnes). This was a Soo Line RR station built in 1892 in NE¼ Sec. 10-141-59, Stewart Twp., four miles SE of Rogers. Some say it was named for Tompkins Harrison Matteson (1813-1884), an American artist famous for his historical paintings. The post office was established October 11, 1895 with Samuel Fletcher (1846-1934) pm. The station was moved to Rogers in 1897, and

the post office closed October 31, 1913 with mail to Roger, as it was then called. (1, 2, 3, 5, 18, 34, 40, 76)

**MAX** (McLean). This was a farm post office established July 13, 1904 with Paul Freitag (1873-1952) as pm, who named it for his son. Max Freitag was a Colonel in the U. S. Army who was stationed in occupied Japan after World War II. Max is a shortened form of Maximillian, a Latin name meaning the greatest. It was located in SW¼ Sec. 18-150-82, Poplar Twp., but in 1907 it moved three miles WNW to SE¼ Sec. 10-150-83, Economy Twp., the site of a new Soo Line RR townsite on the west bank of Elbow Lake. Railroad officials suggested the names Junction and Junction City, but local residents persuaded them to retain the name MAX. It incorporated as a village in 1907, and became a city in 1947 with H. R. Freitag as first mayor. The Zip Code is 58759, and a peak population of 500 was reported in 1930. Peter D. Podhola (1876-1961), Arthur Steinhaus (1881-1950), and Gust Steinhaus (1873-1963) were prominent pioneer businessmen. (1, 2, 3, 18, 19, 28, 33, 40, 79, 193, 389)

**MAXBASS** (Bottineau). This townsite was founded in 1905 as the terminus of the GNRR branch line from Towner, and named for Max Bass, a native of Austria who was the GNRR Commissioner of Immigration, and a promoter of Dunkard settlements throughout ND. He died in Chicago, IL in 1909. MAXBASS was platted in 1905 by the Tallman Townsite Co. in SW¼ Sec. 35-161-81, Hastings Twp. The post office was established August 4, 1905 with John Staub pm. The village incorporated in 1905, and it became a city in 1910, reaching a peak population of 259 in 1950. The elevation is 1513, and the Zip Code is 58760. (1, 2, 18, 33, 34, 40, 79, 101, 153)

**MAXWELL** (McLean). This was a rural post office established June 27, 1905 with Lafayette Maxwell pm at his home in SE¼ Sec. 20-148-79, Medicine Hill Twp., nine miles NE of Turtle Lake. Maxwell is an Anglo-Saxon name meaning from Maccus' pool. Maccus was an ancient Celtic

character whose name is derived from Marcus, in turn derived from Mars, the Roman god of war, whose name means hammer. The post office was discontinued December 31, 1912 with mail to Turtle Lake. (2, 3, 18, 19, 28, 40, 389)

**MAY** (Traill). This was a pioneer settlement developed around the Hudson's Bay Company trading post called ARNOLD'S POST. It was started by Alvin L. Arnold in 1871 in Sec. 31-147-52, Lindaas Twp., just west of present-day Mayville, and named for Mr. Arnold's daughter, May, who is said to have been the first white child born in the area. (2, 3, 187, 225)

**MAYFLOWER** (Hettinger). In 1886 Thomas W. Bicknell led a group of advance scouts into what is now Hettinger County to look for a suitable townsite location for a group of easterners, primarily from VT and MA. Most of the group had previously lived at Vermont City, Dakota Territory, a place now known as Loyalton, SD. They came to SE¼ Sec. 4-135-97, New England Twp., in April 1887, and platted eight blocks which they named MAYFLOWER for the famous ship used by the first group of Pilgrims in 1620. Many of these pioneers were descendants of the *Mayflower* Pilgrims. The post office was established August 26, 1887 with Frank H. Clark pm, and on September 16, 1887 the name was changed to NEW ENGLAND CITY. (2, 3, 18, 25, 40, 385)

**MAYNARD** (McKenzie). Christopher J. Graue, a native of IA, became pm of the SANFORD post office on March 9, 1910, moving that facility to his home in SE¼ Sec. 35-153-94, River View Twp., twenty-eight miles NE of Watford City. Because of confusion with Lansford, he changed the name to MAYNARD on August 25, 1910 to honor his son who farmed two miles to the NW in NW¼ Sec. 22-153-94. Maynard Graue had been named for the family's ancestral home of Maynard, MA, which was named for Amory Maynard (1804-1890), a prominent textile manufacturer. Maynard is a Teutonic name meaning mighty brave. The post office closed March 31, 1913 with mail to Charlson. (1, 2, 3, 10, 18, 19, 40, 53, 228, 415)

*Max about 1908*

**MAYVILLE** (Traill). This post office opened June 20, 1877 with Mrs. Alvin Arnold, nee Helen Peck, pm. It was located in SE¼ Sec. 35-147-53, Viking Twp., just north of present-day Portland, and named for the Arnold's daughter, May. Others say it was named for the Arnolds former home in Mayville, OH, while still others say it was named for Mrs. Anna Marie "May" Weltzin Chantland. John Chantland became pm in 1879 in SW¼ Sec. 31-147-52, Lindaas Twp., two miles to the east, and in 1881 it moved to the new GNRR townsite in Secs. 31 & 32-147-52, and Secs. 5 & 6-146-52, Mayville Twp. Although MAYVILLE lost a bid for the county seat, it developed quickly. It incorporated as a village in 1883, and became a city in 1888 with E. M. Paulson (1855-1920) as mayor. The elevation is 978, the Zip Code is 58257, and a peak population of 2,554 was reached in 1970. Clarence Norman Brunsdale (1891-1978), Governor of ND 1953-1957, was a prominent resident. Mayville State College was founded here in 1890. (1, 2, 3, 10, 25, 29, 33, 40, 52, 79, 187, 225, 359, 393, 414)

**MAZA** (Towner). This is a GNRR station in Sec. 32-157-66, Maza Twp., eight miles south of Cando where Towner, Benson, and Ramsey counties come together. Railroad officials named it for Maza Chante, a Sioux Indian chief known as Indian Heart, who campaigned in the MN Indian Wars, and later ranched south of Devils Lake. The post office was established January 16, 1893 with Lewis J. Ransier pm, and closed December 31, 1964 with mail to Cando. The village, which incorporated in 1922, reached a peak population of 85 in 1920, but declined to just 20 in 1970. It claims several unique features. In 1923 it was the site of the only bank robbery in Towner County, it has never had a bar, and with its official village limits including the entire township, or thirty-six square miles, it once claimed to be the largest incorporated village in area in the nation. (1, 2, 3, 18, 40, 79, 102)

**MAZDA** (Slope). This was a Milwaukee Road RR station in SE¼ Sec. 34-133-105, Hughes Twp., three miles east of Marmarth. It appeared on maps circa 1915-1925, and is said to have been named for the popular brand of light bulbs at that time. The name is derived from Ahuro Mazdao, the supreme god and Lord of Light in the Zoroastrian religion that developed in Persia about 700 B.C. The popular Japanese automobile traces its name to the same source. No development occurred at the site. (1, 3, 5, 408)

**McARTHUR** (Pembina). This was a GNRR loading station in NE¼ Sec. 9-162-51, Joliette Twp., seven miles south of Pembina, named for D. H. McArthur, a local resident. The post office was established May 17, 1904 with Charles H. Hart pm, and closed October 15, 1919 with mail to Pembina. A population of 10 was reported in 1920. The station was removed in 1957. (1, 2, 18, 40, 79, 108)

**McCANNA** (Grand Forks). This GNRR station was built in 1883 in NW¼ Sec. 9-152-55, Elm Grove Twp., eight miles NNW of Larimore, and named for Dan W. McCanna, who came here in 1881 with his son, Simon,

leading a group of settlers from southern MN. The townsite was platted in June 1884, and the post office was established November 20, 1884 with Simon A. McCanna pm. The elevation is 1115, the Zip Code is 58253, and the village, which incorporated in 1887, has maintained a population of just under 100 for many years. (1, 2, 18, 25, 31, 40, 69, 79)

**McCARTHYVILLE** (Pierce). This was an early GNRR construction camp named for foreman Kelly McCarthy. It is thought that it was between Fero and Berwick, but the exact location is unknown. (2, 3)

**McCLUSKY** (Sheridan). This townsite was founded in 1902 in Secs. 8 & 9-146-77, McClusky Twp., and named for William Henderson McClusky, a pioneer settler who came here from Winside, NE. The post office was established February 16, 1903 with Sarah E. Southard pm. In the spring of 1905 the NPRR purchased the NE¼ Sec. 11-146-77 from L. S. Needham, and McCLUSKY moved three miles east to the new location. Arthur Steinbrecker was the first pm at the new townsite. McCLUSKY incorporated as a village in 1908, became the county seat when Sheridan County was formed from the eastern part of McLean County in 1909, and became a city in 1911 with P. R. Thelen mayor. The elevation is 1943, the Zip Code is 58463, and a peak population of 924 was reached in 1940. John E. Davis, Governor of ND 1957-1960, was a longtime resident. McCluskey is an erroneous spelling. (1, 2, 3, 18, 21, 30, 33, 40, 52, 79)

**McCOMB** (McLean). This post office was authorized July 5, 1904 with Ramsey R. McComb pm, who named it for pioneer settler Melvin O. McComb. It was located in SW¼ Sec. 10-147-79, Wise Twp., six miles north of Mercer, but the order was rescinded October 14, 1904. (1, 2, 28, 40)

**McCONNELL** (Pembina). This was a farm post office established in 1882 as BRUCE in NW¼ Sec. 34-163-54, Felson Twp., five miles SW of Neche. On October 31, 1883 pm Robert McConnell renamed it for himself.

When David McFadden became pm on December 23, 1889 he renamed it BRUCE. (2, 3, 40, 108)

**McCULLOUGH** (Divide). This was a farm post office established February 14, 1907 with Frederick J. McCullough pm. It was located in NW¼ Sec. 32-161-97, Frazier Twp., thirteen miles south of Crosby, and closed January 31, 1914 with mail to Plumer. (2, 18, 40, 53)

**McCUMBER** (Rolette). This GNRR townsite was established in 1905 in Sec. 20-160-71, Leonard Twp., and named for Porter James McCumber (1858-1933), a U. S. Senator from ND 1899-1923. The post office was established September 20, 1905 with Tyler O. Ramsland pm. A population of 350 was reported in 1906 when a new townsite called Rolette was founded one mile SE at the junction of the GNRR and the Soo Line RR. McCUMBER literally moved to the new site, and the post office closed December 14, 1907 with mail to Rolette. (2, 3, 39, 40, 123)

**McFADDEN** (Rolette). This was a stage station between Rolette and Davidson in SW¼ Sec. 13-159-70, Island Lake Twp., three miles south of Mylo. It was named for station operator John McFadden, and declined with the coming of the railroad. (2, 3, 123)

**McGOWAN'S FERRY** (Benson). This was a ferry service run by James McGowan in SW¼ Sec. 2-154-67, Riggin Twp., five miles SSW of Churchs Ferry, spanning the Grand, or Mauvais, Coulee. An 1884 atlas shows it one half mile north of here in Sec. 35-155-67, Normanna Twp. (2, 3, 18, 110)

**McGREGOR** (Williams). This post office was established February 9, 1905 with William McGregor (1864-1945) pm. When the GNRR began its Stanley-Grenora branch line in 1910, a townsite was platted just NW of this post office in SW 1/4 Sec. 14-159-95, Sauk Valley Twp., in the extreme NE corner of the county. The townsite was platted in 1910, and the McGREGOR post office relocated to it with a retention of the name. The elevation is 2216, the Zip Code is 58755, and a peak population of 250 was claimed in 1920. (1, 2, 33, 40, 50)

*McClusky January 8, 1910*

**McGUIRE** (Kidder). This was a farm post office established May 26, 1884 with William A. McGuire pm. It was located in NW¼ Sec. 3-137-73, South Manning Twp., about eleven miles SSE of Steele. A population of 23 was reported in 1890, but the post office closed March 8, 1890 with mail to Steele. McQuire is an erroneous spelling. (2, 3, 18, 33, 40, 123, 414)

**McHENCH SIDING** (Cass). This was an early Milwaukee Road RR siding in NE 1/4 Sec. 14-139-49, Barnes Twp., a site now within the city limits of Fargo. It was named for Andrew McHench, who settled in Fargo in 1871, and served as a territorial legislator and the first county Superintendent of Schools. (2, 34, 77, 199)

**McHENRY** (Foster). This townsite was founded in 1899 as the terminus of the NPRR's Sanborn branch line in SE¼ Sec. 5-157-62, McHenry Twp. It was named for E. H. McHenry, Chief Civil Engineer of the NPRR, who is remembered as the designer of the railroad's famous Chinese monad trademark. The post office was established November 24, 1899 with Knut Alfstad pm. The village incorporated in 1903, and reached a peak population of 398 in 1910 with a steady decline to just 113 in 1980. The elevation is 1529, and the Zip Code is 58464. The actual terminus of the branch line is a unique loop just west of town to accomplish turnarounds. The line was abandoned August 1, 1981, and the loop is now preserved as a national historical site. (1, 2, 3, 18, 33, 40, 52, 97)

**McHUGH** (Cavalier). This townsite was founded in Sec. 15-161-60, Elgin Twp., just NW of Langdon, and named for Patrick H. McHugh (1846-1902), a county organizer, territorial legislator, and delegate to the ND Constitutional Convention in 1889. The post office was established January 29, 1885 with Charles B. Nelson pm, and on June 25, 1886 it was relocated to the neighboring townsite of Langdon, which absorbed McHUGH. Mr. McHugh was instrumental in bringing the GNRR into this area, and later served as mayor of Langdon. (2, 3, 18, 25, 40, 209, 216)

**McKENZIE** (Burleigh). This townsite was founded in Secs. 28 & 29-139-77, McKenzie Twp., on the NPRR mainline. The post office was established October 17, 1887 with Benjamin F. Scovil pm, and named for the somewhat notorious politician from Bismarck, Alexander McKenzie (1856-1922). The elevation is 1725, the Zip Code is 58553, and the population has never been much over 100. On July 2, 1965 the post office became a rural branch of Bismarck. (1, 2, 8, 14, 18, 25, 33, 40, 79)

**McKENZIE** (McKenzie). This place appears only on a 1930 roadmap published by the General Drafting Co. on old ND Highway 16, about fifteen miles SSW of Alexander. Like other similar places on this map, it borrows its name from its county, and is a copyright town. (3)

**McKINNEY** (Renville). This rural post office was established January 14, 1889 with Clyde W. Joslyn pm. It was located in SW¼ Sec. 24-161-86, McKinney Twp., three miles NE of Tolley, and named for Otis F. McKinney, a cousin and business partner of the Joslyns. A townsite was begun in Secs. 13 & 14-161-86, one mile to the north, in 1902, and the post office moved there. A population of 200 was claimed about 1910, and the village had several stores, a newspaper, a doctor, and many other luxuries held dear by the pioneer settlers. Without a railroad, however, the town declined, and the post office closed August 15, 1916 with mail to Tolley. The population had declined to just 20 in 1920, but McKINNEY remains an almost legendary ghost town in the hearts of many area residents. The location was picturesque, and its bridge across the Souris River was witness to many early romantic scenes. McKinley is an erroneous spelling. (2, 3, 18, 25, 40, 71, 79, 322)

**McLEAN** (Cavalier). This was a rural post office established January 7, 1892 with Alex McLean pm, who named it for Henry McLean, the chairman of the first county commission who came here from Ontario, Canada. In 1898 a townsite was platted in NE¼ Sec. 24-161-57, South Olga Twp., about nine miles NE of Osnabrock. The site was now owned by Mrs. Lomelia McLean, widow of Alex, but little development occurred, and the post office was moved two miles east into Pembina County on August 27, 1908 with a name change to Concrete. The Cavalier County site was not abandoned, however, and a country store/bar combination still exists today. For many years it was run by Henry Manley, and local residents commonly refer to the place as Hank's Corner. (2, 3, 18, 40, 53, 115, 117)

**McLEAN CORNERS** (Cavalier). This was a rural settlement in Sec. 6-163-63, Byron Twp., seven miles west of Hannah. It was named for Henry McLean (1847-1936), a native of Scotland who came here in 1882 from Ontario, Canada, was the chairman of the first county commission, and served in the state legislature for twenty years. Little development occurred here, and the site was soon abandoned. (2, 3, 215)

**McLEOD** (Ransom). This settlement on the Soo Line RR was founded in 1890 and named SANDOUN. Located in NW¼ Sec. 25-134-53, Sandoun Twp., twelve miles NW of Wyndmere, it changed its name to McLEOD on April 26, 1905 during the term of pm Eric Sovde to honor pioneer realtor J. J. McLeod of this area. The elevation is 1074, the Zip Code is 58057, and the population has been reported as high as 300 on several occasions. The community achieved a bit of notoriety in the early 1980's when it was discovered that the lowest paid full-time teacher in the country was employed at the local school. (1, 2, 3, 18, 40, 79, 201, 206)

**McRAE** (Bottineau). This townsite in Secs. 12 & 13-159-75, Ostby Twp., was founded in 1884 as BENNETT, but within a month had been renamed McRAE for Roderick McRae, who became the pm when the post office was established November 10, 1886. The settlement was on the GNRR, and boasted of a weekly newspaper. On November 9, 1889, one week after ND became a state, the name was changed to WILLOW CITY.

McCrae is an erroneous spelling. (2, 3, 18, 25, 34, 40, 101, 153)

**McRAE** (Grand Forks). This farm post office was established April 21, 1894 with Omund T. Josendahl pm. It was located in Sec. 25-150-53, Pleasant View Twp., nine miles south of Emerado, and named for D. C. McRae, an early teacher at the local rural school. It was relocated to the home of new pm Fannie Johnston in 1899, and closed January 30, 1904 with mail to Northwood. (2, 18, 31, 40, 69, 241)

**McVILLE** (Nelson). This was a rural post office established May 26, 1887 with Fred W. McDougall (1861-1936) pm at a site about two miles north of the present townsite. It closed December 15, 1890 with mail to Bue. It was reestablished May 1, 1894 with F. M. McCracken pm in his country store in NW 1/4 Sec. 26-150-59, Hamlin Twp., virtually the same site as the earlier office. The name was coined to note the presence of many famile with "Mc" names in the area, and is pronounced Mack'-ville. In 1906 the post office moved to the new GNRR townsite in SW¼ Sec. 35-150-59, two miles to the south that had been known as McVILLE STATION. The village incorporated in 1908, and reached a peak population of 626 in 1950. The elevation is 1468, and the Zip Code is 58254. (1, 2, 3, 18, 33, 40, 52, 79, 86, 124, 128, 129)

**McVILLE STATION** (Nelson). This name was applied to the new GNRR station in SW¼ Sec. 35-150-59, Hamlin Twp., to note the rural store and post office of McVILLE two miles to the north. The post office was relocated here in 1906 and the village of McVILLE began to develop. The new site soon became McVILLE, and the old site became known as OLD McVILLE as it gradually became a ghost town. (3, 124, 128)

**MEADOW** (McHenry). This was a farm post office established June 21, 1899 with Klemet K. Hage as the first and only pm. It was located in NE¼ Sec. 10-159-78, Meadow Twp., two miles north of Upham, and named for the township, which was named to describe the locale. The post office closed August 31, 1905, being replaced the following day by the post office at the new GNRR townsite of Upham. (2, 3, 12, 40, 186, 414, 415)

**MEADOW** (Stutsman). A post office was established at MEDINA on August 16, 1888 with Silas G. Guilford pm, who submitted his application as MEADOW, descriptive of the area, but the appointment was approved as MEDINA, a name which had been in use since about 1880. First called ELEVENTH SIDING, then MIDWAY for a short time in 1880, this settlement in Secs. 31 & 32-140-68, Flint Twp., has been MEDINA without objection since 1888. (2, 3, 40)

**MEAGHER** (Walsh). This Soo Line RR siding was built in 1911 in NW¼ Sec. 16-155-55, Eden Twp., two miles west of Conway, and named WILD ROSE. About 1913 the name was changed to MEAGHER, honoring Cornelius Meagher and his son, Edward Patrick Meagher (1880-1941), well known farmers in the area. (1, 3, 75, 293)

125

*McVille about 1915*

**MECKINOCK** (Grand Forks). This was a rural post office established October 7, 1879 with Robert Blakely pm at the site formerly known as BLAKELY'S CROSSING in SE¼ Sec. 20-152-53, Mekinock Twp., four miles SW of present-day Mekinock. The name is a corruption of the Ojibway Indian word *mukekenauk*, meaning turtle, and noting its location in the Turtle River valley. The post office closed February 20, 1882 with mail to Grand Forks. In 1888 the NPRR townsite of Mekinock was founded, using the old name with a slight change in the spelling. (2, 3, 18, 31, 40, 69)

**MEDBERRY** (LaMoure). A rural post office named MEDBERY was located in NW 1/4 Sec. 33-134-63, Wano Twp., five miles ENE of Edgeley, and had a post office 1886-1893. In 1906 the NPRR built a station at this site and named it MEDBERRY, which is believed to be the correct spelling of the last name of pioneer settler Harry M. Medberry. The post office was established October 9, 1906 with William Sorenson pm. A village of 90 people was reported here in 1920, but it gradually became a ghost town. The last elevator burned in August 1951, and the post office closed October 31, 1951 with mail to Edgeley. (1, 3, 40, 143)

**MEDBERY** (LaMoure). This was a rural post office established May 13, 1886 with Hattie A. Medberry pm. It was located in the home of Harry M. Medberry in NW¼ Sec. 33-134-63, Wano Twp., five miles ENE of Edgeley. A small village developed, reporting a population of 25 in 1890, but the post office closed April 13, 1893 with mail to Edgeley. The spelling of the name with just one "r" is assumed to be an error by postal officials that was accepted by local residents. In 1906 the NPRR built a station at this site, naming it MEDBERRY. (3, 40, 79, 143)

**MEDDOW** (McHenry). Enoch Mower (1859-1939) settled in the Towner area in 1889, coming from his native NH. About 1894 he moved to Meadow Twp. (159-78) in the vicinity of present-day Upham, and on September 5, 1896 he was appointed pm of the MEDDOW post office, but the order was rescinded October 17, 1896. The name is assumed to be a spelling error on postal records. Another post office spelled Meadow operated in this area 1899-1905 prior to the founding of Upham. Mr. Mower left this township, settling about two miles north of Towner. (3, 18, 40, 412)

**MEDFORD** (Walsh). This post office was established November 2, 1881 with Sherburn S. Worthing pm. It was located in SE¼ Sec. 26-155-56, Medford Twp., where a small village began to form around the general store run by Bertram W. Carpenter.

The post office moved two miles NNW in 1895 to SW¼ 22-155-56, and in 1905 moved to the Soo Line RR tracks in SW¼ Sec. 25-155-56, where a townsite was platted August 23, 1905. Some say the name came from Medford, WI, the home of local settlers, which was named for Medford, MA, which has an English place name meaning the middle ford. Others say Mr. Worthing named it for his hometown of Medford, MN, which was named by William K. Colling for the ship he sailed on when coming to America. Mr. Worthing had submitted a number of names to postal officials in 1881, with a notation that his preference was Sanbornton, but every name on his list was rejected in favor of MEDFORD. The name was officially changed to FORDVILLE on July 1, 1910, although the post office had already made the change on May 21, 1910. (1, 2, 3, 10, 13, 25, 40, 70, 75, 254, 294)

**MEDINA** (Stutsman). Founded in 1873 in Secs. 31 & 32-140-68, Flint Twp., as ELEVENTH SIDING, this NPRR station was called MIDWAY for a short time in 1880. Later that year NPRR President Jules M. Hannaford renamed it MEDINA by transposing the last two letters of "median". Others say it was named for Medina, NY, which was named for the city in Hejaz, Saudi Arabia, which has a name derived from *Medinahal-nabi*, meaning City of the Prophet, i.e. Mohammed, who fled here in 622 A.D. from Mecca. The post office was established August 16, 1888 with Silas G. Guilford pm, who attempted to change the name to MEADOW, but postal officials rejected this name and Mr. Guilford accepted the established name of MEDINA. The village incorporated in 1906, and it became a city in 1946 with Daniel Preszler Jr. (1900-1964) as mayor. The elevation is 1816,

the Zip Code is 58467, and a peak population of 564 was reached in 1950. MEDINA once called itself "The Biggest Little Town on the N. P." (1, 2, 5, 19, 18, 25, 33, 49, 79, 158, 159)

**MEDORA** (Billings). This townsite was founded in 1883 in Secs. 26 & 27-140-102, Medora Twp., on the NPRR just east of the old settlement of Little Missouri. It was named for Medora von Hoffman, a wealthy NY heiress, by her husband, the Marquis de Mores. The name Medora is traced to an 1814 poem, *The Corsair*, by Lord Byron. The post office was established November 13, 1883 with Charles E. Haupt pm. The elevation is 2290, the Zip Code is 58645, a peak population of 210 was reached in 1930, and it is the county seat of Billings County. President Theodore Roosevelt lived in this area 1883-1886. In the late 1950's Bismarck businessman Harold Schafer began the restoration and promotion of this historic town, and it has become one of the leading tourist attractions in ND. (1, 2, 3, 18, 25, 33, 40, 79, 81, 279, 294)

**MEIDINGER** (McIntosh). This was a farm post office established September 5, 1919 with Sophia Meidinger pm. It was located in the home of Johann R. "John" Meidinger (1858-1921) in SE¼ Sec. 22-131-68, Rosenthal Twp., twelve miles NE of Ashley in the Antelope Valley area. Mr. Meidinger came here with his father, Adam Meidinger, and four brothers in 1886 from Kassel, South Russia, and served five terms as county sheriff. The post office closed December 31, 1920 with mail to Ashley. (2, 3, 18, 40, 134, 211)

**MEKINOCK** (Grand Forks). This NPRR station was founded in 1887 in NE¼ Sec. 1-152-53, Mekinock Twp., and named for its township, which bears an Ojibway Indian name derived from *mukekenauk*, meaning turtle, and noting the station's location in the Turtle River valley. Some say it was named for a township in MN, although no such place could be found. The post office was erroneously established as MACKINOCK on January 30, 1888 with Mathew Ladwell pm, and the spelling error was corrected on February 14, 1888. The elevation is 886, the Zip Code is 58258, and a population of 250 was reported in 1890, with a decline to just 90 in 1981. Olger B. Burtness, a District Judge and benefactor of UND in Grand Forks, was born at this site in 1884, three years before the townsite was founded. (1, 2, 3, 13, 18, 31, 33, 40, 69, 79)

**MELBY** (Dunn). This was a rural community in Sec. 4-144-94, Clay Butte Twp. The post office was established January 22, 1907 with Carl Ludwig Melby pm, who was a school teacher, and later served as Dunn County's first Superintendent of Schools. On

*Medora about 1930*

May 7, 1914 the post office was relocated to the new NPRR townsite of Dunn Center, two miles to the NNW. (2, 18, 40, 223)

**MELBY** (Foster). This was a rural post office established June 21, 1890 with Knut Melby pm. It was located in N½ Sec. 3-147-62, McHenry Twp., one mile east of McHenry, which was established as a NPRR terminus in 1899. The MELBY post office relocated to the new townsite on November 24, 1899, but an attempt to retain the old name was unsuccessful. (2, 3, 40, 97, 240)

**MELLEMVILLE** (Griggs). In 1899 the NPRR established a station in NW¼ Sec. 19-147-59, Tyrol Twp., on land owned by J. E. Mellem, who named the new townsite for himself. Pioneer settlers persuaded him to allow the JESSIE post office to keep its original name when it relocated to the townsite later that year. (3, 18, 40, 284)

**MELVILLE** (Foster). This was a NPRR station established in 1883 in E½ Sec. 35-145-66, Melville Twp., just east of the pioneer settlement of Newport, whose post office moved here on May 2, 1883 with Edgar S. Leavenworth pm. Most sources attribute the name to "Melville D. Carrington", a partner in the Carrington-Casey Land Co., owners of the townsite, but Mr. Carrington's given name was actually Miles. It is more likely that the name was chosen by another partner, Lyman R. Casey, to honor one of the firm's stockholders, Howard Melville Hanna. Melville is a variant of Melvin, a Celtic name meaning servant. The elevation is 1622, and it is the oldest existing settlement in the county. A population of 200 was reported in 1890, but the current population is less than 50. The post office closed April 21, 1967 with mail to Carrington. (1, 2, 3, 18, 25, 40, 97)

**MELVILLE** (Nelson). This place appears on a 1905 map of Nelson County published by the J. P. Lamb Land Co. of Michigan, ND, in SE¼ Sec. 9-149-59, Nesheim Twp., two miles SW of present-day McVille which was founded in 1906. It is assumed that this was an attempt to show the new GNRR townsite of McVille, with a spelling error by the cartographer. (3, 128)

**MENASHA CENTER** (Dickey). This was one of several names used by townsite promoter M. H. Puffer in SW¼ Sec. 32-130-60, Hudson Twp., now the NE section of GUELPH. This name noted the fact that many of the settlers came from Menasha, WI, which was given an Algonquin Indian name meaning island, or thorn. The name had been suggested by the wife of WI Governor Doty. Other names used at the ND site were CENTER, CENTRALIA, CENTROPOLIS, and COLDWATER. (2, 3, 10, 70, 154)

**MENOKEN** (Burleigh). The NPRR built SEVENTEENTH SIDING in 1873 in N½ Sec. 33-139-78, Menoken Twp., and the first settlers called it BLAINE. The post office was established in 1880 as CLARKE'S FARM, and on March 6, 1883 pm Florence Corey changed the name at the suggestion of townsite owner Col. S. G. Magill of Fargo to MENOKEN, an Indian word said to mean thou shalt reap where thou hast sown. Col. Magill platted the townsite in March 1883, at which time the population was about 50. The NPRR did not like the name MENOKEN, and called its station BURLEIGH from September 23, 1891 until it closed in 1957. The Zip Code is 58558, and a peak population of 80 was reached in 1920, with a decline to just 26 in 1983. Alfred Taylor Welch (1868-1934) was the pm 1898-1934, and Nettie J. Dance held the post 1935-1971. Playwright Evertt Phillip "Ev" Miller was born here in 1935. (1, 2, 3, 12, 14, 18, 25, 33, 40, 253)

**MERCER** (McLean). This NPRR station was founded in 1905 in SW¼ Sec. 2-146-79, Mercer Twp., and named for William Henry Harrison Mercer, originally spelled Musser, a native of PA who settled near Painted Woods in 1869 and was a well known rancher in the Missouri River valley for many years. Mercer County is also named for him. The post office was established October 2, 1905 with Nels Oleson pm. The elevation is 1948, the Zip Code is 58559, and a peak population of 250 was reported in both 1930 and 1940. (1, 2, 18, 28, 33, 40, 79, 389)

**MERCER** (Mercer). This was a rural post office established February 13, 1886 with Gertie

Wood pm, who named it for its county, which was named for William Henry Harrison Mercer, a pioneer rancher in the Missouri River valley. It was located in SW¼ Sec. 35-145-85, four miles west of Stanton, and closed January 31, 1888 with mail to Stanton. It reopened April 18, 1888 with Luella Munro pm at her home in NE¼ Sec. 6-144-85, about one-half mile SW of the original site, but closed for good January 30, 1889 with mail to Causey. (2, 3, 25, 40, 240, 414)

**MERCER CITY** (Mercer). This townsite was platted about 1885 by J. J. Luke and A. V. Schallern of the Lutheran Colonization Bureau of Chicago, IL, a group also involved with the founding of New Salem in Morton County. It was located in Sec. 5-144-85, about five miles west of Stanton, and was named for its county, which was named for William Henry Harrison Mercer, a pioneer rancher in the Missouri River valley. Twenty-five lots were sold in MERCER CITY, mostly to buyers from IL, but only George Hawley, later a county commissioner, actually took up residence here as the venture became a ghost town. (2, 64, 121, 232)

**MERIDA** (McLean). This was a Soo Line RR siding built about 1913 in SE¼ Sec. 35-144-81, midway between Wilton and Washburn, and just west of the old Roosevelt siding. Joseph William "Billy" Jennings, later a state legislator, led a group of neighbors in privately building the facility, complete with scales, stockyards, and a small building, as a shipping point for their grain and livestock. The origin of the name is unknown, although it has been speculated that it was named for Merida, the capital of Yucatan, in Mexico, a country much in the news at that time. The siding was removed in 1965. (1, 2, 3, 5, 28, 414, 433)

**MERIDEN** (McLean). This was a rural post office established May 5, 1898 with Carolette Smith Hoffman (1868-1950) as pm, but the order was rescinded June 28, 1898. Mrs. Hoffman, a native of MI, and her husband, Charles Ward Hoffman, were associated with the Fort Berthold Indian Reservation for about fifty years as teachers, benefactors, and administrators. The post office was likely intended to be in the village of Shell Creek in SE¼ Sec. 8-150-91, Shell Creek Twp., about fifteen miles SW of Parshall, where the Hoffmans lived from their marriage in 1895 until 1908. The origin of the name is unknown, although it is found throughout the United States, and traces to Meriden Farms in Dorking, Surrey, England. (3, 28, 33, 37, 40)

**MERL** (Ramsey). This was a farm post office established February 28, 1898 with Sivert H. Oakland (1859-1902) pm. Mr. Oakland, who came here from IA in 1895, also operated a country store at the site, which he named for his daughter, Merl Roselia Oakland (1882-1970), who acted as his assistant. It was located in NW¼ Sec. 12-158-60, Highland Center Twp., in the extreme NE corner of the county. Mr. Oakland's son-in-law, Peder Solberg, became pm in 1902 and closed the facility June 30, 1906 with mail to Nekoma. (2, 3, 40, 75, 103, 247)

**MERRICOURT** (Dickey). This was a farm post office established October 18, 1883 with Bertha V. Mann pm. It was located in SE¼ Sec. 22-132-65, Young Twp., and was named by the pm for a name she had seen in a novel. It is an English place name, and was originally the name of the township as well. In 1891 the Soo Line RR built a townsite in Secs. 25 & 36-132-65, about two miles to the SE, and the post office relocated there. The elevation is 1644, the Zip Code is 58469, and a peak population of 153 was reached in 1940, although a rapid decline has reduced the count to just 17 in 1980. (1, 2, 3, 18, 33, 40, 52, 79, 154, 264, 316)

**MERRIFIELD** (Grand Forks). This was a GNRR station built in 1881 in SW¼ Sec. 31-151-50, Grand Forks Twp., six miles south of Grand Forks. It was named for site owner Webster Merrifield (1852-1916), a native of VT who became a charter faculty member of UND in 1883, and served as its President 1891-1901. The post office was established November 9, 1886 with Hattie M. Thompson pm, and closed June 15, 1895. It reopened October 23, 1895, closed January 2, 1907, reopened March 27, 1907, and closed for good January 31, 1954 with mail in all instances going to Grand Forks. A small village existed at the site for many years, reporting populations of 18 in 1890 and 12 in 1960, but the site is now virtually abandoned. (1, 2, 3, 5, 25, 31, 40, 69, 79)

**MESA** (Williams). This GNRR townsite was founded in 1916 in NE¼ Sec. 13-159-102, Barr Butte Twp., two miles NE of the Howard store and post office. It was at first called MESA, a Spanish word meaning table in reference to a high, flat table land, which described the locale in ND. Margaret Dorothy Schroeder Lyman (1858-1936) was the original townsite owner. When the post office was established December 19, 1916, the name was changed to HANKS. (2, 10, 40, 50)

**METIGOSHE** (Bottineau). This was a rural post office established May 24, 1909 with Charles E. Bergholtz pm. It was located in NW¼ Sec. 1-163-75, Roland Twp., twelve miles NNE of Bottineau on the east shore of Lake Metigoshe. The name was part of the Chippewa Indian name for the lake, *Metigoshe Washegum*, meaning clear water lake surrounded by oaks. The lake's name was suggested by pioneer settler James Dawson as preferable to Fish Lake, or Farquhar Lake, which had been suggested to honor astronomer F. U. Farquhar. The post office was discontinued March 15, 1914 with mail to Bottineau. The Washegum post office on the west shore of the lake, which utilized the other part of the Indian name, was in operation at virtually the same period of time. (1, 2, 3, 18, 40, 153)

**METIGOSHE PARK** (Bottineau). This was a platted resort community in SW¼ Sec. 2-163-75, Roland Twp., on an island in the southern part of the lake. Lots were platted around the shoreline of the island, with a ball field in the middle. It appeared as such only in a 1910 county atlas. (3, 18)

**MICHIGAN** (Nelson). This is the generally used name for MICHIGAN CITY, the first settlement in the county, founded by Edwin

A. Lamb in 1882 in SE¼ Sec. 32-153-58, Michigan City Twp. The post office was established January 2, 1883 with Creighton J. Bondurant pm, and the village incorporated May 12, 1883. The affairs of MICHIGAN have almost always been dominated by members of the Lamb family, although it is said that Mrs. Julia FitzGerald Lamb, the family matriarch, flatly rejected the idea of naming the site Lambville. The elevation is 1523, the Zip Code is 58259, and a peak population of 501 was reached in 1980 as the city has maintained a steady growth. (1, 2, 3, 18, 25, 33, 40, 52, 79, 124, 128)

**MICHIGAN CITY** (Nelson). This GNRR townsite was founded in 1882 by Edwin A. Lamb, who came here from Port Huron, MI with his family. Despite the fact that the Lambs came from the state of MI, some claim the townsite was named for Michigan City, IN. The name is an Indian word of uncertain origin derived from *Mitchisawgyegan* meaning great lake, or *Mishi-maikin-nac*, meaning swimming turtle. It is located in SE¼ Sec. 32-153-58, Michigan City Twp., and was the first settlement in Nelson County. The official name is still MICHIGAN CITY, but the shortened form MICHIGAN has had almost universal usage since pioneer days. (2, 3, 10, 18, 25, 58, 124, 128)

**MICHIGAN SETTLEMENT** (Richland). Warren Spaulding of Hartford, MI was discouraged by the high land prices in southern MI, and came here in 1878. Encouraged by what he found, he led over forty families into Fairmount and DeVillo Townships in April 1879, and this group became known as the MICHIGAN SETTLEMENT. When Mr. Spaulding started a post office in 1880, it was named DeVILLO, and in 1884 was renamed FAIRMOUNT. (2, 3, 147, 355)

**MIDDLE STATION** (Sheridan). This was a stopping point on the Fort Totten-Fort Stevenson trail used during the trail's active era of 1867-1872. The name is descriptive of its location in SW¼ Sec. 13-150-76, Rosenfield Twp., about eleven miles west of Martin, which was approximately midway between the two military posts. The site was chosen for that reason, and also because of the presence of fresh water and brush for protection. The trail, and this site, became obsolete when the NPRR mainline reached Bismarck in 1872. (2, 3, 21, 60)

**MIDLAND** (Pembina). Several longtime residents of Pembina County recall this "place", which actually was the name of a well known baseball team of the early 1900's made up of men from both Hensel and Crystal. (3, 366)

**MIDWAY** (Cass). This was a short-lived NPRR station east of Buffalo in NE 1/4 Sec. 27-140-54, Buffalo Twp., which apparently was named to note its location between Tower City and Buffalo. The site is now abandoned. (2, 34, 77)

**MIDWAY** (Emmons). This place was founded in 1936 by George J. Dockter in NE¼ Sec. 19-132-74, twelve miles east of Linton on the south side of ND Highway 13, and consisted

of a grocery store, bar, gas station, blacksmith shop, and a creamery. The name apparently noted the fact that it was midway between Linton and the junction with ND Highway 3. Katherine Miller assisted Mr. Dockter for many years. Improvements in transportation reduced the feasability of such operations, and Mr. Dockter moved his businesses into Linton in 1957, ending the history of MIDWAY. (3, 34, 66)

**MIDWAY** (McHenry). This was a rural stopping point on ND Highway 14, midway between Towner and Drake at the junction of the county road going west to Verendrye. It was in SE¼ Sec. 17-154-76, and appeared on maps as late as the 1960's. Some believe it was a copyright town. (3, 185)

**MIDWAY** (Ramsey). This GNRR station was founded in 1883 in NW¼ Sec. 17-153-62, Stevens Twp., and named to note the fact that it was midway between Bartlett and Devils Lake. Some say the name noted the fact that the site was built on the middle of the three surveyed routes into the area. When application was made for a post office, this rather generic name was rejected by postal officials, and the post office opened January 14, 1884 as CRARY. (2, 3, 18, 25, 40, 103)

**MIDWAY** (Slope). This was a rural settlement founded in the summer of 1907 in NW¼ Sec. 12-135-100, White Lake Twp., seven miles ENE of Amidon. It was named to note the fact that it was halfway between Belfield and the rural settlement of Stillwater in Bowman County. Others say it was named to note that it was midway between the NPRR and the Milwaukee Road RR, a statement that is not quite as accurate as the first explanation. MIDWAY contained a store, hotel, bank, lumber yard, cream station, and a blacksmith shop. The post office was established June 17, 1907 with Peter Oberg pm. L. M. Engelson purchased the store in 1914 and moved it one mile east to Sec. 7-135-99, Moord Twp., and the rest of the town followed. A population of 40 was reported in 1920, but the post office closed January 31, 1930 with mail to New England. Blacksmith Edwin J. Rotering (1887-1951) was the last resident of MIDWAY. (1, 2, 3, 18, 40, 53, 82)

**MIDWAY** (Stutsman). The NPRR siding built in Secs. 31 & 32-140-68, Flint Twp., in 1873 was first called ELEVENTH SIDING. For a time in 1880 it was called MIDWAY after NPRR officials determined that this place was exactly halfway between the easternmost point of the United States and the westernmost point of Alaska. Later in 1880 the site was renamed MEDINA, and was served by the Eldridge post office until the MEDINA post office opened in 1888. (2, 3, 25, 40, 158)

**MIDWAY** (Traill). A map in the 1881 annual report of the NPRR shows a station called MIDWAY, approximately midway between Mayville and Blanchard, both of which were themselves quite newly-settled townsites at the time. The actual midway point between these two townsites would be in the southern part of Mayville Twp. (146-52), near what would become Murray. MIDWAY, as conceived in 1881, failed to develop. (3, 422)

**MIKKELSON** (Billings). This ranch post office was established July 9, 1894 with Elias E. Mikkelson (1857-1920) pm. It was located on his ranch in Sec. 1-142-100, eighteen miles north of Fryburg. Seven additional pms served the local ranchers in this general area until the post office closed June 30, 1934 with mail to Gorham. Its last location was on the west bank of the Little Missouri River about twenty miles north of Medora. (1, 2, 3, 33, 40, 81)

**MILAN** (Grand Forks). This rural settlement in NE¼ Sec. 20-154-53, Johnstown Twp., was first called MILAN for Milan, PA, the hometown of pioneer settler John Ryan Barker, and likely named for the great city in Italy. The name was also given to the township when it first organized. When the post office was established December 13, 1880 with Mr. Barker as pm, the name was changed to JOHNSTOWN. (2, 3, 13, 40, 69)

**MILITARY SPUR** (Ramsey). This was a GNRR station in SE¼ Sec. 29-153-64, Lake Twp., six miles south of the city of Devils Lake at the northern point of the narrows of Devils Lake, serving military installations on both sides of the lake. The name is found on maps circa 1910-1920, while later maps call it FORT TOTTEN STATION. (3, 18)

**MILL** (Pierce). This was a rural post office established June 1, 1909 with Jacob N. Muehl pm. It was located in NW¼ Sec. 31-152-72, Alexanter Twp., six miles NE of Clifton and six miles NW of Selz, and served the STRASBURG COLONY of about fifty families from South Russia. Strasburg was suggested as the name of this post office, but was already being used by a post office in Emmons County. MILL is said to be a severe Anglicization of the pm's name. The post office closed September 15, 1910 with mail to Esmond. Mills is an erroneous spelling. (2, 3, 18, 40, 114, 414)

**MILLARTON** (Stutsman). This townsite was founded in 1912 as a Midland Continental RR station in Sec. 21-137-64, Severn Twp., between Sydney and Nortonville, and was named for a Belgian investor in the railroad. The post office was established June 24, 1913 with Charles E. Strock pm. Marvin Egstrom was the last depot agent here, and his daughter, Norma Delores Egstrom, achieved great fame in show business as the singer Peggy Lee. A population of 125 was reported in 1920, but the count had declined to just 40 in 1960. The post office, Zip Code 58470, closed in December 1977, although government records did not record this fact until October 13, 1984. (1, 2, 3, 40, 79, 158)

**MILLER** (McLean). In 1903 it was clear that the NPRR was soon going to build into the vicinity of the Turtle Lake post office in NE¼ Sec. 26-147-81, Lake Williams Twp. This rural post office had been established in 1886 by Peter Miller (1827-1924), a native of Ireland who had settled here in 1884 and had served as a county judge. Mr. Miller began promoting this location, and within a few months a machine shop, livery stable, hardware store, and a general store were

operating at the fledgling townsite. Meanwhile Christian Paulson took over the post office and moved it to his land one mile to the SW, where he started a rival townsite called Wanamaker. The NPRR arrived in 1905, but built its station two miles further to the west, and both townsites moved to that site, retaining the name of the old post office, Turtle Lake. (2, 3, 40, 271)

**MILLER** (Ransom). This was a farm post office established April 27, 1899 with Ole H. Miller pm. It was located in Sec. 4-136-57, Preston Twp., eight miles NNE of Fort Ransom, and closed March 31, 1905 with mail to Preston. (2, 3, 18, 40, 201)

**MILLERS** (Foster). This was a Soo Line RR spur and loading station in NW 1/4 Sec. 19-145-64, Buchephalia Twp., four miles SW of Bordulac. It was named for pioneer settler Myron Miller who came here in 1892, and his widow rode on the first train to use the spur. It appeared on maps circa 1910-1950, and often was shown as MILLERS SPUR. A population of 2 was listed in 1930 and 1940. (2, 3, 53, 97)

**MILLERS SPUR** (Foster). This was a Soo Line RR spur and loading station in NW¼ Sec. 19-145-64, Buchephalia Twp., four miles SW of Bordulac. It appeared on maps circa 1910-1950, and was often called simply MILLERS. (2, 3, 18, 97)

**MILLER'S SPUR** (Williams). This was a GNRR spur built in Sec. 17-153-100, Stony Creek Twp., three miles NE of Williston, to serve the Huseby & Ellithorpe Coal Mine located at the site. It was built about 1910 and named for R. N. Miller, manager of the mine. Clarence E. Ellithorpe, one of the mine's owners, was at the time Superintendent of Schools in Williston. The facility appeared on maps circa 1910-1915. (2, 3, 18, 50)

**MILLIZEN** (Hettinger). This post office was authorized March 14, 1908 with H. M. Millizen pm, but the order was rescinded October 8, 1908. The location is unknown. (2, 3, 40)

**MILLSBURGH** (Sargent). This was a rural community in NE¼ Sec. 23-131-57, Harlem Twp., four miles NE of Cogswell. The post office was established July 2, 1883, the same day as Kandiotta, with Robert Timmins pm, who named it for pioneer merchant Simeon Mills. The post office closed November 17, 1886 with mail to Sargent. Most MILLSBURGH residents became pioneers at the new townsite of Harlem. Millsburg is an erroneous spelling. (2, 3, 40, 165, 167)

**MILL SIDING** (Richland). This was a GNRR siding one mile SE of Kindred in Sec. 5-136-50, Walcott Twp. The name referred to a flour mill located at the site. A post office named ULNESS operated here 1898-1905, and later maps showed the site as KINDRED MILL SPUR. (2, 3, 18, 40, 147)

**MILLWOOD** (Dickey). This was a rural community centered in Porter Twp. (132-62), just north of Fullerton. It was named for William Mills, who had settled in eastern Dickey County in 1882, and had once owned

the townsite of Oakes. Frank O. Alin was appointed pm on March 17, 1902, but the order was rescinded. Mr. Alin did, however, succeed in getting the county's first Rural Free Delivery mail route established out of Fullerton to serve this area. (2, 3, 40, 154, 316, 318)

**MILNOR** (Sargent). This townsite was founded in August 1883 in Sec. 9-132-54, Milnor Twp., after negotiations for more land had failed at Linton, three miles to the east. The post office was established October 18, 1883 with Thomas V. Phelps pm. As the temporary terminus of the NPRR branch line from Fergus Falls, MN, this settlement was designated as county seat in 1883, but lost that honor in 1886 to the centrally located townsite of Forman. MILNOR incorporated as a village in 1884, and became a city in 1914 with L. W. Intlehouse mayor. The name was chosen by the NPRR for two of its employees, William Milnor Roberts, the Chief Civil Engineer, and William E. Milnor, the local telegrapher. It is the oldest existing settlement in the county, and had a college for two years before it was relocated to Mayville. The elevation is 1250, the Zip Code is 58060, and a peak population of 850 was reported in 1890. (1, 2, 3, 18, 25, 40, 52, 79, 165, 171)

**MILROY** (McHenry). The SHIGLEY post office was established May 27, 1901 in SE¼ Sec. 18-158-77, Bantry Twp., two miles WNW of Bantry. Pm John F. Shafer received authorization to change the name to HOOSIER on August 8, 1902, but that order was rescinded. On December 12, 1902 the name was changed to MILROY, supposedly to honor General Robert Huston Milroy (1816-1890), a hero of the Mexican and Civil Wars who had been Superintendent of Indian Affairs in Washington Territory 1872-1885. A village in MN was also named for Gen. Milroy in 1902. On July 10, 1905 the post office was relocated to the new GNRR townsite of Bantry, assuming that name. (2, 3, 13, 40, 412, 415)

**MILROY** (McHenry). This was a GNRR station founded about 1907 in NW¼ Sec. 7-157-76, Milroy Twp., seven miles SE of Bantry. It was named for the old rural post office which had relocated to Bantry in 1905. The new MILROY post office was established December 31, 1909 with James E. Bruton pm in his grocery store. Very little development occurred, and the post office closed September 30, 1915 with mail to Bantry. Two elevators remained at the site in 1922, but MILROY is now a vacant townsite. (1, 2, 3, 18, 40, 412)

**MILTON** (Cavalier). This was a rural post office established July 7, 1882 with Donald McDonald pm, who suggested the name Springfield. Instead it was named for Milton, Ontario, Canada, the hometown of pioneer settler Steven Sophar, which was named for Martin Mills. Others say it was named for the famous British author John Milton (1608-1674). Milton is an Old English name meaning from the mill farmstead. The post office was located in NE¼ Sec. 10-159-57, Montrose Twp., until 1885 when it moved one mile NW to NE¼ Sec. 4-159-57. In 1887 the GNRR founded a townsite two miles west in NE¼ Sec.

6-159-57, and the MILTON post office moved there with Joseph Powles pm. A population of 764 was reported here in 1890 at the peak of its initial boom, but the count had declined to 195 in 1980. The village incorporated in 1888, its elevation in 1686, and the Zip Code is 58260. (1, 2, 3, 10, 19, 25, 33, 40, 79, 117, 218)

**MINDEN** (McLean). This Soo Line RR station was built in 1913 in W½ Sec. 23-145-82, Buffalo Lake Twp., between Washburn and Underwood. The site was donated to the railroad by Karl Eichhorst, and named for Minden, Prussia. A townsite was platted here in June 1916, but when the post office was established December 16, 1916 the name was changed to FALKIRK to avoid confusion with Mandan. (2, 3, 28, 40)

**MINER** (Grant). This was a farm post office established December 2, 1908 with John G. Streigel pm. It was located in NE¼ Sec. 18-131-88, Howard Twp., sixteen miles SSE of Elgin, and closed May 15, 1916 with mail to Pretty Rock. The origin of the name is unknown. (1, 2, 3, 17, 40, 176, 177, 415)

**MINERAL SPRINGS** (Slope). This was a rural settlement in SW¼ Sec. 14-133-100, Mineral Springs Twp., twelve miles SSE of Amidon, and named to note the many natural springs in the area that were thought to have medicinal properties. The townsite was owned by Mrs. Bernice V. Bullock, whose daughter Madgie E. Bullock married the local storekeeper, Andrew Larson. The post office was established September 7, 1910 with Henry Fries pm. The town had several stores, a newspaper, and a 1920 population of 75, but when it became obvious that the Milwaukee Road RR would not reach this site, it declined rapidly. The post office closed July 15, 1924 with mail to Buffalo Springs, and the last building at the site was destroyed in a storm in 1955. (1, 2, 3, 40, 53, 79, 82, 400)

**MINISTER** (Logan). This site, Sec. 8-135-67, Gutschmidt Twp., was settled by Germans from Bessarabia, South Russia in 1891, and a settlement called HACKNEY began. In 1903 the name was changed to GACKLE, but in 1904 it was relocated six miles north to the new NPRR townsite. The people who remained at the old site renamed it MINISTER for unknown reasons. A post office was authorized April 26, 1904 with Louis Larsen pm, but the order was rescinded September 27, 1904. The townsite soon became a ghost town. (2, 40, 116)

**MINNEWAKAN** (Ramsey). This was a rural post office established July 21, 1882 with Jason B. Packard pm. It was located in NW¼ Sec. 21-153-63, South Minnewaukan Twp., four miles SE of the city of Devils Lake. The name is a corruption of the Indian name for the lake. In 1883 it moved two miles NW to NE¼ Sec. 18-153-63, the home of new pm William H. Makee, and closed February 13, 1884 with mail to Devils Lake. The name, with a slight change in the spelling, was transferred to the new townsite at the east end of Devils Lake, destined to become the county seat of Benson County. (2, 3, 25, 40, 414)

**MINNEWAUKAN** (Benson). This townsite was founded in 1883 in SE¼ Sec. 15-153-67, West Bay Twp., as one of several sites competing for the important NPRR connection at the west end of Devils Lake. MINNEWAUKAN was the winner, and became the county seat in 1884. The name is based on the Indian name for Devils Lake, *Mini Waukon Chante*, meaning water of bad spirits. Bad referred to the saltiness of the water, not the devil, as misinterpreted by the white man. The post office was established as MINNEWAUKON on March 12, 1884 with Thomas B. Ware pm. The spelling was changed to the commonly used version, MINNEWAUKAN, on August 2, 1909 by pm James M. Cubbison, who operated a drugstore and was the county's first Register of Deeds. The village incorporated in 1897, and became a city in 1898. The elevation is 1483, the Zip Code is 58351, and a peak population of 564 was reached in 1920. (1, 2, 3, 18, 25, 34, 40, 52, 110, 255)

**MINNEWAUKON** (Benson). This post office was established March 12, 1884 with Thomas B. Ware pm in his hardware store, using a corruption of the Indian name for Devils Lake. Most people spelled the name MINNEWAUKAN, however, and on August 2, 1909 pm James M. Cubbison officially changed the spelling to conform with popular demand. (2, 3, 34, 40, 79, 255)

**MINNIE LAKE** (Barnes). This farm post office was established March 29, 1880 with Edwin Priest pm. It was located in SW¼ Sec. 22-142-56, Minnie Lake Twp., eight miles SSE of Pillsbury. The post office and the township were named for the nearby lake, but the origin of the lake's name is unknown. The post office closed June 19, 1897 with mail to Ellsbury. In 1898 it reopened one mile SW, but the name was spelled as one word to comply with new government spelling regulations. (3, 40, 76, 281)

**MINNIELAKE** (Barnes). This farm post office was established February 28, 1898 in NW¼ Sec. 28-142-56, Minnie Lake Twp., one mile SW of the recently closed post office of MINNIE LAKE. The one-word spelling was required to comply with new government spelling regulations. The pm was Wesley Van Steenbergh, who sometimes spelled his name Van Steinburgh. The post office moved three miles NE in 1904, and closed November 30, 1906 with mail to Algeo. (2, 3, 25, 34, 40, 76, 281, 425)

**MINOT** (Ward). This GNRR townsite was founded in 1886 and became known as "The Magic City" because of its rapid growth, quickly covering most of Harrison Twp. (155-83). It was named for Henry Davis Minot (1859-1890), a director of the GNRR who was killed in a train wreck. The post office was established February 12, 1887 with Patrick H. McNamara pm. It incorporated as a city in 1887, replaced Burlington as the county seat of Ward County in 1888, and has grown steadily to a peak population of 32,886 in 1980. The elevation is 1566, the Zip Code is 58701, and it is the site of Minot State University. It should be noted that the correct pronunciation of this city's name is My-Knot. (1, 2, 3, 18, 33, 40, 52, 79, 100)

**MINOT AIR FORCE BASE** (Ward). Groundbreaking for this military facility was held July 12, 1955, and the base was activated February 7, 1957. It ocuupies parts of twelve sections of Waterford Twp. (157-83), and parts of three sections of Tatman Twp. (157-82), at its location about thirteen miles north of Minot, the city for which it is named. It has a classified branch of the Minot post office, sharing its Zip Code of 58701. (33, 34, 40, 100)

**MINOT STOCK YARDS** (Ward). This was a GNRR siding in NE¼ Sec. 20 & NW 1/4 Sec. 21-155-82, Nedrose Twp., three miles east of Minot. It appears on maps circa 1905-1925, and as the name implies was a loading facility for livestock. (3, 18)

**MINTO** (Walsh). This GNRR townsite was founded in 1880 in Sec. 31-156-52, Harriston Twp., and named for either Minto, Wellington County, Ontario, or Hamilton, Minto County, Ontario. Both Canadian place names are for Gilbert Elliott, 3rd Baronet of Minto (1722-1777), an early

*Minot about 1907*

Governor-General of Canada who was a staunch supporter of the British cause in the American Revolution. The post office was established March 15, 1880 with John Ogilvie Brown pm. The elevation is 820, the Zip Code is 58261, and the village, which incorporated in 1883 and became a city in 1903, reached a peak population of 701 in 1910. (1, 2, 3, 18, 25, 33, 40, 45, 52, 75, 79)

**MIRIAM** (Emmons). This settlement dates from about 1887, and is said to have been named for Mrs. Albert B. Peterson, nee Maria Jacobson, who adopted this given name after coming here from Sweden in 1883. Miriam is a Hebrew name meaning rebellious. A townsite was platted in Sec. 34-136-75, just south of present-day Braddock, but the plat was not filed, and the site failed to develop. Merriam is an erroneous spelling. (2, 3, 19, 25, 66, 113)

**MITCHELL'S POST** (Burleigh). This was a trading post established about 1822 by David D. Mitchell on the Missouri River, probably just north of Bismarck near the old townsite of Wogansport. He later established Fort McKenzie in what is now SD. (2, 3, 420)

**MOEN** (Nelson). This was a rural post office established September 29, 1905 with Anders Johannes Moen (1848-1924) pm. It was located in SE¼ Sec. 3-154-58, Sarnia Twp., three miles NE of Whitman. Some say it was named for Lars Moen, who came here as early as 1871 from his home in Freeborn County, MN, while the pm came here in 1882 from Norway. The post office closed May 15, 1907 with mail to Michigan. (2, 18, 40, 124)

**MOFFIT** (Burleigh). This settlement began at the west end of Long Lake in Sec. 17-137-76, Long Lake Twp., as early as 1886, but real development did not begin for several years. The post office was established February 27, 1906 with Knonley F. Moffit (1883-1969) pm, who named it for his father, George Washington Moffit (1862-1903). The elder Mr. Moffit was killed in a train accident in this town which bore his name. In 1909 MOFFIT residents tried to establish a new county from southern Burleigh and northern Emmons counties, but the effort failed. The site is at a junction of NPRR and Soo Line RR lines, but the population has never exceeded the count of 184 reported in 1940. The elevation is 1763, and the Zip Code is 58560. (1, 2, 3, 8, 14, 18, 40, 79, 90)

**MOHALL** (Renville). This GNRR townsite was founded in 1901 in Sec. 13-161-84, Brandon Twp., as HALL, but due to alleged duplication, the name was changed to MOHALL. Both names honor the town's founder, Martin O. Hall (1853-1925), the local newspaperman, who also founded Greene in 1909. The post office was established February 24, 1902 with Mr. Hall as pm. When Renville County was formed in 1910, MOHALL was named the county seat in an election featuring all of the new county's established villages. The elevation is 1648, the Zip Code is 58761, and a peak population of 1,073 was reached in 1950. Thomas H. Moodie, Governor of ND for a short time during the political upheaval of 1935, was a longtime resident of MOHALL. (1, 2, 3, 18, 33, 40, 71, 79, 322)

*Mohall about 1912*

**MOHAWK** (Dunn). This was the last of the three planned townsites, the others being Pembroke and Juniper in McKenzie County, on a proposed GNRR extension from Watford City to New Rockford. Right-of-way negotiations stalled just east of Watford City, and plans for the line were dropped. Mohawk would have been located in Sec. 12-148-97, sixteen miles SE of Watford City, on the south bank of the Little Missouri River in the extreme NW corner of Dunn County. The name is attributed to settlers from Mohawk, NY, which was named for the Algonquin name for their enemy, the Iroquois. The name means cannibals, referring to the Iroquois custom of eating the bodies of captured adversaries. The railroad extension had been planned in 1916, and by 1920 plans for MOHAWK were abandoned. (2, 3, 10, 53)

**MOHLER** (Sargent). This farm post office was established September 13, 1888 with August Schrump pm. It was located in Sec. 30-130-56, Forman Twp., eleven miles west of Rutland. The origin of the name is unknown. The GNRR founded a townsite here in 1890, naming it BROOKLAND. The post office adopted this name on February 15, 1890. (2, 3, 40)

**MOLINE** (McKenzie). This was a rural post office established March 10, 1910 with Earl G. Rose pm. It was located in NE¼ Sec. 28-149-102, Moline Twp., eleven miles SW of Alexander, and named by Mrs. Rose for her uncle, John Moline, who lived in Sweden. The post office closed November 15, 1919 with mail to Alexander. (1, 2, 18, 40, 414)

**MOLTKE** (Burleigh). This was a rural post office established December 31, 1883 with Albert E. Weber pm. It was located in NE¼ Sec. 32-142-79, Ecklund Twp., four miles NNE of Baldwin, and named for Count Helmuth Karl Bernhard von Moltke (1800-1891), a German military leader. The post office closed October 22, 1884 with mail to Cromwell. (2, 5, 13, 14, 25, 40)

**MOLTKE** (Stark). This was the pioneering effort in 1882 of Charles Krauth and Ferdinand Leutz to promote a settlement of Germans. They established their townsite in Sec. 34-140-91, six miles west of Hebron, on the Bismarck-Fort Keogh mail route between the fourth and fifth stations, and named it for Count Helmuth Karl Bernhard von Moltke (1800-1891), a German military leader. The mail route was abandoned shortly after MOLTKE was founded, and lightning destroyed the Krauth-Leutz store in 1883. The townsite was abandoned, and most settlers moved to the new townsite of Hebron. (2, 3, 13, 74, 417)

**MONA** (Cavalier). This was a rural settlement founded in the early 1880's in SE¼ Sec. 21-162-58, Loam Twp., twelve miles NE of Langdon. The post office was established April 2, 1883 with John J. Wood pm, who named it for Mona Jacobson, the daughter of area pioneer Ole Jacobson. Later it was moved one mile NE to NW¼ Sec. 15-162-58, the home of new pm William Hutton. A population of 20 was reported in 1890, and a count of 10 was made in 1920, but settlements of this type could not compete with larger cities, and the post office closed March 30, 1935 with mail to Langdon. (1, 2, 3, 18, 25, 40, 115)

**MONANGO** (Dickey). This Milwaukee Road RR station was founded in 1886 in Sec. 8-131-63, Keystone Twp. Some say the name was coined from the Monongahela River in PA, the home state of many pioneer settlers, while others say it memorializes an Indian child found after the battle of Whitestone Hill in 1863 who was badly injured and sent to IA for treatment. Still others say it is a composite name with no local meaning whatsoever. The post office was established September 18, 1886 with Beriah Magoffin (1843-1924) pm. He and his son Eb were the first two settlers in the new townsite. The elevation is 1507, the Zip Code is 58471, and a peak population of 238 was reached in 1910, with a steady decline to just 59 in 1980. (1, 2, 3, 18, 33, 40, 52, 79, 92, 154, 320)

**MONANGO TRANSFER** (Dickey). This was the junction of the Milwaukee Road RR and the Soo Line RR one mile SE of Monango in SE¼ Sec. 17-131-63, Keystone Twp. No development occurred at the site. (1, 2, 3)

**MONDAK** (Williams). This was a famous and somewhat notorious boom town that owed its existance to the different laws concerning alcoholic beverages that existed in MT and ND at the beginning of the twentieth century. It straddled the border, with the MT side containing most of the businesses, in particular the saloons. It was founded about 1903, and was more or less doomed by national prohibition in 1920. What remained of the townsite was destroyed by fire in 1928. The post office operated 1904-1925 with Jacob Deel as first pm, but it was on the MT side of the border. Officially the ND portion of the townsite in NE¼ Sec. 7-152-104, Buford Twp., was known as EAST MONDAK. (2, 3, 18, 50, 88)

**MONTAIR** (Rolette). The state tuberculosis sanitarium was established in 1909 in Sec. 19-162-72, Hillside Twp., one mile north of Dunseith. Postal service was from Dunseith until December 1, 1922 when a post office was established at the institution with the Superintendent, Dr. John C. Lamont, as the pm. The name is descriptive, being coined from MOuNTain AIR. On January 24, 1923 the name was changed to SAN HAVEN. (2, 3, 40, 123)

**MONTCLAIR** (Griggs). The NPRR established a station in Sec. 20-145-60, Montclair Twp., four miles NNW of Hannaford, in 1882. The post office was established July 11, 1882 with Archibald M. Sinclair pm. It was named for its township, which bore a coined name, MONT, a contraction of mountain to note the hills in the area, and CLAIR, to honor the Sinclair family. Early promotional efforts were directed here, but it soon became apparent that Hannaford would become the dominant townsite in the area. The post office closed November 23, 1886, three days after the Hannaford post office had been established; but MONTCLAIR mail initially went to Helena. (2, 18, 25, 40, 65, 284)

**MONTEREY** (Benson). This rural post office was established August 12, 1903 with Paul J. Moen pm in his store in Sec. 17-151-68, West Antelope Twp., seven miles SE of Maddock. It was named for Monterey, MN, which was named for Monterey, Mexico, the scene of one of the fiercest battles of the Mexian War in 1846. The name is Spanish for king mountain. Mr. Moen was a state legislator 1909-1915. The post office closed December 31, 1905 with mail to Maddock. (2, 3, 13, 18, 40, 239)

**MONTE'S RANCHEROS** (Morton). This is a rural subdivision founded in 1971 in W½ Sec. 8-139-82, nine miles WNW of Mandan by site owner Leo J. Boehm, who named it for his son, Monte Lee Boehm. (3)

**MONTLINE** (Slope). This was a Milwaukee Road RR station in Sec. 31-133-106, Bucklin Twp., just inside the border with MT. The name is coined from MONTana state LINE. It first appeared on maps about 1910, and disappeared during the 1940's. (1, 2, 3, 18, 82)

**MONTPELIER** (Stutsman). This NPRR townsite was platted in 1885 by J. J. Flint and Bailey W. Fuller, both of whom were born in VT. They named it for the capital of their home state, which was named in 1781 by Col. Jacob Davis for Montpellier, France, to show his gratitude for French assistance during the Revolutionary War. This site is in Secs. 11 & 12-137-63, Montpelier Twp., just north of the old townsite of Tarbell, which it absorbed. The post office was moved from Tarbell on April 26, 1886 with Jacob Smith pm. The elevation is 1381, the Zip Code is 58472, and a peak population of 186 was reported in 1920. (1, 2, 3, 10, 33, 40, 45, 52, 79, 158)

**MONTROSE** (Divide). This was a farm post office established June 23, 1906 with Mrs. Anna E. Palmer, widow of Civil War veteran U. H. Palmer, as pm. It was located in NW¼ Sec. 35-160-97, Palmer Twp., twenty miles SSE of Crosby, just above the Williams County line, and named for Montrose, MN, which was named for Montrose, Anguishire, Scotland, a place made famous in the writings of Sir Walter Scott. On July 13, 1910 Mrs. Palmer closed the post office and took over the new post office at Wildrose in Williams County, two miles to the south. (2, 10, 13, 18, 34, 40, 50)

**MOORE** (Ransom). This pioneer settlement was promoted in SE¼ Sec. 26-136-56, Moore Twp., six miles SW of Enderlin, and named for W. W. Moore, an early settler at Lisbon. Little development took place, and the site is now abandoned. It appeared only in an 1884 atlas. (2, 3, 39, 77, 201)

**MOORES GROVE** (Sargent). This was a station on the stage line from Lisbon, and was located in SW¼ Sec. 13-129-58, Southwest Twp., four miles south of Straubville. The post office was established May 3, 1904 with Gearhart F. Moore pm, and was named for the pm and his fine grove of trees in NE¼ Sec. 23-129-58. Eight other members of this family had homesteads in the township. The post office closed August 31, 1904 with mail to Straubville. (2, 40, 165, 415)

**MOORETON** (Richland). This name was adopted April 21, 1884 for the NPRR station of GRIFFIN in Secs. 6 & 7-132-49, Mooreton Twp., and the TRIEST post office in Sec. 6-132-49, which soon developed into a thriving village serving the Antelope Farm, a 17,300-acre bonanza farm owned by Hugh Moore, who also owned several of the businesses in town. At first MOORETON was mostly north of the tracks, but after a fire in 1895 it was rebuilt on the south side of the tracks. The elevation is 961, the Zip Code is 58061, and the village, which incorporated in 1911, reached a peak population of 199 in 1980 as it has avoided the usual pattern of decline experienced by most smaller settlements in ND. A major force in modern MOORETON is George Feneis, who has been an implement dealer, mayor, and fire chief for most of his life, and is one of the most respected men in Richland County. (1, 2, 3, 18, 25, 33, 40, 79, 147, 242)

**MORAINE** (Grand Forks). This was a rural post office established May 26, 1904 with Jesse Lunney pm. It was located in NE¼ Sec. 29-151-56, Moraine Twp., nine miles south of Niagara, and named for its township, which was named by Capt. Simon P. Webster, a Civil War veteran, to note the moraines in the area. A moraine is an area where a ridge of boulders has been left by a receding glacier. The post office closed February 28, 1915 with mail to Larimore. (1, 2, 10, 18, 31, 40)

**MORDEN JUNCTION** (Walsh). This was a GNRR station in SE¼ Sec. 12-157-53, Grafton Twp., just north of Grafton, where the branch line to Walhalla leaves the line to Neche. The Walhalla line was extended into Canada in 1907, with its terminus at Morden, Manitoba, hence the name. (1, 3, 75)

**MORGAN** (Richland). This was an unofficial name for the BARRIE post office when it was located in the home of pm Charles H. Morgan in SW¼ Sec. 20-136-51, Barrie Twp., just west of the original 1878 site. Morgan is a Celtic name meaning born by the sea. Like many of the area's pioneers, Mr. Morgan had come here from Barrie, Ontario, Canada. (2, 3, 40, 147)

**MORGANVILLE** (Mercer). This was a farm post office established September 8, 1884 with Frank C. "Longhaired" Morgan pm. Mr. Morgan, referred to as Morgan Spencer in some accounts, was a man of obvious education who had chosen the frontier life of a trapper and hunter. Some people believed that he was a fugitive from justice. The post office was located in SW¼ Sec. 26-144-88, at the west edge of present-day Beulah, and closed November 12, 1885 with mail to Slaton. Morgansville is an erroneous spelling. (1, 2, 3, 18, 25, 40, 64, 232, 414)

**MORRIS** (Eddy). This was a rural settlement in NW¼ Sec. 20-150-63, Eddy Twp., about nineteen miles NE of New Rockford. The post office was established February 13, 1886 with Thomas P. Morris, a retired soldier from Fort Totten, as pm. Morris is a Latin name meaning dark-skinned. A population of 25 was reported in 1890. Cyrus B. Jackson, Carrie Dutee, and Daniel Dailey succeeded Mr. Morris as pms, and the post office closed October 31, 1908 with mail to Tiffany. (2, 19, 25, 40, 53, 79, 119, 240)

**MORTIMER** (Cass). This GNRR station was built in late 1914 or early 1915 in SW¼ Sec. 16-143-53, Dows Twp., between Erie and Galesburg. The origin of the name is unknown, although the first thing pioneer residents recalled was a sign stating this name, believed to have been erected by GNRR officials. Mortimer is a French/Latin name meaning dweller by the still water, and was the name of one of England's most powerful families in medieval times. J. C. Miller of Page built an elevator here, and it was first managed by Henry Tenneson. A population of 11 was reported in 1930. The elevator burned in 1936, and the station was removed in 1940. (2, 19, 34, 77, 246)

**MORTON** (Cavalier). This was a rural settlement founded in the 1890's in SE¼ Sec. 29-159-61, West Billings Twp., six miles WNW of Nekoma. The post office was established September 1, 1899 with Charles A. Morton pm, who later operated a restaurant in Hampden. MORTON had a dance hall and a baseball field during its heyday. The post office closed September 15, 1905, and was replaced by the Irene post office five miles NNE of here. (2, 3, 18, 40, 247)

**MORTON** (Morton). Frederic Gerard and Robert Henry came to Sec. 28-139-81 in 1872, a site about two miles north of the military post of Fort McKeen. A settlement began which came to be known as MORTON, for Oliver Hazard Perry Throck Morton (1823-1877), a U. S. Senator and former Governor of IN. The post office was established July 16, 1878 with Andrew J. Davis pm in a sod shack near the east end of Main Street in present-day MANDAN. The townsite was named LINCOLN on October 7, 1878, and was renamed MANDAN on December 14, 1878. The MORTON post office adopted the MANDAN name March 3, 1879. (2, 3, 5, 10, 25, 40, 107, 343)

**MOSCOW** (Cavalier). This was a Mennonite settlement in SE¼ Sec. 15-161-61, Waterloo Twp., thirteen miles west of Langdon. It was named for Moscow, Russia, which was founded in 1147 by George Dolgoruki and grew into the capital and metropolis of the Soviet Union. The post office was established April 21, 1894 with Matthew Michlink pm, and closed April 15, 1903 with mail to Langdon. (2, 3, 5, 18, 40)

**MOSE** (Griggs). This NPRR station in Sec. 4-147-61, Bryan Twp., five miles WNW of Binford, was founded in 1899 and called FLORENCE and LEWIS prior to 1904. Postal officials rejected LEWIS due to duplication, and the post office was established October 31, 1904 as MOSE, with Knud K. Alfstad pm. This name honored local lumberyard worker Morris Greenland by using his nickname. The elevation is 1564. The site never experienced any major development, with a peak population of about 25. The post office closed December 30, 1933 with mail to Binford. It reopened November 1, 1934, but closed for good January 31, 1954 with mail to McHenry. (1, 2, 18, 34, 40, 65, 79)

**MOSELLE** (Richland). This was a Soo Line RR siding in Sec. 21-132-51, Danton Twp., three miles SE of Wyndmere. A post office called JASPER existed here for one month in 1883. In 1891 a new post office called FLETCHER was established, and on January 26, 1892 the name was changed to MOSELLE by pm Alex Springer for the river in the Alsace-Lorraine region in Europe. The post office

closed November 30, 1900 with mail to Wyndmere, and all buildings in MOSELLE were soon moved to that new townsite, although the site is still shown on some maps. (1, 2, 3, 18, 40, 79, 147, 248)

**MOSHER** (Golden Valley). This was a farm post office established May 5, 1919 with Henry C. F. Thoemke pm at his home in NE¼ Sec. 34-143-104, Pearl Twp., sixteen miles north of Sentinel Butte. It was named for Alden Mosher who operated the Rafteree post office just west of here 1905-1908. The MOSHER post office closed April 30, 1927 with mail to Beach. (2, 3, 18, 40)

**MOTT** (Hettinger). This townsite on both the Milwaukee Road RR and the NPRR was founded in 1904 by William H. Brown (1860-1943), who also founded Flasher, Haynes, and several towns in MT. It was named for Mr. Brown's secretary, Lillian Mott, later Mrs. C. L. Cummings of Minneapolis, MN, although many sources claim it was named for C. W. Mott, a NPRR official. The post office was established September 17, 1904 with Maurice W. Wilcox pm, replacing the Chase post office. It incorporated as a village in 1910, and became a city in 1928 with George Glenny mayor. When Hettinger County was organized in 1907, MOTT was designated as the county seat. The elevation is 2377, the Zip Code is 58646, and a peak population of 1,583 was reached in 1950. Arnold Bannon, Harry O. Pearce, and Robert E. Trousdale were prominent among its pioneer businessmen. (1, 2, 3, 18, 33, 40, 52, 79, 178, 179, 180, 181)

**MOUND** (Slope). This was a rural community in Sec. 20-134-103, Harper Twp., thirteen miles NE of Marmarth. The post office was established April 21, 1908 with Frances O. (Parks) Pearl (1855-1931) as pm, who named it to note the contour of the surrounding countryside, and to note that she had come here from Pleasant Mounds, Blue Earth County, MN, which was named in 1863 to note a number of drift gravel hills in that area. The first post office was in her sod house. The settlement reported a population of 100 in 1930, which surely included an area much larger than the actual townsite. In 1931 the post office moved two miles west

to the home of new pm Mrs. W. B. "Bud" Conner, and closed November 14, 1936 with mail to Vim. (1, 2, 3, 13, 40, 53, 82, 120)

**MOUNTAIN** (Pembina). This rural community was founded about 1873 in NE¼ Sec. 16-160-56, Thingvalla Twp., by immigrants from Iceland, and was a station on the short-lived Northern Dakota RR. The post office was established September 12, 1873 with Harald Thorlackson pm. The somewhat surprising name results from its location near the Pembina Mountains, whose name is a classic example of relativity when compared to mountain ranges such as the Rockies. The site is on the shore of ancient Lake Agassiz at the edge of the present-day Red River valley. The elevation is 1043, and the Zip Code is 58262. The village incorporated in 1940 with M. F. Bjorson mayor, and reached a peak population of 219 in 1950. (1, 2, 3, 18, 25, 33, 40, 79, 108, 366)

**MOUNTAIN RANGE ESTATES** (Dunn). This is a rural housing development founded in the 1970's in Sec. 25 & E½ Sec. 26-146-97, twelve miles WNW of Killdeer. The name notes its location on the west slope of the Killdeer Mountains. (3, 34)

**MOUNT CARMEL** (Cavalier). This was a rural settlement founded in 1887 in SW¼ Sec. 14 & NE¼ Sec. 22-163-60, Mount Carmel Twp., thirteen miles north of Langdon. It was named by Father Bickland, a local Roman Catholic priest, for the mountain in Israel where the Order of the Lady of Mount Carmel was founded in the twelfth century. Carmel is a Hebrew name meaning cultivated land. The post office was established April 13, 1887 with Jacob Schneider pm. A population of 190 was reported in 1940, which surely included outlying areas, although the townsite itself had a population of about 50 for many years, and still exists although the post office closed April 21, 1967 with mail to Langdon. Mount Carmal is an erroneous spelling. (1, 2, 3, 10, 18, 25, 40, 79)

**MOUNT MORIAH** (Cavalier). This was a Roman Catholic rural settlement founded three miles from Mount Carmel, with which it merged. Mount Moriah is where Abraham was commanded to sacrifice Isaac in Genesis 22:2. (2, 10)

**MOUNT VIEW** (Walsh). This was a pioneer settlement of immigrants from Scotland in SE¼ Sec. 23-158-55, Dundee Twp., two miles WSW of Hoople. The name notes its location on the rim, or shore, of ancient Lake Agassiz. The post office was established August 2, 1880 with Perry G. Ewart pm, and closed March 11, 1884 with mail to Grafton. Mountain View is an erroneous spelling. (2, 3, 25, 40, 75, 79, 392)

**MOUSE RIVER** (McHenry). This was a rural post office established December 17, 1884 with Robert W. Davidson pm. It was located in Sec. 26-153-80, Velva Twp., one mile SE of Velva, and named for the Souris, or Mouse, River on which it was located. The river had been called *Inyan-hdoka-wakpa* by the Indians, meaning river of the rock, but was renamed to note the large number of field mice along its banks. On March 22, 1886 the post office was renamed NICHOLS,

*Mott about 1906*

with the original Nichols post office taking the name Mouse River. (2, 3, 18, 40, 79)

**MOUSE RIVER** (McHenry). This post office was established January 25, 1886 as NICHOLS. On March 22, 1886 it switched names with the original Mouse River post office with Palmer G. Potter continuing as the pm. When settlement began two miles to the west in Sec. 22-153-80, Velva Twp., the post office moved there, taking the name VELVA on November 18, 1893. (2, 3, 18, 40, 415)

**MOUSE RIVER PARK** (Renville). This resort in SW¼ Sec. 2-161-86, McKinney Twp., was established about 1911 by George Sauer of Tolley on land owned by William Grinnell, one of the area's most colorful pioneers who had come here in 1885. It was located on the Mouse River, just west of the historic settlement of McKinney. For many years it was a favorite recreational site for people in all directions, and held the well known Chautauqua festivals periodically. While the site has gradually lost its appeal as a resort for entertainment, it survives as a rural residential area with fifteen families and one cafe listed here in 1981. (3, 18, 55, 322)

**MOWBRAY** (Cavalier). This was an early Canadian port-of-entry in SW¼ Sec. 30-164-61, Mount Carmel Twp., nine miles NE of Wales. Dr. E. I. Donavan, the townsite owner, named it for his hometown of Mowbray, Ontario, Canada, and a sister settlement across the border in Manitoba shared the name. The post office was established December 13, 1909 with Mark J. O'Brien pm, and closed August 31, 1936 with mail to Langdon. A population of 60 was reported in 1920, but the customs station was soon relocated to Maida, five miles to the east on ND Highway 1. (1, 2, 18, 40, 79)

**MOWRER** (McLean). This was a rural post office established October 5, 1903 with Mrs. Fred (Estella) Platt pm. It was located in NW¼ Sec. 11-149-85, Platt Twp., eight miles NW of Garrison, and eight miles SSW of Douglas. The name was chosen by postal officials with no known local significance. Some have suggested that the name honored Frank Roger Mowrer, who served as the United States Ambassador to Japan, China, Belgium, Ethiopia, Italy, and Denmark between 1897-1909. The post office was later moved across the township road to SW¼ Sec. 2-149-85, where new pm G. W. Kinney had a country store. The post office closed June 30, 1908 with mail to Douglas. (2, 3, 5, 18, 28, 40, 389)

**MOYERSVILLE** (Kidder). This was a farm post office established January 16, 1901 with Leonard S. Moyer (1869-1956) pm. It was located in Sec. 12-143-74, Kickapoo Twp., three miles north of Tuttle. The last pm, James George Boyland, closed the post office May 15, 1913 with mail to Tuttle. (1, 2, 18, 40, 91, 122)

**MUDDY** (Burleigh). This place is listed in an 1890 guide of ND as being in Burleigh County, and served by the Bismarck post office. The name apparently is based on the popular nickname for the Missouri River. No other information is available. (3, 25)

**MUGFORD** (Pembina). This was a rural community in SW¼ Sec. 13-160-52, Midland Twp., four miles WSW of Bowesmont, that was named for area settler John Mugford. The post office was established January 5, 1886 with George Hodgson pm, and closed July 31, 1916 with mail to Bowesmont. A population of 25 was reported in 1890. (1, 2, 3, 18, 25, 40, 53, 108)

**MULBERRY** (Kidder). Six families from Mulberry, IN came here in the early 1900's to homestead, naming their rural community NEW MULBERRY, but postal officials shortened the name to MULBERRY to comply with government spelling regulations when the post office was established October 26, 1908 with William I. Slipher pm at his home in SW¼ Sec. 26-143-74, Kickapoo Twp., two miles NW of Tuttle at the west end of Jones Lake. Mulberry, IN was named in 1858 for a tall mulberry tree at that site. The post office closed May 15, 1912 with mail to Moyersville. Mr. Slipher in the meantime had become the pm at the new village of Tuttle. (2, 18, 40, 59, 95, 122)

**MULLEN** (Ransom). This was a farm post office established February 6, 1882 with Martin Svarverud pm. It was located in Sec. 19-136-57, Preston Twp., four miles NNE of Fort Ransom, and named for Mullen, NE, which was named for an official of the Grand Island & Wyoming RR. The post office closed July 7, 1884 with mail to Fort Ransom. The nearby Preston post office operated 1895-1905. Muller is an erroneous spelling. (2, 3, 10, 40, 77, 89, 201)

**MUNICH** (Cavalier). This is a GNRR townsite in NE¼ Sec. 19-160-63, Henderson Twp., named by townsite owner William Budge for Munich, Bavaria, Germany, a metropolis that emerged from obscurity in 1158 when King Henry the Lion selected the town as the site of the royal mint. The post office was established December 12, 1904 with Peter D. Walde pm. The elevation is 1601, the Zip Code is 58352, and the village, which incorporated in 1910, has shown a slow but steady growth, reaching a peak population of 288 in 1980. Quentin Northrop Burdick, a longtime U. S. Senator, was born here in 1908. (1, 2, 3, 5, 18, 33, 40, 79, 110, 253)

**MUNSTER** (Eddy). This was a GNRR loading station built in 1912 on the Surrey cutoff line in SW¼ Sec. 17-149-67, Munster Twp., between New Rockford and Bremen. It was named for its township, which was named for the local school district that had been established in 1884. The origin of the name is unknown, but the school district had been organized at the homestead of Timothy O'Connor, prompting the theory that the name came from the province of Munster in Ireland. An elevator was built in 1913, but that was the extent of the development at this site. Ole H. Olson, ND Governor for six months in 1934, lived just north of MUNSTER. (1, 2, 3, 39, 45, 119, 272)

**MURRAY** (Richland). This was a country store in Sec. 29-129-51, Elma Twp., eight miles SE of Lidgerwood. The post office was established September 14, 1907 with storekeeper Alexander O. Johnson pm, who

chose a name with no known local significance. Murray is a Celtic name meaning seaman. The post office closed April 15, 1914 with mail to Hankinson, and the store was later moved to Hammer, SD. (1, 2, 3, 18, 19, 40, 53, 147, 353)

**MURRAY** (Traill). This name was approved, for unknown reasons, as a name change for the ALHALSTEAD post office and GNRR station in SW¼ Sec. 27-146-52, Mayville Twp., five miles SE of Mayville, on December 23, 1897. The post office closed April 14, 1898, and the name change was rescinded for official purposes only on April 25, 1898. It is believed that the new name was never used by the post office. The GNRR, however, did adopt the name MURRAY as its station name, and the site, consisting of two grain elevators, lasted until about 1940, reporting a population of 10 in 1920. (1, 2, 3, 18, 29, 40, 77)

**MYLO** (Rolette). This Soo Line RR station was founded in 1905 in SW¼ Sec. 31-160-69, Ellsworth Twp., and NW¼ Sec. 6-159-69, Pleasant Valley Twp. The post office was established October 18, 1905 with Thomas H. Blouse pm. The village, which incorporated in 1907, was named for the county's first Roman Catholic priest, Father John E. Malo, with the spelling changed to note the correct pronunciation of his name. Others say it was named for a Soo Line RR official. The Zip Code is 58353, and a peak population of 140 was reached in 1920, with a decline to just 32 in 1980. Roy Mylo "Butch" Wager, the first baby born in the town, became a professional trumpet player with the Phil Harris band, and spent eleven years on the Jack Benny radio program. (1, 2, 3, 18, 33, 40, 52, 68, 79, 123)

**MYRA** (Cass). This was a NPRR loading station built in 1900 in SW¼ Sec. 13-139-53, Gill Twp., five miles SW of Casselton on the Marion branch line. It was named for Myra Smith, the daughter of the original owner of this site. Myra is a Latin name meaning wonderful. No development occurred here. (1, 2, 3, 18, 19, 34, 77)

**MYRTLE** (Burke). This was a rural post office established August 6, 1903 with Neal Van Berkom (1881-1946) pm. It was located in NW¼ Sec. 21-159-92, Garness Twp., three miles NE of Powers Lake. The order was rescinded March 26, 1904 before the post office had gone into operation. The origin of the name is unknown. Mr. Van Berkom was one of seven brothers who homesteaded in this area, but none of them had a wife or daughter named Myrtle. (3, 40, 67)

# N

**NAESATZ** (Mercer). This was a rural post office established September 29, 1916 with J. S. McLaughlin pm. Mr. McLaughlin lived in NE¼ Sec. 20-146-89, but the post office was located in his neighbor's home in SE¼ Sec. 20-146-89, ten miles north of Goldenvalley. The name was a corruption of Neusatz, South Russia, home of many area settlers. The post office closed August 31, 1918 with mail to Goldenvalley. Noesatz is an erroneous spelling. (2, 3, 7, 18, 40, 64)

**NAMELESS** (McKenzie). This was a rural post office established June 21, 1909 with Dora Isabelle Olive Stroud, the wife of legendary rancher Robert Stroud (1868-1931), as pm. It was located in NW¼ Sec. 26-151-103, Sioux Twp., five miles east of Cartwright. Mr. Stroud named it for his former home of Nameless, TX, which had been given this rather humorous name after postal officials had rejected six other suggested names. Nameless, TX had a post office 1880-1890. The NAMELESS, ND post office closed August 31, 1916 with mail to Cartwright, but the Nameless Cemetery still exists in SW¼ Sec. 26-151-103. (1, 2, 3, 18, 40, 84, 227, 414)

**NANSON** (Rolette). This GNRR townsite was platted in 1905 in SE¼ Sec. 23-159-71, Rice Twp., as SELDEN, but almost from the beginning it has been called NANSON by its Norwegian settlers, honoring the Norwegian explorer Fridtjof Nansen (1861-1930), with an Anglicized spelling. The post office was established December 11, 1905 with Olaf H. Johnson pm. The elevation is 1608, and a peak population of 125 was reported in 1920, with a decline to just 25 in 1960. The post office, Zip Code 58354, closed January 9, 1981, although postal records did not show this until June 25, 1982. (1, 2, 3, 5, 18, 33, 40, 79, 123)

**NAPOLEON** (Logan). This Soo Line RR townsite was founded in 1886 in SE¼ Sec. 9-135-72, Bryant Twp., but was relocated shortly afterward to the present site in SW¼ Sec. 17-135-72. The original townsite was platted in 1885 by George H. Cook of Steele, who named it for Napoleon Goodsill (1841-1887), a Steele realtor who was promoting this site. It became the county seat before the first settlers arrived, and survived several challenges for that honor, including an 1899 challenge from King that was settled through judicial action. The Paul post office moved here September 7, 1886 with Walter M. Leonard pm. The elevation is 1955, the Zip Code is 58561, and the population has increased steadily to a peak of 1,088 in 1980. NAPOLEON incorporated as a village in 1914, and became a city in 1947 with John Mitzel mayor. Three generations of the Bryant family published *The Napoleon Homestead* for nearly a century beginning in 1886. Ben Meier, longtime ND Secretary of State, was born here in 1918. (1, 2, 3, 18, 25, 39, 40, 79, 116)

**NARROWS** (Benson). This GNRR station was built in the early 1900's in NW 1/4 Sec. 5-152-64, Mission Twp., and named to note its location on a narrow neck of land extending into the south shore of Devils Lake, where the Casselton branch line crossed the lake on its route to the city of Devils Lake. The post office was established April 6, 1912 with Thure O. Olin pm, and closed September 30, 1913 with mail to Fort Totten. (1, 2, 34, 40)

**NASH** (Walsh). This is a GNRR loading station built in 1890 in SE¼ Sec. 30-158-53, Farmington Twp., six miles NW of Grafton. The post office was established July 11, 1891 with Charles Hanson pm. The Zip Code is 58264, and a peak population of 55 was recorded in 1940. It was named for the Nash brothers, pioneer settlers in the area, who later established a fruit store in Grafton, and a wholesale grocery business in Grand Forks which evolved into the Nash-Finch Company. (1, 2, 18, 39, 40, 75, 79)

**NAUGHTON** (Burleigh). This was a rural post office established February 14, 1901 with Michael Wolf pm. It was located in SW¼ Sec. 6-140-78, Frances Twp., about fourteen miles NE of Bismarck, and named for the adjacent township to the west, which was named for John Patrick Naughton (1846-1928), who settled here in 1882. The post office closed May 31, 1917 with mail to Frances. (2, 8, 12, 18, 40)

**NAVAL TRAINING SCHOOL STATION** (Richland). Postmarks of this name are known from 1943, which show this as a branch of the Wahpeton post office. It is apparent that a postal service was established during World War II for U. S. Navy personnel who were receiving training at the ND State School of Science in SW¼ Sec. 5-132-47, Center Twp., within the city limits of Wahpeton. (3, 18)

**NEBO** (Steele). This was a rural post office established June 25, 1890 with James Savage pm in SE¼ Sec. 12-148-56, Westfield Twp., eight miles NE of Finley. It was named for the Biblical Mount Nebo, elevation 2643, a peak at the north end of the Dead Sea from which Moses viewed the promised land. The name was chosen by postal officials from a list of six submitted by Mr. Savage. The post office closed August 9, 1904 with mail to Hatton. Nebro is an erroneous spelling. (2, 3, 5, 13, 40, 83, 99, 240)

**NECHE** (Pembina). This was a rural post office established May 27, 1873 with John Otten pm in SE¼ Sec. 25-164-54, Felson Twp. Several stories tell of how the name was selected, the most likely being that Charles Cavileer coined it from the Ojibway Indian word *nidji*, meaning friend, neighbor, or one like myself. The post office closed October 29, 1873 with mail to Pembina. It reopened December 6, 1875 with Joseph Daniels pm, and in 1882 moved one mile SE to the new GNRR townsite in SW¼ Sec. 31-164-53, Neche Twp. The village incorporated in 1883, and became a city in 1954 with Howard Hughes as mayor, who shared only his name with the famous billionaire. The elevation is 838, the Zip Code is 58265, and a peak population of 615 was reached in 1940. William L. Walton manufactured automobiles here 1902-1906. Native son Henry Gurke, killed in action during World

*GNRR depot at Neche about 1910*

War II, had a U. S. Navy destroyer named for him. (1, 2, 3, 13, 18, 33, 40, 79, 108, 235)

**NEKOMA** (Cavalier). This Soo Line RR townsite was founded in 1905 in S½ Sec. 22-159-60, Nekoma Twp., and given a Chippewa Indian name meaning I promise to do something. The POLAR post office moved here in 1905 from its original location one mile to the NE, but did not assume the new name until March 2, 1906, when Ozro B. Aldrich replaced Charles Billings as pm. The Zip Code is 58355, and the village incorporated in 1906, reaching a peak population of 191 in 1930. America's only Safeguard ABM and Missile Site Radar military installations are located just NE of Nekoma. (1, 2, 3, 18, 33, 40, 79, 217, 247)

**NELLIE** (Kidder). This was a farm post office established February 27, 1915 with Levi F. Carlson pm. He was one of three brothers who came here from IA. The name honored Nellie Jacobson, step-daughter of Gregorius Severson, the local mail carrier. The post office was located in NW¼ Sec. 4-140-74, Excelsior Twp., nine miles NW of Steele, and closed April 30, 1917 with mail to Steele. (1, 2, 3, 40, 122, 200)

**NELSON** (Kidder). This farm post office was established September 13, 1904 with Berndt Nelson (1875-1945) as pm. Mr. Nelson, a native of Sweden, came here in 1902 and operated the post office at his farm in SE¼ Sec. 32-142-71, Lake Williams Twp., six miles SE of Robinson. E. A. "Swede" Lewis and T. T. Eastburn were the mail carriers for this long-lived post office which closed September 30, 1936 with mail to Dawson. (1, 2, 3, 18, 40, 61, 93, 122)

**NELSON** (Nelson). This place appears on a 1930 road map published by the General Drafting Co., and like several other similar places on this map, it takes its name from its county, which was named for territorial legislator N. E. Nelson. It is on ND Highway 32, midway between Aneta and Petersburg, and is a copyright town. (3)

**NELVIK** (Dickey). This is a rural telephone exchange, prefix 374, in western Dickey County operated by the Dickey Rural Telephone Cooperative since the early 1950's. The name was coined from the names of B. L. NELson of Fullerton and John A. VIKen of Ellendale, the first President and Secretary-Treasurer, respectively, of the Board of Directors of the cooperative. (3, 55)

**NESSON** (Williams). This was a rural post office established June 9, 1886 with Charles Baldwin (1857-1939) pm. It was located in Sec. 11-154-96, Hofflund Twp., thirteen

miles SSE of Ray, on the north bank of the Missouri River, and was the second post office in Williams County. It took its name from the area known as the Nesson Flats, named for Peter Nessen, the owner of the 777 Ranch, who later spelled his name Nesson. In 1896 it moved to NE¼ Sec. 15-154-97, Nesson Valley Twp., and about 1900 moved to Sec. 18-154-96, Hofflund Twp. It was run from several other homes in the immediate area as new pms were appointed, and closed March 15, 1918 with mail to Hofflund. (2, 18, 40, 50, 53)

**NEU GLEUCKSTAHL** (Mercer). *UE ü* This was a rural community in SE Mercer County, centered around a Congregational Church built in 1905 in SE¼ Sec. 14-141-88 under the leadership of Peter Kessler Sr. It was named for Gleuckstal, South Russia, the hometown of many area settlers, with the name meaning lucky valley. The community declined after World War II, and today only a cemetery marks the site. (3, 7, 61)

**NEVA** (Slope). This was a rural post office established September 3, 1907 with Neva M. Woods pm. She was a daughter of pioneer homesteader Joshua Hughes (1853-1928), the namesake of the township, and she was named for the Neva River in Russia, which flows from Lake Ladoga through Leningrad to the Bay of Cronstadt. Leningrad was then known as Saint Petersburg, and was the capital of Czarist Russia. The pm married Frank Woods, who built a hotel in SE¼ Sec. 30-133-105, Hughes Twp., in anticipation of the Milwaukee Road RR. When the railroad arrived later in 1907, they built their station just to the west of the hotel, naming it MARMARTH. The NEVA post office moved to MARMARTH on February 29, 1908, assuming the new name with Mrs. Woods continuing as pm. (2, 3, 5, 40, 82)

**NEWBRE** (Ramsey). This was a farm post office established March 13, 1890 with Orson C. Newbre pm. It was located in SW¼ Sec. 24-155-61, Newbre Twp., five miles WNW of Brocket, and closed August 30, 1902 with mail to Foxlake. (2, 3, 40, 103, 240)

**NEW BUFFALO** (Cass). The NPRR built THIRD SIDING in SW¼ Sec. 19-140-54, Buffalo Twp. About 1875 it was named NEW BUFFALO by Socrates Squires and his daughter, Mrs. Gertrude Talcott, both of whom owned large tracts of land in the area, for Buffalo, NY, the home of NPRR official W. E. Wilkeson, and Mary Strong Wilson, another local landowner. The NY city was named for Buffalo Creek which flows into Lake Erie at this point. Because the large mammal of the prairie is not native to western NY, the origin of the name is not as obvious as one might think. Many feel it is a corruption of the French *beau fleuve*, meaning beautiful river. NEW BUFFALO was platted just NW of the present townsite in 1879. The post office was established October 15, 1878 with Hans B. Strand pm. On June 5, 1883 the name was shortened to BUFFALO. (2, 3, 10, 25, 40, 77, 266)

**NEWBURG** (Bottineau). This GNRR station was founded in 1905 in NE¼ Sec. 6-160-79, Tacoma Twp., and named for Andrew H. Newborg, a pioneer settler in the area, with

a slight change in the spelling. The post office was established September 1, 1905 with Lewis W. Heath pm. The elevation is 1472, the Zip Code is 58762, and the village, which incorporated in 1906, reached a peak population of 158 in 1960. Frederick Sund (1896-1972), a native son of NEWBURG, was a well known inventor and the founder of Sund Manufacturing Co., a major employer in the community. (1, 2, 3, 18, 33, 34, 40, 101, 153)

**NEWBURG** (LaMoure). This was a farm post office established May 9, 1888 with Erick Bjur pm. It was located in NE¼ Sec. 11-133-66, Norden Twp., four miles north of Kulm, and served a pioneer colony of Swedish immigrants. The name was coined to note that this was a new home for those settlers. The post office closed April 9, 1892 with mail to Edgeley. Newberg is an erroneous spelling. (2, 3, 25, 40, 142)

**NEWBURGH** (Steele). This was a rural post office established June 20, 1877 to replace a mail route out of Caledonia. Halvor O. Berg (1828-1881), who led a colony of settlers here in 1871 from Northwood, IA, was the first pm. The name was intended to be New Berg, noting the site as a new home and honoring Mr. Berg, but through a series of events it was corrupted into NEWBURGH. It was located in Sec. 28-148-54, Newburgh Twp., fifteen miles NE of Finley. After Mr. Berg's death, the pm duties were assumed by his youngest son, Joseph (1859-1940), who closed the post office October 21, 1887 with mail to Hatton. (2, 3, 18, 40, 77, 79, 99, 240)

**NEW CHICAGO** (Benson). This site was platted in 1883 by W. C. Riggins and L. W. Harriman in SE¼ Sec. 35-154-67, Riggin Twp., at what was then the west end of Devils Lake. The founders thought the location resembled that of Chicago, IL on Lake Michigan, hence the name. Chicago is an Algonquin Indian word meaning garlic field. The NPRR planned on extending its line through here, but the owners set the price too high, and development shifted to the nearby townsite of West End. One store and two saloons had been built, but NEW CHICAGO soon became a ghost town. (2, 3, 10, 18, 34, 110, 255)

**NEW COLUMBUS** (Burke). When the Soo Line RR founded this townsite in 1906 in NW¼ Sec. 32-163-93, Short Creek Twp., it was unofficially named NEW COLUMBUS to note its proximity to the inland town of COLUMBUS, six miles to the NW. The COLUMBUS post office, however, moved to the new townsite and retained its original name, with the original townsite lingering on as OLD COLUMBUS. (3, 18, 40, 67)

**NEW ENGLAND** (Hettinger). This was the first townsite in Hettinger County by many years, being founded in 1887 as MAYFLOWER, and becoming NEW ENGLAND CITY later that year. On June 8, 1894 new pm Horace W. Smith shortened the name to simply NEW ENGLAND, noting that most early settlers were from VT and MA, two of the New England states. The town by now spread over Secs. 3 & 4-135-97, New England Twp., having grown in a northerly direction from the original plat of eight blocks. The elevation is 2593, the Zip Code is 58647, and the village, which incorporated in 1910, reached a peak population of 1,117 in 1950. The Milwaukee Road RR reached here in 1910, making the village its terminus for the McLaughlin branch line. (1, 2, 3, 10, 18, 33, 40, 76, 178, 179, 385)

**NEW ENGLAND CITY** (Hettinger). This pioneer townsite, the first in the county by many years, was founded in 1887 in Sec. 4-135-97, New England Twp., as MAYFLOWER, but on September 16, 1887, twenty days after the post office had been established, pm Frank H. Clark changed the name to NEW ENGLAND CITY. Most of the first settlers were from VT and MA, two of the so-called New England states. This name was first given to what is now the northeastern United States in 1614 by John Smith of the Virginia colony, and the name was confirmed in 1620 by the King, the same year the Pilgrims began permanent settlement in the region. Although the town did not yet have a railroad, a population of 100 was reported in 1890. On June 8, 1894 Horace W. Smith became the pm, and he shortened the name to NEW ENGLAND. (2, 3, 10, 18, 40, 179, 385)

**NEW FORT BERTHOLD** (McLean). This military post was established June 12, 1867 in NE¼ Sec. 10-147-85, Stevenson Twp., and named for the historic fur trading post about nineteen miles upriver. It was part of the network of forts being established along the Missouri River to protect settlers coming into the area. On July 9, 1867 the fort was renamed FORT STEVENSON by War Department officials. (2, 3, 28)

**NEWHOME** (Stutsman). This was a rural settlement in SW¼ Sec. 7-144-68, Conklin Twp., ten miles NNW of Woodworth. It was named for the valley in which it was located, which was named by the first settlers with an obvious meaning. The valley is noted for its duck hunting. The post office was established May 27, 1899 with Henry I. Heinrichs pm, and was spelled as one word to comply with government spelling regulations, although many maps of the period show the name as two words. At one time NEWHOME had a general store, pool hall, blacksmith shop, livery, and a mill, but after it became apparent that the railroad would bypass the site, it began to decline. The post office closed August 31, 1916 with mail to Sykeston, and the site was abandoned by 1918. (1, 2, 3, 18, 40, 53, 79, 158)

**NEW HRADEC** (Dunn). This community was founded in 1898 in SE¼ Sec. 29-141-96, eleven miles NW of Dickinson in the extreme SW corner of Dunn County. The majority of the settlers were of Bohemian descent, and they named their new home for

Hradec, Bohemia, which bears a name meaning castle. The post office was established February 8, 1908 with Edward Kasal pm, and closed December 15, 1914 with mail to Dickinson. It reopened August 2, 1917 and is still in operation. The Zip Code is 58648, and a peak population of 57 was reported in 1940. New Hardec is an erroneous spelling. (2, 3, 18, 33, 40, 44)

**NEW JERUSALEM** (McLean). This was a rural community founded in June 1882 by twenty-two Jewish families from South Russia that had been sponsored by the Hebrew Emigrant Aid Society of New York City. The name noted the famous city in the Holy Land. Farming was about the only way to make a living at this site in Sec. 16-143-81, Nettle Creek Twp., between Wilton and the Missouri River, and these people had little or no experience in that occupation. The site was abandoned in 1883, and many of the settlers moved to nearby townsites where they became merchants. (2, 3, 28, 33)

**NEW LEIPZIG** (Grant). This two-railroad townsite was founded in 1910 in SE 1/4 Sec. 35-134-90, with the Milwaukee Road RR reaching the site in May, and the NPRR arriving in October. The two railroads are connected at the site by a short spur, the only such structure between Minneapolis, MN and Miles City, MT. The name was chosen to perpetuate the name of the inland town of LEIPZIG, about eleven miles to the NE. The post office was established May 13, 1910 with Mike C. Rausch pm. On January 15, 1912 the name was changed to LAWTHER, but reverted back to NEW LEIPZIG on August 2, 1912. The elevation is 2336, the Zip Code is 58562, and a peak population of 447 was reached in 1950. (1, 2, 3, 17, 33, 40, 52, 79, 176, 177, 358, 414)

**NEWMAN** (Cass). This was a GNRR station built in 1912 in NE¼ Sec. 35-141-51, Rush River Twp., fifteen miles NW of Fargo on the Surrey cutoff line. It was named for Seth Newman, a Fargo attorney, and consisted of a loading platform, elevator, and a passing track. No further development occurred, and the elevator was moved to Wheatland in 1940. The sugar beet station closed in 1963, effectively ending the history of NEWMAN. (1, 2, 3, 34, 77)

**NEW MINNEAPOLIS** (Stutsman). This was a townsite platted in 1884 in Sec. 32-140-65, Eldridge Twp., three miles WSW of Eldridge. Promoters hoped to duplicate the growth of Minneapolis, MN, but the site failed to develop. The MN city was named with a coined word combining MINNEhAha, a Sioux word meaning waterfall which was the heroine of Henry Wadsworth Longfellow's epic poem, and POLIS, Greek for city. (2, 3, 10, 158)

**NEW MULBERRY** (Kidder). The Slipher, Grove, Combs, Buck, Hill, and Van Sickle families came here in the early 1900's from Mulberry, IN to homestead, and a rural community, called "The Hoosier Community" in local slang, began to develop. A post office application was made in 1908 using the settlers chosen name of NEW MULBERRY, but postal officials were not allowing two-word names at the time,

and the facility was approved as MULBERRY. (2, 3, 40, 122)

**NEWPORT** (Burke). This townsite of two blocks was platted in NE¼ Sec. 2-162-88, Lakeview Twp., as a shipping port on the east shore of Des Lacs Lake. The name is said to have been descriptive of its purpose. The post office was established October 4, 1902 with Charles C. Gifford pm. The townsite failed to develop, and the post office moved one mile SE to SW¼ Sec. 12-162-88, where it was, in effect, a farm post office, closing June 30, 1914 with mail to Bowbells. (1, 2, 3, 18, 40, 67, 375)

**NEWPORT** (Foster). This was the first settlement in the county, founded in 1882 in SW¼ Sec. 36-145-66, Melville Twp. The post office was established July 24, 1882 with Edgar S. Leavenworth pm. It was named for Col. R. M. Newport, Treasurer of the NPRR, but when the railroad came through the following year, this site was bypassed due to a dispute over the cost of right-of-way, and everything moved to the new townsite of Melville, just to the west. The post office made the move May 2, 1883 with Mr. Leavenworth continuing as pm. (2, 3, 25, 40, 97)

**NEWPORT** (McHenry). This pioneer settlement was located in Sec. 10-156-76, Newport Twp., just west of present-day Towner on the west bank of the Souris River. The origin of the name is unknown. It is quite possible that a trading post existed here as early as 1862, but the first confirmed development occurred in 1884. The post office was established September 3, 1884 with Charles E. Jones pm. C. F. Anderson and Nels Jacobson operated stores, and the town even had a newspaper for a short time, but the GNRR established its station at Towner in 1886, and NEWPORT quickly declined. The post office closed April 23, 1887 with mail to Towner. (2, 3, 18, 25, 40, 182, 412)

**NEW ROCKFORD** (Eddy). Settlement began in 1882 in Sec. 32-149-66, New Rockford Twp. The pioneer townsites called DUNN'S CREEK, DUNN, and GARRISON all became part of the NPRR townsite of NEW ROCKFORD, which was officially founded in 1883. The name was chosen by Charles E. Gregory for his former home of Rockford, IL, after postal officials had rejected Rockford, Rockville, and Rocky Ford. Some claim the name notes the natural rock ford over the James River at this site. The post office was established September 13, 1883 with Francis A. Sebring pm. It became the county seat in 1885, and unsuccessfully challenged Bismarck for the state capital in 1915. It incorporated as a city in 1912 with George M. Pike as mayor, and reached a peak population of 2,195 in 1930. The GNRR's Surrey cutoff line was built through NEW ROCKFORD in 1912. The elevation is 1533, and the Zip Code is 58356. It has been called "The Midway City" and "Turkey Capital of North Dakota." (2, 3, 40, 119, 272, 273)

**NEW SAINT ANDREWS** (Walsh). This was a NPRR station in NW¼ Sec. 16-158-51, Saint Andrews Twp., four miles NW of the Red River port of Saint Andrew, for which it was named. It was built in 1887, and about 1893 the name was changed to SAINT ANDREWS STATION. A post office operated here 1895-1903 using the name ELORA, after which the site was renamed HERRICK. (2, 3, 34, 40, 75)

**NEW SAINT JOSEPH** (Pembina). This settlement in Sec. 21-163-55, Saint Joseph Twp., seven miles east of Walhalla, was started by settlers who were tired of being flooded by the Pembina River. It was named for its township, with the "New" added to differentiate it from Walhalla, which was originally called Saint Joseph. When the post office was established here in 1887, it was named LEROY. (3, 25, 40, 440)

**NEW SALEM** (Morton). This NPRR townsite in Sec. 21-139-85, Engelter Twp., was founded in 1883 as SALEM, but almost immediately changed its name to NEW SALEM to avoid duplication with a Salem that is now in SD. SALEM is part of the name of the Holy City of Jerusalem, and is generally believed to be derived from shalom, the Hebrew word for peace, with the name being found as early as the reign of Egypt's Amenhotep IV (1375-1354 B.C.). The first settlers were German Lutherans sponsored by a church group in Chicago, IL, and the second wave of settlers were German nationals from Worms, Rohrbach District, South Russia. The post office was established August 24, 1883 with Arthur V. Schallern pm. The elevation is 2188, the Zip Code is 58563, and the city, which incorporated in 1911, has shown a steady growth, reaching a peak population of 1,082 in 1980. To note its dairy industry, the city built the world's largest Holstein cow on a butte just north of town overlooking Interstate 94. (1, 2, 3, 17, 18, 25, 33, 40, 52, 79, 107, 109)

**NEW SANISH** (Mountrail). This was a site in Sec. 23-152-93, Sanish Twp., that was promoted in 1954 by people who were unhappy with the government-sponsored townsite of New Town, which was being built to replace the towns that would become inundated by the backwaters of Garrison Dam. It was about one mile south of the original Sanish townsite, and met with limited success. (2, 3, 72)

**NEWTON** (Dickey). This site in Sec. 31-130-59, Riverdale Twp., just north of Ludden, was the intersection of GNRR and Chicago & NW RR lines. In the 1880's a small settlement named RIVERDALE existed here, but the GNRR station built in 1915 was named for Newton Whitman, who settled at Fargo in 1871 and is credited with growing the first wheat in the area. Newton is an Anglo-Saxon name meaning from the farmstead. The name was soon changed to RIVERDALE when local residents asked to have the old name restored. (2, 3, 18, 19)

**NEWTOWN** (Mountrail). This was the rather generic name coined for the government-sponsored townsite created in the 1950's to replace the towns that would be inundated by the backwaters of Garrison Dam. The post office was established January 1, 1953 with Hulbert J. Olson pm. Local citizens did not like the one-word spelling, and the name was changed to NEW TOWN on May 1, 1953. (3, 40, 72)

**NEW TOWN** (Mountrail). This was the townsite developed by the Sanish-Van Hook Relocation Townsite Corp. with government backing to replace Sanish, Van Hook, and Elbowoods, all of which were being inundated by the backwaters of Garrison Dam in the early 1950's. The site was platted in August 1950, with initial settlement beginning the following month. The name was never officially voted upon, but became generally accepted because of signs in the area that referred to the area as the "New Town Site." Residents did not like the original one-word spelling, NEWTOWN, and the name was officially changed to NEW TOWN on May 1, 1953. Hulbert J. Olson was the first pm, and Paul McCutheon was the first mayor. The Soo Line RR arrived here on September 22, 1953 with Sen. Milton R. Young driving the ceremonial golden spike. The Zip Code is 58763, and it had a population of about 1,000 almost immediately, peaking at 1,586 in 1960. (2, 3, 33, 40, 72)

**NEWVILLE** (Ramsey). This was a farm post office established November 15, 1900 with Jeremiah S. Kenepp pm. It was located in Sec. 6-158-64, Klingstrup Twp., in the extreme NW corner of the county near the border with Towner and Cavalier counties. The name was coined to indicate that this was a new home for the settlers. On November 2, 1904 Lorenzo W. Strong was appointed pm, and he moved the post office to the new Farmers Grain & Shipping Co. RR station in Towner County, four miles NW of the original site, on September 5, 1905. (3, 40, 75)

**NEWVILLE** (Towner). This Farmers Grain & Shipping Co. RR townsite was founded in 1905 in SW¼ Sec. 25-159-65, Victor Twp., six miles SE of Egeland. On September 5, 1905 pm Lorenzo W. Strong moved the NEWVILLE post office to the townsite from his farm home in Ramsey County, four miles to the SE. The name of that post office was accepted as the name of the townsite by railroad officials. A population of 80 was reported in 1920, but the count had declined to just 11 in 1940. The post office closed August 31, 1942 with mail to Egeland, and NEWVILLE disappeared from most maps during the 1960's. (1, 2, 3, 18, 40)

**NEW WARSAW** (Walsh). This townsite was platted in SE¼ Sec. 25-156-52, Harriston Twp., and named by Anton L. Gudajtes for the capital city of Poland, his homeland. Because the government did not accept two-word names at this time, the post office was established June 30, 1894 as WARSAW. (2, 3, 18, 40, 75)

**NEW YORK SETTLEMENT** (Grand Forks). This was the name of the settlement that developed at the BARKER'S STATION stopping point in Sec. 6-152-56, Niagara Twp., on the Grand Forks-Fort Totten trail. Most of the settlers were from Niagara County, NY, that state being named for James, Duke of York (1633-1701), later King James II of England. In 1882 it moved one mile south to the new GNRR townsite, which was named Niagara. (2, 3, 10, 31, 69)

**NEW YORK TOWN** (Kidder). This was a rural community founded in 1883 in the north half of Buckeye Twp. (141-71), and the south half of Lake Williams Twp. (142-71), about ten miles SE of Robinson. Peter D. White (1845-1924) led the first group of settlers, most of whom were from the state of NY. (3, 148)

**NIAGARA** (Grand Forks). This GNRR station was built in 1882 in E½ Sec. 7-152-56, Niagara Twp., one mile south of Barker's Station and the New York Settlement. Most of the settlers were from Niagara County, NY, whose name is a corruption of *Ongniaahra*, meaning bisected bottom lands, the Iroquois Indian settlement at the mouth of the Niagara River. The post office was established February 20, 1883 with Charles M. Leonard pm. The elevation is 1445, the Zip Code is 58266, and the village, which incorporated in 1907, reached a peak population of 207 in 1930, but has declined to just 76 in 1980. (1, 2, 10, 18, 25, 31, 40, 52, 69, 79, 339)

**NICHOLS** (McHenry). This was a rural post office established January 25, 1886 with Palmer G. Potter pm. It was located in NW¼ Sec. 25-153-80, Velva Twp., two miles east of Velva at what is thought to have been the site of SCRIPTOWN, the original county seat. The origin of the name NICHOLS is unknown. On March 22, 1886 this post office switched names with the nearby Mouse River post office, with Mr. Potter continuing as pm in his store, which curiously was called the New Store at Scriptown. Potters Lake, just east of this site, was named for Mr. Potter. (2, 3, 40, 415)

**NICHOLS** (McHenry). The original MOUSE RIVER post office was established December 17, 1884 with Robert W. Davidson pm. On March 22, 1886 it switched names with Nichols, with Mr. Davidson continuing as pm. This second NICHOLS post office operated only until September 14, 1886, when it closed with mail to the new Mouse River post office. (2, 3, 25, 40)

**NICHOLSON** (Sargent). This Soo Line RR townsite was platted in 1883 in NE 1/4 Sec. 6-130-57, Sargent Twp., four miles west of Cogswell. The post office was established January 25, 1886 with the town's namesake, Thomas W. Nicholson, as pm. A population of 32 was reported in 1890, but that was about the extent of the growth. The post office closed February 15, 1922 with mail to Cogswell, and the elevator closed in 1939. (2, 3, 18, 40, 165, 167)

**NICKOLS CROSSING** (Dickey). This was a Soo Line RR station in SW¼ Sec. 24-131-60, Clement Twp., three miles west of Oakes. It was also known as MAHONEY SPUR and NORWAY. This name honored H. S. Nickols, who owned a large farm here in pioneer days and held the township organizational meeting at his home in 1884. (2, 3, 154)

**NILES** (Benson). This GNRR siding was built in NW¼ Sec. 1-155-68, Lake Ibsen Twp., four miles east of Leeds, and named for Niles, MI, which was named for Hezekiah Niles (1777-1839), the author of several books on the American government. Niles is a Finnish name meaning the people's victory. The post office was established February 28,

1898 with Joseph L. Page pm, and closed July 14, 1905 with mail to Leeds. The peak population of 10 was reported in 1920. (2, 5, 10, 18, 19, 34, 40)

**NINA** (Renville). This was a farm post office established April 3, 1903 with Owen H. Moon, who came here in 1901, as pm. He named it for his daughter, whose name means grace in Hebrew, but more recently had become a popular Spanish name meaning little girl. It was located in NW¼ Sec. 8-163-85, Colquhoun Twp., four miles west of Sherwood, with mail coming here from Pleasant, ten miles to the WSW. In 1904 Mr. Moon moved the post office to the new townsite of Sherwood in NE¼ Sec. 12-163-85 without official permission. The Sherwood post office was established January 24, 1905, and the NINA post office closed April 15, 1905 with mail to Sherwood. (2, 3, 18, 19, 40, 71)

**NINETEENTH SIDING** (Morton). This NPRR siding and loading station was built in 1910 in SE¼ Sec. 6-136-79, nineteen miles SE of Mandan. Its name is generally thought to represent the distance from Mandan, although some have suggested that it represented the chronological order of sidings built from Mott to Mandan, which if true would be inconsistent with previous NPRR numbering practices. The post office was established May 12, 1911 as HUFF. (2, 3, 40, 107)

**NINTH SIDING** (Pembina). This NPRR station was founded in 1888 in SE¼ Sec. 11-160-51, Lincoln Twp., as NINTH SIDING, but was named PETTIT shortly after its construction. When the post office opened May 7, 1888, it was renamed BOWESMONT. (3, 40, 414)

**NIOBE** (Ward). This GNRR townsite was founded in 1907 in Sec. 18-160-89, Elmdale Twp., seven miles WNW of Kenmare, and named by the Dakota and Great Northern Townsite Co. for the wife of Amphion, King of Thebes, in Greek mythology. The post office was established March 24, 1908 with Andrew Nelson pm, a position held by Lillian S. Larson 1942-1972. The elevation is 2028, and a peak population of 250 was claimed in 1920, with a rapid decline to just 95 in 1930. The post office, Zip Code 58764, closed May 1, 1974 with mail to Kenmare. (1, 2, 18, 33, 40, 79, 100, 375)

**NISBET** (Oliver). This was a farm post office established April 6, 1904 with John Nisbet, a native of Scotland, as pm. It was located in NE¼ Sec. 9-143-86, Red Butte Twp., ten miles NW of Hannover. It was operated at several locations until 1913 when creamery operator Lars C. J. Wayne became the pm at the original site. The post office closed November 30, 1914 with mail to Hazen. (2, 3, 18, 40, 53, 121, 414)

**NISHU** (McLean). This name was adopted in the early 1920's for the Arikara Indian community in NW¼ Sec. 27-147-88, Nishu Twp., formerly known as ARMSTRONG. The name was of Arikara origin, meaning arrow, and was also the name of the tribal leader known to the white man as Floyd Bear. The post office was established June 2, 1926 with Sidney M. Pearson pm, and

closed June 30, 1934 with mail to Blackwater. It reopened December 11, 1935 with J. H. Bossen pm in SW¼ Sec. 21-147-88, about one mile WNW of the original location, and closed for good on April 30, 1941, with mail again going to Blackwater. The site was inundated by Lake Sakakawea in the 1950's. (2, 18, 28, 40)

**NOBLE** (Cass). This was a rural community in NE¼ Sec. 22-143-49, Noble Twp., six miles NE of Gardner on the west bank of the Red River. It was named for H. W. Noble of Erie, PA, a banker and oil producer with large holdings in the county. The post office was established January 17, 1882 with James Pratt pm, and closed January 31, 1890 with mail to Perley, MN. A population of 41 was reported in 1890. (2, 34, 40, 77)

**NOEL** (Grant). This was a farm post office established April 20, 1901 with Jessie W. Harper pm. It was located in SW¼ Sec. 20-136-87, nine miles NNW of Carson, and closed January 8, 1912 with mail to Carson. Noel is a French/Latin word meaning Christmas, but no explanation is known for its use as the name of this post office. (1, 2, 3, 17, 18, 19, 40, 53, 177)

**NOLAN** (Cass). This GNRR station on the Surrey cutoff line was built in 1911 in SE¼ Sec. 6-142-54, Rich Twp., two miles SE of Page. It was first called BEDFORD, but on August 15, 1944 the name was changed to NOLAN for James Nolan, a prominent pioneer settler in Cass County. Nolan is a Celtic name meaning noble. (2, 19, 34, 77)

**NOLAN CROSSING** (Richland). This was a crossing of the Sheyenne River on the Fort Abercrombie-Fort Ransom trail, first used in 1843 by Norman Kittson and Joseph Rolette. It was located in NW¼ Sec. 32-136-51, Barrie Twp., nine miles west of Walcott, and named for Anthony Nolan, a native of NY who settled here in 1868 after serving at Fort Abercrombie. It was later known as BARRIE CROSSING. (2, 3, 147)

**NOMAD** (McHenry). This place is shown on road maps of 1936 and 1940 published by the H. M. Gousha Company, and appears to

be about thirteen miles north of Granville in Saline Twp. (157-79). The name means wanderer, and it is believed to be a copyright town. (3, 4, 412)

**NOMAD** (Mountrail). This place appears on maps of the early 1970's published by the H. M. Gousha Company in NW¼ Sec. 2-153-88, Spring Coulee Twp., four miles north of Plaza. It is a copyright town, and uses the same name used by the Gousha firm for a copyright town shown in McHenry County about forty years earlier. (3, 34)

**NOME** (Barnes). This NPRR townsite was founded in 1900 in SE¼ Sec. 13-137-57, Thordenskjold Twp., and named for Nome, AK, which had been named in 1898 when townsite officials misinterpreted the word "name" as Nome. The post office was established April 25, 1901 with Charles D. Hackett pm. The townsite was platted in 1901 by Charles Ferguson, and incorporated as a village in 1907, reaching a peak population of 277 in 1940, with a decline to just 67 in 1980. The elevation is 1352, and the Zip Code is 58062. (1, 2, 5, 18, 34, 40, 52, 76, 79, 188)

**NOONAN** (Divide). This GNRR townsite was founded in 1906 in NE¼ Sec. 4-162-95, Coal Field Twp., and named for the Noonan family that had business, farm, and coal interests in the area. The post office was established March 22, 1907 with Henry J. Kotschevar pm. It incorporated as a village in 1929, and was once known as "The White City" because of an ordinance requiring all buildings to be painted white. The elevation is 1956, the Zip Code is 58765, and a peak population of 625 was reached in 1960, although a sharp decline has reduced that figure to just 278 in 1980. ND Supreme Court Associate Justice Gerald Wayne Vander Walle was born here in 1933. (1, 2, 3, 18, 34, 39, 40, 52, 73, 253)

**NORA** (Divide). This was a farm post office established December 18, 1911 with Knute Christopherson pm, who named it for Nora C. Jeffries, a pioneer settler in the area. Nora is derived from the Latin name Honoria, meaning honor, and from the

*Nome about 1907*

Greek name Leonora, meaning light. It was located in SW 1/4 Sec. 14-160-100, Smoky Butte Twp., twenty miles SW of Crosby, and closed October 31, 1917 with mail to Appam. (2, 18, 19, 40)

**NORACONG** (Cavalier). This was a pioneer settlement of the 1880's, said to be in Hope Twp. (163-58), about twenty miles north of Osnabrock. Little is known about its history, or its namesake, L. C. Noracong, an early county official who apparently left for parts unknown without ever having owned land in the county. (2, 3, 33, 249)

**NORD** (Walsh). This was a farm post office established April 12, 1900 with Lewis L. Anderson pm. It was located in SE¼ Sec. 32-155-57, Cleveland Twp., eight miles SSW of Lankin on the border with Nelson County. The area was settled by Norwegians, and *nord* means north in their native language. The post office closed December 15, 1905 with mail to Petersburg. (2, 3, 18, 34, 40, 75, 415)

**NORFOLK** (McHenry). This was a GNRR station founded in 1913 in Sec. 13-152-76, Strege Twp., six miles NE of Drake, and named for Norfolk County, England by GNRR officials. An elevator was built, and a population of 10 was reported in 1920, but development stagnated at that point. (2, 3, 18, 183)

**NORGE** (Divide). This was a rural settlement in SE¼ Sec. 26-163-101, DeWitt Twp., named by its Scandinavian settlers for Norway, which is *Norge*, pronounced Nor-Gay, in their native tongue. This name was the result of a compromise after residents could not decide which of their number to name the town after, having also rejected the first compromise name of Green Valley. The post office was established November 15, 1907 with IL native Irvin R. Smith as pm in his general store. C. H. Hoff, also from IL, had an implement dealership, and William Priest opened a bank. The Soo Line RR established the new townsite of Fortuna one mile to the west in 1913, and the NORGE post office closed October 10, 1913, being replaced the following day by the Fortuna post office. (2, 3, 18, 40, 73)

**NORMA** (Renville). This Soo Line RR townsite was built in NW¼ Sec. 33-161-87, Fairbanks Twp., between Tolley and Kenmare, and named for the daughter of Anton Nelson, a local merchant and pioneer settler in the area. Others say that Soo Line RR agent Ambrose Olson named it for his daughter. Norma is a Latin name meaning the model. The post office was established March 4, 1907 with William E. Shortridge pm in his store, which he had moved here from Lewis. A population of 200 was claimed in 1920, but it is well under 100 today. The post office, Zip Code 58766, closed July 31, 1981. (1, 2, 18, 19, 33, 40, 41, 71)

**NORMAN** (Cass). This was a rural community that developed around the mill run by Carl Norman in SW¼ Sec. 24-137-50, Normanna Twp., four miles east of Kindred. The post office was established November 14, 1873 with Soren Ottis (1841-1919) as pm. Elling Ulness (1866-1954), later affiliated with two post offices bearing his name, was a

storekeeper here. A population of 35 was reported in 1890, but the settlement declined and the post office closed September 5, 1900 with mail to Kindred. (1, 2, 3, 40, 77)

**NORMANNA** (Ransom). This was a rural community in Sec. 28-135-58, Fort Ransom Twp., four miles SW of Fort Ransom, that developed around a creamery built by local farmers in 1903 on land owned by Albert Jacobson. Some say a local Scandinavian settler gave it a name of old country origins, while others say it was named for Normanna Twp. (137-50) in Cass County, which had their original name of Norman altered to avoid duplication with a township of this name in Traill County, while still others say it was named by pm Isaac J. Oliver of Fort Ransom for Normanna, TX, which was originally named San Domingo, but was renamed in 1886 by Norwegian Mennonites with a word said to mean home of the Norsemen. Whatever the source of the name, it soon became a ghost town. (2, 3, 77, 84, 201)

**NORPAK** (Cass). This NPRR station between Casselton and Mapleton was built in 1882 and named GREENE. On May 24, 1912 it was renamed NORPAK, a name coined from NORthern PACific Railroad, with a mild stylizing of the spelling. The site is now a short spur serving an elevator. (1, 2, 18, 34, 77)

**NORTH ALMONT** (Morton). This NPRR station was built in 1946 in W½ Sec. 23-139-86, Caribou Twp., nine miles north of Almont, and four miles west of New Salem. Two elevators were moved from Almont after the NPRR rerouted its mainline, bypassing both Sims and Almont. (3, 34, 109)

**NORTH BRITTON** (Sargent). This name is used for residents of SW Sargent County with telephone prefix 443, part of the exchange in Britton, SD, which was named for Col. Isaac Britton, General Manager of the Dakota & Great Southern RR. (3, 36, 55)

**NORTHBROOK** (Burleigh). This is a contract station of the Bismarck post office established April 2, 1980. It is located in the Northbrook Shopping Center on North Washington Street, officially SW¼ Sec. 28-139-80, Hay Creek Twp. The shopping center opened in 1964, and was given a euphonic name. (3, 34)

**NORTH CARSON** (Grant). This townsite was founded in 1907 in Sec. 12-134-87, Carson Twp., two miles north of the rival townsite of CARSON, which had moved to Sec. 24-134-87 in 1906. NORTH CARSON's biggest industry was a creamery built in 1908. When the NPRR built between the two townsites in 1910, CARSON and NORTH CARSON merged as CARSON in Sec. 13-134-87, midway between the two. August Anderson was the first pm at the new townsite. (2, 3, 40, 173, 176)

**NORTH CENTRAL** (Barnes). On June 3, 1958 voters approved the merger of the Dazey, Rogers, Leal, and five rural school districts into North Central of Barnes District 65. A large twelve-grade school

building was completed in 1963 in NE¼ Sec. 18-142-60, Edna Twp., about midway between Dazey and Rogers. Since that time the site has appeared on some maps as NORTH CENTRAL. (34, 328)

**NORTH CHAUTAUQUA** (Ramsey). This was the post office at the Chautauqua Assembly grounds four miles SW of Devils Lake, on Creels Bay of the lake of the same name. The assembly had begun in 1893 and was generally called CHAUTAUQUA, but the post office was established June 30, 1902 as NORTH CHAUTAUQUA with Idelette Booth as pm. The "north" apparently was added to note its geographic location relative to other assemblies. In 1911 this was the third largest Chautauqua in the country, but interest began to wane, and the last assembly was held in 1929. The area had begun to develop into a residential site, unofficially called Lakewood, and on April 1, 1931 the NORTH CHAUTAUQUA post office changed its name to LAKEWOOD PARK. (1, 2, 5, 18, 40, 103)

**NORTH DICKINSON** (Stark). In 1891 the Guarantee Investment & Trust Co. platted 86 acres in NW¼ Sec. 3-139-96, just north of Dickinson, apparently as a rival townsite. Little development took place, and the area was annexed by Dickinson in 1900, with the old plat being officially abandoned in 1909. The area today is largely residential, lying between the original townsite and Interstate 94, being parts of the Hilliard & Manning Subdivisions. (18, 406)

**NORTHFIELD** (Ramsey). This was a rural settlement founded in 1898 in SW 1/4 Sec. 4-158-62, Northfield Twp., and named for Northfield, MN, which was named for two men of that city, John W. North (1815-1890), an attorney, MN state legislator, member of Constitutional Conventions in both MN and NV, a founder of the University of MN, and Surveyor-General and a Supreme Court Justice in NV, and Ira Stratton Field (1813-1892), a VT legislator who settled in MN and was a farmer and a blacksmith. The post office was established March 4, 1902 with Ole Iverson pm. On July 15, 1903 it moved one mile NE to the new GNRR townsite, with a name change to HAMPDEN. (2, 3, 10, 13, 18, 40, 103)

**NORTH GATE** (Burke). This townsite in Secs. 29 & 30-164-89, North Star Twp., right on the Canadian border, was platted in 1910, but settlement occurred one mile south in NE¼ Sec. 31-164-89, which was platted as NORTH GATE SOUTH. The post office was established at NORTH GATE SOUTH in 1914 as one-word, NORTHGATE. The names are all credited to GNRR officials, who noted its northern location and Canadian port-of-entry status. (3, 18, 40, 79, 83)

**NORTHGATE** (Burke). This post office was established April 14, 1914 with Henry Schweyen pm, who held that position until 1938. It is located in NE¼ Sec. 31-164-89, North Star Twp., at the townsite platted as NORTH GATE SOUTH, noting its location one mile south of the platted, but vacant, townsite of NORTH GATE in Secs. 29 & 30-164-89, right on the Canadian border. The name was chosen by GNRR officials to note its port-of-entry status and its extreme northern location. The site is the connection of the GNRR and the Canadian Grand Trunk RR. The elevation is 1851, and a population of 150 was reported in 1920, with a decline to just 65 in 1960. The post office, Zip Code 58767, closed August 24, 1985. (1, 2, 3, 18, 33, 34, 40, 41, 67, 79, 83)

**NORTH GATE SOUTH** (Burke). This townsite was platted in NE¼ Sec. 31-164-89, North Star Twp., after the original townsite of NORTH GATE, one mile to the north at the Canadian border, was not developed. A post office was established here in 1914 with the one-word name, NORTHGATE, which was soon adopted by the village. (3, 18, 34, 40)

**NORTH GLANAVON** (Emmons). This was a rural community in Twp. 130-79 in SW Emmons County, south of Winona, which was opposite Fort Yates. It flourished about 1900, and was often called COLVILLE for prominent settler William Colville. NORTH GLANAVON referred to Glanavon, a rural community just to the south which had its own post office 1903-1907. (3, 18, 40)

**NORTH HECLA** (Dickey). This name is used for residents of SE Dickey County with telephone prefix 992, part of the exchange in Hecla, SD, which was named for a volcano in Iceland. (3, 36, 55)

**NORTH LEMMON** (Adams). This is a Milwaukee Road RR station in SW¼ Sec. 35-129-92, North Lemmon Twp., which is actually the portion of Lemmon, SD that is north of the state line. Lemmon, SD was named for George E. Lemmon, a wealthy land owner in the area. C. R. Braught was the original owner of the land on the ND side of the border. (2, 3, 18, 34)

**NORTH McINTOSH** (Sioux). This name is used for residents of southern Sioux County with telephone prefix 276, part of the exchange in McIntosh, SD, which was named for the brothers who built the Milwaukee Road RR grade across the Standing Rock Indian Reservation in 1909. (3, 36, 55)

**NORTH McLAUGHLIN** (Sioux). This name is used for residents of SE Sioux County with telephone prefix 827, part of the exchange in McLaughlin, SD, which was named for Col. James McLaughlin, a longtime Indian agent and author. (3, 36, 55)

**NORTH MINNEWAUKAN** (Benson). This was a paper townsite in SE¼ Sec. 10-153-67, West Bay Twp., one mile north of present-day Minnewaukan. During the flurry of activity in 1883-1884 at the west end of Devils Lake, this site was promoted by Benjamin F. Brown, but when the townsite one mile south began to grow, NORTH MINNEWAUKAN was abandoned. Unnamed during its brief "life", the name was coined only after Minnewaukan had established itself as the surviving townsite in the area. (2, 3, 18, 110)

**NORTH MORRISTOWN** (Sioux). This name is used for residents of SW Sioux County with telephone prefix 522, part of the exchange in Morristown, SD, which was

named for Nels P. Morris in 1917. Mr. Morris, a resident of Chicago, IL, was the owner of the Morris Packing Co., owners of the C-7 Ranch at this site, which at the time had 30,000 head of cattle. (3, 36, 55)

**NORTH NEW EFFINGTON** (Richland). This name is used for residents of SW Richland County with telephone prefix 634, part of the exchange in New Effington, SD, which was named for a nearby abandoned townsite in 1913. "Old" Effington had been named for the first girl born in the area, who had been christened Effie. (3, 36, 55)

**NORTH RIVER** (Cass). This is a rural subdivision started in 1973 in SE¼ Sec. 12-140-48, Reed Twp., just north of Fargo, and named to note its location on the west bank of the Red River. A population of 65 was reported in 1980. (3, 34)

**NORTHRUP** (Dunn). This was a farm post office established February 10, 1909 with John Northrup pm. It was located in SW¼ Sec. 15-145-96, Richloam Twp., seven miles west of Killdeer, and closed February 28, 1914 with mail to Fayette. Northrop is an erroneous spelling. (1, 2, 3, 18, 40, 53)

**NORTH VALLEY CITY** (Barnes). This place appears on some modern maps at the junction of county roads about two miles north of Valley City in NE¼ Sec. 16-140-58. The main road continues north to the Sibley resort, while the other road angles westward to Bald Hill Dam. Several commercial ventures have developed at the site. (3, 34)

**NORTH VEBLEN** (Sargent). This name is used for residents of SE Sargent County with telephone prefix 736, part of the exchange in Veblen, SD, which was named for pioneer settler J. E. Veblen, and was once the terminus of a railroad line from Fairmount, ND. (3, 36, 55)

**NORTHVIEW** (Cass). This was a farm post office established March 20, 1882 with Lewis K. Rich pm. It was located between Ayr and Page in E½ Sec. 7-140-54, Buffalo Twp., and closed September 22, 1882. The origin of the name is unknown, although it is undoubtedly of a descriptive nature. (2, 34, 40, 77)

**NORTH VIKING** (Benson). This was a rural post office established April 5, 1892 with Ole H. Myhre pm. It was located in Sec. 5-151-69, South Viking Twp., three miles south of Maddock, and was named for its township, which was named for the legendary Norse pirates. The "north" indicated its relative location to the Viking post office four miles SSE of here in the same township. The post office closed February 4, 1898 with mail to Maddock. (2, 3, 18, 34, 40, 239)

**NORTHWOOD** (Grand Forks). This was a farm post office established December 17, 1879 with Paul C. Johnson pm, who named it for the hometown of most of the area settlers, Northwood, IA. It was located in NE¼ Sec. 18-149-54, Northwood Twp., until 1882 when it moved two miles ENE to the new GNRR townsite in Sec. 9-149-54, which was platted by Thomas O. Hougen, who became the mayor when it incorporated as

a city in 1892. The elevation is 1102, the Zip Code is 58267, and a peak population of 1,240 was reported in 1980 as the city has shown a consistent growth. Dan Leroy Clark Campbell (1877-1966) published *The Northwood Gleaner* from 1899 until his death. (1, 3, 18, 25, 31, 33, 40, 52, 69, 79, 241)

**NORTON** (Grand Forks). This was a GNRR station in Sec. 25-150-51, Allendale Twp., and Sec. 30-150-50, Walle Twp., eleven miles south of Grand Forks, named for George Norton, the owner of the townsite. When the post office was established in 1881, the name was changed to THOMPSON to avoid confusion with Norton, MN. Norton is an Anglo-Saxon name meaning from the north farmstead or village. The station was locally referred to as Norton Station. (2, 3, 19, 31, 40, 69, 276)

**NORTON** (Walsh). This was a rural community in NW¼ Sec. 8-156-57, Norton Twp., two miles NW of the Galt post office, which closed on May 20, 1892. The NORTON post office opened May 21, 1892 with Per E. Peterson pm, and took the name of its township, which was named in 1883 with an Anglicized compromise name after the Norwegian settlers could not decide on Nordford or Nordland. A population of 15 was reported in 1920. The post office closed July 30, 1932 with mail to Adams. (1, 2, 3, 18, 40, 75)

**NORTONVILLE** (LaMoure). This town was founded in 1913 as a station on the Midland Continental RR in Sec. 28-136-64, Kennison Twp., about midway between Edgeley and Jamestown, and named for a Belgian investor in the railroad. The post office was established February 8, 1913 with Edward Withnell pm. The Zip Code is 58473, and the population has generally been about 100. The post office became a rural branch of Jud on September 30, 1963, and changed to a rural branch of Jamestown on May 2, 1964. (2, 3, 33, 40, 158)

**NORUM** (Divide). This farm post office was authorized May 7, 1908 with Ole J. Skjermo pm, who named it for Norum, Sogn og Fjordane, Norway. It was located in SW¼ Sec. 11-163-102, Elkhorn Twp., six miles north of Alkabo. The order was rescinded June 8, 1908. On June 29, 1908 the post office was reestablished as SKERMO, and operated until 1914. Vorum is an erroneous spelling. (3, 40)

**NORVAL** (Nelson). This was a Soo Line RR station in E½ Sec. 18-154-57, Dahlen Twp., four miles west of Dahlen. It was named for Norval, the Scottish shepherd in the 1757 play *Douglas*, written by John Home. It appeared on maps circa 1915-1925, but virtually no development occurred at the site. (1, 3, 5, 19)

**NORWAY** (Dickey). This was a Soo Line RR station in SW¼ Sec. 24-131-60, Clement Twp., three miles west of Oakes. It was called MAHONAY SPUR and NICKOLS CROSSING until 1912, when the name NORWAY began appearing on maps. This was the original name of the township in 1884, and noted the homeland of most area settlers, which bears a name that literally translates as North Kingdom. A population of 5 was reported in 1930. John H. Coulter managed the elevator here for seventeen years. (2, 3, 5, 154)

**NORWAY** (Traill). This was a rural settlement founded in 1871 as GOOSENLAND. It later was centered at the John Anderson farm in SE¼ Sec. 27-146-51, three miles NW of Hillsboro, and was named NORWAY for its township, which was named for the homeland of most area settlers. A post office was established in the area in 1877, but it was first called STONY POINT, and later BLOOMFIELD. (2, 3, 29, 40)

**NORWEGIAN** (McIntosh). This was a rural post office established June 25, 1890 in NW¼ Sec. 21-131-70, Danzig Twp., about two miles NE of Danzig. Martin C. Moen was the pm in his sod house, and he named his office to note the nationality of most of his patrons. The post office closed May 12, 1899 with mail to Ashley. (2, 3, 40, 134, 211)

**NORWICH** (McHenry). This GNRR station was founded in 1901 in Sec. 17-155-80, Norwich Twp., and named for Norwich, England to please stockholders from that country. The English city dates from about 700 A.D., was the site of an early-day mint, and appears in 1002 A.D. as Northwic. While Americans generally pronounce the name Nor'-witch, the English say Nor'-idge. The post office was established February 14, 1901 with Frederick Blocher pm. The elevation is 1531, the Zip Code is 58768, and a peak population of 200 was claimed in 1920, although the count has been well under 100 for the last fifty years. (1, 2, 3, 5, 18, 25, 33, 40, 79, 182)

**NOSODAK** (Sioux). This townsite was planned in 1910 in SE¼ Sec. 35-129-79, in the extreme SE corner of the county on the west bank of the Missouri River just above the SD border. It was to be a station on a new NPRR mainline running from Mandan to Galveston, TX, but this ambitious dream of a north-south railroad died in 1914. Although NOSODAK remained on many maps for about thirty years, it never grew beyond a railroad construction camp. The Western Townsite & Development Company coined the name from NOrth and SOuth DAKota, noting its location. (2, 3, 18, 127, 434)

**NOVA** (Walsh). This was a farm post office established August 1, 1881 with John J. Kratky pm. It was located in Sec. 19-156-54, Prairie Centre Twp., four miles east of Pisek, and given the Latin name for new. The post office closed November 20, 1886 with mail to Conway, although six days later the Veseley post office opened to serve the area. The NOVA post office was reestablished January 26, 1887, but closed for good April 3, 1888 with mail again to Conway. Nora is an erroneous spelling. (2, 3, 25, 40)

**NOWESTA** (Pembina). This was a pioneer settlement in SW¼ Sec. 20-160-51, Lincoln Twp., five miles SW of Bowesmont. The name was coined to note the early-day fur trading posts established in the area by the North West Fur Co. The post office was established November 25, 1885 with Whitfield Douglas pm, and closed January 15, 1919 with mail to Bowesmont. A population of 25 was reported in 1890. (2, 3, 18, 25, 40, 53, 79, 108)

**NUDELMAN** (McLean). This townsite was platted May 17, 1888 in NW¼ Sec. 23-143-81, Nettle Creek Twp., about midway between Wilton and Washburn, and about two miles SE of the settlement called New Jerusalem. It was an attempt by the colony of Russian Jews who had come to this area in 1882 to form their own townsite, and was named for Jacob Nudelman of Chicago, IL, who owned the site. Little development took place, and the venture was abandoned. Reports of a post office at NUDELMAN are not supported by government records, and early guides show the town being served by the Falconer post office. (2, 3, 25, 28, 33, 40, 390)

**NUITA** (Dunn). This was an Indian settlement consisting of a school, a Congregational church, and a Roman Catholic church. It was located one mile above the mouth of the Little Missouri River in Sec. 33-148-91, and given a name of Indian origin, said to mean Mandan. The site is now inundated by Lake Sakakawea. (2, 3)

**NUMEDAHL** (Cavalier). This was a farm post office established June 27, 1898 with Halvor Halvorson pm. It was named for the district and river of Norway, whose name translates as beautiful valley between hills. It was first located in NE¼ Sec. 34-164-58, Hope Twp., nineteen miles NE of Langdon, and later moved to a small village that began to develop just to the west in NW¼ Sec. 34-164-58. A population of 10 was reported in 1920. The post office closed August 31, 1926 with mail to Walhalla. (2, 3, 13, 18, 40, 79, 292)

**OAK CREEK** (Bottineau). This was the first settlement in Bottineau County, founded in the early 1880's when J. B. Sinclair, Alex McClay, Robert Brander and William Hulburt led a group of colonists to SE¼ Sec. 19-162-75, Whitteron Twp., one mile NE of present-day Bottineau. It was named for the creek on which it was located, and was a station on a stage line from Devils Lake, 120 miles to the SE. William H. Kirk, who later operated a resort hotel on Lake Metigoshe, was the first customs agent when OAK CREEK became a Canadian port-of-entry. In 1884 most settlers moved to the new GNRR townsite of Bottineau. (2, 3, 101, 153)

**OAKDALE** (Dunn). This was a rural post office established July 23, 1889 with Michael S. Cuskelly pm. The Cuskelly family came to America from Ireland in 1882, and Mrs. Cuskelly coined the name to note the native oak trees in this region. It was located in SW¼ Sec. 23-146-96, nine miles NW of Killdeer until 1919 when it moved two miles north to NE¼ Sec. 15-146-96, the home of new pm W. F. Sperb. A rural community developed at this site, reporting a population of 30 in 1920. OAKDALE was one of ND's last rural post offices, closing September 30, 1958 with mail to Killdeer. (1, 2, 3, 18, 25, 40, 219, 223)

**OAKES** (Dickey). This NPRR townsite was founded in 1886 in Secs. 20, 21, 28 & 29-131-59, Clement Twp., and named for Thomas Fletcher Oakes, then General Manager of the NPRR, and its President 1888-1893. The post office was established December 6, 1886 with Floyd Hineman pm. It incorporated as a city in 1888, and its first mayor was its most famous citizen, Thomas Frank Marshall (1854-1921), later a U. S. Representative. OAKES became a railroad hub when the Chicago & NW RR arrived in 1886 and the Soo Line RR mainline was built here in 1887. The elevation is 1315, the Zip Code is 58474, and a peak population of 2,110 was reached in 1980. (1, 2, 3, 18, 25, 33, 40, 52, 154, 318, 319)

**OAKES JUNCTION** (LaMoure). The intersection of the NPRR lines in Sec. 11-133-60, LaMoure Twp., five miles east of LaMoure, was called VALLEY JUNCTION when it was built in 1886. On May 17, 1897 the name was changed to OAKES JUNCTION as the Dickey County city grew in regional importance. A post office called INDEPENDENCE operated here 1910-1919, and the railroad station belatedly changed its name to match on November 20, 1919, eight months after the post office had closed. (2, 3, 18, 40)

**OAKLAND** (McHenry). This was a rural post office established April 5, 1892 with Carrie B. Deming pm. It was located in SW¼ Sec. 33-159-76, Willow Creek Twp., seven miles NE of Bantry, near the Stevens Ranch on the east bank of the Souris River. The name is thought to be descriptive. The post office closed June 15, 1912 with mail to Towner. (2, 3, 18, 40, 186)

**OAK SPRINGS** (Rolette). This was a resort platted at the extreme southern end of Lake Upsilon, at a point called Crow Bay in NW¼ Sec. 15-163-71, Hutchinson Twp., five miles west of Saint John. The name is descriptive and euphonic. OAK SPRINGS appeared only in county atlases of 1910 and 1928. (18)

**OAKVILLE** (Barnes). This was a pioneer settlement in Sec. 13-137-58, Oakhill Twp., two miles east of Kathryn. It was named for its township, which was named Oakville in 1889 to describe the locale, and changed its name to Oakhill in 1904. The post office was established April 1, 1891 with Fannie Walker pm in the store run by her husband, Myron O. Walker. Ole Venaas operated a blacksmith shop, but most area settlers chose to live in the NPRR townsite of Kathryn which was founded in 1900. The post office closed February 14, 1906 with mail to Kathryn. (1, 2, 40, 76, 331)

**OAKWOOD** (Walsh). This was an inland settlement in SW¼ Sec. 12-157-52, Oakwood Twp., six miles east of Grafton, and named for its township, which was named to note the many oak trees growing within its boundaries. The post office was established November 4, 1895 with Alex Gagnier pm in his grocery store. The post office closed April 30, 1924 with mail to Grafton, but the settlement survived for many years, reporting a population of 55 as late as 1960. (1, 2, 3, 18, 40, 75)

**OATLAND** (Cass). This GNRR station was built about 1888 in SW¼ Sec. 10-141-53, Empire Twp., six miles ENE of Ayr, and was served by the Ripon post office. The origin of the name is unknown, and in 1895 it was renamed MASON. (2, 3, 18, 25, 77)

**OBERON** (Benson). This NPRR siding in SW¼ Sec. 2-151-67, Oberon Twp., was built in 1885 and named ANTELOPE. The post office was established January 25, 1886 with Vernon B. Mathews pm, who changed the name to OBERON, a name made famous in William Shakespeare's play *A Midsummer Night's Dream*. The name is believed to be of Scandinavian origin, and in mythology Oberon was the king of the fairies and husband of Titania. The Zip Code is 58357, and a peak population of 300 was reported in 1920, with a decline to 156 in 1980. (1, 2, 3, 5, 18, 33, 34, 40, 79, 110)

**OBERWEIS** (Richland). This post office was established February 23, 1882 with Peter Ehr pm, who named it for his birthplace of Oberweis, Saxony, Germany. It was located

in Sec. 7-132-50, Barney Twp., four miles east of Wyndmere at the site of the NPRR loading station called BARNEY STATION. The post office closed September 22, 1884 with mail to Wahpeton. In 1899 a small village named BARNEY was founded at this site. Oberwait is an erroneous spelling. (2, 3, 25, 40, 77, 248, 348)

**ODDENA** (McIntosh). This was a farm post office established May 19, 1894 with Anton Bachmeier pm at his home in NW¼ Sec. 32-130-73, Strassburg Twp., five miles NNW of Zeeland. The consensus choice for the name was Odessa for the major city of South Russia, homeland of many area settlers, but postal officials rejected this name because of anticipated confusion with Odessa, Hand County, SD, which operated 1882-1903. ODDENA, an intentional corruption of Odessa, was accepted. The post office was later moved two miles SE to the home of new pm Johannes Streifel in NW¼ Sec. 3-129-73, Farmers Twp., where it closed July 16, 1898 with mail to Kassel. (2, 3, 40, 211)

**ODELL** (Barnes). This was a NPRR station founded in August 1883 in NE¼ Sec. 6-141-59, Stewart Twp., and Sec. 31-142-59, Rogers Twp., just south of Rogers. It was named for J. T. O'Dell, Assistant General Manager of the NPRR. The name is Old English meaning of the valley, and the omission of the apostrophe was apparently intentional. The post office was established November 5, 1883 with Almond C. Chandler pm. A population of 50 was reported in 1890, but on July 11, 1893 the post office moved to the adjacent townsite of Clive, adopting that name. In 1898 the townsite of Rogers was established, quickly absorbing the five rival townsites here. (2, 3, 19, 25, 40, 76, 328)

**ODEN** (Rolette). This was a rural community of the 1890's in Sec. 35-164-71, Holmes Twp., about twelve miles NNE of Dunseith. Some sources report a post office at the site, but this is not confirmed by government records. It was named for Ole Oden, who came to Rolla in 1893 from Norway and ran a shoe shop before homesteading in Holmes Twp. (2, 3, 33, 123)

**ODENSE** (Morton). This was a farm post office established October 5, 1904 with Hans C. Hanson pm, who named it for Odense, Denmark, which takes its name from the fjord on which it is located. It was first located in SE¼ Sec. 19-135-80, nine miles WSW of Fort Rice, and in 1913 moved one mile NE to NE¼ Sec. 20-135-80, where a country store was run by Daniel O'Neill. Mrs. Ella O'Neill was the last pm, closing the facility October 15, 1917 with mail to Solen. (1, 2, 3, 17, 40, 53, 107)

**ODESSA** (Grant). This NPRR station was founded in 1910 as BIRDSALL, but on July 19, 1911 pm William L. Martin changed the name to ODESSA for the major city in South Russia, homeland of many area settlers, which was founded by the ancient

Greeks who named it Odessus. Located in W½ Sec. 5-133-90, five miles west of New Leipzig, ODESSA once had two elevators, four stores, a pool hall, lumber yard, blacksmith shop, stockyard, church, and several homes. In 1917 the population was reported to be 150, but a sharp decline began shortly after that unofficial count, and the post office closed December 31, 1926 with mail to New Leipzig. In 1976 only two homes remained at the old townsite. (1, 2, 5, 17, 40, 176, 177, 358)

**ODESSA** (Pierce). This was a rural community of German-Russian Roman Catholics centered around the St. Boniface Church in Sec. 24-151-72, Alexanter Twp., about three miles NE of Selz, and named for the principal city of South Russia. The post office was authorized May 11, 1899 with "Conrad Erck" pm, but the order was rescinded February 15, 1900 before it had begun operations. Conrad Erck was not born until April 19, 1900, and the appointment is thought to have been intended for his father, Joseph Erck (1866-1934), who came to SD in 1893 from South Russia, and moved here in 1898. The church is just inside the county line, with the cemetery across the road in Benson County. (2, 3, 40, 149)

**ODESSA** (Ramsey). This townsite was platted November 16, 1882 in Secs. 12 & 13-152-63 and Secs. 7 & 18-152-62, all Odessa Twp. It was created by prominent politicians Alexander Griggs, Col. Oscar M. Towner, Judson LaMoure, and George Walsh as a candidate for the capital of Dakota Territory, which was at the time almost certainly destined to be removed from its first home at Yankton, SD. Col. Towner named it for the great city of South Russia, noting similarities in the locations of the two places, the ND site being on the narrows between Devils Lake proper and Lamoreaux Bay. The territorial capital did get relocated, but to Bismarck, and ODESSA quickly faded, with its few residents receiving mail service from the short-lived Rogers post office. (3, 103)

**ODESSA** (Ramsey). This was a farm post office established April 18, 1905 with Erland Christofferson pm. It was located in Sec. 3-151-62, Odessa Twp., in the extreme southern tip of Ramsey County at the east end of Devils Lake, and named for the historic ghost town of Odessa which had challenged for the territorial capital in 1882. The post office closed August 18, 1906 when Mr. Christofferson became pm at the new GNRR townsite of Hamar, seven miles to the south in Eddy County. (3, 40, 103)

**OELLA** (Sargent). This farm post office was established May 7, 1900 with Winifred S. Howard pm. It was located in Sec. 15-129-56, Taylor Twp., four miles NW of Havana, and named for the nearby lake which had been named for Oella Parson, owner of the land around the lake. The post office closed September 15, 1903 with mail to Havana. Ollea is an erroneous spelling. (2, 3, 40, 165)

**OGDEN** (Divide). This was a farm post office established July 10, 1905 with Fred H. Johncox pm. It was located in SW¼ Sec. 32-164-96, Long Creek Twp., eight miles NE of Crosby, and named for the Ogden family,

pioneers in the Fortuna area. Ogden is a variant of Oakden, an Old English name meaning from the oak-tree valley. The post office closed September 30, 1907 with mail to Crosby. (2, 3, 19, 40, 73, 415)

**OJATA** (Grand Forks). This GNRR townsite was founded in 1880 in Sec. 2 & 11-151-52, Oakville Twp., ten miles west of Grand Forks, and named STICKNEY. This name was unpopular with local residents, and on March 6, 1883 pm Charles Hutchinson changed the name to OJATA, a corruption of the Sioux word *oz-ate*, meaning crossing. A population of 58 was reported in 1890, and 45 people were here as late as 1920, but the village failed to develop beyond that date, and the post office closed May 15, 1936 with mail to Emerado. The site is now abandoned. (1, 2, 3, 18, 25, 31, 40, 69, 79)

**OLANTA** (Mercer). This was a pioneer settlement founded about 1895 in Sec. 15-144-90, and said to have been named for Olanta, PA, which had been founded in 1885. This settlement failed to develop, but in 1909 a new group of settlers came here and founded GOLDENVALLEY. (2, 3)

**OLD CARSON** (Grant). This name was given to the original 1906 townsite of CARSON after 1910, when the NPRR built between it and North Carson, resulting in a new CARSON townsite. OLD CARSON was in Sec. 24-134-87, Carson Twp., one mile south of the new townsite, and was identified in one account as Old South Carson. (2, 3, 173, 177)

**OLD COAL HARBOR** (McLean). This site, the center quarter of Sec. 35-147-84, Coal Harbor Twp., was first settled in 1883 by Canadians who named it VICTORIA. In 1885 the nearby Missouri River port of COAL HARBOR imposed its name on the site when its post office moved here. In 1905 the COAL HARBOR post office moved to the new Soo Line RR townsite of Coleharbor, after which this site became known as OLD COAL HARBOR. By 1914 it was virtually abandoned, with the site owned by H. F. Beerman, although it appeared on some maps into the 1920's. (1, 2, 3, 18)

**OLD COLUMBUS** (Burke). In 1906 most of the inland townsite of COLUMBUS moved to the new Soo Line RR townsite six miles to the SE. The original site in SE¼ Sec. 16-163-94, Forthun Twp., became known as OLD COLUMBUS, and within a few years was a ghost town. (3, 18, 67)

**OLD CROSBY** (Divide). CROSBY moved one mile east to SE¼ Sec. 29-163-97, Fillmore Twp., in 1908. The original site in SE¼ Sec. 30-163-97 became known as OLD CROSBY. (2, 3, 73)

**OLD CROSSING** (Walsh). This was a crossing point of the Red River in Saint Andrew Twp. (158-51), about twelve miles ENE of Grafton, and known to pioneers as early as the 1860's. Job and Frank Herrick settled at OLD CROSSING on July 20, 1870, and many years later were enthusiastic members of the Red River Valley Old Settlers Association. The name OLD CROSSING was coined about the time the nearby townsite of Saint Andrew was founded in the late 1870's. (2, 3, 75, 420)

**OLD FORT ABERCROMBIE** (Richland). This name appears on a 1912 map in Sec. 4-134-48, Abercrombie Twp., just east of the village of Abercrombie, and refers to the ruins of the historic military post. (3, 18)

**OLD FORT ABRAHAM LINCOLN** (Morton). This name appeared on several maps into the 1920's to note the site of the abandoned military post in Sec. 13-138-81, just south of Mandan. The site is now a popular state park, featuring the rebuilt Slant Indian Village, buildings recording the fort's colorful history, and a picnic and camp grounds. Just to the west, atop a high bluff, are three reconstructed block houses and the newly-rebuilt Custer home. (3, 18)

**OLD FORT BUFORD** (Williams). Some maps continued to show the site of FORT BUFORD, Sec. 16-152-104, Buford Twp., into the 1920's, although it had been abandoned in 1895. This name memorialized the original site, which was at the time only the ruins and remnants of the original military post (3, 18, 50)

**OLD FORT CLARK** (Mercer). This name appeared on several maps of the 1880's at the site of the ruins of FORT CLARK, the abandoned fur trading post in SE 1/4 Sec. 36-144-84. (3)

**OLD FORT McKEEN** (Morton). This name appeared on some maps as late as 1920 to note the location of the old abandoned military post in Sec. 13-138-81, just south of Mandan, even though the post had used the name FORT McKEEN for only five months in 1872. The name FORT McKEEN today generally refers to the high bluff just west of ND Highway 1806 which is the site of three reconstructed block houses and the newly-rebuilt Custer home, while FORT LINCOLN generally refers to the Slant Indian Village and museum at the bottom of the bluff on the east side of the road. The entire area is one of ND's most visited state parks. (3, 18)

**OLD FORT PEMBINA** (Pembina). This name appeared on maps circa 1900-1915, and refers to the abandoned military post just south of Pembina in Sec. 16-163-51, Pembina Twp. (3, 18)

**OLD FORT RICE** (Morton). This name appeared on maps as late as 1920, and noted the site of the ruins of the military post in NW¼ Sec. 14-135-79, just south of the village of Fort Rice. (3, 18)

**OLD FORT SEWARD** (Stutsman). FORT SEWARD, the old military post in SE¼ Sec. 26-140-64, Midway Twp., was abandoned in 1877, but appeared on some maps under this name into the early twentieth century. Located in what is now the NW part of the city of Jamestown, the NPRR donated the site to ND in 1925 for use as a historic site. (3, 18)

**OLD FORT STEVENSON** (McLean). FORT STEVENSON, a military post 1867-1883, and an Indian Agency from then until 1894, was shown on many maps into the 1920's as OLD FORT STEVENSON. It was located in NE¼ Sec. 10-147-85, Stevenson Twp., seven miles SW of Garrison, and is now inundated by Lake Sakakakwea. (18, 34)

**OLD FORT UNION** (Williams). Maps as late as 1912 continued to show the ruins of this historic fort as OLD FORT UNION. It was located in SE¼ Sec. 7-152-104, Buford Twp., and was abandoned in 1866. The site is now undergoing a massive reconstruction. (18, 50)

**OLD GARRISON** (Mclean). GARRISON was founded in 1903 by Theodore and Cecil H. Taylor, formerly of Bismarck, in NW¼ Sec. 6-147-84, Coal Harbor Twp. It developed into a thriving little community, but when the Soo Line RR established a townsite five miles NNE of here in 1905, most of the town moved to the new site. The original site became known as OLD GARRISON, and was inundated by Lake Sakakawea in the 1950's. (3, 28, 387)

**OLD LEIPZIG** (Grant). When the LEIPZIG post office closed in 1915, the site in NW¼ Sec. 32-135-89, Leipzig Twp., became known as OLD LEIPZIG, as opposed to New Leipzig, the railroad townsite that had led to the demise of this original settlement. Unlike many such sites, it is not abandoned, even though a commemorative plaque was erected here in 1960 to mark the site. A rural school continues to operate, and the Ebenezer United Church of Christ, built in 1925, continues to hold services each Sunday. (17, 33, 358)

**OLD LUCCA** (Barnes). The townsite of LUCCA moved one mile north to the crossing of the NPRR and the Soo Line RR in 1900. A few residents stayed at the original site in NE¼ Sec. 11-137-56, Raritan Twp., which became known as OLD LUCCA. (3, 118)

**OLD LUDDEN** (Dickey). The pioneer settlement of LUDDEN was founded in 1883 in Secs. 1 & 12-129-60, Lovell Twp. When the site was moved one mile east to the new Chicago & NW RR townsite in 1886, the original site gradually became a ghost town, and during its last years was commonly called OLD LUDDEN. (2, 3, 154)

**OLD MANTADOR** (Richland). This name evolved after 1914 when the townsite of MANTADOR moved to the south side of the Soo Line RR tracks. The original townsite in NE¼ Sec. 8-131-50, Belford Twp., was on the north side of the tracks, and became known as OLD MANTADOR. (2, 3, 147)

**OLD MAYVILLE** (Traill). This name appeared in some accounts of the 1880's, and is thought to refer to the first location of real commercial development at what is now MAYVILLE. About 1879 the Chantland

brothers, Storeland brothers, Mons Knutson, O. P. Lura, and a Mr. Syverud all had businesses in SW¼ Sec. 31-147-52, Lindaas Twp., just west of the present city which began to develop in 1881. (3, 395)

**OLD McCLUSKY** (Sheridan). This townsite was founded in 1902 in Secs. 8 & 9-146-77, McClusky Twp., and named McCLUSKY. The townsite moved to the NPRR tracks in 1905, three miles to the east, and this site became known as OLD McCLUSKY. It soon became a ghost town. (2, 3, 18, 21, 30)

**OLD McVILLE** (Nelson). In 1906 the country store and post office in NW¼ Sec. 26-150-59, Hamlin Twp., known as McVILLE relocated to the GNRR tracks two miles to the south, which had been named McVILLE STATION. The new site adopted the McVILLE name, and the original site became known as OLD McVILLE as it declined into a ghost town. (2, 3, 124)

**OLD STANTON** (Mercer). This name was locally used to name the original townsite of Stanton in N½ Sec. 6-144-84, at the mouth of the Knife River. The townsite had been moved a bit to the south in 1906 to avoid spring floods. The original site was once the Mandan Indian village of Mah-har-ha. (2, 3, 64)

**OLD WESTBY** (Divide). This name was applied to the original site of WESTBY in SW¼ Sec. 23-162-103, Westby Twp., in 1913 when it moved two miles NW to the new Soo Line RR townsite on the MT side of the ND-MT border. (2, 3, 40)

**OLESBERG** (Barnes). This was a farm post office established February 8, 1882 with Ever O. Olesberg pm, who came here in 1878 from Norway. It was located in SE¼ Sec. 24-137-58, Oakhill Twp., two miles SE of Kathryn, and closed September 25, 1885 with mail to Daily. Olesburg and Olsberg are erroneous spellings. (3, 25, 40, 76, 331)

*The site of Olga was part of Pembina County until 1885*

**OLGA** (Cavalier). Founded in 1882 in Sec. 5-161-57, Olga Twp., as SAINT PIERRE, this is the oldest settlement in Cavalier County. The post office was established September 18, 1882 with the town's namesake, Father Cyrille Saint Pierre, as pm, and he changed the name to OLGA at the suggestion of the area's first school teacher, Ernestine Mager, who greatly admired Norway's Princess Olga. Olga is a Teutonic name meaning holy. The village incorporated in 1883, challenged unsuccessfully for the county seat in 1889, and settled into a stable little town of 100 people for many years. Recent decline led to a closing of the post office on July 31, 1958 with mail to Concrete, with mail service

switching to Langdon in 1964. The village, however, continues to survive with most current residents being descendants of the original French-Canadian pioneers. (1, 2, 3, 18, 19, 25, 40, 115, 292)

**OLIVE** (Ward). This was a farm post office established September 23, 1904 with Olive May (Mrs. William) Smith pm. The Smiths lived in SW¼ Sec. 31-152-83, Gassman Twp., eighteen miles SSE of Minot, but the post office was located in the home of Mrs. Smith's mother, Anna Haigh, in SE¼ Sec. 31-152-83, just to the east. Olive is the feminine form of Oliver, a Latin name meaning olive, with an implied meaning of peace. The post office closed April 30, 1910 with mail to Sawyer. (2, 3, 18, 19, 40, 100, 374)

**OLIVIA** (McHenry). This was a pioneer settlement founded in 1900 in Secs. 32 & 33-151-79, Olivia Twp., midway between Butte and Ruso just inside the McHenry County line. It was named by settlers from Olivia, MN, which was named in 1881 by civil engineer Albert Bowman Rogers for a female depot agent in Ortonville, MN. Olivia is a Latinized name symbolizing peace. The townsite was platted in 1913 by the Tri-State Land Co. on the Soo Line RR. The post office was established January 15, 1916 as KONGSBERG, and this gradually became the generally accepted name, although the local general store operated under the name Olivia Cash Store until 1973. (1, 2, 3, 10, 13, 19, 40, 412)

**OLMSTEAD** (Towner). This was a Farmers Grain & Shipping Co. RR station in NE¼ Sec. 6-159-65, Victor Twp., just east of Egeland. The post office was established September 20, 1905 with Albert A. Olmstead pm. Frank Fee operated a general store here for a number of years, and a population of 90 was reported in 1920, but the post office closed November 14, 1925 with mail to Egeland. It seems quite obvious that the site was named for the first pm, but some sources say it was named for Olmsted County, MN, with no explanation for the difference in the spelling. That county was named for David Olmsted (1822-1861), the first mayor of Saint Paul, MN. (1, 2, 3, 10, 13, 18, 40, 79, 197)

**OMEMEE** (Bottineau). This GNRR townsite was founded in 1887 in Sec. 4-160-75, Willow Vale Twp., and named for Omemee, Ontario, Canada, the hometown of George Raye, who became pm when the post office was established April 8, 1890. The name is a corruption of the Ojibway Indian word *omimi*, meaning pigeon or turtle dove, and was selected by postal officials from a list of names submitted by Mr. Raye. In 1903 the town moved to a new site in Secs. 4 & 9-160-75, the junction of the GNRR and Soo Line RR, the later being built in 1905. The village incorporated in 1902, and reported a population of 650 in 1906, but that figure had declined to 332 in 1910, and reached a low of just 5 in 1970. The post office closed April 21, 1967 with mail to Willow City. (1, 2, 3, 13, 34, 40, 52, 79, 101, 153)

**OMIO** (Emmons). This was a rural post office established February 4, 1886 with Abraham L. Raynolds pm at his home in NW¼ Sec.

22-132-76, three miles SE of Linton. Mr. Raynolds also operated the WAYLIN post office at this site for two months in 1886. In 1888 the OMIO post office moved four miles NW to the home of pm Leah Carmichael in SW¼ Sec. 6-132-76, just north of present-day Linton, and in 1892 it was moved eight miles ESE to NE¼ Sec. 20-132-75, the home of pm Libbie Wescott. A Methodist church at this site was a longtime community center. The post office closed December 31, 1914 with mail to Linton. The origin of the name is unknown. (1, 2, 3, 18, 25, 40, 53, 66, 415)

**ONG** (Burleigh). This was a farm post office established August 7, 1902 with Lewis H. Ong pm, who came here in 1901 from IA and purchased the Canfield Ranch in 1902. It was located in SW¼ Sec. 8-142-76, Wing Twp., three miles WSW of Wing, until 1905 when it moved four miles NE to SE¼ Sec. 28-143-76, Richmond Twp., the home of new pm George Feldhausen. The post office closed May 31, 1912 with mail to Wing. Mr. Ong sold his interests in 1915 and returned to IA, later moving to CA. (2, 3, 8, 12, 18, 40, 63)

**ONTARIO** (Wells). In 1884 R. S. Long founded a townsite in Sec. 33-147-71, West Ontario Twp., two miles north of present-day Bowdon, and named it for his hometown of Ontario, Wayne County, NY. The name is a corruption of the Iroquois *ontare io*, meaning lake beautiful, and is the name of one of the Great Lakes and a province of Canada. George Brynjulson was the first settler. The townsite was platted and a Chicago, IL firm built a store with the promise of a free lot for each employee, but when the NPRR bypassed the site, ONTARIO was doomed and today is a plowed field. Mail service was provided by Sykeston, the only post office in the county at the time. (2, 3, 10, 18, 25, 79, 267, 363)

**OPGRAND** (Hettinger). This rural post office was authorized May 13, 1907 with Arnt Opgrand pm, but the order was rescinded September 13, 1907. The exact location is unknown. (2, 3, 40)

**OPS** (Walsh). This was a Soo Line RR station built in the early 1900's in SW¼ Sec. 21-155-54, Ops Twp., about six miles west of Forest River. It was named for its township, which was named for the Roman goddess of plenty and fertility, who was the wife of Saturn and lived on the earth to protect agriculture. Three grain elevators were here in 1910, but the site did not develop beyond that and disappeared from maps in the 1950's. (1, 2, 3, 5, 18, 75)

**ORANGE** (Adams). This was a rural post office established May 7, 1908 with James E. Goforth pm at his farm in SE¼ Sec. 35-129-91, Orange Twp., just above the SD border. Mr. Goforth, a native of MO, used a bit of frontier humor in naming the post office, selecting ORANGE to note its proximity to Lemmon, SD, about six miles to the west. The Milwaukee Road RR built into this area in 1908, and sometime after August 1909 it moved to the new railroad townsite which put it into SD, where it changed its name to Thunder Hawk in December 1910. (3, 18, 40, 189, 414)

**ORANGE** (Grand Forks). Settlers from northern MN came here in 1878, and a post office was established November 12, 1879 in SE¼ Sec. 10-151-54, Arvilla Twp., with Webster Merrifield, who was later prominent in the affairs of the University of North Dakota in Grand Forks, as pm. The name was suggested by James H. Mathews, owner of the nearby New York Farm, to note his former home in Orange County, NY, which was named for the European royal family of Orange-Nassau, which has both Dutch and English branches. In 1882 it moved one mile north to the home of new pm George Hughes in SE¼ Sec. 3-151-54, and later that year it moved two miles east to a new GNRR townsite, adopting the name ARVILLA. (2, 3, 10, 31, 40, 69, 414)

**ORISKA** (Barnes). Founded in 1872 as FOURTH SIDING on the NPRR mainline, and named CARLTON in 1879, confusion with Casselton led to a renaming in 1881 as ORISKA. The post office adopted the new name September 19, 1881 during the term of pm John M. Dennett (1837-1920), who was the main developer of this city. The name is thought to have been taken from the Indian princess heroine of the poet Mrs. Lydia H. Sigourney (1791-1865). Others believe the name is coined from the Oriskaney period of geology, while *The Valley City Times-Record* of June 21, 1936 says it was named for an Indian woman who remained faithful to her white husband after he abandoned her for a woman of his own race. ORISKA is located in Secs. 18 & 19-140-56, Oriska Twp., just west of the original townsite. It incorporated as a village in 1912, and became a city in 1967. The elevation is 1291, the Zip Code is 58063, and a peak population of 217 was reached in 1940. (1, 2, 34, 40, 76, 79, 281)

**ORKNEY** (Pierce). This was a rural mail distribution point in NW¼ Sec. 21-158-70, Wolford Twp., operated by Grace G. Smith, who later married the area's first settler, O. B. Berkness. Mail was brought here from Grasslake. Some sources say this was an official post office, but government records do not confirm this claim. The name came from the islands off the northern coast of Scotland, originally called the Orcades. Many pioneers of this area had come from Canada, and claimed to have ancestry in these islands. In 1905 the GNRR built a line through the site, and a townsite called WOLFORD was established August 8, 1905. (2, 5, 18, 40, 114)

**ORMISTON** (Morton). This was a farm post office established June 6, 1904 with James Ormiston pm, who came to NY in 1882 from his native Scotland before settling here. It was located in E½ Sec. 25-137-85, eighteen miles south of New Salem, and closed June 15, 1905 with mail to New Salem. (2, 17, 40, 107)

**ORR** (Grand Forks). This GNRR station was built in 1882 in SE¼ Sec. 2-153-55, Agnes Twp., four miles south of Inkster. The post office was established February 10, 1885 with John C. Orr pm, a bachelor from IL who homesteaded on what became the townsite. A small village began, reporting a population of 75 in 1890, and reaching a peak population of 150 in 1920. By 1960 the count had declined to just 65, and the post office, Zip Code 58268, closed November 15, 1972 with mail to Inkster. (2, 25, 31, 40, 69, 79)

**ORRIN** (Pierce). This Soo Line RR townsite was founded in 1912 in Sec. 10-153-74, Elling Twp., between Drake and Balta, and named for Orrin Pierce, a traveling salesman and later a grocer in Minot. The new townsite absorbed much of the rural community of Kandel, founded about 1898 by Germans from Russia. The post office was established November 26, 1913 with Ferdinand Senger pm. The elevator closed in 1965, and the school and last store closed in 1972. The post office, Zip Code 58359, continues to operate although the 1984 population was just 35. (2, 23, 40, 114)

**OSAGO** (Nelson). This was a farm post office established January 10, 1890 with Rolf C. Brekken pm. It was located in SW¼ Sec. 13-150-60, Osago Twp., three miles NE of Pekin, and named for its township, whose name is thought to be a corruption or erroneous spelling of Osage, a Sioux tribe originally from the MO area, which through a series of treaties was relocated to OK. The tribal name is derived from their chosen name *Wazhazhe*, the meaning of which is unknown. The post office closed March 3, 1896 with mail to Bue. It reopened July 2, 1901, but closed for good on June 10, 1902 when the order was rescinded. It is widely believed that the reestablished post office never went into actual operation. (2, 3, 10, 40, 124, 240)

**OSCAR** (McLean). This was a rural post office established February 16, 1903 with Gilbert O. Gilbertson pm, who named it for his father, pioneer homesteader Oscar G. Gilbertson. Oscar is a Celtic name meaning leaping warrior. It was located in SW¼ Sec. 10-150-86, Blue Hill Twp., seven miles south of Ryder. A country store was added to the post office in 1904, and the Blue Hill School was built here in 1909. The post office closed May 15, 1909 with mail to Ryder, but the school operated until 1953. OSCAR has been found on maps as late as 1948, and the original post office building still exists. Opear is an erroneous spelling. (1, 2, 3, 18, 19, 28, 40, 277, 389)

**OSGOOD** (Cass). This farm post office between Fargo and Horace was established in 1895 as GARFIELD. On April 29, 1899 pm Christian C. Furnberg changed the name to OSGOOD to honor George S. Osgood, a pioneer who settled here in 1878 and farmed 4,000 acres. Osgood is a Teutonic name meaning divine creator. In 1900 a NPRR station was built, and a village of 30 people was reported in 1920, although the post office had closed July 15, 1911 with mail to Fargo. The station was removed in 1951, and the store, now at the Bonanzaville museum in West Fargo, closed in 1953, leaving the site vacant. (2, 18, 19, 34, 40, 77, 79)

**OSHKOSH** (Wells). This was a farm post office established October 30, 1888 with Albert Lane as the first and only pm. It was located at his home in NE 1/4 Sec. 30-148-70, Oshkosh Twp., two miles south of Fessenden, and named by Welsh settlers from Oshkosh, WI, which was named for Chief Oshkosh (1759-1858), a leader of the Menominee tribe. Frank H. Beans and R. T. Roberts were the area's first settlers, and Robert Griffith served as mail carrier, bringing the mail only on Saturday via a Star Route from Sykeston. The post office closed February 12, 1894 with mail to the new townsite of Fessenden. (2, 3, 10, 18, 25, 40, 54, 79, 364)

**OSNABROCK** (Cavalier). This GNRR townsite was founded in 1882 in NE¼ Sec. 20-160-58, Alma Twp., and named for Osnabrock, Ontario, Canada, which was named for Osnabruck, Germany, a city in Saxony on the Haase River. The post office was established October 25, 1883 with James A. Anderson pm. The elevation is 1625, the Zip Code is 58269, and the village, which incorporated in 1903, reached a peak population of 310 in 1920. (1, 2, 3, 5, 18, 25, 33, 40, 79, 117)

**OSTERDAHL SETTLEMENT** (Cass). Ole Strandvold, a Norwegian who first settled in IA, came to the area north of Fargo in May 1870, and was later responsible for encouraging several of his countrymen in IA to do the same. The settlers were centered in Harwood Twp. (141-49) and Wiser Twp. (142-49). The name of this loosely-knit rural community came from Mr. Strandvold's home in Norway, the Osterdal valley in Hedmark county. From 1873-1899 the area was served by the TRYSIL post office. (2, 3, 40, 77)

**OSTREM** (McIntosh). This was a farm post office established August 8, 1891 with John L. Ostrem pm. It was located in E½ Sec. 8-131-72, Rosenfield Twp., ten miles SW of Wishek, and closed April 15, 1903 with mail to Danzig. (2, 3, 40, 211)

**OSWALD** (Richland). This was a GNRR station built before 1890 in Sec. 20-130-48, DeVillo Twp., six miles west of Fairmount, and served by the post office in that village. A population of 10 was reported in 1920, but the site was abandoned shortly after that date. The origin of the name is unknown, although it is a Teutonic name meaning of god-like power. (2, 3, 19, 25, 147)

**OSWEGO** (Stutsman). This was a NPRR loading station in SW¼ Sec. 36-140-66, Windsor Twp., between Windsor and Eldridge. It was named by settlers from Oswego County, NY, which was named with a corruption of the Iroquois Indian name *osh-we-ge*, meaning the outpouring, which can also be translated as the place where the valley widens. The name was first applied to the mouth of the Oswego River. Little development occurred, and the name is primarily known today as Exit #54 on Interstate 94. (1, 2, 3, 10, 18, 158)

**OTTAWA** (Dickey). This was a name used occasionally for the pioneer settlement of BUSHTOWN, founded in 1883 in Sec. 2-129-60, Port Emma Twp. Later it was known by it most remembered name, PORT EMMA, and the post office here was known as EMMA. The founder of the town, Thomas W. Bush, was from Ontario, Canada, and built a hotel here which he called the Ottawa House for the capital of Canada, which was named for the Algonquin tribe residing there. The name is derived from *adawe*, meaning to trade. A ferry across the James River which operated at this site beginning in 1884 used BUSHTOWN for its name, and the OTTAWA name was virtually forgotten. (2, 3, 10, 154, 264)

**OTTAWA** (Griggs). This was a rural post office established May 7, 1882 with Isaac E. Mills, a county commissioner, as pm. It was first located in Sec. 25-148-59, Pilot Mound Twp., about seven miles NE of Jessie, and named by another county commissioner, N. C. Rukke, for Ottawa, MN, which was named for the Algonquin Indian tribe whose name is a corruption of *adawe*, meaning to trade. In 1884 the post office moved to the home of Mrs. Annie Gunderson in Sec. 24-148-59, and in 1889 it moved to N½ Sec. 31-148-58, Lenora Twp., closing July 30, 1892 with mail to Romness. (2, 10, 13, 25, 40, 65, 284)

**OTTENTON** (Pembina). This was a pioneer townsite promoted by John A. Otten (1844-1934), a Civil War veteran from OH who came here in 1869 as a customs inspector. It was located in SW¼ Sec. 25-164-54, Felson Twp., and was platted in July 1882 by H. S. Donaldson and S. O. McGwin. Reports of a post office are not confirmed by government records, and the town was soon replaced by the GNRR townsite of Neche, one mile to the south. Ottention is a commonly found erroneous spelling. (2, 3, 18, 40, 108, 235)

**OTTER** (Burke). This was a farm post office established June 22, 1903 with Abel M. Gilbert pm. It was located in SW¼ Sec. 19-162-89, Minnesota Twp., four miles north of Bowbells, and named for Otter Tail County, MN, which was named to note the shape of a large lake within its borders. The order was rescinded June 8, 1904 before the post office had gone into actual operation. (2, 3, 40, 100, 415)

**OTTERBERG** (Grant). This was a farm post office established December 16, 1915 with Nettie Otterberg, the daughter of Andrew Otterberg, as pm. It was located in Sec. 34-131-90, seventeen miles south of New Leipzig, and three miles east of the Selma school and post office which had closed in 1913. The OTTERBERG post office closed January 15, 1919 with mail to Pretty Rock. (2, 3, 17, 18, 40, 177)

**OTTER CREEK** (Oliver). This was a rural settlement founded about 1904 in NE¼ Sec. 10-141-86, Bismarck Twp., eight miles SW of Hannover. The post office was established January 18, 1905 with Emanuel Blum pm. It was named for nearby Otter Creek, home to a large population of otters. Its source is a spring in SW Oliver County, and it enters the Knife River near Hazen. A population of 10 was reported in 1920, and 15 residents were listed as late as 1960. Edward Lennick became pm in 1942 and served until the post office closed January 31, 1954 with mail to Hannover, although local residents report that the facility operated unofficially until the fall of 1954. (1, 2, 3, 18, 40, 121)

**OTTER CROSSING** (Burleigh). This was a pre-1872 squatters' settlement at the site of present-day BISMARCK, named for the native animal and the fact that the settlers expected this to be the site of the NPRR crossing of the Missouri River. After the NPRR's arrival, the site was generally known as CARLETON CITY. (2, 3, 343)

**OTTOFY** (Nelson). This was a farm post office established December 31, 1883 with Louis Ottofy pm. It was located in E½ Sec. 7-149-60, Bergen Twp., five miles SW of Pekin. Later it moved to a country store in E½ Sec. 7-149-60, just west of the original site, which was run by new pm John Iverson. A small village began with a population of 25 recorded in 1890. Olaf S. Quam operated a blacksmith shop here for many years. Mrs. Inga Samuelson Steigberg (1872-1958) became the pm in 1903, and closed the post office March 30, 1907 with mail to Deehr. (2, 3, 25, 40, 124, 126, 128)

**OVERHOLT** (Renville). This was a farm post office established October 14, 1896 with Ole Person (1868-1949) pm, who named it for Joe Overholt, the stage driver on the local mail route. It was located in SE¼ Sec. 34-160-85, Grassland Twp., eleven miles SW of Mohall, until 1901 when it moved three miles south to the McLean farm in Callahan Twp. (159-85). The post office closed July 27, 1905 with mail to Grano. (2, 39, 40, 71, 322)

**OVERLY** (Bottineau & Rolette). This Soo Line RR station was founded in 1905 in E½ Sec. 13-160-74, Cecil Twp., at the eastern edge of Bottineau County. Five blocks were platted some years later in SW¼ Sec. 18-160-73, Kohlmeier Twp., Rolette County, making OVERLY a two-county townsite. Some say it was named for Hans Overlie, a pioneer settler, with a corruption of the spelling, while others say it was named by Soo Line RR officials to note the one-day layover by their crews at this site, or for one of their officials. The post office was established August 21, 1905 with Jay O. Smith pm. The Zip Code is 58360, and the village, which incorporated in 1906, reached a peak population of 193 in 1920, but has declined to just 25 in 1980. (1, 2, 18, 33, 34, 40, 79, 101, 153)

**OWEGO** (Ransom). Capt. Lafayette Hadley of Owego, NY began preparations in 1869 for a settlement on the Sheyenne River in Dakota Territory. In 1871 twelve log cabins were built in SW¼ Sec. 11-135-53, Owego Twp., just inside the Ransom County line, making this the first civilian settlement in the county. The post office was established September 1, 1871 with James C. Felch pm, and it closed June 16, 1873 with mail to Fort Abercrombie after Indians burned most of the town. It reopened August 18, 1873, and closed July 6, 1874 with mail again to Fort Abercrombie. It reopened October 19, 1874 with W. F. Baughn pm at the new townsite two miles SW in NE¼ Sec. 16-135-53. A population of 64 was reported in 1871, but the 1890 count was just 14. The post office closed for good April 14, 1906 with mail to Sheldon. Owego is an Iroquois Indian word meaning the place that widens. (2, 3, 10, 25, 40, 85, 201, 204, 206)

**OWENS** (McHenry). This was a rural post office established March 27, 1907 with William A. Bokovy pm. It was located in NE¼ Sec. 24-151-78, Cottonwood Lake Twp., three miles NW of Kief, and named for site owner David T. Owens, although some sources say it was named for W. P. Owens, said to be a promoter of the Kief townsite. The post office closed November 30, 1907 with mail to Drake. (2, 3, 18, 40, 412)

# P

*Page about 1910*

**PACE** (McLean). This was a farm post office established September 23, 1904 with Robert E. Sharp pm. It was located in NW¼ Sec. 28-144-80, Heaton Twp., ten miles ESE of Washburn, and named for area settler James C. Pace. The post office was discontinued February 29, 1908 with mail to Washburn. (2, 3, 18, 28, 40, 389)

**PADDINGTON** (Divide). This was a farm post office established October 1, 1908 with Walter G. Inman pm, replacing the FORTIER post office which had closed the previous day. It was located in NE¼ Sec. 18-160-96, Hayland Twp., seventeen miles SE of Crosby, and one mile north of FORTIER. The name was coined to honor pioneer settler S. A. Paddon. For a time it was thought that this site would become a new GNRR townsite, and a newspaper, *The Willow Lake Wave*, was established as part of this anticipation. The railroad bypassed PADDINGTON to the south, and this area's townsite became Wildrose, a few miles to the SW in Williams County. The post office closed November 30, 1912 with mail to Upland. (2, 3, 18, 34, 40, 50, 53, 73)

**PAGE** (Cass). This GNRR station was founded in 1881 in Sec. 31-143-54, Page Twp., and named by Col. M. B. Morton, a major area landowner, for his brother-in-law, Egbert S. Page of Des Moines, IA. In the early days the site was sometimes called PAGE CITY. The post office was established March 17, 1882 with Frank Longstaff pm. The village incorporated in 1903, and reached a peak population of 482 in 1950. The elevation is 1165, and the Zip Code is 58064. Louis B. Hanna (1861-1948), a U. S. Representative and Governor of ND, was a longtime PAGE merchant and banker. (1, 2, 18, 25, 33, 40, 52, 77, 79, 308)

**PAGE CITY** (Cass). This name was used at times by the GNRR and others as an alternative name for PAGE. By 1900 the shorter name had become almost universally used. (3, 18, 77)

**PAINTED WOODS** (Burleigh). This historic place was settled in 1867 and can claim to be the first settlement in Burleigh County. It was located in N½ Sec. 26-142-81, Painted Woods Twp., about nine miles SW of Wilton, and owes its name to an Indian legend about an intertribal romance that resulted in the ending of a truce designating this area as neutral ground. Slain bodies were placed in the cottonwood trees. The bark of the trees was stripped away, and as the dead trees bleached in the sun, their trunks were used to paint propaganda about threats and victories. The Indian name for the site was *Can-So-Yapi*, meaning they make the wood red. An 1851 fire destroyed the grove of dead trees. The post office was established May 5, 1879 with Sven A. Peterson pm. He served until 1914 when his daughter, Martha Peterson Witmore, assumed the position and served until the facility closed April 30, 1920 with mail to Baldwin. A population of 200 reported in 1890 would seem to be a gross exaggeration. (1, 2, 3, 8, 9, 12, 14, 18, 25, 40)

**PAISLEY** (Burke). This was a grain elevator in NW¼ Sec. 7-163-88, Lakeview Twp., twelve miles NE of Bowbells on the shore of Upper Des Lacs Lake when that lake was used by commercial shippers. It was named for Paisley, Ontario, Canada, which was named for Paisley, Scotland, a manufacturing center seven miles SW of Glasgow. It had been founded by the Romans as Vanduara, and came to be known as Passeleth during medieval times. The post office was established April 3, 1903 with Malcolm Blue pm, and closed July 15, 1907 with mail to Patterson. (2, 5, 18, 40, 67)

**PALDA** (Mountrail). This was a farm post office established September 26, 1902 with Charles Wesley Hyde pm. It was located in SW¼ Sec. 5-154-89, Oakland Twp., about fourteen miles SE of Stanley, and named by local Republican party chairman J. S. Murphy for Leo J. Palda, a well known Minot attorney. It was served by a Star Route from Palermo, and closed November 30, 1906 with mail to Epworth. (2, 40, 72)

**PALERMO** (Mountrail). This GNRR townsite was founded in 1901 in NE¼ Sec. 14-156-90, Palermo Twp. The post office was established February 28, 1902 with John C. Hoff pm, who platted the townsite later that year. Although the town was settled largely by people of Norwegian ancestry, it was named for the capital of Sicily to honor Italians who had worked on the railroad in the area. Some say that Mr. Hoff selected the name from a favorite play, William Shakespeare's *The Merchant of Venice*. The village incorporated in 1908, and reached a peak population of 205 in 1930. The elevation is 2201, and the Zip Code is 58769. (1, 2, 18, 33, 40, 72, 79)

**PAOLI** (Bowman). This was a much-moved rural post office established January 24, 1900 with Mrs. Clark (Bertha) Green pm, and was first located on unsurveyed land about eight miles SW of Bowman. The Greens came from Paoli, WI, which was named for Paoli, IN, which was named for Paoli, PA, which was named for Pasquale de Paoli (1725-1807), a Corsican patriot who led an unsuccessful revolt 1755-1768 against the Genoese. In 1902 the post office moved to the home of Cynthia A. Stark in SE¼ Sec. 13-131-105, twenty-four miles west of Bowman. Mrs. Stark had tried to establish the Cynthia post office here in 1898. In 1904 the post office moved to the Minnie Bankey home in NW¼ Sec. 29-131-103, Hart Twp., six miles east of Bowman. In 1909 it moved six miles SE to the home of Sadie Bankey in SE¼ Sec. 1-130-103, Amor Twp., and in 1913 it moved two miles south to the Mabel Thompson home in SE¼ Sec. 24-130-103. The post office closed November 30, 1914 with mail to Bowman. (1, 2, 3, 5, 10, 18, 40, 70, 120, 414)

**PARADISE** (Grant). This was a farm post office established May 3, 1907 with George W. Wiese pm. It was located in SW¼ Sec. 28-131-87, Schultz Twp., nineteen miles south of Carson, and named for Paradise

Flats, the local name for this region which referred to the settlers evaluation of their surroundings. In 1917 the post office moved two miles east to the home of new pm L. L. Sutliff in Sec. 26-131-87, where mail was received three times weekly from Morristown, SD. The post office closed February 28, 1935 with mail to Watauga, SD. (1, 2, 3, 17, 18, 40, 127, 176, 177)

**PARADISE** (Ward). This Soo Line RR station appeared on maps circa 1895-1905 in Burlington Twp. (155-84), just NW of Burlington, and is believed to have served a small coal mine. The origin of the name is unknown. (3, 414)

**PARIS** (Stutsman). This was a rural post office established April 3, 1903 with Joseph Elmer Wiant pm, who named it for the local school district which had been named by a local French immigrant named Jandell for the capital city of his homeland. That great city was called Lutetia in ancient times, and Julius Caesar wrote that its residents were called the Parisii, a Celtic name meaning boat people. This post office was located in E½ Sec. 34-142-67, Paris Twp., eight miles SE of Woodworth, and closed May 31, 1908 with mail to Clare. (2, 3, 5, 40, 158, 160, 415)

**PARK** (McLean). This was a farm post office established December 14, 1903 with Mrs. John (Hannah) Park as its first and only pm. It was located in SE 1/4 Sec. 25-150-80, Otis Twp., five miles SE of Ruso, and closed January 31, 1910 with mail to Ruso. Park Twp. (145-79) was named for Mr. Park, who came to McLean County in 1892. (2, 18, 28, 40)

**PARK** (Pembina). This was a pioneer Icelandic settlement founded in 1879 in Sec. 2-159-56, Gardar Twp., two miles NE of Gardar. It was named for its scenic view, and when the post office was established in 1883 the name was changed to PARKTOWN. (2, 40, 108)

**PARKHURST** (Nelson). This post office was established December 27, 1881, replacing the old Stump post office. It was located in the home of pm Henry Ashton Fox in NE¼ Sec. 11-151-60, Wamduska Twp., eight miles NNE of Pekin, and three miles NNE of Stump. The origin of the name is unknown. On June 20, 1882 the post office was moved two miles SW to the home of new pm Cicero T. Harris, who renamed it Harrisburgh. (3, 34, 40, 124, 415)

**PARKHURST** (Stutsman). This NPRR station was founded in 1882 in NW¼ Sec. 3-140-64, Midway Twp., five miles NNW of Jamestown, and named ARCTIC. Development was slow, and the post office closed in 1885. It reopened June 21, 1899 with Mary McGinnis pm. The original name had never been popular for obvious reasons, and the post office was renamed PARKHURST for unknown reasons after postal officials had rejected the name McGinnis. Some say it was named for local settler A. G. Parkhurst, while others say it was named for H. W. Parkhurst, a NPRR civil engineer who had been in charge of the construction of the NPRR bridge over the Missouri River at Bismarck. The site again had little development, and the post office closed May 5, 1900 with mail to Jamestown,

although the station appeared on some maps into the 1940's. (1, 2, 3, 25, 40, 79, 158, 414, 416)

**PARKIN** (Morton). This was at first a mail station built in 1880 on the Bismarck-Fort Yates route in Sec. 28-136-80, six miles SW of Huff, and named for the Parkin brothers, Henry Sidney and Walter Stevenson, who came here from Pittsburgh, PA in 1872. Walter Parkin (1856-1914) was the post trader at Fort Yates 1889-1903. A post office was established at PARKIN on January 15, 1902 with John Ellison pm, and it closed May 15, 1914 with mail to Huff. An attempt was made in 1915 to name a new NPRR townsite Parkin, but the name was objected to by government officials, and it was renamed Breien. (1, 2, 3, 17, 18, 40, 79, 107, 343)

**PARKIN** (Morton). This was a NPRR townsite founded in 1915 in NW¼ Sec. 36-134-82, New Hope Twp., and named for Walter Stevenson Parkin (1856-1914), one of the two well known brothers who ranched in the area, and a former post trader at Fort Yates. The name commemorated the recently-closed nearby rural post office, but early in 1916 the name of the townsite was changed to BREIEN. (1, 2, 3, 40, 107, 343)

**PARK RIVER** (Walsh). This was a farm post office established April 28, 1879 with William McKenzie pm. It was located in NE¼ Sec. 1-157-52, Oakwood Twp., six miles ENE of Grafton, and named to note its location on the Park River, which was named by pioneer fur trader Alexander Henry to note the corrals, or parks, that the Assiniboine Indians had built on its banks into which they would herd wild animals, allowing them to be killed at close range. In early 1882 it moved two miles SW to the home of new pm Adelord R. Loranger in NW¼ Sec. 13-157-52, and closed July 11, 1882 with mail to Grafton. (3, 6, 40, 79, 414)

**PARK RIVER** (Walsh). This GNRR townsite was founded in 1884 in Secs. 21 & 28-157-55, Kensington Twp., and named to note its location on the Park River. The post office

was established September 15, 1884 with Charles Hatherly Honey pm. It incorporated as a village later that year, and became a city in 1896 with Hiram A. Libby as mayor. The elevation is 1003, the Zip Code is 58270, and a peak population of 1,858 was reached in 1980. Prominent early residents included Roger Allin, the 4th Governor of ND, Samuel Holland (1859-1937), who manufactured automobiles in PARK RIVER, and Elizabeth Preston Anderson, an author and WCTU activist. Heber L. Edwards (1897-1962), ND Adjutant General 1937-1962, was born here. (1, 2, 3, 18, 25, 33, 40, 75, 79, 356, 414)

**PARK RIVER JUNCTION** (Grand Forks). A GNRR line was built to Park River in 1884, and this station was built at its junction with the mainline in NE¼ Sec. 3-151-55, Larimore Twp., two miles NW of Larimore. When the branch line was extended to Hannah in 1897, this station was renamed HANNAH JUNCTION. (3, 18, 25, 31)

**PARK RIVER POST** (Walsh). This was an early fur trading post built in September 1800 by Alexander Henry of the North West Fur Co., and abandoned May 17, 1801 in favor of a new site downriver near present-day Pembina. It was located in Sec. 36-158-51, Saint Andrew Twp., just above the mouth of the Park River, and just south of the old settlement of Saint Andrew. Early French trappers had called the river the Little Salt because of its salinity, but Mr. Henry renamed it to note the corrals, or parks, built by the Assiniboine Indians for herding wild animals, allowing them to be killed at close range. The post was sometimes called HENRY'S POST. (2, 3, 75)

**PARKTOWN** (Pembina). This was an Icelandic settlement in NW¼ Sec. 2-159-56, Gardar Twp., two miles NE of Gardar. Founded in 1879 as PARK for its scenic view, the post office was established April 17, 1883 as PARKTOWN with Robert Thexton pm. On March 2, 1887 the name was changed to THEXTON. (2, 3, 25, 40, 108)

**PARSHALL** (Mountrail). This Soo Line RR

*Park River about 1940*

townsite was founded in 1914 in Sec. 25-152-90, Parshall Twp., and named for George Parshall, a Hidatsa Indian who had surveyed the townsite and was a mail stage driver in the area. The post office was established February 16, 1914 with Mrs. Gertrude M. Larin pm. The village incorporated in 1915, and it became a city in 1917 with Scott J. Hurst mayor. The Zip Code is 58770, and it reached a peak population of 1,246 in 1970. Paul A. Broste has his world famous rock museum here. On February 15, 1936 PARSHALL recorded a temperature of -60°F, a state record low, and on July 12, 1936, less than five months later, the temperature hit 112°F, a variance that is believed to be a world record. (2, 3, 33, 39, 40, 52, 72, 79, 289)

**PASCAL** (McIntosh). This was a proposed Soo Line RR townsite between Wishek and Ashley during a flurry of activity in 1911. Located in Secs. 7 & 8-131-70, Danzig Twp., most settlers instead went to the revitalized settlement of Danzig, about two miles to the south. A post office did get established here on February 24, 1911 with Robert S. Wilson pm, but it closed September 27, 1912 with mail to Danzig. Pascal is a Hebrew name meaning pass over, referring to the religious festival, but no one knows why it was chosen for this townsite. Some have speculated that it was named for the French religious writer Blaise Pascal (1623-1662). Paschal is an erroneous spelling. (2, 3, 5, 18, 19, 40, 53, 211)

**PASHA** (Towner). This was a Soo Line RR loading station in SW¼ Sec. 35-162-67, Armourdale Twp., six miles SE of Armourdale and three miles SW of Rocklake. C. Borgerding owned the site in 1909. The origin of the name is unknown. It appeared on maps circa 1910-1925, but no development occurred. (1, 2, 18)

**PAST** (Stutsman). This was a farm post office established March 6, 1901 with William H. Past pm. It was located in SW¼ Sec. 8-141-67, Valley Spring Twp., twelve miles NE of Medina, and closed September 30, 1902 with mail to Medina. (2, 3, 40, 158, 415)

**PATTERSON** (Burke). This townsite was founded in 1901 in SW¼ Sec. 26-163-88, Lakeview Twp., fourteen miles NE of Bowbells. Nine blocks were platted, but little development occurred. The post office was established July 2, 1901 with Fred A. Patterson pm, and closed May 15, 1909 with mail to Newport. (1, 2, 3, 18, 34, 40, 53, 67, 375)

**PAUL** (Logan). This rural post office was established June 2, 1884 with James A. Weed pm, and was the first in Logan County. The Weeds came here from Saint Paul, MN, and Col. Wilbur F. Steele of Steele suggested the name as a remembrance of their hometown. The MN capital city was named for the apostle Paul, the missionary from Tarsus who died in 67 A.D. Paul is a Latin name meaning little. Mrs. Augusta Larson Weed replaced her husband as pm in 1885. PAUL was located in SW¼ Sec. 10-135-72, Bryant Twp., and when the city of Napoleon was founded two miles SW in 1886, development shifted to that new Soo Line

RR townsite. PAUL post office closed September 7, 1886 when it relocated to Napoleon. (2, 3, 10, 18, 19, 40, 116)

**PAULSON** (Divide). This was a GNRR siding in SW¼ Sec. 34-163-96, Long Creek Twp., between Crosby and Noonan, and was named for local resident Steen Paulson (1876-1965). The post office was established November 23, 1916 with Eugene Morgan pm. W. L. Peale managed a grain elevator at the site, which claimed a population of 50 in 1920, but the post office closed December 15, 1920 with mail to Kermit. The elevator burned to the ground in 1934, leaving the site virtually vacant. (2, 3, 40, 73)

**PAULSON** (Dunn). Erland Overlie Paulson (1858-1928) came to MN in 1880 from his native Norway. In 1894 he settled in SW¼ Sec. 3-142-93, Myron Twp., about sixteen miles north of Taylor, at one of the few natural crossings of the Knife River. His home became a popular stopping place for food, water, and lodging, and the immediate area was widely known by his surname. Mr. Paulson's descendants continue to live in this area. (2, 3, 34, 223)

**PEAK** (Barnes). This NPRR station was built in 1884 in Sec. 20-140-57, Alta Twp., between Valley City and Oriska. It is located on the summit of Alta Ridge at the east edge of the Sheyenne River valley, so named because its elevation of 1454 is more than 200 feet higher than the 1218 elevation at Valley City. On July 29, 1923 the name was changed to ALTA, although a nearby elevator built in 1915 continues to use the original name. The site still appears on some maps. (2, 3, 34)

**PEARCE** (Grant). This was a rural post office established May 18, 1906 with Asa Levi Pearce pm. It was located in NW¼ Sec. 8-133-83, Freda Twp., one mile east of Freda and eight miles NNW of Shields. In 1910 the post office was moved one mile SW to the home of new pm Herman H. Hanson in NW¼ Sec. 18-133-83. It closed November 11, 1910 when it was replaced by the post office at the new Milwaukee Road RR townsite of Freda. (2, 3, 40, 177, 414, 415)

**PEARL** (Mountrail). This was a ranch post office established July 16, 1906 with Henry E. Schultz pm. It was located in SE¼ Sec. 24-155-93, Debing Twp., six miles SSW of Ross, and named for the Pearl Valley in which it was located. The valley was named for Charles H. Pearl, a meat dealer from Dickinson who had a large sheep ranch in this area. Pearl is a name derived from the Latin name for the gem, so called because many examples are pear shaped. The post office closed January 31, 1908 with mail to Ross. There were persistent rumors that shortages had been found in the postal receipts. (2, 19, 40, 72)

**PEARSON** (Grand Forks). This was a farm post office established April 6, 1880 with William Sheppard pm. It was located in NE¼ Sec. 6-152-50, Falconer Twp., seven miles NNW of Grand Forks, and named for William Pearson, who purchased the quarter section immediately to the west of

Mr. Sheppard's land on the same date, June 8, 1880. Others say it was named for Pearson, WI. The post office closed February 7, 1882 with mail to Grand Forks. Pierson is an erroneous spelling. (2, 3, 25, 31, 40)

**PEEBLER** (Ward). This was a farm post office established July 1, 1902 with John W. Peebler pm. It was located in NE¼ Sec. 26-157-81, Margaret Twp., fifteen miles NE of Minot. On February 3, 1903 it moved one mile SE to the home of new pm William H. Allen in SE¼ Sec. 25-157-81. On November 9, 1903 Mr. Allen moved the post office one mile NE to the new GNRR townsite of Deering in NW¼ Sec. 30-157-80, Deering Twp., McHenry County, adopting the new name. (2, 3, 40, 100, 414, 415)

**PEERLESS** (Mountrail). This was a farm post office established August 27, 1907 with James M. Fortner pm. It was located in Sec. 31-155-89, McAlmond Twp., about seven miles SW of the discontinued Palda post office, which is said to have closed because the pm had become too involved with his store to have time for the post office. The origin of the name is unknown, although it was at the time a popular brand name for automobiles, motor oil, etc. The post office closed May 31, 1910 with mail to Epworth. (2, 3, 18, 40, 72)

**PEHL SPUR** (Dickey). This was a GNRR siding and loading station built in 1905 in SE¼ Sec. 18-129-63, Ellendale Twp., between Ellendale and Forbes. It was at first called EDDVILLE, but was soon renamed PEHL SPUR. Both names honored local landowner Edward Pehl, whose father Andrew Pehl had homesteaded here in 1883. The siding was shown on maps until the 1930's. (2, 3, 154)

**PEKIN** (Nelson). This GNRR station was founded in 1906 in SE¼ Sec. 22-150-60, Osago Twp., and named by settlers from Pekin, IL, which was named for Pekin (Peking), China because it was thought that the site was exactly halfway around the world from China. The post office was established August 13, 1906 with Peter P. Idsvoog pm. The elevation is 1472, the Zip Code is 58361, and the village, which incorporated in 1912, reached a peak population of 229 in 1940, but declined to just 96 in 1980. (2, 3, 18, 33, 40, 52, 79, 124, 128)

**PELICAN** (Burleigh). This was a farm post office established May 9, 1905 with Nels M. Christianson pm. He was also the president of the local school board. It was located in SW¼ Sec. 12-144-77, Schrunk Twp., twelve miles NE of Regan, and named for nearby Pelican Lake, so called because it was a favorite nesting place for pelicans. The post office closed December 31, 1913 with mail to Regan. (2, 8, 12, 18, 40, 63)

**PELTO** (Nelson). This was a farm post office established November 4, 1895 with Charles Laski pm. The name honored John Pelto, originally Peltonen (1884-1982), a native of Finland who came here in 1887 as a child and was a popular young boy in the area. Pelto is Finnish for plowed field. The post office closed June 29, 1907 with mail to Brocket. The Soo Line RR built a station

*Pekin about 1915*

here in 1912 and reused the old name. A small village developed at the site, Secs. 9, 10, 15 & 16-154-59, Enterprise Twp., twelve miles north of Mapes, and the post office reopened November 30, 1923. PELTO declined, and the post office closed May 31, 1957 with mail again to Brocket. The last population report in 1960 showed just 19 residents in town. (2, 18, 39, 40, 79, 124, 128)

**PEMBINA** (Pembina). This historic city is the oldest settlement in ND, founded about 1843 by members of the Selkirk colonies near Winnipeg. Among the well known pioneers here were Norman W. Kittson, a fur trader who established the post office on May 18, 1850, Charles Cavileer, Kittson's assistant and a customs agent, and Joseph Rolette. Mr. Kittson chose the name, which is a corruption of the Chippewa word *anepeminan*, meaning summer berry in reference to the cranberries growing in the area. Several other versions of the derivation exist. PEMBINA was named as county seat in 1867, but lost that honor to Cavalier in 1911. The elevation is 805, the Zip Code is 58271, and the city, which incorporated in 1885, claimed a population of 1,000 in 1890, but has stabilized at about 700 during the twentieth century. The city is located in Sec. 4-163-51, Pembina Twp., near the extreme NE corner of ND. Albert J. Christianson was mayor of PEMBINA 1931-1970, and served in the state legislature 1953-1967. (1, 2, 3, 13, 33, 40, 52, 79, 108)

**PEMBINA HOUSE** (Pembina). This was an alternate name for FORT PAUBIAN, the fur trading post built by Alexander Henry in 1801 in Sec. 4-163-51. It closed in 1823, but later this site just north of the confluence of the Pembina and Red Rivers became the city of Pembina. (2, 3, 108, 365)

**PEMBINA RIVER** (Pembina). An 1890 guide to ND lists this place as being in Pembina County, and served by the Walhalla post office. No other information is availble. (25)

**PEMBROKE** (McKenzie). This was to be a GNRR station built in 1913 in Sec. 35-150-98, Schafer Twp., just south of

Schafer. A local rancher named it for his hometown of Pembroke, ME, which was named for Pembroke, Wales. Pembroke is a Welsh name meaning from the headland. Railroad construction stopped at Watford City, and PEMBROKE failed to develop. (2, 3, 5, 18, 19, 39)

**PENDENNIS** (Benson). This NPRR loading station was built in the early 1900's in SW¼ Sec. 1-152-71, Rich Valley Twp., between Esmond and Hesper. It was named for Arthur Pendennis, the fictional hero of *His Fortunes and Misfortunes* by William Makepeace Thackeray (1811-1863), the British author. No development occurred at the site. (2, 5, 18, 34)

**PENDROY** (McHenry). This was the second post office in McHenry County, established May 23, 1884 with James Martin Pendroy (1834-1899) pm at his home in Sec. 17-154-78, Falsen Twp., three miles north of Verendrye. The Pendroy family came here in 1882 from Guthrie, IA, and many of its members were influential in county affairs. Levi Bootes Pendroy (1861-1954) was once the county treasurer. Following the death of James M. Pendroy, Thomas Donnel became pm, closing the facility October 31, 1903 with mail to Velva. In 1884 a colony of Negroes from Chicago moved here. After the first winter only J. H. Vaughn chose to remain, operating his general store. He died in 1886, having become a most beloved citizen of this community, and was buried with honors in the local cemetery. (2, 3, 25, 34, 40, 79, 94, 412)

**PENEQUA** (Ransom). This was a farm post office established April 21, 1881 with Thomas B. Quaw pm. It was located in Sec. 34-133-57, Alleghany Twp., seven miles SE of Englevale. The origin of the name is unknown, but it would seem to be based on the name of the pm. The post office closed February 4, 1885 with mail to Vivian. Penegrea is an erroneous spelling. (2, 3, 25, 39, 77, 201)

**PENN** (Ramsey). This GNRR townsite was platted in 1882 in NW¼ Sec. 25-155-66,

Coulee Twp., and named LAURENS, apparently for townsite owner Fred Lau. The tracks were built in 1883 and the station was renamed PENN for the English city just NW of London. Development was very slow with the post office not being established until December 21, 1888 with Gustav H. Gessner (1862-1939) as pm, and the GNRR station did not become operational until July 1900. The elevation is 1472, the Zip Code is 58362, and a peak population of 150 was reported in 1920. (1, 2, 18, 33, 40, 79, 103)

**PENNEL STATION** (Billings). This was a station on an overland stage route in the 1870's. It was located in Sec. 10-139-102, five miles south of Medora on the east bank of the Little Missouri River. The name came from the stage driver who is said to have erected a building at this site, which is today a tourist trail ride facility. (2, 3, 34, 81)

**PENNINGTON** (Pembina). This name is shown at a "new settlement" in Sec. 4-161-54, Cavalier Twp., in 1875, the year the first settlers arrived. The name undoubtedly honors John L. Pennington, the NC publisher who served as Governor of Dakota Territory 1874-1878. During the next two years pioneers John Bechtel and George A. Douglas promoted the adjacent townsites of CAVALIER (after Tongue River had been rejected), and DEWEY, which became DOUGLAS POINT. On July 30, 1877 the DOUGLAS POINT post office closed and the site became the city of CAVALIER. (3, 15, 414)

**PENNYHILL** (Rolette). This was a rural post office established November 14, 1900 with Dugald McKellar pm. It was located in Sec. 14-159-73, South Valley Twp., twelve miles WSW of Rolette, and named for the nearby hills which folklore says were named by Father Campeau of Willow City, who remarked, "I don't see how anyone could make a penny in those hills—penny hills, that should be a good name for them." A small village was promoted here, but Beric Cote's blacksmith shop was about the extent of any development. The post office closed December 31, 1904 with mail to Denver. Penny Hills was the commonly used spelling for this place, but the post office was required by the government to use a one-word spelling. (2, 3, 33, 40, 123)

**PERELLA** (Burke). This was a GNRR loading station built in Sec. 32-163-89, North Star Twp., seven miles north of Bowbells. The origin of the name is unknown. It appeared on maps circa 1915-1965. (1, 2, 34, 67)

**PERESEVERS** (Williams). This was an erroneous spelling entered in government postal records as the name of the PERSEVERE post office when it was established May 23, 1912. The incorrect spelling was not used at the site, and the records were later corrected. (40)

**PERLEY** (McLean). This post office was established as DODGEN in 1890 in McLean County. In 1898 it moved into McHenry County, but returned to McLean County in 1900. Emma Perley became pm December 13, 1902 at the home of her husband, Edwin, in SW¼ Sec. 5-150-79, Butte Twp., and on

September 7, 1904 the name was changed to PERLEY. The post office closed December 31, 1907 with mail to Ruso. (2, 3, 28, 40, 414)

**PERRY** (Sargent). This Soo Line RR station was located in Sec. 6-130-54, Shuman Twp., seven miles east of Forman. Theories abound about the origin of the name. Some say it was named for Dickey County attorney Ebenezer P. Perry. Others say it was named for local farmer Perry Johnson. Still other claim it was named for Perry, IL, Perry, MI, or Perry County, MO, all of which were named for Oliver Hazard Perry (1785-1819), the famous naval officer. Perry is an Old English name meaning the pear tree. The post office was established February 1, 1893 with Chresten C. Nundahl pm. A small village began, but a boom never occurred. The post office closed April 15, 1912 with mail to Ransom. (1, 2, 3, 10, 19, 25, 40, 46, 165)

**PERRY** (Walsh). This was a farm post office established April 7, 1880 with John T. Daley pm. It was located in SE¼ Sec. 9-157-54, Fertile Twp., nine miles west of Grafton. Halvor Johnson, who helped secure the post office, named it for his former home of Perry, WI, which was named for Oliver Hazard Perry (1785-1819), the naval hero of the War of 1812. The post office closed April 13, 1883 with mail to Grafton. (2, 40, 70, 75)

**PERSEVERE** (Williams). This was a rural post office established May 23, 1912 with Emma Elton pm. It was located in SW¼ Sec. 28-156-103, Bull Butte Twp., eighteen miles NW of Williston. Emma Erickson, who came here from MN and married John Elton in 1904, named the post office to describe the strong characteristics of self-survival among the pioneers in this area. The post office closed May 31, 1914 with mail to Williston. Postal officials recorded the name of this post office as PERESEVERS, but the spelling was soon corrected and the erroneous name was probably never used at the site. (2, 3, 40, 50, 53)

**PERSIS** (Cass). This NPRR station was built in 1900 in NE¼ Sec. 7-139-52, Everest Twp., four miles SW of Casselton on the Marion branch line. It was named by R. H. Watson, a NPRR official, for his secretary, Miss Edith Persis Howes. Persis is a Greek name meaning woman from Persia, and is found in the Bible as the woman praised by St. Paul for her good works. The station was removed in 1951. (2, 18, 19, 34, 77)

**PERTH** (Grand Forks). This was a rural post office established November 2, 1881 with Alexander Stewart (1832-1921) pm, who was also the first assessor of Lakeville Twp. It was located in NE¼ Sec. 22-153-52, Lakeville Twp., six miles WSW of Manvel, and named by settlers from Perth, Ontario, Canada, which was named for Perthshire, Scotland, which was originally known as St. Johnstown. The Stewart family had emigrated to Canada in 1836, and many of them came here in 1879-1880. The post office closed March 23, 1882 with mail to Manvel. (2, 3, 5, 10, 40, 69, 79, 238)

**PERTH** (Towner). This GNRR station was founded in 1889 in Sec. 5-160-68, Grainfield Twp. The post office was established July 23, 1889 with Robert J. Laird pm, who also owned the townsite and named it for his former hometown of Perth, Ontario, Canada. The elevation is 1736, the Zip Code is 58363, and the village, which incorporated in 1905, reached a peak population of 221 in 1910, with a steady decline to just 20 in 1980. The post office became a rural branch of Bisbee on May 31, 1973. (1, 2, 10, 18, 25, 33, 40, 52)

**PETERS** (Kidder). This was a farm post office established March 8, 1886 with Richard C. Peters pm. It was located in SW¼ Sec. 12-140-73, Allen Twp., eight miles NE of Steele, and closed May 25, 1887 with mail to Steele. (2, 3, 25, 40, 414)

**PETERS** (Logan). This Soo Line RR loading station was built in 1912 in Sec. 11-134-72, Starkey Twp., at the site of the 1887 speculative townsite of LOWRY, midway between Napoleon and Burnstad. The new station was named for Hans Peters, who came here from IA in 1909 and sold land to the railroad for this siding. Mr. Peters moved to MN in 1936. The Peters Elevator was built in 1914, and a population of 20 was reported in 1920. The old elevator was moved into Napoleon in 1952, and it was destroyed by fire in 1977. (2, 39, 53, 116, 335)

**PETERSBERG** (Nelson). This GNRR station was founded in 1882 in NW¼ Sec. 6-152-57, Petersburg Twp. Levi H. Peterson and M. N. Johnson founded the townsite, and Mr. Peterson won a coin flip with Mr. Johnson for the rights to name the town, chosing an Anglicized version of the name of his birthplace of Petersborg, Telemark, Norway. The post office was established March 6, 1883 with Mr. Peterson as pm, and on December 18, 1884 the name was changed to PETERSBURG. (2, 3, 18, 40, 124, 126, 128)

**PETERSBURG** (Nelson). The GNRR townsite of PETERSBERG was founded in 1882 in NW¼ Sec. 6-152-57, Petersburg Twp. On December 18, 1884 pm Levi H. Peterson changed the name to PETERSBURG, supposedly because virtually everyone was spelling the name in this manner. The elevation is 1526, the Zip Code is 58272, and the village, which incorporated in 1906, reached a peak population of 367 in 1920. (1, 2, 18, 25, 33, 40, 52, 79, 124, 126, 128)

**PETERSEN** (Cass). This was a rural post office established June 28, 1890 with Edward A. Pfettscher pm. It was located in NW¼ Sec. 20-138-54, Eldred Twp., two miles ESE of Alice, and named for Sonnick Petersen, who came here in 1877 from Denmark and is considered to be the first settler in Alice. Some sources say it was named for Charles A. Peterson, a settler in Howes Twp. Early references mention a Petersen post office just west of present-day Alice, which probably is in reference to the mail drop known as Wadeson. On June 15, 1901 the PETERSEN post office and the Wadeson mail drop were closed, being replaced by the post office at the new NPRR townsite of Alice. Peterson is an erroneous spelling. (2, 3, 18, 40, 77, 310)

**PETREL** (Adams). This Milwaukee Road RR townsite was founded in 1908 in S ½ Sec. 35-129-93, Gilstrap Twp., nine miles ESE of Haynes, and just inside the ND border. It was named for the stormy petrel, a long-winged pigeon common to the area. On October 29, 1908 pm Louis A. Sattler moved his THEBES post office into this townsite, adopting the new name. The post office closed September 30, 1939 with mail to Lemmon, SD, although there were 65 people reported here as late as 1960. Petral is an erroneous spelling. (2, 18, 34, 40, 79)

**PETREL** (Bowman). This Milwaukee Road RR station was established in 1907 when a boxcar depot was positioned along the tracks in NW¼ Sec. 26-132-104, Rhame Twp., just west of the present townsite of RHAME. The post office was established February 8, 1908 with Allen G. Elliott pm, and named for the long-winged pigeon common to the area. On June 5, 1908 the name was changed to RHAME. (2, 3, 40, 120, 389)

**PETTIBONE** (Kidder). This NPRR station was founded in 1910 in NW¼ Sec. 14-142-70, Pettibone Twp., and named by Lee C. Pettibone (1863-1936) for himself. Mr. Pettibone was a Dawson businessman and NPRR official who was repsonsible for most townsite names on both the Pingree-Wilton and Mandan-Killdeer branch lines. The post office was established September 1, 1910 with John H. Gambs pm, replacing the rural post offices of Gerber and Roundlake. The elevation is 1856, the Zip Code is 58475, and a peak population of 260 was reached in 1920, with a decline to 127 in 1980. (1, 2, 18, 33, 40, 61, 79, 122, 314, 315)

**PETTIS** (Renville). This post office was established June 22, 1903 with Charles H. Pettis pm, but the order was rescinded February 16, 1904. It was located in SW¼ Sec. 23-163-84, Eden Valley Twp., five miles SE of Sherwood on Cut Bank Creek. (2, 3, 40, 442)

**PETTIT** (Pembina). A new NPRR townsite was founded in 1888 in SE¼ Sec. 11-160-51, Lincoln Twp., and was known as NINTH SIDING until being christened PETTIT for unknown reasons. Volney S. Waldo was well into the process of securing a post office when the nearby BOWESMOUNT facility closed. He opted to reuse this name, with a slight change in the spelling, and on May 7, 1888 the new BOWESMONT post office opened at this site. (3, 18, 40, 414)

**PHILLIPS SETTLEMENT** (Stutsman). The first settlers in the area came in 1879, but the rural community here took its name from the brothers Ward R. and Willis A. Phillips, who filed in the NW¼ and SW 1/4, respectively, of Sec. 28-141-65, Hidden Twp., twelve miles NNW of Eldridge on October 12, 1880. (2, 3, 18, 158, 415)

**PHOENIX** (Burleigh). This was a farm post office established September 15, 1903 with George F. Spang pm. It was located in NW¼ Sec. 32-144-75, Hazel Grove Twp., seven miles NNE of Wing, and named for the adjacent township to the south, which was named for the legendary bird of mythology who lived five hundred years, burned itself to ashes on a pyre, and rose from those ashes to live again. Thomas P. Wilkinson, Thomas Wedmore, and David Spang served as pms as the facility moved about in the immediate area before closing May 15, 1912 with mail to Stark. (2, 3, 4, 8, 12, 18, 40, 63)

**PICKARDSVILLE** (Sheridan). This NPRR station was founded in 1916 in NW¼ Sec. 14 & NE¼ Sec. 15-146-78, Pickard Twp., seven miles west of McClusky. It was named for William Henry Pickard (1845-1936), a pioneer settler in SW¼ Sec. 12-146-78, two miles to the NE, who came here in 1903 and was said to be the only Civil War veteran to settle in Sheridan County. He served under Gen. William T. Sherman on the famous march to the sea, and came here from Winside, NE, which was also the hometown of William H. McClusky. The post office was established January 10, 1917 with James C. Murphy pm, who was a storekeeper and the brother-in-law of Mr. Pickard. The townsite name was misspelled from the start as PICKARDVILLE, so on July 6, 1917 the pm officially changed the spelling to match what was apparently the public's preference. (1, 2, 3, 18, 21, 30, 40)

**PICKARDVILLE** (Sheridan). This NPRR station was founded in 1916 in NW¼ Sec. 14 & NE¼ Sec. 15-146-78, Pickard Twp., and named PICKARDSVILLE for William H. Pickard, a Civil War veteran from NE. The post office was established January 10, 1917 with James C. Murphy pm, but the name was so frequently misspelled as PICKARDVILLE that Mr. Murphy changed the spelling on July 6, 1917 to match what apparently was the public's preference. The site never experienced any major development, and the post office closed June 30, 1957 with mail to McClusky. Curiously, the peak population of 23 was reported in 1960. (1, 2, 3, 18, 21, 30, 40)

**PICK CITY** (Mercer). This was one of the few Garrison Dam boom towns to even be considered on the west side of the Missouri River. It was founded in 1947 in W½ Sec. 36-147-85, one mile west of the dam, and named for General Lewis A. Pick, Chief of the Corps of Engineers, United States Army, and the author of the Pick-Sloan plan for Missouri River development. It reported a population of 294 in 1950 at the height of construction on the dam, then went into a period of decline. In recent years it has become a center for recreational activities on Lake Sakakawea, and reported a population of 182 in 1980. It has never had a post office. (2, 3, 18, 34, 39, 40, 52)

**PICKERT** (Steele). This rural post office in Sec. 7-146-56, Easton Twp., two miles south of Finley, was established in 1882 as GRAIN, but when James A. Pickert became pm on June 22, 1883 he changed the name to PICKERT. This site was part of the Pickert Bonanza Farm, and also doubled as a hotel on the Caledonia-Carrington stage route. On March 18, 1896 the name was changed to EASTON, and the following year the post office was moved into the new GNRR townsite of Finley. The PICKERT name was reborn later that year as the name of a GNRR siding two miles SE of the original site, which developed into a small village. (2, 3, 18, 40, 77, 79, 99, 240, 326)

**PICKERT** (Steele). This GNRR siding, often called PICKERT SIDING, was built in 1896 in SW¼ Sec. 21-146-56, Easton Twp., five miles SSE of Finley, and two miles SE of the rural post office of Easton, which had been called Pickert until March 18, 1896. A new PICKERT post office was established November 23, 1896 with Rozel F. Pickert pm, and closed April 30, 1900 with mail to Sherbrooke. Settlement began here in 1908, and the post office was reestablished October 27, 1908 with A. J. Hornecker (1883-1952) pm. He retired on June 30, 1951, and the post office closed as well with mail to Finley. The population never exceeded 30, but a few people continue to live in PICKERT, and the place still appears on some maps. (2, 3, 18, 25, 40, 79, 99, 326)

**PICKERT SIDING** (Steele). This GNRR siding was built in 1896 in SW¼ Sec. 21-146-56, Easton Twp., and named for the Pickert family, whose 5,760-acre farm was served by this facility. A post office named simply PICKERT operated here 1896-1900 with Rozel F. Pickert pm, and the name had previously been used by a nearby rural post office 1883-1896. Settlement began in 1908, and the village of PICKERT developed at PICKERT SIDING. (2, 99, 326)

**PICTON** (Towner). This was a farm post office established October 15, 1887 with Richard Cowan pm. It was located in SW¼ Sec. 20-163-68, Picton Twp., six miles SW of Hansboro, and named by pioneer settler Eben Young for his hometown of Picton, Nova Scotia, Canada, which was named for Sir Thomas Picton (1758-1815), an English general who was killed at the Battle of Waterloo. Some say it was named for Picton, Ontario, Canada, which was named for the same man. The post office was discontinued April 15, 1912 with mail to Rolla. Piston is an erroneous spelling. (2, 3, 5, 18, 25, 40, 240)

**PIERCE** (Burleigh). This was a NPRR siding in N½ Sec. 7-138-79, Apple Creek Twp., four miles east of Bismarck. It was named for either Gilbert A. Pierce, a Governor of Dakota Territory, Gerald Pierce, an area pioneer, or Pierce Blewett, a railroad official. Pierce is an Anglo-French variant of Peter, a Greek name meaning rock. Members of the Barrett family have owned the site for many decades. The siding appeared on maps circa 1905-1920. (1, 2, 8, 14, 18, 19)

**PIERCE** (Slope). This was a rural post office established October 25, 1911 with Henry H. Prain pm. It was located in SE¼ Sec. 2-133-99, Woodberry Twp., fifteen miles SE of Amidon, and served the community known as RENO. The post office name honored the brothers Charles (1890-1965), Michael T. (1880-1965), Frank, and Jack Pierce, and their sister Mary Pierce, all of whom homesteaded in the area. Their father had come to America in 1870 from Ireland. The townsite, which used both names interchangeably, was owned by John Curley and reported a population of 20 in 1920. Forrest V. Pafford was appointed pm in 1912, and Godfrew Nelson assumed the post in 1916, closing the facility October 31, 1922 with mail to Amidon. Mr. Nelson ran a store in conjunction with the post office, and he and subsequent owners George Waller and Thomas Stafford operated the store until 1943. The Pierce Congregational Church,

built in 1965, perpetuates the name. (1, 2, 3, 40, 53, 82, 381)

**PIERSON** (Adams). This was a farm post office established January 29, 1909 with James Arthur Pierson (1880-1951) pm. It was located in SW¼ Sec. 20-132-96, Cedar Twp., twelve miles NNE of Bucyrus on Chanta Peta Creek. In 1914 it moved three miles south to NE¼ Sec. 5-131-96, Argonne Twp., the home of new pm Arvilla M. Dennis. The post office closed November 30, 1914 with mail to Bucyrus. (2, 3, 18, 34, 40, 53, 189, 414)

**PIERSON** (Dickey). This was a farm post office established January 29, 1898 with Angelina Pierson pm. It was located in NW¼ Sec. 19-130-64, Albion Twp., about ten miles SW of Monango on the land homesteaded by her husband, James R. Pierson, in 1883. The post office closed November 15, 1902 with mail to Monango. It reopened March 28, 1903, but closed for good May 14, 1904 with mail again to Monango. (2, 40, 154, 264)

**PIGEON POINT** (Ransom). This was a stage station in Sec. 19-135-53, Owego Twp., on the overland trail near the pioneer village of Owego on the south bank of the Sheyenne River in the NE corner of the county. It was established in 1867 by David Faribault, a French-Chippewa halfbreed who came here with his wife, an Arickaree. It was sometimes called FARIBAULT, and closed in 1872. (2, 85, 201, 204, 206)

**PILLSBURY** (Barnes). This GNRR station was founded in July 1910 in NE¼ Sec. 17-143-56, Ellsbury Twp., on the Surrey cutoff line, and named by townsite owner C. O. Smith for Alfred F. Pillsbury, an official of the famous milling firm of that name in Minneapolis, MN. The post office was established December 14, 1911 with Lemuel B. Smith pm. The elevation is 1281, the Zip Code is 58065, and the village, which incorporated in 1921, reached a peak population of 260 in 1930, but has declined sharply to a low of just 46 in 1980. Fred Keyes operated a general store here for 63 years. (1, 2, 33, 34, 40, 76, 79)

**PILOT** (Grand Forks). This was a pioneer settlement in SW¼ Sec. 29-153-55, Agnes Twp., seven miles NE of Niagara. It was named by settlers from Pilot Grove Twp., Faribault County, MN, which was named in 1864 for a grove of native timber that was used by pioneers as a navigational landmark before roads were built. A post office was established December 23, 1880 with James Christensen pm, serving the nearby stage stop known as Bachelor's Grove. It closed May 31, 1881 with mail to Hegton. It also operated June 20, 1881 to January 12, 1882 with mail to Hegton,

April 13, 1882 to December 3, 1884 with mail to Larimore, and January 1, 1899 to June 30, 1939 when it closed for good with mail to McCanna. (1, 2, 13, 25, 40, 69)

**PINE** (Slope). This was a farm post office established September 4, 1908 with Elias Kostenbader pm. It was located in Sec. 20-133-98, Cedar Creek Twp., eighteen miles SE of Amidon, and named to note the scrub pines growing in the area. On October 19, 1911 it moved two miles south to the home of new pm Jens Rise (1874-1966), whose house in SW¼ Sec. 32-133-98 was the first frame house built in the county. On March 30, 1914 it moved one mile NE to the home of Carl Gustofson in NE¼ Sec. 32-133-98, and closed June 15, 1915 with mail to Scranton. The Kostenbader's sod house is now just a pile of dirt, the Rise house is still standing, but is vacant and delapidated, and the Gustofson house has been moved to the nearby F. R. Schaar farm where is it used as a shed. (1, 2, 3, 40, 82)

**PINGREE** (Stutsman). This NPRR station was founded in 1881 in NW¼ Sec. 34-143-65, Pingree Twp., and named for Hazen Senter Pingree (1842-1901), a pioneer potato farmer in this area who returned to MI and served as that state's Governor 1897-1900, and was mayor of Detroit 1900-1901. Others say it was named for David Pingree, probably a relative, who came here in 1881 from Salem, MA. The post office was established October 26, 1882 with Daniel A. Piercy pm. It incorporated as a village in 1917, and became a city in 1968 with Paul Messner mayor. It had a brief flurry of activity in 1911 when it became the railhead of the NPRR's new Pingree-Wilton branch line that was promoted and developed by local resident Edward Swearingen (1868-1950). The elevation is 1547, the Zip Code is 58476, and a peak population of 286 was reached in 1920. (1, 2, 5, 18, 25, 33, 40, 52, 79, 158, 160)

**PINKHAM** (Cass). This GNRR siding was built in 1912 and named REED. It was located in SE¼ Sec. 19-140-49, Reed Twp., six miles NW of Fargo on the Surrey cutoff line. On October 1, 1930 the name was changed to PINKHAM, honoring N. B. Pinkham, a homesteader in this area who served in the first state legislature. The station was removed in 1964, although it remained on some maps into the 1970's. (2, 34, 52, 77)

**PINTO** (Oliver). This was a farm post office established July 6, 1907 with Tillman P. Arnoldy pm at his home in NW¼ Sec. 34-143-85, Pleasant Valley Twp., four miles north of Hannover. The name Albers is crossed out on the post office application, with PINTO written in. Folklore says that two postal officials were at the T. H. Albers home trying to select a name for this post office when a spotted horse came up to a water tank. They asked what kind of horse it was, and upon hearing that it was a pinto, decided that that should be the name of this post office. Pinto is a Spanish-American word meaning spotted. In 1909 the post office moved one mile east to the John Kirby farm where Ellen Kirby was pm. It closed August 31, 1913 with mail to Hannover. (2, 3, 4, 18, 33, 40, 53, 79, 121, 414)

**PIPESTEM** (Stutsman). This place is shown on an 1882 county map in Sec. 7-143-66, Pipestem Valley Twp., ten miles WNW of Pingree or one mile north of the old Vashti townsite. It is thought that it was a paper townsite planned in anticipation of NPRR expansion NW from Jamestown. It owed its name to the Pipestem Creek, which was named to note its use by Indians as a source of stone for making pipes, although some sources say it was named by cartographers to describe the shape of its path from Wells County to Jamestown, where it flows into the James River. (3, 158, 414)

**PISEK** (Walsh). This GNRR station was founded in 1882 in NE¼ Sec. 28-156-55, Rushford Twp., but most of the later development occurred just across the section line in SE¼ Sec. 21-156-55. It was named by Bohemian settlers for their hometown, which bears a Bohemian name meaning sand. The post office was established June 8, 1887 with Joseph Lovcik pm, who platted the townsite in 1890. The elevation is 1006, the Zip Code is 58273, and a peak population of 312 was reaported in 1910. The village incorporated in 1898 with Frank Paul Rumreich (1847-1909) as president of the village board, and it became a city in 1968. St. John's Nepomucene Catholic Church features a large painting by the famous Czech artist, Alfons Mucha (1860-1939). (1, 2, 3, 18, 25, 33, 40, 75, 79, 254)

**PITCAIRN** (Richland). This was a GNRR station in SE¼ Sec. 9-134-49, Abercrombie Twp., midway between Galchutt and Colfax. Abercrombie banker A. K. Tweto and Christ Twedt organized the Pitcairn Wheel Elevator here in 1900, and the facility was used to market wheat for over fifty years. Erick Thoe operated a store at the site for a number of years. The name is said to honor John Pitcairn (1740-1775), a British soldier of the Revolutionary War who was killed at Bunker Hill, although it seems more likely that the name might have been borrowed from the remote island in the Pacific Ocean made famous for its role in the mutiny of the *H. M. S. Bounty*. The site was shown on maps into the 1970's. (2, 3, 5, 18, 147)

**PITTS** (Ward). This was a farm post office established April 4, 1908 with William A. Pitts pm. It was located in SE¼ Sec. 7-153-84, Torning Twp., fifteen miles SW of Minot, and closed January 31, 1914 with mail to Grelland. (2, 3, 18, 40, 100, 374)

**PITTSBURG** (Pembina). This was a farm post office founded in 1880 as PITTSBURGH, and moved to the NPRR townsite in Sec. 35-160-51, Lincoln Twp., in 1887. On February 9, 1892 pm James S. Douglas changed the spelling to PITTSBURG to comply with new government spelling regulations for geographic names. The post office closed June 15, 1910 with mail to Drayton, and the last population figure was a report of just 2 in 1930. The station was removed in 1957, leaving the site virtually vacant. (1, 2, 3, 18, 40, 108)

**PITTSBURGH** (Pembina). This was a farm post office established February 9, 1880 with Margaret A. Biggerstaff pm. It was located in NW¼ Sec. 12-159-51, Drayton Twp., on

the Red River four miles north of Drayton. In 1887 it was relocated two miles NW to Sec. 35-160-51, Lincoln Twp., the site of a new NPRR townsite. Development was very slow with a peak population of just 15 being reported in 1890. On February 9, 1892 the name was changed to PITTSBURG to comply with new government spelling regulations for geographic names. The origin of the name is unknown, but most sources speculate that it was named for the great industrial city of PA, which was named for William Pitt, 1st Earl of Chatham (1708-1778), the great English statesman. (2, 3, 10, 25, 40, 108)

**PLANO** (Barnes). This was a farm post office established February 12, 1896 with George A. Williams pm. It was located in Sec. 30-138-61, Meadow Lake Twp., twelve miles NW of Litchville, and named with a Spanish word meaning flat land, descriptive of the location. The post office closed December 31, 1904 with mail to Marion. (2, 10, 18, 34, 40, 76)

**PLANO** (Walsh). This NPRR townsite was founded in 1887 in SE¼ Sec. 28-156-53, Walsh Centre Twp., and named with a Spanish word meaning flat land, descriptive of the location. This name was rejected by postal officials who feared confusion with Plana, a post office 1887-1927 near Aberdeen, in what is now SD. On November 23, 1888 the post office was established as VOSS. (3, 40, 75)

**PLAZA** (Mountrail). This Soo Line townsite was officially founded July 20, 1906 as the terminus of a branch line from Max. It was located in SW¼ Sec. 35-153-88, Spring Coulee Twp., with additions in NE¼ Sec. 5-152-88, Plaza Twp., and was named to note the central plaza within the business district. The post office was established September 8, 1906 with Vern L. Shaw pm. The village incorporated in 1910, and it became a city in 1951 with Roy Sandstrom mayor. The Soo Line RR extended its line to Sanish in 1914, starting at Prairie Junction SE of town, creating the appearance that PLAZA was located on a spur of the railroad. The Zip Code is 58771, and a peak population of 408 was reached in 1930. Walter J. Maddock (1880-1951), Governor of ND 1928-1929, was a resident of PLAZA. (1, 2, 3, 18, 33, 40, 72, 79, 290, 291)

**PLEASANT** (Renville). This was a rural community located in SW¼ Sec. 15-163-87, Stafford Twp., thirteen miles NNW of Tolley. The first mail service was provided from Elmore, Saskatchewan, Canada in an example of international cooperation. The post office was established May 5, 1898 with James Harkness pm, who gave it a name he felt was descriptive of the site. In 1903 it moved two miles SE to the Hans O. Johnson home in NE¼ Sec. 26-163-87. A small village, complete with a saloon and a blacksmith shop, began to develop, and a population of 10 was reported in 1920, but the post office closed April 15, 1921 with mail to Tolley. (1, 2, 3, 18, 40, 71)

**PLEASANT LAKE** (Benson). This GNRR station was founded in 1886 in SW¼ Sec. 4-156-71, Pleasant Lake Twp., just north of

*Plaza about 1910*

Pleasant Lake, which had been named by GNRR President James J. Hill. Local Indians had called it Broken Bone Lake due to their use of the site for slaughtering buffalo. The post office was established June 11, 1887 with Calvin B. Holbrook pm. The elevation is 1608, and a peak population of 100 was claimed in 1920, although in recent years the town has been less than half that size. The post office, Zip Code 58364, closed September 30, 1984. (1, 2, 3, 18, 25, 33, 34, 40, 237)

**PLEASANT VALLEY SIDING** (Stark). This site was reached in 1871 during a preliminary NPRR survey, and when the railroad reached here in 1880 it was named PLEASANT VALLEY SIDING to describe the area. It was located in SW¼ Sec. 3-139-96, and by early 1881 had a population of about 50. Emil F. Messersmith, an NPRR employee, was the first permanent settler. When the post office was established October 6, 1881, the name was changed to DICKINSON. (2, 3, 18, 25, 406)

**PLEASANTVIEW** (Foster). This rural post office was established June 21, 1898 with William H. Grasser pm. It was located in SE¼ Sec. 12-145-62, Eastman Twp., about six miles SE of Glenfield, and named to note the view from the hilltop home of the pm. On March 11, 1904 the post office was moved two miles NE, which put it into Griggs County, where it was discontinued in 1906. (2, 40, 97)

**PLEASANTVIEW** (Griggs). This was a rural post office established in 1898 in Foster County. On March 11, 1904 it was moved two miles NE to NW¼ Sec. 6-145-61, Mabel Twp., Griggs County, two miles WNW of Sutton, the home of new pm William Watson. The post office closed July 21, 1906 with mail to Courtenay. Many maps of the period spell the name as two words. (2, 18, 40, 65, 97)

**PLUMER** (Divide). This was a rural community in NW¼ Sec. 16-161-98, Plumer Twp., eleven miles SW of Crosby. A post office was established December 28, 1906

with Thomas Plumer Schell pm. An early county atlas lists this person as James Plumer Schell. Others say it was named for Gus Plumer, a wagon maker who worked with local railroad crews. The Schell family operated a general store here, and a population of 10 was reported in 1920, but the Schells moved to Ambrose in 1922, and the post office closed January 15, 1923 with mail to Crosby. Mr. Schell died in 1951. (1, 2, 3, 18, 40, 73, 79)

**PLYMOUTH** (Ransom). This site, Sec. 11-135-57, Springer Twp., eight miles NW of Lisbon, was originally a town called FOREST CITY which failed along with the railroad which had given it its birth. A townsite did develop here a few years later, but it was called WISNER. When the post office was established November 15, 1880 with Abraham Russell pm, it was called PLYMOUTH. This name ultimately traces to the city in England, known as Tamarworth and Sutton before 1438, which is famous as the departure point of the Pilgrims in 1620. It is said that the promoter of the townsite, J. E. Wisner, was somehow connected to the English city. The settlement reported a population of 50 in 1890, but declined after that, and the post office closed May 31, 1905 with mail to Lisbon. (2, 3, 5, 10, 13, 18, 25, 40, 77, 201, 202, 204)

**POINT MICHAEL** (Pembina). This was a fur trading post built in 1859 in SE 1/4 Sec. 30-164-53, Felson Twp., just north of present-day Neche. It was on a crossroads of the Pembina-Walhalla trail, and was operated by Charles Grant. It is sometimes called Grant's House or Grant's Place in historical accounts. The origin of POINT MICHAEL is unknown. The site was abandoned in 1878 as the fur trade declined, and the building burned in 1880. (1, 3, 235)

**POINT PLEASANT** (Burleigh). This was another of the unofficial names for the settlement forming at the terminus of the NPRR mainline at the Missouri River, which soon became BISMARCK. The name is descriptive, and somewhat unrealistic for what must have been a rather bleak, uncivilized location in 1871-1872. (2, 3)

**POKERVILLE** (Traill). This was a highly unofficial, but frequently used name for the south part of early MAYVILLE located in NW¼ Sec. 5-146-52, Mayville Twp. The Grandin family, who had owned the northern part of the townsite, did not like saloons and related facilities on their land, so all such enterprises were located in the southern part of town. Locals coined this name for that area, based on the name of the popular card game played in the saloons. (3, 395)

**POLAND** (Walsh). This was a Soo Line RR station built in 1903 in SE¼ Sec. 32-155-51, Walshville Twp., six miles east of Ardoch. It was named by settlers from Poland, with the name being suggested by area pioneers Frank Nice and Joseph Michalski. The country takes its name from the Polani, an ancient tribe living in that area of eastern Europe. The post office was established January 13, 1906 with Andrew Hobbs pm in his general store, and it closed April 30, 1919 with mail to Ardoch. The only population figure reported was a count of 1 in 1940. (1, 2, 5, 18, 40, 75)

**POLAR** (Cavalier). This was a rural post office established May 31, 1898 with Charles Billings pm. It was located in Sec. 14-159-60, Nekoma Twp., and named for Polar, WI, which was named for Hiram B. Polar, an Indian trader and prospector who came to northern WI in 1861 and lived among the Indians for many years. In 1905 the post office was relocated to the new Soo Line RR townsite of NEKOMA in S½ Sec. 22-159-60, and it assumed this name on March 2, 1906. The original site, one mile to the NE, is the location of the Safeguard ABM and Missile Site Radar (MSR) military installation, the only ones of their type in the nation. (2, 3, 18, 40, 53, 70, 217, 247)

**POLEGE** (Williams). This was a farm post office established February 9, 1904 with Emil Polege pm. It was located in NE¼ Sec. 9-157-97, Champion Twp., seven miles NNW of Ray. In 1905 Ole A. Hill (1849-1941) became pm and the post office moved to his home in SW¼ Sec. 28-158-97, New Home Twp., three miles north of the original site. It closed August 14, 1909 with mail to Angie. Polega is an erroneous spelling. (2, 3, 40, 50, 415)

**PONDEROSA** (Sioux). This is a settlement created in the 1960's just west of Fort Yates in Secs. 11 & 14-130-80. Fort Yates Community College is located here. The name was taken from the ficticious ranch home of the Cartwright family on the NBC television show *Bonanza*, which was very popular at the time. PONDEROSA is Spanish for heavy. (3, 34, 127)

**PORCUPINE** (Sioux). This is an old Indian settlement in Secs. 29, 30, 31 & 32-132-83, on the east bank of the Cannonball River opposite Selfridge. It dates from about 1895, and was named for nearby Porcupine Creek. Some say the creek was named for a Sioux chief, while others say it notes the large population of porcupines in the area. The name of the animal, a large rodent noted for its stiff, sharp bristles, is a corruption of the Middle English *porkepin*, which is derived from the latin *porcus*, meaning pig, and *spina*, meaning spine. (3, 4, 127, 434)

**PORTAL** (Burke). This Soo Line RR division point was founded in 1893 in Secs. 30 & 31-164-92, Soo Twp., and Secs. 25 & 36-164-92, Portal Twp. It has long been a major port of entry into Canada, hence the name which was coined by Soo Line RR officials. The post office was established October 16, 1893 with Horace G. Prairie pm. It was platted in 1899, incorporated as a village in 1905, and became a city in 1914. It actually straddles the international boundary, with the northern portion of the town being the city of North Portal, Saskatchewan. The elevation is 1954, the Zip Code is 58772, and a peak population of 567 was recorded in 1913, with a decline to 228 in 1980. (1, 2, 18, 40, 67)

**PORT EMMA** (Dickey). Founded in 1883 in NE¼ Sec. 2-129-60, Port Emma Twp., and known as BUSHTOWN and OTTAWA, the name PORT EMMA came into general usage about 1884. It was coined by founder Thomas W. Bush to note its being a port on the James River, actually a ferry across the river, and to honor his new bride, the former Emma Williams, the first woman homesteader in the area. When the railroad built on the opposite side of the river, this historic pioneer town was doomed, and many of its residents moved to the new railroad townsite of Ludden. A post office named EMMA operated here 1883-1887. (2, 3, 18, 40, 154, 264)

**PORT EMMA** (Dickey). This GNRR station was built in the early 1900's in SW 1/4 Sec. 35-130-60, Hudson Twp., and named for the ghost town of Port Emma one mile to the south. It was served by the Ludden post office, and was found on maps into the 1960's. Some early maps call it Port Emma Station. (2, 3, 18, 25, 154, 264)

**PORTERVILLE** (LaMoure). This site was established as early as 1880 by the brothers Charles and Arthur Porter. They built a loading station for the newly arrived NPRR in 1886, but the name was changed to ADRIAN before any real development began. PORTERVILLE was in NW¼ Sec. 13-136-63, Adrian Twp., now the site of the local stockyards. (3, 138)

**PORTLAND** (Traill). This townsite was founded in the early 1880's by the GNRR as a rival to the NPRR townsite of Mayville two miles to the east. It is located in Secs. 35 & 36-147-53, Viking Twp., and Sec. 2-146-53, Roseville Twp. The post office was established January 19, 1882 with Dr. James D. McKenzie pm, and the following year the town incorporated as a village. In 1885 the first insurance company in Dakota Territory was chartered here. The elevation is 970, the Zip Code is 58274, and a peak population of 641 was recorded in 1950. The name is said to note the fact that railroad officials thought it was midway between Portland, ME and Portland, OR, both of which were named for Portland, Dorsetshire, England. (1, 2, 10, 18, 25, 29, 33, 40, 52, 79, 187)

**PORTLAND JUNCTION** (Traill). This is the name of the junction of GNRR lines through Portland and Mayville in SE¼ Sec. 11-147-53, Viking Twp., about four miles north of Portland. A townsite was platted, and an elevator and potato warehouse were built, but little development took place beyond that. The ENGER post office operated here 1910-1912. (2, 18, 29, 40, 187)

**PORTLAND PEMBINA CEMENT COMPANY** (Cavalier). Thomas D. Campbell and Daniel F. Bell of Grand Forks established the Northern Dakota RR in 1908 to connect the cement mines in this area with the GNRR at Edinburg, twenty-one miles to the south. This site, Secs. 25 & 26-161-57, South Olga Twp., was the terminus of the line, and was one mile SW of the townsite of Concrete. Portland cement was first made in Aspdin, England in 1824, and was named to note the similarity in color to the oolitic limestone found on the nearby island of Portland. Introduced into the United States in 1880, it swept the engineering and architectural fields by storm. This ND site, however, proved to be economically unfeasible, and the venture was closed in 1922. (5, 18, 39, 75, 117)

**PORTNER** (Kidder). This was a rural post office established November 22, 1916 with Mrs. Byron W. (Isabella) Dexter pm. The site, NE¼ Sec. 4-137-72, Bunker Twp., eleven miles south of Dawson, was previously a mail drop known as DEXTER. The name of the post office honored Sherman B. Portner, who came from PA in 1884 and homesteaded in SE¼ Sec. 2-137-73, South Manning Twp., three miles west of the post office, which closed June 30, 1919 with mail to Dawson. (1, 2, 3, 18, 40, 414)

**POSTVILLE** (Burke). This was a farm post office established May 4, 1900 with William Henry Post (1847-1934) as pm. It was located in SE¼ Sec. 25-163-91, Soo Twp. On May 31, 1901 it moved one mile SE to the new Soo Line RR townsite of Flaxton, adopting this name with Mr. Post continuing as the pm. (2, 40, 67)

**POSTVILLE** (Sargent). This was a pioneer settlement, the first in the county, founded in 1879 in SE¼ Sec. 11-131-53, Herman Twp., on the east bank of the Wild Rice River seven miles north of Geneseo. It was named for Ezra D. Post, the county's first white settler, who began an unofficial post office here in 1880, which he called HERMAN. In 1881 the post office was officially established with the name HAMLIN. (2, 39, 40)

**POTSDAM** (Dickey). This Milwaukee Road RR townsite was founded in 1886 in NE¼ Sec. 11-132-64, Potsdam Twp., between Monango and Edgeley, and named for its township, which was named by local German settlers for Potsdam, Germany, a city sixteen miles SW of Berlin noted for its many beautiful parks and the royal palace. A six-block townsite was platted on the east side of the tracks, but little development occurred. In 1917 the name was changed to POTTS because of anti-German sentiments during World War I. (1, 2, 3, 12, 13, 18, 154)

**POTTS** (Dickey). This Milwaukee Road RR townsite was founded in 1886 as POTSDAM, and was located in NE¼ Sec. 11-132-64, Potsdam Twp., between Monango and Edgeley. In 1917 the name was changed to POTTS because of anti-German sentiments during World War I. Little development occurred here, and it disappeared from maps about 1950. (2, 3, 18, 154)

**POWELL** (Grand Forks). This was a GNRR siding and loading station built in 1907 in NW¼ Sec. 8-151-51, Brenna Twp., five miles west of Grand Forks. An elevator was built here in 1916, but it was destroyed by fire in 1945. A population of 10 was reported in 1920. James E. Earl (1887-1959) was the longtime elevator manager. The name honors Arthur D. Powell, a GNRR brakeman killed in an accident at Shawnee in 1906, although some claim the name simply notes several Powell families living in the area. Powell is a Celtic name meaning descendant of Howel, who was an ancient Welsh king whose name meant alert. (2, 18, 19, 31, 69)

**POWER** (Richland). This was a rural community in NW¼ Sec. 33-136-52, Helendale Twp., on the north shore of the Sheyenne River about thirteen miles west of Walcott. The post office was established May 1, 1886 with William A. Power pm, although the office was technically named for his brother, James B. Power, a prominent NPRR and GNRR official, land owner, and the second President of ND Agricultural College in Fargo. A country store operated here for years, and a population of 25 was reported in 1890, but no major development occurred, and the post office closed June 15, 1915 with mail to Leonard. (1, 2, 18, 25, 40, 79, 147, 243)

**POWERS LAKE** (Burke). This townsite was founded in 1906 in SW¼ Sec. 29-159-92, Garness Twp., and named for John Joseph Powers, a pioneer area rancher who came here in the 1890's, and for the lake on whose shores it was located. On April 2, 1906 Ole H. Garnes moved his nearby Garnes post office to the townsite, and continued to serve as pm using the new name. In 1909 the town was moved two miles WNW to Sec. 25-159-93, Colville Twp., the site of a new GNRR station on the Stanley-Grenora branch line. The village incorporated in 1910, and it became a city in 1935 with A. E. Anderson as mayor. The elevation is 2205, the Zip Code is 58773, and a peak population of 633 was reached in 1960. It calls itself the "Queen City of the Northwest." (1, 2, 3, 18, 33, 34, 40, 52, 67, 79, 376)

**PRAHA** (Walsh). This was a rural community in Sec. 16-155-57, Cleveland Twp., about six miles SSW of Lankin. The post office was established May 7, 1883 with William Ruzicka pm. Most of the settlers were from Bohemia, and they named their community for the capital of their homeland, Prague, as it is spelled in their native tongue. The post office closed May 31, 1907 with mail to Medford. (1, 2, 3, 25, 40, 75)

**PRAIRIE** (Stutsman). This was a rural post office established February 17, 1900 with Mary C. Chadduck pm. It was located in Sec. 2-141-66, Deer Lake Twp., and was given a name descriptive of its location. It closed August 14, 1909 with mail to Deer Lake. (2, 12, 39, 40, 53, 158)

**PRAIRIE JUNCTION** (Mountrail). This site, Secs. 11 & 14-152-88, Plaza Twp., about three miles SE of Plaza, notes the point on the Max-Plaza line of the Soo Line RR from which it was extended to Sanish in 1914, giving the impression that the original terminus of Plaza is located at the end of a short spur. The name is descriptive, and no settlement ever occurred here. (1, 2, 3, 12, 39, 72)

**PRAIRIE ROSE** (Cass). This was one of the new cities of the 1970's, incorporated April 3, 1979 primarily to avoid annexation by larger cities, in this case Fargo. PRAIRIE ROSE, named for the state flower, is in NW¼ Sec. 35-139-49, Barnes Twp., just south of Fargo on the east side of Interstate 29, and south of 40th Avenue South. It began as Lean's Estates Subdivision, an outlying residential development on land owned by Earle J. and Evelyn Lean. This city's principal distinction is that the vote for incorporation took place on the very day that Governor Arthur A. Link signed a bill raising the minimum population required for incorporation as a city from 50 to 150. PRAIRIE ROSE at the time had a population of 64, resulting in a flurry of legal opinions from the Attorney General's office. (3, 34)

**PRAIRIE VALLEY** (McKenzie). Since about 1953 the rural community in Wilbur Twp. (153-101), fifteen miles north of Alexander, has been known by this descriptive name, although many still use the original name of ROSSELAND. (2, 3)

**PRATT** (McHenry). This was a rural post office established October 1, 1900 with William H. Pratt pm. The township was also named for him when it organized in 1902. It was located in SW¼ Sec. 28-159-80, Pratt Twp., about thirteen miles west of Upham, and closed April 30, 1907 with mail to Eckman. (2, 3, 18, 40, 75, 186)

**PRATTFORD** (Pembina). This was a rural post office established May 27, 1887 with Alexander Pratt pm. The "ford" noted the home of Mr. Pratt in Sec. 24-161-52, Carlisle Twp., about seven miles SE of Hamilton, which was at a crossing point of a long slough. William H. Willis (1846-1930) was the second pm, and he was succeeded by Robert Menzies who closed the facility March 31, 1910 with mail to Hamilton. Prattsford is an erroneous spelling. (2, 3, 18, 25, 33, 40, 108, 146)

**PRESTON** (Ransom). This was a rural post office established June 14, 1895 with Charles J. O. Jacobson pm in his country store. It was located in SE¼ Sec. 20-136-57, Preston Twp., four miles NNE of Fort Ransom and just east of the old post office of Mullen, and named for its township, which was named by settlers from Preston, MN, which was named by town founder John Kaercher for Luther Preston, one of his employees who became the first pm. Some sources say it was named for Col. John Preston, the Treasurer of VA. Preston is an Old English name meaning from the domain of the church. The post office closed December 15, 1905 with mail to Fort Ransom. (2, 10, 13, 19, 40, 201)

**PRESTON** (Traill). This was a GNRR loading station in Sec. 12-144-52, Greenfield Twp., about three miles south of Blanchard. The name came from Brown Bros. & Preston, the realtors who owned the site. A projected village here never developed. The only population report was a count of just 2 in 1930. (2, 18, 29, 77)

**PRETTY ROCK** (Grant). This was a rural community founded in 1906 fifteen miles south of Elgin. The post office was established May 13, 1907 with John T. Whitehead pm. His wife, Margaret, acutally performed the duties, and named the post office for Pretty Rock Butte in Secs. 27, 28, 33 & 34-131-89, Pretty Rock Twp. The post office was first located in NW¼ Sec. 8-131-89, and in 1908 moved one mile SW to NE¼ Sec. 18-131-89, the home of Robert C. Breckinridge. In 1917 it moved two miles north to the home of Fae C. Parr in SE¼ Sec. 6-131-89. In 1918 it returned to the Breckinridge home with Mrs. Jennie L. Breckinridge as pm. In 1920 it returned to the Parr home, with Della Parr as pm. Finally, in 1934 it moved to the Bertha Churchill home in SW¼ Sec. 8-131-89, just south of the original site, and closed August 31, 1940 with mail to Lemmon, SD. The community once had a town hall, a school, and even a newspaper, *The Pretty Rock Sentinel*, published by Fred Schoenrigel in 1909, but after being bypassed by the NPRR development came to a virtual halt. (1, 2, 3, 17, 18, 40, 111, 176, 177, 358, 414)

**PRICE** (Oliver). This NPRR station was founded in 1911 in SE¼ Sec. 28-142-81, Manley Twp., and named by NPRR surveyors for William Price (1867-1952), from whom they had acquired the right-of-way. Mr. Price was appointed pm when the post office was established March 9, 1915. The townsite was platted in 1917 by A. D. Gaines, but after reaching a peak population of 50 in 1920, it declined to a virtual ghost town. The post office closed July 7, 1961 with mail to Hensler. (1, 2, 3, 39, 40, 79, 121)

**PRIMROSE** (Steele). Gilbert K. Jordet settled in Sec. 7-146-54, Primrose Twp., about twelve miles ESE of Finley, in 1885. A post office was established here on November 4, 1895 with Mr. Jordet as pm, who named the office for its township which had been named by settlers from Primrose, Dane County, WI, which was named in 1848 by Mrs. R. Speers for the song *On Primrose Hill*. Primrose is derived from the Latin for first rose. The post office closed April 18, 1899 with mail to Sherbrooke. (2, 19, 40, 70, 99)

**PROHIBITION CITY** (Morton). The small settlement of Moltke in Stark County was destroyed by fire in 1883, and later that year Hebron was founded nearby. In between, this rather bizarre townsite was promoted by a Rev. Bradley, who had several blocks platted in SW¼ Sec. 32-140-90, Custer Twp., one mile SW of Hebron. He chose the name, claiming it would attract some of his female parishioners as well as temperance advocates from the east. Little interest was shown, and Rev. Bradley moved on without paying his surveyor for his services. (3, 428)

**PROSPER** (Cass). This was a GNRR townsite platted in 1911 in N½ Sec. 8-140-50, Raymond Twp., about six miles NNE of Mapleton. A post office was established February 26, 1913 with Henry L. Hanson pm. GNRR officials or local settlers were responsible for the name which notes the prosperous farms in the area. The elevation is 904, and a population of about 50 has been here during most of its existance. Albert H. Waa became pm in 1927 and served until the post office closed April 5, 1968 with mail to Harwood. (1, 2, 33, 34, 40, 77, 79)

**PROSPERITY** (Renville). This was a rural community that served as a mail drop for local residents, although no official post office ever existed here. Albert A. Taylor supplied this service at his home in SE¼ Sec. 12-163-86, Prosperity Twp., about six miles west of Sherwood. The name was borrowed from its township, which had been named by pioneer settler Sam Fuller to note the crops, which were the best he had ever seen. The mail service ended about 1902. (1, 3, 40, 71)

**PULASKI** (Walsh). This was a rural community in SW¼ Sec. 30 & NW¼ Sec. 31-156-51, Pulaski Twp., named for its township, which was named for Count Casimir Pulaski (1748-1779), the Polish military genius who was a hero of the American Revolution. It was located just east of WARSAW, and is now considered to be a part of that community. (3, 5, 75)

**PURCELL** (Slope). This was a farm post office established March 12, 1908 with George F. Purcell pm. It was located in SW¼ Sec. 32-135-100, White Lake Twp., three miles SE of Amidon. Mr. Purcell operated a grocery store in conjunction with the post office, which closed December 31, 1914 with mail to Amidon. (1, 2, 3, 40, 53, 82)

**PURDON** (Mountrail). This was a GNRR station in White Earth Twp. (157-94), between Tioga and White Earth. The origin of the name is unknown, and it appears only on maps circa 1910-1925. (1, 2, 3, 18, 39, 377)

**PURSIAN** (Kidder). This was a rural post office established March 13, 1905 with John Barta (1881-1961) pm. It was located in SE¼ Sec. 24-137-74, Baker Twp., about thirteen miles SSW of Steele, and closed March 31, 1913 with mail to Kintyre. The name was taken from nearby Pursian Lake which was a popular resort for area residents for many years. The lake was named for Frank Pursian, a carpenter who had settled in Steele in 1883, although some insist that it was named for Gen. John J. Pershing, the hero of World War I, with a corruption of the spelling. (2, 3, 18, 40, 113, 116, 122)

# Q

QUAY (Rolette). This was a farm post office established April 21, 1890 with Ole W. Martin pm. It was located in NE¼ Sec. 7-160-71, Leonard Twp., three miles NW of Rolette, and closed April 29, 1892 with mail to Rolla. The origin of the name is unknown, although it has been suggested that it was named for Mathew Stanley Quay (1833-1904), a U. S. Senator from PA at the time. (2, 3)

QUESTAD (Renville). This was a farm post office established December 30, 1901 with Ingwald M. Questad pm at his home in SE¼ Sec. 30-158-84, Muskego Twp., nine miles NE of Carpio. Martin A. Pederson had a country store at the site for a number of years, and A. B. Crow operated a butcher shop. The post office closed May 31, 1909 with mail to Carpio. Questadt is an erroneous spelling. (2, 3, 40, 71, 322)

*Quincy postmark of 1880 with erroneous county designation*

QUINCY (Traill). This village developed at the site of the ELM RIVER STATION and post office in the center of Sec. 26-144-49, Elm River Twp., in the extreme SE corner of the county. The post office changed its name from ELM RIVER to QUINCY on February 16, 1880 with George H. F. Johnson pm, and it is apparent from the postmark used at this time that there was some confusion as to which county it was in. The new name came from Quincy, IL, which was named for President John Quincy Adams (1767-1848). Quincy is an Old French/Latin name meaning from the place owned by the fifth son. At first the village thrived, having an estimated population of 200 in 1883, but when it was bypassed by the GNRR it began to decline, reporting a population of just 30 in 1890. The post office closed July 15, 1896 with mail to Hendrum, MN. The hotel was torn down in 1920, the church was moved away in 1949, and only a cemetery marks this historic site today. (2, 3, 10, 18, 19, 25, 29, 40, 79, 187, 240)

QUINION (Billings). This rural post office was established February 25, 1910 with Lydia B. Townsend pm. Her suggested name of O-Y Ranch was rejected by postal officials, who then accepted the name QUINION, honoring H. Chris Quinion, a native of VT who came here in 1885 and started the Q-Bar Ranch on Magpie Creek north of Fryburg. It was located in SE ¼ Sec. 13-144-100, twenty-nine miles NNE of Medora near the McKenzie County line until 1911 when it moved one mile west to SE ¼ Sec. 14-144-100, the home of new pm Florence M. Mason. Elizora M. Desmouth became the pm in 1916, holding this position until 1918 when the post office moved one mile NE to SW ¼ Sec. 12-144-100, the home of new pm Frank O. Pierce. It closed July 14, 1923 with mail to Fairfield. (1, 2, 40, 53, 81, 414)

# R

**RAFTEREE** (Golden Valley). This was a farm post office established May 9, 1905 with Alden Mosher pm. It was located in NW¼ Sec. 34-143-104, Pearl Twp., seventeen miles north of Sentinel Butte, and is thought to have been named for Jim Raftery, a pioneer rancher in Sec. 8-141-105, who came here from WI. The post office closed May 31, 1908 with mail to Sentinel Butte. Rafletree is an erroneous spelling. (2, 3, 18, 40, 80)

**RAGGED BUTTES** (McKenzie). This was a transient workers camp at the Bird Head Cattle Co. in Sec. 5-150-101, Alex Twp., named for the nearby Ragged Buttes, so named because of their profile against the horizon. The townsite of Alexander was founded at this site in 1905. (3, 229, 230)

**RAGUS** (Pembina). This place appears in recent commercial guides of ND. No other information is available. (3)

**RAINY BUTTE** (Slope). A post office and grocery store were opened March 9, 1907 in a dug-out sod house in SE¼ Sec. 32-135-99, Moord Twp., about eleven miles SSE of Amidon. Burton Scott Covell (1864-1922) was the pm, and he named the facility for the nearby buttes, which had been named by drivers on the Dickinson-Belle Fourche stage line to note the slow-drying gumbo roads in the area. The post office closed December 15, 1914 with mail to Pierce. It reopened June 15, 1915 in the home of pm Robert B. Ware in NW¼ Sec. 2-134-99, Hume Twp., six miles east of the original site. A small village began, but the only population reported was a count of 10 in 1920. The post office closed for good April 30, 1932 with mail to New England. (1, 2, 18, 40, 53, 82)

**RALEIGH** (Grant). This Milwaukee Road RR townsite was founded in 1910 in SE¼ Sec. 1 & NE¼ Sec. 12-133-85, Raleigh Twp., and supposedly named for Sir Walter Raleigh (1552-1618), the English adventurer. Raleigh is an Old English name meaning from the deer meadow. The post office opened October 1, 1910 when Dogtooth pm Charles C. Leonard moved his store to the new townsite. A wave of Germans from Russia, who had originally settled near Strasburg in Emmons County, moved here, and a population of 200 was reported in 1920. The elevation is 2038, and the Zip Code is 58564. The post office became a rural branch of Flasher on December 3, 1965. (1, 2, 3, 17, 19, 33, 40, 79, 176, 177)

**RALSTON** (Ward). This was a GNRR station in Sec. 16-155-84, Burlington Twp., eight miles WNW of Minot. The Old English name meaning from Ralph's estate has no known local significance. It appears on maps circa 1910-1925. Ralstad is an erroneous spelling. (1, 2, 3, 18, 19, 100, 377)

**RAMONA** (Stutsman). This NPRR station was founded in 1914 in Sec. 5-142-67, Paris Twp., six miles east of Woodworth. Six blocks were platted by the State Center Land Co., and an official of that firm named it for his daughter. Ramona is a Teutonic name meaning wise protectress. The name was popularized by Helen Hunt Jackson's 1884 novel of that name. When the post office was established November 5, 1915, the name was changed to GOLDWIN. (2, 19, 40, 158)

**RAMSEY** (Ramsey). This was a Soo Line RR station built in 1913 in Sec. 13-154-66, Pelican Twp., about four miles south of Penn. A post office was established January 31, 1914 with Thor G. Nestegard pm, and closed July 15, 1924 with mail to Devils Lake. A population of 10 was reported in 1920. It was named for its county, which was named by settlers from Ramsey County, MN, which was named for Alexander Ramsey (1815-1903), the Governor of MN during the Civil War, and later a U. S. Senator and Secretary of War. Ramsey is a Teutonic name meaning from Ram's island, Ram being a name meaning strong. (2, 13, 19, 39, 40, 103)

**RAMSEY** (Ramsey). This place appears on a 1930 roadmap published by the General Drafting Company. It is about seven miles SE of Starkweather, and is a copyright town. (3)

**RAND** (Dunn). This was a farm post office established May 17, 1892 with George E. Rand pm. It was located in SW¼ Sec. 2-143-96, two miles west of Manning, and closed January 25, 1896 with mail to Dickinson. (2, 3, 40, 414)

**RANGELEY** (McHenry). This was a GNRR townsite founded in 1912 on the Surrey cutoff line, and probably named for Rangeley, ME, which was named for Squire Rangeley of Yorkshire, England, who owned the site when it was founded in 1825. It was located in W½ Sec. 30-153-76, Lake George Twp., seven miles SE of Karlsruhe. RANGELEY had a depot, a store run by the Myhre family, and an elevator, which was closed in 1960 and torn down in 1965, but no post office. It reported populations of 10 in 1920, and 8 in both 1930 and 1940. Rangely is an erroneous spelling. (1, 2, 3, 18, 34, 78, 412)

**RANGER** (Slope). This was a rural post office established January 29, 1912 with Margaret Miller pm. It was located at the home of Ralph Sheriff in SE¼ Sec. 30-136-102, Ranger Twp., eleven miles NW of Amidon, and named for a nearby ranger station in the Dakota National Forest, created November 24, 1908 by proclamation of President Theodore Roosevelt. The post office was housed in a converted sheep wagon, and served about ten patrons. In 1916 it moved two miles NE to the home of Bert Sargent in W½ Sec. 22-136-102, and later moved to SE¼ Sec. 18-136-102. Bess Lebo, later Mrs. Bruce Austin, was the last pm, closing RANGER on September 15, 1942 with mail to Amidon. (1, 2, 3, 33, 40, 79, 82)

**RANKIN** (Kidder). This was a NPRR siding in Secs. 13, 14 & 23-139-74, Pleasant Hill Twp., three miles west of Steele. It was named for Dr. J. A. Rankin, a surgeon at Carrington and later at Jamestown, who was associated with the NPRR. No settlement occurred at the site. (2, 18, 97, 122)

**RANSOM** (Sargent). This townsite was founded in 1882 in SE¼ Sec. 1-130-54, Rutland Twp., two miles north of Cayuga, and named for Fort Ransom, which was named for Gen. Thomas E. G. Ransom (1834-1864). The post office was established June 29, 1882 with David G. Cobb pm, and closed June 21, 1887 with mail to Kandiotta. It reopened August 12, 1887, and closed December 15, 1894 with mail to Cayuga. It opened for the third time on April 3, 1895, and closed for good April 30, 1915 with mail again to Cayuga. The townsite had a reported population of 100 in 1890, but most of its settlers moved to nearby Cayuga to be nearer to the railroad. It was sometimes called Ransom City to differentiate it from Ransom County. By the 1940's RANSOM had become a ghost town. (2, 3, 5, 6, 10, 18, 25, 34, 40, 165)

**RAUB** (McLean). This place was founded as a rural post office October 2, 1912 with Miss Nellie Alice Taylor (1878-1951) pm. It was located on the Jacob Raub farm in NW¼ Sec. 23-149-89, Loquemont Twp., about three miles south of the present townsite. In 1915 it was moved to Sec. 8-149-89, the site of a country store run by A. P. Blonde. The next year it moved to Sec. 19-149-89, a new townsite promoted by the new pm, Timothy C. Veum. Jacob Raub (1875-1948), the namesake of the townsite and post office, had come here from Raub, IN, which had been named for A. D. Raub, his grandfather, in 1872. A population of 150 was claimed in 1920, but a 1978 count showed just 5 residents of RAUB. The post office, Zip Code 58774, closed October 15, 1979 with mail to Roseglen, although government records did not record this fact until November 12, 1985. (2, 3, 28, 33, 40, 41, 79, 95, 289)

**RAWLINGS** (Burleigh). This was a rural post office established June 27, 1898 with Edward Rawlings pm. It was located in SW¼ Sec. 6-141-79, Crofte Twp., about two miles north of Baldwin. August Olston became the pm in 1900 in NW¼ Sec. 18-141-79, and closed November 16, 1901 after the establishment of Baldwin on the Soo Line RR. (2, 3, 8, 14, 18, 40, 414)

**RAWSON** (McKenzie). This GNRR station was founded in 1910 in SW¼ Sec. 7-150-100, Arnegard Twp., between Alexander and Arnegard. It was named for Willis C. Rawson, a hardware and implement dealer from Williston, who owned the townsite. The post office was established March 21, 1914 with Henry E. Baumann pm. The elevation is 2257, and the post office, Zip Code 58848, closed December 30, 1972 with mail to Alexander. (1, 2, 3, 40, 52, 79)

**RAY** (Williams). This GNRR townsite was founded in 1901 in SW¼ Sec. 9-156-97, Equality Twp., and named for Ray Payton, a pioneer settler, or for William Ray, a GNRR official and friend of James J. Hill. Ray is an Old French name meaning kingly. The post office was established March 18, 1902 with Glen R. Byrkett pm. RAY incorporated as a city in 1914 with Dr. Walter Byron Scott (1873-1943), a pioneer physician, as mayor. The elevation is 2270, the Zip Code is 58849, and a peak population of 1,049 was reached in 1960 as the city experienced growth during the 1950's oil boom in the Williston Basin. (1, 2, 3, 18, 19, 25, 33, 40, 50, 52, 79)

**RAYMOND** (Cass). This name surfaced in the 1960's as Exit #84 on Interstate 94, four miles east of Mapleton at the corner of Secs. 4, 5, 8 & 9-139-50, Mapleton Twp. The exit provides highway access to the residents of Raymond Twp. (140-50), just to the north. The township was named for a pioneer settler named Raymond, who later was involved in law enforcement. (3, 18, 77)

**RAYMOND** (Oliver). This townsite was platted in SW¼ Sec. 19-143-81, Sanger Twp., on the west bank of the Missouri River two miles NNW of the original site of Sanger. When Oliver County organized in 1885 RAYMOND became the county seat, although Sanger was at the time much more developed, including such luxuries as a post office. Because there already was a Raymond in Clark County in what is now SD, the county seat required a name change to secure its own post office. Lewisburg and Clarksville, obviously selected to honor Lewis & Clark of expedition fame, were rejected, and on May 18, 1885 RAYMOND became SANGER. However, this change was found to be illegal, and the name reverted back to RAYMOND. Meanwhile, very little settlement was taking place here, and on May 20, 1888 the county seat was moved to Sanger, and RAYMOND became a ghost town. The name honored Tom Raymond, a buffalo hunter who settled here in the 1870's. (2, 3, 40, 121)

**RECTOR** (Nelson). This was a GNRR loading station built in 1902 in SW¼ Sec. 22-154-60, Clara Twp., about eight miles north of Lakota. A depot and stockyards were built here, but a planned townsite never materialized. Robert J. Gardiner (1867-1941) was the original owner of the site. The origin of the name is unknown. (2, 124)

**RED SPRING** (Mercer). This place appeared on an 1882 map of Dakota Territory in NW¼ Sec. 31-146-84, on the west bank of the Missouri River approximately midway between Mannhaven and Stanton. No other information is available. (3, 414)

**REE** (Mercer). This rural community was founded in 1908 in NW¼ Sec. 4-146-88, fourteen miles north of Zap on the south bank of the Missouri River. It was at first called STOELTINGTON, but on August 27,

1909 pm Henry G. Klindworth changed the name to REE, a local nickname for the Arikara tribe who had a village near this site. It declined after being bypassed by the railroad, reporting a 1920 population of just 40. The post office closed October 15, 1929 with mail to Beulah. In the 1930's the Beaver Creek Store in SW¼ Sec. 5-146-88, one mile SW of the original site, listed its location as REE, but the entire area is now inundated by Lake Sakakawea. (1, 2, 3, 18, 40, 64, 232)

**REED** (Cass). This was a GNRR siding built in 1912 in SE¼ Sec. 19-140-49, Reed Twp., six miles NW of Fargo on the Surrey cutoff line. It was named for its township, which was named for A. L. Reed, a pioneer who settled here in 1871. Reed is an Old English name meaning red-haired, or of a ruddy complexion. The name was changed to PINKHAM on October 1, 1930. (2, 19, 34, 77)

**REED** (McLean). This was a rural post office established October 30, 1882 with James M. Reed pm. Mr. Reed, a Civil War veteran, homesteaded in NE¼ Sec. 29-143-81, Nettle Creek Twp., seven miles WNW of Wilton. The post office closed April 14, 1884 with mail to Falconer, which was established one mile to the SE on this date. (2, 3, 18, 28, 40)

**REEDER** (Adams). This Milwaukee Road RR station was founded in 1908 in Secs. 4 & 9-130-98, Reeder Twp., and named for E. O. Reeder, Assistant Chief Engineer of the railroad. The post office was authorized May 29, 1908, but the rural post office of LEFF had moved to this site on March 16, 1908, and the new name was not used until after July 1, 1908. Henry W. O'Dell was the first pm. The elevation is 2806, the Zip Code is 58469, and the peak population of 395 was reached in 1930. Dr. Thorlief L. Stangbye (1884-1972) practiced dentistry here for 27 years, and then practiced 28 years in nearby Mott. Marvell F. Peterson, ND Superintendent of Public Instruction 1951-1980 was born here. (1, 2, 18, 33, 34, 40, 79, 189, 262)

**REEVES** (Stutsman). This was a NPRR station in NW¼ Sec. 13-139-63, Homer Twp., seven miles SE of Jamestown, named for Bud Reeves, a local politician who is remembered for persuading the large Minneapolis, MN grain firms to contribute to the support of rural schools in this area. No development occurred in REEVES. (2, 18, 158)

**REGAN** (Burleigh). This NPRR townsite was founded in 1911 on the Pingree-Wilton line in Sec. 35-143-78, Estherville Twp. The name honors J. Austin Regan of Fessenden, an official of the Dakota Land & Townsite Co. Regan is a Celtic name meaning kingly. The post office was established October 5, 1911 with Lillian Ong, the daughter of Lewis Ong, a former rural pm in this area, as the pm. The elevation is 2051, the Zip Code is 58477, and the peak population of 202 was reached in 1920, with a decline to just 71 in 1980. Axel H. Lundberg (1880-1948) was a well known pioneer grocer and merchant here. (1, 2, 12, 14, 18, 19, 33, 40, 52, 79)

**REGENT** (Hettinger). This Milwaukee Road RR station was founded in October 1910 in Sec. 13-134-95, Indian Creek Twp. The post office was established May 21, 1910 with Absalm Switzer pm. Railroad officials gave it a regal-sounding name thinking it would become the county seat. Early in its history REGENT was billed as "The Queen City" and "The Wonder City." The elevation is 2461, the Zip Code is 58650, and the village, which incorporated in 1911, reached a peak population of 405 in 1950. Byron L. Dorgan, a ND Tax Commissioner and Congressman, was born in REGENT. (1, 2, 3, 33, 40, 44, 178, 179, 253)

**REILE'S ACRES** (Cass). This is a rural subdivision in SE¼ Sec. 21-140-49, Reed Twp., six miles NW of downtown Fargo. It began in 1973 on land owned by Reinhold Reile, incorporated as a city in 1978 when its population was 147, and reported a 1980 population of 191. (3, 18, 34)

**RELIANCE** (Burke). This was a GNRR station in SE¼ Sec. 5-162-92, Vale Twp., three miles WNW of Lignite. The origin of the name is unknown. C. M. Hanson was the owner of the site, but little development occurred and it disappeared from most maps during the 1920's. (2, 3, 18, 34, 67)

**REMICK** (Kidder). This place appears on a 1936 roadmap published by the H. M. Gousha Company as a rural community about twelve miles south of Steele, just north of the junction of Kidder, Logan, and Emmons counties. Many local residents believe that it was a copyright town, although some speculate that it might have been a rural community named in Anglicized form for either William Remmich, who settled in the area in 1905 and moved to Steele in 1934, or Michael Roemmich, another pioneer of the area. (3, 61, 122)

**REMICK** (Morton). This place appears on roadmaps published by the H. M. Gousha Co. in 1936 and 1940 in Sec. 33-137-86, seven miles SSW of Almont. It is thought to be a copyright town. (3)

**RENNIE** (Burke). This was a rural post office established August 21, 1903 with Nels Johnson (1868-1939) pm. His brother, Syver O. Johnson, was his assistant. The post office building was built by John Monson in SW¼ Sec. 26-162-91, Dale Twp., four miles SE of Lignite, and named for John R. Rennie, who had lived in the township for many years. The post office closed October 15, 1909 with mail to Lignite. (2, 18, 40, 67)

**RENO** (Grand Forks). This was a rural community on the Forest River in SE 1/4 Sec. 2-154-54, Strabane Twp., four miles NE of Inkster. Leonard and J. R. "Bob" Wagar were the first settlers, coming here about 1878. The settlement consisted of a general store, blacksmith shop, tavern, and a post office, which was established December 8, 1881 with John McDonald (1844-1921) pm. It was bypassed in 1881 by the GNRR and in 1885 by the NPRR, and quickly declined. The post office closed November 12, 1885 with mail to Forest River. It is said to have been named for Marcus Albert Reno (1835-1889), an officer under Gen. George

161

A. Custer who escaped death at the Battle of the Little Big Horn in 1876, but was cited for cowardice and dismissed from the military. (2, 5, 18, 25, 31, 40, 69, 337, 338)

**RENO** (Pierce). This was a rural post office established June 13, 1901 with Charles M. West pm, located in SW¼ Sec. 19-155-72, Reno Valley Twp., eleven miles south of Rugby. In 1903 Charles H. Olive assumed the pm position, and opened a store in conjunction with the post office which closed January 31, 1905 with mail to Rugby. It was named for its township, which was named for unknown reasons. (2, 18, 40, 114, 149)

**RENO** (Slope). This was a rural community founded in anticipation of the Milwaukee Road RR, which never came. It was centered in Woodberry Twp., (133-99), fifteen miles SE of Amidon, and is said to have been named for Major Marcus A. Reno, a controversial figure of the Battle of the Little Big Horn. A post office was established here in 1911, operating until 1922, but it was called PIERCE. The RENO name continued to be used by many local residents, and the community's baseball team barnstormed under this name. (2, 3, 40, 82)

**RENVILLE** (Bottineau). This was a rural post office established January 6, 1902 with Frank A. McDonald pm. It was located in Sec. 10-161-82, Renville Twp., at the site of the ARRETON post office which had been authorized the previous year, but was soon rescinded. The RENVILLE post office and its township were named for Joseph Renville (c.1799-1846), a pioneer trader, scout, and trapper. In 1903 the post office moved one mile south to Sec. 15-161-82, the home of new pm William Freeman, and closed September 28, 1906 with mail to Maxbass. (2, 3, 13, 18, 34, 40, 75, 153)

**RENVILLE** (Dunn). This was a country store in SW¼ Sec. 30-144-93, seven miles SSW of Halliday. A post office was established February 8, 1911 with Sten Williams pm. Many area settlers came from Renville County, MN, which was named for Joseph Renville (c.1799-1846), a pioneer trader, scout, and trapper. Mr. Williams later moved to Arthur, and the facility was taken over by Andrew J. Johnson. The post office closed April 30, 1918 with mail to Center. (1, 2, 3, 10, 18, 40, 223)

**REPUBLIC** (Mercer). This was a NPRR spur built in 1922 in Sec. 19-144-88, two miles east of Zap to serve the Republic Coal Co. mine at the site, which was owned by the Minneapolis, MN firm. (2, 3)

**REVERE** (Griggs). The GNRR established this townsite in the spring of 1913 on its newly-built Surrey cutoff line. It is located in NE¼ Sec. 29-145-60, Helena Twp., seven miles NW of Hannaford, and named for a Mr. Revere, an easterner with interests in the GNRR and the Revere-Sutton Realty Co., which had large holdings in the area. Others say it was named for Paul Revere, the Revolutionary War hero. The post office was established May 6, 1913 with Cromwell W. Broom pm. The site never experienced a boom, with a peak population of just 50 in 1920, and the post office closed October 15,

1955 with mail to Sutton. It was claimed that this was the only town on the GNRR with its depot on the south side of the tracks. (2, 33, 40, 65, 79)

**REVERS** (Benson). This place appears on a 1920 map published by the Clason Map Co. in the SW corner of Wood Lake Twp. (151-64), five miles SW of Tokio. Although a Reeves Lake is nearby, REVERS is thought to be a copyright town. (1, 3, 34, 110)

**REYNOLDS** (Grand Forks & Traill). This GNRR station was founded in 1880 in SW¼ Sec. 31-149-50, Americus Twp., Grand Forks County and NW¼ Sec. 1-148-51, Buxton Twp., Traill County. Dr. Henry A. Reynolds, a temperance advocate, platted the townsite in 1880, and became the pm when the post office was established May 26, 1881. The city, which has maintained a population of about 300 for most of its history, incorporated in 1892 with C. L. Taft as mayor. Main Street is the county line, and the population has been quite equally divided between the two counties. The elevation is 910, and the post office, Zip Code 58275, is located on the Grand Forks County side of Main Street. (1, 2, 3, 25, 31, 33, 40, 69, 77, 187, 340)

**RHAME** (Bowman). This Milwaukee Road RR station was established in 1907 as PETREL, and on June 5, 1908 pm Allen G. Elliott changed the name to RHAME, for Mitchell Davison Rhame (1846-1913), the district engineer for the railroad who lived in Minneapolis, MN. His grandfather came to America from Austria in 1816, and changed his name from Rehm to Rhame about 1818. It is located in NW 1/4 Sec. 26-132-104, Rhame Twp., just east of the original site of PETREL, and at an elevation of 3184 is the highest settlement in ND. The Zip Code is 58651, and the village, which incorporated in 1913, reached a peak population of 356 in 1930. (1, 2, 3, 18, 34, 40, 79, 120, 382, 384)

**RHEIN** (Oliver). This was a rural post office established July 16, 1906 with Peter Bumann pm. It is said to have been named

for the Rhine River in Germany, using its German spelling. It was located in NW¼ Sec. 13-142-87, Bert Twp., nine miles west of Hannover, and closed May 31, 1908 with mail to Otter Creek. It reopened April 9, 1910 with Ollie Jeglum pm at his home two miles west of the original site, and in 1917 moved to the nearby home of new pm August F. Miller, closing April 15, 1918 with mail to Beulah. (2, 3, 5, 33, 40, 53, 121)

**RHODES** (Benson). The NPRR built the terminus of its Oberon branch line in 1901 in Secs. 27, 34 & 35-153-71, Esmond Twp., naming it for John Cecil Rhodes (1853-1902), the British statesman and African colonial baron who established the Rhodes scholarships. The post office was established here as ESMOND in 1901, but the railroad continued using the original name to avoid confusion with Esmond, SD. Local residents preferred the post office name, and by 1903 usage of the RHODES name had ceased. (2, 5, 34)

**RICELAKE** (Ward). This was a farm post office established December 15, 1898 with John R. Rice (1864-1944) as the first and only pm. Mr. Rice came to America in 1882 from his native Norway, and arrived in this area as a laborer with a GNRR construction crew. The post office was located in SE¼ Sec. 3-152-85, Rice Lake Twp., nine miles SW of Minot, and named for Rice Lake, which was also named for Mr. Rice. It closed June 30, 1899 with mail to Minot when Mr. Rice decided to try his luck at ranching in MT. During the 1920's this site was a popular resort. (2, 3, 40, 100, 277, 414)

**RICEVILLE** (Cass). This was a settlement of French-Canadians that evolved near the old mission of Holy Cross. It was located in S½ Sec. 24-138-49, Stanley Twp., and named for the nearby Wild Rice River, which was named by French explorers who noted wild rice, or oats, growing along its banks. A post office was established November 17, 1881 with August Duvert pm, and the Milwaukee Road RR arrived in 1883. When the townsite was platted in 1884, it was filed as WILD RICE, and the post office adopted this name February 7, 1884. (2, 3, 25, 34, 40, 77)

*Rhame school about 1911*

**RICHARDTON** (Stark). This NPRR station was founded in 1881 in Sec. 5-139-92, and named SPRING VALLEY. In 1882 it was renamed by Oscar L. Richard (1855-1954) for his relative, C. B. Richard, Passenger Agent for the Hamburg-American Steamship Co. of New York City, a company promoting German-Russian settlement in this area. The post office was established June 15, 1883 with merchant Adolph Norberg pm. The elevation is 2487, the Zip Code is 58652, and the village, which incorporated in 1906, reached a peak population of 799 in 1970. It became a city in 1935 with Fred Born Sr. (1883-1953) mayor. Assumption Abbey, a Roman Catholic monastery, was founded here in 1899, and matured under the guidance of Bishop Vincent dePaul Wehrle (1855-1941), who was the first Abbot 1903-1910. Its famous twin-tower cathedral was built in 1906. (1, 2, 3, 18, 25, 33, 40, 52, 74, 79, 245)

**RICHBURG** (Bottineau). This pioneer townsite was platted in 1898 in SW¼ Sec. 28-163-80, Richburg Twp., and named for its township, which was named to note the hoped for success of its pioneers. The post office was established January 8, 1900 with Jules Beaudoin pm. August Soucie operated a general store at the site, but in 1903 the GNRR townsite of Westhope was founded two miles to the west, and most of RICHBURG moved there. The post office closed February 13, 1904 with mail to Westhope. (2, 3, 40, 101, 153)

**RICHFIELD** (Richland). This was a farm post office established October 27, 1902 with Ole A. Nelson pm. It was located in NE¼ Sec. 27-135-52, Sheyenne Twp., about fifteen miles NNW of Wyndmere, and closed May 15, 1905 with mail to Homestead when Mr. Nelson moved away. The name was chosen by the pm to note the good farm land in the area. (2, 3, 18, 40, 147)

**RICHMOND** (Walsh). This was a farm post office established August 7, 1879 with William Ritchey pm, who is said to have coined this name from his own. Richmond is a Teutonic name meaning mighty protector, and was made famous by Charles Lennox, 1st Duke of Richmond (1672-1723), and Charles Lennox, 3rd Duke of Richmond (1735-1806). Most places of this name in America are named for one of these two men. On January 7, 1890 the post office was relocated to the new townsite of Hoople, two miles to the west. (2, 3, 19, 25, 40, 45, 75)

**RICHVILLE** (Logan). This was a rural post office established February 25, 1892 with Michael R. Farrell pm at his country store in Sec. 21-135-70, German Twp., thirteen miles east of Napoleon. It was named by local settlers from Richville, MI, which was named for the fine farmland in that area.

It had been founded in 1851 by German Lutherans as Frankenhilf, but this name was unpopular with non-German residents due to difficulty with both the spelling and the pronunciation. Mr. Farrell was authorized to change the name to BELDEN on April 18, 1892, but no action was taken and the order was rescinded January 28, 1895. John Goehring was appointed pm of RICHVILLE on February 4, 1895, moving the facility to his home in NE¼ Sec. 22-136-70, six miles to the north. The post office closed April 2, 1906 with mail to Napoleon. (2, 3, 18, 39, 40, 46, 116)

**RICHVILLE** (Richland). Morgan T. Rich arrived here about 1864, and about 1869 began a settlement in Sec. 5-132-47, Center Twp., naming it for himself. The county was also named for Mr. Rich when it organized in 1873. A post office was established December 1, 1871 with Folsom Dow pm, and on October 13, 1873 the name was changed to CHAHINKAPA. This Indian name was quite popular with local citizens, but was difficult to spell and pronounce, and on July 24, 1874 the name was changed to WAHPETON. (2, 3, 40, 243, 346)

**RIDER** (Golden Valley). This NPRR siding was built in SW¼ Sec. 24-140-103, Sentinel Twp., five miles west of Medora, and named WALDON. About 1914 the name was changed to RIDERS to honor the cowboys of the area. During the 1940's the name generally became simply RIDER, and disappeared altogether during the 1960's as little development ever occurred at this site. (3, 34)

**RIDERS** (Golden Valley). This NPRR siding was built in SW¼ Sec. 24-140-103, Sentinel Twp. five miles west of Medora, and named WALDON. About 1914 it was renamed RIDERS, supposedly a gesture by the NPRR to honor the cowboys of the region. It was later known as simply RIDER and disappeared from most maps in the 1960's. (1, 2, 3, 34)

**RIDGEFIELD** (Cavalier). This was a rural post office established April 7, 1884 with Herman P. Steifvator pm. It was located in NE¼ Sec. 17-161-58, Hay Twp., nine miles east of Langdon. Mr. Steifvator wanted to name the post office Hull, for mail carrier A. A. Hull, but this name was rejected for unknown reasons. Although it appears that postal officials selected the name RIDGEFIELD, others credit the name to pioneer settler James Wait, who noted the farms along a ridge, the Pembina Escarpment. A population of 10 was reported in 1890, but the post office closed April 7, 1894 with mail to Langdon, having operated exactly ten years. (2, 3, 18, 25, 40, 117, 249, 414)

**RIGA** (McHenry). This GNRR station was founded in 1901 in NW¼ Sec. 33-156-78, Riga Twp., between Granville and Denbigh. The post office was established June 27, 1902 with Jens G. Springer pm, and closed March 30, 1918 with mail to Granville. A population of 30 was reported in 1920, but only two houses mark the site today. The name came from the capital city of Latvia, which at that time was part of the Czarist Russian province of Livonia. (2, 3, 5, 18, 40, 182)

**RING** (Bowman). This was a ranch post office established April 22, 1912 with Oluf M. Ring pm. Mr. Ring (1865-1946) came to America from Norway in 1889, and settled here in 1910. The post office was located in NE¼ Sec. 24-129-103, Grand River Twp., about eighteen miles SW of Bowman, and closed July 15, 1919 with mail to Swartwood. (1, 2, 3, 18, 34, 40, 120)

**RIO** (Stutsman). This settlement began about 1879 in NE¼ Sec. 6-141-64, Buchanan Twp., between Jamestown and Pingree. The NPRR soon built through the area, and a post office was established August 10, 1887 with James A. Buchanan pm. The preferred name of Buchanan was not available due to its current usage by a rural post office in Emmons County, so it was named for Rio, WI, hometown of the Buchanan family, which had been founded in 1852, with pm Delos Bundy requesting the name Ohio, which was misread by postal officials as Rio. Rio is Spanish for river, although this had nothing whatsoever to do with the erroneous naming of the WI townsite. The Emmons County post office of Buchanan closed on June 15, 1894, and when word of this reached RIO the process began to change the name. On September 6, 1894 the site finally became BUCHANAN. (2, 3, 10, 25, 40, 70, 158, 240)

**RIPLEY** (Sargent). This farm post office was established April 24, 1884 with Samuel J. Bromley pm. It was located in NW¼ Sec. 14-131-57, Harlem Twp., two miles west of Cogswell on the Lisbon stage trail, and named by settlers from Ripley County, IN, which was named for Eleazar Wheelock Ripley (1782-1839), a politician from MA who was a General in the War of 1812, and later was a Congressman from LA. Ripley is an Anglo-Saxon name meaning the shouter. The post office closed November 15, 1887 with mail to Sargent. (2, 5, 10, 19, 25, 40, 165)

**RIPON** (Cass). This townsite was first settled in 1876, and in 1881 the GNRR built a station in SW¼ Sec. 4-140-53, Wheatland Twp., just SE of Absaraka. A townsite was platted and great progress was predicted, but the site was found to drain poorly, and most settlers moved to Absaraka. A post office was established March 8, 1882 with John A. Smith pm, closing January 15, 1895 with mail to Absaraka. The townsite was officially abandoned in 1890. Edgar L. Sears, the town's founder, named it for his hometown of Ripon, WI, which was named for Ripon, West Yorkshire, England. Others claim it was named directly for the English city. (2, 10, 18, 40, 77, 79)

**RIPPEL** (Morton). This was a NPRR siding

built in 1936 in Sec. 2-138-81, midway between Mandan and Fort Lincoln State Park. It existed for only a few years, and was built to serve a stockyards owned by R. Peter Rippel (1892-1960), a Mandan developer and cattle buyer who opened a sausage factory in Mandan in 1934 with his brother, John. Ripple is an erroneous spelling. (2, 3)

**RISING** (McHenry). This was a GNRR loading station built in Sec. 8-156-80, Kottke Valley Twp., between Deering and Granville. No development took place here, and the origin of the name is unknown. (1, 2, 3, 18)

**RITA** (Cass). This was a GNRR station built in 1893 in S½ Sec. 10-138-53, Walburg Twp., as the terminus of the twelve-mile branch line from Addison. It was named by Eben Chaffee of the Amenia-Sharon Land Co. for his niece, Rita Chaffee. Rita is a Greek name meaning a pearl. In 1894 the name was changed to CHAFFEE. (2, 19, 34, 77)

**RIVAL** (Burke). This was a Soo Line RR townsite named to note its status as a rival of the nearby GNRR townsite of Lignite. It was located in Secs. 33 & 34-163-92, Portal Twp., three miles WNW of Lignite, and was the terminus of the branch line from Flaxton. The post office was established May 17, 1907 with Chester L. Teisinger pm, and closed May 17, 1909 with mail to Columbus. (1, 2, 18, 34, 40, 79)

**RIVER BEND** (Cass). This is a platted subdivision founded in the 1970's in SW¼ Sec. 19-138-49, Stanley Twp., one mile SW of Horace. The name notes its location on a bend of the Sheyenne River. (3, 34)

**RIVERDALE** (Cass). Paul and Ivan Berg developed a trailer court in the 1970's in SE¼ Sec. 6-138-49, Stanley Twp., three miles north of Horace, and by 1976 it had twenty-four homes on site. Originally known as the Horse Shoe Bend Trailer Court, it was platted as RIVERDALE, noting its location on the Sheyenne River. (3, 34, 77)

**RIVERDALE** (Dickey). This was a rural settlement founded in the 1880's in Sec. 31-130-59, Riverdale Twp., and named for its township which was named to note the James River which flowed through the area. A population of 25 was reported in 1890, but the site quickly declined, never having a post office. In 1915 the GNRR built a station here, this site now being the junction of its line with the Chicago & NW RR. The station was first called NEWTON, but the old name was soon restored by popular demand. It was served by the Guelph post office. (2, 3, 25, 40)

**RIVERDALE** (McLean). This was the principal boom town resulting from the construction of Garrison Dam which officially began October 4, 1947. The first settlement occurred in 1946, and the name was chosen by Mrs. T. O. Lervick of Granville, whose name was chosen from 20,000 entries in a statewide contest. The site was in Sec. 2-146-84, North Hancock Twp., on land that had been owned 1902-1946 by Espy Ash. The post office was established December 3, 1947 with Mrs. Nellie P. Johnson pm. President Dwight David Eisenhower visited here in 1953 to dedicate the completed dam. A population of 4,033 was reported in August 1954, but it has declined since the completion of the dam, reporting a count of just 545 in 1970. The Zip Code is 58565. The federal government withdrew from the administration of the town in 1986, and it is now an incorporated city of ND. (2, 3, 28, 33, 40)

**RIVERDALE JUNCTION** (McLean). This is the junction of the Soo Line RR east of Riverdale and the spur that serves that city. It is located at Sec. 31-147-82, Linder Twp., near the Garrison Dam boom town of Gateway. Mike Overlee was a well known bar owner at this site during its heydey in the 1950's. (2, 28)

**RIVER LANDING** (Burleigh). This name was used in the 1870's through the 1890's to identify the Missouri River boat landing just west of Bismarck in Sec. 31-139-81, Hay Creek Twp. The docks were on the east bank of the river, just north of the NPRR bridge, and just south of the present-day dock used by the modern stern-wheeler *Far West*, named for the famous river boat piloted by Capt. Grant Marsh. (3, 25, 34)

**RIVERSIDE** (Cass). This settlement was known as SHEYENNE STOCKYARDS, HAGGART'S, HAGGARTS, and HAGGART in the 1870's and 1880's. New growth in the 1920's led to the founding of WEST FARGO. This name was transferred to the much larger neighbor to the south, South West Fargo, in 1967, with this place becoming WEST FARGO INDUSTRIAL PARK, a name never popular with local citizens. Mayor Luvern Eid began a campaign to change the name, and on September 17, 1974 Mayor Geraldine Walz proclaimed the city to be renamed RIVERSIDE, noting its location on the banks of the Sheyenne River. The city has grown from a population of 104 in 1970 to 465 in 1980, and is served by the West Fargo post office. (3, 77, 210)

**RIVERVIEW HEIGHTS** (Morton). This rural housing development began in the 1970's in S½ Sec. 4-139-81, about four miles north of Mandan. The name describes its location on the bluffs overlooking the Missouri River. (3)

**RIVIERE PEMBINATI** (Pembina). This was an alternate name for CHABOILLEZ POST, the historic fur trading post of 1797-1798 at the site of present-day Pembina. The name is French for Pembina River. (2, 3, 108)

**ROACH** (McLean). This was a stopping point on the Velva-Coal Harbor stage route located in SW¼ Sec. 10-147-84, Coal Harbor Twp., about five miles north of Riverdale. A post office was established April 10, 1895 with Mary A. Staley pm, and closed August 15, 1902 with mail to Coal Harbor. The name honors William N. Roach of Larimore, who was that city's mayor 1883-1887, a territorial delegate to Congress, and the unsuccessful candidate for Governor in 1889 and 1890. The site is now inundated by Lake Sakakawea. (2, 3, 28, 40)

**ROACH** (Ward). This was a GNRR station in NW¼ Sec. 14-156-87, Passport Twp., four miles WNW of Berthold. It was named for James Roach, a prominent realtor, banker, and onetime mayor of Minot. The site never saw any real development, yet appeared on maps from about 1905 into the 1960's. (1, 2, 3, 100, 372)

**ROBINSON** (Kidder). This NPRR townsite was founded in 1911 on the Pingree-Wilton line in SE¼ Sec. 3-142-72, Robinson Twp., and named for John F. Robinson (1875-1923), President of the First National Bank in Steele. The post office was established May 13, 1911 with William F. Legler (1864-1942) pm. The elevation is 1792, the Zip Code is 58478, and the village, which incorporated in 1929, reached a peak population of 185 in 1930. Verne Wells came to ROBINSON in 1922 and established banking and civic leadership traditions that are now in their third generation. The village experienced a brief frenzy in 1925 when it was thought that oil had been discovered nearby. Vernon Liedtke (1912-1957), a world famous circus star, was born here. (1, 2, 3, 18, 40, 93)

*Robinson, Kidder County, about 1913*

**ROBINSON** (McLean). This was a farm post office established August 10, 1903 with Mrs. Nancy J. Frederickson pm. It was located in NW¼ Sec. 28-148-86, Emmet Twp., twelve miles WSW of Garrison, and named for George and John Robinson, brothers who were pioneers in the area. On September 2, 1905 the name was changed to EMMET. (2, 28, 40, 387)

**ROBINSON** (Ward). This was a farm post office established July 29, 1895 with George L. Robinson pm. It was located in SE¼ Sec. 20-152-81, Brillian Twp., nine miles south of Sawyer. James L. Robinson became pm two months later, serving until January 1897, when D. S. Bennett took over. The post office closed April 8, 1897 with mail to Velva. (3, 40, 100, 414)

**ROCHESTER** (Cass). This was a NPRR station in Sec. 10-143-55, Rochester Twp., six miles NW of Page. It was named for its township, which has a name that ultimately traces to Rochester, Kent, England, an ancient city founded by the Romans. Chester is derived from the Latin *castra*, meaning a camp or fortified place. A post office was established June 8, 1882 with William C. Whisnaud pm, and closed April 22, 1884 with mail to Colgate. (3, 25, 34, 40, 45, 77)

**ROCK HAVEN** (Morton). This was a United States government boat landing in Sec. 14-139-81, three miles north of Mandan. It consisted of a series of long wooden piers built into the Missouri River at a place considered to be the best landing on the river. The name noted the natural ledges of rock that stabilized the banks, and the fact that this made the site a haven from spring ice breakups. The landing had its peak during the 1880's and 1890's, and declined as the steamboat era ended. (2, 3, 107, 343)

**ROCK HAVEN HEIGHTS** (Morton). This is a rural subdivision founded in 1980 in SW¼ Sec. 10-139-81, three miles north of Mandan. The name notes its location on the bluffs overlooking the site of the historic Missouri River port of Rock Haven. (3)

**ROCK ISLAND** (Ramsey). This was a trading post founded about 1819 in Lake Twp. (153-64), just south of the city of Devils Lake. The name honored founder Augustus Rock, a French-Canadian who came here a few years after the Scotsman Duncan Graham. Both Rock Island and Grahams Island became peninsulae due to the receding waters of Devils Lake. Mr. Rock's grandson, G. H. Faribault, was the farm manager at Fort Totten as late as 1871. (2, 3, 421)

**ROCK ISLAND** (Ramsey). By order of the President of the United States, a large tract of land comprising all or parts of Secs. 19, 20, 21, 28, 29 & 33-153-64, Creel Twp., south of the city of Devils Lake, was set aside as a wood reserve for use at nearby Fort Totten. The reserve was generally called ROCK ISLAND for the long abandoned trading post founded here in 1819 by Augustus Rock. Fort Totten closed in 1890 and the reserve became a National Guard training center the following year, using several names before adopting the name CAMP GRAFTON in 1924. (2, 3, 103)

*Hotel Keeney, Rocklake, about 1912*

**ROCK ISLAND MILITARY RESERVATION** (Ramsey). After being officially nameless for six years, the National Guard training center south of the city of Devils Lake was given this lengthy name in 1922, commemorating the name of the 1819 trading post at the site, which became a government wood reserve 1881-1890. In 1924 the facility unofficially became known as CAMP GRAFTON, with this name becoming official in 1952. (2, 3)

**ROCKLAKE** (Towner). This was a farm post office established February 28, 1898 with Wilber Johnson pm. It was located in NW¼ Sec. 29-162-66, Rock Lake Twp., and named for the lake on whose shore it was located. Early French explorers had named the lake noting the many rocks on its shores. The GNRR built a station in Secs. 6 & 7-161-66, Virginia Twp., three miles SSW of this post office in 1904, and proposed naming it Keeneyville for J. B. Keeney, but Mr. Keeney suggested using the existing name of ROCKLAKE, whose post office moved here in 1905 with John Eller pm. The elevation is 1551, the Zip Code is 58365, and the village, which incorporated in 1906, reached a peak population of 385 in 1950. The official name is ROCKLAKE, but nearly all maps, including the current official state issue, use the two-word spelling. (1, 2, 3, 18, 33, 40, 79, 192)

**ROCKPORT** (Barnes). George H. Ellsbury, manager of the Charlemagne Tower interests, founded this townsite before 1880 in NE¼ Sec. 21-143-56, Ellsbury Twp., two miles SE of Pillsbury. The origin of the name is unknown, and when the post office was established December 20, 1880, it was named ELLSBURY. (3, 34, 40, 425)

**ROCKSPRING** (Dunn). This was a rural post office established March 8, 1898 in Sec. 29-143-94, ten miles SE of Dunn Center. Ole Peterson (1846-1911) was the pm, and E. O. Baker operated a general store at the site. The post office closed March 31, 1913 with mail to Emerson. The name noted the cold water springs coming from rocks near the store. Rock Spring and Rock Springs are erroneous spellings. (2, 3, 18, 40, 223)

**ROGER** (Barnes). This Soo Line RR station was founded in October 1897 in Sec. 31-142-59, Rogers Twp., at a junction with a NPRR line. The name was intended to be ROGERS, but an error by a postal official resulted in the post office being established as ROGER on April 25, 1898 with Nels Larson pm. The error was corrected July 13, 1917. (1, 3, 40, 76)

**ROGERS** (Barnes). This townsite in SE¼ Sec. 31-142-59, Rogers Twp., was platted in 1898 and named for Joseph H. Rogers, its owner who came here in 1897. Some say it was named by G. J. Parker, a merchant in nearby Clive, for A. R. Rogers, a Minneapolis, MN lumber dealer. When the post office was established in 1898, the name was erroneously approved as ROGER, and it was not changed until July 13, 1917 when Lora E. Moore was the pm. The elevation is 1445, the Zip Code is 58479, and the village, which incorporated in 1915, reached a peak population of 174 in 1940. Located at the junction of Soo Line RR and NPRR lines, ROGERS absorbed the nearby communities of Lowry, Odell, Booth, Clive, and Mattison. (1, 2, 3, 18, 33, 34, 40, 52, 76, 79)

**ROGERS** (Ramsey). This was a rural post office established November 23, 1882 with Richard H. Rogers pm. It was located in Sec. 34-153-63, South Minnewaukan Twp., about four miles SW of Crary, and closed August 18, 1887 with mail to Crary. (2, 3, 40, 103)

**ROHRVILLE** (Ramsey). This Soo Line RR station was built in 1913 in Sec. 13-154-62, Ontario Twp., five miles NW of Crary. No development occurred at the site, and it never had a post office. It was named for Andrew Rohr, who came here from Norway and owned the site. A population of 10 was reported in 1920, and it later became a ghost town, but 5 people were again living in ROHRVILLE in 1982. (2, 39, 40, 103)

**ROKIWAN CAMP** (Stutsman). This was a boys' summer camp of eight acres established in 1923 on the NW shore of Spiritwood Lake in NE¼ Sec. 36-142-63, Ashland Twp., eleven miles east of Buchanan. It was named for the two sponsoring Jamestown service clubs, the ROtary International and the KIWANis Club. (2, 3, 34, 79)

**ROLETTE** (Rolette). This city was founded in 1905 at the junction of the GNRR and the Soo Line RR in Secs. 20, 21, 28 & 29-160-71, Leonard Twp. The post office was established July 10, 1905 with Albert E. Hurst pm. The elevation is 1630, the Zip Code is 58366, and the village, which incorporated in 1930, reached a peak population of 704 in 1970. It was named for its county, which was named for Joseph Rolette (1820-1871), an almost legendary character associated with the early fur trade in Pembina, who is remembered in MN as the man who stole the bill that would have moved the state capital from St. Paul to St. Peter. (1, 2, 13, 40, 52, 123)

**ROLLA** (Rolette). This GNRR station was founded in 1888 in NW¼ Sec. 16 & NE¼ Sec. 17-162-69, Mount Pleasant Twp. Some say it was named by Dr. Richard D. Cowan, a pioneer physician, by coining it from the county name. Others say it was named for Rolla Noyes, a lawyer in Grand Forks who was associated with the GNRR. Still others say it was named for Rolla, MO, which likewise has many explanations for its name. The post office was established November 9, 1888 with David C. Boyd pm, who operated the facility from his building in the old townsite of BOYDTON one mile to the NW. In October 1893 new pm Andrew Smith moved the post office to the ROLLA townsite, which bills itself as the "Jewel City of America," and in 1890 was made the new county seat, replacing Saint John. The elevation is 1838, the Zip Code is 58367, and it reached a peak population of 1,486 in 1980. ROLLA incorporated as a village in 1891, and became a city in 1907. (1, 2, 3, 10, 18, 25, 33, 40, 52, 79, 123, 397)

**ROLSON** (Divide). This was a rural post office established June 4, 1907 with Dahl L. Melby pm. It was located in NE¼ Sec. 19-162-102, Westby Twp., six miles NW of Alkabo, and was named for Otto Rolson, who lived about five miles to the SE in NW¼ Sec. 10-161-102, Daneville Twp. The post office closed May 31, 1913 with mail to Skermo. (2, 3, 18, 40, 415)

**ROME** (Pembina). A 1890 guide to ND lists this place as being in Pembina County, and served by the Bowesmont post office. No other information is available. (25)

**ROMFO** (Cavalier). This was a rural settlement in SE¼ Sec. 14-160-58, Alma Twp., three miles ENE of Osnabrock. The post office was established October 10, 1882 with Olaf J. Romfo pm in his country store. A population of 30 was reported in 1890, but the settlement declined and the post office closed July 12, 1895 with mail to Osnabrock. (2, 3, 25, 40, 117)

**ROMNESS** (Griggs). Peter Matheson and John Hogenson settled here in 1880, and a rural post office was established November 21, 1883 with Mr. Matheson as pm. It was located in Sec. 16-147-58, Romness Twp., eight miles east of Jessie, and named for Romness, Telemarken, Norway, the birthplace of the pm's wife. Mr. Hogenson

became pm in 1887, and the post office closed May 15, 1903 with mail to Cooperstown. (2, 3, 25, 40, 65, 240, 284)

**RONDA** (Mercer). This was a rural post office established May 27, 1907 with John Kaufman pm. It was located in SW¼ Sec. 28-144-89, three miles SW of Zap, and said to have been named for a female resident of the area. In 1911 it moved one mile north to SW¼ Sec. 20-144-89, and closed September 15, 1913 with mail to Bowdish. (2, 18, 40, 53, 64, 414)

**RONESS** (Mountrail). This GNRR siding was founded in the 1880's in NE¼ Sec. 14-156-89, McGahan Twp. as DELTA. When settlement began in 1904 it was first called RONESS, for unknown reasons, but the name was soon changed to BLENHEIM. The post office was established in 1905 as GRENADA, but this name was unpopular with many local residents, who began calling the town HANLEY. This name was rejected by postal officials, and on October 21, 1905 the name was changed to BLAISDELL. (2, 40, 72)

**RONEY** (McLean). This was a farm post office and country store in SW¼ Sec. 23-148-86, Emmet Twp., about ten miles WSW of Garrison. The post office opened March 16, 1905 with E. Jennie Roney pm, and closed December 31, 1909 with mail to Garrison. (2, 3, 18, 28, 40, 278)

**ROOP** (Emmons). This was a farm post office established August 21, 1884 with Joseph N. Roop pm at his farm in NW¼ Sec. 22-135-75, about four miles south of Braddock. Mr. Roop, who was born near Berlin, Germany, and came here in 1883, was killed by a bull on September 24, 1892. A small settlement began, reporting a population of 22 in 1890, but the post office closed March 15, 1900 with mail to Braddock. (2, 3, 25, 40, 66, 96)

**ROOSEVELT** (McLean). This was a Soo Line RR siding built in 1902 in SE¼ Sec. 36-144-81, about midway between Wilton and Washburn. Gen. William D. Washburn planned it as a service point for the Washburn Lignite Coal Co., and named it for President Theodore Roosevelt (1858-1919). Some years later it was replaced by the Merida siding about one mile to the west, which was primarily an agricultural facility. The ROOSEVELT site is now within the Lost Lake National Wildlife Refuge. (2, 3, 10, 28, 414)

**ROOSEVELT** (Wells). This was a farm post office established June 2, 1905 with Michael Rasmussen pm, who named it for President Theodore Roosevelt (1858-1919), who had lived in the Badlands in the 1880's, and was a great favorite of many state residents. It

was located in Sec. 29-145-69, Johnson Twp., nine miles SSW of Sykeston, and closed April 30, 1908 with mail to Sykeston. (2, 3, 40, 53, 79, 364)

**ROPER** (Hettinger). This place appears on a 1930 roadmap published by the General Drafting Co. It is shown about fifteen miles north of Mott, approximately in Campbell Twp. (136-93), and is thought to be a copyright town. (3)

**ROSA LAKE** (Cavalier). This place challenged for the county seat in 1889, and finished a distant third in a four-way race, beating Lemon, but trailing the winner, Langdon, and Olga. The location of ROSA LAKE is unknown, although it might have been in the Munich area as the Klein post office that was established near Munich in 1898 was submitted as Rosa. Others feel it was to be a compromise site that had no reason to develop after losing the county seat challenge. (3, 115, 414)

**ROSEBUD** (Morton). This was a rural community in NE¼ Sec. 7-140-84, nine miles NNE of New Salem, and named for the Rosebud Sioux Indians. Others say the name noted the wild flowers of the area. The post office was established March 15, 1904 with Emil C. Otte pm. For many years the major business here was the Rosebud Creamery Co., managed by the Tellman family, with Ole Sorby as the first butter maker. A population of 10 was reported in 1920. August T. Oellerman ran the post office for many years, and his widow, Lisetta Mueller Oellerman took over following his death in 1925, closing the facility December 31, 1936 with mail to Judson. (2, 3, 17, 18, 40, 107, 109)

**ROSEDALE** (Cass). This was a name given to the new NPRR townsite in NW¼ Sec. 24-142-52, Arthur Twp. in 1881, honoring Rose Gunkel, a sister of prominent local settler Carl Julius Gunkel. This name is considered by some to have been unofficial, as the present name, ARTHUR, was used virtually from the first day of the new settlement. (2, 3, 265)

**ROSEDALE** (Towner). This was a farm post office established September 16, 1901 with Edward N. Huffman pm. It was located in SW¼ Sec. 23-161-66, Virginia Twp., four miles SE of Rocklake, and thought to have been named to note the prairie roses in a nearby valley. The post office closed February 28, 1906 with mail to Ellison. (2, 3, 18, 40)

**ROSEGLEN** (McLean). Settlers arrived here about 1902 and got their mail from Oscar. On March 16, 1904 a post office was established in the home of pm Johannes "John" H. Snippen (1880-1960) in NW¼ Sec. 13-149-87, Roseglen Twp. Mr. Snippen submitted Glennon, Glenwood, Hill, Kolden, Rostad, Shea and Snippen as suggested names to postal officials, and all were rejected. He then combined "rose", inspired from a seed catalog, and "glen", from his neighbors, Patrick and Mike Glennon, who were the area's first settlers, and ROSEGLEN was accepted as the name. When new land was opened to settlement by whites in 1916, the post office moved four miles ESE to the platted townsite called BATESVILLE in Sec. 5-149-87. An expected railroad never came, but the village continues to exist with a population of about 50, and the post office, Zip Code 58775, still operates. (2, 28, 33, 40, 79, 277, 278)

**ROSEHILL** (Cavalier). This was a Mennonite settlement founded in 1897 in Sec. 12-160-62, Henderson Twp., six miles NE of Munich. The post office was established January 10, 1900 with Henry D. Ewert pm in the Mennonite Brethren Church, which was located near a high hill covered with wild prairie roses, hence the name. Some say Henry Newhold named it for a region in South Russia. The post office closed December 12, 1909 with mail to Munich. (2, 18, 40, 53, 212)

**ROSENFELD** (Hettinger). This was a rural post office established May 23, 1906 with Juliana Muller pm. It was located in NE¼ Sec. 6-135-91, Walker Twp., fourteen miles NE of Mott, and named by settlers from Rosenfeld, Akkerman District, Bessarabia. Some sources claim it was named for President Theodore Roosevelt, with a severe corruption of the name because of the existance of a Roosevelt post office in Wells County. A name change to WILLA was approved March 15, 1907, but the order was rescinded. The change was approved again on June 11, 1907, and on that date the post office moved one-half mile west to the home of new pm Johannes Schmitt, and became WILLA. (2, 3, 18, 23, 40, 181)

**ROSENTAL** (Emmons). This was a pioneer community of Germans from Russia in Strasburg Twp. (131-76), just NW of present-day Strasburg. The first settlers came from Rosental, Kischinew District, Bessarabia. (3, 23)

**ROSE POINT** (Walsh). This was a pioneer Red River stage station in SE¼ Sec. 28-158-51, Saint Andrew Twp., ten miles NE of Grafton, and three miles west of the later settlement of Saint Andrew. It was named for Frank Rose, the operator of a stage station just south of Pembina. Antoine Girard and Jacob Reinhart, later the first sheriff of Walsh County, explored this area in 1866, and settlement began about 1870. The post office was established October 6, 1871 with Ezra B. Andrus pm, and closed July 28, 1873 with mail to Grand Forks. (2, 3, 18, 40, 75, 79, 414)

**ROSE VALLEY** (Cass). This was a rural community covering much of Gunkel Twp. (142-51), and named for Rose Gunkel, the sister of Carl Julius Gunkel, for whom the township was named. The name is also descriptive of its location near the Elm River, and is perpetuated by a cemetery in SE¼ Sec. 2-142-51. (3, 77, 265)

**ROSEVILLE** (Traill). This was a GNRR station five miles south of Portland in SE¼ Sec. 22-146-53, Roseville Twp. It was named for its township, which was named by Christian Monson in 1880 to note the many wild prairie roses in bloom at the time. No settlement occurred at the site. (2, 18, 25, 29)

**ROSS** (Foster). A 1890 guide to ND shows this NPRR station in SW¼ Sec. 18-146-67, Wyard Twp., between Sykeston and Carrington on the west bank of Pipestem Creek. It is believed to be a cartographer's error, with the correct location being one mile west in Wells County. (3, 25)

**ROSS** (Mountrail). This GNRR townsite was founded in 1887 in Secs. 20 & 29-156-92, Ross Twp. The post office was established June 2, 1902 with Arthur S. DeLance, the first state legislator from the county, as pm. Some say it was named for Ross H. McEnany, a GNRR employee who surveyed this site, while others say it was named for Ross Davidson, a Minot banker and realtor. Ross is a Teutonic name meaning horse. A water tank and siding had been built here in 1887, but no further development occurred until settlement began in 1902. The elevation is 2291, the Zip Code is 58776, and a peak population of 225 was reported in 1920. Among the early settlers were immigrants from Syria, and their mosque built in 1930 is considered to be the first Moslem house of worship in the United States. Ruth Olson Meiers, the first female Lt. Governor of ND, was a resident of ROSS. (1, 2, 3, 18, 19, 25, 33, 40, 72)

**ROSS** (Wells). This was a NPRR station built before 1890 in SE¼ Sec. 13-146-68, Bilodeau Twp., five miles east of Sykeston, and named for the NPRR superintendent at Duluth, MN. When a townsite called Ross was founded in 1902 in Mountrail County, some confusion developed, and on August 27, 1903 this station changed its name to DOVER. (2, 3, 18, 363)

**ROSSELAND** (McKenzie). This name has been associated for many years with the rural community around the country church in Sec. 22-153-101, Wilbur Twp., fifteen miles north of Alexander, and named for the maiden name of Mrs. Anton Nelson, an area pioneer. About 1953 the community began using the name PRAIRIE VALLEY, although the original name is still in use as well. (2, 3)

**ROTH** (Bottineau). This GNRR station in Secs. 29 & 32-163-78, Scandia Twp., was founded in 1904 and platted as FALDET. The station name was changed to ROTH in 1905, honoring pioneer settler Martin Rothe with a change in the spelling. Folklore tells of a mixup, either by GNRR officials or by the Secretary of State, that resulted in the names of this site and Carbury being reversed. Further confusion occurred when the post office was established as HEWITT on May 22, 1907. On May 14, 1908 the post office changed its name to ROTH to match the name of the railroad station, with new pm John W. Reep given credit for clearing up the inconsistency. The elevation is 1508, and a peak population of 80 was reported in 1920. The post office closed August 14, 1964 with mail to Souris. (1, 2, 3, 18, 34, 40, 79, 101, 153, 380)

**ROTHVILLE** (McKenzie). This was a rural post office established November 2, 1906 with Edward M. Roth pm, who then decided to decline the appointment. Mr. Roth's home was in SE¼ Sec. 26-152-102, Elk Twp., eight miles NNW of Alexander. Edward L. Penson was appointed pm when the post office was again authorized on March 12, 1907, with the facility located in SE¼ Sec. 19-152-101, Poe Twp., three miles NE of the Roth home, and nine miles north of Alexander. It closed January 31, 1910 with mail to Wilbur. (2, 3, 34, 40, 415)

**ROTTERDAM** (McIntosh). This was a farm post office established March 3, 1893 with Johann Rott Jr. pm. It was located in SW¼ Sec. 11-131-68, Rosenthal Twp., fourteen miles NE of Ashley. Some say the name was coined from the name of the pm, while others say it was named for the Dutch city, which has no known local connection. The post office closed May 22, 1897 with mail to Ashley. (2, 3, 12, 34, 40, 211)

**ROUEN** (Mountrail). The GNRR station built in the late 1880's in NE¼ Sec. 14-156-89, McGahan Twp., was first called DELTA, then during 1904-1905 was briefly called RONESS, BLENHEIM, GRENADA, and HANLEY. In 1905 the name was supposedly fixed as BLAISDELL, but a 1909 map of Ward County shows this place as both BLAISDELL and ROUEN. The latter name, which undoubtedly came from Rouen, France, had been submitted by pm William F. Thompson when the post office was established in early 1905, and although the name was rejected it is apparent that its use at the site continued for some time. (2, 3, 40, 414)

**ROUGHRIDER ESTATES** (Morton). This is a rural residential development founded in 1974 in SE¼ Sec. 12-139-82, five miles NW of Mandan, and named to commemorate the Roughriders, the 1898 Spanish-American War heros led by Col. Theodore Roosevelt. The housing project was sponsored by Mor-Gran-Sou Rural Electric Cooperative of Flasher. (3)

**ROUNDLAKE** (Kidder). This farm post office was established April 29, 1908 with Fannie L. Phelps pm. It was located in N½ Sec. 12-142-70, Pettibone Twp., one mile NE of Pettibone, and named for the nearby lake whose name described its shape. The one-word spelling was done to comply with government specifications for place names. The post office closed October 31, 1910 with mail to Gerber. (2, 18, 40, 122)

**ROUND PRAIRIE** (Williams). This is a rural community in Round Prairie Twp. (154-103 & 104), west of Williston on the MT border. The Scott post office served this area 1906-1912, which takes its name from the round rocks found on the prairie, said to be the largest field stones in ND. In recent years this name referred to a telephone exchange of the Northwest Mutual Aid Telephone Corporation. (3, 50, 55)

**ROUSES** (Ward). This was a Soo Line RR loading station in NW¼ Sec. 33-160-88, Kenmare Twp., one mile SE of Kenmare. It was named for Augustine Rouse, a pioneer of the area who was the pm at Lignite, Ward County, and was killed in a gunfight in 1896. The station primarily served a small coal mine which Mr. Rouse had helped to develop. (2, 3, 18, 100)

**RUBY** (McKenzie). This was a rural post office established November 10, 1910 with Ben. L. Green pm in his home in SW¼ Sec.

167

33-149-104, thirteen miles SSW of Cartwright. Postal officials rejected the name Cheney, after which it was named for Ruby Lowe Anderson, a local rancher's wife. Ruby is a Latin name meaning red, and is usually associated with the gem stone of this name. On February 17, 1912 the post office moved two miles SW to the home of Silas R. Bryant, who changed the name to BENNIEPIER. (2, 3, 19, 40)

**RUBY** (Nelson). This farm post office was established December 14, 1886 with Alfred V. Fuller pm. The origin of the name is unknown. It was located in SE¼ Sec. 21-150-57, Rugh Twp., eight miles NE of Aneta, and closed September 14, 1905 with mail to Aneta. (2, 3, 18, 25, 40, 124, 128)

**RUDE** (Williams). This farm post office was established July 17, 1906 with Holm Olson Studsrud (1865-1954) pm at his home in NW¼ Sec. 8-159-97, Hazel Twp., three miles SW of Wildrose. Mr. Studsrud came to America from Norway in 1883, went back to his homeland in 1889, and returned to America in 1891, settling in Williams County in 1906. It is thought that the post office's name was coined from the pm's name, *rud* being Norwegian for a clearing in the woods for a building. The post office closed November 30, 1909 with mail to Montrose. (2, 18, 40, 50)

**RUDSER** (Divide). This post office was established February 23, 1906 with Peter Rudser pm. It was located in the country store opened by Mr. Rudser in 1905 in Sec. 36-160-100, Smokey Butte Twp., twenty-five miles SW of Crosby near the Williams County Line. It closed March 15, 1917 with mail to Zahl. (2, 3, 18, 34, 40, 73, 79)

**RUGBY** (Pierce). This GNRR station was platted as RUGBY JUNCTION, but since its founding in 1886 has been almost universally called simply RUGBY, for Rugby, Warwickshire, England. This was one of many GNRR stations that were given English names. The post office was established December 6, 1886 with Nels Jacobsen pm. It is the county seat of Pierce County, and a stone monument built in 1931 marks the site as the geographical center of North America. The elevation is 1567, the Zip Code is 58368, and a peak population of 3,343 was reached in 1980. RUGBY incorporated as a village in 1897, and became a city in 1905 with A. H. Jones mayor. (1, 2, 10, 40, 44, 52, 114)

**RUGBY JUNCTION** (Pierce). This site in Secs. 1 & 2-156-73, Christenson Twp., was the junction of the GNRR main line and its branch to Antler. The townsite was platted in July 1886 by Comstock & White of Moorhead, MN, and named RUGBY

JUNCTION, but the shortened name RUGBY has seen almost universal usage since its beginning. (3, 114)

**RUGH** (Nelson). This farm post office was established November 17, 1884 with Charles H. Rugh pm. It was located in Sec. 21-150-57, Rugh Twp., eight miles NNE of Aneta, and closed December 16, 1885 with mail to Adler. Two days short of a year later, the Ruby post office was established in the same section. (2, 3, 40, 124)

**RURAL** (Morton). This was a farm post office established April 18, 1905 with Henry Schrink pm, who named it to note its rural location. It was located in SW¼ Sec. 4-137-82, ten miles SW of Mandan, and closed July 31, 1908 with mail to Strain. (2, 3, 17, 40, 107)

**RUSCOE** (Ransom). This farm post office was established July 13, 1881 with Lyman E. Truesdell pm. It was located in NW¼ Sec. 6-133-56, Bale Twp., seven miles SW of Lisbon, and closed January 31, 1883 with mail to Lisbon. The origin of the name is unknown. (2, 40, 201)

**RUSHLAKE** (Cavalier). This was a rural settlement in SW¼ Sec. 31-163-61, Dresden Twp., named for nearby Rush Lake, which was named to note the ten-foot rushes growing along its banks. The post office was established December 17, 1897 with Amos Abbott pm, who used the one-word spelling to comply with government spelling regulations. On April 25, 1899 the name was changed to WALES. (2, 3, 18, 40)

**RUSH RIVER** (Cass). This was a GNRR townsite planned in Sec. 27-142-53, Erie Twp., and named for the river that flows through the area. A section house was built and timetables were printed showing this station, but site owner Donald Viestenz apparently did not have the influence of Frank L. Williams and George S. Churchill, who persuaded the railroad to relocate the townsite two miles north to what became Erie. (25, 77)

**RUSO** (McLean). This Soo Line RR station was founded in 1906 in Sec. 5-150-80, Otis Twp.,

just SE of the border point shared by McLean, Ward, and McHenry counties. The post office was established December 1, 1906 with Edwin J. Burgess pm. The village incorporated in 1909, and by 1910 reported a population of 141, with a doctor, newspaper, and many other luxuries often missing in new townsites. Since that time, however, RUSO has been in decline, and had just 12 residents in 1980. The post office, Zip Code 58778, remains open. The name is said to be a Russian word meaning south of us, while others say it was coined from SOuth RUssia, the homeland of many area settlers. (1, 2, 18, 28, 33, 40, 52, 79)

**RUSSELL** (Bottineau). This farm post office was established August 21, 1901 with Austin C. Russell pm on his farm in NE¼ Sec. 30-160-79, Tacoma Twp. Mr. Russell came here in 1883 from Ontario, Canada, and was the chairman of the first county commission. Russell is a Latin name meaning red-haired. In 1905 it was relocated to the new Soo Line RR townsite in NW¼ Sec. 20-160-79, one mile to the NE. The villaged incorporated in 1905, and recorded a peak population of 161 in 1910, but the 1970 count was just 14. The post office closed February 7, 1958 with mail to Newburg. (1, 2, 3, 18, 19, 34, 40, 52, 75, 101, 153)

**RUSSELL** (LaMoure). This was a farm post office established June 11, 1884 with Ella Fidelia Walter pm. It was located in SW¼ Sec. 28-135-63, Russell Twp., midway between Dickey and Edgeley, and named for its township, which was named for Russell Root, grandfather of the pm's husband, Guy Walter. The petition for the post office had requested the name Russellville, but postal officials shortened it to RUSSELL. A small community began, reporting a population of 30 in 1890, but it declined and the post office closed January 23, 1899 with mail to Dickey. (2, 3, 25, 40, 410, 414)

**RUTHVILLE** (Ward). This townsite was founded in 1931 by William Mackenroth (1880-1935), who named it for his daughter Ruth, later Mrs. Herbert Rhoades of Sun City, AZ. Ruth is a Hebrew name meaning beauty. It is located at the junction of Secs. 1 & 2-156-83, Eureka Twp., and Secs. 31 &

*Rutland about 1910*

32-157-82, Tatman Twp., ten miles north of Minot. It is two miles south of the main entrance to Minot Air Force Base, and has enjoyed many economic benefits since the opening of the military facility in the 1950's. (19, 34, 100)

**RUTLAND** (Sargent). This GNRR townsite was founded in 1887 in SW¼ Sec. 19-130-54, Ransom Twp., and SE¼ Sec. 24-130-55, Rutland Twp. It was first called STEWART in honor of Albert H. Stewart who donated the townsite, but when Mr. Stewart established the post office on February 23, 1887, he renamed it RUTLAND for his hometown in VT, which was named for Rutland, Worcestershire, England by John Murray, founder of the VT city. Most VT towns were indirectly named for living English nobility, in this case being John Manners, 3rd Duke of Rutland (1696-1779). The elevation is 1216, the Zip Code is 58067, and a peak population of 309 was reached in 1950. (1, 2, 3, 10, 25, 33, 40, 45, 52, 434)

**RUTTEN** (Ramsey). This farm post office was established November 1, 1887 with Francis Michael Hubert "Frank" Rutten pm. It was located in N½ Sec. 5-154-62, Ontario Twp., eight miles north of Crary, and closed November 29, 1902 with mail to Crary. (2, 25, 40, 103, 240)

**RYBERG** (Burleigh). Anton Alfred Ryberg Sr. (1860-1942) came to Dakota in 1881 from his native Sweden, and homesteaded in NE¼ Sec. 24-140-79, Naughton Twp., twelve miles NW of Bismarck in 1883. He lived here until 1889, when he went to work for the railroad for a few years. During the 1883-1889 period, several contemporary accounts mention a RYBERG post office. This is not confirmed by government records, and it is likely that the Ryberg farmhouse was actually a mail distribution point. Mr. Ryberg later returned to Burleigh County, farming north of Menoken. (3, 9, 12, 40)

**RYDER** (Billings). This was a pioneer NPRR construction camp just west of Medora, and named for Mose Ryder, the operator of a saloon serving the laborers. (2, 3)

**RYDER** (Ward). This farm post office was established June 26, 1903 with Austin Gray pm. It was located in SE¼ Sec. 24-151-86, Ryder Twp., and named for Arthur F. Ryder of Minot, who had loaned his sheeplined coat to a postal inspector who was traveling to this site during cold weather. In 1906 the post office was moved to the new Soo Line RR townsite in Sec. 10-151-86, two miles NW of the original site. Pm Ole J. Bye of the nearby Bye post office took over the Ryder post office after it moved to the townsite. The village incorporated in 1907, and it became a city in 1968 with Donald L. Morris mayor. The Zip Code is 58779, and a peak population of 483 was reached in 1920. (2, 18, 40, 52, 79, 100, 277)

# S

**SAFFORD** (Traill). This GNRR station was founded in 1880 in NE¼ Sec. 5-144-50, Kelso Twp., and named for Larkin S. Safford, who came here in 1875 from ME and farmed 1,400 acres with his brother-in-law, Augustus L. Wentworth. The post office was established January 3, 1881 with Mr. Wentworth as pm, whose suggested name of Ludlow was rejected by postal officials, and the townsite was platted later that year by A. A. White. On February 1, 1882 the name was changed to KELSO. (3, 29, 40, 187, 414)

**SAGINAW** (Towner). This rural post office was established January 8, 1900 with Spencer W. Stout pm. He came here in 1898 from Saginaw, MI, which was given an Ojibway Indian name meaning the place of the Sacs, or Sauks. It was located in NW¼ Sec. 23-162-66, Rock Lake Twp., six miles NE of Rocklake, and closed May 31, 1908 with mail to Rocklake. (2, 10, 18, 40, 46)

**SAINT ANDREW** (Walsh). This was the post office serving the Red River townsite of SAINT ANDREWS. No explanation of the spelling difference is known, but it probably was the result of a frequent rejection of possessive-type names by postal officials. The post office was established October 20, 1880 with Lewis E. Booker pm. John B. Symons became pm in 1882, and he was followed by William McConnell in 1886. The post office closed July 28, 1891 with mail to Drayton. It reopened September 9, 1892 with Thomas J. Mahoney pm, but the town was declining rapidly by this time, and the post office closed for good November 30, 1903 with mail again to Drayton. (2, 3, 18, 25, 40, 75)

**SAINT ANDREWS** (Walsh). This was a pioneer settlement on the Red River founded about 1879 in SW¼ Sec. 25-158-51, Saint Andrews Twp., in the extreme NE corner of Walsh County. It was named for Saint Andrews, New Brunswick, Canada, which was named by a French priest who set the Cross of St. Andrew on the site. St. Andrew is the patron saint of Scotland. The townsite was platted in 1880 by the Red River Transportation Co., but after being bypassed by the GNRR and NPRR, and seeing a general decline in riverboat traffic, the site declined. The 1890 population was just 32, and by the early 1900's it had become a ghost town, with the site returned to farmland. The post office at this townsite operated 1880-1903, and was called SAINT ANDREW. (2, 3, 10, 40, 75)

**SAINT ANDREWS STATION** (Walsh). This was a NPRR station built in 1887 in NW¼ Sec. 16-158-51, Saint Andrews Twp., four miles NW of the Red River port of Saint Andrews. It was first called NEW SAINT ANDREWS, but adopted this name about 1893. A post office called ELORA operated here 1895-1903, after which the station was renamed HERRICK. (3, 40, 75)

**SAINT ANTHONY** (Logan). This was a rural community founded in 1905 in NW 1/4 Sec. 24-133-73, fourteen miles SSW of Napoleon. St. Anthony's Catholic Church was built in 1905, with a parish house added in 1908, and the town hall was built in 1911. Joseph Job and Martin Dillman erected rival stores in 1913. Mr. Job died during the flu epidemic of 1918, and Mr. Dillman sold his store to Michael Sperle, who ran it until it burned in the 1920's. The site was abandoned in the 1960's. (3, 34)

**SAINT ANTHONY** (Morton). This is a rural settlement in SE¼ Sec. 6 & NE 1/4 Sec. 7-136-81, fourteen miles south of Mandan. It was founded about 1890 and called LITTLE HEART, but by 1896 it had adopted the name of its Roman Catholic church. Anthony is a Latin name meaning beyond praise, and St. Anthony is the patron saint of Italy. The post office was established January 14, 1902 with Rev. Henry Braunagel pm. The elevation is 1783, the Zip Code is 58566, and a peak population of 130 was reported in 1930. (1, 2, 3, 18, 19, 23, 33, 40, 107, 414)

**SAINT BENEDICT** (Cass). This is a small village founded in 1879 in Secs. 34 & 35-138-49, Stanley Twp., three miles SE of Horace. It was named for St. Benedict (1748-1783), founder of the Roman Catholic order of this name, who was born Joseph Labre in France. Benedict is a Latin name meaning blessed. This community replaced the old mission of Holy Cross in Sec. 13-138-49. Father A. F. Bernier was the first resident priest in 1881, and several stores were established, but nearby Horace received most of the area's development. (3, 19, 34, 77, 83, 309)

**SAINT BONIFACE** (Logan). This was a rural community founded in 1905 in NE 1/4 Sec. 29-134-73, Weigel Twp., nine miles SW of Napoleon, and named for the rural Roman Catholic church established by seventeen families of Germans from Russia. Sebastian Burgad opened a store just to the north in SE¼ Sec. 20-134-73, selling it to Anton Wangler and his son-in-law, Benedict Fettig, in 1917. The store burned in 1921 and was not rebuilt. (3, 34, 113)

**SAINT CARL** (Ward). This farm post office was the second to be established in Ward County, and its purpose was primarily to increase the number of post offices in the Souris River valley to justify a regular mail route to Burlington. It opened February 18, 1885 with Olaf Carl Larson as the first and only pm in NW¼ Sec. 4-154-82, Sundre Twp., about five miles SE of Minot. The name was chosen by James Johnson of Burlington to honor the pm. The "saint" part of the name is explained by a bit of folklore. Mr. Larson is said to have protested the addition to his given name, and Mr. Johnson is said to have responded, "Well, you're a saint, ain't ya?" Carl is a variant of Charles, a Teutonic name meaning man. The post office was

discontinued March 27, 1891 with mail to Minot. (2, 3, 19, 25, 40, 100)

**SAINT CLAUDE** (Rolette). This was a Roman Catholic mission, chapel, and school established in May 1882 in Sec. 3-163-70, Baxter Twp., two miles north of Saint John. Father John Malo directed the mission until 1884. A small settlement began, which today is considered to be the first white settlement in the county, and it today marked as a historic site. Claude is a Latin name meaning lame. Some sources spell the name Saint Claud, and others add "Mission" as part of the name. (2, 3, 123)

**SAINT ELIZABETH** (Stark). This was an unofficial name for the German-Hungarian community twelve miles south of Gladstone. The name comes from the sod church built here by Roman Catholic settlers in 1899. Occasionally the site was called SCHNELLREICH, but in 1911 the post office was established as LEFOR, which became the uncontested name of the community. (3, 74)

**SAINT GEORGE** (LaMoure). This was a pioneer townsite founded in 1882 by Richard Sykes, an Englishman who left his mark at many places in ND, particularly at Sykeston, his namesake townsite. This townsite was located in SE¼ Sec. 33-134-64, Nora Twp., two miles NW of Edgeley, and named for the patron saint of England. George is a Greek name meaning farmer. The post office was established June 16, 1884 with John B. Kesler pm at his store. When the Milwaukee Road RR established the new townsite of Edgeley in 1886, most of SAINT GEORGE quickly relocated there. The post office transferred its operations to Edgeley on November 16, 1886. (2, 3, 25, 40, 140)

**SAINT GERTRUDE'S** (Grant). This is a rural community in E½ Sec. 5-132-85 and SW¼ Sec. 35-133-85, Raleigh Twp., five miles SSW of Raleigh. Roman Catholic Germans from Russia came here about 1905, and St. Gertrude's Parish was formed in 1913, with a parochial school added to the church a few years later. A high school was built in 1960 which flourished for about twenty years, but declining enrollment, even with the recruitment of boarding students, caused the school to close in the 1980's. (3, 34, 106)

**SAINT JOE** (Ramsey). This was a Farmers Grain & Shipping Co. RR station built in 1905 in NE¼ Sec. 17-158-64, Klingstrup Twp., four miles NW of Starkweather. It was named for Joseph M. Kelly (1859-1936), a founder of the railroad, who came to the Devils Lake area in 1883 from his native Quebec, Canada. At one time the site included two grain elevators, a loading platform, a school, and several houses, but only one elevator remains at the site today. (34, 103)

**SAINT JOHN** (Rolette). This early settlement

in Sec. 15-163-70, Baxter Twp., was called SAINT JOHN'S until November 17, 1892, when the name was changed to SAINT JOHN to comply with new government spelling regulations. The village incorporated in 1903, and it has had a population of about 400 for most of the twentieth century, peaking at 517 in 1940. The elevation is 1945, and the Zip Code is 58369. (3, 40, 52, 123)

**SAINT JOHN'S** (Rolette). This settlement began in 1843 as a trading post in Sec. 15-163-70, Baxter Twp. When the nearby Roman Catholic mission school of Saint Claude began in 1882, this site again attracted settlers, and the post office was established August 7, 1882 with William Brunelle pm. Some say the name was selected by pioneer settler F. H. A. Bourassa for his hometown of Saint John, Quebec, Canada, while others say Father John Malo named it for St. John the Baptist. Although the official name was SAINT JOHN'S, known postmarks omit the apostrophe. The GNRR reached the site and made it the terminus of its branch line from Churchs Ferry, and a population of 150 was reported in 1890. On November 17, 1892 the name of the post office was changed to SAINT JOHN to comply with new government spelling regulations. (2, 3, 40, 79, 123)

**SAINT JOSEPH** (Grant). This rural community was founded in 1893 twelve miles south of Glen Ullin. It took its name from the local Roman Catholic church built in 1899 in Sec. 26-137-88, and named for the husband of the Virgin Mary. Joseph is a Hebrew name meaning he shall add. The post office was established May 13, 1907 with Frank W. McDonald pm, with that facility located in the country store of S. A. Davis in S½ Sec. 20-137-88, two miles west of the church. The post office closed March 31, 1919 with mail to Glen Ullin, and the store closed in 1922. The church operated until 1977, when it became affiliated with the Sacred Heart Church in Glen Ullin. (1, 2, 3, 13, 17, 18, 19, 40, 53, 105, 165, 176, 177)

**SAINT JOSEPH** (Pembina). This settlement was founded as early as 1845 by Father George A. Belcourt, the famous missionary, in Sec. 21-163-56, Walhalla Twp., and took its name from the church built by Fr. Belcourt. It was commonly known by its slang name, St. Joe. The post office was established January 26, 1855 with Charles Grant (1824-1888) as pm, when the site was still in Minnesota Territory. It closed October 21, 1863, but reopened January 17, 1865. As one of the oldest settlements in ND, it claims a number of firsts. The first printing press in ND was brought here in 1853, and the first flour mill in the state was built here in 1856. A customs office opened in 1870. On July 21, 1871 the name was changed to WALHALLA. (2, 25, 40, 79, 108, 292)

**SAINT MARTIN** (Dunn). This was a Roman Catholic settlement centered around St. Martin's Catholic Church in NE¼ Sec. 20-143-91, seven miles SSW of Dodge. The post office was established April 18, 1908 in the home of pm Joseph Jacobs, a native of South Russia who came here in 1897, in Sec. 18-143-91, but the order was rescinded November 25, 1908. (3, 40)

**SAINT MICHAEL** (Benson). White people were in this Indian community as early as 1874. A Roman Catholic mission was founded here by nuns from Montreal, Quebec, Canada, and named for St. Michael, the Chief of the Celestial Hierarchy. Michael is a Hebrew name meaning like unto the Lord. Major William H. Forbes was the first Indian Agent here. It is located in E½ Sec. 17-152-64, Mission Twp., on the GNRR five miles NW of Tokio. The post office was established February 25, 1932 with Damian A. Preske pm. The Zip Code is 58370, and a population of 50 was reported in 1960. (2, 18, 19, 33, 34, 40, 110)

**SAINT MICHAEL'S** (Emmons). This is a rural community founded in 1914 in SW 1/4 Sec. 22-133-74, seventeen miles ENE of Linton, and named for the rural Roman Catholic church at this site, which was dedicated in September 1915 on the Sunday closest to the feast of Saint Michael the archangel. Leo and Christian Kuntz operated a store just south of the church in NW¼ Sec. 27-133-74 beginning about 1920, and the community is sometimes called KUNTZ. Other stores were later opened by Daniel Kuhn and Joseph A. Gefreh. A parish hall was built in 1948, and the community continues to serve the people of east central Emmons County. (3, 18, 34, 66)

**SAINT ONA** (Billings). A map included in the 1881 NPRR annual report shows a station called SAINT ONA between Little Missouri and Sully Springs. No other information is available. (3)

**SAINT PIERRE** (Cavalier). This was the first settlement in Cavalier County, founded in early 1882 in Sec. 5-161-57, Olga Twp., and named for Father Cyrille Saint Pierre, the local Roman Catholic priest. His last name is the French equivalent of Saint Peter, considered to be the first pope. When he became the pm later in the year, the site was renamed OLGA. (2, 3, 19, 40, 115)

**SAINT PIUS** (Stark). St. Pius Catholic Church, named for Pope Pius V (1504-1572), born Michele Ghislieri, was built in 1910 in SE¼ Sec. 13-137-97, fourteen miles SSW of Dickinson. A rural community called SCHEFIELD developed, and on June 6, 1913 a townsite was platted and named for the church. Development was very slow, and SCHEFIELD became the more commonly-used name for the site. (3, 5, 18, 74)

**SAINT STEPHENS CHURCH** (Stark). This is a rural community centered around St. Stephen's Church in NW¼ Sec. 21-137-92, fourteen miles south of Richardton, which was named for St. Stephen (d. 1038), the Hungarian king who introduced Christianity to his people. An earlier St. Stephen is considered to be the first Christian martyr. Stephen is a Greek name

meaning a crown. The settlers were primarily Roman Catholics of German-Hungarian ancestry, and the first masses were held in 1900. The Spalding post office operated one mile SW of here 1900-1903. The first resident priest was Fr. Anthony Nussbaumer in 1928. A new brick church building was built in 1951 under the direction of Fr. James Reilly, O.S.B. (3, 5, 18, 19, 34, 44, 74)

**SAINT THOMAS** (Pembina). This GNRR townsite was founded in 1881 in Secs. 3, 4, & 10-159-53, Saint Thomas Twp., and named by settlers from Saint Thomas, Ontario, Canada, which was named for Col. Thomas Talbot (1771-1853), a colonizer of Canada who is credited with establishing many Canadian townsites. Thomas is a Hebrew name meaning the twin. The post office was established July 25, 1881 with Thomas J. Lemon pm. The city incorporated in 1885, and a peak population of 850 was reported in 1890, with the 1980 count being a respectable 528. The elevation is 847, and the Zip Code is 58276. Native sons include Edward K. Thompson, onetime Editor of *Life* magazine and the founder of *The Smithsonian* magazine, and Thomas E. Whelan, U. S. Ambassador to Nicaragua 1951-1961. (1, 2, 10, 18, 19, 25, 33, 40, 52, 79, 108)

**SAINT VINCENT** (Morton). This was a rural community founded in 1888 in NW 1/4 Sec. 2-139-83, Sweet Briar Twp., twelve miles WNW of Mandan. The community has also been called CROWN BUTTE. The local Roman Catholic church was first called St. Margaret's, but was renamed to honor Bishop Vincent Wehrle (1855-1941), a native of Switzerland who was the first Bishop of the Bismarck Diocese, and a promoter of Assumption Abbey at Richardton. The post office was established October 20, 1908 with Henry Pfau pm, and closed June 15, 1914 with mail to Sweetbriar. It reopened July 30, 1917, but closed for good December 14, 1918 with mail again to Sweetbriar. The only population report was a count of 12 in 1908. (1, 2, 3, 17, 18, 34, 40, 53, 107, 414)

**SALEM** (Morton). This NPRR townsite was founded in 1883 in Sec. 21-139-85, Engelter Twp., and named for the Biblical city of Salem, which is an Anglicized form of the Hebrew word *shalom*, meaning peace, and is a part of the name Jerusalem, meaning city of peace. Others say the name means dead. When it was learned that there already was a Salem in what is now SD, the settlers changed the name to NEW SALEM. (2, 3, 10, 79, 109)

**SALINE** (McHenry). This was a farm post office established July 11, 1901 with Elizabeth B. Huston pm. It was located in NE¼ Sec. 7-157-79, Saline Twp., seven miles ENE of Deering near Deep Creek. The township's name notes the existence of salt in the area, which was an important commodity for the early settlers, both as a food preservative and as a salt lick for their cattle. The post office closed March 31, 1909 with mail to Deering. Mount Carmel Methodist Camp was located near this site from 1907-1956 at a place called Grogan's Grove. (2, 3, 10, 18, 40, 187)

**SALT LAKE** (Walsh). This was a rural community centered in Martin Twp. (158-52), just NE of Grafton, and named for Salt Lake in Sec. 36-158-52. The lake's name is no doubt taken from the nearby Park River, orginally called the Little Salt River. The settlement became the NPRR townsite of Cashel in 1887, although the Salt Lake Rural Telephone Company perpetuated the old name until 1961. (3, 75)

**SALYARDS** (Ward). Several maps circa 1900 show a Soo Line RR loading station named SALYARDS in Sec. 14-155-83, Harrison Twp., in the NW part of the city of Minot. The name honored H. T. Salyards, founder of the Minot Mercantile Co. and a pioneer in local political and banking affairs. (2, 3, 414)

**SAMS** (Bottineau). This was a farm post office established January 23, 1902 with Samuel Lewis pm, with the post office taking the possessive form of his nickname and the township taking his family name. Samuel is a Hebrew name meaning asked of God. It was located in Sec. 30-160-81, Lewis Twp., six miles SE of Maxbass. It moved three miles closer to that city in 1905, and closed June 2, 1906 with mail to Hurd. (2, 3, 19, 40, 101, 153)

**SANBORN** (Barnes). The NPRR built this station in 1877 in SW¼ Sec. 14-140-60, Potter Twp., between Sixth Siding (Hobart) and Seventh Siding (Eckelson). Townsite promoter Louis S. Lenham platted the site in 1879, and the post office was established May 15, 1879 with G. T. Bauder pm, who named it for George G. Sanborn, Treasurer of the NPRR. Sanborn is an Old English name meaning from the sandy brook. Mr. Bauder's wife, Lizzie, actually performed the duties at the post office. The elevation is 1468, the Zip Code is 58480, and the village, which incorporated in 1884, reached a peak population of 675 in 1890, but has declined to a count of 239 in 1980. (1, 2, 3, 18, 19, 25, 34, 40, 52, 76, 79, 330)

**SANDCREEK** (Slope). This was a farm post office established June 21, 1898 with Edwin B. Brewster pm. It was the second post office in what is now Slope County, and received its mail from Medora, about fifty miles to the north. It was located in NE¼ Sec. 34-134-101, Chalky Butte Twp., ten miles south of Amidon, and was named for nearby Sand Creek. The post office closed December 15, 1909 with mail to Purcell. (1, 2, 3, 40, 82, 400, 414)

**SAND CREEK STATION** (Slope). This was the ninth station on the Bismarck-Fort Keogh stage route established in 1878. It was located on Sand Creek in SE 1/4 Sec. 14-135-102, Sand Creek Twp., six miles north of Amidon, and closed in 1882 after the completion of the NPRR mainline. (2, 3, 82)

**SANDERS** (Grant). This was a rural post office established August 27, 1907 with Dr. Charles B. Saunders, a physician who died in 1910, as pm at his home in SE¼ Sec. 12-133-88, Rock Twp., two miles SW of Leith. The spelling of the post office name as SANDERS is unexplained. Both Saunders and Sanders are Greek names

meaning son of Alexander, which means helper of mankind. On September 9, 1908 Jeppe G. Andersen took over the post office at his home in NW 1/4 Sec. 24-133-88, two miles to the south, and operated it until it closed February 28, 1911 with mail to Elm. During his tenure as pm, local references called this post office ANDERSEN, but official records indicate that Mr. Andersen continued to use the original name. Saunders is an erroneous spelling of the post office name. (2, 3, 18, 19, 40, 177, 414)

**SANDLIE** (Divide). This was a ranch post office established June 6, 1906 with Clara Isaacson (1874-1957) pm. She came here in 1900 with her husband, Hawkin Isaacson (1861-1931). It was located in NE¼ Sec. 26-160-103, Fertile Valley Twp., fourteen miles SSW of Alkabo, and closed March 31, 1913 with mail to Fertile. It was named for the Isaacson's hometown in Norway. Sandie is an erroneous spelling. (1, 2, 18, 40, 73, 415)

**SANDOUN** (Ransom). This Soo Line RR townsite was founded in 1890 in Sec. 25-134-53, Sandoun Twp., and named for its township, which is a coined word noting the sand dunes in the area. The post office was established May 23, 1892 with Llewellyn King pm. On April 26, 1905 the name was changed to McLEOD, officially to avoid confusion with Sanborn, but it was widely known that local residents were unhappy with the old name because of its negative connotations. Sandown is an erroneous spelling. (2, 3, 18, 40, 79, 85, 240)

**SANDY'S CORNER** (Walsh). This was a pioneer settlement in SE¼ Sec. 36-156-53, Walsh Centre Twp., first settled in the 1870's and abandoned in 1880 when the GNRR townsite of Minto was founded one mile to the ENE. The name is said to be coined from the landowner at the site, Alex "Sandy" Thomson, a native of Scotland, and the fact that it is near the corner of four townships, Walsh Centre, Harriston, Forest River, and Ardoch. (1, 2, 3, 75)

**SANFORD** (McKenzie). This was a rural post office established April 13, 1907 with Silas Morton, a native of PA who was nearly seventy years of age, as pm. It was located in SW¼ Sec. 26-153-95, Elm Tree Twp., one mile south of Charlson, and named for the many Sanford families in the area, particularly Paul and William J. Sanford, neighbors of Mr. Morton. Christopher J. Graue became pm on March 9, 1910, and moved the post office seven miles ESE to his home in SE¼ Sec. 35-153-94, River View Twp. Because of confusion with Lansford, the name was changed to MAYNARD on August 25, 1910. (2, 3, 18, 40, 228, 229, 414, 415)

**SANGER** (Oliver). This was a pioneer Missouri River town founded by George Sanger (1830-1920) and his brother, Charles Henry Sanger, in 1879 in SW¼ Sec. 32-143-81, Sanger Twp. The post office was established June 6, 1881 with George Sanger pm. In 1885 the county seat of Raymond, two miles NNW of here, changed its name to Sanger as part of the requirements for securing a post office, but the change was quickly ruled to be illegal, and this town got its name back, replacing Raymond as the county seat in 1888. Charles P. Thurston became pm on May 17, 1890, and he changed the name to BENTLEY. On September 23, 1891 George Sanger again became the pm, and he restored the SANGER name. It remained the county seat until 1902 when it was replaced by the new townsite of Center. In 1909 Robert Livingston platted a new townsite at the NPRR grade in NW¼ Sec. 30-143-81, just south of the old Raymond townsite. An early boom produced a population of 100 in 1920, but the 1985 count was just 3. The post office closed July 31, 1964 with mail to Hensler. (1, 2, 3, 18, 25, 40, 79, 121)

**SAN HAVEN** (Rolette). The state tuberculosis sanitarium was authorized in 1909, and was built on a hill just north of Dunseith in Sec. 19-162-72, opening in 1912. A post office named MONTAIR was established here in 1922, and on January 24, 1923 pm Dr. John C. Lamont changed the name to SAN HAVEN, coined from the Latin word *sanitas*, meaning health, and haven to describe its worth to its patients. The Zip Code is 58371, but as of 1988 plans are well under way to close the facility, which undoubtedly will terminate the post office as well. (2, 3, 33, 40, 79, 123)

**SANISH** (Mountrail). This Soo Line RR townsite was founded in 1914 when their Max branch line was extended beyond the temporary terminus of Plaza. It was named by Charles W. Hoffman, an official at the Fort Berthold Indian Reservation, for the Arikara word meaning real people, or object. The correct pronunciation of the Indian word is saw-nish, but san-ish became the commonly used pronunciation from the beginning. The post office was established January 29, 1915 with William F. Thompson pm. The village incorporated in 1917, a bridge was built across the Missouri River in 1927, and a peak population of 463 was reached in 1930, but the building of the Garrison Dam after World War II led to the demise of this settlement. The village dissolved its incorporation charter on April 29, 1953 with M. H. Aubol as the last mayor, and most citizens relocated to the government-sponsored New Town, two miles to the NW. A few people continue to reside in "new" SANISH near the old townsite, which sometimes resurfaces when the level of the reservoir drops. The post office, Zip Code 58780, closed May 2, 1980, although this fact was not recorded by the government until September 30, 1984. (1, 2, 3, 33, 40, 41, 72, 253)

**SANSAHVILLE** (Bottineau). This was a rural post office established March 17, 1888 with Norman A. Stewart pm. It was located in NE¼ Sec. 26-162-77, Peabody Twp., six miles west of Bottineau, and named for a

*Sanish in the late 1940's*

pioneer settler who operated a small store in his home. The post office closed November 24, 1896 with mail to Bottineau. Sausaville and Susahville are erroneous spellings. (2, 3, 25, 40, 153, 240, 379, 415)

**SARATOGA** (LaMoure). This pioneer settlement began about 1881, and was named by settlers from Saratoga, NY, which bears a Mohawk Indian name meaning springs from the hillside, descriptive of the NY location. It was located in Sec. 3-135-62, Roscoe Twp., near the James River boat landing called DICKEY'S LANDING. The post office was established September 5, 1881 with William E. Mansfield pm. The NPRR built into this section in 1884, and a new townsite called DICKEY was founded. The SARATOGA post office relocated to DICKEY on October 28, 1884. (2, 10, 18, 25, 40, 139)

**SARATOGA SPRINGS** (LaMoure). Several contemporary maps show SARATOGA SPRINGS in Sec. 3-135-62, Roscoe Twp., the site of the pioneer settlement whose post office was called SARATOGA. (3, 414)

**SARDIS** (Nelson). This Soo Line RR station was built in SW¼ Sec. 13-154-60, Clara Twp., ten miles west of Whitman near the junction with the GNRR. Martin Loken (1863-1911), a native of Norway, owned the site. The name is said to commemorate the ancient city of Sardis, Asia Minor, mentioned in the Bible. No development occurred at the site, which was shown on maps circa 1905-1925. Saidis is an erroneous spelling. (1, 2, 3, 5, 124)

**SARGEANT** (Sargent). This was a farm post office established June 1, 1883 with Willis W. Bradley pm. It was located in SE¼ Sec. 4-131-55, Dunbar Twp., six miles NNE of Forman, and named for Malcolm L. Sargeant, who settled about thirty miles to the east in Richland County in 1879, and apparently was an acquaintance of Mr. Bradley. On August 20, 1883 the post office was replaced by the facility at the new townsite of Dunbar, two miles to the SW, with Mr. Bradley continuing as the pm. (2, 40, 165, 167, 414)

**SARGENT** (Sargent). This townsite was established in early 1883 as BLACKSTONE, but on December 31, 1883 the name of the post office was changed to SARGENT with Ford D. Benton continuing as the pm. It was located in NW¼ Sec. 13-130-57, Sargent Twp., and named along with its county and township for Col. H. E. Sargent, General Manager of the NPRR. A population of 75 was reported in 1890, but the proposed NPRR line through here never materialized, and after a Soo Line RR townsite named Cogswell was founded two miles to the north, most of SARGENT relocated there within a few months. The post office closed August 27, 1890 with mail to Cogswell. (2, 3, 40, 165, 167)

**SARLES** (Cavalier & Towner). This GNRR station was founded in 1905 in NW 1/4 Sec. 18-163-64, Cypress Twp., Cavalier County, and has grown slightly into Sec. 13-163-65, Dash Twp., Towner County. It was named for newly elected Gov. Elmore Yocum Sarles (1859-1929), who came here July 4, 1906 to give the Independence Day address. The post office was established November 25, 1905 with William Woods pm. The elevation is 1586, the Zip Code is 58372, and the village, which incorporated in 1906, reached a peak population of 383 in 1930. D. W. Elves was the customs agent at the Canadian port-of-entry 1905-1940. SARLES is the hometown of Allen I. Olson, ND Attorney General 1973-1981 and Governor 1981-1985. (1, 2, 3, 18, 33, 40, 52, 79, 208)

**SARLES** (Walsh). This Soo Line RR station was founded in 1905 in Secs. 13 & 14-157-58, Adams Twp., and named for newly elected Gov. Elmore Yocum Sarles. A community in Cavalier County had just chosen this name, so this community became ADAMS, retaining the name of the rural post office that relocated to the railroad townsite. (1, 2, 3, 18, 40, 75)

**SARNIA** (Nelson). This was a farm post office established January 15, 1898 with Engebret L. Nestegard pm. It was located in NW¼ Sec. 5-154-58, Sarnia Twp., two miles NW of Whitman, and named for Sarnia, Ontario, Canada, which was named in 1835 by Sir John Colborne, Lt. Governor of Canada, for his former home, the island of Guernsey in the English Channel, which had been named Sarnia by the ancient Romans. On September 26, 1898 the post office moved two miles NE to the home of new pm Knut O. Loken in NE¼ Sec. 32-155-58, Perth Twp., Walsh County. (2, 3, 10, 18, 40, 53, 75, 414, 415)

**SARNIA** (Walsh). This was a farm post office established January 15, 1898 in Nelson County. On September 26, 1898 it moved two miles NE to NE¼ Sec. 32-155-58, Perth Twp., the home of new pm Knut O. Loken. It later moved one mile SW to the home of Tosten M. Lillehaugen (1847-1934) in SE¼ Sec. 31-155-58, just above the Nelson County line near the original site. The post office closed March 15, 1914 with mail to Brocket. (1, 2, 3, 40, 75, 415)

**SATHER** (Burleigh). This was a farm post office established June 12, 1901 with Ole Sather pm. It was located in NW¼ Sec. 18-140-80, Burnt Creek Twp., ten miles NNW of Bismarck. Mr. Sather came here in 1882 from Norway with his parents and brothers, was a school district official, and in 1908 organized a rural telephone company, which was renamed in his honor in 1929, eventually being absorbed by Northwestern Bell in 1974. The post office was on the Painted Woods rural mail route with Charles K. Kupitz carrier, and closed November 15, 1911 with mail to Wogansport. (2, 3, 8, 12, 18, 40)

**SAUNDERS** (Cass). This was a Milwaukee Road RR station built in late 1883 in Sec. 1-138-49, Stanley Twp., six miles south of Fargo, and named for A. H. and O. A. Saunders, owners of the site. Saunders is a Greek name meaning son of Alexander. The post office was established September 5, 1895 with John G. Steen pm, and closed September 30, 1905 with mail to Wild Rice. A population of 10 was reported in 1920. The station was removed in December 1940. Sanders is an erroneous spelling. (1, 2, 3, 18, 19, 25, 34, 40, 77)

**SAUNDERSVILLE** (Wells). William and Fannie Saunders filed a plat September 20, 1915 for the city of SAUNDERSVILLE in NE¼ Sec. 20-150-72, Wells Twp., two miles NE of Harvey, and just west of the Sheyenne River Academy, a Seventh Day Adventist school built in 1904. Several oldtimers of the area tell of a thriving little city, but only a handful of lots were ever sold and rumors of a post office are not confirmed by government records. Active promotion of the townsite had ended by 1925, and the few houses that were built there were faculty homes for teachers at the school, which closed its doors in 1977, moving to the newly-built Dakota Adventist Academy north of Bismarck. The town, however, has never been legally dissolved, and continues to appear in county atlases. (3, 18, 68, 363)

**SAWYER** (Ward). This is a Soo Line RR townsite in NW¼ Sec. 11-153-81, Sawyer Twp. Some say it was named for an official of the railroad, while others say it was named for a Col. Sawyer, an authority on horse racing. The name is of Celtic origin, and means a cutter of wood. The Echo post office moved here April 26, 1898 with Fred L. Hartleib (1873-1919) as pm. The elevation is 1525, the Zip Code is 58781, and the village, which incorporated in 1908, reached a peak population of 420 in 1980. (1, 2, 18, 19, 33, 40, 79, 100, 373)

**SAXONY** (Cass). This GNRR station was built in 1897 in E½ Sec. 29-140-52, Casselton Twp., just west of Casselton on the Devils Lake branch line. It was named for the province of Germany founded in 880 A.D. by the Saxons, a Teutonic tribe whose name means swordsmen. The station was removed in December 1940. (1, 2, 3, 5, 18, 34, 77)

**SCATTER VILLAGE** (McLean). This was a settlement that began in 1933 in NE 1/4 Sec. 5-147-90, Elbowoods Twp., during the construction of the Four Bears Bridge. The name made light of the haphazard layout of the site. The town is now inundated by Lake Sakakawea. (2, 3, 28)

**SCHAFER** (McKenzie). This place began as a rural post office established November 28, 1899 with Charles E. Shafer pm. It was named for the pm, with the addition of the "c" credited to G. B. Metzger (1851-1930), said to be the first settler in the area, who had seen Mr. Shafer's name misspelled so many times that he thought the post office name should reflect the incorrect form of the name. It was located in NE¼ Sec. 23-150-98, Schafer Twp., five miles east of Watford City, and was involved in the battles for the county seat in 1905-1906, capturing the honor in 1906 from Alexander. This resulted in a boom period, with the town reporting a population of 225 in 1920. The GNRR planned to extend its line from Watford City through Schafer to New Rockford, but high land acquisition costs caused the railroad to drop these plans, resulting in a rapid decline for SCHAFER, now destined to be without a railroad. On June 1, 1941 the county seat was moved to Watford City, and SCHAFER soon became a ghost town. John K. Diehm became pm in 1909, and held that position until the post office closed September 30, 1941 with mail to Watford City. The founder's son, George F. Shafer (1888-1948), was Governor of ND 1929-1932. (1, 2, 3, 18, 40, 79, 229, 414)

**SCHAIBLE** (Cass). This NPRR siding was built in 1881 in NW¼ Sec. 33-138-50, Warren Twp., and named LEECHES. In 1887 it was renamed WARREN and a small village began to develop. On May 31, 1908 the NPRR named the station SCHAIBLE, the maiden name of the wife of George Hall, a NPRR official. Because of difficulty with the spelling and the pronunciation, and because the post office continued to use the WARREN name, the station name was changed back to WARREN on July 25, 1915. (1, 2, 18, 34, 40, 303)

**SCHALLER** (Grant). This was a farm post office established March 16, 1908 with John C. Schaller pm at his home in NE¼ Sec. 22-132-85, seven miles south of Raleigh. In 1912 it moved one mile NE to the home of new pm Nina Preston in SE¼ Sec. 14-132-85, and in 1917 it moved four miles south to the home of new pm Mrs. Fannie A. Angell in SW¼ Sec. 2-131-85. The post office closed January 31, 1921 with mail to

Shields. Scheller is an erroneous spelling. (1, 2, 3, 17, 18, 34, 40, 53, 176, 177, 414)

**SCHAPERA** (Ramsey). This was a farm post office established August 24, 1887 with Josef Schapera pm. It was located in NE¼ Sec. 5-156-63, Harding Twp., nine miles NE of Webster. On December 23, 1889 it moved four miles SE and was renamed IOLA. (2, 3, 25, 40, 103, 414)

**SCHEFIELD** (Stark). This was a rural community founded in 1911 in SE¼ Sec. 13-137-97, fourteen miles SSW of Dickinson near the St. Pius Catholic Church which had been built in 1910, with the community sometimes being called SAINT PIUS. The post office was established as SCHEFIELD on August 17, 1911 with Peter Jahner pm, and closed September 15, 1922 with mail to New England. A population of 25 was reported as late as 1960. The name is said to be a corruption of *schoenfeld*, German for beautiful field. (2, 3, 18, 40, 44, 74)

**SCHMALZ** (Morton). This was a farm post office established June 13, 1906 with John J. Schmalz pm. Schmalz is German for grease or lard. It was located in SW¼ Sec. 32-140-83, six miles NE of Judson, and closed August 31, 1907 with mail to Sweetbriar. (2, 3, 34, 40, 415)

**SCHMIDT** (Morton). This was a NPRR siding and loading station built in 1909 in Sec. 20-137-80, twelve miles SE of Mandan on land owned by Joseph Schmidt (1850-1940), who came here in 1881 from Austria. His son, whose name of Mikel was often Anglicized as Michael, became the pm when the post office established February 27, 1913. A population of 10 was reported here in 1920, but the post office closed March 31, 1924 with mail to Mandan. Michael Schmidt (1890-1942) was murdered by an ex-convict whom he had hired to work at the local elevator. SCHMIDT became a ghost town, and the railroad tracks were removed in 1967. (2, 3, 17, 18, 40, 79, 107)

**SCHMIDT** (Sheridan). This was a farm post office established April 19, 1901 with Ludwig Schmidt Sr. pm. It was located in NE¼ Sec. 30-149-74, Berlin Twp., ten miles SSW of Martin, and closed November 29, 1902 with mail to Harvey. (2, 3, 40, 415)

**SCHNEBLY** (Adams). This was a rural post office established June 4, 1907 with Henry L. Schnebly pm in his sod house in NE¼ Sec. 7-130-95, Duck Creek Twp., seven miles north of Hettinger. The post office closed July 15, 1909 with mail to Hettinger. Schnelby and Schnebley are erroneous spellings. (2, 3, 18, 40, 77, 190)

**SCHNELLREICH** (Stark). This was an unofficial name for the German-Hungarian colony twelve miles south of Gladstone, centered in Sec. 17-137-94. The name is German for get rich quick, noting both the hopes and the humor of the pioneers. When the local Roman Catholic church was built of sod in 1899, the community adopted its name of SAINT ELIZABETH. When the post office was established in 1911 as LEFOR, this name became universally used by its people. (3, 44, 74)

**SCHURMEIER** (Grand Forks). This was a

GNRR station built in 1881 in S½ Sec. 7-152-50, Falconer Twp., between Grand Forks and Manvel. It was named for J. H. Schurmeier, a wagon maker from Saint Paul, MN, who owned land along the right-of-way at this site. The buildings at SCHURMEIER were moved to other sites after a few years, but the siding was used into the 1930's. The site is now vacant. (2, 3, 18, 25, 31, 69)

**SCHUTZ** (Hettinger). This was a farm post office established October 2, 1905 with Charles E. Schutz, a native of South Russia who came here in 1905, as pm. Schutz is German for shelter. It was located in NE¼ Sec. 32-136-91, Odessa Twp., twelve miles north of Burt, but the order was rescinded April 19, 1906 before the post office had gone into operation. Schultz is an erroneous spelling. (2, 3, 18, 40)

**SCHUYLER** (Benson). This NPRR station was founded in June 1901 in SW¼ Sec. 30-152-68, Aurora Twp., four miles ESE of Maddock. It was platted by the owner of the townsite, William H. S. Schuyler. Later that year the name was changed to FLORA because of alleged duplication of the name SCHUYLER on NPRR lines. (2, 18, 34, 110, 239)

**SCORIA** (Billings). This was a NPRR station built on the mainline in Sec. 5-139-101, five miles SE of Medora. It was named for the reddish-colored rock common to the area, which was formed by clay, sand, and shale baking around the burning coal veins. The elevation is 2509. No development took place, and the area was served at all times by the Medora post office. (1, 2, 18, 25, 34, 79, 81)

**SCOTIA** (Bottineau). This was a rural settlement founded in 1895 in Sec. 31-163-79, Scotia Twp., on the east bank of the Souris River. A ferry service across the river was the first economic venture at this place, which was named for its township, which was given the poetic name for Scotland by pioneer settlers from that country. The post office was established April 5, 1895 with William C. Gourley pm in his store. On December 17, 1903 the post office moved three miles SW to the new GNRR townsite of Westhope, assuming the new name. (2, 3, 40, 101, 153)

**SCOTT** (Ramsey). This was a pioneer settlement at the head of Teller's Bay. Because of fluctuating water levels, and the fact that the site was unsurveyed at the time of its existance, the exact location of SCOTT is not positively identified, but it probably was in, or very near, Sec. 22-154-65, Grand Harbor Twp., two miles south of present-day Grand Harbor. The post office was established July 24, 1882 with Ever Wagness pm, who suggested the name Arthur. This was rejected in favor of SCOTT, said to be for a Lt. Scott. The name literally refers to the Scottish people, and is variously interpreted as tattoed, or wanderers. The site failed to develop, and the post office closed December 6, 1882 with mail to Swan, which fourteen days later was itself replaced by the Grand Harbor post office. (2, 3, 18, 19, 34, 40, 103, 414, 415)

**SCOTT** (Williams). This was a farm post office established March 21, 1906 with Adah Amsterberg Scott pm. She was the wife of Ed Scott (1861-1942), a pioneer of the area. It was located in NW¼ Sec. 19-154-103, Round Prairie Twp., eight miles NW of Trenton, and closed November 30, 1912 with mail to Trenton. (2, 3, 18, 40, 50, 53)

**SCOTT'S** (Barnes). In 1893 the ASHTABULA post office moved to Sec. 2-142-58, Ashtabula Twp., the site of an anticipated railroad townsite. Nothing came of the venture, but local people began calling the site SCOTT'S for pm James Scott, although the post office kept the original name until it closed in 1913. (3, 40, 76)

**SCOUTEN'S ADDITION TO ECKELSON** (Barnes). This is the official name for the new townsite of ECKELSON in SE¼ Sec. 14-140-61, Eckelson Twp., two miles west of the original NPRR townsite of this name. The village was moved here in 1897 because of the steep grade at the original site. Burton Scouten, who came here in 1885 from Towanda, PA, was the owner of the new site. (2, 3, 76)

**SCOVILL** (Ransom). This rural post office was established September 28, 1880 with Patrick Devitt pm in NW¼ Sec. 32-134-54, Scovill Twp., nine miles ESE of Lisbon. It was named for Charles Merritt Scovill and his wife, Olivia H. Scovill, who came here in 1880 from NY. The post office closed January 31, 1905 with mail to Milnor. Scoville is an erroneous spelling. (2, 18, 40, 94, 171)

**SCOW** (Traill). This pioneer post office was established October 6, 1879 with Ole G. Hangen pm, and closed September 14, 1880 with mail to Trysil. The location is unknown, although most references point towards Traill County as the site. It is said to have been named for the Schow family with a modification of the spelling. The Schows came to America in 1867 from Norway, and were among the first pioneers in the Red River valley in 1870. A grandson, Martin Schow (1892-1977), moved to Regent in 1911 where he was a prominent resident for many years. (2, 3, 40, 179)

**SCRANTON** (Bowman). This Milwaukee Road RR townsite was founded in 1907 in SE¼ Sec. 23 & NE¼ Sec. 26-131-100, Scranton Twp., and named for Scranton, PA because both towns were the centers of coal mining districts. The PA city was founded in 1788 as Slocum Hollow, and was known as Lackawanna, Harrison, and Scrantonia before adopting its current name in 1851 to honor Selden T. Scranton and his brother, George Whitfield Scranton (1811-1861), as well as their cousin, Joseph H. Scranton (1813-1872), area ironworks developers. The ND post office was established October 3, 1907 with Alice Radebaugh pm. The elevation is 2770, the Zip Code is 58653, and a peak population of 416 was reached in 1980. SCRANTON incorporated as a village in 1909, and became a city in 1937. Warren Christopher, chief American negotiator during the Iranian hostage crisis of 1979-1981, was born here in 1925. (1, 2, 3, 5, 10, 18, 34, 40, 79, 120, 381)

**SCRIPTOWN** (McHenry). This pioneer townsite was promoted in 1881 by Johnson Nickeus, a prominent Jamestown attorney, who named it hoping that it would become a valuable site when the NPRR arrived. This never happened, but the town did have a brief moment of glory. Although it was little more than a couple log buildings, SCRIPTOWN was named as the county seat when McHenry County organized in 1884, holding that honor until Towner was founded in 1886. Allan Mitchell "managed" the log cabin court house, and George Cameron, the first Superintendent of Schools, had a two-room log hotel. C. M. Sivyer was the storekeeper. Within a few years the site was abandoned in favor of nearby Velva. Although some ruins were existing as late as the 1920's, the exact site of SCRIPTOWN is not positively known, the best guess being in the NW¼ Sec. 25-153-80, Velva Twp., two miles east of Velva. Scripton is an erroneous spelling. (2, 3, 18, 79, 182, 279, 412)

**SEABORN** (Stutsman). This was a farm post office established September 14, 1907 with Thomas Seaborn, who came here in 1903, as pm. It was located in NW 1/4 Sec. 10-143-68, Wadsworth Twp., five miles NNE of Woodworth, and closed December 21, 1912 with mail to Woodworth, although it continued to appear on maps into the late 1930's. Seeborn is an erroneous spelling. (1, 2, 3, 18, 40, 158)

**SEARING** (McKenzie). This was a farm post office established July 25, 1916 with Thomas C. Taylor pm. It was located in NW¼ Sec. 10-147-103, thirty-three miles SW of Watford City, and named for the site owner, Julius Searing Taylor, after Taylor had been rejected because of duplication in Stark County. The post office closed March 15, 1921 with mail to Alexander. It reopened February 7, 1922 in SE¼ Sec. 2-146-103, seven miles SSE of the original site as SEARING, but only after a name change to Dean had been rejected. In 1928 it moved one mile NW to SE¼ Sec. 28-147-103, and operated until pm Annie Kemna closed the facility September 30, 1952 with mail to Sidney, MT. A population of 3 was reported in 1940. (2, 3, 40, 227, 414, 434)

**SECOND CROSSING OF THE SHEYENNE** (Barnes). The NPRR arrived here in 1872 and christened the site with this generic name to note that they had previously crossed the Sheyenne River just west of Fargo. When the siding was built it was renamed FIFTH SIDING. The first permanent settlers named the place WAHPETON, which was changed in 1874 to WORTHINGTON. Finally, in 1878, the name was changed to VALLEY CITY, and it has grown into the metropolis of Barnes County. Donald D. McFadgen and James Morrison had settled here before the arrival of the NPRR, and are considered to be the first settlers in VALLEY CITY. The first mail received at this place carried the address "2X Sheyenne." (2, 3, 76, 275)

**SECOND SIDING** (Cass). This NPRR station was built in 1872 and named to note the chronological order of sidings as they were built westward from Fargo. It was located in SE¼ Sec. 27-140-53, Wheatland Twp., and was renamed WHEATLAND in 1878. (2, 34, 77)

**SECOND SIDING** (Morton). This NPRR station was built in 1880 in SW¼ Sec. 25-139-86, Caribou Twp., three miles SW of New Salem. It was named to note the chronological order of sidings as they were built westward from Mandan. By 1884 it had been renamed BLUE GRASS by NPRR officials to note the wide-bladed, blue-colored bunch grass common to the area. (2, 3)

**SEDALIA** (Morton). This was a NPRR station built before 1890 in SW¼ Sec. 19-139-84, Dettman Twp., about midway between New Salem and Judson. It appeared on maps until the 1920's, although little development ever occurred here. It is thought that the name was suggested by Herman Friese, who came to America from Germany in 1882 and lived just south of the station. Mr. Friese lived in MO before coming to Morton County, and selected the name of the MO city that would become famous as the home of ragtime composer Scott Joplin. Sedalia, MO was founded by Gen. George R. Smith in 1856, who named it for his daughter, Sarah Elvira Smith, whose nickname was Sed, which was Latinized with the suffix "alia" to follow the fashion of the day. (1, 2, 3, 5, 10, 18, 25, 107, 121)

**SEDAN** (McHenry). This was a farm post office established May 12, 1905 with Felix Eberle pm. It was located in NW¼ Sec. 8-153-77, Regstad Twp., three miles NE of Karlsruhe, and named for Sedan, KS, which was named for Sedan, France, the site of a famous battle of the Franco-Prussian War in 1870 which led to the formation of the French Republic. The post office closed May 31, 1909 with mail to Balfour. (2, 10, 13, 18, 40, 53)

**SELDEN** (Rolette). This GNRR townsite in SE¼ Sec. 23-159-71, Rice Twp., was platted in 1905 as SELDEN, but it appears that the name was never in general use at the site. Selden is a Teutonic name meaning from the valley manor. The GNRR was fond of naming its townsites with British names, and it has been suggested that this name honored John Selden (1584-1654), an English statesman. The site was settled primarily by Norwegians who renamed it NANSON. (2, 3, 5, 18, 19, 123)

**SELFRIDGE** (Sioux). This Milwaukee Road RR station was founded in 1911 in NE¼ Sec. 34-130-82. Several theories exist as to the origin of its name. Some say it is descriptive of the ridge of hills in the area. Others say it was named for a Milwaukee Road RR official. Another theory is that it was named for Lt. Thomas E. Selfridge, a U. S. Army pilot who is considered to be the first fatality in aviation history in 1908. Yet another theory is that it was named for Thomas Oliver Selfridge (1804-1902), or his son, Thomas Oliver Selfridge Jr., both famous officers in the U. S. Navy. The post office was established May 20, 1912 with Eben W. Philput pm. The village incorporated in 1919 with lumber dealer Fred Rott as board president, and it became a city in 1968 with Grant Krebs as mayor. The elevation is 2183, the Zip Code is 58568, and a peak population of 371 was reached in 1960. (1, 2, 3, 5, 33, 40, 79, 127, 368)

**SELMA** (Grant). This was a farm post office

established May 27, 1907 with Frank Schrader pm, who named it for his daughter, Selma, who later married Charles Grease and lived in Sioux Falls, SD. Selma is a Teutonic name meaning fair. The post office was located in SW¼ Sec. 21-130-90, Schrader Twp., twenty-one miles south of New Leipzig on the north bank of the Cedar River. In 1909 Robert F. Anderson became the pm, moving the post office five miles NNW to his farm in NE¼ Sec. 32-131-90. It closed October 31, 1913 with mail to Pretty Rock. (1, 2, 3, 17, 18, 19, 40, 177, 358, 414)

**SELZ** (Emmons). This was a rural community of Roman Catholic Germans from Russia founded in the summer of 1885, and named for their former home of Selz, South Russia, a Kherson District settlement founded in 1808. The post office was established April 13, 1896 with Anton F. Vetter pm at his home in SW¼ Sec. 26-130-74, five miles ENE of Hague, and closed May 30, 1903 with mail to Hague, whose post office had recently been established by Franz Wolf, a former pm of SELZ. (2, 3, 23, 34, 40, 66)

**SELZ** (Pierce). This townsite was founded in 1910 by the Northern Town & Land Co. in NW¼ Sec. 33-151-72, Hagel Twp., as DALLAS. Postal officials objected to this name, and the post office was established October 25, 1910 as SELZ with Rochus Sanders pm. Mr. Sanders is credited with selecting the name, which according to some was for the author Charles Alden Selz, whose name was actually Charles Alden Seltzer, while a more likely explanation is that he named it for Selz, South Russia, the hometown of many area settlers. The GNRR's Surrey cutoff line arrived in 1912. The elevation is 1608, the Zip Code is 58373, and a peak population of 160 was recorded in 1920. (1, 2, 3, 33, 40, 68, 79, 114)

**SENECA** (Sargent). This GNRR station was founded in 1886 and named for Seneca County, NY, the home of many local settlers. The Seneca Indians lived in western NY, and were one of the five nations of the Iroquois, with their name said to mean stony area. It was located in Sec. 18-130-53, Kingston Twp., but because of anticipated confusion with Seneca, Faulk County, in what is now SD, the name was changed to CAYUGA in 1887. (2, 3, 10, 25)

**SENESCHAL** (McKenzie). This was a rural post office established May 12, 1911 with Charles H. Holliday pm. It was located in SE¼ Sec. 28-154-97, Twin Valley Twp., twenty-four miles NNE of Watford City on the south bank of the Missouri River, near the trading post and ferry service run by Capt. Edw. H. Seneschal, for whom it was named after Mr. Holliday's suggested name of WHITE CITY was rejected by postal officials. Capt. Seneschal's ferry was sunk during the spring 1917 icebreaking of the Missouri River. The post office was taken over by Ovid C. Parks in 1915, and by Guy R. Renbarger, a native of IN, in 1916, when it moved four miles ENE to Sec. 23-154-97. The post office closed October 31, 1918 with mail to Banks. (1, 2, 3, 40, 414, 415)

**SENNEF** (Dunn). This was a rural post office established August 24, 1915 with Charles

E. Senff pm at his home in NE¼ Sec. 4-141-91, about sixteen miles south of Dodge. It is thought that the variation in the spelling was intentional as part of an effort to assure the correct pronunciation. The name, nevertheless, was often misspelled with Senf, Sennf, and Sneff being the most frequently encountered versions. The post office closed December 30, 1916 with mail to Marshall. (2, 3, 18, 40, 223)

**SENTINEL BUTTE** (Golden Valley). The NPRR reached here in late 1880 and built a station in SE¼ Sec. 19-140-104, Sentinel Twp., which was named for the flat-topped butte three miles to the SE, elevation 3430, which was named to honor two Arikara Indian sentinels who were killed here in 1864 by the Sioux. The post office was established February 18, 1886 with Thomas F. Ives pm. The townsite did not develop, however, until the early 1900's. It was platted in June 1902, and incorporated as a village in 1913. The elevation is 2731, the Zip Code is 58654, and a peak population of 292 was recorded in 1920, with a decline to just 86 in 1980. Father Elwood Cassedy founded the well known Home on the Range for Boys near here in 1949. (1, 2, 3, 18, 25, 33, 40, 44, 79, 80)

**SERGIUS** (Bottineau). This rural post office was established May 11, 1900 with Sara E. Gaulke pm at her home in NW¼ Sec. 29-162-80, Sergius Twp., six miles SSW of Westhope. The township and this post office were named for Sergius Gaulke, the first baby born in the area. Sergius is an ancient Roman name of unknown meaning. The post office closed September 29, 1906 with mail to Westhope. (1, 2, 18, 19, 34, 40, 75, 101, 153)

**SEROCO** (Oliver). This was a rural post office established June 26, 1908 with Martin J. Staigle as the first and only pm. The name was coined from the first letters of the giant mail order and retail firm headquartered in Chicago, IL, the SEars, ROebuck & COmpany. It was located in SW¼ Sec. 24-143-83, Nebo Twp., about nine miles NE of Center, and closed August 15, 1925 with mail to Hensler. (2, 40, 79, 121, 414)

**SEVEN LAKES** (Cavalier). This was a rural settlement that began about 1884 in NE¼ Sec. 1-163-60, Mount Carmel Twp., fifteen miles north of Langdon. Its name noted the fact that there were seven small lakes in the area. Later in 1884 the Maida post office was established one mile to the west of SEVEN LAKES. (2, 3, 18, 40)

**SEVENTEENTH SIDING** (Burleigh). This NPRR siding was built in 1873 in Sec. 33-139-78, Menoken Twp., and named for

the chronological order of sidings built westward from Fargo. The first settlers called it BLAINE, and a post office was established in 1880 as CLARKE'S FARM, although all known postmarks read CLARKE FARM. The post office was renamed MENOKEN in 1883, but the NPRR did not like this name, and called their station BURLEIGH from 1891 until it closed in 1957. (2, 3, 18, 40, 153)

**SEVENTH SIDING** (Barnes). This NPRR station was built in 1872 in S½ Sec. 18-140-60, Potter Twp., and given the generic name noting the chronological order of sidings as they were built westward from Fargo. When settlement began in the early 1880's, it was renamed ECKELSON. (2, 76)

**SEVEN TREES** (Richland). This was a mail relay station of the 1870's on the Fort Abercrombie military trail that was named for a nearby grove of seven cottonwood trees on the open prairie. It was located in Sec. 16-136-51, Barrie Twp., near the Barrie Crossing of the Sheyenne River. (2, 3, 147)

**SEWALL STATION** (Richland). This was the Milwaukee Road RR station in Sec. 20-130-47, Fairmount Twp., which was the site of the village of FAIRMOUNT. The origin of this name is unknown, and on May 9, 1887 the railroad changed the station's name to FAIRMOUNT to match that of the village. (2, 25, 354)

**SEYMOUR** (Richland). This post office was established January 9, 1888 with Charles S. Moores pm. It was located in NW¼ Sec. 14-130-51, Moran Twp., seven miles west of Hankinson, and named for Homer Seymour, a pioneer settler in Richland County. Seymour is a French name meaning the moorist saint, and an Old English name meaning famed at sea. The post office closed October 31, 1902 with mail to Hankinson. Both the GNRR and Soo Line RR built lines through this site, and for many years a station named STILES existed here. (2, 3, 19, 25, 40, 414)

**SHAFER** (McKenzie). Many early-1900's sources and maps show SHAFER in NE 1/4 Sec. 23-150-98, Schafer Twp., named for Charles E. Shafer (1851-1930), the founder of this settlement who was the head of a prominent family that included a son, George, who would later serve as Governor of ND. Although this spelling is technically correct, it is said that another pioneer, G. B. Metzger, suggested using SCHAFER to coincide with the frequently-seen erroneous spelling, and the incorrect version became the official name of the townsite. (2, 3, 18, 44, 177)

**SHANLEY** (Grant). This NPRR townsite in Sec. 22-134-89, Minnie Twp., was named for John Shanley, the first Roman Catholic Bishop of ND 1889-1909, who had recently died. Because of anticipated confusion with Stanley, the name was changed to ELGIN in 1910, although its telegraph call remained "SY". (2, 3, 18, 44, 177)

**SHANTAPEDA** (Morton). This was the second stage station out of Bismarck on the Bismarck-Deadwood trail laid out in 1876. Ample evidence remains to identify a crossing of Louse Creek, a branch of Chanta Peta Creek in NW¼ Sec. 3-135-84, Fair Valley Twp., six miles north of Flasher, and it is likely that the station was at or very near this crossing. The name is a corrupted version of the larger creek, which has a Sioux name meaning fire heart. The spelling seems to come from the same school of thought that resulted in the Sheyenne, as opposed to the Cheyenne, River in eastern ND. (3, 79, 418)

**SHARLOW** (Stutsman). This was a farm post office established April 13, 1887 with Newton M. Brown pm. It was located in SW¼ Sec. 10-137-65, Sharlow Twp., five miles west of Millarton, and named for its township, which was named for pioneer settler James L. Sharlow, who came here from Davenport, IA in 1881. His niece, Myrna Sharlow, an international opera star, was born in the township in 1893. The post office closed June 15, 1910 with mail to Jamestown. (2, 3, 18, 25, 40, 79, 158, 240, 415)

**SHARON** (Steele). This was a farm post office established August 6, 1889 with Anna Wilcox Duncan pm at the farm home of her husband, Peter T. Duncan, in SE¼ Sec. 26-148-57, Sharon Twp. Mrs. Duncan submitted the township name after postal officials had rejected Trenton and Wilcox. The name SHARON was transferred from Sharon, WI, which was named for Sharon, NY. Both the WI and ND settlements were promoted by the Sharon-Amenia Land Co., which took its name from Sharon and Amenia, NY, and both names were adopted by ND townsites. In 1896 the GNRR founded a townsite just SW of here in NW¼ Sec. 35-148-57, and the post office moved there with a retention of the name. The village incorporated in 1908, and became a city in 1966 with Alfred Klabo as first mayor. The elevation is 1516, the Zip Code is 58277, and a peak population of 371 was reached in 1940. Native sons of SHARON include Albert Paulsen, the inventor of the spring and valve action used on modern trumpets and cornets, Hjalmer Curtis Nygaard (1906-1963), a U. S. Representative 1961-1963, and Albert C. Bakken, a longtime First District Judge. (1, 2, 18, 33, 40, 52, 70, 79, 99, 240, 326)

**SHAW** (Wells). This place is shown on a United States map published by the Geographical Publishing Co., and included in a 1941 atlas by Capper Publications, Inc. of Topeka, KS. It appears to be the western terminus of the NPRR branch line from Carrington, which actually terminates at Turtle Lake in McLean County. SHAW is shown about due north of Dawson, placing it in the vicinity of Chaseley, and is assumed to be either a cartographer's error or a copyright town. (3)

**SHAWNEE** (Grand Forks). This was a GNRR station built in 1882 in SW¼ Sec. 30-152-55, Elm Grove Twp., six miles NW of Larimore, whose post office served the site until the SHAWNEE post office was established September 6, 1902 with John Solseng pm. The name honored pioneer settler Erving Shaw, with an obvious reference to the Shawnee Indians, an Algonquin tribe whose name is said to mean southerner. A population of 15 was reported in 1920, but

the post office closed May 31, 1923 with mail to McCanna. (1, 2, 10, 18, 25, 31, 40, 69, 79)

**SHELDON** (Ransom). On June 22, 1881 pm Barnabus D. Wilcox of Jenksville in Cass County purchased a townsite in Secs. 17 & 20-136-54, Greene Twp., six miles to the south, for $3200, naming it JENKSVILLE. Within a few days he sold it to E. E. Sheldon for $3800, and Mr. Sheldon renamed it for himself. The post office was established July 20, 1881 with Karl E. Rudd pm in his store, replacing the old Jenksville post office on that date, and the NPRR arrived in SHELDON in 1882. The village incorporated in 1884, and quickly became famous as a hotbed of amateur baseball, winning the state title in 1895. Lynn Bernard "Line Drive" Nelson (1905-1955), a major league baseball player 1930-1940, was born and raised here. The elevation is 1101, the Zip Code is 58068, and a peak population of 358 was recorded in 1910, although an unofficial count of 480 was claimed in 1921. (1, 2, 3, 18, 33, 40, 79, 85, 201, 250)

**SHELDON JUNCTION** (Ransom). This site is the junction of the NPRR's Fargo-Streeter line, and the Soo Line RR's Hankinson-Enderlin line, and is located in Sec. 24-136-55, Liberty Twp., two miles SW of Sheldon, hence the name. Despite being the junction of two important railroad lines, the site never attracted any development. About 1910 maps began showing the site as CROSSING, and since about 1915 the name WILLARD has been used for the junction. (3, 18, 85)

**SHELL** (Mountrail). This was a farm post office established December 12, 1905 with Edwin Burdick pm. It was named for nearby Shell Creek, which early French explorers had named Coquille, meaning shell, to note the many shells in its bed. It was located in SE¼ Sec. 34-153-89, Shell Twp., seven miles west of Plaza, and closed May 31, 1911 with mail to Plaza. (2, 18, 40, 72, 79, 289)

**SHELL CREEK** (McLean). This was a Hidatsa Indian village in SE¼ Sec. 8-150-91, Shell Creek Twp., nine miles south of Van Hook. The creek was named Coquille, meaning shell, by early French explorers to note the many shells in its bed. The village consisted of a few stores, a dance hall, school, two churches, and other buildings, but it was abandoned in 1954 when the site was inundated by the backwaters of the Garrison Dam. (2, 3, 28)

**SHENFORD** (Ransom). This was a pioneer settlement in Sec. 32-135-54, Shenford Twp., eight miles ENE of Lisbon. William F. Bascom came here in 1879 and coined the name to note the nearby crossing of the Sheyenne River, where it is only SHIN-deep, and can be easily FORDed. Although petitions were submitted as Shinford, the post office was established as SHENFORD on August 2, 1880 with Mr. Bascom as pm. The actual crossing of the river is just to the south in Sec. 6-134-54, Shenford Twp., and is shown on some early maps as Shen's Ford. A population of 200 was claimed in 1884, which had to have been a wild exaggeration. The village had a store, blacksmith shop, elevator, and a true count of 15 residents in

1890. On January 21, 1892 the post office moved to the new townsite of Anselm four miles to the north, assuming that name. (2, 3, 25, 40, 77, 85, 201, 204, 206)

**SHEPARD** (Griggs). This was a NPRR siding built in 1901 in SW¼ Sec. 12-145-59, Ball Hill Twp., four miles south of Cooperstown. NPRR officials named it for Finley Shepard, a secretary to J. W. Kendrick, General Manager of the NPRR. Shepard is an Anglo-Saxon name meaning, as one would expect, a shepherd. A small settlement began, but the population never exceeded 10. Jorgen Soma and Martin Ueland, the latter being the namesake of a well known dam in the county, owned the Shepard Farmers Elevator Co. here for many years. (2, 3, 18, 19, 65, 79)

**SHEPARD** (Pembina). This was a farm post office established January 26, 1885 with James Shepard pm, whose suggested name of Banda was rejected by postal officials. It was located in NW¼ Sec. 17-159-55, Crystal Twp., four miles west of Crystal, and closed March 31, 1887 with mail to Stokesville. It reopened June 8, 1887 at the home of new pm Alexander Robertson in SE¼ Sec. 4-159-55, two miles NE of the original site. Mr. Robertson applied for the post office as Westbrook, but postal officials rejected this in favor of the old name. It operated as SHEPARD until closing for good July 14, 1894 with mail to Crystal. (2, 3, 25, 40, 240)

**SHERBROOKE** (Steele). This townsite was platted in 1884 by Dustin P. Baldwin, owner of the townsite, who named it for his hometown of Sherbrooke, Quebec, Canada, which was named for Sir John Coape Sherbrooke (1764-1830), Governor-General of Canada 1816-1818. Because of its central location, the county seat was moved here from Hope in 1885, and the post office was established August 24, 1885 with Matthew Cavanaugh pm. Rumors of a railroad surfaced in both 1887 and 1914, but neither materialized, and SHERBROOKE began to decline. The county seat was moved to Finley in 1918, and the post office closed November 15, 1919 with mail to Hope. A population of 100 had been reported in 1890, but the 1972 count was just 2. Clarence Norman Brunsdale (1891-1978), Governor of ND 1951-1957, was born here. (1, 2, 10, 18, 25, 40, 79, 99, 326)

**SHERMAN** (Pierce). This GNRR station was established in 1886 in NE¼ Sec. 1-156-74, Ness Twp., six miles west of Rugby, and named for local settler John Sherman. Sherman is an Old English name meaning a shearer of the nap of woolen cloth. Little development took place here until 1900, and when the post office was established in 1901, it was renamed TUNBRIDGE. (2, 3, 19, 114)

**SHERWOOD** (Renville). This GNRR townsite was founded in September 1904 as the terminus of the Granville line in NE¼ Sec. 12-163-85, Colquhoun Twp. The name honored Sherwood H. Sleeper, a Mohall banker who had once owned the townsite. Sherwood is an Old English name meaning from the bright forest, and a forest of this name is famous because of the legend of Robin Hood. The Nina post office moved here in 1904 without official permission, and continued to operate for three months after pm Minnie Alexander moved the Bolaker post office here with the government's blessing on January 24, 1905, taking the new name. The village, a Canadian port-of-entry, incorporated in 1916. The elevation is 1649, the Zip Code is 58782, and a peak population of 455 was reached in 1930. The post office was destroyed by fire on October 30, 1980, and equipment from the Charlson post office in McKenzie County, which closed November 14, 1980, was sent here to hasten the restoration of mail service in SHERWOOD. (1, 2, 3, 18, 19, 33, 40, 71, 79)

**SHEYENNE** (Barnes). This was a farm post office established April 13, 1881 with James Daily pm, who named it for the nearby Sheyenne River. It was located in Sec. 35-138-58, Nelson Twp., three miles north of Kathryn. On March 28, 1882 it moved one mile south and was renamed DAILY by new pm Ole P. Hjelde. (2, 3, 40, 76, 79, 118, 331)

**SHEYENNE** (Eddy). Settlement began here in 1883, and the NPRR reached the site in 1884. The post office was established May 27, 1887 with John W. Richter pm. It was located in Sec. 9-150-66, Gates Twp., and replaced the old Gates post office which was just SSW of the new townsite. The name honors the Cheyenne Indians, whose tribal name is derived from the Sioux word *Sha-i-e-na*, meaning enemy or people of an alien tongue. The spelling is said to be the result of an early typographical error relating to the Sheyenne River, which has been perpetuated. It became an incorporated city in 1926, and reached an official peak population of 469 in 1950, although unofficial counts were higher in the early 1900's. The elevation is 1480, and the Zip Code is 58374. (1, 2, 3, 40, 79, 112)

**SHEYENNE STOCKYARDS** (Cass). This was a NPRR station in Sec. 5-139-49, Barnes Twp., where a siding and spur were built in the 1870's to serve a large cattle operation. From 1874-1875 the site was served by the HAGGART'S post office, and it has developed into the present city of RIVERSIDE. (2, 3, 34, 40, 77)

**SHIELDS** (Grant). This was a rural post office established September 16, 1896 with Nathaniel John Shields pm at his home in Sec. 18-132-83, Shields Twp. In 1901 it moved two miles south to SE¼ Sec. 30-132-83, where new pm Joshua M. Murphy ran a country store on the NW bank of the Cannonball River. The Milwaukee Road RR reached the site in 1910, platting a townsite in Secs. 19 & 30-132-83, and Secs. 24 & 25-132-84. The new townsite experienced an initial boom, boasting of a bank and a newspaper, and began calling itself "The Gateway City of Southern Grant County." The elevation is 1807, and a population of 250 was reported in 1920, with a decline to just 99 in 1950. James Rodenbaugh was the local depot agent 1913-1960. The post office, Zip Code 58569, became a rural branch of Flasher on July 2, 1965. (1, 2, 3, 18, 33, 34, 40, 107, 175, 176)

**SHIGLEY** (McHenry). This was a farm post office established May 27, 1901 with John

F. Shafer pm at his home in SE¼ Sec. 18-158-77, Bantry Twp., two miles WNW of Bantry. The origin of the name is unknown. On August 8, 1902 a name change to HOOSIER was authorized, but the order was rescinded before it could be implemented. On December 12, 1902 the name was changed to MILROY. (3, 40, 412, 415)

**SHOLLSMADE** (Slope). This was a farm post office established September 2, 1908 with Mrs. Einar (Inga) Sholl pm. It was located in SW¼ Sec. 14-136-99, Dovre Twp., thirteen miles NE of Amidon. The "made" is said to have been an erroneous spelling of "maid", noting the Sholls four children, all girls. Einar Sholl (1867-1914) operated a store at the site, and after his death his widow continued the operation. The store went out of business in 1919, and Mrs. Sholl moved the post office into the basement of the Dovre School in SE 1/4 Sec. 16-136-99, one mile to the west. The post office closed May 31, 1921 with mail to South Heart, and Mrs. Sholl moved to Dickinson. (1, 2, 3, 18, 40, 53, 82, 414)

**SHOOFLY** (Morton). This was the third of three new NPRR sidings built in 1946 when the mainline was rebuilt between New Salem and Glen Ullin. SHOOFLY was located in W½ Sec. 26-139-88, Curlew Twp., four miles east of Glen Ullin. A shoofly is any of several plants said to repel flies, and later became the name of a child's rocking chair built to resemble an animal. Why this name was chosen for the siding is unknown. North Almont became a grain-loading facility and Dengate became familiar as the name of an exit on Interstate 94, but SHOOFLY saw no development whatsoever, and has been forgotten. (3, 34, 414)

**SIBLEY** (Barnes). This was an old resort spot known as SIBLEY'S TRAIL RESORT, referring to the location in E½ Sec. 12-143-58, Sibley Trail Twp., on the west bank of Lake Ashtabula near the trail used in 1863 by Gen. Henry Hastings Sibley (1811-1891) during his campaign against the Sioux. Mr. and Mrs. Ed Hagglund started a permanent settlement here on May 30, 1954 which was called simply SIBLEY. A rural branch of the Dazey post office opened on February 15, 1964 with James Dahl as officer-in-charge. It shared Zip Code 58429 with its parent office, and operated until May 6, 1966. The summer population reaches about 75, and the official 1980 population was 21. (2, 5, 19, 34, 40, 41, 328)

**SIBLEY** (Burleigh). Maps in the 1876 and 1877 NPRR annual reports show a town called SIBLEY just south of Bismarck, probably still within Lincoln Twp. (138-80). It is

thought that this was a proposed townsite named in honor of Gen. H. H. Sibley that did not develop and was forgotten. (3, 422)

**SIBLEY** (Cass). This farm post office was established in 1876 in Richland County. On September 10, 1879 it moved two miles north to SE¼ Sec. 29-137-50, Normanna Twp., Cass County, the home of new pm Albert Vangsness. In 1880 the GNRR built a line through this site and founded a townsite named KINDRED. The SIBLEY post office adopted the new name on May 18, 1881. (3, 40, 77, 305)

**SIBLEY** (Richland). This was a farm post office established May 22, 1876 with Eric Benson pm, who named it for Gen. Henry Hastings Sibley, who passed through this area on his 1863 campaign against the Sioux. It was located in SW 1/4 Sec. 6-136-50, Walcott Twp., just west of the Ulness post office which would be established in 1898. The SIBLEY post office moved about two miles north on September 10, 1879 to the Albert Vangsness farm, which was in Cass County, and the following year the site became the GNRR station of KINDRED. (2, 3, 25, 40)

**SIBLEYBUTTE** (Burleigh). This was a farm post office established August 14, 1900 with Harvey E. Smith pm. It was located in NW¼ Sec. 14-140-77, Sibley Butte Twp., about six miles NNE of McKenzie, and named for the butte in SW¼ Sec. 11-140-77, which was named for Gen. Henry Hastings Sibley (1811-1891), who passed near here on his 1863 Indian expedition. The one-word spelling was necessary to comply with existing government regulations for geographic names. The post office moved four miles ENE to SE¼ Sec. 8-140-76, Christiania Twp., the home of new pm Vernard O. Savage, and closed July 15, 1910 with mail to Sterling. (1, 2, 3, 5, 8, 10, 12, 18, 40, 79, 414)

**SIBLEY'S CROSSING** (Barnes). Although no settlement ever occurred here, this site in SW¼ Sec. 18-143-57, Baldwin Twp., was well known to early explorers, military personnel, and settlers as a crossing point of the Sheyenne River. The Sibley Expedition used it on July 16, 1863, and used it again on August 13, 1863 on the return march. It is about sixteen miles north of Valley City, and a stone marker identifies the site today. (2, 3, 79)

**SIBLEY'S TRAIL RESORT** (Barnes). This is an early resort area in E½ Sec. 12-143-58, Sibley Trail Twp., named for its township which is crossed by the trail used in 1863 by Gen. H. H. Sibley during his Indian campaign. A permanent settlement began here in 1954 which was called SIBLEY. (2, 34, 328)

**SIDNEY** (Cass). This was a NPRR station founded in 1882 in Secs. 30 & 31-140-52, Casselton Twp., three miles west of Casselton. A 160-acre site was platted in November 1882, and promoters claimed it would replace Casselton. The post office was established September 25, 1882 with Russell B. McVay pm, but it closed September 28, 1883 with mail to Casselton. The GNRR crossed the site, giving it two-railroad status, but this line was removed in 1893 as no development occurred. The origin of the name is unknown, although it is a name derived from the ancient Phoenician city of Sidon, which is Hebrew for ensnare. The name of the station was changed to GLACIS on November 19, 1905. (2, 3, 19, 25, 40, 77)

SIDNEY (Towner). This was a farm post office established August 30, 1887 with James Dunphy pm, who named it for his hometown of Sidney, Nova Scotia, Canada. It was located in NW¼ Sec. 6-163-67, Sidney Twp., two miles north of Hansboro, and closed April 2, 1906 with mail to Hansboro. (2, 18, 25, 40)

SIFTON (Kidder). This was a NPRR siding built in 1905 in S½ Sec. 7-139-72, Sibley Twp., five miles east of Steele. It was first called GROUSE, but on January 1, 1909 the name was changed to SIFTON to honor Dr. J. W. Sifton, a Jamestown surgeon associated with the NPRR. The siding appeared on maps until the 1940's. (1, 2, 18, 122)

SIG (McLean). This was a rural post office established July 15, 1921 with Arnljot Sigurd Kjelstrup pm. It was located in SE¼ Sec. 11-150-91, Shell Creek Twp., in the extreme NW end of the county on the Fort Berthold Indian Reservation. Chief Poor Wolf selected the name which was the nickname of the pm, a longtime storekeeper here who was a great friend of the Indian people. The post office closed March 15, 1927 with mail to Van Hook, but the site remained on many maps until it was inundated by Lake Sakakawea in the 1950's. (2, 3, 28, 40, 414)

SILO (Oliver). This post office was established March 9, 1907 in the farm home of pm George Maxwell in SW¼ Sec. 28-143-82, Marysville Twp., about five miles west of Sanger. It had been authorized as DAISY one month earlier, but that order was rescinded by postal officials who became concerned about possible confusion with Dazey in Barnes County. Mr. Maxwell then named the post office for the cylindrical farm storage buildings common in the area. The word is of Spanish origin. The post office closed February 28, 1914 with mail to Seroco. (2, 3, 4, 18, 40, 53, 121)

SILVA (Pierce). This Soo Line RR station was founded in 1912 in SW¼ Sec. 9-154-72, Elverum Twp., between Balta and Fillmore. Townsite owner John Magnuson Nygren (1858-1934) is said to have named it for a town in Sweden. Silva is Latin for forest. The post office was established June 9, 1913 with Hans Morque pm. A population of 125 was reached in 1920, but SILVA has had less than 100 residents ever since. Gladys Romine Lunde, pm since 1937, retired in August 1978 and the post office, Zip Code 58375, closed at that time, but the government did not record the closing until December 15, 1984. Native son Julius Thompson, who died in 1955, was billed as the "World's Tallest Man", measuring 8'7" in height, and weighing 460 lbs. (2, 3, 33, 40, 41, 79, 114, 149)

SILVER CITY (McLean). This was the first of the many boom towns that began with the

construction of the Garrison Dam. O. H. Burgeson, the honorary "mayor", started this town in September 1945 and named it to note that all the buildings were painted silver. By 1947 the town had three bars and 425 people, but the establishment of Riverdale siphoned off most of this place's opportunities for official recognition. It was located in Sec. 31-147-83, Coleharbor Twp., two miles NE of Riverdale. (2, 28)

SILVERLEAF (Dickey). This was a GNRR flag station built in 1887 in SW¼ Sec. 6-129-61, Ada Twp., seven miles east of Ellendale. GNRR officials named it for the shrub, silverberry, common to the area, which has leaves that are silvery on both sides and fragrant yellow flowers. Others say that Dan Keenan, a pioneer settler, cut the label from an empty can of "Silverleaf" lard and nailed it to the boxcar that had been placed at the new site as a temporary depot. The post office was established October 17, 1887 with Wilder B. McTorrey pm. A small village began, but the population never exceeded 50. The post office closed December 31, 1938 with mail to Ellendale. The two-word spelling, Silver Leaf, is incorrect. (1, 2, 3, 18, 40, 79, 154, 264)

SILVER STRIP (Williams). This contract station of the Williston post office opened April 1, 1966 and shared Zip Code 58801 with the parent office. It closed January 22, 1983. (3, 33, 40)

SILVISTA (Walsh). This was a farm post office established April 6, 1883 with James F. Berry pm at his home in SE¼ Sec. 24-158-58, Silvesta Twp., nine miles WNW of Edinburg. The name is coined from the Latin words meaning view of the woods, descriptive of the locale. The township originally spelled its name like the post office, which closed June 15, 1904 with mail to Edinburg. (2, 3, 18, 40, 75)

SIMCOE (McHenry). This GNRR station was built in SE¼ Sec. 18-154-79, Hendrickson Twp., seven miles SSW of Granville, and named by railroad officials for Simcoe, Ontario, Canada, which was named for John Graves Simcoe (1752-1806), a British veteran of the Revolutionary War who was later Lt. Governor of Upper Canada. He is credited with opening up large areas of Canada for settlement, although his tactics earned him many enemies. The post office was established September 14, 1910 with Martin J. Bredvold pm, and closed January 31, 1954 with mail to Granville. A small village developed, but the population was never much more than 20. (2, 3, 5, 10, 18, 33, 40, 79)

SIMS (Morton). This NPRR townsite was founded in 1883 in E½ Sec. 11 & W½ Sec. 12-138-86, Sims Twp., at the site of CARBON, a brickmaking community four miles north of Almont. It was named for George V. Sims, a NPRR official in New York City, although some say it was named for Capt. W. H. Sims, a Missouri River boat pilot. The post office was established May 2, 1883 with Theodore Shenkenberg pm. SIMS experienced an incredible initial boom as a coal mining center, reporting a population of over 1,000 in 1884. The 1890 federal census reported a population of 400,

but the count had declined to just 98 in 1940. When the NPRR rerouted its mainline in 1946, SIMS was bypassed and the town was doomed. The post office closed October 31, 1947 with mail to Almont. A population of 1 was reported in 1975, and SIMS, elevation 1982, is now one of ND's most remarkable ghost towns. (1, 2, 3, 17, 18, 25, 40, 79, 107)

SITKA (McLean). This was another of the boom towns that began with the construction of the Garrison Dam. SITKA was founded in 1947 in NW¼ Sec. 5-146-83, Longfellow Twp., just east of Big Bend, under the direction of H. C. McNulty. 200 people lived here that first year, and the town had two grocery stores and a cafe, but like the others it lost most of its influence when the government started the town of Riverdale. Nelson Haakenstad named the town for Sitka, AK where he had recently visited. That historic village was founded by Alexander Baranov of the Russian Army in 1799, and was first called New Archangel. The Sitka Indians were a native tribe whose name was Tlingit for by the sea, and most of them lived at this settlement. (2, 5, 10, 28)

SIXTEENTH SIDING (Burleigh). This NPRR siding was built in 1873 in Secs. 32 & 33-139-76, Sterling Twp., and given a name noting the chronological order of the sidings as they were built westward from Fargo. For a time it was called BALLVILLE, but when the post office was established in 1882, the name was changed to STERLING. (2, 3, 8, 18, 40, 153)

SIXTH SIDING (Barnes). This NPRR station was built in 1872 in SE¼ Sec. 17-140-59, Hobart Twp., and named to note the chronological order as the sidings were built westward from Fargo. In 1882 it was renamed HOBART, but little development occurred, and the station was removed in the spring of 1925. (2, 34, 76, 330)

SKAAR (McKenzie). This was a rural community founded in 1912 in Sec. 22-145-105, Loyal Twp., thirty-eight miles west of Grassy Butte in the extreme SW corner of the county, and named for local rancher Edward Skaar. K. P. Hetzler started a country store here in 1912, and the post office was established June 5, 1915 with Nancy Clements pm. A population of 30 was reported in 1920. The post office closed February 28, 1955 with mail to Sidney, MT, and the store and its contents were sold at auction June 23, 1955. SKAAR still appears on some maps. (2, 3, 18, 40, 414)

SKERMO (Divide). This was a farm post office in SW¼ Sec. 11-163-102, Elkhorn Twp., six miles north of Alkabo. It was authorized May 7, 1908 as NORUM with Ole J. Skjermo pm, but the order was rescinded. It was reestablished June 29, 1908 as SKERMO, and named for the pm, with the "j" omitted in an attempt to Anglicize the name. The post office was located on the NW shore of Skjermo Lake, also named for the pm, and closed April 30, 1914 with mail to Alkabo. Shermo is an erroneous spelling. (2, 3, 18, 40)

SKOGMO (Sheridan). This was a rural community founded in 1903 in NE¼ Sec.

20-149-76, Cransville Twp., fifteen miles north of McClusky. The post office was established October 4, 1904 with John T. Skogmo pm, and closed March 31, 1932 with mail to Kief. The store run by Harold O. Ostrom was destroyed by fire about 1940, when the population of the town was just 6. SKOGMO became a ghost town, and the site is now a plowed field with no traces of the former settlement to be found. (1, 2, 3, 18, 21, 40, 79, 414)

**SLABTOWN** (Sioux). This is a small village in Sec. 15-131-80, four miles north of Fort Yates near Proposal Hill. The origin of the name is unknown. (3, 127)

**SLATON** (Mercer). This was a rural community centered at the farm of James R. Slaton in SE¼ Sec. 2-144-86, four miles ENE of Hazen on the south bank of the Knife River. The post office was established January 29, 1885 with Mr. Slaton as pm, and closed April 14, 1891 with mail to Causey. A population of 25 was reported in 1890. (2, 3, 25, 40, 64, 415)

**SLAUGHTER** (Burleigh). This was a rural community in SW¼ Sec. 10-142-79, Ecklund Twp., six miles ESE of Wilton. Originally called SOLITUDE, the name was changed to SLAUGHTER when the post office was established March 9, 1886 with Mrs. Linda Warfel Slaughter (1843-1911) of Bismarck as pm. John C. Ecklund (1857-1945), the namesake of the township, became the resident pm in 1886, and Axel H. Olson assumed the post in 1892. A population of 26 was reported in 1890, and its was becoming an important point in northern Burleigh County, but the founding of the Soo Line RR station of Wilton led to its demise. The post office closed January 31, 1908 with mail to Wilton. (1, 2, 3, 18, 25, 40, 79, 414)

**SLOPE** (Slope). A 1930 road map published by the General Drafting Co. shows this place about twelve miles NW of Amidon on the south bank of the Little Missouri River. It was named for its county, which was named to note the general eastward slope of the terrain toward the Missouri River, and like other similar places on this map, it is a copyright town. (3, 10)

**SLOPE CENTER** (Slope). This post office began as HOLTON in 1908, and moved to the Ed Hess store in NW¼ Sec. 2-134-102, Slope Center Twp., seven miles WSW of Amidon in 1910. George F. Giese was pm at both locations, and renamed the facility for himself when it moved to the Hess store. William F. Hess became pm in 1913, but the post office closed in 1914, after which the site generally became known as HESS. Mr. Giese reestablished the post office in the store on January 10, 1917, naming it SLOPE CENTER for its township, which is named to note its location within the county. L. L. Moore became pm in 1920, moving the post office two miles NW to his home in NW¼ Sec. 34-135-102, West Sand Creek Twp., but in 1921 it moved back to the Hess store. A population of 10 was reported in 1920. The post office closed November 30, 1923 with mail to Bessie. (1, 2, 3, 40, 79, 414)

**SLOPTOWN** (Sioux). This is an abandoned Indian village in Sec. 36-134-82, just across the Cannonball River from Breien near the St. Gabriel Episcopal Mission. The settlement never had an official name, but local residents often used this derogatory title. (3, 127)

**SLOTTEN** (Richland). This was a GNRR loading station in SE¼ Sec. 35-133-48, Dwight Twp., three miles NW of Wahpeton, and appeared on maps circa 1910-1920. It was named for Andrew Slotten (1840-1902), who came to MN from Norway in 1867, and moved to Richland County in the early 1880's. He was a member of the 1889 state Constitutional Convention, served in the state legislature, and was on the state railroad commission. His portrait hangs in the offices of the Public Service Commission in Bismarck. Slotton is an erroneous spelling. (1, 2, 3, 147, 351)

**SMISHEK** (Burke). This was a farm post office established June 28, 1906 with Joseph J. Smishek pm. It was located in NE¼ Sec. 35-160-93, Cleary Twp., twelve miles SSE of Columbus. The post office was destroyed by fire on September 16, 1910, and the facility was then moved four miles NNE to the John B. Swanson home in SW¼ Sec. 7-160-92, Lucy Twp. The name was changed to VILLA on January 1, 1911, but nearby Smishek Lake and the Smishek Lake State Game Management Area perpetuate the original name. (2, 3, 18, 34, 40, 67, 376)

**SMITH** (Mountrail). This was a townsite platted in 1913 just east of Wabek in SE¼ Sec. 21-152-88, Plaza Twp., in anticipation of the Soo Line RR and a rumored extension of a GNRR line from Watford City to New Rockford. The Soo Line RR bypassed SMITH later that year, establishing Wabek, and the plans for the new GNRR line were abandoned, resulting in SMITH being stillborn. Local residents sometimes called it SMITHVILLE. It was likely named for George J. Smith, the newspaperman at nearby Plaza, but some believe it was named for Ole and Roy Smith, father and son, who had homesteaded in Sec. 30-152-88. (3, 72, 289, 291)

**SMITHS** (Ward). This was a Soo Line RR coal loading station in NE¼ Sec. 13-160-89, Elmdale Twp., one mile NW of Kenmare. It was named for Louie and Clinton Smith, founders of the Smith strip mine in Smith Coulee, and appeared on maps circa 1915-1925. The site is now abandoned. (1, 2, 3, 18, 100, 375)

**SMITHVILLE** (Mountrail). This was a locally used name for SMITH, the townsite platted just east of Wabek in SE¼ Sec. 21-152-88, Plaza Twp. It was conceived in anticipation of two new railroad lines, but one bypassed the site, and the other was not built. No development ever occurred here. (72)

**SMUGGLER'S POINT** (Pembina). This was a famous pioneer locale on the trail between Pembina and Walhalla in Sec. 29-164-53, Felson Twp., one mile NE of Neche. It was the only point where the heavily wooded valley of the Pembina River straddled the border with Canada, and therefore offered smugglers a natural cover to perform their affairs. William H. Moorhead operated a store and tavern here 1864-1878. (2, 3, 25, 108)

**SNAKE** (McLean). This was a rural post office established March 29, 1895 with William Lacy pm, who came here about 1887. It was located in NW¼ Sec. 24-147-84, Coal Harbor Twp., five miles west of Coleharbor, and was named for nearby Snake Creek, noted for its large population of garter snakes. The post office closed December 16, 1896 with mail to Roach, and the site is now inundated by Lake Sakakawea. (2, 3, 28, 34, 40, 415)

**SNAKE** (McLean). This Soo Line RR station appears on a circa-1905 map as the first station west of Max on the new branch line to Plaza, which was later extended to Sanish. It was probably planned in Rosemount Twp. (150-84), but the site was not developed. (3, 34)

**SNOOK** (Divide). This post office was authorized February 15, 1908 in Williams County with Holmes O. Snook pm, but the order was rescinded November 25, 1908. The exact location is unknown, but it is thought to have been in the eastern half of Divide County, which separated from Williams County in 1910. (2, 3, 18, 40, 415)

**SNOW** (Billings). This was a rural post office established November 25, 1908 with Lucy A. Snow pm. The post office was named for her after postal officials had rejected the name Indian Springs. She had homesteaded in NE¼ Sec. 32-143-98, five miles east of Fairfield, before her marriage to rancher Bob Snow, and is remembered as a nurse. In 1913 the post office moved two miles south to a townsite that was developing in SE¼ Sec. 20-143-98. Eight pms served this town of one store, a pool hall, and 10 people. Pm John A. Sivak closed the post office July 31, 1943 with mail to Gorham. (1, 2, 40, 53, 81)

**SNYDER** (Towner). This was a farm post office established February 18, 1886 with Jared M. Snyder pm. It was located in NE¼ Sec. 18-160-66, Crocus Twp., thirteen miles north of Cando on the south shore of Snyder Lake. A rural community apparently developed, as SNYDER reported a population of 25 in 1890, but the post office closed October 22, 1890 with mail to Cando, and disappeared from maps before the dawn of the twentieth century. (2, 18, 25, 40)

**SODHOUSE** (Rolette). This was a farm post office established May 29, 1891 with Ingebret M. Ingebretson pm. It was located in a sod house, as the name implies, in SW¼ Sec. 34-160-71, Leonard Twp., three miles SE of Rolette. Mr. Ingebretson came to Rolette County from MN in 1885, and served on the county commission. The post office closed May 19, 1894 with mail to Island Lake. (2, 3, 18, 40, 123)

**SOFIA** (Mercer). This was a farm post office established January 25, 1906 with David D. Mitchell, a native of MI, as pm at him home in NE¼ Sec. 8-145-89, six miles NNE of Goldenvalley. It moved two miles WNW in 1909 to SW¼ Sec. 6-145-89, the home of new pm Mrs. Mary Dewitt, and closed December 10, 1913 with mail to Goldenvalley. The origin of the name is unknown, although it is a Greek name meaning wisdom. Some have speculated that it may have been named for the capital of Bulgaria, which was founded about 809 A.D. as Ulpia Serdica, and was later named for St. Sophia. (2, 3, 5, 18, 19, 40, 64, 414)

**SOGN** (Nelson). This was a rural post office established August 10, 1887 with Nils E. Slinde pm. It was located in the country store operated by N. O. Haugen in NE¼ Sec. 28-150-58, Field Twp., four miles NE of McVille. The name, which means parish in Norwegian, was selected by settlers from Sogn og Fjordane, in south central Norway. A population of 12 was reported in 1890. In 1898 the post office moved one-half mile NE to SW¼ Sec. 22-150-58, and closed August 15, 1905 with mail to Aneta. (2, 18, 25, 40, 124, 128, 414)

**SOLEN** (Sioux). This NPRR townsite was founded in 1910 in Sec. 30-134-80, and named for Mrs. Mary Louise Van Solen, a pioneer settler who was the first school teacher on the Standing Rock Indian Reservation. She was the daughter of Honore Picotte, a French nobleman who came here in 1825 to engage in the fur trade, and his wife Alma, a full-blooded Sioux whose Indian name was Wambdiantapiwin, meaning eagle woman all look at. She was also the sister of Mrs. H. S. Parkin, the wife of the well known Morton County rancher. P. A. Thian, a NPRR official, is credited with suggesting the name SOLEN. The post office was established February 9, 1911 with Alma M. Rogers pm. The elevation is 1696, the Zip Code is 58570, and a peak population of 250 was claimed for a period of about thirty years beginning in 1935, but the official 1980 count was just 137. (1, 2, 3, 18, 33, 40, 79, 127, 434)

**SOLITUDE** (Burleigh). This was a rural community in Sec. 10-142-79, Ecklund Twp., six miles ESE of present-day Wilton. In 1886 the famous Slaughter family of Bismarck promoted the establishment of a post office here, primarily as a means of establishing a mail route from Bismarck to the north, and Mrs. Linda Warfel Slaughter christened it SOLITUDE to describe its peaceful, rural setting. Postal officials approved the establishment of the post office March 9, 1886 with Mrs. Slaughter as the pm, but renamed it SLAUGHTER in her honor. (2, 3, 18, 40)

**SOMBER** (Bottineau). This was a rural post office established April 15, 1904 with Rudolph T. Jacobsen pm. It was located in NW¼ Sec. 3-163-74, Homen Twp., thirteen miles NE of Bottineau, and named to note its isolated location. In 1905 it moved two miles east to the country store operated by new pm Frank W. Seidel in NW¼ Sec. 1-163-74. On June 21, 1908 the store was robbed, Mr. Seidel and his niece were killed, and the store/post office was set afire. The

post office was officially closed August 31, 1908 with mail to Ackworth. (2, 3, 40, 53, 153, 379, 414, 415)

**SONORA** (Richland). This was a NPRR station at the corner of Secs. 17, 18, 19 & 20-130-48, DeVillo Twp., seven miles west of Fairmount. Why the name was chosen is unknown, but it is a Spanish word meaning grand, in the feminine form, and probably is traced to the state of Sonora, Mexico, along the United States border. A post office named THEED operated here 1891-1906. A population of 25 was reported in 1920, and the site was still shown on some maps into the 1970's. (1, 2, 3, 10, 18, 25, 147)

**SOPER** (Cavalier). This was a rural post office established June 11, 1888 with John D. Soper pm in his general store. He came here in 1882 from Canada, and later operated a store in Loma. The SOPER post office was located in SE 1/4 Sec. 23-159-59, Osnabrock Twp., seven miles SSW of Osnabrock, and closed October 15, 1906 with mail to Fairdale. (2, 18, 25, 40, 247)

**SORKNESS** (Mountrail). A farm post office was authorized June 22, 1903 with Henry O. Sorkness pm, but the order was rescinded. It would have been located in NW¼ Sec. 1-157-93, Sorkness Twp., seven miles NE of White Earth. Mr. Sorkness and his brother, George Sorkness (1875-1962), came here in 1902 from Ashby, MN, where their Norwegian-born father had settled. The post office was reestablished October 16, 1903 with Frank J. Haines pm at his home in SW 1/4 Sec. 35-158-93, Powers Lake Twp., just across the section line from the Sorkness home, and closed February 28, 1911 with mail to White Earth. (3, 18, 40, 67, 72)

**SOURIS** (Bottineau). This GNRR station was founded in 1901 in SW¼ Sec. 29-163-77, Haram Twp., and was the terminus of this branch line until it was extended in 1903. It was named for the nearby Souris River, which was named by early French explorers who encountered large hords of field mice while camped on its banks. The post office was established July 19, 1901 with John Jenks pm, and its Zip Code is 58783. The village incorporated in 1907, and is said to have reached a population of 800 in 1903 at the height of its original boom as a terminus, but its highest official population was just 169 in 1920. (1, 2, 10, 18, 33, 40, 52, 79, 101)

**SOURIS CITY** (McHenry). This was a pioneer settlement promoted by Edmund Hackett, the first mayor of Bismarck, in Sec. 31-156-76, Newport Twp., six miles SW of Towner on the banks of the Souris River. A brief flurry of activity took place in 1882, mostly promotional, but the site declined when it became obvious that the NPRR would never reach the area. It was sometimes called HACKETT FALLS. (2, 18, 412)

**SOUTHAM** (Ramsey). This was a Soo Line RR station built in 1912 in NE¼ Sec. 13-154-62, Ontario Twp., seven miles NE of Crary. The name is said to be for Fred Southam, a local landowner, or for a Miss Southam, presumably his daughter, who married a

man named Chamberlain. The post office was established May 17, 1913 with Martin Johnson pm, and closed December 30, 1965 with mail to Crary. A population of 200 was claimed in 1920, but the count had declined to just 60 in 1960. (1, 2, 40, 79, 103)

**SOUTH DICKINSON** (Stark). A 10.82-acre site was platted by John McDonough in 1886, apparently as a rival townsite to Dickinson. SOUTH DICKINSON was located in NW¼ Sec. 10-139-96, on the south side of the NPRR tracks opposite Dickinson, but development was slow, and the platted area was annexed by the city of Dickinson in 1900. (18, 406)

**SOUTHDOWN** (Stutsman). This was a NPRR station located in N½ Sec. 2-139-69, Saint Paul Twp., three miles west of Medina. It was named for the Southdown breed of sheep, which originated in England and was named for the South Downs, a range of hills. The name appeared on maps circa 1910-1950, but little development ever occurred at the site. (3, 4, 18, 45, 158)

**SOUTH HEART** (Stark). This NPRR townsite was founded in May 1881 in SW¼ Sec. 11-139-98, South Heart Twp., and named to note its location at the mouth of the South Fork of the Heart River. The post office was established October 18, 1883 with Bernard O. Finger pm. A new townsite was platted in May 1908 in SW¼ Sec. 12 & N½ Sec. 13-139-98, about one mile east of the original site. The elevation is 2499, the Zip Code is 58655, and a peak population of 297 was reached in 1980 as the village has more than tripled in size since 1960. (1, 2, 3, 18, 25, 33, 40, 74, 79, 81)

**SOUTH MOREAU** (Burleigh). This place is listed in an 1890 guide to ND as being in Burleigh County, and served by the Bismarck post office. It is thought that it actually referred to a place in the area drained by the Moreau River of western SD, whose north and south forks converge in SW Perkins County, entering the Missouri River south of Mobridge. The name honors a French trader who lived at its mouth, and was later killed by his Cheyenne wife. Lewis and Clark refer to the river as Murow Creek in their journal. (3, 25, 36)

**SOUTH PEMBINA** (Pembina). This was a platted townsite in Sec. 4-163-51, Pembina Twp., south of the Pembina River and the original townsite of Pembina. Its status as a separate entity was short-lived, if at all, and it is now a part of the city of Pembina. (3, 18)

**SOUTH PRAIRIE** (Emmons). This was a farm post office established April 21, 1892 with Celia J. Flick pm. It was located in the home of her husband, Capt. Martin Flick, in NW¼ Sec. 6-131-76, Strasburg Twp., five miles south of Linton. The name is descriptive, with the "south" apparently noting its location in the southern part of the county. The post office closed April 22, 1899 with mail to Tirsbol. (2, 3, 40, 66)

**SOUTH PRAIRIE** (Ward). This is a rural community located primarily in Secs. 23, 24, 25 & 26-153-83, Freedom Twp., twelve miles south of Minot at the junction of US

Highway 83 and ND Highway 23. It was generally known as STRINGTOWN until adopting this name, descriptive of its location on the prairie south of Minot, after World War II. A U. S. Air Force radar base operated 1951-1979 at a site two miles south of here, and remains a landmark for area residents. (3, 18, 34, 100, 374)

**SOUTH WASHINGTON** (Grand Forks). This was a contract station of the Grand Forks post office established November 1, 1958, and discontinued October 28, 1978. It was named for the street on which it was located in Sec. 9-151-50, Grand Forks Twp., within the city limits of Grand Forks, and shared Zip Code 58201 with its parent office. (3, 33, 40)

**SOUTH WEST FARGO** (Cass). This settlement in SW¼ Sec. 8-139-49, Barnes Twp., began in 1936 on the south side of US Highway 10, just south of West Fargo, hence the name. Within months the population was 540, and the village incorporated in 1937 with Ole Anderson mayor. The West Fargo post office was physically moved here in 1948, retaining the old name. The population of SOUTH WEST FARGO reached 3,328 in 1960. On June 7, 1967 the name WEST FARGO was transferred to this city, with the old West Fargo becoming West Fargo Industrial Park. Southwest Fargo is an erroneous spelling. (2, 3, 77, 210)

**SOUTH WILTON** (Burleigh). This is the portion of the city of Wilton platted in N½ Sec. 2-142-80, Ecklund Twp., Burleigh County, which actually is incorporated as a part of Wilton proper. It was laid out in October 1899 on land owned by Jacob Killian, and two of the streets were named for his daughters, Louise and Minnie. The 1970 population was 116, compared to 579 people living in the McLean County portion of town. (2, 3, 14, 18, 34)

**SPAIN** (Steele). Postal records show a SPAIN post office established June 12, 1888 with Frank Stevens pm, but later rescinded without the date of the action being listed. It has been speculated that the entry may have been made erroneously on the listings for Dakota Territory, while others think that the pm might have been a Benjamin F. (probably Franklin) Stevens who had a tree claim in SE¼ Sec. 18-144-56, Carpenter Twp., midway between Hope and Luverne in 1880. (2, 3, 40, 415)

**SPALDING** (Hettinger). This post office was authorized October 2, 1905 with Thomas Sarver pm, but he declined the appointment and the order was rescinded April 19, 1906. A Spalding post office, named for Cass County politician Burleigh F. Spalding, existed in Stark County 1900-1903 fifteen miles south of Richardton, and it is thought

that the 1905-1906 action was an unsuccessful effort to reestablish it in Hettinger County. In 1907 a Thomas R. Sarver, believed to be the same man, became the first pm at Gilstrap, which was located east of Haynes in Gilstrap Twp. (129-93), near the SD border in what is now Adams County. In 1908 he became the pm at Howser in Campbell Twp. (136-93), about thirteen miles north of Mott, and just SW of the old Spalding post office in Stark County. (3, 40, 414, 432)

**SPALDING** (Stark). This was a ranch post office established August 24, 1900 with Peter Kilzer pm. It was located in SE¼ Sec. 20-137-92, fifteen miles south of Richardton, and named for Burleigh F. Spalding, a member of the 1889 State Constitutional Convention from Cass County. The post office closed November 14, 1903 with mail to Richardton. (2, 3, 18, 34, 50, 53)

**SPANGLER** (Rolette). This was a farm post office established June 15, 1901 with Virginia Spangler as the first and only pm. It was located in SE¼ Sec. 34-164-71, Hutchinson Twp., eight miles NW of Saint John, and closed August 15, 1906 with mail to Carpenter. (2, 3, 40, 123, 415)

**SPAULDING'S FERRY** (Benson). John Spaulding and his sons, Martin and Frank, settled in E½ Sec. 13-154-67, Riggin Twp., about midway between Minnewaukan and Churchs Ferry, in the 1880's. They ran a general store and a ferry service across the Grand, or Mauvais, Coulee for a number of years before moving to the Turtle Mountains. Some sources call this place Spaulding. (2, 34, 110)

**SPEARINVILLE** (McKenzie). This was a rural post office established February 24, 1908 with Willard W. Spearin pm. It was located in SE¼ Sec. 20-151-102, Charbon Twp., ten miles WNW of Alexander until 1910, when it moved five miles north to SE¼ Sec. 29-152-102, Elk Twp. The post office closed October 31, 1912 with mail to Alexander. (1, 2, 3, 40, 53, 227, 414, 415)

**SPEEDWAY** (Ward). This was a tourist camp, featuring a cafe and gas station, located in Sec. 18-155-83, Harrison Twp., about five miles west of Minot near the junction of US Highways 2 and 52. The name honored Irving "Speed" Wallace, a descendant of the founders of nearby Burlington who was involved in the promotion of SPEEDWAY. Mr. Wallace was a freelance writer and automobile racing enthusiast. SPEEDWAY appeared on maps from about 1940 until the mid-1950's. (3, 34, 442)

**SPENCER** (Burke & Ward). This is a rural telephone exchange, prefix 848, located SW of Kenmare in parts of Burke and Ward counties. It is named for Spencer Twp., Ward County (159-89), which some say was named for local pioneers, while others say it was named for Charles A. M. Spencer (1850-1933), ND Attorney General 1891-1892. (3, 34, 52, 55)

**SPERRY** (Richland). This was a Milwaukee Road RR station in SW¼ Sec. 17-135-48, Eagle Twp., four miles NW of Abercrombie. The post office was established December

21, 1892 with William Enloe Sperry, the manager of the elevator, as pm. About 1910 the station name was changed to ENLOE, and on March 12, 1913 the post office adopted the new name as well. (2, 3, 18, 40, 147, 345)

**SPIRAL** (Burke). This was a Soo Line RR station in N½ Sec. 25-161-89, Bowbells Twp., five miles SW of Bowbells, which appeared on maps circa 1905-1925. It has been stated that the name described the shape of the railroad spur at the site, but old county atlases show the standard double track at the site, which served a nearby coal mine and also included stock yards and a loading dock for cattle. The livestock facilities were later moved into Kenmare. (1, 2, 3, 18, 34, 67, 375)

**SPIRITWOOD** (Stutsman). Founded by the NPRR in 1873 as EIGHTH SIDING in Secs. 15 & 22-140-62, Spiritwood Twp., settlement began here in 1879. B. S. Russell, Cuyler Adams, and Charles D. Francis platted the townsite in 1879, and the post office was established June 19, 1879 with Mr. Francis as pm. The name was taken from the nearby lake and bonanza farm, both of which bore a name noting a Sioux legend about the maiden Minneawawa who plunged into the waters to join her slain lover. The Indian name for the lake is *Minnieskaya*, meaning water with the foam on top. The elevation is 1500, the Zip Code is 58481, and a peak population of 286 was reached in 1940. Rupert Dumond led a party of settlers from here into Canada in 1912, founding the city of Spiritwood, Saskatchewan. (1, 2, 18, 25, 33, 40, 79, 83, 158)

**SPIRITWOOD LAKE** (Stutsman). This city was incorporated in 1975 in S½ Sec. 31-142-62, Gray Twp., on the south shore of Spiritwood Lake. The area was a resort community in territorial days, first being called Gray, and later Community, but many residents now live here on a permanent basis. The 1980 population was 50. (3, 158)

**SPRAGUE LAKE** (Sargent). This rural community was founded in 1883 in Sec. 35-130-55, Rutland Twp., three miles SW of Rutland, on the east shore of Lake Sprague, which was named for pioneer settler William Sprague. Mr. Sprague was about to petition for a post office when development shifted to the new GNRR townsite of Rutland. Some sources show the name simply as Sprague. (2, 3, 25, 165, 240)

**SPRING** (Burleigh). This place is listed in an 1890 guide to ND as being in Burleigh County, and served by the Bismarck post office. No other information is available. (3, 25)

**SPRINGBROOK** (Williams). This name was first applied to a pioneer settlement in Sec. 18-155-99, Springbrook Twp. A rival townsite three miles ENE in Sec. 10-155-99 was begun about 1903, taking the name EAST SPRINGBROOK. When the GNRR chose the latter site for their station, the name SPRINGBROOK was transferred to EAST SPRINGBROOK. The post office was established May 8, 1903 with Jacob L. Kingston pm. The townsite was originally owned by Phillander Pollack, and its name noted the numerous springs in the area. It incorporated as a village in 1916 with Charles Ulrich as first mayor. The elevation is 2071, the Zip Code is 58850, and a peak population of 105 was recorded in 1930. Spring Brook is an erroneous spelling. (1, 2, 3, 18, 33, 40, 50, 52)

**SPRINGBUTTE** (Adams). This was a rural post office established April 3, 1912 with Walter C. Howard pm, who was a native of PA and came here in 1907. It was located in NE¼ Sec. 28-131-92, Cedar Butte Twp., seventeen miles NE of Haynes, and was named for the nearby butte. The post office closed July 31, 1915 with mail to Lemmon, SD. Although enforcement of the one-word rule for place names had been lifted, the SPRINGBUTTE post office used the one-word form for its name, and it is incorrect to spell it as two words. (2, 3, 18, 40, 53)

**SPRING COULEE** (McLean). This was an early rural community founded about 1878 by Charles Weller in SE¼ Sec. 12-145-83, Basto Twp., fourteen miles NW of Washburn. The name noted some springs on the Weller homestead, which was in a coulee. Reports of a post office are not supported by government records. When Mr. Weller did in fact establish a post office here on February 26, 1883, he was appointed as the pm and named it for himself. Spring Cooley is an erroneous spelling. (2, 3, 25, 28, 40)

**SPRING GROVE** (Stutsman). This is a platted resort area in NW¼ Sec. 31-142-62, Gray Twp., on the north shore of Spiritwood Lake. It dates from the 1920's, and was named to note the native trees at the site and the natural spring water found here. Governor William Langer built a governor's cottage here in 1933 which is still used by state personnel. SPRING GROVE is sometimes called STUTSMAN COUNTY MEMORIAL PARK. (2, 3, 158)

**SPRING HILL** (Dickey). Jacob L. Findley and W. H. Findley came here in the early 1880's, and promoted a townsite at the foot of the escarpment of the Coteau du Missouri near some natural springs, hence the name SPRING HILL. The Findleys land was in Secs. 9, 10 & 11-129-65, Lorraine Twp., about four miles NW of Forbes, but their plans failed to materialize. (2, 3)

**SPRING VALLEY** (Bowman). This post office was established July 7, 1911 with Ole Lewison pm, replacing the Victor post office two miles to the SW. The new site, NW¼ Sec. 4-129-101, Minnehaha Twp., inspired the descriptive name, being in the Grand River valley twelve miles SE of Bowman. The post office closed July 31, 1913 with mail to Bowman. (18, 40, 53, 120)

**SPRING VALLEY** (Stark). This NPRR station was founded in 1881 in Sec. 5-139-92, with the name credited to Herman L. Breum, who first settled near Gladstone, but moved here when he discovered a natural spring. In 1882 the name was changed to RICHARDTON. (2, 3, 74, 245)

**SPRING VALLEY** (Stutsman). This was a farm post office established May 27, 1903 with George Henry Putnam pm, and given

a name descriptive of the locale. It was located in NW¼ Sec. 36-142-68, Strong Twp., six miles SSE of Woodworth. In 1906 it moved two miles SE to SW¼ Sec. 8-141-67, Valley Spring Twp., the home of new pm William H. Past, previously associated with the Past post office. The following year it moved one mile SW to the home of John H. Nally in SE¼ Sec. 18-141-67, and in 1908 it moved two miles WNW to the home of pm J. A. Rosencrantz in SW¼ Sec. 12-141-68, Iosco Twp., who closed the post office May 31, 1910 with mail to Medina. Valley Springs is an erroneous name with obvious influences from the township in which this post office was once located. (2, 18, 40, 158, 414, 415)

**SPUR** (Morton). This place, presumably a spur of the NPRR at Mandan, is listed in an 1890 guide to ND, with the notation that it was served by the post office at Fort Abraham Lincoln. (3, 25)

**SPUR 11** (Barnes). An atlas published in 1922 by John Thomas shows this place on the Soo Line RR between Lanona and Cuba, approximately in the NW corner of Cuba Twp. (139-57), about eight miles SE of Valley City. The map itself is thought to date from about 1905, and it is thought that SPUR 11 was a proposed facility that attracted the attention of a cartographer, but failed to develop. (3, 34)

**SPUR 562** (Burke). This was a Soo Line RR siding in NE¼ Sec. 33-163-94, Forthun Twp., one mile east of Atcoal and four miles west of Columbus. Hans G. Nordrum owned the land at this facility, which was used for only a few years in the early twentieth century as a loading station for grain and cattle. The name indicated the mileage from the beginning of the railroad line in Saint Paul, MN. (3, 18, 67, 375)

**SQUARE BUTTE** (Morton). This was a ranch post office established June 6, 1881 with George W. Harmon pm. It was located in SE¼ Sec. 6-140-81, ten miles NNW of Mandan in the extreme NE corner of the county, and just north of the later Harmon station on the NPRR. The suggested name of Harmon was rejected by postal officials, after which it was named for the nearby butte, also called Flat Top Butte, which has nearly a section of land on its top. The post office closed October 13, 1882 with mail to Mandan. (2, 3, 25, 40, 107, 414)

**SQUAW GAP** (McKenzie). This is the name of a rural community in SW McKenzie County, centered in one of the most sparsely settled regions in the state. The name notes a local rock formation said to resemble an Indian squaw carrying a papoose, and its location in a gap in the hills. SQUAW GAP achieved national attention in 1971 when it became one of the last regions in the country to receive telephone service. (3, 55)

**SQUIRES** (Williams). This was a rural post office established September 23, 1904 with Herman A. Squires, who came here in 1904, as the pm. It was located in NE¼ Sec. 22-155-103, Hebron Twp., fourteen miles NW of Williston. Lena Zemliska (1873-1947), a pioneer female rural mail carrier, brought the mail once per week from

Williston. The post office closed May 31, 1914. (2, 18, 40, 50)

**STADY** (Divide). This was a rural settlement founded in 1907 in SE¼ Sec. 31-161-100, Alexandria Twp., and named for pioneer homesteader Alice M. Stady. The post office was established July 18, 1907 with George Hanson pm. In 1909 it moved one mile SW to NE¼ Sec. 3-160-101, Sioux Trail Twp., where it was a stopping point for many years on old US Highway 85. A population of 60 was reported in 1920, but the count had declined to just 11 in 1940 as the highway was relocated a few miles to the east, leaving STADY isolated from the flow of traffic. The post office closed January 31, 1955 with mail to Zahl, and the town disappeared from maps during the 1960's. (1, 2, 3, 18, 33, 40)

**STAFFORD** (Emmons). The Milwaukee Road RR established a townsite in S½ Sec. 26-131-76, Strasburg Twp., in 1902 and called it STAFFORD for unknown reasons. At the request of local settlers the name was changed to STRASBURG later in the year. (18, 66)

**STAMMEN** (Ward). This was a farm post office established January 7, 1896 with Hubert Heinen pm, who had entered the name Saint Mary on his application. This name was rejected, and the post office was then named for prominent local cattleman John Stammen, a native of Germany who came to America in 1868. Many members of his family lived in the area. The post office was located in NE¼ Sec. 28-157-84, Saint Mary's Twp., nine miles NW of Burlington on the west bank of the Souris River, and closed December 30, 1899 with mail to Burlington. Hammen is an erroneous spelling. (2, 3, 40, 100, 414)

**STAMPEDE** (Burke). This GNRR townsite was founded in 1907 in NW¼ Sec. 3-162-93, Fay Twp., as a rival townsite to Columbus, two miles to the NE. The name is a Spanish word meaning to run blindly, and was chosen for its romantic western flavor. The townsite was platted by the Dakota and Great Northern Townsite Co. in 1907, and the post office was established April 25, 1908 with John G. Peterson pm. Ole Bonsness, Glenn Vinson, and Samuel Heggen started an elevator, and Henry Boe ran a general store, but development stalled at that point. The post office closed January 15, 1919 with mail to Columbus. A population of 15 was reported in 1920, and 13 were counted in 1930, but STAMPEDE is now a ghost town. (1, 2, 3, 18, 34, 40, 79)

**STANDARD SPUR** (Williams). This was a GNRR spur built in Sec. 17-153-100, Stony Creek Twp., three miles NE of Williston, to serve the Holland Coal Mine operated by the Holland brothers. The name came from the brand name of loading scales installed at the site. Miller's Spur was also in this section, and operated at the same approximate time. (2, 3, 18, 50)

**STANDINGROCK** (Ransom). This was a rural post office established March 15, 1881 with Gilbert Hanson pm. It was located in NE¼ Sec. 12-136-58, Northland Twp., six miles north of Fort Ransom, and named for the glacial drift boulder near here in SW¼ Sec. 6-136-57, Preston Twp., that projects four feet out of the ground, and was named by Gen. H. H. Sibley when he passed the site on his 1863 Indian expedition. The Indians called it *Inyan Bisdata*. The post office closed July 14, 1884 with mail to Olesburg. The name is often found in references as two words, which is correct for the rock itself, but technically incorrect for the post office. (2, 3, 25, 40, 77, 201, 204)

**STANDING ROCK** (Sioux). This pioneer outpost was located in N½ Sec. 7-130-79, just NE of the military post of Fort Yates. It was named for the nearby upright stone called *Inyan Bisdata* by the Sioux, who considered it a sacred monument said to represent a mother and child turned into stone. The post office was established August 21, 1875 with Mrs. M. L. DeGray pm. On May 7, 1879 it was replaced by the post office at FORT YATES. The Standing Rock Agency Boarding School was later built at this site. (3, 15, 40, 127)

**STANDY** (Richland). This was a rural post office established July 26, 1895 with Ole K. Standy, who came here about 1881 from Vang, Norway, as the pm. It was located in SW¼ Sec. 30-135-51, Viking Twp., thirteen miles west of Colfax, in Mr. Standy's general store, and closed May 15, 1905 with mail to Homestead. (1, 2, 18, 40, 147)

**STANLEY** (Mountrail). A post office was established here July 3, 1899 with Edsell H. Sikes, later a state senator, as pm, but development did not begin until 1902 when George W. Wilson (1858-1935) platted the townsite. The name honored Col. King Stanley, a pioneer in the area, although some say it was named for David Sloane Stanley, the former Commandant of Fort Berthold. Stanley is an Old English name meaning dweller at the stony area. It is located in Sec. 21-156-91, Idaho Twp., and incorporated as a city in 1909 with Frank Alger mayor. It was chosen as Mountrail County seat in the 1910 election. The elevation is 2259, the Zip Code is 58784, and a peak population of 1,795 was reached in 1960. (1, 2, 5, 18, 19, 25, 33, 40, 52, 72, 79)

**STANLEY LINE JUNCTION** (Mountrail). This is a GNRR junction built in 1914 in Sec. 22-156-91, Idaho Twp., two miles east of Stanley, where the Grenora branch line begins. (1, 3, 72)

**STANTON** (Mercer). This Missouri River settlement was founded in 1883 in Sec. 6-144-84, and named by James and Thomas McGrath for the maiden name of their mother. Others say it was named for Edwin McMasters Stanton (1814-1869), Secretary of War during the Civil War. Stanton is an Old English name meaning from the stone dwelling. The original townsite was at the mouth of the Knife River, but it was moved slightly to the south in 1906 to avoid spring floods. The post office was established December 4, 1882 with James McGrath pm, and it became the county seat when Mercer County organized in 1884. The elevation is 1722, the Zip Code is 58571, and the village, which incorporated in 1909, reached a peak population of 626 in 1980, having grown steadily since the energy boom of the 1960's. Harold Schafer, the well known Bismarck businessman and promoter of Medora, was born here in 1912. (1, 2, 3, 19, 25, 33, 40, 52, 64, 79, 232, 253)

**STANWICK** (Hettinger). This was a Milwaukee Road RR station in SE¼ Sec. 26-134-94, Farina Twp., five miles ESE of Regent. The origin of the name is unknown, and little development occurred at the site. It appeared on maps circa 1910-1940. (1, 2, 3, 18, 181)

**STAR** (McHenry). This was a farm post office established May 12, 1898 with Ole A. Melhouse pm at his home in SE¼ Sec. 22-155-77, six miles SE of Denbigh. It was named for *The Turtle Mountain Star*, a newspaper published at Rolla, after postal officials had rejected the name Norway. In 1902 it moved one-half mile SE to the home of new pm John Brooten in NW¼ Sec. 26-155-77, and the following year it moved two miles SW to SE¼ Sec. 28-155-77, the home of new pm Theodore Rom. The post office closed August 31, 1911 with mail to Denbigh. (1, 2, 3, 18, 40, 414)

**STARK** (Burleigh). This was a farm post office established August 18, 1904 with William H. Stark, a native of PA who also operated a country store, as pm. It was located in SE¼ Sec. 8-144-75, Hazel Grove Twp., twelve miles NNE of Wing, and was named for Walter H. Stark, a son of the pm who was the first white child born in the township. Some say it was named for George Stark, the namesake of Stark County, who was the General Manager of the NPRR. The post office closed June 30, 1914 with mail to Wing. (1, 2, 8, 9, 12, 18, 40, 63)

**STARKWEATHER** (Ramsey). This was a farm post office established February 18, 1886 with James H. Boden pm, who named it for James E. Starkweather, a local homesteader who returned to his native MI about 1901, after postal officials had rejected the use of his own name. It was located on Mr. Boden's farm in NW¼ Sec. 8-157-64, Hammer Twp., until 1902 when a new townsite was founded three miles ENE in NW¼ Sec. 2-157-64, on the Farmers Grain & Shipping Co. RR, which initially called it DAVISVILLE. The first plans were to move the Evanston post office here, but local citizens thought that that name was too common, and asked the STARKWEATHER post office to relocate to the townsite. Pm Mrs. Frank (Amy C.) Maurer accepted this request, but kept the facility at her home in SW¼ Sec. 33-158-64, Klingstrup Twp., two miles WNW of the townsite until about 1909. The Zip Code is 58377, the village incorporated in 1903, and reached a peak population of 312 in 1930. Ralph J. Erickstad, Chief Justice of the ND Supreme Court 1973-date, was born here in 1922. (1, 2, 3, 18, 33, 40, 52, 79, 103, 253, 414)

**STAR LAKE SPUR** (Richland). This was a NPRR siding in Sec. 5-132-52, Wyndmere Twp., five miles WNW of Wyndmere. It was named for nearby Star Lake, so named because of its shape. The siding appeared on maps circa 1910-1920. (2, 3, 18, 147)

**STATE HOSPITAL** (Stutsman). This facility was authorized in 1883, and opened in 1885 just south of Jamestown in Sec. 6-139-63, Homer Twp. Some thirty years later the name was applied to an adjacent station of the Midland Continental RR. (3, 52)

**STATE UNIVERSITY STATION** (Cass). This post office was known as AGRICULTURAL COLLEGE, and operated as an independent facility 1897-1925. It was known as AGRICULTURAL COLLEGE STATION during 1925-1960, when it operated as a branch of the Fargo post office, taking the name STATE UNIVERSITY STATION on December 8, 1960 to note the institution's name change from ND Agricultural College to ND State University of Agriculture and Applied Sciences. It shared Zip Code 58102 with the Fargo post office, and ended its contract station status on January 26, 1980. (3, 33, 34, 40, 41, 77)

**STATION** (Barnes). This was a Soo Line RR station in NW¼ Sec. 21-140-58, just north of the NPRR highline bridge at the northern edge of Valley City. Most maps show the site with the name VALLEY CITY STATION. (3, 18)

*Stanley about 1908*

**STEBBINS** (Grant). This was a ranch post office established July 18, 1907 with Ella B. Stebbins pm on the ranch owned by her husband, G. H. Stebbins, in NW¼ Sec. 32-132-86, thirteen miles SW of Raleigh on the North Fork of the Cannonball River. In 1910 it moved two miles east to NW¼ Sec. 34-132-86, the home of new pm Mary J. Brisbane, and two years later it moved one mile NE to the home of Mrs. Sadie J. Frederick in Sec. 26-132-86. In 1917 it moved two miles south to NE¼ Sec. 2-131-86, Cannonball Twp., the home of O. C. and Harriet P. Gross, where Mrs. Gross was the new pm. Mail was received twice weekly from Brisbane until the post office closed April 30, 1921 with mail to Raleigh. (1, 2, 3, 17, 18, 33, 40, 177, 414)

**STEELE** (Kidder). The NPRR built FOURTEENTH SIDING in 1872 in SE¼ Sec. 17-139-73, Woodlawn Twp., and Col. Wilbur Fisk Steele (1844-1917), who came here in 1877 from NY, began his dream town in 1880. The post office was established June 10, 1880 with Col. Steele as pm, the site was platted in 1881, and it became the county seat in 1882. Hopes of becoming the capital of Dakota Territory in 1883, however, met with failure, as Bismarck won that political contest, even though Col. Steele had personally financed the construction of what would have been the territorial capital, but instead became the county court house. Col. Steele served in the first state legislature before moving back to NY. STEELE became an incorporated city in 1883, and reached a population of 700 by 1890. The elevation is 1857, the Zip Code is 58482, and a peak population of 847 was reached in 1960. (1, 2, 3, 18, 25, 33, 40, 52, 59, 79, 122)

**STEELE** (Mountrail). This was an alternate name for CHIDA, which was apparently a mail drop for local residents on the farm of Samuel Steele in SE ¼ Sec. 18-158-91, Lostwood Twp., four miles NNW of what would become the townsite of Lostwood. It is stated by many sources that a post office existed here, but government records do not support this claim. The STEELE name could not have been used for the post office in any case, as this was the name of the county seat of Kidder County. When a post office was opened in this area in 1907, it was named Lostwood. (2, 3, 33, 40, 72)

**STEELE'S FARM** (Kidder). This was a NPRR spur built in 1878 in SW¼ Sec. 16-139-73, Woodlawn Twp., to serve the model farm of Col. Wilbur Fisk Steele (1844-1917). The site was served by the Bismarck post office until the townsite of Steele was founded in 1880 adjacent to this site. (25, 122)

**STEIDL** (Logan). This was a farm post office established July 20, 1889 with Joseph Steidel pm, who named it for his father, Jacob Steidel, who had come here in 1885 from Quincy, Traill County, having come to that pioneer settlement in 1884 from his native Austria. The family name of Steidel was changed to STEIDL by postal officials without explanation. It was located in SE¼ Sec. 8-134-71, Red Lake Twp., eight miles SE of Napoleon, and closed July 5, 1894 with mail to Napoleon. (2, 3, 40, 116, 414)

*Steele about 1910*

**STELLA** (Williams). This was a farm post office established July 20, 1907 with Andrew J. Aaberg pm. He named it for Stella Steen, who homesteaded in the adjoining section in 1907 and later that year became his bride. Stella is Latin for star. It was located in NE¼ Sec. 36-159-98, Big Stone Twp., six miles SW of Wildrose. Mr. Aaberg died in 1909, and the post office moved one mile NE to the home of new pm Joseph A. Smiley in NW¼ Sec. 30-159-97, Hazel Twp. The post office closed November 30, 1912 with mail to Wildrose. (2, 3, 18, 19, 40, 50, 414)

**STENVICK** (McLean). This was a rural post office established May 20, 1903 with Fred Parmer, a native of IN, as pm. The facility never went into operation, although no rescinding entry was made in government records, and the origin of the name is unknown. The Parmer home was in SE¼ Sec. 18-150-85, Douglas Twp., about five miles SW of present-day Douglas. Stenwick is an erroneous spelling. (2, 3, 33, 40)

**STERLING** (Burleigh). This NPRR station was built in 1873 and named SIXTEENTH SIDING. The first settlers arrived about 1880 and called the place BALLVILLE, but the post office was established September 27, 1882 with Oscar Ball pm, and renamed STERLING, for Sterling, IL, which had been formed in 1839 when Samuel Sterling combined the pioneer settlements of Chatham and Harrisburg. The townsite was platted in December 1882, and for a time the population was about 200, but it has been only about half of that figure during recent years. The elevation is 1834, and the Zip Code is 58572. It is more familiar than most towns its size due to its location at the junction of Interstate 94 and US Highway 83. (1, 2, 3, 8, 10, 14, 18, 25, 33, 40, 79)

**STEVEN** (Wells). This place appears on a 1961 road map published by the H. M. Gousha Company approximately in Sec. 23-145-72, Silver Lake Twp., seven miles south of Chaseley. The site is very near the location of Velda, and both are believed to be copyright towns. (3, 34)

**STEVENSON** (Grant). This was a farm post office established July 31, 1894 with Donald Stevenson (1833-1908) pm on his ranch in Morton County. Following his death, the post office was taken over by Peter Port on December 4, 1908. Mr. Port's large ranch was adjacent to the Stevenson ranch, but his home three miles to the SW in SE¼ Sec. 3-132-83 was in what is now Grant County. Rev. Elon J. Reed became the pm in 1910 at his home in NW¼ Sec. 10-132-83, just SW of the Port home. His wife, Gertrude C. Reed, assumed the position in 1916, and closed the facility November 15, 1916 with mail to Timmer, from which it had been getting its mail three times weekly. (1, 2, 3, 17, 18, 40, 53, 107, 414)

**STEVENSON** (Morton). This was a ranch post office established July 31, 1894 with Donald Stevenson (1833-1908) pm. A native of Scotland, he had come to Dakota Territory as early as 1863 to make his living supplying the military, first from a base at Pembina and after 1872 from Bismarck. He operated the Bismarck-Deadwood stage line 1876-1883, and then settled at the crossing of the Cannonball River in 1885. The post office was located on his ranch in SW¼ Sec. 21-133-82, Stevenson Twp., four miles SW of Breien. On December 4, 1908 the post office was relocated three miles SW to the home of new pm Peter Port in SE¼ Sec. 3-132-83, in what is now Grant County. (1, 2, 3, 17, 18, 40, 107, 414)

**STEVENSON'S** (Richland). This was a NPRR loading station in Secs. 9 & 10-132-48, Center Twp., four miles west of Wahpeton, and named by Eugene Moore, who came here in 1870, for his wife, Polly Stevenson Moore. It appeared on maps circa 1905-1930, and is occasionally spelled as Stevenson or Stevenson's Siding. (1, 2, 3, 18, 147)

**STEWART** (Grand Forks). This was a farm post office established February 23, 1886 with Mary H. "May" Mitchell pm. It was located in NW¼ Sec. 7-149-52, Union Twp., ten miles east of Northwood, and named for Joseph M. Stewart, the editor of *The Goose River Farmer*, a newspaper published at

Mayville. Mrs. Mitchell, a widow with a teenage daughter, came here in 1885 from VT. The post office closed January 6, 1887 with mail to Northwood. (2, 3, 25, 40, 415)

**STEWART** (Sargent). This was a proposed name for the GNRR townsite in SW 1/4 Sec. 19-130-54, Rutland Twp. The name honored local pioneer Albert H. Stewart, but when he became the first pm on February 23, 1887, he changed the name to RUTLAND. (2, 3, 40)

**STEWARTSDALE** (Burleigh). This was a rural post office established July 2, 1883 with Donald A. Stewart (1838-1906), a native of Scotland, as pm. It was located in SE¼ Sec. 2-137-79, Missouri Twp., ten miles SE of Bismarck. Some years later the Soo Line RR built a line through this area, and a station and elevator were built at the site, although no further development occurred. The post office closed July 31, 1917 with mail to Bismarck. Stewartsdale is a frequently found erroneous spelling. (1, 2, 3, 8, 12, 18, 40, 79, 240, 414)

**STICKNEY** (Grand Forks). This GNRR townsite was founded in 1880 in Secs. 2 & 11-151-52, Oakville Twp., ten miles west of Grand Forks, and named for Alpheus B. Stickney, a GNRR official who in 1882 organized the Union Stock Yards in Saint Paul, MN. The post office was established August 19, 1880 with James W. Hunter pm. The townsite was built largely on the north side of the tracks in Sec. 2-151-52, and when development began on the south side of the tracks in Sec. 11-151-52, a movement was initiated to change the name, which had bad connotations in an area plagued by gumbo quagmires following any rainfall. On March 6, 1883 the name was changed to OJATA. (2, 13, 31, 40, 69)

**STILES** (Richland). This was a junction of virtually parallel lines of the GNRR and Soo Line RR in Sec. 14-130-51, Moran Twp., between Hankinson and Lidgerwood. A station existed here for many years bearing the name of E. A. and Alfred Stiles, original owners of the right-of-way. A population of 35 was reported in 1890, and a count of 32 was made in 1930, but the site declined after World War II and disappeared from most maps during the 1960's. The SEYMOUR post office operated at this site 1888-1902. (1, 2, 3, 18, 25, 40)

**STILL** (Burleigh). This was a NPRR station built in 1911 in Sec. 36-143-79, Grass Lake Twp., between Wilton and Regan, and named for H. E. Still, Assistant General Freight Agent for the NPRR. A small village with a store, elevator, blacksmith shop, and about 10 people existed here for many years, but the town never had a post office, and today is marked by one small building. (1, 2, 3, 12, 14)

**STILLWATER** (Bowman). This was a rural settlement in SE¼ Sec. 15-132-100, Stillwater Twp., seven miles north of Scranton. It was named for its township, which was named by settlers from Stillwater, MN, which was named to note the stillness of the water in nearby McKusick's Lake and Lily Lake, and also for Stillwater, ME, the hometown of the founder, John McKusick. The ME town was named for the nearby river whose name notes that its current is slower than that of the Penobscot River. The post office was established October 25, 1904 with Samuel A. Bobb pm, and closed April 30, 1917 with mail to Scranton. STILLWATER was well known for its hotel which catered to cross-country travelers. (1, 2, 3, 10, 13, 18, 34, 40, 53, 120, 386)

**STILWELL** (Cavalier). This rural post office was established August 17, 1889 with Joseph B. Radford pm, who named it for the family in whose home it was located in NW¼ Sec. 3-162-59, Harvey Twp., the very same section in which the Lemon post office had existed 1883-1888. A small settlement began in Secs 3 & 4-162-59, reporting a population of 30 in 1890, but the 1920 count was just 10, and pm C. H. Radford closed the post office September 15, 1920 with mail to Langdon, ten miles to the SW. Stillwell is an erroneous spelling. (1, 2, 3, 18, 40, 414)

**STIRUM** (Sargent). This NPRR townsite was founded in 1900 in Secs. 27 & 34-132-57, Vivian Twp., and absorbed much of the pioneer townsite of Harlem to the south. It was named for Fredrik Wilhelm Count Limburg Stirum, a German investor in the NPRR who visited this nameless station in 1900 with Artur von Gwinner as a guest of the railroad. He lived in Sweden after World War II, and confirmed this story in a 1949 letter. Folklore says that the name came from the NPRR foreman who would "stir-um up" each morning for work. The post office was established June 22, 1901 with Earl Albertson pm. The elevation is 1375, and a population of 113 was reported in the special census of 1923, but it had declined to under 100 by 1940. Velma Anderson became pm in 1949, and retired February 10, 1978. The post office, Zip Code 58069, closed on that date, although government records still have not recorded this fact. Styrum is an erroneous spelling. (1, 2, 3, 10, 18, 40, 79, 165, 171, 172, 414)

**STOCK YARDS** (Ward). This was a GNRR siding in NE¼ Sec. 20 & NW¼ Sec. 21-155-82, Nedrose Twp., three miles east of Minot. It appeared on maps circa 1905-1925, usually as MINOT STOCK YARDS. (3, 18, 100)

**STOCK YARDS** (Ward). This place appeared as a NPRR station in Orlien Twp. (152-87) in a 1911 brochure published by the railroad, and was apparently a cattle loading facility. By its position, it is assumed that this was a predecessor of MAKOTI, which was founded in that year in Sec. 27-152-87. (3, 432)

**STOELTINGTON** (Mercer). This was a rural community founded in 1908 in SW 1/4 Sec. 4-147-88, fourteen miles north of Zap on the south bank of the Missouri River. It was named for Benjamin Stoelting, a native of WI who came here in 1906, operated a lumber yard, and served on the county commission. The post office was established December 2, 1908 with C. B. Heinemeyer pm, and changed its name to REE on August 27, 1909. (2, 3, 18, 40, 232)

**STOKESVILLE** (Pembina). This was a pioneer settlement of Roman Catholics in SE¼ Sec. 12-159-56, Gardar Twp., four miles NE of Gardar. The post office was established December 11, 1885 with George Stokes pm, and closed April 30, 1903 with mail to Gardar. A population of 50 was reported in 1890. (2, 25, 40, 414)

**STOLTZVILLE** (Ramsey). The GNRR townsite in NE¼ Sec. 24-157-61, Fancher Twp., was founded in 1901 as STOLTZVILLE, named for townsite owner F. H. Stoltz, but when the post office was established July 19, 1901, the name was changed to EDMORE. The nearby rural post office of Lunde considered changing its name to Stoltzville, but it closed August 31, 1901 with mail to Edmore. (3, 40, 103)

**STONE** (Morton). This was a farm post office established April 22, 1907 with Mrs. Edith M. Wilson pm. It was located in NE¼ Sec. 26-137-83, sixteen miles SW of Mandan, and is said to have been named for N. E. Stone, a farmer near Flasher in NE¼ Sec. 11-134-84, Flasher Twp., after the pm's suggested name of Wilson was rejected because of duplication in Kidder County. In 1909 the post office moved three miles WNW to the home of new pm O. J. Carlson in SE 1/4 Sec. 20-137-83, and closed July 31, 1913 with mail to Mandan. (2, 3, 17, 18, 40, 414, 415)

**STONEVILLE** (Slope). Frank P. Stone, a young man from RI, came to the Badlands country about 1878, and made a living ranching and marketing buffalo hides at Sully Springs. Some early accounts mention a STONEVILLE post office at his home near the confluence of Box Elder Creek and the Little Missouri River, thought to have been in Sec. 17-136-102, Ranger Twp., about fifteen miles NW of Amidon, but postal records do not support this claim. The entire region was unsurveyed at this time, so the exact location is subject to debate. Mr. Stone's son, Almon C. Stone (1876-1951), was the Sheriff of Golden Valley County 1923-1927. (2, 3, 40, 80, 421)

**STONY POINT** (Traill). This was a rural post office established June 20, 1877 with Rev. Jonas Ostlund, a Methodist minister, as pm. It was located in NE¼ Sec. 33-146-51, Norway Twp., five miles WNW of Hillsboro, and named for the nearby prairie landmark, a huge boulder twenty feet in diameter at the edge of ancient Lake Agassiz. Local legends say it dropped from the sky. Rev. Ostlund (1827-1914) came to Chicago, IL in 1855 from Sweden, moved to Dakota Territory in the 1860's, and was one of the first county commissioners of Traill County. On March 24, 1879 the name of the post office was changed to BLOOMFIELD. (2, 18, 25, 40, 187, 395)

**STORDAHL** (Williams). This was a rural post office established November 24, 1903 with

Edward O. Salveson (1869-1953) pm. It was located in NE¼ Sec. 25-159-97, Hazel Twp., near the Stordahl Lutheran Church, and about five miles SE of Wildrose. The name came from Stjordahlen, Norway, which can be translated as big meadow, the name of the adjoining township, and was selected after postal officials rejected the name Arne. In 1908 the post office moved four miles ESE to SW¼ Sec. 27-159-96, Big Meadow Twp., the home of new pm Dr. J. K. W. Dillon, and two years later it moved two miles NW to NW¼ Sec. 29-159-96, the home of pm C. J. Helle. The post office closed January 15, 1913 with mail to Wildrose. (2, 40, 50, 414)

**STORLIE** (Cavalier). This was a rural post office established April 6, 1899 with Martin Martinson pm at his home in NW¼ Sec. 26-159-62, Storlie Twp., six miles SE of Alsen. It was later moved to the home of new pm Halvor O. Storlie in SW¼ Sec. 21-160-62, Gordon Twp. Both the post office and the township were named for Mr. Storlie. On August 31, 1905 the post office moved to the new Soo Line RR townsite of Alsen, adopting the new name. Starlie is an erroneous spelling. (2, 3, 18, 40, 75, 212)

**STOUGHTON** (Grand Forks). This was a farm post office established March 3, 1893 with Nathan Dayton Stoughton pm. Postal officials had rejected Mr. Stoughton's suggested name of Greenwood, for pioneer settler Joseph Greenwood, because of duplication in what is now SD. It was located in NE¼ Sec. 3-154-51, Turtle River Twp., eight miles north of Manvel in the extreme NE corner of the county, and closed February 28, 1905 with mail to Walshville. (2, 31, 40, 69, 238)

**STOVER** (Ramsey). This GNRR station was built in NW¼ Sec. 5-156-60, Lawton Twp., five miles NNW of Lawton. It appeared on maps circa 1905-1925, but no development occurred at the site. The name is thought to have been chosen to honor Torgen J. Staver, a pioneer settler in the area, with an error in the spelling. (2, 18, 103)

**STOWERS** (Adams). This was a farm post office established March 19, 1907 with Mason B. Stowers pm, with the name said to honor the pm and Charles E. Stowers, both of whom came here in 1906. It was located in NW¼ Sec. 29-130-91, South Fork Twp., nineteen miles ENE of Haynes on the south bank of the Cedar River. Charles E. Stowers became pm in 1918, and a population of 10 was reported in 1920, but the post office closed December 31, 1920 with mail to Thunderhawk, SD. (2, 18, 34, 40)

**STRABANE** (Bottineau). The GNRR first planned this townsite in 1903 in Sec. 33-163-79, Scotia Twp., and named it for Strabane, county Tyrone, Northern Ireland. The name was not popular with the Norwegian immigrants in the area, and when real settlement began in 1904, it was renamed LANDA. (2, 38, 101, 153)

**STRABANE** (Grand Forks). This was a rural post office established December 5, 1881 with Edward Miller pm in SW¼ Sec. 22-154-54, Strabane Twp., five miles WSW of Johnstown. Mr. Miller is said to have

claimed that the name meant I stray in Latin, but it was later discovered that he had come here from Strabane, Ontario, Canada, which was named for Strabane, county Tyrone, Northern Ireland. The post office closed June 10, 1886 with mail to Johnstown. (2, 3, 18, 25, 38, 40, 69, 414)

**STRAHON** (Golden Valley). Guy L. Strahon, a young rancher from SD, came to ND about 1904 and homesteaded in 1906 in NE¼ Sec. 28-138-104, Garner Twp., twelve miles south of Sentinel Butte, and just north of the homestead of his brother, Clinton E. Strahon, who had come here a year earlier. Guy Strahon was appointed pm of the STRAHON post office on May 19, 1908, but the order was rescinded October 31, 1908. In 1910 Guy Strahon sold his interests to his brother, and returned to SD. For many years a rural school in the area was known by this family name. (3, 40, 80, 415)

**STRAIN** (Morton). This was a country store in NW¼ Sec. 8-136-82, five miles west of Saint Anthony, run by James Jacob Strain (1870-1927), a native of IL who came here in 1902 and served in the state legislature 1919-1923. He was appointed pm of the post office here on June 16, 1904, which was named STRAIN after postal officials had rejected Mr. Strain's suggested name of Jims. William F. Crozier became pm in 1913 at his home in SW¼ Sec. 8-136-82, and closed the post office June 30, 1914 with mail to Saint Anthony. (1, 2, 3, 17, 18, 40, 52, 107, 414)

**STRANGE SIDING** (Burke). This was a Soo Line RR siding built in 1913 in NE 1/4 Sec. 15-162-90, Carter Twp., between Flaxton and Bowbells. In that year a 3.8-acre site was sold to the railroad by Moses Souther, and a 1914 atlas shows the site owned by George Gann and C. A. White, with the facility called "Spur Loading Platform." The origin of the name STRANGE SIDING is unknown. (2, 3, 18)

**STRASBURG** (Emmons). This Milwaukee Road RR townsite was founded in S½ Sec. 26-131-76, Strasburg Twp., in 1902 and named STAFFORD. The area had been settled in 1888 by Germans from Strasburg, South Russia, which had been founded in 1808 by Roman Catholic settlers from Strasburg, Alsace, now a part of France. The local settlers asked that the name be changed to STRASBURG, and railroad officials approved the request. The post office was established April 29, 1903 with Egiti Keller pm, who moved his Tirsbol post office to the new townsite. The village incorporated in 1908, and became a city in 1941. The elevation is 1805, the Zip Code is 58573, and it reached a peak population of 994 in 1940. Lawrence Welk, the famous band leader and television personality, was born here in 1903. (1, 2, 3, 18, 23, 33, 40, 66, 79, 403, 404)

**STRASBURG COLONY** (Pierce). This was a rural community in Alexanter Twp. (152-72), SW of Esmond, consisting of about fifty families from South Russia, who used the name of a settlement in their homeland. Because of duplication with Strasburg in Emmons County, the post office was established in 1909 as MILL. (3, 40, 414)

**STRATE** (Cavalier). Many early accounts mention a STRATE post office, which undoubtedly refer to the GERTRUDE post office whose first pm in 1883 was John J. Strate. It was later located in Sec. 25-159-58, Osford Twp., five miles SW of Milton, where George and Martin Strate operated a country store in which the post office was housed. (3, 117, 218)

**STRAUBVILLE** (Sargent). This GNRR station was founded in 1886 in SW¼ Sec. 25-130-58, Jackson Twp., and named for Joseph W. Straub, the area's first settler in 1883. The post office was established August 31, 1887 with Henry Straub as pm. Major development never occurred in STRAUB-VILLE, and the population was never more than 40. The post office, Zip Code 58070, closed August 19, 1984. (2, 18, 25, 40, 41, 167)

**STRAWBERRY LAKE** (McLean). This is a resort community in NE¼ Sec. 2-149-80, Horseshoe Valley Twp., and SE¼ Sec. 35-150-80, Otis Twp., about twelve miles south of Velva, which was named for the long lake around which it is located. The lake was an important landmark on the military trail between Fort Totten and Fort Stevenson, but modern interest in it began in 1932 when a dam was built at its south end to stabilize the water level. In the early 1950's Neena Steenerson opened a tavern and restaurant at the south end of the lake, and by 1953, when a second dam was built, the area had developed into a popular resort. It first appeared on road maps in the late 1970's, and current telephone listings show about fifty families, a few businesses, and a fire department at the site. (3, 28, 34, 55)

**STREETER** (Stutsman). This NPRR station was founded in 1905 as the terminus of its branch line from Edgeley. It is located in NW¼ Sec. 26-137-69, Streeter Twp., and was named for Col. Darwin Reed Streeter (1848-1918), the editor of the *Emmons County Record* at Linton. Others say it was named for J. B. Streeter, and still others say it was named for Streator, IL, with no explanation for the difference in the spelling. The post office was established March 2, 1906 with Alex Anderson (1872-1936) pm, replacing the rural post office of Bloomenfield on that date. The village incorporated in 1916, and it became a city in 1950 with Oscar Seher as mayor. The elevation is 1953, the Zip Code is 58483, and a peak population of 711 was reported in 1930. (1, 2, 3, 18, 33, 40, 52, 66, 79, 158, 162)

**STREHLOW** (Hettinger). This was a rural community founded in the 1890's in Strehlow Twp. (134-97), about eight miles south of New England. The name honored Alfred Strehlow, a local sheep and cattle rancher in partnership with Casper Getz. Reports of a post office are not supported by government records. (2, 3, 40, 74)

**STRINGTOWN** (Ward). This name was applied to the rural community centered in SW¼ Sec. 24-153-83, Freedom Twp., twelve miles south of Minot, which was the site of a country store operated by Margaret Witham. The name is credited to Effie Caswell, who noted how the settlement was strung out for about six miles along County Road 18. The place later took the name SOUTH PRAIRIE. (3, 18, 100, 374)

**STROUD** (McKenzie). This was a rural post office, the first in McKenzie County, established October 3, 1895 with Jeffrey Edward Hanley (1864-1945) as pm. It was located in NE¼ Sec. 1-152-101, ten miles NNE of Alexander near what was called Baker's Ferry. The name honored Joseph G. Stroud, who had come to this area from TX with his brother, Robert W. Stroud. The post office moved several times within this general area as six additional pms served the patrons of the region, and closed July 15, 1913 with mail to Williston. (1, 2, 3, 18, 40, 227, 228, 414, 415, 432)

**STUART** (Slope). This was a farm post office established May 23, 1910 with Rev. Charles W. Anthony pm, who named it for James G. Stuart, a pioneer rancher who came here in 1902 from VA, but left before 1910 for NM. It was located in SE¼ Sec. 4-135-106, West Yule Twp., about thirty miles WNW of Amidon in the extreme NW corner of the county. In 1916 it moved six miles SE to Sec. 18-135-105, East Yule Twp., the home of new pm Julius G. Dryden, and closed April 30, 1925 with mail to Ollie, MT. (1, 2, 3, 40, 53, 82)

**STUMP** (Nelson). The post office serving the mail station called STUMP LAKE in SE¼ Sec. 27-151-60, Wamduska Twp., five miles NE of Tolna, was established June 14, 1880 with Homer E. Smith pm, who called it simply STUMP. His son, Warren Smith, was the mail carrier. On December 27, 1881 the STUMP post office was replaced by the Parkhurst post office located three miles NNE of this site. (25, 40, 124, 415)

**STUMP LAKE** (Nelson). This was a pioneer settlement in SE¼ Sec. 27-151-60, Wamduska Twp., on the NE shore of Stump Lake, named to note the stumps of a prehistoric forest protruding from the water. French explorers called it Chicot Lake, meaning stump. It began as a station on the Grand Forks-Fort Totten mail route, and became STUMP when the post office was established June 14, 1880. (2, 40, 79, 124, 415)

**STURGIS** (Morton). This was a settlement promoted by Ben Ash in Sec. 2-138-81, just north of Fort Abraham Lincoln. It was founded in 1877 and named for Lt. J. G. Sturgis, who had been killed in 1876 at the Battle of the Little Big Horn. STURGIS was on the Bismarck-Deadwood trail, and can be considered as a predecessor of Mandan. Sturgis, SD was founded in 1878, and named for Lt. Sturgis' father, Major Samuel D. Sturgis, commander of nearby Fort Meade at the time. (2, 3, 10, 36, 107)

**STUTSMAN COUNTY MEMORIAL PARK** (Stutsman). This is an alternate name for SPRING GROVE, the platted resort in NW¼ Sec. 31-142-62, Gray Twp., on the north shore of Spiritwood Lake. (2, 3, 158)

**SULLY'S HILL** (Benson). This is a national game preserve of 994 acres just NE of Fort Totten on the south shore of Devils Lake. Located in Secs. 9, 10, 15 & 16-152-65, it was

Baker's Ferry near the Stroud post office was not for the faint of heart

named for General Alfred H. Sully (1821-1879), a leader of many Indian campaigns in the Dakotas. It was administered by the National Park Service 1914-1931, at which time control was transferred to the U. S. Fish and Wildlife Service. (2, 3, 5, 10, 18, 34, 79, 110, 414)

**SULLY SPRINGS** (Billings). This was a NPRR station built before 1890 in Sec. 11-139-101, West Fryburg Twp., four miles west of Fryburg. It was named for Gen. Alfred H. Sully (1821-1879), who had camped near here in 1864 during one of his Indian campaigns. The name also notes several natural springs in the area. It was served by the Medora post office until its own post office was established July 23, 1909 with W. W. Williamson pm, and closed March 31, 1922 with mail to Fryburg. The elevation is 2599, and development was always so minimal that no population figure was ever reported. (1, 2, 3, 5, 18, 25, 34, 40, 81, 414)

**SUMMIT** (Billings). A settlement of railroad construction workers developed in NE¼ Sec. 9-139-100, East Fryburg Twp., in 1879 and was named FOGARTY. In 1883 the name was changed to SUMMIT to note its location at the summit of the plains just before the terrain begins to descend into the Badlands of the Little Missouri River valley. When the

post office was established May 13, 1911, the name was changed to FRYBURG. (2, 3, 34, 40, 81)

**SUNNY** (Morton). This NPRR station was built before 1890 in NW¼ Sec. 30-139-81, three miles west of Mandan, and named SUNNYSIDE to describe its location in the Heart River valley. A depot was built at the site about 1908 and named SUNNY. Little development took place, and the station was later abandoned. (1, 2, 3, 17, 18, 79)

**SUNNYSIDE** (Morton). This NPRR station was built before 1890 in NW¼ Sec. 30-139-81, three miles west of Mandan, and given a name descriptive of its location in the Heart River valley. A depot was built about 1908 with the name shortened to SUNNY. No development occurred, and the station was later abandoned. (2, 3, 25, 79, 240)

**SUNNY SLOPE** (Ward). This is a rural subdivision founded in the 1960's in SE¼ Sec. 24-155-82, Nedrose Twp., about two miles SW of Surrey, and just south of US Highway 2. The name is descriptive of the location. (3, 34)

**SUPERIOR** (Bottineau). This was a farm post office established October 23, 1899 with Henry Vaughn pm. It was named for the

*NPRR depot at Sunny about 1909*

largest of the Great Lakes, called *Kitchigumi* by the Indians, and named Lake Superior by the white man because of its size. Many settlers in the area had come from MN, which probably influenced the name selection. It was first located in SW¼ Sec. 7-160-78, Stone Creek Twp., three miles west of Kramer, and moved four miles NW in 1901 to the home of new pm John L. Banks in NW¼ Sec. 23-161-78, Starbuck Twp. Later that year Mr. Banks moved the facility four miles NW to SW¼ Sec. 7-161-78. The following year the post office moved to the home of new pm Ludvig John Larson in SE¼ Sec. 32-161-78, about two miles north of the original site, and closed August 15, 1905 with mail to Ely. (2, 3, 10, 13, 40, 75, 101, 153, 414)

**SURREY** (Ward). This GNRR townsite was promoted by Max Bass, the railroad's immigration agent, in 1894 in Sec. 19-155-81, Surrey Twp., and named for Surrey, England by railroad officials. Settlement began in 1900, and the post office was established June 18, 1900 with George W. Burke pm. The town became a household word in ND in 1911 when it was made the terminus of the GNRR's new Surrey cutoff line from Fargo. The elevation is 1473, and the Zip Code is 58785. The village did not incorporate until 1951, when the population was about 150. Since that time it has become a favorite location for people who work in Minot, but wish to live in a smaller town, and its 1980 population reached a peak of 998. Surry is an erroneous spelling. (1, 2, 3, 33, 40, 79, 100)

**SUTTON** (Griggs). The GNRR founded this townsite in the spring of 1910 in SE¼ Sec. 4-145-61, Mabel Twp., as a station on its projected cutoff line from Fargo to Surrey, and reached the site on May 22, 1912. GNRR officials named it for John Sutton (1861-1945), a local farmer who had provided lodging for the construction crews. Sutton is an Old English name meaning from the south village, or south town. The post office was established January 6, 1913 with Proctor W. Rice pm. The Zip Code is 58484, and the population has remained at about 150 for many years. (2, 5, 19, 33, 40, 65, 79)

**SVEA** (Barnes). This was a rural settlement in SW¼ Sec. 28-138-60, Svea Twp., seven miles NW of Litchville. The post office was established July 13, 1889 with John Peter Herman Appelquist pm. The name was chosen by settlers from Svea Twp., Kittson County, MN, which was given the poetic name for Sweden, where it is sometimes seen as a feminine version of the name Sven. The post office closed May 14, 1904 with mail to Litchville, but a high school operated here until 1963. Besides the township, the name is perpetuated by a picnic grounds at the site. (2, 3, 13, 18, 34, 40, 76, 414)

**SVENBY** (Barnes). This was a farm post office established July 13, 1889 with Louis Berg pm. The name is Swedish for young village. It was located in SE¼ Sec. 22-137-58, Oak Hill Twp., one mile SW of Kathryn, and moved two miles SW in 1891 to NW¼ Sec. 34-137-58, the home of new pm Bergsvend B. Thorud. The post office closed September 29, 1900 with mail to Kathryn. It is an interesting coincidence that the two rural post offices in Barnes County that begin with "Sv" were established on the same date. (2, 3, 40, 76, 414)

**SVERDRUP** (McLean). This rural community was founded in 1882 in Sec. 5-143-81, Nettle Creek Twp., on the east bank of the Missouri River four miles SE of Washburn. The settlers, mostly of Scandinavian origin, came here from Hudson, WI, and named their new home HUDSON COLONY, but in 1883 they changed the name to SVERDRUP for Johan Sverdrup (1816-1892), the Prime Minister of Norway 1884-1889. Little development occurred, and most of the settlers relocated to Washburn, where the First Lutheran Church congregation is considered to be the continuation of the SVERDRUP settlement. (3, 34, 390)

**SVOLD** (Pembina). This was an Icelandic settlement that began in 1897 in SE¼ Sec. 31-162-55, Advance Twp., eight miles west of Cavalier. The name is that of an island mentioned in the Scandinavian sagas where a battle was fought September 9, 1000 A.D. between Norwegian Vikings and a coalition of Denmark, Sweden, and England. The exact location of this island is unknown, but many scholars believe it is an island off the NW coast of Germany. The name was selected from a list of names submitted to postal officials who wanted a name with little chance of duplication. The post office was established May 5, 1899 with Halldor Vivatson pm in his country store, which was a local landmark for many years. The post office closed June 30, 1943 with mail to Akra, but a population of 11 was reported at SVOLD as late as 1960. (1, 2, 3, 18, 40, 79, 108)

**SWAN** (Ramsey). This was a rural post office established September 12, 1882 with Michael E. Donohue pm, and named for local settler A. E. Swan. It was located in NE¼ Sec. 27-154-65, Grand Harbor Twp., at the head of Teller's Bay, and apparently very close to the existing post office of Scott. On December 6, 1882 the SWAN post office absorbed the Scott post office, but fourteen days later on December 20, 1882, the SWAN post office closed, and was replaced by the facility at the new townsite of Grand Harbor, two miles to the north, with Mr. Donohue continuing as pm. (2, 3, 25, 40, 103, 414, 415)

**SWAN CREEK** (Cass). A settlement known as GOOSE CREEK was founded in Sec. 35-140-52, Casselton Twp., about 1870, but when the NPRR sent Mike Smith here in 1873 to experiment with shelter belts, the place was called SWAN CREEK. Both names noted the nearby creek, called *Aux Ontardes* by French explorers to note the wild geese, or swans, that fed and nested on its banks. In 1876 the site was renamed CASSTOWN, and later that year became CASSELTON. (2, 77, 299, 300)

**SWARTWOOD** (Bowman). This was a farm post office established July 16, 1908 with LeRoy Swartwood as pm. He was a nephew of territorial legislator William Bowman, for whom the county was named. The post office was first located in Sec. 33-129-100, Minnehaha Twp., sixteen miles SSE of Bowman, but it was relocated several times until November 26, 1921, when it moved into SD, where it closed February 28, 1923 with mail to Bowman. (1, 2, 3, 18, 34, 40, 53, 120)

**SWASTIKA** (Sioux). This was a rural community in SE¼ Sec. 27-130-86, on the south bank of Cedar Creek about twenty-four miles west of Selfridge. The post office was established June 16, 1912 with James C. Smith pm, and closed December 31, 1923 with mail to McIntosh, SD. A population of 10 was reported in 1920. Mr. Smith's suggested name, Cedar Valley, was rejected by postal officials, after which it was named for the ancient symbol that has been found in use from Scandinavia to the Middle East, with a similar device being used by various Indian tribes in both North and South

America. It was usually used as a symbol for good luck, but the swastika has fallen from favor since it was used by Nazi Germany. (2, 3, 5, 40, 79, 127, 414)

**SWEDEN** (Mountrail). This was a farm post office established August 21, 1903 with August Walters pm. It was located in NE¼ Sec. 11-157-90, Clearwater Twp., seven miles NNW of Palermo, and named to honor the Swedish homesteaders in the area. Sweden is derived from Swealand, one of the three divisions of ancient Scandinavia. Carl Bergland became pm in 1905, moving the post office to his farm in SE¼ Sec. 1-157-90. Hans Scheldrup was the mail carrier, bringing it from Palermo. He was an expert skier, and often used this method of travel during winter months. The post office closed May 15, 1909 with mail to Palermo. (2, 3, 5, 18, 40, 72)

**SWEDEN** (Walsh). This was a farm post office established April 28, 1879 with John Magnus Almen pm, who named it for his homeland. Later that year it moved to the country store operated by William McKenzie and A. A. Blekken in Sec. 36-158-54, Glenwood Twp., one mile WSW of Nash. The post office closed August 21, 1882 with mail to Grafton. (1, 2, 40, 75)

**SWEDISH SETTLEMENT** (Walsh). This name was given to a colony of fourteen families from Sweden who settled in Dewey Twp. (157-59), a few miles south of Fairdale, in the early 1900's. (75)

**SWEET BRIAR** (Morton). This NPRR station was built in 1879 in SW¼ Sec. 27 & SE¼ Sec. 28-139-83, Sweet Briar Twp., sixteen miles west of Mandan, and named for the nearby creek which was named for the eglantine, a thorny, rose-like shrub in the area. Most early development was at Marmot, a few miles to the east, but as that community stagnated SWEET BRIAR began to grow. The Marmot post office moved here June 3, 1886 with George V. Gilman becoming the pm. On January 17, 1896 the name was changed to SWEETBRIAR to comply with new government spelling regulations. (3, 40, 79)

**SWEETBRIAR** (Morton). This post office was established June 3, 1886 as SWEET BRIAR, but pm James J. Lane changed to a one-word spelling on January 17, 1896 to comply with new government regulations for place names. The elevation is 1824, and a population of 100 was reported in 1920. A steady decline followed, and pm Ervin Siefert closed the post office on June 17, 1949 with mail to Mandan. A population of 1 was reported in 1976. (1, 2, 3, 17, 18, 25, 40, 107)

**SWEETWATER** (Ramsey). This was a GNRR station built in 1902 in SW¼ Sec. 27-155-64, Freshwater Twp., seven miles north of Devils Lake. The name came from the lake just east of the station, which had been named to note the sweet taste of its water. Joshua Coykendall (1818-1887) and his son Fredrick (1856-1922) settled here in 1882, and a townsite was promoted, but the railroad station was about the extent of its development. SWEETWATER disappeared from maps in the 1940's, and the site is now vacant. (3, 18, 103)

**SYDNA** (Ransom). This was a farm post office established August 4, 1882 with James C. Lanegan pm, who named it for his daughter Sydna. She later married John L. Tanner, who played a major role in the organization of this township. It was located in NE¼ Sec. 20-133-54, Sydna Twp., four miles NW of Milnor, and closed January 21, 1884 with mail to Milnor. Some sources erroneously place this post office in Sargent County. (2, 3, 40, 171, 201)

**SYDNEY** (Stutsman). This was a Midland Continental RR station founded in 1912 in NW¼ Sec. 33-138-64, Sydney Twp., and named for Herbert Sydney Duncombe, a lawyer who was an organizer of the railroad. Several sources erroneously claim that it was named for Sidney, NE. The post office was established August 26, 1913 with Ludwig H. Lewis pm. A village of 60 people was reported in 1920, but the population had declined to just 17 in 1960. The post office, Zip Code 58485, closed January 4, 1974 with mail to Jamestown. (2, 3, 35, 40, 158)

**SYKESTON** (Wells). This NPRR townsite was the namesake of promoter Richard Sykes, a wealthy Englishman who founded several towns in the state. SYKESTON dates from 1883, although an 1882 map by Wells & Dudley shows "Sykes" at this site in Sec. 13-146-69, Sykeston Twp. For several years it was the terminus of the NPRR, and was the county seat until 1894. The post office was established October 11, 1883 with Harry L. Durbrow pm. The village incorporated in 1905, and it became a city in 1925 with O. J. Lundby (1885-1950) as mayor. The elevation is 1653, the Zip Code is 58486, and a peak population of 367 was reached in 1920. SYKESTON was the first settlement in Wells County, and Lake Hiawatha, created here in 1899, is considered to be the first artificial lake in ND. (1, 2, 3, 18, 25, 33, 40, 52, 79, 268, 414)

**SYLVAN** (Morton). This was a pioneer NPRR townsite founded as GRINNELL in the early 1880's in SW¼ Sec. 6-138-82, four miles ESE of Sweetbriar. It is believed to have been named for Sylvane Ferris, a pioneer rancher near Medora and an associate of Theodore Roosevelt. Some say the name comes from the Latin *silva*, noting its location along the wooded Sweet Briar Creek. The post office was established April 25, 1883 with DeWitt C. Grinnell pm, but little development occurred, and it closed November 5, 1883 with mail to Marmot. (2, 3, 25, 40, 414)

**SYLVAN GLEN** (Rolette). This site in NE¼ Sec. 13-162-73, Gilbert Twp., three miles north of Dunseith, was platted July 25, 1906 around a small lake with hopes that it would develop into a summer resort. Dr. C. M. Wagner of Dunseith was its promoter, and he gave it an idyllic name coined from the Latin *silva*, meaning forest, and the Celtic *glen*, meaning valley. It flourished for a few years, but was vacated in 1917. (2, 10, 19, 123)

# T

**TAFT** (Slope). This was a ranch post office established October 5, 1908 with Sarah Wood Bard pm on the ranch of her husband, Walter E. Bard, who came here in 1907 from Minneapolis, MN and died in 1910. The name was chosen to honor William Howard Taft (1857-1930), who was at the time the Republican candidate for President of the United States and the current Vice President under President Theodore Roosevelt. The post office was located in SE¼ Sec. 12-136-100, Peaceful Valley Twp., eleven miles NE of Amidon, and closed January 15, 1914 with mail to Gaylord. (2, 3, 18, 40, 82, 414)

**TAFT** (Traill). This is a GNRR station in SW¼ Sec. 17 & SE¼ Sec. 18-146-50, Eldorado Twp., between Hillsboro and Cummings. The site is mentioned in an 1890 guide of ND as GUNDIN FARM, and appears on a 1904 map as CLARKE. This name first appeared about 1910, and was selected to honor William Howard Taft (1857-1930), President of the United States 1909-1913, and Chief Justice of the US Supreme Court 1921-1930. He is the only person to have held both positions. A village of about 15 people was here in 1920, and a count of 8 was made in 1960, but the village has never had a post office or developed beyond an elevator and related buildings. (2, 3, 10, 18, 25, 29, 187)

**TAGUS** (Mountrail). This GNRR station in SW¼ Sec. 12-156-88, Egan Twp., was first known as WALLACE when founded in 1900. Due to confusion with Wallace, ID, the name was changed to TAGUS. Some say it was named for an early settler named Taguson, while others say it was named for the Tagus River in Spain to please Spanish laborers working on the railroad at the time. The post office was established January 30, 1901 with Edward O. Sjaastad pm. The village incorporated in 1908 and reached a peak population of 140 in 1940, but declined to just 14 in 1970. Michael C. Egan (1879-1963) published *The Tagus Mirror* for a few years. The post office, Zip Code 58786, closed May 6, 1966 with mail to Berthold, and the last business in town closed in 1976. (2, 18, 40, 72, 79)

**TANSEM** (Divide). This was a farm post office established December 18, 1911 with Peter Tansem pm. It was located in SW¼ Sec. 23-162-100, Lincoln Valley Twp., eight miles SE of Fortuna. Andrew F. Hanson became the pm in 1918, and closed the facility August 14, 1920 with mail to Colgan. (2, 3, 34, 40, 414)

**TAPPEN** (Kidder). The NPRR established TWELFTH SIDING in 1872 in Secs. 9 & 10-139-71, Tappen Twp. Sheppard Tappen and John Van Dusen arrived in 1878 and began the 10,240-acre bonanza farm which they named Troy Farm, with the loading facilities at TWELFTH SIDING taking the name TROY FARM SIDING. A settlement began in 1882, which was named to honor

*Tappen about 1918*

Mr. Tappen. The post office was established May 25, 1882 with Alfred Birchett pm, and by 1883 the new townsite had 115 residents. The elevation is 1789, the Zip Code is 58487, and the village, which incorporated in 1914, reached a peak population of 379 in 1950. (1, 2, 18, 25, 33, 40, 52, 62, 79, 122, 148)

**TARA** (Steele). This was a farm post office established June 25, 1890 with Samuel Salisbury pm. It was located on the Thomas Underwood farm in SW¼ Sec. 5-148-56, Westfield Twp., eleven miles north of Finley near the Grand Forks County line. It is thought that the name came from the famous hill and village in Ireland which was the seat of royal power for centuries. The name is Gaelic for crag or tower, and is most familiar to Americans as the name of the fictional plantation in Margaret Mitchell's *Gone With The Wind*. The post office closed March 25, 1898 with mail to Nebo. (2, 3, 13, 19, 40, 99)

**TARBELL** (Stutsman). This was a rural post office established July 25, 1881 with Mrs. Elliot A. Tarbell pm. It was located in NE¼ Sec. 14-137-63, Montpelier Twp., and named for J. R. Tarbell, who came here in 1879. Postal officials rejected the suggested name of Elm Wood, citing possible confusion with Elm River, even though that Traill County post office had recently changed its name to Quincy. When the NPRR townsite of Montpelier was platted just to the north in 1885, all development shifted there. The TARBELL post office was relocated to Montpelier on April 26, 1886. (2, 3, 18, 40, 158, 414)

**TARSUS** (Bottineau). This was a rural post office established September 14, 1886 with Alexis Breault pm in NE¼ Sec. 5-161-74, Lordsburg Twp., eight miles SE of Bottineau. The name is traced to the ancient city of Tarsus, Turkey, the birthplace of St.

Paul, although the post office name came directly from the local Tarsus Catholic Church, completed in 1887. A small village developed around the country store of Joseph Trudel, and a population of 30 was reported in 1890. The village declined, and the post office closed January 31, 1920 with mail to Bottineau. (1, 2, 3, 18, 25, 40, 79, 101, 152)

**TASCO** (Bottineau). This was a Soo Line RR siding built in 1908 in Sec. 18-160-74, Cecil Twp., five miles west of Overly. Tasco means clay earth, and the name was supposedly transferred here from Tasco, KS, but that town was called Guy until 1923. Three elevators were built at the site, and one operated into the 1940's, but little settlement ever occurred here, and the site never had a post office. It disappeared from maps during the 1960's. (2, 3, 18, 34, 101, 153)

**TASKER** (Ward). This post office was established December 29, 1904 with Benjamin B. Tasker pm. It was located in NE¼ Sec. 30-156-84, Kirkelie Twp., at the site of the VANDERWALKER station which served a coal mine five miles NW of Burlington. The post office closed November 15, 1917 with mail to Burlington. (2, 3, 18, 40, 100)

**TATMAN** (Ward). This GNRR station appeared only on some maps of the 1950's in Waterford Twp. (157-83), and was the terminus of a short spur from a point just east of Minot called J. D. Switch. It was apparently named for Tatman Twp. (157-82), and the line is believed to have been built to transport materials needed for the construction of the Minot Air Force Base. (3, 34)

**TAYLOR** (Stark). This NPRR station was founded in 1881 in N½ Sec. 33-140-93,

Taylor Twp., and named ANTELOPE. On September 4, 1882 it was renamed by Lyman N. Cary, General Land Agent of the NPRR at Mandan and a promoter of the site, for his friend David Russell Taylor (1846-1926), a native of VT who was also a NPRR official at Mandan, later founding a well known drugstore in that city. ANTELOPE pm John M. Tracey (1850-1921) continued in that position after the name change. The elevation is 2512, the Zip Code is 58656, and the village, which incorporated in 1912, reached a peak population of 285 in 1920. Richard Elkin, a longtime ND Public Service Commissioner, was born here in 1932. (1, 2, 18, 25, 33, 40, 74, 79, 263, 407)

**TELL** (Emmons). This was a rural community founded by Swedish immigrants in 1888, and named for the Tell Lutheran Church in SW¼ Sec. 27-135-74, Tell Twp., eight miles SE of Braddock. Some sources say the name came from Tell, TX, but that settlement was not founded until 1905. A rural school was built here in 1893 by Olof Pehrson, who became pm of the TELL post office when it was established April 23, 1894 in his home in SW¼ Sec. 28-135-74, one mile east of the church. Charles H. Pearson became the pm in 1903, and the post office closed April 25, 1908 with mail to Braddock. (2, 3, 18, 40, 66, 84, 113, 414)

**TEMPELTON** (Emmons). This 13-block townsite was platted in May 1908 by the brothers Franz and Balthazar Tempel on their land in NE¼ Sec. 5-133-76, McCulley Twp., on the east side of the NPRR tracks opposite LARVIK. LARVIK had previously been known as GODKIN and BROFY, and the whole situation of rival townsites proved confusing even then, with the *Emmons County Record* reporting on August 11, 1910 that, "The name of Brofy, a small station nine miles from Linton on the NP branch, has been changed to Tempeltonville." This was not quite accurate, but on May 9, 1911 TEMPELTON and LARVIK did merge as TEMVIK. (2, 3, 18, 23, 66)

**TEMPLE** (Williams). This is a GNRR station in SE¼ Sec. 27-157-96, Golden Valley Twp., five miles west of Tioga, and one-half mile west of Haarstad, which it replaced in 1908. The name was chosen by GNRR officials with no known local significance. The Harstaad post office moved here on March 12, 1908, with Ole G. Haarstad continuing as the pm. The townsite began to develop into a thriving little village, reporting a population of 90 in 1920, but the count declined to just 25 in 1960. Pm Hugo Nelson closed the post office, Zip Code 58851, on April 30, 1965 with mail to Tioga. (1, 2, 18, 40, 41, 50)

**TEMVIK** (Emmons). This NPRR townsite in NE¼ Sec. 5-133-76, McCulley Twp., was founded in 1904 as GODKIN, and its first post office was named BROFY. In 1908 the name was changed to LARVIK, and a rival townsite called TEMPELTON was platted on the opposite side of the tracks. After three years of spirited competition, the two merged as TEMVIK, borrowing from both names after postal officials rejected the name Union City. The TEMVIK post office opened May 9, 1911 with Ezra P. Zunkel pm.

The elevation is 1950, and the village once claimed a population of about 200, but the 1960 count was just 45. The post office, Zip Code 58574, closed March 8, 1968 with mail to Linton. (1, 2, 3, 18, 33, 34, 40, 66, 79)

**TENT CITY** (Cass). This was an unofficial name for the squatters settlement near the site of the NPRR crossing of the Red River into Dakota Territory, and noted the type of home used by the settlers. TENT CITY later became CENTRALIA, and on February 13, 1872 it was renamed FARGO. (2, 3)

**TENTH SIDING** (Stutsman). The NPRR built this siding in 1872 in Sec. 35-140-65, Eldridge Twp., and named it to note the chronological order as sidings were built westward from Fargo. Settlement began in 1879 and the site was renamed BURTON, but the following year the name was changed to ELDRIDGE. (2, 153, 158)

**TENT TOWN** (Ward). The name of this GNRR construction camp in Harrison Twp. (155-83), just west of Minot, described its temporary structures. Founded in 1886, it was promoted as a rival townsite to Minot, but by the following year it had been completely absorbed by its rapidly-growing neighbor. (3, 371, 442)

**TERRELL** (Ward). Nathan Terrell and Fred M. Lang opened a country store about 1883 in NE¼ Sec. 11-153-81, Sawyer Twp., just east of present-day Sawyer. Early accounts indicate that a mail distribution service was conducted here, but reports of a post office are not supported by government records. Mr. Terrell did open a post office here in 1886, but it was named BLACK. (2, 3, 40, 100)

**TEWAUKON** (Sargent). This pioneer settlement was located on the north shore of Lake Tewaukon in SW¼ Sec. 5-129-53, Kingston Twp., five miles SE of Cayuga. The lake bears an Indian name meaning skunk. It was called Polecat Lake on Judson's 1838 map, and was called Makah Lake on Nicollet's 1839 map. John Longie settled here in 1878 and is considered to be the county's first farmer. The post office was established November 21, 1883 with James Ross pm, and closed January 31, 1903 with mail to Cayuga. A population of 25 was reported in 1890, but TEWAUKON failed to attract a railroad and became a ghost town. (2, 3, 40, 79, 165)

**THACKERAY** (Stutsman). This place is listed in an 1890 guide of ND as being in Stutsman County, and served by the Windsor post office. No other information is available for THACKERAY, which probably was named for William Makepeace Thackeray (1811-1863), the British novelist. (3, 5, 25)

**THATCHER** (Dickey). The THATCHER post office was established March 19, 1887 with Harry Holderness pm, eleven days after the GUELPH post office had been established. THATCHER was in NW¼ Sec. 5-129-60, Port Emma Twp., which today is the main part of the city of GUELPH. The name honored the three Thatcher families who came here from Menasha, WI, and local

references refer to the place as THATCHERVILLE. The post office closed April 24, 1889 with the notation "no papers" on government records. (3, 40, 154)

**THATCHERVILLE** (Dickey). This was a settlement in NW¼ Sec. 5-129-60, Port Emma Twp., where a post office called THATCHER was authorized in 1887. The site is now the SE portion of GUELPH. (2, 3, 40, 154)

**THEBES** (Adams). This was a rural post office established May 22, 1908 with Louis A. Sattler pm. It was located in SW¼ Sec. 35-129-93, Gilstrap Twp., nine miles ESE of Haynes, and just above the SD border. The name came from either the ancient city of Egypt or one of the same name in Greece. On October 29, 1908 the post office moved to the adjacent Milwaukee Road RR townsite of PETREL. (2, 3, 4, 5, 40, 414)

**THE COLONY** (Ransom). This generic name was synonymous with OWEGO, the pioneer settlement on the Sheyenne River 1869-1874 near the Richland County line. This name was found on some contemporary maps, but does not appear to have ever been used by local settlers. (3, 153, 201)

**THE CROSSING** (Burleigh). The NPRR reached the Missouri River in Lincoln Twp. (138-80) in 1872, and christened the location as THE CROSSING. The great engineering effort required to span the river and financial troubles within the NPRR delayed the actual crossing for several years, but THE CROSSING soon became the village of EDWINTON, which was renamed BISMARCK in 1873. (2, 3, 18)

**THE CROSSING** (Cass). When the NPRR crossed the Red River into Dakota Territory in 1871, they gave the location this generic name. The site, NE¼ Sec. 7-139-48, Barnes Twp., was called TENT CITY by the squatters who set up makeshift homes here, then CENTRALIA, and finally in 1872 it was named FARGO and developed into the metropolis of ND. (2, 3, 77)

**THEED** (Richland). This was a rural post office established July 2, 1891 with Nick Schultheis pm, who named it for his neighbor Henry Theede, with a change in the spelling. It was located in SE¼ Sec. 18-130-48, DeVillo Twp., at the site of the NPRR station called SONORA. The Theedes came here in 1881 from WI, and were prominent farmers in the area. A son, Alton Theede (1876-1965), was a longtime merchant here, and married the first white child born in Hankinson. The post office closed September 29, 1906 with mail to Fairmount. (2, 3, 18, 40, 147, 354)

**THE END OF THE TRACK** (Ramsey). The GNRR reached the NE¼ Sec. 25-153-61, Bartlett Twp., just into Ramsey County, in the fall of 1882, and ceased construction of their mainline for the winter. Even though it was common knowledge that construction would resume in a few months, the site became an overnight boomtown, reaching a population of between 1,000 and 2,000 within weeks. It was at first given this generic name, but on January 4, 1883 the post office was established, taking the name BARTLETT. (2, 3, 18, 40, 103)

**THE FORKS** (Ward). This initial settlement was made in May 1883 in NW¼ Sec. 1-155-84, Burlington Twp., one-half mile NE of Burlington, by a party of settlers led by Joseph Lynn Colton, most recently from Lisbon. The site was at the forks of the Des Lacs and Souris Rivers, but later that summer the settlers moved to higher ground, founding the first village in Ward County, COLTON, which later was renamed BURLINGTON. (2, 3, 18, 100, 371)

**THEISEN** (Billings). This was a rural post office established October 22, 1918 with John A. Kumer pm. His name is also found in various records as Kumar and Koomer. It was located in NW¼ Sec. 6-143-98, four miles NE of Fairfield, and was named for Father Theodore Theisen of the Immaculate Conception Catholic Church in Sec. 12-143-99, one mile SW of the post office, which closed December 31, 1920 with mail to Snow. (1, 2, 33, 40, 81, 414)

**THELEN** (Golden Valley). This was a NPRR townsite platted in 1916 in SE 1/4 Sec. 31-139-105, Beach Twp., seven miles SSE of Beach, and named for John M. Thelen, the original owner of the site. Lots were sold September 25, 1916, and a population of 15 was reported in 1920. The post office was established July 21, 1920 with Troy E. Beach pm, and closed July 30, 1921 with mail to Beach. August Brockmeyer ran a blacksmith shop here for a number of years, but the 1930 population was only 4, and the town soon disappeared. Thelan is an erroneous spelling. (2, 3, 18, 34, 40, 80)

**THE SLIDE** (McLean). This was a natural landmark known to early travelers on the upper Missouri River. It was located in Sec. 36-150-91, eleven miles west of Raub, and is listed in an 1890 guide to ND as an apparent settlement, with mail service coming from Fort Berthold. The site is now inundated by Lake Sakakawea. (3, 25, 417)

**THEXTON** (Pembina). This Icelandic settlement was founded in 1879 in SW 1/4 Sec. 2-159-56, Gardar Twp., two miles NE of Gardar, and called PARK. The post office was established in 1883 as PARKTOWN, but on March 2, 1887 pm Robert Thexton renamed it for himself. It closed November 16, 1892 with mail to Saint Thomas. Phexton is an erroneous spelling. (2, 3, 25, 40, 240, 414)

**THIAN** (Grant). This was a NPRR siding in NE¼ Sec. 11-134-86, Thian Twp., six miles east of Carson, and named for P. A. Thian, valuation officer of the railroad. The town never had a post office, or much development of any kind, but it did, strangely enough, have a high school 1936-1938, graduating just 8 students. Thain is an erroneous spelling. (1, 2, 3, 17, 79, 174, 176, 177)

**THIERS** (Williams). This was a rural post office established November 25, 1908 with Zed Campbell, who came here from IN, as pm. It was located in SW¼ Sec. 21-157-103, Strandahl Twp., twenty-five miles NW of Williston near the MT border, and closed June 30, 1913 with mail to Bonetrail. It is said that the name honored Louis Adolphe Thiers (1797-1877), the President of France 1871-1873, who was instrumental in

negotiating a peace treaty with Chancellor Otto von Bismarck of Germany. (2, 3, 5, 18, 40, 50)

**THIRD SIDING** (Cass). This NPRR station was built in 1872 in SW¼ Sec. 19-140-54, Buffalo Twp., and named to note the chronological numbering of the sidings as they were built westward from Fargo. An early NPRR map shows this place as BUFF, and about 1875 it was named NEW BUFFALO, becoming BUFFALO in 1883. (2, 3, 34, 153)

**THIRTEENTH SIDING** (Kidder). This NPRR siding was built in 1872 in Sec. 10-139-72, Sibley Twp., and named to note the chronological numbering of the sidings as they were built westward from Fargo. A townsite began here in 1880, taking the name DAWSON. (2, 3, 18, 61, 122)

**THIRTYMILE** (Hettinger). This name appears on maps circa 1910 in Sec. 6-133-91, Cannonball Twp., on the NPRR about seven miles east of Mott. The name notes nearby Thirty Mile Creek which was named to note that it was thirty miles south of the NPRR mainline. The townsite of ALTON, later renamed BURT, was founded here before the end of 1910. (2, 3, 18, 178)

**THOMAS** (Mercer). This was a rural post office established July 15, 1909 with Thomas P. Farrington pm, and given his first name, which is of Hebrew origin and means the twin. It was located in SW¼ Sec. 30-144-87, one mile east of Beulah. On February 21, 1910 the name was changed to FARRINGTON. (2, 3, 19, 40, 414)

**THOMPSON** (Grand Forks). Settlers were here as early as 1874, and the GNRR station built here in 1879 was named for townsite owner George Norton. When a post office application was submitted December 14, 1880, postal officials rejected NORTON because of possible confusion with Norton, MN. The post office was established January 26, 1881 with Albert Thompson pm, who renamed it for himself and his brother, Robert. Others say the new name honored Alec Thompson, a pioneer businessman. It straddled Sec. 25-150-51, Allendale Twp., and Sec. 30-150-50, Walle Twp., and incorporated as a village in 1923. The Zip Code is 58278, and a peak population of 785 was reported in 1980, almost triple what the count had been in 1970 as the city began to attract residents who worked in nearby Grand Forks, but preferred to live in a smaller town. (2, 18, 25, 31, 33, 40, 69, 79, 276)

**THOMPSON'S LANDING** (Ramsey). This place appeared on an 1884 map in SE¼ Sec. 12-153-65, Grand Harbor Twp., four miles SW of Devils Lake, and opposite Heerman's

Landing on Creel Bay. Several Thompson families were pioneers in the Devils Lake region, and it cannot be determined which one was associated with this steamboat landing. (3, 34)

**THOMSON'S GROVE** (Grand Forks). This was a stage stop on the Grand Forks-Fort Totten trail in Sec. 30-153-55, Agnes Twp., two miles NW of McCanna. The name honored pioneer settlers Thomas and Gulick Thomson, and noted the many trees along the nearby Turtle River. After 1879 this site was generally known as BACHELOR'S GROVE. (2, 31, 69)

**THOR** (Bottineau). This was a farm post office established July 29, 1899 with John Gunder Vedquam pm. He was a native of Norway, coming here in 1887, and named the post office for Thor, the Norse god of thunder. It was located in SE¼ Sec. 35-162-79, Eidsvold Twp., six miles SSE of Landa, and closed January 31, 1906 with mail to Landa. (2, 18, 19, 34, 40, 101, 153)

**THORNE** (Rolette). This GNRR station was platted by Burchfield and Galbraith in 1905 in S½ Sec. 25-161-72, Russell Twp., seven miles NW of Rolette, and named for Samuel Thorne, an associate of GNRR President James J. Hill. Local folklore says it was so named because it was a thorn in the side of Dunseith, or to note the many prairie roses in the area, with THORNE chosen because local residents didn't like the name Rose. The post office was established August 29, 1905, but pm-to-be Homer E. Smith declined the appointment. The position was accepted by Frank P. Peltier, who opened the post office on October 13, 1905. The elevation is 2309, and the village, which incorporated in 1907, reached a peak population of 105 in 1910, but declined to just 38 in 1930. The post office, Zip Code 58378, closed October 22, 1965 with mail to Rolette. (1, 2, 3, 18, 40, 41, 79, 123)

**THORSON** (Burke). This was a rural post office established October 27, 1905 with Ole Andershaug Olson pm. It was located in SW¼ Sec. 28-160-94, Thorson Twp., six miles NW of Battleview, and named for its township, which was named for D. H. Thorson, a local homesteader. Claus Albert Nelson became pm in 1908 at his home in NE¼ Sec. 29-160-94, and he was succeeded by Jemmey Hanson in 1909. On July 26, 1910 the post office was moved about two miles NW to the home of new pm August Person, which was in Divide County. (2, 3, 18, 40, 67, 73, 414)

**THORSON** (Divide). This rural post office was established October 27, 1905 in Burke County. On July 26, 1910 it was moved about two miles NW to the farm home of new pm August Person in SE¼ Sec. 13-160-95, Stoneview Twp., about eight miles north of McGregor. After its move into Divide County, Henry B. Bye, who lived in SE¼ Sec. 12-160-95, one mile north of the post office, was hired as the mail carrier. The post office closed June 30, 1912 with mail to McGregor. (3, 18, 40, 73, 414)

**TICEVILLE** (Dickey). This rural settlement was founded in 1883 in NE¼ Sec. 31-129-59, Lovell Twp., five miles SSE of Ludden, and named KAYTOWN. When the post office was established October 18, 1883 with Edward F. Kay pm, it was renamed TICEVILLE to avoid confusion with Keystone. The new name honored Henry A. Tice of Columbia, SD, who was known as "the guardian angel of the squatters." The post office was on the mail route from Columbia to Port Emma, and closed January 9, 1888 with mail to Ludden. (2, 3, 18, 40, 154, 264, 414)

**TIEBELL** (Sheridan). This was a rural post office established December 9, 1903 with Joseph Teibel Sr., who came here in 1902, as pm. No explanation is given for the variation in the spelling. It was located in NW¼ Sec. 34-145-77, Johns Lake Twp., about thirteen miles NNE of Regan, and just above the Burleigh County line. The orders for both the Wehr post office and this facility were rescinded on July 6, 1904, before either had gone into operation. (2, 40, 415)

**TIFFANY** (Eddy). This was the first settlement in Eddy County, and was founded in SE¼ Sec. 29-149-64, Tiffany Twp., about twelve miles east of New Rockford. The name honored B. C. Tiffany, Registrar of the U. S. Land Office at Grand Forks during the 1880's. The post office was established October 23, 1882 with Cyrus H. Culver pm. Sixty families from Chautauqua, NY came here in 1882, but by 1890 the population was only about 50, and the post office closed August 31, 1917 with mail to Brantford. (2, 18, 25, 40, 79, 112, 119)

**TILDEN** (Benson). This Soo Line RR station was built in 1912 in SE¼ Sec. 15-154-67, Riggin Twp., six miles north of Minnewaukan, and named for Tilden, IL, which was named for Samuel Jones Tilden (1814-1886), a Governor of NY and the unsuccessful Democratic candidate for President in 1876. Little development occurred at the site, although an elevator operated until 1981, when manager Fred Malmedal retired after forty years of service. A population of 8 was listed in 1960. The station appeared as Tilden Station on some maps. (2, 3, 5, 18, 34, 110)

**TILTON'S FORT** (Mercer). This was an alternate name for the fur trading post called FORT TILTON, operated by the American Fur Co. 1822-1824 between Fort Clark and present-day Stanton. (2, 3, 417)

**TILTON'S POST** (Mercer). This was an alternate name for the somewhat obscure FORT TILTON of 1822-1824, a fur trading post between Fort Clark and present-day Stanton. (2, 3, 417)

**TIMMER** (Morton). This NPRR townsite was founded in 1910 in NE¼ Sec. 5-133-82, three miles WSW of Breien, and named for Charles L. Timmerman (1860-1914), a pioneer area rancher, merchant in Sims, and banker in Mandan, who promoted development along NPRR lines throughout western ND. The post office was established July 21, 1910 with newspaperman Bert H. Finch pm, replacing the Finch post office just NW of the townsite. A prosperous little community began to develop, but the population never exceeded 100. The

elevation is 1760, and the population declined to just 15 in 1940. The post office closed April 30, 1954 with mail to Solen, and TIMMER is now deserted. (1, 2, 3, 17, 40, 79, 107, 343)

**TIOGA** (Williams). This GNRR station was founded in 1902 in Sec. 27-157-95, Tioga Twp., and named by settlers from Tioga, NY, which was given an Iroquois Indian name meaning peaceful valley. The post office was established December 5, 1902 with Nels W. Simon (1865-1933) pm. The elevation is 2240, the Zip Code is 58852, and the village incorporated in 1909. Oil was discovered April 4, 1951 on the Clarence Iverson farm eight miles south of town, and TIOGA became the center of the Williston Basin oil boom. Its population went from 456 in 1950 to 2,087 in 1960, with the 1980 population being 1,595 as oil production and exploration has stabilized. (1, 2, 3, 18, 25, 33, 40, 50, 52, 79)

**TIPPERARY** (Cavalier). This was a GNRR station built in 1907 in Sec. 25-164-57, Fremont Twp., in the extreme NE corner of the county. It served as a port-of-entry for the newly-built extension of the GNRR from Walhalla to the Canadian border with a connection to Morden, Manitoba, and was opposite the Canadian port-of-entry station called Haskett. Very little development occurred at the site, although it appeared on some maps into the 1940's. Like many other GNRR stations, this place was given a British place name with no local significance, in this case taking its name from the county in southern Ireland. (1, 3, 34, 420)

**TIRSBOL** (Emmons). This was a farm post office established May 3, 1898 with Egiti Keller pm. It was located in NE¼ Sec. 23-131-76, Strasburg Twp., one mile north of Strasburg, and named for Tiraspol, Cherson District, South Russia, the Roman Catholic diocese in the old country for many area settlers. No explanation is given for the change in the spelling. The suggested name of Elsas was rejected by postal officials. On April 29, 1903 Mr. Keller moved his post office one mile south to the new Milwaukee Road RR townsite of Strasburg, adopting the new name. (2, 3, 18, 23, 40, 66, 414)

**TOBACCO GARDEN** (McKenzie). This name dates from 1869 when it was a woodyard for river boats in Secs. 23, 24 & 25-154-97, Twin Valley Twp., on the south bank of the Missouri River twenty miles NNE of Watford City. The name was developed from the Sioux and Assiniboine Indian name for the creek at this site. The Indians used the same word for tobacco and reeds, and the white man erroneously translated their name as tobacco, when the Indians were actually noting the reeds that grew in profusion here. The site is now inundated by Lake Sakakawea, but the name is perpetuated by the Tobacco Garden Creek State Game Management Area where the creek now enters the reservoir. (2, 3, 34, 79, 229)

**TOBACCO GARDEN** (McKenzie). This was a rural post office established December 22, 1906 with Rev. Peder G. Arnstad (1871-1948) as pm. Rev. Arnstad, a Lutheran minister,

was born in Norway and came here from MN in 1905. The post office was located in N½ Sec. 10-151-98, Garden Twp., eight miles NNE of Watford City, and named for the nearby creek and the boat landing at the creek's mouth. Preliminary application forms show this post office as Garden, but postal officials apparently ignored the one-word tradition and allowed the two-word historic place name to be used. The post office closed October 31, 1916 with mail to Schafer. (1, 2, 3, 18, 40, 79, 229, 414)

**TODD** (Williams). This was a GNRR loading station built in 1888 in NE¼ Sec. 11-153-102, Trenton Twp., between Williston and Trenton, and named for Boyd Todd, a pioneer rancher in the area. No development occurred at the site, and it was abandoned in 1930. (2, 18, 50)

**TOKIO** (Benson). This GNRR station was established in 1906 in SW¼ Sec. 2-151-64, Wood Lake Twp., and named by a GNRR official for the Indian word *to-ki*, meaning gracious gift. It is only natural that some insist that it was named for Tokyo, Japan. The post office opened January 26, 1907 with Victor Ruth pm. The elevation is 1502, the Zip Code is 58379, and a peak population of 112 was reported in both 1930 and 1940. (1, 2, 18, 33, 34, 40, 79)

**TOLLEY** (Renville). This Soo Line RR townsite was founded in 1905 in NE 1/4 Sec. 33-161-86, McKinney Twp., and named for townsite founder Eli C. Tolley, a Soo Line RR official much in the forefront of area development. The site absorbed much of the old settlement of Joslyn, including the post office, which transferred here on December 19, 1905 with Henry Ludke continuing as the pm. Later the historic village of McKinney declined in favor of TOLLEY, which had the advantages offered by a railroad. The Zip Code is 58787, and a peak population of 325 was reached in 1920, with a steady decline to just 103 in 1980. (2, 18, 33, 40, 71, 79, 322)

**TOLNA** (Nelson). This GNRR townsite was founded in 1906 in Secs. 10 & 11-150-61, Dayton Twp., and named for Tolna Tallman, the eldest daughter of the townsite owner, a Mr. Tallman from Willmar, MN. Streets in the new town were named for Mr. Tallman's other daughters. Others say it was named for Tolna, Hungary. The post office was established August 11, 1906 with Edward Hollander pm. The village incorporated in 1907, and is known as "The Turkey Capital of North Dakota." The elevation is 1462, the Zip Code is 58380, and a peak population of 291 was reached in 1960. Obert C. Teigen (1908-1978), an Associate and Chief Justice of the ND Supreme Court 1959-1973, was born here. (1, 2, 18, 33, 40, 52, 79, 124, 132, 263)

**TOMEY** (Walsh). This was a farm post office established June 25, 1886 with Thomas Healey pm, who was also a pioneer school teacher in the area. The name was based on the pm's childhood nickname. Nels T. Hedalen, a state legislator, was later the pm here for ten years. It was first located in Sec. 29-155-56, Medford Twp., five miles west of Fordville. In 1899 it moved one mile NW to the home of new pm Knud G. Morstad in

SE¼ Sec. 19-155-56, and closed May 31, 1907 with mail to the new townsite of Medford. (2, 18, 40, 75, 240, 293, 414)

**TOMLINSON** (Eddy). This rural post office was established June 22, 1883 with Alva D. Tomlinson pm. It was located three miles north of New Rockford in SE¼ Sec. 17-149-66, New Rockford Twp., and closed November 12, 1885 with mail to New Rockford. (2, 40, 112, 119, 414)

**TONGUE** (Pembina). An 1882 map shows this settlement in SW¼ Sec. 15-161-56, Beaulieu Twp., two miles west of Hallson. It was just north of the Tongue River, which was named by Indians who thought its crooked course was like a white man's tongue. Little development occurred here, although some evidence of buildings can still be found. (3, 18, 414, 439, 440)

**TOTTEN** (Benson). This NPRR station was built in 1885 in Sec. 15-152-67, Lallie Twp., and called FORT TOTTEN STATION for the military post nine miles to the east. The name was shortened to TOTTEN in July 1887, and in 1889 it was renamed LALLIE. (2, 3, 25, 34)

**TOUGH TIMBER** (McLean). This was a pioneer Missouri River townsite founded about 1880 in NW¼ Sec. 29-146-84, North Hancock Twp., just below the present-day Garrison Dam. The name is thought to be descriptive of the stands of trees on the river bottoms. It was replaced in 1886 by the new townsite of Hancock one mile to the north. (2, 3, 28)

**TOWANDA** (Sargent). This was a Soo Line RR station in SE¼ Sec. 31-131-56, Bowen Twp., and NE¼ Sec. 6-130-56, Forman Twp., two miles east of Cogswell. The post office was established March 17, 1888 with George C. Passage pm, who named it for his hometown of Towanda, NY. *Towanda* is an Algonquin word meaning place of burial. The post office closed July 12, 1888 with mail to Forman, but reopened November 28, 1894. A store and elevator were built at the site, but it quickly declined and the post office closed for good August 31, 1900 with mail to Cogswell. The site is now vacant. (1, 2, 10, 18, 25, 40, 165, 167)

**TOWER CITY** (Cass). This NPRR station was officially founded on August 19, 1879 in S½ Sec. 19-140-55, Tower Twp. The name was selected by George H. Ellsbury (1840-1907) to honor Charlemagne Tower Sr. (1809-1889), a NPRR official and the former owner of the site. Mr. Tower suggested changing the name of the townsite to Ellsbury, but Mr. Ellsbury declined the honor. Tower City, PA and Tower, MN were also named for Mr. Tower. The post office was established May 5, 1879 with Edgar Chapman pm. The elevation is 1194, the Zip Code is 58071, and the village, which incorporated in 1881, reported a population of 800 in 1883, but has declined to just 295 in 1980. The Baptist Church operated Tower University here 1886-1888. (1, 2, 3, 5, 13, 18, 25, 34, 40, 77, 79, 199, 280)

**TOWNER** (McHenry). This city was founded in 1886 in SE¼ Sec. 10 & W½ Sec. 11-156-76, Newport Twp., and named for

Col. Oscar M. Towner (1842-1897), a Confederate veteran of the Civil War who played major roles in the development of Grand Forks and McHenry counties. Towner County is also named in his honor. The post office was established December 11, 1886 with Robert McCombs pm. It replaced Scriptown as county seat in 1886, incorporated as a village in 1892, and became a city in 1904. The elevation is 1490, the Zip Code is 58788, and a peak population of 955 was reached in 1950. It bills itself as the "Cattle Capital of North Dakota." (1, 2, 3, 18, 25, 33, 40, 52, 79, 185, 342, 412)

**TRACY** (Ramsey). This was a GNRR station in NW¼ Sec. 23-153-62, Stevens Twp., possibly named for Tracy, MN, which was named for John F. Tracy, former President of the Chicago & NW RR. Tracy is an Anglo-Saxon name meaning courageous. It was located two miles ESE of present-day Crary, and seven miles WNW of Bartlett. L. D. Bissell opened a store at the site, and his clerk, William J. McIntyre was appointed pm when the post office was established August 24, 1883. The site failed to develop, and the post office closed May 21, 1886 with mail to Crary. (2, 3, 13, 18, 19, 25, 40, 103)

**TRAILL CENTRE** (Traill). This townsite was founded in 1883 in SE¼ Sec. 36-147-53, Viking Twp., and NE¼ Sec. 1-146-53, Roseville Twp., midway between Mayville and Portland, and was an early example of cooperation between these two rival townsites. The name was borrowed from its county which was named for Walter John Strickland Traill (1847-1938), and "Centre" to note its central position in what was then Traill County. The spelling was in the romantic style in vogue at the time. The purpose of TRAILL CENTRE was to present a unified front in the effort to remove the county seat from Caledonia. TRAILL CENTRE won a special election on April 19, 1883, but court action the following year reversed the outcome due to irregularities. It was technically the county seat for a few months while the litigation was in progress, but the court house never actually left Caledonia, and a change in the county boundary in 1887 eliminated the site's geographic advantage. Caledonia did eventually lose the county seat in 1890, but it went to Hillsboro, and the little development that had occurred at TRAILL CENTRE soon relocated to one of its two more established neighbor cities. (2, 3, 29, 77, 187, 225, 359)

**TRENTON** (Williams). This GNRR station was founded in 1894 in SW¼ Sec. 17-153-102, Trenton Twp., and named to honor stockholders from Trenton, NJ, which was named for its founder, William Trent. Trent is an English name meaning dweller by the river, and is derived from the Latin

meaning swift running. Some claim the name notes the Trenton period of geology. The townsite was originally owned by W. H. Denny, the first mayor of Williston. The post office was established March 26, 1903 with Lorenzo J. Ezell pm. The Zip Code is 58853, and the village has maintained a population of about 100 for many years, with many of its residents being American Indians. Fred J. Wilkinson (1867-1945) was a prominent pioneer merchant. (2, 10, 18, 19, 40, 50)

**TRIER** (Cavalier). This was a rural post office established July 1, 1899 with Dominick Schuler pm, whose last name is sometimes recorded as Shuler. It was located adjacent to the township hall in SW¼ Sec. 20-160-64, Trier Twp., three miles north of Calio, and named for the ancient city of western Germany, homeland of many area settlers. The post office closed August 31, 1906 with mail to Calio. (2, 3, 18, 38, 40, 75, 414)

**TRIEST** (Richland). This NPRR station was founded in 1882 in Sec. 6-132-49, Mooreton Twp. The post office was established October 23, 1882 with Matthias Butala as pm, who named it for his hometown of Triest, then a seaport of the Austro-Hungarian empire, and now a city jointly administered by Italy and Yugoslavia. It is at the head of the Adriatic Sea, and in ancient times it was called Tergesteum. Mr. Butala built the first home and store at this site, and on April 21, 1884 changed the name of the post office to MOORETON. The NPRR apparently didn't like the new name, for they soon began calling their station GRIFFIN until yielding to popular demand, which had almost universally embraced the MOORETON name. (2, 3, 5, 40, 147, 242)

**TROTTERS** (Golden Valley). This rural community dates from about 1903 when settlers arrived near the source of Smith Creek. The post office was established May 7, 1904 with Francis L. "Lee" Trotters pm. It was located in NW¼ Sec. 23-144-105, Henry Twp., but moved in 1906 to NE¼ Sec. 6-144-104, Pearl Twp. It later moved one mile west to NW¼ Sec. 6-144-104, where H. H. Burchette became the pm. Leonard Hall has been the pm since 1959. The Zip Code is 58657, and the community is one of the most remote in ND, being over twenty miles from the nearest town of Beach. (2, 3, 33, 34, 40, 79, 80, 414)

**TROY** (Mercer). Dr. Norman E. Vredenburg platted this townsite in 1911 in Sec. 25-144-88, and named it for his hometown of Troy, NY, which was named for the ancient city in Asia Minor made famous in the poetry of Homer. The NPRR arrived in 1914 and renamed the site BEULAH. The old name is perpetuated by a park in the southern part of the city. (2, 3, 10, 64)

**TROY FARM SIDING** (Kidder). This NPRR siding was built in 1872 in Secs. 9 & 10-139-71, Tappen Twp., and named TWELFTH SIDING. In 1878 two speculators, Sheppard Tappen and John Van Dusen, arrived from Troy, NY to operate a 10,240-acre bonanza farm centered around the siding, and named their venture the Troy Farm for their hometown, and the NPRR renamed the siding to match. In 1882 a settlement began here, and the name was changed to honor Mr. Tappen. (2, 10, 18, 25, 79, 122, 147, 148)

**TRUAX** (Mercer). This was a settlement consisting of several houses, buildings, and a school that developed at the site of the Dakota Star Mine in SW¼ Sec. 21-145-86, five miles north of Hazen. The name honored Elmer Truax Sr., founder of the Truax-Traer Coal Co., operators of the mine, which had a privately-owned railroad spur built to the mine mouth. The mine opened in 1944 and flourished for many years until declining production forced its abandonment in 1966. (3, 34, 435)

**TRUAX** (Williams). This was a rural post office established May 13, 1903 with Charles L. Gemberling, a native of PA, as pm. It was located in SW¼ Sec. 8-154-98, Truax Twp., about seven miles SSE of Epping, and named for James W. Truax (1836-1902), a Williams County judge 1898-1902. Some claim it was named for John Truax of Hastings, MN, who is said to have run a portable saloon for the railroad construction crews. The post office closed July 15, 1909 with mail to Wheelock. (2, 3, 18, 40, 50, 53)

**TRURO** (Bottineau). This was a GNRR townsite founded in 1903 in SW¼ Sec. 7-160-83, Blaine Twp., about six miles NW of Lansford, and named by settlers from the Truro hills area on Cape Cod, MA, with that name tracing to Truro, Cornwall, England. The townsite was owned by the Dakota Development Co., but their efforts proved unsuccessful, with the 1920 count of 10 being its only population report. The post office was established June 1, 1906 with Franklin E. Ingram pm, and closed August 31, 1916 with mail to Lansford. (1, 2, 3, 10, 40, 45, 101)

**TRYGG** (Burleigh). This was a farm post office established January 31, 1905 with Wallace H. Lee pm. It was located in NW¼ Sec. 18-142-77, Rock Hill Twp., three miles SE of Regan, and after postal officials rejected the names Pulford and Lees, it was named for Trygg Twp. (141-77), just to the south, which was named for the brothers Charles J., Andrew, and David Trygg who came to America in 1886 from Sweden and homesteaded in Trygg Twp. in 1905. *Trygg* is Swedish for safe, or calm. Roy D. Young became pm in 1907 at his home in NW¼ Sec. 8-142-77, and the post office closed December 31, 1911 with mail to Canfield. (2, 12, 18, 40, 63, 414)

**TRYSIL** (Cass). This was a rural post office established September 2, 1873 with Ole Strandvold pm, who named it for his birthplace of Trysil, Osterdalen, Norway. Henry Hanson was the mail carrier for this pioneer post office which was located in NE¼ Sec. 25-142-49, Wiser Twp., about three miles north of Argusville. The post office closed November 21, 1899 with mail to Georgetown, MN. Mr. Strandvold was an experienced newspaperman, and was influential in promoting a group of Norwegians in IA to come here, forming what was known as the OSTERDAHL SETTLEMENT. (2, 25, 40, 77)

**TUNBRIDGE** (Pierce). This GNRR station was built in 1886 in NE¼ Sec. 1-156-74,

Ness Twp., six miles west of Rugby, and called SHERMAN. When the post office was established October 21, 1901 with Ole L. Ohnstad pm, the name was changed to TUNBRIDGE, for Tunbridge Wells, England. The change was made by GNRR officials who were naming most of their townsites on the mainline for places in England to please their English stockholders. The elevation is 1512, and a population of 75 was recorded in 1920. Nels Tweet was the pm 1920-1950, and his wife Augusta followed him in the position, closing the post office June 30, 1955 with mail to Rugby. (1, 2, 3, 18, 40, 114)

**TURTLE CREEK** (McLean). This place appeared in an 1890 guide to ND, stating that it was in Burleigh County and served by the Washburn post office. This is thought to be a reference to the old Turtle Valley post office of 1874-1882 which predated the founding of Washburn. This area was in Burleigh County during this time, later becoming a part of McLean County. (3, 25)

**TURTLE LAKE** (McLean). This was a farm post office established January 25, 1886 with Peter Miller pm at his home in NE¼ Sec. 26-147-81, Lake Williams Twp. The post office was actually on the south shore of Lake Williams, but it was named for Turtle Lake, three mile WNW of here, which was named for its shape. In 1903 it moved one mile SW to SE¼ Sec. 27-147-81, the home of new pm Christian Paulson (1876-1938). In 1905 the new NPRR terminus station was founded in SE¼ Sec. 29-147-81, and after considerable competition and political maneuvering, the TURTLE LAKE post office moved to the townsite with a retention of the name. The elevation is 1899, the Zip Code is 58575, and a peak population of 839 was reached in 1950. It incorporated as a village in 1916, and became a city in 1946 with Gus Samuelson as mayor. (1, 2, 3, 25, 28, 33, 40, 79, 271)

**TURTLE MOUNTAIN** (Rolette). This was the name given to the Indian mission started in 1883 in NE¼ Sec. 20-162-70, Couture Twp., noting its location in the Turtle Mountains on the Turtle Mountain Indian Reservation. The mountains were named because they are said to resemble a turtle's back when viewed from a distance. Some say the explorer Verendrye selected the name, while others credit the name to government cartographers. In 1888 the mission was renamed BELCOURT for the pioneer Roman Catholic missionary, Father George Belcourt. (2, 3, 10, 79, 123)

**TURTLE RIVER** (Grand Forks). This was a rural community in SE¼ Sec. 35-154-51, Turtle River Twp., three miles NE of Manvel, and just west of the townsites of CHRISTIANI and BELLEVUE. The post office was established November 7, 1877 with Melvin D. Chappell pm, and closed February 20, 1882. It reopened April 5, 1882 with August Christiani pm, and closed October 31, 1892. It opened for the third time on December 1, 1892 with Albert Lindsey pm, and closed April 30, 1900. It opened for the fourth time on May 13, 1901 with George Henderson Stead pm, and closed for good on November 29, 1902, with the mail going to Manvel after each closing.

A population of 50 was reported in 1890, but the site is virtually vacant today. It was named for its township, which was named for the river which flows through it. (2, 3, 25, 40, 69, 238)

**TURTLE RIVER STATION** (Grand Forks). This was a stage station on the Fort Abercrombie-Fort Garry, Manitoba, Canada trail, built in 1879 in NE¼ Sec. 15-153-51, Ferry Twp., and named for the river which flows through the site. When the GNRR arrived in 1881, they changed the name to MANVEL. (2, 238)

**TURTLE VALLEY** (McLean). This was a popular stopping point on the trail between Bismarck and Fort Stevenson in the 1870's. It was located in Sec. 30-144-81, Satterlund Twp., just SE of present-day Washburn, and was the home of George Grafton Rhude (1849-1920), the first white settler in McLean County. The post office was established October 31, 1874 with Mr. Rhude as pm, who named it for the valley in which it was located, and closed September 4, 1882 when Mr. Rhude became pm at the new townsite of Washburn. He served in that position only until October 19, 1882, when John S. Veeder became the pm. Turkey Valley is an erroneous spelling. (2, 3, 28, 40)

**TUTTLE** (Kidder). This NPRR townsite was founded in 1911 in SE¼ Sec. 1-142-74, Tuttle Twp., and named for Col. William P. Tuttle (1847-1924), a somewhat notorious realtor, financier, and politician who lived in Dawson 1905-1914, and served as a state legislator. The post office was established May 12, 1911 with John J. Levi pm. The elevation is 1478, the Zip Code is 58488, and the village, which incorporated in 1916, reached a peak population of 383 in 1930, with a decline to just 199 in 1980. (1, 2, 3, 18, 40, 52, 61, 79, 122, 313)

**TWALA** (Rolette). This was a rural post office established June 7, 1888 with Charles E. Cleveland pm in SW¼ Sec. 4-160-73, Kohlmeier Twp., about eight miles SSW of Dunseith. The pm and his sister, Mrs. Lena Lee, are credited with suggesting the name, which is said to have been a character in a book they had just read. Christian F. Cleveland became pm in 1903 at his home just across the section line in NE¼ Sec. 9-160-73, and closed the post office January 31, 1906 with mail to Overly. Tivala is an erroneous spelling. (2, 40, 123)

**TWELFTH SIDING** (Kidder). The NPRR built this siding in 1872 in Secs. 9 & 10-139-71, Tappen Twp., and named it to note the chronological order of sidings as they were built westward from Fargo. It was named TROY FARM SIDING in 1878, and became the village of TAPPEN in 1882. (3, 18)

**TWIN BUTTES** (Bowman). When a townsite began to develop in Sec. 11-131-102, Bowman Twp., in 1907, it was called TWIN BUTTES, noting the two flat-topped buttes just to the north. The site apparently was called EDEN for a time, but the post office was established July 26, 1907 as LOWDEN. On October 19, 1907 the name was changed to BOWMAN. (2, 3, 18, 34, 40, 120)

*Tuttle about 1912*

**TWIN BUTTES** (Dunn). This is an Indian agency settlement for the southern portion of the Fort Berthold Indian Reservation. It was founded in the 1950's in SW¼ Sec. 26-147-91 when the backwaters of the Garrison Dam had begun to inundate the old river bottom villages. (3)

**TWIST** (Wells). This was a farm post office established February 28, 1898 with Jesse D. Twist as the first and only pm at his home in SW¼ Sec. 4-149-68, Bremen Twp. A son, David R. Twist, was a prominent figure in county affairs for many years, and his wife, Mary Gardner Bower Twist, achieved some fame as an author. The post office closed April 30, 1909 with mail to Cathay, and the following year the townsite of Bremen was founded just west of this site as a station on the GNRR's new Surrey cutoff line. (2, 3, 18, 40, 79, 364)

**TYLER** (Richland). This townsite was purchased and platted in 1884 by Richard S. Tyler of Fargo, a realtor with large holdings in the area south of Fargo. Tyler is an Old English name meaning maker of tiles or bricks. The Milwaukee Road RR reached the site in Sec. 20-131-47, Summit Twp., about seven miles south of Wahpeton, but no major development ever occurred. The post office was established June 29, 1891 with Charles G. Rebstock pm, and closed May 31, 1958 with mail to Wahpeton. A peak population of 40 was reported in 1930, but only three families continued to reside here in 1975. (2, 3, 18, 19, 40, 147)

**TYNER** (Pembina). This was a rural community in SE¼ Sec. 6-162-54, Cavalier Twp., about seven miles NNW of Cavalier. The post office was established July 7, 1881 with Andrew T. Carr pm. The post office moved across the section line in 1884 to SW¼ Sec. 5-162-54, the home of new pm Robert John Currie, and a population of 20 was reported in 1890. The origin of the name is unknown, although some have suggested that it was named for James Noble Tyner (1826-1904), Postmaster General of the United States when this post office was established. His son, A. H. Tyner, was active in the development of the Red River valley. The post office closed November 30, 1912 with mail to Cavalier. (2, 3, 5, 18, 25, 40, 243)

**TYSON** (Richland). This was a rural post office established June 15, 1892 with Samuel E. Tyson pm, with the name technically honoring the pm's father, William Tyson (1807-1884), who had accompanied his sons here from IL in the early 1880's. Tyson is a Teutonic name meaning son of the Teuton, or German. Some say it is derived from Dyson, or Dionysos, the Greek god of wine. The post office was located in NW¼ Sec. 33-129-49, Greendale Twp., about eight miles SSE of Hankinson, and closed November 18, 1892 with mail to Hankinson. The post office operated just a little more than five months, but the area is still known locally as Tysonville or Tysonvale. (2, 3, 19, 40, 147)

# U

**UKRAINA** (Billings). This rural community began about 1905 around St. Demetrius Ukrainian Catholic Church in SE¼ Sec. 4-141-98, sixteen miles NE of Medora. Most of the settlers were from the Ukraine, hence the name, which means frontier in both Russian and Polish. A post office was established May 15, 1912 with Joe Malkowski pm. In 1921 the post office was moved to Sec. 10-141-99, and in 1928 again moved to Sec. 2-141-99. A townsite was promoted by Dmetro Repetowski (1859-1942), but little development occurred. A population of 35 was reported in 1930. John Palachuk, according to government records, closed the post office November 14, 1931 with mail to Belfield, but postmarks exist from UKRAINA dated as late as 1933. Only the cemetery remains to mark the site today. (1, 2, 3, 5, 33, 40, 53, 81)

**ULNESS** (Dickey). This was a rural post office established December 19, 1883 with Elling O. Ulness (1866-1954) as pm. It was located in SW¼ Sec. 24-132-60, River Valley Twp., just south of Glover, which was founded in 1887 on the NPRR. On January 26, 1887 the ULNESS post office closed, and Mr. Ulness became pm at Glover. He left in 1888, and in 1898 began another Ulness post office in Richland County. (2, 3, 40, 154, 264, 318, 414)

**ULNESS** (Richland). Elling O. Ulness had operated a post office in Dickey County 1883-1887. On May 14, 1898 he was appointed pm of a new post office in Sec. 5-136-50, Walcott Twp., two miles SE of Kindred near the GNRR tracks, where a siding was built, known alternately as KINDRED MILL SPUR or MILL SIDING. Elling Ulness moved to Wilton in 1903, and his brother, Engebret (1864-1921), became pm. The ULNESS post office closed November 15, 1905 with mail to Kindred. (2, 3, 18, 40, 147)

**UMBRIA** (Rolette). A Soo Line RR loading station called INA was built in 1905 in NW¼ Sec. 28-160-70, Union Twp., and for a time a small village and post office existed there. Sometime after 1910, probably around 1930, the name was changed to UMBRIA, which is the name of a province in ancient Italy. (2, 3, 123).

**UNDERWOOD** (McLean). This Soo Line RR townsite was founded in 1903 in Secs. 20 & 21-146-82, Underwood Twp., and named for Fred D. Underwood, Soo Line RR Vice President, who lived at the time in Enderlin. He later moved back east and served as President of the Erie RR. The town was platted in July 1903, and the post office opened August 10, 1903 with Rose A. Ward pm. The village incorporated in 1908, the Zip Code is 58576, and the population reached a peak of 1,343 in 1980 as a result of the boom in the energy industry. The well known artist and religious leader, Clell G. Gannon, was raised here. (2, 3, 18, 23, 28, 40, 79)

**UNION** (Cavalier). Settlement began here in 1881, and the GNRR reached the site, SE¼ Sec. 26-159-57, Montrose Twp., in 1887. The name was suggested by pioneer settler Henry Felix (1835-1906), a Civil War veteran, who wanted to note that the union still existed. When the post office was established September 5, 1890, pm Edward H. Thrugstad submitted several names to postal officials, who chose the existing name from the list. The population of UNION has never exceeded 75, with a 1960 count of just 26. The school closed in 1961, and the Lutheran church closed in 1977, but the post office, Zip Code 58279, continues to operate. (1, 2, 3, 18, 33, 40, 79, 117)

**UNION CENTER** (McKenzie). In 1931 Peter Hanson opened a garage and repair shop in NW¼ Sec. 2-151-96, Blue Butte Twp., about twenty miles NE of Watford City. By the following year the site had become somewhat of a community center, and that fall leaders of the local Farmers Union gave it its name. In October 1934 pm Catherine Schuman moved the KEENE post office, five miles to the north, to UNION CENTER, and within a short time the KEENE name had come into general usage here. (2, 3, 18, 228)

**UNION VALLEY** (Williams). This is a rural community centered around the Union Valley School in NW¼ Sec. 12-152-103, Buford Twp., near Buford. The name commemorates nearby Fort Union, and also notes the togetherness of the residents, who are almost cut off from the rest of the township by a bend in the Missouri River. (3, 50)

**UNIVERSITY** (Grand Forks). A post office was established April 12, 1890 on the campus of the University of North Dakota with Professor Earle S. Babcock pm. It was located in Sec. 5-151-50, Grand Forks Twp., which at the time was west of the city of Grand Forks. The GNRR built a station at the site, using this name on its company literature. On January 31, 1921 the post office lost its independent status, becoming a classified station of the Grand Forks post office, officially known as UNIVERSITY STATION. (2, 3, 18, 25, 33, 40, 69)

**UNIVERSITY STATION** (Grand Forks). The UNIVERSITY post office, which had operated at the University of North Dakota since 1890, became a classified station of the Grand Forks post office on January 31, 1921, with the name UNIVERSITY STATION. It operated under this arrangement until closing January 26, 1980. In later years it was housed in Twamley Hall and shared Zip Code 58201 with Grand Forks. (2, 18, 25, 31, 40)

**UPHAM** (McHenry). This GNRR station was founded in June 1905 in SW¼ Sec. 22-159-78, Meadow Twp., and named for Dr. Warren Upham (1850-1934), longtime Superintendent of the Minnesota Historical Society. He was the author of the standard book on Minnesota place names, and it is likely that this is the only instance where a town was named after such a writer. The post office was established Septmeber 1, 1905 with Nelson J. Kenyon pm. Raymond C. Long later held this post for 46 years in two tenures. The village incorporated in 1908, its elevation is 1460, the Zip Code is 58789, and a peak population of 403 was reached in 1950. Andrew L. Freeman, a leader in rural electrification, was born here in 1909. (1, 2, 3, 5, 13, 33, 40, 186, 262)

**UPLAND** (Divide). This was a farm post office established May 12, 1911 with Adolph M. Engelson pm. It was located in NW¼ Sec. 20-161-96, Upland Twp., and named for its township, which has a name describing its location on the north-south continental divide. The post office, twelve miles SE of Crosby, was discontinued April 30, 1914 with mail to Wildrose. (2, 3, 40, 53)

**URBANA** (Barnes). This site was chosen in 1881 along the NPRR mainline in NW¼ Sec. 20-140-61, Eckelson Twp., although the station was not built until July 1886. An elevator was built in 1903, and the post office opened April 22, 1907 with Everett T. Phelps pm. George Whipple and Albert Sayre platted the townsite in 1910, but most settlers had left by 1913. The post office closed January 15, 1923 with mail to Spiritwood, and the school closed in 1962, making the settlement a virtual ghost town. URBANA, elevation 1493, was named for Urbana, IL, which was named using a form of the Latin word for city. (1, 2, 10, 34, 40, 76)

**UTOPIA** (Bowman). This was a farm post office established October 9, 1907 with Henry T. Thompson, who lived here 1906-1922, as pm. It was located in NW 1/4 Sec. 14-132-104, Rhame Twp., two miles north of Rhame, and named for Utopia, TX. Utopia is a fictional land in the political romance *De Optimo Republicae Stati, Deque Nova Insula Utopia*, written in 1615 by Sir Thomas More. The work has been cited as the source of modern socialistic philosophy, and the name has also become a term used to describe a perfect place. In truth, the word is of Greek origin, and means no place. The post office authorization was rescinded January 24, 1908 before it had gone into operation, an ironic realization of the meaning of the name. (2, 3, 5, 18, 34, 40, 120)

**UXBRIDGE** (Barnes). Settlers arrived here in 1882, and a rural post office was established November 20, 1883 with Joseph J. Bascom pm. It was located in NW¼ Sec. 14-142-61, Uxbridge Twp., and closed December 28, 1892 with mail going to the new Soo Line RR townsite of Leal, about three miles to the SW. A rural school continued to operate here until 1957. The name was chosen by settlers from Uxbridge, Ontario, Canada, which was named for Uxbridge, Middlesex, England. (2, 3, 10, 40, 76, 240, 269)

# V

**VADA** (Dunn). This was a rural post office established September 14, 1910 with Mrs. Louisa Powers pm. It was located in NW¼ Sec. 6-146-96, thirteen miles NW of Killdeer, and closed September 30, 1912 with mail to Oakdale. It is said that VADA was named for Vada, KY, but the latter place did not exist until the 1930's. (2, 3, 18, 40, 53, 87)

**VALBORG** (Adams). This post office was authorized November 15, 1907, the same date as the Leff post office. Both were in the immediate vicinity of what would become the Milwaukee Road RR townsite of Reeder in 1908, and for reasons unknown, Leff became the operating post office, with VALBORG's authorization rescinded January 15, 1908. Jacob L. Hjort, who would have been the pm, named the post office for his daughter. A native of Minneapolis, MN, Mr. Hjort came here in 1907 for health reasons, and engaged in farming, banking, and real estate work, but his main claim to fame in Reeder was his influence as a former professional musician. He encouraged and inspired the pioneers of the area to participate in almost countless musical and theatrical groups. Mr. Hjort and the village were featured in an article in the May 15, 1915 issue of *Etude Music Magazine*. (2, 3, 40, 189)

**VALHALL** (Wells). This was a farm post office established April 25, 1891 with Peter M. Mattson as the first and only pm. It was located in Sec. 35-150-68, Valhalla Twp., five miles NE of Bremen, and closed November 11, 1892 with mail to New Rockford. The name was coined from the name of its township, which was named by Scandinavian settlers for Valhalla, the home of Odin, king of the gods in Norse mythology. (2, 3, 18, 40, 79, 112, 364)

**VALLEY CITY** (Barnes). Founded by the NPRR in 1872, this place was called SECOND CROSSING OF THE SHEYENNE, FIFTH SIDING, and WAHPETON before the year was over. In 1874 it was named WORTHINGTON, but confusion with Worthington, MN resulted in another name change to VALLEY CITY, descriptive of its location in the Sheyenne River valley, on May 10, 1878. Christian Anderson was the pm at that time. The new name was suggested by Joel S. Weiser (1834-1925), later a mayor and state legislator. It is the county seat of Barnes County, incorporated as a village in 1881, and became a city in 1883 with C. A. Benson as mayor. The elevation is 1218, the Zip Code is 58072, and a peak population of 7,843 was recorded in 1970. It is on the mainlines of the NPRR and Soo Line RR, and is the site of the famous highline trestle. A state college was established here in 1890. Frank White, a Governor of North Dakota and Treasurer of the United States, and George Mason, founder of the American Motors Corporation, were natives of VALLEY CITY. (1, 2, 3, 18, 25, 34, 40, 76, 79, 275)

*Valley City about 1955*

**VALLEY CITY STATION** (Barnes). This was a Soo Line RR station in NW¼ Sec. 21-140-58, just north of the NPRR highline bridge at the north end of Valley City. Prior to 1915, some maps show the place as simply STATION. (1, 3, 18, 25, 34)

**VALLEY JUNCTION** (LaMoure). This NPRR junction was built in 1886 in Sec. 11-133-60, LaMoure Twp., five miles east of LaMoure, whose post office served the region. This was the intersection of the Fargo-Streeter line and the newly-built LaMoure-Oakes line, known as the Valley Line, due to its location in the James River valley. In 1897 the name was changed to OAKES JUNCTION, and in 1919 it was renamed INDEPENDENCE, the name of a post office that had been established here in 1910. (2, 3, 18, 25, 240)

**VALMONT** (Cavalier). This was a rural settlement in NE¼ Sec. 32-164-57, Fremont Twp., twenty-two miles NE of Langdon in the extreme NE corner of the county. Its name was coined from its location in the Pembina River VALley, and its township, FreMONT. The post office was established February 23, 1892 with Jens G. Bjornstadt pm, but it closed October 8, 1892 with mail to Vang. (2, 40, 249)

**VANCE** (Cass). This was a GNRR junction station built in 1912 in NW¼ Sec. 13-141-52, Amenia Twp., two miles north of Amenia. The site marked the point where the old GNRR Casselton-Mayville line was crossed by the newly-built Surrey cutoff line. The station was named for the George H. Vance family which lived nearby. One son, Wallace, was the signal tower operator at the station, and another son, Ralph, was the railway mail clerk here. No development occurred at the site. (1, 2, 34, 77)

**VANDALIA** (Williams). This was a pioneer country store in NW¼ Sec. 19-159-99, Rock Island Twp., three miles west of Alamo. A post office was established January 25, 1906 with Arthur T. Gause, owner of the store, as pm. He named it for Vandalia, MO, which bears a popular Latinized form of Vandal, a Germanic tribe known for their savagery. The place name has been popular throughout the country despite its derivation. The pm's father, Dr. William C. Gause (1844-1921), was a pioneer physician in the area. The post office delivered mail twice weekly, but closed November 30, 1913, when the store was moved into the nearby townsite of Appam. (2, 10, 18, 40, 50)

**VANDERWALKER** (Ward). This was a Soo Line RR loading station in NE¼ Sec. 30-156-84, Kirkelie Twp., five miles NW of Burlington, serving a small coal mine. A post office called TASKER operated here 1904-1917. Mr. Vanderwalker was the local mine manager. A population of 30 was reported in 1920, but the site was soon vacated. (1, 2, 3, 18, 100)

**VANG** (Cavalier). This pioneer settlement was founded in SW¼ Sec. 26 & NE¼ Sec. 34-163-58, Hope Twp., fourteen miles NE of Langdon. The post office was established October 15, 1887 with John Dahlvang pm, who coined its name from his own. A population of 25 was reported in 1890, a peak of 30 residents were counted in 1920, and 15 citizens were reported as late as 1940, but the post office closed October 31, 1935 with mail to Langdon, and the town disappeared from maps in the 1960's. (1, 2, 3, 18, 25, 40, 79, 116, 292)

**VAN HOOK** (Mountrail). This Soo Line RR station was founded in 1914 in NW 1/4 Sec.

32-152-91, Van Hook Twp., and named for Fred Van Hook, who led a party of surveyors into the area in 1911 after it had been opened for white settlement by President Taft. Mr. Van Hook lived in the Ryder area until 1937 when he moved to Yakima, WA. The post office was established January 19, 1915 with John W. George pm. The village incorporated in 1915, and reached a population of 372 in 1930. Its rapid growth gave it the nickname "The City of Speed." Garrison Dam backwaters led to its demise in the 1950's, most residents moving to the government-sponsored city of New Town. The village charter was dissolved April 30, 1953, and the post office closed August 15, 1953 with mail to New Town. The site is now deserted, and has been converted into a park. (2, 3, 33, 40, 52, 72)

**VAN PELTS** (Richland). This was a NPRR station and siding in W½ Sec. 2-131-49, Brandenburg Twp., two miles north of Great Bend. The origin of the name is unknown. It appeared on maps circa 1905-1920. (2, 3, 347)

**VANVILLE** (Burke). This is a long-lived rural community named for the Van Vorst families that made up a major portion of the population. The post office was established November 13, 1905 with Frank E. Drinkwater, who also published a newspaper here 1904-1909, as pm at his home in SW¼ Sec. 26-159-91, Vanville Twp. The facility was later located in the homes of pm John Van Vorst, SE¼ Sec. 27-159-91, pm F. E. Van Vorst, Sec. 34-159-91, and pm Mrs. Paul Kelly, NW¼ Sec. 23-159-91, who closed the post office November 15, 1922 with mail to Lostwood. Population figures, peaking at 171 in 1920, were for the entire township. (1, 2, 3, 18, 34, 40, 67, 376)

**VASHTI** (Stutsman). This was a NPRR station in Sec. 19-143-66, Pipestem Valley Twp., eight miles west of Pingree. It was named by Rev. Levi Jarvis, a retired Methodist minister who lived in the area, for his wife, Mollie Vashti Jarvis. *Vashti* is a Persian name meaning beautiful. The post office was established August 11, 1916 with Peter H. Boileau pm, and closed March 15, 1955 with mail to Pingree. The village once had a school, general store, and a grain elevator, and reached a peak population of 40 in 1930. (1, 2, 18, 19, 33, 40, 79, 158)

**VEBLEN JUNCTION** (Richland). A short-lived railroad, the Fairmount & Veblen, was built in 1913, and shortly thereafter was absorbed by the Soo Line RR. The two lines ran parallel to Sec. 22-130-48, DeVillo Twp., four miles west of Fairmount, where the F & V angled south into SD. This point became known as VEBLEN JUNCTION, or V Junction in local slang, named for its terminus city in SD, which was named in 1900 for pioneer settler J. E. Veblen. (3, 36)

**VEDA** (Sargent). The Soo Line RR townsite of Alicia and the GNRR townsite of Geneseo were just one-half mile apart, and in 1904 J. D. Hazlett platted a townsite on his land between the two in Sec. 13-130-53, Kingston Twp., naming it for his daughter, Veda. This is a Sanskrit name meaning knowledge or understanding. This only added to the confusion caused by the adjacent townsites,

rather than solving it as Mr. Hazlett had hoped, and his townsite was stillborn. Ultimately Geneseo became the dominant townsite, with Alicia joining VEDA as an anecdote of history. (2, 3, 4, 5, 18, 19, 165)

**VELDA** (Wells). This place appears on several road maps of the 1970's published by the H. M. Gousha Company, approximately three miles south of Chaseley in NE¼ Sec. 3-145-72, Silver Lake Twp., a site owned by Aldean and Marcia Gross at the time. Earlier the Gousha company placed STEVEN just north of this site, and both are believed to be copyright towns. (3, 34)

**VELVA** (McHenry). This settlement began in 1886 as the second MOUSE RIVER post office in SE¼ Sec. 22-153-80, Velva Twp. The name was changed in 1893 to VELVA by Soo Line RR officials, noting the velvet-like appearance of the Souris River valley at this site. The post office adopted the name November 18, 1893 with John Downing pm. The elevation is 1511, the Zip Code is 58790, and a peak population of 1,330 was reached in 1960. The village incorporated in 1902, and it became a city in 1905 with Gust Livdahl mayor. Television newsman Eric Severaid was born here in 1912. Ernest M. Sands, who became mayor in 1961, was North Dakota Lt. Governor 1981-1985. VELVA bills itself as the "Charolais Capital of North Dakota." (1, 2, 3, 18, 33, 40, 79, 279, 412)

**VENLO** (Ransom). This Soo Line RR townsite was founded in 1891 in Sec. 22-135-54, Shenford Twp., seven miles SSE of Sheldon, and named for Venlo, Limburg, Netherlands, which dates from circa 90 A.D., and has a modern history dating from 1272. The name is derived from *veen-loe*, which can be translated as the land surrounded by water. Folklore says that VENLO, ND was named for the fact that Indians used this place to avoid the wind, i.e. wind-low. Development was very slow here. The post office was established January 18, 1922 with Albert E. Carter pm, and it closed March 15, 1950 with mail to Enderlin. A population of 15 was still here in 1960, but today just one decaying building remains to mark the site. (1, 2, 3, 18, 38, 40, 85, 201, 204)

**VENTURIA** (McIntosh). The Soo Line RR established this townsite in 1901, and the name was selected by John H. Wishek of Ashley, using a name he saw on a boxcar. Ventura is Spanish for happiness or fortune, but the Latinized spelling used here is unexplained. Jacob J. Wiedmann (1870-1914) was named pm when the post office was established November 27, 1901, and his brother John was pm for 34 years following Jacob's death. It is located in Secs. 10 & 15-129-71, Johnstown Twp., and was incorporated as a village in 1913. The elevation is 2072, the Zip Code is 58489, and a peak population of 257 was reached in 1940. (1, 2, 3, 10, 18, 40, 79, 134, 135)

**VERA** (Cavalier). This was a rural post office established October 1, 1900 with Louis Foise pm. The origin of the name, Latin for true, and a popular female name, is unknown. It was located in Sec. 20-163-64, Cypress Twp., one mile SE of Sarles, and closed December 15, 1905, twenty days after the

establishment of the Sarles post office, although mail at first went to Woodbridge, a nearby rural post office, which itself merged with Sarles in 1906. (2, 3, 19, 40)

**VERENDRYE** (McHenry). This GNRR station was founded in 1912 in Sec. 31-154-78, Falsen Twp., on the Surrey cutoff line midway between Simcoe and Karlsruhe. It was originally named FALSEN, but on March 1, 1925 the name was changed to VERENDRYE to honor Pierre de la Verendrye (1685-1749), the French explorer who in 1738 led the first party of white men into what is now ND. The village never exceeded 100 in population, and the post office closed November 5, 1965 with mail to Bergen. (2, 3, 13, 40)

**VERNER** (Sargent). This Soo Line RR siding was built in 1883 in NW¼ Sec. 29-131-58, Verner Twp., two miles north of the rural community of Babcock, both of which were named for pioneer settler Luther Verner Babcock, a county judge 1884-1886. The post office was established November 21, 1883 with George B. Phifer pm. The village, six miles north of Straubville, recorded a population of 27 in 1890, but declined after that. The post office closed October 28, 1896 with mail to Oakes. (2, 40, 165, 240)

**VERONA** (LaMoure). This NPRR station was founded in 1883 in Sec. 2-133-59, Ovid Twp., and named MATSON. When the post office was established June 25, 1886 with James J. Stephens pm, the name was changed to VERONA at the suggestion of a settler from Verona, MI, which was named for the nearby Verona Mining Co. The name is ultimately traced to the city and province in northern Italy, made famous in the play *Two Gentlemen of Verona* by William Shakespeare. The village incorporated in 1905, and became a city in 1968. The elevation is 1408, the Zip Code is 58490, and a peak population of 258 was recorded in 1920. A unique situation existed 1907-1911 when this small town had three newspapers competing with one another. (1, 2, 3, 13, 18, 25, 33, 40, 46, 52, 79, 150)

**VERSIPPI** (Stark). This was a rural community centered around the Versippi School, which existed at several area sites until a brick structure was built in 1917 in NE¼ Sec. 10-140-95, eight miles NE of Dickinson. It was located on the Green River, but because this name was already associated with several other places in the county, a new name was coined by area resident William Powers, combining the French word *vert*, meaning green, as in Vermont, and *sippi*, derived from the almost universal Indian word *cebe*, meaning water, as in Mississippi. Although it was a public school, most area residents were Roman Catholic, and the community began to decline in the 1960's following the establishment of Dickinson Trinity High School. (3, 10, 18, 34, 74)

**VESELEY** (Walsh). This was a farm post office established November 26, 1886 with Mathias Houska pm. It was located in NE¼ Sec. 9-156-54, Prairie Centre Twp., seven miles east of Pisek. The name was transferred from Veseli, Bohemia, hometown of many area settlers, and means jolly. The post office closed December 15, 1887 with mail to Grafton. (2, 3, 25, 40, 75)

**VESELEYVILLE** (Walsh). This townsite was founded in 1891 in NW¼ Sec. 23-156-54, Prairie Centre Twp., two miles SE of the old Veseley post office, from which it borrowed its name, meaning jolly in Bohemian. Five blocks were platted, and the post office opened July 15, 1891 with Vaclav Dusek pm, closing May 31, 1906 with mail to Grafton. It reopened November 5, 1906, operating until May 31, 1943 with mail again to Grafton. Populations of 150 were reported in both 1950 and 1960, which surely included outlying areas, as the village itself was never that large. (1, 2, 3, 4, 18, 50, 75)

**VESTA** (Walsh). This was a rural settlement in SW¼ Sec. 18-157-57, Vesta Twp., two miles south of Adams. The post office was established December 4, 1883 with Paul Halvorsen pm. The name was chosen by settlers from Vesta Twp., Redwood County, MN, which was named by pioneer settler F. V. Hotchkiss for Vesta, Roman goddess of the home hearth fire. In 1897 it was moved four miles ENE to SW¼ Sec. 11-157-57, where the Soo Line RR built in 1905, but the proposed townsite failed to develop. The post office closed August 31, 1905 with mail to Park River. (1, 2, 3, 13, 18, 40, 75, 79)

**VICTOR** (Bowman). This site was at one time a stage stop in the pre-railroad days. A post office was established July 31, 1908 with Charles Victor Hook pm, who named it for his son, Victor. The name is derived from the Latin word meaning conqueror. It was located in NE¼ Sec. 18-129-101, Minnehaha Twp., fifteen miles SE of Bowman, and closed July 7, 1911, being replaced by the Spring Valley post office two miles to the NE. (2, 3, 18, 19, 40)

**VICTORIA** (McLean). This pioneer settlement was founded in 1883 in the center quarter of Sec. 35-147-84, Coal Harbor Twp., by settlers from Prince Edward Island, Canada, who named it for Queen Victoria (1819-1901). It was one mile east of the Missouri River port of COAL HARBOR, which had been established the previous year. In 1885 the post office at COAL HARBOR was relocated to VICTORIA, and this site began to be called by the post office name, with VICTORIA quickly disappearing from general usage. In 1905 the COAL HARBOR post office moved seven miles ENE to the new Soo Line RR townsite called Coleharbor, although it continued to use the old spelling until 1923. (2, 3, 10, 28, 40, 387)

**VIENNA** (Grant). This was a proposed townsite on the Dickinson, Lefor, and New Leipzig RR of 1917, named for the capital of Austria, apparently to compliment the neighboring proposed townsite of Budapest. It was to be located in SW¼ Sec. 9-135-90 near the old settlement of Leipzig, or about nine miles NNW of New Leipzig, on land owned by Johann Titz, but the town died when the railroad project was abandoned. (3, 18, 74)

**VIGNESS** (Burleigh). This was a rural settlement centered in SW¼ Sec. 30-142-79, Ecklund Twp., northeast of Baldwin. It was named for Carl L. Vigness, who is said to have maintained a mail drop here. Reports of a post office at the site in 1904 are not confirmed by government records. Mr. Vigness was later county Superintendent of Schools. (2, 3, 18, 33, 40)

**VIK** (Pembina). This was a pioneer settlement in NW¼ Sec. 16-160-56, Thingvalla Twp., founded about 1873 by Rev. Pall Thorlakson, who derived this name from *vikur-bygd*, meaning parish in the cove. Some say it was named for Lars Vik, a pioneer in Fillmore County, MN. In 1881 the name was changed to MOUNTAIN. (2, 3, 366)

**VIKING** (Benson). This rural village was founded in the 1880's in NE¼ Sec. 33-151-69, South Viking Twp., and named for its township, which was named by Timan L. Quarve for the legendary Norse sea pirates. It was eight miles SSE of Maddock, and at one time had a store, church, and a post office established October 4, 1888 with Mr. Quarve as pm. The village declined and it became a ghost town. The post office closed April 14, 1906 with mail to Maddock. (2, 3, 18, 25, 50, 53, 79, 239, 240)

**VIKING** (Wells). This GNRR station was founded in 1910 in SE¼ Sec. 32-150-69, Norway Lake Twp., and named for the legendary Norwegian adventurers of the middle ages. The post office was established March 3, 1911 with Frank Schroeder pm. The name was unpopular with the local settlers, most of whom were Germans, and was often confused with other places, past and present, so about 1912 a movement began to change the name to HAMBURG. On May 29, 1913 the name was changed to HAMBERG, a sort of ethnic compromise. (2, 3, 18, 40, 79, 364)

**VILLA** (Burke). This rural post office was established as SMISHEK in 1906, and when the original post office building was destroyed by fire on September 16, 1910, the facility was moved to the John B. Swanson home in SW¼ Sec. 7-160-92, Lucy Twp., ten miles SE of Columbus. On January 1, 1911 the name was changed to VILLA, a Spanish word meaning town. Mr. Swanson (1878-1965) also operated a small country store at this site. The post office was discontinued June 30, 1914 with mail to Powers Lake. (1, 2, 3, 10, 18, 40, 67, 376)

**VILLARD** (McHenry). This was the first settlement in McHenry County, founded in 1882 by Edmund Hackett in NW¼ Sec. 4-154-77, Villard Twp., and named for NPRR President Henry Villard (1835-1900) in hopes of luring the railroad to build into the area. Mr. Villard was later a partner of Thomas Alva Edison, and his wife was the daughter of abolitionist William Lloyd Garrison. The post office was established June 2, 1882 with George Hofmann pm. Richard H. Copeland, the second pm, started a newspaper, and later was engaged in this business in Washburn. A population of 38 was reported in 1890, but when a railroad failed to reach the site, it declined as a townsite. After 1902 the post office was located at several sites, mostly in Falsen Twp. (154-78), and closed August 31, 1911

with mail to Denbigh. Villas is an erroneous spelling. (1, 2, 3, 13, 25, 30, 53, 79, 182, 184, 412, 415)

**VIM** (Slope). This was a rural post office established September 28, 1920 with William Lamb pm, who added a room to his home in SE¼ Sec. 18-136-103, Bullion View Twp., to house the facility. Mr. Lamb (1870-1959) chose the Latin word meaning strength for the name of the post office, noting the vitality of his patrons. He moved to Beach in 1923, and Thomas Finneman became pm, moving the post office to his home in N½ Sec. 20-136-103, one mile SE of the Lamb home. In 1937 Mrs. Beila Flowers Foust, the bride of a Texas cowboy, Patterson C. Foust, became the pm in Sec. 16-136-103. The VIM post office, located about seventeen miles WNW of Amidon, closed February 29, 1944 with mail to Rhame. (2, 3, 4, 40, 82, 382, 384, 434)

**VIRDEN** (Rolette). This was a farm post office established June 26, 1900 with Elias Gingerich pm. It was located in NW¼ Sec. 25-160-70, Union Twp., two miles NW of Mylo, and closed January 3, 1901 with mail to Perth. The origin of the name is unknown, although it has been suggested that it was named for Virden, IL. (2, 3, 40, 123, 415)

**VIVIAN** (Sargent). This was a rural post office established May 7, 1883 with Adam C. Smith pm. It was located in NW¼ Sec. 4-132-57, Vivian Twp., four miles north of Stirum, and is said to have been named by Mrs. Smith for her hometown. Vivian is a Latin name meaning lively. The post office later moved to the home of Mrs. Ella C. Rusco in SE¼ Sec. 10-132-57, but closed May 16, 1887 with mail to Harlem. (2, 19, 25, 40, 172)

**VOLGA** (Traill). This was a GNRR loading station in NE¼ Sec. 11-145-52, Blanchard Twp., four miles NW of Blanchard. It was named for Volga, IA, which was named for the 2,200 mile long river in Russia. The site included an elevator and a school. It appeared on maps circa 1910-1930. (1, 2, 3, 5, 18, 29, 77)

**VOLTAIRE** (McHenry). This Soo Line RR station was founded in 1900 in NE 1/4 Sec. 1-152-80, Brown Twp., and NW¼ Sec. 6-152-79, Voltaire Twp. The post office was established January 21, 1901 with Ole Ranum pm. The village incorporated in 1929. The elevation is 1587, the Zip Code is 58792, and the peak official population of 101 was reached in 1940. Most sources state that the name was chosen by Soo Line RR officials to honor the French writer, Jean Francois Marie Arouet Voltaire (1694-1778), although others claim that it was named for an early settler. (1, 2, 3, 4, 5, 18, 33, 40, 52)

**VOSS** (Walsh). This NPRR townsite was founded in 1887 in SE¼ Sec. 28-156-53, Walsh Centre Twp., and named PLANO. This name was rejected by postal officials, and on November 23, 1888 the post office was established as VOSS, with Frank E. Vorachek pm. Town founder Andrew Heron named it for his birthplace of Vossongen, Norway. Two blocks were platted in 1892, but the village, which never incorporated, failed to ever report a population greater than 60. The post office, Zip Code 58280, closed January 8, 1983 with mail to Minto. (1, 2, 3, 18, 25, 33, 40, 75, 79)

# W

**WABEK** (Mountrail). This Soo Line RR townsite was founded in 1914 when the railroad began to extend its Max branch line beyond Plaza to Sanish. It was located in SW¼ Sec. 21-152-88, Plaza Twp., three miles south of Plaza, and given an Indian name thought to refer to nearby Shell Creek. The post office was established July 7, 1917 with Rasmus J. Torgerson pm. The village incorporated in 1918, but this status was dissolved in 1966 as the population dropped from a 1930 high of 46 to just 14 in 1960. In 1924-1925 the village boasted of a radio station, appropriately with the call letters WABK. In 1979 only a bar remained in operation at this site. (2, 40, 72, 291)

**WADE** (Grant). This was a rural post office located in NW¼ Sec. 32-131-85, thirteen miles SW of Shields. It was established January 15, 1898 with William Vose Wade (1851-1927) pm. Mr. Wade, a native of Plymouth, MA, came to Emmons County in 1872, and was its first sheriff in 1883. He moved to Grant County in 1890, establishing the Anchor Ranch. He was a longtime official of the Standing Rock Indian Agency, and was a charter county commissioner when Grant County organized in 1916. Wade is an Anglo-Saxon name meaning one who wanders. The post office closed October 30, 1920 with mail to Shields. (1, 2, 3, 17, 19, 40, 96, 173, 176)

**WADESON** (Cass). This was a rural settlement in Sec. 13-138-55, Clifton Twp., named for John Wadeson, a pioneer settler in the area. Some sources list this as a post office, but government records do not confirm this claim. It is thought that about 1893 Mr. Wadeson did establish a mail drop in association with the nearby Petersen post office. When the NPRR built through this area in 1900, a new townsite named Alice was founded, and WADESON became the western part of that city. (2, 3, 18, 34, 40, 77, 118)

**WAGAR** (McHenry). This was a rural post office established July 25, 1898 with Anson Peters pm in his grocery store located in NE¼ Sec. 27-157-77, Wagar Twp., six miles NNE of Denbigh. It was named for the Wagar family, many of whom lived in the township. The patriarch was James Wagar (1869-1958), a native of Ontario, Canada, who came here in 1893. Mr. Peters moved to Alberta, Canada, and the post office closed March 31, 1903 with mail to Denbigh. It reopened May 20, 1903 with Oscar Wagar pm at his home in SE¼ Sec. 23-157-77, two miles SW of the original site, closing November 30, 1905 with mail again to Denbigh. (2, 3, 18, 40, 412)

**WAHPETON** (Barnes). First called SECOND CROSSING OF THE SHEYENNE, and then FIFTH SIDING, this NPRR townsite was given its third name of 1872 when local settlers began calling the place WAHPETON, a Sioux Indian word meaning

*Wahpeton about 1908*

place of many leaves. The site was platted by Charles Scott and Richard Chavey in Sec. 21-140-58, but legal problems over title to the land, and lack of recognition by NPRR officials caused the development to stagnate. In 1874 it was replatted as WORTHINGTON, and a final name change in 1878 resulted in VALLEY CITY. (2, 153, 275)

**WAHPETON** (Richland). The metropolis and county seat of Richland County, this settlement was founded in 1869 as RICHVILLE, and in 1873 was renamed CHAHINKAPA. The current name was adopted July 24, 1874 by pm Hugh R. Blanding. It incorporated as a village in 1881, and became a city in 1884. The elevation is 962, the Zip Code is 58075, and a peak population of 9,065 was recorded in 1980 as the city has shown a rapid growth in recent years. The well known Rosemeade pottery, named for a township in Ransom County whose name is a contraction of Rose Meadows, was made here 1940-1956. Steve Myhra, a professional football player, was born here in 1934. WAHPETON is derived from the Sioux *wa-qpe-tong-wong*, meaning village of many leaves, or dweller among the deciduous trees. (1, 2, 3, 18, 25, 33, 40, 79, 262)

**WAHPETON JUNCTION** (Richland). Several commercial atlases list this place, which is believed to be the junction of GNRR lines from Casselton and Moorhead, MN in NW¼ Sec. 7-132-47, Center Twp., just west of Wahpeton. (3)

**WALCOTT** (Richland). This GNRR townsite was founded in 1880 by Frank E. Walcott, a native of MA who later moved to IA. It is located in Sec. 35-136-50, Walcott Twp., and was platted by J. W. Blanding. The post office was established January 6, 1881 with Mr. Walcott as pm. Walcott is an Old

English name meaning dweller in the walled cottage. The elevation is 950, the Zip Code is 58077, and the village, which incorporated in 1880, reached a peak population of 375 in 1930, declining to 186 in 1980. (1, 2, 3, 18, 19, 33, 40, 77, 79, 147, 243)

**WALDEN** (Cass). This GNRR loading station was built in 1912 in SE¼ Sec. 30-143-55, Rochester Twp., six miles west of Page on the Surrey cutoff line. It is thought to have been named for the famous Walden Pond in MA, known by most through the writings of Henry David Thoreau. Walden is a common English place name, derived from the Teutonic word meaning mighty, and an Old English name meaning from the wooded valley. A population of 10 has been reported at various times over the years, and in 1965 the site still had two operating elevators, although one of these shut down in 1975 and was demolished. (1, 2, 13, 19, 34, 45, 77)

**WALDON** (Golden Valley). This NPRR siding appears on maps circa 1905-1912 in SW¼ Sec. 24-140-103, Sentinel Twp., five miles west of Medora. The origin of the name is unknown. Later maps show the site as RIDER or RIDERS, and while it remained on some maps into the 1960's, the siding never saw any significant development. (2, 3, 18)

**WALDORF** (Ward). This was a twelve block townsite platted in SE¼ Sec. 30 & SW¼ Sec. 29-155-82, Nedrose Twp., two miles SE of Minot. It appears only in a 1915 county atlas, and was probably named for Edward Waldorf, who had extensive holdings of land between Minot and Velva. Waldorf, Germany, is the ancestral home of the wealthy Astor family, and for this reason is a commonly found name throughout the United States. (3, 18)

**WALES** (Burleigh). This was a rural post office established May 21, 1886 with Dr. Benjamin Franklin Slaughter (1842-1896) as pm, primarily as a means of creating a rural route from Bismarck to the Slaughter post office located farther north, which was officially run by Dr. Slaughter's wife. They were residents of Bismarck, and held the pm positions just long enough for them to get established. WALES was located in NE¼ Sec. 24-140-80, Burnt Creek Twp., nine miles NNE of Bismarck, near what was known as the Burleigh County Poor Farm. The proposed name for this facility was Mount Hope, but the Slaughters renamed it for a postal official to compliment his decision to rename the Solitude post office as Slaughter. A population of 25 was reported in 1890, but when the post office building burned to the ground on July 26, 1892 the facility closed with mail to Bismarck. The official date for closing was August 15, 1892, and WALES quickly disappeared from the scene. (2, 3, 25, 34, 40, 240, 414)

**WALES** (Cavalier). This was a GNRR station in SW¼ Sec. 31-163-61, Dresden Twp., the site of the RUSHLAKE post office, which adopted this name on April 25, 1899 with Augustus H. Koehinstedt pm. GNRR President James J. Hill chose the name, a major political division of Great Britain, to please British stockholders of the railroad. The elevation is 1572, the Zip Code is 58281, and a peak population of 400 was claimed in 1920, but a steady decline has reduced the count to just 74 in 1980. (1, 2, 3, 18, 40, 52, 79)

**WALHALLA** (Pembina). Founded in the 1840's as SAINT JOSEPH, the name was changed to WALHALLA on July 21, 1871 when George W. Reed was pm. The name is an Anglicized version of Valhalla, the home of the gods in Norse mythology, and was suggested by an army officer or by local resident George Emmerling, or by J. W. Taylor, U. S. Consul at Winnipeg, to note the beauty of the area. The GNRR extended its branch line from Grafton to this point in 1898. The elevation is 966, the Zip Code is 58282, and a peak population of 1,471 was reached in 1970. (1, 2, 3, 18, 25, 33, 40, 52, 79, 108, 292)

**WALKER** (Steele). This was a rival townsite of GILBERT, and was founded in late 1896 in NE¼ Sec. 31-147-56, Finley Twp. It is said that it was named for a Bishop Walker, who traveled the state giving sermons from the back of a railroad car. Because of duplication on its lines, the GNRR changed the name to FINLEY, and in 1897 it absorbed GILBERT. (3, 99, 326)

**WALKERTOWN** (McLean). This was a pioneer townsite in SW¼ Sec. 21-146-84, North Hancock Twp., three miles SSW of Riverdale, and named for James Walker, who in 1878 was the first white settler in the area. Opposite Stanton, it was an important supplier of wood for the Missouri River steamboats. The post office was established October 10, 1882 with Thomas J. Mann pm, and the townsite was platted by E. T. Winston in 1883. The post office closed July 24, 1886, being replaced by the new townsite of Hancock one mile to the SW. (2, 28, 40)

**WALLACE** (Kidder). This was a farm post office established February 14, 1901 with Joseph Wallace Chinworth pm. It was first located in NE¼ Sec. 30-144-71, Wallace Twp., eight miles NNE of Robinson, and named for its township, which was named for Robert E. Wallace, who settled here in 1880 and later was a banker in Jamestown. Others say both the post office and the township were named for Mr. Chinworth. Wallace is a Teutonic name, meaning a Welshman, which in the context of day, meant a foreigner. In 1904 the post office was moved to the home of D. J. Mahoney in SE¼ Sec. 14-144-72, North Merkel Twp., and in 1905 it moved to the country store of pm Harry L. Miller in NW¼ Sec. 14-144-72. Mrs. Stephen F. Stickel became pm in 1910, and the post office closed August 15, 1912 with mail to Bowdon. (1, 2, 18, 19, 40, 93, 122)

**WALLACE** (McHenry). This was a rural settlement in SE¼ Sec. 17-154-78, Falsen Twp., seven miles NW of Karlsruhe. George H. McKay ran a general store at the site in 1886, which was about the extent of its development. The origin of the name is unknown. (3, 412)

**WALLACE** (Mountrail). This GNRR station was founded about 1900 in SW¼ Sec. 12-156-88, Egan Twp., and was served by the Des Lacs post office. The origin of the name is unknown. Because of confusion with Wallace, ID, the name was changed to TAGUS in 1901. (2, 3, 25, 72)

**WALLACE GROVE** (Stutsman). This is a platted resort area on the SE shore of Spiritwood Lake in SE¼ Sec. 31 & SW¼ Sec. 32-142-62, Gray Twp. The origin of the name is unknown. (3, 34)

**WALLE** (Grand Forks). This was a rural post office established October 4, 1878 with Ole Olson Upsahl pm. It was located in Sec. 25-150-50, Walle Twp., six miles east of Thompson, with mail coming from there once each week. It was named for its township, which was named by Olav N. Loiland (1842-1933) and his brothers, who were the first permanent settlers here, coming from Valle, Satesdalen, Norway. The post office closed November 15, 1902 with mail to Thompson. (2, 3, 18, 25, 31, 40, 69, 240, 276)

**WALSHVILLE** (Walsh). This inland town was the second settlement in Walsh County, being founded in 1877 in SE¼ Sec. 22-155-51, Walshville Twp., seven miles ENE of Ardoch. It was named for its county, which was named for George H. Walsh, a newspaperman and politician in Grand Forks. The post office was established May 17, 1878 with Charles G. Williams pm, with the facility being located in the tavern operated by Augustus Williams, the town's first settler. It was on the Grand Forks-Winnipeg stage line, but after it was bypassed by the GNRR it began to decline. The post office closed January 31, 1914 with mail to Ardoch. (1, 2, 3, 18, 25, 40, 53, 75)

**WALTER** (Renville). Wilson Walter erected a building in SW¼ Sec. 12-158-82, Ensign Twp., in 1902 to house his country store. On September 20, 1902 a post office was added with Mr. Walter as pm. Walter is a Teutonic name meaning mighty warrior. When the GNRR townsite of GLENBURN was founded in 1903 just one mile SW of here, Mr. Walter moved his operation to the new townsite, adopting GLENBURN as the name of his post office on October 9, 1903. (2, 3, 19, 39, 40, 71, 323)

**WALUM** (Griggs). This NPRR station built in September 1902 was first called GUNDERSON when development began in 1900, but the name was soon changed to WALUM, honoring Martinus O. Wallum, a prosperous farmer adjacent to the site. The variation in the spelling is said to have been done by a postal official who preferred his version of Mr. Wallum's name. The post office was established November 7, 1904 with Martin J. Mossing pm, and the village was platted May 17, 1905 in Secs. 29 & 30-144-59, Greenfield Twp. WALUM never had a boom period, with a peak population of 100 being claimed in 1920, but an actual count of just 30 in 1960. The elevation is 1454, and the post office, Zip Code 58491, closed August 1, 1973 with mail to Hannaford. (1, 2, 33, 40, 65, 79)

**WAMDUSKA** (Nelson). Located in NW¼ Sec. 6-151-60, Wamduska Twp., about midway between Lakota and Tolna, this attempt at founding a townsite was a magnificent failure. It was conceived in April 1882 in anticipation of the GNRR. Forty blocks were platted and about fifty buildings were constructed, including the Wamduska House, a 42-room hotel. The post office was established July 11, 1882 with Emery Mapes Jr. pm. The name came from nearby Stump, or Wamduska, Lake, which likely was once the eastern part of Devils Lake. *Wamduska* is a Sioux word meaning when on the water, oh look. The GNRR bypassed the site to the north by ten miles, and the town was doomed. The post office closed March 8, 1887 with mail to Lakota. It operated again July 16, 1904 as a rural post office at the same site, but closed for good January 31, 1908 with mail again to Lakota. The townsite was officially abandoned in 1916, and the hotel was demolished in 1954. (2, 3, 25, 40, 53, 126, 425)

**WANAMAKER** (McLean). This townsite was promoted in 1903 by Christian Paulson, who had just moved the Turtle Lake rural post office to his land in SE 1/4 Sec. 27-147-81, Lake Williams Twp. The site was one mile SW of Miller, a townsite promoted by pioneer settler Peter Miller. WANAMAKER, named for an investor from Columbus, OH, tempted the livery stable and hardware store away from Miller, and a two-story bank was built, but when the NPRR arrived in 1905, they built the railroad two miles beyond WANAMAKER, supposedly because of pending legal actions, and both speculative townsites relocated to the new railroad townsite, which adopted the name of the old post office, Turtle Lake. (2, 3, 28, 40, 271)

**WANESKA PARK** (Stutsman). This is a platted resort area on the north shore of Spiritwood Lake in NE¼ Sec. 31-142-62, Gray Twp. The name is a corruption of the Ojibway word *wanashkobia*, meaning a basin of water. (3, 13, 34)

**WANO** (LaMoure). This was a farm post office established February 18, 1886 with Wells Wano Wilcox pm. It was only in operation for seven months, closing September 25, 1886 with mail to Medbery. WANO was in SW¼ Sec. 26-134-63, Wano Twp., about seven miles NE of Edgeley. (2, 3, 40, 143)

**WARD** (Ward). This place is shown on a 1930 roadmap published by the General Drafting Co. on old ND Highway 28, about midway between Berthold and Ryder, probably in Tolgen Twp. (154-86), near the old Hesnault post office. It apparently takes its name from the county, named for either J. P. or Mark Ward, both territorial legislators, and is a copyright town inserted on the map to detect unlawful copying by competitors. (3, 18)

**WARNER** (Richland). This NPRR station was built in 1899 in Sec. 7-132-51, Danton Twp., and named supposedly for George Worner, a pioneer settler, with no explanation for the variation in spelling. Warner is a Teutonic name meaning guarding warrior. The siding was just SE of Wyndmere, and the name was changed to BERNDT in October 1915. It was dismantled in 1943. (2, 3, 18, 19)

**WARNTON** (Morton). This was a rural post office established August 7, 1879 with John S. Warn pm. It was near exposed coal veins used by the locomotives of the newly-built NPRR, and the suggested name was Coal Bank Station, which was rejected by postal officials. WARNTON was located in NE¼ Sec. 29-139-85, Engelter Twp., one mile SW of New Salem, and closed October 19, 1880 with mail to Bismarck. (2, 3, 25, 40, 107, 414)

**WARREN** (Cass). This NPRR siding was built in 1881 in NW¼ Sec. 33-138-50, Warren Twp., three miles NE of Davenport, and named LEECHES. On April 10, 1887 it was renamed by Theo. Warnecke for his hometown of Warren, MN, which was named for Charles H. Warren, the local railroad agent. Warren is a Teutonic name meaning game warden. The post office was established February 25, 1892 with Lewis Olsen pm. A small village developed, peaking at a population of 60 in 1920, although the post office had closed October 31, 1918 with mail to Davenport. On May 31, 1908 the NPRR renamed the station SCHAIBLE, restoring the WARREN name on July 25, 1915. Only an elevator, store, and a few houses remain. (1, 2, 3, 10, 13, 19, 25, 34, 40, 77, 79, 303)

**WARREN'S BANKS STATION** (Morton). This was the second relay station on the Bismarck-Fort Keogh mail route established in 1878. It was located in NE¼ Sec. 29-139-84, Dettman Twp., two miles west of Judson, and named for the nearby coal banks owned by John Warren, who furnished gravel and buffalo meat to the NPRR crews building the mainline westward from Mandan. When this line was completed in 1882, the mail route and the relay station were abandoned. (2, 3, 18)

**WARSAW** (Walsh). This rural townsite was platted as NEW WARSAW in SE¼ Sec. 25-156-52, Harriston Twp., and named by Anton L. Gudajtes for the capital city of Poland, his homeland. The government did

*Washburn Main Street in the 1950's*

not accept two-word names at the time, and the post office was established as WARSAW on June 30, 1894 with Mr. Gudajtes pm. The community, which never incorporated, has never had a population exceeding 100, but continues to survive, largely due to the presence of the magnificent St. Stanislaus Catholic Church built in 1900. The church was badly damaged by fire on October 19, 1978, but restoration was begun in short order and completed in 1980. The post office closed January 31, 1935 with mail to Minto. (1, 2, 3, 18, 40, 75)

**WARWICK** (Benson). This GNRR station was established in 1906 in SW¼ Sec. 34-151-63, Warwick Twp., and named for Richard Neville, Earl of Warwick (c.1428-1471), known as "The King Maker." Warwick is a Teutonic name meaning protecting ruler. The post office opened January 26, 1907, the same day as neighboring Tokio, with Christian O. Ness pm. The elevation is 1474, the Zip Code is 58381, and a peak population of 190 was given in 1920 with a decline to just 108 in 1980. (1, 2, 5, 18, 19, 34, 40, 52, 110)

**WASA** (Barnes). This was a farm post office established June 22, 1882 with Emil Djuberg pm at the home of his father, A. J. Djuberg, in SW¼ Sec. 3-138-60, Svea Twp., ten miles south of Sanborn. It is thought to have been named for Vaasa, Finland, with an Anglicized spelling. The post office closed September 25, 1885 with mail to Sanborn. (2, 3, 25, 38, 40, 76)

**WASHBURN** (McLean). This Missouri River townsite was founded in 1882 and named for Cadwallader Colden Washburn (1818-1882), a Civil War General, Congressman, and Governor of WI. He was also the brother of William D. Washburn, who several years later would be active in various pursuits in this area, including the founding of Wilton. The post office was established September 4, 1882 with George G. Rhude pm, who had operated the old Turtle Valley post office just SE of WASHBURN. "King" John Satterlund (1851-1930) was among the city's pioneer

leaders. WASHBURN was designated McLean County seat when the county organized in 1883, and it incorporated as a city in 1902, the year the Soo Line RR arrived. A long-awaited highway bridge over the Missouri River opened in 1971. The Zip Code is 58577, and the recent boom in the energy industry swelled the 1980 population to 1,766, more than double the 1970 count. Admiral Homer N. Wallin, born in 1893, and artist Gary P. Miller, born in 1935, are natives of WASHBURN. (1, 2, 3, 25, 33, 40, 79, 121)

**WASHEGUM** (Bottineau). This rural post office replaced the Somber post office, eight miles ESE, which had closed August 31, 1908 after its pm had been killed and the building set afire by thieves. WASHEGUM opened July 15, 1909 with Arthur W. Burnett pm at his hotel-store in SE¼ Sec. 34-164-75, Roland Twp., on the west shore of Lake Metigoshe. The name is part of the Chippewa name for the lake, *metigoshe washegum*, meaning clear water lake surrounded by oaks. The post office closed April 30, 1914 with mail to Bottineau. (1, 2, 3, 18, 40, 101, 153)

**WASSAIC** (Mountrail). This was a GNRR station built in 1914 in NE¼ Sec. 25-157-91, James Hill Twp., six miles north of Stanley on the Grenora branch line. It was on land owned by John Anderson (1872-1949), and is said to have been named for Wassaic, NY. Another GNRR station, BELAIR, was in the same area, and may have been an alternate name for this site. (1, 2, 3, 72)

**WATERLOO** (Benson). This was a rural post office established November 30, 1898 with Ella C. Moen pm, who named it for her hometown of Waterloo, IA, which was named for Waterloo, Belgium, famous as the site of Gen. Arthur Wellesley's defeat of Napoleon Bonaparte in 1815. It was located in NE¼ Sec. 5-151-69, South Viking Twp., two miles south of Maddock, and replaced the old North Viking post office which had closed February 4, 1898. WATERLOO closed August 31, 1901 with mail to Viking. (2, 3, 10, 40)

**WATER TANK** (Bottineau). This was a GNRR service station in Sec. 5-162-79, Eidsvold Twp., between Landa and Westhope. It appears on maps circa 1905-1920, and was sometimes called FRANCE. (2, 3, 101)

**WATER TANK** (Grand Forks). This was a GNRR service station in SW¼ Sec. 31-149-50, Americus Twp., at the north edge of Reynolds, used for replenishing the water supply of their steam locomotives. (3, 18, 69)

**WATER TANK** (McHenry). This site is shown on maps circa 1910-1925 just west of Towner in NE¼ Sec. 10 & NW¼ Sec. 11-156-76, Newport Twp. It consisted of a large GNRR service facility, including coal docks, an engine stall, and the water tank which was in Sec. 11. (3, 18)

**WATER TANK** (Richland). This was a Soo Line RR service point in Sec. 11-130-50, Brightwood Twp., just north of Hankinson. (3)

**WATFORD** (McKenzie). This GNRR townsite was first called BANKS, but the name was changed in 1914 to WATFORD at the suggestion of Dr. Vaughan G. Morris, the town's first physician, for his hometown of Watford, Ontario, Canada, which was named for Watford, Hartfordshire, England. The post office was established December 8, 1914 with John C. Zeller pm. Because of negotiation problems, the GNRR line was terminated here, making the new town's importance even greater. It incorporated as a village June 7, 1915. Because of confusion with Wolford in Pierce County, the name was changed to WATFORD CITY on May 13, 1916. (2, 3, 18, 40, 79, 229)

**WATFORD CITY** (McKenzie). This GNRR terminus city was founded in 1913 as BANKS, but was soon thereafter renamed WATFORD. Because of confusion with Wolford in Pierce County, it was renamed WATFORD CITY on May 13, 1916. John C. Zeller (1881-1960) continued as pm. The village became a city in 1934 with Dr. Harry U. Winner as first mayor, and in 1941 it defeated Alexander for county seat honors, taking the court house away from Schafer. The elevation is 2084, the Zip Code is 58854, and a peak population of 2,114 was reached in 1980. Historian and author Erling Nicolai Rolfsrud and former Lt. Governor and Labor Commissioner Orville West "Ike" Hagen are natives of WATFORD CITY. (1, 2, 3, 18, 33, 40, 52, 229, 253)

**WATROUS** (Hettinger). This Milwaukee Road RR loading station was built in NE¼ Sec. 23-133-92, Brittian Twp., seven miles ESE of Mott. A post office was established October 29, 1910 with Mrs. G. K. Jordet pm, although the duties of the office were usually performed by Frances Pew. John Hallam became pm in 1918, and L. H. Boknecht assumed the office on May 31, 1923, closing the facility on May 31, 1923 with mail to Bentley. Some say the name was borrowed from the Watrous Fire Engine Manufacturing Co., while others say it was named for Watrous Twp., Koochiching County, MN, which was named for Charles B. Watrous, a sawmill operator who had come from PA. A small village was here for a few years, reporting a population of 15 in

1920. The elevator still exists under private ownership. (2, 13, 40, 79, 179, 180, 181)

**WATSON** (Cass). This was a rural settlement in NE¼ Sec. 34-138-53, Walburg Twp., three miles SSE of Chaffee on the north bank of the Maple River. A post office was established January 21, 1879 with Peter Walburg pm, and named for J. S. Watson, a major area landowner who was an attorney in Fargo and often represented the NPRR in its litigation. Watson is a contraction for son of Walter. The post office was discontinued September 14, 1900 with mail to Leonard. (1, 2, 18, 19, 25, 40, 77, 301)

**WAYLIN** (Emmons). This was a rural post office established February 18, 1886 with Abraham L. Raynolds pm, fourteen days after he had been appointed pm of OMIO. Both post offices were located in his home in NW¼ Sec. 22-132-76, three miles SE of Linton. The WAYLIN post office closed April 7, 1886 with Mr. Raynolds continuing as the OMIO pm. The origin of the name is unknown. (3, 34, 40, 66, 415)

**WAYNE** (Ward). This was a coal mining settlement in SE¼ Sec. 4-157-83, Waterford Twp., fifteen miles NNW of Minot near the Renville County line. A post office was established June 22, 1903 with William H. Rouse pm, and it closed June 30, 1908 with mail to Lynch. The origin of the name, which is a diminutive of Wainwright, an Old English name meaning wagon maker, is unknown. (2, 19, 40, 53, 100, 415)

**WEAVER** (Cavalier). This was a GNRR station built about 1901 in SW¼ Sec. 13-159-63, Banner Twp., three miles SW of Alsen, and named for its founder, Andrew J. Weaver. The post office was established May 2, 1902 with Robert G. Paxman pm, and it closed July 31, 1953 with mail to Munich. A population of 40 was reported in 1920, but the site never experienced any real development and disappeared from maps during the 1960's. (2, 3, 18, 40, 79)

**WEBER** (Sargent). This GNRR station was founded in 1883 in Secs. 30 & 31-129-55, Weber Twp., and named for Henry Weber, who came to WI from Germany in 1850, and came here in 1883. Because of confusion with other stations with similar names, WEBER was renamed HAVANA in 1886. (2, 18, 170)

**WEBSTER** (Ramsey). This Farmers Grain & Shipping Co. RR townsite was founded in 1903 in SE¼ Sec. 33-156-64, Webster Twp., and NE¼ Sec. 4-155-64, Freshwater Twp. Some say it was named for Webster LaPlant, who in 1882 was the area's first settler, while others say it was named for William Webster (1838-1921), who came here in 1883 from Scotland. Webster is an Old English name meaning weaver. The post office was established January 30, 1903 with William D. Millar pm. The elevation is 1474, the Zip Code is 58382, and the village reached a peak population of 280 in 1940, although a count made in 1982 showed just 58 residents. H. Kent Jones, a longtime state legislator and Agriculture Commissioner, was born here in 1926. (1, 2, 18, 33, 40, 79, 103)

**WEHR** (Sheridan). This was a rural post office established January 13, 1904 with Christian Wehr pm. It was located in NW¼ Sec. 31-150-77, in the extreme NW corner of the county, about six miles SE of Butte. The post office orders for both WEHR and Tiebell were rescinded on July 6, 1904, before either had gone into actual operation. (3, 40, 415)

**WEIBLE** (Traill). This was a rural post office established October 29, 1883 with J. S. Weible pm, serving the GREENFIELD station of the GNRR. The post office was located on the east side of the tracks in Sec. 24-144-52, Greenfield Twp., six miles south of Blanchard, and closed December 18, 1883 with mail to Hunter. It reopened July 8, 1884 with Bryan L. Hill pm, operating until November 30, 1909 when mail was sent to Blanchard. GREENFIELD station is still shown on some maps. (2, 3, 18, 25, 29, 40, 77)

**WEIGHTMAN** (Adams). This was a rural post office established April 22, 1908 with Urban H. Weightman pm. It was located in SE¼ Sec. 3-130-91, South Fork Twp., twenty-two miles NE of Haynes, and closed September 30, 1911 with mail to Stowers. (3, 18, 34, 40, 414)

**WELBY** (Mountrail). This was a farm post office established April 12, 1900 with William Henson pm. It was located in SE¼ Sec. 26-154-94, seventeen miles south of White Earth on the north shore of the Missouri River. The origin of the name is unknown. Welby is a Scandinavian name meaning from the farm by the spring. The post office closed March 30, 1907 with mail to Chilcot. (2, 19, 40, 72)

**WELCH** (Logan). This was a rural post office established October 4, 1904 with Eunice D. Cline pm at her home in SW¼ Sec. 24-133-68, Lautt Twp., four miles west of Fredonia, and two miles NNE of Guyson. The post office order was rescinded January 25, 1905 before it had gone into operation. The origin of the name is unknown. (2, 3, 40)

**WELCH SPUR** (Burleigh). This was a Soo Line RR siding in S½ Sec. 4-137-78, Telfer Twp., near the present-day Dutton Airfield about eight miles south of Menoken. It was named for Oliver P. Welch (1861-1936), George A. Welch (1866-1918), and Aurie D. Welch (1871-1951), area pioneers. It appears on maps circa 1910-1940, occassionally as simply Welch. (2, 3, 8, 12, 14, 18)

**WELFORD** (Pembina). This was a farm post office established January 5, 1886 with Thomas Welford pm. Welford is an Old English name meaning from the spring by the ford. It was located in NW¼ Sec. 7-163-52, Pembina Twp., seven miles SE of Neche. A rural community developed, reporting a population of 25 in 1890. The post office closed July 30, 1904 with mail to Neche. (2, 3, 18, 19, 25, 40, 53, 108, 240)

**WELLER** (McLean). This was a rural post office established February 26, 1883 with Charles Weller, a Civil War veteran who settled here 1878 and promoted a community called Spring Coulee, as pm. It was located in NE¼ Sec. 12-145-83, Basto Twp., fourteen miles NW of Washburn, and later moved to SE¼ Sec. 1-145-83, and Sec. 10-145-83, both in the same immediate area. The post office closed April 15, 1903 with mail to Washburn. It reopened May 27, 1903, closing for good October 31, 1906 with mail to Underwood. A population of 20 was reported in 1890. (2, 3, 25, 28, 40, 121, 389, 390)

**WELLERVILLE** (McLean). This was a townsite platted in May 1883 in SE¼ Sec. 1-145-83, Basto Twp., three miles SW of Underwood. It was named for Charles Weller, the pm at the nearby farm post office of Weller who was the first settler in the area. Sixteen blocks were staked off, but no settlers arrived. (1, 2, 28)

**WELLS** (Oliver). This was a farm post office established October 20, 1906 with Allen B. Wells pm. It was located in SE¼ Sec. 9-142-83, Center Twp., five miles ENE of Center, and closed November 15, 1909 with mail to Gaines. (3, 40, 53, 121)

**WELLS** (Wells). This was a farm post office established March 25, 1890 with Gottfried Schlechter pm. It was located in Sec. 7-148-70, Oshkosh Twp., and named for its county, which was named for Edward P. Wells, a territorial legislator and promoter of the James River valley. The site was reached by the Soo Line RR in 1893, and on November 23, 1893 the post office was replaced by the facility in the new townsite which was named FESSENDEN. Wells is an Old English name meaning dweller by the springs. (2, 3, 19, 40, 54, 79, 364)

**WELLSBURG** (Wells). This GNRR station was founded in 1910 in NW¼ Sec. 9-150-71, Fram Twp., on the Surrey cutoff line. It was named for its county, which was named for Edward P. Wells, a territorial legislator from Jamestown. The post office was established April 1, 1913 with Jacob Heil pm. The elevation is 1600, and a peak population of 150 was reported in 1920, with a steep decline to a count of just 14 in 1981. The post office closed August 25, 1967 with mail to Harvey. (1, 2, 10, 33, 40, 68, 79)

**WERNER** (Dunn). This NPRR townsite was founded in 1914 in SW¼ Sec. 19-145-92, six miles west of Halliday. Local settlers wanted to name it Three Springs, but NPRR townsite agent Lee C. Pettibone named it instead for John Steinman Werner (1862-1932), who came to ND in 1883 from NY, and was the banker in Mr. Pettibone's hometown of Dawson. The village incorporated in 1917, but the post office was not established until May 15, 1919 with Agnes D. Bessire pm. A peak population of 213 was reported in 1930, but the town declined after that, counting just 21 residents in 1970. The post office closed June 3, 1966 with mail to Halliday, and the city charter was dissolved November 1, 1971, this action having been approved by a 7-2 vote on September 7, 1971. Arthur Kummer's service station was the last business in town, closing with his death in 1970, and Robert Odum was the last mayor. (1, 2, 3, 18, 40, 52, 79)

**WEST ACRES** (Morton). This is a rural subdivision founded in 1975 in SW 1/4 Sec. 16 & SE¼ Sec. 17-139-83, Sweet Briar Twp.,

fifteen miles WNW of Mandan. Albert G. Kovash, the developer, named it to describe the location. (3)

**WEST BONETRAILL** (Williams). Ole Koppang established this townsite in NE 1/4 Sec. 26-157-103, Strandahl Twp., six miles WSW of Bonetrail. It was midway between Bonetrail and the Thiers post office, which was seemingly a good location in the 1910 era, but a country store was the extent of its development. (50)

**WEST BORDULAC** (Foster). This was a platted area located in SE¼ Sec. 10-145-65, Bordulac Twp., just west of Bordulac. It is thought that this was to be a rival townsite, but no development occurred except for a row of houses. In cold weather the curls of smoke rising from their chimneys gave the place a local slang name, Smoky Row. (97)

**WESTBORO** (Dickey). This farm post office was established December 31, 1884 with George J. Bolles pm at his home in McPherson County, in what is now SD. He gave it a name noting that it was in the western part of the country, although some sources say it was named for Westboro, MA. On May 19, 1888 it was relocated to the farm home of new pm Patrick M. McShane in SE¼ Sec. 32-129-64, Elm Twp., three miles east of Forbes, in what is now Dickey County, ND. A population of 12 was listed in 1890, although no indication has been found that WESTBORO was ever a settlement. The post office closed September 15, 1900 with mail to Ellendale. (2, 3, 18, 25, 40, 45, 154, 316, 414)

**WESTBY** (Divide). This was a rural settlement in SW¼ Sec. 23-162-103, Westby Twp., which was given a coined name, "west" noting its location in the extreme western part of ND, and *by*, Danish for town. The post office was established July 1, 1910 with James Hanson pm. Oliver Sannerud opened a general store, and Harold Borg established a bank, but when the Soo Line RR came through the area in 1913, they bypassed WESTBY by about two miles to the north. Most businesses moved to the new railroad townsite, which was mostly in Sec. 9-162-103, Sheridan County, MT, although a small portion of the town is in SW¼ Sec. 10-162-103, inside the ND line. About 1913, but possibly as late as 1916, the post office moved to the new site on the MT side of the border, becoming Westby, MT, making its name something of a contradiction. The original site, two miles to the SE, became known as OLD WESTBY. (1, 2, 3, 34, 40, 88)

**WESTBY** (Pierce). This was a rural post office established March 20, 1902 with Simon Westby pm. It was located in SW¼ Sec. 3-158-71, Juniata Twp., thirteen miles NE of Rugby near the Rolette County line. The post office closed February 28, 1906 with mail to Rugby. (2, 3, 18, 40, 114, 414)

**WEST CLIMAX** (Traill). This name is used for residents of NE Traill County with telephone prefix 856, part of the exchange in Climax, MN, which was named for Climax Tobacco, a popular product of pioneers days. The word is of Greek origin, meaning the highest point of attainment. (3, 13, 55)

**WEST COMSTOCK** (Cass). This name is used for residents of SE Cass County with telephone prefix 588, part of the exchange in Comstock, MN, which was named for Solomon Gilman Comstock, a politician from Moorhead, MN. (3, 13, 55)

**WESTEDGE** (Barnes). This village was platted November 27, 1901 by Sever L. Retan in NE¼ Sec. 14-137-59, Spring Creek Twp., where a post office had been established April 18, 1901 with William J. Westergaard pm. Its name noted the location on the west edge of the Sheyenne River valley. Many local residents spelled the name as two words. The post office closed June 15, 1904 with mail to Hastings, which had relocated just one mile to the west of WESTEDGE. (2, 3, 40, 76)

**WEST END** (Benson). This townsite was platted in May 1883 by Orlando Brown in SE¼ Sec. 3-153-67, West Bay Twp., which at the time was the western end of Devils Lake. It was one of several speculative sites awaiting the arrival of the NPRR. E. F. Sibley started a newspaper, *The West End News*, and a 400-foot wharf was built into the lake to handle steamboat traffic, but the railroad bypassed the site and the lake receded away from the wharf. WEST END quickly became a ghost town. (2, 3, 110, 255, 425)

**WESTERHEIM** (Golden Valley). This was a rural post office established June 10, 1913 with Henry Morris pm, although his wife, Minnie, actually performed the duties of the office. It was housed in a country store with a dance hall on the second floor, first located in SW¼ Sec. 20-142-103, thirteen miles NE of Sentinel Butte, and moved short distances at least three times during its existance. The name is said to be coined, with a German touch, to mean western home. Sam Pendleton, Reuben Hershey, William Conboy, and Charles Lowman ran the operation until the post office closed January 31, 1935 with mail to Sentinel Butte. A population of 50 was claimed in 1930, which seems to be an exaggeration. In later years the old building was destroyed by fire. (1, 2, 3, 18, 40, 80)

**WEST FARGO** (Cass). This settlement in Sec. 5-139-49, Barnes Twp., originated in the 1870's as SHEYENNE STOCKYARDS, served by post offices called HAGGART'S, HAGGARTS, and HAGGART sporadically from 1874-1885. Settlement began about 1920 around the Armour Meat Packing Co. plant, and was named WEST FARGO to note its location with respect to Fargo. A post office was established March 23, 1926 with Oden O. Ganslow pm, and in 1948 it moved to a different building which was across US Highway 10 in the neighboring city of South West Fargo, although it retained the original name. A population of 159 was reported in 1930, and the following year it incorporated as a village with Joseph Jameson as mayor. South West Fargo meanwhile was growing rapidly, and on June 7, 1967 it took the West Fargo name, with the older village becoming WEST FARGO INDUSTRIAL PARK, a name never popular with local residents. On September 17, 1974, it became the city of RIVERSIDE. (1, 2, 3, 33, 34, 40, 77, 210)

**WEST FARGO** (Cass). This settlement began in 1936 just south of US Highway 10 and the village of West Fargo, taking the name SOUTH WEST FARGO. It quickly grew to be much larger than its older neighbor, which was essentially a company town. The West Fargo post office was physically moved to SOUTH WEST FARGO in 1948, which took the name WEST FARGO on June 7, 1967, with the former West Fargo becoming West Fargo Industrial Park. The new WEST FARGO continued to grow, reaching a population of 10,080 in 1980, making it a major component of the Fargo-Moorhead metropolitan area. The 1967 name change was largely due to the efforts of mayor Clayton A. Lodoen, a powerful political figure here for many years. (3, 210)

**WEST FARGO INDUSTRIAL PARK** (Cass). This settlement dates from the early 1870's, and has had the names SHEYENNE STOCKYARDS, HAGGART'S, HAGGARTS, and HAGGART. During the 1920's it became known as WEST FARGO, but on June 7, 1967 this name was transferred to the much larger city of South West Fargo, with this settlement taking the name WEST FARGO INDUSTRIAL PARK. Luvern Eid was the mayor, and faced the task of replacing this unpopular name. On August 28, 1974 a name change to RIVERSIDE was approved, becoming official September 17, 1974. A population of 104 was reported in 1970. (3, 34, 77, 210)

**WESTFIELD** (Emmons). This is a Dutch settlement founded in 1884, eleven miles west of Hague, and locally known as the "Wooden Shoe Community." The name came from settlers who had previously lived in Westfield, IA, which was named to note its rural setting and the fact that it is the most western town in IA. The post office was established February 18, 1888 with Henry Van Beek pm in his store located in S½ Sec. 33-130-76, while just south across the section line in N½ Sec. 4-129-76 are a school, church and parsonage. The elevation is 1885, and the village, which never incorporated, has reported a population of about 40 for most of the twentieth century. The post office closed December 30, 1964 with mail to Hague. (1, 2, 3, 18, 34, 40, 66)

**WEST FLASHER** (Morton). Four blocks were platted in NE¼ Sec. 4-134-84, Flasher Twp., just west of Flasher, about 1910. The area ultimately was absorbed by the existing community. (3, 18)

**WEST HALSTAD** (Traill). This name is used for residents of eastern Traill County with telephone prefix 457, part of the exchange in Halstad, MN, which was named for Ole Halstad, a pioneer settler who came from Norway. (3, 13, 55)

**WESTHOPE** (Bottineau). This GNRR station was founded in 1903 in Secs. 26 & 27-163-80, Richburg Twp., and within a short time it had absorbed the rural communities of Richburg, Scotia, and Sergius. The Scotia post office moved here December 17, 1903 with George Fulwiler pm. It incorporated as a city in 1906, and reached a peak population of 824 in 1960, helped by the discovery of oil nearby in the 1950's. The elevation is 1506, and the Zip Code is 58793.

WESTHOPE calls itself "The City of Trees," but its name was coined from an earlier slogan, "Hope of the West," credited to GNRR officials to promote prosperity for the new townsite. (1, 2, 3, 18, 33, 34, 40, 52, 79, 101, 153)

**WEST LaMOURE** (LaMoure). This townsite was platted by F. B. Folsom of Fargo in Sec. 2-133-61, Bean Twp., on the west bank of the James River opposite LaMoure on the east bank. The NPRR began their branch to Jamestown on the east side of the river, and this townsite was abandoned. (2, 3, 25)

**WEST MAXBASS** (Bottineau). This townsite was platted in NE¼ Sec. 5-160-81, Lewis Twp., just SW of Maxbass, and was promoted as a rival townsite to the GNRR terminus, but little development took place. It appeared only in a 1910 county atlas, but residents of Maxbass delighted in claiming that they had the only suburb in the county. (3, 18, 153)

**WEST NIELSVILLE** (Traill). This name is used for residents of eastern Traill County with telephone prefix 942, part of the exchange in Nielsville, MN, which was named by the GNRR for one of its officials. (3, 13, 55)

**WESTON** (Dickey). This was a stage stop on the route from Ellendale to points in the eastern part of ND. It was located in NE¼ Sec. 21-129-61, Ada Twp., ten miles ESE of Ellendale, and named for Elmer W. Weston, who came here in 1883 from NY and later was in the newspaper and insurance businesses in Oakes. The post office was established October 18, 1883 with Allan W. Burnham pm, and it closed April 23, 1887 with mail to Ludden. (2, 3, 40, 264)

**WEST OSLO** (Grand Forks). This name is used for residents of NE Grand Forks County with telephone prefix 699, part of the exchange in Oslo, MN, which was named for the capital of Norway. (3, 13, 55)

**WEST PERLEY** (Cass). This name is used for residents of NE Cass County with telephone prefix 860, part of the exchange in Perley, MN, which was named for George Edmund Perley of Moorhead, MN, a lawyer and state legislator. (3, 13, 55)

**WEST PRAIRIE** (Griggs). This was a pioneer rural community in northern Griggs County centered around the homestead of Jens C. Thinglestad (1861-1933) in NW¼ Sec. 30-148-59, Pilot Mound Twp. The name was taken from the local church, which was named to note its location on the prairie west of the Sheyenne River. (2, 65)

**WEST SHELLY** (Traill). This name is used for residents of eastern Traill County with telephone prefix 887, part of the exchange in Shelly, MN, which was named for John Shelly, a pioneer settler, in 1896. Mr. Shelly was later a prominent citizen of Duluth, MN. (3, 13, 55)

**WESTVIEW** (Pembina). This was a rural post office established July 25, 1881 with Thomas West pm, with the name said to be coined from that of the pm. It was located in SE¼ Sec. 14-162-55, Advance Twp., one

mile NNW of Backoo, and closed March 23, 1882 with mail to Cavalier. West View is an erroneous spelling. (2, 3, 25, 34, 40, 414)

**WEST WILLISTON** (Williams). This name appears on plats of the development in Secs. 19 & 30-154-101, Williston Twp., four miles SW of Williston at the junction of US Highways 2 and 85. (3)

**WHEATLAND** (Cass). This NPRR station was built in 1872 in SE¼ Sec. 27-140-53, Wheatland Twp., and named SECOND SIDING. The post office was established May 6, 1878 with William D. Murray pm, and named WHEATLAND to note the fields of wheat on the large bonanza farms in the area. Townsite owner Hannah K. Brown of Cortland, NY had the site platted in November 1878. The elevation is 1016, the Zip Code is 58079, and a peak population of 450 was claimed in 1890, with a decline to about 100 residents today. (1, 2, 3, 18, 25, 34, 40, 77, 79, 270)

**WHEATON** (Steele). This place is listed in an 1890 guide to ND, stating that it was in Steele County and served by the Hope post office. No other information is available. (3, 25, 99)

**WHEELER** (Renville). This was a rural post office established June 27, 1903 with Leslie James McCormick pm. It was located in SW¼ Sec. 2-160-84, Clay Twp., three miles SE of Mohall, and named for one of its employees. The post office was discontinued October 15, 1904 with mail to Mohall. (2, 40, 71, 414)

**WHEELOCK** (Williams). This GNRR townsite was founded in 1902 in NW¼ Sec. 35-156-98, Wheelock Twp. The post office was established August 1, 1902 with James W. Maloney, the townsite owner, as pm. The town was named for Ralph W. Wheelock, an editorial writer with *The Minneapolis Tribune* who had written a nice article about the new townsite. WHEELOCK was platted in 1902, and incorporated as a village in 1916. The elevation is 2387, making this the highest GNRR station in ND. A peak population of 115 was recorded in 1930, but by 1970 only 21 people resided here. The post office, Zip Code 58855, became a rural branch of Ray on February 25, 1966. (1, 2, 3, 18, 40, 50, 79)

**WHETSTONE** (Dunn). This was a rural community about ten miles west of Killdeer, settled primarily by Norwegians, who built the Dovre Lutheran Church in 1918 in NW¼ Sec. 24-145-97. Named for J. F. "Jack" Whetstone, the first mayor of Killdeer, the community reported a population of 10 in 1920. Others say it was named for the stone used by Indians to sharpen the edges of their tools. The church was used on a regular basis until 1941, when it became affiliated with St. John's Lutheran Church of Killdeer under the name Whetstone Chapel. The cemetery, christened Haven of Rest in 1959, remains to mark the site of WHETSTONE. (2, 3, 4, 34, 79, 223, 399)

**WHISKEY POINT** (Burleigh). This was one of the unofficial names used in the Bismarck area prior to 1872. This name referred to what was more generally known as POINT PLEASANT, opposite Fort Abraham

Lincoln, and noted the availibility of liquor here. (2, 3)

**WHITBY** (Wells). This was a farm post office established February 27, 1890 with William Montgomery pm. It was located in SE¼ Sec. 17-149-72, Forward Twp., three miles SE of Harvey, and named by the pm for his hometown of Whitby, Ontario, Canada, which was named for Whitby, Yorkshire, England. Whitby is a Scandinavian name meaning from the white dwellings. When the new Soo Line RR townsite of Harvey began in 1892, plans were made to move this post office to that site. Postal officials approved the relocation and name change effective August 31, 1893 with Carl W. Brauer pm, but the change order was rescinded September 16, 1893. On October 2, 1893 the move was achieved, with Miss Sara L. Beaubier becoming the new pm. (2, 3, 5, 10, 19, 40, 68, 79, 240)

**WHITEAKER** (Divide). This was a farm post office established February 21, 1905 with Edith R. Whiteaker pm. It was located on the farm of Hiram C. Whiteaker in NW¼ Sec. 1-161-98, Plumer Twp., eight miles SSW of Crosby, and closed February 29, 1908 with mail to Plumer. (2, 3, 40)

**WHITE CITY** (McKenzie). Capt. Ed Seneschal came to McKenzie County in 1910 from Fort Pierre, SD and founded a townsite in NW¼ Sec. 28-154-97, Twin Valley Twp., twenty-four miles NNE of Watford City, naming it WHITE CITY because all of its buildings were painted this color. In 1911 the Seneschal post office was established just to the SE, taking this name only after postal officials had rejected WHITE CITY, which continued to see local usage. (3, 414)

**WHITE EARTH** (Mountrail). This GNRR townsite was founded in 1887 in NW¼ Sec. 36-157-94, White Earth Twp., but settlers were here as early as 1883. It is the oldest community in Mountrail County. The name came from the nearby creek, which was named for a translation of the Indian word *maskawapa*, meaning white clay sand. The Hidatsa tribe called the area *u-ka-ta-ka-zis*, meaning white earth. The post office was established March 14, 1888 with Newton B. Eustis pm, but it closed December 14, 1892 with mail to Williston. It reopened September 19, 1893 with Phil Porger pm. The townsite was platted in 1891, and has an elevation of 2097. A peak population of 272 was recorded in 1940, but steady decline has reduced the count to just 99 in 1980. (1, 2, 18, 25, 33, 40, 67, 72, 79)

**WHITE HOUSE** (McKenzie). This name is found in early accounts to denote a building in Sec. 6-152-100, adjacent to the Stroud post office, that served for a short time in 1905 as the first McKenzie County court house. The county seat status was never officially recognized, and within a few weeks Alexander received the honor. Some sources call this place Stone House, thought to be erroneous. (3, 79, 229)

**WHITE SHIELD** (McLean). This is a government-built village centered around a school in Sec. 2-148-88, White Shield Twp., six miles south of Roseglen. It was founded

in 1954 to replace the town of Elbowoods which was inundated by Lake Sakakawea. The name honors White Shield, a famous chief of the Arikara, and a onetime scout for Gen. George A. Custer. Albert Waubaunsee was the first principal of the school. Reports of a short-lived post office here in the mid-1980's are unconfirmed. (3, 28, 278)

**WHITE SPUR** (Bottineau). This was a Soo Line RR siding built in 1911 in SW 1/4 Sec. 9-160-77, Elysian Twp., five miles east of Kramer. It was named for A. H. White, a promoter of the site. Two elevators were built here, and in 1920 a population of 5 was listed, but everything was later dismantled. Some maps show the place as Spur 531. (1, 2, 3, 34, 101)

**WHITMAN** (Nelson). This Soo Line RR station was built in 1912 in NW¼ Sec. 16-154-58, Sarnia Twp., fourteen miles NE of Lakota. It was named for E. A. Whitman, Chief Civil Engineer for the railroad, and a brother-in-law of President Kroeze of Jamestown College. The post office was established December 20, 1912 with Clara F. Sell pm. A small village of about 100 residents existed for many years until a recent decline. Evelyn Shirek Rysavy became the pm in 1949, and retired from the post in August 1981, at which time the post office, Zip Code 58283, closed as well, although government records did not record the closing until April 16, 1982. (1, 2, 33, 40, 79, 124, 128)

**WHITNEY** (Renville). This was a farm post office established December 19, 1903 with John W. Abbott pm. J. A. Juno was the mail carrier. It was located in SW¼ Sec. 4-162-85, Hamerly Twp., seven miles SW of Sherwood. The origin of the name is unknown. Whitney is an Anglo-Saxon name meaning from the white island. A star route six times weekly was established out of Mohall in 1904, and the post office relocated to Sec. 30-163-84, Eden Valley Twp. For a time this site had a country store, blacksmith shop, and land office in addition to the post office, which closed January 15, 1906 with mail to Sherwood. (2, 19, 40, 71)

**WHYNOT** (Grand Forks). This was a country store run by Erik K. Larsgaard in SE¼ Sec. 29-149-49, Bentru Twp., eight miles east of Reynolds in the extreme SE corner of the county. Settlers wondered why Mr. Larsgaard was erecting the store on his land, and he would always answer, "Why not?" He painted this statement in large letters on the front of the store to attract attention. When he established a rural post office in the store on May 6, 1892, the choice of name was easy. In 1900 it moved one mile NW to SW¼ Sec. 21-149-49, the home of new pm John H. Alfson, and closed January 15, 1907 with mail to Reynolds. (2, 3, 18, 31, 40, 69)

**WILBUR** (McKenzie). This was a rural post office established February 27, 1905 with Wilbur H. Rogers pm. Wilbur is an Anglo-Saxon name meaning beloved stronghold. It was located in NE¼ Sec. 9-153-101, Wilbur Twp., three miles SW of Williston on the south bank of the Missouri River. It moved two miles south in 1910 to NW¼ Sec. 14-153-101, and closed November 30, 1912 with mail to Williston. (1, 2, 3, 18, 40, 53, 414)

**WILDER** (Cass). This was a rural post office established April 21, 1892 with Thomas J. Wilder pm, but the order was rescinded November 25, 1893 with the entry "no papers" in government records. The exact location is unknown. (3, 40)

**WILD RICE** (Cass). This community of French-Canadians was founded as RICEVILLE in S½ Sec. 21-138-49, Stanley Twp., just south of the old mission of Holy Cross. When the townsite was platted in 1884 by Richard S. Tyler, he called the place WILD RICE for the nearby river, which had been called *Folles Avoine* by early French explorers, noting the wild rice, or oats, growing along its banks. The post office adopted this name on February 7, 1884 when George D. Brown, credited with starting the state's first cheese factory, was pm. The elevation is 911, the Zip Code is 58080, and a peak population of 75 was claimed in 1890 and 1920. The post office closed October 15, 1970 with mail to Horace. In 1975 it was said that this was the only settlement in Cass County that could not be reached by a paved road. (1, 2, 3, 10, 18, 25, 33, 40, 41, 77, 79, 309, 311)

**WILD ROSE** (Walsh). This was a Soo Line RR siding built in 1911 in NW¼ Sec. 16-155-55, Eden Twp., two miles west of Conway, although a large curve in the tracks made the actual rail distance closer to four miles. The name notes the flowers in the area. About 1913 the name was changed to MEAGHER. (2, 3, 18, 75, 254, 293)

**WILDROSE** (Williams). This was a GNRR townsite founded in 1909 in Sec. 10-159-97, Hazel Twp. It absorbed the old post offices of Paddington and Montrose. It was planned that the Montrose name would be transferred here, but it was duplicated on GNRR lines, and officials of the railroad selected a new name noting the wild roses in bloom at the site. The post office was established July 13, 1910 with Anna Eliza Eastruan Palmer (1850-1938), the former pm at Montrose, assuming the pm position here. The site was platted in 1910, and became an incorporated village in 1913, with William Bickford Mathews (1872-1936) as mayor. Its elevation is 2240, and the Zip Code is 58795. Until 1916 it was the terminus of the branch line, and billed itself as the largest primary grain market in the United States. A peak population of 518 was reached in 1930. (1, 2, 33, 39, 40, 50, 52, 79)

**WILEY** (Bottineau). This place appears on current Hearne Brothers maps, just NE of the Soo Line RR-GNRR junction at Lansford. Local residents have no knowledge of such a place, and an official of the map company hedges on the fact that it is a copyright town. An elevator in this area was long associated with Henry Willis, but no positive connection between this facility and the map place name can be made. (3, 378)

**WILLA** (Hettinger). Pm Juliana Muller of ROSENFELD was authorized to change the name of that post office to WILLA on March 16, 1907 due to confusion with Roosevelt in Wells County, but the order was rescinded. On June 11, 1907 the name change was made, but with Johannes Schmitt as the new pm, and at a new site, NW¼ Sec. 6-135-91, Walker Twp., one-half mile west of ROSENFELD. Willa is an Anglo-Saxon name meaning desired, and was chosen by postal officials from a list of alternative names, having rejected the local favorite of North Star. The site developed into a small village with a store and a blacksmith shop, and reported a population of 10 in 1920. The post office closed July 15, 1930 with mail to Burt. (2, 3, 18, 19, 40, 181)

**WILLARD** (Ransom). This junction of the NPRR and Soo Line RR in Sec. 24-136-55, Liberty Twp., two miles SW of Sheldon, was at first called SHELDON JUNCTION, and then about 1910 was renamed CROSSING. About 1915 the name WILLARD was used as the name of the site for unknown reasons. It is a Teutonic name meaning resolutely brave. Some maps show WILLARD midway between the actual junction and Enderlin, which is three miles to the NW on the Soo Line RR. (1, 2, 3, 18, 19)

**WILLDO** (Towner). This was a farm post office established March 31, 1890 with Adolphus Evenden pm. It was located in Sec. 14-159-65, Victor Twp., five miles SE of Egeland. Postal officials rejected the suggested name, Norton, so WILLDO was chosen by local settlers as a pun to compliment their county seat of Cando. The post office closed January 10, 1895, being replaced on that date by the Lewis post office. (2, 18, 40, 197, 414)

**WILLIA** (Williams). This is one of several places that are found on a 1930 roadmap published by the General Drafting Co. for the White Eagle Oil Co. Most of these places duplicate the county names, and it is safe to say that this one was intended to be Williams, but was truncated by a cartographer's error. It is shown on old ND Highway 42 about midway between Corinth and Epping, and is believed to be a copyright town. (3)

**WILLIAMS** (Cass). This GNRR station was founded in 1880 in SW¼ Sec. 15 & NW¼ Sec. 22-138-51, Addison Twp., one mile NW of Davenport. It was named for H. M. Williams, whose bonanza farm was served by the station. The post office was established April 5, 1881 with Fred Schimmel pm, and it closed March 23, 1882 with mail to Wahpeton. Two weeks later the Davenport post office was established to serve this area. In 1882 WILLIAMS was renamed ADDISON. (2, 3, 40, 77, 303)

**WILLIAMS** (Golden Valley). This was a farm post office established March 12, 1908 with George Christensen pm. It was located in S½ Sec. 34-137-105, eight miles SE of Golva, and closed February 28, 1914 with mail to Alpha. Okley Cripps, who lived in W½ Sec. 33-137-105, was the mail carrier. The origin of the name is unknown. (2, 3, 18, 40, 53)

**WILLIAMS** (Kidder). This NPRR siding was built in 1915 in Sec. 12-142-71, Lake Williams Twp., between Robinson and Pettibone, and named for the nearby lake, which had been named for pioneer settler Jeremiah D. Williams. A settlement began the following year as LAKE WILLIAMS because the original name had been rejected by postal officials, supposedly because of duplication, although the Williams post office in Golden Valley County had closed in 1914. This site was sometimes called Williams Siding. (2, 18, 40, 122)

**WILLIAMS** (McKenzie). This was a rural post office established March 19, 1906 with John E. "Jack" Williams (1861-1937), who came here in 1898, as pm. It was located in SE¼ Sec. 13-149-96, Bear Den Twp., nineteen miles ESE of Watford City, and closed May 31, 1907 with mail to Schafer. (2, 3, 40, 229)

**WILLIAMSPORT** (Emmons). This inland village was founded in 1883 in N½ Sec. 15-135-76, Hazelton Twp., three miles NE of Hazelton. The townsite was platted in August 1883 by the first settlers, most of whom came from Ashland, OH. The post office was established September 7, 1883 with Daniel R. Williams pm. He was the first Register of Deeds in Burleigh County and the first warden of the State Penitentiary, and later was the first Register of Deeds in Emmons County. The "port" was said to be added for euphonic purposes only, as the town had neither rail or water connections. When Emmons County organized in 1883, WILLIAMSPORT was made the county seat, but this honor was lost to Linton in the election of 1898. During its heyday this was quite a town, reporting a population of 155 in 1890, but after being bypassed by the NPRR it rapidly declined. The post office closed December 10, 1903 with mail to Hazelton, and today the site is marked only by a few ruins of demolished buildings. (3, 3, 18, 25, 40, 66, 96)

**WILLISTON** (Williams). This GNRR station was founded in 1887 at Sidetrack #25 in Secs. 13, 14, 23 & 24-154-101, Williston Twp., and named for Daniel Willis James, a GNRR stockholder and good friend of GNRR President James J. Hill. Willis means son of William, a name derived from the Norse word for helmet. The Little Muddy post office moved here July 12, 1887 with Winfield Scott Dunn as pm. It incorporated as a village in 1894, became a city in 1904, and is the county seat of Williams County. The elevation is 1877, the Zip Code is 58801, and a peak population of 13,354 was recorded in 1980 as the city has shown a steady growth since its founding. Among the people who have called WILLISTON their home are Usher L. Burdick (1879-1960), a longtime leader in state and national politics, and Phil

Jackson, a well known collegiate and professional basketball player. (1, 2, 3, 19, 25, 33, 40, 50, 52, 79)

**WILLMEN** (Dunn). This was a rural post office established December 1, 1913 with Oscar B. Hanson pm. It was located in SE¼ Sec. 18-142-97, thirteen miles SW of Manning near the source of Crooked Creek, and named for the pm's son, Cyrus Willmen Hanson. The post office was discontinued December 15, 1938 with mail to Dickinson. (1, 2, 3, 18, 40, 223)

**WILLOW** (Griggs). This was a rural post office established January 4, 1883 with Harry Clark pm at his home in NW¼ Sec. 16-148-60, Willow Twp. This spelling is used on all known postmarks and on most maps of the period, but postal records show the name as WILLOWS. (2, 3, 40, 240, 284)

**WILLOW CITY** (Bottineau). This settlement was founded in 1884 in Secs. 12 & 13-159-75, Ostby Twp., as BENNETT, and within a month it was renamed McRAE. The post office was established using this name in 1886, but on November 9, 1889 the name was changed to WILLOW CITY by new pm Charles O. Romansen, noting the creek which flows through the area, so named because of the many willow trees along its banks. The village incorporated in 1890, and it became a city in 1906 with Peter E. Sandlie as mayor. The elevation is 1471, the Zip Code is 58384, and it reached its peak population of 623 in 1910. (1, 2, 3, 18, 33, 34, 40, 52, 75, 79, 101, 153)

**WILLOW CREEK** (Cass). This is a residential subdivision platted in the late 1970's in SE¼ Sec. 10-139-50, Mapleton Twp., four miles WSW of West Fargo. The name is descriptive of its locale. (3, 34)

**WILLOW CREEK** (Rolette). At first the settlement at the junction of the GNRR and Soo Line RR in SE¼ Sec. 20-160-71, Leonard Twp., was called WILLOW CREEK, for the nearby creek, but the name was changed to ROLETTE in early 1905. (2, 3, 123)

**WILLOW LAKE** (Rolette). A post office called JUNO had been authorized in 1904 just south of here, but the order was rescinded. Shortly thereafter, Simon Johnson, in SW¼ Sec. 6-162-73, Gilbert Twp., seven miles NW of Dunseith, applied for a post office called WILLOW LAKE for the nearby lake, which is the source of Willow Creek. This name was rejected due to a government ban on two-word place names. On January 25, 1905 Mr. Johnson was appointed as the pm of a new post office, but it adopted the original name of JUNO, operating until 1914. (2, 3, 40, 123)

**WILLOWS** (Griggs). This was a rural post office established January 4, 1883 with Harry

Clark pm. The name noted nearby Red Willow Lake, so named because of the many willow trees growing along its banks. It was located in NW 1/4 Sec. 16-148-60, Willow Twp., about seven miles NW of Jessie. Although postal records clearly spell the name as WILLOWS, all known postmarks and most maps of the period show the site as WILLOW. On July 7, 1892 it was relocated three miles SE and renamed COTTONWOOD. (2, 3, 25, 33, 40, 65, 240, 284)

**WILMA** (Barnes). This was a farm post office established November 26, 1900 with Jacob Steiner pm. The origin of the name is unknown. It was located in SW¼ Sec. 8-143-57, Baldwin Twp., six miles west of Pillsbury, and closed September 15, 1906 with mail to Dazey. Wilna is an erroneous spelling. (2, 18, 34, 40, 76)

**WILSON** (Kidder). This was a rural community centered around a post office established December 18, 1906 in NW¼ Sec. 18-142-72, Robinson Twp., four miles SW of Robinson. William F. Wilson, who came here in 1905, was the pm, and E. H. Wilson, who came here in 1900 from PA, operated a livestock agency. Paul M. Mark, a native of WI, had a blacksmith shop. Wilson means son of William, which is derived from the Norse word meaning helmet. After the NPRR's Pingree-Wilton line was built in 1911, local businesses moved to the new townsite of Robinson. The post office closed December 31, 1912 with mail to Robinson. (2, 3, 18, 19, 40, 122)

**WILSON'S SIDING** (Benson). This GNRR siding was built in 1883 in SE¼ Sec. 19-156-69, York Twp., and named for George Wilson, owner of the site, who lived to be 99 years of age. Development started here in 1886, and the site was renamed YORK. Willson's Siding is an erroneous spelling. (2, 3, 18, 34, 236, 257)

**WILTON** (Burleigh & McLean). This Soo Line RR townsite was founded May 10, 1899 by General William Drew Washburn, who named it for his birthplace of Wilton, ME, which was named for Wilton, NH, which was named for Wilton, Wiltshire, England, a famous carpet manufacturing center. Wilton is an Old English name meaning from the farmstead by the spring. The post office was established January 10, 1900 with Philip K. Eastman (1867-1949) pm. The village incorporated in 1902 and it became a city in 1912. For many years the city was a coal mining center, reaching a peak population of 1,001 in 1930. After a decline it has rebounded to a 1980 count of 950 residents, many of whom commute to Bismarck. The elevation is 2177, and the Zip Code is 58579. It is located in Sec. 35-143-80, McLean County, and Sec. 2-142-80, Ecklund Twp., Burleigh County, with the larger portion of the city being in McLean County. (1, 2, 5, 10, 13, 19, 28, 33, 40, 94)

**WIMBLEDON** (Barnes). As early as 1882 this location, SW¼ Sec. 30-143-61, Pierce Twp., had been known as GIBSON. When the Soo Line RR reached here in 1893, they renamed it WIMBLEDON for the borough of London, England, famous for its annual tennis tournament. The name means

stronghold of the bold friend. The Midland Continental RR arrived here in 1913, giving the town a two-railroad status. The post office was established July 26, 1893 with Tollef (or Joseph) S. Tollefson pm. It became a village in 1899 with John L. More (1863-1945) as board president. It was platted in December 1893, has an elevation of 1486, and the Zip Code is 58492. The peak population of 571 was reached in 1910, and the city likes to refer to itself as the second largest settlement in Barnes County, albeit far behind Valley City. (1, 2, 3, 18, 34, 40, 76, 269)

**WINAL** (LaMoure). This was a planned Midland Continental RR station in N 1/2 Sec. 27-134-64, Nora Twp., two miles north of Edgeley. No development occurred at the site, and the origin of the name is unknown. (3)

**WINANS** (Mountrail). This was a GNRR loading station in Sec. 19-156-90, Palermo Twp., five miles east of Stanley. It is thought to have been named for Ross Winans (1796-1877), the inventor of the camel-back locomotive and the eight-wheeled railroad car, or his son, Thomas DeKay Winans (1820-1878), who with his brother William helped to build the first railroad in Czarist Russia. No development took place at this site. Wimans is an erroneous spelling. (1, 2, 3, 5, 18, 39, 72)

**WINCHESTER** (Emmons). This was a pioneer townsite promoted by Charles Bumstead and Nathaniel Gillett in Sec. 1-132-77, just NW of present-day Linton. It was named for Walter H. Winchester, a District Judge at Bismarck, although some claim it was named by local gunsmith Benjamin Losey, father-in-law of Mr. Bumstead, for the Winchester repeating rifle. The post office was established August 21, 1884 with Mr. Gillett as pm, and a population of 47 was reported in 1890. John Parker opened a cheese factory, but development slowed, and the post office closed January 15, 1900 with mail to Linton. It reopened February 17, 1900 about four miles to the west at the home of John Henderson, and the facility, now a farm post office, moved two more times in the same general area before closing for good December 15, 1909 with mail to Hartford. (2, 3, 25, 40, 66, 79, 240, 415)

**WINDSOR** (Stutsman). This site, Sec. 32-140-66, Windsor Twp., was marked by the NPRR in 1872, but settlement did not begin until 1882. The townsite owner, G. A. Jeffrey, named it for his hometown of Windsor, Ontario, Canada. Some state that it was named for H. H. Windsor, a Saint Paul, MN printer who did the early NPRR timetables. Still others say it was named by Abraham Coats, who came here in 1883 from Windsor, Berkshire, England, which is the ultimate source of this name in all cases. Windsor is a Teutonic name meaning at the bend of the river. The post office was established November 5, 1883 with George W. Nast pm. The elevation is 1864, and the population of this unincorporated village never exceeded 100. The post office, Zip Code 58493, closed January 10, 1975 with mail to Cleveland. The post office building was moved to an outdoor museum in Jamestown. (1, 2, 3, 10, 18, 19, 25, 33, 40, 41, 79, 158)

**WINES** (McHenry). This was a farm post office established February 25, 1888 with Frederick Melhoff pm in his country store located in SE¼ Sec. 22-159-77, Mouse River Twp., ten miles NE of Bantry. Some say it was named for the vines growing along the Souris River in the area, while others say that local Icelandic settlers coined the name from Vinland, the Viking name for America. The post office closed February 28, 1902 with mail to Ely. Mr. Melhoff moved his store to Upham in 1906. (2, 3, 25, 40, 186, 412)

**WING** (Burleigh). This NPRR townsite was founded in 1910 in Secs. 2 & 11-142-76, Wing Twp., on the new Pingree-Wilton branch line. It was named for Charles Kleber Wing (1851-1917), a native of VT who came to ND in 1881 and laid out the townsites of McClusky, Wing, Pingree, Robinson, and Regan. The post office was established April 15, 1911 with Leslie B. Draper pm. The village incorporated in 1921 with Fred H. Scallon as mayor. Axel Soder (1882-1962), a native of Sweden, served as mayor of WING for thirty-five years. The elevation is 1904, the Zip Code is 58494, and a peak population of 303 was reached in 1960. (1, 2, 3, 8, 14, 18, 33, 40, 52, 63, 97)

**WINIFRED** (Renville). This was a farm post office established June 22, 1903 on the Frank Thornton farm in SE¼ Sec. 19-162-84, Hurley Twp., seven miles NW of Mohall, with Sarah A. Thornton pm. In 1904 it was part of a Star Route from Mohall, with mail delivery six days each week. The origin of the name, a Teutonic name meaning friend of peace, is unknown. The post office closed January 15, 1907 with mail to Mohall. (2, 19, 40, 71)

**WINNEBAGO** (Slope). This was a farm post office established July 20, 1909 with Charles B. Williams (1861-1917) pm. Mr. Williams was a native of WI, coming here from IA, and is considered to be the first ND fatality of the great influenza epidemic of 1917-1918. He named the post office for Lake Winnebago in his native state, which bears the name of a Sioux Indian tribe whose name means fish eaters, or people who live in filthy water. The post office was to be located in the sod house of his son, Frood B. Williams, in NW¼ Sec. 8-134-101, Sand Creek Twp., five miles SW of Amidon, and just north of Black Butte, but the order was rescinded January 8, 1910. (3, 10, 34, 40, 82)

**WINONA** (Emmons). This settlement dates from the 1870's, and was founded primarily to cater to the off-duty wants of soldiers stationed across the Missouri River at Fort Yates. It was located in SW¼ Sec. 5 & NW¼ Sec. 8-130-79, at the mouth of Cat-tail Creek, and was named by Fort Yates post trader H. F. Douglas with a Winnebago Sioux word meaning first-born child, if a girl. The name has since become popular as a girl's name among white people. The post office was established May 19, 1884 with James G. Pitts pm, who later served as county auditor and treasurer. This notorious town, known as "The Devil's Colony," had an 1890 population of 150, with a newspaper, hotel, and at least nine saloons, complete with gambling and other attractions operating outside of the law. The post office closed December 30, 1939, and the site is now inundated by Lake Oahe. (1, 2, 3, 10, 13, 18, 25, 40, 66, 79, 403)

**WINSTON LANDING** (McLean). This was an early Missouri River boat landing in Sec. 29-146-84, twelve miles west of Underwood, and was named for E.T. Winston, once the post trader at Fort Stevenson, who ranched near this site. There is some evidence that the actual docks were, at least for a time, located on the Mercer County side of the river. (3, 417)

**WIPRUD** (McLean). This rural post office was established September 3, 1902 as CASEY in SW¼ Sec. 17-148-80, Wiprud Twp., eight miles north of Turtle Lake on the SW shore of Crooked Lake. On July 25, 1904 the post office was taken over by Stener T. Wiprud, a native of Norway, who with his brother operated a country store at this site. They changed the name of the post office to WIPRUD on that date, and operated it until May 31, 1914 when mail went to Turtle Lake. Wiprad is an erroneous spelling. (2, 3, 18, 28, 40, 389)

**WIRCH** (Dickey). This was a farm post office established June 12, 1900 with John Wirch Sr., who came here about 1887 from South Russia, as the first and only pm. It was located in SW¼ Sec. 15-130-66, Spring Valley Twp., twelve miles NW of Forbes. Mr. Wirch, a longtime county commissioner, later added a store to his complex. The post office served much of the NW quarter of the county for many years, closing May 15, 1933 with mail to Forbes. (1, 2, 18, 40, 154, 316, 317, 414)

**WISHEK** (McIntosh). Settlers were here as early as 1885, but development did not start until the Soo Line RR townsite was platted in October 1898 in Secs. 9, 10, 15, & 16-132-71, Youngstown Twp., and named for John H. Wishek (1855-1932), a rancher, politician and promoter living in Ashley. The post office was established November 29, 1898 with Martin E. Pratt pm. WISHEK became an incorporated village in 1907 and a city in 1930 with H. E. Timm as first mayor. The elevation is 2010, the Zip Code is 58495, and a peak population of 1,342 was reached in 1980 as the city continues a slow, but steady growth. (2, 3, 23, 33, 34, 40, 79, 134, 137)

**WISNER** (Burleigh). This was a farm post office established May 16, 1901 with James H. Johnson pm. It was located in SW¼ Sec. 34-143-78, Estherville Twp., one mile west of Regan, and is generally assumed to have been named for J. E. Wisner, the land baron and inventor from Ransom County. The post office closed May 31, 1907 with mail to Canfield. (2, 3, 12, 18, 40, 414)

**WISNER** (Ransom). J. E. Wisner came here in 1880 and was a great promoter of the entire Sheyenne River valley. A native of NY, he built a flour mill, laid out a townsite, promoted a stillborn railroad, and invented a farm implement that made him a wealthy man for his time. The railroad townsite in Sec. 11-135-57 was known as FOREST CITY, and the effort failed. A little later a second effort attracted a few settlers, with the site now called WISNER, although the post office that operated here 1880-1885 was called PLYMOUTH. (2, 3, 18, 39, 40, 77, 201, 205)

**WITTING** (Bottineau). This was a farm post office established February 28, 1896 with George W. Witting, who came here in 1893, as pm. It was located in NE¼ Sec. 22-160-77, Elysian Twp., six miles ESE of Kramer, and closed September 30, 1902 with mail to Willow City. (2, 34, 40, 101, 153)

**WITTMAYER** (Sheridan). This was a farm post office established January 17, 1900 with John Wittmayer pm. It was located in

NE¼ Sec. 20-147-74, Boone Twp., four miles north of Goodrich. Mail was carried here from Harvey by horseback. The post office closed September 30, 1902 with mail to Goodrich. Whitmeyer, Whittmeyer, and Wittmeyer are erroneous spellings. (2, 3, 21, 40)

**WOBURN** (Burke). This GNRR townsite was established in Sec. 25-162-91, Dale Twp., between Lignite and Coteau, and named for Woburn, Bedfordshire, England by GNRR officials, who were naming many of their new stations with decidedly English names to please stockholders from that country. The post office was authorized May 27, 1907 with George W. Carey pm, but the order was rescinded. A second authorization was made, and the post office opened June 26, 1908 with Henry J. A. Mularky pm. The village incorporated in 1934, but the peak population was just 19 in 1940. The post office closed November 30, 1947 with mail to Flaxton. (1, 2, 3, 34, 40, 52, 67, 79)

**WOGANSPORT** (Burleigh). This was a Missouri River boat landing in NW¼ Sec. 30-141-80, Glenview Twp., six miles SSW of Baldwin. A post office was established March 3, 1882 with Henry P. Wogan pm. Known locally as "Professor" Wogan, he envisioned a great city here, and attempted to establish a university at the site. Although it would seem quite obvious that WOGANSPORT was named for him, some sources say it was named for Thomas Wagonman, another promoter of this site. A less controversial figure who lived here was Frank Russo Simons (1858-1936), who served as the pm 1893-1895, and was a plant researcher of some reknown. He lined the "streets" of the town with trees, which still roughly define the layout of the settlement. The post office closed May 30, 1915 with mail to Baldwin. Wogonsport is an erroneous spelling. (1, 2, 3, 8, 9, 12, 18, 40, 79)

**WOIWODE** (Richland). This was a pioneer settlement in SE¼ Sec. 4-131-50, Belford Twp., two miles SE of Mantador. A post office was established February 2, 1881 with Charles Woiwode pm, and closed August 31, 1887 with mail to Hankinson. Woiwode is derived from the Slavonic *Wojwode*, meaning leader in war. The title has been used from Poland to Bulgaria by princes, generals, and government officials. (3, 5, 40, 77, 147)

**WOLF** (Benson). This was a farm post office established June 1, 1900 with Iver A. Bakken pm. It was located in NE¼ Sec. 6-154-69, Butte Valley Twp., nine miles south of York. The origin of the name is unknown. The post office was discontinued July 30, 1904 with mail to York. Wolfe is an erroneous spelling. (2, 3, 18, 34, 40, 236)

**WOLF BUTTE** (Adams). This rural post office was established February 2, 1907 with William N. Worra pm. It was located in Secs. 22 & 23-130-97, Bucyrus Twp., and was named for the nearby butte in Sec. 23-131-97, Wolf Butte Twp., so named because of the wolf dens on its side. On September 14, 1907 the name was changed to DOLAN coincident with its becoming a station on the Milwaukee Road RR. That

*Wishek about 1925*

name proved to be confusing with Doland, SD, so in 1908 the name was changed to BUCYRUS. (2, 3, 40, 189)

**WOLF BUTTE** (Adams). A post office of this name existed for a few months in 1907, which in 1908 evolved into the railroad townsite of Bucyrus. The WOLF BUTTE name was reused when a post office was established February 5, 1908 with Lewis O. Richardson pm. This post office was strictly a rural facility, and was located in NW¼ Sec. 26-131-97, Wolf Butte Twp., five miles north of Bucyrus, and like the former, named for the nearby butte which was just one-half mile to the NE. It was discontinued July 31, 1916 with mail to Bucyrus, although the name is perpetuated by a church built near here in 1913. (2, 3, 18, 34, 40, 79, 189)

**WOLF CREEK** (Rolette). This was a rural community founded in 1898 and named for its township, which was named for the creek that flows through it. This area was populated by many wolves in the early days. When a post office was established September 7, 1898 in NW¼ Sec. 26-160-72, Wolf Creek Twp., four miles west of Rolette, it was named FISHER. (2, 3, 40, 123)

**WOLFF** (Dickey). This was a farm post office established February 9, 1911 with John Wolff (1868-1940) pm. He was a native of South Russia who had homesteaded here in 1888. It was located in SW¼ Sec. 29-129-66, Albertha Twp., nine miles WNW of Forbes, and closed January 15, 1913 with mail to Forbes. (2, 3, 40, 53, 154, 264, 316, 317)

**WOLFORD** (Pierce). This GNRR townsite was founded in 1905 in NW¼ Sec. 21-158-70, Wolford Twp., at the site of the rural mail distribution point called ORKNEY. The post office was established August 8, 1905 with Grace G. Smith pm, having performed these duties in an unofficial capacity at ORKNEY for ten years. It is said that the new name was chosen by a GNRR official for a friend living in the area, but others say it was named for an official of the Dakota Development Co. of Willmar, MN, owners of the townsite. The elevation is 1624, the Zip Code is 58385, and a peak population of 206 was reported in 1940, with higher unofficial figures being quoted in earlier years. (1, 2, 18, 33, 40, 79, 114)

**WOLSETH** (Ward). This GNRR station was founded in 1915 in SW¼ Sec. 3-157-81, Margaret Twp., seven miles SE of Glenburn. The post office was established May 23, 1916 with William R. White pm, and named for Gunder T. Wolseth (1872-1950), who came to MN in 1893 from Norway, and moved here in 1902. He donated the land for the townsite. A small village began, but the 1920 population of 25 was never exceeded. The post office, Zip Code 58796, closed November 30, 1972 with mail to Glenburn. Walseth is an erroneous spelling. (2, 3, 33, 40, 79, 100)

**WOODBRIDGE** (Cavalier). This was a rural community founded in 1883 in SW 1/4 Sec. 36-164-64, Cypress Twp., six miles NE of Sarles at the Canadian border. The post office was established March 9, 1887 with William Hazlitt pm in his roadside tavern. The name was coined from the name of

William WOODs, later the first pm at Sarles, and BRIDGE, noting the crossing of nearby Cypress Creek. Some say it was named for a Mrs. Woodbridge who visited at the pm's home just before the post office was established. A population of 100 was claimed in 1890, and a school was built in 1892, but the establishment of the GNRR townsite of Sarles in 1905 led to the decline of WOODBRIDGE. The post office closed September 29, 1906 with mail to Sarles, and the school building was moved there in 1918. (1, 2, 3, 25, 40, 208, 240)

**WOODHULL** (Richland). This was a Milwaukee Road RR station in SW¼ Sec. 1-133-48, Dwight Twp., eight miles NW of Wahpeton. A post office was established June 30, 1893 with Henry E. Wiedeman pm, closing August 31, 1893 with mail to Wahpeton. It reopened December 23, 1895, and operated until April 30, 1914 when mail again went to Wahpeton. It was named for Col. John W. Woodhull, a Civil War veteran who came here in 1887, and sold the right-of-way for this station. (1, 2, 3, 18, 25, 40, 79)

**WOOD LAKE** (Benson). This was the dream of F. C. Louden, a resident of nearby Tokio, who hoped to develop this site into a settlement and pleasure resort. It was platted in 1915 in NW¼ Sec. 15-151-64, Wood Lake Twp., on the NE shore of Wood Lake, two miles SW of Tokio. A pavilion, tobaggon slide, and several support buildings were built, but the lure of the place wore off, and the site today is a Kiwanis Club boys' camp. (3, 18)

**WOODRUFF** (Richland). This was a NPRR loading station and spur built before 1890 in SE¼ Sec. 34-132-49, Mooreton Twp., three miles north of Great Bend, which provided this site with mail service. It was named for T. S. Woodruff, who came here in 1879 and was part owner of an elevator in Wahpeton. It disappeared from maps in the 1920's. (1, 2, 3, 18, 25)

**WOODS** (Cass). This was a NPRR loading station built in 1882 in Sec. 13-137-52, Leonard Twp., six miles SW of Davenport. It was named for Isaac Woods, owner of a large grain storage terminal here, this being the main reason for the station's existance. A post office was established March 9, 1888 with Sam Rustad pm, closing February 15, 1954 with mail to Leonard. A small village existed for many years, reaching a peak population of 30 in 1920. (1, 2, 25, 34, 40, 77, 79)

**WOODVILLE** (Grand Forks). This was a rural settlement in NE¼ Sec. 11-154-52, Levant Twp., eight miles NW of Manvel. A post office was established May 18, 1881 with William A. Woods pm, closing August 6, 1883 with mail to Ardoch. (2, 3, 25, 31, 40)

**WOODWARD** (Bottineau). This was a pioneer settlement founded in 1883 in Sec. 33-164-75, Roland Twp., eight miles NNE of Bottineau. It was named for Fremont M. Woodward and Rollin O. Woodward, who built the area's first grist and saw mills in December 1883, and built a flour mill here in 1885. When the site failed to develop, the Woodwards moved to Willow City, where they were in the elevator business.

Woodward is an Old English name meaning forester. (2, 153, 415)

**WOODWORTH** (Stutsman). This NPRR townsite was founded in 1911 in SW¼ Sec. 4-142-68, Strong Twp., and named for J. G. Woodworth, Traffic Manager and Vice President of the NPRR. On August 4, 1911 the Gem post office just north of the site was moved here with Hans J. Hanson as pm. Garfield Wilson was the original owner of the townsite, which incorporated as a village in 1916. The elevation is 2035, the Zip Code is 58496, and a peak population of 297 was recorded in 1920, with a decline to just 140 in 1980. (1, 2, 18, 33, 40, 52, 79, 158)

**WORMS** (Grant). This was a farm post office established January 16, 1906 with Jacob Haring Sr. pm. It was located in NW¼ Sec. 12-137-90, fifteen miles SW of Glen Ullin, and named for the ancient city of Germany, known in Roman times as Borbetomagus, and later as Augusta Vangionum. Attila the Hun destroyed the city, but it was rebuilt in 486 A.D. In 1912 the post office moved four miles SSW to NE¼ Sec. 34-137-90, where new pm Gottlieb Roth ran a country store on the bank of the Heart River. The post office closed May 31, 1914 with mail to Saint Joseph, and the store closed in 1916. (1, 2, 3, 5, 17, 40, 177, 414)

**WORTHINGTON** (Barnes). Built by the NPRR in 1872 in Sec. 21-140-58 and called SECOND CROSSING OF THE SHEYENNE, FIFTH SIDING, and WAHPETON all during that first year, real development began in 1874, and when the post office was established June 18, 1874 with Thomas Connors pm, it was named WORTHINGTON for townsite promoter George Worthington. Worthington is an Anglo-Saxon name meaning from the riverside. There was confusion with Worthington, MN, so on May 10, 1878 the name was changed to VALLEY CITY. (2, 3, 19, 40, 76, 275)

**WRIGHT** (Dickey). This was a rural post office established July 31, 1884 with Wilson M. Wright, who came here in 1882 from NY, as pm. Wright is an Anglo-Saxon name meaning carpenter. It was located in Mr. Wright's home, the first building in the township, in NE¼ Sec. 12-132-61, Wright Twp., twelve miles NW of Oakes. Later the post office was moved to Sec. 2-132-61, where his daughter Jessie was pm, and it was later moved back to Sec. 12-132-61 with Peter Jergenson pm. The post office closed February 28, 1901 with mail to Glover. (2, 19, 25, 40, 154, 240, 264)

**WYE** (Rolette). This was a resort platted at the NE end of Lake Upsilon in NE¼ Sec. 3-163-71, Hutchinson Twp., five miles west of Saint John. The lake at this end resembles the letter "Y" in shape, as does the Greek letter Upsilon, hence the name. It appears in county atlases of 1910 and 1928. (2, 18)

**WYLIE** (Stark). This townsite was proposed in 1917 as a station on the Dickinson, Lefor, & New Leipzig RR, which failed to be built. It was to be located in Sec. 23-137-98, Simpson Twp., about sixteen miles SW of Dickinson, near the Daglum post office, and would have been the terminus of a short spur westward from Adie. The origin of the name is unknown. (3, 18, 74)

**WYNDMERE** (Richland). This NPRR townsite was founded in 1883 in Secs. 1 & 12-132-52, Wyndmere Twp., and named for Windermere Lake, Westmorelandshire, England, whose name is derived from *wynd*, or narrow lane, and *mere*, a pool or lake. The post office was established January 7, 1884 with William F. Hilliard pm. The Soo Line RR crossed the NPRR tracks here in 1888, and a place called EAST WYNDMERE began to develop in Secs. 6 & 7-132-51, Danton Twp., in 1899. The following year most WYNDMERE buildings were moved to the new site, which adopted the old name and incorporated as a village in 1902, becoming a city in 1959 with Edwin L. Anderson (1925-1971) as mayor. The elevation is 1065, the Zip Code is 58081, and the city, known as the "Corn Capital of North Dakota," reached a peak population of 644 in 1960. (1, 2, 3, 25, 40, 77, 79, 147, 248)

# Y

**YANDELL** (Barnes). This place appears on 1940-1961 roadmaps in SW¼ Sec. 1-138-61, Meadow Lake Twp., ten miles SSW of Eckelson, and is believed to be a copyright town. The 1882 paper townsite of Clark City was about one mile SW of the location of YANDELL. (3, 34)

**YORK** (Benson). This GNRR station was built in 1883 and called WILSON'S SIDING. When development began in 1886 it was renamed for York, England by GNRR President James J. Hill. York is derived from the Latin *eboracum*, meaning the yew, an ancient sacred tree. The post office was established May 27, 1887 with Miss Cora Wilson pm. The village did not incorporate until 1954, and while the population was once said to be in excess of 300, the 1980 count was just 69. The elevation is 1618, and the Zip Code is 58386. (1, 2, 5, 18, 19, 25, 33, 40, 79, 110, 236, 257)

**YORKTOWN** (Dickey). This pioneer settlement was founded in April 1883 by settlers from NY and named EMPIRE CITY. It was located in SW¼ Sec. 17-131-61, Yorktown Twp., three miles east of Fullerton. This name was rejected by postal officials, and the post office opened as YORKTOWN on June 22, 1883 with George A. White pm. NY was named for James, Duke of York and Albany (1633-1701), later King James II of England. A population of 50 was reported in 1890, but by then the site had been bypassed by the Soo Line RR, and most of the residents were preparing to move to Fullerton. The post office closed May 15, 1905 with mail to Fullerton. (2, 10, 19, 25, 40, 45, 154, 264, 316)

**YOUNG** (Pembina). This rural post office was established March 20, 1882 with Samuel Young pm. It was located in SW¼ Sec. 32-161-56, Beaulieu Twp., one mile SE of Concrete, until 1887 when new pm Martin West moved it two miles NW to SE¼ Sec. 30-161-56. A rural community began, reporting a population of 25 in 1890, but the site failed to develop beyond that modest beginning, and the post office closed May 3, 1892 with mail to Mountain. (2, 3, 25, 33, 40, 108, 414)

**YOUNG** (Walsh). This was a farm post office established April 27, 1898 with John Matejcek pm. It was located in SE¼ Sec. 27-156-57, Norton Twp., and named for George W. Young (1866-1947), a lawyer and school board member in Park River. Mrs. Young, the former Minnie Nicklin, was the first baby born in Kensington Twp. (157-55). The post office closed July 27, 1905, being replaced on that date by the facility at the new Soo Line RR station of Lankin, two miles to the ENE. (2, 3, 18, 40, 75)

**YOUNG MAN'S BUTTE SIDING** (Stark). This NPRR siding was built in 1881 in Sec. 18-139-91, twelve miles SW of Hebron, and at first was called FIFTH SIDING. Later that year it was renamed to note the historic butte two miles to the NW, which was named to note the story of a young Indian brave of the Crow tribe who was the last survivor of a party of 106 doing battle with the Sioux. To avoid being captured, he climbed to the top of the butte, chanted his death song, and killed himself. This act was greatly revered by the Indians, who made the butte his memorial. Rufus S. Brookings came here in 1880 from ME as the first permanent white settler in the county, and established the Oakdale Farm. In 1882 the station was renamed ANTELOPE. (2, 3, 74, 245)

**YOUNG MAN'S BUTTE STATION** (Stark). This was the fifth station on the Bismarck-Fort Keogh mail route, established in 1878 in NE¼ Sec. 10-139-92, two miles SE of Richardton, and named for nearby Young Man's Butte, the highest point in Stark County. The site was used as a construction camp by NPRR work crews in 1879-1880, and once had 50-60 cabins. When railroad traffic became a regular occurrence in 1882, the mail route stations quickly lost their importance and were abandoned. (2, 3, 74, 245, 417)

**YOUNGSTOWN** (McIntosh). This was a ranch post office established November 20, 1885 with Martin H. Young, who settled here in 1884, as pm. The name is said to honor both the pm and George Young, the owner of a local cattle and horse ranch. The post office closed July 31, 1895 with mail to Norwegian, but reopened September 14, 1895 with Martin Elmer Pratt (1863-1932) pm. In 1898 Mr. Pratt became the pm at the new Soo Line RR townsite of Wishek nearby, and the YOUNGSTOWN post office closed January 24, 1899 with mail to Wishek. The site of YOUNGSTOWN in SW¼ Sec. 14-132-71, Youngstown Twp., is today the Wishek air strip. (2, 3, 40, 134, 137, 211)

**YOUNGTOWN** (Morton). This rural community was founded in 1898 when David M. Young opened a creamery in N½ Sec. 15-140-85, seven miles north of New Salem. The post office was established July 10, 1899 with Mr. Young as pm. A thriving little village developed, reporting a population as high as 75 in 1940. John Holle (1878-1968) ran the post office 1907-1948, and for many years Charles Klusman managed the Garfield Creamery Co. The site declined after this creamery was destroyed by fire on August 30, 1945. The post office closed July 15, 1953 with mail to New Salem, and the 1960 population was just 8. Unlike many such places, however, YOUNGTOWN continues to exist, although it is ignored by the current official state roadmap. Youngstown is an erroneous spelling. (1, 2, 3, 17, 18, 40, 79, 107, 109)

**YPSILANTI** (Stutsman). This NPRR station was founded in 1882 in Sec. 7-138-63, Ypsilanti Twp., and Sec. 12-138-62, Corwin Twp., although the site had been a stage stop on the Jamestown-LaMoure line as early as 1879. William Hartley Colby named it for his hometown of Ypsilanti, MI, which was named for the Greek patriot Demetrius Ypsilanti (1793-1832) by Judge Augustus Brevoort Woodward of Detroit in 1825. The post office was established May 29, 1882 with Mr. Hartley as pm. The Zip Code is 58497, and the village, which never incorporated, has generally had a population of about 100. (1, 2, 10, 18, 25, 33, 40, 46, 79, 158, 164)

**YUCCA** (Oliver). This post office was established January 26, 1901 with Carl Engler pm in SE¼ Sec. 8-141-82, Butte Twp., eight miles SE of Center near the old HEART RANCH trading post. The name was suggested by local resident Mrs. R. H. Walker for the yucca lily, or Spanish bayonet, a plant which was abundant in the area. Mr. Engler submitted the names Lawton, Presto, Coyote, Squareton, and YUCCA to postal officials, who chose the latter name. The post office operated at several locations in the area until it closed January 31, 1929 with mail to Center. It reopened September 7, 1929 with Oliver M. Whitmer pm in NE¼ Sec. 8-141-82, and three years later it moved two miles east to a townsite in NW¼ Sec. 10-141-82, on ND Highway 25. An exaggerated population of 100 was reported in 1930, while a count of just 4 was made in 1940. The pm at the townsite was Otis A. Tye (1860-1946), who closed the facility December 31, 1945 with mail to Mandan. The Yucca Rodeo, first held here in 1927, was a popular attraction for many years. (1, 2, 3, 40, 79, 121, 414)

**YULE** (Slope). Sir John Pender, a wealthy Englishman, founded the Yule Ranch in 1883 as part of his Little Missouri Land & Stock Co., sending an Irishman, Gregor Lang, to manage it. This event roughly coincided with the beginnings of the Marquis de Mores' ventures in Medora, and it is known that Mr. Lang and the Marquis became acquaintances and friends. No clear explanation of the YULE name has surfaced, although it has logically been assumed that it somehow referred to the Christmas season. Postal officials may have chosen the name, as they substituted it for the suggested name of Langrange when the post office application was submitted in 1891. The post office was established July 13, 1891 with Miss Sophia C. Lang as pm in NW¼ Sec. 22-136-104, Wilkens Twp., the site of the main ranch buildings about thirteen miles NW of Amidon near the Little Missouri River. Lincoln A. Lang, Janet Lang, and William G. Lang held the pm position until 1908, when the Langs moved to Baker, MT. The post office was then taken over by Alf Benson, who closed the facility March 31, 1910 with mail to Alpha. (2, 3, 18, 40, 80, 82, 414)

# Z

**ZACHMEIER FLATS** (Morton). This is a rural subdivision founded in 1975 in W½ Sec. 3-139-81, three miles north of Mandan on the west bank of the Missouri River. The name honors owner/developer Francis Zachmeier and notes its location in the river bottoms. (3)

**ZAHL** (Williams). This was a farm post office established April 18, 1905 with J. Erick Dohnstreick (1877-1954) pm, who named it for his uncle, Frederick Rudolph "Doc" Zahl (1865-1918), who came here in 1886, served as a county commissioner and mayor of Williston, and operated the largest ranch in ND. *Zahl* is German for number. The post office was located in NW¼ Sec. 30-159-100, Blue Ridge Twp., until 1916 when pm Zita Colwell Brannon (1885-1973) moved it about two miles west to NE¼ Sec. 26-159-101, Scoria Twp., the new GNRR townsite on the Stanley-Grenora line. The Zip Code is 58856, and a population of 250 was claimed in 1920. (2, 3, 40, 50, 79)

**ZAP** (Mercer). This NPRR townsite was founded in 1913 in SW¼ Sec. 14-144-89. The post office was established June 20, 1914 with Della Thompson, later Mrs. Frank Tysver, as pm. The elevation is 1859, the Zip Code is 58580, and the village, which incorporated in 1917 and became a city in 1966, reached a peak population of 574 in 1940. After townsite owner Jacob Kraft declined the honor of having the townsite named for himself, the name ZAP was adopted on May 29, 1913 with many explanations about its origin. Some sources say the name was transferred from a coal mining community in Scotland, while others say it was named for Edward Zapp, a prominent banker in Saint Cloud, MN. Local folklore says that a man named Zap stepped forward after Mr. Kraft withdrew his name from consideration. Others suggest that the name was coined from a town in South Russia, the homeland of many area residents, with the most likely being Zaporozh've. Converting from Cyrillic to Arabic letters, the Russian word for west is *zap*. ZAP received national attention on May 10, 1969 when several thousand college students converged on the city for the so-called "Zap-In." (1, 2, 3, 18, 33, 40, 64, 79)

**ZEELAND** (McIntosh). Christian Bauer, Friedrich Ellwein, and Heinrich Hafner came here in 1884, and a townsite was started in 1902 along the tracks of the Milwaukee Road RR in Secs. 21 & 28-129-73, Farmers-Zeeland Twp. The post office was established October 24, 1902 with Christian Hafner pm. ZEELAND was named by local Dutch settlers for Zeeland province in the Netherlands. The name means sea land, and evidence exists that the ND site was once under water, making the name quite appropriate. The elevation is 2012, the Zip Code is 58581, and a peak population of 489 was reached in 1940. ZEELAND became a village in 1906 and a city in 1946 with M. M. Braun as first mayor. Longtime Public Service Commissioner Ben Wolf was born here in 1907. (1, 2, 3, 10, 23, 40, 44, 79, 134, 136, 263)

**ZENITH** (Stark). This was a NPRR station in SW¼ Sec. 6-139-98, South Heart Twp., five miles WNW of South Heart. It served a coal mine owned by Henry Truelson, who named it for Duluth, MN, the "Zenith City." This sobriquet, officially "The Zenith City of the Unsalted Seas," originated with an 1868 speech given by Dr. Thomas Foster (1818-1903), who founded that city's first newspaper in 1869. The post office was established October 23, 1903 with Ida M. Truelson pm, and closed December 31, 1942 with mail to Belfield. The elevation is 2525. A population of 80 was reported in 1920, but the 1940 count was just 20, and the site disappeared from most maps during the 1960's. (1, 2, 3, 13, 18, 40, 74)

**ZERBA** (Pembina). This place appears on several maps circa 1905-1915 on the NPRR line just north of Bowesmont in Lincoln Twp. (160-51). It is thought to have been some sort of service facility for the locomotives. The origin of the name is unknown. (3, 432)

**ZION** (Cass). This was a rural post office established June 9, 1890 with William Henschel pm. It was located in NE¼ Sec. 13-138-53, Walburg Twp., two miles east of Chaffee, and closed September 30, 1895 with mail to Chaffee. Postal officials rejected the name Henschel, probably because of anticipated confusion with Hensel in Pembina County, after which the pm, a member of the Evangelical Association, named it for the city of the chosen people. Zion is the highest point in Jerusalem, praised for its beauty in Psalms 48, and is the utopia envisioned in Judaism. The name has had a great popularity with German people throughout the world. (1, 2, 4, 13, 40, 77, 414)

**ZION** (Richland). This is a rural community started in 1881 in Secs. 27 & 28-135-50, Colfax Twp., four miles west of Colfax. Jacob and Adolph Ista were the first settlers, and the community has revolved around the Zion Evangelical Church. (18, 147, 349)

**ZION** (Towner). This was the first settlement of Dunkard colonists in ND, and when the pioneer settlers arrived March 28, 1894, their community was referred to as the DUNKER COLONY. John R. Peters led the group from Walkerton, IN to a site eight miles west of Cando under the sponsorship of F. L. Thompson, a Cando businessman, and Max Bass, the GNRR immigration agent. Mr. Peters established the post office July 1, 1899 in NW¼ Sec. 24-158-68, Zion Twp., which he named for the township, which had been given this popular Biblical name by the colonists. A small village developed, reporting a population of 20 in 1920. Later pms were Clarence E. Joseph, Melvin R. Zentz, and James B. Griffin, but the post office closed March 31, 1921 with mail to Cando. The last remaining buildings were destroyed by fire in 1975, leaving only a cemetery to mark the site. (1, 2, 3, 4, 18, 40, 102, 414)

# County Index

Adams
Bentley
Bucyrus
Cannon
Cedar
Chandler
Chantapeta
Cook

**ADAMS COUNTY** was established March 13, 1885, and organized April 17, 1907 with the county seat being placed in Hettinger. It was named for John Quincy Adams (1848-1919), the general land and townsite agent for the Milwaukee Road RR, who was a distant relative of Presidents John and John Quincy Adams. The area is 989 square miles, and a peak population of 6,343 was reported in 1930, with a decline to just 3,584 in 1980. (3, 10, 27, 52, 57, 189, 190)

| | | | |
|---|---|---|---|
| Dolan | Leff | Schnebly |
| Gadsden | Leigh | Springbutte |
| Gilstrap | Lloyd | Stowers |
| Groat | North Lemmon | Thebes |
| Haynes | Orange | Valborg |
| Hendley | Petrel | Weightman |
| Hettinger | Pierson | Wolf Butte |
| Lake View | Reeder | Wolf Butte |

Abbotts
Alderman
Algeo
Alta
Ashtabula
Baird
Barnes
Berea
Binghamton
Birch
Booth
Brackett
Burbank
Camp Arnold
Camp Corning
Camp Johnson
Camp Libby
Camp Sheardown
Camp Smith
Camp Weiser
Carlton
Charleston
Clark City
Clive
Cuba
Daily

**BARNES COUNTY** was established January 14, 1875 and named for Alanson H. Barnes (1818-1890), Judge of the First Judicial District of Dakota Territory, who discovered a scheme by Governor John A. Burbank to enlarge his personal fortune through the misuse of government funds. The county seat was placed in Worthington, which was renamed Valley City in 1878. The area is 1,479 square miles, and a peak population of 18,804 was reported in 1930, with a decline to just 13,960 in 1980. (3, 10, 24, 27, 52, 57, 76)

| | | |
|---|---|---|
| Dazey | Leal | Seventh Siding |
| Eastedge | Litchville | Sheyenne |
| Eckelson | Logan | Sibley |
| Edna | Lowry | Sibley's Crossing |
| Ellsbury | Lucca | Sibley's Trail |
| Faust | Matteson | Resort |
| Fifth Siding | Minnie Lake | Sixth Siding |
| Fingal | Minnielake | Spur 11 |
| Fisher | Nome | Svea |
| Fourth Siding | North Central | Svenby |
| Frazier | North Valley City | Urbana |
| Gibson | Oakville | Uxbridge |
| Gorman | Odell | Valley City |
| Gragreen | Old Lucca | Valley City Station |
| Hackett | Olesburg | Station |
| Harvard | Oriska | Wahpeton |
| Hastings | Peak | Wasa |
| High Bridge | Pillsbury | Westedge |
| Hilltown | Plano | Wilma |
| Hobart | Rockport | Wimbledon |
| Ivan | Roger | Worthington |
| Kathryn | Rogers | Yandell |
| Kibby | Sanborn | |
| Koldok | Scott's | |
| Lake Eckelson | Scouten's Addition to Eckelson | |
| Lanona | Second Crossing of the Sheyenne | |

Abbottsford
Albert
Antelope
Baker
Barker
Barker
Brinsmade
Comstock
Devil's Lake Agency
Ellwood
Esmond
Fillmore
Fishlake
Flora
Fort Totten
Fort Totten
Fort Totten Station

**BENSON COUNTY** was established March 9, 1883, and organized June 9, 1883. It was named for Bertil W. Benson, a Valley City merchant and land dealer, who came to America from Norway in 1875. He was elected to the Territorial Legislature in 1883, and is said to have been instrumental in some boundary manipulations that led to the formation of this county. After some spirited competition, the county seat was placed at Minnewaukan. The area is 1,368 square miles, and a peak population of 13,327 was reached in 1930, with a decline to just 7,944 in 1980. (3, 10, 24, 27, 52, 57, 110, 255)

| | | |
|---|---|---|
| Genin | Maddock | Schuyler |
| Goa | Malloy | Spaulding's Ferry |
| Graham | McGowan's Ferry | Sully's Hill |
| Grahams Island | Minnewaukan | Tilden |
| Graham's Island | Minnewaukon | Tokio |
| Hannaford | Monterey | Totten |
| Harlow | Narrows | Viking |
| Hesper | New Chicago | Warwick |
| Iron Heart | Niles | Waterloo |
| Josephine | North Minnewaukan | West End |
| Kahler | North Viking | Wilson's Siding |
| Klara | Oberon | Wolf |
| Knox | Pendennis | Wood Lake |
| Lake Ibsen | Pleasant Lake | York |
| Lallie | Revers | |
| Larose | Rhodes | |
| Leeds | Saint Michael | |

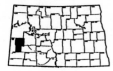

**BILLINGS COUNTY** was established February 10, 1879 during the construction of the NPRR mainline from Mandan to the west coast, and named for the President of the railroad, Frederick K. Billings (1823-1890). Its most historic era occurred during the early 1880's when such notables as the Marquis de Mores and Theodore Roosevelt resided here, although the county did not organize until 1886, with the county seat being placed in Medora. A population of 10,186 was reported in 1910, but BILLINGS COUNTY at this time included what are now Slope and Golden Valley counties. Since 1915 its area has been 1,168 square miles, and a peak population of 3,140 was reported in 1930. Its 1980 population was just 1,138, making it the least populated county in ND. (3, 10, 27, 52, 57, 81)

| | | | |
|---|---|---|---|
| Cedar Canyon | Hanly | Quinion | Summit |
| Comba | Little Missouri | Ryder | Theisen |
| Fairfield | Little Missouri Cantonment | Saint Ona | Ukraina |
| Fogarty | Medora | Scoria | |
| Fryburg | Mikkelson | Snow | |
| Gorham | Pennel Station | Sully Springs | |

**BOTTINEAU COUNTY** was established January 4, 1873, but did not organize until July 22, 1884, when the county seat was placed in Bottineau. Both the county and the city were named for Pierre Bottineau (1812-1895), a pioneer guide, hunter, interpreter, and frontiersman, who is often considered to be the first white child born in what is now ND, although in fact he was a Metis of French-Canadian and Chippewa Indian ancestry. The area is 1,699 square miles, and a peak population of 17,295 was reached in 1910, with a decline to just 9,239 in 1980. (3, 10, 27, 52, 57, 100, 101)

| | | | |
|---|---|---|---|
| Antler | France | Little Fargo | Sergius |
| Arnedo | Gardena | Lordsburg | Somber |
| Arreton | Gordon | Maltby | Souris |
| Belmar | Gravly | Markillie | Strabane |
| Bennett | Haase | Maxbass | Superior |
| Bjelland | Hewitt | McRae | Tarsus |
| Bottineau | Hunskor | Metigoshe | Tasco |
| Brand's Subdivision | Hurd | Metigoshe Park | Thor |
| Carbury | Jefferson | Newburg | Truro |
| Cordelia | Kirk | Oak Creek | Washegum |
| Dana's Grove | Knudson | Omemee | Water Tank |
| Deep | Kramer | Overly | Westhope |
| Dokken | Kuroki | Renville | West Maxbass |
| Dunning | Lake Metigoshe | Richburg | White Spur |
| East Souris | Lake Metigoshe Park | Roth | Wiley |
| Eckman | Landa | Russell | Willow City |
| Ely | Lansford | Sams | Witting |
| Faldet | Lauda | Sansahville | Woodward |
| Forfar | Lilac | Scotia | |

**BOWMAN COUNTY** was established March 8, 1883, but early settlement was virtually nonexistent, with a population of just 6 in 1890. Homesteaders began arriving about the turn of the century, and the county organized July 5, 1907 with the county seat being placed in Bowman. It is generally stated that both the city and county were named for William Bowman, a territorial legislator, although many believe that the honor belongs to Edward W. Bowman, an official of the Chicago, Milwaukee, & Puget Sound RR. The area is 1,170 square miles, and a peak population of 5,119 was reached in 1930. Since that time the county's population has been quite stable, with a population of 4,229 being reported in 1980. (3, 10, 27, 52, 57, 120)

| | | | |
|---|---|---|---|
| Adelaide | Cynthia | Haley | Ring |
| Amor | Delahunt | Ingomar | Scranton |
| Ash | Duval | Ives | Spring Valley |
| Atkinson | Eden | Kirk | Stillwater |
| Austin | Fischbein | Ladd | Swartwood |
| Badland | Fort Dilts | Langberg | Twin Buttes |
| Beaver | Galey | Lowden | Utopia |
| Bowman | Gascoyne | Paoli | Victor |
| Buffalo Springs | Graceville | Petrel | |
| Concord | Griffin | Rhame | |

**BURKE COUNTY** was created July 6, 1910 from the NW part of Ward County, and the county seat was placed in Bowbells. It was named for John Burke (1859-1937), a state legislator who served as ND Governor 1907-1913, and Treasurer of the United States under President Woodrow Wilson. Gov. Burke's statue stands in the United States Capitol in Washington, DC. The county's area is 1,121 square miles, and a peak population of 9,998 was reached in 1930, with a decline to just 3,822 in 1980. (3, 10, 27, 52, 57, 67)

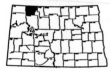

| | | | |
|---|---|---|---|
| Atcoal | Larson | Paisley | Spiral |
| Battleview | Lignite | Patterson | Spur 562 |
| Bowbells | Macroom | Perella | Stampede |
| Columbus | Myrtle | Portal | Strange Siding |
| Coteau | New Columbus | Postville | Thorson |
| Fern | Newport | Powers Lake | Vanville |
| Flaxton | Northgate | Reliance | Villa |
| Garnes | North Gate | Rennie | Woburn |
| Goss | North Gate South | Rival | |
| Hobo Kingdom | Old Columbus | Smishek | |
| Kincaid | Otter | Spencer | |

**BURLEIGH COUNTY** was established January 4, 1873, and organized September 25, 1873 with the county seat being placed at the NPRR terminus of Bismarck. It was named for Dr. Walter Atwood Burleigh (1820-1896), a physician, lawyer, Indian agent, and territorial delegate to Congress. The area is 1,648 square miles, and its population has increased with each federal census, reaching a count of 53,811 in 1980. (3, 10, 12, 27, 52, 57)

| | | | |
|---|---|---|---|
| Aetna | Camp Chaska | Isaac | Rawlings |
| Alta | Camp Greeley | Junction Switch | Regan |
| Andrews | Camp Hancock | Kirkwood | River Landing |
| Angora | Camp Schoenemann | Lakeview | Ryberg |
| Apple Creek | Camp Slaughter | Langhorne | Sather |
| Appleton | Camp Stees | Lein | Seventeenth Siding |
| Apple Valley | Canfield | Lincoln | Sibley |
| Arena | Carleton City | Linden | Sibleybutte |
| Arnold | Chapin | Livona | Sixteenth Siding |
| Baldwin | Chase | Long Lake City | Slaughter |
| Ballville | Clarke Farm | Macomber | Solitude |
| Barron | Clarke's Farm | Magnus | South Moreau |
| Bessoba | Conger | Maine | South Wilton |
| Bismarck | Crofte | McKenzie | Spring |
| Bismark | Cromwell | Menoken | Stark |
| Blaine | Cumberland | Mitchell's Post | Sterling |
| Bohan | Driscoll | Moffit | Stewartsdale |
| Brewers Corners | Dry Forks | Moltke | Still |
| Brittin | Edberg | Muddy | The Crossing |
| Brookfield | Edwinton | Naughton | Trygg |
| Burdick | Fort Lincoln | Northbrook | Vigness |
| Burleigh | Frances | Ong | Wales |
| Burleigh | Geneva | Otter Crossing | Welch Spur |
| Burleigh City | Glascock | Painted Woods | Whiskey Point |
| Burnt Creek | Grass Lake | Pelican | Wilton |
| Campagna | Grove | Phoenix | Wing |
| Camp Banks | Harriet | Pierce | Wisner |
| Camp Braden | Hay Creek | Point Pleasant | Wogansport |

**CASS COUNTY** was established January 4, 1873, and organized October 27, 1873 with the county seat being placed in Fargo. It was named for George Washington Cass (1810-1888), a nephew of onetime MI Governor Lewis Cass. George W. Cass served as President of the NPRR 1872-1875, after which he was a major investor in the famous bonanza farms run by Oliver Dalrymple. The area is 1,749 square miles, and the population has grown steadily to a peak of 88,247 in 1980, making it the most populous county in ND. (3, 10, 27, 52, 57, 77, 199)

| | | | |
|---|---|---|---|
| Absaraka | Embden | Leonard | Rochester |
| Addison | Erie | Lynchburg | Rosedale |
| Agricultural College | Erie Junction | Magnolia | Rose Valley |
| Agricultural College Spur | Everest | Malette | Rush River |
| Agricultural College Station | Fabian | Maple | Saint Benedict |
| Alice | Fairground | Maple River | Saunders |
| Amenia | Fargo | Mapleton | Saxony |
| American Settlement | Fife | Mason | Schaible |
| Argusville | Fleming | Mason Junction | Second Siding |
| Arthur | Frontier | McHench Siding | Sheyenne Stockyards |
| Aye | Gardner | Midway | Sibley |
| Ayr | Garfield | Mortimer | Sidney |
| Bedford | Gill | Myra | South West Fargo |
| Bogusville | Glacis | New Buffalo | State University Station |
| Briarwood | Goose Creek | Newman | Swan Creek |
| Buff | Goshen | Noble | Tent City |
| Buffalo | Grandin | Nolan | The Crossing |
| Camp Ambler | Greene | Norman | Third Siding |
| Camp Stevens | Haggart | Norpak | Tower City |
| Canaan | Haggarts | North River | Trysil |
| Canfield | Haggart's | Northview | Vance |
| Casselton | Hartley | Oatland | Wadeson |
| Casstown | Harwood | Osgood | Walden |
| Centralia | Hickson | Osterdahl Settlement | Warren |
| Chaffee | Hill | Page | Watson |
| Chase | Holy Cross | Page City | West Comstock |
| Cotter | Horace | Persis | West Fargo |
| Cotters | Horace Station | Petersen | West Fargo |
| Cowan | Howes | Pinkham | West Fargo Industrial Park |
| Dakota City | Hunter | Prairie Rose | West Perley |
| Dalrymple | Hyland Park | Prosper | Wheatland |
| Dartmoor | Jenksville | Raymond | Wilder |
| Davenport | Kego | Reed | Wild Rice |
| Delno | Kibby | Reile's Acres | Williams |
| Dunlop | Kibbyville | Riceville | Willow Creek |
| Durbin | Kindred | Ripon | Woods |
| Eldred | Kruegersville | Rita | Zion |
| Elgin | Langers | River Bend | |
| Elizabeth | Larson | Riverdale | |
| Embden | Leeches | Riverside | |

**CAVALIER COUNTY** was established January 4, 1873, and organized July 8, 1885 with the county seat placed in Langdon. It is generally assumed that it was named for Charles Turner Cavileer (1818-1902), a well known politician and promoter from Pembina, with a Gallicized spelling. The area is 1,513 square miles, and a peak population of 15,659 was reached in 1910, with a decline to just 7,636 in 1980. (3, 10, 27, 52, 57, 216)

Alma
Alsen
Ambro
Austin
Bac
Banner
Beaulieu
Brickmine
Byron
Calio
Calvin
Cavalier
Clyde
Cypress
Daniels
Dresden
Easby
East Osnabrock
Elgin
Elkwood
Ellerton

Elmpoint
Empire
Etna
Fairview
Gertrude
Glenila
Grace
Gresham
Hanna
Hannah
Homen
Hove Mobile Park
Irene
Klein
Langdon
Lemon
Loma
Mack
Maida
Marie
McHugh

McLean
McLean Corners
Milton
Mona
Morton
Moscow
Mount Carmel
Mount Moriah
Mowbray
Munich
Nekoma
Noracong
Numedahl
Olga
Osnabrock
Polar
Portland Pembina Cement
    Company
Ridgefield
Romfo
Rosa Lake

Rosehill
Rushlake
Saint Pierre
Sarles
Seven Lakes
Soper
Stilwell
Storlie
Strate
Tipperary
Trier
Union
Valmont
Vang
Vera
Wales
Weaver
Woodbridge

**DICKEY COUNTY** was established March 5, 1881, and organized the following year with the county seat placed in Ellendale. It was named for Alfred M. Dickey (1846-1901), a prominent land dealer who served as the first Lt. Governor of ND. Others claim it was named for Valley City attorney George H. Dickey or a somewhat elusive railroad official. The area is 1,144 square miles, and a peak population of 10,877 was reached in 1930, with a decline to just 6,976 in 1970. The 1980 population was 7,207. (3, 10, 27, 52, 57, 154, 158)

Albertha
Baldwin
Bear Creek
Boynton
Bushtown
Center
Centralia
Centropolis
Clement
Coldwater
Coraton
Crescent Hill
DeCora
Duane
Dundas
Eaton
Eddville

Ellendale
Emma
Empire City
Forbes
Fullerton
Glover
Guelph
Hillsdale
Hudson
Janet
Kaytown
Keyes Spur
Keystone
Keystone City
Kilbernie
Lorraine
Ludden

Mahonay Spur
Maple River Tank
Menasha Center
Merricourt
Millwood
Monango
Monango Transfer
Nelvik
Newton
Nickols Crossing
North Hecla
Norway
Oakes
Old Ludden
Ottawa
Pehl Spur
Pierson

Port Emma
Port Emma
Potsdam
Potts
Riverdale
Silverleaf
Spring Hill
Thatcher
Thatcherville
Ticeville
Ulness
Westboro
Weston
Wirch
Wolff
Wright
Yorktown

**DIVIDE COUNTY** was approved by a vote of the people on November 8, 1910, and organized December 9, 1910. The county seat was temporarily placed in Crosby, with this location officially approved in the election of 1912. The name was suggested by Williston attorney George A. Gilmore to note its division from Williams County, although some state that the name notes the Coteau du Missouri which runs through the county and is a north-south continental divide. The area is 1,303 square miles, and a peak population of 9,637 was reached in 1920, with a decline to just 3,494 in 1980. (3, 10, 27, 50, 52, 57, 73)

Alkabo
Ambrose
Bounty
Buttercup
Clinton
Colgan
Crosby
Daneville
Divide
East Westby
Ella

Fertile
Fortier
Fortuna
Garfield
Happy
Imperial
Juno
Kermit
Knoff
Lee
McCullough

Montrose
Noonan
Nora
Norge
Norum
Ogden
Old Crosby
Old Westby
Paddington
Paulson
Plumer

Rolson
Rudser
Sandlie
Skermo
Snook
Stady
Tansem
Thorson
Upland
Westby
Whiteaker

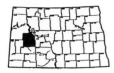

**DUNN COUNTY** was established March 9, 1883 and named by territorial legislator Eratus A. Williams for John Piatt Dunn (1839-1917), a prominent pioneer of Bismarck. The county went through a number of boundary changes before being organized January 18, 1908 with the county seat located in Manning, a small inland community which continues to survive challenges for the honor. The area is 2,068 square miles, and a peak population of 9,566 was reached in 1930, with a decline to just 4,627 in 1980. (3, 10, 24, 27, 52, 57)

Acorn
Bailey
Baldt
Brooks
Collins
Connolly
Dodge
Dunn
Dunn Center
Edgar
Elmgrove
Emerson

Fayette
Glen Laurel
Gorder
Halliday
Hanks
Harte
Hartinger
Hirschville
Independence
June
Kildeer
Killdeer

Kniferiver
Knife River
Libby Butte
Loring
Manning
Marshall
Melby
Mohawk
Mountain Range Estates
New Hradec
Northrup
Nuita

Oakdale
Paulson
Rand
Renville
Rockspring
Saint Martin
Sennef
Twin Buttes
Vada
Werner
Whetstone
Willmen

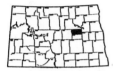

**EDDY COUNTY** was established in a special election on March 31, 1885 when voters chose to split from Foster County, and organized April 27, 1885 with the county seat being placed in New Rockford. It was named for Fargo banker and developer Ezra B. Eddy (1830-1885), who had recently died. The area is 651 square miles, and a peak population of 6,493 was reached in 1920, with a decline to just 3,554 in 1980. (3, 10, 27, 41, 52, 57, 112, 119, 272)

Barker
Brantford
Brenner
Buell
Dallas
Divide

Dundas
Dunn
Dunn's Creek
Eddy
Ferdinand
Freeborn

Garrison
Gates
Hamar
Morris
Munster
New Rockford

Sheyenne
Tiffany
Tomlinson

**EMMONS COUNTY** was established February 10, 1879 and named by territorial legislator Erastus A. Williams for James A. Emmons (1843-1919), a Missouri River boat captain who came to Bismarck in 1872 as the post trader at Camp Hancock. The county organized November 9, 1883 with the county seat being placed in Williamsport. As settlers moved into the southern part of the county a move was made to relocate the court house to a more centralized location, and in the general election of 1898 the new townsite of Linton was chosen, with the actual move occurring in 1899. The area is 1,546 square miles, and a peak population of 12,467 was reached in 1930, with a decline to just 5,877 in 1980. (3, 10, 24, 27, 52, 57, 66)

Armstrong
Ashgrove
Barker
Bobtown
Braddock
Brennan's Landing
Brofy
Buchanan
Casselman
Campbell
Camp Shields
Colville
Corbinsville
Dale
Dakem
Dana
Danbury

East Linton
Elzas
Emmonsburg
Ethel
Exeter
Fremont
Gayton
Gayton Landing
Glanavon
Glencoe
Godkin
Grassna
Hague
Hampton
Hartford
Hazelton
Hazen

Hebbard
Hoe
Hull
Kertzman
Kintyre
Kuntz
Kurtzman
Larvik
Larvik
Linton
Livona
Marie
Mars Junction
Mastel
Midway
Miriam
North Glanavon

Omio
Roop
Rosental
Saint Michael's
Selz
South Prairie
Stafford
Strasburg
Tell
Tempelton
Temvik
Tirsbol
Waylin
Westfield
Williamsport
Winchester
Winona

**FOSTER COUNTY** was established January 4, 1873 and organized October 11, 1883 with the county seat being placed in Carrington. It was named for James S. Foster, who came to Mitchell (now South Dakota) in 1864, and served as Commissioner of Immigration for Dakota Territory. The area is 644 square miles, and a peak population of 6,353 was reached in 1930, with a decline to just 4,611 in 1980. (3, 10, 27, 52, 57, 97)

Annie
Barlow
Bordulac
Camp Forbes
Camp Hall
Camp Kimball
Camp Olin
Carrington

Chaffees
Chaffee Spur
Chihaun
Cline
Ewen
Farquer
Garland
Glenfield

Grace City
Guptill
Haven
Juanita
Larrabee
Lemert
Maria
McHenry

Melby
Melville
Millers
Millers Spur
Newport
Pleasantview
Ross
West Bordulac

**GOLDEN VALLEY COUNTY** came into existance on November 11, 1912 when voters chose to separate from Billings County, placing the county seat at Beach. The name was largely promotional, and noted the golden fields of grass and wheat in the area. The "valley" is thought to have been purely euphonic, as the local terrain is actually a high plateau. The Golden Valley Land and Cattle Co. was a major land owner in the county, and some claim the county was named for the company. The area is 1,014 square miles, and a peak population of 4,832 was reported in 1920, with a decline to just 2,391 in 1980. (3, 10, 27, 52, 57, 80)

Alpha
Andrews
Arvid
Beach
Bonnie View
Brenizer

Buelsdale
Burkey
Chama
DeMores
East Carlyle
Golva

Mosher
Rafteree
Rider
Riders
Sentinel Butte
Strahon

Thelen
Trotters
Waldon
Westerheim
Williams

**GRAND FORKS COUNTY** was established January 4, 1873, and organized March 2, 1875 with the county seat being placed in the city of Grand Forks. Both the city and the county were named to note the confluence of the Red Lake River and the Red River of the North, which early French explorers had called *Les Grandes Fourches*. The area is 1,438 square miles, and the population has increased with each federal census to a high of 66,100 in 1980. (3, 10, 27, 52, 57, 69)

Aae
Arvilla
Bachelor's Grove
Barker's Station
Belleville
Bean
Bellevue
Bentru
Bjorn
Blakely's Crossing
Blooming
Bolack
Bushnell Park
Cable
Camp Sill
Chester
Christiani
Clinton
Dahl
Danish Settlement ·
Edisons
Emerado
Enerson

Fairlawn
Fergus
Flushing
Gilby
Grand Forks
Grand Forks Air Force Base
Grand Forks Junction
Hall
Hannah Junction
Hanson
Hegton
Holmes
Honeyford
Hubbard Pit
Inkster
Johnstown
Kellys
Kelly's Station
Kempton
Lakewood
Laramore
Larimore
Levant

Logan Center
Mackinock
Manvel
Mathie
McCanna
McRae
Meckinock
Mekinock
Merrifield
Milan
Moraine
New York Settlement
Niagara
Northwood
Norton
Ojata
Orange
Orr
Park River Junction
Pearson
Perth
Pilot
Powell

Reno
Reynolds
Schurmeier
Shawnee
South Washington
Stewart
Stickney
Stoughton
Strabane
Thompson
Thomson's Grove
Turtle River
Turtle River Station
University
University Station
Walle
Water Tank
West Oslo
Whynot
Woodville

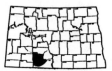

**GRANT COUNTY** was approved by voters in the November 7, 1916 general election, and officially separated from Morton County on November 25, 1916 with the county seat being placed in Carson. It was named for General Ulysses Simpson Grant (1822-1885), Commander of the Union forces during the Civil War, and President of the United States 1869-1877. It is the newest county in ND, and the only one which has a namesake in SD. The area is 1,666 square miles, and a peak population of 10,134 was reached in 1930, with a decline to just 4,274 in 1980. (3, 10, 27, 52, 57)

Andersen
Berlin
Birdsall
Brisbane
Cannon Ball
Carl
Carson
Dogtooth
Elgin
Elm
Esther
Fleak
Freda
Green Valley

Heart
Heil
Howe
Janesburg
Kaiser
Kary
Kenyon
Kuck
Landon
Lark
Larkee
Lawther
Lawther
Leipzig

Leith
Miner
New Leipzig
Noel
North Carson
Odessa
Old Carson
Old Leipzig
Otterberg
Paradise
Pearce
Pretty Rock
Raleigh
Saint Gertrude's

Saint Joseph
Sanders
Schaller
Selma
Shanley
Shields
Stebbins
Stevenson
Thian
Vienna
Wade
Worms

**GRIGGS COUNTY** was established February 18, 1881, and organized June 16, 1882 with the county seat being placed in Hope. This townsite was destined to become part of the newly-created Steele County, so on November 7, 1882 the court house was moved to Cooperstown. The county was named for Alexander Griggs (1838-1903), a Red River steamboat captain and prominent pioneer of Grand Forks. The area is 714 square miles, and a peak population of 7,402 was reported in 1920, with a decline to just 3,714 in 1980. (3, 10, 27, 52, 57, 199, 283, 284, 341)

Binford
Blooming Prairie
Camp Atchison
Camp Burt
Camp Pope
Camp Rusten
Cooperstown
Cottonwood
Durham

Fairview
Florence
Gallatin
Gunderson
Hannaford
Helena
Jessie
Karnak
Lewis

Lovell
Lybeck
Mail Station
Mardell
Mellemville
Montclair
Mose
Ottawa
Pleasantview

Revere
Romness
Shepard
Sutton
Walum
West Prairie
Willow
Willows

**HETTINGER COUNTY** was established March 9, 1883, and organized April 17, 1907 with the county seat being placed in Mott. Territorial legislator Erastus A. Williams chose the name to honor his father-in-law, Mathias K. Hettinger (1810-1890) of Freeport, IL. The area is 1,135 square miles, and a peak population of 8,796 was reached in 1930, with a decline to just 4,275 in 1980. (3, 10, 27, 52, 57, 178, 385)

| | | | |
|---|---|---|---|
| Acklin | Coalbank | Jordan | Roper |
| Alden | Coal City | Kennedy | Rosenfeld |
| Alton | Edton | Liberty | Schutz |
| Bentley | Graber | Mayflower | Spalding |
| Berry | Havelock | Millizen | Stanwick |
| Budapest | Hettinger | Mott | Strehlow |
| Burt | Hoosier | New England | Thirtymile |
| Cedar | Horswill | New England City | Watrous |
| Chase | Howser | Opgrand | Willa |
| Church | Inez | Regent | |

**KIDDER COUNTY** was established January 4, 1873, and organized March 22, 1881 with the county seat being placed at Steele. It was named for Jefferson Parish Kidder (1815-1883), a lawyer who served as a state legislator, Attorney General, and Lt. Governor in his native VT, was a state legislator in MN, and then served as the Dakota Territorial delegate to Congress and as an Associate Justice on the territorial Supreme Court. The area is 1,377 square miles, and a peak population of 8,031 was reached in 1930, with a decline to just 3,833 in 1980. (3, 10, 24, 27, 52, 57, 59) ← *BIBLIOGRAPHY*

| | | | |
|---|---|---|---|
| Bostonia | Dexter | Long Lake | Roundlake |
| Bunker | Fifteenth Siding | McGuire | Sifton |
| Camp Grassick | Fourteenth Siding | Moyersville | Steele |
| Camp Kennedy | Frettim | Mulberry | Steele's Farm |
| Camp Pfaender | Geneva | Nellie | Tappen |
| Camp Sibley | Grouse | Nelson | Thirteenth Siding |
| Camp Whitney | Hasselbrock | New Mulberry | Troy Farm Siding |
| Camp Williston | Heffernan | New York Town | Tuttle |
| Carlson | Hinger | Peters | Twelfth Siding |
| Carlsondale | Kidder | Pettibone | Wallace |
| Crystal Springs | Ladoga | Portner | Williams |
| Crystalsprings | Lake Williams | Pursian | Wilson |
| Dawson | Lamoine | Rankin | |
| Dell | Langedahl | Remick | |
| DeMorris | Lendrum | Robinson | |

**LaMOURE COUNTY** was established January 4, 1873, and organized October 22, 1881 with the county seat being placed in Grand Rapids. In 1886 the court house was relocated to the city of LaMoure, which like the county was named for Judson LaMoure (1839-1918), a prominent territorial and state legislator. The area is 1,147 square miles, and a peak population of 11,564 was reached in 1920, with a decline to just 6,473 in 1980. (3, 10, 27, 52, 57, 144)

| | | | |
|---|---|---|---|
| Adrian | Elmo | Jud | Porterville |
| Alfred | Floyd | Kulm | Russell |
| Benson | Fox | Lakeview | Saint George |
| Benson Corners | Franklin | LaMoure | Saratoga |
| Berlin | Grand Rapids | Litchville | Valley Junction |
| Colben | Griswold | Marion | Verona |
| Deasam | Gunthorp | Matson | Wano |
| Deisem | Hamlet | Medberry | West LaMoure |
| Dickey | Hettinger | Medbery | Winal |
| Dickey's Landing | Ibsen | Newburg | |
| Edgeley | Independence | Nortonville | |
| Edgeley Junction | Ione | Oakes Junction | |

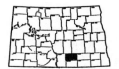

**LOGAN COUNTY** was established January 4, 1873, and organized September 1, 1884 with the fledgling townsite of Napoleon designated as the county seat. On January 17, 1899 the court house was technically relocated to King, which had defeated Napoleon for the honors in the 1898 general election, but the results of this election were overturned by the courts, and Napoleon was restored as the county seat on September 30, 1899. The county was named for Gen. John Alexander Logan (1826-1886), a Civil War veteran from IL who served as a Congressman and U. S. Senator, and was the unsuccessful Republican candidate for Vice President in 1884. Counties in CO, KS, NE, and OK are also named in his honor. The ND county has an area of 1,003 square miles, and reached a peak population of 8,089 in 1930, with a decline to just 3,493 in 1980. (3, 10, 27, 52, 57, 116)

| | | | |
|---|---|---|---|
| Beaver Creek | Fredonia | King | Peters |
| Beaver Lake | Fryar | Lehr | Richville |
| Belden | Gackle | Lowry | Saint Anthony |
| Belden | Gage City | Minister | Saint Boniface |
| Burnstad | Guyson | Napoleon | Steidl |
| Denevitz | Hackney | Paul | Welch |

**McHENRY COUNTY** was established January 4, 1873, and organized February 19, 1885. The pioneer settlement of Villard had claimed to be the county seat as early as 1884, but county organizers awarded the court house to Scriptown, which consisted of little more than a few log buildings. In 1886 the county seat was moved to the new GNRR townsite of Towner. The county was named for James McHenry, a pioneer resident of Vermillion, in what is now SD. The area is 1,890 square miles, and a peak population of 17,637 was reached in 1910, with a decline to just 7,745 in 1980. (3, 10, 27, 52, 57, 412)

| | | | |
|---|---|---|---|
| Alta | Falsen | Midway | Saline |
| Amy | Funston | Milroy | Scriptown |
| Anamoose | Genoa | Milroy | Sedan |
| Balfour | Granville | Mouse River | Shigley |
| Bantry | Gravel Pit | Mouse River | Simcoe |
| Bergen | Guthrie | Newport | Souris City |
| Berwick | Hackett Falls | Nichols | Star |
| Brushlake | Henrico | Nichols | Towner |
| Buffalo Lodge Park | Hoosier | Nomad | Upham |
| Carder | Kaluga | Norfolk | Velva |
| Caughey | Karlsruhe | Norwich | Verendrye |
| Chicota | Kief | Oakland | Villard |
| Cliffdale | Kongsberg | Olivia | Voltaire |
| Deepriver | Lane | Owens | Wagar |
| Deering | Lilla | Pendroy | Wallace |
| Denbigh | Linusville | Pratt | Water Tank |
| Dogden | Martha | Rangeley | Wines |
| Drake | Meadow | Riga | |
| Ely | Meddow | Rising | |

**McINTOSH COUNTY** was established March 9, 1883, and organized October 4, 1884 with the county seat being placed in Hoskins, at the time the only settlement in the county. In November 1887 the court house was moved to the new Soo Line RR townsite of Ashley. The county was named for E. H. McIntosh, a prominent territorial legislator. The area is 1,003 square miles, and a peak population of 9,621 was reached in 1930, with a decline to just 4,800 in 1980. (3, 10, 27, 52, 57, 211)

| | | | |
|---|---|---|---|
| Ashley | Hellwig | Lowell Valley | Rotterdam |
| Bensville | Hoskins | Ludwig Heins Corner | Venturia |
| Bischof | Jewell | Meidinger | Wishek |
| Coldwater | Kassel | Norwegian | Youngstown |
| Danzig | Koeppel | Oddena | Zeeland |
| Giedt | Lehr | Ostrem | |
| Gohring | Lowell | Pascal | |

**McKENZIE COUNTY** was established March 8, 1883, and named by Erastus A. Williams for the powerful and somewhat notorious Bismarck politician, Alexander McKenzie (1856-1922), who was a major force in the affairs of the Dakotas throughout his lifetime. The county organized in 1905, and the first county seat was at what is usually called White House, near the Stroud post office. This action was never officially recognized, and on May 13, 1905 the court house was awarded to Alexander. Residents of Schafer managed to gain the county seat in 1906, but after the GNRR abandoned their plans to build their line through here to New Rockford, this townsite declined, and on June 1, 1941 the county seat was moved to Watford City. The area is 2,847 square miles, making the county the largest in ND. A peak population of 9,709 was reached in 1930, and after dropping to just 6,127 in 1970, the population has rebounded to 7,132 in 1980 largely on the strength of energy development. (3, 10, 27, 52, 57, 226, 229)

| | | | |
|---|---|---|---|
| Alexander | Dore | Juniper | Schafer |
| Almira | Earl | Keene | Searing |
| Arnegard | East Fairview | Kinsley | Seneschal |
| Banks | East Sidney | Leakey | Shafer |
| Banks | Elidah | Loyal | Skaar |
| Beicegel | Elk Landing | Mandaree | Spearinville |
| Benniepier | Elsworth | Mary | Squaw Gap |
| Berg | Estes | Maynard | Stroud |
| Bicycle | Farland | McKenzie | Tobacco Garden |
| Bluebell | Fort Gilbert | Moline | Tobacco Garden |
| Blueshale | Fort Henry | Nameless | Union Center |
| Camp Barbour | Glasser | Pembroke | Watford |
| Cartwright | Goodall | Prairie Valley | Watford City |
| Cathmere | Grant | Ragged Buttes | White City |
| Catlin | Grassy Butte | Rawson | White House |
| Charbonneau | Green | Rothville | Wilbur |
| Charlson | Hardy Beet Siding | Rosseland | Williams |
| Cherry | Joe | Ruby | |
| Croff | Johnsons Corners | Sanford | |

**McLEAN COUNTY** was established March 8, 1883, and organized November 1, 1883 with the county seat being placed in Washburn. It was named for John A. McLean (1849-1916), the mayor of Bismarck at the time whose son, Harry, became a famous builder of bridges and dams, and donated the statue of the pioneers on the mall of the State Capitol. The area is 2,289 square miles, and a peak population of 18,824 was reached in 1950 during the construction of the Garrison Dam, with a decline to 11,251 in 1970. The count increased to 12,288 in 1980 as the county experienced growth with the energy industry boom. (3, 10, 27, 52, 57)

| | | | |
|---|---|---|---|
| Aldridge | Elbowoods | Max | Scatter Village |
| American City | Elm Point | Maxwell | Shell Creek |
| Amundsville | Emmet | McComb | Sig |
| Arickaree | Endres | Mercer | Silver City |
| Armstrong | Energy | Merida | Sitka |
| Arvidson | Erickson | Meriden | Snake |
| Basto | Ethel | Miller | Snake |
| Batesville | Falconer | Minden | Spring Coulee |
| Bayfield | Falkirk | Mowrer | Stenvick |
| Benedict | Fort Atkinson | New Fort Berthold | Strawberry Lake |
| Big Bend | Fort Berthold | New Jerusalem | Sverdrup |
| Bitumia | Fort Berthold | Nishu | The Slide |
| Blackwater | Fort Mandan | Nudelman | Tough Timber |
| Butte | Fort Stevenson | Old Coal Harbor | Turtle Creek |
| Byers | Fort Stevenson | Old Fort Stevenson | Turtle Lake |
| Casey | Gady | Old Garrison | Turtle Valley |
| Chitutah | Garrison | Oscar | Underwood |
| Coal Harbor | Gateway | Pace | Victoria |
| Coal Lake | Greatstone | Park | Walkertown |
| Coleharbor | Hancock | Perley | Wanamaker |
| Conkling | Hiddenwood | Raub | Washburn |
| Cremerville | Huberton | Reed | Weller |
| Custer | Hudson Colony | Riverdale | Wellerville |
| Dakota City | Ingersoll | Riverdale Junction | White Shield |
| Darling | Jeanette | Roach | Wilton |
| Dillingham | Jeannette | Robinson | Winston Landing |
| Dogden | Johnson | Roney | Wiprud |
| Dogden | Kapeto | Roosevelt | |
| Douglas | Lucky Mound | Roseglen | |
| Eastman | Malcolm | Ruso | |

**MERCER COUNTY** was established January 14, 1875 and named by Erastus A. Williams for William Henry Harrison Mercer (1844-1901), a well known pioneer of the Missouri River valley who came to Dakota Territory in 1869. The county organized August 22, 1884 and placed the county seat in Stanton, which has survived several challenges from larger, more centrally located cities in the county. The area is 1,042 square miles, and a peak population of 9,611 was reached in 1930. By 1970 the population had declined to just 6,175, but the county was at the center of energy development in the 1970's, and the 1980 count increased by more than 50% to 9,421. (3, 9, 10, 27, 52, 57, 232)

| | | | |
|---|---|---|---|
| Alderin | Farrington | Krem | Republic |
| Arcis | Fort Clark | Kronthal | Ronda |
| Beaumont | Fort Defiance | Mannhaven | Slaton |
| Benton | Fort Lewis | Mercer | Sofia |
| Beulah | Fort Lisa | Mercer City | Stanton |
| Big Bend | Fort Primeau | Morgansville | Stoeltington |
| Bowdish | Fort Tilton | Naesatz | Thomas |
| Broncho | Fort Vanderburgh | Neu Gleuckstahl | Tilton's Fort |
| Cambridge | Friedenthal | Olanta | Tilton's Post |
| Causey | Gilma | Old Fort Clark | Troy |
| Deapolis | Goldenvalley | Old Stanton | Truax |
| Defiance | Hazen | Pick City | Zap |
| Dixboro | Hub | Red Spring | |
| Expansion | Kasmer | Ree | |

**MORTON COUNTY** was established January 8, 1873 and named for Oliver Hazard Perry Throck Morton (1823-1877), a U. S. Senator and Governor of IN. The county organized February 28, 1881 and placed the county seat in Mandan. The area is 1,933 square miles, although prior to World War I the county had been the largest in the state, including present-day Grant and Sioux counties. The 1910 population of 25,289 was, in effect, a total for these three counties. Since assuming its present boundaries in 1916, the county has maintained a steady population of about 20,000, although recent growth for the city of Mandan resulted in a 1980 population of 24,951. (3, 10, 27, 52, 57)

| | | | |
|---|---|---|---|
| Almont | Flasher | Lincoln | Rural |
| Baby Mine | Fort Abraham Lincoln | Little Heart | Saint Anthony |
| Bahm | Fort McKeen | Little Heart | Saint Vincent |
| Barnes | Fort Rice | Littleheart | Salem |
| Berrier | Fort Rice | Little Heart | Schmalz |
| Bethel | Fort Rice Landing | Lynwood | Schmidt |
| Blue Grass | Fort Sauerkraut | Lyons | Second Siding |
| Bluegrass | Fourth Station | Mandan | Sedalia |
| Bly's Mine | Gall | Mantahni | Shantapeda |
| Breien | Geck | Marmot | Shoofly |
| Burgess | Glenullen | Monte's Rancheros | Sims |
| Camp Greene | Glen Ullin | Morton | Spur |
| Cannon | Glenullin | New Salem | Square Butte |
| Cannon Ball | Grinnell | Nineteenth Siding | Stevenson |
| Carbon | Gwyther | North Almont | Stone |
| Cold Spring | Hailstone Creek Station | Odense | Strain |
| County Line | Harmon | Old Fort Abraham Lincoln | Sturgis |
| Creamery | Haymarsh | Old Fort McKeen | Sunny |
| Crown Butte | Heart River Station | Old Fort Rice | Sunnyside |
| Curlew | Hebron | Ormiston | Sweet Briar |
| Cushman | Hobson | Parkin | Sweetbriar |
| Cynch | Huff | Parkin | Sylvan |
| Dayton | Inverlac | Prohibition City | Timmer |
| Dengate | Iowa City | Remick | Warnton |
| DeVaul | Jennie | Rippel | Warren's Banks Station |
| Diamond | Judson | Riverview Heights | West Acres |
| Duke Spur | Knife River | Rock Haven | West Flasher |
| Eagles Nest | Kovash | Rock Haven Heights | Youngtown |
| Fallon | Kurtz | Rosebud | Zachmeier Flats |
| Finch | Lidstrom | Roughrider Estates | |

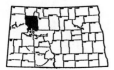

**MOUNTRAIL COUNTY** was established January 4, 1873, and most early references show it as "Mountraille", the correct spelling the name of its namesake, Joseph Mountraille, a Metis voyageur, scout, and frontiersman. A petition to organize the county from Ward County was filed March 29, 1907, but various delays resulted in the county not officially coming into existance until the election of November 8, 1910, with Stanley as the county seat. The area is 1,914 square miles, and a peak population of 13,544 was reached in 1930, with a decline to just 7,663 in 1980. (3, 10, 27, 52, 57, 72)

| | | | |
|---|---|---|---|
| Amanda | Fort Kipp | New Sanish | Shell |
| Baskin | Fort Maneury | Newtown | Smith |
| Belair | Grenada | New Town | Smithville |
| Belden | Hall's Trading Post | Nomad | Sorkness |
| Blaisdell | Hanley | Palda | Stanley |
| Blenheim | Hannons | Palermo | Stanley Line Junction |
| Brookbank | Henley | Parshall | Steele |
| Chester | Hills | Pearl | Sweden |
| Chida | Indiana | Peerless | Tagus |
| Chilcot | Jardine | Plaza | Van Hook |
| Coulee | Kipp's Post | Prairie Junction | Wabek |
| Delta | Leland | Purdon | Wallace |
| Dymond | Lostwood | Roness | Wassaic |
| Ellefson | Lundsvalley | Ross | Welby |
| Elton | Manitou | Rouen | White Earth |
| Epworth | Mansfield | Sanish | Winans |

**NELSON COUNTY** was established March 9, 1883, and organized June 9, 1883 with the county seat being placed in Lakota. It was named for Nelson E. Nelson (1830-1913), who came to Pembina as a customs inspector in 1869, and was the father-in-law of Judson LaMoure. The area is 1,008 square miles, and a peak population of 10,362 was reached in 1920, with a decline to just 5,241 in 1980. (3, 10, 27, 52, 57, 124, 127, 420)

| | | | |
|---|---|---|---|
| Adler | Finland | Michigan | Rector |
| Aneta | Harrisburg | Michigan City | Ruby |
| Ashem | Harrisburgh | Moen | Rugh |
| Baconville | Hoiland | Nelson | Sardis |
| Bolken | Jacobson | Norval | Sarnia |
| Bue | Kloten | Old McVille | Sogn |
| Coryell | Lakota | Osago | Stump |
| Crosier | Lee | Ottofy | Stump Lake |
| Dahlen | Liberal | Parkhurst | Tolna |
| Dayou | Mapes | Pekin | Wamduska |
| Deehr | McVille | Pelto | Whitman |
| Dissmore | McVille Station | Petersberg | |
| East Michigan City | Melville | Petersburg | |

**OLIVER COUNTY** was established March 12, 1885, and organized May 18, 1885 with the county seat being placed in Raymond, a Missouri River townsite that was virtually nonexistent. Attempts at developing this site proved unsuccessful, and in 1888 the court house was relocated to the nearby settlement of Sanger. As homesteaders filed on the interior land, efforts began to move the county seat to a more centrally located site, and on November 4, 1902 the court house was moved to the new townsite of Center. The county was named for Harry S. Oliver (1855-1909), a territorial legislator from Lisbon. The area is 720 square miles, and a peak population of 4,425 was reached in 1920, with a decline to just 2,322 in 1970. Energy development resulted in a slight growth to 2,504 in 1980. (3, 10, 27, 52, 57, 121)

| | | | |
|---|---|---|---|
| Aplin | Darmstadt | Heart Ranch | Price |
| Aster | Ellis | Hensler | Raymond |
| Bentley | Evans | Hult | Rhein |
| Butte | Fort Clark | Klein | Sanger |
| Center | Gaines | Lone Tree | Seroco |
| Churchtown | Gainesville | Mathias | Silo |
| Cordes | Germantown | Nisbet | Wells |
| County Line | Hannover | Otter Creek | Yucca |
| Daisy | Harmon | Pinto | |

**PEMBINA COUNTY**, the cradle of civilization in ND, was officially established January 9, 1867, although it had existed in concept for more than twenty years at that time, originally as a part of Minnesota Territory. The county organized August 12, 1867 with the county seat being placed in Pembina. Both the city and the county bear a corruption of the Chippewa word *anepeminan*, meaning summer berry in reference to the cranberries growing in the area. On December 15, 1911 the court house was moved to the more centrally located city of Cavalier. The area is 1,124 square miles, and a peak population of 17,869 was reached in 1900, with a decline to 10,386 in 1980. (3, 10, 27, 52, 57, 108, 366)

| | | | |
|---|---|---|---|
| Akra | Douglas Point | Kelvin | Pittsburg |
| Alma | Drayton | Langton | Pittsburgh |
| Backoo | Ernest | Leroy | Point Michael |
| Baltimore | Eyford | Leroy's Trading Post | Prattford |
| Bathgate | Fleece | Leyden | Ragus |
| Bay Center | Fort Daer | Little Lake | Riviere Pembinati |
| Bay Centre | Fort George H. Thomas | Little Salt | Rome |
| Bayview | Fort Gibraltar | McArthur | Saint Joseph |
| Beaulieu | Fort Paubian | McConnell | Saint Thomas |
| Boundary Line | Fort Pembina | Midland | Shepard |
| Bowesmont | Gardar | Mountain | Smuggler's Point |
| Bowesmount | Garder | Mugford | South Pembina |
| Bruce | Glasston | Neche | Stokesville |
| Camp Comfort | Grund | New Saint Joseph | Svold |
| Canton | Hair Hills | Ninth Siding | Thexton |
| Carlisle | Hallson | Nowesta | Tongue |
| Carl's Point | Hamilton | Old Fort Pembina | Tyner |
| Cavalier | Hastings Landing | Ottenton | Vik |
| Cavileer | Hensel | Park | Walhalla |
| Chaboillez Post | Huron City | Parktown | Welford |
| Concrete | Hyde Park | Pembina | Westview |
| Cooley | Hydepark | Pembina House | Young |
| Crystal | International Boundary | Pembina River | Zerba |
| Dewey | Johnson's Siding | Pennington | |
| Dimock | Joliette | Pettit | |

**PIERCE COUNTY** was established March 11, 1887, and organized April 11, 1889 with the county seat being placed in Rugby. It was named for Gilbert Ashville Pierce (1829-1901), a Civil War veteran and newspaperman, who served as Governor of Dakota Territory 1884-1887, and later was a U. S. Senator and the Minister to Portugal. The area is 1,053 square miles, and a peak population of 9,740 was reached in 1910, with a decline to just 6,175 in 1980. (3, 10, 27, 52, 57)

| | | | |
|---|---|---|---|
| Annis | Denney | Juniata | Rugby Junction |
| Aylmer | Dubay | Kandel | Selz |
| Balta | Egan | Leverich | Sherman |
| Barton | Elling | McCarthyville | Silva |
| Beyrout | Fero | Mill | Strasburg Colony |
| Brazil | Fulda | Odessa | Tunbridge |
| Cecil | Girard | Orkney | Westby |
| Clifton | Grasslake | Orrin | Wolford |
| Dallas | Hong | Reno | |
| Davidson | Hurricane Lake | Rugby | |

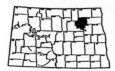

**RAMSEY COUNTY** was established January 4, 1873, and organized January 25, 1883 with the county seat being placed in Creel City, which the following year was renamed Devils Lake. It was named for Alexander Ramsey (1815-1903), the first Governor of Minnesota Territory, who later served as that state's Governor, a U. S. Senator, and Secretary of War under President Rutherford B. Hayes. He is also the namesake of Ramsey County, MN, the site of Saint Paul. The area is 1,214 square miles, and a peak population of 16,252 was reached in 1930. The 1980 population was 13,026. (3, 10, 27, 52, 57)

Bartlett
Benzion
Brocket
Camp Burke
Camp Gilbert C. Grafton
Camp Grafton
Camp Hanna
Camp Lawton
Camp Miller
Cato
Chautauqua
Church
Church's Ferry
Churchs Ferry
City of Devils Lake
Crary
Creel City
Creelsburgh
Dana's Grove
Darby
Davisville

DeGroat
Degroat
Derrick
Devils Lake
Doyon
Dudley
Edmore
Elmo
Essex
Evanston
Finland
Fort Totten Station
Fox Lake
Foxlake
Garske
Grand Harbor
Greenwood
Hampden
Heerman's Landing
Iola
Jackson

Jerusalem
Keith
Kildahl
Lake City
Lakewood Park
Laurens
Lawton
Locke
Lunde
Merl
Midway
Military Spur
Minnewakan
Newbre
Newville
North Chautauqua
Northfield
Odessa
Odessa
Penn
Ramsey

Ramsey
Rock Island
Rock Island
Rock Island Military
    Reservation
Rogers
Rohrville
Rutten
Saint Joe
Schapera
Scott
Southam
Starkweather
Stoltzville
Stover
Swan
Sweetwater
The End of the Track
Thompson's Landing
Tracy
Webster

**RANSOM COUNTY** was established January 4, 1873, and organized April 4, 1881 with the county seat being placed in Lisbon. It was named for Fort Ransom, located within its borders, which was named for Gen. Thomas Edward Greenfield Ransom (1834-1864), a Union casualty of the Civil War. The area is 863 square miles, and a peak population of 11,618 was reached in 1920, with a decline to just 6,714 in 1980. (3, 10, 27, 52, 57, 206)

Aliceton
Anselm
Bonnersville
Brockway
Buttzville
Camp Hayes
Camp Wharton
Camp Wilson
Coburn
Crossing
Elliott
Enderlin

Englevale
Faribault
Forest City
Fort Ransom
Fort Ransom
Greenriver
Griswold
Hayes
Jenksville
Kidville
Lisbon
Little Norway

Marshall
McLeod
Miller
Moore
Mullen
Normanna
Owego
Penequa
Pigeon Point
Plymouth
Preston
Ruscoe

Sandoun
Scovill
Sheldon
Sheldon Junction
Shenford
Standingrock
Sydna
The Colony
Venlo
Willard
Wisner

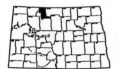

**RENVILLE COUNTY** was established January 4, 1873, but because of a lack of settlers failed to develop, and became a part of Ward County. On November 20, 1908 the people voted to organize a new county, and an executive proclamation of July 6, 1910 officially recognized this election with the county seat being placed in Mohall. It was named for Gabriel Renville, a pioneer fur trader, although many sources state that it was named for the legendary frontiersman, Joseph Renville (c.1799-1846). The area is 901 square miles, and a peak population of 7,840 was reached in 1910, with a decline to just 3,591 in 1980. (3, 10, 27, 52, 57)

Barber
Bolaker
Chola
Edson
Error
Geth
Glenburn
Glenn
Grano

Greene
Half Way House
Hall
Hammerfest
Joslyn
Lewis
Lincoln
Lorain
Loraine

Luzon
Markillie
McKinney
Mohall
Mouse River Park
Nina
Norma
Overholt
Pettis

Pleasant
Prosperity
Questad
Sherwood
Tolley
Walter
Wheeler
Whitney
Winifred

**RICHLAND COUNTY** was established January 4, 1873, and organized November 25, 1873 with the county seat being placed in Chahinkapa, which was renamed Wahpeton the following year. It was named for Morgan T. Rich (1832-1898), a prominent pioneer of the county. The area is 1,449 square miles, and a peak population of 21,008 was reached in 1930, with a decline to 18,089 in 1970. The recent growth of Wahpeton resulted in an increase to 19,197 in 1980. (3, 10, 27, 52, 57)

| | | | |
|---|---|---|---|
| Abercrombie | Downing | LaMars | Sewall Station |
| Adams | Dwight | Lehigh | Seymour |
| Antelope | East Wyndmere | Lidgerwood | Sibley |
| Barney | Ellsworth Station | Lithia | Slotten |
| Barney Station | Enloe | Lone Tree | Sonora |
| Barrett | Fairmount | Lovdokken | Sperry |
| Barrie | Fairview Junction | Lurgan | Standy |
| Barrie Crossing | Farmington | Mantador | Star Lake Spur |
| Bayne | Fletcher | Mathews | Stevenson's |
| Belmont | Florine | Michigan Settlement | Stiles |
| Berlin | Fort Abercrombie | Mill Siding | Theed |
| Berndt | Fort Hankinson | Mooreton | Triest |
| Blackmer | Galchutt | Morgan | Tyler |
| Brightwood | Glenora | Moselle | Tyson |
| Camp Chase | Great Bend | Murray | Ulness |
| Camp Edgerton | Greatbend | Naval Training School Station | Van Pelts |
| Camp Hackett | Greenman's Spur | Nolan Crossing | Veblen Junction |
| Camp Libby | Griffin | North New Effington | Wahpeton |
| Camp Tattersall | Hankinson | North Veblen | Wahpeton Junction |
| Chahinkapa | Homestead | Oberweis | Walcott |
| Christine | Ingram | Old Fort Abercrombie | Warner |
| Colfax | Jasper | Old Mantador | Water Tank |
| Crossing | Junkers | Oswald | Woiwode |
| Danton | Kelly | Pitcairn | Woodhull |
| DeVillo | Keystone Junction | Power | Woodruff |
| DeVillo | Kindred Mill Spur | Richfield | Wyndmere |
| Devillo | Kloeppel | Richville | Zion |
| Dexter | Kongsberg | Seven Trees | |

**ROLETTE COUNTY** was established January 4, 1873, and organized October 14, 1884 with the county seat being placed in Dunseith. In 1886 it was moved to Saint John's, and in 1890 it was moved to Rolla, the present location. The county was named for Joseph "Jolly Joe" Rolette (1820-1871), a native of WI whose June 1868 homestead in Pembina County was the first in ND. He was a pioneer frontiersman who was widely known throughout MN and Dakota Territory. The area is 913 square miles, and a peak population of 12,583 was reached in 1940. The 1980 count is 12,177, as ROLETTE COUNTY is one of the few ND counties without a major city to maintain a stable population in recent years. (3, 10, 27, 52, 57, 123)

| | | | |
|---|---|---|---|
| Ackworth | Dion Lake | Kelvin | Saint John |
| Agate | Done Workin Beach | Kringen | Saint John's |
| Alcide | Dunseith | Lake Laureat | San Haven |
| Bachelor | Eagles Nest | Little Chicago of the West | Selden |
| Barby | Elisa | Mars | Sodhouse |
| Belcourt | Fisher | McCumber | Spangler |
| Benoit | Fonda | McFadden | Sylvan Glen |
| Berdella | Galloway | Montair | Thorne |
| Bertha | Gronna | Mylo | Turtle Mountain |
| Birchwood | Hanson | Nanson | Twala |
| Birchwood Park | Helium | Oak Springs | Umbria |
| Bollinger | Hillside | Oden | Virden |
| Boundary | Hutchinsonville | Overly | Willow Creek |
| Boydton | Ina | Pennyhill | Willow Lake |
| Calmar | Island Lake | Quay | Wolf Creek |
| Calvin | Kincaid | Rolette | Wye |
| Carpenter | Jarves | Rolla | |
| Denver | Juno | Saint Claude | |

**SARGENT COUNTY** was established March 3, 1883, and organized October 8, 1883 with the county seat being placed in Milnor. The court house was moved to the centrally located townsite of Forman in 1886. The county was named for Gen. Homer E. Sargent, an official of the NPRR who was actively interested in the promotion of this region. The area is 855 square miles, and a peak population of 9,655 was reached in 1920, with a decline to just 5,512 in 1980. (3, 10, 27, 52, 57, 165, 171)

| | | | |
|---|---|---|---|
| Alden | Dunbar | Kandiotta | Rutland |
| Alicia | Elizabeth | Klepol | Sargeant |
| Babcock | End of the Track | Lewis | Sargent |
| Belle Plaine | Forman | Linton | Seneca |
| Blackstone | Forsby | Manning | Sprague Lake |
| Brampton | Geneseo | Millsburgh | Stewart |
| Brookland | Goetz | Milnor | Stirum |
| Camp Buell | Graball | Mohler | Straubville |
| Camp Parker | Gwinner | Moores Grove | Tewaukon |
| Cayuga | Hamlin | Nicholson | Towanda |
| Cogswell | Hample | North Britton | Veda |
| Coryell | Harlem | Oella | Verner |
| Crete | Harvard | Perry | Vivian |
| Crossing | Havana | Postville | Weber |
| DeLamere | Herman | Ransom | |
| Delamere | Hoving | Ripley | |

**SHERIDAN COUNTY** was established January 4, 1873, but no settlement occurred and the region was absorbed by McLean County. In the general election of November 3, 1908 the people voted to create the county again from the eastern portion of McLean County. It organized the following January with the county seat being placed in McClusky. The county was named for Gen. Philip Henry Sheridan (1831-1888) of Civil War fame. The area is 996 square miles, and a peak population of 8,103 was reported in 1910, with a steady decline to just 2,812 in 1980. (3, 10, 21, 27, 52, 57) *BIBLIOGRAPHY*

| | | | |
|---|---|---|---|
| Bass Station | Denhoff | Lincoln Valley | Pickardville |
| Berlin | Dudley | Martin | Schmidt |
| Blaine | Goodrich | McClusky | Skogmo |
| Casselman | Herr | Middle Station | Tiebell |
| Clark | Lamont | Old McClusky | Wehr |
| Curtis | Lincoln | Pickardsville | Wittmayer |

**SIOUX COUNTY** was established by proclamation of Gov. Louis B. Hanna on September 3, 1914, and organized January 14, 1915 with the county seat being placed in Fort Yates. Its entire area of 1,114 square miles comprises the ND portion of the Standing Rock Indian Reservation, and the county takes its name from the principal tribe residing here, the Sioux, whose name is derived from the Chippewa word *Nadowe-is-iw*, meaning snakes or enemies. The peak population of 4,687 was reached in 1930, and the 1980 count of 3,633 reflects a level that has been maintained for about forty years. (3, 10, 27, 52, 57, 127)

| | | | |
|---|---|---|---|
| Belden | Fort Yates | North Morristown | Sloptown |
| Cannon Ball | Fort Yates | Nosodak | Solen |
| Cannon Ball Junction | Goose Camp | Ponderosa | Standing Rock |
| Carignan | Hekton | Porcupine | Swastika |
| Cedar River | North McIntosh | Selfridge | |
| Chadwick | North McLaughlin | Slabtown | |

**SLOPE COUNTY** was established by a vote of the people on November 3, 1914, having formerly been the southern part of Billings County. It organized on January 14, 1915 with the county seat being placed in Amidon. The name notes the general eastward slope of the terrain, with the entire SW part of ND often referred to as the Missouri Slope. The area is 1,226 square miles, and a peak population of 4,940 was reached in 1920, with a decline to just 1,171 in 1980. (3, 10,27, 52, 57, 82)

| | | | |
|---|---|---|---|
| Amidon | Demores | Mineral Springs | Sand Creek Station |
| Austin | Desart | Montline | Shollsmade |
| Badland | DeSart | Mound | Slope |
| Berger | Giese | Neva | Slope Center |
| Bessie | Hess | Pierce | Stoneville |
| Bierman | Holton | Pine | Stuart |
| Billings | Hume | Purcell | Taft |
| Burdette | Little Missouri Station | Rainy Butte | Vim |
| Calcite | Marmarth | Ranger | Winnebago |
| Chenoweth | Mazda | Reno | Yule |
| Cookranch | Midway | Sandcreek | |

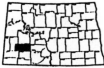

**STARK COUNTY** was established February 10, 1879, and organized May 25, 1882 with the county seat being placed in Dickinson. It was named for George Stark, General Manager of the NPRR, whose mainline crosses the entire length of the county. The area is 1,356 square miles, and the population has grown steadily to a peak of 23,703 in 1980. (3, 10, 27, 52, 57, 74)

Adie
Antelope
Antelope
Antelope Station
Belfield
Boyle
Camp Houstin
Daglum
Dickinson
Double Wall Station
Eland

Fifth Siding
Fort Hannifin
Gaylord
Gladstone
Green River
Green River Station
Hungary
Keogh
Knife River
Knowlton
Lefor

Lehigh
Moltke
North Dickinson
Pleasant Valley Siding
Richardton
Saint Elizabeth
Saint Pius
Saint Stephen
Schefield
Schnellreich
South Dickinson

South Heart
Spalding
Spring Valley
Taylor
Versippi
Wylie
Young Man's Butte Siding
Young Man's Butte Station
Zenith

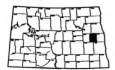

**STEELE COUNTY** was established March 8, 1883 from portions of Traill and Griggs counties. It organized June 13, 1883 with the county seat being placed in Hope, which had once been the county seat of Griggs County. A desire for a more centrally located court house led to the establishment of Sherbrooke, which became the county seat on May 19, 1885, but this site never attracted a railroad, and on December 16, 1918 the court house was moved to the nearby GNRR townsite of Finley. Many different explanations exist concerning the name of the county. Most sources say that it was named for either J. A. Steele, President of the Red River Land Co., or Edward H. Steele, a prominent pioneer settler, while others say it was named for Franklin Steele (1813-1880), a promoter of this area who was a distinguished resident of Minneapolis, MN. The area is 710 square miles, and a peak population of 7,616 was reached in 1910, with a decline to just 3,112 in 1980. (3, 10, 27, 52, 57, 79, 233, 327)

Bellevyria
Blabon
Colgate
Easton
Finley
Gilbert
Golden Lake

Grain
Hope
Interlaken
Lake Tobiason
Little Fork
Luverne
Mardell

Nebo
Newburgh
Pickert
Pickert
Pickert Siding
Primrose
Sharon

Sherbrooke
Spain
Tara
Walker
Wheaton

**STUTSMAN COUNTY** was established January 4, 1873, and organized June 10, 1873 with the county seat being placed in Jamestown. It was named for Enos Stutsman (1826-1874), a distinguished Dakota Territory legislator who served as Speaker of the House 1867-1868. The area is 2,274 square miles, and a peak population of 26,100 was reached in 1930. The 1980 population was 24,159 as the growth of Jamestown has virtually offset declines in the rural areas. (3, 10, 27, 52, 57, 158)

Albion
Alsop
Arctic
Arrowwood
Atwill
Barnett
Beaver
Beaver Creek
Berner
Bloom
Bloomenfield
Bremer's Ranch
Buchanan
Burton
Camp Gilfillan
Camp Grant
Camp Sykes
Camp Thomas
Clarke
Clayton Ranch
Clementsville
Cleveland
Community
Corinne
Courtenay
Courtney
Deer Lake

Don
Donovan
Durham
Durkee
Durum
Durupts
Edmunds
Eighth Siding
Eldridge
Eldrige
Eleventh Siding
Esler
Fancher
Fort Cross
Fort Seward
Fried
Gem
Gerber
Gingrey
Goldwin
Gray
Hettinger
Homer
Horn
Hurning
Hyland Park
Jamestown

Jamestown Junction
Jenkins
Jim
Lake Johnson
Karlopolis
Kensal
Klose
Klose Siding
Klose's Spur
Lakeview Park
Lees Ranch
Lippert
Marston
Marstonmoor
Meadow
Medina
Midway
Millarton
Montpelier
Newhome
New Minneapolis
Old Fort Seward
Oswego
Paris
Parkhurst
Past
Phillips Settlement

Pingree
Pipestem Prairie
Ramona
Reeves
Rio
Rokiwan Camp
Seaborn
Sharlow
Southdown
Spiritwood
Spiritwood Lake
Spring Grove
Spring Valley
State Hospital
Streeter
Stutsman County Memorial
   Park
Sydney
Tarbell
Tenth Siding
Thackeray
Vashti
Wallace Grove
Waneska Park
Windsor
Woodworth
Ypsilanti

**TOWNER COUNTY** was established March 8, 1883, and organized January 24, 1884. There were no townsites in the county at that time, and it took the pioneers a month of spirited political debate to choose a site for the county seat, with its name, Cando, reflecting the determination of the winners. The name of the county was chosen by Gov. Nehemiah Ordway to honor Col. Oscar M. Towner (1842-1897), a territorial legislator who was a Confederate veteran of the Civil War. The area is 1,044 square miles, and a peak population of 8,963 was reached in 1910, with a decline to just 4,048 in 1980. (3, 10, 27, 52, 57, 102)

Antwerp
Armourdale
Arndt
Balton
Bement
Beston
Big Coulee
Bisbee
Brumbaugh
Cando
Cecil
Clarena

Considine
Coolin
Crocus
Dash
Dunker
Colony
Egeland
Ellison
Elsberry
Evanston
Fernwood
Gleason

Hansboro
Hanson
Hyland
Jarvis
LaCrosse
Lakeview
Lansing
Lewis
Maza
Newville
Olmstead
Pasha

Perth
Picton
Rocklake
Rosedale
Saginaw
Sarles
Sidney
Snyder
Willdo
Zion

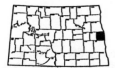

**TRAILL COUNTY** was established January 12, 1875, and organized February 23, 1875 with the county seat placed in Goose River, which on August 19, 1875 changed its name to Caledonia. Several attempts were made to relocate the court house to a more central location, and the move was finally accomplished in 1896 when Hillsboro became the new county seat. The county was named for Walter John Strickland Traill (1847-1938), a Canadian who came to the area in 1866 as an employee of the Hudson's Bay Company, and was prominent in the early affairs of the county. He moved to MT in the 1880's, and lived his last years in British Columbia. The area is 861 square miles, and a peak population of 12,600 was reached in 1930. Situated between Fargo and Grand Forks, the county has not experienced as sharp of a decline as many rural counties, reporting a population of 9,629 in 1980. (3, 10, 27, 52, 57, 187)

Alhalstead
Alton
Alton Junction
Ames
Arnold's Post
Bellmont
Belmont
Blanchard
Bloomfield
Brown's Landing
Buxton
Caledonia
Carlton
Clarke
Clifford
Comstock
Cumings

Cummings
Dalry
Duane
Elm River
Elm River Station
Enger
Eyresville
Fork
Frog Point
Galesburg
Goosenland
Goose Rapids
Goose River
Grandin
Grant River
Greenfield
Green River

Gundin Farm
Hague
Hague
Hartsland
Hatton
Hill City
Hillsboro
Junction
Kelso
Little Chicago
May
Mayville
Midway
Murray
Norway
Old Mayville
Pokerville

Portland
Portland Junction
Preston
Quincy
Reynolds
Roseville
Safford
Scow
Stony Point
Taft
Traill Centre
Volga
Weible
West Climax
West Halstad
West Nielsville
West Shelly

**WALSH COUNTY** was established February 8, 1881, and organized August 30, 1881 with the county seat placed in Grafton. It was named for George H. Walsh (1845-1913), a newspaperman and politician in Grand Forks. The area is 1,287 square miles, and a peak population of 20,747 was reached in 1940, with a decline to 15,381 in 1980. (3, 10, 27, 52, 57, 75)

Acton
Adams
Amor
Ardoch
Ardock
Auburn
Auburn Station
Bechyne
Butler
Cashel
Clare
Conway
Conway
Dewar
Dundee
Eden
Edinburg
Edinburgh
Elora
Fairchild
Fairdale
Fertile
Fordville

Forest River
Galt
Garfield
Geoff
Grafton
Henry's Post
Herrick
Herriott
Hoople
Kellogg
Kelly's Point
Kelner
Kensington
Kerry
Kimball
Kinloss
Lambert
Lampton
Lankin
Latona
Linstad
Lomice
Louren

Mandt
Meagher
Medford
Minto
Morden Junction
Mount View
Nash
New Saint Andrews
New Warsaw
Nord
Norton
Nova
Oakwood
Old Crossing
Ops
Park River
Park River
Park River Post
Perry
Pisek
Plano
Poland
Praha

Pulaski
Richmond
Rose Point
Saint Andrew
Saint Andrews
Saint Andrews Station
Salt Lake
Sandy's Corner
Sarles
Sarnia
Silvista
Sweden
Swedish Settlement
Tomey
Veseley
Veseleyville
Vesta
Voss
Walshville
Warsaw
Wild Rose
Young

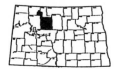

**WARD COUNTY** was established November 23, 1885, and organized April 14, 1885 with the county seat placed in Burlington, at the time the only settlement in the county. In 1888 it moved to the new GNRR divison point of Minot, which would soon become one of ND's four major cities. The county was named for Mark Ward of Kimball, SD, a territorial legislator who chaired the Committee on Counties during the 1885 session. The county was once one of the largest in the state's history, and was known as Imperial Ward County, but the establishment of Mountrail, Burke, and Renville counties reduced its size to a still formidable 2,048 square miles. A unique feature of WARD COUNTY is its "gooseneck" extending NW from the main part of the county, which was the result of political maneuvering by officials in Burke and Renville counties who wished to prevent Kenmare from becoming a county seat. The peak population of 58,560 was reached in 1970, with a slight decline to 58,392 in 1980. (3, 10, 27, 52, 57, 371)

| | | | |
|---|---|---|---|
| Amor | Fairview Gardens | Logan | Salyards |
| Aurelia | Floradale | Lone Tree | Sawyer |
| Baden | Foxholm | Lonetree | Smiths |
| Berthold | Galva | Lynch | South Prairie |
| Bison Spur | Gassman | Makoti | Speedway |
| Black | Goetz | Martells | Spencer |
| Burlington | Gooler | Minot | Stammen |
| Bye | Grelland | Minot Air Force Base | Stock Yards |
| Caithness | Hagen | Minot Stock Yards | Stock Yards |
| Carpio | Harrison | Niobe | Stringtown |
| Centerville | Hartland | Olive | Sunny Slope |
| Colton | H. B. Junction | Paradise | Surrey |
| Davis | Hecker | Peebler | Tasker |
| DeKalb | Hesnault | Pitts | Tatman |
| Des Lacs | J. D. Switch | Ralston | Tent Town |
| Deslacs | Jerome | Ricelake | Terrell |
| Donnybrook | Kenaston | Roach | The Forks |
| Douglas | Kenmare | Robinson | Vanderwalker |
| Downtown | LaFollette | Rouses | Waldorf |
| Drady | Liberty | Ruthville | Ward |
| Echo | Lignite | Ryder | Wayne |
| Enterprise | Lloyd's Spur | Saint Carl | Wolseth |

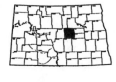

**WELLS COUNTY** was established as Gingras County on January 4, 1873. The name was changed on February 26, 1881 to honor Edward Payson Wells (1847-1936) of Jamestown, a prominent territorial legislator. It organized June 24, 1884 with the county seat placed in Sykeston, the only settlement in the county. On November 16, 1894 the court house was moved to the more centrally located townsite of Fessenden. The area is 1,293 square miles, and a peak population of 13,285 was reached in 1930, with a decline to just 6,983 in 1980. (3, 10, 27, 52, 57, 79, 268) *BIBLIOGRAPHY*

| | | | |
|---|---|---|---|
| Bowdon | Fessenden | Jim River Crossing | Steven |
| Bremen | Gwynne | Kiner | Sykeston |
| Cathay | Gwynne City | Manfred | Twist |
| Chaseley | Hamberg | Ontario | Valhall |
| Chess Crossing | Hamburg | Oshkosh | Velda |
| Delger | Harvey | Roosevelt | Viking |
| Doland | Heaton | Ross | Wells |
| Dover | Heimdal | Saundersville | Wellsburg |
| Eden | Hurdsfield | Shaw | Whitby |
| Emrick | | | |

**WILLIAMS COUNTY** was established January 8, 1873 in the general area of present-day Mercer and Dunn counties, but the name later was applied to the unorganized counties of Buford and Flannery. The county seat is at Williston, and since the separation of Divide County in 1910, its area has been 2,138 square miles. The name honors Erastus Appleman Williams (1850-1930), a territorial legislator and mayor of Bismarck, who was instrumental in the naming of many counties in ND. The population has generally increased over the years, with a peak population of 22,237 reported in 1980. (3, 10, 27, 52, 57)

| | | | |
|---|---|---|---|
| Alamo | Gambetta | Marley | Stella |
| Angie | Gladys | Marmon | Stordahl |
| Appam | Grenora | McGregor | Temple |
| Avoca | Grinnell | Mesa | Thiers |
| Baqual | Grinnell's Landing | Miller's Spur | Tioga |
| Bonetraill | Haarstad | Mondak | Todd |
| Buford | Hamlet | Nesson | Trenton |
| Corinth | Hankey | Old Fort Buford | Truax |
| Cottonwood | Hanks | Old Fort Union | Union Valley |
| Cottonwood Lake | Harold Petersons | Peresevers | Vandalia |
| Dow | Harry | Persevere | West Bonetraill |
| East Mondak | Higley | Polege | West Williston |
| East Springbrook | Hofflund | Ray | Wheelock |
| Epping | Howard | Round Prairie | Wildrose |
| Fort Buford | Junket | Rude | Willia |
| Fort Lloyd | Keys Cove | Scott | Williston |
| Fort Mortimer | Leighton | Silver Strip | Zahl |
| Fort Union | Little Muddy | Spring Brook | |
| Fort William | Lyndale | Squires | |
| Frederickson | Manger | Standard Spur | |

native of Evansville, MN, coming here in 1906, and he named the post office to note his view of an Indian battle field several miles to the south. Later research at the site turned up many Indian relics, but the site proved to be an abandoned Hidatsa village with no concrete evidence of any battle being fought here. In 1911 the post office was moved three miles SSW to Sw¼ Sec. 23-159-94, the site of a new GNRR townsite, which adopted this name. The elevation is 2197, the Zip Code is 58714, and a peak population of 100 was reported in 1920, with a decline to 52 in 1930, at which level it has remained for many years. (1, 2, 3, 18, 34, 40, 67)

**BAY CENTER** (Pembina). This was a farm post office established December 20, 1882 with Wentworth J. Dumble pm. The origin of the name is unknown, and seems to have no descriptive significance. It was first located in NE¼ Sec. 5-163-55, Saint Joseph Twp., seven miles NE of Walhalla. In 1885 it moved across the section line to NW¼ Sec. 4-163-55, the home of new pm Andrew J. Lindsay. In 1888 it moved two miles WNW to the home of pm William H. Best in SW¼ Sec. 31-164-55, Saint Joseph Twp., who spelled the name as BAY CENTRE. In 1894 it again moved, this time a bit to the east in SE¼ Sec. 31-164-55, the home of Albert Noice, who restored the BAY CENTER spelling to comply with new government regulations for place names. The post office closed January 15, 1906 with mail to Walhalla. (2, 3, 18, 25, 40, 45, 235, 414)

**BAY CENTRE** (Pembina). William H. Best was appointed as the pm of what was officially known as the BAY CENTER post office in 1888 at his home in SW¼ Sec. 31-164-55, Saint Joseph Twp., six miles NE of Walhalla. His Site Report filed July 30, 1888 shows the "romantic" spelling, BAY CENTRE, which apparently went unnoticed by postal officials. When Albert Noice became pm in 1894, the original, and official, spelling was restored in part, no doubt, due to newly enacted government regulations for place names. Several postmarks are known from the Best tenure, all showing BAY CENTRE, indicating that he had clearly intended to alter the spelling, and had carried out his plans. (3, 40, 414)

**BAYFIELD** (McLean). This was a farm post office established November 17, 1905 with James Fielding pm. It was located in SE¼ Sec. 20-146-80, five miles south of Turtle Lake and named for Bayfield County, WI, which also has a county seat named Washburn, named for the same C. C. Washburn that the McLean County city is named for. The WI county was named for Henry W. Bayfield, a British naval officer. The post office closed March 15, 1907 with

mail to Turtle Lake. (2, 3, 5, 10, 28, 40, 70, 414)

**BAYNE** (Richland). This was a NPRR loading station in Sec. 11-131-50, Belford Twp., that was the terminus of a thirteen-mile spur into the 7,000 acre Keystone Farm on the Wild Rice River. It operated during the 1890's, then was dismantled. The origin of the name is unknown. (2, 18)

**BAYVIEW** (Pembina). This was a pioneer settlement founded in 1879 by Isaac Foster in Sec. 3-162-53, Bathgate Twp., and named to note the view of a bay, actually a bend in the Tongue River. When the post office was established November 2, 1881, it was renamed BATHGATE. (2, 18, 108)

**BEACH** (Golden Valley). The NPRR built a section house here in 1881 and named it for Capt. Warren C. Beach of the 11th Infantry, U. S. Army, who had escorted the first railroad surveyors through this area in 1880. Settlement began in 1900, and by 1910 a city of 1,003 people spread across Secs. 23, 24, 25 & 26-140-106, Beach Twp. The post office was established October 27, 1902 with Frank E. Heath pm. The village incorporated in 1908, it became a city in 1909, and when Golden Valley County organized in 1912, BEACH was named as the county seat. The elevation is 2779, the Zip Code is 58621, and a peak population of 1,460 was reached in 1960. (1, 2, 3, 18, 33, 40, 80, 369, 370)

**BEAN** (Grand Forks). This was a NPRR station founded in 1887 in NE¼ Sec. 32-153-53, Gilby Twp., three miles south of Gilby, and named for S. S. Bean, who came here in 1886 and built an elevator at the site. A post office was established March 29, 1888 with Samuel White pm, and it was discontinued April 27, 1891 with mail to Gilby. In 1882 the post office was reestablished, but it was named HONEYFORD for new pm William J. "Bob" Honeyford. The station continued using the BEAN name until 1906, when it changed to the more frequently used HONEYFORD. (2, 25, 31, 40, 69, 240, 338)

*Beach about 1925*

**BEAR CREEK** (Dickey). This was a relay stage station on the line from Jamestown to Columbia, SD built in 1880. It was located at the corner of Secs. 4, 5, 8 & 9-131-59, Bear Creek Twp., just north of Oakes. The township and this station were named for Bear Creek, which had been named in 1839 by the explorers Nicollet and Fremont. The Indian name for this creek translated as the place where the grizzly bear has his den. (2, 3, 18, 154)

**BEAULIEU** (Cavalier). This historic settlement was founded about 1880 in NW¼ Sec. 26-162-57, North Olga Twp., and named for Paul H. Beaulieu, a descendant of the famous fur trader Joseph Beaulieu, who had come here in the 1830's from WI. The name is French, and can be translated as beautiful place. The post office was established July 11, 1882 with James R. Copeland pm. A thriving little village developed, and the general stores of Alex Montpetit and the Xerxa brothers are remembered by many. A population of 39 was reported as late as 1930, but the post office closed July 31, 1935 with mail to Walhalla, six miles to the NE, and the site is now largely abandoned. Bealieu is an erroneous spelling. (2, 3, 18, 40, 79, 115, 292)

**BEAULIEU** (Pembina). The 1884 Andreas Historical Atlas of Dakota Territory shows this place in NW¼ Sec. 18-162-56, LaMoure Twp., two miles NE of the pioneer settlement of this name in Cavalier County. A 1890 map published by Rand-McNally also shows it in Pembina County. It is assumed that these two locations were one and the same, but no explanation has been found for the dual locations. (3, 18, 25)

HEDEMARKEN COLLECTIBLES is proud to announce the publication of NORTH DAKOTA PLACE NAMES by Douglas A. Wick.

Ten years in the making, NORTH DAKOTA PLACE NAMES represents a comprehensive study of more than three thousand past and present place names, with each name receiving separate treatment. Typical entries include exact locations, origins of the names, prominent residents, populations, elevations, postal history, etc. The main body of the book is fully cross-referenced and indexed by county.

Unlike many books of this type, NORTH DAKOTA PLACE NAMES is profusely illustrated with rare photographs, picture post cards, and postmarks from leading private collections. Most of the illustrations are published here for the first time.

The author, an accountant by profession, is a well known North Dakota hobbyist whose interests include history, deltiology, genealogy, and travel. He has been a frequent writer and speaker on subjects as diverse as philately and classic motor cars. His thorough review of virtually every North Dakota local history book, personal visitations to each of the fifty-three counties, and discussions with countless local citizens have combined to produce what should be the definitive work on this subject for many years to come.

NORTH DAKOTA PLACE NAMES is printed on high quality paper with a full 8 1/2" x 11" inch format. The 248 pages are attractively hardbound to provide years of service. It is offered with the standard HEDEMARKEN COLLECTIBLES guarantee - if for any reason you are unsatisfied with NORTH DAKOTA PLACE NAMES, simply return it within ten days for a prompt refund.

Please share this important offer with others who are interested in North Dakota history and heritage.

HEDEMARKEN COLLECTIBLES
P. O. Box 7399 - Northbrook Station
Bismarck, ND 58502
Telephone: (701) 258-5794

Yes, send _____ copies of NORTH DAKOTA PLACE NAMES at $29.95 plus $2.50 for postage and handling. Bismarck and Devils Lake residents must include 7% sales tax, and other North Dakota residents must include 5% sales tax. In other words, the cost per book by mail for Bismarck and Devils Lake residents is $34.72. The cost per book to other North Dakota residents is $34.40. The cost per book for out of state orders is $32.45.

My Check or Money Order for $ _____ is enclosed.

Name _____

Address _____

City _____ State _____ Zip Code _____

"...the most thorough book of its kind, a "must" on every North Dakotan's centennial reading list." - North Dakota REC Magazine, January 1989
"...comprehensive study of more than three thousand past and present place names" - The Good Stuff, November 1988
"...the best book of its type - for any state" - E.P., Arizona
"...the most comprehensive study...in the state" - The Leader-News Dec. 8, 1988
"...a new book just for you" - The Bismarck Tribune Dec. 25, 1988
"...a corker! Why don't you write one for Montana?" - B.M., Montana

# North Dakota Place Names

## Douglas A. Wick

Cannon Ball
Beulah
Ops
Bicycle
Hamar
MANDAN
Anamoose
Pembina
Napoleon
Echo Buttzville
Strasburg
Phoenix Max
Paris Berlin
Tioga
Fargo
Worms
Carpio
Bismarck
Zap Wahpeton
Dogtooth Killdeer
Skermo Nameless
Hoople Cando
Munich
Blabon
Bottineau
Williston
Whynot
Happy
Larimore
Hoskins
Karnak Sykeston
Jamestown
Nosodak
Rugby
Gragreen
HOE
Kandiotta
Mott Kibby
Ypsilanti Dickinson
Trier
Thor
Makoti
Omemee
Trotters
Abercrombie
Budapest
Versippi Mondak
Dogden Lowell
Mohall
AUBURN
Paoli
Aae
Elbowoods
Bac
Twist
Yule
Moscow Sogn
Tobacco Garden
Joe
Goa Wing
Snow
Ottofy
Hong
Beyrout
Sig New Hradec
Ong
Dash Tokio
Baltimore Forbar
Venlo Noel Pleasant
Coal City
Mugford
Ina Keogh
Lakota
Odessa
Minot
Chicota
HARLEM
Veseley
Orange
Grand Forks
Rugby
Yucca
Enderlin
Krem
Persevere
Gladys
Monango
Warsaw
Saunders
Seaborn
Herr
Lisbon
Metigoshe
Hub
Silo
Price Maddock

# Bibliography

**BOOKS, PAMPHLETS, & BROCHURES without specific author(s):**

1. Clason's No. Dakota Green Guide. The Clason Map Co., Chicago & Denver. Undated (circa 1920).

4. Webster's Seventh New Collegiate Dictionary. G. & C. Merriam Company, Springfield, MA. 1967.

5. The Americana. The Americana Company, New York, NY. 1914.

7. Beulah 1914-1964. Jubilee Book Committee.

8. Directory of Bismarck and Burleigh County. The Bismarck Tribune. 1910.

17. Mandan City and Morton and Grant Counties, N.D. 1917-1918. Keiter Directory Co., Norfolk, NE. 1917.

18. George T. Ogle Co. Various county atlases, circa 1910-1915, et al.

24. North Dakota. Northern Pacific Railroad Co. 1922.

25. Pocket Map and Shippers' Guide of North Dakota. Rand, McNally & Co., Chicago & New York. 1890.

26. Various travel guides. German Travel Bureau, New York, NY. 1933, 1934.

27. The World Almanac and Book of Facts. Newspaper Enterprise Association, Cleveland & New York. 1972.

32. Who's Who in the Central States. The Mayflower Publishing Co., Inc. Washington, DC. 1929.

33. Directory of Post Offices. U. S. Postal Service. 1973.

34. Midwest Atlas Co., Fergus Falls, MN. Various county atlases circa 1960-1985, et al.

37. Connecticut State Register and Manual. The Peiper Press, Inc., Wallingford, CT. 1950.

38. Ideal World Atlas. Hammond Incorporated, Maplewood, NJ. 1971.

50. The Wonder of Williams. The Williams County Historical Society 1976.

52. North Dakota Blue Book. Secretary of State, Bismarck, ND. Various editions.

54. Fessenden Diamond Jubilee Book 1968. The Book and Biography Committee.

58. Brocket Diamond Jubilee 1900-1975. Ness Printing Co., Devils Lake, ND. 1975.

59. Steele Centennial, One Hundred Years of Progress 1881-1981.

61. Dawson Centennial 1880-1980. Book Committee 1980.

62. Tappen 1878-1966, 88 Years of Progress. Tappen Historical Association 1966.

63. Our Pioneers, The Wing Area 1892-1976. Wing Bicentennial Committee.

65. Griggs County History 1879-1976. Griggs County Historical Society 1976.

67. Pioneers and Progress. Burke County and White Earth Historical Society 1972.

68. Growing With Pride. Harvey 75th Jubilee Committee 1981.

69. Grand Forks County Heritage Book (2 vols.). Grand Forks Heritage Book Committee 1976.

71. Renville County History. Renville County Old Settler's Association 1976.

72. Tales of Mighty Mountrail. Moutrail County Historical Society 1979.

73. Divide County History. History Book Committee 1974.

75. Walsh Heritage (4 vols.). Walsh County Historical Society 1976.

76. Barnes County History. Barnes County Historical Society Inc. 1976.

77. Rural Cass County. The Cass County Historical Society, Inc., West Fargo, ND. 1976.

81. Echoing Trails, Billings County History. Billings County Historical Society 1979.

82. Slope Saga. Slope Sage Committee, Slope County, ND. 1976.

85. Sheldon Community History. Enderlin Independent Printing, Enderlin, ND. 1981.

90. Moffit, North Dakota 75 Years 1905-1980. The History Committee.

91. 50th Anniversary Tuttle, North Dakota 1911-1961. The Tuttle Jubilee Board of Directors 1961.

92. The Banner City Monango 1886-1986. The Monango Centennial Committee 1985.

93. Golden Jubilee Robinson, North Dakota 1911-1961. History Committee of the Robinson Jubilee.

97. A History of Foster County. Foster County History Book Committee 1983.

99. Steele County 1883-1983. Steele County Historical Society, Finley, ND. 1983.

100. People, Places, & Events, Minot & Ward County, 100 Years of Magic. Minot-Ward County Centennial Commission 1986.

101. The People of Bottineau County. Centennial Book Committee 1984.

102. Cando and Surrounding Eight Rural Areas. Cando Centennial Committee 1984.

103. Ramsey County 1883-1983 (3 vols.). Lake Region Chautauqua Corporation 1982.

104. Hebron, North Dakota 1885-1985. Hebron Centennial Incorporated 1984.

105. Glen Ullin Yesteryears 1883-1983. Glen Ullin Historical Society 1983.

106. Flasher 75th Jubilee Book. 1976.

108. Pembina County, North Dakota Heritage '76 Then and Now. Pembina County Historical Society, Cavalier, ND. 1975.

109. New Salem 1883-1983. Centennial Book Committee 1983.

110. Pioneers and Progress, Minnewaukan, N.Dak. and Countryside. Minnewaukan History Book Committee 1983.

111. Elgin, North Dakota 1910-1985. Elgin Diamond Jubilee Book Committee.

112. Our Heritage 1883-1980 Sheyenne Area. Sheyenne Historical Society 1980.

114. Pierce County and Rugby, North Dakota 1886-1986. Prairie Publishing, Inc., Rugby, ND. 1986.

115. History of Olga, North Dakota and Our Lady of the Sacred Heart Church 1882-1982. Associated Printers, Grafton, ND. 1982.

116. Napoleon, N.D. 1884-1984. Centennial Committee 1984.

117. A Century of Area History 1882-1982 Milton, North Dakota. Milton Area Historical Committee.

118. Fingal, North Dakota 1980. Fingal Community History Committee, Fingal, ND. 1980.

119. A Century of Sowers, A Harvest of Heritage, New Rockford, Eddy County, North Dakota 1883-1983. Centennial History Committee 1983.

120. Prairie Tales. Rural Area Development Committee, Bowman County, ND 1965.

122. Diamond Jubilee Steele, N.Dak. 1881-1956. Jubilee Executive Committee.

124. Nelson County History (2 vols.). Wold Printing Co., Inc., Larimore, ND. 1985.

126. Petersburg Area Heritage Book. Petersburg Centennial Book Committee 1981.

128. Michigan City, North Dakota Centennial 1883-1983. Wold Printing, Inc., Larimore, ND. 1983.

129. McVille, North Dakota 1906-1981. History Book Committee 1981.

130. Lakota 100 Years 1883 to 1983. Lakota History Committee 1983.

131. Action in Aneta 1896-1971. Aneta Boosters Club 1971.

132. Tolna and Tolna Community Bicentennial History 1906-1976. The Tolna Bicentennial Book Committee 1976.

133. Lehr Diamond Jubilee 1898-1973. Book Committee, Quality Printing Company, Bismarck, ND. 1973.

134. Ashley's Golden Jubilee 1888-1938. Ashley Golden Jubilee Committee 1938.

135. Venturia Golden Jubilee 1901-1951. Anniversary Club, Ashley Tribune, Ashley, ND. 1951.

136. Zeeland 1902-1977. Jubilee Committee.

137. Wishek Golden Jubilee 1898-1948. Executive Committee Wishek Golden Jubilee.

138. A History of Adrian, North Dakota 1885-1985. The Litchville Bulletin, Litchville, ND. 1985.

139. Once In A Hundred—Dickey, N.Dak. 1882-1982. Dickey Centennial History Book Committee 1982.

140. Area Survey For Edgeley, North Dakota. Edgeley Lions Club & Otter Tail Power Co. 1964.

141. Diamond Jubilee Jud, North Dakota 1980.

142. Kulm, N.Dak. 1892 to 1957. Kulm Lions Club 1957.

143. Gone But Not Forgotten—Deisem, Franklin, Medbery. 1986.

144. A History of LaMoure, North Dakota 1882-1982. LaMoure Centennial Book Committee 1982.

145. Our Community—Prairie to Present—Marion, N.Dak. 1900-1975. Marion Diamond Jubilee History Committee.

146. Fondly We Remember. Hamilton Book Committee 1980.

147. A History of Richland County. Richland County Historical Society 1977.

149. Esmond Diamond Jubilee 1901-1976. Herald Press, Harvey, ND 1976.

150. A History of Verona, North Dakota 1883-1983. The Verona Centennial Book Committee 1983.

151. Adrian 1885-1976. The Litchville Bulletin, Litchville, ND. 1976.

153. Historical Highlights of Bottineau County. Bottineau County Historical Society, Bottineau, ND. 1977.

156. Cleveland, North Dakota Centennial 1982.

159. Diamond Jubilee Medina, North Dakota 1899-1974. The Medina Historical Committee 1974.

160. Pingree 1880-1980. Pingree Centennial Committee 1980.

162. Diamond Jubilee Streeter, N.D. 1905-1980. The Historical Committee 1980.

163. Ypsilanti and Community 1976. Booklet Committee 1976.

164. Ypsilanti Centennial 1882-1982. Ypsilanti Centennial Commitee 1982.

167. Recollections Cogswell, North Dakota 1886-1986 Centennial. Cogswell Centennial Committee, Cogswell, ND. 1986.

168. Forman, North Dakota. Women's Literary Club of Forman & Otter Tail Power Co. 1966.

169. Gwinner 1900-1975.

170. Havana Centennial Book 1883-1983. The Havana Centennial Committee 1983.

171. 100 Years of Milnor Memories 1883-1983. J & M Printing, Inc., Gwinner, ND. 1982.

172. Stirum Diamond Jubilee 1907-1982. Stirum Diamond Jubilee Committee 1982.

173. Grant County's Silver Jubilee and Old Settlers' Picnic. Carson Commercial Club 1941.

174. 50th Anniversary Carson, North Dakota 1910-1960.

175. Carson, N.D. 75th Diamond Jubilee 1910-1985. Carson Diamond Jubilee Committee.

176. Grant County, North Dakota. The Carson Press, Carson, ND. 1925.

177. Prairie Pioneers of Grant County, N.D. Bicentennial Edition 1976.

179. Regent Reviews 1910-1985. The Book Committee 1985.

180. Mott, North Dakota The First 75 Years 1907-1982. 75th Anniversary Committee, Press Print, Mott, ND. 1982.

185. Towner, North Dakota Community Fact Survey. Towner Association of Commerce, Towner Industrial Development Assn., & Otter Tail Power Co.

186. Upham Diamond Jubilee 1905-1980. Upham Commercial Club 1980.

187. Traill County History (2 vols.). Traill County Historical Society & Red River Valley Historical Society 1976.

190. Our Heritage, The First 75 Years, Hettinger Diamond Jubilee 1907-1982. Hettinger Diamond Jubilee Committee 1982.

191. Reeder Diamond Jubilee 1908-1983. Record Print, Hettinger, ND. 1983.

192. Rocklake History from 1905 to 1980. The Printer, Langdon, ND. 1980.

193. Golden Jubilee 1906-1956 Max, North Dakota. Max Civic Club 1956.

196. Marking the 50th Anniversary of the Founding of Hansboro, N.D. 1905-1955.

197. Egeland 50th Anniversary 1905-1955.

198. Rolla, North Dakota. Rolla Commercial Club & Otter Tail Power Co. 1967.

199. History of The Red River Valley (2 vols.). Herald Printing Co., Grand Forks, ND. 1909.

200. Driscoll, North Dakota 1883-1970. Gay 30's Committee.

202. Lisbon 1880-1980. History Book Committee, Lisbon, ND. 1980.

204. Enderlin Diamond Jubilee 1891-1966. The Anniversary Committee, Enderlin, ND. 1966.

205. Industries of Lisbon. Clipper Steam Printing and Publishing House, Lisbon, Dakota. 1883.

208. Sarles 1905-1980. The Printer, Langdon, ND. 1980.

209. Langdon, North Dakota Diamond Jubilee 1888-1963. Langdon Jubilee Committee 1963.

210. West Fargo—Riverside History Thru the Years to '76. The Bicentennial West Fargo-Riverside History Book Committee 1976.

212. Alsen Diamond Jubilee 1980. Ness Printing Co., Devils Lake, ND. 1980.

214. Dresden 75th Anniversary 1897-1972.

215. Hannah 1896-1971. Historical Committee 1971.

216. Langdon, North Dakota 1888-1988. Langdon Centennial Book Committee 1986.

218. Seventy-five Years Down Memory Lane At Milton, Cavalier County, North Dakota 1887-1962.

219. Report of the Killdeer Mountain Park Commission. 1919.

221. Halliday Anniversary Book 1914-1964. The Book Committee 1964.

222. 50th Golden Anniversary 1914-1964 Dodge, North Dakota. The Committee 1964.

223. Dauntless Dunn 1970. Committee of Seven.

225. Mayville, N.Dak. Diamond Jubilee 1881-1956.

227. Cartwright Area History. Cartwright, ND. 1976.

229. Watford City, North Dakota Golden Jubilee 1914-1964. Golden Jubilee Book Committee.

231. Hazen Tomorrow A Plan. Hazen Planning and Zoning Commission & Hazen City Commission 1979.

233. Hope Through The Century 1882-1982. Hope Centennial Committee, Hope, ND. 1982.

234. Braddock, N.D. 1884-1984.

235. Proudly We Speak, A History of Neche, Bathgate, Bruce and Hyde Park. Neche/Bathgate History Book Committee, Neche, ND. 1976.

236. Our Heritage, Leeds, York 1886-1986. Leeds History Book Committee, Leeds, ND. 1986.

238. From Trails to Tribute, Manvel Centennial 1882-1982. Tri-County Press, Grand Forks, ND. 1982.
239. Maddock Diamond Jubilee 1901-1976. Herald Press, Harvey, ND. 1977.
240. Hatton Centennial 1884 to 1984 A Century of Change. Hatton Centennial Committee 1983.
241. A Century of Progress, Northwood 1984. Centennial Book Committee.
242. Mooreton History 1884-1984. Mooreton Centennial Book Committee 1984.
244. Gladstone Centennial 1882-1982. Gladstone Centennial Committee 1982.
246. Footprints Across the Prairie Galesburg Centennial 1882-1982.
248. Wyndmere Centennial 1985. Wyndmere Centennial Committee, Wyndmere, ND. 1985.
250. Leonard Centennial 1881-1981. Cass County Reporter Print 1981.
253. Sanish Silver Anniversary Jubilee 1915-1940. The Anniversary Committee 1940.
254. Pisek The First Century. Pisek Centennial Book Committee, Pisek, ND. 1982.
256. History of the Knox Community. 1976.
257. Seventy-five Years Leeds & York 1886-1961. Diamond Jubilee Committee 1961.
258. Golden Jubilee Harlow 1912-1962. Harlow Golden Jubilee Executive Committee.
260. The Fort Totten Historic Site. North Dakota Bicentennial Commission & State Historical Society of North Dakota 1976.
264. Granary of the Plains Guelph, North Dakota 1883-1983. Guelph Centennial Committee, Guelph, ND. 1983.
265. One Hundred Years With Arthur 1882-1982. Centennial Book Committee 1982.
266. Buffalo Our Town on the Prairie Centennial Edition 1880-1980. Buffalo Centennial Committee 1980.
267. Bowdon Diamond Jubilee 1899-1974.
268. The First 100 Sykeston, North Dakota Centennial 1883-1983. Centennial Book Committee 1983.
270. Wheatland Centennial 1879-1979. Wheatland Centennial Committee 1979.
272. A Community Fact Survey New Rockford, North Dakota. New Rockford Civic Assn., et al & Otter Tail Power Co. 1965.
273. Agriculture, Eddy County, North Dakota. Hugh Peoples, New Rockford, ND. 1915.
275. Valley City—City of Five Names 1883-1983. Valley City Times-Record, Valley City, ND. 1983.
276. Memories of Yesterday Thompson Centennial 1881-1981. Tri-County Press, Grand Forks, ND. 1981.
277. Ryder, North Dakota Diamond Jubilee 1906-1981. The Book Committee 1981.
278. Golden Jubilee 1917-1967 Roseglen, North Dakota. Roseglen Community Club 1967.
283. Area Fact Survey Cooperstown, North Dakota. Cooperstown Commercial Club & Otter Tail Power Co. 1966.
284. Cooperstown, North Dakota 1882-1982. Centennial Book Committee.
285. 75th Anniversary of Binford, North Dakota 1906-1981. Binford Diamond Jubilee Committee 1981.
286. Hannaford, North Dakota 1906 and 1981. Two Rivers Printing Inc.
288. Berwick Memories 1911-1960.
289. Parshall 1914-1964 The City With A Big Future. The Historical Committee 1964.
290. Plaza's Golden Jubilee 1906-1956.
291. Plaza Diamond Jubilee 1906-1981. Missouri Valley Publishing, Inc., Garrison, ND. 1981.
292. Walhalla Quasquicentennial Anniversary 1848-1973.
295. Douglas, North Dakota 1906-1981.
296. Absaraka Centennial, Absaraka, North Dakota. 1982.
297. Our Community, 100 Years of Caring and Sharing, Ayr, North Dakota 1883-1983.
298. Hunter, North Dakota Bicentennial Community 1976. Hunter Bicentennial Committee 1976.
299. Casselton, North Dakota Community Fact Survey. Casselton Community Club & Otter Tail Power Co. 1967.
300. Casselton, North Dakota 1879-1979. Casselton Community Club 1979.
301. Fargo Souvenir 1897. Record Publishing Co., Fargo, ND. 1897.
302. Kindred, North Dakota Area Fact Survey. Community Betterment Committee & Otter Tail Power Co. 1967.
303. Davenport Centennial 1882-1982. Cass County Reporter Print 1982.
304. Mapleton Centennial 1876-1976. Centennial Committee 1976.
305. Gardner Centennial 1882-1982. Centennial Commission 1982.
306. Kindred Centennial 1880-1980.
307. Diamond Jubilee Fargo 1875-1950. Fargo Diamond Jubilee Committee, The Pierce Co., Fargo, ND. 1950.
308. Our Page 1882-1957. North Dakota Institute For Regional Studies, Fargo, ND. 1958.
309. They Planted Their Roots Deep, Horace 100 Years. History Committee 1973.
310. Alice, North Dakota 1900-1975. History Committee 1975.
311. Wild Rice Settlers Reunion June 8, 1975.
314. Pettibone, N.Dak. 1910-1960. Pettibone Golden Jubilee Committee.
315. Pettibone, North Dakota 1910-1985.
316. A Century of Memories Ellendale, North Dakota 1882-1982.
317. Forbes 1905-1980. Forbes Jubilee Committee 1980.
318. Oakes, North Dakota 1886-1986. Oakes Centennial Book Committee 1986.
319. Community Fact Survey of Oakes, North Dakota. Oakes Commercial Club & Otter Tail Power Co. 1965.
320. Whitestone Battlefield A History From 1863 to 1976. Whitestone Battlefield Celebration Committee.
323. Diamond Jubilee 1904-1979 Glenburn, North Dakota. Diamond Jubilee Committee 1979.
324. The Call Of The West. The Carrington Weekly Independent 1909.
326. Finley 75th Diamond Jubilee 1897-1972.
327. Hope of the Prairie, 75th Anniversary 1882-1957. Hope Jubilee Committee 1957.
328. Dazey, Our Heritage. Dazey History Committee 1983.
329. Community Fact Survey, Litchville, North Dakota. Litchville Commercial Club & Otter Tail Power Co. 1966.
330. 100 Years of Happenings in Sanborn 1879-1979. Litchville Bulletin, Litchville, ND. 1979.
331. Kathryn, North Dakota 75th Anniversary 1900-1975. Kathryn, ND. 1976.
333. Litchville, 75 Years and Growing 1900-1975. Litchville Bulletin, Litchville, ND. 1975.
334. Fredonia Diamond Jubilee 1904-1979. Jubilee History Book Committee 1979.
335. Own A Home In Logan County, North Dakota. Normanden Publishing Co., Grand Forks, ND. C.1920.
336. Emerado Centennial 1882-1982. Centennial Book Committee, Wold Publishing Co., Larimore, ND. 1982.
338. Gilby Chronicle 1887-1987. Gilby Centennial Committee, Gilby, ND. 1986.
339. Historical Booklet. Niagara Community Historical Society 1973.
341. They Came To Stay, Grand Forks, North Dakota Centennial 1874-1974. Grand Forks Centennial Corporations 1974.
342. Larimore Centennial 1881-1981. Souvenir Booklet Committee 1981.
345. A Centennial History of the City of Christine and Eagle Township. Centennial History Book Committee 1983.
354. Them Wuz The Days! Fairmount, North Dakota History 1883-1983. Centennial Committee, Fairmount, ND. 1983.
356. Park River—100 Years 1884-1984. Centennial Book Committee 1984.
357. Butte, North Dakota 1906-1981. History Book Committee.
358. New Leipzig, North Dakota 1910-1985 Book of Memories 75th Jubilee.
359. A Saga of Two Cities—A History of Mayville-Portland 1881-1981. Centennial Book Committee 1981.
360. Hankinson, ND Centennial 1986. Hankinson Centennial Committee 1985.
362. Lidgerwood—Yesterday, Today & Tomorrow 1886-1986. Lidgerwood Centennial Committee, Lidgerwood, ND. 1985.
366. Pembina County Centennial 1867-1967. Pembina Centennial Committee 1967.
368. Selfridge, North Dakota Seventy-five Diamond Years 1911-1986.
369. Beach, North Dakota Community Survey. North Dakota Economic Development Commission, Bismarck, ND. 1961.
370. Beach, North Dakota Diamond Jubilee 1984. Beach Diamond Jubilee Committee 1984.
371. Burlington Centennial 1883-1983. Burlington Historical Committee 1983.
372. Berthold, North Dakota 75th Anniversary. 75th Anniversary Committee 1975.
373. Ward County 75th Jubilee. Ward County Diamond Jubilee 1961.
374. People of the Prairie. South Prairie History Committee 1982.
375. Seventy-five Years of Kenmare and the Gooseneck Area. Diamond Jubilee Committee 1972.
376. A History of Powers Lake 75th Jubilee 1984. History Committee, Burke County Tribune 1984.
378. Reflections of Lansford, North Dakota and Community. Lansford 1976 Bicentennial Committee.
379. Diamond Jubilee 1884-1959, A Brief History of the County of Bottineau, North Dakota. Diamond Anniversary Publication Committee 1959.
381. Scranton Through The Years 1908-1983. 75th Anniversary Committee 1983.
382. Rhame, N.D. The First 75 Years 1908-1983. Bowman County Pioneer 1983.
383. This Bowman Community. Bowman Commercial Club 1960.
384. Rhame, North Dakota 1908-1958. Friendly City Club 1958.
385. New England, N.D. Centennial 1886-1986. Richtman's Printing, Bismarck & Fargo, ND. 1986.
388. Garrison 50th Anniversary 1905-1955. Historical Commitee 1955.
389. Grasp This Opportunity In North Dakota. Klein-Johnson Lumber Co., Washburn, ND. 1914.
391. Area Fact Survey Hoople, North Dakota. Hoople Community Betterment Committee & Otter Tail Power Co. 1964.
392. Edinburg's 75th Anniversary 1882-1957. Record Printers, Grafton, ND.
394. Prairie Portraits, Clifford, North Dakota. Clifford Centennial Committee 1981.
396. Hillsboro, North Dakota The First Hundred Years.
397. Rolla, North Dakota. Rolla Commercial Club & Otter Tail Power Co. 1967.
398. A Brief Look At Dunseith, North Dakota. Otter Tail Power Co. 1960.
399. Killdeer, North Dakota 40th Anniversary. The Publicity Committee 1954.
400. The Chenoweth Trailblazers. Sunshine Homemakers Club 1972.
401. History of Hazelton 75th Anniversary. The Jubilee Committee 1978.
404. Area Fact Survey of Strasburg, North Dakota. Strasburg Civic Club et al 1966.
407. Prairie Notes—Taylor, North Dakota Centennial 1881-1981. Taylor Centennial Book Committee.
410. Edgeley, N.D. 1887-1987. Edgeley Centennial Committee 1986.
412. McHenry County Centennial.
413. The Banner. North Dakota School For The Deaf, Devils Lake, ND, May 1952.
417. North Dakota History. State Historical Society of North Dakota, Bismarck, ND (various issues).
419. North Dakota—The American Guide Series. State Historical Society of North Dakota & WPA. 1938.
422. Northern Pacific Railroad Co. Annual Reports 1870-1896.
425. Profiles of the Past Pillsbury, North Dakota 1912-1987. Valley City Times-Record, Valley City, ND. 1987.
427. New Leipzig's 50th Anniversary 1960. 50th Anniversary Committee.
429. Map of the Missouri River. Missouri River Commission 1892-1895.
432. Western North Dakota. Northern Pacific Railway 1911.
433. Biennial Report of the Secretary of State of North Dakota (various issues).
435. Noonan Diamond Jubilee 1906-1981.
441. Souvenir of the Golden Jubilee of SS. Peter and Paul Parish in Bechyn (sic), N.D. 1936.

**BOOKS, PAMPHLETS, & BROCHURES with specific author(s):**

2. Williams, Mary Ann Barnes. Origins of North Dakota Place Names. 1966.
9. Bird, George F. & Taylor, Edwin J. Jr. History of the City of Bismarck, North Dakota. Bismarck Centennial Association 1972.
10. Harder, Kelsie B. (Ed.). Illustrated Dictionary of Place Names, United States and Canada. Van Nostrad Reinhold Company, New York, NY. 1976.
12. Bauman, Beth Hughes & Jackman, Dorothy J. Burleigh County: Prairie Trails To Hi-Ways. Bismarck-Mandan Genealogical and Historical Society. 1978.
13. Upham, Warren. Minnesota Geographic Names. Minnesota Historical Society. 1920, 1969.
15. Rolfsrud, Erling Nicolai. The Story of North Dakota. Lantern Books, Alexandria, MN. 1963.
19. Ames, Winthrop. What Shall We Name The Baby? Pocket Books, New York, NY. 1963.
21. Wills, Jim (Ed.). Sheridan County Heritage '76. McClusky Gazette 1976.
23. Sallet, Richard. Russian-German Settlements in the United States. North Dakota Institute for Regional Studies, Fargo, ND. 1974.
35. Fitzpatrick, Lilian L. Nebraska Place-Names. University of Nebraska Press, Lincoln, NE. 1960.
36. Sneve, Virginia Driving Hawk (Ed.). South Dakota Geographic Names. Brevet Press, Sioux Falls, SD. 1973.
41. Govern, Robert W. & Lounsbury, Jay W. Discontinued and Renamed Post Offices in the Zip Code Era 1963-1981.
42. Pearce, T. M. (Ed.). New Mexico Place Names. University of New Mexico Press, Albuquerque, NM. 1965.
43. Walters, George J. Wir Wollen Deutsche Bleigen.
44. Aberle, Msgr. George P. From The Steppes to the Prairies. Bismarck Tribune, Bismarck, ND.
45. Swift, Esther Munroe. Vermont Place-Names. The Stephen Greene Press, Brattleboro, VT. 1977.
46. Romig, Walter. Michigan Place Names. C. 1970.
48. Cairns, Robert (Ed.). The Orange Disc, Spring 1982. The Gulf Corporation.
57. Kane, Joseph Nathan. The American Counties. Scarecrow Press, New York, NY. 1962.
64. Heinemeyer, C. B. & Janssen, Mrs. Ben. History of Mercer County, North Dakota. Hazen Star, Hazen, ND. 1960.
66. Woods, Ellen & Wenzel, Euvagh (Eds.). A History of Emmons County. Emmons County Historical Society 1976.
70. Gard, Robert E. & Sorden, L. G. The Romance of Wisconsin Place Names. October House, New York, NY. 1968.
74. Thompson, Earlene & Dohrmann, Mrs. Clarence (Eds.). Stark County Heritage and Destiny. Stark County Historical Society, Dickinson, ND. 1978.
78. Rutherford, Phillip R. The Dictionary of Maine Place Names. Bond Wheelwright Co., Freeport, ME. 1970.
79. Spokesfield, Walter E. The History of Wells County, North Dakota and Its Pioneers. 1929.
80. Dietz, Herman F. (Ed.). Golden Valley County Pioneers. Sentinel Butte Bicentennial Group 1976.
83. Russell, E. T. What's in a Name, The Story Behind Saskatchewan Place Names. Western Producer Prairie Books, Saskatoon, SA. 1973.
84. Tarpley, Fred. 1001 Texas Place Names. University of Texas Press, Austin, TX. 1980.

Thank you for ordering NORTH DAKOTA PLACE NAMES. We hope that it meets with your expectations. If not, simply return the book for a full refund.

HEDEMARKEN COLLECTIBLES is primarily an international mail order firm specializing in postal history and picture post cards for collectors.

If you have material for sale that is similar to these illustrations or those in NORTH DAKOTA PLACE NAMES, we would appreciate the opportunity to make an offer. We handle material from all fifty states, Canada, railroads, military, etc., as well as some foreign material.

HEDEMARKEN COLLECTIBLES
P. O. Box 7399 - Northbrook Station
Bismarck, North Dakota 58502

87. Rennick, Robert M. Kentucky Place Names. The University Press of Kentucky, Lexington, KY. 1984.
88. Cheney, Robert Carkeek. Names on the Face of Montana. Mountain Press Publishing Co., Missoula, MT. 1983.
89. Perkey, Elton A. Perkey's Nebraska Place Names. Nebraska State Historical Society, Lincoln, NE. 1982.
94. Hennessy, W. B. History of North Dakota. Bismarck Tribune Co., Bismarck, ND. 1910.
95. Baker, Ronald L. & Carmony, Marvin. Indiana Place Names. Indiana University Press, Bloomington, IN. 1975.
96. Geil, Dewey Manila. Dakota Pioneer History. 1970.
98. Shirk, George H. Oklahoma Place Names. University of Oklahoma Press, Noramn, OK. 1965.
107. Peterson, Marion Plath (Ed.). Morton Prairie Roots. The Morton County Historical Society 1975.
113. Dickson, Mrs. Leonard & Kuipers, Mrs. Carl (Eds.). 75th Anniversary of Kintyre, North Dakota 1904-1979.
121. Reuther, Peg, Bueligen, Millie, & Tellman, Debra (Eds.). Oliver County 1885-1985.
123. Law, Laura Thompson. History of Rolette County, North Dakota and Yarns of the Pioneers. The Lund Press, Inc., Minneapolis, MN. 1953.
125. Tweten, D. Jerome. Grand Forks—A Pictorial History. The Donning Company/Publishers, Norfolk, VA. 1986.
127. Hinton, May E. South of the Cannonball. Washburn Printing Center, Grand Forks, ND. 1984.
152. Sandness, Mrs. Joel. The History of LaMoure. LaMoure Chronicle 1957.
154. Black, R. M. (Ed.). A History of Dickey County, North Dakota. Dickey County Historical Society, Ellendale, ND. 1930.
155. Chenery, Mrs. Jennie M. The Early History of Jamestown. Jamestown, ND. 1900.
157. Cushing, Mrs. W. F. Jamestown and Stutsman County, North Dakota. Jamestown Commercial Club 1915.
158. Smorada, James & Forrest, Lois. Century of Stories, Jamestown, ND, Stutsman County. Fort Seward Historical Society, Inc. 1983.
161. Snape, William. History of Kensal. The Carrington Record, Carrington, ND. 1910.
165. Thorfinnson, Snorri M. Sargent County History. Sargent County Commissioners, Forman, ND. 1977.
166. White, L. H. Cogswell and Sargent County, North Dakota. 1903.
178. Shults, Ralph (Ed.). 50th Anniversary, Hettinger County, North Dakota. Mott Pioneer Press, Mott, ND. 1957.
181. Bern, Enid. Our Hettinger County Heritage. Pioneer Press, Mott, ND. 1975.
182. Brooks, Carol Henke. Granville, A Community Which Refuses to Die. McHenry County Journal-Register, Velva, ND. 1976.
183. Cantlon, Cleo (Ed.). Prairie Patchwork. McHenry County Journal-Register, Velva, ND. 1977.
184. Cantlon, Cleo. Seedstock: An Improper History of Early Balfour. Linnertz Publications, Velva, ND. 1975.
188. Erickson, Marjorie & Olson, Gertrude. Pioneer Sons and Daughters, History of Adams County. Dakota Buttes Historical Society, Hettinger, ND. 1980.
189. Erickson, Mrs. Harley & Merwin, Mrs. Dan (Eds.). Prairie Pioneers, A Story of Adams County. Dakota Buttes Historical Society, Hettinger, ND. 1976.
194. Barton, Helen L. Braddock 1883-1944 In The Hands of Time. Bismarck Tribune, Bismarck, ND. 1944.
195. Hadler, Mabel Jacques. History of Arndt, Towner County, North Dakota. 1943.
201. Thorfinnson, Snorri M. Ransom County History. Ransom County Historical Society 1975.
203. Taylor, Ardis. The Skanings Revisited. J & M Printing, Gwinner, ND. 1982.
206. Schunk. Albert H. (Posthumous). History of the Schunk Family and Community. Edna Wiltse Schunk 1961.
207. Thorfinnson, Snorri M. Fort Ransom Area History 1878-1978.
211. Wishek, Nina Farley. Along the Trails of Yesterday, A History of McIntosh County. Ashley Tribune, Ashley, ND. 1941.
213. Hahn, Emma. Yesteryears of Dresden. The Printer, Langdon, ND. 1979.
217. Parker, Mrs. P. C. Nekoma, North Dakota 1906-1976.
220. Faser, Elmer. A General History of Halliday, North Dakota 1900-1940.
224. Miller, Michael M. (Ed.). Moments to Remember Strasburg 1976. Strasburg Schools Alumni Association 1976.
226. Svore, Hedvig Clausen. Lest We Forget. 1959.
228. Berntson, Norma E. As The Sod Was Turned. Fairview, MT. 1959.
230. Svore, Hedvig Clausen. From Dreams To Reality. 1954.
237. Newgard, Thomas P. Knox Area History. Knight Printing, Fargo, ND. 1977.
243. Crandall, Horace B. A History of Richland County. Colfax, Dakota. 1886.
245. Gengler, John (Ed.). Richardton Heritage, A History of Richardton, North Dakota. Assumption Abbey Press, Richardton, ND. 1983.
247. Melland, Gail Haugen (Ed.). Our Heritage Nekoma, North Dakota 1905-1980. Nekoma Book Committee, Nekoma, ND. 1980.
251. Kay, John L. & Smith, Chester M. Jr. Pennsylvania Postal History. Quarterman Publications, Lawrence, MA. 1976.
255. McPhillips, Henry T. (Pub.). Minnewaukan Illustrated. Pioneer Print, Larimore, ND. 1901.
259. Foy, Susan Rolle. Memories of Brinsmade, North Dakota. Fargo, ND. 1976.
261. McCormick, John Michael. The History of Fort Totten 1867-1890. Masters thesis, University of North Dakota 1972.
262. White, Hugh L. (Pub.). Who's Who For North Dakota. North Dakota State Historical Society, Bismarck, ND. 1954, 1958.
263. Brand, Wayne L. & Hector, James C. (Eds.). North Dakota Decision Makers. Analytical Statistics Inc., Fargo, ND. 1972.
269. Blinsky, Kathleen. Wimbledon History 1893-1968. Wimbledon, ND. 1968.
271. Braun, W. L. (Ed.). Turtle Lake, North Dakota 50th Anniversary. Turtle Lake Commercial Club 1955.
274. Brown, Ann M. Billings County T Y (9th Issue). 1938.
279. Holm, Donald R. Reunion Summer. Explorer Publications, Ltd., Beaverton, OR. 1972.
280. Petersen, Allen J. Tower City, North Dakota Centennial 1879-1979. The Centennial Book Committee 1979.
281. Conway, John A. (Ed.). Oriska, North Dakota Centennial 1881-1981. Oriska History Committee, Oriska, ND. 1980.
282. Nye, Marinda & Lorenz, Agnes. Heritage of Lawton, North Dakota and Surrounding Area. Ness Printing Co., Devils Lake, ND. 1976.
293. Ness, G. K. History of Fordville and Surrounding Area. Ness Press, Fordville, ND. 1973.
294. Goplen, Arnold O. DeMores State Historic Site, Medora, North Dakota. National Park Service 1938.
312. Patera, Alan H. & Gallagher, John S. The Post Offices of Minnesota. The Depot, Burtonsville, MD. 1978.
322. Hembree, Blanche. Fate, Destiny, Necessity on Renville's Prairies. 1977.
325. Mitzel, Mrs. Balzer & Edwardson, Mrs. Edward. Blabon, A Link to our Past. 1982.
331. Saugstad, C. Norman. Kathryn, North Dakota 75th Anniversary 1900-1975.
332. Arvidson, Robert T. My Native Land. Wimbledon, ND. 1940.
337. Romberg, Harry J. (Posthumous). Early History Along The Forest River In Grand Forks County. 1974.
340. Weber, Clara. Reynolds City Centennial 1880-1980. Reynolds Homemakers Club 1980.
343. Fristad, Palma. Historic Mandan and Morton County. Mandan, ND. 1970.
344. Mitskog, Mrs. Fritz. A History of Colfax and Area. Richland County Historical Society 1970.
346. Callan, F. G. A History of Richland County, North Dakota. Globe Gazette, Wahpeton, ND. 1938.
347. Berndt, Lois. A History of Brandenburg Township. Richland County Historical Society 1981.
348. Biegert, Mrs. Ernest. A History of the City of Barney. 1975.
349. Blumer, Mrs. Harold. A History of the Town of Colfax and Colfax Township. Richland County Historical Society 1973.
350. Goerger, Edd. Some of the History of Danton Twp. Richland County Historical Society 1975.
351. Wold, Mrs. Earl. Dwight Township, It's Past and Present. 1979.
352. Quamme, Lillian Knudson. The Centennial Review of Dwight, North Dakota. 1974.
353. Riemann, Henrietta Klar. A History of Elma Township. 1976.
355. Luick, A. W. Early History of Fairmount. Richland County Historical Society 1974.
361. Olson, Mrs. LaVerne. A History of Homestead Township. Richland County Historical Society 1973.
363. Levorsen, Barbara. The Quiet Conquest. Hawley Herald, Hawley, MN. 1974.
364. Eldredge, Mary (Ed.). Wells County, North Dakota 1884-1984. Eldredge Publishing Co., Harvey, ND. 1984.
365. Steffan, Bernard R. & Parker, Lloyd B. Pembina, North Dakota's Oldest Settlement. Pembina Community Club 1957.
367. Lee, Charles H. The Long Ago. Semi-Weekly Mountaineer Print, Walhalla, ND. 1898.
377. Milloy, James S. Northwest North Dakota Wants 100,000 More Neighbors. Circa 1910.
380. Redal, Olav. A History of the Norwegian Settlement, Northern Bottineau County, North Dakota. Forfatterens Forlag 1917.
387. Sprunk, Larry J. The Garrison History Book. Historical & Archaelogical Surveys, Inc., Garrison, ND. 1980.
390. Williams, Mary Ann Barnes. Pioneer Days of Washburn, North Dakota and Vicinity. Washburn Leader, Washburn, ND. 1936.
393. Beal, Leonard. Centennial of Traill County 1875-1975. Hillsboro, ND. 1975.
395. Burner, Thea & Brasel, Merilla. Pillars of Time, A History of Pioneering on the Goose River. 1980.
403. Miller, Michael M. As We Reminisce. Strasburg Schools Alumni Association, Strasburg, ND. 1967.
405. Oder, Naomi Buckley. Glencoe Stage Run. 1976.
406. Cole, Janell (Ed.). Centennial Roundup, A History of Dickinson, North Dakota. Assumption Abbey Press, Richardton, ND. 1982.
408. Nicholson, Tim. Car Badges Of The World. American Heritage Press, New York, NY. 1970.
409. Gartner, Mrs. Anton. History of Fort Rice, North Dakota. 1974.
411. Daniels, Arthur M. A Journal Of Sibley's Indian Expedition. James D. Thueson (Pub.), Minneapolis, MN. 1980.
416. Smalley, Eugene Virgil. History of the Northern Pacific Railroad. G. P. Putnam's Sons, New York, NY. 1883.
418. Holst, Vernon S. A Story Of The 1876 Bismarck To Deadwood Trail. Butte County Historical Society 1983.
420. Lounsberry, Col. Clement A. Early History of North Dakota. Liberty Press, Washington, DC. 1919.
421. Crawford, Lewis F. History of North Dakota. The American Historical Society, Inc., Chicago & New York. 1931.
423. Lounsberry, Col. Clement A. The Record. C. A. Lounsberry (Pub.), Fargo, ND. 1895-1905.
426. Schweigert, Kurt. Historic Sites Cultural Resource Inventory In The Devils Lake Region. Department of Anthropology and Archaeology, University of North Dakota, Grand Forks. 1977.
428. Berg, Jane & Elmer, Kathy. In The Beginning Hebron, North Dakota 1876-1912. 1978.
430. Glasrud, Clarence A. (Ed.). Roy Johnson's Red River Valley. Red River Valley Historical Society 1982.
431. Pearce, W. D. List of Fargo Division Stations Showing Origins of the Station Names. Northern Pacific Railway 1944.
438. Innis, Ben. Sagas of the Smoky-Water. Centennial Press, Williston, ND. 1985.

**SOURCE INFORMATION:**

3. Personal on-site observation, and conversations and communications with local residents.
40. Register of Post Office Appointments 1837-1972.
55. Telephone Books (various).
60. Walter Essig, Bismarck, ND.
252. A. Carlisle Stevens, Dimock, PA.
414. U. S. Post Office Dept. Reports of Site Locations 1837-1950.
415. Official Records, U. S. Dept. of the Interior, Bureau of Land Management. Dakota Tract Books. Billings, MT.
424. Renae Kimball, Bismarck, ND.
434. North Dakota Writers' Project Records. WPA 1937-1940.
436. James Benjaminson, Walhalla, ND.
437. Peter J. Hillman, Cavalier, ND.
439. Arni Johnson, Cavalier, ND.
440. Frances W. Branchaud, Cavalier, ND.
442. Dr. George M. Christensen, Minot, ND.

238

87. Rennick, Robert M. Kentucky Place Names. The University Press of Kentucky, Lexington, KY. 1984.

88. Cheney, Robert Carkeek. Names on the Face of Montana. Mountain Press Publishing Co., Missoula, MT. 1983.

89. Perkey, Elton A. Perkey's Nebraska Place Names. Nebraska State Historical Society, Lincoln, NE. 1982.

94. Hennessy, W. B. History of North Dakota. Bismarck Tribune Co., Bismarck, ND. 1910.

95. Baker, Ronald L. & Carmony, Marvin. Indiana Place Names. Indiana University Press, Bloomington, IN. 1975.

96. Geil, Dewey Manila. Dakota Pioneer History. 1970.

98. Shirk, George H. Oklahoma Place Names. University of Oklahoma Press, Noramn, OK. 1965.

107. Peterson, Marion Plath (Ed.). Morton Prairie Roots. The Morton County Historical Society 1975.

113. Dickson, Mrs. Leonard & Kuipers, Mrs. Carl (Eds.). 75th Anniversary of Kintyre, North Dakota 1904-1979.

121. Reuther, Peg, Bueligen, Millie, & Tellman, Debra (Eds.). Oliver County 1885-1985.

123. Law, Laura Thompson. History of Rolette County, North Dakota and Yarns of the Pioneers. The Lund Press, Inc., Minneapolis, MN. 1953.

125. Tweten, D. Jerome. Grand Forks—A Pictorial History. The Donning Company/Publishers, Norfolk, VA. 1986.

127. Hinton, May E. South of the Cannonball. Washburn Printing Center, Grand Forks, ND. 1984.

152. Sandness, Mrs. Joel. The History of LaMoure. LaMoure Chronicle 1957.

154. Black, R. M. (Ed.). A History of Dickey County, North Dakota. Dickey County Historical Society, Ellendale, ND. 1930.

155. Chenery, Mrs. Jennie M. The Early History of Jamestown. Jamestown, ND. 1900.

157. Cushing, Mrs. W. F. Jamestown and Stutsman County, North Dakota. Jamestown Commercial Club 1915.

158. Smorada, James & Forrest, Lois. Century of Stories, Jamestown, ND, Stutsman County. Fort Seward Historical Society, Inc. 1983.

161. Snape, William. History of Kensal. The Carrington Record, Carrington, ND. 1910.

165. Thorfinnson, Snorri M. Sargent County History. Sargent County Commissioners, Forman, ND. 1977.

166. White, L. H. Cogswell and Sargent County, North Dakota. 1903.

178. Shults, Ralph (Ed.). 50th Anniversary, Hettinger County, North Dakota. Mott Pioneer Press, Mott, ND. 1957.

181. Bern, Enid. Our Hettinger County Heritage. Pioneer Press, Mott, ND. 1975.

182. Brooks, Carol Henke. Granville, A Community Which Refuses to Die. McHenry County Journal-Register, Velva, ND. 1976.

183. Cantlon, Cleo (Ed.). Prairie Patchwork. McHenry County Journal-Register, Velva, ND. 1977.

184. Cantlon, Cleo. Seedstock: An Improper History of Early Balfour. Linnertz Publications, Velva, ND. 1975.

188. Erickson, Marjorie & Olson, Gertrude. Pioneer Sons and Daughters, History of Adams County. Dakota Buttes Historical Society, Hettinger, ND. 1980.

189. Erickson, Mrs. Harley & Merwin, Mrs. Dan (Eds.). Prairie Pioneers, A Story of Adams County. Dakota Buttes Historical Society, Hettinger, ND. 1976.

194. Barton, Helen L. Braddock 1883-1944 In The Hands of Time. Bismarck Tribune, Bismarck, ND. 1944.

195. Hadler, Mabel Jacques. History of Arndt, Towner County, North Dakota. 1943.

201. Thorfinnson, Snorri M. Ransom County History. Ransom County Historical Society 1975.

203. Taylor, Ardis. The Skanings Revisited. J & M Printing, Gwinner, ND. 1982.

206. Schunk. Albert H. (Posthumous). History of the Schunk Family and Community. Edna Wiltse Schunk 1961.

207. Thorfinnson, Snorri M. Fort Ransom Area History 1878-1978.

211. Wishek, Nina Farley. Along the Trails of Yesterday, A History of McIntosh County. Ashley Tribune, Ashley, ND. 1941.

213. Hahn, Emma. Yesteryears of Dresden. The Printer, Langdon, ND. 1979.

217. Parker, Mrs. P. C. Nekoma, North Dakota 1906-1976.

220. Faser, Elmer. A General History of Halliday, North Dakota 1900-1940.

224. Miller, Michael M. (Ed.). Moments to Remember Strasburg 1976. Strasburg Schools Alumni Association 1976.

226. Svore, Hedvig Clausen. Lest We Forget. 1959.

228. Berntson, Norma E. As The Sod Was Turned. Fairview, MT. 1959.

230. Svore, Hedvig Clausen. From Dreams To Reality. 1954.

237. Newgard, Thomas P. Knox Area History. Knight Printing, Fargo, ND. 1977.

243. Crandall, Horace B. A History of Richland County. Colfax, Dakota. 1886.

245. Gengler, John (Ed.). Richardton Heritage, A History of Richardton, North Dakota. Assumption Abbey Press, Richardton, ND. 1983.

247. Melland, Gail Haugen (Ed.). Our Heritage Nekoma, North Dakota 1905-1980. Nekoma Book Committee, Nekoma, ND. 1980.

251. Kay, John L. & Smith, Chester M. Jr. Pennsylvania Postal History. Quarterman Publications, Lawrence, MA. 1976.

255. McPhillips, Henry T. (Pub.). Minnewaukan Illustrated. Pioneer Print, Larimore, ND. 1901.

259. Foy, Susan Rolle. Memories of Brinsmade, North Dakota. Fargo, ND. 1976.

261. McCormick, John Michael. The History of Fort Totten 1867-1890. Masters thesis, University of North Dakota 1972.

262. White, Hugh L. (Pub.). Who's Who For North Dakota. North Dakota State Historical Society, Bismarck, ND. 1954, 1958.

263. Brand, Wayne L. & Hector, James C. (Eds.). North Dakota Decision Makers. Analytical Statistics Inc., Fargo, ND. 1972.

269. Blinsky, Kathleen. Wimbledon History 1893-1968. Wimbledon, ND. 1968.

271. Braun, W. L. (Ed.). Turtle Lake, North Dakota 50th Anniversary. Turtle Lake Commercial Club 1955.

274. Brown, Ann M. Billings County T Y (9th Issue). 1938.

279. Holm, Donald R. Reunion Summer. Explorer Publications, Ltd., Beaverton, OR. 1972.

280. Petersen, Allen J. Tower City, North Dakota Centennial 1879-1979. The Centennial Book Committee 1979.

281. Conway, John A. (Ed.). Oriska, North Dakota Centennial 1881-1981. Oriska History Committee, Oriska, ND. 1980.

282. Nye, Marinda & Lorenz, Agnes. Heritage of Lawton, North Dakota and Surrounding Area. Ness Printing Co., Devils Lake, ND. 1976.

293. Ness, G. K. History of Fordville and Surrounding Area. Ness Press, Fordville, ND. 1973.

294. Goplen, Arnold O. DeMores State Historic Site, Medora, North Dakota. National Park Service 1938.

312. Patera, Alan H. & Gallagher, John S. The Post Offices of Minnesota. The Depot, Burtonsville, MD. 1978.

322. Hembree, Blanche. Fate, Destiny, Necessity on Renville's Prairies. 1977.

325. Mitzel, Mrs. Balzer & Edwardson, Mrs. Edward. Blabon, A Link to our Past. 1982.

331. Saugstad, C. Norman. Kathryn, North Dakota 75th Anniversary 1900-1975.

332. Arvidson, Robert T. My Native Land. Wimbledon, ND. 1940.

337. Romberg, Harry J. (Posthumous). Early History Along The Forest River In Grand Forks County. 1974.

340. Weber, Clara. Reynolds City Centennial 1880-1980. Reynolds Homemakers Club 1980.

343. Fristad, Palma. Historic Mandan and Morton County. Mandan, ND. 1970.

344. Mitskog, Mrs. Fritz. A History of Colfax and Area. Richland County Historical Society 1970.

346. Callan, F. G. A History of Richland County, North Dakota. Globe Gazette, Wahpeton, ND. 1938.

347. Berndt, Lois. A History of Brandenburg Township. Richland County Historical Society 1981.

348. Biegert, Mrs. Ernest. A History of the City of Barney. 1975.

349. Blumer, Mrs. Harold. A History of the Town of Colfax and Colfax Township. Richland County Historical Society 1973.

350. Goerger, Edd. Some of the History of Danton Twp. Richland County Historical Society 1975.

351. Wold, Mrs. Earl. Dwight Township, It's Past and Present. 1979.

352. Quamme, Lillian Knudson. The Centennial Review of Dwight, North Dakota. 1974.

353. Riemann, Henrietta Klar. A History of Elma Township. 1976.

355. Luick, A. W. Early History of Fairmount. Richland County Historical Society 1974.

361. Olson, Mrs. LaVerne. A History of Homestead Township. Richland County Historical Society 1973.

363. Levorsen, Barbara. The Quiet Conquest. Hawley Herald, Hawley, MN. 1974.

364. Eldredge, Mary (Ed.). Wells County, North Dakota 1884-1984. Eldredge Publishing Co., Harvey, ND. 1984.

365. Steffan, Bernard R. & Parker, Lloyd B. Pembina, North Dakota's Oldest Settlement. Pembina Community Club 1957.

367. Lee, Charles H. The Long Ago. Semi-Weekly Mountaineer Print, Walhalla, ND. 1898.

377. Milloy, James S. Northwest North Dakota Wants 100,000 More Neighbors. Circa 1910.

380. Redal, Olav. A History of the Norwegian Settlement, Northern Bottineau County, North Dakota. Forfatterens Forlag 1917.

387. Sprunk, Larry J. The Garrison History Book. Historical & Archaeological Surveys, Inc., Garrison, ND. 1980.

390. Williams, Mary Ann Barnes. Pioneer Days of Washburn, North Dakota and Vicinity. Washburn Leader, Washburn, ND. 1936.

393. Beal, Leonard. Centennial of Traill County 1875-1975. Hillsboro, ND. 1975.

395. Burner, Thea & Brasel, Merilla. Pillars of Time, A History of Pioneering on the Goose River. 1980.

403. Miller, Michael M. As We Reminisce. Strasburg Schools Alumni Association, Strasburg, ND. 1967.

405. Oder, Naomi Buckley. Glencoe Stage Run. 1976.

406. Cole, Janell (Ed.). Centennial Roundup, A History of Dickinson, North Dakota. Assumption Abbey Press, Richardton, ND. 1982.

408. Nicholson, Tim. Car Badges Of The World. American Heritage Press, New York, NY. 1970.

409. Gartner, Mrs. Anton. History of Fort Rice, North Dakota. 1974.

411. Daniels, Arthur M. A Journal Of Sibley's Indian Expedition. James D. Thueson (Pub.), Minneapolis, MN. 1980.

416. Smalley, Eugene Virgil. History of the Northern Pacific Railroad. G. P. Putnam's Sons, New York, NY. 1883.

418. Holst, Vernon S. A Story Of The 1876 Bismarck To Deadwood Trail. Butte County Historical Society 1983.

420. Lounsberry, Col. Clement A. Early History of North Dakota. Liberty Press, Washington, DC. 1919.

421. Crawford, Lewis F. History of North Dakota. The American Historical Society, Inc., Chicago & New York. 1931.

423. Lounsberry, Col. Clement A. The Record. C. A. Lounsberry (Pub.), Fargo, ND. 1895-1905.

426. Schweigert, Kurt. Historic Sites Cultural Resource Inventory In The Devils Lake Region. Department of Anthropology and Archaeology, University of North Dakota, Grand Forks. 1977.

428. Berg, Jane & Elmer, Kathy. In The Beginning Hebron, North Dakota 1876-1912. 1978.

430. Glasrud, Clarence A. (Ed.). Roy Johnson's Red River Valley. Red River Valley Historical Society 1982.

431. Pearce, W. D. List of Fargo Division Stations Showing Origins of the Station Names. Northern Pacific Railway 1944.

438. Innis, Ben. Sagas of the Smoky-Water. Centennial Press, Williston, ND. 1985.

**SOURCE INFORMATION:**

3. Personal on-site observation, and conversations and communications with local residents.

40. Register of Post Office Appointments 1837-1972.

55. Telephone Books (various).

60. Walter Essig, Bismarck, ND.

252. A. Carlisle Stevens, Dimock, PA.

414. U. S. Post Office Dept. Reports of Site Locations 1837-1950.

415. Official Records, U. S. Dept. of the Interior, Bureau of Land Management. Dakota Tract Books. Billings, MT.

424. Renae Kimball, Bismarck, ND.

434. North Dakota Writers' Project Records. WPA 1937-1940.

436. James Benjaminson, Walhalla, ND.

437. Peter J. Hillman, Cavalier, ND.

439. Arni Johnson, Cavalier, ND.

440. Frances W. Branchaud, Cavalier, ND.

442. Dr. George M. Christensen, Minot, ND.

STREET VIEW, McALLEN, TEX.

U.S. ARMY
709
SEP 26
1944
POSTAL SERVICE

CORDOVA
DEC
22
1937
ALASKA

BISMARCK
AUG
31
A.M.
1959
W. VA.

Thank you for ordering NORTH DAKOTA PLACE NAMES.
We hope that it meets with your expectations.  If
not, simply return the book for a full refund.

HEDEMARKEN COLLECTIBLES is primarily an international mail order firm specializing in postal
history and picture post cards for collectors.

If you have material for sale that is similar to
these illustrations or those in NORTH DAKOTA PLACE
NAMES, we would appreciate the opportunity to make
an offer.  We handle material from all fifty states,
Canada, railroads, military, etc., as well as some
foreign material.

HEDEMARKEN COLLECTIBLES
P. O. Box 7399 - Northbrook Station
Bismarck, North Dakota   58502

NINEVEH JUN
OCT
5
1932
N. Y.

BOSTON
NOV
18
1 P M
1881
MASS

LEITERSBURG RURAL
AUG
6
A.M.
1907
HAGERSTOWN,

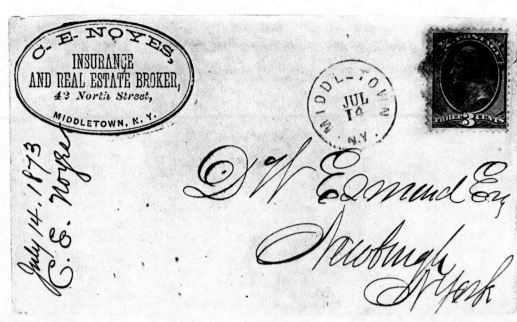

C. E. NOYES,
INSURANCE
AND REAL ESTATE BROKER,
42 North Street,
MIDDLETOWN, N. Y.

MIDDLE-TOWN
JUL
14
N.Y.

THREE 3 CENTS

July 14. 1873
C. E. Noyes

**The Poppke Collection**

*Gift of Herb Poppke*

The Libraries
North Dakota State University
PO Box 5599
Fargo, ND 58105-5599 USA
701-231-8416
www.ndsu.nodak.edu/gerrus

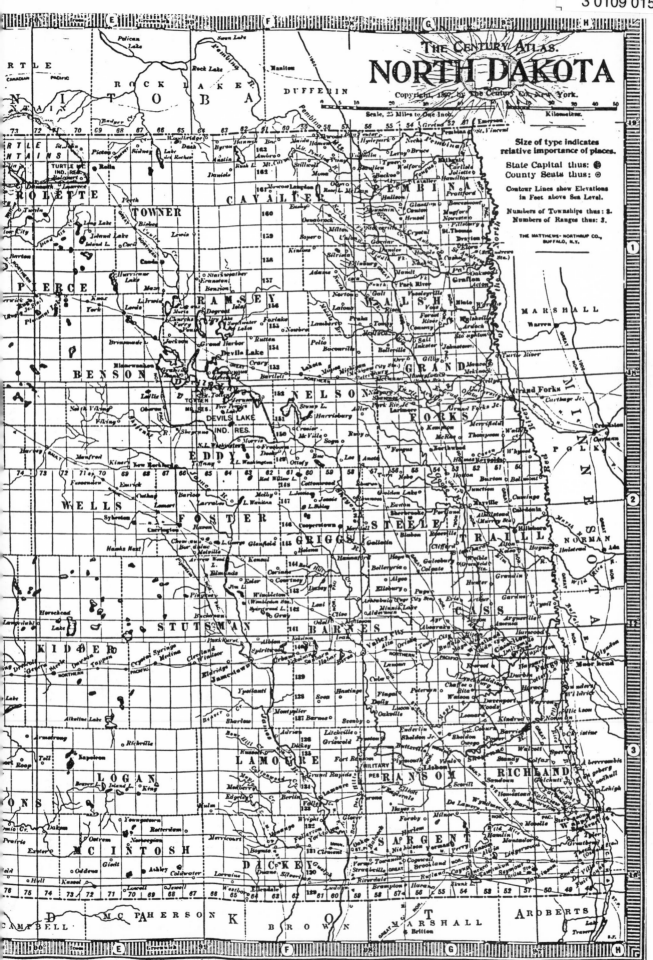

THE CENTURY ATLAS.

# NORTH DAKOTA

Copyright, 1897, by The Century Co., New York.

Scale, 25 Miles to One Inch.

Kilometers.

Size of type indicates relative importance of places.

State Capital thus: ⊛
County Seats thus: ⊚

Contour Lines show Elevations in Feet above Sea Level.

Numbers of Townships thus: 2.
Numbers of Ranges thus: 3.

THE MATTHEWS-NORTHRUP CO.,
BUFFALO, N.Y.